The Cherry Red Non-League Newsdesk Annual 2006

by

James Wright

CONTENTS

MISCELLANEOUS

Compiled by
James Wright
Non-League Newsdesk
6 Harp Chase
Taunton
Somerset TA1 3RY
(Tel: 07786 636659 Fax: 01823 324938)
Email: james@nlnewsdesk.co.uk

Designed & Set by
Nigel Davis
Broomhouse Farmhouse
George Nympton
South Molton
Devon EX36 4JF
(Tel: 01769 572257/ 07768 204784)
Email: NigelDavis@aol.com or NLNAnnual@aol.com

Published by
James Wright

Printed by
Bath Press Ltd
Lower Bristol Road
Bath BA2 3BL
Tel: 01225 428101
www.cpi-group.net
Email: enquiries@bathpress.co.uk

ISBN 0-9539198-6-2

Front Cover

Grays Athletic's skipper Stuart Thurgood gets the better of York City's Mark Convery during their 3-0 FA Cup 1st Round victory at the Kit Kat Stadium on November 5th 2005
Photo: Gavin Ellis (www.tgsphoto.co.uk)

REAL FOOTBALL

I don't know about you but I'm glad that over-hyped World Cup nonsense is over. Actually (glancing up intermittently from my lap top as I toiled on this book) I enjoyed the early stages more that I expected I would. But come the knock-out phase I was distinctly bored, largely by the realisation that most ties would be won by the side whose diving was the more convincing or whose nerve held best in the lottery of penalties.

I was aghast to learn that the face value of one ticket for a potentially meaningless group match cost more than the aggregate of the eight I procured on the streets when I hitch-hiked my way round Italia '90. How in just sixteen years has the "Game of the People" been taken so far away from the people? Whilst stadia are full of international rich kids posing with their expensive gadgetry, the "people" are condemned to the dreaded "Big Screen." Aaaargh – those two words sum up for me so much of what is wrong with the game in 2006!

My stepson pulled on his England shirt for each match and trotted down the pub "for the atmosphere". Atmosphere! In a pub! Full of lagered-up, know-nothing chavs trying to out-partisan each other. Do me a favour! Bring on real football, played and watched by real people on real grounds. It is a long time since I've wanted a summer to end so quickly.

Welcome to the seventh edition of the Cherry Red Non-League Newsdesk Annual. This summer has seen another re-organisation of the National League System with the addition of an extra division at Step Four and the further expansion of the Nationwide Conference to 24 teams in its top flight.

This has of course resulted in somewhat more inter-league shuffling than normal, and we hope you will find all the information you require on this within these pages. At a quite early stage of the summer we realised that our proposed publication date of July 24th was perhaps a little optimistic, so we pushed back a week to July 31st. We hope this means that the book is that much more comprehensive and accurate than it would otherwise have been. Nonetheless, there will doubtless be some late changes to the league line-ups after we go to press. There always are. As ever we will try to post these on the website in the early weeks of the season.

I would like to express our gratitude to Iain McNay of Cherry Red Records for again sponsoring this title. And I would also like to thank everyone who has provided me with the pieces from which to assemble this 304 page jigsaw, be it by submitting batches of scores weekly to merely answering a query about a ground address. I've tried to list you all in the Contributors section. If I have inadvertently omitted someone, please do not take offence.

Enjoy your season, and I hope I may bump into you at "real" ground somewhere over the next ten months.

JAMES WRIGHT

CONTRIBUTORS

Roy Ainge, Roger Allen, Bruce Badcock, Martin Bayliss, Jim Bean, Paul Beard, Chris Berezai, Jeremy Biggs, Paul Birkitt, Daniel Braddock, David Braithwaite, Ron Bridges, Martin Bryant, Tim Burgin, Ann Camm, Alan Charlton, Steve Clark, Tom Clark, Alan Constable, Ian Craid, Greg Cunningham, William Davies, John Deal, Richard Durrant, Rolant Ellis, Barbara Ely, Denis Emery, Robert Errington, Margaret Errington, Alun Foulkes, Peter Francis, Bill Gardner, Arthur Green, James Greenwood, Tony Griffiths, Rob Grillo, Ian Hallett, Norman Harvey, David Herbert, Phil Hiscox, Stephen Hosmer, Frank Hunt, Robert Hurst, David Jarrett, Geoff Jenkins, Dennis Johnson, David Johnson, Neil Johnson, Philip Jones, Graham Jones, Neil Juggins, Brian King, Russell Lax, Paul Lenaghan, Phil Lewis, David Lumley, David Marsay, Adrian Marson, Chris McCullough, Mark McIntyre, Warren McMahon, Peter Miles, Mervyn Miles, Jim Milner, Phil Mitcham, Andrew Moffat, Andy Molden, John Mugridge, David Munday, Jane Phillips, Michael Piatek, Phil Platt, Derrick Procter, Hilary Redmond, Brian Redmond, Philip Rhodes, Paul Rivers, Mark Rozzier, Richard Rundle, Mike Sampson, Del Saunders, Trevor Scorah, John Shenton, Bob Sinclair, Jim Stanway, Mike Stokes, Rob Sutherland, Trevor Syms, Mel Thomas, David Ward, Alan Watkins, Jon Weaver, Scott White, Jim Wicks, Chris Wight, David Wilcox, Mike Wilson, Jeff Worrall

SOME CONVENTIONS USED WITHIN THIS BOOK

Results grids

W-L: Points awarded to home side
L-W: Points awarded to away side
n/a: Game not scheduled, or not played due to one side having withdrawn
M: Scoreline awarded by management committee
(e.g. 0M0 denotes a goalless draw awarded for an unplayed game)

Some standard abbreviations

aet: after extra time
INT: Intermediate
INV: Invitation
OB: Old Boys
PF: Playing Field or Playing Fields
Res.: Reserves
Rgrs: Rangers
Utd: United
Wdrs: Wanderers

Inter-league movement

Promoted/relegated clubs are listed in alphabetical preference with abbreviations showing the origin of the move:-
(E) – Expelled; (F) – Folded; (P) – Promoted; (R) – Relegated; (S) – Switched;
(W) – Withdrew after season ended;
(WN) – Withdrew playing no games;
(WS) – Withdrew during the course of the season

League tables

All tables are final.
Total points and goal adjustments (eg -2g) are shown before the playing record.

Order of entries

The leagues in this book appear alphabetically.

Cup competitions

Penalty shoot-out scores are indicated in parentheses, the first listed side's score preceding the second listed side.
So (3-4p) means the second listed side won 4-3 on penalties.
Some Welsh cup results are only recorded after penalties and are denoted as such.

Sponsors

Sponsors names have been dropped.
This is for alphabetical ease of reference, and historical continuity only.
Non-League football is indebted to its many sponsors, and their generosity is recognised in a separate section starting at page 274.

CAPITAL COUNTIES FEEDER LEAGUES TROPHY

For Isthmian feeder clubs not entered in the FA Vase
Sponsored by Anagram Records – part of Cherry Red

FIRST ROUND

Bedmond Sports & Social 4 MK Scot 0
Buntingford Town 3 Markyate 0
Chipperfield Corinthians 0 **Spelthorne Sports** 1
Sandridge Rovers (w/o) v Winslow United (scr.)
Sheerwater 1 **Bushey Rangers** 3
Sun Postal Sports 3 **Hinton** 3 *aet* (3-4p)
The 61 FC (Luton) 1 Farleigh Rovers 0
Wormley Rovers 3 Amersham Town 0 *aet*

SECOND ROUND

Bethnal Green United 4 The 61 FC (Luton) 2
Codicote 2 Buntingford Town 1
Crown & Manor 4 Little Munden 2
Epping 2 Kent Athletic 2 *aet* (4-3p)
Evergreen 0 **Frenford Senior** 5
Feltham 2 London Lions 1 *aet*
Hadley 3 Bushey Rangers 0
Manford Way 3 Bedmond Sports & Social 0
Metropolitan Police Bushey 1 **Brache Sparta** 2
Sandridge Rovers 1 Hinton 0
Spelthorne Sports 4 Hatfield Town 3
Takeley 3 Walthamstow Avenue & Pennant 1
White Ensign 2 New Bradwell St Peter 1
White Notley 4 Elliott Star 2
Whitewebbs 1 Stony Stratford Town 0
Wormley Rovers 0 **London Tigers** 2

THIRD ROUND

Codicote 0 **Epping** 3
Feltham 1 **White Ensign** 2
Hadley 2 Frenford Senior 0
London Tigers 0 **Manford Way** 4
Sandridge Rovers 4 Bethnal Green United 3
Spelthorne Sports 0 **Crown & Manor** 0 *aet* (3-4p)
White Notley 3 Brache Sparta 1
Whitewebbs 2 Takeley 1

QUARTER-FINALS

Crown & Manor 0 **White Notley** 2
Epping 0 **Manford Way** 3
Hadley 2 **White Ensign** 4 *aet*
Whitewebbs 2 Sandridge Rovers 2 *aet* (4-1p)

SEMI-FINALS

Manford Way 2 Whitewebbs 2 *aet* (3-2p)
White Ensign 3 White Notley 1 *aet*

FINAL

(April 17th at Welwyn Garden City)
White Ensign 1 Manford Way 0

AMATEUR FOOTBALL ALLIANCE

AMATEUR COMBINATION

	Albanian	Bealonians	Hale End Athletic	Honourable Artillery Company	Latymer Old Boys	Old Aloysians	Old Hamptonians	Old Meadonians	Parkfield	UCL Academicals
Albanian		1-1	3-1	2-1	2-2	1-0	2-0	1-5	2-0	2-1
Bealonians	2-1	*P*	0-2	3-3	3-0	4-0	3-3	0-4	0-1	2-0
Hale End Athletic	1-3	0-1	*R*	2-7	3-1	1-4	0-1	0-5	1-0	0-5
Honourable Artillery Company	7-1	3-0	2-1	*E*	9-0	0-0	1-1	1-2	5-0	6-0
Latymer Old Boys	3-4	0-0	1-4	2-4	*M*	0-3	0-5	1-5	2-2	0-3
Old Aloysians	2-4	1-2	3-2	0-3	7-1		0-5	2-5	2-4	2-1
Old Hamptonians	2-1	0-1	2-1	2-1	7-1	3-0	*D*	0-0	3-0	4-3
Old Meadonians	2-2	0-0	0-0	2-2	11-3	1-0	1-0	*I*	5-0	1-1
Parkfield	2-1	1-4	3-0	1-4	5-0	2-2	1-2	1-2	*V*	0-2
UCL Academicals	1-2	2-0	1-2	0-3	1-2	2-0	1-2	1-2	1-1	

Premier Division		P	W	D	L	F	A	Pts
Old Meadonians		18	12	6	0	53	15	42
Old Hamptonians		18	12	3	3	42	17	39
Honourable Artillery Company		18	11	4	3	62	19	37
Albanian		18	10	3	5	35	33	33
Bealonians		18	8	5	5	26	22	29
Parkfield		18	5	3	10	24	38	18
UCL Academicals		18	5	2	11	26	31	17
Old Aloysians		18	5	2	11	28	41	17
Hale End Athletic		18	5	1	12	21	42	16
Latymer Old Boys	*-3*	18	1	3	14	19	78	3

Senior Division One	P	W	D	L	F	A	Pts
Southgate County	18	12	3	3	51	26	39
Old Parmiterians	18	11	5	2	41	18	38
Enfield Old Grammarians	18	11	4	3	44	23	37
Glyn Old Boys	18	9	2	7	46	30	29
Old Salvatorians	18	8	5	5	43	36	29
Old Danes	18	6	6	6	24	34	24
Wood Green Old Boys	18	5	2	11	26	40	17
Old Tiffinians	18	4	3	11	22	38	15
Old Wokingians	18	4	2	12	27	45	14
Old Ignatian	18	3	2	13	16	50	11

Senior Division Two	P	W	D	L	F	A	Pts
Sinjuns Grammarians	20	15	3	2	71	32	48
Old Challoners	20	14	3	3	50	26	45
Economicals	20	13	2	5	56	30	41
Old Suttonians	20	12	4	4	54	36	40
Clapham Old Xaverians	20	11	2	7	45	32	35
Shene Old Grammarians	20	9	4	7	50	47	31
Old Vaughanians	20	6	2	12	31	44	20
Old Aloysians Res.	20	4	4	12	35	49	16
Old Dorkinians	20	3	4	13	38	57	13
Old Tenisonians	20	2	6	12	39	58	12
Old Isleworthians	20	2	4	14	22	80	10

Senior Division Three North		P	W	D	L	F	A	Pts
Old Meadonians Res.		18	12	3	3	46	21	39
Old Salvatorians Res.		18	12	3	3	50	27	39
Albanian Res.		18	12	1	5	50	32	37
UCL Academicals Res.		18	11	2	5	40	20	35
Hale End Athletic Res.		18	9	3	6	50	36	30
Old Minchendenians		18	6	5	7	48	49	23
Old Manorians		18	6	3	9	32	42	21
Parkfield Res.		18	4	3	11	37	42	15
Old Buckwellians		18	4	2	12	29	54	14
Pegasus	*-1*	18	1	1	16	16	75	3

Senior Division Three South	P	W	D	L	F	A	Pts
Kings Old Boys	20	14	4	2	65	26	46
Old Paulines	20	11	4	5	54	34	37
Wandsworth Borough	20	11	4	5	52	38	37
Old Hamptonians Res.	20	9	4	7	35	35	31
Hampstead Heathens	20	7	7	6	40	39	28
Fitzwilliam Old Boys	20	8	4	8	40	41	28
Old Guildfordians	20	8	3	9	34	37	27
John Fisher Old Boys	20	8	2	10	41	48	26
Reigatians	20	5	4	11	35	42	19
Queen Mary Coll. Old Boys	20	5	2	13	29	42	17
Old Sedcopians	20	4	2	14	27	70	14

(Lower divisions in "Other Leagues" section – page 230)

ARTHURIAN LEAGUE

	Lancing Old Boys	Old Bradfieldians	Old Brentwoods	Old Carthusians	Old Chigwellians	Old Etonians	Old Foresters	Old Harrovians	Old Reptonians	Old Salopians
Lancing Old Boys		5-2	1-1	2-5	4-0	0-3	3-1	2-4	3-0	1-1
Old Bradfieldians	1-4	*P*	0-1	0-8	3-0	4-5	1-2	0-4	3-2	2-6
Old Brentwoods	3-0	2-1	*R*	1-4	7-1	2-1	2-1	1-6	5-0	1-5
Old Carthusians	2-1	4-1	2-1	*E*	6-0	3-1	3-0	4-1	4-1	3-2
Old Chigwellians	0-2	0-3	0-3	0-8	*M*	2-4	1-2	2-3	2-2	1-1
Old Etonians	2-2	6-0	0-3	0-0	5-0		1-0	2-2	4-0	4-1
Old Foresters	2-3	7-2	1-1	3-2	0-1	2-5	*D*	3-0	5-2	5-3
Old Harrovians	3-0	8-0	2-1	5-3	7-0	1-2	7-0	*I*	5-0	0-3
Old Reptonians	2-2	1-0	1-1	2-4	6-3	1-6	3-3	0-7	*V*	2-2
Old Salopians	1-1	0-0	0-0	1-3	3-1	1-1	3-3	3-5	6-0	

Premier Division		P	W	D	L	F	A	Pts
Old Carthusians		18	15	1	2	68	22	46
Old Harrovians		18	13	1	4	70	26	40
Old Etonians		18	11	4	3	52	24	37
Old Brentwoods		18	9	4	5	36	26	31
Lancing Old Boys		18	7	5	6	36	33	26
Old Foresters		18	7	3	8	40	43	24
Old Salopians		18	5	8	5	42	33	23
Old Reptonians	*-3*	18	2	5	11	25	65	8
Old Bradfieldians	*-3*	18	3	1	14	23	65	7
Old Chigwellians		18	1	2	15	14	69	5

Division One		P	W	D	L	F	A	Pts
Old Westminsters		14	9	3	2	40	24	30
Old Cholmeleians		14	9	0	5	29	23	27
Old Aldenhamians		14	7	4	3	40	27	25
Old Wykehamists		14	5	5	4	23	19	20
Old Malvernians		14	4	3	7	23	29	15
Old Haileyburians		14	2	7	5	23	27	13
Old Tonbridgians	*-3*	14	4	1	9	29	41	10
Old Haberdashers	*-18*	14	4	1	9	24	41	-5

Division Two		P	W	D	L	F	A	Pts
Old Salopians Res.		16	10	2	4	49	29	32
Old Foresters Res.		16	10	2	4	46	29	32
Old Etonians 'C'		16	9	2	5	31	26	29
Old Chigwellians Res.		16	7	3	6	38	28	24
Old Carthusians Res.		16	7	3	6	35	29	24
Old Etonians Res.		16	5	5	6	25	39	20
Old Westminsters Res.		16	5	2	9	30	41	17
Old Carthusians 'C'		16	5	1	10	20	40	16
Old Cholmeleians Res.	*-3*	16	3	2	11	21	34	8

Division Three	P	W	D	L	F	A	Pts
Old Brentwoods Res.	12	9	1	2	43	18	28
Old Radleians	12	8	2	2	33	16	26
Old Bradfieldians Res.	12	6	1	5	29	30	19
Old Wellingtonians	12	4	2	6	25	33	14
Old Aldenhamians Res.	12	4	2	6	26	36	14
Lancing Old Boys Res.	12	2	4	6	23	33	10
Old Brentwoods 'C'	12	1	4	7	16	29	7

Division Four		P	W	D	L	F	A	Pts
Old Chigwellians 'C'		14	10	2	2	33	16	32
Old Oundelians		14	8	1	5	32	17	25
Old Foresters 'C'		14	8	1	5	32	22	25
Old Malvernians Res.	*-3*	14	7	2	5	30	29	20
Old Eastbournians		14	6	1	7	29	23	19
Old Brentwoods 'B'		14	5	2	7	25	21	17
Old Berkhamstedians		14	5	1	8	29	36	16
Old Cholmeleians 'C'		14	1	2	11	11	57	5

Division Five		P	W	D	L	F	A	Pts
Old Westminsters 'C'		15	9	2	4	31	21	29
Old Harrovians Res.		15	7	4	4	30	32	25
Old Chigwellians 'B'		15	6	5	4	24	14	23
Old Wykehamists Res.	*-3*	15	8	1	6	32	25	22
Old Foresters 'B'		15	5	2	8	25	25	17
Old Cholmeleians 'B'	*-9*	15	2	2	11	20	45	-1

SOUTHERN AMATEUR LEAGUE

	Broomfield	Civil Service	E. Barnet Old Gramms	Nottsborough	Old Actonians Assoc.	Old Esthameians	Old Lyonians	Old Owens	Old Salesians	West Wickham	Winchmore Hill
Broomfield	*S*	0-2	3-1	0-2	0-0	3-3	3-1	2-0	2-1	0-7	2-1
Civil Service	5-2	*E*	2-2	0-2	1-1	4-5	1-1	0-4	1-2	0-1	0-2
East Barnet Old Grammarians	0-0	1-6	*N*	0-2	1-0	3-0	5-2	1-3	3-1	1-1	0-2
Nottsborough	0-0	4-0	4-2	*I*	5-1	3-3	3-1	2-1	1-0	2-2	2-1
Old Actonians Association	1-1	1-1	0-1	0-4	*O*	1-1	6-2	0-5	4-3	0-1	0-2
Old Esthameians	0-2	1-1	1-1	0-2	1-1	*R*	1-1	0-2	1-1	1-1	2-3
Old Lyonians	1-0	3-5	0-3	2-1	2-1	1-2		1-3	1-0	0-3	0-1
Old Owens	5-0	2-1	1-0	2-0	4-0	6-0	1-2		1-2	3-1	3-2
Old Salesians	2-2	2-1	1-1	3-3	2-0	2-0	3-1	2-2	*O*	0-1	0-3
West Wickham	2-4	3-0	4-1	1-1	2-1	3-0	4-0	1-0	1-1	*N*	0-0
Winchmore Hill	1-0	1-0	1-0	1-0	2-0	1-1	1-0	2-3	4-0	0-2	*E*

Senior Division One	P	W	D	L	F	A	Pts
Old Owens	20	14	1	5	51	19	43
West Wickham	20	12	6	2	41	15	42
Nottsborough	20	12	5	3	43	20	41
Winchmore Hill	20	13	2	5	31	15	41
Broomfield	20	7	6	7	26	35	27
Old Salesians	20	6	6	8	28	33	24
East Barnet Old Grammarians	20	6	5	9	27	34	23
Civil Service	20	4	5	11	31	40	17
Old Lyonians	20	5	2	13	22	47	17
Old Esthameians	20	2	10	8	23	42	16
Old Actonians Association	20	2	6	12	18	41	12

Senior Division Two	P	W	D	L	F	A	Pts
Alleyn Old Boys	20	12	2	6	48	26	38
Old Wilsonians	20	11	5	4	38	26	38
Norsemen	20	11	3	6	44	24	36
Ibis	20	11	2	7	51	42	35
Carshalton	20	8	6	6	46	41	30
Bank of England	20	7	5	8	31	33	26
Weirside Rangers	20	7	5	8	37	41	26
Polytechnic	20	7	4	9	36	39	25
HSBC	20	7	4	9	24	31	25
South Bank Cuaco	20	4	3	13	33	53	15
Old Finchleians	20	4	3	13	28	60	15

Senior Division Three	P	W	D	L	F	A	Pts
Merton	20	13	3	4	58	26	42
BB Eagles	20	11	7	2	55	27	40
Alexandra Park	20	12	3	5	59	35	39
Old Westminster Citizens	20	10	6	4	44	37	36
Old Parkonians	20	9	5	6	50	38	32
Crouch End Vampires	20	8	3	9	38	45	27
Old Stationers	20	7	4	9	46	52	25
Old Latymerians	20	7	2	11	27	43	23
Lloyds TSB Bank	20	6	3	11	39	62	21
Kew Association	20	3	3	14	28	59	12
Southgate Olympic	20	2	5	13	25	45	11

Intermediate Division One		P	W	D	L	F	A	Pts
Old Actonians Assoc. Res.		20	11	5	4	50	29	38
Old Owens Res.		20	11	5	4	43	29	38
E. Barnet Old Gramms Res.		20	10	2	8	50	41	32
Winchmore Hill Res.		20	9	4	7	34	30	31
Polytechnic Res.		20	8	5	7	46	47	29
Nottsborough Res.		20	7	7	6	46	34	28
Civil Service Res.		20	8	4	8	26	29	28
Old Finchleians Res.		20	6	4	10	41	50	22
West Wickham Res.		20	5	7	8	30	40	22
Norsemen Res.		20	4	6	10	31	50	18
Old Esthameians Res.	-2	20	4	5	11	35	53	15

Intermediate Division Two	P	W	D	L	F	A	Pts
Old Wilsonians Res.	20	14	4	2	48	21	46
HSBC Res.	20	12	3	5	46	41	39
Carshalton Res.	20	10	3	7	47	37	33
BB Eagles Res.	20	9	4	7	40	33	31
Old Salesians Res.	20	8	5	7	40	37	29
Weirside Rangers Res.	20	7	4	9	38	38	25
Bank of England Res.	20	6	5	9	31	41	23
Alleyn Old Boys Res.	20	6	4	10	38	45	22
Merton Res.	20	3	11	6	25	29	20
Alexandra Park Res.	20	5	5	10	34	44	20
Old Stationers Res.	20	2	8	10	32	53	14

Intermediate Division Three		P	W	D	L	F	A	Pts
Old Westminster Citizens Res.		20	13	4	3	76	32	43
Broomfield Res.		20	12	3	5	49	46	39
South Bank Cuaco Res.		20	11	5	4	52	30	38
Old Parkonians Res.		20	10	4	6	49	34	34
Southgate Olympic Res.		20	9	4	7	49	42	31
Old Latymerians Res.		20	9	3	8	46	50	30
Old Lyonians Res.		20	7	4	9	31	28	25
Ibis Res.		20	7	1	12	39	53	22
Crouch End Vampires Res.		20	6	3	11	47	61	21
Lloyds TSB Bank Res.		20	4	2	14	28	67	14
Kew Association Res.	-7	20	4	3	13	26	49	8

(Lower divisions in "Other Leagues" section – page 248)

AMATEUR FOOTBALL ALLIANCE SENIOR CUP

QUALIFYING ROUND

Alleyn Old Boys 4 Hampstead Heathens 0
Bank of England 4 Lancing Old Boys 0
Carshalton 5 Queen Mary College Old Boys 0
Honourable Artillery Company 6 Old Vaughanians 2
Ibis 0 **West Wickham** 2
London Welsh 2 **Old Manorians** 4
Merton 0 **Albanian** 3
Old Addeyans 2 **Old Actonians Association** 3
Old Buckwellians 3 **Old Parmiterians** 5
Old Edmontonians 0 **South Bank Cuaco** 1
Old Esthameians 3 Mount Pleasant Post Office 2
Old Ignatian 2 **Alexandra Park** 3
Old Latymerians 2 Crouch End Vampires 2 *aet* (4-1p)
Old Lyonians 1 **HSBC** 4
Old Parkonians 0 **Old Challoners** 2
Old Salopians 3 **Old Suttonians** 2
(Old Salopians expelled)
Old Tenisonians 1 **Old Camdenians** 2
Old Uxonians 2 **East Barnet Old Grammarians** 5
Old Westminster Citizens 3 **Old Tiffinians** 4
Old Woodhouseians 2 Hale End Athletic 1
Parkfield 2 Kew Association 0
University of Hertfordshire 2 **Cardinal Manning Old Boys** 6
Wandsworth Borough 1 **Enfield Old Grammarians** 5
Weirside Rangers 3 Old Minchendenians 2
Winchmore Hill 3 Latymer Old Boys 0

FIRST ROUND

Alleyn Old Boys 4 Glyn Old Boys 0
Bank of England 2 Brent 0
BB Eagles 1 **Southgate Olympic** 2
Bradfield Old Boys 0 **Civil Service** 5
Centymca 1 Old Actonians Association 0
Chislehurst Sports 1 **William Fitt** 3
Enfield Old Grammarians (w/o) v Old Chigwellians (scr.)
Lloyds TSB Bank 2 **Broomfield** 6
Norsemen 7 Old Manorians 2
Nottsborough 4 Bealonians 1
Old Aloysians 3 Old Latymerians 2
Old Camdenians 1 **Bromleians Sports** 3
Old Challoners 0 **Polytechnic** 1
Old Danes 0 **South Bank Cuaco** 3
Old Esthameians 6 Old Sedcopians 1
Old Foresters 2 **Old Brentwoods** 8
Old Guildfordians 4 Cardinal Manning Old Boys 2
Old Hamptonians 5 Old Wokingians 1
Old Isleworthians 3 Old Stationers 2
Old Meadonians 2 Alexandra Park 0
Old Parmiterians 0 **Albanian** 3
Old Reptonians 2 **Old Wilsonians** 4
Old Salesians 0 **Old Owens** 1 *aet*
Old Suttonians 1 Carshalton 0
Old Woodhouseians 0 **Wake Green Amateurs** 4
Sinjuns Grammarians 3 **East Barnet Old Grammarians** 4
Southgate County 6 Old Tiffinians 3
UCL Academicals 2 HSBC 0
Weirside Rangers 4 Old Salvatorians 2
West Wickham 3 Honourable Artillery Company 2
Winchmore Hill 4 Parkfield 1
Wood Green Old Boys 4 **Old Finchleians** 5

SECOND ROUND

Albanian 3 **Polytechnic** 5
Alleyn Old Boys 5 **East Barnet Old Grammarians** 6 *aet*
Bank of England 1 **Wake Green Amateurs** 2
Bromleians Sports 2 Nottsborough 1
Broomfield 2 UCL Academicals 1
Centymca 0 **West Wickham** 4
Enfield Old Grammarians 1 **Winchmore Hill** 3
Norsemen 1 Civil Service 1 *aet* (4-2p)
Old Esthameians 2 Old Brentwoods 1
Old Finchleians 0 **Old Owens** 4
Old Hamptonians 2 Old Guildfordians 0
Old Isleworthians 1 **William Fitt** 2
Old Meadonians 2 Old Aloysians 1
Old Wilsonians 2 Weirside Rangers 2 *aet* (3-2p)
South Bank Cuaco 1 Southgate Olympic 1 *aet* (5-4p)
Southgate County 2 Old Suttonians 0

THIRD ROUND

Broomfield 2 **East Barnet Old Grammarians** 2 *aet* (2-4p)
Norsemen 0 **West Wickham** 4
Old Meadonians 3 Bromleians Sports 1
Polytechnic 3 Old Hamptonians 2
South Bank Cuaco 4 Old Wilsonians 1
Wake Green Amateurs 5 Southgate County 0
William Fitt 1 **Old Owens** 3
Winchmore Hill 4 Old Esthameians 1

QUARTER-FINALS

Old Meadonians 4 East Barnet Old Grammarians 1
Polytechnic 2 **Wake Green Amateurs** 3
South Bank Cuaco 0 **Old Owens** 2
West Wickham 0 **Winchmore Hill** 1

SEMI-FINALS
(both at HSBC)

Old Meadonians 1 **Old Owens** 1 *aet* (2-4p)
Wake Green Amateurs 0 **Winchmore Hill** 4

FINAL
(April 8th at Norsemen)

Winchmore Hill 1 Old Owens 0

ANGLIAN COMBINATION

	Acle United	Attleborough Town	Beccles Town	Blofield United	Brandon Town	Cromer Town	Gorleston Res.	Halvergate United	Lowestoft Town Res.	North Walsham Town	Norwich Union	Sheringham	Sprowston Athletic	St Andrews	Watton United	Wroxham Res.
Acle United	*P*	4-1	3-1	3-0	2-1	3-6	5-3	2-0	3-2	5-2	6-0	2-1	5-1	2-1	3-2	2-3
Attleborough Town	0-1	*R*	1-3	0-3	2-2	2-4	2-2	2-4	1-3	5-3	1-1	5-2	3-2	8-2	2-3	4-2
Beccles Town	3-2	2-1	*E*	0-1	1-2	1-1	2-3	0-1	0-2	6-1	5-0	3-2	8-1	6-0	3-1	6-1
Blofield United	2-1	3-0	4-1	*M*	3-1	1-1	5-0	4-1	2-0	3-3	6-0	2-1	0-1	6-2	4-1	5-1
Brandon Town	4-0	2-0	1-1	2-5	*I*	4-2	3-0	0-0	1-0	3-1	4-2	1-3	3-2	3-0	3-0	3-2
Cromer Town	2-0	5-0	6-0	3-2	2-2	*E*	3-2	1-1	3-2	3-0	4-0	1-1	4-2	7-0	8-1	2-1
Gorleston Res.	1-3	2-0	0-2	1-6	0-2	0-8	*R*	1-5	1-4	2-2	4-2	1-5	1-2	4-3	0-3	2-0
Halvergate United	2-4	3-1	3-2	3-3	0-1	2-4	6-0		2-0	2-1	2-1	0-1	4-0	2-0	1-1	2-0
Lowestoft Town Res.	3-3	2-2	1-2	0-2	1-1	1-2	6-3	2-0	*D*	4-1	1-3	3-1	2-2	2-1	9-0	4-2
North Walsham Town	1-1	1-4	1-1	0-5	4-3	0-2	5-0	0-3	0-2	*I*	1-0	1-2	3-5	2-1	0-2	2-1
Norwich Union	0-1	3-1	2-0	0-10	1-4	1-1	1-0	1-2	3-0	3-2	*V*	0-2	0-2	3-0	2-0	2-1
Sheringham	3-1	6-1	6-0	3-4	1-1	2-2	2-1	1-1	1-3	5-1	5-0	*I*	2-2	1-2	3-5	5-3
Sprowston Athletic	4-3	3-0	2-2	2-5	2-2	2-4	4-5	5-2	3-1	3-6	1-2	5-5	*S*	3-0	2-4	3-3
St Andrews	0-3	1-1	1-0	1-1	2-2	2-6	2-0	0-1	0-0	1-0	1-1	1-1	0-0	*I*	3-0	2-1
Watton United	2-3	1-2	0-1	2-2	1-2	1-5	1-5	2-2	1-1	1-9	0-1	1-4	1-6	3-1	*O*	1-1
Wroxham Res.	1-4	2-1	1-2	1-3	3-2	3-5	3-1	2-0	2-3	0-2	4-0	0-1	1-0	2-1	5-4	*N*

Premier Division		P	W	D	L	F	A	Pts
Cromer Town		30	22	7	1	107	39	73
Blofield United		30	22	5	3	102	35	71
Acle United		30	20	2	8	80	52	62
Brandon Town		30	16	8	6	65	43	56
Halvergate United		30	15	6	9	57	42	51
Sheringham		30	14	7	9	78	53	49
Beccles Town		30	14	4	12	64	51	46
Lowestoft Town Res.		30	13	6	11	64	48	45
Sprowston Athletic		30	10	7	13	72	81	37
Norwich Union		30	11	3	16	35	71	36
Wroxham Res.		30	9	2	19	52	74	29
North Walsham Town		30	8	4	18	55	78	28
Attleborough Town		30	7	5	18	53	77	26
St Andrews		30	6	7	17	31	71	25
Watton United		30	6	5	19	45	93	23
Gorleston Res.	*-3*	30	7	2	21	45	97	20

MUMMERY CUP

(Premier and Division One teams)

FIRST ROUND

Beccles Town 3 Gorleston Res. 0
Brandon Town 6 Mattishall 4
Cromer Town 5 Halvergate United 3
Dereham Town Res. 3 Dersingham Rovers 0 *aet*
Hempnall 1 **North Walsham Town** 3
Hindringham 1 **Blofield United** 2
Holt United 2 Wroxham Res. 1
Horsford United 1 **Scole United** 2
Lowestoft Town Res. 6 Watton United 1
Mulbarton United 2 Attleborough Town 1
Sheringham 3 Sprowston Wanderers 2
Sprowston Athletic 3 Loddon United 1
St Andrews 2 Aylsham Wanderers 1
Stalham Town 1 Acle United 1 *aet* (4-2p)
Wells Town (scr.) v **Norwich Union** (w/o)
Wymondham Town 1 **Southwold Town** 3

ANGLIAN COMBINATION PREMIER DIVISION CONSTITUTION 2006-07

ACLE UNITED .... Bridewell Lane, Acle, Norwich NR13 3RA 01493 751379
ATTLEBOROUGH TOWN............ Recreation Ground, Station Road, Attleborough NR17 2AS 01953 455365
BECCLES TOWN .... College Meadow, Beccles NR34 7FA 07729 782817
BLOFIELD UNITED.............................. Old Yarmouth Road, Blofield, Norwich NR13 4LE.............................. 01603 712576
BRANDON TOWN .... Remembrance Playing Field, Church Road, Brandon IP27 0JB.............................. 01842 813177
CROMER TOWN.............................. Cabbell Park, Mill Road, Cromer NR27 0AD 01263 512185
DERSINGHAM ROVERS ...... Behind Feathers Hotel, Manor Road, Dersingham, King's Lynn PE31 6LN.............................. 01485 542707
HALVERGATE UNITED.............................. Playing Field, Wickhampton Road, Halvergate NR13 3BQ.............................. 01493 700349
LOWESTOFT TOWN RESERVES......... Crown Meadow, Love Road, Lowestoft NR32 2PA 01502 573818
MATTISHALL .... Mattishall Playing Fields, South Green, Mattishall, Norwich NR20 3JY 01362 850246
NORTH WALSHAM TOWN........... Sports Centre, Greens Road, North Walsham NR28 0HW.............................. 01692 406888
NORWICH UNION .... Pinebanks, White Farm Lane, Harvey Lane, Thorpe 01603 434457
SHERINGHAM .... Weybourne Road, Sheringham NR26 8WD 01263 824804
SPROWSTON ATHLETIC... Sprowston Sports & Social Club, Blue Boar Lane, Sprowston, Norwich NR7 8RJ 01603 427688
ST ANDREWS............. Thorpe Recreation Ground, Laundry Lane, Thorpe St Andrew, Thorpe NR7 0XQ 01603 300316
WROXHAM .... Trafford Park, Skinners Lane, Wroxham NR12 8SJ 01603 783538

IN: Dersingham Rovers (P), Mattishall (P)
OUT: Gorleston Reserves (F), Watton United (R)

	Aylsham Wanderers	Dereham Town Res.	Dersingham Rovers	Hempnall	Hindringham	Holt United	Horsford United	Loddon United	Mattishall	Mulbarton United	Scole United	Southwold Town	Sprowston Wanderers	Stalham Town	Wells Town	Wymondham Town
Aylsham Wanderers		1-1	2-6	4-2	1-0	2-1	2-4	2-0	0-5	4-3	3-2	3-7	1-1	3-4	2-3	1-0
Dereham Town Res.	1-2		1-2	0-1	2-0	2-0	0-1	3-1	1-0	0-0	3-0	0-4	0-3	3-2	3-1	0-0
Dersingham Rovers	8-0	3-1	*D*	5-0	3-0	5-0	5-0	3-0	2-1	8-1	3-2	0-2	1-2	3-1	2-2	4-2
Hempnall	0-0	1-0	1-1	*I*	1-2	0-1	5-0	0-0	1-3	2-0	3-0	2-0	2-1	0-0	0-0	1-1
Hindringham	6-0	1-1	4-2	2-1	*V*	8-1	4-0	5-1	3-0	2-1	4-0	1-3	1-2	0-1	0-1	1-1
Holt United	3-1	2-2	3-5	0-2	1-2	*I*	3-2	1-1	0-2	3-1	2-1	1-2	1-2	1-2	2-4	1-1
Horsford United	1-0	2-0	2-5	2-0	3-0	0-3	*S*	0-1	0-0	1-1	0-4	0-2	2-0	0-1	2-3	2-2
Loddon United	2-1	1-1	3-3	3-0	2-2	1-3	1-1	*I*	0-1	4-1	2-1	1-0	3-1	2-2	2-0	2-0
Mattishall	2-2	2-0	3-2	1-0	1-0	4-0	5-1	2-0	*O*	1-0	2-0	3-0	1-1	3-3	0-0	0-0
Mulbarton United	2-1	0-1	3-3	2-1	1-1	2-1	2-0	1-1	0-2	*N*	1-2	2-2	1-4	2-4	0-0	1-0
Scole United	1-5	1-0	1-3	1-1	2-0	1-4	3-0	3-3	0-3	0-2		1-0	2-0	0-4	0-3	0-2
Southwold Town	1-2	4-3	4-2	0-2	1-2	3-0	6-0	4-1	1-1	2-1	0-3	*O*	2-0	2-1	3-0	2-0
Sprowston Wanderers	1-1	1-0	1-0	5-0	2-2	2-0	3-0	2-1	2-2	5-0	1-2	2-0	*N*	4-1	1-1	3-1
Stalham Town	1-1	2-1	0-1	1-3	1-3	0-2	1-1	1-1	1-2	4-3	1-1	1-2	2-5	*E*	1-1	3-0
Wells Town	2-0	3-1	0-2	1-1	3-0	1-1	1-2	0-0	2-0	2-0	2-0	1-2	2-1	3-0		1-3
Wymondham Town	2-1	1-0	2-1	2-1	0-0	4-1	1-1	2-2	1-1	0-0	2-0	2-2	1-1	2-3	2-2	

Division One	P	W	D	L	F	A	Pts
Dersingham Rovers	30	19	4	7	93	44	61
Mattishall	30	17	9	4	53	23	60
Southwold Town	30	18	3	9	63	38	57
Sprowston Wanderers	30	16	7	7	59	33	55
Wells Town	30	13	10	7	45	33	49
Hindringham	30	13	6	11	56	39	45
Loddon United	30	9	12	9	42	46	39
Wymondham Town	30	8	14	8	37	38	38
Hempnall	30	10	8	12	34	38	38
Stalham Town	30	10	8	12	49	55	38
Aylsham Wanderers	30	10	6	14	48	72	36
Holt United	30	9	4	17	42	65	31
Dereham Town Res.	30	8	6	16	31	42	30
Scole United	30	9	3	18	34	59	30
Horsford United	30	8	6	16	30	64	30
Mulbarton United	30	6	8	16	34	61	26

SECOND ROUND

Brandon Town 7 Stalham Town 1
Cromer Town 4 Holt United 1
Dereham Town Res. 3 Southwold Town 2
Lowestoft Town Res. 1 **North Walsham Town** 2
Mulbarton United 2 **Beccles Town** 5
Scole United 0 **Blofield United** 2
Sheringham 0 **Norwich Union** 1
Sprowston Athletic 3 **St Andrews** 3 *aet* (4-5p)

QUARTER-FINALS

Beccles Town 3 St Andrews 0
Blofield United 2 **Dereham Town Res.** 2 *aet* (3-4p)
Brandon Town 5 North Walsham Town 1
Norwich Union 0 **Cromer Town** 4

SEMI-FINALS

Brandon Town 2 Dereham Town Res. 1
Cromer Town 2 Beccles Town 1

FINAL

(April 17th at Wroxham)
Brandon Town 1 **Cromer Town** 1 *aet* (3-4p)

DON FROST MEMORIAL CUP

(Premier Division champions v Mummery Cup holders)

(August 23rd at Norwich United)
Blofield United 1 **Acle United** 2

ANGLIAN COMBINATION DIVISION ONE CONSTITUTION 2006-07

AYLSHAM WANDERERS .... Sir Williams Lane, Aylsham, Norwich NR11 6AN .... None
DEREHAM TOWN RESERVES .... Aldiss Park, Norwich Road, Dereham NR20 3AL 01362 690460
GAYTON UNITED .... Lime Kiln Road, Gayton, King's Lynn PE32 1QB .... None
HEMPNALL .... Bungay Road, Hempnall, Norwich NR15 2NG 01508 498086
HINDRINGHAM .... Wells Road, Hindringham, Fakenham NR21 0PL .... None
HOLT UNITED .... Gaunts Common, Holt, Wimborne BH21 4JN 01263 711217
LODDON UNITED .... George Lane Playing Fields, Loddon, Norwich NR14 6NB 01508 528497
LONG STRATTON .... Manor Road Playing Fields, Long Stratton, Norwich NR15 2XR .... None
MUNDFORD .... The Glebe, Mundford, Thetford IP26 5EJ .... None
SCOLE UNITED .... Ransome Avenue Playing Field, Scole, Diss IP21 4EA 01379 741204
SOUTHWOLD TOWN .... Southwold Common, Southwold .... None
SPROWSTON WANDERERS .... Sprowston Cricket Club, Barkers Lane, Sprowston, Norwich NR7 8QZ 01603 404042
STALHAM TOWN .... Rivers Park, Stepping Stone Lane, Stalham, Norwich NR12 9EP .... None
WATTON UNITED .... Watton Playing Field, Dereham Road, Watton, Thetford IP25 6EZ 01953 881281
WELLS TOWN .... Beach Road, Wells-next-the-Sea NR23 1DR 01328 710907
WYMONDHAM TOWN .... Kings Head Meadow, Wymondham NR18 0LB 01953 607326

***IN:** Gayton United (P), Long Stratton (P), Mundford (P), Watton United (R)*
***OUT:** Dersingham Rovers (P), Horsford United (R), Mattishall (P), Mulbarton United (F)*

	Anglian Windows	Bungay Town	Caister United	Corton	Fakenham Town Res.	Gayton United	Great Yarmouth Town Res.	Hellesdon	Long Stratton	Mundford	Norwich St Johns	Poringland Wanderers	Reepham Town	Swaffham Town Res.	Thorpe Rovers	Wortwell
Anglian Windows		1-0	5-1	1-2	6-1	6-2	2-3	4-0	1-3	0-2	5-4	2-2	0-0	2-2	1-1	4-2
Bungay Town	0-1		4-3	4-0	4-0	1-1	7-1	3-0	1-0	0-2	1-2	0-4	2-2	3-1	2-2	2-1
Caister United	3-2	2-2	*D*	0-2	1-5	4-0	5-2	6-2	1-2	5-1	1-5	2-0	4-1	3-0	2-0	0-0
Corton	2-3	0-0	4-0	*I*	1-3	1-0	1-5	0-1	0-2	0-2	2-2	5-1	4-0	3-2	3-0	0-0
Fakenham Town Res.	0-1	1-0	1-2	2-2	*V*	1-6	3-2	2-1	0-1	5-0	6-1	2-3	3-0	2-1	0-2	2-2
Gayton United	4-2	3-1	1-1	4-0	6-6	*I*	3-0	3-2	1-0	2-1	2-0	2-1	4-3	1-1	1-2	7-4
Great Yarmouth Town Res.	4-0	4-1	2-4	1-3	2-3	0-5	*S*	4-2	0-2	0-1	4-1	4-1	1-1	1-1	1-2	3-1
Hellesdon	1-0	0-2	2-4	2-5	1-0	2-3	4-4	*I*	0-3	1-3	3-1	0-4	2-2	6-1	0-2	1-1
Long Stratton	2-2	1-0	2-1	6-1	4-5	0-6	1-0	4-0	*O*	2-0	0-2	1-2	3-4	3-1	3-0	1-0
Mundford	6-2	2-1	4-2	1-2	7-0	1-0	1-1	2-0	1-0	*N*	2-1	3-1	1-1	5-0	2-0	1-0
Norwich St Johns	1-2	1-0	3-2	1-4	4-1	0-2	2-1	2-0	1-1	4-2		1-5	2-1	4-6	1-3	1-1
Poringland Wanderers	0-0	1-2	2-1	4-0	3-1	2-5	1-3	2-0	1-2	5-0	1-2	*T*	0-3	0-3	5-1	1-1
Reepham Town	2-2	2-1	3-0	1-1	2-3	3-0	3-4	0-4	1-3	0-4	1-3	3-3	*W*	2-1	1-3	1-2
Swaffham Town Res.	1-2	3-2	1-5	2-1	4-2	3-3	1-2	4-4	3-5	0-2	4-2	1-4	3-1	*O*	4-2	0-2
Thorpe Rovers	2-0	4-2	7-1	1-5	3-0	2-2	2-2	0-1	2-1	0-2	1-1	1-3	0-4	4-1		2-2
Wortwell	3-2	3-2	4-3	1-1	2-0	1-0	0-3	3-1	1-2	1-4	1-4	2-0	2-0	1-0	5-3	

Division Two		P	W	D	L	F	A	Pts
Mundford		30	21	2	7	65	36	65
Long Stratton		30	19	2	9	60	38	59
Gayton United		30	17	6	7	79	51	57
Corton		30	13	6	11	55	52	45
Wortwell		30	12	8	10	49	51	44
Poringland Wanderers		30	13	4	13	62	53	43
Anglian Windows		30	12	7	11	61	56	43
Norwich St Johns		30	13	4	13	59	65	43
Caister United		30	13	3	14	69	69	42
Thorpe Rovers		30	12	6	12	54	58	42
Great Yarmouth Town Res.		30	12	5	13	64	64	41
Fakenham Town Res.		30	12	3	15	60	74	39
Bungay Town		30	10	5	15	50	48	35
Reepham Town		30	7	8	15	48	65	29
Swaffham Town Res.	*-3*	30	8	5	17	55	79	26
Hellesdon		30	7	4	19	43	74	25

CYRIL BALLYN CUP

(Division Two, Three, Four, Five and Six first teams and external league reserve sides)

FIRST ROUND

Fakenham Town Res. 3 Thorpe Village 1
Foster Athletic 3 **Thetford Town Res.** 3 *aet* (3-4p)
Great Yarmouth Town Res. 8 Harleston Town 1
Newton Flotman 0 **Downham Town Res.** 1
Norwich United Res. 2 Gayton United 1

SECOND ROUND

Anglian Windows 4 City of Norwich School OBU 3
Beccles Caxton 2 **Kirkley Res. 4**
Bradenham Wanderers 2 **Swaffham Town Res.** 3
Bungay Town 3 **Wortwell** 5
Caister United 1 **Great Yarmouth Town Res.** 3
East Harling 3 Thetford Rovers 3 aet (3-1p)
Easton 3 Morley Village 0
Fakenham Town Res. 2 Norwich St Johns 0
Foulsham 3 Reepham Town 2
Long Stratton 1 **Thorpe Rovers** 2
Martham 2 **Norwich CEYMS** 4
Mundford 2 Thetford Town Res. 1
Necton SSC 2 Downham Town Res. 1

ANGLIAN COMBINATION DIVISION TWO CONSTITUTION 2006-07

ANGLIAN WINDOWS.................. Horsford Manor, Cromer Road, Norwich NR5 8AP 01603 404723
BUNGAY TOWN........................... Maltings Meadow, Ditchingham, Bungay 01986 894028
CAISTER UNITED .... Caister Playing Fields, off Allendale Road, Caister-on-Sea NR30 5ES .... None
CORTON.................................... Village Playing Field, Long Lane, Corton .... None
DOWNHAM TOWN RESERVES ... Memorial Playing Field, Lynn Road, Downham Market PE38 9QG .... None
FAKENHAM TOWN RESERVES .... Clipbush Park, Clipbush Lane, Fakenham NR21 8SW 01366 388424
GREAT YARMOUTH TOWN RESERVES ...Wellesley Road Rec Ground, Sandown Road, Great Yarmouth NR30 1EY 01328 856222
HORSFORD UNITED........................ Holt Road, Horsford NR10 3DN........................ 01493 843373
KIRKLEY RESERVES .... Kirkley Recreation Ground, Walmer Road, Lowestoft NR33 8HZ .... None
NORWICH CEYMS .... Hilltops Sports Centre, Main Road, Swardeston, Norwich NR14 8DU 01502 513549
NORWICH ST JOHNS .... Cringleford Recreation Ground, Oakfields Road, Cringleford 01508 578826
NORWICH UNITED RESERVES ... Plantation Park, off Plantation Road, Blofield, Norwich NR13 4PL .... None
PORINGLAND WANDERERS. . Poringland Memorial Field, The Footpath, Poringland, Norwich NR14 7RF 01603 716963
REEPHAM TOWN.......................... Stimpsons Piece Rec Ground, Reepham, Norwich 01508 495198
THORPE ROVERS .... Dussindale Park, Pound Lane, Thorpe NR7 0SR............................ None
WORTWELL .... Wortwell Playing Field, opposite Bell PH, High Road, Wortwell, Harleston IP20 0HH .... None

IN: Downham Town Reserves (P), Horsford United (R), Kirkley Reserves (P), Norwich CEYMS (P), Norwich United Reserves (P)
OUT: Gayton United (P), Hellesdon (R), Long Stratton (P), Mundford (P), Swaffham Town Reserves (R)

	Acle United Res.	City of Norwich SOBU	Downham Town Res.	Foster Athletic	Harleston Town	Hempnall Res.	Kirkley Res.	Morley Village	Necton SSC	Norwich CEYMS	Norwich United Res.	Oulton Broad & Notleys	South Walsham	Sprowston Athletic Res.	Thetford Town Res.	Thorpe Village
Acle United Res.		9-2	0-1	1-0	3-1	2-1	1-6	4-1	12-0	0-0	2-4	1-1	2-3	6-2	3-0	2-1
City of Norwich SOBU	3-1	*D*	1-3	2-1	5-0	1-0	0-3	2-6	7-1	1-2	1-3	0-2	4-1	4-2	2-2	1-1
Downham Town Res.	1-3	4-0	*I*	1-0	2-1	2-2	1-6	5-2	7-0	0-1	1-0	1-1	2-1	2-2	0-2	6-1
Foster Athletic	3-2	3-1	1-1	*V*	5-2	2-1	0-4	4-5	2-0	1-1	2-1	2-0	2-2	6-0	1-0	4-3
Harleston Town	1-7	2-4	1-2	0-2	*I*	1-6	1-9	1-1	3-4	2-2	0-7	0-3	3-3	1-5	1-2	1-2
Hempnall Res.	3-2	8-2	2-2	6-1	5-0	*S*	0-4	0-5	8-2	0-0	3-1	3-2	4-1	3-5	8-0	3-1
Kirkley Res.	3-2	6-1	5-1	4-0	3-0	4-0	*I*	7-0	3-1	2-0	2-1	6-1	5-1	4-0	1-1	12-0
Morley Village	2-3	1-2	1-9	1-6	3-0	3-2	1-0	*O*	1-4	0-8	1-2	3-0	2-3	2-5	3-3	0-1
Necton SSC	0-4	3-4	0-2	3-5	5-2	0-3	2-13	3-5	*N*	0-7	0-3	3-1	2-1	4-3	0-1	2-3
Norwich CEYMS	2-2	4-2	2-3	3-1	4-0	8-0	1-2	5-2	3-0		3-2	8-1	1-1	2-1	3-4	1-1
Norwich United Res.	2-1	1-1	3-1	2-0	3-2	2-2	0-6	0-0	3-0	4-1	*T*	0-1	6-0	3-0	6-0	1-0
Oulton Broad & Notleys	0-6	2-3	0-3	1-4	4-1	4-1	1-5	3-4	6-2	1-5	1-4	*H*	0-2	1-3	0-1	0-0
South Walsham	1-3	5-5	2-3	1-0	0-2	7-5	0-7	3-5	2-3	0-4	4-3	2-0	*R*	4-1	1-1	1-2
Sprowston Athletic Res.	0-5	1-3	1-5	3-1	4-3	1-4	2-2	4-4	5-1	2-6	0-3	2-3	1-2	*E*	3-0	3-2
Thetford Town Res.	0-1	0-0	2-2	2-1	3-4	4-2	0-7	2-2	4-3	1-4	1-2	8-0	1-2	6-1	*E*	0-1
Thorpe Village	1-1	1-1	1-1	2-1	1-1	1-2	0-4	3-1	4-2	0-4	1-3	0-1	3-0	2-2	0-0	

Norwich United Res. 4 **Poringland Wanderers** 5
Oulton Broad & Notleys 1 **Corton** 2
South Walsham 0 **Hellesdon** 2

THIRD ROUND

Anglian Windows 3 Swaffham Town Res. 2
East Harling 3 Thorpe Rovers 2
Easton 1 **Mundford** 3 *aet*
Fakenham Town Res. 2 Norwich CEYMS 0
Foulsham 2 **Hellesdon** 4
Kirkley Res. 6 Great Yarmouth Town Res. 0
Necton SSC 0 **Poringland Wanderers** 5
Wortwell 2 Corton 1

QUARTER-FINALS

Anglian Windows 2 **Fakenham Town Res.** 3
East Harling 0 **Mundford** 2
Hellesdon 1 **Poringland Wanderers** 2
Kirkley Res. 4 Wortwell 0

SEMI-FINALS

Fakenham Town Res. 1 **Poringland Wanderers** 2
Kirkley Res. 2 Mundford 0 *aet*

FINAL

(May 1st at Norwich United)
Poringland Wanderers 1 Kirkley Res. 0

Division Three		P	W	D	L	F	A	Pts
Kirkley Res.		30	27	2	1	145	19	83
Norwich CEYMS		30	18	7	5	95	36	61
Norwich United Res.		30	19	3	8	75	37	60
Downham Town Res.		30	17	7	6	74	44	58
Acle United Res.		30	17	4	9	91	45	55
Foster Athletic		30	14	3	13	61	55	45
Hempnall Res.	*-3*	30	14	4	12	87	70	43
City of Norwich SOBU		30	12	6	12	65	78	42
Thetford Town Res.		30	10	8	12	51	64	38
Thorpe Village		30	9	9	12	39	61	36
Morley Village		30	10	5	15	67	94	35
South Walsham	*-3*	30	10	5	15	56	82	32
Sprowston Athletic Res.		30	9	4	17	64	94	31
Oulton Broad & Notleys		30	8	3	19	41	83	27
Necton SSC		30	7	0	23	50	127	21
Harleston Town	*-3*	30	2	4	24	37	109	7

ANGLIAN COMBINATION DIVISION THREE CONSTITUTION 2006-07

ACLE UNITED RESERVES .... Bridewell Lane, Acle, Norwich NR13 3RA 01493 751372
BECCLES CAXTON.................. Caxton Meadow, Adj. Beccles Station, Beccles NR34 9QH.................... 01502 712829
BECCLES TOWN RESERVES .... College Meadow, Beccles NR34 7FA.................................... 01502 712221
BRANDON TOWN RESERVES ...... Remembrance Playing Field, Church Road, Brandon IP27 0JB.................... 01842 813177
CITY OF NORWICH SOBU .... Britannia Barracks, Mousehold, Norwich.................................... None
HELLESDON .... Hellesdon Community Centre, Wood View Road, Hellesdon, Norwich NR6 5QB 01603 427675
HEMPNALL RESERVES.................. Bungay Road, Hempnall, Norwich NR15 2NG.................................... 01508 498086
MARTHAM............. Coronation Recreation Ground, Rollesby Road, Martham, Great Yarmouth NR29 4SP 01493 740252
MATTISHALL RESERVES ...... Mattishall Playing Fields, South Green, Mattishall, Norwich NR20 3JY 01362 850246
MORLEY VILLAGE.................. Golf Links Road, Morley St Peter, Wymondham NR18 9SU .... None
OULTON BROAD & NOTLEYS .... Kirkley Recreation Ground, Walmer Road, Lowestoft NR33 8HZ.............................. None
SOUTH WALSHAM.................. The Playing Field, South Walsham.................................... None
SPROWSTON ATHLETIC RESERVES . . .Sprowston Sports & Social Club, Blue Boar Lane, Sprowston, Norwich NR7 8RJ 01603 427688
SWAFFHAM TOWN RESERVES........ Shoemakers Lane, off Cley Road, Swaffham PE37 7NT.................... 01760 722700
THORPE VILLAGE .... Thorpe Recreation Ground, Laundry Lane, Thorpe St Andrew, Norwich NR7 0XQ 01603 300316
WEST LYNN SSC .... West Lynn Sports & Social Club, St Peters Road, West Lynn PE34 3LB 01553 761646

IN: Beccles Caxton (P), Beccles Town Reserves (P), Brandon Town Reserves (P), Hellesdon (R), Martham (P), Mattishall Reserves (P), Swaffham Town Reserves (R)
OUT: Downham Town Reserves (P), Harleston Town (R), Kirkley Reserves (P), Necton SSC (R), Norwich CEYMS (P), Norwich United Reserves (P), Thetford Town Reserves (S – Eastern Counties League Reserve Division North)
Foster Athletic become West Lynn SSC

	Attleborough Town Res.	Beccles Caxton	Beccles Town Res.	Blofield United Res.	Bradenham Wanderers	Brandon Town Res.	Bungay Town Res.	Cromer Town Res.	Halvergate United Res.	Hindringham Res.	Loddon United Res.	Martham	Mattishall Res.	Newton Flotman	Norwich Union Res.	St Andrews Res.
Attleborough Town Res.		0-4	0-1	4-2	1-2	2-3	2-3	3-2	0-4	1-2	2-2	1-1	1-7	0-2	2-2	2-2
Beccles Caxton	3-0	*D*	3-2	3-1	3-0	3-0	3-1	1-1	5-0	2-3	4-1	2-3	2-1	8-2	2-0	5-0
Beccles Town Res.	1-2	1-4	*I*	4-1	3-0	0-3	7-1	3-2	1-0	5-0	2-0	3-5	1-1	3-2	3-3	3-1
Blofield United Res.	3-2	0-4	1-1	*V*	1-1	2-2	4-0	4-2	1-1	1-3	1-3	0-1	0-2	12-1	1-1	3-2
Bradenham Wanderers	0-6	1-2	1-3	3-3	*I*	0-2	7-3	3-0	4-2	3-2	1-3	4-3	0-4	2-0	0-2	1-2
Brandon Town Res.	3-1	0-2	0-1	3-1	6-1	*S*	3-3	4-0	1-0	3-2	4-2	1-2	3-0	1-1	1-0	1-3
Bungay Town Res.	5-3	0-8	2-2	1-6	1-2	2-4	*I*	1-1	3-4	4-0	7-1	0-4	1-5	3-1	1-2	3-1
Cromer Town Res.	5-1	1-4	5-2	1-3	1-1	3-0	3-2	*O*	1-2	1-2	5-2	1-3	4-2	3-0	2-3	1-4
Halvergate United Res.	4-2	3-4	4-0	2-2	0-1	3-8	2-1	2-2	*N*	3-2	1-4	1-0	0-3	1-5	1-0	1-2
Hindringham Res.	3-2	1-1	1-3	3-1	3-3	1-3	6-0	4-5	0-1		4-1	2-3	3-2	5-1	3-3	1-2
Loddon United Res.	5-0	2-3	1-2	3-0	5-1	3-1	0-4	2-1	5-2	2-2		1-1	0-1	1-1	0-3	0-3
Martham	6-1	3-2	4-1	5-0	5-1	4-2	4-0	3-1	3-0	2-2	3-0	*F*	0-2	3-1	0-2	2-1
Mattishall Res.	2-3	2-2	2-2	4-1	2-2	2-1	3-5	5-2	2-0	2-2	4-0	1-2	*O*	1-0	1-0	4-2
Newton Flotman	1-2	0-2	2-3	0-4	2-0	0-3	1-4	3-3	2-7	1-2	1-5	2-3	6-9	*U*	0-1	1-2
Norwich Union Res.	1-2	0-0	1-0	0-1	3-2	2-2	0-1	0-3	5-0	0-2	2-1	2-2	0-4	16-0	*R*	1-4
St Andrews Res.	3-1	0-2	0-2	1-2	1-4	0-1	1-0	0-2	3-1	0-4	0-2	0-4	0-6	0-0	3-2	

Division Four		P	W	D	L	F	A	Pts
Beccles Caxton		**30**	**23**	**4**	**3**	**93**	**29**	**73**
Martham		**30**	**22**	**4**	**4**	**84**	**37**	**70**
Mattishall Res.		**30**	**18**	**5**	**7**	**86**	**45**	**59**
Brandon Town Res.		**30**	**17**	**4**	**9**	**69**	**46**	**55**
Beccles Town Res.		**30**	**16**	**5**	**9**	**65**	**52**	**53**
Hindringham Res.		**30**	**13**	**6**	**11**	**70**	**61**	**45**
Norwich Union Res.		**30**	**11**	**7**	**12**	**57**	**44**	**40**
St Andrews Res.		**30**	**12**	**2**	**16**	**43**	**62**	**38**
Blofield United Res.		**30**	**10**	**7**	**13**	**62**	**63**	**37**
Loddon United Res.		**30**	**11**	**4**	**15**	**57**	**66**	**37**
Bradenham Wanderers		**30**	**10**	**5**	**15**	**51**	**74**	**35**
Halvergate Utd Res.	*-3*	**30**	**11**	**3**	**16**	**52**	**72**	**33**
Bungay Town Res.		**30**	**10**	**3**	**17**	**62**	**90**	**33**
Cromer Town Res.	*-3*	**30**	**10**	**5**	**15**	**64**	**69**	**32**
Attleborough Town Res.		**30**	**7**	**4**	**19**	**49**	**84**	**25**
Newton Flotman		**30**	**3**	**4**	**23**	**39**	**109**	**13**

C S MORLEY

(Anglian Combination club reserve teams)

FINAL

(April 28th at Wroxham)

Brandon Town Res. 3 **Mattishall Res.** 4 *aet*

Division Five		P	W	D	L	F	A	Pts
Thetford Rovers		28	19	4	5	102	43	61
Caister United Res.		28	17	3	8	78	54	54
Wymondham Town Res.		28	15	7	6	58	45	52
Wells Town Res.	*-3*	28	16	6	6	72	33	51
Norwich St Johns Res.		28	11	8	9	55	44	41
Sprowston Wanderers Res.	*-6*	28	13	6	9	63	58	39
Watton United Res.	*-6*	28	14	3	11	53	49	39
North Walsham Town Res.		28	11	3	14	63	70	36
Stalham Town Res.		28	11	1	16	58	74	34
Sheringham Res.	*-6*	28	12	1	15	74	69	31
Aylsham Wanderers Res.	*-3*	28	8	8	12	58	77	29
Scole United Res.	*-6*	28	8	7	13	51	58	25
Mundford Res.		28	6	6	16	49	72	24
Thorpe Village Res.		28	6	4	18	30	88	22
Gayton United Res.	*-18*	28	6	7	15	42	72	7

Division Six		P	W	D	L	F	A	Pts
Foulsham		26	21	3	2	97	28	66
Easton		26	21	2	3	87	29	65
East Harling		26	20	2	4	132	30	62
Dersingham Rovers Res.		26	17	1	8	78	47	52
Mulbarton United Res.	*-3*	26	15	3	8	48	42	45
Norwich CEYMS Res.		26	11	3	12	50	76	36
Wortwell Res.		26	9	6	11	53	59	33
Long Stratton Res.		26	9	6	11	45	64	33
CNSOBU Res.		26	9	3	14	40	58	30
Thorpe Rovers Res.	*-6*	26	8	2	16	47	82	20
Reepham Town Res.		26	5	4	17	35	77	19
Holt United Res.	*-6*	26	6	5	15	44	71	17
Horsford United Res.	*-3*	26	5	3	18	32	75	15
Poringland Wanderers Res.	*-3*	26	3	3	20	33	83	9

Harleston Town Res. – record expunged
Newton Flotman Res. – record expunged

ANGLIAN COMBINATION DIVISION FOUR CONSTITUTION 2006-07

BLOFIELD UNITED RESERVES .... **Old Yarmouth Road, Blofield, Norwich NR13 4LE** **01603 712576**
BRADENHAM WANDERERS .... **Hale Road, Bradenham, Thetford IP25 7RA** .... **None**
BUNGAY TOWN RESERVES .... **Maltings Meadow, Ditchingham, Bungay** **01986 894028**
CAISTER UNITED RESERVES ... **Caister Playing Fields, off Allendale Road, Caister-on-Sea NR30 5ES** .... **None**
CROMER TOWN RESERVES .... **Cabbell Park, Mill Road, Cromer NR27 0AD** **01263 512185**
HALVERGATE UNITED RESERVES .. **Playing Field, Wickhampton Road, Halvergate NR13 3BQ** **01493 700349**
HARLESTON TOWN .... **Rec & Memorial Leisure Centre, Wilderness Lane, Harleston IP20 9DD** **01379 854519**
HINDRINGHAM RESERVES .... **Wells Road, Hindringham, Fakenham NR21 0PL** **01328 878608**
LODDON UNITED RESERVES .... **George Lane Playing Fields, Loddon, Norwich NR14 6NB** **01508 528497**
NECTON SSC .... **Necton Playing Field, Tuns Road, Necton PE37 8EH** .... **None**
NORWICH ST JOHNS RESERVES ... **Cringleford Recreation Ground, Oakfields Road, Cringleford** .... **None**
NORWICH UNION RESERVES .... **Pinebanks, White Farm Lane, Harvey Lane, Thorpe** **01603 434457**
ST ANDREWS RESERVES .. **Thorpe Recreation Ground, Laundry Lane, Thorpe St Andrew, Thorpe NR7 0XQ** **01603 300316**
THETFORD ROVERS .... **Euston Park, Euston, near Thetford** .... **None**
WELLS TOWN RESERVES .... **Beach Road, Wells-next-the-Sea NR23 1DR** **01328 710907**
WYMONDHAM TOWN RESERVES .... **Kings Head Meadow, Wymondham NR18 0LB** **01953 607326**

***IN:** Caister United Reserves (P), Harleston Town (R), Necton SSC (R), Norwich St Johns Reserves (P), Thetford Rovers (P), Wells Town Reserves (P), Wymondham Town Reserves (P)*
***OUT:** Attleborough Town (R), Beccles Caxton (P), Beccles Town Reserves (P), Brandon Town Reserves (P), Martham (P), Mattishall Reserves (P), Newton Flotman (R)*

BEDFORD & DISTRICT LEAGUE

	AFC Kempston Town	Bedford SA	Blunham	Caldecote	Campton	Dunton	Ickwell & Old Warden	Oakley Sports	Riseley Sports	Sandy	Three H'shoes Renhold	Turvey	Westoning Rec. Club	Wilhamstead
AFC Kempston Town		5-0	1-2	0-1	0-3	3-0	2-1	4-1	0-1	4-0	0-0	4-1	2-4	3-2
Bedford SA	0-4	*P*	0-6	1-2	2-4	2-5	1-4	0-0	2-2	2-1	3-2	4-4	2-3	0-1
Blunham	2-3	6-4	*R*	1-2	5-1	5-1	2-1	3-2	1-0	3-2	4-0	1-0	4-0	7-1
Caldecote	1-2	7-1	5-3	*E*	3-3	2-0	2-2	4-0	0-0	4-1	5-4	1-4	2-1	2-1
Campton	3-5	3-3	3-0	0-2	*M*	3-1	2-5	5-3	4-0	4-0	2-1	4-2	2-1	4-3
Dunton	1-1	1-2	1-2	0-3	1-2	*I*	3-3	1-2	2-2	0-1	2-0	3-1	3-0	1-2
Ickwell & Old Warden	2-2	6-1	0-0	1-1	1-1	0-1	*E*	3-0	4-3	3-2	W-L	5-2	3-0	2-2
Oakley Sports	0-4	2-3	2-4	2-3	0-2	4-2	5-3	*R*	2-3	4-2	1-1	1-1	5-1	0-2
Riseley Sports	2-2	1-4	2-4	1-2	4-1	2-1	1-4	3-2		4-1	2-3	1-2	3-0	1-3
Sandy	1-3	0-2	1-4	0-1	1-6	2-0	0-1	4-3	3-1		2-3	1-3	1-2	4-0
Three Horseshoes Renhold	0-2	3-0	W-L	2-2	2-1	1-4	2-6	2-1	1-3	1-1	*D*	1-0	4-2	3-4
Turvey	0-4	1-2	4-2	1-7	0-3	1-3	1-2	1-3	1-1	3-0	4-2	*I*	3-4	1-2
Westoning Recreation Club	1-4	0-1	1-6	2-2	2-0	1-5	1-2	0-4	4-2	2-4	4-4	2-5	*V*	2-4
Wilhamstead	3-1	4-1	1-2	0-1	2-2	1-2	0-2	0-1	3-1	0-2	1-3	2-1	2-1	

BRITANNIA CUP

FIRST ROUND
Ickwell & Old Warden 3 Dunton 2
Oakley Sports 1 **Wilshamstead** 2
Sandy 0 **Caldecote** 5
Three Horseshoes Renhold 1 **Riseley Sports** 2
Turvey 5 Bedford SA 1
Westoning Recreation Club 3 AFC Kempston Town 2

QUARTER-FINALS
Caldecote 3 Riseley Sports 1
Ickwell & Old Warden 0 **Campton** 2 *aet*
Turvey 1 **Westoning Recreation Club** 3
Wilshamstead 5 Blunham 1

SEMI-FINALS
Campton 2 Wilshamstead 1
Westoning Recreation Club 1 **Caldecote** 7

FINAL
(May 1st at Biggleswade United)
Caldecote 3 Campton 0

Premier Division	Ded.	P	W	D	L	F	A	Pts
Caldecote		26	18	6	2	67	33	42
Blunham		26	19	1	6	79	38	39
Ickwell & Old Warden		26	15	7	4	66	37	37
AFC Kempston Town		26	16	4	6	65	32	36
Campton		26	15	4	7	68	49	34
Wilhamstead		26	12	2	12	46	50	26
Three Horseshoes Renhold		26	9	5	12	45	56	23
Dunton		26	9	3	14	44	48	21
Riseley Sports		26	8	5	13	46	56	21
Bedford SA		26	8	4	14	43	77	20
Oakley Sports		26	8	3	15	50	61	19
Turvey		26	7	3	16	47	65	17
Sandy		26	7	1	18	37	63	15
Westoning Rec Club	*-2*	26	6	2	18	41	79	12

Associate Division One	P	W	D	L	F	A	Pts
Caldecote Res.	20	14	4	2	70	31	32
Westoning Recreation Club Res.	20	12	4	4	56	33	28
AFC Kempston Town Res.	20	11	2	7	58	45	24
Blunham Res.	20	10	4	6	48	45	24
Sandy Res.	20	9	3	8	41	39	21
Woburn Res.	20	7	6	7	54	46	20
Ickwell & Old Warden Res.	20	7	3	10	42	52	17
Bedford SA Res.	20	6	5	9	45	62	17
Dunton Res.	20	6	4	10	45	62	16
Wilshamstead Res.	20	5	4	11	60	65	14
Riseley Sports Res.	20	2	3	15	40	79	7

Associate Division Two	Ded.	P	W	D	L	F	A	Pts
Exel United		18	14	3	1	83	30	31
Caldecote 'A'		18	13	1	4	88	29	27
Meppershall Jurassic Res.		18	11	1	6	67	37	23
Stewartby Village		18	10	3	5	50	38	23
Oakley Sports Res.		18	8	4	6	52	44	20
Blue Chip		18	7	5	6	60	50	19
Sandy 'A'		18	5	2	11	48	58	12
Marsh Leys		18	5	0	13	27	78	10
Flitwick Town Res.	*-2*	18	4	2	12	33	74	8
Lidlington United Res.		18	1	3	14	22	92	5

WATSON SHIELD FINAL *(April 28th at Wootton Blue Cross)*
Caldecote Res. 2 AFC Kempston Town Res. 2 *aet* (4-3p)

Division One	Ded.	P	W	D	L	F	A	Pts
Henlow Italians		22	20	2	0	95	15	42
Sharnbrook		22	15	3	4	55	29	33
Luton Borough		22	11	8	3	57	35	30
Bedford Corinthians		22	11	5	6	62	50	27
Flitwick Town		22	7	7	8	53	55	21
Woburn		22	8	4	10	51	51	20
Stevington		22	6	5	11	40	49	17
Reddings Wood		22	5	6	11	40	56	16
Kempston		22	6	4	12	44	74	16
Meppershall Jurassic		22	5	4	13	51	78	14
Denbigh Hall S & S Bletchley	*-2*	22	6	3	13	32	60	13
Campton Res.		22	3	7	12	29	57	13

CENTENARY CUP FINAL
(April 29th at Biggleswade United)
Henlow Italians 2 Bedford Corinthians 1

Division Two	Ded.	P	W	D	L	F	A	Pts
Marston Social		26	19	5	2	95	26	43
Blunham Village		26	19	3	4	89	35	41
Royal Oak Kempston		26	17	5	4	68	32	39
Biggleswade Athletic		26	15	2	9	82	43	32
Marston Shelton Rovers		26	15	1	10	71	49	31
Great Barford		26	14	1	11	57	43	29
Mulberry Bush	*-2*	25	14	2	9	79	49	28
Lidlington United		26	11	1	14	49	65	23
Sugar Loaf Meppershall	*-2*	25	9	6	10	56	48	22
Bedford Albion		26	8	3	15	54	84	19
Twinwoods Thistle		26	7	2	17	52	87	16
Russell Park United		26	5	3	18	46	99	13
Potton Wanderers		26	5	2	19	33	84	12
Newnham Athletic		26	4	2	20	39	126	10

(Mulberry Bush v Sugar Loaf Meppershall not played)

JUBILEE CUP FINAL
(April 29th at Biggleswade United)
Marston Social 2 Biggleswade Athletic 0

BEDFORD & DISTRICT LEAGUE PREMIER DIVISION CONSTITUTION 2006-07

AFC KEMPSTON TOWN .... Hillgrounds Road, Kempston, Bedford MK42 8QU 01234 852346
BEDFORD SA .... Cople Playing Fields, Cople, Bedford MK44 3TP .... None
BLUNHAM .... The Playing Fields, Blunham Road, Moggerhanger, Sandy MK44 3RG .... None
CALDECOTE .... Harvey Close, Upper Caldecote, Biggleswade SG18 9BQ .... None
CAMPTON .... The Recreation Ground, Church Road, Campton SG17 5BN .... None
HENLOW ITALIANS .... Henlow Park, Groveside, Henlow Village SG16 6AW .... None
ICKWELL & OLD WARDEN .... Ickwell Green, Ickwell, Biggleswade SG18 9EF .... None
LUTON OLD BOYS .... Luton Regional Sports Centre, St Thomas's Road, Stopsley, Luton LU2 7XP 01582 453919
MELTIS CORINTHIANS .... Meltis Sports Club, Miller Road, Bedford MK42 9NY 01234 352872
OAKLEY SPORTS .... Oakley Village Sports Centre, Oakley, Bedford MK43 7RG .... None
RISELEY SPORTS .... Gold Street, Riseley MK44 1EG .... None
SANDY .... Recreation Ground, Bedford Road, Sandy SG19 1BW .... None
SHARNBROOK .... Playing Fields, Lodge Road, Sharnbrook MK44 1JP .... None
TURVEY .... Grove Road, Turvey MK43 8EK .... None
WESTONING RECREATION CLUB .... Recreation Ground, Greenfield Road, Westoning MK45 5JP .... None
WILHAMSTEAD .... Jubilee Playing Fields, Bedford Road, Wilshamstead MK45 3HN .... None

IN: Henlow Italians (P), Luton Borough (P), Meltis Corinthians formerly Bedford Corinthians (P), Sharnbrook (P)
OUT: Dunton (F), Three Horseshoes Renhold (R)

CAMBRIDGESHIRE COUNTY LEAGUE

	Cambridge University Press	Cottenham United	Eaton Socon	Fordham	Great Paxton	Great Shelford	Hemingford United	Histon 'A'	Linton Granta	Littleport Town	Newmarket Town Res.	Over Sports	Sawston United	Somersham Town	Waterbeach
Cambridge University Press		3-0	4-1	1-3	8-1	2-5	3-2	1-2	5-3	1-1	3-0	0-3	0-1	4-0	3-1
Cottenham United	3-0		4-0	3-2	2-2	2-0	1-0	3-3	2-0	1-3	4-1	3-5	1-1	4-1	1-4
Eaton Socon	2-3	3-2	*P*	3-1	1-2	2-1	6-1	0-2	5-3	1-3	0-7	1-2	0-8	2-0	1-1
Fordham	2-2	0-3	2-4	*R*	3-1	2-4	4-0	2-0	3-1	0-0	3-1	0-1	0-4	2-2	0-0
Great Paxton	2-4	1-4	1-1	2-3	*E*	3-1	2-2	1-0	6-3	2-4	1-3	0-4	0-2	5-1	2-4
Great Shelford	4-1	1-2	4-1	4-1	0-0	*M*	2-0	2-0	1-0	4-0	1-1	4-0	0-1	4-0	2-0
Hemingford United	1-7	2-8	3-1	2-4	2-5	0-4	*I*	1-6	0-1	1-1	1-1	3-1	0-3	2-0	1-2
Histon 'A'	1-2	2-3	2-1	2-2	0-3	1-4	5-1	*E*	1-0	0-1	3-2	1-3	0-5	2-0	1-1
Linton Granta	0-7	2-5	1-3	0-1	3-1	2-3	1-2	2-1	*R*	1-3	1-0	0-2	2-0	4-5	1-2
Littleport Town	1-2	1-0	3-0	3-0	1-3	1-2	6-2	1-0	3-1		0-1	2-0	1-2	2-0	1-0
Newmarket Town Res.	2-2	1-3	2-3	1-1	2-2	1-0	3-0	1-3	2-1	4-1	*D*	0-2	0-1	3-1	0-0
Over Sports	2-4	1-1	3-0	0-3	1-2	0-1	4-1	2-2	1-1	2-1	4-1	*I*	3-3	5-0	2-1
Sawston United	1-1	3-1	5-2	4-0	3-0	1-4	3-1	8-1	2-0	4-0	5-0	0-3	*V*	3-0	2-0
Somersham Town	1-4	0-2	2-0	2-2	1-1	2-0	3-2	1-2	5-1	2-3	0-2	1-3	0-2		3-0
Waterbeach	2-0	1-1	1-0	2-0	3-0	1-5	2-1	2-4	0-1	2-2	0-0	2-1	0-3	6-2	

Premier Division	P	W	D	L	F	A	Pts
Sawston United	28	22	3	3	80	20	69
Great Shelford	28	19	2	7	67	27	59
Cottenham United	28	16	5	7	69	43	53
Cambridge University Press	28	16	4	8	77	47	52
Over Sports	28	16	4	8	60	38	52
Littleport Town	28	15	4	9	49	38	49
Waterbeach	28	11	7	10	40	40	40
Fordham	28	10	7	11	46	52	37
Histon 'A'	28	11	4	13	47	55	37
Newmarket Town Res.	28	9	7	12	42	46	34
Great Paxton	28	9	6	13	51	66	33
Eaton Socon	28	9	2	17	44	73	29
Somersham Town	28	6	3	19	35	72	21
Linton Granta	28	6	1	21	36	71	19
Hemingford United	28	4	3	21	34	89	15

PREMIER DIVISION CUP

FIRST ROUND

Cambridge University Press (w/o) v Tuddenham Rovers (scr.)
Cottenham United 0 **Fordham** 2
Eaton Socon 5 Somersham Town 0
Histon 'A' 4 **Great Paxton** 7
Newmarket Town Res. 0 **Linton Granta** 2
Over Sports 6 Hemingford United 1
Sawston United 2 Great Shelford 1
Waterbeach 1 **Littleport Town** 3

QUARTER-FINALS

Cambridge University Press 0 **Sawston United** 3
Fordham 2 **Great Paxton** 2 *aet* (4-5p)
Littleport Town 5 Eaton Socon 0
Over Sports 5 Linton Granta 1

SEMI-FINALS

Littleport Town 2 Sawston United 1
Over Sports 6 Great Paxton 0

FINAL

(May 16th at Histon)
Over Sports 2 Littleport Town 1 *aet*

CAMBRIDGESHIRE COUNTY LEAGUE PREMIER DIVISION CONSTITUTION 2006-07

CAMBRIDGE UNIVERSITY PRESS . . CUP Sports Ground, Shaftesbury Road, Cambridge CB2 2BS . . . . . None
COTTENHAM UNITED . . . . . Lambs Lane, Cottenham, Cambridge CB4 8TA 01954 250873
EATON SOCON . . . . . River Road, Eaton Ford, St Neots PE19 7AU . . . . . None
FORDHAM. . . . . Recreational Ground, Carter Street, Fordham, Ely CB7 5JT. . . . . None
GREAT PAXTON . . . . . Recreation Ground, High Street, Great Paxton, St Neots PE19 6RG. . . . . None
GREAT SHELFORD . . . . . Recreation Ground, Woollards Lane, Great Shelford CB2 5LZ. 01223 842590
HISTON 'A'. . . . . The Glassworld Stadium, Bridge Road, Impington, Cambridge CB4 9PH 01223 237373
LINTON GRANTA. . . . . Recreation Ground, Meadow Lane, Linton, Cambridge CB1 6HX . . . . . None
LITTLEPORT TOWN . . . . . Sports Centre, Camel Road, Littleport, Ely CB6 1EW. . . . . None
NEEDINGWORTH UNITED . . . . . Mill Field, Holywell Road, Needingworth PE27 4TF . . . . . None
NEWMARKET TOWN RESERVES . . Cricket Field Road, off New Cheveley Road, Newmarket CB8 8BG. 01638 663637
OVER SPORTS . . . . . Over Recreation Ground, The Doles, Over CB4 5NW. . . . . None
SAWSTON UNITED. . . . . Spicers Sports Ground, New Road, Sawston CB2 4BN . . . . . None
SOMERSHAM TOWN . . . . . West End Ground, St Ives Road, Somersham, Huntingdon PE28 3ET 01487 843384
WATERBEACH. . . . . Reacreation Ground, Waterbeach . . . . . None
WICKHAMBROOK. . . . . Recreation Ground, Cemetary Hill, Wickhambrook . . . . . None
IN: Needingworth United (P), Wickhambrook (P)
OUT: Hemingford United (R), Tuddenham Rovers (WN)

	Bluntisham Rangers	Brampton	Foxton	Gamlingay United	Girton United	Grampian	Hardwick	Hundon	Lakenheath	Mildenhall Town Res.	Needingworth United	Soham Town Rangers Res.	West Wratting	Wickhambrook	Wisbech Town Res.
Bluntisham Rangers		1-0	2-2	2-4	1-0	1-0	0-3	1-4	1-5	2-1	0-4	1-1	1-1	2-3	1-3
Brampton	0-2		1-5	0-0	2-2	6-1	2-0	3-0	0-1	0-0	2-3	2-5	2-1	0-4	0-0
Foxton	3-1	3-6	*S*	2-0	5-1	4-0	1-2	0-1	3-2	2-1	2-1	0-3	1-2	2-3	0-3
Gamlingay United	3-2	2-1	5-1	*E*	0-3	1-0	0-0	1-3	3-4	0-1	0-4	1-5	0-1	2-3	1-0
Girton United	0-2	1-1	4-0	3-0	*N*	1-2	0-1	0-1	2-1	2-0	1-1	2-1	0-0	0-0	2-3
Grampian	3-1	3-2	0-4	4-3	3-3	*I*	2-4	1-4	4-0	0-0	0-3	2-6	0-1	1-3	2-1
Hardwick	1-0	1-1	1-0	2-1	1-0	5-2	*O*	2-1	3-1	2-2	2-3	0-1	1-2	1-3	3-5
Hundon	2-1	3-0	3-1	1-8	0-1	1-2	1-2	*R*	0-3	0-3	4-2	1-3	4-0	1-1	0-5
Lakenheath	2-3	8-2	1-4	2-1	0-3	7-4	4-2	3-2		1-1	1-6	1-4	2-3	3-0	1-1
Mildenhall Town Res.	1-1	4-0	5-1	3-2	2-0	3-1	2-1	1-2	2-0	*D*	1-1	2-1	1-1	2-2	2-0
Needingworth United	4-0	1-1	4-0	2-0	2-1	13-0	2-0	4-1	4-2	0-1	*I*	4-0	1-2	3-1	1-2
Soham Town Rangers Res.	3-4	4-1	1-1	1-0	2-0	2-1	1-1	1-1	2-3	1-1	0-5	*V*	3-0	2-3	3-0
West Wratting	2-2	10-0	2-1	5-0	2-4	5-1	0-3	0-1	3-1	3-2	0-1	1-0		2-2	0-3
Wickhambrook	1-1	3-3	3-1	1-1	1-0	5-0	3-1	2-0	2-2	2-0	1-0	2-1	5-1	*A*	1-4
Wisbech Town Res.	0-0	2-1	6-1	2-0	3-0	2-0	4-0	1-3	6-2	1-1	4-1	6-1	1-1	1-3	

Senior Division A		P	W	D	L	F	A	Pts
Wickhambrook		28	17	8	3	63	37	59
Needingworth United		28	18	3	7	80	29	57
Wisbech Town Res.		28	17	5	6	69	31	56
Mildenhall Town Res.		28	12	10	6	45	29	46
West Wratting		28	13	6	9	51	43	45
Soham Town Rangers Res.		28	13	5	10	58	46	44
Hardwick		28	13	4	11	45	44	43
Hundon		28	13	2	13	45	52	41
Lakenheath		28	11	3	14	63	71	36
Foxton		28	10	2	16	50	64	32
Bluntisham Rangers		28	8	7	13	36	56	31
Girton United	*-3*	28	9	6	13	36	37	30
Gamlingay United		28	7	3	18	39	58	24
Brampton		28	5	8	15	39	70	23
Grampian	*-6*	28	7	2	19	39	91	17

WILLIAM COCKELL CUP

(Senior A teams)

FIRST ROUND

Brampton 2 Gamlingay United 1

Foxton 1 Girton United 0

Grampian 1 Needingworth United 0

Hardwick (w/o) v Bassingbourn (scr.)

Lakenheath 3 Bluntisham Rangers 2

West Wratting 3 **Hundon** 5

Wickhambrook 2 Soham Town Rangers Res. 1

Wisbech Town Res. 3 Mildenhall Town Res. 1

QUARTER-FINALS

Foxton 4 Brampton 0

Hundon 2 Wickhambrook 0

Lakenheath 2 **Hardwick** 3

Wisbech Town Res. 3 Grampian 2

SEMI-FINALS

Hardwick 0 **Foxton** 1

Wisbech Town Res. 2 Hundon 0

FINAL

(May 8th at Cambridge City)

Foxton 2 Wisbech Town Res. 1

CAMBRIDGESHIRE COUNTY LEAGUE SENIOR DIVISION A CONSTITUTION 2006-07

BLUNTISHAM RANGERS .... Mill Lane, Bluntisham, Huntingdon PE28 3LR .... None
BRAMPTON.................. Thrapston Road Playing Fields, Brampton, Huntingdon PE28 4NL.................. None
ELY CITY RESERVES .... The Unwin Ground, Downham Road, Ely CB6 2SH 01353 662035
FOXTON.................. Recreation Ground, Foxton.................. None
FULBOURN INSTITUTE.................. Fulbourn Recreation, Home End, Fulbourn CB1 5BS.................. None
GAMLINGAY UNITED .... Gamlingay Village College, Station Road, Gamlingay SG19 3HD .... None
GIRTON UNITED .... Girton Recreation, Cambridge Road, Girton CB3 0FH .... None
GRAMPIAN .... Sports Ground, Grampian Foods, Little Wratting CB9 7TD .... None
HARDWICK .... Egremont Road, Hardwick, Cambridge CB3 7XR .... None
HEMINGFORD UNITED ... Memorial Playing Fields, Manor Road, Hemingford Grey, Huntingdon PE28 9BX.................. None
HUNDON.................. North Street, Hundon CO10 8EE .... None
LAKENHEATH.................. The Nest, Wings Road, Lakenheath IP27 9HW.................. None
MILDENHALL TOWN RESERVES.......... Recreation Way, Mildenhall, Bury St Edmunds IP28 7EL.................. 01638 713449
SOHAM TOWN RANGERS RESERVES....... Julius Martins Lane, Soham, Ely CB7 5EQ 01353 720732/722139
WEST WRATTING .... Recreation Ground, Bull Lane, West Wratting CB1 5NJ.................. None
WISBECH TOWN RESERVES .... Fenland Park, Lerowe Road, Wisbech PE13 3QL 01945 584176

IN: Ely City Reserves (P), Fulbourn Institute (W – Eastern Counties League Division One), Hemingford United (R)
OUT: Bassingbourn (WN), Needingworth United (P), Wickhambrook (P)

	Castle Camps	Cherry Hinton	Comberton United	Debden	Ely City Res.	Ely Crusaders	Fulbourn Institute Res.	Great Chesterford	Haddenham Rovers	J M Sports	Milton	Sawston United Res.	Soham United	Swavesey Institute	West Row Gunners	Willingham
Castle Camps		2-1	0-1	1-1	0-4	1-0	2-1	3-1	1-1	0-1	3-3	2-3	1-4	6-4	1-1	3-3
Cherry Hinton	1-0		1-6	3-2	1-1	3-8	0-3	2-2	1-3	1-1	4-3	1-0	1-2	2-2	1-0	4-1
Comberton United	2-4	2-3	*S*	3-0	2-1	2-3	0-5	3-0	2-0	5-2	0-0	3-2	4-2	1-2	0-0	1-3
Debden	0-2	4-1	2-0	*E*	2-3	2-5	0-4	1-1	3-2	2-1	2-2	1-1	5-0	4-1	1-1	2-0
Ely City Res.	2-1	4-1	0-0	5-1	*N*	2-1	0-2	4-0	3-1	2-0	7-1	1-1	2-2	5-1	3-0	3-1
Ely Crusaders	4-3	2-0	1-4	4-0	2-2	*I*	2-0	4-3	2-2	3-1	0-0	4-2	3-0	2-2	1-1	5-0
Fulbourn Institute Res.	2-1	3-2	1-3	2-1	0-0	9-1	*O*	4-2	1-1	2-1	2-1	1-0	4-0	4-0	1-0	2-0
Great Chesterford	0-6	2-4	1-3	1-2	0-1	1-5	1-4	*R*	0-5	2-4	1-2	1-1	4-1	2-1	1-2	4-1
Haddenham Rovers	2-1	3-1	0-1	6-3	0-3	0-3	0-0	0-2		3-1	1-0	2-2	1-1	4-0	0-2	1-4
J M Sports	1-2	5-2	1-4	4-2	1-3	1-3	0-5	3-5	2-1	*D*	2-3	3-1	4-1	3-3	2-1	3-3
Milton	3-0	1-2	2-2	1-3	2-4	3-2	0-3	7-0	0-4	2-1	*I*	2-2	2-1	1-0	3-1	0-3
Sawston United Res.	0-2	0-2	4-1	0-2	0-4	4-5	3-2	5-2	3-1	1-1	0-2	*V*	5-1	1-3	1-6	2-5
Soham United	3-2	4-5	2-1	2-5	0-4	2-4	0-1	6-2	1-3	2-1	2-1	0-0		2-1	0-1	3-6
Swavesey Institute	1-1	0-3	3-0	0-0	0-6	2-0	0-3	6-0	0-5	4-3	1-6	3-2	2-1	*B*	2-2	0-1
West Row Gunners	3-2	1-3	2-1	1-1	0-1	3-2	1-1	5-2	3-1	0-0	1-1	3-0	4-2	0-0		0-2
Willingham	1-2	1-2	2-5	2-2	0-3	3-4	1-5	4-0	1-1	2-4	1-0	5-0	5-2	4-2	5-3	

Senior Division B	P	W	D	L	F	A	Pts
Ely City Res.	30	22	6	2	83	23	72
Fulbourn Institute Res.	30	22	4	4	77	23	70
Ely Crusaders	30	18	5	7	85	58	59
Comberton United	30	15	4	11	62	49	49
Cherry Hinton	30	14	4	12	58	68	46
West Row Gunners	30	11	10	9	48	41	43
Willingham	30	13	4	13	70	68	43
Debden	30	11	8	11	56	59	41
Haddenham Rovers	30	11	7	12	54	47	40
Milton	30	11	7	12	54	55	40
Castle Camps	30	11	6	13	55	54	39
J M Sports	30	9	5	16	57	70	32
Swavesey Institute	30	8	7	15	46	74	31
Soham United	30	8	3	19	49	84	27
Sawston United Res.	30	6	7	17	46	71	25
Great Chesterford	30	5	3	22	43	99	18

PERCY OLDHAM CUP

(Senior B teams)

FIRST ROUND

Cherry Hinton 1 **Haddenham Rovers** 4
Comberton United 3 Willingham 2
Debden 5 West Row Gunners 1
Ely City Res. 5 Sawston United Res. 1
Fulbourn Institute Res. 2 **Castle Camps** 2 *aet* (4-5p)
Great Chesterford 4 J M Sports 1
Soham United 2 **Ely Crusaders** 3
Swavesey Institute 1 **Milton** 1 *aet* (7-8p)

QUARTER-FINALS

Castle Camps 2 **Ely City Res.** 5
Comberton United 1 Milton 0
Debden 3 Haddenham Rovers 3 *aet* (6-5p)
Great Chesterford 2 **Ely Crusaders** 6

SEMI-FINALS

Ely City Res. 1 Comberton United 0
Ely Crusaders 4 **Debden** 4 *aet* (3-4p)

FINAL

(May 10th at Cambridge City)
Ely City Res. 2 Debden 1

CAMBRIDGESHIRE COUNTY LEAGUE SENIOR DIVISION B CONSTITUTION 2006-07

BARTON MILLS .... Village Green, Barton Mills, Bury St Edmunds, Suffolk IP28 6AA .... None
CASTLE CAMPS .... Recreation Ground, Bumpstead Road, Castle Camps .... None
CHERRY HINTON .... Recreation Ground, Cherry Hinton, Cambridge .... None
COMBERTON UNITED .... Recreation Ground, Hines Lane, Comberton CB3 7BZ .... None
DEBDEN .... Recreation Ground, High Street, Debden, Saffron Walden CB11 3LE .... None
ELY CRUSADERS .... Paradise Sports Centre, Newnham Street, Ely CB7 4PE 01353 667580
HADDENHAM ROVERS .... Hop Row, Haddenham, Ely CB6 3SR .... None
J M SPORTS .... J M Sports & Social Club, Cambridge 01763 253731
MILTON .... Milton Recreation Ground, The Sycamores, Milton .... None
OUTWELL SWIFTS .... The Nest, Wisbech Road, Outwell PE14 8PE .... None
SOHAM UNITED .... Qua Fen Common, Soham, Ely CB6 5DH .... None
SWAVESEY INSTITUTE .... The Green, High Street, Swavesey CB4 5QU .... None
WEST ROW GUNNERS .... Chapel Row, West Row, Bury St Edmunds IP28 8PA .... None
WEST WRATTING RESERVES .... Recreation Ground, Bull Lane, West Wratting CB1 5NJ .... None
WHITTLESFORD UNITED .... The Lawn, Whittlesford CB2 4NG .... None
WILLINGHAM .... Recreation Ground, West Fen Road, Willingham .... None

IN: Barton Mills (P – Division One B), Outwells Swifts (P – Division One B), West Wratting Reserves (P – Division One A), Whittlesford United (P – Division One A)

OUT: Ely City Reserves (P), Fulbourn Institute Reserves (R – Division One B), Great Chesterford (R – Division One A), Sawston United Reserves (R – Division One A)

Division One A	P	W	D	L	F	A	Pts
Whittlesford United	26	22	2	2	83	26	68
West Wratting Res.	26	16	5	5	64	36	53
Barrington	26	15	3	8	54	43	48
Tuddenham Rovers Res.	26	15	2	9	69	38	47
Saffron Crocus	26	14	4	8	74	45	46
Fowlmere	26	11	5	10	51	45	38
Litlington Athletic	26	10	8	8	51	45	38
Sawston Rovers	26	11	3	12	56	47	36
Great Shelford Res.	26	10	4	12	53	64	34
Steeple Bumpstead	26	9	4	13	41	43	31
Fulbourn Institute 'A'	26	8	5	13	37	51	29
Camden United	26	7	5	14	46	68	26
Linton Granta Res.	26	6	3	17	30	71	21
Melbourn	26	0	3	23	24	111	3

Division One B	P	W	D	L	F	A	Pts
Outwell Swifts	26	17	5	4	77	43	56
Barton Mills	26	16	2	8	54	49	50
Cottenham United Res.	26	14	3	9	52	42	45
St Ives Rangers	26	14	3	9	57	52	45
Godmanchester Rovers Res.	26	11	7	8	44	32	40
Waterbeach Res.	26	11	6	9	51	34	39
March Town United Res.	26	9	7	10	68	70	34
Great Paxton Res.	26	9	5	12	52	53	32
Eaton Socon Res.	26	9	5	12	62	64	32
Buckden	26	9	5	12	48	53	32
Bottisham Sports	26	8	5	13	32	49	29
Gransden Chequers	26	7	7	12	38	53	28
Littleport Town Res.	26	8	4	14	30	49	28
Hemingford United Res.	26	7	2	17	30	52	23

DIVISION ONE CHAMPIONSHIP PLAY-OFF *(May 16th at Whittlesford United)* **Whittlesford United** 3 Outwell Swifts 1

Division Two A	P	W	D	L	F	A	Pts
Helions Bumpstead	24	19	3	2	85	18	60
Girton United Res.	24	19	3	2	85	30	60
Cambridge Univ Press Res.	24	14	3	7	52	31	45
Comberton United Res.	24	13	5	6	73	39	44
Thaxted	24	13	2	9	63	48	41
Duxford United	24	10	4	10	48	46	34
Balsham	24	7	7	10	54	59	28
Cambourne Rovers	24	8	4	12	32	40	28
Grampian Res. *-3*	24	8	1	15	39	68	22
Papworth	24	5	6	13	29	71	21
Foxton Res. *-3*	24	6	5	13	34	52	20
Mott MacDonald	24	5	3	16	26	76	18
Great Chesterford Res.	24	5	2	17	36	78	17

Cherry Hinton Res. – record expunged

Division Two B	P	W	D	L	F	A	Pts
Fenstanton	26	19	5	2	73	25	62
Huntingdon United RGE	26	20	1	5	86	28	61
Needingworth United Res.	26	17	3	6	61	28	54
Longstanton	26	15	2	9	78	60	47
Sutton United	26	13	5	8	80	64	44
St Ives Town Res.	26	10	9	7	69	52	39
Stretham Hotspurs	26	10	4	12	52	51	34
Over Sports Res.	26	11	1	14	42	50	34
Lode	26	10	4	12	54	67	34
Ely City 'A'	26	8	5	13	44	58	29
Bluntisham Rangers Res.	26	8	2	16	31	74	26
Milton Res.	26	6	5	15	42	65	23
Isleham United	26	7	1	18	46	74	22
Somersham Town Res.	26	3	3	20	29	91	12

DIVISION TWO CHAMPIONSHIP PLAY-OFF *(May 16th at Helions Bumpstead)* **Helions Bumpstead** 6 Fenstanton 3

CREAKE CHARITY SHIELD FINAL *(May 9th at Cambridge City)* **St Ives Town Res.** 2 Buckden 1

Division Three A	P	W	D	L	F	A	Pts
Hardwick Res.	26	20	5	1	70	24	65
Camden United Res.	26	17	3	6	76	48	54
Gamlingay United Res.	26	17	0	9	73	50	51
Wilbraham	26	14	5	7	84	40	47
Withersfield	26	13	8	5	69	50	47
Bassingbourn Res.	26	13	5	8	59	50	44
Whittlesford United Res.	26	10	5	11	51	54	35
Ashdon Villa	26	10	3	13	43	59	33
Great Chishill	26	9	3	14	58	60	30
Castle Camps Res.	26	8	4	14	43	62	28
Abington United	26	8	4	14	51	80	28
Hempstead United	26	8	3	15	73	87	27
Orwell *-3*	26	6	0	20	28	60	15
Sawston United 'A'	26	4	2	20	39	93	14

Division Three B	P	W	D	L	F	A	Pts
Newmarket White Lion	26	18	6	2	110	35	60
Witchford	26	18	2	6	92	40	56
Wisbech St Mary	26	16	8	2	72	32	56
Brampton Res.	26	14	2	10	64	44	44
Huntingdon Utd RGE Res.	26	12	7	7	79	59	43
The Vine	26	12	7	7	65	55	43
Fordham Res.	26	13	2	11	70	59	41
Lakenheath Res.	26	11	3	12	64	60	36
Dullingham	26	9	6	11	52	78	33
Hemingfords United 'A'	26	7	8	11	47	71	29
Cottenham United 'A'	26	8	4	14	59	76	28
Soham United Res.	26	5	6	15	47	74	21
Little Downham Swifts	26	5	1	20	37	114	16
West Row Gunners Res.	26	2	2	22	36	97	8

DIVISION THREE CHAMPIONSHIP PLAY-OFF *(May 17th at Hardwick)* **Hardwick Res.** (w/o) v Newmarket White Lion (scr.)

JOHN ABLETT CUP *(May 11th at Cambridge City)* **Withersfield** 2 Whittlesford United 1

Division Four A	P	W	D	L	F	A	Pts
Steeple Morden	26	18	3	5	81	41	57
Harston	26	18	1	7	51	32	55
Elsworth Sports	26	17	3	6	73	38	54
Eaton Socon 'A'	26	16	1	9	79	51	49
J M Sports Res.	26	14	5	7	74	62	47
Sawston Rovers Res.	26	11	6	9	57	50	39
Cambridge Univ. Press 'A'	26	11	2	13	55	57	35
Hundon Res.	26	9	7	10	44	45	34
Saffron Crocus Res.	26	10	4	12	38	45	34
Fowlmere Res.	26	10	4	12	44	63	34
Steeple Bumpstead Res.	26	7	3	16	47	66	24
Linton Granta 'A'	26	7	2	17	31	71	23
Hardwick 'A' *-6*	26	8	4	14	47	56	22
Comberton United 'A'	26	2	3	21	36	80	9

Division Four B	P	W	D	L	F	A	Pts
Wisbech St Mary Res.	26	22	1	3	149	36	67
St Ives Town 'A'	26	14	6	6	81	40	48
Pymore	26	14	6	6	76	58	48
Sutton United Res.	26	10	11	5	73	63	41
Mepal Sports	26	11	5	10	70	56	38
Burwell Swifts	26	11	5	10	58	60	38
Willingham Res.	26	10	7	9	69	56	37
Swavesey Institute Res.	26	10	6	10	56	49	36
Barton Mills Res.	26	10	6	10	49	56	36
Ely Crusaders Res.	26	8	7	11	41	66	31
Exning Athletic	26	8	3	15	59	92	27
Milton 'A'	26	7	5	14	48	82	26
Haddenham Rovers Res. *-3*	26	6	4	16	39	74	19
Wicken Amateurs	26	3	4	19	44	124	13

DIVISION FOUR CHAMPIONSHIP PLAY-OFF *(May 20th at Steeple Morden)* Steeple Morden 0 **Wisbech St Mary Res.** 1

Division Five A	P	W	D	L	F	A	Pts
Figleaves	28	21	3	4	96	42	66
Fulbourn Spts & Soc. Club	28	21	0	7	84	40	63
Hundon 'A'	28	19	4	5	78	51	61
Litlington Athletic Res.	28	16	6	6	73	42	54
Saffron Rangers	28	17	2	9	88	62	53
Bottisham Sports Res.	28	14	2	12	70	56	44
Lode Res.	28	14	1	13	88	59	43
Steeple Morden Res.	28	13	4	11	63	58	43
Dalehead Foods	28	13	3	12	73	68	42
Barrington Res.	28	12	1	15	63	71	37
Barton	28	9	3	16	55	86	30
Papworth Res.	28	7	3	18	51	98	24
Duxford United Res.	28	6	4	18	48	69	22
Newport Veterans	28	4	2	22	32	98	14
Gransden Chequers Res.	28	2	6	20	40	102	12

Division Five B	P	W	D	L	F	A	Pts
Newmarket Town 'A'	26	21	4	1	121	35	67
March Rangers	26	19	3	4	105	49	60
Wisbech St Mary 'A'	26	19	3	4	71	31	60
Earith United	26	14	5	7	85	55	47
Fenstanton Res.	26	14	3	9	70	46	45
Burwell Swifts Res.	26	13	2	11	66	46	41
Outwell Swifts Res.	26	11	3	12	41	58	36
Isleham United Res.	26	9	7	10	67	58	34
Walsoken United	26	9	2	15	52	78	29
Littleport Town 'A'	26	8	2	16	41	71	26
Cottenham United 'B'	26	5	8	13	44	78	23
The Vine Res.	26	5	3	18	47	95	18
Little D'ham Swifts Res. *-3*	26	5	5	16	43	78	17
Coldham United	26	4	2	20	32	107	14

DIVISION FIVE CHAMPIONSHIP PLAY-OFF *(May 16th at Figleaves)* Figleaves 0 **Newmarket Town 'A'** 0 *aet* (3-1p)

REG HAIGH/ALEX PECK CUP *(May 12th at Cambridge City)* **Newmarket Town 'A'** 3 Wisbech St Mary 'A' 3 *aet* (5-4p)

CENTRAL MIDLANDS LEAGUE

Note – AFC Barnsley withdrew during the course of the season Their results are shown herein but are expunged from the league table	AFC Barnsley	Appleby Frod. Ath.	Barton Town OB	Blackwell Miners W.	Bolsover Town	Clipstone Welfqre	Dinnington Town	Dunkirk	Gedling Miners W.	Graham St. Prims	Greenwood Meadows	Heanor Town	Holbrook Miners W.	Kimberley Town	Nettleham	Pinxton	Radcliffe Olympic	Radford	Rainworth Miners W.	Rolls Royce Leisure	Sandiacre Town	Southwell City
AFC Barnsley		3-2	3-1	9-1	n/a	2-0	2-2	1-3	1-0	4-2	n/a	3-2	n/a	2-0	n/a	8-1	2-0	0-0	6-1	2-1	4-2	n/a
Appleby Frodingham Ath.	0-1		1-6	1-2	1-0	0-2	1-0	0-0	2-1	1-2	4-1	1-1	1-0	2-2	1-1	0-2	1-1	1-1	1-2	1-0	0-1	2-0
Barton Town Old Boys	n/a	4-0		6-0	3-1	2-1	2-3	1-0	2-1	3-2	5-0	0-2	1-0	2-0	3-0	5-0	1-2	4-0	0-0	5-2	3-3	4-2
Blackwell Miners Welfare	1-3	2-1	1-5	*S*	5-2	1-1	3-2	2-1	1-0	2-1	2-1	1-3	1-4	3-8	1-3	2-0	1-3	1-3	3-1	2-1	3-1	1-1
Bolsover Town	0-7	0-2	2-3	1-1	*U*	0-2	0-5	0-2	0-1	5-2	1-2	1-2	2-1	1-1	3-0	0-2	1-1	0-2	0-0	2-1	2-3	0-0
Clipstone Welfare	3-1	3-1	1-2	2-2	3-1	*P*	1-2	0-1	1-1	0-1	2-3	0-1	0-3	2-0	1-1	0-1	1-0	2-0	3-0	2-2	1-2	4-0
Dinnington Town	3-1	0-1	2-1	2-1	0-0	4-1	*R*	4-0	2-0	4-1	3-3	0-0	1-1	2-2	4-2	1-0	2-0	1-0	2-1	2-0	3-1	0-1
Dunkirk	1-1	3-2	1-4	2-1	2-1	6-2	0-3	*E*	2-2	3-1	3-0	2-0	1-1	2-1	0-1	3-1	0-1	2-0	1-0	1-3	0-1	0-0
Gedling Miners Welfare	3-1	3-1	1-0	2-1	3-1	1-3	0-2	0-0	*M*	3-1	2-0	1-1	3-1	4-1	4-0	3-3	4-0	3-3	3-1	2-0	4-2	1-2
Graham Street Prims	n/a	0-3	2-4	6-1	1-1	2-3	0-3	1-5	2-2	*E*	0-2	0-4	1-2	0-1	0-1	2-2	2-1	1-3	2-0	3-1	2-0	1-0
Greenwood Meadows	0-6	0-1	0-3	1-4	1-2	1-1	0-3	1-2	1-5	4-3		2-2	0-1	3-1	3-2	1-0	3-3	1-2	2-4	3-1	1-1	1-1
Heanor Town	n/a	3-0	2-3	6-0	0-0	1-0	0-1	0-0	3-0	2-2	4-1	*D*	0-1	2-0	1-0	2-1	1-0	1-0	3-1	2-2	1-1	0-1
Holbrook Miners Welfare	1-1	1-0	1-1	2-1	4-1	2-0	3-2	1-2	1-1	2-2	2-1	3-0	*I*	1-0	7-1	4-2	2-0	0-2	2-2	2-1	2-1	1-1
Kimberley Town	n/a	2-0	0-5	0-1	2-3	4-0	0-3	0-0	1-5	5-4	2-2	3-0	1-3	*V*	3-3	1-2	2-4	2-2	0-2	1-3	3-2	1-1
Nettleham	1-1	4-3	0-2	2-3	0-1	1-4	0-1	1-0	2-3	1-2	2-1	1-1	0-2	1-2	*I*	2-3	2-1	0-3	1-3	0-0	1-2	0-2
Pinxton	2-4	0-3	0-3	3-2	0-2	2-0	0-2	1-0	1-3	1-0	1-0	0-4	0-0	1-1	1-3	*S*	0-4	1-5	1-3	1-2	3-0	1-3
Radcliffe Olympic	n/a	1-0	1-1	5-0	1-2	2-0	1-3	0-4	0-0	1-4	7-2	0-0	6-2	3-1	2-1	2-2	*I*	1-1	0-1	0-2	1-1	2-1
Radford	3-0	1-0	1-2	3-0	8-1	4-1	3-2	3-2	2-1	1-0	0-2	0-0	0-0	3-0	0-0	0-0	3-2	*O*	0-3	1-1	3-1	0-2
Rainworth Miners Welfare	n/a	2-0	2-4	1-0	4-0	0-2	0-1	2-0	0-1	5-1	4-0	1-3	1-1	4-1	0-0	3-1	1-1	4-2	*N*	4-0	1-1	2-1
Rolls Royce Leisure	2-1	3-2	0-4	2-1	0-0	2-1	1-3	1-8	2-0	0-1	0-1	4-2	0-1	3-3	1-2	0-0	1-1	4-1	2-1		0-2	0-3
Sandiacre Town	2-4	2-2	2-3	1-2	6-2	0-4	2-1	0-5	3-3	4-3	2-3	1-1	0-3	2-1	6-1	0-1	2-1	0-0	0-2	0-0		0-5
Southwell City	2-3	1-0	2-0	3-2	2-0	3-1	1-1	1-0	3-0	4-1	1-1	3-0	2-0	1-1	2-0	5-2	0-2	0-2	2-0	1-0	0-2	

Supreme Division		P	W	D	L	F	A	Pts
Barton Town Old Boys		40	30	4	6	112	41	94
Dinnington Town		40	27	6	7	82	34	87
Holbrook Miners Welfare		40	22	10	8	70	42	76
Southwell City		40	22	9	9	64	36	75
Gedling Miners Welfare		40	19	10	11	77	54	67
Heanor Town		40	18	13	9	61	38	67
Radford		40	19	10	11	68	49	67
Dunkirk		40	19	7	14	66	44	64
Rainworth Miners Welfare		40	19	7	14	68	48	64
Radcliffe Olympic		40	14	11	15	64	58	53
Blackwell Miners Welfare		40	16	4	20	63	93	52
Sandiacre Town		40	13	10	17	61	77	49
Clipstone Welfare		40	14	6	20	58	62	48
Appleby Frodingham Athletic		40	12	7	21	44	60	43
Pinxton	*-1*	40	12	7	21	43	76	42
Rolls Royce Leisure	*-3*	40	11	9	20	48	72	39
Graham Street Prims		40	11	5	24	62	90	38
Greenwood Meadows	*-3*	40	11	8	21	55	89	38
Bolsover Town		40	9	9	22	42	79	36
Kimberley Town		40	8	11	21	60	87	35
Nettleham		40	9	7	24	43	82	34

AFC Barnsley – record expunged

Reserve Premier Division		P	W	D	L	F	A	Pts
Arnold Town Res.		34	25	5	4	123	48	80
Southwell City Res.		34	21	6	7	84	57	69
Retford United Res.		34	17	10	7	84	43	61
Holbrook M W Res.	*+2*	34	17	8	9	76	60	61
Nettleham Res.		34	16	5	13	62	45	53
Rainworth Miners W Res.		34	15	8	11	69	59	53
Radford Res.		34	14	11	9	68	58	53
Dunkirk Res.		34	15	6	13	60	48	51
Heanor Town Res.	*-1*	34	13	8	13	82	70	46
Sandiacre Town Res.		34	13	6	15	59	62	45
Bilborough Pelican Res.		34	13	6	15	83	88	45
Clipstone Welfare Res.		34	13	5	16	64	79	44
Teversal Res.		34	12	5	17	56	66	41
Carlton Town 'A'		34	12	3	19	57	101	39
Forest Town Res.		34	10	6	18	39	65	36
Radcliffe Olympic Res.		34	9	8	17	49	63	35
Thoresby Coll. Welfare Res.		34	6	7	21	34	78	25
Graham Street Prims Res.		34	6	5	23	49	108	23

CENTRAL MIDLANDS LEAGUE SUPREME DIVISION CONSTITUTION 2006-07

APPLEBY FRODINGHAM ATHLETIC .. Brumby Hall Sports Ground (Corus), Ashby Road, Scunthorpe DN16 1AA........ 01724 843024
ASKERN WELFARE .... Welfare Sports Ground, Manor Way, Askern, Doncaster DN6 0AL.................. 01302 700957
BARTON TOWN OLD BOYS...... The Euronics Ground, Marsh Lane, Barton-on-Humber DN15 5HB..................... 07900 105204
BILBOROUGH PELICAN......... Brian Wakefield Sports Ground, Lenton Lane, Nottingham NG7 2SA 0115 986 8255
BLACKWELL MINERS WELFARE... Sports Ground, Primrose Hill, Blackwell, Alfreton DE55 5JF 01773 811295
BOTTESFORD TOWN............ Birch Park, Ontario Road, Bottesford, Scunthorpe DN17 2TQ 01724 871883
CLIPSTONE WELFARE.......... Lido Ground, Clipstone Road East, Clipstone, Mansfield NG21 9AZ 01623 477978
DUNKIRK................. Ron Steel Sports Ground, Lenton Lane, Clifton Bridge, Nottingham NG7 2SA.......... 0115 985 0803
GEDLING MINERS WELFARE.... Plains Social Club, Plains Road, Mapperley, Nottingham NG3 5RH 0115 926 6300
GRAHAM STREET PRIMS...... Asterdale Sports Centre, Borrowash Road, Spondon, Derby DE21 7PH 01332 668656
GREENWOOD MEADOWS .... Lenton Lane, Clifton Bridge, Nottingham 0115 986 5913
HEANOR TOWN..................... The Town Ground, Mayfield Avenue, Heanor DE75 7EN 01773 713742
HOLBROOK MINERS WELFARE .... Welfare Ground, Shaw Lane, Holbrook DE56 0TG................................ 01332 880259
KIMBERLEY TOWN .... The Stag Ground, Nottingham Road, Kimberley NG16 2ND 0115 938 2788
NETTLEHAM .... Mulsanne Park, Field Close, Nettleham, Lincoln LN2 2RX.......................... 01522 750007
RADCLIFFE OLYMPIC ..... Recreational Ground,Wharf Lane, Radcliffe-on-Trent, Nottingham NG12 2AN.......................... None
RADFORD .... Selhurst Street, Off Radford Road, Radford, Nottingham NG7 5EH 0115 942 3250
RAINWORTH MINERS WELFARE .. Welfare Ground, Kirklington Road, Rainworth, Mansfield NG21 0JY.................... 01623 792495
ROLLS ROYCE LEISURE .... Rolls Royce Sports & Social, Watnall Road, Hucknall NG15 6EU 0115 963 2380
SOUTHWELL CITY........... War Memorial Recreation Ground, Bishops Drive, Southwell NG25 0JP......................... 01636 814386

IN: Askern Welfare (P), Bilborough Pelican (P), Bottesford Town (P)

OUT: AFC Barnsley (WS), Bolsover Town (R), Dinnington Town (P – Northern Counties East League Division One), Pinxton (R), Sandiacre Town (R)

	Askern Welfare	Bentley Colliery	Bilborough Pelican	Blidworth Welfare	Bottesford Town	Forest Town	Grimsby Borough	Harworth CI	Hatfield Main	Kiverton Park	LSS Lucarly's	Matlock United	Newark Flowserve	Newark Town	Ollerton Town	Santos	Thoresby CW	Thorne Colliery	Welbeck Welfare	Yorkshire Main
Askern Welfare		0-1	1-3	4-1	0-1	4-0	0-0	2-0	6-0	4-1	0-2	1-0	3-0	5-1	3-0	1-0	7-0	4-0	6-1	2-1
Bentley Colliery	1-1		3-1	2-1	3-2	3-0	3-2	2-0	3-3	4-1	2-3	3-0	1-2	1-4	0-3	1-1	3-0	2-4	2-1	0-3
Bilborough Pelican	3-1	0-2	*P*	4-0	1-1	3-2	6-3	1-0	6-0	2-0	2-0	1-0	3-1	2-3	1-1	2-3	4-0	1-2	2-0	7-1
Blidworth Welfare	0-3	2-2	1-2	*R*	0-4	1-1	0-3	2-2	1-3	1-0	1-2	1-0	1-0	0-1	1-2	1-2	1-2	1-3	1-2	0-0
Bottesford Town	2-1	4-1	2-2	1-1	*E*	5-0	0-0	4-1	6-0	1-1	3-2	5-1	2-0	1-1	2-1	5-1	6-0	5-1	3-1	2-3
Forest Town	2-2	1-2	1-3	3-2	2-0	*M*	1-3	2-0	4-0	0-1	0-4	1-1	0-1	1-1	3-2	0-4	0-2	3-4	3-0	4-0
Grimsby Borough	0-3	6-0	2-0	5-0	0-2	2-2	*I*	2-2	2-1	1-1	1-3	0-3	1-0	3-3	0-3	4-1	1-1	3-2	5-2	4-1
Harworth Colliery Institute	0-3	0-4	0-6	2-4	1-6	0-3	1-4	*E*	0-4	1-1	1-4	0-0	1-1	2-0	0-0	1-1	1-2	2-5	4-2	1-1
Hatfield Main	1-2	0-5	0-2	2-1	0-0	0-4	2-4	1-1	*R*	1-1	2-4	0-1	3-1	1-2	0-0	1-2	5-0	2-7	1-3	0-0
Kiverton Park	2-4	6-0	2-5	4-0	0-3	0-2	1-0	0-1	4-1		0-1	0-0	0-1	5-0	1-0	0-0	0-0	6-2	2-2	3-1
LSS Lucarly's	1-3	1-0	0-2	2-1	2-1	2-2	1-2	6-0	2-0	1-2	*D*	0-0	1-2	1-1	5-1	2-2	6-1	13-3	4-0	5-2
Matlock United	2-0	0-1	4-4	2-0	2-4	3-3	1-3	1-0	1-1	3-2	0-2	*I*	1-2	1-1	2-0	1-0	3-1	1-4	2-2	1-3
Newark Flowserve	0-3	3-5	1-4	1-0	2-1	2-1	2-4	0-0	6-0	2-1	3-3	2-1	*V*	1-0	1-1	1-4	1-1	2-2	6-2	2-1
Newark Town	0-1	1-0	2-2	2-1	3-1	4-0	0-1	2-1	0-2	3-1	2-1	4-1	1-1	*I*	1-1	0-0	5-1	2-0	1-3	4-0
Ollerton Town	0-2	1-2	1-2	3-0	1-2	6-1	1-0	4-1	2-1	4-1	3-1	4-3	4-2	2-0	*S*	1-2	2-1	3-3	1-2	3-1
Santos	1-3	5-1	2-4	0-1	1-3	0-0	2-2	0-2	6-0	3-1	3-3	2-2	1-2	2-1	5-1	*I*	8-1	4-2	3-1	2-4
Thoresby Colliery Welfare	0-3	1-3	1-4	3-5	0-0	1-0	2-4	0-0	1-4	0-1	1-4	0-2	2-4	1-2	2-1	2-4	*O*	3-2	2-0	3-2
Thorne Colliery	3-2	1-6	2-4	4-0	1-4	3-1	2-3	1-0	5-1	2-2	2-1	1-0	2-1	2-0	0-2	1-2	3-0	*N*	4-1	3-2
Welbeck Welfare	2-1	0-4	1-9	3-6	1-2	0-3	0-7	2-0	2-2	2-3	3-4	2-4	4-1	2-4	3-2	1-3	7-1	3-4		0-2
Yorkshire Main	1-8	0-6	0-6	3-4	0-5	1-1	0-6	0-0	3-0	1-1	0-3	1-2	2-1	1-0	0-4	1-6	6-0	3-4	4-0	

Premier Division		P	W	D	L	F	A	Pts
Bilborough Pelican		38	27	5	6	116	46	86
Askern Welfare		38	26	3	9	99	33	81
Bottesford Town		38	24	8	6	101	38	80
LSS Lucarly's		38	22	6	10	102	54	72
Grimsby Borough		38	21	8	9	93	55	71
Bentley Colliery	*-1*	38	22	4	12	84	64	69
Thorne Colliery		38	21	3	14	96	95	66
Santos	*+2*	38	18	9	11	88	60	65
Newark Town		38	17	9	12	62	52	60
Ollerton Town		38	17	6	15	71	57	57
Newark Flowserve		38	16	7	15	61	67	55
Kiveton Park	*-4*	38	12	10	16	58	59	42
Forest Town	*-1*	38	11	9	18	57	72	41
Matlock United	*-6*	38	12	10	16	52	61	40
Yorkshire Main		38	10	6	22	55	103	36
Hatfield Main	*+2*	38	7	8	23	45	100	31
Thoresby Colliery Welfare	*+2*	38	8	5	25	39	114	31
Welbeck Welfare		38	9	3	26	63	118	30
Blidworth Welfare		38	8	5	25	44	84	29
Harworth Colliery Institute		38	4	12	22	29	83	24

Reserve Division One		P	W	D	L	F	A	Pts
Santos Res.	*+3*	26	21	2	3	64	25	68
Appleby Frodingham Ath. Res.		26	18	2	6	80	40	56
Welbeck Welfare Res.	*+2*	26	15	3	8	91	55	50
Newark Flowserve Res.		26	15	4	7	75	36	49
Bottesford Town Res.		26	15	3	8	71	33	48
Bolsover Town Res.		26	13	5	8	70	50	44
Bilborough Pelican 'A'	*-3*	26	13	5	8	47	36	41
Blidworth Welfare Res.		26	11	2	13	42	62	35
Blackwell M Welfare Res.	*-1*	26	9	4	13	52	60	30
Ollerton Town Res.		26	9	3	14	29	72	30
Matlock United Res.		26	9	1	16	47	71	28
Newark Town Res.		26	5	4	17	54	79	19
Sandiacre Town 'A'		26	4	2	20	29	92	14
Kimberley Town Res.		26	3	4	19	42	82	13

RESERVES CUP FINAL

FINAL

(April 12th at Nettleham)

Bottesford Town Res. 2 **Retford United Res.** 3

CENTRAL MIDLANDS LEAGUE PREMIER DIVISION CONSTITUTION 2006-07

BENTLEY COLLIERY .... Bentley Miners Welfare, The Avenue, Bentley, Doncaster DN5 0NP 01302 874420
BLIDWORTH WELFARE ... Blidworth Recreation Centre, Mansfield Road, Blidworth, Mansfield NG21 0LR 01623 793361
BOLSOVER TOWN .... Bolsover Town Sports & Social Club, Moor Lane, Bolsover, Chesterfield S44 6EW 01246 822449
CALVERTON MINERS WELFARE .. Calverton Miners Welfare, Hollinwood Lane, Calverton NG14 6NR 0115 965 4390
FOREST TOWN .... Forest Town Academy, Clipstone Road West, Forest To, Mansfield NG19 0EE 01623 624678
GRIMSBY BOROUGH .... Grimsby Institute Ground, Nunns Corner, Laceby Road, Grimsby 07890 318054
HARWORTH COLLIERY INSTITUTE .. Recreation Ground, Scrooby Road, Bircotes, Doncaster DN11 8JT 01302 750614
HATFIELD MAIN .... Dunscroft Welfare Ground, Broadway, Dunscroft, Doncaster DN7 4HD 01302 841326
KIVETON PARK .... Kiveton Park Miners Welfare, Hard Lane, Kiveton Park, Sheffield S26 6NB 07763 467979
LOUTH UNITED .... Park Avenue, Louth LN11 8BY 01507 607351
NEWARK FLOWSERVE .... Lowfields Works, Hawton Lane, New Balderton, Newark NG24 3EH 01636 494780
NEWARK TOWN .... Collingham FC, Station Road, Collingham NG23 7RA 01636 892303
OLLERTON TOWN .... The Lane, Walesby Lane, New Ollerton, Newark NG22 9UX .... None
PINXTON .... Welfare Ground, Wharf Road, Pinxton NG16 6NY 07989 324249
SANDIACRE TOWN .... St Giles Park, Stanton Road, Sandiacre NG10 5EP 0115 939 2880
THORESBY COLLIERY WELFARE .. Thoresby Colliery Sports Ground, Fourth Avenue, Edwinstowe NG21 9NS 07802 417987
THORNE COLLIERY .... Moorends Welfare, Grange Road, Moorends, Thorne, Doncaster DN8 4LU 07855 545221
WELBECK WELFARE .... Colliery Ground, Elkesley Road, Meden Vale, Warsop, Mansfield NG20 9PS 07863 568576
YORKSHIRE MAIN .... Yorkshire Main Miners Welfare, Edlington Lane, Edlington, Doncaster DN12 1DA 01709 864075

IN: Bolsover Town (R), Calverton Miners Welfare (P – Notts Senior League), Louth United (P – Lincolnshire League), Pinxton (R), Sandiacre Town (R)

OUT: Askern Welfare (P), Bilborough Pelican (P), Bottesford Town (P), LSS Lucarly's (S – Humber Premier League Division One), Matlock United (W), Santos (F)

LEAGUE CUP

FIRST ROUND

Bottesford Town 0 **Blidworth Welfare** 1
Clipstone Welfare 8 Thorne Colliery 4
Dunkirk 1 Forest Town 1
Forest Town 3 Dunkirk 0 *replay*
Kimberley Town 4 LSS Lucarly's 3
Kiveton Park 1 Holbrook Miners Welfare 0
Nettleham 0 **Southwell City** 1
Newark Town 2 Newark Flowserve 1
Pinxton 2 Harworth Colliery Institute 0
Santos 1 **Barton Town Old Boys** 3
Yorkshire Main 0 **AFC Barnsley** 4

SECOND ROUND

Barton Town Old Boys 0 Grimsby Borough 0
Grimsby Borough 1 Barton Town Old Boys 0 *replay*
Bilborough Pelican 4 Blackwell Miners Welfare 0
Bolsover Town 1 Radford 0
Clipstone Welfare 2 Pinxton 0
Gedling Miners Welfare 1 **Dinnington Town** 3
Hatfield Main 4 Graham Street Prims 1
Heanor Town 2 Greenwood Meadows 1
Kimberley Town 2 Forest Town 0
Kiveton Park 2 Rolls Royce Leisure 1
Matlock United 1 **Askern Welfare** 2
Newark Town 0 **Bentley Colliery** 2
Ollerton Town 2 **AFC Barnsley** 4
Radcliffe Olympic 1 **Welbeck Welfare** 2
Sandiacre Town 3 Appleby Frodingham Athletic 0
Southwell City 0 Rainworth Miners Welfare 0
Rainworth Miners Welfare 1 **Southwell City** 4 *replay*
Thoresby Colliery Welfare 2 Blidworth Welfare 1

THIRD ROUND

Askern Welfare 2 Sandiacre Town 1
Bentley Colliery 0 **Dinnington Town** 3
Bilborough Pelican 2 Kimberley Town 1
Bolsover Town 3 Welbeck Welfare 3
Welbeck Welfare 5 Bolsover Town 4 *aet replay*
Grimsby Borough 0 Southwell City 0
Southwell City 0 **Grimsby Borough** 2 *replay*
Heanor Town 0 **Clipstone Welfare** 1
Kiveton Park 1 AFC Barnsley 0
Thoresby Colliery Welfare 2 Hatfield Main 0

QUARTER-FINALS

Askern Welfare 2 Grimsby Borough 2
Grimsby Borough 2 **Askern Welfare** 4 *aet replay*
Bilborough Pelican 5 Welbeck Welfare 2
Clipstone Welfare 3 Kiveton Park 0
Thoresby Colliery Welfare 0 Dinnington Town 0
Dinnington Town 0 Thoresby Colliery Welfare 0 *aet* (5-4p) *replay*

SEMI-FINALS

Askern Welfare 1 Clipstone Welfare 0
(at Harworth Colliery Institute)
Dinnington Town 2 Bilborough Pelican 1
(at Rainworth Miners Welfare)

FINAL

(May 7th at Alfreton Town)
Dinnington Town 2 Askern Welfare 1

FLOODLIGHT TROPHY

FIRST ROUND

AFC Barnsley 3 Blidworth Welfare 1
Askern Welfare 4 Southwell City 1
Barton Town Old Boys 3 Bottesford Town 0
Gedling Miners Welfare 0 **Rainworth Miners Welfare** 2
Graham Street Prims 3 Nettleham 2
Heanor Town 1 Blackwell Miners Welfare 1
Blackwell Miners Welfare 2 Heanor Town 1 *replay*
Holbrook Miners Welfare 10 Newark Town 0
Kimberley Town 0 Greenwood Meadows 2
(Greenwood Meadows expelled)
Rolls Royce Leisure 1 Appleby Frodingham Athletic 0
Sandiacre Town 4 Clipstone Welfare 1

SECOND ROUND

AFC Barnsley 2 Kimberley Town 1
Askern Welfare 0 **Barton Town Old Boys** 3
Blackwell Miners Welfare 1 **Rolls Royce Leisure** 2
Hatfield Main 1 **Sandiacre Town** 5
Holbrook Miners Welfare 1 Dinnington Town 1
Dinnington Town 4 Holbrook Miners Welfare 1 *replay*
Radcliffe Olympic 2 Dunkirk 1
Radford 0 Harworth Colliery Institute 0
Harworth Colliery Institute 0 **Radford** 1 *replay*
Rainworth Miners Welfare 4 Graham Street Prims 2

QUARTER-FINALS

Barton Town Old Boys 1 **Rainworth Miners Welfare** 2
Dinnington Town (w/o) v AFC Barnsley (scr.)
Radcliffe Olympic 1 **Radford** 3
Sandiacre Town 2 Rolls Royce Leisure 0

SEMI-FINALS

(played over two legs)
Radford 1 Dinnington Town 2,
Dinnington Town 0 **Radford** 2
Rainworth Miners Welfare 1 Sandiacre Town 1,
Sandiacre Town 5 Rainworth Miners Welfare 0

FINAL

(April 5th at Dunkirk)
Radford 1 Sandiacre Town 0

COMBINED COUNTIES LEAGUE

	Ash United	Bedfont	Bedfont Green	Chessington & Hook Utd	Chipstead	Cobham	Colliers Wood United	Cove	Farnham Town	Feltham	Frimley Green	Godalming Town	Guildford United	Horley Town	Merstham	Mole Valley Predators	North Greenford United	Raynes Park Vale	Reading Town	Sandhurst Town	Southall	Westfield
Ash United		1-2	2-1	0-1	5-1	0-1	2-1	2-0	2-0	3-0	1-1	3-5	3-0	2-0	0-0	6-0	1-0	3-3	2-2	1-1	0-2	3-0
Bedfont	1-2		4-2	1-1	2-0	0-0	2-2	1-0	7-0	1-0	6-2	1-2	4-0	2-0	1-3	4-2	2-1	1-2	1-1	1-4	n/a	1-1
Bedfont Green	1-4	1-1		2-6	2-1	2-1	2-3	1-1	0-1	1-2	2-2	2-6	4-1	0-1	1-4	4-1	1-2	1-6	2-1	0-2	1-3	2-1
Chessington & Hook United	0-1	4-0	4-1	*P*	0-0	3-3	2-0	1-2	2-0	6-1	5-1	0-1	0-0	0-0	0-0	1-4	3-0	2-1	1-1	1-1	2-3	4-0
Chipstead	2-0	0-0	5-1	2-2	*R*	2-1	0-1	3-3	3-0	4-0	0-2	2-4	2-1	1-1	0-2	1-3	1-1	1-2	2-1	0-0	0-2	2-0
Cobham	0-1	1-0	1-2	1-0	1-4	*E*	2-3	1-0	3-1	1-2	1-1	0-2	2-3	2-2	0-2	4-0	0-2	3-0	1-1	1-2	n/a	0-1
Colliers Wood United	4-2	1-0	1-3	3-4	3-1	4-2	*M*	2-0	2-2	4-0	5-2	0-3	4-0	0-1	0-2	5-1	4-1	2-0	4-0	1-1	3-3	2-4
Cove	3-2	2-2	2-2	4-4	0-2	0-3	0-2	*I*	2-1	3-0	1-0	0-1	6-3	2-2	0-4	0-3	2-0	1-2	0-2	0-2	2-2	2-2
Farnham Town	0-1	0-3	1-1	0-8	1-1	3-3	1-6	0-0	*E*	0-3	3-1	1-5	1-5	3-4	0-1	3-0	1-1	1-1	2-2	0-0	n/a	2-2
Feltham	2-1	0-1	0-2	0-2	4-1	1-1	5-3	1-2	1-0	*R*	1-2	1-2	1-4	1-1	0-2	2-3	0-0	1-4	3-1	2-4	3-3	1-1
Frimley Green	0-4	0-3	3-2	1-0	3-1	0-1	2-1	1-1	2-0	2-2		1-1	1-2	2-1	0-1	1-2	0-1	4-0	1-1	1-0	n/a	0-4
Godalming Town	1-1	0-2	4-0	5-1	0-0	1-0	3-2	5-0	1-0	3-0	3-3	*D*	3-0	1-2	0-0	5-0	3-1	1-0	1-1	3-2	4-0	2-0
Guildford United	2-1	0-2	0-3	0-0	1-1	1-2	3-1	1-1	2-1	3-3	0-1	1-4	*I*	3-4	1-0	2-2	1-4	0-0	0-4	2-2	3-1	4-0
Horley Town	1-1	1-0	3-2	1-3	2-0	2-0	0-2	4-0	1-2	2-0	3-0	1-0	0-0	*V*	2-0	0-0	1-0	3-1	0-1	0-4	1-0	0-1
Merstham	0-1	4-0	3-0	1-0	2-0	1-0	1-1	2-2	2-1	0-2	4-0	1-1	2-0	1-0	*I*	3-1	2-4	5-2	0-0	1-0	1-0	3-1
Mole Valley Predators	2-1	1-1	0-1	0-5	1-2	3-2	2-1	3-4	4-0	3-2	3-1	1-7	0-1	2-0	0-1	*S*	2-2	2-0	4-2	0-3	1-3	0-4
North Greenford United	2-3	2-1	2-3	1-1	1-2	1-2	2-3	5-3	1-2	4-0	2-0	0-1	4-1	1-1	0-0	0-4	*I*	6-0	2-6	5-1	1-2	1-5
Raynes Park Vale	1-0	1-2	3-1	2-1	2-3	0-5	2-4	5-1	3-2	3-2	3-0	1-4	4-1	1-2	3-1	4-2	5-2	*O*	1-0	0-7	0-3	1-2
Reading Town	0-2	0-3	5-2	0-2	3-0	5-2	0-3	1-2	3-1	4-0	2-1	1-2	2-1	0-1	1-0	2-0	1-2	0-2	*N*	2-3	n/a	0-0
Sandhurst Town	1-2	1-1	3-0	3-1	3-2	1-1	2-1	5-2	1-1	3-1	3-0	1-2	3-0	0-2	0-2	2-2	0-2	1-0	2-4		7-1	2-2
Southall	1-0	2-2	n/a	n/a	3-2	n/a	n/a	n/a	5-1	3-2	n/a	3-0	2-2	n/a	n/a	n/a	n/a	n/a	1-0	n/a		4-2
Westfield	1-1	0-2	2-0	2-1	4-1	1-0	1-2	0-1	5-0	3-2	2-0	0-1	1-3	0-2	1-1	1-2	1-4	2-0	1-2	1-1	1-2	

Note – Southall withdrew during the course of the season; their results are shown above but are expunged from the league table

Premier Division		P	W	D	L	F	A	Pts
Godalming Town		40	30	7	3	99	33	97
Merstham		40	24	9	7	64	26	81
Ash United		40	21	8	11	73	43	71
Colliers Wood United		40	22	4	14	93	63	70
Horley Town		40	20	9	11	54	41	69
Bedfont		40	19	10	11	69	45	67
Sandhurst Town		40	18	12	10	77	50	66
Chessington & Hook United	*-4*	40	17	12	11	82	46	59
Raynes Park Vale		40	18	3	19	71	82	57
Reading Town		40	15	9	16	65	59	54
Westfield		40	15	9	16	60	58	54
Mole Valley Predators		40	16	5	19	65	90	53
North Greenford United		40	15	7	18	72	70	52
Chipstead		40	13	10	17	56	65	49
Cobham		40	12	8	20	55	60	44
Cove		40	11	11	18	55	83	44
Guildford United		40	11	9	20	53	83	42
Frimley Green		40	11	8	21	45	78	41
Bedfont Green		40	12	5	23	60	95	41
Feltham		40	9	6	25	49	90	33
Farnham Town		40	5	11	24	38	95	26

Southall – record expunged

Reserve Premier Division		P	W	D	L	F	A	Pts
Raynes Park Vale Res.		26	20	5	1	71	30	65
Colliers Wood United Res.		26	18	3	5	73	38	57
Sandhurst Town Res.		26	17	3	6	55	24	54
Ash United Res.		26	13	5	8	53	36	44
Westfield Res.		26	12	4	10	50	37	40
Bedfont Green Res.	*-3*	26	13	2	11	48	41	38
Cobham Res.	*-1*	26	11	5	10	53	46	37
Chessington/Hook Utd Res.		26	10	5	11	50	46	35
Cove Res.		26	8	5	13	37	52	29
Hartley Wintney Res.		26	8	5	13	51	69	29
Farnham Town Res.		26	8	3	15	40	70	27
Frimley Green Res.		26	7	2	17	31	68	23
Egham Town Res.		26	7	1	18	36	63	22
Mole Valley Predators Res.		26	2	8	16	31	59	14

Reserve Division One	P	W	D	L	F	A	Pts
Bookham Res.	20	16	2	2	73	18	50
Staines Lammas Res.	20	16	2	2	58	17	50
Warlingham Res.	20	14	2	4	56	26	44
Coney Hall Res.	20	14	2	4	51	24	44
Farleigh Rovers Res.	20	11	0	9	42	27	33
Crescent Rovers Res.	20	11	0	9	50	36	33
Worcester Park Res.	20	6	1	13	33	38	19
Merrow Res.	20	6	0	14	28	52	18
Tongham Res.	20	6	0	14	29	58	18
Sheerwater Res.	20	3	1	16	21	79	10
Chobham Res.	20	2	0	18	23	89	6

Monotype Res. & Netherne Res. – records expunged

COMBINED COUNTIES LEAGUE PREMIER DIVISION CONSTITUTION 2006-07

ASH UNITED	Youngs Drive, Shawfield Road, Ash, near Aldershot GU12 6RE	01252 345757
BANSTEAD ATHLETIC	Merland Rise, Tadworth KT20 5JG	01737 350982
BEDFONT	The Orchard, Hatton Road, Bedfont TW14 9QT	020 8890 7264
BEDFONT GREEN	Avenue Park, Western Avenue, Greenford UB6 8GA *(or groundshare at Yeading FC)*	020 8578 2706
BOOKHAM	Dorking FC, Meadowbank, Mill Lane, Dorking RH4 1DX	01306 88412
CAMBERLEY TOWN	Krooner Park, Krooner Road, off Frimley Road, Camberley GU15 2QP	01276 65392
CHERTSEY TOWN	Alwyns Lane, Chertsey KT16 9DW	01932 561774/571792
CHESSINGTON & HOOK UNITED	Chalky Lane, Chessington KT9 2PW	01372 745777
CHIPSTEAD	High Road, Chipstead CR5 3SF	01737 553250
COBHAM	Leg O'Mutton Field, Anvil Lane, Downsbridge Road, Cobham KT11 3BD	01932 865959
COLLIERS WOOD UNITED	Wibbandune Sports Ground, Robin Hood Way, Kingston SW20 0AA	020 8942 8062
COVE	Oak Farm, 7 Squirrel Lane, Cove, Farnborough GU14 8PB	01252 543615
DORKING	Meadowbank, Mill Lane, Dorking RH4 1DX	01306 884112
EGHAM TOWN	Runnymede Stadium, Tempest Road, Egham TW20 8HX	01784 435226/436466
EPSOM & EWELL	Banstead Athletic FC, Merland Rise, Tadworth KT20 5JG	01737 350982
GUILDFORD CITY	Spectrum Leisure Centre, Parkway, Guildford GU1 1UP	01483 443322
MERSTHAM	Merstham Recreation Ground, Weldon Way, Merstham RH1 3PF	01737 644046
NORTH GREENFORD UNITED	Berkeley Fields, Berkeley Avenue, Greenford	020 8422 8923
RAYNES PARK VALE	Princes Georges Playing Field, Grand Drive, Raynes Park SW20 9LN	020 8540 8843
READING TOWN	Scours Lane, Tilehurst, Reading RG30 6AY	0118 945 3555
SANDHURST TOWN	Bottom Meadow, Memorial Park, Yorktown Road, Sandhurst GU47 9BJ	01252 878768
WEMBLEY	Vale Farm, Watford Road, Sudbury, Wembley HA0 4UR	020 8904 8169/8908 5461
WESTFIELD	Woking Park, off Elmbridge Lane, Kingfield, Woking GU22 7AA	01483 771106

IN: Banstead Athletic (R – Isthmian League Division One), Bookham (P), Camberley Town (S – Isthmian League Division Two), Chertsey Town (S – Isthmian League Division Two), Dorking (S – Isthmian League Division Two), Egham Town (S – Isthmian League Division Two), Epsom & Ewell (S – Isthmian League Division Two), Wembley (S – Isthmian League Division Two)

OUT: Farnham Town (R), Feltham (R), Frimley Green (R), Godalming Town (P – Isthmian League Division One South), Horley Town (R), Mole Valley Predators (W), Southall (WS – Middlesex County League Premier Division)

Guildford United become Guildford City

LEAGUE CUP

FIRST ROUND

Colliers Wood United 4 Warlingham 2
Horley Town 4 Bookham 0
Merstham 0 Farleigh Rovers 0 *aet* (3-2p)
Netherne 0 **Hartley Wintney** 8
North Greenford United (w/o) v Ditton (scr.)
Sheerwater 0 **Reading Town** 4
Shottermill & Haslemere 1 **Hanworth Villa** 0
(Shottermill & Haslemere expelled)
Southall 8 Chobham 2
Staines Lammas 1 **Tongham** 2

SECOND ROUND

AFC Wallingford 4 Coney Hall 1
Chessington & Hook United (w/o) v Seelec Delta (scr.)
Chipstead 0 **Godalming Town** 4
Cobham 2 Guildford United 1
Cove 4 Ash United 3
Crescent Rovers 1 **Merstham** 4
Farnham Town 3 **Worcester Park** 4
Feltham 2 Merrow 1
Frimley Green 0 **Colliers Wood United** 1
Hanworth Villa 3 Mole Valley Predators 2
Hartley Wintney 4 Bedfont Green 0
Horley Town 1 **Southall** 2
Reading Town 1 **North Greenford United** 2
Sandhurst Town 2 Monotype 0
Tongham 4 Raynes Park Vale 0
Westfield 2 Bedfont 1 *aet*

THIRD ROUND

AFC Wallingford 2 Cove 1 *aet*
Colliers Wood United 1 **North Greenford United** 2
Feltham 3 Hartley Wintney 0
Hanworth Villa 2 Worcester Park 5
(Worcester Park expelled)
Merstham 3 Cobham 1
Southall 0 **Sandhurst Town** 2
Tongham 1 **Godalming Town** 2
Westfield 2 Chessington & Hook United 1

QUARTER-FINALS

AFC Wallingford 1 **Hanworth Villa** 3
Feltham 4 **North Greenford United** 5 *aet*
Sandhurst Town 2 **Merstham** 3
Westfield 0 **Godalming Town** 2

SEMI-FINALS

Merstham 4 Hanworth Villa 0
North Greenford United 0 **Godalming Town** 1 *aet*

FINAL

(April 28th at Woking)
Godalming Town 4 Merstham 0

PREMIER RESERVE CUP

FINAL

(April 12th at Bedfont)
Ash United Res. 1 Sandhurst Town Res. 0

RESERVE DIVISION ONE CUP

FINAL

(May 3rd at Merstham)
Warlingham Res. 5 Bookham Res. 1

RESERVES SHIELD

FINAL

(May 9th at Ash United)
Cobham Res. 3 Staines Lammas Res. 2

	AFC Wallingford	Bookham	Chobham	Coney Hall	Crescent Rovers	Farleigh Rovers	Hanworth Villa	Hartley Wintney	Merrow	Monotype	Netherne Village	Sheerwater	Shottermill & Haslemere	Staines Lammas	Tongham	Warlingham	Worcester Park
AFC Wallingford		1-2	6-0	4-1	5-1	1-0	2-1	3-2	4-0	3-1	3-2	2-0	1-0	7-0	4-3	0-2	5-1
Bookham	2-3		1-1	3-2	5-0	4-2	2-5	2-0	8-0	6-0	3-2	4-1	3-0	0-0	5-1	2-2	1-1
Chobham	1-4	0-8	*D*	0-3	3-3	0-2	1-4	0-2	0-1	0-2	4-1	0-2	4-4	0-3	1-4	1-4	4-1
Coney Hall	2-3	2-3	13-0	*I*	1-3	5-2	2-2	1-1	3-0	6-1	5-1	5-3	3-1	4-2	3-3	1-2	4-1
Crescent Rovers	1-1	3-5	2-3	0-1	*V*	1-1	4-3	6-0	2-0	0-3	4-1	2-0	1-0	2-0	0-4	1-0	1-4
Farleigh Rovers	1-2	0-2	3-1	2-1	1-0	*I*	2-6	2-4	3-2	2-3	4-1	1-1	2-0	2-1	2-3	3-4	0-1
Hanworth Villa	2-1	1-3	6-1	3-3	5-0	1-3	*S*	1-3	2-1	2-1	1-0	4-2	6-0	0-1	1-2	2-0	1-1
Hartley Wintney	2-0	1-1	1-0	1-0	3-0	2-0	2-2	*I*	4-0	1-2	6-0	4-0	6-0	2-1	1-4	3-1	3-0
Merrow	1-5	0-4	3-2	1-5	2-2	0-3	3-1	2-4	*O*	0-4	6-1	2-3	4-0	2-4	1-6	3-4	1-5
Monotype	1-1	0-9	0-0	1-3	0-2	1-1	1-7	0-2	3-0	*N*	2-2	5-1	3-5	1-3	0-7	0-2	1-2
Netherne Village	0-5	0-9	4-5	2-5	0-3	2-2	0-7	1-2	6-0	0-3		5-3	0-2	2-1	0-5	0-5	0-4
Sheerwater	1-0	1-1	3-0	0-0	1-0	1-2	1-5	0-2	3-3	3-1	2-1		3-1	1-4	1-5	0-3	2-3
Shottermill & Haslemere	0-2	0-8	0-1	0-6	0-4	1-3	1-2	2-1	2-4	1-1	4-1	4-2	*O*	3-4	2-4	1-8	0-0
Staines Lammas	0-4	0-3	2-0	0-0	3-2	2-2	1-2	3-4	2-1	3-3	7-1	1-2	3-1	*N*	1-2	4-5	0-1
Tongham	1-4	0-2	9-1	3-3	1-3	1-2	5-3	0-2	10-1	5-1	9-1	10-1	3-0	3-1	*E*	2-3	1-1
Warlingham	5-0	2-0	2-0	4-1	3-3	2-0	1-1	6-3	6-1	1-0	9-1	2-0	2-1	5-1	4-0		2-1
Worcester Park	2-4	2-2	5-0	4-1	6-0	1-0	3-5	4-0	3-2	9-0	2-0	8-0	3-0	3-0	3-2	1-1	

Division One		P	W	D	L	F	A	Pts
Warlingham		32	25	4	3	102	37	79
AFC Wallingford		32	24	2	6	90	38	74
Bookham		32	22	7	3	113	33	73
Worcester Park		32	19	6	7	86	43	63
Hartley Wintney	*-3*	32	21	3	8	74	44	63
Tongham		32	19	3	10	118	58	60
Hanworth Villa		32	18	5	9	94	53	59
Coney Hall		32	15	7	10	95	56	52
Farleigh Rovers		32	13	5	14	55	57	44
Crescent Rovers		32	13	5	14	56	65	44
Staines Lammas		32	11	4	17	58	70	37
Sheerwater		32	9	4	19	44	90	31
Monotype		32	8	6	18	45	89	30
Merrow		32	6	2	24	47	114	20
Chobham		32	5	4	23	34	108	19
Shottermill & Haslemere		32	5	3	24	36	98	18
Netherne Village		32	3	2	27	38	132	11

DIVISION ONE CUP

FIRST ROUND

Ditton (scr.) v **Merrow** (w/o)
Sheerwater 0 **Hanworth Villa** 2
Worcester Park 3 Shottermill & Haslemere 3 *aet* (5-4p)

SECOND ROUND

Crescent Rovers 0 **Bookham** 2
Farleigh Rovers 0 **Hanworth Villa** 1
Merrow 2 AFC Wallingford 1
Monotype 4 **Hartley Wintney** 6
Netherne (w/o) v Seelec Delta (scr.)
Staines Lammas 4 Chobham 2
Tongham 1 **Coney Hall** 4
Worcester Park 2 Warlingham 2 *aet* (4-3p)

QUARTER-FINALS

Bookham 4 Merrow 1
Coney Hall 4 Hartley Wintney 0
Hanworth Villa 0 **Worcester Park** 2
Netherne 1 **Staines Lammas** 5

SEMI-FINALS

Bookham 1 **Worcester Park** 2
Staines Lammas 1 **Coney Hall** 3

FINAL

(April 26th at Tooting & Mitcham United)
Coney Hall 3 Worcester Park 0

COMBINED COUNTIES LEAGUE DIVISION ONE CONSTITUTION 2006-07

CB HOUNSLOW UNITED .... Osterley Sports Club, Tentelow Lane, Osterley, Southall UB2 4LW 020 8574 3774
CHOBHAM .... Chobham Recreation Ground, Station Road, Chobham GU24 8AZ 01276 857876
CONEY HALL .... Tie Pigs Lane, Coney Hall, West Wichkam BR4 9BT 020 8462 9103
COULSDON TOWN .... Woodplace Lane, Coulsdon CR5 1NB 01737 557509
CRESCENT ROVERS .... Wallington Sports/Social Club, Mollison Drive, Wallington SM6 9BY 020 8647 2558
FARLEIGH ROVERS .... Parsonage Field, Harrow Road, Farleigh, Warlingham CR6 9EY 01884 626483
FARNHAM TOWN .... Memorial Ground, West Street, Farnham GU9 7DY 01252 715305
FELTHAM .... Hampton & Richmond Borough FC, The Beveree, Beaver Close, Station Road, Hampton TW12 2BX 020 8941 2838
FRIMLEY GREEN .... Frimley Green Rec. Ground, Frimley Green Road, Frimley Green, Camberley GU16 6LL 01252 835089
HANWORTH VILLA .... Rectory Meadow, Park Road, Hounslow Road, Hanworth 020 8831 9391
HARTLEY WINTNEY .... Memorial Playing Fields, Green Lane, Hartley Wintney RG27 8HD 01252 843586
HORLEY TOWN .... The New Defence, Court Lodge Road, Horley RH6 8RS 01293 822000
MERROW .... The Urnfield, Downside Road, Guildford GU4 8PH .... None
SALFORDS .... Coulsdon Town FC, Woodplace Lane, Coulsdon CR5 1NB 01737 557509
SHEERWATER .... Blackmore Crescent, Sheerwater Estate, Woking GU21 5NW .... None
SOUTH PARK .... Snoxhall Fields, Knowle Lane, Cranleigh, Surrey GU6 8JW 01483 275295
STAINES LAMMAS .... Laleham Recreation Ground, The Broadway, Laleham, Staines TW18 1RX 01784 465204
TONGHAM .... Recreation Ground, Poyle Road, Tongham GU10 1BS .... None
WARLINGHAM .... Warlingham Sports Club, Church Road, Warlingham CR6 9PR 01883 622943
WORCESTER PARK .... Skinners Field, Green Lane, Worcester Park KT4 8AJ 020 8337 4995

IN: CB Hounslow United (P – Middlesex County League Premier Division), Farnham Town (R), Feltham (R), Frimley Green (R), Horley Town (R), South Park (P – Crawley & District League Premier Division)

OUT: AFC Wallingford (S – Hellenic League Premier Division), Bookham (P), Ditton (WN), Seelec Delta (WN), Shottermill & Haslemere (R – Surrey Intermediate League (West) Premier Division)

Monotype become Salfords, Netherne Village become Coulsdon Town

CORNWALL COMBINATION

	Falmouth Tn Res.	Goonhavern Res.	Hayle	Helston Athletic	Holmans SC	Illogan RBL	Ludgvan	Mousehole	Mullion	Newquay Res.	Penryn Ath. Res.	Penzance Res.	Perranporth	Perranwell	RNAS Culdrose	St Agnes	St Ives Town	St Just	Truro City Res.	Wendron CC Utd
Falmouth Town Res.		1-0	2-3	1-3	1-3	2-0	1-0	0-0	4-1	1-0	3-1	2-2	2-0	0-0	1-3	3-2	0-2	2-1	n/a	2-0
Goonhavern Res.	1-3		1-4	0-1	0-1	2-1	0-4	0-3	0-5	1-1	1-5	2-1	1-3	2-4	2-1	0-1	0-5	0-7	2-3	3-4
Hayle	3-2	6-0		2-1	1-1	3-0	2-2	1-2	5-0	5-0	1-1	2-0	4-1	2-1	2-1	1-3	0-0	2-1	2-4	0-1
Helston Athletic	6-1	5-1	3-1		2-2	1-2	1-1	3-2	3-0	2-0	2-1	2-2	3-1	0-2	3-1	0-1	1-3	1-0	1-4	2-0
Holmans Sports Club	1-0	3-0	1-3	1-4		3-3	3-2	1-1	2-1	7-0	1-1	1-0	5-0	0-1	0-0	0-1	1-1	4-0	0-0	3-0
Illogan RBL	1-5	2-1	3-1	1-2	1-1		2-1	2-3	5-2	2-1	1-4	1-1	1-0	0-3	4-2	0-2	4-0	3-0	2-1	3-1
Ludgvan	3-1	4-2	0-2	2-2	1-0	3-1		4-1	3-1	3-2	5-0	2-0	2-2	2-0	0-0	1-2	1-6	1-1	0-2	1-2
Mousehole	3-0	4-0	1-0	4-2	1-1	1-3	0-0		3-1	1-3	1-0	4-2	2-0	2-1	2-1	0-0	1-0	4-0	1-3	0-3
Mullion	1-2	3-2	1-1	0-3	1-1	1-4	1-1	0-1		8-1	2-4	5-6	1-1	0-1	2-2	1-1	1-1	2-0	1-2	0-3
Newquay Res.	1-4	1-0	1-5	1-3	1-6	0-2	3-1	2-1	2-0		1-2	4-4	0-2	0-2	6-0	3-7	0-1	6-1	2-3	0-2
Penryn Athletic Res.	3-2	9-1	1-2	2-1	1-2	0-3	1-0	2-1	4-2	6-0		4-3	0-2	3-1	1-1	1-4	0-0	2-0	0-2	1-1
Penzance Res.	0-2	4-3	0-1	1-1	8-0	1-3	2-4	0-0	1-3	0-0	1-0		1-1	0-0	3-2	0-2	0-4	4-2	1-1	1-3
Perranporth	1-1	1-2	0-2	1-2	2-3	4-1	0-2	1-0	4-0	1-2	1-2	1-1		1-2	3-1	1-1	0-0	0-0	0-0	0-5
Perranwell	3-3	2-1	1-1	1-1	1-1	4-4	4-1	3-1	4-1	5-1	1-1	5-0	4-3		5-1	0-2	1-1	1-1	2-1	1-1
RNAS Culdrose	1-2	2-1	1-4	1-2	3-1	3-1	2-2	1-2	1-3	3-1	1-2	2-3	0-2	0-1		2-6	1-3	1-2	1-4	n/a
St Agnes	3-2	2-0	1-3	3-3	6-2	5-0	5-2	1-1	3-2	7-0	2-2	5-1	2-0	0-0	4-1		1-5	1-2	2-4	4-3
St Ives Town	1-2	1-0	0-0	0-2	2-1	0-1	0-2	0-0	3-0	6-0	1-0	4-0	5-0	0-0	0-2	1-3		0-1	0-2	5-1
St Just	1-4	2-0	1-0	1-0	2-1	0-1	1-1	1-2	2-4	4-2	0-1	0-0	0-0	0-3	0-2	0-4	2-2		1-4	0-5
Truro City Res.	2-0	3-0	2-0	n/a	4-1	3-0	0-1	3-0	8-0	2-1	3-1	7-0	0-1	1-2	1-2	2-1	5-1	6-0		2-3
Wendron CC United	7-5	7-0	0-3	7-2	1-1	1-1	1-4	4-1	2-2	1-0	3-2	5-0	2-0	1-3	1-1	3-0	2-1	0-0	0-1	

GEORGE EVELY CUP

(Cornwall Comb. Cup winners v E Cornwall Prem. Lge Cup winners)

(May 7th at Penryn Athletic)

Truro City Res. 1 Godolphin Atlantic 0

		P	W	D	L	F	A	Pts
Truro City Res.		36	26	3	7	95	32	81
St Agnes		38	24	7	7	100	52	79
Hayle		38	22	7	9	80	41	73
Perranwell	*-1*	38	20	13	5	75	40	72
Helston Athletic		37	20	7	10	76	54	67
Wendron CC Utd	*-3*	37	20	7	10	86	55	64
Mousehole		38	18	8	12	57	49	62
Illogan RBL		38	19	5	14	69	68	62
Falmouth Town Res.		37	18	5	14	69	63	59
St Ives Town		38	16	10	12	65	38	58
Ludgvan		38	16	10	12	69	56	58
Penryn Athletic Res.		38	17	7	14	71	59	58
Holmans Sports Club		38	14	13	11	66	57	55
Perranporth		38	9	10	19	41	62	37
St Just		38	9	8	21	37	76	35
Penzance Res.		38	7	12	19	54	90	33
RNAS Culdrose		37	8	6	23	50	82	30
Mullion		38	7	8	23	59	96	29
Newquay Res.		38	8	3	27	49	111	27
Goonhavern Res.		38	4	1	33	32	119	13

Falmouth Town Res. v Truro City Res. – not played
RNAS Culdrose v Wendron CC United – not played
Truro City Res. v Newquay Res. – not played

LEAGUE CUP

PRELIMINARY ROUND

Illogan RBL 3 Holmans S C 1
Ludgvan 1 **St Ives Town** 2
Mousehole 5 Falmouth Tn Res. 2
Perranwell 0 RNAS Culdrose 0
RNAS Culdrose 1 **Perranwell** 6 *replay*

FIRST ROUND

Goonhavern Res. 1 **Penzance Res.** 2
Hayle 1 **Wendron CC United** 4
Mousehole 1 **Illogan RBL** 5
Newquay Res. 0 **St Ives Town** 3
Penryn Athletic Res. 3 St Agnes 0
Perranporth 2 Mullion 2
Mullion 2 Perranporth 1 *replay*
Perranwell 2 **Helston Athletic** 4
St Just 0 **Truro City Res.** 2

QUARTER-FINALS

Helston Athletic 2 Penryn Athletic Res. 1
Illogan RBL 0 Mullion 0
Mullion 0 **Illogan RBL** 2 *replay*
Truro City Res. 4 Penzance Res. 0
Wendron CC Utd 0 **St Ives Tn** 2

SEMI-FINALS

Helston Athletic 1 **Illogan RBL** 3 *(at Hayle)*
St Ives Town 0 **Truro City Res.** 2 *(at Illogan RBL)*

FINAL

(April 16th at Helston Athletic)
Illogan RBL 0 **Truro City Res.** 2

SUPPLEMENTARY CUP

(Teams eliminated in the Preliminary and First Round of the League Cup)

PRELIMINARY ROUND

Goonhavern Res. 1 **Mousehole** 4
Perranporth 2 Falmouth Town Res. 2
Falmouth Town Res. 1 **Perranporth** 2 *replay*
Perranwell 3 **Holmans S C** 4
St Agnes 2 Newquay Res. 0

QUARTER-FINALS

Ludgvan 3 Mousehole 1
RNAS Culdrose 1 **Holmans Sports Club** 4
St Agnes 1 Perranporth 0
St Just 0 **Hayle** 2

SEMI-FINALS

Holmans Sports Club 2 Hayle 1 *(at Illogan RBL)*
Ludgvan 3 St Agnes 2 *(at Hayle)*

FINAL *(May 21st at Penzance)*
Holmans Spts Club 3 Ludgvan 1

CORNWALL COMBINATION CONSTITUTION 2006-07

FALMOUTH TOWN RESERVES ...... Bickland Park, Bickland Water Road, Falmouth TR11 4PB 01326 377736
HAYLE ...... Trevassack Park, Viaduct Hill, Hayle TR27 4HT 01736 757157
HELSTON ATHLETIC ...... Kellaway Parc, Clodgy Lane, Helston TR13 8BN 01326 573742
HOLMANS SPORTS CLUB ...... Blaythorne Memorial Sports Ground, Pendarves, Camborne TR14 7QG 01209 713631
ILLOGAN RBL ...... Oxland Park, Richards Lane, Illogan, Redruth TR16 4HA 01209 216488
LUDGVAN ...... Ludgvan Community Centre, Fairfield, Ludgvan TR20 8ES 01736 740774
MOUSEHOLE ...... Trungle Parc, Paul, Penzance TR19 6XB ...... None
MULLION ...... Clifden Parc, Clifden Close, Mullion, Helston TR12 7EQ 01326 240676
NEWQUAY RESERVES ...... Mount Wise, Clevedon Road, Newquay TR7 2BU 01637 872935
PENRYN ATHLETIC RESERVES ...... Kernick, Kernick Road, Penryn TR10 8NT 01326 375182
PENZANCE RESERVES ...... Penlee Park, Alexandra Place, Penzance TR18 4NE 01736 361964
PERRANPORTH ...... Budnick Estate, Perranporth TR6 0DB 01872 575000
PERRANWELL ...... King George V Playing Field, School Hill, Perranwell Station TR3 7LA 01872 870202
RNAS CULDROSE ...... Sports Field, RNAS Culdrose, Helston TR12 7RH 01326 574121x7167
ST AGNES ...... Enys Park, West Polperro, St Agnes TR5 0SS 01872 553673
ST DAY ...... Vogue, St Day, Redruth TR16 5NP ...... None
ST IVES TOWN ...... The Saltings, Lelant TR6 3DL ...... None
ST JUST ...... Lafrowda Park, St Just, Penzance TR19 7RY 01736 788503
TRURO CITY RESERVES ...... Treyew Road, Truro TR1 2TH 01872 278853
WENDRON CC UNITED ...... Underlane, Carnkie 01209 860946

IN: St Day (P – Falmouth-Helston League Division One)
OUT: Goonhavern Reserves (R – Mining League Division One)

CYMRU ALLIANCE

	Bala Town	Bodedern	Buckley Town	Flint Town United	Glantraeth	Gresford Athletic	Guilsfield	Halkyn United	Holyhead Hotspurs	Holywell Town	Lex XI	Llandudno Town	Llandyrnog United	Llanfairpwll	Llangefni Town	Penrhyncoch	Queens Park	Ruthin Town
Bala Town		1-3	1-1	0-1	1-4	4-0	2-2	5-0	3-1	2-1	6-1	2-2	2-1	5-3	1-2	6-2	0-3	1-1
Bodedern	1-1		0-3	2-2	0-4	1-3	1-1	2-1	2-0	2-0	0-1	1-2	1-4	2-1	1-0	3-1	1-0	2-1
Buckley Town	2-2	5-1		0-3	2-3	0-0	2-1	1-0	3-0	5-1	6-5	3-5	4-2	1-2	0-2	4-0	6-0	2-1
Flint Town United	2-0	2-1	0-0		0-0	5-0	4-1	2-1	0-0	0-0	2-2	1-1	2-4	4-1	1-1	5-3	4-0	2-5
Glantraeth	3-0	4-0	3-1	0-1		3-1	2-2	6-2	5-1	5-2	3-1	4-2	5-0	4-2	1-1	3-0	3-0	0-0
Gresford Athletic	0-2	0-1	0-1	1-2	3-2		0-2	3-3	1-1	2-2	2-1	0-2	2-0	2-2	2-2	2-5	1-1	1-3
Guilsfield	1-1	0-0	3-3	3-3	2-2	2-0		2-0	5-0	3-3	5-1	2-1	2-0	2-0	1-6	0-1	4-0	4-0
Halkyn United	2-1	0-1	3-3	0-3	2-1	1-0	3-4		1-0	2-2	2-2	1-3	2-2	2-3	1-5	3-4	2-2	2-2
Holyhead Hotspurs	2-3	0-4	0-1	1-4	1-2	1-2	3-0	1-0		5-3	1-1	0-3	0-1	3-0	3-0	4-1	2-0	1-1
Holywell Town	0-2	0-1	2-5	1-1	1-0	1-4	0-0	2-1	4-4		1-3	1-1	2-2	5-0	1-1	3-0	1-2	2-2
Lex XI	1-3	2-1	3-5	3-2	3-0	1-1	2-2	3-2	3-1	4-2		3-2	2-4	1-3	1-3	1-3	2-2	2-1
Llandudno Town	1-1	7-0	1-2	0-2	0-2	2-1	0-2	3-1	0-0	3-0	3-3		3-0	2-1	1-0	1-2	4-0	0-2
Llandyrnog United	0-1	3-2	1-2	2-3	1-1	2-4	1-5	1-1	1-1	1-0	0-0	2-2		0-1	1-3	1-3	1-0	2-2
Llanfairpwll	4-0	3-1	2-4	1-4	0-2	3-0	0-4	3-2	3-3	2-2	3-0	1-2	4-2		4-0	1-4	1-2	2-2
Llangefni Town	3-2	2-0	2-2	3-3	1-2	2-1	0-2	6-0	1-1	4-1	0-4	1-2	2-1	1-0		4-1	1-0	0-1
Penrhyncoch	0-1	3-1	3-1	1-1	0-2	1-1	2-4	1-3	6-1	0-2	0-5	0-1	0-3	1-1	3-2		1-1	5-2
Queens Park	2-1	0-0	0-4	2-3	0-0	2-3	1-0	2-1	3-1	1-0	3-3	0-1	0-2	3-0	0-4	2-1		1-0
Ruthin Town	0-0	1-1	0-1	0-3	3-2	1-2	0-0	2-0	0-1	2-1	1-2	1-1	0-3	1-1	1-3	3-4	1-1	

		P	W	D	L	F	A	Pts
Glantraeth		34	21	7	6	83	36	70
Buckley Town		34	20	7	7	85	52	67
Flint Town United	*-3*	34	19	12	3	77	40	66
Guilsfield		34	16	12	6	73	44	60
Llangefni Town		34	17	7	10	68	46	58
Llandudno Town	*-3*	34	17	8	9	64	42	56
Bala Town		34	14	9	11	63	52	51
Lex XI		34	13	9	12	72	75	48
Bodedern		34	13	6	15	40	58	45
Penrhyncoch		34	13	4	17	62	78	43
Queens Park		34	11	8	15	36	59	41
Llanfairpwll		34	11	6	17	58	73	39
Llandyrnog United		34	10	8	16	51	64	38
Gresford Athletic		34	9	9	16	45	64	36
Ruthin Town		34	7	13	14	43	55	34
Holyhead Hotspurs		34	8	9	17	44	67	33
Holywell Town	*-3*	34	5	12	17	49	72	24
Halkyn United		34	5	8	21	47	83	23

LEAGUE CUP

PRELIMINARY ROUND

Flint Town United 2 Llandudno Town 1 *aet*

Penrhyncoch 0 **Buckley Town** 3

FIRST ROUND

Buckley Town 1 **Halkyn Utd** 2

Flint Town United 0 **Guilsfield** 3

Holyhead Hotspurs 1 **Gresford Athletic** 2 *aet*

Llanfairpwll 1 **Bodedern** 1 *aet* (1-3p)

Llandyrnog United 3 Lex XI 1

Llangefni Tn 2 **Bala Tn** 3 *aet*

Queens Park 3 **Glantraeth** 4

Ruthin Town 2 Holywell Town 0

QUARTER-FINALS

Bodedern 1 **Gresford Athletic** 4

Guilsfield 1 **Glantraeth** 2

Llandyrnog United 2 Halkyn United 2 *aet* (4-2p)

Ruthin Town 1 **Bala Town** 2

SEMI-FINALS

Bala Town 3 Gresford Athletic 1 *(at Lex XI)*

Llandyrnog United 0 **Glantraeth** 1 *(at Llandudno Town)*

FINAL

(May 6th at Llandudno Town)

Glantraeth 0 Bala Town 0 *aet* (5-3p)

CYMRU ALLIANCE CONSTITUTION 2006-07

BALA TOWN .... Maes Tegid, Castle Street, Bala LL23 7YB .... None
BODEDERN .... Cae r Ysgol, Holyhead Road, Bodedern LL65 3SU .... None
BUCKLEY TOWN .... Globe Way, Liverpool Way, Buckley CH7 3LL .... None
FLINT TOWN UNITED .... Cae Y Castell, March Lane, Flint CH6 5PJ 01352 730982
GLANTRAETH .... Trefdraeth, Bodorgan, LL62 5EU 01407 840401
GRESFORD ATHLETIC........ Clapper Lane, Gresford, Wrexham LL12 8RW .... None
GUILSFIELD........ Community Centre, Guilsfield, Welshpool SY21 9ND........ None
HOLYHEAD HOTSPURS........ New Oval, Leisure Centre, Kingsland, Holyhead LL65 2YE 01407 764111
LEX XI .... Stansty Park, Summerhill, Wrexham LL11 4YG........ 01978 261148
LLANDUDNO TOWN........ Maesdu Park, Builder Street, Llandudno LL30 1HH 01492 860945
LLANDYRNOG UNITED .... Swyn Y Nant, Llandyrnog, Denbigh LL16 4HB .... None
LLANFAIRPWLL .... Rear of Post Office, Ffordd Caergybi, Llanfairpwllgwyngyll LL61 5YG .... None
LLANGEFNI TOWN .... Cae Bob Parry, Talwrn Road, Llangefni LL77 7LP........ None
MYNYDD ISA........ Argoed Sports Field, Snowden Avenue, Bryn-y-Baal, Mold CH7 6SZ .... None
PENRHYNCOCH .... Cae Baker, Penrhynchoch, Aberystwyth SY23 3XH 01970 828992
PRESTATYN TOWN .... Bastion Road, Prestatyn........ 01745 856905
QUEENS PARK........ Queensway Athletics Stadium, Montgomery Road, Wrexham LL13 8UH 01978 261182
RHYL........ Belle Vue, Grange Road, Rhyl LL18 4BT........ 01745 338327
RUTHIN TOWN .... Memorial Playing Fields, Park Road, Ruthin LL15 1NB........ None

IN: Mynydd Isa (P – Welsh National League (Wrexham Area) Premier Division), Prestatyn Town (P – Welsh Alliance)

OUT: Halkyn United (R – Welsh Alliance), Holywell Town (R – Welsh Alliance)

DEVON COUNTY LEAGUE

	Alphington	Appledore	Buckland Athletic	Budleigh Salterton	Crediton United	Cullompton Rangers	Dartmouth	Elburton Villa	Holsworthy	Ivybridge Town	Newton Abbot	Newton Abbot Spurs	Ottery St Mary	Plymstock United	St Loyes	Stoke Gabriel	Teignmouth	Totnes & Dartington	University of Exeter	Vospers Oak Villa
Alphington		2-0	4-1	3-2	1-5	3-3	1-3	1-3	2-1	3-1	2-1	3-0	1-2	0-5	3-0	1-2	3-2	2-2	2-1	1-5
Appledore	0-2		2-1	0-4	1-0	6-1	0-3	2-1	1-3	0-2	2-1	1-1	1-3	0-1	2-1	2-2	4-2	1-3	2-1	4-0
Buckland Athletic	3-3	1-0		3-2	3-1	1-0	1-2	1-1	4-5	0-2	2-1	3-1	0-1	0-3	0-0	4-0	1-1	1-1	1-4	3-2
Budleigh Salterton	3-1	5-0	3-1		2-1	2-1	5-2	3-0	1-3	0-2	0-4	1-1	1-0	2-1	3-1	3-1	1-3	3-3	1-2	5-1
Crediton United	4-0	2-1	4-2	0-2		1-2	0-1	1-0	3-2	0-3	3-2	2-1	0-0	0-1	1-0	2-1	1-2	2-1	3-7	3-1
Cullompton Rangers	0-1	2-1	1-3	0-1	1-0		0-7	1-3	6-1	1-4	1-4	0-2	1-2	0-1	5-0	3-0	1-4	0-7	1-2	1-1
Dartmouth	1-0	6-0	4-3	3-0	0-0	0-0		3-2	3-5	2-3	1-0	2-1	2-2	2-4	2-0	3-2	3-2	0-3	2-0	0-0
Elburton Villa	2-0	5-0	3-0	1-1	0-0	1-6	1-3		0-2	0-2	0-1	2-2	1-4	2-0	4-1	6-0	0-2	0-3	1-0	1-0
Holsworthy	3-0	1-0	6-1	3-2	5-3	1-1	0-1	3-3		0-1	2-1	2-1	5-2	2-0	6-1	3-0	4-2	0-2	1-1	2-1
Ivybridge Town	4-1	2-1	1-3	2-0	2-1	8-1	2-1	4-2	6-1		1-1	2-0	3-0	3-1	10-1	6-1	1-1	3-1	2-1	2-2
Newton Abbot	1-0	5-1	5-1	4-2	1-0	5-3	0-2	0-2	2-2	1-3		0-3	1-1	1-2	4-0	2-0	2-1	2-1	4-1	3-0
Newton Abbot Spurs	2-2	5-0	2-1	1-2	8-0	3-2	3-1	2-1	2-1	1-1	4-2		0-3	0-3	3-1	2-0	1-1	2-1	2-1	2-1
Ottery St Mary	1-0	2-0	1-3	5-4	1-2	2-1	2-0	4-3	1-4	3-1	1-2	1-4		0-0	0-0	8-1	2-2	3-4	2-1	3-1
Plymstock United	5-0	8-0	5-0	0-2	1-0	4-0	1-1	2-0	1-1	1-7	1-1	3-0	1-1		5-2	6-3	9-3	1-1	3-0	1-2
St Loyes	0-3	3-1	1-4	1-4	1-1	2-1	2-7	0-1	2-3	1-3	2-6	1-2	0-2	0-2		0-4	0-1	1-4	0-1	2-3
Stoke Gabriel	2-2	2-5	3-1	1-2	1-3	1-2	1-1	0-1	1-2	1-8	0-6	2-2	0-4	1-1	3-1		1-3	1-3	1-3	1-2
Teignmouth	5-0	2-0	1-1	1-1	5-0	4-1	4-0	1-2	2-3	3-4	1-1	4-2	2-4	0-0	4-1	4-0		2-2	2-0	4-2
Totnes & Dartington SC	0-0	1-0	0-2	2-2	1-0	2-3	5-3	0-0	0-1	0-1	0-4	3-2	2-6	0-2	5-0	5-1	0-1		3-1	4-1
University of Exeter	4-3	3-1	5-1	0-1	1-2	2-3	0-1	2-1	3-1	0-6	0-1	1-3	2-5	1-4	3-0	1-1	4-1	7-0		0-2
Vospers Oak Villa	0-0	6-3	1-2	1-0	1-2	3-0	1-1	2-3	4-0	1-4	1-1	1-2	4-1	3-4	2-2	4-0	4-5	1-3	1-0	

		P	W	D	L	F	A	Pts
Ivybridge Town		38	31	4	3	122	38	97
Plymstock United		38	23	8	7	93	41	77
Holsworthy		38	23	5	10	90	67	74
Ottery St Mary		38	21	7	10	85	60	70
Dartmouth		38	21	7	10	79	56	70
Newton Abbot		38	20	6	12	83	49	66
Budleigh Salterton		38	20	5	13	78	59	65
Newton Abbot Spurs		38	19	7	12	75	58	64
Teignmouth		38	18	9	11	90	66	63
Totnes & Dartington SC		38	17	8	13	78	62	59
Elburton Villa	*+3*	38	15	6	17	59	59	54
Crediton United		38	16	4	18	53	65	52
Buckland Athletic		38	14	6	18	63	82	48
Alphington		38	13	7	18	56	79	46
Vospers Oak Villa		38	12	7	19	68	75	43
University of Exeter	*-4*	38	14	2	22	66	71	40
Cullompton Rangers		38	10	4	24	56	95	34
Appledore		38	10	2	26	45	95	32
Stoke Gabriel		38	4	6	28	42	117	18
St Loyes		38	2	4	32	31	118	10

CHARITY SHIELD

(League Champions v League Cup holders)

(August 7th at Buckland Athletic)

Teignmouth 2 Totnes & Dartington SC 1

LEAGUE CUP

FIRST ROUND

Ivybridge Town 6 Appledore 0
Newton Abbot 5 Stoke Gabriel 1
Teignmouth 2 Alphington 0
Totnes & Dartington SC 3 Cullompton Rangers 1

SECOND ROUND

Buckland Athletic 1 Vospers Oak Villa 0
Crediton United 0 **Newton Abbot** 2
Dartmouth 2 University of Exeter 1
Holsworthy 3 Budleigh Salterton 2
Newton Abbot Spurs 1 **Elburton Villa** 2 *aet*
Ottery St Mary 1 Totnes & Dartington SC 0
St Loyes 1 **Plymstock United** 5
Teignmouth 1 **Ivybridge Town** 2

QUARTER-FINALS

Holsworthy 3 Newton Abbot 2 *aet*
Ivybridge Town 4 Buckland Athletic 0
Ottery St Mary 5 Elburton Villa 1
Plymstock United 3 Dartmouth 0

SEMI-FINALS

Holsworthy 2 **Ottery St Mary** 5 *(at Cullompton Rangers)*
Ivybridge Town 1 **Plymstock United** 2 *(at Newton Abbot)*

FINAL

(May 1st at Crediton United)
Plymstock United 2 Ottery St Mary 1

DEVON COUNTY LEAGUE CONSTITUTION 2006-07

ALPHINGTON	The Chronicles, Alphington, Exeter EX2 8SW	01392 279556
APPLEDORE	Marshford, Churchill Way, Appledore EX39 1PA	01237 477099
BUCKLAND ATHLETIC	Homers Heath, Kingskerswell Road, Newton Abbot TQ12 5JU	01626 362602
BUDLEIGH SALTERTON	Greenway Lane, Budleigh Salterton EX9 6SG	01395 443850
CREDITON UNITED	Lords Meadow, Commercial Road, Crediton EX17 1ER	01363 774671
CULLOMPTON RANGERS	Speeds Meadow, Duke Street, Cullompton EX15 1DW	01884 33090
DARTMOUTH	Longcross, Townstall Road, Dartmouth TQ5 9LW	01803 832902
ELBURTON VILLA	Haye Road, Elburton, Plymouth PL9 8AR	01752 480025
HOLSWORTHY	Upcott Field, North Road, Holsworthy EX22 6HF	01409 254295
IVYBRIDGE TOWN	Erme Valley, Ivybridge PL21 9GX	01752 896686
NEWTON ABBOT	Coach Road Stadium, Coach Road, Newton Abbot TQ12 5DS	01626 335011
NEWTON ABBOT SPURS	Recreation Ground, Marsh Road, Newton Abbot TQ12 2AR	01626 365343
OTTERY ST MARY	Washbrook Meadows, Butts Road, Ottery St Mary EX11 1EL	01404 813539
PLYMSTOCK UNITED	Dean Cross, Dean Cross Road, Plymstock PL9 7AZ	01752 406776
STOKE GABRIEL	C J Churchward Memorial Ground, Broadley Lane, Stoke Gabriel, Totnes TQ9 6RR	01803 782223
TEIGNMOUTH	Coombe Valley, Coombe Lane, Teignmouth TQ14 9EZ	01626 776688
TOTNES & DARTINGTON SC	Foxhole Sports Ground, Dartington TQ9 6EB	01803 868032
UNIVERSITY OF EXETER	University Sports Ground, Topsham EX4 4QJ	01392 264452
VOSPERS OAK VILLA	The Mill, Ferndale Road, Weston Mill, Plymouth PL2 2EL	01752 363352
WITHERIDGE	Sports Field, Fore Street, Witheridge, Tiverton EX16 8PS	01884 861511

IN: Witheridge (P – Devon & Exeter League Premier Division)
OUT: St Loyes (R – Devon & Exeter League Premier Division)

DEVON & EXETER LEAGUE

	Axminster Town	Buckland Athletic Res.	Cullompton Rangers Res.	Exeter Civil Service	Exmouth Town Res.	Feniton	Hatherleigh Town	Heavitree Social United	Pinhoe	Seaton Town	Sidmouth Town	St Martins	Thorverton	Topsham Town	University of Exeter Res.	Witheridge
Axminster Town	*P*	2-0	0-2	0-0	1-1	4-1	2-3	1-2	0-2	3-2	2-1	1-1	2-1	2-1	3-0	1-2
Buckland Athletic Res.	1-0	*R*	0-0	0-2	3-3	2-2	0-1	2-2	5-2	0-0	1-5	2-1	0-1	2-0	1-0	2-2
Cullompton Rangers Res.	0-4	0-2	*E*	1-5	1-2	0-1	3-2	1-1	3-2	2-2	4-3	3-3	1-3	1-5	2-3	0-2
Exeter Civil Service	0-2	3-1	7-1	*M*	3-1	2-1	4-0	2-3	1-2	4-0	2-3	5-1	5-2	2-0	0-3	4-0
Exmouth Town Res.	1-1	6-0	1-2	1-1	*I*	0-4	3-1	2-3	1-4	0-0	0-1	1-2	0-0	1-0	1-1	0-2
Feniton	6-1	2-1	4-2	3-1	5-2	*E*	3-2	3-2	0-0	2-1	4-1	1-4	3-2	4-0	1-0	1-1
Hatherleigh Town	1-2	3-1	1-1	1-2	1-3	4-3	*R*	0-1	1-2	3-3	3-2	2-2	0-4	4-1	0-2	2-1
Heavitree Social United	3-0	1-0	3-2	1-1	2-2	2-2	2-1		3-2	1-0	2-1	2-2	1-1	1-0	3-1	0-0
Pinhoe	2-1	3-3	2-0	2-4	5-4	1-0	2-1	1-2	*D*	1-1	5-1	0-1	2-0	2-4	2-2	0-7
Seaton Town	0-4	3-0	2-0	0-2	0-2	2-2	2-2	0-4	1-2	*I*	1-2	0-0	0-1	2-1	2-1	1-2
Sidmouth Town	2-1	1-1	1-3	5-1	1-3	4-5	1-1	1-4	4-0	4-2	*V*	0-1	2-0	2-0	2-0	1-2
St Martins	2-2	1-2	4-1	2-1	5-3	3-2	2-1	1-4	3-1	7-0	2-3	*I*	3-1	4-1	5-1	1-3
Thorverton	4-1	1-0	3-3	2-1	4-0	1-1	1-0	1-1	7-1	2-1	2-2	3-1	*S*	2-0	4-2	1-1
Topsham Town	3-1	1-6	3-1	0-2	2-3	2-2	2-0	1-5	4-2	2-3	2-3	2-2	3-4	*I*	2-2	0-2
University of Exeter Res.	0-0	5-0	0-2	2-1	2-1	4-3	4-0	1-2	2-3	0-1	1-2	0-5	3-0	3-2	*O*	4-1
Witheridge	2-3	4-0	3-0	3-1	0-0	2-1	1-2	2-2	5-1	3-1	3-0	2-0	2-0	2-2	4-1	*N*

Premier Division		P	W	D	L	F	A	Pts
Heavitree Social United		30	19	10	1	65	34	67
Witheridge	*-4*	30	18	7	5	66	32	57
St Martins		30	15	7	8	71	50	52
Feniton		30	15	7	8	72	53	52
Thorverton		30	15	7	8	58	42	52
Exeter Civil Service	*-4*	30	16	3	11	69	43	47
Sidmouth Town		30	14	3	13	61	58	45
Pinhoe		30	13	4	13	56	71	43
Axminster Town		30	12	6	12	47	46	42
University of Exeter Res.		30	11	4	15	50	55	37
Exmouth Town Res.		30	8	9	13	48	57	33
Buckland Athletic Res.		30	8	8	14	38	57	32
Hatherleigh Town		30	8	5	17	43	62	29
Cullompton Rangers Res.		30	7	6	17	42	74	27
Seaton Town		30	6	8	16	33	59	26
Topsham Town	*-2*	30	6	4	20	46	72	20

Senior Division One		P	W	D	L	F	A	Pts
Okehampton Argyle		26	20	4	2	102	35	64
Clyst Valley		26	15	5	6	53	23	50
Beer Albion		26	14	4	8	64	43	46
Exeter Civil Service Res.		26	11	7	8	47	53	40
Broadclyst Social Club		26	10	9	7	42	44	39
Westexe Rovers		26	10	6	10	25	26	36
Bickleigh		26	8	11	7	41	37	35
Halwill		26	10	4	12	49	54	34
Exeter St Thomas	*-4*	26	8	9	9	32	42	29
Newtown		26	8	5	13	35	47	29
Wellington Town Res.	*-2*	26	7	9	10	40	42	28
North Tawton		26	6	7	13	38	51	25
Willand Rovers Res.	*-1*	26	5	8	13	23	45	22
Sidmouth Town Res.		26	5	2	19	25	74	17

DEVON & EXETER LEAGUE PREMIER DIVISION CONSTITUTION 2006-07

AXMINSTER TOWN .... **Sector Lane, Axminster EX13 5BP** .... **None**
BEER ALBION .... **Furzebrake, Stovar Long Lane, Beer EX12 3DY** .... **None**
CLYST VALLEY .... **Winslade Park, Exmouth Road, Clyst St Mary** .... **None**
CULLOMPTON RANGERS RESERVES .. **Speeds Meadow, Duke Street, Cullompton EX15 1DW** **01884 33090**
EXETER CIVIL SERVICE .... **Foxhayes, Exwick, Exeter EX4 2BQ** **01392 273976**
EXMOUTH TOWN .... **King George V Ground, Southern Road, Exmouth EX8 3EE** **01395 263348**
FENITON .... **Station Road, Feniton, Honiton EX14 3DF** **01404 850835**
HATHERLEIGH TOWN .... **The Sportsfield, Okehampton Road, Hatherleigh, Okehampton** **01837 810346**
HEAVITREE SOCIAL UNITED .... **Wingfield Park, East Wonford Hill, Exeter EX1 3BS** **01392 273020**
OKEHAMPTON ARGYLE .... **Simmons Park, Mill Road, Okehampton** **01837 53997**
PINHOE .... **Station Road, Pinhoe, Exeter EX1 3SA** .... **None**
SIDMOUTH TOWN .... **Manstone Recreation Ground, Manstone Lane, Sidmouth EX10 9TS** **01395 577087**
ST LOYES .... **St Loyes College, Millbrook Lane, Topsham Road, Exeter EX2 6EP** .... **None**
ST MARTINS .... **Minster Park, Exminster Hospital, Exminster** **01392 823909**
THORVERTON .... **Recreation Playing Field, Riaddon Road, Thorverton, Exeter** .... **None**
UNIVERSITY OF EXETER RESERVES ...... **University Sports Ground, Topsham EX4 4QJ** **01392 264452**

IN: Beer Albion (P), Clyst Valley (P), Okehampton Argyle (P), St Loyes (R – Devon County League)

OUT: Buckland Athletic Reserves (S – South Devon League Premier Division), Seaton Town (R), Topsham Town (R), Witheridge (P – Devon County League)

Exmouth Town Reserves become Exmouth Town

Senior Division Two	P	W	D	L	F	A	Pts
Culm United	26	20	2	4	108	44	62
Exmouth Amateurs	26	19	3	4	65	34	60
Heavitree Harriers	26	18	4	4	87	30	58
Budleigh Salterton Res.	26	16	5	5	71	35	53
Alphington Res. *-4*	26	14	2	10	67	51	40
Honiton Town	26	11	4	11	64	39	37
Kentisbeare	26	11	4	11	66	66	37
Univ of Exeter 'A' *-1*	26	11	2	13	57	43	34
Elmore Res.	26	10	2	14	62	74	32
Sandford	26	9	3	14	55	78	30
Lympstone	26	8	5	13	40	69	29
Lapford	26	7	2	17	48	72	23
Topsham Town Res.	26	6	3	17	44	108	21
Motel Rangers & Offwell	26	1	1	24	26	117	4

Senior Division Three	P	W	D	L	F	A	Pts
University of Exeter 'B'	26	21	2	3	93	22	65
East Budleigh	26	18	5	3	81	28	59
Barnstaple Town Res.	26	14	7	5	62	39	49
Otterton	26	15	3	8	59	38	48
Dawlish Town Res.	26	14	4	8	61	32	46
Heavitree Social Utd Res.	26	13	2	11	70	60	41
Newtown Res.	26	11	5	10	61	44	38
Lifton *-2*	26	11	3	12	74	78	34
Colyton	26	9	5	12	48	65	32
Newton St Cyres	26	8	2	16	44	66	26
St Loyes Res. *-1*	26	7	3	16	41	104	23
Tedburn St Mary	26	6	3	17	58	86	21
Winkleigh	26	5	6	15	46	86	21
Dunkeswell Rovers	26	4	2	20	46	96	14

Senior Division Four	P	W	D	L	F	A	Pts
Bow AAC	26	21	3	2	101	30	66
Sidbury United	26	17	6	3	54	27	57
Upottery	26	15	2	9	73	45	47
Seaton Town Res.	26	12	4	10	55	50	40
Pinhoe Res. *-2*	26	12	4	10	49	72	38
South Zeal United	26	11	4	11	54	53	37
Tipton St John *-2*	26	8	10	8	51	50	32
Westexe Rovers Res.	26	10	2	14	55	63	32
Bampton	26	8	7	11	50	57	31
Sampford Peverell	26	8	5	13	48	58	29
Exmouth Amateurs Res.	26	7	7	12	33	52	28
Crescent	26	8	3	15	49	64	27
Woodbury	26	7	3	16	46	77	24
Oakwood	26	7	2	17	31	51	23

Senior Division Five	P	W	D	L	F	A	Pts
Beacon Knights	26	21	4	1	93	30	67
Morchard Bishop	26	19	2	5	90	33	59
Uplowman Athletic	26	14	6	6	93	39	48
Bickleigh Res. *-1*	26	14	4	8	85	54	45
Broadclyst Social Club Res.	26	12	6	8	55	43	42
Crediton United Res.	26	13	3	10	79	68	42
Alphington `A'	26	11	8	7	73	59	41
Kentisbeare Res.	26	11	4	11	62	63	37
Axminster Town Res.	26	10	6	10	51	52	36
St Martins Res.	26	9	3	14	42	68	30
Witheridge Res.	26	6	3	17	44	71	21
Lympstone Res.	26	5	3	18	37	99	18
Exmouth Amateurs 'A' *-1*	26	5	2	19	35	100	16
Cullompton Rangers 'A'	26	3	4	19	30	90	13

Intermediate Division One	P	W	D	L	F	A	Pts
Newtown 'A'	24	16	5	3	65	32	53
Clyst Valley Res.	24	15	3	6	55	40	48
Thorverton Res.	24	12	6	6	47	28	42
Phoenix Club	24	12	5	7	63	36	41
Colaton Raleigh	24	11	7	6	68	43	40
Okehampton Argyle Res.	24	11	6	7	50	40	39
Legends *-2*	24	11	5	8	73	44	36
Sidbury United Res.	24	9	5	10	28	35	32
North Tawton Res.	24	9	3	12	43	38	30
Lord's XI	24	9	2	13	47	74	29
Up & Under *-1*	24	8	1	15	41	82	24
Cheriton Fitzpaine	24	7	2	15	44	77	23
Northlew *-4*	24	0	2	22	19	74	-2

Intermediate Division Two	P	W	D	L	F	A	Pts
Dawlish United	26	18	3	5	84	37	57
Dawlish Town 'A'	26	17	3	6	88	40	54
Feniton Res.	26	16	5	5	77	47	53
Silverton *-4*	26	16	4	6	64	39	48
Countess Wear Dynamoes	26	13	6	7	78	52	45
Awliscombe United	26	10	6	10	62	59	36
Met Office	26	10	6	10	44	47	36
Culmstock	26	10	4	12	64	78	34
Culm United Res.	26	10	3	13	49	60	33
Honiton Town Res. *-1*	26	7	5	14	40	60	25
Axminster Town 'A'	26	7	2	17	30	68	23
Heavitree/Wonf'd USC *-6*	26	8	3	15	62	86	21
Beer Albion Res. *-2*	26	6	5	15	38	67	21
Hatherleigh Town Res.	26	5	3	18	33	73	18

Intermediate Division Three	P	W	D	L	F	A	Pts
Heavitree Harriers Res.	26	18	6	2	104	46	60
Uplowman Athletic Res.	26	16	9	1	90	40	57
Axmouth United	26	16	6	4	73	38	54
Tedburn St Mary Res.	26	13	5	8	60	46	44
Bow AAC Res.	26	11	10	5	71	60	43
Bradninch	26	12	6	8	66	58	42
AFC Sidford	26	10	6	10	51	54	36
Priory	26	10	3	13	50	55	33
Lapford Res.	26	8	4	14	48	78	28
Colyton Res. *-1*	26	7	7	12	58	63	27
Follygate & Inwardleigh	26	6	4	16	53	65	22
Amory Argyle	26	5	5	16	44	69	20
Motel & Offwell Res. *-1*	26	5	4	17	50	96	18
Winkleigh Res.	26	3	9	14	50	100	18

Intermediate Division Four	P	W	D	L	F	A	Pts
Alphington 'B'	26	21	1	4	116	39	64
East Budleigh Res.	26	18	3	5	64	25	57
Seaton Town 'A'	26	17	3	6	73	54	54
Newton St Cyres Res.	26	15	6	5	69	46	51
Halwill Res.	25	15	5	5	84	36	50
Crediton United 'A'	26	12	3	11	66	68	39
Honiton Town 'A'	26	11	4	11	67	59	37
Bampton Res.	26	9	7	10	51	57	34
Otterton Res.	26	9	3	14	51	65	30
Okehampton Argyle 'A' *-1*	26	10	1	15	55	72	30
Langdon	26	8	5	13	69	79	29
Sandford Res. *-2*	26	4	9	13	43	80	19
Awliscombe Res. *-4*	26	4	3	19	31	96	11
Tedburn St Mary 'A' *-2*	25	0	3	22	22	85	1

Tedburn St Mary 'A' v Halwill Res. – not played

DORSET COUNTY LEAGUE

	Allendale	Barwick & Stoford	Chickerell United	Corfe Mullen United	Easton United	Gillingham Town Res.	Poole Borough Res.	Poole Town Res.	Portland United Res.	Shaftesbury Res.	Sturminster Marshall	Weymouth United	Wimborne Town Res.	Witchampton United
Allendale		1-2	1-0	4-0	6-1	5-0	1-3	2-2	7-0	2-1	0-4	2-1	2-2	1-1
Barwick & Stoford	2-4		0-2	1-0	0-2	3-2	2-2	1-0	1-1	6-2	1-3	1-6	0-0	3-5
Chickerell United	2-1	2-0	*S*	1-2	0-1	1-2	1-1	2-1	2-0	6-0	1-3	2-1	1-2	6-0
Corfe Mullen United	0-5	2-2	0-3	*E*	5-1	0-2	1-3	4-3	3-2	3-0	2-2	0-0	0-4	0-1
Easton United	6-0	2-0	1-3	4-1	*N*	1-3	0-5	1-3	1-1	4-0	2-2	4-0	1-2	0-1
Gillingham Town Res.	1-0	2-1	0-4	3-6	2-5	*I*	0-2	1-0	0-1	1-2	5-1	1-4	1-5	0-3
Poole Borough Res.	0-1	2-0	1-3	0-1	4-4	7-0	*O*	1-2	6-0	3-2	0-2	0-0	0-2	0-1
Poole Town Res.	1-2	0-1	0-2	3-3	2-1	0-1	3-4	*R*	3-1	4-2	1-3	2-1	1-3	1-0
Portland United Res.	1-3	4-1	0-6	0-4	1-1	5-3	0-3	2-3		1-1	2-4	6-2	0-3	2-4
Shaftesbury Res.	3-3	0-3	1-2	0-1	2-1	0-2	2-2	3-2	1-3	*D*	1-4	1-8	1-3	1-2
Sturminster Marshall	1-0	2-3	2-1	7-0	6-3	5-1	3-1	7-1	2-2	3-1	*I*	5-0	1-0	3-1
Weymouth United	0-5	2-1	1-1	0-0	3-3	3-1	2-2	3-1	4-1	5-2	2-5	*V*	0-1	2-2
Wimborne Town Res.	0-1	3-3	3-4	4-0	6-1	8-1	1-0	3-3	1-0	7-0	0-3	3-2		4-1
Witchampton United	2-1	4-1	0-5	0-0	0-3	1-2	0-4	1-3	3-0	4-2	0-4	7-1	2-3	

Senior Division	P	W	D	L	F	A	Pts
Sturminster Marshall	26	21	3	2	87	31	66
Wimborne Town Res.	26	18	4	4	73	29	58
Chickerell United	26	17	2	7	63	24	53
Allendale	26	14	4	8	60	36	46
Poole Borough Res.	26	11	6	9	56	34	39
Witchampton United	26	12	3	11	46	52	39
Corfe Mullen United	26	9	6	11	38	55	33
Easton United	26	9	5	12	54	58	32
Weymouth United	26	8	7	11	53	59	31
Poole Town Res.	26	9	3	14	45	55	30
Gillingham Town Res.	26	10	0	16	37	73	30
Barwick & Stoford	26	8	5	13	39	55	29
Portland United Res.	26	5	5	16	36	72	20
Shaftesbury Res.	26	3	3	20	31	85	12

DORSET COUNTY LEAGUE SENIOR DIVISION CONSTITUTION 2006-07

ALLENDALE .... Redcotts Recreation Ground, School Lane, Wimborne BH21 1HQ .... None
CHICKERELL UNITED .... Weymouth College, Cranford Avenue, Weymouth DT4 7LQ 01305 208892
DORCHESTER YMCA .... Recreation Ground, Weymouth Avenue, Dorchester DT1 2RZ .... None
EASTON UNITED .... Grove Road Playing Field, Easton, Portland .... None
MORETON .... Recreation Field, Dick o'the Banks Road, Crossways DT2 8BJ .... None
OKEFORD UNITED .... Recreation Ground, Okeford Fitzpaine .... None
STALBRIDGE .... The Park, Park Grove, Stalbridge DT10 2RA .... None
TINTINHULL .... The Village Green, Tintinhull, Yeovil .... None
WAREHAM RANGERS .... Purbeck Sports Centre, Worgret Road, Wareham BH20 4PH 01929 556454
WEYMOUTH SPARTANS .... Redlands Sports Ground, Dorchester Road, Weymouth DT3 5AP .... None
WEYMOUTH SPORTS .... The Marsh (Main Pitch), Weymouth *(or Weymouth College)* .... None
WEYMOUTH UNITED .... Redlands Sports Ground, Dorchester Road, Weymouth DT3 5AP .... None
WINCANTON SPORTS .... Wincanton Sports Ground, Moor Lane, Wincanton BA9 9EJ 01963 31815
WITCHAMPTON UNITED .... Crichel Park, Witchampton 01258 840986

IN: Dorchester YMCA (P), Moreton (P), Okeford United (P), Stalbridge (P), Wareham Rangers (R – Dorset Premier League), Weymouth Spartans (P), Weymouth Sports (P), Wincanton Sports (formerly Wincanton Town) (S – Somerset County League Division Two)

OUT: Corfe Mullen United (F), Gillingham Town Reserves (S – Reserve Division), Poole Borough Reserves (S – Reserve Division), Poole Town Reserves (S – Wessex League Combination Division One), Portland United Reserves (S – Reserve Division), Shaftesbury Reserves (S – Reserve Division), Sturminster Marshall (P – Dorset Premier League), Wimborne Town Reserves (S – Wessex League Combination Division One)

Barwick & Stoford become Tintinhull

Division One		P	W	D	L	F	A	Pts
Moreton		26	18	2	6	58	39	56
Okeford United		26	16	6	4	68	36	54
Chickerell United Res.		26	15	6	5	67	38	51
Stalbridge		26	16	2	8	59	39	50
Weymouth Sports		26	13	10	3	65	37	49
Wallisdown Sports		26	11	7	8	60	45	40
Sturminster Newton United Res.		26	7	12	7	34	38	33
Dorchester YMCA		26	10	3	13	45	56	33
Weymouth Spartans		26	9	5	12	51	54	32
Blandford United Res.		26	8	5	13	35	55	29
Bishop's Caundle		26	7	3	16	34	64	24
Sherborne Town Res.	-1	25	7	2	16	40	56	22
Allendale Res.		26	4	5	17	37	66	17
Cobham Sports Res.		25	4	4	17	32	62	16

Cobham Sports Res. v Sherborne Town Res. – not played

Division Two		P	W	D	L	F	A	Pts
AC Matravers		18	13	2	3	58	24	41
Lytchett Red Triangle		18	13	2	3	50	19	41
Purbeck Panthers		18	11	3	4	57	31	36
Kangaroos		18	10	3	5	54	30	33
Bere Regis		18	7	4	7	35	34	25
Broadmayne		18	7	3	8	45	51	24
Easton United Res.		18	4	6	8	33	40	18
Wareham Rangers Res.	-1	18	3	4	11	31	49	12
Cranborne Res.		18	3	3	12	20	64	12
AFC Hurst		18	3	2	13	24	65	11

CUP FINAL *(May 6th at Poole Borough)*
Purbeck Panthers 4 AC Matravers 0

Division Three North & East	P	W	D	L	F	A	Pts
Ferndown Sports	20	17	2	1	79	22	53
Stourpaine Res.	20	14	2	4	63	29	44
Gillingham Town 'A'	20	14	1	5	85	28	43
Corfe Mullen United Res.	20	13	3	4	82	29	42
Handley Sports	20	11	2	7	52	30	35
Child Okeford	20	9	1	10	48	52	28
Stalbridge Res.	20	6	3	11	63	68	21
Linthorpe	20	5	4	11	42	65	19
Sturminster Marshall Res.	20	6	1	13	38	69	19
Shaftesbury 'A'	20	2	4	14	33	84	10
Milborne St Andrew	20	1	1	18	16	125	4

CUP FINAL *(May 6th at Poole Borough)*
Gillingham Town 'A' 1 Ferndown Sports 0

Division Three South & West	P	W	D	L	F	A	Pts
Corfe Castle	18	14	2	2	65	20	44
Swanage Town & Herston Res.	18	13	2	3	52	27	41
Poundbury	18	10	3	5	57	34	33
Piddletrenthide United	18	9	3	6	48	26	30
Wyke Regis Social Club	18	9	3	6	49	47	30
The Excise House	18	7	2	9	44	44	23
Winfrith	18	6	2	10	44	59	20
Barwick & Stoford Res.	18	4	2	12	28	51	14
Piddlehinton United	18	4	1	13	34	67	13
ABRO Bovington	18	4	0	14	37	83	12

CUP FINAL *(May 11th at Milborne St Andrew)*
The Excise House 1 Corfe Castle 0

Division Four North & East	P	W	D	L	F	A	Pts
Witchampton United Res.	14	11	0	3	37	15	33
Stickland United	14	9	1	4	42	19	28
Lytchett Red Triangle Res.	14	7	3	4	31	25	24
AC Matravers Res.	14	6	4	4	37	25	22
Donhead United	14	6	1	7	29	34	19
Okeford United Res.	14	4	2	8	26	40	14
Sturminster Newton United 'A'	14	3	3	8	24	48	12
Quayside	14	2	2	10	24	44	8

CUP FINAL *(April 29th at Milborne St Andrew)*
Witchampton United Res. 2 Stickland United 2 *aet* (4-2p)

Division Four South & West		P	W	D	L	F	A	Pts
Antelope Hotel Wareham		16	13	3	0	86	22	42
Chickerell United 'A'		16	8	3	5	40	31	27
Railway Tavern Weymouth	-3	16	8	4	4	45	36	25
Crossways		16	8	1	7	37	45	25
Puddletown		16	7	3	6	46	34	24
Maiden Newton & Cattistock		16	7	3	6	47	41	24
Dorchester YMCA Res.		16	4	4	8	33	59	16
Swanage Town & Herston 'A'		16	3	1	12	21	42	10
Weymouth Spartans Res.		16	1	4	11	33	78	7

CUP FINAL *(May 9th at Milborne St Andrews)*
Chickerell United 'A' 4 Crossways 2

DORSET PREMIER LEAGUE

	Blandford United	Bournemouth Sports	Bridport Res.	Cobham Sports	Cranborne	Dorchester Town Res.	Dorchester United	Gillingham Town	Hamworthy Recreation	Hamworthy United Res.	Holt United	Poole Borough	Sherborne Town	Stourpaine	Sturminster Newton Utd	Swanage Tn & Herston	Wareham Rangers	Westland Sports
Blandford United		1-3	0-1	3-4	2-1	1-2	1-3	2-4	1-1	2-1	3-1	1-5	1-3	2-0	0-3	1-1	3-1	2-1
Bournemouth Sports	4-0		8-1	0-0	2-0	0-3	2-1	1-3	0-2	1-1	1-2	3-1	0-4	1-0	1-2	0-3	2-1	1-3
Bridport Res.	2-0	1-1		0-2	2-0	0-2	0-1	2-0	2-4	0-3	2-2	3-0	0-2	1-2	1-2	2-0	1-1	2-1
Cobham Sports	1-2	5-0	3-0		0-3	1-3	6-5	1-1	1-3	1-3	0-4	3-1	1-3	2-3	1-2	6-2	1-1	1-1
Cranborne	3-1	2-1	1-1	3-0		0-1	1-6	0-1	0-1	0-0	1-4	0-1	0-4	2-4	0-2	2-1	2-2	0-0
Dorchester Town Res.	2-1	1-0	2-1	1-1	2-0		4-0	3-1	3-0	2-1	0-2	1-1	1-6	6-2	0-1	0-1	3-0	5-0
Dorchester United	2-1	6-0	4-2	2-1	3-0	0-2		2-0	2-0	1-1	0-1	0-1	3-1	6-2	1-2	1-2	8-0	3-1
Gillingham Town	3-1	0-0	1-1	1-3	4-0	2-0	2-2		4-2	2-0	0-2	6-0	3-0	1-1	1-0	2-2	1-1	1-2
Hamworthy Recreation	1-0	1-1	3-0	3-1	2-2	0-2	2-2	0-3		0-3	3-1	1-2	4-2	0-0	3-4	5-1	4-1	0-1
Hamworthy United Res.	4-3	2-1	2-0	2-0	4-1	0-4	5-1	2-3	4-1		0-4	4-5	1-4	3-2	3-0	2-1	2-1	0-0
Holt United	1-0	2-3	0-1	3-0	2-0	3-1	2-0	1-1	1-0	3-0		1-1	3-0	1-0	2-0	5-0	3-1	4-1
Poole Borough	6-0	1-4	2-3	2-1	3-0	1-1	3-1	3-3	2-1	0-4	0-2		2-3	0-2	4-1	2-2	5-0	3-0
Sherborne Town	3-0	1-2	2-1	4-0	6-0	3-3	1-1	2-2	0-2	1-1	1-2	4-2		10-0	4-0	4-1	3-2	3-0
Stourpaine	1-1	4-2	0-0	3-1	3-2	1-3	1-1	1-6	1-4	3-1	0-6	2-8	0-2		2-2	0-4	4-2	3-1
Sturminster Newton United	1-1	0-2	2-1	2-3	1-1	1-1	1-1	0-2	0-1	2-4	1-2	0-3	2-5	1-3		3-2	3-1	1-3
Swanage Town & Herston	3-1	0-5	2-3	2-2	2-0	0-2	1-0	0-2	1-1	1-1	0-3	0-3	2-5	3-2	0-1		4-2	4-4
Wareham Rangers	2-2	1-1	1-2	2-2	1-1	1-4	6-0	0-1	0-4	0-4	0-3	3-2	0-3	1-4	2-1	0-1		1-5
Westland Sports	0-2	5-0	2-0	4-3	2-0	3-1	1-3	0-4	1-1	3-2	1-1	2-0	1-1	6-0	4-1	1-1	1-1	

		P	W	D	L	F	A	Pts
Holt United		34	26	4	4	79	22	82
Sherborne Town		34	22	5	7	100	43	71
Dorchester Town Res.		34	22	5	7	71	35	71
Gillingham Town		34	18	10	6	71	37	64
Hamworthy United Res.	*-3*	34	17	6	11	70	53	54
Hamworthy Recreation		34	15	7	12	60	49	52
Dorchester United		34	15	6	13	72	56	51
Westland Sports		34	14	9	11	61	55	51
Poole Borough	*-3*	34	16	5	13	75	62	50
Bournemouth Sports		34	13	6	15	53	60	45
Stourpaine		34	12	6	16	56	92	42
Bridport Res.		34	11	6	17	39	58	39
Sturminster Newton Utd	*-3*	34	12	5	17	45	65	38
Swanage Town & Herston	*-3*	34	10	8	16	50	73	35
Cobham Sports	*-3*	34	9	7	18	58	74	31
Blandford United		34	8	5	21	42	74	29
Cranborne		34	5	7	22	28	71	22
Wareham Rangers		34	3	9	22	39	90	18

EDGAR MAIDMENT CHARITY SHIELD

(League Champions v League Cup holders)

(August 13th at Hamworthy Recreation)

Hamworthy Recreation 0 **Poole Borough** 3

LEAGUE CUP

FIRST ROUND

Dorchester United 2 Cobham Sports 1
Cranborne 2 **Gillingham Town** 3

SECOND ROUND

Bridport Res. 1 Sturminster Newton Utd 0 *aet*
Dorchester Town Res. 2 Blandford United 0
Dorchester United 2 Swanage Town & Herston 1
Hamworthy Recreation 1 Gillingham Town 0
Hamworthy United Res. 0 Westland Sports 0 *aet*
Westland Sports 1 **Hamworthy United Res.** 2
Poole Borough 0 **Holt United** 0 *aet*
(Poole Borough expelled)
Stourpaine 1 **Bournemouth Sports** 2
Wareham Rangers 1 **Sherborne Town** 4

QUARTER-FINALS

Dorchester Town Res. 1 Bournemouth Sports 1 *aet*
Bournemouth Sports 2 **Dorchester Town Res.** 4
Dorchester United 3 Bridport Res. 0
Hamworthy Recreation 3 Hamworthy United Res. 1
Sherborne Town 0 **Holt United** 2

SEMI-FINALS

Hamworthy Recreation 1 **Dorchester United** 2 *aet*
Holt United 2 Dorchester Town Res. 1 *aet*

FINAL *(April 26th at Dorchester Town)*

Holt United 2 Dorchester United 1 *aet*

DORSET PREMIER LEAGUE CONSTITUTION 2006-07

BLANDFORD UNITED .... Recreation Ground, Park Road, Blandford Forum DT11 7BX .... None
BOURNEMOUTH SPORTS CM ..... Bournemouth Sports Club, Chapel Gate, East Parley BH23 6BD 01202 581933
BRIDPORT RESERVES .... St Marys Field, Skilling Hill Road, Bridport DT6 5LN 01308 423834
COBHAM SPORTS .... Merley Park, Merley Lane, Wimborne BH21 .... 01202 885773
CRANBORNE .... Recreation Ground, Penny's Lane, Cranborne, Wimborne BH21 5QE .... None
DORCHESTER TOWN RESERVES .. The Avenue Stadium, Weymouth Avenue, Dorchester DT1 2RY 01305 262451
DORCHESTER UNITED .... Sandringham Sports Centre, Armada Way, Dorchester DT1 2TN .... None
GILLINGHAM TOWN .... Hardings Lane, Gillingham SP8 4HX 01747 823673
HAMWORTHY RECREATION .. Hamworthy Recreation Club, Magna Road, Canford Magna, Wimborne BH21 3AP 01202 881922
HAMWORTHY UNITED RESERVES .. The County Ground, Blandford Close, Hamworthy, Poole BH15 4BF 01202 674974
HOLT UNITED .... Gaunts Common, Holt, Wimborne BH21 4JR 01258 840379
POOLE BOROUGH .... Turlin Moor Recreation Ground, Blandford Moor, Hamworthy, Poole BH21 5XX ... Club Office: 01202 674973
PORTLAND UNITED .... New Grove Corner, Grove Road, Portland DT5 1DP 01305 861489
STOURPAINE .... Dick Draper Memorial Fields, Stourpaine, Blandford Forum .... None
STURMINSTER MARSHALL .... Churchill Close, Sturminster Marshall BH21 4BQ .... None
STURMINSTER NEWTON UNITED .. Barnetts Field, Honeymead Lane, Sturminster Newton DT10 7EW 01258 471406
SWANAGE TOWN & HERSTON .... Day's Park, off De Moulham Road, Swanage BH19 2JW 01929 424673
WESTLAND SPORTS .... Alvington Lane, Yeovil BA22 8UX .... None

***IN:** Sturminster Marshall (P – Dorset County League Senior Division), Portland United (R – Wessex League Division One)*
***OUT:** Sherborne Town (P – Western League Division One), Wareham Rangers (R – Dorset County League Senior Division)*
Bournemouth Sports become Bournemouth Sports CM

DURHAM ALLIANCE

	Ashbrooke Belford	Birtley Town Res.	Brandon Prince Bishop	Ebchester	Hartlepool The Office	Hartlepool Town	Herrington Colliery Welfate	Newton Aycliffe	Seaham Tn Community	Shildon Railway	Silksworth CC	Simonside Social Club	Thornley	Wheatley Hill WMC	Whitehill
Ashbrooke Belford		3-0	2-1	1-0	8-1	2-2	2-0	4-1	1-0	2-0	1-4	4-1	3-0	5-1	1-1
Birtley Town Res.	1-2		4-4	1-4	6-3	5-2	3-3	4-4	3-5	1-0	4-2	2-2	5-3	3-6	1-6
Brandon Prince Bish	0-6	2-1		2-3	8-1	1-2	4-1	7-2	5-3	1-1	3-2	8-1	3-1	2-6	0-2
Ebchester	0-5	1-2	0-1		1-1	4-5	2-1	2-2	1-4	2-2	0-4	0-4	4-4	0-2	0-2
H'pool The Office	1-10	2-2	1-4	1-1		0-7	4-4	3-3	4-3	0-2	0-6	2-3	4-5	1-0	0-5
Hartlepool Town	3-4	3-2	0-4	6-2	4-1		2-1	1-2	3-4	1-1	0-1	2-2	2-2	0-0	1-1
Herrington CW	0-3	2-0	3-0	3-1	4-0	3-2		2-3	5-4	2-1	2-2	1-2	5-2	0-4	1-2
Newton Aycliffe	1-3	3-4	0-3	6-3	5-0	2-1	4-3		0-3	1-2	3-1	3-2	10-3	1-0	1-2
Seaham Tn Comm.	0-6	1-4	4-0	1-3	7-1	3-4	1-0	1-4		2-3	1-3	3-2	4-1	2-3	1-7
Shildon Railway	1-3	0-5	0-3	1-1	1-3	1-0	1-1	1-3	5-2		2-1	6-5	3-3	0-3	4-4
Silksworth CC	0-2	1-1	0-0	4-3	1-0	2-1	2-1	1-0	1-1	2-1		1-2	3-3	2-2	1-5
Simonside S Club	2-4	2-5	4-3	6-1	5-2	2-2	2-3	2-2	1-4	1-1	5-1		1-5	5-4	0-1
Thornley	1-4	4-1	0-1	3-3	6-1	1-3	1-3	2-3	2-4	2-7	1-3	1-1		1-1	1-5
Wheatley Hill WMC	0-1	6-3	8-3	2-1	4-1	4-0	2-3	2-1	5-3	5-1	4-1	2-0	4-0		2-3
Whitehill	3-3	3-0	3-2	0-1	8-0	0-0	0-2	4-3	4-3	6-2	1-0	4-1	5-0	7-2	

		P	W	D	L	F	A	Pts
Ashbrooke Belford		28	24	3	1	95	25	75
Whitehill		28	21	5	2	94	33	68
Wheatley Hill WMC		28	17	3	8	84	50	54
Brandon Prince Bishop		28	14	3	11	75	61	45
Silksworth CC		28	12	6	10	52	49	42
Newton Aycliffe	*-3*	28	13	4	11	73	66	40
Herrington Colliery Welfare		28	12	4	12	59	56	40
Birtley Town Res.		28	10	6	12	73	79	36
Hartlepool Town		28	9	8	11	59	57	35
Seaham Town Community		28	11	1	16	74	81	34
Simonside Social Club		28	9	6	13	66	77	33
Shildon Railway		28	8	8	12	50	65	32
Ebchester		28	5	7	16	44	76	22
Thornley	*-3*	28	4	7	17	58	96	16
Hartlepool The Office		28	3	5	20	38	123	14

LEAGUE CUP

FIRST ROUND

Brandon Prince Bishop 3 Ashbrooke Belford 2
Hartlepool The Office 1 Seaham Town Community 0
Newton Aycliffe 3 Herrington C W 2
Silksworth CC 2 **Whitehill** 4
Simonside Social Club 5 Ebchester 4
Thornley 5 Hartlepool Town 3
Wheatley Hill WMC 6 Shildon R'way 2

QUARTER-FINALS

Birtley Town 3 **Simonside S C** 4
Brandon Prince Bishop 6 Thornley 2
Wheatley Hill WMC 5 Newton Aycliffe 1
Whitehill 6 Hartlepool The Office 2

SEMI-FINALS

Brandon Prince Bishop 5 Whitehill 0
Wheatley Hill WMC 3 Simonside S C 1

FINAL

(March 20th at Chester-le-Street Town)
Brandon Prince Bishop 5 Wheatley Hill WMC 0

CLEM SMITH BOWL

FIRST ROUND

Ashbrooke Belford 3 Whitehill 2
Ebchester 0 **Brandon Prince Bishop** 3
Hartlepool The Office 1 **Birtley Tn Res.** 3
Newton Aycliffe 6 Herrington Colliery Welfare 1
Shildon Railway 0 **Wheatley Hill WMC** 1
Silksworth CC 6 **Seaham Town Community** 7
Thornley 1 **Simonside Social Club** 8

QUARTER-FINALS

Birtley Tn Res. 1 **Wheatley Hill WMC** 4
Brandon Prince Bishop 3 Hartlepool Town 2
Seaham Town Community 0 **Ashbrooke Belford** 1
Simonside S C 5 Newton Aycliffe 3

SEMI-FINALS

Brandon Prince Bishop 1 **Simonside Social Club** 2
Wheatley Hill WMC 2 **Ashbrooke Belford** 5

FINAL

(March 22nd at Chester-le-Street Town)
Simonside S C 2 **Ashbrooke Belford** 3

MARK BLAKE MEMORIAL TROPHY

FIRST ROUND

Birtley Town Res. 2 **Ebchester** 4
Hartlepool Tn 1 Simonside Soc. Club 0
Seaham Tn Comm. 4 H'pool The Office 1
Shildon Railway 2 Thornley 1

SEMI-FINALS

Ebchester 5 Shildon Railway 2
Hartlepool Tn 1 Seaham Tn Community 0

FINAL

(April 10th at Chester-le-Street Town)
Ebchester 1 Hartlepool Town 1 *aet* (4-2p)

DURHAM ALLIANCE CONSTITUTION 2006-07

ASHBROOKE BELFORD	Silksworth Park, Silksworth, Sunderland	None
BIRTLEY TOWN RESERVES	Birtley Sports Complex, Durham Road, Birtley, Chester-le-Street DH3 2TB	None
BLACKHALL	Welfare Park, Blackhall TS27 4LX	None
BRANDON PRINCE BISHOP	Dorlonco Villas, Browney Lane, Meadowfield DH7 8HT	None
EBCHESTER CONSETT	Crookhall, Consett DH8 7LR	None
FATFIELD	Northumbria Centre, Stephenson Road, Washington NE37 3HR	0191 219 3390
FERRYHILL ATHLETIC	Dean Bank Recreation Cent, Ferryhill DL17 8PP	None
HARTLEPOOL TOWN	Grayfields, Jesmond Road, Hartlepool TS26 0HN	None
HERRINGTON COLLIERY WELFARE	Welfare Park, New Herrington, Houghton-le-Spring DH4 4LR	None
NEWTON AYCLIFFE	Newton Aycliffe Sports Club, Moore Lane, Newton Aycliffe DL5 5AG	01325 300324
RYTON RESERVES	Kingsley Park, Stannerford Road, Crawcock, Ryton NE40 3SN	0191 413 4448
SEAHAM TOWN COMMUNITY	Dawdon Welfare Park, Green Drive, Dawdon, Seaham SR7 7XL	None
SHILDON RAILWAY	Shildon Railway Sports & Social Club, Hackworth Street, Shildon DL4 1XL	None
SILKSWORTH CC	Silksworth Welfare Park, Silksworth, Sunderland	None
SIMONSIDE SOCIAL CLUB	Cleadon Recreation Ground, Sunderland Road, South Shields	None
THORNLEY	Thornley Colliery Welfare, Ashfield Grove, Thornley	None
WHEATLEY HILL WMC	Old Fire Station, Quetlaw Road, Wheatley Hill DH6 3SB	None
WHITEHILL	Riverside Ground, Chester-le-Street	None

IN: Blackhall (P – Hartlepool Churches League), Fatfield (N), Ferryhill Athletic (S – Wearside League), Ryton Reserves (N)
OUT: Hartlepool The Office (F)

EAST CORNWALL PREMIER LEAGUE

	Biscovey	Bodmin Res.	Callington Res.	Camelford	Dobwalls	Foxhole Stars	Godolphin Atl.	Launceston Res.	Liskeard Res.	Nanpean Rvrs	Padstow Utd	Probus	Roche	Saltash U Res.	St Cleer	St Dennis	St Stephen	Sticker	Torpoint Res.	Wadebridge Res.
Biscovey		3-4	6-0	1-3	1-2	0-3	1-3	1-1	5-3	2-3	3-2	1-2	2-1	3-4	2-0	2-2	2-2	0-5	2-2	0-3
Bodmin Town Res.	4-2		2-5	3-1	3-2	0-2	1-3	3-2	1-0	2-1	0-0	1-0	2-1	1-3	3-1	0-1	4-0	0-0	1-6	2-2
Callington Town Res.	3-3	0-3		0-1	2-0	0-3	7-1	2-2	1-7	3-0	1-1	1-1	3-0	1-4	2-0	1-2	2-1	2-5	0-3	3-3
Camelford	2-1	1-3	4-2		1-3	3-1	3-1	4-3	0-2	2-0	0-0	0-1	2-1	0-1	4-4	1-2	3-0	1-4	5-1	0-1
Dobwalls	4-3	5-2	2-0	2-2		3-3	1-1	0-1	1-1	5-1	4-3	1-3	5-0	2-3	5-0	5-2	2-1	1-2	2-0	3-1
Foxhole Stars	3-0	2-1	5-1	1-0	1-3		2-1	1-2	2-0	2-1	4-2	2-1	1-2	0-0	3-2	2-1	5-1	3-1	0-2	1-4
Godolphin Atlantic	2-0	3-2	4-1	1-2	2-1	5-3		1-0	1-1	1-0	4-0	4-2	4-0	2-2	7-1	3-0	2-1	1-1	1-3	1-1
Launceston Res.	4-0	3-0	1-0	3-2	1-2	0-3	3-4		1-2	4-0	1-1	2-1	4-1	2-6	6-1	0-5	1-3	2-2	1-1	1-1
Liskeard Athletic Res.	5-1	0-1	3-1	0-1	1-1	1-2	0-3	0-4		1-1	1-1	3-3	0-1	1-1	3-1	2-1	5-0	4-1	2-2	1-2
Nanpean Rovers	1-3	2-1	1-4	2-1	3-1	1-2	1-3	1-3	0-6		2-2	0-2	1-1	0-4	1-2	1-2	2-0	0-2	6-0	2-4
Padstow United	4-3	3-1	0-2	0-0	2-2	2-1	2-1	1-0	1-2	2-2		0-1	2-0	1-1	4-3	4-1	3-3	2-2	4-1	1-1
Probus	3-0	3-1	2-0	4-0	1-0	4-2	1-0	5-1	1-2	2-1	4-3		0-0	1-0	4-1	1-0	2-1	5-0	3-1	6-2
Roche	0-1	0-1	1-1	2-3	4-7	1-1	1-5	0-1	0-4	2-2	3-2	0-2		2-3	1-0	0-0	2-1	4-1	0-1	3-2
Saltash United Res.	8-1	2-1	6-0	3-1	2-0	3-1	2-1	2-1	2-0	5-0	1-0	2-1	3-1		2-1	3-0	1-0	4-1	8-1	1-3
St Cleer	1-1	0-1	2-6	1-7	0-1	0-2	0-3	0-1	1-0	1-2	1-2	0-3	4-1	0-2		1-4	1-2	1-6	2-2	1-2
St Dennis	4-0	1-0	5-0	1-2	0-0	2-0	1-2	0-1	1-2	7-1	1-0	0-0	3-1	1-2	1-2		4-2	5-1	2-0	1-2
St Stephen	1-2	2-3	1-1	1-4	0-4	2-1	1-2	2-4	1-1	0-1	4-3	2-2	2-1	0-2	1-0	3-2		1-2	4-0	1-4
Sticker	2-1	5-4	2-2	0-0	1-7	2-2	4-0	3-1	2-0	3-2	1-2	2-1	3-1	0-2	8-0	1-0	3-1		5-0	2-0
Torpoint Athletic Res.	2-1	5-0	2-3	2-0	3-4	2-3	1-4	1-2	0-4	5-0	6-0	1-1	3-0	0-6	7-0	2-0	4-1	1-1		0-4
Wadebridge Town Res.	1-1	1-0	1-3	0-2	1-1	0-3	3-3	1-1	2-4	2-1	1-4	1-2	3-0	1-3	4-0	1-0	4-0	3-0	6-1	

FRED BINKS MEMORIAL TROPHY

(League Cup Preliminary and First Round losers)

FINAL *(May 21st at St Dennis)*
Foxhole Stars 5 St Stephen 2

		P	W	D	L	F	A	Pts
Saltash United Res.		38	32	4	2	109	32	100
Probus	*-3*	38	25	6	7	81	38	78
Godolphin Atlantic		38	23	6	9	90	56	75
Foxhole Stars		38	22	4	12	78	56	70
Dobwalls		38	20	8	10	94	58	68
Sticker		38	20	8	10	86	66	68
Wadebridge Town Res.		38	18	9	11	78	59	63
Camelford		38	18	5	15	68	58	59
Launceston Res.		38	17	7	14	71	63	58
Liskeard Athletic Res.		38	16	9	13	74	51	57
St Dennis		38	16	4	18	65	51	52
Bodmin Town Res.	*-3*	38	17	3	18	62	73	51
Padstow United		38	12	13	13	66	69	49
Torpoint Athletic Res.		38	14	6	18	74	88	48
Callington Town Res.		38	12	8	18	66	90	44
Biscovey		38	8	7	23	61	99	31
St Stephen		38	8	5	25	49	91	29
Nanpean Rovers		38	8	5	25	46	94	29
Roche		38	7	6	25	39	85	27
St Cleer		38	4	3	31	36	116	15

LEAGUE CUP

PRELIMINARY ROUND
Saltash United Res. 3 St Stephen 0
St Cleer 1 **Godolphin Atlantic** 5 *aet*
St Dennis 3 Roche 0
Sticker 6 Torpoint Athletic Res. 1

FIRST ROUND
Biscovey 3 **Godolphin Atlantic** 5
Bodmin Town Res. 2 **Camelford** 4 *aet*
(at Camelford)
Foxhole Stars 2 **Liskeard Ath Res.** 3 *aet*
Nanpean Rovers 1 **Callington Tn Res.** 2
Saltash United Res. 2 Probus 0
St Dennis 3 Padstow United 1
Sticker 2 Launceston Res. 0
Wadebridge Town Res. 1 **Dobwalls** 4

QUARTER-FINALS
Camelford 0 **Sticker** 4
Dobwalls 2 St Dennis 2 *aet*
St Dennis 2 **Dobwalls** 3 *replay*
Godolphin Atlantic (w/o) v Callington Town Res. (scr.)
Liskeard Ath Res. 0 **Saltash Utd Res.** 1

SEMI-FINALS
Godolphin Atlantic 2 Dobwalls 0
(at Sticker)
Saltash United Res. 3 Sticker 0
(at Nanpean Rovers)

FINAL
(April 16th at Liskeard Athletic)
Saltash United Res. 1 Godolphin Atlantic 1

FINAL REPLAY
(April 23rd at Liskeard Athletic)
Godolphin Atlantic 2 Saltash Utd Res. 1

WWW.NLNEWSDESK.CO.UK

EAST CORNWALL (formerly PREMIER) LEAGUE PREMIER DIVISION CONSTITUTION 2006-07

BODMIN TOWN RESERVES .... Priory Park, Bodmin PL31 2PP 01208 78165
CAMELFORD .... Trefew Park, Camelford .... None
DOBWALLS .... Lantoom Park, Duloe Road, Dobwalls PL14 4LR .... None
FOXHOLE STARS .... Goverseth Playing Fields, Goverseth Terrace, Foxhole PL26 7XX 01726 824615
GODOLPHIN ATLANTIC .... Godolphin Way, Newquay TR7 3BU .... None
LAUNCESTON RESERVES .... Pennygillam, Pennygillam Industrial Estate, Launceston PL15 7ED 01566 773279
LISKEARD ATHLETIC RESERVES .... Lux Park, Coldstyle Lane, Liskeard PL14 3HZ 01579 342665
PADSTOW UNITED .... Wadebridge Road, Padstow .... None
PROBUS .... Recreation Ground, Probus .... None
SALTASH UNITED RESERVES .... Kimberley Stadium, Callington Road, Saltash PL12 6DX 01752 845746
ST DENNIS .... Boscawen Park, St Dennis PL6 8AP 01726 822635
STICKER .... Ennis Farm, St Stephen Road, Sticker 01726 71003
TORPOINT ATHLETIC RESERVES .... The Mill, Mill Lane, Torpoint PL11 2RE 01752 812889
WADEBRIDGE TOWN RESERVES .... Bodieve Park, Bodieve Road, Wadebridge PL27 6EA 01208 812537

IN: Top fourteen clubs in league in 2006-07

EAST CORNWALL (formerly PREMIER) LEAGUE DIVISION ONE CONSTITUTION 2006-07

BISCOVEY .... Par Athletics Track, Moorland Road, Par, St Austell PL24 2PB .... None
BUDE TOWN .... Broadclose, Bude EX23 8DR .... None
CALLINGTON TOWN RESERVES .. The Marsh, Callington Community College, Launceston Road, Callington PL17 7DR 01579 382647
HOLSWORTHY RESERVES .... Upcott Field, North Road, Holsworthy EX22 6HF 01409 254295
LANREATH .... Rally Park, Lanreath Village Hall, Lanreath .... None
LIFTON .... Recreation Ground, Lifton .... None
MORWENSTOW .... Playing Field, Shop, Morwenstow, Bude EX23 9SQ .... None
NANPEAN ROVERS .... Victoria Park, Victoria Bottoms, Nanpean PL26 7YE 01726 823435
ROCHE .... Trezaise Road, Roche, St Austell PL26 8HD 01726 890718
ST BLAZEY RESERVES .... Blaise Park, Station Road, St Blazey PL24 2ND 01726 814110
ST COLUMB MAJOR .... Recreation Ground, St Columb Major TR9 6RP .... None
ST STEPHEN .... Trethosa Road, St Stephen, St Austell PL26 7PZ .... None
TAMARSIDE .... Parkway Sports & Social Club, Ernesettle Lane, Ernesettle, Plymouth PL5 2EY .... None
TAVISTOCK RESERVES .... Langsford Park, Crowndale Road, Tavistock PL19 8DD 01822 614447

IN: Bottom six clubs in league in 2006-07, Bude Town (Duchy League Premier Division), Holsworthy Reserves (North Devon League Premier Division), Lanreath (Duchy League Premier Division), Lifton (Devon & Exeter League Senior Division Three), Morwenstow (North Devon League Premier Division), St Blazey Reserves (Duchy League Premier Division), St Columb Major (Duchy League Premier Division), Tamarside (Plymouth & West Devon Combination Premier Division), Tavistock Reserves (Plymouth & West Devon Combination Senior Division)
OUT: St Cleer (W – Duchy League Division Two)

EASTERN COUNTIES LEAGUE

	AFC Sudbury	Bury Town	Cam. City Res.	Clacton Town	Dereham Town	Diss Town	Halstead Town	Harwich & P.	Histon Res.	Ipswich Wdrs	King's Lynn Res.	Kirkley	Leiston	Lowestoft Tn	Mildenhall Tn	Needham Mkt	Newmarket Tn	Norwich Utd	Soham T R	Wisbech Town	Woodbridge	Wroxham
AFC Sudbury		1-0	6-0	6-1	2-2	4-2	5-2	1-0	3-1	0-4	4-3	3-1	4-1	1-0	5-0	2-0	5-0	2-0	0-1	1-3	3-1	0-4
Bury Town	2-1		2-0	5-0	2-1	4-0	5-0	5-1	2-0	2-0	1-1	5-0	1-0	1-0	1-2	3-0	2-1	3-1	1-3	0-1	7-2	5-0
Cambridge City Res.	2-1	2-5		6-1	1-5	0-5	2-2	3-1	1-2	2-1	1-1	3-1	0-5	0-4	0-2	1-6	0-2	0-3	3-2	3-4	3-2	1-1
Clacton Town	0-5	1-8	0-4	*P*	1-6	0-8	0-2	1-2	1-3	0-6	0-0	2-4	0-4	0-7	3-5	0-5	1-4	0-2	0-5	0-7	0-4	1-3
Dereham Town	1-4	1-0	4-2	8-0	*R*	3-0	2-1	4-1	1-2	1-2	3-0	3-2	3-0	4-2	2-3	1-1	0-2	0-1	2-2	1-1	1-2	2-0
Diss Town	1-5	0-1	4-0	4-1	0-5	*E*	1-1	2-1	3-1	0-1	5-1	3-2	1-2	2-1	7-3	1-3	1-2	3-1	1-3	1-0	2-1	0-0
Halstead Town	1-4	1-1	4-2	9-2	4-1	1-4	*M*	2-0	4-1	1-7	2-2	3-8	2-6	0-2	0-7	1-2	0-0	2-1	1-0	2-3	2-1	0-1
Harwich & Parkeston	1-1	1-4	1-0	3-0	0-7	2-1	0-4	*I*	1-2	1-2	2-3	1-2	1-5	0-4	0-6	0-2	1-2	2-1	1-0	2-0	3-0	0-3
Histon Res.	2-3	2-0	2-1	2-0	2-4	2-2	2-4	3-2	*E*	0-1	2-1	2-5	3-3	0-7	1-3	0-3	1-1	1-1	0-0	1-5	3-2	2-2
Ipswich Wanderers	0-2	0-0	3-0	4-0	2-2	2-1	1-0	0-1	0-1	*R*	1-0	1-1	3-1	1-1	0-1	1-1	2-0	2-0	3-1	1-3	0-0	3-0
King's Lynn Res.	2-4	1-1	2-2	5-0	1-1	9-6	3-1	1-1	1-1	2-1		2-2	1-1	1-5	0-3	2-1	4-1	1-0	0-1	0-4	0-1	0-3
Kirkley	1-2	0-2	0-1	1-0	2-1	1-2	0-0	2-0	4-2	0-2	2-1	*D*	1-1	0-1	1-1	1-2	2-0	2-0	0-6	1-2	3-0	1-3
Leiston	4-2	0-1	4-1	3-0	1-5	4-2	3-0	2-1	0-4	1-0	2-3	0-1	*I*	4-2	2-1	1-0	1-1	3-1	0-1	2-2	3-0	1-2
Lowestoft Town	0-3	3-0	3-2	4-0	3-1	1-0	3-0	2-0	1-1	3-1	3-1	3-1	5-1	*V*	4-0	2-1	9-0	5-0	4-1	4-3	3-1	2-1
Mildenhall Town	1-6	1-1	1-1	3-0	2-2	0-1	5-1	3-0	2-3	5-3	3-2	3-1	2-0	1-1	*I*	0-0	2-0	5-1	1-1	2-1	0-0	4-3
Needham Market	2-2	0-1	2-0	5-0	5-1	2-1	6-0	1-0	1-1	1-2	3-1	0-1	2-1	3-2	2-3	*S*	1-1	0-0	0-0	3-1	2-1	0-1
Newmarket Town	2-4	0-4	2-2	4-0	2-1	2-2	2-1	0-2	2-1	0-1	1-3	2-0	1-5	0-4	4-2	0-3	*I*	2-3	1-5	0-2	1-2	0-2
Norwich United	2-1	1-5	1-1	1-0	1-1	2-3	3-0	3-1	3-3	0-2	0-2	0-1	2-6	1-3	1-5	0-2	0-1	*O*	2-1	1-1	2-3	0-1
Soham Town Rangers	2-1	0-2	0-2	1-0	3-1	1-2	2-2	8-1	2-2	0-1	0-0	1-1	4-2	1-2	2-2	3-0	1-0	2-1	*N*	1-0	3-2	2-2
Wisbech Town	1-1	0-1	4-2	4-2	1-1	2-3	7-1	3-1	1-0	1-0	2-1	4-0	3-1	0-3	2-1	0-0	1-4	3-2	1-1		3-1	4-2
Woodbridge Town	1-1	2-1	4-1	3-1	0-0	1-2	8-3	2-1	1-4	0-1	1-1	3-0	0-2	3-3	1-4	0-3	4-2	1-0	2-1	1-4		0-2
Wroxham	2-3	1-3	2-2	4-1	1-4	0-0	9-0	3-1	0-3	2-1	0-3	3-1	0-1	2-0	2-0	2-3	4-1	0-2	2-1	0-4	2-0	

Premier Division	P	W	D	L	F	A	Pts
Lowestoft Town	42	30	4	8	121	43	94
Bury Town	42	29	5	8	100	32	92
AFC Sudbury	42	28	5	9	114	56	89
Wisbech Town	42	25	7	10	98	55	82
Mildenhall Town	42	23	9	10	100	68	78
Needham Market	42	22	9	11	79	41	75
Ipswich Wanderers	42	23	6	13	69	38	75
Wroxham	42	21	6	15	77	62	69
Leiston	42	21	5	16	89	69	68
Soham Town Rangers	42	18	11	13	75	51	65
Diss Town	42	20	5	17	89	78	65
Dereham Town	42	18	10	14	99	64	64
Histon Res.	42	15	11	16	71	84	56
Kirkley	42	15	6	21	60	76	51
King's Lynn Res.	42	12	13	17	68	78	49
Woodbridge Town	42	14	6	22	64	83	48
Newmarket Town	42	13	6	23	53	91	45
Halstead Town	42	11	7	24	67	124	40
Cambridge City Res.	42	10	8	24	60	107	38
Norwich United	42	10	6	26	47	82	36
Harwich & Parkeston	42	10	2	30	41	100	32
Clacton Town	42	0	1	41	20	179	1

EASTERN COUNTIES LEAGUE PREMIER DIVISION CONSTITUTION 2006-07

CLACTON TOWN .... Rush Green Bowl, Rush Green Road, Clacton-on-Sea CO16 7BQ 01255 432590
CRC .... Cambridge United FC, Abbey Stadium, Newmarket Road, Cambridge CB5 8LN 01223 566500
DEREHAM TOWN .... Aldiss Park, Norwich Road, Dereham NR20 3AL 01362 690460
DISS TOWN .... Brewers Green Lane, Diss IP22 4DQ 01379 651223
FELIXSTOWE & WALTON UNITED .... Town Ground, Dellwood Avenue, Felixstowe IP11 9HT 01394 282917
HALSTEAD TOWN .... Rosemary Lane, Broton Industrial Estate, Halstead CO9 1HR 01787 472082
HARWICH & PARKESTON .... Royal Oak, Main Road, Dovercourt, Harwich CO12 4AX 01255 503643
HISTON RESERVES .... The Glassworld Stadium, Bridge Road, Impington, Cambridge CB4 9PH 01223 237373
IPSWICH WANDERERS .... SEH Sports Centre, Humberdoucy Lane, Ipswich IP4 3PB 01473 728581
KING'S LYNN RESERVES .... The Walks Stadium, Tennyson Road, King's Lynn PE30 5PB 01553 760060
KIRKLEY .... Kirkley Recreation Ground, Walmer Road, Lowestoft NR33 8HZ 01502 513549
LEISTON .... LTAA, Victory Road, Leiston IP16 4DQ 01728 830308
LOWESTOFT TOWN .... Crown Meadow, Love Road, Lowestoft NR32 2PA 01502 573818
MILDENHALL TOWN .... Recreation Way, Mildenhall, Bury St Edmunds IP28 7EL 01638 713449
NEEDHAM MARKET .... Bloomfields, Quinton Road, Needham Market IP6 8DA 01449 721000
NEWMARKET TOWN .... Cricket Field Road, off New Cheveley Road, Newmarket CB8 8BG 01638 663637
NORWICH UNITED .... Plantation Park, off Plantation Road, Blofield, Norwich NR13 4PL 01603 716963
SOHAM TOWN RANGERS .... Julius Martins Lane, Soham, Ely CB7 5EQ 01353 720732
STANWAY ROVERS .... Hawthorns, New Farm Road, Stanway, Colchester CO3 0PG 01206 578187
WISBECH TOWN .... Fenland Park, Lerowe Road, Wisbech PE13 3QL 01945 584176
WOODBRIDGE TOWN .... Notcutts Park, Fynn Road, off Seckford Hall Lane, Woodbridge IP12 4DA 01394 385308
WROXHAM .... Trafford Park, Skinners Lane, Wroxham NR12 8SJ 01603 783538

IN: Felixstowe & Walton United (P), Stanway Rovers (P)

OUT: AFC Sudbury (P – Isthmian League Division One North), Bury Town (P – Isthmian League Division One North), Cambridge City Reserves (W)

	Cornard United	Debenham Leisure C	Downham Town	Ely City	Fakenham Town	Felixstowe & W. Utd	Fulbourn Institute	Godmanchester Rovers	Gorleston	Great Yarmouth Town	Hadleigh United	Haverhill Rovers	Long Melford	March Town United	Saffron Walden Town	Stanway Rovers	Stowmarket Town	Swaffham Town	Thetford Town	Tiptree United	Walsham-le-Willows	Whitton United
Cornard United		1-0	5-1	1-2	2-2	4-2	3-4	0-4	0-4	3-1	2-0	1-2	1-1	2-4	3-2	3-6	4-2	1-4	2-3	1-2	1-2	0-5
Debenham Leisure Centre	1-0		4-2	1-0	3-1	0-4	0-1	1-1	0-0	1-0	2-1	2-3	3-2	2-2	3-2	1-1	3-3	0-2	1-1	2-3	1-2	0-2
Downham Town	0-2	0-0		1-0	0-1	0-3	1-4	1-2	2-1	0-5	0-1	0-1	1-1	0-0	3-0	0-7	5-2	1-1	0-1	1-3	0-2	2-1
Ely City	2-0	3-0	7-1		1-1	2-0	4-0	3-1	2-1	3-0	1-1	1-3	1-1	1-1	1-2	1-2	1-1	3-0	2-0	3-6	4-0	1-4
Fakenham Town	2-4	2-0	1-1	1-1		0-1	2-2	2-0	2-1	1-0	1-2	2-2	2-4	2-1	0-1	1-2	3-0	1-1	2-1	3-2	0-2	0-1
Felixstowe & Walton United	2-0	6-1	6-1	0-0	3-0	*D*	2-3	3-1	2-0	3-0	4-2	1-0	5-2	6-0	1-0	2-1	3-1	1-1	4-1	2-1	2-3	2-0
Fulbourn Institute	1-0	5-0	4-0	3-0	5-1	2-3	*I*	1-0	3-1	1-1	1-0	1-2	7-2	7-0	3-1	1-0	3-0	3-3	4-0	1-6	2-1	2-0
Godmanchester Rovers	2-1	1-2	1-1	2-8	2-2	0-1	2-2	*V*	1-0	0-2	1-0	1-1	1-1	1-0	2-3	1-2	4-0	0-3	2-0	0-4	1-2	2-2
Gorleston	0-3	1-3	2-3	4-4	0-1	2-2	2-6	0-2	*I*	0-2	1-0	1-3	1-0	3-0	0-1	0-2	1-0	2-3	2-2	1-6	1-1	2-1
Great Yarmouth Town	0-0	3-0	1-1	1-2	1-4	0-2	1-3	1-2	1-1	*S*	0-0	1-0	2-0	3-0	0-2	0-5	2-1	2-1	2-2	1-4	1-1	1-3
Hadleigh United	1-1	3-4	1-1	2-2	0-0	1-4	0-3	2-1	1-3	1-1	*I*	3-1	1-1	1-0	1-1	0-3	1-1	1-3	3-1	0-4	2-2	1-2
Haverhill Rovers	4-2	1-2	3-1	3-1	3-1	3-2	0-1	3-4	0-0	3-1	1-0	*O*	3-1	2-0	2-2	1-4	3-0	1-0	3-2	5-2	2-2	0-2
Long Melford	3-0	0-1	1-3	0-1	3-3	1-4	1-2	0-3	3-0	2-5	1-1	0-3	*N*	1-0	2-2	1-2	5-2	2-2	1-1	2-0	0-1	2-0
March Town United	3-1	0-2	1-2	2-3	0-3	2-4	0-2	1-0	1-3	0-0	2-0	3-1	1-0		1-4	0-1	2-1	3-2	4-2	0-3	1-4	1-1
Saffron Walden Town	1-0	2-2	3-0	2-2	2-2	0-1	1-2	0-0	0-0	2-0	4-1	1-1	0-3	2-1	*O*	1-0	0-1	0-1	3-0	0-1	0-0	2-3
Stanway Rovers	4-1	0-1	4-0	2-3	1-0	4-1	3-2	6-0	0-0	2-0	1-0	2-0	2-1	3-1	5-0	*N*	5-1	3-0	2-0	1-1	1-0	5-0
Stowmarket Town	3-1	2-4	5-3	3-2	0-3	1-2	0-1	1-1	2-2	0-2	2-0	2-0	1-2	1-1	2-4	1-2	*E*	3-0	3-0	0-2	1-5	1-2
Swaffham Town	1-0	2-2	1-0	6-1	1-3	2-2	7-2	1-1	2-2	2-0	2-2	1-1	2-0	3-2	2-1	1-2	3-0		6-2	1-4	2-4	3-6
Thetford Town	1-2	2-1	3-0	2-3	1-3	0-6	2-6	2-1	1-1	1-4	3-0	0-6	2-2	2-0	1-1	0-3	2-2	1-1		1-5	0-4	0-0
Tiptree United	7-0	0-2	3-1	4-0	2-0	5-1	3-1	3-1	1-3	0-2	4-1	3-1	5-1	4-3	5-1	0-1	2-2	3-4	5-0		0-2	2-2
Walsham-le-Willows	2-0	1-1	4-0	0-2	7-1	0-0	5-0	2-0	3-0	1-1	4-0	2-0	4-1	3-1	0-0	0-2	3-6	0-3	8-1	1-2		1-3
Whitton United	3-1	2-1	1-1	3-4	3-2	1-2	0-2	3-1	2-1	0-3	2-0	2-0	3-2	3-1	4-0	2-2	1-3	3-4	4-0	1-3	0-0	

Division One		P	W	D	L	F	A	Pts
Stanway Rovers		42	33	4	5	106	29	103
Felixstowe & Walton United		42	30	5	7	107	48	95
Fulbourn Institute		42	30	4	8	109	60	94
Tiptree United		42	29	3	10	125	56	90
Walsham-le-Willows		42	23	10	9	91	46	79
Whitton United		42	22	7	13	83	63	73
Ely City		42	20	10	12	88	68	70
Haverhill Rovers		42	21	7	14	77	60	70
Swaffham Town		42	19	12	11	90	71	69
Debenham Leisure Centre		42	17	10	15	60	70	61
Fakenham Town		42	15	11	16	64	69	56
Saffron Walden Town		42	14	12	16	56	62	54
Great Yarmouth Town		42	14	10	18	54	60	52
Godmanchester Rovers		42	12	10	20	53	73	46
Long Melford		42	9	11	22	59	84	38
Stowmarket Town		42	10	8	24	63	95	38
Cornard United		42	11	4	27	59	96	37
Gorleston	*-4*	42	9	12	21	50	74	35
March Town United		42	9	6	27	46	91	33
Downham Town		42	8	9	25	41	99	33
Hadleigh United		42	6	13	23	38	78	31
Thetford Town		42	7	10	25	47	114	31

EASTERN COUNTIES LEAGUE DIVISION ONE CONSTITUTION 2006-07

CORNARD UNITED............. Blackhouse Lane Sport Ground, Great Cornard, Sudbury CO10 0NL.............. 01787 376719
DEBENHAM LEISURE CENTRE .... Gracechurch Street, Debenham, Stowmarket IP14 6BY.............. 01728 861101
DOWNHAM TOWN .... Memorial Playing Field, Lynn Road, Downham Market PE38 9QG.............. 01366 388424
ELY CITY .... The Unwin Ground, Downham Road, Ely CB6 2SH 01353 662035
FAKENHAM TOWN .... Clipbush Park, Clipbush Lane, Fakenham NR21 8SW.............. 01328 856222/855859
GODMANCHESTER ROVERS .... Bearscroft Lane, Godmanchester PE29 2LQ.............. 07950 367417
GORLESTON .... Emerald Park, Wood Farm Lane, Gorleston NR31 9AQ.............. 01493 602802
GREAT YARMOUTH TOWN... Wellesley Road Rec Ground, Sandown Road, Great Yarmouth NR30 1EY.............. 01493 843373
HADLEIGH UNITED .... Millfield, Tinkers Lane, off Duke Street, Hadleigh IP7 5NG.............. 01473 822165
HAVERHILL ROVERS .... Hamlet Croft, Hamlet Road, Haverhill CB9 8LH.............. 01440 712396
LONG MELFORD .... Stoneylands Stadium, New Road, Long Melford CO10 9JY 01787 312187
MARCH TOWN UNITED .... GER Sports Ground, Robin Goodfellows Lane, March PE15 8HS.............. 01354 653073
SAFFRON WALDEN TOWN.................. Catons Lane, Saffron Walden CB10 2DU.............. 01799 522789
STOWMARKET TOWN.................. Greens Meadow, Bury Road, Stowmarket IP14 1JQ.............. 01449 612533
SWAFFHAM TOWN................. Shoemakers Lane, off Cley Road, Swaffham PE37 7NT.............. 01760 722700
THETFORD TOWN .... Recreation Ground, Mundford Road, Thetford IP24 1NB.............. 01842 766120
TIPTREE UNITED....................... Chapel Road, Tiptree, near Colchester CO5 0RA.............. 01621 815213
WALSHAM-LE-WILLOWS...... Walsham Sports Club, Summer Road, Walsham-le-Willows IP31 3AH.............. 01359 259298
WHITTON UNITED............. King George V Playing Fields, Old Norwich Road, Ipswich IP6 6LE.............. 01473 464030

OUT: Felixstowe & Walton United (P), Fulbourn Institute (W – Cambridgeshire County League Senior Division A), Stanway Rovers (P)

LEAGUE CUP

PRELIMINARY ROUND

Cornard United 2 **Tiptree United** 6
Debenham Leisure Centre 0 **Stowmarket Town** 3
Dereham Town 1 Downham Town 0
Godmanchester Rovers 1 **Mildenhall Town** 2
Kirkley 1 **Great Yarmouth Town** 2
March Town United 2 **Soham Town Rangers** 4 *aet*
Needham Market 3 Ipswich Wanderers 3 *aet* (6-5p)
Newmarket Town 1 Wisbech Town 0
Norwich United 0 **Gorleston** 2
Stanway Rovers 2 Long Melford 1 *aet*
Walsham-le-Willows 2 **Woodbridge Town** 3
Whitton United 2 **Harwich & Parkeston** 6

FIRST ROUND

Bury Town 1 Needham Market 0
Cambridge City Res. 2 Ely City 1
Dereham Town 1 **Swaffham Town** 3
Diss Town 5 Thetford Town 0
Felixstowe & Walton United 2 Stowmarket Town 1
Great Yarmouth Town 2 Fakenham Town 1
Hadleigh United 2 **Harwich & Parkeston** 4 *aet*
Halstead Town 2 Haverhill Rovers 1
Histon Res. 2 **Soham Town Rangers** 6
King's Lynn Res. 7 Wroxham 4 *aet*
Leiston 2 Woodbridge Town 2 *aet* (9-8p)
Lowestoft Town 3 Gorleston 1
Mildenhall Town 3 Saffron Walden Town 0
Newmarket Town 4 **Fulbourn Institute** 6
Stanway Rovers 2 **AFC Sudbury** 3
Tiptree United 5 Clacton Town 0

SECOND ROUND

Bury Town 4 Soham Town Rangers 3
Diss Town 8 Swaffham Town 2
Felixstowe & Walton United 1 **Lowestoft Town** 5
Halstead Town 0 **Tiptree United** 3
Harwich & Parkeston 1 **AFC Sudbury** 2
King's Lynn Res. 3 Cambridge City Res. 2
Leiston 3 Great Yarmouth Town 1
Mildenhall Town 2 Fulbourn Institute 0

QUARTER-FINALS

Bury Town 3 **AFC Sudbury** 4 *aet*
Diss Town 1 **King's Lynn Res.** 3
Lowestoft Town 2 Leiston 1
Tiptree United 2 **Mildenhall Town** 5

SEMI-FINALS

Lowestoft Town 2 King's Lynn Res. 0
Mildenhall Town 1 **AFC Sudbury** 2 *aet*

FINAL

(May 10th at Diss Town)

AFC Sudbury 2 Lowestoft Town 1

DIVISION ONE CUP

PRELIMINARY ROUND

Debenham Leisure Centre 1 **Cornard United** 4
Fakenham Town 4 Thetford Town 0
Felixstowe & Walton United 2 Hadleigh United 1
Godmanchester Rovers 2 **March Town United** 4
Walsham-le-Willows 3 Fulbourn Institute 1
Whitton United 4 Haverhill Rovers 1

FIRST ROUND

Cornard United 2 **Stanway Rovers** 5 *aet*
Fakenham Town 1 Downham Town 0
Felixstowe & Walton United 3 Long Melford 2
March Town United 4 Great Yarmouth Town 1
Saffron Walden Town 0 **Tiptree United** 1
Swaffham Town 2 Gorleston 1
Walsham-le-Willows 2 Ely City 1
Whitton United 2 **Stowmarket Town** 4

QUARTER-FINALS

Fakenham Town 1 Walsham-le-Willows 0
Felixstowe & Walton United 0 **Tiptree United** 1
Stanway Rovers 2 Stowmarket Town 1
Swaffham Town 3 March Town United 2

SEMI-FINALS

Fakenham Town 2 Swaffham Town 1
Tiptree United 1 **Stanway Rovers** 1 *aet* (2-4p)

FINAL *(May 1st at Mildenhall Town)*

Fakenham Town 3 Stanway Rovers 2 *aet*

Reserve Division (North)	P	W	D	L	F	A	Pts
Felixstowe/Walton Utd Res.	18	11	3	4	54	23	36
Walsham-le-Willows Res.	18	9	6	3	33	16	33
Woodbridge Town Res.	18	8	5	5	38	29	29
Diss Town Res.	18	8	5	5	34	29	29
Stowmarket Town Res.	18	9	2	7	29	33	29
Whitton United Res.	18	7	4	7	34	25	25
Leiston Res.	18	5	3	10	27	31	18
Ipswich Wanderers Res.	18	5	3	10	30	47	18
Needham Market Res.	18	4	5	9	19	37	17
Hadleigh United Res.	18	3	6	9	19	47	15

Reserve Division (South)	P	W	D	L	F	A	Pts
AFC Sudbury Res.	20	14	3	3	64	21	45
Stanway Rovers Res.	20	13	3	4	57	25	42
Tiptree United Res.	20	12	3	5	71	37	39
Haverhill Rovers Res.	20	11	4	5	57	30	37
Braintree Town Res.	20	9	3	8	36	52	30
Halstead Town Res.	20	8	3	9	42	33	27
Harwich & Parkeston Res.	20	7	5	8	52	32	26
Wivenhoe Town Res. *-3*	20	8	4	8	46	37	25
Long Melford Res.	20	5	5	10	31	44	20
Cornard United Res.	20	3	3	14	22	86	12
Clacton Town Res.	20	1	2	17	22	103	5

RESERVES CUP

FINAL

(April 19th at Hadleigh United)

Wivenhoe Town Res. 2 Harwich & Parkeston Res. 1

RESERVES CHAMPIONSHIP

(Reserve Div (Nth) champions v Reserve Div (Sth) champions)

(May 3rd at Whitton United)

Felixstowe & Walton United Res. 3 AFC Sudbury Res. 1

ESSEX OLYMPIAN LEAGUE

	Bishop's Stortford Swifts	Debden Sports	Epping	Frenford Senior	Harold Wood Athletic	Kelvedon Hatch	Manford Way	Old Chelmsfordians	Roydon	Takeley	White Ensign	White Notley
Bishop's Stortford Swifts	*D*	0-1	1-0	1-3	1-1	2-1	1-1	4-0	2-0	2-1	2-1	2-3
Debden Sports	0-2	*I*	1-1	1-2	0-3	0-3	0-0	1-2	1-4	2-0	2-8	0-3
Epping	1-1	1-2	*V*	0-2	0-0	0-1	2-0	3-3	1-3	1-2	0-0	2-1
Frenford Senior	0-4	3-0	3-0	*I*	1-1	2-1	2-0	5-4	5-1	3-1	1-2	2-2
Harold Wood Athletic	1-0	2-1	2-0	1-1	*S*	1-0	2-0	2-1	4-0	2-1	3-2	3-2
Kelvedon Hatch	2-2	1-0	2-2	0-1	1-0	*I*	0-4	1-1	3-1	1-2	0-3	2-3
Manford Way	2-1	3-0	6-1	0-1	0-1	0-1	*O*	4-1	4-0	3-2	0-1	2-3
Old Chelmsfordians	1-0	3-0	1-1	1-1	0-1	0-1	1-3	*N*	2-0	1-3	1-4	0-4
Roydon	1-0	2-0	0-3	1-1	0-2	0-1	1-1	1-0		2-2	2-1	1-0
Takeley	0-4	2-0	1-1	2-2	1-4	1-1	0-3	0-0	1-0	*O*	1-1	0-3
White Ensign	1-2	4-1	3-0	1-0	2-4	1-3	3-0	W-L	2-0	4-1	*N*	1-3
White Notley	2-0	3-0	1-2	0-1	0-1	3-0	2-1	2-1	3-1	3-2	3-3	*E*

Division One	P	W	D	L	F	A	Pts
Harold Wood Athletic	22	17	4	1	41	14	55
Frenford Senior	22	13	6	3	42	24	45
White Notley	22	14	2	6	49	27	44
White Ensign	22	12	3	7	48	29	39
Bishop's Stortford Swifts	22	10	4	8	34	23	34
Kelvedon Hatch	22	9	4	9	26	29	31
Manford Way	22	9	3	10	37	26	30
Roydon	22	7	3	12	21	39	24
Takeley	22	5	6	11	26	43	21
Epping	22	4	8	10	22	36	20
Old Chelmsfordians	22	4	5	13	24	41	17
Debden Sports	22	3	2	17	13	52	11

SENIOR CHALLENGE CUP

(Division One champions v Senior Cup holders)

(August 13th at White Ensign)

White Ensign 7 Shenfield Association 0

ESSEX OLYMPIAN LEAGUE DIVISION ONE CONSTITUTION 2006-07

BISHOP'S STORTFORD SWIFTS . . Silver Leys, Hadham Road (A1250), Bishop's Stortford CM23 2QE 01279 658941
CANNING TOWN . . . . . Gooseleys Playing Fields, St Albans Avenue, East Ham E6 6HQ . . . . . None
EPPING . . . . . Stonards Hill Rec Ground, Tidy's Lane, Epping CM16 6SP . . . . . None
FRENFORD SENIOR . . . . . Oakfields Sports Ground, Forest Road, Barkingside IG6 3HD 020 8500 1998
GALLEYWOOD . . . . . Clarkes Field, Slades Lane, Galleywood, Chelmsford CM2 8RW 01245 352975
HAROLD WOOD ATHLETIC . . . . Harold Wood Recreation Park, Harold View, Harold Wood RM3 0LX 01708 348827
KELVEDON HATCH . . . . . New Hall, School Road, Kelvedon Hatch, Brentwood CM15 0DH 01277 372153
MANFORD WAY . . . . . London Marathon Sports Ground, Forest Road, Hainault IG6 3HJ 020 8500 3486
MOUNTNESSING . . . . Henderson Sports & Social Club, Kenilworth Avenue, Harold Park, Romford RM3 9NE 01708 343019
ROYDON . . . . . Roydon Playing Fields, Harlow Road, Roydon, Harlow CM19 5HE . . . . . None
TAKELEY . . . . . Station Road (adjacent to rail bridge), Takeley, Bishop's Stortford CM22 6SG 01279 870404
WHITE ENSIGN . . . . Borough Football Combination HQ, Eastwoodbury Lane, Southend-on-Sea SS2 6XG . . . . . None
WHITE NOTLEY . . . . . Oak Farm, Faulkbourne, Witham 01376 519864

IN: Canning Town (P), Galleywood (P), Mountnessing (P)
OUT: Debden Sports (W), Old Chelmsfordians (R)

SENIOR CUP

(All teams from Divisions One, Two and Three)

FIRST ROUND

Bishop's Stortford Swifts 2 **White Ensign** 4
Canning Town 2 Great Baddow 0
Debden Sports 1 **Barnston** 2
Herongate Athletic 3 **Writtle** 3 *aet* (3-4p)
Hutton 5 Basildon Town 2
Metropolitan Police Chigwell 2 Upminster 1
Old Chelmsfordians 0 **Galleywood** 3
Ongar Town 0 **Manford Way** 3
Roydon 2 Epping 1
Ryan 1 **Leigh Ramblers** 3

SECOND ROUND

Barnston 2 **Runwell Hospital** 4 *aet*
Benfleet 4 Writtle 0
Broomfield 0 **Faces** 1
Frenford Senior 7 Westhamians 2
Kelvedon Hatch 5 Hannakins Farm 0
Leigh Ramblers 0 **White Notley** 3
Leytonstone United 1 **Hutton** 1 *aet* (2-4p)
Manford Way 6 Ramsden 1
Marconi Athletic (scr.) v **Stambridge United** (w/o)
Rayleigh Town 0 **Galleywood** 1
Roydon 1 **Canning Town** 2
Sandon Royals 1 Mountnessing 0
Shenfield Association 0 **Harold Wood Athletic** 1
Springfield 2 **Shell Club Corringham** 4 *aet*
Takeley 4 Metropolitan Police Chigwell 1
White Ensign 5 Linford Wanderers 0

THIRD ROUND

Canning Town 1 Stambridge United 0
Faces 10 Runwell Hospital 0
Frenford Senior 1 Manford Way 0
Galleywood 3 Shell Club Corringham 2
Harold Wood Athletic 2 Kelvedon Hatch 1
Hutton 1 **White Notley** 3
Takeley 4 Sandon Royals 1
White Ensign 2 Benfleet 1

QUARTER-FINALS

Galleywood 0 **Canning Town** 1
Harold Wood Athletic 3 Frenford Senior 1
Takeley 1 **White Ensign** 3
White Notley 4 Faces 0

SEMI-FINALS

Harold Wood Athletic 1 White Notley 0 *aet*
White Ensign 2 Canning Town 1

FINAL

(May 16th at Billericay Town)

Harold Wood Athletic 2 White Ensign 0

	Benfleet	Broomfield	Canning Town	Faces	Galleywood	Herongate Athletic	Linford Wanderers	Mountnessing	Rayleigh Town	Ryan	Sandon Royals	Shell Club Corringham	Shenfield Association	Springfield	Stambridge United
Benfleet		W-L	0-1	3-2	1-0	0-1	4-1	1-4	2-4	2-3	2-0	4-5	2-1	0-2	0-2
Broomfield	1-5	*D*	0-3	1-3	2-3	1-2	1-2	1-2	2-3	3-1	1-0	1-1	0-1	0-2	0-0
Canning Town	3-2	3-2	*I*	0-1	2-0	1-0	2-1	1-2	5-2	1-0	3-1	6-1	4-0	4-1	3-2
Faces	1-1	2-0	3-3	*V*	2-3	3-2	9-1	2-1	3-1	3-2	0-0	3-1	1-1	1-1	2-0
Galleywood	2-0	2-0	1-1	0-1	*I*	3-2	6-1	1-2	2-1	2-1	1-1	2-0	3-0	0-2	2-0
Herongate Athletic	2-1	0-2	0-4	1-2	0-1	*S*	0-0	0-2	0-3	1-1	1-1	0-2	0-2	1-1	0-1
Linford Wanderers	5-1	0-1	0-6	1-1	0-5	L-W	*I*	2-6	2-3	L-W	1-2	1-1	1-1	3-3	3-4
Mountnessing	3-1	6-2	2-1	0-3	2-2	0-2	10-0	*O*	2-2	3-0	1-0	1-0	4-1	1-3	1-3
Rayleigh Town	0-0	1-0	3-3	4-1	0-1	0-0	2-2	3-2	*N*	2-2	2-0	2-0	4-5	0-1	0-3
Ryan	3-2	1-0	1-5	1-4	4-4	5-1	8-1	1-2	3-2		1-1	3-3	1-0	1-0	2-2
Sandon Royals	1-2	3-1	2-0	1-0	1-2	1-1	4-1	0-1	3-1	1-1		0-1	W-L	0-1	1-1
Shell Club Corringham	3-3	2-0	0-0	2-3	1-2	3-1	2-1	1-0	3-2	6-6	1-0	*T*	1-2	3-1	2-2
Shenfield Association	1-4	1-1	0-2	5-1	2-2	0-1	3-0	0-4	0-2	0-3	2-2	4-1	*W*	1-1	1-2
Springfield	3-3	3-3	2-3	0-1	2-0	1-1	1-0	0-1	0-2	1-2	0-1	1-1	2-2	*O*	4-1
Stambridge United	2-1	1-0	0-1	1-1	0-2	1-1	1-1	0-5	2-0	3-0	0-4	W-L	0-1	0-1	

Division Two		P	W	D	L	F	A	Pts
Canning Town	*+2*	28	20	4	4	71	29	66
Mountnessing		28	19	2	7	70	33	59
Galleywood		28	17	5	6	54	31	56
Faces	*-2*	28	16	7	5	59	37	53
Springfield	*+2*	28	10	9	9	40	36	41
Ryan		28	11	8	9	57	55	41
Stambridge United		28	11	7	10	34	39	40
Rayleigh Town		28	11	6	11	51	49	39
Shell Club Corringham		28	10	8	10	47	51	38
Sandon Royals		28	9	8	11	31	29	35
Benfleet		28	9	4	15	47	56	31
Shenfield Association		28	8	7	13	37	49	31
Herongate Athletic		28	6	8	14	21	42	26
Broomfield		28	4	4	20	26	53	16
Linford Wanderers		28	2	7	19	31	87	13

ESSEX OLYMPIAN LEAGUE DIVISION TWO CONSTITUTION 2006-07

BENFLEET................ The Club House, Woodside Extension, Manor Road, Benfleet, Rayleigh SS7 4BG 01268 743957
FACES .... Ford Sports & Social Club, Aldbrough Road South, Newbury Park, Ilford IG3 8HG 020 8590 3797
HERONGATE ATHLETIC......... Adjacent to 77 Billericay Road, Herongate, Brentwood CM13 3PU 01277 811260
LEIGH RAMBLERS................. Belfairs Park, Eastwood Road North, Leigh-on-Sea SS9 4LR.............. 01702 421077
OLD CHELMSFORDIANS .... Lawford Lane, Roxwell Road, Chelmsford CM1 2NS............. 01245 420442
ONGAR TOWN.................... Love Lane, High Street, Ongar CM5 9BL............. 01277 363838
RAYLEIGH TOWN............ Rayleigh Town Sports & Social Club, London Road, Rayleigh SS6 9HR............. 01268 784001
RYAN.......................... Old Parmiters Sports Ground, 102a Nelson Road, Chingford E4 9AS .... None
SANDON ROYALS .... Sandon Sports Club, Rectory Chase, Sandon, Chelmsford CM2 7SQ 01245 476626
SHELL CLUB CORRINGHAM .... Shell Club, Springhouse Road, Corringham SS17 7QT 01375 673100
SHENFIELD ASSOCIATION................ The Drive, Warley, Brentwood CM13 3BH .... None
SPRINGFIELD .... Springfield Hall Park, Arun Close, Springfield, Chelmsford CM1 7QE .... None
STAMBRIDGE UNITED .. Stambridge Recreation Ground, Rochford Rd, Great Stambridge, Rochford SS4 2AX............. 01702 258988
UPMINSTER .... Hall Lane Playing Fields, Hall Lane, Upminster, Romford RM14 1AU............. 01708 220320

IN: Leigh Ramblers (P), Old Chelmsfordians (R), Ongar Town (P), Upminster (P)
OUT: Broomfield (R), Canning Town (P), Galleywood (P), Linford Wanderers (R), Mountnessing (P)

DENNY KING MEMORIAL CUP

(All teams eliminated from Rounds One and Two of the Senior Cup)

FIRST ROUND

Basildon Town 1 **Rayleigh Town** 5
Bishop's Stortford Swifts 4 Herongate Athletic 0
Broomfield 0 **Ongar Town** 2
Leigh Ramblers 6 Metropolitan Police Chigwell 1
Linford Wanderers (w/o) v Great Baddow (scr.)
Mountnessing 1 **Roydon** 1 *aet* (4-5p)
Shenfield Association 4 Ramsden 1
Springfield 3 **Epping** 4 *aet*
Writtle 3 Ryan 1

SECOND ROUND

Barnston 2 **Westhamians** 3
Bishop's Stortford Swifts 3 Debden Sports 0
Leigh Ramblers 3 **Epping** 3 *aet* (2-4p)
Leytonstone United 2 Old Chelmsfordians 1
Ongar Town 3 Writtle 1
Roydon 7 Linford Wanderers 1
Shenfield Association 0 **Rayleigh Town** 3
Upminster 5 Hannakins Farm 1

THIRD ROUND

Epping 2 Bishop's Stortford Swifts 0
Leytonstone United 1 Westhamians 0
Ongar Town 2 Upminster 0 *aet*
Roydon 1 **Rayleigh Town** 3 *aet*

SEMI-FINALS

Epping 6 Rayleigh Town 2
Leytonstone United 2 **Ongar Town** 3

FINAL

(May 27th at White Notley)
Epping 5 Ongar Town 2

	Barnston	Basildon Town	Great Baddow	Hannakins Farm	Hutton	Leigh Ramblers	Leytonstone	Marconi Athletic	Met Police Chigwell	Ongar Town	Ramsden	Runwell Hospital	Upminster	Westhamians	Writtle
Barnston	*D*	1-2	1-1	2-4	1-5	1-4	0-5	1-0	0-1	2-2	4-2	5-2	0-5	1-0	1-0
Basildon Town	3-4	*I*	2-0	4-4	3-0	1-1	4-2	n/a	1-1	1-5	3-3	5-3	2-1	1-4	0-1
Great Baddow	2-2	0-1	*V*	0-1	3-0	0-2	0-0	n/a	1-2	1-2	2-2	2-1	1-2	7-0	1-2
Hannakins Farm	5-5	2-2	2-1	*I*	3-5	0-1	2-2	n/a	4-2	1-2	3-1	1-1	2-5	2-4	1-1
Hutton	3-1	3-1	L-W	3-3	*S*	0-3	2-1	n/a	1-1	1-5	3-2	0-0	1-2	0-3	2-3
Leigh Ramblers	3-0	3-0	1-1	1-1	1-1	*I*	0-2	n/a	3-2	2-5	0-1	2-1	0-0	2-0	2-1
Leytonstone United	4-1	3-2	0-1	4-3	0-1	2-0	*O*	n/a	2-1	2-2	1-1	2-2	2-1	3-3	2-0
Marconi Athletic	n/a	n/a	n/a	n/a	n/a	n/a	n/a	*N*	n/a	n/a	n/a	n/a	n/a	n/a	n/a
Metropolitan Police Chigwell	3-0	4-0	0-0	4-2	1-1	5-4	2-2	n/a		3-1	2-1	3-3	0-2	1-1	3-2
Ongar Town	5-2	4-1	2-0	2-1	4-1	5-0	3-0	n/a	3-1		1-0	2-0	2-2	5-2	3-2
Ramsden	5-0	4-2	2-5	0-3	0-2	3-1	0-3	n/a	0-1	4-4	*T*	1-4	4-8	3-3	4-2
Runwell Hospital	5-0	1-3	2-0	0-1	3-3	1-2	1-1	n/a	3-7	2-2	3-2	*H*	1-2	0-2	0-1
Upminster	7-2	0-4	2-1	0-6	4-1	3-3	2-1	n/a	1-0	2-4	2-1	1-0	*R*	2-0	2-0
Westhamians	2-3	1-0	1-1	1-4	1-1	1-2	1-1	n/a	3-1	0-4	1-3	1-2	2-1	*E*	3-3
Writtle	1-1	0-0	1-1	1-2	1-4	1-1	2-2	n/a	3-0	3-4	2-2	4-1	0-1	5-2	*E*

Division Three	P	W	D	L	F	A	Pts
Ongar Town	26	20	5	1	83	36	65
Upminster	26	17	3	6	60	40	54
Leigh Ramblers	26	12	7	7	44	38	43
Leytonstone United	26	10	10	6	49	37	40
Metropolitan Pol. Chigwell	26	11	7	8	51	44	40
Hannakins Farm	26	10	8	8	63	54	38
Hutton	26	9	7	10	44	50	34
Basildon Town	26	9	6	11	48	55	33
Writtle	26	7	8	11	42	45	29
Westhamians	26	7	7	12	42	58	28
Great Baddow	26	6	8	12	32	33	26
Ramsden	26	6	6	14	51	65	24
Barnston	26	6	5	15	40	81	23
Runwell Hospital	26	5	7	14	42	55	22

Marconi Athletic – record expunged

ESSEX OLYMPIAN LEAGUE DIVISION THREE CONSTITUTION 2006-07

BARNSTON	High Easter Road, Barnston, Dunmow CM6 1LZ	01371 876364
BASILDON TOWN	GEC Avionics Sports Ground, Gardiners Lane South, Gardiners Way, Basildon SS14 3AP	01268 883128
BROOMFIELD	The Angel Meadow, Main Road, Broomfield, Chelmsford CM1 7AH	01245 443819
GREAT BADDOW	Great Baddow Rec, Baddow Road, Great Baddow, Chelmsford CM2 9RL	01245 475899
HANNAKINS FARM	Hannakins Farm, Rosebay Avenue, Billicay CM12 0SY	01277 630851
HUTTON	Polo Fields, Hall Green Lane, Hutton, Brentwood CM13 2QT	01277 262257
LEYTONSTONE UNITED	Ilford Wanderers RFC, Forest Road, Hainault IG6 3HJ	020 8500 4622
LINFORD WANDERERS	Lakeside Pitches, Thurrock RM20 2ZL	None
M & B CLUB	M & B Sports & Social Club, Dagenham Road, Dagenham RM10	020 8919 2427
METROPOLITAN POLICE CHIGWELL	Met Police Sports Club, High Road, Chigwell IG7 6BD	020 8500 1017
POTTER STREET	Minton Lane, Church Langley Country Park, Harlow	None
RAMSDEN	Nursery Sports Ground, Downham Road, Ramsden Heath, Billericay CM11 1PU	01268 711502
RUNWELL HOSPITAL	Runwell Hospital, Runwell Chase, Wickford SS11 7QE	01268 562967
WESTHAMIANS	Fairlop Oak Playing Fields, Forest Road, Hainault IG6 3HT	None
WRITTLE	Paradise Road Playing Fields, Writtle, Chelmsford CM1 3HW	01245 420332

IN: Broomfield (R), Linford Wanderers (R), M & B Club (P – Essex Business Houses League Premier Division), Potter Street (P – Mid-Essex League Premier Division)

OUT: Leigh Ramblers (P), Marconi Athletic (WS), Ongar Town (P), Upminster (P)

Reserve Division One		P	W	D	L	F	A	Pts
Frenford Senior Res.		24	19	3	2	72	18	60
Manford Way Res.		24	16	3	5	58	20	51
Harold Wood Res.	*-3*	24	15	1	8	59	27	43
Canning Town Res.		24	12	4	8	56	38	40
B Stortford Swifts Res.		24	12	2	10	48	39	38
White Ensign Res.	*+3*	24	9	6	9	39	33	36
Epping Res.		24	9	7	8	36	32	34
Rayleigh Town Res.		24	7	7	10	28	48	28
Shenfield Assn Res.		24	8	3	13	36	52	27
Ryan Res.		24	6	5	13	44	66	23
Debden Sports Res.	*-3*	24	7	4	13	28	57	22
Shell Club Corr Res.	*+3*	24	5	4	15	27	67	22
Takeley Res.		24	6	1	17	35	69	19

Reserve Division Two	P	W	D	L	F	A	Pts
Galleywood Res.	24	15	7	2	83	33	52
Old Chelmsfordian Res.	24	13	8	3	57	35	47
White Notley Res.	24	12	7	5	54	28	43
Kelvedon Hatch Res.	24	13	3	8	35	28	42
Met Pol Chigwell Res.	24	10	7	7	42	29	37
Herongate Athletic Res.	24	10	7	7	42	34	37
Sandon Royals Res.	24	10	3	11	28	37	33
Hutton Res.	24	8	8	8	42	38	32
Upminster Res.	24	7	6	11	44	51	27
Linford Wanderers Res.	24	6	6	12	38	55	24
Ramsden Res.	24	6	3	15	33	60	21
Leigh Ramblers Res.	24	6	3	15	31	62	21
Broomfield Res.	24	4	4	16	29	68	16

Reserve Division Three	P	W	D	L	F	A	Pts
Hannakins Farm Res.	24	19	2	3	82	19	59
Runwell Hospital Res.	24	16	4	4	72	32	52
Roydon Res.	24	16	2	6	67	37	50
Faces Res.	24	11	4	9	71	49	37
Westhamians Res.	24	11	4	9	50	52	37
Great Baddow Res.	24	11	2	11	50	49	35
Leytonstone United Res.	24	10	2	12	45	51	32
Basildon Town Res.	24	8	7	9	44	51	31
Springfield Res.	24	10	1	13	57	79	31
Benfleet Res.	24	8	5	11	43	55	29
Mountnessing Res.	24	8	3	13	48	56	27
Writtle Res.	24	6	0	18	34	73	18
Barnston Res.	24	3	2	19	32	92	11

RESERVE DIVISIONS CHALLENGE CUP

(Reserve Div One champions v Reserve Div Cup holders)

(August 13th at White Ensign)

Manford Way Res. 1 **Harold Wood Athletic Res.** 3

RESERVE DIVISIONS CUP

(All Reserve Division teams)

(May 10th at Witham Town)

Manford Way Res. 0 **Harold Wood Athletic Res.** 1

ESSEX SENIOR LEAGUE

	AFC Hornchurch	Barkingside	Basildon United	Bowers & Pitsea	Brentwood Town	Burnham Ramblers	Concord Rangers	Eton Manor	Hullbridge Sports	London APSA	Romford	Sawbridgeworth Town	Southend Manor	Stansted	Tilbury	Waltham Abbey
AFC Hornchurch		1-0	3-0	3-1	4-1	4-0	3-3	3-0	4-1	1-0	3-0	1-0	2-0	1-2	1-1	1-0
Barkingside	1-4		3-0	1-0	2-1	1-4	1-0	3-2	3-1	1-1	2-0	1-1	4-0	2-2	2-2	0-0
Basildon United	2-4	0-2		4-3	2-1	1-6	0-3	2-2	2-2	1-4	2-1	2-2	1-2	4-2	3-2	0-3
Bowers & Pitsea	0-1	1-3	0-2		0-3	1-0	1-2	2-4	3-2	1-1	2-0	1-4	1-4	2-1	1-1	0-1
Brentwood Town	0-3	2-0	0-2	2-2		1-3	1-0	3-0	2-2	4-1	4-1	0-3	3-0	4-0	1-2	3-0
Burnham Ramblers	2-3	3-0	5-2	5-3	1-1		2-0	1-2	3-2	4-1	1-1	0-0	7-1	2-3	3-1	2-1
Concord Rangers	0-1	0-1	0-2	2-0	2-0	1-3		0-0	2-1	0-2	0-0	1-0	2-0	0-0	0-1	4-3
Eton Manor	1-2	0-1	3-1	3-3	0-2	1-1	0-4		0-0	1-0	1-1	0-2	1-4	2-2	1-4	1-3
Hullbridge Sports	0-4	0-2	6-2	1-0	1-1	2-2	2-1	1-3		2-1	3-1	2-2	0-2	0-1	0-1	2-5
London APSA	2-2	0-0	4-4	3-1	2-0	1-1	0-1	2-2	2-1		1-1	0-1	1-2	2-2	0-1	0-4
Romford	0-2	2-3	2-2	0-2	2-2	2-2	1-3	3-2	3-0	0-0		1-1	1-1	4-1	1-3	1-1
Sawbridgeworth Town	1-3	0-0	1-1	4-1	0-0	3-1	0-1	1-0	3-0	1-1	3-2		5-0	1-0	0-1	4-1
Southend Manor	1-3	1-1	3-1	0-2	0-2	1-1	1-2	0-2	0-1	1-2	1-2	1-1		4-1	2-1	1-0
Stansted	0-2	1-3	2-2	0-1	1-1	0-2	0-1	1-0	2-2	0-1	0-1	2-1	1-1		2-3	0-3
Tilbury	1-2	1-1	5-0	3-1	3-0	3-4	1-1	2-0	2-1	8-1	1-2	2-2	2-0	4-2		1-3
Waltham Abbey	1-0	0-0	0-0	5-0	2-1	1-1	5-0	3-1	1-0	4-0	5-2	2-0	4-3	3-0	0-0	

		P	W	D	L	F	A	Pts
AFC Hornchurch		30	25	3	2	71	21	78
Waltham Abbey		30	18	6	6	64	28	60
Tilbury		30	16	7	7	63	37	55
Barkingside		30	15	10	5	44	30	55
Burnham Ramblers		30	15	9	6	72	44	54
Sawbridgeworth Town		30	12	11	7	47	28	47
Concord Rangers		30	14	5	11	36	32	47
Brentwood Town		30	11	7	12	46	41	40
London APSA		30	7	11	12	36	52	32
Southend Manor		30	9	5	16	37	57	32
Basildon United	*-1*	30	8	8	14	47	76	31
Romford		30	6	11	13	38	54	29
Eton Manor		30	6	8	16	35	57	26
Hullbridge Sports		30	6	7	17	38	60	25
Bowers & Pitsea		30	7	4	19	36	65	25
Stansted		30	5	8	17	31	59	23

ESSEX SENIOR LEAGUE CONSTITUTION 2006-07

BARKING .... **Mayesbrook Park, Lodge Avenue, Dagenham RM8 2JY** **020 8595 6511**
BARKINGSIDE .... **Redbridge FC, Oakside Stadium, Station Road, Barkingside, Ilford IG6 1NB** **020 8550 3611**
BASILDON UNITED .... **The Stadium, Gardiners Close, Gardiners Lane, Basildon SS14 3AN** **01268 520268**
BEAUMONT ATHLETIC .... **Mile End Stadium, Rhodeswell Road, Burdett Road, Poplar E14 7TW** **020 8980 1885**
BOWERS & PITSEA ...... **Ken Salmon Stadium, Crown Avenue, off Kenneth Road, Pitsea, Basildon SS14 2BE** **01268 452068**
BRENTWOOD TOWN .... **The Arena, Brentwood Centre, Doddinghurst Road, Brentwood CM15 9NN** **01277 215151 Ext.713**
BURNHAM RAMBLERS .... **Leslie Field, Springfield Road, Burnham-on-Crouch CM0 8TE** **01621 784383**
CLAPTON .... **Old Spotted Dog Ground, Upton Lane, Forest Gate E7 9NP** **020 8472 0822**
CONCORD RANGERS .... **Thames Road Stadium, Thames Road, Canvey Island SS8 0HH** **01268 691780**
ETON MANOR .... **Tilbury FC, Chadfields, St Chad's Road, Tilbury RM18 8NL** **01375 843093**
HULLBRIDGE SPORTS .... **Lower Road, Hullbridge, Hockley SS5 6BJ** **01702 230420**
LONDON APSA .... **Terence Macmillan Stadium, 281 Prince Regents Lane, Plaistow, London E13 8SD** **01708 349597**
ROMFORD .... **Ford Sports & Social Club, Rush Green Road, Rush Green, Romford RM7 OLU** **01708 737457**
SAWBRIDGEWORTH TOWN .... **Crofters End, West Road, Sawbridgeworth CM21 0DE** **01279 722039**
SOUTHEND MANOR .... **Southchurch Park Arena, Lifstan Way, Southend-on-Sea SS1 2TH** **01702 615577**
STANSTED .... **Hargrave Park, Cambridge Road, Stansted CM24 8DL** **01279 812897**

IN: Barking (N), Beaumont Athletic (P – Essex Business House League Division One), Clapton (S – Isthmian League Division Two)

OUT: AFC Hornchurch (P – Isthmian League Division One North), Tilbury (P – Isthmian League Division One North), Waltham Abbey (P – Isthmian League Division One North)

LEAGUE CUP

GROUP A

	P	W	D	L	F	A	Pts
Brentwood Town	6	3	1	2	8	8	10
Burnham Ramblers	6	3	0	3	14	8	9
Southend Manor	6	2	2	2	6	9	8
Sawbridgeworth Town	6	2	1	3	7	10	7

Brentwood Town 2 Burnham Ramblers 0
Brentwood Town 1 Sawbridgeworth Town 2
Brentwood Town 2 Southend Manor 1
Burnham Ramblers 5 Brentwood Town 1
Burnham Ramblers 1 Sawbridgeworth Town 2
Burnham Ramblers 5 Southend Manor 1
Sawbridgeworth Town 0 Brentwood Town 2
Sawbridgeworth Town 1 Burnham Ramblers 3
Sawbridgeworth Town 1 Southend Manor 2
Southend Manor 0 Brentwood Town 0
Southend Manor 1 Burnham Ramblers 0
Southend Manor 1 Sawbridgeworth Town 1

GROUP B

	P	W	D	L	F	A	Pts
Eton Manor	6	3	1	2	9	5	10
Romford	6	2	2	2	6	4	8
Stansted	6	2	2	2	5	9	8
Bowers & Pitsea	6	2	1	3	5	7	7

Bowers & Pitsea 0 Eton Manor 1
Bowers & Pitsea 0 Romford 0
Bowers & Pitsea 3 Stansted 1
Eton Manor 1 Bowers & Pitsea 2
Eton Manor 2 Romford 1
Eton Manor 1 Stansted 1
Romford 3 Bowers & Pitsea 0
Romford 1 Eton Manor 0
Romford 1 Stansted 1
Stansted 1 Bowers & Pitsea 0
Stansted 0 Eton Manor 4
Stansted 1 Romford 0

GROUP C

	P	W	D	L	F	A	Pts
AFC Hornchurch	6	6	0	0	23	6	18
Tilbury	6	3	0	3	12	9	9
Hullbridge Sports	6	2	1	3	10	17	7
London APSA	6	0	1	5	5	18	1

AFC Hornchurch 6 Hullbridge Sports 2
AFC Hornchurch 5 London APSA 1
AFC Hornchurch 3 Tilbury 1
Hullbridge Sports 1 AFC Hornchurch 5
Hullbridge Sports 2 London APSA 0
Hullbridge Sports 2 Tilbury 1
London APSA 1 AFC Hornchurch 2
London APSA 2 Hullbridge Sports 2
London APSA 1 Tilbury 2
Tilbury 0 AFC Hornchurch 2
Tilbury 3 Hullbridge Sports 1
Tilbury 5 London APSA 0

GROUP D

	P	W	D	L	F	A	Pts
Barkingside	6	3	2	1	9	6	11
Basildon United	6	2	2	2	7	6	8
Concord Rangers	6	2	2	2	7	7	8
Waltham Abbey	6	1	2	3	5	9	5

Barkingside 0 Basildon United 0
Barkingside 2 Concord Rangers 1
Barkingside 3 Waltham Abbey 1
Basildon United 1 Barkingside 2
Basildon United 1 Concord Rangers 2
Basildon United 2 Waltham Abbey 0
Concord Rangers 2 Barkingside 1
Concord Rangers 1 Basildon United 1
Concord Rangers 1 Waltham Abbey 1
Waltham Abbey 1 Barkingside 1
Waltham Abbey 1 Basildon United 2
Waltham Abbey 1 Concord Rangers 0

Top two teams from each group qualify for knockout stage

QUARTER-FINALS
(played over two legs)

Basildon United 0 Burnham Ramblers 2, **Burnham Ramblers** 1 Basildon United 0
Brentwood Town 1 Eton Manor 0, Eton Manor 0 **Brentwood Town** 5
Romford 2 Barkingside 0, Barkingside 2 **Romford** 1
Tilbury 2 AFC Hornchurch 2, **AFC Hornchurch** 1 Tilbury 0

SEMI-FINALS
(played over two legs)

AFC Hornchurch 1 Romford 0, Romford v **AFC Hornchurch** *(Romford expelled)*
Brentwood Town 0 Burnham Ramblers 0, Burnham Ramblers 1 **Brentwood Town** 2

FINAL
(May 1st at Grays Athletic)

AFC Hornchurch 2 Brentwood Town 0

GORDON BRASTED MEMORIAL TROPHY

FIRST ROUND

AFC Hornchurch 2 Brentwood Town 0 *aet*
Barkingside 1 Bowers & Pitsea 0 *aet*
Basildon United 3 Stansted 0
Concord Rangers 2 Southend Manor 1
Eton Manor 2 **Burnham Ramblers** 4
Hullbridge Sports 1 **Romford** 3
London APSA 0 Waltham Abbey 0 *aet* (3-4p)
(Waltham Abbey expelled)
Tilbury 3 Sawbridgeworth Town 2 *aet*

QUARTER-FINALS

AFC Hornchurch 1 London APSA 0
Barkingside 2 Concord Rangers 0
Burnham Ramblers 2 Basildon United 1
Tilbury 2 Romford 1

SEMI-FINALS

Barkingside 4 Burnham Ramblers 1
Tilbury 2 **AFC Hornchurch** 2 *aet* (3-4p)

FINAL *(April 15th at Burnham Ramblers)*

AFC Hornchurch 1 Barkingside 0

ESSEX & SUFFOLK BORDER LEAGUE

	Alresford Colne Rangers	Bury Town Res.	Coggeshall Town	Dedham Old Boys	Earls Colne	Essex University	Gas Recreation	Hatfield Peverel	Kelvedon Social	Lawford Lads	Little Oakley	Mistley United	St Osyth	Walton Town	Weeley Athletic	West Bergholt
Alresford Colne Rangers	*P*	1-3	1-2	2-1	0-6	0-5	0-3	1-2	2-1	0-1	2-2	0-0	2-0	2-1	1-4	1-2
Bury Town Res.	2-5	*R*	4-0	3-1	2-2	3-1	2-1	3-0	7-0	3-1	2-1	W-L	1-2	3-1	0-0	2-1
Coggeshall Town	2-3	2-1	*E*	1-3	2-6	3-1	0-5	2-2	1-2	0-2	2-1	2-2	3-2	0-2	1-1	1-4
Dedham Old Boys	1-2	0-2	2-5	*M*	2-1	3-1	1-1	1-0	5-2	0-2	1-2	0-0	1-2	2-1	2-0	0-0
Earls Colne	1-1	0-2	3-2	1-1	*I*	2-2	1-5	1-2	7-1	2-0	2-1	0-3	4-4	1-1	1-5	1-1
Essex University	1-1	3-3	4-2	0-0	1-3	*E*	2-3	0-3	1-0	3-3	0-0	3-2	3-2	4-1	1-2	0-2
Gas Recreation	3-2	1-1	3-1	3-1	3-2	3-2	*R*	2-1	3-1	2-2	2-2	2-1	3-2	2-2	3-1	2-3
Hatfield Peverel	4-1	0-2	1-0	5-0	2-3	0-2	2-0		0-0	1-0	1-2	1-2	2-5	0-1	1-0	0-2
Kelvedon Social	1-7	0-1	2-5	0-1	1-3	0-6	0-2	1-3	*D*	1-3	1-2	2-4	1-4	0-5	1-3	0-4
Lawford Lads	3-2	5-0	1-0	1-0	4-1	3-2	2-6	W-L	9-0	*I*	3-1	1-3	1-3	3-1	3-1	1-2
Little Oakley	3-0	0-4	9-2	3-1	1-0	W-L	0-1	4-2	4-1	0-3	*V*	0-6	1-6	0-0	1-3	1-3
Mistley United	0-0	0-0	7-0	1-0	3-3	4-0	4-0	1-1	3-0	0-0	0-0	*I*	3-1	2-1	0-0	2-3
St Osyth	1-0	1-2	0-0	0-1	1-2	1-2	2-2	7-1	3-2	0-1	0-2	0-1	*S*	1-2	5-2	1-4
Walton Town	3-1	3-2	0-0	1-2	2-0	3-0	2-2	2-4	8-1	0-1	1-3	0-0	2-1	*I*	1-2	1-4
Weeley Athletic	1-0	3-0	0-1	0-1	3-0	2-0	0-2	0-1	3-2	3-0	4-0	3-1	1-1	3-0	*O*	2-1
West Bergholt	1-1	2-2	2-3	4-1	1-5	1-3	1-4	2-1	4-1	6-1	4-2	2-1	1-3	8-0	4-2	*N*

Premier Division		P	W	D	L	F	A	Pts
Gas Recreation		30	19	7	4	74	43	64
West Bergholt		30	19	4	7	79	45	61
Bury Town Res.		30	18	6	6	62	37	60
Lawford Lads		30	18	3	9	60	43	57
Weeley Athletic		30	16	4	10	54	35	52
Mistley United		30	13	11	6	56	25	50
Earls Colne	*+3*	30	11	8	11	64	59	44
Hatfield Peverel		30	12	3	15	43	47	39
Little Oakley	*-3*	30	12	5	13	48	57	38
Dedham Old Boys		30	11	5	14	35	46	38
St Osyth		30	11	4	15	61	53	37
Essex University		30	10	6	14	53	55	36
Walton Town		30	10	6	14	48	54	36
Coggeshall Town		30	9	5	16	45	76	32
Alresford Colne Rangers		30	8	6	16	41	60	30
Kelvedon Social		30	1	1	28	25	113	4

A V LEE MEMORIAL TROPHY

(Premier Division champions v League Cup holders)

(August 29th at Gas Recreation)

Gas Recreation 3 West Bergholt 2

ESSEX & SUFFOLK BORDER LEAGUE PREMIER DIVISION CONSTITUTION 2006-07

ALRESFORD COLNE RANGERS .... Ford Lane, Alresford, Colchester CO7 8AY 07796 036467
COGGESHALL TOWN .... The Crops, West Street, Coggeshall CO15 .... 01376 562843
DEDHAM OLD BOYS .... The Old Grammar School, Royal Square, Dedham, Colchester CO7 6AA 01206 322302
EARLS COLNE .... Green Farm Meadow, Halstead Road, Earls Colne, Colchester CO6 2NG 01787 223584
ESSEX UNIVERSITY .... Wivenhoe Town FC, Broad Lane Sports Ground, Wivenhoe CO7 7HA 01206 825380
GAS RECREATION .... Bromley Road, Colchester CO4 3JF 01206 860383
GREAT BENTLEY .... The Green, Great Bentley, Colchester CO7 8LX 01206 251532
HATFIELD PEVEREL .... Strutt Memorial Field, Maldon Road, Hatfield Peverel CM3 2JP .... None
LAWFORD LADS .... School Lane, Lawford, Manningtree CO11 2JA 01206 397211
LITTLE OAKLEY .... War Memorial Club Ground, Little Oakley 01255 880370
MISTLEY UNITED .... Furze Hill, Shrubland Road, Mistley CO11 1HS 01206 392714
ST OSYTH .... Cowley Park, Mill Street, St Osyth, Clacton-on-Sea CO16 8EJ .... None
TIPTREE HEATH .... Colchester Road, Tiptree CO5 0EX 07889 463004
WALTON TOWN .... Frinton Playing Fields, Jubilee Way, Frinton-on-Sea CO13 0AP .... None
WEELEY ATHLETIC .... Weeley Playing Fields, Clacton Road, Weeley, Clacton-on-Sea CO16 9DH .... None
WEST BERGHOLT .... Lorkin Daniel Field, Lexden Road, West Bergholt, Colchester CO6 3BW 01206 241525

IN: Great Bentley (P), Tiptree Heath (P)

OUT: Bury Town Reserves (S – Eastern Counties League Reserve Division North), Kelvedon Social (R)

	Alresford Colne Rangers Res.	Boxted Lodgers	Bradfield Rovers	Bures United	Coggeshall Res.	Dedham Old Boys Res.	Gas Recreation Res.	Glemsford & Cavendish Utd	Gosfield United	Great Bentley	Mersea Island	St Johns (Clacton)	Tiptree Heath	Weeley Athletic Res.	West Bergholt Res.	Witham Town Res.
Alresford Colne Rangers Res.		0-1	2-3	3-3	2-4	2-1	1-2	1-0	2-5	0-7	0-5	1-2	0-2	1-1	0-2	0-0
Boxted Lodgers	4-1		1-4	4-4	1-0	1-0	2-1	2-1	2-2	2-4	0-1	n/a	2-3	1-0	3-3	1-2
Bradfield Rovers	4-0	1-1	*D*	1-2	1-3	4-1	3-3	3-0	3-1	3-2	1-3	10-1	2-4	1-1	2-3	0-1
Bures United	3-0	2-2	3-2	*I*	0-4	1-1	5-1	2-0	4-0	0-6	2-3	3-1	0-5	2-2	3-5	1-6
Coggeshall Res.	2-0	0-1	1-1	0-4	*V*	7-0	4-1	3-0	1-1	1-2	3-3	n/a	1-3	0-2	2-6	3-0
Dedham Old Boys Res.	3-2	2-3	1-1	2-2	3-1	*I*	2-1	4-0	0-5	0-1	0-1	n/a	3-2	5-1	0-1	0-1
Gas Recreation Res.	1-0	2-1	4-3	1-0	0-4	3-2	*S*	2-1	2-2	3-1	2-0	n/a	1-3	4-1	1-0	0-2
Glemsford & Cavendish United	3-0	1-2	2-2	1-3	1-1	3-4	1-2	*I*	0-5	1-7	1-4	n/a	0-2	0-3	2-3	2-6
Gosfield United	6-1	4-0	3-0	0-2	2-2	5-0	0-1	7-3	*O*	0-4	7-2	n/a	2-2	4-0	2-2	1-2
Great Bentley	7-2	1-1	1-1	4-2	1-1	4-1	1-1	1-0	4-0	*N*	5-0	n/a	6-1	3-0	0-0	1-6
Mersea Island	5-1	5-0	4-2	2-2	2-2	0-0	3-4	2-1	0-3	1-2		n/a	2-0	1-0	7-3	0-3
St Johns (Clacton)	n/a	n/a	n/a	n/a	n/a	1-3	2-2	4-5	n/a	n/a	n/a	*O*	1-6	n/a	3-1	n/a
Tiptree Heath	4-0	5-1	3-0	2-1	5-1	3-0	5-1	4-1	2-0	2-0	2-3	n/a	*N*	6-0	3-0	1-5
Weeley Athletic Res.	0-2	2-1	1-0	1-2	0-0	3-3	2-3	1-3	2-1	2-4	3-1	n/a	0-2	*E*	1-2	0-3
West Bergholt Res.	2-2	1-1	2-1	2-4	2-2	0-3	3-1	2-0	1-9	0-8	1-5	n/a	1-2	7-1		1-2
Witham Town Res.	3-1	4-0	2-1	4-2	4-0	6-1	2-1	3-0	3-3	9-1	3-3	n/a	4-0	3-0	3-0	

Note – St Johns (Clacton) withdrew during the course of the season
Their results are shown above but are expunged from the league table

Division One		P	W	D	L	F	A	Pts
Witham Town Res.	*-3*	28	24	3	1	92	24	72
Tiptree Heath		28	21	1	6	78	37	64
Great Bentley		28	18	5	5	88	40	59
Mersea Island		28	15	5	8	68	53	50
Gas Recreation Res.	*-3*	28	15	3	10	49	54	45
Gosfield United		28	12	7	9	80	47	43
Bures United		28	11	7	10	61	64	40
Coggeshall Town Res.	*+3*	28	9	9	10	53	48	39
West Bergholt Res.		28	11	6	11	55	70	39
Boxted Lodgers		28	10	7	11	41	56	37
Bradfield Rovers	*+6*	28	7	7	14	50	55	34
Dedham Old Boys Res.		28	8	5	15	42	64	29
Weeley Athletic Res.	*-3*	28	6	5	17	30	65	20
Alresford Colne Rangers Res.		28	3	4	21	26	83	13
Glemsford & Cavendish United		28	2	2	24	28	81	8

St Johns (Clacton) – record expunged

LEAGUE CUP

FIRST ROUND

Alresford Colne Rangers 2 **Little Oakley** 2 *aet* (3-4p)
Boxted Lodgers 0 **Bures United** 1
Brightlingsea Regent 3 **Glemsford & Cavendish Utd** 4 *aet*
Coggeshall Town 2 **Earls Colne** 3
Essex University 1 **Witham Town Res.** 3
Foxash Social 1 **Mersea Island** 5
Gas Recreation 3 West Suffolk College 2
Gosfield United 2 St Johns (Clacton) 0
Hatfield Peverel 0 **Dedham Old Boys** 3
Hedinghams United 1 **Tiptree Heath** 1 *aet* (1-2p)
Lawford Lads 1 Bury Town Res. 0
Mistley United 4 Great Bentley 2 *aet*
Sudbury Athletic 3 Kelvedon Social 1
Weeley Athletic 2 **St Osyth** 3 *aet*
West Bergholt 3 Bradfield Rovers 0

ESSEX & SUFFOLK BORDER LEAGUE DIVISION ONE CONSTITUTION 2006-07

ALRESFORD COLNE RANGERS RESERVES . . Ford Lane, Alresford, Colchester CO7 8AY. 07796 036467
BOXTED LODGERS. . . . . The Playing Field, Cage Lane, Boxted, Colchester CO4 5RE. 01206 271969
BRADFIELD ROVERS . . . . The Playing Field, The Street, Bradfield, Manningtree CO11 2UU . . . . None
BRIGHTLINGSEA REGENT . . . . North Road, Brightlingsea, Colchester CO7 0PL. 01206 304199
BURES UNITED. . . . . Recreation Ground, Nayland Road, Bures CO8 5BX . . . . None
COGGESHALL TOWN RESERVES. . . . . . . The Crops, West Street, Coggeshall CO15. . . . . 01376 562843
DEDHAM OLD BOYS RESERVES . . The Old Grammar School, Royal Square, Dedham, Colchester CO7 6AA. 01206 322302
GAS RECREATION RESERVES . . . . Bromley Road, Colchester CO4 3JF 01206 860383
GLEMSFORD & CAVENDISH UNITED . . Memorial Hall, Melford Road, Cavendish CO10 8AA. . . . . None
GOSFIELD UNITED . . . . The Playing Field, Gosfield, Halstead. . . . . None
KELVEDON SOCIAL. . . . . The Chase, High Street, Kelvedon, Colchester CO5 9JD. 01376 572240
MERSEA ISLAND . . . . The Glebe, Colchester Road, West Mersea CO5 8JZ 01206 385216
MISTLEY UNITED RESERVES . . . . Furze Hill, Shrubland Road, Mistley CO11 1HS 01206 392714
WEELEY ATHLETIC RESERVES . . Weeley Playing Fields, Clacton Road, Weeley, Clacton-on-Sea CO16 9DH . . . . None
WEST BERGHOLT RESERVES . . Lorkin Daniel Field, Lexden Road, West Bergholt, Colchester CO6 3BW 01206 241525
WEST SUFFOLK COLLEGE . . . . Out Risbygate, Bury St Edmunds IP33 3RL. 01284 701301

IN: Brightlingsea Regent (P), Kelvedon Social (R), Mistley United Reserves (P), West Suffolk College (P)

OUT: Great Bentley (P), Severalls Athletic (WN), Tiptree Heath (P), St Johns (Clacton) (WS), Witham Town Reserves (S – Eastern Counties League Reserve Division South)

	Boxted Lodgers Res.	Brightlingsea Regent	Bures United Res.	Earls Colne Res.	Foxash Social	Great Bentley Res.	Hatfield Peverel Res.	Hedinghams United	Kelvedon Social Res.	Lawford Lads Res.	Little Oakley Res.	Mersea Island Res.	Mistley United Res.	St Osyth Res.	Sudbury Athletic	West Suffolk College
Boxted Lodgers Res.		0-6	2-0	1-2	1-1	0-3	5-1	5-2	7-2	2-3	1-1	2-2	2-4	W-L	1-2	0-3
Brightlingsea Regent	1-1		7-1	1-0	4-0	1-2	4-0	4-1	4-2	3-2	2-2	4-2	4-3	W-L	3-2	0-1
Bures United Res.	3-1	1-2	*D*	1-4	0-1	2-5	2-3	1-1	2-5	2-1	0-3	2-0	1-1	W-L	2-3	1-4
Earls Colne Res.	3-1	0-1	1-2	*I*	3-3	4-1	3-0	3-2	L-W	3-1	0-0	2-0	4-3	2-1	3-1	2-3
Foxash Social	6-2	0-3	2-0	1-2	*V*	1-0	5-3	3-4	3-1	0-1	1-0	1-2	5-1	3-2	0-2	1-2
Great Bentley Res.	0-1	0-4	2-1	1-2	0-2	*I*	2-0	1-1	1-4	1-1	2-3	2-3	1-1	0-0	0-1	1-0
Hatfield Peverel Res.	3-0	0-7	W-L	1-3	0-1	0-2	*S*	2-1	7-3	0-0	0-3	1-0	0-1	4-4	2-1	0-3
Hedinghams United	5-2	1-5	6-7	3-2	2-2	1-4	3-2	*I*	8-1	3-1	1-2	1-1	4-2	3-2	3-3	0-0
Kelvedon Social Res.	2-4	2-4	1-1	3-1	2-1	0-3	2-1	2-0	*O*	1-4	4-3	3-2	1-2	0-5	1-1	0-5
Lawford Lads Res.	5-2	0-4	2-0	1-1	0-2	0-1	5-1	1-3	3-1	*N*	0-4	4-0	1-3	1-2	1-2	1-3
Little Oakley Res.	1-2	1-3	1-0	1-1	1-2	4-0	4-2	2-1	4-2	1-2		2-2	2-0	6-2	0-2	0-1
Mersea Island Res.	2-7	1-5	1-5	0-3	1-5	1-3	2-0	0-5	W-L	0-7	0-5	*T*	1-1	5-2	0-3	1-1
Mistley United Res.	3-0	4-6	4-2	2-1	0-1	2-1	2-0	2-1	5-0	2-1	2-1	9-2	*W*	3-2	W-L	1-3
St Osyth Res.	9-1	2-3	5-2	0-1	L-W	L-W	2-2	L-W	4-2	5-1	2-2	3-2	1-2	*O*	L-W	0-5
Sudbury Athletic	5-0	0-4	0-0	0-2	3-3	L-W	W-L	8-3	5-1	2-0	0-1	1-2	L-W	1-2		0-8
West Suffolk College	5-0	4-2	5-0	1-2	2-2	1-2	6-2	2-1	6-1	1-0	1-0	W-L	2-3	3-2	2-5	

Division Two	P	W	D	L	F	A	Pts
Brightlingsea Regent	30	25	2	3	101	35	77
West Suffolk College	30	22	3	5	83	30	69
Mistley United Res.	30	19	3	8	68	50	60
Earls Colne Res.	30	18	4	8	60	36	58
Foxash Social	30	16	5	9	58	44	53
Little Oakley Res.	30	14	6	10	60	38	48
Sudbury Athletic	30	14	4	12	53	44	46
Great Bentley Res.	30	14	4	12	41	41	46
Hedinghams United +2	30	11	6	13	70	72	41
Lawford Lads Res.	30	10	3	17	50	55	33
Boxted Lodgers Res.	30	9	4	17	53	85	31
Kelvedon Social Res.	30	9	2	19	49	96	29
St Osyth Res.	30	8	4	18	59	54	28
Bures United Res.	30	7	4	19	41	73	25
Hatfield Peverel Res.	30	7	3	20	37	76	24
Mersea Island Res. *-1*	30	6	5	19	35	89	22

SECOND ROUND

Bures United 1 **Sudbury Athletic** 2
Dedham Old Boys 3 Tiptree Heath 1
Earls Colne 2 Gosfield United 2 *aet* (3-1p)
Gas Recreation 4 Little Oakley 2
Glemsford & Cavendish United 0 **Mistley United** 4
Lawford Lads 4 St Osyth 0
Walton Town 5 West Bergholt 4
Witham Town Res. 2 Mersea Island 2 *aet* (5-4p)

QUARTER-FINALS

Earls Colne 5 Dedham Old Boys 4
Gas Recreation 3 Walton Town 0
Lawford Lads 7 Sudbury Athletic 0
Mistley United 2 **Witham Town Res.** 3

SEMI-FINALS

Gas Recreation 4 Earls Colne 0
Witham Town Res. 0 **Lawford Lads** 1

FINAL

(April 19th at AFC Sudbury)
Gas Recreation 3 Lawford Lads 2

RESERVES CUP

FINAL *(April 26th at Wivenhoe Town)*
Little Oakley Res. 4 Mistley United Res. 3

ESSEX & SUFFOLK BORDER LEAGUE DIVISION TWO CONSTITUTION 2006-07

BOXTED LODGERS RESERVES...... The Playing Field, Cage Lane, Boxted, Colchester CO4 5RE........ 01206 271969
BRIGHTLINGSEA REGENT RESERVES ... North Road, Brightlingsea, Colchester CO7 0PL........ 01206 304199
BURES UNITED RESERVES............. Recreation Ground, Nayland Road, Bures CO8 5BX .... None
EARLS COLNE RESERVES .... Green Farm Meadow, Halstead Road, Earls Colne, Colchester CO6 2NG 01787 223584
FOXASH SOCIAL............. Foxash Playing Field, Harwich Road, Lawford, Manningtree CO11 2LP........ 01206 231309
GREAT BENTLEY RESERVES .... The Green, Great Bentley, Colchester CO7 8LX........ 01206 251532
GREAT BRADFORDS................ Notley Sports Centre, Notley Road, Braintree CM7 1WX 01376 323873
HATFIELD PEVEREL RESERVES .. Strutt Memorial Field, Maldon Road, Hatfield Peverel CM3 2JP .... None
HEDINGHAMS UNITED......... Lawn Meadow, Yeldham Road, Sible Hedingham, Halstead CO9 3QJ........ None
HOLLAND................ Eastcliff Sports Ground, Dulwich Road, Holland-on-Sea, Clacton CO15 5HR........ 01255 814874
KELVEDON SOCIAL RESERVES ...... The Chase, High Street, Kelvedon, Colchester CO5 9JD........ 01376 572240
LAWFORD LADS RESERVES .... School Lane, Lawford, Manningtree CO11 2JA 01206 397211
LITTLE OAKLEY RESERVES............ War Memorial Club Ground, Little Oakley........ 01255 880370
MERSEA ISLAND RESERVES .... The Glebe, Colchester Road, West Mersea CO5 8JZ 01206 385216
SUDBURY ATHLETIC.............. Lucas Social Club, Alexandra Road, Sudbury CO10 2XH........ 01787 881143
WALTON TOWN RESERVES....... Frinton Playing Fields, Jubilee Way, Frinton-on-Sea CO13 0AP .... None

IN: Brightlingsea Regent Reserves (N), Great Bradfords (N), Holland (N), Walton Town Reserves (N)

OUT: Brightlingsea Regent (P), Coggeshall Town Res. (WN), Mistley United Reserves (P), St Osyth Reserves (W), West Suffolk College (P)

FOOTBALL CONFERENCE

	Accrington Stanley	Aldershot Town	Altrincham	Burton Albion	Cambridge United	Canvey Island	Crawley Town	Dagenham & Redbridge	Exeter City	Forest Green Rovers	Gravesend & Northfleet	Grays Athletic	Halifax Town	Hereford United	Kidderminster Harriers	Morecambe	Scarborough	Southport	Stevenage Borough	Tamworth	Woking	York City
Accrington Stanley		3-2	1-0	2-1	1-0	1-0	4-2	1-0	1-2	2-0	1-1	2-3	1-1	2-1	2-0	2-0	1-0	4-0	1-1	2-1	2-1	2-1
Aldershot Town	1-4	*F*	0-2	1-1	1-3	2-2	3-2	3-1	1-0	2-1	3-2	0-3	3-1	0-1	1-0	2-0	0-1	2-0	2-2	0-2	1-1	2-1
Altrincham	0-1	5-1	*O*	1-2	2-1	0-1	1-1	0-5	1-1	2-1	2-2	0-2	1-2	0-1	3-0	2-0	1-1	1-0	1-1	2-0	0-4	0-3
Burton Albion	0-2	1-2	1-0	*O*	2-0	1-2	3-1	2-2	2-0	1-0	0-0	1-1	1-2	0-1	1-0	0-4	2-1	0-0	3-1	1-1	1-1	0-0
Cambridge United	3-1	0-2	4-0	2-2	*T*	3-1	2-1	1-2	2-1	2-2	1-1	1-1	1-1	2-1	0-2	2-2	2-1	2-1	1-0	2-1	0-2	2-0
Canvey Island	0-2	2-1	1-1	0-2	1-1	*B*	1-0	1-2	1-1	1-1	1-2	2-1	0-1	1-1	2-1	3-3	1-0	2-1	1-1	1-2	0-2	1-1
Crawley Town	0-1	2-0	2-0	1-1	1-0	3-1	*A*	0-0	0-2	1-0	1-2	1-3	2-2	0-2	2-0	1-3	2-0	2-0	1-2	3-0	2-2	0-1
Dagenham & Redbridge	1-2	2-0	2-4	3-1	1-0	2-2	0-3	*L*	2-2	1-1	1-2	1-2	1-0	0-1	3-0	3-1	0-2	3-1	2-2	2-1	1-3	0-2
Exeter City	1-3	4-0	3-1	1-2	4-0	0-2	4-0	3-1	*L*	0-0	1-0	1-2	4-2	1-2	1-0	2-0	1-1	5-0	0-2	3-0	1-1	1-3
Forest Green Rovers	1-1	4-2	5-0	1-0	1-0	1-2	2-2	0-3	0-0		0-0	1-2	2-2	2-2	0-0	1-0	5-1	1-2	2-0	1-3	0-3	1-2
Gravesend & Northfleet	1-3	0-3	2-0	0-1	0-0	2-0	1-1	1-3	0-2	2-0		1-3	4-0	1-2	1-2	1-0	0-0	2-1	0-2	2-0	2-0	2-2
Grays Athletic	1-2	2-1	1-1	2-3	5-3	1-2	1-0	0-4	3-0	2-2	6-1	*C*	1-1	2-2	2-2	1-2	5-0	1-1	2-2	5-0	2-2	1-1
Halifax Town	2-2	1-1	2-0	1-0	1-0	0-2	2-2	3-0	2-0	1-0	2-0	2-1	*O*	2-1	0-0	0-0	1-0	2-1	1-1	4-0	1-0	1-0
Hereford United	2-2	2-1	0-0	2-0	3-0	1-1	2-1	1-1	0-2	1-1	1-1	0-2	1-0	*N*	0-1	1-0	4-0	1-1	2-0	1-0	4-0	1-0
Kidderminster Harriers	2-0	1-4	1-1	0-1	1-0	3-2	1-0	3-1	1-2	1-3	0-2	0-5	0-1	1-1	*F*	1-0	2-1	1-1	0-0	0-1	2-1	0-0
Morecambe	3-2	5-2	2-0	3-1	0-1	1-0	3-0	2-0	2-2	3-2	3-0	3-0	1-0	2-2	2-0	*E*	0-3	0-0	4-1	0-0	3-1	2-0
Scarborough	2-2	2-2	1-2	3-0	1-2	1-2	1-2	0-1	0-1	1-0	3-1	2-7	2-0	0-1	1-1	0-1	*R*	0-1	1-1	0-0	1-1	2-2
Southport	2-0	0-1	1-1	3-2	2-2	2-0	0-2	1-2	0-3	3-1	1-0	1-4	0-2	1-2	1-4	0-3	0-2	*E*	3-2	1-1	1-0	1-4
Stevenage Borough	3-1	2-1	3-0	2-3	3-1	3-0	2-1	2-1	2-0	2-1	2-0	0-1	1-0	0-0	3-1	1-0	2-0	0-1	*N*	3-1	1-1	1-1
Tamworth	1-2	2-1	1-1	1-1	1-1	1-0	0-0	2-2	1-1	0-0	1-0	2-2	1-2	0-1	1-1	0-3	0-1	0-0	2-0	*C*	0-1	0-3
Woking	0-1	1-2	3-1	2-2	0-1	1-1	0-0	0-0	1-0	2-1	1-3	1-1	2-2	1-1	0-1	0-1	4-0	1-0	3-2	5-0	*E*	2-0
York City	2-4	3-2	5-0	0-1	1-0	2-1	0-0	1-1	4-2	5-1	1-0	1-2	0-2	1-3	2-2	1-1	3-1	0-0	0-1	2-1	2-1	

			HOME					AWAY					TOTAL					
		P	W	D	L	F	A	W	D	L	F	A	W	D	L	F	A	Pts
Accrington Stanley		42	16	3	2	38	17	12	4	5	38	28	28	7	7	76	45	91
Hereford United		42	11	7	3	30	14	11	7	3	29	19	22	14	6	59	33	80
Grays Athletic		42	7	9	5	46	32	14	4	3	48	23	21	13	8	94	55	76
Halifax Town		42	14	6	1	31	11	7	6	8	24	29	21	12	9	55	40	75
Morecambe		42	15	4	2	44	17	7	4	10	24	24	22	8	12	68	41	74
Stevenage Borough		42	15	3	3	38	15	4	9	8	24	32	19	12	11	62	47	69
Exeter City		42	11	3	7	41	22	7	6	8	24	26	18	9	15	65	48	63
York City		42	10	5	6	36	26	7	7	7	27	22	17	12	13	63	48	63
Burton Albion		42	8	7	6	23	21	8	5	8	27	31	16	12	14	50	52	60
Dagenham & Redbridge		42	8	4	9	31	32	8	6	7	32	27	16	10	16	63	59	58
Woking		42	8	7	6	30	20	6	7	8	28	27	14	14	14	58	47	56
Cambridge United		42	11	6	4	35	25	4	4	13	16	32	15	10	17	51	57	55
Aldershot Town		42	10	4	7	30	30	6	2	13	31	44	16	6	20	61	74	54
Canvey Island		42	6	8	7	23	27	7	4	10	24	31	13	12	17	47	58	51
Kidderminster Harriers		42	8	5	8	21	27	5	6	10	18	28	13	11	18	39	55	50
Gravesend & Northfleet		42	8	4	9	25	25	5	6	10	20	32	13	10	19	45	57	49
Crawley Town		42	9	4	8	27	22	3	7	11	21	33	12	11	19	48	55	47
Southport		42	7	3	11	24	38	3	7	11	12	30	10	10	22	36	68	40
Forest Green Rovers		42	7	7	7	31	27	1	7	13	18	35	8	14	20	49	62	38
Tamworth		42	4	10	7	17	23	4	4	13	15	40	8	14	20	32	63	38
Scarborough		42	4	7	10	24	30	5	3	13	16	36	9	10	23	40	66	37
Altrincham	*-18*	42	7	5	9	25	30	3	6	12	15	41	10	11	21	40	71	23

PLAY-OFFS

SEMI-FINALS *(1st leg)*

(May 6th) Halifax Town 3 Grays Athletic 2 ***Att*** 3,848
(May 7th) Morecambe 1 Hereford United 1 ***Att*** 5,208

SEMI-FINALS *(2nd leg)*

(May 10th) Grays Athletic 2 **Halifax Town** 2 ***Att*** 2,886
(May 11th) **Hereford Utd** 3 Morecambe 2 *aet* ***Att*** 6,278

FINAL

(May 20th at Leicester City)

Halifax Town 2 **Hereford United** 3 *aet* ***Att*** 15,499

DATES & GATES

	Accrington Stanley	Aldershot Town	Altrincham	Burton Albion	Cambridge United	Canvey Island	Crawley Town	Dagenham & Redbridge	Exeter City	Forest Green Rovers	Gravesend & Northfleet	Grays Athletic	Hereford United	Hereford United	Kidderminster Harriers	Morecambe	Scarborough	Southport	Stevenage Borough	Tamworth	Woking	York City
Accrington Stanley		20 Sep *1,114*	3 Dec *1,436*	25 Feb *1,946*	21 Jan *1,837*	13 Aug *1,012*	17 Sep *1,365*	11 Feb *2,156*	27 Aug *1,312*	18 Nov *1,506*	1 Oct *1,206*	1 Apr *2,642*	2 Jan *3,014*	7 Oct *1,603*	10 Dec *1,366*	20 Feb *3,041*	17 Apr *3,320*	26 Nov *1,630*	18 Mar *2,119*	22 Apr *3,014*	3 Sep *959*	29 Oct *2,193*
Aldershot Town	7 Mar *1,645*		27 Aug *2,235*	18 Feb *2,248*	8 Apr *2,198*	24 Jan *1,800*	5 Sep *2,371*	11 Mar *2,010*	2 Jan *3,136*	26 Nov *2,290*	12 Nov *2,415*	17 Apr *1,879*	21 Jan *2,417*	27 Sep *2,656*	15 Oct *2,315*	25 Feb *1,868*	25 Mar *2,245*	10 Dec *2,066*	17 Sep *2,563*	13 Aug *2,641*	22 Apr *2,704*	24 Sep *2,470*
Altrincham	16 Aug *1,264*	28 Jan *1,115*		25 Mar *1,214*	11 Feb *1,151*	11 Mar *903*	1 Oct *819*	10 Sep *876*	12 Nov *1,366*	20 Aug *804*	8 Apr *688*	22 Apr *917*	21 Feb *1,139*	15 Apr *1,251*	2 Jan *1,165*	29 Aug *1,447*	20 Sep *862*	15 Oct *1,225*	7 Jan *914*	26 Nov *824*	10 Dec *825*	4 Apr *1,237*
Burton Albion	10 Sep *1,374*	2 Oct *1,493*	30 Oct *1,375*		21 Feb *1,577*	27 Aug *1,423*	19 Nov *1,353*	25 Apr *1,235*	10 Feb *1,924*	22 Apr *2,331*	10 Dec *1,733*	13 Aug *1,654*	24 Jan *1,540*	18 Mar *2,512*	26 Nov *1,847*	20 Sep *1,352*	3 Sep *1,336*	18 Apr *1,488*	8 Oct *1,319*	2 Jan *2,680*	21 Jan *2,061*	1 Apr *2,605*
Cambridge United	20 Aug *2,730*	19 Nov *2,905*	24 Sep *2,199*	27 Sep *2,298*		31 Dec *2,594*	29 Oct *2,413*	29 Apr *3,161*	4 Apr *2,358*	7 Jan *2,344*	28 Jan *2,459*	7 Mar *1,821*	18 Mar *2,288*	16 Aug *2,924*	29 Aug *3,161*	1 Apr *2,129*	3 Dec *2,809*	18 Feb *2,310*	26 Dec *3,697*	7 Oct *2,606*	17 Sep *2,345*	14 Apr *3,188*
Canvey Island	7 Jan *962*	16 Aug *1,210*	8 Oct *835*	28 Jan *741*	26 Nov *842*		25 Feb *698*	29 Aug *1,458*	22 Apr *641*	1 Apr *426*	20 Aug *1,070*	2 Jan *1,445*	10 Dec *664*	18 Feb *784*	14 Apr *621*	29 Oct *480*	17 Sep *744*	24 Sep *727*	27 Sep *832*	19 Nov *646*	4 Apr *358*	18 Mar *754*
Crawley Town	4 Mar *1,361*	15 Apr *1,764*	18 Feb *1,085*	8 Apr *1,341*	25 Mar *1,472*	10 Sep *1,335*		16 Aug *1,734*	15 Oct *2,454*	18 Mar *1,067*	26 Nov *1,426*	24 Sep *1,471*	22 Apr *1,285*	20 Aug *1,842*	27 Sep *1,012*	28 Jan *1,253*	11 Mar *1,181*	12 Nov *2,055*	29 Aug *2,019*	10 Dec *1,448*	2 Jan *2,073*	7 Jan *1,514*
Dagenham & Redbridge	24 Sep *1,331*	9 Oct *1,512*	11 Apr *1,058*	17 Sep *1,149*	10 Dec *1,271*	17 Apr *1,139*	28 Mar *932*		3 Sep *1,372*	29 Oct *1,325*	2 Jan *1,405*	27 Sep *2,017*	1 Apr *1,078*	19 Nov *1,294*	22 Apr *1,038*	18 Mar *960*	27 Aug *1,074*	13 Aug *1,265*	18 Feb *1,427*	21 Jan *1,352*	26 Nov *1,138*	7 Mar *973*
Exeter City	30 Jan *4,624*	26 Dec *4,989*	1 Apr *3,134*	24 Sep *4,025*	10 Sep *3,407*	3 Dec *3,465*	25 Apr *1,782*	15 Apr *3,186*		29 Aug *4,696*	7 Jan *3,396*	19 Nov *6,682*	8 Oct *3,154*	30 Dec *4,433*	16 Aug *4,194*	20 Aug *3,978*	29 Apr *3,382*	4 Mar *3,485*	14 Mar *3,026*	29 Oct *3,369*	27 Sep *3,082*	18 Feb *3,381*
Forest Green Rovers	7 Apr *1,187*	31 Dec *1,051*	21 Jan *995*	13 Dec *548*	13 Aug *1,112*	12 Nov *678*	20 Sep *916*	25 Mar *625*	17 Apr *1,334*		21 Feb *582*	2 Sep *1,152*	27 Aug *905*	26 Dec *1,957*	4 Mar *1,033*	1 Oct *802*	11 Feb *732*	11 Mar *846*	29 Apr *1,510*	24 Jan *788*	15 Oct *875*	10 Sep *889*
Gravesend & Northfleet	17 Feb *1,616*	1 Apr *1,131*	19 Nov *1,091*	29 Apr *912*	27 Aug *1,379*	20 Jan *1,560*	28 Feb *698*	26 Dec *1,391*	13 Aug *1,578*	27 Sep *706*		4 Apr *1,245*	17 Sep *918*	7 Mar *618*	24 Sep *1,054*	3 Dec *1,172*	25 Feb *930*	3 Sep *813*	29 Oct *1,372*	18 Mar *841*	17 Apr *776*	8 Oct *1,133*
Grays Athletic	12 Nov *1,985*	29 Aug *1,869*	6 Dec *1,028*	31 Jan *858*	20 Sep *1,543*	27 Dec *2,910*	11 Feb *1,038*	21 Feb *1,065*	10 Apr *1,369*	15 Apr *1,205*	16 Aug *1,562*		1 Oct *1,807*	28 Jan *1,528*	10 Sep *1,316*	29 Apr *1,950*	15 Oct *1,515*	25 Apr *918*	31 Dec *1,214*	4 Mar *1,117*	11 Mar *1,256*	20 Aug *1,272*
Halifax Town	26 Dec *2,688*	20 Aug *1,571*	27 Sep *1,453*	16 Aug *1,681*	15 Oct *1,621*	29 Apr *2,049*	3 Dec *1,616*	12 Nov *1,532*	11 Mar *2,104*	28 Jan *1,284*	25 Apr *1,680*	18 Feb *1,666*		24 Sep *1,559*	4 Feb *1,544*	9 Jan *1,962*	30 Dec *1,682*	8 Apr *1,791*	14 Apr *2,253*	10 Sep *1,453*	28 Mar *1,465*	29 Aug *2,078*
Hereford United	11 Mar *4,497*	21 Feb *2,205*	3 Sep *2,318*	15 Oct *2,493*	31 Jan *2,142*	1 Oct *2,500*	21 Jan *2,782*	8 Apr *2,561*	26 Nov *3,754*	2 Jan *3,507*	20 Sep *2,396*	27 Aug *2,997*	11 Feb *2,555*		25 Mar *4,223*	17 Sep *2,422*	13 Aug *3,105*	22 Apr *2,547*	27 Feb *2,394*	17 Apr *2,809*	12 Nov *2,498*	10 Dec *1,950*
Kidderminster Harriers	29 Apr *1,934*	18 Mar *1,630*	26 Dec *2,206*	30 Dec *1,749*	17 Apr *1,665*	2 Sep *1,842*	21 Feb *1,302*	3 Dec *1,559*	5 Nov *1,869*	17 Sep *1,818*	11 Feb *1,575*	28 Mar *1,220*	20 Sep *1,566*	29 Oct *3,241*		8 Oct *1,461*	21 Jan *1,740*	27 Aug *1,753*	1 Apr *1,490*	1 Oct *1,961*	13 Aug *1,926*	19 Nov *1,768*
Morecambe	27 Sep *2,162*	10 Sep *1,429*	17 Apr *2,118*	4 Feb *1,855*	12 Nov *1,648*	25 Mar *1,471*	27 Aug *1,473*	15 Oct *1,718*	21 Jan *2,073*	18 Feb *1,486*	22 Apr *1,991*	10 Dec *1,785*	13 Aug *2,150*	4 Apr *1,699*	11 Mar *1,662*		24 Jan *1,478*	2 Jan *2,788*	24 Sep *1,738*	3 Sep *1,413*	8 Apr *1,468*	26 Nov *1,778*
Scarborough	29 Aug *1,541*	29 Oct *1,682*	4 Feb *1,405*	15 Apr *1,808*	22 Apr *1,831*	21 Mar *1,153*	8 Oct *1,257*	28 Jan *1,505*	10 Dec *1,428*	24 Sep *1,341*	10 Sep *1,207*	19 Apr *1,560*	26 Nov *1,843*	7 Jan *1,582*	20 Aug *1,401*	16 Aug *1,759*		27 Sep *1,280*	19 Nov *1,152*	11 Apr *1,648*	18 Feb *1,278*	2 Jan *4,057*
Southport	21 Mar *1,414*	29 Apr *1,709*	18 Mar *1,278*	29 Aug *1,253*	1 Oct *1,204*	11 Feb *901*	1 Apr *1,308*	7 Jan *1,002*	17 Sep *1,423*	7 Oct *1,087*	15 Apr *1,301*	29 Oct *1,148*	19 Nov *1,402*	14 Mar *1,057*	28 Jan *1,076*	26 Dec *1,807*	14 Jan *1,035*		20 Aug *1,007*	20 Sep *1,012*	10 Apr *1,054*	16 Aug *1,646*
Stevenage Borough	15 Oct *2,141*	4 Feb *2,010*	13 Aug *2,008*	11 Mar *2,081*	2 Jan *3,463*	21 Feb *1,403*	17 Apr *2,410*	5 Oct *2,447*	20 Sep *2,445*	10 Dec *1,771*	25 Mar *1,873*	26 Nov *2,753*	3 Sep *1,682*	10 Sep *2,404*	12 Nov *2,207*	11 Feb *2,068*	8 Apr *1,861*	21 Jan *2,231*		27 Aug *1,635*	24 Jan *2,152*	22 Apr *2,701*
Tamworth	10 Jan *1,094*	4 Apr *914*	31 Dec *1,064*	26 Dec *2,151*	11 Mar *1,325*	8 Apr *1,156*	29 Apr *1,545*	20 Aug *1,040*	28 Mar *823*	16 Aug *1,258*	15 Oct *1,003*	17 Sep *1,078*	25 Feb *1,672*	29 Aug *1,744*	18 Feb *1,278*	15 Apr *1,176*	12 Nov *1,165*	25 Mar *1,442*	28 Jan *1,228*		24 Sep *1,021*	27 Sep *1,005*
Woking	15 Apr *2,665*	21 Mar *3,244*	29 Apr *1,650*	20 Aug *1,692*	4 Mar *2,066*	20 Sep *1,543*	26 Dec *2,643*	31 Dec *1,806*	21 Feb *1,536*	25 Apr *890*	29 Aug *1,770*	8 Oct *1,995*	29 Oct *2,054*	1 Apr *1,929*	7 Jan *1,514*	19 Nov *2,069*	1 Oct *1,840*	10 Sep *1,477*	16 Aug *2,592*	11 Feb *2,030*		28 Jan *1,938*
York City	25 Mar *3,912*	12 Feb *2,401*	17 Sep *2,643*	12 Nov *2,411*	2 Sep *2,666*	15 Oct *3,070*	13 Aug *2,276*	20 Sep *2,927*	1 Oct *3,503*	25 Feb *2,314*	11 Mar *2,902*	21 Jan *2,461*	17 Apr *4,084*	29 Apr *2,755*	9 Apr *3,376*	31 Dec *2,172*	26 Dec *4,921*	24 Jan *2,176*	10 Jan *2,325*	21 Feb *2,153*	26 Aug *2,302*	

FOOTBALL CONFERENCE

CONSTITUTION FOR 2006-07

ALDERSHOT TOWN
Recreation Ground, High Street, Aldershot, Hampshire GU11 1TW
Tel: 01252 337065 Fax: 01252 324347
Manager: Terry Brown www.theshots.co.uk Colours: Red

ALTRINCHAM
Moss Lane, Altrincham, Cheshire WA15 8AP
Tel: 0161 928 1045 Fax: 0161 926 9934
Manager: Graham Heathcote www.altrinchamfc.com Colours: Red, white & black

BURTON ALBION
Pirelli Stadium, Princess Way, Burton-on-Trent, Staffordshire DE13 0AR
Tel: 0870 190 0060 Fax: 01283 523199
Manager: Nigel Clough www.burtonalbionfc.co.uk Colours: Yellow & black

CAMBRIDGE UNITED
Abbey Stadium, Newmarket Road, Cambridge, Cambridgeshire CB5 8LN
Tel: 01223 566500 Fax: 01223 566502
Manager: Rob Newman www.cambridge-united.co.uk Colours: Amber & black

CRAWLEY TOWN
Broadfield Stadium, Brighton Road, Crawley, West Sussex RH11 9RX
Tel: 01293 410000 Club: 01293 410001 Fax: 01293 410002
Manager: John Hollins www.ctfc.net Colours: Red

DAGENHAM & REDBRIDGE
Glyn Hopkin Stadium, Victoria Road, Dagenham, Essex RM10 7XL
Tel: 020 8592 7194 Club: 020 8592 1549 Fax: 020 8593 7227
Manager: John Still www.daggers.co.uk Colours: Red & white

EXETER CITY
St James Park, Stadium Way, Exeter, Devon EX4 6PX
Tel: 01392 411243 Fax: 01392 413959
Manager: Paul Tisdale www.exetercityfc.co.uk Colours: Red, white & black

FOREST GREEN ROVERS
The Lawn, Nympsfield Road, Forest Green, Nailsworth, Gloucestershire GL6 0ET
Tel: 01453 834860 Fax: 01453 835291
Manager: Gary Owers www.fgrfc.co.uk Colours: Black & white

GRAVESEND & NORTHFLEET
Stonebridge Road, Northfleet, Gravesend, Kent DA11 9GN
Tel: 01474 533796 Fax: 01474 327754
Manager: Liam Daish www.gnfc.co.uk Colours: Red & white

GRAYS ATHLETIC
Recreation Ground, Bridge Road, Grays, Essex RM17 6BZ
Tel: 01375 377753 Club: 01375 391649 Fax: 01375 377753
Manager: Frank Gray www.graysathletic.co.uk Colours: Sky blue

HALIFAX TOWN
The Shay Stadium, Shaw Hill, Halifax, West Yorkshire HX1 2YS
Tel: 01422 341222 Ticket Office: 01422 353423 Fax: 01422 349487
Manager: Chris Wilder www.halifaxafc.co.uk Colours: Blue & white

KIDDERMINSTER HARRIERS
Aggborough Stadium, Hoo Road, Kidderminster, Worcestershire DY10 1NB
Tel: 01562 823931 Fax: 01562 827329
Manager: Mark Yates www.harriers.co.uk Colours: Red & white

MORECAMBE
Christie Park, Lancaster Road, Morecambe, Lancashire LA4 5TJ
Tel: 01524 411797 Fax: 01524 832230
Manager: Sammy McIlroy www.morecambefc.com Colours: Red, white & black

NORTHWICH VICTORIA
Victoria Stadium, Wincham Avenue, Wincham, Northwich, Cheshire CW9 6GB
Tel: 01606 41450 Fax: 01606 330577
Manager: Steve Burr www.nvfc.co.uk Colours: Green & white

OXFORD UNITED
The Kassam Stadium, Grenoble Road, Oxford, Oxfordshire OX4 4XP
Tel: 01865 337500 Fax: 01865 337555
Manager: Jim Smith www.oufc.co.uk Colours: Yellow & navy blue

RUSHDEN & DIAMONDS
Nene Park, Diamond Way, Irthlingborough, Northants NN9 5QF
Tel: 01933 652000 Fax: 01933 650418
Manager: Paul Hart www.thediamondsfc.com Colours: Red

SOUTHPORT
Haig Avenue, Southport, Merseyside PR8 6JZ
Tel: 01704 533422 Club: 01704 530182 Fax: 01704 533455
Manager: Paul Cook www.southportfc.net Colours: Yellow & black

ST ALBANS CITY
Clarence Park, York Road, St Albans, Hertfordshire AL1 4PL
Tel: 01727 864296 Club: 01727 866819 Fax: 01727 866235
Manager: Colin Lippiatt www.sacfc.co.uk Colours: Yellow & blue

STAFFORD RANGERS
Marston Road, Stafford, Staffordshire ST16 3BX
Tel: 01785 602430 Fax: 01785 602431
Manager: Phil Robinson www.srfc.co.uk Colours: Black & white

STEVENAGE BOROUGH
Broadhall Way Stadium, Broadhall Way, Stevenage, Herts SG2 8RH
Tel: 01438 223223 Fax: 01438 743666
Manager: Mark Stimson www.stevenageborofc.com Colours: White & red

TAMWORTH
The Lamb Ground, Kettlebrook, Tamworth, Staffordshire B77 1AA
Tel: 01827 65798 Fax: 01827 62236
Manager: Mark Cooper www.thelambs.co.uk Colours: Red

WEYMOUTH
Wessex Stadium, Radipole Lane, Weymouth, Dorset DT4 9XJ
Tel: 01305 785558 Fax: 01305 766658
Manager: Garry Hill www.theterras.co.uk Colours: Claret, blue & white

WOKING
Kingfield, Kingfield Road, Woking, Surrey GU22 9AA
Tel: 01483 772470 Fax: 01483 888423
Manager: Glenn Cockerill www.wokingfc.co.uk Colours: Red, white & black

YORK CITY
Kit Kat Crescent, Grosvenor Road, York, North Yorkshire YO30 7AQ
Tel: 01904 624447 Fax: 01904 631457
Manager: Billy McEwan www.ycfc.net Colours: Red & white

IN: Northwich Victoria (P – Football Conference North), Oxford United (R – Football League Division Two), Rushden & Diamonds (R – Football League Division Two), St Albans City (P – Football Conference South), Stafford Rangers (P – Football Conference North), Weymouth (P – Football Conference South)
OUT: Accrington Stanley (P – Football League Division Two), Canvey Island (W – Isthmian League Divisiom One North), Hereford United (P – Football League Division Two), Scarborough (R – Football Conference North)

	Alfreton Town	Barrow	Droylsden	Gainsborough Trinity	Harrogate Town	Hednesford Town	Hinckley United	Hucknall Town	Hyde United	Kettering Town	Lancaster City	Leigh RMI	Moor Green	Northwich Victoria	Nuneaton Borough	Redditch United	Stafford Rangers	Stalybridge Celtic	Vauxhall Motors	Worcester City	Workington	Worksop Town
Alfreton Town		2-1	1-3	1-2	4-1	3-2	1-1	1-1	2-0	1-1	0-2	1-1	1-1	2-4	1-0	2-1	2-1	0-0	1-2	1-0	1-3	2-1
Barrow	2-2		2-0	3-1	3-1	3-1	2-5	2-0	2-2	0-1	1-4	3-1	2-2	1-1	0-3	1-1	1-1	4-2	0-2	0-2	6-1	1-0
Droylsden	1-0	2-2		1-2	2-1	1-1	3-1	2-3	1-0	3-1	6-1	4-1	3-0	4-3	2-2	2-1	2-1	1-0	4-0	3-0	2-3	3-1
Gainsborough Trinity	2-2	3-2	2-2	*C*	0-2	1-1	1-2	3-2	0-3	0-2	1-0	2-1	2-2	1-2	1-2	2-2	1-1	1-0	1-1	0-1	0-0	2-0
Harrogate Town	1-0	2-1	1-1	2-0	*O*	2-3	2-1	1-0	1-0	1-1	3-1	3-0	3-0	0-2	2-0	1-1	0-2	1-0	2-1	4-1	1-1	2-0
Hednesford Town	1-0	0-3	0-1	1-1	0-4	*N*	3-4	1-1	0-2	2-2	1-0	1-3	1-2	1-4	0-0	1-1	0-2	1-1	0-1	0-4	0-0	2-1
Hinckley United	2-2	1-0	1-1	1-0	1-3	1-2	*F*	3-1	2-1	1-1	3-3	5-1	1-2	1-3	0-1	1-1	0-1	1-1	2-1	1-3	0-0	3-0
Hucknall Town	1-0	2-1	2-0	4-1	4-1	2-2	0-2	*E*	1-3	1-1	0-0	2-2	2-2	3-2	0-1	4-1	0-2	2-1	1-2	1-2	1-0	0-0
Hyde United	2-3	2-2	2-2	2-0	3-1	4-2	0-1	0-0	*R*	3-0	2-4	3-3	3-2	1-3	1-0	1-3	1-3	1-3	2-3	4-0	1-1	1-1
Kettering Town	1-0	1-3	1-0	1-2	0-2	4-0	2-2	0-0	3-2	*E*	2-0	4-0	0-3	2-0	3-0	4-0	0-1	4-1	1-0	2-1	2-1	1-0
Lancaster City	2-2	3-0	2-2	2-3	2-1	1-0	2-2	0-1	1-3	0-1	*N*	2-0	3-3	1-2	1-1	1-0	1-1	2-2	1-0	0-0	0-1	2-1
Leigh RMI	0-0	1-1	0-1	0-0	3-1	0-0	1-0	2-1	1-1	0-2	1-2	*C*	1-3	2-1	1-0	2-1	1-3	2-1	1-1	1-4	0-1	0-1
Moor Green	0-0	1-1	1-1	1-1	2-2	1-2	1-1	2-4	1-2	1-1	3-1	4-1	*E*	1-2	0-4	2-1	0-1	1-1	2-1	1-1	1-4	1-0
Northwich Victoria	1-1	2-0	2-1	2-0	3-0	8-0	2-0	2-0	1-2	3-1	3-2	1-0	1-1		2-2	5-1	3-1	1-0	3-1	0-1	4-1	4-1
Nuneaton Borough	1-0	2-1	2-2	3-1	4-0	3-2	2-0	2-2	1-0	2-2	3-0	3-1	2-2	1-2	*N*	2-1	1-1	0-0	3-2	0-0	3-1	3-1
Redditch United	1-0	2-1	4-1	1-1	1-3	1-2	1-1	1-1	1-1	2-1	0-1	1-2	0-1	1-2	3-0	*O*	0-1	1-4	3-0	2-2	3-6	0-3
Stafford Rangers	1-0	3-1	0-0	3-0	0-1	1-1	2-3	2-0	1-0	1-3	3-0	0-0	1-3	2-0	2-0	3-0	*R*	1-0	3-0	1-1	2-2	4-2
Stalybridge Celtic	3-0	2-1	1-1	1-0	3-1	3-0	1-1	2-1	1-2	2-0	2-1	6-1	4-1	3-3	2-0	5-1	2-3	*T*	2-1	2-3	2-1	2-1
Vauxhall Motors	3-1	0-1	2-4	1-2	0-2	0-0	0-1	0-2	0-2	1-1	1-0	4-4	1-2	0-3	1-2	1-2	1-3	4-2	*H*	1-0	2-1	5-2
Worcester City	2-2	1-0	1-2	2-1	2-0	6-2	0-0	0-1	2-2	2-0	2-0	2-0	0-2	0-1	0-1	2-2	1-1	0-1	0-0		1-1	1-1
Workington	2-0	0-0	2-1	2-0	2-4	2-0	1-1	1-1	1-0	3-2	1-1	0-0	1-4	5-2	0-2	1-2	0-1	1-2	1-2	2-2		1-2
Worksop Town	1-1	2-1	3-2	1-1	1-0	3-3	0-0	2-1	1-1	2-1	2-0	3-3	0-2	1-2	0-4	1-1	0-1	2-1	1-1	0-3	1-2	

Conference North			HOME					AWAY					TOTAL					
		P	**W**	**D**	**L**	**F**	**A**	**W**	**D**	**L**	**F**	**A**	**W**	**D**	**L**	**F**	**A**	**Pts**
Northwich Victoria		42	16	3	2	53	16	13	2	6	44	33	29	5	8	97	49	92
Stafford Rangers		42	12	5	4	36	17	13	5	3	32	17	25	10	7	68	34	85
Nuneaton Borough		42	13	7	1	43	21	9	4	8	25	22	22	11	9	68	43	77
Droylsden		42	15	3	3	52	24	5	9	7	28	32	20	12	10	80	56	72
Harrogate Town		42	14	4	3	35	16	8	1	12	31	40	22	5	15	66	56	71
Kettering Town		42	14	2	5	38	18	5	8	8	25	31	19	10	13	63	49	67
Stalybridge Celtic		42	15	3	3	51	23	4	6	11	23	31	19	9	14	74	54	66
Worcester City		42	7	8	6	27	20	9	6	6	31	26	16	14	12	58	46	62
Moor Green		42	5	9	7	27	32	10	7	4	40	32	15	16	11	67	64	61
Hinckley United		42	7	7	7	31	28	7	9	5	29	27	14	16	12	60	55	58
Hyde United		42	7	6	8	39	37	8	5	8	29	24	15	11	16	68	61	56
Hucknall Town		42	9	6	6	33	26	5	7	9	23	29	14	13	15	56	55	55
Workington		42	7	6	8	29	29	7	7	7	31	33	14	13	15	60	62	55
Barrow		42	9	6	6	39	33	3	5	13	23	34	12	11	19	62	67	47
Lancaster City		42	7	8	6	29	26	5	3	13	23	40	12	11	19	52	66	47
Gainsborough Trinity		42	6	8	7	26	30	5	5	11	19	35	11	13	18	45	65	46
Alfreton Town		42	9	6	6	30	28	1	9	11	16	30	10	15	17	46	58	45
Vauxhall Motors		42	6	3	12	28	37	6	4	11	22	34	12	7	23	50	71	43
Worksop Town		42	7	8	6	27	31	3	3	15	19	40	10	11	21	46	71	41
Redditch United		42	6	5	10	29	34	3	7	11	24	44	9	12	21	53	78	39
Leigh RMI	*-1*	42	7	6	8	20	25	2	7	12	25	54	9	13	20	45	79	39
Hednesford Town		42	3	7	11	16	37	4	7	10	26	50	7	14	21	42	87	35

PLAY-OFFS

SEMI-FINALS

(May 1st) Nuneaton Borough 0 **Droylsden** 1 ***Att*** 2,005

(May 2nd) **Stafford Rangers** 1 Harrogate Town 0 ***Att*** 1,665

FINAL

(May 6th at Burton Albion)

Stafford Rangers 1 Droylesden 1 *aet* (5-3p) ***Att*** 2,704

DATES & GATES	Alfreton Town	Barrow	Droylsden	Gainsborough Trinity	Harrogate Town	Hednesford Town	Hinckley United	Hucknall Town	Hyde United	Kettering Town	Lancaster City	Leigh RMI	Moor Green	Northwich Victoria	Nuneaton Borough	Redditch United	Stafford Rangers	Stalybridge Celtic	Vauxhall Motors	Worcester City	Workington	Worksop Town
Alfreton Town		18 Feb *287*	4 Feb *271*	29 Apr *301*	28 Feb *217*	14 Jan *336*	4 Mar *344*	26 Dec *564*	17 Apr *281*	6 Dec *575*	3 Sep *279*	18 Oct *224*	12 Nov *267*	27 Aug *385*	8 Apr *436*	10 Sep *219*	11 Mar *480*	15 Oct *388*	13 Aug *283*	7 Feb *256*	14 Mar *257*	21 Jan *367*
Barrow	15 Nov *755*		25 Feb *892*	11 Feb *852*	21 Feb *672*	13 Aug *1,031*	1 Oct *981*	17 Apr *689*	3 Sep *920*	8 Apr *801*	2 Jan *1,301*	27 Aug *1,074*	5 Nov *714*	21 Jan *1,007*	22 Apr *752*	10 Dec *839*	19 Nov *907*	17 Sep *1,057*	11 Apr *630*	11 Mar *962*	6 Sep *1,308*	25 Mar *852*
Droylsden	1 Oct *319*	10 Sep *354*		14 Nov *320*	25 Mar *382*	31 Dec *352*	11 Feb *397*	3 Sep *336*	20 Feb *761*	11 Mar *419*	8 Apr *319*	14 Jan *285*	21 Jan *342*	26 Dec *601*	13 Aug *398*	3 Apr *279*	5 Nov *473*	29 Apr *1,302*	27 Aug *275*	17 Apr *468*	12 Dec *246*	8 Oct *272*
Gainsborough Trinity	10 Dec *337*	15 Oct *385*	18 Feb *300*		8 Nov *270*	27 Aug *362*	10 Sep *363*	25 Mar *335*	5 Nov *429*	22 Apr *457*	19 Nov *306*	3 Sep *259*	13 Aug *317*	14 Mar *255*	17 Dec *373*	4 Feb *306*	8 Apr *418*	18 Oct *412*	17 Apr *284*	21 Jan *378*	11 Mar *337*	2 Jan *647*
Harrogate Town	18 Mar *468*	18 Oct *425*	12 Nov *433*	11 Apr *376*		19 Apr *335*	29 Oct *432*	14 Jan *515*	13 Aug *371*	17 Sep *437*	22 Apr *435*	2 Jan *428*	27 Aug *301*	24 Jan *502*	21 Jan *602*	18 Feb *432*	10 Dec *505*	21 Mar *462*	15 Oct *365*	3 Sep *319*	25 Feb *433*	17 Apr *442*
Hednesford Town	15 Aug *640*	7 Jan *475*	22 Apr *434*	28 Jan *472*	19 Nov *521*		20 Aug *620*	7 Nov *434*	8 Apr *362*	14 Nov *992*	23 Jan *438*	3 Apr *492*	20 Feb *454*	10 Sep *660*	2 Jan *1,011*	15 Apr *552*	1 Oct *1,452*	29 Aug *816*	10 Dec *397*	25 Mar *510*	11 Feb *438*	11 Mar *478*
Hinckley United	17 Sep *611*	4 Feb *467*	15 Oct *578*	25 Feb *481*	11 Mar *563*	21 Jan *719*		27 Aug *671*	19 Nov *569*	2 Jan *1,322*	13 Aug *559*	17 Apr *461*	8 Oct *442*	3 Sep *703*	10 Dec *2,278*	18 Oct *442*	25 Mar *715*	18 Feb *506*	22 Apr *651*	24 Jan *470*	5 Nov *567*	8 Apr *528*
Hucknall Town	2 Jan *909*	29 Aug *551*	15 Apr *356*	12 Nov *407*	16 Aug *520*	7 Mar *281*	28 Jan *459*		17 Dec *337*	21 Feb *508*	10 Dec *404*	22 Apr *304*	1 Oct *386*	29 Oct *620*	17 Sep *625*	3 Dec *397*	7 Jan *601*	1 Apr *394*	18 Mar *271*	25 Feb *360*	20 Aug *421*	11 Feb *480*
Hyde United	29 Aug *433*	14 Apr *503*	17 Oct *633*	17 Sep *416*	7 Jan *404*	3 Dec *334*	1 Apr *402*	18 Feb *501*		28 Jan *520*	15 Oct *351*	12 Nov *436*	29 Apr *261*	18 Mar *667*	4 Feb *507*	29 Oct *422*	20 Aug *412*	26 Dec *1,087*	6 Mar *301*	31 Dec *401*	15 Aug *422*	22 Oct *313*
Kettering Town	11 Apr *918*	3 Dec *1,272*	29 Oct *2,060*	28 Feb *906*	4 Mar *1,238*	18 Feb *1,282*	26 Dec *1,444*	18 Oct *1,067*	27 Aug *905*		21 Jan *1,592*	15 Oct *1,211*	24 Jan *1,108*	4 Feb *1,154*	17 Apr *1,205*	18 Mar *911*	10 Sep *966*	12 Nov *1,478*	1 Apr *1,006*	13 Aug *962*	29 Apr *974*	3 Sep *817*
Lancaster City	15 Apr *254*	26 Dec *702*	3 Dec *271*	1 Apr *229*	6 Apr *192*	18 Mar *259*	7 Jan *264*	29 Apr *353*	11 Feb *352*	20 Aug *317*		7 Mar *246*	22 Oct *293*	12 Nov *513*	25 Feb *403*	28 Jan *249*	29 Aug *375*	16 Aug *346*	29 Oct *281*	1 Oct *282*	20 Apr *265*	17 Sep *257*
Leigh RMI	21 Feb *148*	28 Jan *301*	16 Aug *245*	15 Apr *125*	26 Dec *177*	17 Sep *301*	29 Aug *232*	30 Dec *181*	24 Mar *195*	11 Feb *225*	10 Jan *225*		11 Mar *175*	29 Apr *639*	24 Jan *201*	7 Jan *178*	22 Oct *301*	20 Aug *304*	24 Feb *185*	8 Apr *185*	1 Oct *183*	4 Nov *186*
Moor Green	24 Mar *226*	18 Mar *187*	20 Aug *139*	7 Jan *177*	28 Jan *192*	18 Oct *233*	4 Apr *205*	4 Feb *221*	10 Dec *177*	16 Aug *359*	18 Feb *216*	29 Oct *170*		1 Apr *384*	15 Oct *530*	2 Jan *171*	15 Apr *393*	25 Feb *193*	3 Dec *202*	17 Sep *311*	29 Aug *230*	22 Ap *210*
Northwich Victoria	28 Jan *1,017*	20 Aug *711*	2 Jan *1,106*	16 Aug *669*	8 Apr *1,032*	25 Feb *855*	15 Apr *1,250*	11 Mar *1,020*	7 Feb *850*	1 Oct *909*	25 Mar *1,027*	10 Dec *755*	19 Nov *737*		8 Nov *1,119*	29 Aug *784*	22 Apr *3,154*	28 Feb *834*	17 Sep *778*	11 Feb *1,062*	28 Mar *729*	21 Feb *579*
Nuneaton Borough	31 Jan *1,108*	30 Dec *902*	14 Mar *629*	18 Mar *879*	20 Aug *724*	26 Dec *1,254*	29 Apr *1,301*	4 Mar *1,012*	1 Oct *1,113*	29 Aug *1,049*	10 Sep *716*	1 Apr *1,082*	11 Feb *1,118*	11 Apr *1,296*		16 Aug *920*	28 Jan *2,183*	29 Oct *818*	12 Nov *810*	21 Feb *801*	15 Apr *1,003*	6 Dec *675*
Redditch United	25 Feb *369*	29 Apr *751*	17 Sep *301*	1 Oct *332*	17 Dec *226*	3 Sep *381*	21 Feb *200*	8 Apr *323*	11 Mar *339*	22 Nov *752*	27 Aug *562*	13 Aug *316*	26 Dec *406*	17 Apr *703*	14 Jan *644*		11 Feb *546*	5 Nov *354*	21 Jan *365*	20 Dec *451*	22 Oct *325*	19 Nov *332*
Stafford Rangers	29 Oct *913*	1 Apr *956*	18 Mar *785*	3 Dec *704*	29 Apr *808*	14 Mar *1,519*	12 Nov *964*	13 Aug *634*	21 Jan *935*	28 Mar *745*	17 Apr *949*	18 Feb *1,035*	3 Sep *729*	31 Dec *1,677*	27 Aug *1,063*	15 Oct *744*		7 Mar *561*	18 Oct *552*	26 Dec *1,372*	17 Sep *737*	14 Feb *783*
Stalybridge Celtic	11 Feb *499*	25 Apr *492*	10 Dec *863*	21 Feb *327*	1 Oct *647*	17 Apr *511*	22 Oct *478*	19 Nov *561*	2 Jan *1,243*	25 Mar *589*	13 Apr *308*	21 Jan *560*	10 Sep *385*	13 Aug *533*	11 Mar *572*	22 Apr *521*	8 Nov *519*		3 Sep *417*	4 Apr *380*	8 Apr *423*	27 Aug *506*
Vauxhall Motors	7 Jan *197*	16 Aug *305*	28 Jan *230*	29 Aug *155*	11 Feb *164*	29 Apr *316*	31 Dec *174*	5 Nov *200*	6 Dec *188*	19 Nov *383*	11 Mar *220*	10 Sep *155*	8 Apr *168*	4 Apr *529*	25 Mar *234*	20 Aug *186*	21 Feb *198*	15 Apr *262*		10 Jan *186*	26 Dec *180*	1 Oct *201*
Worcester City	1 Apr *860*	29 Oct *1,019*	29 Aug *816*	20 Aug *738*	15 Apr *923*	12 Nov *1,278*	15 Aug *1,064*	10 Sep *734*	22 Apr *803*	7 Jan *867*	4 Feb *745*	13 Feb *818*	13 Mar *969*	15 Oct *951*	17 Oct *922*	6 Mar *1,060*	2 Jan *1,228*	18 Mar *742*	18 Feb *905*		28 Jan *931*	10 Dec *806*
Workington	22 Apr *380*	7 Mar *542*	1 Apr *414*	29 Oct *434*	10 Sep *475*	15 Oct *385*	18 Mar *475*	21 Jan *580*	14 Jan *491*	10 Dec *437*	18 Oct *479*	4 Feb *502*	17 Apr *392*	18 Feb *476*	3 Sep *611*	12 Nov *487*	11 Apr *495*	3 Dec *458*	2 Jan *562*	27 Aug *503*		13 Aug *517*
Worksop Town	20 Aug *496*	12 Nov *407*	21 Mar *285*	26 Dec *615*	29 Aug *342*	29 Oct *446*	3 Dec *376*	15 Oct *501*	10 Sep *276*	15 Apr *468*	25 Apr *314*	18 Mar *296*	30 Dec *284*	18 Oct *446*	18 Feb *522*	1 Apr *370*	16 Aug *519*	28 Jan *506*	14 Mar *316*	29 Apr *390*	7 Jan *315*	

FOOTBALL CONFERENCE NORTH

CONSTITUTION FOR 2006-07

ALFRETON TOWN

Impact Arena, North Street, Alfreton, Derbyshire DE55 7FZ
Tel: 01773 830277 Club: 01773 832819 Fax: 01773 836164
Manager: Gary Mills www.alfretontownfc.com Colours: Red

BARROW

Holker Street Stadium, Wilkie Road, Barrow-in-Furness, Cumbria LA14 5UW
Tel: 01229 820346 Fax: 01229 820346
Manager: Phil Wilson www.barrowafc.com Colours: Blue & white

BLYTH SPARTANS

Croft Park, Plessey Road, Blyth, Northumberland NE24 3JE
Tel: 01670 352373 Club: 01670 354818 Fax: 01670 545592
Manager: Harry Dunn www.blythspartansafc.co.uk Colours: Green & white

DROYLSDEN

Butchers Arms, Market Street, Droylsden, Manchester M43 7AY
Tel: 0161 370 1426 Club: 0161 301 1352 Fax: 0161 370 8341
Manager: David Pace www.droylsdenfc.co.uk Colours: Red & black

FARSLEY CELTIC

Throstle Nest, Newlands, Farsley, Pudsey, Leeds, West Yorkshire LS28 5BE
Tel: 0113 255 7292 Fax: 0113 257 1058
Manager: Lee Sinnott www.farsleyceltic.co.uk Colours: Blue

GAINSBOROUGH TRINITY

The Northolme, North Street, Gainsborough, Lincolnshire DN21 2QN
Tel: 01427 613295 Fax: 01427 613295
Manager: Paul Mitchell www.gainsboroughtrinity.com Colours: Blue & white

HARROGATE TOWN

Wetherby Road, Harrogate, North Yorkshire HG2 7SA
Tel: 01423 880675 Fax: 01423 880675
Manager: Neil Aspin www.harrogatetown.com Colours: Yellow & black

HINCKLEY UNITED

The Marstons Stadium, Leicester Road, Hinckley, Leicestershire LE10 3DR
Tel: 01455 840088 Fax: 01455 840088
Manager: Dean Thomas www.hinckleyunitedfc.org Colours: Red & blue

HUCKNALL TOWN

Watnall Road, Hucknall, Nottinghamshire NG15 6EY
Tel: 0115 963 0206 Club: 0115 956 1253 Fax: 0115 963 0716
Manager: Kevin Wilson www.devoted.to/hucknalltownfc Colours: Yellow & black

HYDE UNITED

Tameside Stadium, Ewens Fields, Walker Lane, Hyde, Cheshire SK14 2SB
Tel: 0161 368 1031 Club: 0161 368 1621 Fax: 0161 367 7273
Manager: Steve Waywell www.hydeunited.co.uk Colours: Red & white

KETTERING TOWN

Rockingham Road, Kettering, Northants NN16 9AW
Tel: 01536 483028 Clubhouse: 01536 410962 Fax: 01536 412273
Manager: Morell Maison www.ketteringtownfc.co.uk Colours: Red & black

LANCASTER CITY
Giant Axe, West Road, Lancaster, Lancashire LA1 5PE
Tel: 01524 382238 Club: 01524 843500 Fax: 01524 382238
Manager: Gary Finlay www.lancastercityfc.com Colours: Sky blue

LEIGH RMI
Hilton Park, Kirkhall Lane, Leigh, Lancashire WN7 1RN
Tel: 01942 743743 Fax: 01942 719266
Manager: Andy Nelson www.leighrmi-mad.co.uk Colours: Red & white

MOOR GREEN
Solihull Borough FC, Damson Park, Damson Parkway, Solihull, West Midlands B91 2PP
Tel: 0121 705 6770 Fax: 0121 711 4045
Manager: Bob Faulkner www.moorgreenfc.co.uk Colours: Sky & navy blue

NUNEATON BOROUGH
Manor Park, Beaumont Road, Nuneaton, Warwickshire CV11 5HD
Tel: 024 7638 5738 Fax: 024 7634 2690
Manager: Roger Ashby www.nbafc.net Colours: White & blue

REDDITCH UNITED
Valley Stadium, Bromsgrove Road, Redditch, Worcestershire B97 4RN
Tel: 01527 67450 Fax: 01527 60611
Manager: Gary Whild www.thisisrufc.co.uk Colours: Red

SCARBOROUGH
McCain Stadium, Seamer Road, Scarborough, North Yorkshire YO12 4HF
Tel: 01723 375094 Fax: 01723 366211
Manager: Mark Patterson www.scarboroughfc.co.uk Colours: Red, white & black

STALYBRIDGE CELTIC
Bower Fold, Mottram Road, Stalybridge, Cheshire SK15 2RT
Tel: 0161 338 2828 Club: 0161 338 8443 Fax: 0161 338 8256
Manager: John Reed www.stalybridgeceltic.co.uk Colours: Blue & white

VAUXHALL MOTORS
Vauxhall Sports Ground, Rivacre Road, Hooton, Ellesmere Port, South Wirral CH66 1NJ
Tel: 0151 328 1114 Club: 0151 327 2294 0151 328 1114
Manager: Carl Macauley www.vmfc.com Colours: White & navy blue

WORCESTER CITY
St George's Lane, Barbourne, Worcester, Worcestershire WR1 1QT
Tel: 01905 23003 Fax: 01905 26668
Manager: Andy Preece www.worcestercityfc.co.uk Colours: Blue & white

WORKINGTON
Borough Park, Workington, Cumbria CA14 2DT
Tel: 01900 602871 Fax: 01900 67432
Manager: Tommy Cassidy www.workingtonreds.co.uk Colours: Red

WORKSOP TOWN
Babbage Way, Sandy Lane, Worksop, Nottinghamshire S80 1TN
Tel: 01909 501911 Fax: 01909 501911
Manager: Ronnie Glavin www.worksoptownfc.co.uk Colours: Yellow & black

IN: Blyth Spartans (P – Northern Premier League Premier Division), Farsley Celtic (P – Northern Premier League Premier Division), Scarborough (R)
OUT: Hednesford Town (R – Northern Premier League Premier Division), Northwich Victoria (P), Stafford Rangers (P)

	Basingstoke Town	Bishop's Stortford	Bognor Regis Town	Cambridge City	Carshalton Athletic	Dorchester Town	Eastbourne Borough	Eastleigh	Farnborough Town	Havant & Waterlooville	Hayes	Histon	Lewes	Maidenhead United	Newport County	St Albans City	Sutton United	Thurrock	Welling United	Weston-super-Mare	Weymouth	Yeading
Basingstoke Town		1-1	2-3	0-5	2-1	2-0	2-2	0-1	0-1	2-1	1-1	0-1	1-5	0-1	1-0	1-1	2-0	0-3	2-2	2-1	0-3	0-4
Bishop's Stortford	1-1		2-1	1-3	3-3	5-2	0-1	4-1	1-1	1-3	1-0	5-0	0-3	1-0	0-1	1-3	2-1	2-2	1-1	2-3	0-2	2-1
Bognor Regis Town	2-1	2-2		4-2	1-1	1-1	2-1	2-0	0-1	0-1	1-1	3-1	2-2	8-1	1-1	2-1	0-0	0-1	0-0	0-1	0-2	0-2
Cambridge City	1-0	1-1	2-0	*C*	0-0	1-2	2-3	2-1	0-2	0-0	3-1	3-1	0-2	3-0	0-2	4-3	3-0	6-0	0-0	3-0	1-3	0-2
Carshalton Athletic	1-2	0-0	1-1	0-2	*O*	3-1	2-2	1-3	2-2	1-3	1-2	0-0	2-2	0-1	1-0	0-2	0-0	0-0	1-0	1-1	2-1	2-2
Dorchester Town	2-1	1-3	3-5	1-0	2-0	*N*	3-0	1-3	1-1	1-1	2-2	0-3	2-2	1-3	2-2	1-4	0-5	2-0	0-3	1-2	2-0	4-0
Eastbourne Borough	2-3	1-1	0-0	1-1	1-1	1-1	*F*	0-1	0-1	2-2	0-0	1-1	3-1	3-3	2-0	1-1	2-1	0-0	1-1	1-3	0-2	2-1
Eastleigh	0-3	0-1	1-0	1-1	3-1	1-2	2-1	*E*	2-0	2-6	2-1	1-2	2-0	2-1	2-0	0-2	2-0	3-0	1-3	4-1	2-0	0-3
Farnborough Town	1-0	3-0	2-1	0-3	4-0	0-1	2-3	1-0	*R*	4-1	0-0	0-2	2-2	3-1	2-1	0-0	2-1	0-0	1-0	5-0	0-1	1-0
Havant & Waterlooville	2-0	2-2	1-0	1-1	1-1	1-0	1-0	2-1	1-0	*E*	1-1	3-1	1-0	2-1	1-2	0-1	0-1	1-2	0-0	3-2	2-1	3-0
Hayes	1-2	2-0	1-2	2-0	1-2	0-1	0-2	1-0	0-1	1-2	*N*	2-1	2-2	2-1	3-2	0-1	2-1	0-1	1-3	4-1	1-2	0-1
Histon	2-0	3-2	2-2	1-0	0-1	4-1	3-1	1-0	3-6	3-1	2-3	*C*	1-1	3-0	2-3	0-5	3-0	3-1	1-1	1-1	2-1	1-0
Lewes	3-0	2-1	1-1	2-2	2-1	3-2	1-0	1-2	6-2	0-2	2-1	0-3	*E*	2-2	1-0	0-2	2-0	0-0	2-1	5-2	2-3	1-0
Maidenhead United	0-0	2-2	1-2	0-5	0-2	2-3	2-6	2-2	1-2	3-1	2-1	1-4	0-1		1-1	0-4	2-0	1-3	2-4	2-4	0-0	1-2
Newport County	2-0	1-0	1-0	0-2	4-1	0-2	1-1	0-2	1-2	2-3	1-0	0-1	2-3	3-0	*S*	1-3	1-0	3-4	2-2	2-2	0-3	1-3
St Albans City	3-1	3-0	2-0	2-4	3-0	2-0	5-0	2-4	2-2	2-0	1-0	1-0	2-0	4-0	1-0	*O*	3-1	3-2	3-1	1-2	4-0	5-2
Sutton United	0-1	1-1	1-0	3-2	1-1	1-0	2-0	0-3	1-0	1-1	2-1	1-1	1-5	4-1	1-1	4-0	*U*	1-1	2-1	1-2	0-3	0-0
Thurrock	4-1	2-1	3-0	0-3	2-1	0-1	1-0	3-1	0-2	0-2	1-1	1-2	2-3	1-2	4-2	2-1	5-3	*T*	1-1	0-1	1-2	0-1
Welling United	3-2	0-0	2-0	1-1	2-0	4-3	1-2	2-1	1-0	2-2	1-0	1-1	2-1	3-3	1-1	3-1	0-0	1-1	*H*	1-0	1-0	0-1
Weston-super-Mare	4-3	0-1	2-2	1-3	2-0	0-4	1-0	1-4	1-1	1-3	1-1	1-4	1-2	1-1	2-1	3-1	2-3	0-5	0-1		1-3	0-3
Weymouth	1-1	3-1	2-0	1-1	4-0	1-0	2-1	2-0	1-2	1-0	5-1	1-0	2-0	4-0	4-0	3-2	3-1	2-0	2-1	2-1		1-1
Yeading	0-4	0-0	0-3	1-2	3-4	0-1	1-1	2-2	0-3	2-0	2-3	1-0	0-3	0-2	1-2	2-2	0-2	1-1	1-0	1-2	0-1	

Conference South			HOME					AWAY					TOTAL					
		P	**W**	**D**	**L**	**F**	**A**	**W**	**D**	**L**	**F**	**A**	**W**	**D**	**L**	**F**	**A**	**Pts**
Weymouth	*-4*	42	17	3	1	47	13	13	1	7	33	21	30	4	8	80	34	90
St Albans City		42	17	1	3	54	19	10	4	7	40	28	27	5	10	94	47	86
Farnborough Town		42	12	4	5	33	17	11	5	5	32	24	23	9	10	65	41	78
Lewes		42	12	4	5	38	27	9	6	6	40	30	21	10	11	78	57	73
Histon		42	12	4	5	41	30	9	4	8	29	26	21	8	13	70	56	71
Havant & Waterlooville	*-3*	42	12	5	4	29	17	9	5	7	35	31	21	10	11	64	48	70
Cambridge City	*-3*	42	10	4	7	35	23	10	6	5	43	23	20	10	12	78	46	67
Eastleigh		42	12	1	8	33	28	9	2	10	32	30	21	3	18	65	58	66
Welling United		42	11	8	2	32	20	5	9	7	26	24	16	17	9	58	44	65
Thurrock		42	9	2	10	33	31	7	8	6	27	29	16	10	16	60	60	58
Dorchester Town		42	7	5	9	32	40	9	2	10	28	32	16	7	19	60	72	55
Bognor Regis Town		42	7	8	6	31	23	5	5	11	23	32	12	13	17	54	55	49
Sutton United		42	9	7	5	28	25	4	3	14	20	36	13	10	19	48	61	49
Weston-super-Mare		42	5	4	12	25	46	9	3	9	32	42	14	7	21	57	88	49
Bishop's Stortford		42	8	5	8	35	33	3	10	8	20	30	11	15	16	55	63	48
Yeading		42	3	5	13	18	38	10	3	8	29	24	13	8	21	47	62	47
Eastbourne Borough		42	4	12	5	24	25	6	4	11	27	36	10	16	16	51	61	46
Newport County		42	7	3	11	28	34	5	5	11	22	33	12	8	22	50	67	44
Basingstoke Town		42	6	5	10	21	37	6	3	12	26	35	12	8	22	47	72	44
Hayes		42	8	1	12	26	28	3	8	10	21	32	11	9	22	47	60	42
Carshalton Athletic		42	4	10	7	21	27	4	6	11	21	41	8	16	18	42	68	40
Maidenhead United	*-2*	42	3	5	13	25	49	5	4	12	24	50	8	9	25	49	99	31

PLAY-OFFS

SEMI-FINAL

(May 1st) Farnborough Town 0 **Histon** 3 ***Att*** 1,081

(Lewes ground not graded for Football Conference National Division)

FINAL

(May 7th at Stevenage Borough)

St Albans City 2 Histon 0 ***Att*** 3,175

DATES & GATES

DATES & GATES	Basingstoke Town	Bishop's Stortford	Bognor Regis Town	Cambridge City	Carshalton Athletic	Dorchester Town	Eastbourne Borough	Eastleigh	Farnborough Town	Havant & Waterlooville	Hayes	Histon	Lewes	Maidenhead United	Newport County	St Albans City	Sutton United	Thurrock	Welling United	Weston-super-Mare	Weymouth	Yeading
Basingstoke Town		11 Feb *320*	10 Dec *287*	25 Feb *301*	3 Sep *304*	13 Aug *388*	21 Jan *346*	2 Jan *507*	17 Sep *706*	17 Dec *298*	22 Apr *390*	17 Apr *293*	11 Mar *280*	8 Apr *345*	5 Nov *471*	27 Aug *440*	1 Oct *437*	25 Mar *268*	22 Nov *202*	14 Feb *224*	8 Nov *557*	19 Nov *285*
Bishop's Stortford	15 Oct *340*		18 Feb *330*	14 Mar *384*	15 Feb *289*	21 Jan *267*	13 Aug *307*	17 Apr *270*	3 Sep *363*	19 Nov *307*	25 Feb *314*	15 Nov *342*	5 Nov *312*	18 Oct *231*	25 Mar *370*	2 Jan *512*	17 Sep *364*	11 Mar *304*	10 Dec *309*	27 Aug *267*	22 Apr *1,016*	8 Apr *302*
Bognor Regis Town	29 Apr *329*	22 Oct *326*		17 Sep *417*	17 Apr *305*	31 Jan *385*	27 Aug *481*	3 Sep *340*	5 Nov *486*	26 Dec *481*	11 Feb *341*	25 Mar *220*	21 Feb *341*	8 Nov *312*	11 Mar *425*	21 Jan *402*	25 Feb *331*	19 Nov *360*	1 Oct *442*	14 Mar *256*	8 Apr *802*	13 Aug *358*
Cambridge City	10 Sep *433*	1 Oct *1,052*	4 Mar *628*		8 Apr *504*	27 Aug *411*	3 Sep *386*	19 Nov *525*	10 Dec *709*	25 Apr *245*	21 Feb *279*	2 Jan *1,542*	25 Mar *585*	21 Jan *535*	22 Apr *507*	14 Feb *472*	17 Jan *379*	8 Nov *427*	11 Feb *542*	13 Aug *387*	29 Nov *429*	17 Apr *370*
Carshalton Athletic	15 Apr *386*	16 Aug *326*	29 Aug *297*	3 Dec *297*		1 Apr *348*	7 Mar *246*	11 Feb *338*	25 Feb *402*	22 Oct *342*	12 Nov *313*	1 Oct *212*	20 Aug *336*	17 Sep *278*	7 Jan *431*	29 Oct *367*	26 Dec *1,056*	31 Dec *299*	21 Feb *236*	18 Mar *266*	28 Jan *513*	29 Apr *474*
Dorchester Town	7 Jan *521*	20 Aug *472*	16 Aug *488*	28 Jan *465*	19 Nov *428*		10 Dec *522*	8 Apr *461*	4 Apr *429*	8 Nov *345*	1 Oct *426*	22 Apr *417*	1 Nov *380*	5 Nov *459*	21 Feb *452*	17 Sep *506*	29 Aug *534*	11 Feb *452*	15 Apr *526*	25 Feb *453*	2 Jan *3,006*	11 Mar *402*
Eastbourne Borough	20 Aug *704*	7 Jan *538*	28 Jan *704*	15 Apr *538*	8 Nov *547*	29 Apr *578*		11 Mar *503*	8 Apr *512*	25 Mar *447*	22 Nov *434*	19 Nov *603*	26 Dec *1,066*	31 Dec *676*	1 Oct *580*	25 Feb *605*	4 Apr *458*	16 Aug *711*	29 Aug *674*	17 Sep *558*	11 Feb *802*	18 Mar *435*
Eastleigh	26 Dec *506*	29 Aug *386*	15 Apr *525*	11 Apr *364*	15 Oct *343*	3 Dec *352*	29 Oct *409*		19 Oct *502*	29 Apr *652*	7 Jan *356*	4 Mar *356*	1 Feb *213*	18 Feb *368*	20 Aug *578*	18 Mar *357*	12 Nov *513*	28 Jan *312*	10 Sep *287*	4 Apr *257*	17 Aug *782*	4 Feb *312*
Farnborough Town	4 Mar *619*	14 Apr *696*	18 Mar *465*	29 Apr *510*	10 Sep *484*	12 Nov *604*	3 Dec *524*	21 Feb *377*		1 Oct *566*	16 Aug *669*	11 Feb *484*	7 Jan *566*	26 Dec *610*	29 Aug *610*	1 Apr *699*	28 Jan *540*	20 Aug *480*	21 Mar *383*	29 Oct *526*	10 Jan *781*	31 Dec *504*
Havant & Waterlooville	17 Oct *410*	1 Apr *428*	2 Jan *757*	29 Oct *474*	10 Apr *407*	6 Mar *399*	12 Nov *474*	10 Dec *668*	4 Feb *602*		20 Aug *349*	10 Sep *418*	29 Aug *411*	15 Oct *453*	28 Jan *524*	22 Apr *502*	15 Aug *500*	15 Apr *377*	18 Mar *494*	3 Dec *370*	7 Jan *1,163*	4 Mar *401*
Hayes	31 Dec *213*	10 Sep *202*	15 Oct *215*	18 Oct *209*	25 Mar *203*	4 Feb *160*	18 Feb *205*	13 Aug *229*	14 Jan *244*	21 Jan *184*		11 Mar *190*	8 Apr *167*	27 Aug *243*	8 Nov *264*	3 Sep *262*	29 Apr *389*	5 Nov *192*	4 Mar *214*	25 Apr *174*	24 Jan *302*	26 Dec *417*
Histon	29 Aug *441*	26 Apr *691*	12 Nov *489*	26 Dec *1,711*	4 Feb *454*	31 Dec *548*	1 Apr *571*	17 Sep *424*	15 Oct *791*	25 Feb *552*	29 Oct *453*		28 Jan *425*	29 Apr *893*	15 Apr *1,092*	11 Jan *494*	18 Mar *409*	15 Mar *261*	17 Aug *367*	18 Feb *438*	20 Aug *489*	18 Oct *346*
Lewes	29 Oct *448*	18 Mar *395*	19 Oct *612*	12 Nov *586*	21 Jan *553*	18 Feb *405*	2 Jan *1,193*	22 Apr *435*	13 Aug *620*	17 Apr *527*	20 Dec *356*	27 Aug *478*		4 Sep *485*	10 Sep *485*	4 Feb *555*	8 Mar *305*	4 Mar *452*	1 Apr *660*	15 Oct *459*	10 Dec *705*	14 Jan *449*
Maidenhead United	31 Jan *395*	21 Feb *183*	4 Apr *165*	20 Aug *309*	4 Mar *405*	18 Mar *285*	22 Apr *217*	22 Oct *315*	2 Jan *411*	11 Feb *251*	28 Jan *315*	10 Dec *235*	15 Apr *307*		16 Aug *434*	12 Nov *326*	7 Jan *322*	29 Aug *223*	29 Oct *306*	1 Apr *208*	1 Oct *402*	10 Sep *284*
Newport County	18 Mar *504*	12 Nov *649*	29 Oct *604*	8 Feb *522*	13 Aug *886*	19 Oct *587*	4 Feb *548*	21 Jan *675*	17 Apr *1,059*	27 Aug *720*	5 Apr *702*	4 Sep *604*	25 Feb *534*	14 Jan *625*		18 Feb *665*	1 Apr *632*	29 Apr *1,148*	18 Jan *602*	26 Dec *754*	17 Sep *724*	15 Oct *703*
St Albans City	28 Jan *526*	26 Dec *658*	20 Aug *311*	16 Aug *413*	11 Mar *562*	4 Mar *647*	10 Sep *405*	5 Nov *513*	19 Nov *557*	31 Dec *560*	15 Apr *977*	8 Apr *863*	1 Oct *541*	25 Mar *835*	22 Oct *531*		11 Feb *639*	21 Feb *354*	7 Jan *560*	29 Apr *853*	29 Aug *526*	8 Nov *331*
Sutton United	4 Feb *453*	4 Mar *487*	10 Sep *536*	18 Feb *518*	2 Jan *950*	17 Apr *502*	18 Oct *493*	25 Mar *482*	27 Aug *693*	14 Jan *536*	10 Dec *494*	7 Feb *367*	8 Nov *628*	13 Aug *510*	19 Nov *581*	15 Oct *640*		8 Apr *517*	22 Apr *525*	3 Sep *562*	11 Mar *668*	21 Jan *502*
Thurrock	12 Nov *187*	29 Oct *294*	1 Apr *193*	6 Mar *218*	22 Apr *187*	15 Oct *221*	14 Jan *235*	27 Aug *227*	21 Jan *294*	3 Sep *218*	18 Mar *159*	13 Aug *278*	17 Sep *289*	17 Apr *184*	10 Dec *231*	17 Oct *281*	3 Dec *276*		3 Jan *422*	4 Feb *182*	25 Feb *301*	18 Feb *165*
Welling United	18 Feb *537*	29 Apr *512*	7 Feb *417*	15 Oct *811*	18 Oct *462*	3 Sep *447*	17 Apr *603*	25 Feb *523*	8 Nov *726*	13 Dec *520*	17 Sep *572*	28 Feb *500*	19 Nov *713*	11 Mar *646*	8 Apr *629*	13 Aug *552*	31 Dec *718*	26 Dec *705*		21 Jan *671*	25 Mar *905*	27 Aug *566*
Weston-super-Mare	17 Aug *309*	28 Jan *186*	22 Apr *245*	7 Jan *276*	5 Nov *229*	10 Sep *373*	4 Mar *236*	9 Nov *252*	11 Mar *317*	8 Apr *240*	29 Aug *389*	23 Nov *180*	11 Feb *261*	19 Nov *237*	2 Jan *680*	10 Dec *260*	15 Apr *231*	1 Oct *271*	20 Aug *315*		22 Feb *613*	12 Apr *149*
Weymouth	14 Mar *1,802*	31 Dec *1,452*	3 Dec *1,308*	18 Mar *1,765*	27 Aug *1,370*	26 Dec *4,029*	15 Oct *1,252*	14 Jan *1,557*	18 Feb *2,058*	13 Aug *1,521*	1 Apr *1,727*	21 Jan *1,629*	29 Apr *4,071*	4 Feb *1,406*	4 Mar *2,110*	17 Apr *5,022*	29 Oct *1,703*	10 Sep *1,029*	12 Nov *1,706*	6 Dec *1,221*		3 Sep *1,024*
Yeading	1 Apr *191*	3 Dec *169*	7 Jan *177*	29 Aug *201*	10 Dec *146*	29 Oct *132*	20 Dec *133*	1 Oct *143*	22 Apr *258*	17 Sep *199*	2 Jan *601*	21 Feb *102*	16 Aug *230*	25 Feb *189*	11 Feb *201*	7 Mar *132*	20 Aug *225*	22 Nov *140*	28 Jan *189*	12 Nov *135*	15 Apr *502*	

FOOTBALL CONFERENCE SOUTH

CONSTITUTION FOR 2006-07

BASINGSTOKE TOWN
The Camrose Ground, Western Way, Basingstoke, Hampshire RG22 6EZ
Tel: 01256 327575 Boardroom: 01256 325063 Fax: 01256 869997
Manager: Ernie Howe www.btfc.co.uk Colours: Blue & yellow

BEDFORD TOWN
The New Eyrie, Meadow Lane, Cardington, Bedford, Bedfordshire MK44 3LW
Tel: 01234 838448 Fax: 01234 831990
Manager: Nicky Platnauer www.bedfordeagles.net Colours: Blue

BISHOP'S STORTFORD
Woodside Park, Dunmow Road, Bishop's Stortford, Hertfordshire CM23 5RG
Tel: 08700 339930 Fax: 08700 339931
Manager: Martin Hayes www.bsfc.co.uk Colours: Blue & white

BOGNOR REGIS TOWN
Nyewood Lane, Bognor Regis, West Sussex PO21 2TY
Tel: 01243 822325 Fax: 01243 866151
Manager: Jack Pearce www.therocks.co.uk Colours: White & green

BRAINTREE TOWN
Cressing Road Stadium, Clockhouse Way, Braintree, Essex CM7 6RD
Tel: 01376 345617 Fax: 01376 323369
Manager: George Borg Colours: Yellow
www.ukclubnet.co.uk/members/footballclubs/braintreefc

CAMBRIDGE CITY
City Ground, Milton Road, Cambridge, Cambridgeshire CB4 1UY
Tel: 01223 357973 Fax: 01223 351582
Manager: Gary Roberts www.cambridgecityfc.com Colours: White & black

DORCHESTER TOWN
The Avenue Stadium, Weymouth Avenue, Dorchester, Dorset DT1 2RY
Tel: 01305 262451 Fax: 01305 267623
Manager: t.b.a. www.the-magpies.net Colours: Black & white

EASTBOURNE BOROUGH
Langney Sports Club, Priory Lane, Eastbourne, East Sussex BN23 7QH
Tel: 01323 743561 Fax: 01323 743561
Manager: Garry Wilson www.eastbourneboroughfc.co.uk Colours: Red & black

EASTLEIGH
Silverlake Stadium, Ten Acres, Stoneham Lane, North Stoneham, Eastleigh, Hampshire SO50 9HT
Tel: 023 8061 3361 Fax: 023 8061 2379
Manager: Paul Doswell www.eastleighfc.net Colours: White & navy blue

FARNBOROUGH TOWN
Cherrywood Road, Farnborough, Hampshire GU14 8UD
Tel: 01252 541469 Fax: 01252 372640
Manager: Ian McDonald www.farnboroughtownfc.com Colours: Red & white

FISHER ATHLETIC
Dulwich Hamlet FC, Champion Hill Stadium, Dog Kennel Hill, East Dulwich, London SE22 8BD
Tel: 020 7274 2707
Manager: Justin Edinburgh www.fisherathletic.co.uk Colours: Black & white

HAVANT & WATERLOOVILLE
Westleigh Park, Martin Road, Havant, Hampshire PO9 5TH
Tel: 023 9278 7822 Club: 023 9278 7855 Fax: 023 9226 2367
Manager: Ian Baird www.havantandwaterlooville.net Colours: White

HAYES
Townfield House, Church Road, Hayes, Middlesex UB3 2LE
Tel: 020 8573 2075 Fax: 020 8573 2075
Manager: Kevin Hill www.hayesfc.net Colours: Red, white & black

HISTON
The Glassworld Stadium, Bridge Road, Impington, Cambridge, Cambridgeshire CB4 9PH
Tel: 01223 237373 Fax: 01223 872246
Manager: Steve Fallon www.histonfc.co.uk Colours: Red & black

LEWES
The Dripping Pan, Mountfield Road, Lewes, East Sussex BN7 1XN
Tel: 01273 472100 Fax: 01273 472100
Manager: Steve King www.lewesfc.com Colours: Red & black

NEWPORT COUNTY
Newport Stadium, Langland Way, Spytty Park, Newport, Gwent NP19 4PT
Tel: 01633 662262 Stadium: 01633 671815 Fax: 01633 666107
Manager: Peter Beadle www.newport-county.co.uk Colours: Amber & black

SALISBURY CITY
The Raymond McEnhill Stadium, Partridge Way, Old Sarum, Salisbury, Wiltshire SP4 6PU
Tel: 01722 326454 Fax: 01722 323100
Manager: Nick Holmes www.salisburycity-fc.co.uk Colours: White & black

SUTTON UNITED
Borough Sports Ground, Gander Green Lane, Sutton, Surrey SM1 2EY
Tel: 020 8644 4440 Fax: 020 8644 5120
Manager: Ian Hazel www.suttonunited.net Colours: Chocolate & amber

THURROCK
Thurrock Hotel, Ship Lane, Grays, Essex RM19 1YN
Tel: 01708 865492 Club: 01708 865492 Fax: 01708 868863
Manager: Hakan Ramis-Hayrettin www.thurrockfc.co.uk Colours: Yellow & green

WELLING UNITED
Park View Road, Welling, Kent DA16 1SY
Tel: 020 8301 1196 Fax: 020 8301 5676
Manager: Adrian Pennock www.wellingunited.co.uk Colours: Red & white

WESTON-SUPER-MARE
Winterstoke Road, Weston-super-Mare, North Somerset BS24 9AA
Tel: 01934 621618 Fax: 01934 622704
Manager: Frank Gregan www.westonsupermarefc.co.uk Colours: White & blue

YEADING
The Warren, Beaconsfield Road, Hayes, Middlesex UB4 0SL
Tel: 020 8848 7369 Clubhouse: 020 8846 7362 Fax: 020 8848 1200
Manager: Johnson Hippolyte www.yeadingfc.co.uk Colours: Red & black

IN: Bedford Town (P – Southern League Premier Division), Braintree Town (P – Isthmian League Premier Division), Fisher Athletic (P – Isthmian League Premier Division), Salisbury City (P – Southern League Premier Division)
OUT: Carshalton Athletic (R – Isthmian League Premier Division), Maidenhead United (R – Southern League Premier Division), St Albans City (P), Weymouth (P)

FOOTBALL LEAGUE TROPHY

(Football League One and Two clubs including those relegated to the Football Conference in 2005, and the top eight Football Conference finishers with a Football League graded ground)

NORTHERN SECTION FIRST ROUND

Barnsley 2 **Doncaster Rovers** 5 ***Att*** *4,095*
Blackpool 4 Wrexham 3 *aet* ***Att*** *3,239*
Boston United 2 Huddersfield Town 1 ***Att*** *1,593*
Cambridge United 3 Chester City 0 ***Att*** *1,224*
Grimsby Town 1 **Morecambe** 1 *aet* (3-4p) ***Att*** *1,131*
Halifax Town 6 Bury 1 ***Att*** *1,191*
Kidderminster Harriers 2 Darlington 1 ***Att*** *696*
Macclesfield Town 2 Chesterfield 0 ***Att*** *796*
Mansfield Town 0 **Hereford United** 1 ***Att*** *1,393*
Oldham Athletic 1 **Carlisle United** 1 *aet* (5-6p) ***Att*** *2,226*
Rochdale 3 Stockport County 1 ***Att*** *1,683*
Rotherham United 3 Accrington Stanley 3 *aet* (3-2p) ***Att*** *1,888*
Scunthorpe United 1 Hartlepool United 0 ***Att*** *2,028*
Tranmere Rovers 2 Lincoln City 1 ***Att*** *3,210*

SOUTHERN SECTION FIRST ROUND

AFC Bournemouth 4 Aldershot Town 1 ***Att*** *2,657*
Barnet 3 Bristol City 2 ***Att*** *1,031*
Brentford 1 **Oxford United** 1 *aet* (3-4p) ***Att*** *1,785*
Gillingham 2 Crawley Town 0 *aet* ***Att*** *1,988*
Leyton Orient 2 Yeovil Town 0 ***Att*** *958*
Milton Keynes Dons 3 Exeter City 2 ***Att*** *2,745*
Northampton Town 5 Notts County 2 ***Att*** *2,041*
Peterborough United 2 Bristol Rovers 1 *aet* ***Att*** *1,477*
Rushden & Diamonds 1 Southend United 0 ***Att*** *1,300*
Shrewsbury Town 0 **Cheltenham Town** 2 ***Att*** *2,146*
Swindon Town 2 Stevenage Borough 0 ***Att*** *1,771*
Torquay United 1 **Swansea City** 3 ***Att*** *1,025*
Woking 3 Nottingham Forest 2 ***Att*** *3,127*
Wycombe Wanderers 2 Dagenham & Redbridge 1 *aet* ***Att*** *1,094*

NORTHERN SECTION SECOND ROUND

Boston United 0 **Kidderminster Harriers** 3 ***Att*** *1,131*
Cambridge United 3 Doncaster Rovers 2 ***Att*** *1,435*
Carlisle United 2 Blackpool 1 ***Att*** *2,987*
Halifax Town 1 **Scunthorpe United** 3 ***Att*** *1,124*
Hereford United 2 Port Vale 1 *aet* ***Att*** *1,355*
Morecambe 0 **Bradford City** 1 ***Att*** *1,649*
Rotherham United 1 **Macclesfield Town** 2 ***Att*** *1,646*
Tranmere Rovers 3 Rochdale 2 ***Att*** *2,867*

SOUTHERN SECTION SECOND ROUND

Barnet 0 **Milton Keynes Dons** 3 ***Att*** *991*
Colchester United 3 Northampton Town 2 *aet* ***Att*** *1,719*
Gillingham 2 **Wycombe Wanderers** 2 *aet* (1-3p) ***Att*** *2,111*
Oxford United 1 Leyton Orient 0 ***Att*** *1,521*
Peterborough United 2 Swindon Town 1 ***Att*** *959*
Swansea City 4 Rushden & Diamonds 2 ***Att*** *5,321*
Walsall 1 AFC Bournemouth 0 ***Att*** *2,031*
Woking 1 **Cheltenham Town** 5 *aet* ***Att*** *883*

NORTHERN SECTION QUARTER-FINALS

Macclesfield Town 4 Cambridge United 2 ***Att*** *860*
Hereford United 2 Scunthorpe United 0 ***Att*** *1,452*
Kidderminster Harriers 2 Bradford City 1 ***Att*** *1,276*
Tranmere Rovers 0 **Carlisle United** 0 *aet* (10-11p) ***Att*** *3,054*

SOUTHERN SECTION QUARTER-FINALS

Cheltenham Town 2 Oxford United 1 ***Att*** *1,825*
Milton Keynes Dons 1 **Colchester United** 2 ***Att*** *2,649*
Swansea City 3 Peterborough United 1 *aet* ***Att*** *5,474*
Walsall 3 Wycombe Wanderers 2 ***Att*** *2,571*

NORTHERN SECTION SEMI-FINALS

Carlisle United 1 Kidderminster Harriers 0 ***Att*** *4,432*
Macclesfield Town 2 Hereford United 0 ***Att*** *1,315*

SOUTHERN SECTION SEMI-FINALS

Cheltenham Town 0 **Colchester United** 1 ***Att*** *2,243*
Swansea City 2 Walsall 2 *aet* (6-5p) ***Att*** *6,670*

NORTHERN SECTION FINAL

(played over two legs)
Carlisle United 2 Macclesfield Town 1 ***Att*** *5,706*
Macclesfield Town 3 **Carlisle United** 2 *aet (Carlisle United win on away goals rule)* ***Att*** *3,598*

SOUTHERN SECTION FINAL

(played over two legs)
Swansea City 1 Colchester United 0 ***Att*** *7,285*
Colchester United 1 **Swansea City** 2 ***Att*** *3,236*

FINAL

(May 2nd at Millennium Stadium)
Swansea City 2 Carlisle United 1 ***Att*** *42,028*

GLOUCESTERSHIRE COUNTY LEAGUE

	AXA	DRG Stapleton	Ellwood	Hardwicke	Henbury Old Boys	Highridge United	Kings Stanley	Lydney Town	Patchway Town	Pucklechurch Sports	Roman Glass St Glass	Sea Mills Park	Taverners	Thornbury Town	Totterdown Port of B	Wotton Rovers	Yate Town Res.
AXA		4-2	1-1	4-4	1-4	0-2	3-1	1-2	2-4	4-1	1-2	3-1	2-4	3-2	1-1	6-1	1-1
DRG Stapleton	2-2		3-2	1-0	2-3	1-2	1-0	2-3	2-2	3-2	1-2	1-2	1-2	0-1	3-3	4-2	1-2
Ellwood	3-2	3-1		1-0	3-0	0-0	1-1	1-1	0-0	4-0	6-1	3-2	1-1	2-5	1-2	8-0	0-1
Hardwicke	2-4	2-2	1-2		0-1	2-2	1-2	2-1	0-3	1-1	3-0	2-1	2-4	1-2	3-1	3-1	1-0
Henbury Old Boys	2-1	2-0	1-2	0-5		0-4	1-1	1-1	1-1	5-3	2-0	3-1	1-1	3-1	2-0	1-2	1-2
Highridge United	2-1	5-0	0-0	3-2	1-0		0-2	1-1	0-1	1-0	1-2	6-2	0-1	2-1	2-1	4-0	2-0
Kings Stanley	0-2	2-0	2-2	2-5	0-1	2-3		1-4	1-4	0-0	0-4	3-0	1-1	1-5	0-1	7-1	3-0
Lydney Town	3-0	3-0	4-2	6-0	1-1	4-2	2-0		3-1	2-1	1-1	5-0	1-0	1-2	4-0	5-1	2-0
Patchway Town	0-1	2-0	2-0	3-1	1-2	0-3	0-2	1-4		1-0	0-2	5-0	1-0	0-0	1-1	2-0	2-1
Pucklechurch Sports	0-2	1-1	0-2	1-3	3-4	0-4	4-3	0-1	0-1		1-1	3-0	2-3	1-2	0-4	2-2	0-3
Roman Glass St George	2-0	4-2	0-0	0-3	0-2	1-2	4-2	1-3	0-3	1-0		2-0	3-1	3-0	1-1	4-0	0-2
Sea Mills Park	1-1	5-0	2-1	2-2	0-5	0-5	2-6	1-6	1-2	2-0	2-1		1-2	0-3	1-5	0-2	2-6
Taverners	2-0	7-3	2-0	4-1	1-1	1-5	4-1	1-1	3-1	3-2	2-1	1-2		1-2	0-2	0-1	1-1
Thornbury Town	0-0	1-3	0-2	2-3	1-2	2-1	1-3	1-3	2-1	3-1	1-2	2-2	1-0		1-2	6-2	2-2
Totterdown Port of Bristol	2-0	7-0	0-3	2-2	3-1	3-3	2-2	1-3	1-2	2-1	2-1	2-0	4-0	5-1		3-1	2-2
Wotton Rovers	3-1	1-1	0-3	1-2	1-2	0-4	2-4	0-4	1-5	0-1	1-3	0-0	0-3	2-2	2-5		0-3
Yate Town Res.	2-2	0-1	0-1	2-1	2-1	1-1	1-1	2-2	5-3	4-0	2-0	4-1	1-0	2-1	2-0	5-1	

		P	W	D	L	F	A	Pts
Lydney Town		32	23	7	2	87	28	76
Highridge United		32	20	6	6	73	31	66
Yate Town Res.		32	17	8	7	61	36	59
Totterdown Port of Bristol		32	16	8	8	70	46	56
Patchway Town		32	17	5	10	55	39	56
Ellwood		32	15	9	8	60	35	54
Taverners		32	15	6	11	56	46	51
Henbury Old Boys	-7	32	17	6	9	56	45	50
Roman Glass St George		32	15	4	13	49	47	49
Thornbury Town		32	13	5	14	56	56	44
Hardwicke		32	12	6	14	60	61	42
AXA		32	10	8	14	56	59	38
Kings Stanley		32	10	7	15	56	62	37
DRG Stapleton		32	7	6	19	44	79	27
Sea Mills Park		32	6	4	22	36	92	22
Wotton Rovers		32	4	4	24	31	103	16
Pucklechurch Sports		32	3	5	24	31	72	14

LES JAMES MEMORI AL CUP

PRELIMINARY ROUND

Highridge United 2 Taverners 1

FIRST ROUND

AXA 2 DRG Stapleton 0
Henbury Old Boys 3 Kings Stanley 1
Highridge United 7 Sea Mills Park 1
Patchway Town 0 **Lydney Town** 1
Pucklechurch Sports 0 **Totterdown Port of Bristol** 2
Roman Glass St George 0 **Hardwicke** 1
Wotton Rovers 1 **Thornbury Town** 2
Yate Town Res. 0 **Ellwood** 1

QUARTER-FINALS

AXA 2 Thornbury Town 1
Hardwicke 1 **Henbury Old Boys** 2
Highridge United 5 Totterdown Port of Bristol 1
Lydney Town 4 Ellwood 0

SEMI-FINALS

AXA 1 **Highridge United** 3 *(at Yate Town)*
Lydney Town 1 Henbury Old Boys 1 (4-3p) *(at Yate Town)*

FINAL

(April 12th at Yate Town)
Lydney Town 0 **Highridge United** 1

GLOUCESTERSHIRE COUNTY LEAGUE CONSTITUTION 2006-07

AXA .... **Cribbs Causeway, Bristol BS10 7TT** **0117 950 2303**
BERKELEY TOWN .... **Station Road, Berkeley GL13 9AJ** .... **None**
DRG STAPLETON .... **Frenchay Park Road, Frenchay, Bristol BS16 1HY** .... **None**
ELLWOOD .... **Bromley Road, Ellwood, Coleford GL16 7LZ** **01594 832927**
HANHAM ATHLETIC .... **Vicarage Road Playing Fields, Hanham, Bristol BS15 3AH** .... **None**
HARDWICKE .... **Green Lane, Hardwicke, Gloucester GL2 4QA** **01452 720587**
HENBURY OLD BOYS .... **Lorain Walk, Henbury, Bristol BS10 7AS** **0117 959 0475**
HIGHRIDGE UNITED .... **Lakemead Grove, Highridge, Bristol BS13 8EA** **0117 978 4878**
KINGS STANLEY .... **Marling Close, Kings Stanley GL5 5AQ** **01453 828975**
PATCHWAY TOWN .... **Scott Park, Coniston Road, Patchway, Bristol BS34 5JR** **0117 949 3952**
PUCKLECHURCH SPORTS .. **Pucklechurch Recreation Ground, St Aldams Drive, Pucklechurch, Bristol BS16 9QQ** **0117 937 2102**
ROMAN GLASS ST GEORGE .... **Bell Hill, Whiteway Road, St George, Bristol BS5 7RW** **0117 983 7707**
SEA MILLS PARK .... **Napier Miles Road, Lawrence Weston, Bristol BS11 0UU** .... **None**
TAVERNERS .... **Highwood School, Spring Hill, Nailsworth GL6 0LU** .... **None**
THORNBURY TOWN .... **Mundy Playing Fields, Kington Lane, Thornbury BS35 1NB** .... **None**
TOTTERDOWN PORT OF BRISTOL .. **City & Port of Bristol SC, Nibley Road, Shirehampton, Bristol BS11 9XW** **0117 982 3927**
WOTTON ROVERS .... **Synwell Playing Fields, Synwell Lane, Wotton-under-Edge GL12 7HQ** **01453 842929**
YATE TOWN RESERVES .... **Lodge Road, Yate, Bristol BS17 5LE** **01454 228103**

***IN:** Berkeley Town (P – Gloucestershire Northern Senior League Division One), Hanham Athletic (P – Bristol Premier Combination Premier Division)*
***OUT:** Lydney Town (P – Hellenic League Division One West)*

GLOUCESTERSHIRE NORTHERN SENIOR LEAGUE

	Berkeley Town	Bourton Rovers	Brimscombe & Thrupp	Broadwell Amateurs	Brockworth Albion	Cam Bulldogs	Chalford	Cheltenham Civil Service	Huntley	Kingswood	Longlevens	Sharpness	Shortwood United Res.	Tetbury Town	Viney St Swithins	Warden Hill United
Berkeley Town		0-0	2-2	1-2	2-0	2-1	3-0	4-2	2-1	3-0	3-1	2-1	2-2	1-3	6-1	4-0
Bourton Rovers	0-4		1-3	2-2	2-0	1-1	1-1	1-2	2-0	2-2	0-1	1-2	2-4	0-1	3-2	3-0
Brimscombe & Thrupp	1-2	3-0	*D*	0-1	0-0	2-0	4-0	3-4	1-6	2-0	1-2	2-2	2-2	0-1	5-0	1-0
Broadwell Amateurs	0-1	2-0	1-0	*I*	0-1	2-0	9-0	1-1	4-1	1-4	2-1	0-0	3-0	3-0	1-0	2-1
Brockworth Albion	1-3	1-2	0-0	0-0	*V*	2-2	1-0	1-1	1-4	0-1	4-1	0-6	1-0	3-2	0-0	2-0
Cam Bulldogs	0-2	2-2	2-1	2-1	3-1	*I*	8-0	2-1	3-1	0-1	3-4	2-0	8-1	2-0	3-0	2-0
Chalford	0-2	0-4	0-2	0-9	1-2	0-6	*S*	0-2	1-3	0-10	0-5	0-6	0-2	0-5	4-2	6-1
Cheltenham Civil Service	2-1	4-0	3-1	2-0	4-1	0-1	6-0	*I*	1-2	3-0	2-2	1-3	0-0	2-2	2-3	1-1
Huntley	1-4	5-2	1-2	1-1	0-4	1-3	5-1	4-2	*O*	3-3	1-3	1-2	0-0	1-3	1-2	0-1
Kingswood	1-3	6-1	3-0	1-3	7-1	2-3	3-1	4-2	1-0	*N*	1-2	1-1	3-2	1-2	1-0	2-1
Longlevens	0-5	4-3	0-1	3-1	6-1	0-1	11-0	0-2	2-0	3-2		1-0	3-1	3-1	3-1	7-0
Sharpness	0-4	3-2	5-1	0-0	0-0	2-1	9-0	3-2	2-2	2-0	3-4	*O*	3-2	1-1	4-0	5-1
Shortwood United Res.	2-1	1-2	4-3	0-1	2-0	0-2	3-1	0-1	2-1	0-7	0-4	1-3	*N*	2-1	3-0	3-1
Tetbury Town	1-0	4-0	3-2	0-1	3-0	4-0	5-2	1-2	4-1	6-0	1-1	1-0	2-2	*E*	3-0	7-0
Viney St Swithins	0-4	1-1	1-2	0-3	1-0	2-2	9-0	1-4	1-4	1-2	1-5	1-6	1-3	2-1		5-1
Warden Hill United	2-3	3-1	0-4	0-3	0-3	0-2	4-0	1-1	0-2	3-0	0-4	2-2	1-2	2-0	1-3	

Division One		P	W	D	L	F	A	Pts
Berkeley Town		30	22	3	5	76	27	69
Longlevens		30	21	2	7	86	41	65
Broadwell Amateurs		30	18	6	6	59	22	60
Sharpness		30	16	8	6	76	36	56
Tetbury Town		30	17	4	9	68	34	55
Cam Bulldogs	*-3*	30	18	4	8	67	35	55
Cheltenham Civil Service		30	14	7	9	62	43	49
Kingswood		30	15	3	12	69	51	48
Brimscombe & Thrupp		30	12	5	13	51	46	41
Shortwood United Res.		30	12	5	13	46	59	41
Brockworth Albion		30	9	7	14	31	53	34
Huntley		30	9	4	17	53	60	31
Bourton Rovers		30	7	7	16	41	64	28
Viney St Swithins	*-3g -3*	30	7	3	20	38	78	21
Warden Hill United		30	5	3	22	27	80	18
Chalford		30	2	1	27	18	142	7

REG DAVIS MEMORIAL CUP

FIRST ROUND

Berkeley Town 7 Horsley United 0
Bourton Rovers 0 **Bishops Cleeve Res.** 1
Bredon 1 **Cheltenham Civil Service** 3
Brimscombe & Thrupp 1 **Kingswood** 3
Broadwell Amateurs 3 Mitcheldean 1
Brockworth Albion (scr.) v **Tuffley Rovers Res.** (w/o)
Charfield 0 Cam Bulldogs 1 *(Cam Bulldogs expelled)*
Dursley Town 8 Chalford 0
Gala Wilton 0 **Longlevens** 2
Huntley 1 Smiths Athletic 1 (2-1p)
Sharpness 1 **Shortwood United Res.** 3
Staunton & Corse 1 **Longford** 2
Tetbury Town 4 Stonehouse Freeway 1
Viney St Swithins 1 **Lydbrook Athletic** 1 (0-3p)
Warden Hill United 1 Newton Heath 1 (4-2p)
Whitecroft 1 **Mushet & Coalway** 2

GLOUCESTERSHIRE NORTHERN SENIOR LEAGUE DIVISION ONE CONSTITUTION 2006-07

BISHOPS CLEEVE RESERVES .... Kayte Lane, Bishops Cleeve, Cheltenham GL52 3PD 07866 077291
BOURTON ROVERS .... Rissington Road, Bourton-on-the-Water, Cheltenham GL54 2DZ 01451 821977
BRIMSCOMBE & THRUPP .... The Meadow, London Road, Brimscombe, Stroud GL5 2QE 01453 885039
BROADWELL AMATEURS .... The Hawthornes, Poolway Road, Broadwell, Coleford GL16 7BE 01594 837347
BROCKWORTH ALBION .... Parton Road, Churchdown GL3 2JH .... None
CAM BULLDOGS .... Recreation Ground, Everlands, Cam, Dursley GL11 5NL 01453 546736
CHELTENHAM CIVIL SERVICE .. Civil Service Sports Ground, Tewkesbury Road, Uckington, Cheltenham GL51 9SX 01242 680424
HUNTLEY .... Recreation Ground, Huntley .... None
KINGSWOOD .... Wickwar Road, Kingswood, Wotton-under-Edge GL12 8RF 07836 734020
LONGLEVENS .... Longford Lane, Longlevens, Gloucester GL2 9EU 01452 530388
LYDBROOK ATHLETIC .... Reeds Sports Ground, Lydbrook .... None
SHARPNESS .... Berkeley Vale Community School, Sharpness .... None
SHORTWOOD UNITED RESERVES .... Meadowbank, Shortwood, Nailsworth, Stroud GL6 0SJ 01453 833936
TETBURY TOWN .... Preston Park, Cirencester Road, Tetbury GL8 8EZ .... None
TUFFLEY ROVERS .... Glevum Park, Lower Tuffley Lane, Gloucester GL2 6DT 01452 423402
VINEY ST SWITHINS .... Viney Sports & Social Club, Viney Hill, Lydney GL15 4NF 01594 510658

IN: Bishops Cleeve Reserves (P), Lydbrook Athletic (P), Tuffley Rovers (formerly Tuffley Rovers Reserves) (P)

OUT: Berkeley Town (P – Gloucestershire County League), Chalford (R), Warden Hill United (F)

	Bishops Cleeve Res.	Bredon	Charfield	Dursley Town	Gala Wilton	Horsley United	Longford	Lydbrook Athletic	Mitcheldean	Mushet & Coalway	Newton Heath	Smiths Athletic	Staunton & Corse	Stonehouse Freeway	Tuffley Rovers Res.	Whitecroft
Bishops Cleeve Res.		1-0	2-1	2-2	5-2	1-1	3-1	2-1	4-0	2-0	3-1	1-2	11-0	1-0	3-0	5-1
Bredon	0-3		2-1	2-1	2-2	1-1	0-0	0-0	1-1	4-0	0-1	2-1	2-0	6-1	1-3	3-0
Charfield	2-2	1-2	*D*	1-1	1-2	6-2	1-1	1-3	3-2	5-1	3-0	1-2	4-1	2-3	2-6	7-0
Dursley Town	3-2	5-2	2-0	*I*	2-3	4-2	2-2	2-2	3-0	3-1	1-1	3-2	4-0	3-0	1-4	3-1
Gala Wilton	1-4	3-1	1-3	3-1	*V*	5-0	1-5	0-1	2-0	5-0	1-2	1-1	0-0	4-2	1-3	7-0
Horsley United	0-6	1-5	0-2	0-3	1-0	*I*	0-1	0-3	1-2	3-1	1-2	0-2	1-2	0-0	0-4	0-0
Longford	0-1	1-1	1-3	1-3	4-0	4-0	*S*	0-2	2-0	3-0	1-2	2-2	1-1	2-2	0-2	3-0
Lydbrook Athletic	2-2	3-2	2-2	2-0	0-2	16-0	3-1	*I*	3-2	5-0	3-0	0-2	7-0	4-0	0-0	9-1
Mitcheldean	1-4	2-1	0-1	2-1	5-3	4-0	5-1	0-2	*O*	5-0	0-2	1-3	2-1	1-1	1-1	3-0
Mushet & Coalway	0-9	1-0	2-0	2-5	3-5	2-4	1-6	0-4	1-3	*N*	1-3	0-1	3-0	3-6	0-1	2-1
Newton Heath	2-0	3-0	2-0	3-0	5-1	6-0	2-1	1-3	1-1	2-2		2-1	3-1	3-0	1-0	2-1
Smiths Athletic	0-0	0-4	6-1	0-1	1-2	4-0	1-2	0-1	2-0	4-0	1-0	*T*	2-4	2-0	0-0	1-1
Staunton & Corse	1-4	0-3	0-4	0-5	1-4	2-2	0-5	0-5	0-2	5-0	4-7	2-1	*W*	0-4	0-2	4-2
Stonehouse Freeway	0-4	1-1	3-4	3-0	1-1	8-2	4-2	1-4	3-2	4-1	2-2	0-2	3-0	*O*	0-2	9-3
Tuffley Rovers Res.	3-1	2-0	9-0	0-0	2-1	2-1	5-1	0-0	4-1	9-0	0-0	2-0	5-0	2-0		8-1
Whitecroft	0-6	1-2	1-8	2-7	2-7	0-0	1-3	1-7	2-2	2-1	0-3	0-4	0-2	2-4	1-6	

SECOND ROUND

Bishops Cleeve Res. 3 Huntley 1
Broadwell Amateurs 5 Mushet & Coalway 0
Cheltenham Civil Service 3 Charfield 0
Dursley Town 2 **Longlevens** 4
Lydbrook Athletic 4 Longford 2
Shortwood United Res. 2 Berkeley Town 2 (5-4p)
Tuffley Rovers Res. 1 **Kingswood** 2
Warden Hill United 0 **Tetbury Town** 4

QUARTER-FINALS

Broadwell Amateurs 0 **Bishops Cleeve Res.** 1
Lydbrook Athletic 4 Longlevens 2
Shortwood United Res. 0 **Cheltenham Civil Service** 0 (2-3p)
Tetbury Town 1 **Kingswood** 1 (4-5p)

SEMI-FINALS

Bishops Cleeve Res. 6 Kingswood 1
Lydbrook Athletic 3 Cheltenham Civil Service 0

FINAL

(September 21st at Tuffley Rovers)
Bishops Cleeve Res. 0 **Lydbrook Athletic** 2

Division Two	P	W	D	L	F	A	Pts
Tuffley Rovers Res.	30	22	6	2	87	17	72
Lydbrook Athletic	30	21	6	3	97	22	69
Bishops Cleeve Res.	30	21	5	4	94	27	68
Newton Heath	30	20	5	5	64	32	65
Dursley Town	30	16	6	8	71	45	54
Smiths Athletic	30	14	5	11	50	33	47
Gala Wilton	30	14	4	12	70	58	46
Bredon	30	12	7	11	50	40	43
Charfield	30	13	4	13	70	61	43
Longford	30	11	7	12	57	48	40
Stonehouse Freeway	30	11	6	13	65	65	39
Mitcheldean	30	11	5	14	50	53	38
Staunton & Corse	30	6	3	21	31	98	21
Horsley United	30	3	6	21	23	98	15
Mushet & Coalway	30	4	1	25	28	109	13
Whitecroft	30	1	4	25	27	128	7

GLOUCESTERSHIRE NORTHERN LEAGUE DIVISION TWO CONSTITUTION 2006-07

ASHTON KEYNES .... Bradstone Sports Ground, Rixon Gate, Ashton Keynes, Swindon SN6 6PH .... None
BREDON .... Main Road, Bredon, Tewkesbury GL20 7EG 01684 773152
CHALFORD .... Chalford Sports & Social Club, Chalford Hill, Stroud GL6 8BD 01453 884214
CHARFIELD .... Charfield Memorial Hall, Charfield 01454 260204
DURSLEY TOWN .... Memorial Ground, Kingshill Road, Dursley GL11 4BJ 01453 546122
GALA WILTON .... Gala Club, Fairmile Gardens, Longford, Gloucester GL2 9EB .... None
HARROW HILL RESERVES .... Larksfield Road, Harrow Hill, Drybrook GL17 9JP 01594 543873
LONGFORD .... Playing Field, Longford Lane, Gloucester GL2 9EU .... None
MITCHELDEAN .... Townsend Playing Fields, Mitcheldean .... None
MUSHET & COALWAY .... Coalway Recreation Ground, Coalway .... None
NEWTON HEATH .... Whaddon Road Recreation Ground, Whaddon Road, Cheltenham .... None
SLIMBRIDGE RESERVES .... Wisloe Road, Cambridge GL2 7AF 01453 890361
SMITHS ATHLETIC .... Dowty Rotol Sports Ground, Hatherley Lane, Staverton, Cheltenham GL51 4NF 01242 525515
STAR .... Kayte Lane, Bishops Cleeve, Cheltenham GL52 3PD .... None
STAUNTON & CORSE .... Gloucester Road, Corse, Gloucester GL19 3RQ .... None
STONEHOUSE FREEWAY .... Oldends Lane, Stonehouse GL10 2DG .... None

IN: Ashton Keynes (P – Cirencester League), Chalford (R), Harrow Hill Reserves (P – North Gloucestershire League), Star (P – Cheltenham Association League Division One), Slimbridge Reserves (P – Stroud & District League Division One)

OUT: Bishops Cleeve Reserves (P), Horsley United (R), Lydbrook Athletic (P), Tuffley Rovers (formerly Tuffley Rovers Reserves) (P), Whitecroft (R)

GWENT COUNTY LEAGUE

	Aberbargoed Buds	Abercarn United	Albion Rovers	Blaenavon Blues	Clydach Wasps	Coed Eva Athletic	Cwmffrwdoer Sports	Mardy	Newport Corinthians	Panteg	RTB Ebbw Vale	Spencer Youth & Boys	Trinant	Undy Athletic	West Pontnewydd
Aberbargoed Buds		4-2	4-0	1-1	4-1	7-1	1-0	2-3	4-3	1-3	4-3	2-0	4-0	2-0	4-2
Abercarn United	1-6	*D*	5-5	2-2	3-2	4-0	1-4	0-1	4-2	3-1	2-1	2-0	3-1	2-0	3-2
Albion Rovers	1-5	0-3	*I*	1-3	2-5	2-1	0-5	1-5	4-3	2-2	2-1	3-2	1-1	2-1	2-0
Blaenavon Blues	4-1	4-1	5-1	*V*	2-2	3-3	3-1	1-1	2-0	3-1	9-0	1-1	7-1	5-1	2-3
Clydach Wasps	1-1	2-0	2-2	0-5	*I*	2-2	2-3	1-1	3-3	1-1	4-1	2-0	3-0	3-6	1-3
Coed Eva Athletic	1-2	3-5	2-3	2-5	5-3	*S*	1-2	3-6	3-2	3-1	2-2	2-3	6-3	2-4	2-2
Cwmffrwdoer Sports	4-4	1-2	3-4	2-3	1-1	1-2	*I*	3-3	0-1	5-4	3-3	5-1	3-1	2-2	1-3
Mardy	1-3	4-1	6-0	3-2	4-3	6-1	4-2	*O*	0-1	1-3	6-2	4-3	3-4	4-1	2-1
Newport Corinthians	0-2	1-2	1-1	2-5	1-2	1-0	2-3	0-3	*N*	4-2	2-2	1-2	2-2	4-2	1-1
Panteg	0-6	0-1	2-2	1-1	1-2	1-0	0-1	2-3	3-1		0-0	0-2	3-2	4-3	0-1
RTB Ebbw Vale	1-5	0-2	2-2	0-4	0-0	3-2	0-8	0-2	0-4	0-3		0-9	1-5	3-4	0-3
Spencer Youth & Boys	2-5	0-1	7-2	1-3	3-1	5-2	2-0	4-1	4-1	3-1	3-0	*O*	3-2	1-3	2-0
Trinant	1-2	1-0	5-4	2-5	2-1	1-3	2-3	1-2	2-2	2-0	1-1	2-0	*N*	2-3	1-2
Undy Athletic	1-4	2-3	0-0	1-2	4-3	2-6	4-3	0-3	2-0	0-2	1-2	0-3	3-2	*E*	1-5
West Pontnewydd	2-2	1-2	4-0	2-5	1-0	1-2	4-3	0-3	3-1	2-2	1-0	2-2	2-2	0-1	

Division One	P	W	D	L	F	A	Pts
Aberbargoed Buds	28	21	4	3	92	39	67
Blaenavon Blues	28	19	7	2	97	37	64
Mardy	28	20	3	5	85	45	63
Abercarn United	28	18	2	8	60	50	56
Spencer Youth & Boys	28	15	2	11	68	48	47
West Pontnewydd	28	12	6	10	53	47	42
Cwmffrwdoer Sports	28	11	5	12	72	60	38
Undy Athletic	28	10	2	16	52	74	32
Albion Rovers	28	8	8	12	49	85	32
Clydach Wasps	28	7	9	12	53	61	30
Panteg	28	8	6	14	43	55	30
Coed Eva Athletic	28	8	4	16	62	82	28
Trinant	28	7	5	16	51	72	26
Newport Corinthians	28	6	6	16	46	63	24
RTB Ebbw Vale	28	2	7	19	28	93	13

LEAGUE CUP

FIRST ROUND

AC Pontymister 2 **Rogerstone Welfare** 4
Abergavenny Thursdays 0 **Coed Eva Athletic** 1
Abertillery 1 **Spencer Youth & Boys** 5
Abertillery Bluebirds 12 Lucus Cwmbran 4
Blaenavon Blues 4 Lliswerry 1
Caldicot Castle 4 Mardy 2
Clydach Wasps 4 Tranch 1
Ebbw Vale Town 0 **Panteg** 1
Garnlydarn Athletic 2 **Undy Athletic** 4
Llanhilleth Athletic 3 Cwmffrwdoer Sports 2
Pentwynmawr Athletic 1 **Newport Civil Service** 5
PILCS 2 RTB Ebbw Vale 0
Trethomas Bluebirds 0 **Aberbargoed Buds** 1

SECOND ROUND

Aberbargoed Buds 0 **Clydach Wasps** 1
Abercarn United 0 **Newport Corinthians** 2
Abertillery Bluebirds 3 Monmouth Town 1
Albion Rovers 1 **Coed Eva Athletic** 2
Cefn Fforest 4 Blaenavon Blues 2
Christchurch Hamdden 1 **Caldicot Castle** 3
Crusaders 2 **Undy Athletic** 3
Crickhowell 4 Cromwell Youth 3
FC Dugout (scr.) v **Trinant** (w/o)

GWENT COUNTY LEAGUE DIVISION ONE CONSTITUTION 2006-07

ABERCARN UNITED .... Welfare Ground, Abercarn 01495 243047
ALBION ROVERS .... Kimberley Park, Malpas Road, Newport .... None
BLAENAVON BLUES .... Recreation Ground, Blaenavon, Pontypool .... None
CLYDACH WASPS .... Recreation Ground, Clydach .... None
COED EVA ATHLETIC .... Cwmbran Park, Wesley Street, Cwmbran NP44 3LX 01633 485491
CWMFFRWDOER SPORTS .... Cwmffrwdoer Sports Ground, Gwenhalt Industrial Estate, Cwmffrwdoer .... None
MARDY .... Mardy Playing Field, Mardy .... None
MONMOUTH TOWN .... Sports Ground, Monmouth 01600 772389
NEWPORT CIVIL SERVICE .... Civil Service Sports Ground, Shannon Road, Bettws NP20 7LX 01633 855576
PANTEG .... Panteg House, Greenhill Road, Griffithstown NP4 5BE 01495 763605
SPENCER YOUTH & BOYS .... Ringland Park, Newport NP18 2TA .... None
TREOWEN STARS .... Bush Park, Newbridge 01495 248249
TRINANT .... Trinant Recreation, Trinant, Caerphilly .... None
UNDY ATHLETIC .... Undy Playing Fields, Undy, Caldicot NP26 3EN 01633 881352
WEST PONTNEWYDD .... The Birches, West Pontynewydd, Pontypool .... None

IN: Monmouth Town (P), Newport Civil Service (P), Treowen Stars (R – Welsh League Division Three)
OUT: Aberbargoed Buds (P – Welsh League Division Three), Newport Corinthians (R), RTB Ebbw Vale (R)

	Abertillery	Abertillery Bluebirds	Cefn Fforest	Christchurch Hamdden	Cromwell Youth	Garnlydan Athletic	Llanhilleth Athletic	Lliswerry	Lucas Cwmbran	Monmouth Town	Newport Civil Service	Pentwynmawr Athletic	Race	Rogerstone Athletic	Tranch
Abertillery		1-2	2-1	3-2	0-2	6-2	2-2	1-1	1-3	2-3	2-4	0-4	6-0	0-1	4-1
Abertillery Bluebirds	1-2	*D*	1-0	5-0	2-2	3-2	2-3	4-0	3-2	2-4	1-2	4-2	1-1	3-0	3-2
Cefn Fforest	5-1	1-2	*I*	3-0	1-1	2-2	0-6	2-1	4-2	1-4	3-5	3-1	4-4	0-2	3-4
Christchurch Hamdden	3-1	0-1	1-4	*V*	1-1	5M0	1-4	0-3	0-4	0-3	0M5	3-6	1-2	4-1	2-2
Cromwell Youth	2-1	0-2	1-3	3-0	*I*	8-3	2-3	1-1	3-3	0-1	4-2	6-1	3-2	2-0	3-1
Garnlydan Athletic	4-3	0-7	0-1	4-2	2-4	*S*	2-9	2-4	3-0	3-2	0-1	3-8	1-2	2-5	3-4
Llanhilleth Athletic	5-0	3-1	1-1	4-0	2-0	6-1	*I*	2-2	0-1	1-1	3-0	0-2	1-1	3-2	1-1
Lliswerry	1-1	0-1	0-0	2-1	0-3	0-2	0-2	*O*	5-1	1-1	1-1	2-1	2-2	3-1	4-3
Lucas Cwmbran	2-2	2-2	1-2	5M0	1-3	4-2	2-2	2-3	*N*	1-4	2-1	2-1	2-2	1-1	2-1
Monmouth Town	11-0	2-1	3-4	5-0	2-1	6-2	4-1	0-2	1-2		1-0	6-2	5-1	2-1	4-1
Newport Civil Service	1-3	3-2	2-1	2-0	1-0	6-1	2-2	2-0	4-2	3-1		5-0	2-0	2-0	5-0
Pentwynmawr Athletic	5-0	1-6	1-2	3-1	2-5	6-2	0-2	0-1	1-1	1-8	3-2	*T*	3-6	1-1	1-3
Race	5-0	3-4	2-1	3-1	2-2	3-2	3-3	1-2	1-2	2-3	2-1	0-1	*W*	2-3	3-2
Rogerstone Welfare	6-0	4-0	2-0	4-2	0-2	1-4	1-1	0-1	2-0	1-2	1-4	2-3	3-2	*O*	2-1
Tranch	5-1	3-4	3-1	5-4	1-2	6-2	4-1	1-1	1-1	3-1	0-4	3-3	6-3	4-0	

Fairfield 0 **Spencer Youth & Boys** 1
PILCS 0 **Sebastopol** 1
Race 3 Panteg 2
Rogerstone Welfare 3 Newport Civil Service 2
Sudbrook Cricket Club 5 **New Inn** 6
West Pontnewydd 5 Thornwell Red & White 2
Whiteheads 3 **Llanhilleth Athletic** 6

THIRD ROUND

Abertillery Bluebirds 4 Rogerstone Welfare 0
Crickhowell 1 **Coed Eva Athletic** 3
Llanhilleth Athletic 4 Cefn Fforest 1
New Inn 1 **West Pontnewydd** 4
Newport Corinthians 0 **Spencer Youth & Boys** 5
Race 1 Caldicot Castle 0
Sebastopol 3 **Trinant** 4
Undy Athletic 4 **Clydach Wasps** 6

QUARTER-FINALS

Abertillery Bluebirds 1 **Spencer Youth & Boys** 2 *aet*
Llanhilleth Athletic 7 Clydach Wasps 0
Race 1 **Coed Eva Athletic** 3
Trinant 1 **West Pontnewydd** 2

SEMI-FINALS

Coed Eva Athletic 2 Spencer Youth & Boys 1
(at Sudbrook Cricket Club)
Llanhilleth Athletic 1 West Pontnewydd 0 *(at Undy Athletic)*

FINAL

(May 12th at Abergavenny Thursdays)
Coed Eva Athletic 3 Llanhilleth Athletic 1

Division Two	P	W	D	L	F	A	Pts
Monmouth Town	28	20	2	6	90	39	62
Newport Civil Service	28	19	2	7	72	35	59
Abertillery Bluebirds	28	17	3	8	70	45	54
Llanhilleth Athletic	28	14	10	4	73	38	52
Cromwell Youth	28	15	6	7	66	40	51
Lliswerry	28	12	9	7	43	38	45
Tranch	28	11	5	12	71	68	38
Cefn Fforest	28	11	5	12	53	55	38
Lucas Cwmbran	28	10	8	10	53	55	38
Rogerstone Welfare	28	11	3	14	47	51	36
Race	28	9	7	12	60	67	34
Pentwynmawr Athletic	28	10	3	15	63	79	33
Abertillery	28	7	4	17	45	84	25
Garnlydan Athletic	28	6	1	21	56	114	19
Christchurch Hamdden	28	3	2	23	34	88	11

GWENT COUNTY LEAGUE DIVISION TWO CONSTITUTION 2006-07

ABERTILLERY .... Woodland Field, Cwmtillery, Abertillery NP13 1LA 01495 215676
ABERTILLERY BLUEBIRDS .... Cwmnantygroes Field, Six Bells, Abertillery NP13 2PR 01495 213999
CEFN FFOREST .... Welfare Ground, Cefn Forest .... None
CROMWELL YOUTH .... Hartridge Comprehensive School, Ringland Way, Newport NP18 2TA .... None
FC DUGOUT .... Hilltop Stadium, Darby Crescent, Hilltop, Ebbw Vale NP23 6QG 01495 302071
LLANHILLETH ATHLETIC .... Llanhilleth Park, Llanhilleth 01495 217840
LLISWERRY .... Spytty Park, Newport NP9 0RH 01633 281087
LUCAS CWMBRAN .... Lucas Sports Ground, Cwmbran 01633 861624
NEWPORT CORINTHIANS .... Coronation Park, Newport 01633 274717
PENTWYNMAWR ATHLETIC .... Welfare Ground, Pentwynmawr, Newbridge 01495 243403
RTB EBBW VALE .... Eugene Cross Park, Pontygof, Ebbw Vale NP23 5AZ 01495 302995
RACE .... Pontypool College, Pontypool 01495 763656
ROGERSTONE WELFARE .... Welfare Ground, Rogerstone, Newport .... None
TRANCH .... Tranch Playing Fields, Tranch .... None
TRETHOMAS BLUEBIRDS .... Llanfabon Drive, Trethomas, Caerphilly CF83 8GJ .... None

***IN:** FC Dugout (P), Newport Corinthians (R), RTB Ebbw Vale (R), Trethomas Bluebirds (P)*
***OUT:** Christchurch Hamdden (R), Garnlydan Athletic (R), Monmouth Town (P), Newport Civil Service (P)*

	AC Pontymister	Abergavenny Thursdays	Caldicot Castle	Crickhowell	Crusaders	Ebbw Vale Town	FC Dugout	Fairfield United	New Inn	PILCS	Sebastopol	Sudbrook Cricket Club	Thornwell Red & White	Trethomas Bluebirds	Whiteheads
AC Pontymister	*D*	3-2	2-3	2-2	3-0	5-0	1-3	2-2	4-2	4-3	3-1	2-6	4-0	0-4	0-0
Abergavenny Thursdays	3-1	*I*	0-2	1-0	0-4	3-1	1-4	0-0	3-1	3-3	1-7	4-2	0-3	1-2	1-1
Caldicot Castle	4-4	0-1	*V*	1-2	5-1	3-1	1-4	2-2	0-0	5-0	1-2	1-0	3-1	5-1	2-0
Crickhowell	1-0	4-1	1-3	*I*	2-1	0-1	1-2	0-1	0-2	2-4	1-0	0-3	2-0	2-2	4-1
Crusaders	0-3	2-1	0-0	0-1	*S*	1-1	1-2	1-1	2-1	0-1	1-1	0-3	2-2	2-5	6-0
Ebbw Vale Town	1-1	1-2	0-2	1-3	1-2	*I*	0-4	0-3	1-2	0-2	1-7	2-4	0-2	1-7	1-2
FC Dugout	4-2	4-1	3-3	1-0	1-0	4-2	*O*	1-1	5M0	4-0	4-4	0-2	1-1	2-2	4-3
Fairfield United	0-0	5-2	3-1	1-0	4-1	0-4	1-3	*N*	1-2	0-0	1-3	2-2	3-1	4-4	1-2
New Inn	4-3	1-6	0-1	1-1	2-0	2-1	1-3	2-1		1-0	4-1	3-2	2-0	3-2	2-3
PILCS	3-1	6-3	1-3	4-1	0-2	2-0	0-3	1-2	3-0		2-1	1-2	2-4	3-1	2-3
Sebastopol	0-4	0-1	2-3	5-3	2-1	5-0	1-1	4-0	2-2	0-4	*T*	0-1	5-1	2-3	7-2
Sudbrook Cricket Club	3-2	4-1	2-2	2-1	2-0	4-1	2-2	1-0	4-0	5-1	1-3	*H*	3-2	1-0	4-2
Thornwell Red & White	0-3	0-2	0-4	2-7	3-3	0-1	2-5	2-3	0-2	0-4	4-3	4-2	*R*	2-5	2-2
Trethomas Bluebirds	1-4	3-1	5-2	8-1	5-1	4-0	2-0	1-0	2-0	3-2	6-3	4-2	3-2	*E*	11-0
Whiteheads	0-6	0-4	0-2	3-1	3-2	2-1	3-2	3-3	2-3	2-5	2-1	1-2	4-2	2-8	*E*

Division Three	P	W	D	L	F	A	Pts
Trethomas Bluebirds	28	20	3	5	104	48	63
FC Dugout	28	18	7	3	76	38	61
Sudbrook Cricket Club	28	19	3	6	71	41	60
Caldicot Castle	28	16	6	6	64	38	54
New Inn	28	14	3	11	45	53	45
AC Pontymister	28	12	6	10	69	52	42
PILCS	28	13	2	13	59	55	41
Sebastopol	28	11	4	13	72	58	37
Fairfield United	28	9	10	9	45	45	37
Abergavenny Thursdays	28	11	3	14	49	64	36
Whiteheads	28	10	4	14	48	89	34
Crickhowell	28	10	3	15	43	53	33
Crusaders	28	6	6	16	36	55	24
Thornwell Red & White	28	5	4	19	42	80	19
Ebbw Vale Town	28	3	2	23	24	78	11

GWENT COUNTY LEAGUE DIVISION THREE CONSTITUTION 2006-07

AC PONTYMISTER .... Pontymister Recreation Ground, Pontymister, Caerphilly NP11 6LT .... None
ABERGAVENNY THURSDAYS .... Penypound Stadium, Abergavenny 01873 853906
CALDICOT CASTLE .... Caldicot Castle Grounds, Caldicot NP26 4HU 01291 431584
CHRISTCHURCH HAMDDEN .... Glebelands Sports Stadium, Bank Street, Newport NP19 7HF .... None
CRICKHOWELL .... Elvicta Estate, Brecon Road, Crickhowell .... None
CRUSADERS .... Fields Park, Newbridge, Newport NP11 3NQ .... None
FAIRFIELD UNITED .... Garndiffaith Ravine, Pontypool 01495 773745
GARNLYDAN ATHLETIC .... Recreation Ground, Garnlydan, Ebbw Vale 01495 306952
MALPAS GLADIATOR .... Westfield, Darwin Drive, Malpas .... None
NEW INN .... Woodfield Road Arena, New Inn, Pontypool NP4 0PS 01495 755169
PILCS .... PILCS Sports & Social Club, New Road, Griffithstown, Pontypool NP4 0TL 01495 762039
SEBASTOPOL .... The Ruffetts, Pontnewynydd, Sebastopol, Pontypool 01495 763719
SUDBROOK CRICKET CLUB .... Deepweir, Caldicot NP26 5JG .... None
THORNWELL RED & WHITE .... Thornwell Park, Chepstow .... None
UNDERWOOD SPORTS & SOCIAL .... Larch Grove, Newport NP20 6JB .... None
WHITEHEADS .... Whiteheads Sports Ground, Park View, Bassaleg NP10 8LA 01633 893227

***IN:** Christchurch Hamdden (R), Garnlydan Athletic (R), Malpas Gladiator (Newport & District League Premier Division X), Underwood Sports & Social (East Gwent League Division One)*

***OUT:** FC Dugout (P), Ebbw Vale Town (R – North Gwent League Premier Division), Trethomas Bluebirds (P)*

HAMPSHIRE LEAGUE

	AFC Wolversdene Irons	Broughton	Durley	East Lodge	Fair Oak	Hamble Club Res.	Ludgershall Sports	Ludwig Leisure Basingstoke	Lyndhurst STJs	M & T Awbridge	Mottisfont	Netley Central Sports Res.	QK Southampton Res.	Sporting BTC	Stockbridge Res.	Upham	Winchester City 'A'
AFC Wolversdene Irons		3-0	1-1	0-1	2-0	4-1	1-3	3-1	0-3	1-4	1-2	1-2	5-0	2-3	2-3	1-2	1-4
Broughton	0-2		1-4	2-3	3-4	8-0	4-1	0-3	1-2	0-5	2-5	3-3	3-1	2-1	1-2	1-5	3-0
Durley	4-1	2-1		2-3	2-1	9-0	0-3	2-1	4-3	2-1	2-2	1-1	6-0	2-1	2-1	2-0	4-2
East Lodge	2-1	3-0	3-3		5-2	10-0	3-2	0-0	3-2	2-0	0-1	1-2	8-1	2-5	8-0	0-2	4-0
Fair Oak	2-1	2-5	1-3	1-2		0-3	3-5	2-6	2-1	1-4	0-4	5-2	0-3	0-1	2-1	1-2	2-3
Hamble Club Res.	2-2	0-7	0-8	2-1	0-2		0-5	1-1	0-5	1-7	1-8	2-2	0-1	0-3	3-1	2-6	0-6
Ludgershall Sports	3-1	1-0	1-2	1-0	3-2	9-0		1-3	0-0	2-3	0-7	3-1	7-0	0-6	3-2	1-1	1-1
Ludwig Leisure Basingstoke	3-1	2-2	2-3	1-1	1-0	9-0	4-0		3-1	2-3	1-4	2-1	6-1	2-1	2-1	2-2	4-2
Lyndhurst STJs	3-1	2-1	2-1	3-3	0-2	3-1	4-2	2-0		3-0	1-1	0-5	5-2	1-1	2-1	2-2	2-2
M & T Awbridge	2-2	0-2	0-5	0-2	4-2	6-0	2-2	2-2	1-3		0-4	2-0	4-0	0-0	2-3	2-3	0-3
Mottisfont	5-0	5-1	1-0	2-0	3-0	4-0	5-1	3-2	1-1	0-0		6-0	6-0	2-2	3-3	1-1	2-0
Netley Central Sports Res.	W-L	3-3	0-6	2-2	4-1	4-1	3-1	2-2	1-1	2-0	0-2		4-1	5-3	2-5	3-2	3-3
QK Southampton Res.	3-1	2-4	2-3	0-1	2-2	1-3	1-1	0-1	1-5	0-1	0-9	3-7		0-6	0-3	0-16	1-8
Sporting BTC	3-0	4-0	6-1	1-3	3-1	12-0	1-1	4-1	2-1	1-0	1-1	1-0	0-2		2-1	0-3	6-1
Stockbridge Res.	2-4	4-1	3-4	1-5	3-0	4-3	1-1	2-4	0-3	1-1	0-4	1-4	10-0	2-2		1-3	0-5
Upham	5-0	7-2	3-1	5-1	0-0	6-2	3-1	6-0	2-3	5-2	0-4	5-2	5-0	2-1	1-0		6-3
Winchester City 'A'	1-2	3-0	1-2	0-2	1-3	11-0	3-4	4-1	0-2	1-1	0-6	2-1	2-0	0-1	0-2	2-2	

	P	W	D	L	F	A	Pts
Mottisfont	32	24	8	0	113	20	80
Upham	32	22	6	4	113	43	72
Durley	32	22	4	6	93	48	70
East Lodge	32	19	5	8	84	44	62
Sporting BTC	32	18	6	8	84	38	60
Lyndhurst STJs	32	17	8	7	71	46	59
Ludwig Leisure Basingstoke	32	15	7	10	74	57	52
Netley Central Sports Res.	32	13	8	11	71	71	47
Ludgershall Sports	32	13	7	12	69	67	46
M & T Awbridge	32	11	7	14	59	57	40
Winchester City 'A'	32	11	5	16	74	68	38
Stockbridge Res.	32	10	4	18	64	79	34
Broughton	32	9	3	20	63	84	30
AFC Wolversdene Irons	32	8	3	21	47	70	27
Fair Oak	32	8	2	22	46	82	26
Hamble Club Res.	32	4	3	25	28	165	15
QK Southampton Res.	32	4	2	26	28	142	14

LEAGUE CUP

FIRST ROUND

Durley 7 Broughton 1

SECOND ROUND

AFC Wolversdene Irons 2 Netley Central Sports Res. 2 *aet* (3-2p)
Ludwig Leisure Basingstoke (w/o) v Fair Oak (scr.)
Lyndhurst STJs 2 Upham 1
M & T Awbridge 12 Hamble Club Res. 0
QK Southampton Res. 0 **Mottisfont** 6
Sporting BTC 3 East Lodge 0
Stockbridge Res. 0 **Durley** 5
Winchester City 'A' 4 Ludgershall Sports 3

QUARTER-FINALS

Durley 1 **Sporting BTC** 1 *aet* (3-5p)
M & T Awbridge 3 Ludwig Leisure Basingstoke 1
Mottisfont 1 Lyndhurst STJs 0
Winchester City 'A' 0 **AFC Wolversdene Irons** 4

SEMI-FINALS

M & T Awbridge 0 **Sporting BTC** 1
Mottisfont 3 AFC Wolversdene Irons 0

FINAL

(May 3rd at Hamble ASSC)
Sporting BTC 1 **Mottisfont** 2

HAMPSHIRE LEAGUE CONSTITUTION 2006-07

AFC WOLVERSDENE IRONS .... Charlton Sports & Leisure Centre, West Portway, Andover SP10 3LF.......... None
BROUGHTON.......... The Sportsfield, Buckholt Road, Broughton, Stockbridge SO20 8DA 01794 301150
DURLEY .... Kytes Lane, Durley, Southampton SO32 2AE .... None
EAST LODGE.......... Langstone Harbour Sports Ground, Eastern Road, Portsmouth.......... 023 9282 4798
FAIR OAK .... Lapstone Park, Pavilion Close, Botley Road, Fair Oak .... None
FOUR MARKS .... The Recreation Ground, Upland Lane, Four Marks .... None
LUDGERSHALL SPORTS .... Astor Crescent, Ludgershall, Andover SP11 9RG 01264 398200
LUDWIG LEISURE BASINGSTOKE .. Basingstoke Cricket Club, Mays Bounty, Fairfields, Basingstoke RG21 3DR .... None
LYNDHURST STJS .... Wellands Road, Lyndhurst SO43 7AD .... None
MICHELMERSH & TIMSBURY.. Michelmersh & Timsbury Sports Pavilion, Mannyngham Way, Timsbury, Romsey SO51 0NJ .. 01794 368955
MOTTISFONT .... Bengers Lane, Mottisfont.......... None
NETLEY CENTRAL SPORTS .. Netley Recreation Ground, Station Road, Netley Abbey, Southampton SO21 5AH.......... 023 8045 2267
OVER WALLOP .... Over Wallop Playing Field, Salisbury Lane, Over Wallop, Stockbridge SO20 8JJ .... None
SPORTING BTC.......... Hardmoor, Stoneham Lane, Eastleigh 02380 617574
UPHAM .... Worthies Sports & Social, Lovedon Lane, Kings Worthy, Winchester SO23 7NJ 01962 880457
WINCHESTER CASTLE.......... Hampshire Cricket Ground, Petersfield Road, Winchester.......... None

IN: Four Marks (P – Aldershot & District League Senior Division), Netley Central Sports (R – Wessex League Division Three)
OUT: Hamble Club Reserves (S – Southampton League Combination), Netley Central Sports Reserves (S – Southampton League Combination), QK Southampton Reserves (S – Southampton League Combination)
M & T Awbridge become Michelmersh & Timsbury, Stockbridge Reserves merge with Over Wallop (Andover & District League Division Two) to become Over Wallop, Winchester City 'A' become Winchester Castle

HELLENIC LEAGUE

Note – Tuffley Rovers withdrew during the course of the season Their results are shown herein but are expunged from the league table	Abingdon Town	Abingdon Utd	Almondsbury	Ardley United	Bishops Cleeve	Carterton	Chipping Nort.	Didcot Town	Fairford Town	Henley Town	Highworth Tn	Hungerford Tn	Kidlington	Milton United	North Leigh	Pegasus Juniors	Shortwood Utd	Shrivenham	Slimbridge	Tuffley Rovers	Wantage Town	Witney United
Abingdon Town		0-5	0-2	0-3	1-3	1-3	1-0	1-2	4-2	1-1	0-0	1-0	1-0	2-2	1-3	1-1	2-2	1-2	2-2	n/a	0-0	1-6
Abingdon United	1-0		0-1	2-3	1-2	1-0	0-2	1-3	3-1	4-0	5-1	0-0	3-0	0-2	1-1	3-1	2-0	4-1	2-1	n/a	3-1	1-0
Almondsbury Town	1-1	2-4		0-1	0-1	0-1	4-4	1-0	3-0	2-1	1-2	0-1	3-1	0-0	1-1	3-3	0-3	2-0	0-1	n/a	3-1	1-3
Ardley United	6-3	2-2	2-0	*P*	1-2	0-2	5-1	3-5	1-1	3-0	2-2	2-3	3-0	0-0	1-0	1-0	0-1	1-4	2-0	n/a	1-2	0-1
Bishops Cleeve	7-0	1-5	2-0	4-2	*R*	3-2	5-1	1-1	3-0	3-0	4-1	5-0	1-0	6-2	3-1	3-0	3-0	1-2	1-4	n/a	3-2	2-2
Carterton	3-0	0-1	4-2	2-1	2-1	*E*	3-0	2-1	2-0	2-1	2-1	4-1	3-2	0-2	0-3	0-1	4-0	2-2	0-5	n/a	0-1	0-2
Chipping Norton Town	0-3	2-3	0-2	0-2	2-8	1-6	*M*	0-3	2-2	2-1	0-1	3-1	2-0	5-1	0-3	1-1	0-2	1-1	1-4	n/a	1-1	0-2
Didcot Town	4-0	3-1	4-0	4-1	1-1	3-1	3-0	*I*	5-0	4-0	0-0	3-0	3-2	6-1	1-0	7-0	5-3	3-0	2-0	n/a	5-1	4-0
Fairford Town	3-1	1-0	2-3	1-2	1-5	2-0	2-1	0-1	*E*	0-1	0-0	0-1	2-1	0-2	0-3	3-1	0-2	1-2	2-1	n/a	2-2	0-2
Henley Town	0-3	0-3	1-2	0-4	1-5	0-2	0-0	0-2	0-2	*R*	2-1	0-1	5-1	1-4	1-3	1-1	1-4	0-1	0-2	n/a	0-4	2-3
Highworth Town	4-2	1-3	1-1	1-1	1-2	1-4	1-1	1-3	2-1	4-0		2-1	6-0	2-1	1-1	0-4	7-0	1-4	2-2	n/a	0-4	1-2
Hungerford Town	0-0	0-1	2-1	1-3	1-1	1-2	3-1	1-2	0-0	2-2	1-0	*D*	1-0	0-0	0-1	1-1	2-0	0-2	2-0	n/a	3-1	0-4
Kidlington	0-1	0-3	0-1	1-3	3-1	0-1	3-0	2-4	3-1	2-0	2-3	0-0	*I*	0-4	0-4	2-1	0-4	1-5	0-6	n/a	1-3	2-1
Milton United	0-1	1-3	1-0	2-3	1-2	1-1	2-1	1-3	6-2	2-0	0-3	3-0	1-4	*V*	1-2	3-5	0-0	4-1	1-1	0-0	2-3	0-3
North Leigh	3-2	2-0	4-1	1-0	1-2	2-2	2-0	0-4	3-0	2-1	1-0	3-0	4-2	0-1	*I*	5-0	2-0	1-3	0-4	n/a	2-0	1-1
Pegasus Juniors	1-1	0-2	2-1	4-1	1-3	0-3	3-1	2-3	2-1	0-1	3-1	2-0	4-1	0-0	0-1	*S*	1-1	2-1	1-1	n/a	3-2	1-1
Shortwood United	1-0	0-2	3-1	1-1	0-4	1-5	2-4	0-4	2-2	0-1	2-3	1-0	4-0	1-2	1-3	5-0	*I*	0-0	0-2	n/a	1-2	3-5
Shrivenham	7-0	0-5	2-1	5-0	1-2	3-0	3-1	0-4	0-3	5-1	0-1	3-1	4-1	3-1	1-3	3-0	2-0	*O*	2-0	n/a	2-2	0-0
Slimbridge	4-1	0-2	3-1	3-1	1-0	1-0	6-2	1-3	1-0	6-1	1-0	3-0	8-3	1-1	1-1	3-0	2-1	1-0	*N*	n/a	3-4	3-1
Tuffley Rovers	n/a	n/a	n/a	3-4	n/a	n/a	n/a	n/a	n/a	n/a	n/a	n/a	n/a	n/a	n/a	n/a	0-1	n/a	n/a		n/a	n/a
Wantage Town	3-2	1-5	0-2	1-2	0-0	2-1	1-0	1-0	0-1	3-0	2-2	3-0	2-1	4-3	3-2	1-1	2-3	2-4	3-1	n/a		3-1
Witney United	1-3	4-1	2-1	1-0	0-2	1-2	3-0	2-6	0-1	7-1	7-1	5-0	2-1	0-1	0-3	2-0	3-1	4-1	0-1	n/a	4-0	

Premier Division	P	W	D	L	F	A	Pts
Didcot Town	40	34	3	3	124	31	105
Bishops Cleeve	40	29	5	6	108	45	92
Abingdon United	40	27	3	10	88	40	84
North Leigh	40	25	6	9	78	40	81
Slimbridge	40	24	6	10	90	45	78
Witney United	40	23	4	13	88	51	73
Carterton	40	23	3	14	73	51	72
Shrivenham	40	22	5	13	82	58	71
Wantage Town	40	19	7	14	73	70	64
Ardley United	40	18	6	16	70	63	60
Milton United	40	14	9	17	62	69	51
Highworth Town	40	13	10	17	62	72	49
Pegasus Juniors	40	12	11	17	53	74	47
Almondsbury Town	40	13	6	21	50	64	45
Shortwood United	40	12	6	22	55	79	42
Hungerford Town	40	11	8	21	31	65	41
Fairford Town	40	11	6	23	42	73	39
Abingdon Town	40	9	10	21	45	88	37
Chipping Norton Town	40	6	7	27	43	99	25
Kidlington	40	7	1	32	42	108	22
Henley Town	40	5	4	31	28	102	19

Tuffley Rovers – record expunged

Reserve Division One		P	W	D	L	F	A	Pts
Didcot Town Res.		32	25	3	4	106	37	78
Henley Town Res.		32	17	7	8	61	52	58
Finchampstead Res.		32	17	5	10	74	56	56
Badshot Lea Res.		32	15	6	11	75	71	51
Abingdon United Res.		32	14	8	10	66	52	50
Hungerford Town Res.		32	14	6	12	58	56	48
Wantage Town Res.		32	13	8	11	58	63	47
Kidlington Res.		32	13	7	12	60	52	46
Carterton Res.		32	13	5	14	60	65	44
Fairford Town Res.	*-1*	32	13	4	15	52	62	42
North Leigh Res.		32	10	10	12	63	57	40
Binfield Res.		32	11	6	15	59	56	39
Cheltenham Saracens Res.		32	12	3	17	43	60	39
Wootton Bassett Town Res.		32	11	4	17	53	60	37
Milton United Res.		32	10	5	17	52	74	35
Highworth Town Res.		32	8	7	17	62	91	31
Headington Amateurs Res.		32	6	6	20	40	78	24

HELLENIC LEAGUE PREMIER DIVISION CONSTITUTION 2006-07

AFC WALLINGFORD........... Wallingford Sports Park, Hithercroft Road, Wallingford OX10 9RB 01491 835044
ABINGDON TOWN .... Culham Road, Abingdon OX14 3HP.. 01235 521684
ALMONDSBURY TOWN .... Oakland Park, Gloucester Road, Almondsbury, Bristol BS32 4AG 01454 612220
ARDLEY UNITED .... The Playing Field, Fritwell Road, Ardley, Bicester OX27 7NS 01869 345597
BICESTER TOWN.................................. Sports Ground, Oxford Road, Bicester OX26 2AD 01869 241036
CARTERTON .... Kilkenny Lane, Swinbrook Road, Carterton OX18 1DP................................ 01993 842410
CHIPPING NORTON TOWN .... Walterbush Road, Chipping Norton OX7 5DP.. 01608 645311
FAIRFORD TOWN .... Cinder Lane, London Road, Fairford GL7 4AX 01285 712071
HARROW HILL .... Larksfield Road, Harrow Hill, Drybrook GL17 9JP 01594 543873
HIGHWORTH TOWN .... The Elms Recreation Ground, Highworth, Swindon SN6 7HU 01793 766263
HOUNSLOW BOROUGH ...... Ruislip Manor FC, Grosvenor Vale, off West End Road, Ruislip HA4 6JQ 01895 676168/6374
HUNGERFORD TOWN .... War Memorial Ground, Bulpit Lane, Hungerford RG17 0AY 01488 682939
KIDLINGTON .... Yarnton Road, Kidlington OX5 1AT.. 01865 841526
MILTON UNITED.............. The Sports Field, Potash Lane, Milton Heights, Abingdon OX13 6AG........................ 01235 832999
NORTH LEIGH .... Eynsham Park, Woodstock Road, North Leigh, Witney OX8 6PW 01993 881427
PEGASUS JUNIORS............... Hereford Leisure Centre, Holmer Road, Hereford HR4 9UD...................................... 01432 278178
SHORTWOOD UNITED .... Meadowbank, Shortwood, Nailsworth, Stroud GL6 0SJ............................... 01453 833936
SHRIVENHAM.......................... Recreation Ground, Highworth Road, Shrivenham, Swindon SN6 8BJ.......................... 01793 784453
SLIMBRIDGE.. Wisloe Road, Cambridge GL2 7AF 01453 890361
THAME UNITED .... AFC Wallingford, Wallingford Sports Park, Hithercroft Road, Wallingford OX10 9RB 01491 835044
WANTAGE TOWN............................. Alfredian Park, Manor Road, Wantage OX12 8DW 01235 764781
WITNEY UNITED.......................... Marriotts Stadium, Downs Road, Culbridge, Witney OX29 7WT............................ 01993 848558

***IN:** AFC Wallingford (P – Combined Counties League Division One), Bicester Town (P – Division One East), Harrow Hill (P – Division One West), Hounslow Borough (P – Division One East), Thame United (R – Southern League Division One West)*

***OUT:** Abingdon United (P – Southern League Division One South & West), Bishops Cleeve (P – Southern League Division One Midlands), Didcot Town (P – Southern League Division One South & West), Henley Town (R – Division One East), Tuffley Rovers (WS)*

	Badshot Lea	Banbury United Res.	Bicester Town	Binfield	Bisley Sports	Chalfont Wasps	Chinnor	Englefield Green Rovers	Eton Wick	Finchampstead	Holyport	Hounslow Borough	Kintbury Rangers	Oxford Quarry Nomads	Penn & Tylers Green	Prestwood	Rayners Lane	Wokingham & Emmbrook
Badshot Lea	*D*	1-2	3-1	1-5	4-2	2-2	3-0	0-4	7-1	1-1	1-1	2-4	2-5	1-3	2-3	5-2	1-4	2-2
Banbury United Res.	1-5	*I*	1-2	1-4	0-7	1-2	2-2	2-5	0-2	2-2	4-2	1-2	1-1	2-1	0-1	1-1	0-2	0-2
Bicester Town	0-0	4-1	*V*	0-3	1-2	2-2	3-2	0-0	3-3	1-1	6-1	1-0	1-0	2-0	5-2	6-0	3-2	3-3
Binfield	2-4	6-0	0-1	*I*	1-1	0-1	3-0	2-1	0-0	5-4	2-3	0-4	0-1	2-0	2-1	3-0	2-1	0-1
Bisley Sports	2-0	4-1	2-3	2-0	*S*	0-1	2-0	2-1	7-2	1-1	3-2	0-3	4-3	4-0	4-4	8-0	3-1	1-2
Chalfont Wasps	0-2	5-0	3-1	2-1	2-0	*I*	7-0	2-3	3-0	4-1	5-4	4-1	1-0	1-3	0-0	2-1	3-4	1-2
Chinnor	1-5	3-0	0-2	0-4	1-4	0-3	*O*	0-4	2-4	1-2	0-0	1-4	1-3	3-0	0-2	2-0	4-2	2-5
Englefield Green Rovers	3-1	5-1	1-1	1-2	1-2	2-1	1-0	*N*	3-0	1-0	2-0	1-1	1-2	4-1	2-1	4-2	7-1	0-1
Eton Wick	3-1	2-0	1-3	3-2	1-1	4-3	0-0	0-1		2-1	5-0	0-2	2-5	6-0	0-3	1-1	5-0	4-0
Finchampstead	0-0	5-1	1-3	0-1	3-0	1-2	1-0	0-1	2-3	*O*	3-2	0-0	0-2	3-4	0-4	6-0	3-2	0-2
Holyport	0-6	4-1	1-3	1-3	4-2	0-2	0-0	1-3	2-3	4-1	*N*	3-2	1-6	3-1	0-1	2-1	2-2	2-5
Hounslow Borough	9-3	6-0	0-0	3-2	1-2	3-1	3-3	7-1	2-0	6-4	2-1	*E*	2-1	3-1	3-2	5-0	2-1	4-2
Kintbury Rangers	1-2	2-0	0-1	0-2	0-0	2-7	4-1	4-0	4-1	1-0	5-2	1-0		1-2	2-1	9-0	7-0	3-3
Oxford Quarry Nomads	4-3	6-0	0-5	3-1	3-2	1-2	3-0	1-1	4-0	1-1	1-5	1-0	2-2	*(E*	0-1	5-0	5-1	1-4
Penn & Tylers Green	4-3	4-0	0-4	0-3	3-0	3-1	1-0	3-1	0-3	2-1	2-1	1-5	3-0	4-0	*A*	7-1	2-0	0-1
Prestwood	0-5	1-2	0-6	0-3	1-4	0-2	2-5	0-6	1-4	0-5	0-2	1-3	1-2	3-3	0-0	*S*	1-6	0-5
Rayners Lane	1-0	2-0	0-1	1-3	1-2	3-1	1-0	5-0	1-5	1-2	0-2	1-6	2-1	3-6	1-3	2-3	*T)*	2-0
Wokingham & Emmbrook	1-3	5-1	1-0	3-1	0-1	2-2	2-0	0-2	0-3	0-3	7-0	3-1	2-1	8-1	1-1	6-1	5-1	

Division One (East)	P	W	D	L	F	A	Pts
Hounslow Borough	**34**	**23**	**4**	**7**	**99**	**45**	**73**
Bicester Town	**34**	**21**	**8**	**5**	**78**	**36**	**71**
Wokingham & Emmbrook	**34**	**21**	**5**	**8**	**86**	**47**	**68**
Chalfont Wasps	**34**	**20**	**4**	**10**	**80**	**49**	**64**
Englefield Green Rovers	**34**	**20**	**4**	**10**	**73**	**46**	**64**
Penn & Tylers Green	**34**	**20**	**4**	**10**	**69**	**46**	**64**
Bisley Sports	**34**	**19**	**5**	**10**	**81**	**51**	**62**
Binfield	**34**	**19**	**2**	**13**	**70**	**44**	**59**
Kintbury Rangers	**34**	**18**	**4**	**12**	**81**	**48**	**58**
Eton Wick	**34**	**17**	**5**	**12**	**73**	**64**	**56**
Oxford Quarry Nomads	**34**	**14**	**4**	**16**	**67**	**81**	**46**
Badshot Lea	**34**	**13**	**6**	**15**	**81**	**74**	**45**
Finchampstead	**34**	**10**	**7**	**17**	**58**	**60**	**37**
Holyport	**34**	**10**	**4**	**20**	**58**	**90**	**34**
Rayners Lane	**34**	**11**	**1**	**22**	**57**	**90**	**34**
Chinnor	**34**	**5**	**5**	**24**	**34**	**82**	**20**
Banbury United Res.	**34**	**4**	**4**	**26**	**29**	**108**	**16**
Prestwood	**34**	**1**	**4**	**29**	**24**	**137**	**7**

Reserve Division Two (East)	P	W	D	L	F	A	Pts
Bisley Sports Res. *-1*	20	15	2	3	67	26	46
Wokingham/Emmbrook Res. *-3*	20	15	2	3	66	20	44
Rayners Lane Res.	20	14	1	5	60	36	43
Penn & Tylers Green Res. *-3*	20	12	3	5	46	27	36
Hounslow Borough Res.	20	9	2	9	41	42	29
Englefield Green Rovers Res	20	5	7	8	28	41	22
Chinnor Res.	20	6	4	10	29	43	22
Chalfont Wasps Res.	20	6	3	11	36	43	21
Eton Wick Res.	20	5	3	12	29	49	18
Prestwood Res.	20	4	2	14	31	62	14
Holyport Res.	20	1	7	12	21	65	10

ANNUAL CHALLENGE MATCH

(April 5th at Didcot Town)

Division One East XI 2 Division One West XI 1

HELLENIC LEAGUE DIVISION ONE EAST CONSTITUTION 2006-07

BADSHOT LEA........................ Recreation Ground, Badshot Lea, Farnham GU9 9LB 01252 316076
BINFIELD........................ Stubbs Hill, Binfield, Bracknell RG42 4NN 01344 860822
BISLEY SPORTS........................ James Walker Sports Centre, Church Lane, Bisley GU24 9ED .... None
CHALFONT WASPS .... Playing Fields, Bowstridge Lane, Chalfont St Giles HP8 4DF........................ 01494 875050
CHINNOR .... Station Road, Chinnor OX39 4QQ........................ None
ENGLEFIELD GREEN ROVERS ... Coopers Hill Sports Ground, Coopers Hill Lane, Englefield Green TW20 0JX........................ 01784 435666
ETON WICK........................ Haywards Mead, Eton Wick, Windsor SL4 6JN 01753 852749
FINCHAMPSTEAD .... Memorial Ground, Finchampstead Park, Finchampstead RG11 4JR........................ 0118 973 2890
HEADINGTON AMATEURS .... Recreation Ground, Barton, Oxford OX3 9LA........................ 01865 760489
HENLEY TOWN........................ Triangle Ground, Mill Lane, Henley-on-Thames RG9 4HB 01491 411083
HOLYPORT .... Braywick Sports Centre, Braywick Road, Maidenhead SL6 1BN .... None
KINTBURY RANGERS .... Inkpen Road, Kintbury, Hungerford RG17 9UA........................ 01488 657001
MARLOW UNITED.... Flackwell Heath FC, Wilks Park, Magpie Lane, Flackwell Heath, High Wycombe HP10 9EA 01628 523892
OXFORD QUARRY NOMADS .... Oxford City FC, Court Place Farm, Marsh Lane, Marston OX3 0NQ 01865 744493/742492
PENN & TYLERS GREEN .... French School Meadows, Elm Road, Penn HP10 8LG........................ 01494 815346
PRESTWOOD........... Prestwood Sports Centre, Honor End Lane, Prestwood, Great Missenden HP16 9HG 01494 865946
RAYNERS LANE........................ Tithe Farm Social Club, 151 Rayners Lane, South Harrow HA2 0XH 020 8868 8724
WOKINGHAM & EMMBROOK .. Emmbrook Sports Ground, Lowther Road, Emmbrook, Wokingham RG41 1JB 01189 780209

IN: Headington Amateurs (S – Hellenic League Division One West), Henley Town (R), Marlow United (P – Reading League Senior Division)

OUT: Banbury United Res. (S – Hellenic League Division One West), Bicester Town (P), Hounslow Borough (P)

	Cheltenham Saracens	Cirencester United	Clanfield	Cricklade Town	Easington Sports	Harrow Hill	Headington Amateurs	Hook Norton	Letcombe	Malmesbury Victoria	Middle Barton	Old Woodstock Town	Pewsey Vale	Purton	Ross Town	Trowbridge Town	Tytherington Rocks	Winterbourne United	Wooton Bassett Town
Cheltenham Saracens		3-0	1-0	2-3	0-0	0-0	1-2	2-0	1-1	4-0	n/a	1-0	0-4	0-0	5-1	0-0	2-1	1-1	1-0
Cirencester United	1-1	*D*	1-0	2-1	3-0	0-1	2-3	6-3	0-2	1-2	n/a	1-2	0-3	4-0	2-2	2-2	0-1	2-2	2-2
Clanfield	1-1	3-0	*I*	1-0	0-3	1-2	1-3	4-1	0-3	1-2	n/a	0-4	1-2	1-0	1-0	2-3	0-2	1-4	1-3
Cricklade Town	2-2	0-3	3-0	*V*	3-2	1-1	1-1	2-1	1-3	0-3	n/a	3-5	2-1	4-1	2-4	2-1	1-3	1-4	1-1
Easington Sports	0-3	1-3	1-1	2-3	*I*	1-3	2-2	0-2	0-1	1-2	n/a	2-1	3-0	1-2	0-0	0-4	1-1	0-2	1-1
Harrow Hill	0-2	2-0	2-0	3-1	3-2	*S*	2-3	1-1	2-0	2-1	4-1	1-1	4-2	3-2	1-4	0-0	3-0	3-3	0-1
Headington Amateurs	1-1	0-1	3-0	0-1	1-2	2-1	*I*	2-0	0-0	3-1	n/a	2-0	1-0	1-1	2-0	4-0	2-4	1-2	1-0
Hook Norton	2-2	4-0	4-0	1-0	2-3	2-3	2-2	*O*	5-1	1-0	n/a	2-3	3-2	4-0	1-0	2-0	1-0	0-7	0-2
Letcombe	1-3	3-2	6-4	1-2	4-1	0-2	2-3	1-1	*N*	2-0	n/a	2-1	2-1	1-1	5-0	0-0	1-2	0-2	0-2
Malmesbury Victoria	1-1	0-1	2-1	2-4	1-1	0-2	0-0	3-3	1-0		n/a	1-3	1-1	3-1	3-0	1-2	5-3	1-1	0-2
Middle Barton	n/a	n/a	n/a	1-9	1-3	n/a	n/a	n/a	n/a	n/a	*O*	n/a	n/a	0-1	n/a	n/a	n/a	n/a	n/a
Old Woodstock Town	3-2	4-2	0-0	2-0	2-0	0-1	2-2	2-1	0-1	1-0	n/a	*N*	3-1	1-1	3-1	1-1	1-8	0-3	1-0
Pewsey Vale	2-1	3-0	2-1	3-1	1-1	0-1	1-3	2-0	2-0	3-3	n/a	1-0	*E*	6-1	2-2	0-2	1-1	2-1	2-1
Purton	2-0	3-2	1-1	0-0	1-1	3-0	0-1	1-1	0-4	0-2	n/a	2-2	1-0		3-0	0-3	1-3	0-2	0-1
Ross Town	1-5	1-3	2-1	1-4	1-5	0-7	1-4	1-3	0-1	3-2	n/a	0-1	2-1	1-3	*(W*	3-7	0-5	0-1	0-5
Trowbridge Town	1-2	3-2	5-0	4-0	3-0	1-1	1-3	1-0	2-1	1-1	n/a	2-0	0-0	2-1	4-2	*E*	7-2	1-2	1-0
Tytherington Rocks	1-2	1-0	3-2	3-2	4-0	1-1	2-0	1-2	0-0	2-5	n/a	0-4	3-2	4-1	6-1	4-0	*S*	4-2	0-0
Winterbourne United	5-1	6-1	4-0	3-2	5-0	3-1	2-0	3-1	2-1	4-0	n/a	1-1	5-0	2-0	3-1	5-0	2-3	*T)*	1-3
Wooton Bassett Town	3-1	0-1	1-0	1-2	6-0	2-2	3-1	1-1	2-1	1-1	n/a	1-1	1-1	3-0	2-1	1-1	2-1	4-3	

Note – Middle Barton withdrew during the course of the season
Their results are shown above but are expunged from the league table

Division One (West)		P	W	D	L	F	A	Pts
Winterbourne United		34	24	5	5	98	36	77
Harrow Hill		34	18	9	7	61	40	63
Tytherington Rocks		34	19	5	10	79	54	62
Headington Amateurs		34	18	8	8	59	39	62
Wootton Bassett Town		34	17	10	7	58	30	61
Trowbridge Town		34	17	9	8	65	44	60
Old Woodstock Town		34	16	8	10	55	46	56
Cheltenham Saracens		34	14	12	8	54	40	54
Letcombe		34	14	6	14	51	45	48
Pewsey Vale		34	13	7	14	54	51	46
Hook Norton		34	13	7	14	57	58	46
Cricklade Town		34	13	5	16	55	67	44
Malmesbury Victoria		34	11	9	14	50	56	42
Cirencester United		34	11	5	18	50	64	38
Purton	*-3*	34	7	9	18	33	64	27
Easington Sports		34	6	9	19	37	71	27
Clanfield		34	5	4	25	30	74	19
Ross Town		34	5	3	26	36	103	18

Middle Barton – record expunged

Reserve Division Two (West)	P	W	D	L	F	A	Pts
Oxford Quarry Nomads Res.	22	16	3	3	74	46	51
Cirencester United Res.	22	15	4	3	75	23	49
Old Woodstock Town Res.	22	13	3	6	54	31	42
Ardley United Res.	22	12	3	7	41	30	39
Shrivenham Res.	22	10	9	3	43	35	39
Abingdon Town Res.	22	9	3	10	41	53	30
Witney United Res.	22	8	3	11	42	47	27
Easington Sports Res.	22	7	2	13	42	59	23
Letcombe Res.	22	6	5	11	23	41	23
Cricklade Town Res.	22	6	4	12	36	62	22
Clanfield Res.	22	5	6	11	33	47	21
Hook Norton Res.	22	2	1	19	35	65	7

RESERVES CUP

FINAL

(May 3rd at Shrivenham)

Wokingham & Emmbrook Res. 3 Fairford Town Res. 2

HELLENIC LEAGUE DIVISION ONE WEST CONSTITUTION 2006-07

BANBURY UNITED RESERVES .... Spencer Stadium, Station Approach, Banbury OX16 5TA 01295 263354
CHELTENHAM SARACENS .... Petersfield Park, Tewkesbury Road, Gloucester GL51 8JL 01242 584134
CIRENCESTER UNITED .... Cirencester Town FC, Corinium Stadium, Kingshill Lane, Cirencester GL7 1XG 01285 654543
CLANFIELD .... Radcot Road, Clanfield, Faringdon SN7 8DT 01367 810314
CRICKLADE TOWN .... Cricklade Leisure Centre, Stones Lane, Cricklade SN6 6JW 01793 750011
EASINGTON SPORTS .... Addison Road, Easington Estate, Banbury OX16 9DH 01295 257006
HOOK NORTON .... The Playfields, The Bourne, Hook Norton OX15 5PB 01608 737132
LETCOMBE .... Bassett Road, Letcombe Regis, Wantage OX12 9LJ 01235 768685
LYDNEY TOWN .... Recreation Trust Ground, Lydney 01594 844523
MALMESBURY VICTORIA .... Flying Monk Ground, Gloucester Road, Malmesbury SN16 0AJ 01666 822141
OLD WOODSTOCK TOWN .... New Road, Woodstock OX20 1PD .... None
PEWSEY VALE .... Recreation Ground, Kings Corner, Ball Road, Pewsey SN9 5GF 01672 562990
PURTON .... The Red House, Church Street, Purton SN5 4DT 01793 770262
ROSS TOWN .... Ross Sports Centre, The Riverside, Wilton, Ross-on-Wye HR9 6AA 07787 573080
TROWBRIDGE TOWN .... Woodmarsh, North Bradley, Trowbridge BA14 0SA .... None
TYTHERINGTON ROCKS ... Hardwicke Playing Fields, Woodlands Road, Tytherington, Wotton-under-Edge GL12 8UU .... None
WINTERBOURNE UNITED .... The Rec, Parkside Avenue, Winterbourne, Bristol BS36 1LZ 01454 850059
WOOTTON BASSETT TOWN... Gerard Buxton Sports Ground, Rylands Way, Wootton Bassett SN4 8AY 01793 853880

IN: Banbury United Res. (S – Hellenic League Division One East), Lydney Town (Gloucestershire County League)

OUT: Harrow Hill (P), Headington Amateurs (S – Hellenic League Division One East), Middle Barton (WS – Oxfordshire Senior League Division One)

LEAGUE CUP

(All teams in league)

PRELIMINARY ROUND
Binfield 0 **Ardley United** 4
Carterton 3 Bisley Sports 0
Chipping Norton Town 0 **Almondsbury Town** 4
Clanfield 0 **Fairford Town** 1
Finchampstead 2 Englefield Green Rovers 1
Henley Town 1 **Badshot Lea** 2
Highworth Town 1 Easington Sports 0
Holyport 1 **Chalfont Wasps** 4
Hounslow Borough 1 **Abingdon United** 3
Hungerford Town 2 Abingdon Town 1
Middle Barton (scr.) v **Harrow Hill** (w/o)
Milton United 0 **North Leigh** 2
Old Woodstock Town 2 Bishops Cleeve 0
Oxford Quarry Nomads 3 Rayners Lane 1
Pegasus Juniors 2 Headington Amateurs 0
Penn & Tylers Green 2 **Kintbury Rangers** 3
Prestwood 0 **Kidlington** 3
Purton 2 **Pewsey Vale** 3 *aet*
Ross Town 0 **Shrivenham** 7
Shortwood United 4 Cheltenham Saracens 2
Slimbridge (w/o) v Tuffley Rovers (scr.)
Trowbridge Town 1 **Tytherington Rocks** 3
Wantage Town 2 Bicester Town 1
Winterbourne United 3 Cricklade Town 0
Witney United 4 Chinnor 2 *aet*
Wokingham & Emmbrook 6 Banbury United Res. 0
Wootton Bassett Town 2 Cirencester United 2 *aet* (5-4p)

FIRST ROUND
Abingdon United 3 Witney United 1
Badshot Lea 2 Ardley United 2
Ardley United 3 Badshot Lea 1 *replay*
Carterton 0 **Didcot Town** 2
Eton Wick 1 **Finchampstead** 2
Highworth Town 4 Hook Norton 2
Kidlington 2 **Chalfont Wasps** 8
Kintbury Rangers 5 Oxford Quarry Nomads 2
Letcombe 2 Malmesbury Victoria 1
North Leigh 3 Almondsbury Town 1
Old Woodstock Town 2 Pegasus Juniors 1
Pewsey Vale 1 **Tytherington Rocks** 2
Shortwood United 0 **Fairford Town** 1
Shrivenham 0 **Harrow Hill** 2
Slimbridge 1 Hungerford Town 0
Wantage Town 5 Wokingham & Emmbrook 1
Wootton Bassett Town 1 **Winterbourne United** 4

SECOND ROUND
Abingdon United 1 **Tytherington Rocks** 2
Ardley United 2 Harrow Hill 0
Chalfont Wasps 1 **Didcot Town** 2
Fairford Town 1 **North Leigh** 6
Kintbury Rangers 3 Winterbourne United 1
Letcombe 4 Old Woodstock Town 1
Slimbridge 3 Highworth Town 0
Wantage Town 2 **Finchampstead** 3

QUARTER-FINALS
Ardley United 3 Kintbury Rangers 0
North Leigh 0 **Didcot Town** 4
Slimbridge 4 Finchampstead 0
Tytherington Rocks 1 Letcombe 0

SEMI-FINALS
(played over two legs)
Ardley United 2 Tytherington Rocks 0, Tytherington Rocks 1 **Ardley United** 1
Didcot Town 2 Slimbridge 1, Slimbridge 1 Didcot Town 1

FINAL
(May 6th at Carterton)
Didcot Town 5 Ardley United 0

SUPPLEMENTARY CUP

(League Cup Preliminary and First Round losers)

PRELIMINARY ROUND

Abingdon Town 2 Hungerford Town 0
Almondsbury Town 1 **Bishops Cleeve** 3
Bicester Town 5 Holyport 0
Binfield 3 Chinnor 0
Chipping Norton Town 4 Malmesbury Victoria 1
Cirencester United 0 **Cricklade Town** 2
Hook Norton 4 Easington Sports 2
Shortwood United 1 **Witney United** 2
Wokingham & Emmbrook 4 Prestwood 1

FIRST ROUND

Banbury United Res. 1 **Wokingham & Emmbrook** 3
Binfield 1 **Henley Town** 2
Bishops Cleeve 3 Witney United 2
Carterton 0 **Wootton Bassett Town** 1
Chipping Norton Town 3 Bicester Town 1
Cricklade Town 2 Clanfield 1
Englefield Green Rovers 0 **Badshot Lea** 2
Eton Wick 0 **Hounslow Borough** 2
Headington Amateurs 1 **Bisley Sports** 3
Hook Norton 1 **Shrivenham** 3
Kidlington 1 **Oxford Quarry Nomads** 3
Pegasus Juniors 5 Ross Town 1
Penn & Tylers Green 3 Abingdon Town 1
Pewsey Vale 2 **Purton** 5
Rayners Lane 1 **Milton United** 2
Trowbridge Town 4 **Cheltenham Saracens** 0
(Trowbridge Town expelled)

SECOND ROUND

Badshot Lea 2 Bishops Cleeve 0 *aet*
Cheltenham Saracens 0 **Milton United** 1
Henley Town 0 **Cricklade Town** 1
Hounslow Borough 0 **Chipping Norton Town** 3
Oxford Quarry Nomads 3 Shrivenham 0
Pegasus Juniors 2 **Bisley Sports** 2 *aet* (4-5p)
Penn & Tylers Green 0 Wokingham & Emmbrook 0 *aet* (3-2p)
Wootton Bassett Town 2 Purton 1

QUARTER-FINALS

Badshot Lea 1 Chipping Norton Town 0
Cricklade Town 0 Bisley Sports 0 *aet* (8-7p)
Oxford Quarry Nomads 1 **Milton United** 2
Penn & Tylers Green 2 Wootton Bassett Town 0

SEMI-FINALS

(played over two legs)

Cricklade Town 1 Penn & Tylers Green 1, **Penn & Tylers Green** 2 Cricklade Town 1
Milton United 3 Badshot Lea 0, **Badshot Lea** 4 Milton United 0 *aet*

FINAL

(May 1st at Ardley United)

Badshot Lea 2 Penn & Tylers Green 0

NORMAN MATTHEWS FLOODLIGHT CUP

PRELIMINARY ROUND

Abingdon Town 2 **Penn & Tylers Green** 2 *aet* (4-5p)
Harrow Hill 0 **Slimbridge** 1
Highworth Town 1 **Witney United** 4

FIRST ROUND

Almondsbury Town 0 **Witney United** 1
Ardley United 4 Banbury United Res. 0
Bicester Town 2 Kidlington 1 *aet*
Carterton 0 **Penn & Tylers Green** 1
Cheltenham Saracens 0 **Fairford Town** 3
Cirencester United 2 Pegasus Juniors 1
Didcot Town 0 **Kintbury Rangers** 3
Finchampstead 2 Badshot Lea 1
Henley Town 1 **Abingdon United** 4
Malmesbury Victoria 0 **Wantage Town** 6
Milton United 0 **Hungerford Town** 1
Oxford Quarry Nomads 3 Chipping Norton Town 2 *aet*
Pewsey Vale 1 **Bishops Cleeve** 5
Shrivenham 3 North Leigh 2
Slimbridge 2 Wootton Bassett Town 0

SECOND ROUND

Abingdon United 1 Bishops Cleeve 2
(Bishops Cleeve expelled)
Ardley United 3 Bicester Town 0
Cirencester United 1 **Penn & Tylers Green** 2
Fairford Town 2 **Hungerford Town** 3
Kintbury Rangers 3 Shrivenham 2
Oxford Quarry Nomads 1 **Slimbridge** 4
Wantage Town 3 Finchampstead 1
Witney United 5 Shortwood United 1

QUARTER-FINALS

Abingdon United 1 **Wantage Town** 3
Ardley United 5 Penn & Tylers Green 1
Kintbury Rangers 4 Hungerford Town 1
Witney United 1 **Slimbridge** 2

SEMI-FINALS

(played over two legs)

Kintbury Rangers 2 Ardley United 2,
Ardley United 2 Kintbury Rangers 0
Wantage Town 0 Slimbridge 1,
Slimbridge 2 Wantage Town 0

FINAL

(played over two legs)

(April 6th)

Slimbridge 0 Ardley United 0

(April 13th)

Ardley United 1 **Slimbridge** 3

HERTS SENIOR COUNTY LEAGUE

	Bedmond Sports & Social	Buntingford Town	Bushey Rangers	Chipperfield Corinthians	Codicote	Elliott Star	Evergreen	Hadley	Hatfield Town	Hinton	Little Munden	London Lions	Metropolitan Police Bushey	Sandridge Rovers	Whitewebbs	Wormley Rovers
Bedmond Sports & Social	*P*	2-1	3-1	2-0	W-L	4-2	1-2	0-4	1-0	2-2	1-2	0-0	1-2	2-0	0-3	1-1
Buntingford Town	4-2	*R*	W-L	1-2	1-1	1-1	2-0	2-2	0-3	3-2	4-2	5-1	4-2	1-1	1-0	1-2
Bushey Rangers	1-0	0-0	*E*	2-1	3-0	1-0	2-0	0-3	4-1	0-1	3-2	0-3	1-4	2-2	1-2	1-0
Chipperfield Corinthians	2-1	2-3	1-4	*M*	1-1	4-2	4-2	2-1	0-3	0-2	3-3	1-1	0-2	1-2	0-2	1-2
Codicote	4-2	6-0	1-3	2-1	*I*	2-4	3-1	3-3	2-3	5-3	4-2	0-3	2-1	0-1	2-0	2-2
Elliott Star	0-3	1-4	0-6	4-0	1-2	*E*	4-3	3-1	2-2	2-3	2-3	0-2	0-4	4-1	0-1	2-1
Evergreen	0-5	0-2	2-1	2-2	0-1	1-4	*R*	1-6	0-4	0-1	4-4	3-2	2-3	2-1	0-4	8-4
Hadley	2-2	1-0	2-0	4-0	1-5	3-2	4-1		1-2	1-1	4-1	0-0	1-2	0-0	1-1	0-0
Hatfield Town	1-3	1-0	6-0	7-1	1-2	3-1	8-1	0-1	*D*	4-3	4-1	3-2	2-1	3-2	3-2	1-1
Hinton	0-3	1-1	2-2	3-3	2-0	3-0	2-2	3-1	1-3	*I*	5-0	1-0	3-1	0-2	1-3	0-4
Little Munden	3-3	0-2	2-1	3-3	1-0	3-1	2-1	1-1	0-4	1-1	*V*	1-0	1-1	0-5	1-3	2-2
London Lions	3-2	1-2	0-2	2-0	2-2	2-6	8-0	0-2	1-8	7-2	2-2	*I*	1-1	0-0	0-3	2-0
Metropolitan Police Bushey	5-3	4-1	3-2	4-3	0-3	2-3	4-2	2-4	2-3	3-3	3-3	3-0	*S*	0-2	2-3	1-1
Sandridge Rovers	0-2	1-2	2-1	5-3	2-0	2-2	3-1	0-1	1-1	1-1	2-1	0-1	3-4	*I*	0-3	4-1
Whitewebbs	2-1	0-2	2-2	2-0	3-0	3-0	9-1	0-0	5-0	3-1	2-1	3-1	3-1	2-0	*O*	4-0
Wormley Rovers	2-2	2-1	3-0	1-2	5-3	2-2	1-2	0-2	3-2	1-4	0-3	0-1	2-1	3-4	0-3	*N*

Premier Division		P	W	D	L	F	A	Pts
Whitewebbs		30	23	3	4	76	22	72
Hatfield Town		30	20	3	7	86	44	63
Hadley		30	14	10	6	57	34	52
Buntingford Town		30	15	6	9	51	43	51
Bedmond Sports & Social	*+3*	30	12	6	12	54	49	45
Metropolitan Police Bushey		30	13	5	12	68	62	44
Codicote		30	13	5	12	58	52	44
Hinton		30	11	9	10	57	58	42
Sandridge Rovers	*-3*	30	12	7	11	49	44	40
Bushey Rangers		30	12	4	14	46	48	40
London Lions		30	10	7	13	48	52	37
Little Munden	*+3*	30	8	10	12	51	71	37
Wormley Rovers		30	8	8	14	46	62	32
Elliott Star		30	9	4	17	55	72	31
Chipperfield Corinthians		30	6	6	18	43	75	24
Evergreen	*-3*	30	6	3	21	44	101	18

Reserve Division One	P	W	D	L	F	A	Pts
Bedmond Sports & Social Res.	24	19	4	1	76	22	61
Hadley Res.	24	19	1	4	79	30	58
Hatfield Town Res.	24	14	3	7	69	61	45
Buntingford Town Res.	24	11	5	8	50	40	38
Standon & Puckeridge Res.	24	11	5	8	53	51	38
Elliott Star Res.	24	10	3	11	58	54	33
London Lions Res.	24	9	3	12	55	51	30
Codicote Res.	24	8	6	10	52	55	30
Hinton Res.	24	8	5	11	42	62	29
Buckhurst Hill Res.	24	8	3	13	39	60	27
Metropolitan Police Bushey Res.	24	5	10	9	43	56	25
Evergreen Res.	24	4	4	16	32	62	16
Old Parmiterians Res.	24	2	4	18	24	68	10

FLOODLIGHT CUP

FINAL

(May 6th at Buntingford Town)

Buntingford Town 5 Buckhurst Hill 1

RESERVES CUP

FINAL

(April 29th at Sandridge Rovers)

Bedmond Sports & Social Res. 4 Hadley 1

HERTS SENIOR COUNTY LEAGUE PREMIER DIVISION CONSTITUTION 2006-07

BEDMOND SPORTS & SOCIAL	**Toms Lane Recreation Ground, Toms Lane, Bedmond, Abbots Langley WD5 0RA**	**01923 267991**
BUNTINGFORD TOWN	**Sainsburys Depot Sports Ground, London Road, Buntingford SG9 9JR**	**None**
BUSHEY RANGERS	**Moatfield, Bournehall Lane, Bushey WD23 3JU**	**020 8386 1875**
CODICOTE	**John Clements Memorial Ground, Bury Lane, Codicote SG4 8XX**	**01438 821072**
ELLIOTT STAR	**Pursley Football Ground, London Road, Shenley, Radlett WD7 9EN**	**None**
HADLEY	**Hadley Sports Ground, Brickfield Lane, Arkley, Barnet**	**020 8449 1144**
HATFIELD TOWN	**Birchwood Leisure Centre, Longmead, Birchwood, Hatfield AL10 0AS**	**01707 270772**
HERTFORD HEATH	**The Playing Field, Trinity Road, Hertford Heath SG13 7QR**	**None**
HINTON	**Holtwhites Sports & Social, Kirkland Drive, Enfield EN2 0RU**	**020 8363 4449**
KNEBWORTH	**The Recreation Ground, Watton Road, Knebworth, Stevenage SG3 6AH.**	**None**
LONDON LIONS	**Laing Sports, Rowley Lane, Barnet EN5 3HW**	**020 8441 6051**
METROPOLITAN POLICE BUSHEY	**Met. Police Sports Club, Aldenham Road, Bushey, Watford WD2 3TR**	**01923 243947**
SANDRIDGE ROVERS	**Spencer Recreation Ground, Sandridge, St Albans AL4 9BZ.**	**01727 835506**
STANDON & PUCKERIDGE	**Station Road, Standon, near Ware SG11 1QW.**	**01920 823460**
WHITEWEBBS	**The Whitewebbs Centre, Whitewebbs Lane, Enfield EN2 9HH.**	**01992 760716**
WORMLEY ROVERS	**Wormley Sports Club, Church Lane, Wormley EN10 7QF.**	**01992 460650**

IN: Hertford Heath (P), Knebworth (P), Standon & Puckeridge (P)

OUT: Chipperfield Corinthians (R), Evergreen (R), Little Munden (R)

	Allenburys Sports	Bovingdon	Buckhurst Hill	Croxley Guild	Cuffley	Hertford Heath	Knebworth	Lemsford	Loughton	North Mymms	Old Parmiterians	Sarratt	St Peters	Standon & Puck.
Allenburys Sports		2-0	1-7	2-0	1-3	1-2	2-6	4-2	2-0	0-3	3-1	1-3	1-2	1-1
Bovingdon	4-1	*D*	2-0	6-1	1-3	3-4	1-1	5-4	8-1	5-0	2-1	4-1	1-0	1-2
Buckhurst Hill	4-1	3-2	*I*	1-3	W-L	1-0	0-2	1-2	1-1	4-2	3-1	1-1	4-1	2-3
Croxley Guild	2-4	0-11	0-2	*V*	2-0	3-3	3-5	W-L	1-3	3-0	1-2	2-1	1-3	0-2
Cuffley	1-3	0-3	1-3	0-3	*I*	1-0	0-4	0-3	1-4	1-0	2-3	1-1	2-2	2-6
Hertford Heath	4-2	3-2	7-4	5-1	3-2	*S*	4-1	1-1	2-1	3-0	3-1	3-0	4-0	3-2
Knebworth	3-1	4-5	3-1	1-1	5-0	4-0	*I*	2-3	1-1	2-0	2-1	1-0	2-0	2-5
Lemsford	4-4	2-1	5-2	6-3	5-0	4-4	2-5	*O*	0-1	3-1	1-0	1-3	6-2	5-1
Loughton	3-2	0-1	2-2	2-3	2-5	0-4	1-0	0-1	*N*	1-1	4-2	7-5	0-1	1-3
North Mymms	W-L	2-7	2-2	3-0	1-0	0-3	2-4	0-0	2-6		0-2	3-2	1-3	1-3
Old Parmiterians	W-L	3-2	3-3	5-3	2-2	0-5	2-2	1-1	0-4	1-3	*O*	1-2	1-3	1-2
Sarratt	5-1	1-3	4-1	2-1	5-1	1-2	3-2	6-0	4-2	3-2	1-2	*N*	2-2	2-3
St Peters	1-3	1-2	1-1	1-0	1-3	1-1	0-5	2-0	0-0	1-1	5-2	4-0	*E*	3-1
Standon & Puckeridge	7-2	6-3	4-1	5-2	4-0	3-2	4-4	6-0	2-2	3-2	5-1	1-0	1-1	

Reserve Division Two		P	W	D	L	F	A	Pts
Lemsford Res.		24	17	2	5	68	40	53
Bovingdon Res.		24	15	5	4	72	34	50
Knebworth Res.		24	15	4	5	76	40	49
Sandridge Rovers Res.	+3	24	14	3	7	53	42	48
Whitewebbs Res.	+2	24	11	4	9	54	51	39
Bushey Rangers Res.	*-1*	24	12	3	9	67	46	38
Croxley Guild Res.		24	11	3	10	46	46	36
Cuffley Res.		24	7	6	11	42	58	27
Allenburys Sports Res.		24	7	5	12	35	55	26
North Mymms Res.		24	8	1	15	38	74	25
Chipperfield Corinthians Res.		24	6	4	14	30	53	22
Sarratt Res.	-3	24	5	5	14	55	77	17
Wormley Rovers Res.		24	3	5	16	34	54	14

Division One		P	W	D	L	F	A	Pts
Standon & Puckeridge		26	19	4	3	85	44	61
Hertford Heath	*-3*	26	18	4	4	75	39	55
Knebworth		26	15	5	6	73	42	50
Bovingdon		26	16	1	9	85	46	49
Lemsford	*-3*	26	12	5	9	61	55	38
St Peters		26	10	7	9	41	45	37
Sarratt		26	11	3	12	58	52	36
Buckhurst Hill		26	10	6	10	54	54	36
Loughton		26	9	6	11	49	54	33
Cuffley	*+6*	26	6	3	17	31	67	27
Allenburys Sports		26	8	2	16	45	68	26
Old Parmiterians		26	7	4	15	39	64	25
Croxley Guild		26	7	2	17	39	75	23
North Mymms		26	6	4	16	32	62	22

AUBREY CUP

FIRST ROUND

Allenburys Spts 4 London Lions 2
Buckhurst Hill 0 **Sandridge Rvrs** 4
Buntingford Town 7 Metropolitan Police Bushey 1
Codicote 5 Cuffley 1
Croxley Guild 3 Bovingdon 2 *aet*
Elliott Star 1 Bushey Rangers 0
Evergreen 3 Chipperfield Corinthians 2
(at Chipperfield Corinthians)
Hertford Heath 1 **St Peters** 0
(Hertford Heath expelled)
Lemsford 4 Loughton 0
Little Munden 0 **Hinton** 3
North Mymms 1 **Hadley** 4
Sarratt 3 Old Parmiterians 2
Standon & Puck. 3 Knebworth 0
Wormley Rovers 0 **Hatfield Tn** 5

SECOND ROUND

Buntingford Town 3 St Peters 0
Codicote 6 Croxley Guild 1
Elliott Star 0 **Hadley** 4
Evergreen 0 **Sarratt** 1
Hinton 2 **Allenburys Sports** 3
Lemsford 3 **Hatfield Town** 4
Standon & Puckeridge 2 **Bedmond Sports & Social** 4 *aet*
Whitewebbs 2 Sandridge Rovers 0

QUARTER-FINALS

Bedmond Sports & Social 1 Whitewebbs 0
Codicote 3 Sarratt 0
Hadley 1 Allenburys Sports 0
Hatfield Town 2 **Buntingford Town** 2 *aet* (3-5p)

SEMI-FINALS

Bedmond Sports & Social 0 **Hadley** 1
Buntingford Town 2 Codicote 1

FINAL *(May 1st at Ware)*

Hadley 1 Buntingford Town 0

CHAIRMAN'S CUP

(Teams near end of season with fewest league games remaining)

GROUP A

	P	W	D	L	F	A	Pts
North Mymms	3	3	0	0	5	0	9
Croxley Guild	3	2	0	1	4	2	6
St Peters	3	0	1	2	0	3	1
Old Parmiterians	3	0	1	2	1	5	1

Croxley Guild 0 North Mymms 1
Croxley Guild 2 St Peters 0
North Mymms 3 Old Parmiterians 0
Old Parmiterians 1 Croxley Guild 2
St Peters 0 North Mymms 1
St Peters 0 Old Parmiterians 0

GROUP B

	P	W	D	L	F	A	Pts
Buckhurst Hill	3	3	0	0	9	3	9
Lemsford	3	2	0	1	8	8	6
Cuffley	3	1	0	2	6	7	3
Loughton	3	0	0	3	3	8	0

Buckhurst Hill 2 Cuffley 1
Buckhurst Hill 5 Lemsford 2
Lemsford 3 Cuffley 2
Loughton 0 Buckhurst Hill 2
Loughton 2 Cuffley 3
Loughton 1 Lemsford 3

SEMI-FINALS

Buckhurst Hill 5 Croxley Guild 1
North Mymms 2 Lemsford 0

FINAL

(April 22nd at Lemsford)

North Mymms 2 **Buckhurst Hill** 2 *aet* (4-5p)

HERTS SENIOR COUNTY LEAGUE DIVISION ONE CONSTITUTION 2006-07

ALLENBURYS SPORTS	Glaxo Smith Kline, Westfield, Park Road, Ware SG12 0DP	None
BOVINGDON	Green Lane, Bovingdon, Hemel Hempstead HP3 0LB	01442 832628
BUCKHURST HILL	Roding Lane, Buckhurst Hill IG9 5BJ	020 8504 1189
CHIPPERFIELD CORINTHIANS	Queens Street, Chipperfield, Kings Langley WD4 9BT	01923 269554
CROXLEY GUILD	Croxley Guild of Sport, The Green, Croxley Green, Rickmansworth WD3 3HT	01923 770534
CUFFLEY	King George's Playing Fields, Northaw Road East, Cuffley EN6 4LL	07815 174434
EVERGREEN	South Way, Kings Langley, Abbots Langley WD5 0JL	01923 267812
LEMSFORD	Gosling Sports Park, Stanboroug Road, Welwyn Garden City AL8 6XE	01707 331056
LITTLE MUNDEN	Wormley Rovers FC, Church Lane, Wormley EN10 7QF	01992 460650
LOUGHTON	Avondale Close, Loughton IG10 3DH	None
MILL END SPORTS	King George V Playing Fields, Shepherds Lane, Mill End, Rickmansworth WD3 8JN	01923 776392
NORTH MYMMS	Welham Green Recreation, Dellsome Lane, North Mymms, Hatfield AL9 7DY	01707 266972/260338
OLD PARMITERIANS	Parmiters School, High Elms Lane, Garston, Watford WD25 0JU	01923 682805
PARK STREET VILLAGE	St Peters FC, William Bird Playing Fields, Toulmin Drive, St Albans AL3 6DX	01727 852401
SARRATT	King George V Playing Fields, King Georges Avenue, Sarratt	None
ST PETERS	William Bird Playing Fields, Toulmin Drive, St Albans AL3 6DX	01727 852401
WODSON PARK	Wodson Park Spts & Rec. Centre, Wadesmill Road, Ware SG12 0UQ	01920 487091

IN: Chipperfield Corinthians (R), Evergreen (R), Little Munden (R), Mill End Sports (P – West Herts League Premier Division), Park Street Village (P – Mid-Herts League Premier Division), Wodson Park (P – Hertford & District League Premier Division)
OUT: Hertford Heath (P), Knebworth (P), Standon & Puckeridge (P)

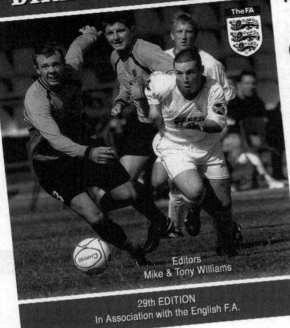

HUMBER PREMIER LEAGUE

	Beverley Town	Bridlington Tn Res.	Driffield	Easington United	Hedon Rangers	Hedon United	Hessle Rangers	Hornsea Town	Hutton Cranswick United	Pocklington Town	Reckitts	Sculcoates Amateurs	St Andrews Sutton	Westella/Willerby	Withernsea
Beverley Town		0-2	6-0	2-3	4-2	4-1	4-2	0-3	5-3	2-0	1-2	2-2	n/a	1-0	1-1
Bridlington Town Res.	2-2		5-3	1-1	0-5	2-0	1-2	0-2	0-4	2-1	0-3	0-4	n/a	0-4	5-3
Driffield	2-1	1-1	*P*	0-2	2-2	0-2	1-4	0-0	2-3	0-1	1-3	1-3	n/a	2-2	5-3
Easington United	1-1	3-2	2-2	*R*	4-1	1-0	0-2	1-1	1-1	0-4	1-6	3-5	n/a	1-1	5-0
Hedon Rangers	0-4	0-1	2-0	1-2	*E*	1-7	2-3	6-1	1-3	3-1	1-3	1-5	n/a	2-2	1-3
Hedon United	1-2	0-2	1-1	0-1	3-3	*M*	1-2	2-2	0-5	1-2	1-7	2-4	n/a	1-1	2-3
Hessle Rangers	0-1	2-1	4-0	1-1	8-0	2-0	*I*	2-0	0-1	3-1	0-3	1-7	n/a	3-1	4-2
Hornsea Town	1-1	1-0	0-2	1-2	4-0	4-1	1-0	*E*	2-0	0-2	0-7	1-3	n/a	0-4	1-2
Hutton Cranswick United	2-2	3-1	4-2	7-0	2-0	4-0	1-0	4-1	*R*	0-0	0-1	0-2	n/a	0-1	5-2
Pocklington Town	3-0	2-0	3-0	1-2	2-0	5-0	0-0	0-0	0-1		1-2	1-0	5-0	5-0	2-0
Reckitts	2-0	2-1	3-1	2-2	3-0	3-0	1-0	1-1	1-2	1-1	*D*	3-1	n/a	4-1	7-0
Sculcoates Amateurs	2-1	1-0	1-1	1-2	5-2	1-2	2-2	3-0	3-1	2-0	2-2	*I*	n/a	1-1	4-1
St Andrews Sutton	n/a	n/a	n/a	n/a	n/a	n/a	n/a	n/a	n/a	n/a	n/a	n/a	*V*	n/a	n/a
Westella & Willerby	1-0	3-0	3-4	3-1	3-1	1-0	1-3	2-0	1-1	3-2	1-0	2-3	n/a		6-0
Withernsea	2-4	2-2	1-2	1-6	0-6	3-2	1-1	1-2	3-8	1-5	1-6	0-8	n/a	0-2	

Note – St Andrews Sutton withdrew during the course of the season
Their results are shown above but are expunged from the league table

Premier Division	P	W	D	L	F	A	Pts
Reckitts	26	20	4	2	78	20	64
Sculcoates Amateurs	26	17	5	4	75	32	56
Hutton Cranswick United	26	16	4	6	65	31	52
Hessle Rangers	26	14	4	8	51	34	46
Westella & Willerby	26	13	6	7	50	35	45
Easington United	26	12	8	6	48	47	44
Pocklington Town	26	13	4	9	45	23	43
Beverley Town	26	11	6	9	51	40	39
Hornsea Town	26	8	6	12	29	46	30
Bridlington Town Res.	26	7	4	15	31	54	25
Driffield	26	5	7	14	35	62	22
Hedon Rangers	26	5	3	18	43	75	18
Withernsea	26	4	3	19	36	102	15
Hedon United	26	3	4	19	30	66	13

St Andrews Sutton – record expunged

LEAGUE CUP

FIRST ROUND

AFC Charleston 1 **Pinefleet Wolfreton** 3
Barton Town Old Boys Res. 0 **Anlaby United** 2
Bransholme Athletic 4 **Discount Carpets** 5
Driffield 4 Brandesburton 0
East Hull Amateurs 2 **North Ferriby United Res.** 6
Hedon United 1 **Malet Lambert YC** 2

SECOND ROUND

Anlaby United 6 Withernsea 3
Driffield 1 Malet Lambert YC 0
Pinefleet Wolfreton 5 Discount Carpets 3
St Andrews Police Club 1 **North Ferriby United Res.** 3

THIRD ROUND

Beverley Town 4 Pinefleet Wolfreton 0
Bridlington Town Res. 0 **Hedon Rangers** 2
Driffield 2 **Hutton Cranswick United** 4 *aet*

HUMBER PREMIER LEAGUE PREMIER DIVISION CONSTITUTION 2006-07

BARTON TOWN OLD BOYS RESERVES..... Marsh Lane, Barton-on-Humber DN15 5HB 07900 105204
BEVERLEY TOWN.................... Recreation Ground, Norwood, Beverley HU17 9HW 01482 862520
BRIDLINGTON TOWN RESERVES .... Queensgate Stadium, Queensgate, Bridlington YO16 5LN............................ 01262 606879
DRIFFIELD .... Allotment Lane, Driffield.................................... None
EASINGTON UNITED.................. Low Farm, Beck Street, Easington, Hull HU12 0TT.................................... None
HEDON RANGERS.................. Destiny Fitness, Staithes Road, Hedon, Hull HU12 8DX............................ 01482 896113
HEDON UNITED.......................... Drapers Lane, Hedon, Hull HU12 8BG............................ 07709 321686
HESSLE RANGERS................. Blackburn Leisure, Prescott Avenue, Brough HU15 1BB .... None
HORNSEA TOWN .... Hollis Recreation Ground, Atwick Road, Hornsea HU18 1EL .... None
HUTTON CRANSWICK UNITED........ Rotsea Lane, Hutton Cranswick, Driffield YO25 9QG.................................... None
NORTH FERRIBY UNITED RESERVES . . Humberside Police Sports Ground, Inglemire Lane, Hull HU6 8JG 01482 326111x2317
POCKLINGTON TOWN..................... The Balk, Pocklington, York YO42 2NZ 01759 303638
RECKITTS .... Humberside Police Sports Ground, Inglemire Lane, Hull HU6 8JG............ 01482 326111x2317
SCULCOATES AMATEURS.... Hull & East Riding Sports Ground, Chanterlands Avenue, Hull HU5 4ED................ 01482 342156
WESTELLA & WILLERBY............... Hull YPI, Chanterlands Avenue, Hull HU5 4EF .... None
WITHERNSEA .... Hull Road, Withernsea HU19 2EG.................................... None

IN: Barton Town Old Boys Reserves (P), North Ferriby United Reserves (P)
OUT: St Andrews Sutton (WS)

	AFC Charleston	Anlaby United	Barton Town Old Boys Res.	Brandesburton	Bransholme Athletic	Discount Carpets	East Hull Amateurs	Malet Lambert YC	North Ferriby United Res.	Pinefleet Wolfreton	St Andrews Police Club
AFC Charleston		1-4	4-4	1-1	3-0	4-1	0-3	0-4	1-5	3-3	2-7
Anlaby United	3-1		0-0	3-2	2-1	2-4	1-2	4-0	1-0	1-1	4-1
Barton Town Old Boys Res.	2-0	2-0	*D*	2-0	3-1	4-1	5-1	2-4	0-1	1-0	4-1
Brandesburton	2-5	0-3	1-2	*I*	3-2	3-4	3-3	3-3	2-5	1-2	6-1
Bransholme Athletic	2-2	3-2	1-3	4-2	*V*	2-3	1-1	1-1	3-5	1-3	1-0
Discount Carpets	1-1	4-1	3-2	4-3	4-1		2-1	0-1	0-2	2-0	1-1
East Hull Amateurs	0-2	0-1	2-2	1-3	4-1	0-2	*O*	2-3	0-2	0-2	0-2
Malet Lambert YC	2-3	1-3	1-4	0-1	0-0	2-2	2-0	*N*	2-2	0-0	1-1
North Ferriby United Res.	0-0	0-1	3-2	5-0	4-5	3-1	3-1	6-0	*E*	1-2	4-0
Pinefleet Wolfreton	1-2	1-1	4-4	2-1	4-3	1-3	3-2	3-3	3-3		4-0
St Andrews Police Club	2-3	2-3	1-3	0-2	1-1	3-2	3-1	1-2	1-1	0-3	

Hessle Rangers 2 Anlaby United 1 *aet*
Hornsea Town 1 Easington United 0
North Ferriby United Res. 5 Westella & Willerby 3 *aet*
Reckitts 1 **Sculcoates Amateurs** 2

FOURTH ROUND

Hedon Rangers 1 **Beverley Town** 2
Hessle Rangers 2 Pocklington Town 1
Hutton Cranswick United 2 Hornsea Town 0
Sculcoates Amateurs 1 North Ferriby United Res. 0

SEMI-FINALS

Beverley Town 0 **Hutton Cranswick United** 2
(at Bridlington Town)
Sculcoates Amateurs 3 Hessle Rangers 0
(at Hull University)

FINAL

(April 28th at North Ferriby United)
Sculcoates Amateurs 1 Hutton Cranswick United 0

Division One		P	W	D	L	F	A	Pts
North Ferriby United Res.		20	12	4	4	55	25	40
Barton Town Old Boys Res.		20	12	4	4	51	29	40
Anlaby United		20	12	3	5	40	26	39
Discount Carpets		20	11	3	6	44	37	36
Pinefleet Wolfreton		20	9	7	4	42	32	34
Malet Lambert YC		20	6	8	6	32	38	26
AFC Charleston	*-3*	20	7	6	7	38	47	24
Brandesburton		20	5	3	12	39	52	18
Bransholme Athletic		20	4	5	11	34	50	17
St Andrews Police Club		20	4	4	12	28	48	16
East Hull Amateurs		20	3	3	14	24	43	12

HUMBER PREMIER LEAGUE DIVISION ONE CONSTITUTION 2006-07

AFC CHARLESTON. . . . . Springhead Lane, Willerby Road, Hull HU5 5YJ. . . . . None
ANLABY UNITED. . . . . Swanland Playing Fields, West Leys Road, West Ella, Hull HU10 7SF . . . . None
BRANDESBURTON. . . . . Brandesburton Playing Fields, Catwick Lane, Brandesburton, Driffield YO25 8SB . . . . None
BRANSHOLME ATHLETIC . . . . Hull University, Inglemire Lane, Hull 01482 466000
DISCOUNT CARPETS . . . . Brooklands Park, Chamberlain Road, Hull . . . . None
EAST HULL AMATEURS. . . . . Brooklands Park, Chamberlain Road, Hull HU8 8DU. 01482 794193
HALL ROAD RANGERS RESERVES . . Dene Park, Dene Close, Beverley Road, Dunswell HU6 0AB 01482 850101
LSS LUCARLY'S . . . . Wilton Road, Humberston, Grimsby DN36 4AW. 01472 812936
LONG RISTON. . . . . Long Riston Playing Fields, Long Riston . . . . None
MALET LAMBERT YC. . . . . James Reckitt Avenue, Hull. . . . . None
NORTH CAVE . . . . North Cave Playing Field, North Cave . . . . None
PINEFLEET WOLFRETON . . . . . Marist RU Club, Cranbrook Avenue, Cottingham Road, Hull HU6 7TT. 01482 859216
SMITH & NEPHEW. . . . . Hull University, Inglemire Lane, Hull . . . . None
ST ANDREWS POLICE CLUB . . . . . Humberside Police Sports Ground, Inglemire Lane, Hull HU6 8JG 01482 326111x2317

IN: Hall Road Rangers Reserves (P – East Riding County Amateur League Division One), Long Riston (P – East Riding County Amateur League Premier Division), LSS Lucarly's (S – Central Midlands League Premier Division), North Cave (P – East Riding County Amateur League Premier Division), Smith & Nephew (P – Hull Sunday League)

OUT: Barton Town Old Boys Reserves (P), North Ferriby United Reserves (P)

ISTHMIAN LEAGUE

	AFC Wimbledon	Billericay Town	Braintree Town	Bromley	Chelmsford City	East Thurrock United	Fisher Athletic	Folkestone Invicta	Hampton/Richmond Boro'	Harrow Borough	Hendon	Heybridge Swifts	Leyton	Maldon Town	Margate	Redbridge	Slough Town	Staines Town	Walton & Hersham	Wealdstone	Windsor & Eton	Worthing
AFC Wimbledon		1-1	1-1	1-1	0-1	3-2	1-0	4-1	0-4	2-1	2-1	1-0	0-0	3-0	1-2	5-0	2-2	1-1	2-1	1-1	1-1	1-2
Billericay Town	2-1		1-1	2-2	4-2	1-3	1-3	2-0	1-2	3-1	1-0	1-2	2-2	2-3	4-1	1-0	3-1	1-1	0-2	2-0	3-0	1-1
Braintree Town	0-0	2-0		3-1	2-1	1-0	3-2	3-0	2-1	3-0	1-0	3-0	1-1	1-1	1-0	2-0	2-1	3-1	3-1	2-0	3-0	4-2
Bromley	2-0	1-0	1-1	*P*	1-1	1-1	1-2	3-3	2-0	1-1	3-1	2-1	1-2	2-1	2-2	1-0	2-3	1-1	1-0	1-1	4-1	1-2
Chelmsford City	1-0	2-1	0-2	3-2	*R*	2-4	0-2	0-1	3-3	3-0	3-0	0-2	1-1	1-2	1-0	2-1	2-0	4-4	1-1	0-0	2-1	1-0
East Thurrock United	1-1	0-3	1-3	1-0	3-0	*E*	2-5	0-2	1-2	3-2	3-0	0-4	1-3	1-1	3-1	2-0	3-2	0-2	1-0	2-0	0-2	5-1
Fisher Athletic	0-1	0-2	1-1	0-0	3-3	1-2	*M*	0-0	4-3	4-1	0-1	2-0	4-1	1-1	2-1	3-1	1-2	2-1	2-0	2-1	2-0	2-2
Folkestone Invicta	1-0	1-0	0-0	1-0	1-1	1-0	0-1	*I*	1-2	2-1	1-2	0-2	2-2	2-0	1-1	1-0	3-0	0-2	3-1	5-2	1-0	1-2
Hampton/Richmond Borough	2-1	0-1	0-1	0-0	3-0	1-0	0-3	3-1	*E*	1-3	3-1	0-5	4-2	1-2	0-1	3-1	3-2	2-1	2-0	3-0	4-0	1-2
Harrow Borough	1-2	1-1	1-0	2-0	2-1	5-4	0-2	5-0	0-2	*R*	1-1	1-2	3-3	1-1	0-0	0-0	2-1	1-4	1-2	1-2	2-1	2-2
Hendon	0-1	2-2	1-2	2-1	0-0	0-0	1-2	0-0	0-2	2-1		0-1	4-0	1-1	1-2	2-0	1-1	1-2	1-1	0-3	1-2	2-2
Heybridge Swifts	1-1	0-0	0-3	1-0	2-0	0-1	1-2	2-0	2-1	2-1	3-0	*D*	1-0	2-0	2-0	2-0	1-0	4-2	2-1	1-3	2-0	1-1
Leyton	1-2	1-3	0-1	0-1	5-1	1-2	3-4	1-1	1-1	0-1	2-0	0-1	*I*	4-2	0-2	4-0	1-2	0-2	0-1	1-2	2-1	1-0
Maldon Town	0-2	0-2	2-3	0-2	0-1	3-2	0-3	1-0	1-2	1-4	2-2	0-1	0-2	*V*	1-1	2-1	0-2	2-2	1-2	2-4	1-2	2-0
Margate	0-1	1-1	1-1	1-1	0-1	2-1	1-1	1-1	3-2	0-0	4-2	1-2	0-1	1-0	*I*	0-0	2-2	2-5	2-4	1-0	1-1	0-0
Redbridge	0-3	0-5	0-1	3-2	1-2	0-1	0-5	0-2	0-2	0-1	0-2	1-2	0-4	0-0	3-1	*S*	1-4	1-2	1-3	2-3	1-1	3-2
Slough Town	0-2	0-2	2-1	2-2	0-1	1-2	0-4	2-0	0-1	5-2	0-2	1-2	0-0	4-1	2-2	3-2	*I*	1-2	0-2	3-2	3-3	0-3
Staines Town	0-3	1-2	1-1	1-2	3-0	1-0	2-0	2-2	0-1	0-1	2-0	5-1	2-3	1-1	2-1	2-2	2-1	*O*	2-1	1-3	1-0	0-1
Walton & Hersham	0-2	0-0	3-2	0-1	2-2	1-0	0-1	0-3	2-0	3-1	1-0	2-1	2-0	3-0	1-1	2-1	0-1	0-2	*N*	1-0	3-2	2-3
Wealdstone	1-5	1-1	2-3	1-2	1-2	0-2	1-2	1-2	1-2	4-1	4-5	3-4	1-0	0-2	0-4	6-1	2-2	1-2	1-3		4-2	2-1
Windsor & Eton	0-4	1-0	0-1	0-1	1-2	0-0	1-4	1-0	1-3	0-1	1-1	3-4	2-0	0-0	0-1	1-0	0-3	1-2	1-1	0-3		2-1
Worthing	0-2	2-4	2-0	1-2	1-3	1-0	4-0	1-0	2-1	3-0	1-1	4-1	0-3	2-1	1-1	5-1	4-2	2-2	0-0	3-1	2-1	

Premier Division		HOME					AWAY					TOTAL					
	P	W	D	L	F	A	W	D	L	F	A	W	D	L	F	A	Pts
Braintree Town	42	18	3	0	45	12	10	7	4	29	20	28	10	4	74	32	94
Heybridge Swifts	42	14	3	4	32	16	14	0	7	38	30	28	3	11	70	46	87
Fisher Athletic	42	10	6	5	36	24	16	1	4	48	22	26	7	9	84	46	85
AFC Wimbledon	42	9	8	4	33	23	13	3	5	34	13	22	11	9	67	36	77
Hampton & Richmond Boro'	42	12	1	8	36	27	12	2	7	37	27	24	3	15	73	54	75
Staines Town	42	9	4	8	31	26	11	6	4	43	30	20	10	12	74	56	70
Billericay Town	42	10	5	6	38	28	9	7	5	31	17	19	12	11	69	45	69
Worthing	42	12	4	5	41	26	7	6	8	30	34	19	10	13	71	60	67
Walton & Hersham	42	11	3	7	28	23	8	4	9	27	27	19	7	16	55	50	64
Chelmsford City	42	10	5	6	32	27	8	5	8	25	35	18	10	14	57	62	64
Bromley	42	9	8	4	34	24	7	6	8	23	25	16	14	12	57	49	62
East Thurrock United	42	10	2	9	33	34	8	3	10	27	26	18	5	19	60	60	59
Folkestone Invicta	42	11	4	6	28	19	5	6	10	19	32	16	10	16	47	51	58
Margate	42	5	10	6	24	27	6	7	8	25	28	11	17	14	49	55	50
Leyton	42	6	2	13	28	30	7	7	7	30	31	13	9	20	58	61	48
Harrow Borough	42	7	7	7	32	31	6	2	13	24	42	13	9	20	56	73	48
Slough Town	42	6	4	11	29	38	7	4	10	34	37	13	8	21	63	75	47
Wealdstone	42	5	2	14	37	48	8	3	10	31	34	13	5	24	68	82	44
Hendon	42	4	8	9	22	26	5	4	12	22	38	9	12	21	44	64	39
Maldon Town	42	4	3	14	21	40	4	8	9	20	33	8	11	23	41	73	35
Windsor & Eton	42	5	4	12	16	32	3	4	14	21	43	8	8	26	37	75	32
Redbridge	42	3	2	16	17	48	0	3	18	11	49	3	5	34	28	97	14

PLAY-OFFS

SEMI-FINALS

(May 1st) Heybridge Swifts 1 **Hampton & Richmond Borough** 1 *aet* (2-4p) ***Att*** 622

(May 2nd) **Fisher Athletic** 2 AFC Wimbledon 1 ***Att*** 2,274

FINAL

(May 6th at Fisher Athletic)

Fisher Athletic 3 Hampton & Richmond Borough 0 ***Att*** 900

DATES & GATES

	AFC Wimbledon	Billericay Town	Braintree Town	Bromley	Chelmsford City	East Thurrock United	Fisher Athletic	Folkestone Invicta	Hampton & Richmond	Harrow Borough	Hendon	Heybridge Swifts	Leyton	Maldon Town	Margate	Redbridge	Slough Town	Staines Town	Walton & Hersham	Wealdstone	Windsor & Eton	Worthing
AFC Wimbledon		8 Oct *2,445*	7 Feb *2,615*	6 Sep *2,563*	11 Mar *2,762*	15 Apr *2,706*	22 Oct *2,745*	20 Aug *3,002*	1 Apr *3,315*	29 Apr *3,044*	10 Dec *2,693*	18 Mar *2,455*	3 Dec *2,470*	5 Nov *2,528*	11 Feb *2,540*	22 Nov *2,093*	28 Jan *2,859*	29 Aug *2,754*	26 Dec *2,969*	4 Oct *2,464*	18 Feb *3,158*	17 Sep *2,642*
Billericay Town	8 Apr *1,180*		13 Dec *371*	11 Mar *503*	29 Aug *980*	10 Dec *458*	1 Oct *511*	14 Jan *513*	29 Apr *1,020*	14 Apr *422*	18 Feb *447*	4 Feb *540*	11 Oct *368*	6 Sep *524*	25 Mar *512*	26 Dec *461*	20 Aug *522*	28 Jan *423*	17 Sep *484*	5 Nov *472*	22 Nov *241*	26 Nov *421*
Braintree Town	4 Mar *1,916*	25 Feb *703*		10 Jan *409*	26 Dec *967*	14 Jan *504*	3 Dec *510*	19 Nov *413*	4 Oct *422*	1 Apr *510*	20 Aug *317*	25 Oct *487*	20 Sep *318*	29 Aug *406*	29 Oct *478*	17 Sep *322*	14 Apr *875*	11 Feb *517*	29 Apr *961*	18 Mar *503*	10 Dec *316*	28 Jan *557*
Bromley	25 Oct *1,235*	19 Nov *403*	8 Apr *431*		20 Aug *499*	28 Jan *345*	17 Jan *510*	29 Aug *409*	25 Feb *312*	11 Feb *321*	15 Apr *272*	4 Mar *322*	25 Mar *331*	17 Sep *405*	20 Sep *362*	22 Apr *268*	3 Dec *378*	29 Oct *402*	14 Jan *363*	17 Dec *374*	1 Oct *344*	27 Dec *480*
Chelmsford City	19 Nov *878*	2 Jan *2,998*	17 Apr *1,495*	7 Jan *1,663*		18 Mar *757*	17 Dec *401*	19 Sep *286*	3 Dec *392*	29 Oct *418*	8 Mar *502*	22 Aug *515*	21 Jan *1,485*	11 Feb *1,236*	3 Mar *853*	1 Apr *748*	25 Feb *1,006*	24 Oct *350*	3 Oct *282*	27 Aug *360*	3 Sep *316*	22 Apr *611*
East Thurrock United	3 Sep *778*	24 Sep *258*	23 Aug *165*	27 Aug *162*	1 Oct *246*		17 Apr *124*	25 Mar *151*	29 Oct *158*	25 Oct *125*	11 Feb *148*	2 Jan *179*	19 Nov *103*	8 Apr *107*	3 Dec *161*	31 Jan *84*	20 Sep *175*	4 Mar *114*	28 Mar *91*	21 Jan *162*	14 Feb *95*	11 Oct *132*
Fisher Athletic	25 Feb *1,036*	18 Mar *208*	4 Feb *378*	1 Apr *246*	29 Apr *208*	26 Dec *138*		29 Oct *152*	19 Sep *234*	17 Sep *134*	14 Jan *170*	3 Oct *184*	4 Mar *112*	28 Jan *116*	24 Oct *192*	20 Aug *120*	19 Nov *160*	15 Apr *139*	10 Dec *144*	28 Nov *170*	26 Nov *116*	29 Aug *206*
Folkestone Invicta	7 Jan *1,048*	26 Sep *242*	11 Mar *370*	2 Jan *369*	21 Nov *304*	3 Oct *251*	18 Feb *427*		21 Jan *405*	18 Mar *346*	5 Dec *239*	3 Sep *256*	27 Aug *286*	30 Jan *248*	17 Apr *574*	27 Feb *274*	28 Nov *263*	17 Dec *263*	1 Apr *405*	22 Apr *384*	4 Feb *417*	5 Sep *241*
Hampton/Richmond Boro'	11 Oct *2,520*	17 Dec *302*	25 Mar *439*	6 Dec *203*	4 Feb *357*	18 Feb *228*	22 Nov *376*	17 Sep *292*		14 Jan *291*	22 Oct *287*	4 Apr *303*	1 Oct *222*	22 Apr *295*	8 Apr *320*	15 Apr *273*	29 Aug *303*	26 Dec *463*	20 Aug *291*	6 Sep *373*	5 Nov *308*	11 Mar *291*
Harrow Borough	21 Mar *611*	3 Sep *144*	6 Dec *111*	24 Jan *113*	18 Feb *193*	6 Sep *130*	21 Jan *150*	1 Oct *147*	23 Aug *165*		11 Mar *190*	7 Jan *140*	2 Jan *144*	22 Nov *94*	27 Aug *212*	22 Oct *163*	22 Apr *220*	25 Mar *137*	4 Feb *158*	18 Apr *547*	8 Apr *141*	5 Nov *185*
Hendon	22 Apr *1,444*	29 Oct *248*	7 Jan *222*	3 Sep *179*	8 Apr *265*	24 Jan *134*	23 Aug *216*	25 Feb *157*	27 Aug *167*	19 Nov *210*		21 Jan *202*	17 Apr *195*	11 Oct *151*	17 Dec *221*	4 Feb *173*	4 Mar *241*	20 Sep *141*	25 Oct *180*	2 Jan *380*	25 Mar *235*	1 Oct *191*
Heybridge Swifts	1 Oct *816*	3 Dec *281*	6 Sep *326*	5 Nov *213*	14 Jan *604*	29 Aug *188*	25 Mar *269*	14 Apr *312*	11 Feb *237*	20 Aug *185*	17 Sep *188*		8 Apr *260*	26 Dec *529*	6 Dec *141*	11 Mar *264*	17 Dec *201*	22 Apr *227*	21 Mar *175*	22 Nov *143*	22 Oct *199*	18 Feb *246*
Leyton	4 Feb *718*	1 Apr *135*	22 Nov *115*	4 Oct *142*	17 Sep *150*	11 Mar *35*	5 Nov *112*	28 Jan *84*	18 Mar *56*	29 Aug *178*	26 Dec *128*	21 Feb *59*		22 Oct *78*	22 Apr *104*	18 Feb *88*	14 Jan *137*	20 Aug *204*	15 Apr *79*	26 Nov *150*	18 Oct *50*	17 Dec *78*
Maldon Town	23 Aug *528*	25 Oct *201*	2 Jan *404*	21 Jan *133*	26 Nov *403*	8 Oct *120*	27 Aug *104*	4 Mar *175*	10 Dec *140*	20 Sep *186*	1 Apr *107*	17 Apr *360*	25 Feb *123*		7 Jan *131*	4 Oct *156*	18 Mar *119*	19 Nov *115*	29 Oct *174*	3 Sep *196*	29 Apr *76*	4 Feb *121*
Margate	7 Mar *776*	4 Oct *807*	18 Feb *678*	22 Nov *401*	5 Nov *759*	4 Feb *491*	6 Sep *812*	26 Dec *902*	26 Nov *505*	28 Jan *535*	29 Apr *701*	1 Apr *557*	10 Dec *505*	20 Aug *1,280*		29 Aug *1,010*	17 Sep *871*	14 Jan *593*	18 Mar *508*	22 Oct *708*	4 Apr *456*	15 Apr *628*
Redbridge	20 Sep *489*	17 Apr *204*	21 Jan *168*	10 Dec *117*	14 Feb *184*	29 Apr *65*	7 Jan *140*	11 Feb *93*	3 Sep *60*	25 Feb *53*	3 Dec *94*	19 Nov *75*	1 Nov *94*	25 Mar *66*	2 Jan *154*		25 Oct *101*	1 Oct *41*	4 Mar *84*	23 Aug *162*	27 Aug *94*	8 Apr *101*
Slough Town	27 Aug *1,264*	7 Jan *308*	3 Sep *260*	4 Feb *294*	22 Oct *340*	22 Nov *191*	11 Mar *293*	8 Apr *289*	2 Jan *448*	10 Dec *333*	5 Nov *291*	29 Apr *274*	23 Aug *246*	1 Oct *303*	21 Jan *346*	6 Sep *248*		11 Oct *274*	26 Nov *311*	18 Feb *412*	17 Apr *508*	25 Mar *258*
Staines Town	2 Jan *2,285*	27 Aug *301*	24 Jan *284*	18 Feb *251*	6 Sep *264*	5 Nov *220*	3 Sep *219*	29 Apr *226*	11 Apr *588*	4 Oct *343*	22 Nov *176*	10 Dec *173*	7 Jan *178*	11 Mar *207*	23 Aug *314*	18 Mar *191*	1 Apr *376*		7 Feb *412*	4 Feb *315*	21 Jan *289*	22 Oct *280*
Walton & Hersham	17 Apr *1,975*	21 Jan *302*	17 Dec *159*	23 Aug *175*	25 Mar *219*	22 Oct *147*	22 Apr *138*	11 Oct *173*	7 Jan *301*	3 Dec *160*	6 Sep *192*	27 Aug *126*	3 Sep *126*	18 Feb *151*	1 Oct *262*	5 Nov *156*	11 Feb *275*	7 Apr *401*		11 Mar *229*	2 Jan *220*	13 Dec *182*
Wealdstone	25 Mar *1,009*	4 Apr *255*	1 Oct *305*	29 Apr *307*	28 Jan *344*	17 Sep *327*	8 Apr *302*	9 Dec *251*	25 Oct *253*	26 Dec *469*	31 Aug *355*	20 Sep *227*	11 Feb *238*	14 Apr *311*	25 Feb *280*	14 Jan *308*	29 Oct *380*	3 Dec *265*	10 Jan *274*		10 Oct *243*	20 Aug *315*
Windsor & Eton	29 Oct *1,012*	28 Mar *124*	22 Apr *147*	18 Mar *132*	15 Apr *136*	20 Aug *131*	11 Feb *128*	3 Dec *100*	4 Mar *169*	14 Mar *85*	4 Oct *135*	25 Feb *122*	25 Oct *104*	17 Dec *86*	19 Nov *154*	28 Jan *103*	26 Dec *609*	17 Sep *180*	29 Aug *144*	1 Apr *210*		14 Jan *173*
Worthing	21 Jan *2,253*	11 Feb *502*	27 Aug *369*	17 Apr *532*	10 Dec *504*	1 Apr *459*	2 Jan *765*	25 Oct *408*	19 Nov *640*	28 Mar *227*	18 Mar *394*	29 Oct *451*	29 Apr *346*	3 Dec *414*	3 Sep *404*	6 Dec *260*	4 Oct *436*	25 Feb *411*	20 Sep *408*	7 Jan *602*	23 Aug *346*	

ISTHMIAN LEAGUE PREMIER DIVISION

CONSTITUTION FOR 2006-07

AFC WIMBLEDON

The Fans' Stadium, Kingsmeadow, Jack Goodchild Way, 422a Kingston Road, Kingston-upon-Thames, Surrey KT1 3PB
Tel: 020 8547 3528
Manager: Dave Anderson www.afcwimbledon.co.uk Colours: Blue

ASHFORD TOWN (MIDDX)

Short Lane Stadium, Short Lane, Stanwell, Staines, Middlesex TW19 7BH
Tel: 01784 245908 Colours: Tangerine, white & black
Manager: Dave Kent www.ashfordtownmxfootballclub.co.uk

BILLERICAY TOWN

New Lodge, Blunts Wall Road, Billericay, Essex CM12 9SA
Tel: 01277 655177 Club: 01277 652188
Manager: Matt Jones www.billericaytownfc.co.uk Colours: Blue & white

BOREHAM WOOD

Meadow Park, Broughinge Road, Boreham Wood, Hertfordshire WD6 5AL
Tel: 020 8953 5097 Club: 020 8207 7982 Fax: 020 8207 7982
Manager: Steve Cook Colours: White & black
www.web-teams.co.uk/Home.asp?team=borehamwoodfc

BROMLEY

The Clive Christian Stadium, Hayes Lane, Bromley, Kent BR2 9EF
Tel: 020 8460 5291 Fax: 020 8313 3992
Manager: Mark Goldberg www.bromleyfc.net Colours: White & black

CARSHALTON ATHLETIC

War Memorial Sports Ground, Colston Avenue, Carshalton, Surrey SM5 2PW
Tel: 020 8642 8658 Fax: 020 8643 0999
Manager: Dave Garland www.carshaltonathletic.org Colours: White & maroon

CHELMSFORD CITY

Melbourne Stadium, Salerno Way, Chelmsford, Essex CM1 2EH
Tel: 01245 290959
Manager: Jeff King www.chelmsfordcityfc.com Colours: Claret

EAST THURROCK UNITED

Rookery Hill, Corringham, Stanford-le-Hope, Essex SS17 9LB
Tel: 01375 382999 Boardroom: 01375 641009 Fax: 01375 641009
Manager: Lee Patterson www.eastthurrockunited.co.uk Colours: Amber & black

FOLKESTONE INVICTA

Buzzlines Stadium, Cheriton Road Sports Ground, Folkestone, Kent CT20 5JU
Tel: 01303 257461 Fax: 01303 255541
Manager: Neil Cugley www.folkestoneinvicta.co.uk Colours: Black & amber

HAMPTON & RICHMOND BOROUGH

Beveree Stadium, Beaver Close, Station Road, Hampton, Middlesex TW12 2BX
Tel: 020 8941 2838 Boardroom: 020 8941 4936 Fax/Club: 020 8979 2456
Manager: Alan Devonshire www.hamptonfc.com Colours: Red & blue

HARROW BOROUGH

Earlsmead Stadium, Carlyon Avenue, South Harrow, Middlesex HA2 8SS
Tel: 0870 609 1959 Fax: 020 8423 0159
Manager: David Howell www.harrowboro.com Colours: Red

HENDON
Claremont Road, Brent Cross, London NW2 1AE
Tel: 020 8201 9494 Club: 020 8455 9185 Fax: 020 8905 5966
Manager: Gary McCann www.hendonfc.net Colours: White & green

HEYBRIDGE SWIFTS
Scraley Road, Heybridge, Maldon, Essex CM9 8JA
Tel: 01621 852978 Club: 01621 852978
Manager: Brian Statham www.heybridgeswifts.com Colours: Black & white

HORSHAM
Queen Street, Horsham, West Sussex RH12 5AD
Tel: 01403 252310 Boardroom: 01403 255787
Manager: John Maggs www.horshamfc.co.uk Colours: Amber & green

LEYTON
Leyton Stadium, 282 Lea Bridge Road, Leyton, London E10 7LD
Tel: 020 8988 7642 Club: 020 8988 7642
Manager: John Sitton www.leytonfc.co.uk Colours: Blue & white

MARGATE
Hartsdown Park, Hartsdown Road, Margate, Kent CT9 5QZ
Tel: 01843 221769 Fax: 01843 221769
Manager: Robin Trott www.margate-fc.com Colours: Royal blue & white

RAMSGATE
Southwood Stadium, Prices Avenue, Ramsgate, Kent CT11 0AN
Tel: 01843 591662
Manager: Jim Ward www.ramsgate-fc.co.uk Colours: Red

SLOUGH TOWN
Windsor & Eton FC, Stag Meadow, St Leonards Road, Windsor, Berkshire SL4 3DR
Tel: 01753 860656 Fax: 01753 860656
Manager: Eddie Denton www.sloughtownfc.net Colours: Yellow & navy blue

STAINES TOWN
Wheatsheaf Park, Wheatsheaf Lane, Staines, Middlesex TW18 2PD
Tel: 01784 225943
Manager: Steve Cordery www.stainesmassive.co.uk Colours: Old gold & blue

TONBRIDGE ANGELS
Longmead Stadium, Darenth Avenue, Tonbridge, Kent TN10 3JW
Tel: 01732 352477 Club: 01732 352417
Manager: Tony Dolby www.tonbridgeafc.co.uk Colours: Black & white

WALTON & HERSHAM
Sports Ground, Stompond Lane, Walton-on-Thames, Surrey KT12 1HF
Tel: 01932 244967 Boardroom: 01932 245363 Fax: 01932 885814
Manager: Alan Dowson www.waltonandhershamfc.org.uk Colours: Red

WORTHING
Woodside Road, Worthing, West Sussex BN14 7HQ
Tel: 01903 239575 Fax: 01903 239575
Manager: Danny Bloor www.worthingfc.com Colours: Red

***IN:** Ashford Town (Middx) (P – Southern League Division One West), Boreham Wood (P – Southern League Division One East), Carshalton Athletic (R – Football Conference South), Horsham (P), Ramsgate (P), Tonbridge Angels (P)*

***OUT:** Braintree Town (P – Football Conference South), Fisher Athletic (P – Football Conference South), Maldon Town (R – Division One North), Redbridge (R – Division One North), Wealdstone (S – Southern League Premier Division), Windsor & Eton (Southern League Division One South & West)*

	Ashford Town	Banstead Athletic	Bashley	Burgess Hill Town	Corinthian-Casuals	Cray Wanderers	Croydon Athletic	Dover Athletic	Dulwich Hamlet	Fleet Town	Hastings United	Horsham	Kingstonian	Leatherhead	Lymington & New Milton	Metropolitan Police	Molesey	Newport IOW	Ramsgate	Tonbridge Angels	Tooting & Mitcham Utd	Walton Casuals	Whyteleafe
Ashford Town		1-1	2-0	1-0	3-1	0-3	0-1	3-2	1-2	0-2	2-2	0-7	2-1	0-0	0-5	1-2	1-3	0-1	0-3	2-3	0-2	1-1	1-2
Banstead Athletic	0-1		1-2	1-0	2-1	0-2	2-0	2-1	1-1	1-1	1-2	0-3	0-4	1-2	0-1	1-0	0-0	3-0	2-2	0-2	0-4	3-3	1-1
Bashley	1-1	3-1		2-1	3-1	3-2	3-1	0-2	0-3	0-5	0-0	1-1	3-2	0-1	2-1	3-4	2-1	3-0	0-1	0-0	1-2	5-2	1-0
Burgess Hill Town	5-0	2-2	0-1		1-3	1-4	1-1	0-1	2-0	3-2	1-2	0-3	1-3	2-2	3-0	0-3	3-1	5-0	1-2	1-2	2-1	3-3	1-0
Corinthian-Casuals	0-1	0-0	1-3	0-1		1-2	0-3	0-5	1-4	3-1	0-2	0-1	0-0	3-0	1-2	0-0	2-0	1-1	0-1	1-1	1-5	3-4	3-0
Cray Wanderers	2-0	2-1	2-2	3-0	3-2	*D*	2-2	3-1	2-1	0-2	0-2	2-1	1-3	3-3	2-5	2-1	3-3	0-3	0-1	2-0	3-3	1-0	3-1
Croydon Athletic	2-0	1-0	0-1	0-0	0-0	2-1	*I*	0-0	3-0	1-1	0-1	1-1	3-1	1-1	1-1	2-1	2-0	1-0	0-3	3-2	3-0	3-1	1-1
Dover Athletic	1-0	1-0	2-1	3-3	4-0	2-1	1-1	*V*	2-1	1-1	2-3	0-0	1-1	1-0	5-1	0-3	1-0	1-0	1-1	0-0	4-0	2-1	4-1
Dulwich Hamlet	2-0	3-1	0-1	3-0	2-0	1-0	1-0	0-0	*I*	0-1	2-0	2-2	0-1	0-1	0-0	1-2	0-1	1-2	3-3	1-3	2-0	1-0	1-0
Fleet Town	1-0	1-0	1-1	1-1	1-0	3-3	1-3	1-2	1-0	*S*	1-0	1-0	3-3	1-1	2-0	1-1	1-1	1-2	0-0	1-0	0-4	0-2	0-0
Hastings United	2-0	3-5	0-2	2-1	3-0	4-0	1-0	4-0	1-4	0-0	*I*	2-3	3-3	1-1	0-1	2-1	3-0	0-1	1-1	0-3	3-2	3-4	3-1
Horsham	3-3	2-0	7-1	3-3	1-0	3-0	1-1	2-3	2-1	4-1	0-0	*O*	2-2	2-1	4-0	1-3	5-0	2-1	2-1	1-0	1-6	3-1	2-1
Kingstonian	2-4	0-0	1-0	3-2	2-2	2-2	2-0	2-2	1-2	1-3	2-0	1-2	*N*	2-1	5-0	2-0	2-1	0-1	1-1	1-2	2-2	4-0	3-1
Leatherhead	1-1	4-0	0-1	2-0	3-2	3-0	2-1	0-0	0-1	0-0	1-2	2-4	0-0		1-1	2-0	5-4	1-0	1-2	4-1	0-3	2-1	2-1
Lymington/New Milton	2-1	3-0	0-1	3-0	2-0	0-3	0-2	1-1	0-1	1-1	0-0	3-1	2-4	0-1		0-3	0-3	4-0	0-3	1-2	1-1	3-3	1-2
Metropolitan Police	2-1	4-3	2-1	3-0	3-1	1-0	2-0	1-2	1-0	3-0	0-0	4-1	0-0	2-1	1-1	*O*	0-1	5-1	1-0	2-3	0-1	1-0	3-1
Molesey	1-1	2-1	2-0	1-1	1-1	0-2	0-1	2-1	1-1	3-1	0-1	1-3	2-3	0-1	2-7	3-2	*N*	3-0	0-2	1-1	0-1	5-1	0-0
Newport IOW	1-1	0-2	1-1	0-2	0-0	2-6	1-2	1-1	2-4	2-2	2-2	0-1	1-3	2-2	3-3	0-0	0-1	*E*	0-0	0-1	1-2	2-5	0-2
Ramsgate	0-0	1-1	2-4	1-0	3-1	2-0	0-1	3-2	0-0	2-0	2-1	1-0	3-3	0-0	5-0	4-1	7-1	6-0		3-3	3-2	0-1	5-1
Tonbridge Angels	3-1	1-0	1-1	2-1	3-1	1-0	2-1	0-0	2-0	1-1	1-0	0-1	1-0	1-4	3-1	0-1	2-0	7-0	2-1		2-3	1-2	0-2
Tooting & Mitcham Utd	2-2	1-1	2-1	2-2	6-0	3-4	1-2	2-0	0-2	4-0	4-1	2-3	0-1	2-1	3-2	1-1	4-3	3-1	1-1	0-2		3-0	1-1
Walton Casuals	1-0	2-2	1-1	5-1	1-0	0-1	1-2	0-2	1-0	2-2	2-3	2-2	0-1	0-3	2-0	1-0	1-1	4-1	0-1	3-1	2-1		0-0
Whyteleafe	3-2	1-0	1-1	6-0	1-2	3-3	1-1	0-2	1-1	0-0	2-0	1-1	0-2	1-1	2-2	1-2	3-1	3-2	0-1	0-3	0-1	1-2	

Division One		HOME					AWAY					TOTAL					
	P	W	D	L	F	A	W	D	L	F	A	W	D	L	F	A	Pts
Ramsgate	44	13	6	3	53	22	11	8	3	31	16	24	14	6	84	38	86
Horsham	44	14	5	3	53	29	11	6	5	41	26	25	11	8	94	55	86
Tonbridge Angels	44	13	3	6	36	21	11	5	6	35	27	24	8	12	71	48	80
Metropolitan Police	44	15	3	4	41	18	9	4	9	31	28	24	7	13	72	46	79
Dover Athletic	44	13	7	2	39	19	8	7	7	30	27	21	14	9	69	46	77
Tooting & Mitcham United	44	10	6	6	47	31	12	3	7	46	31	22	9	13	93	62	75
Kingstonian	44	10	6	6	41	28	10	8	4	41	28	20	14	10	82	56	74
Croydon Athletic	44	11	8	3	30	16	9	5	8	26	25	20	13	11	56	41	73
Bashley	44	11	4	7	36	32	9	6	7	27	29	20	10	14	63	61	70
Leatherhead	44	11	5	6	36	25	7	9	6	28	25	18	14	12	64	50	68
Cray Wanderers	44	11	5	6	41	37	9	3	10	39	37	20	8	16	80	74	68
Hastings United	44	10	4	8	41	33	9	6	7	24	25	19	10	15	65	58	67
Dulwich Hamlet	44	10	4	8	26	18	9	4	9	29	25	19	8	17	55	43	65
Fleet Town	44	8	9	5	23	24	5	10	7	27	32	13	19	12	50	56	58
Walton Casuals	44	9	6	7	32	26	7	4	11	36	49	16	10	18	68	75	58
Lymington & New Milton	44	6	5	11	27	33	6	6	10	34	47	12	11	21	61	80	47
Molesey	44	7	6	9	30	32	5	4	13	26	47	12	10	22	56	79	46
Whyteleafe	44	6	8	8	31	30	4	6	12	19	36	10	14	20	50	66	44
Burgess Hill Town	44	8	4	10	38	36	2	6	14	19	47	10	10	24	57	83	40
Banstead Athletic	44	6	6	10	22	33	2	7	13	21	38	8	13	23	43	71	37
Ashford Town	44	5	4	13	21	44	3	7	12	20	37	8	11	25	41	81	35
Newport IOW	44	0	10	12	21	43	6	1	15	17	54	6	11	27	38	97	29
Corinthian-Casuals	44	4	5	13	21	37	2	4	16	18	48	6	9	29	39	85	27

PLAY-OFFS

SEMI-FINALS *(May 1st)*

Metropolitan Police 0 **Dover Athletic** 1 *Att* 492

Tonbridge Angels 2 Tooting & Mitcham Utd 0 *Att* 707

FINAL

(May 6th at Tonbridge Angels)

Tonbridge Angels 3 Dover Athletic 2 *Att* 1,853

OUT: All were switched to the newly formed Division One South except for Bashley (S – Southern League Division One South and West), Horsham (P), Lymington & New Milton (S – Southern League Division One South and West), Newport IOW (S – Southern League Division One South and West), Ramsgate (P), Tonbridge Angels (P), Waltham Forest (S – Division One North)

DATES & GATES	Ashford Tow	Banstead Athletic	Bashley	Burgess Hill Town	Corinthian-Casuals	Cray Wanderers	Croydon Athletic	Dover Athleti	Dulwich Hamlet	Fleet Town	Hastings United	Horsham	Kingstonian	Leatherhead	Lymington & New Milton	Metropolitan Police	Molesey	Newport IOW	Ramsgate	Tonbridge Angels	Tooting & Mitcham Utd	Walton Casuals	Whyteleafe
Ashford Town		3 Dec *141*	8 Apr *142*	29 Oct *183*	4 Oct *126*	22 Nov *105*	4 Apr *169*	2 Jan *691*	7 Mar *93*	19 Nov *162*	17 Apr *311*	25 Mar *241*	20 Sep *178*	11 Feb *205*	4 Mar *147*	7 Jan *157*	29 Apr *163*	3 Sep *136*	10 Dec *241*	21 Jan *352*	1 Oct *217*	24 Sep *185*	23 Aug *222*
Banstead Athletic	4 Feb *46*		18 Feb *61*	2 Jan *89*	22 Oct *71*	17 Dec *68*	8 Oct *58*	6 Dec *143*	27 Sep *92*	18 Mar *53*	2 Sep *152*	11 Mar *161*	28 Feb *147*	17 Apr *148*	28 Mar *35*	26 Nov *61*	7 Jan *63*	22 Apr *103*	1 Nov *67*	23 Aug *118*	5 Nov *167*	21 Jan *67*	29 Nov *82*
Bashley	8 Oct *59*	29 Oct *88*		24 Sep *78*	22 Apr *97*	4 Mar *88*	19 Nov *62*	3 Sep *103*	25 Feb *105*	25 Oct *62*	3 Dec *91*	17 Dec *98*	1 Apr *212*	23 Aug *130*	26 Dec *351*	15 Nov *68*	28 Mar *57*	2 Jan *118*	18 Mar *102*	11 Feb *152*	21 Jan *174*	12 Nov *55*	7 Jan *97*
Burgess Hill Town	18 Feb *156*	29 Aug *196*	22 Mar *82*		5 Nov *175*	15 Apr *172*	22 Apr *168*	11 Mar *243*	14 Jan *151*	28 Jan *151*	25 Mar *251*	26 Dec *394*	17 Sep *254*	5 Oct *161*	17 Dec *170*	1 Oct *151*	4 Feb *152*	1 Mar *131*	20 Aug *212*	8 Apr *261*	22 Oct *229*	11 Apr *93*	7 Dec *128*
Corinthian-Casuals	1 Apr *132*	25 Feb *90*	10 Dec *77*	4 Mar *104*		7 Mar *50*	7 Feb *86*	15 Nov *142*	19 Nov *117*	29 Oct *86*	23 Aug *96*	29 Nov *112*	8 Oct *301*	3 Sep *117*	21 Jan *87*	3 Jan *106*	17 Apr *114*	26 Nov *71*	27 Sep *84*	29 Apr *183*	6 Dec *121*	7 Jan *103*	4 Feb *102*
Cray Wanderers	6 Dec *112*	29 Apr *123*	5 Nov *85*	10 Jan *110*	1 Nov *112*		18 Mar *107*	14 Feb *202*	1 Apr *179*	27 Sep *52*	21 Jan *205*	28 Feb *117*	20 Dec *163*	10 Dec *118*	7 Jan *97*	23 Aug *134*	18 Jan *123*	4 Feb *121*	11 Mar *167*	17 Apr *232*	2 Jan *214*	3 Sep *96*	18 Feb *128*
Croydon Athletic	22 Oct *60*	8 Apr *98*	11 Mar *91*	10 Dec *97*	28 Feb *98*	1 Oct *90*		31 Jan *150*	29 Nov *90*	29 Apr *63*	4 Oct *91*	18 Feb *141*	1 Nov *121*	5 Nov *101*	3 Sep *72*	21 Jan *95*	6 Dec *101*	7 Jan *76*	13 Dec *89*	25 Mar *253*	24 Sep *191*	23 Aug *76*	17 Apr *136*
Dover Athletic	29 Aug *772*	12 Nov *701*	28 Jan *609*	19 Nov *791*	15 Apr *905*	20 Sep *1,001*	11 Feb *734*		20 Aug *704*	10 Dec *711*	7 Mar *449*	14 Jan *839*	14 Mar *583*	25 Mar *629*	29 Oct *752*	25 Feb *604*	4 Mar *693*	1 Oct *804*	26 Dec *1,734*	25 Oct *1,248*	8 Apr *841*	4 Oct *815*	29 Apr *1,039*
Dulwich Hamlet	1 Nov *148*	25 Mar *289*	22 Oct *196*	23 Aug *255*	11 Mar *244*	4 Oct *172*	20 Sep *177*	7 Jan *315*		14 Feb *167*	11 Feb *279*	8 Apr *341*	18 Feb *328*	1 Oct *260*	3 Dec *209*	22 Apr *286*	2 Jan *240*	24 Jan *186*	28 Feb *239*	3 Sep *285*	17 Apr *411*	5 Nov *229*	21 Jan *256*
Fleet Town	11 Mar *151*	1 Oct *143*	28 Feb *101*	3 Sep *119*	18 Feb *109*	25 Mar *140*	17 Dec *79*	22 Apr *287*	6 Dec *85*		13 Dec *101*	1 Nov *122*	5 Nov *204*	21 Jan *135*	2 Jan *135*	4 Feb *108*	23 Aug *120*	17 Apr *95*	17 Jan *93*	7 Jan *201*	4 Oct *182*	8 Apr *135*	26 Nov *65*
Hastings United	26 Dec *353*	28 Jan *280*	4 Feb *242*	27 Sep *200*	14 Jan *324*	17 Sep *326*	1 Apr *339*	1 Nov *501*	26 Nov *286*	15 Apr *380*		29 Aug *372*	29 Apr *588*	22 Oct *329*	24 Sep *314*	6 Dec *195*	18 Mar *297*	5 Nov *359*	29 Nov *215*	10 Dec *390*	11 Mar *345*	18 Feb *239*	28 Feb *235*
Horsham	27 Sep *210*	19 Nov *716*	29 Apr *563*	17 Apr *550*	20 Sep *202*	25 Oct *230*	29 Oct *341*	23 Aug *366*	15 Nov *238*	11 Apr *328*	2 Jan *440*		18 Mar *502*	3 Dec *407*	10 Sep *251*	3 Sep *287*	10 Dec *296*	21 Jan *320*	1 Apr *707*	4 Mar *522*	7 Jan *419*	11 Feb *322*	24 Sep *348*
Kingstonian	6 Feb *273*	24 Oct *290*	3 Oct *249*	21 Jan *354*	8 Apr *344*	25 Feb *346*	6 Mar *284*	4 Feb *450*	29 Oct *379*	4 Mar *344*	27 Mar *313*	1 Oct *442*		7 Jan *419*	22 Apr *531*	25 Mar *387*	3 Sep *288*	22 Aug *357*	5 Dec *275*	7 Nov *304*	9 Jan *421*	17 Apr *310*	2 Jan *329*
Leatherhead	26 Nov *201*	27 Dec *227*	14 Jan *195*	1 Apr *193*	28 Jan *220*	22 Apr *207*	18 Oct *150*	11 Apr *270*	18 Mar *203*	17 Sep *208*	25 Feb *205*	4 Feb *321*	20 Aug *465*		4 Apr *126*	19 Nov *206*	12 Nov *219*	6 Dec *129*	15 Apr *246*	29 Oct *315*	29 Nov *247*	17 Dec *195*	15 Nov *204*
Lymington/New M	5 Nov *117*	14 Apr *152*	17 Apr *251*	29 Apr *141*	17 Sep *114*	20 Aug *146*	28 Jan *93*	18 Feb *143*	4 Feb *129*	13 Sep *100*	8 Apr *162*	12 Nov *124*	10 Dec *186*	1 Nov *101*		4 Oct *118*	8 Nov *99*	25 Mar *111*	26 Nov *115*	1 Oct *208*	28 Feb *101*	22 Oct *105*	11 Mar *109*
Metropolitan Police	20 Aug *112*	11 Feb *111*	15 Apr *92*	18 Mar *109*	24 Jan *81*	14 Jan *102*	17 Sep *104*	22 Oct *221*	10 Dec *134*	3 Dec *102*	7 Feb *85*	28 Jan *158*	17 Jan *324*	11 Mar *238*	1 Apr *111*		14 Mar *156*	18 Feb *91*	29 Apr *333*	20 Sep *135*	1 Nov *211*	28 Feb *86*	4 Nov *165*
Molesey	17 Dec *105*	20 Aug *100*	26 Nov *92*	24 Jan *103*	26 Dec *141*	11 Feb *65*	21 Feb *80*	5 Nov *165*	29 Aug *120*	14 Jan *109*	1 Oct *130*	22 Apr *302*	28 Jan *300*	28 Feb *110*	20 Sep *88*	8 Apr *150*		11 Mar *85*	17 Sep *105*	4 Oct *175*	18 Feb *220*	24 Mar *215*	22 Oct *120*
Newport IOW	28 Jan *153*	10 Dec *161*	29 Aug *182*	26 Oct *209*	11 Feb *177*	3 Dec *131*	20 Aug *172*	18 Mar *225*	15 Apr *176*	27 Dec *184*	4 Mar *212*	17 Sep *217*	14 Jan *296*	23 Nov *127*	28 Sep *114*	29 Oct *154*	19 Nov *129*		22 Feb *123*	25 Feb *201*	29 Apr *237*	21 Sep *134*	1 Apr *193*
Ramsgate	22 Apr *573*	7 Mar *150*	1 Oct *206*	7 Jan *231*	25 Mar *343*	19 Nov *236*	4 Mar *307*	17 Apr *1,121*	25 Oct *222*	25 Feb *274*	20 Sep *243*	4 Oct *176*	22 Nov *224*	10 Jan *242*	11 Feb *307*	17 Dec *210*	21 Jan *311*	8 Apr *299*		2 Jan *449*	23 Aug *244*	3 Dec *220*	3 Sep *196*
Tonbridge Angels	17 Sep *383*	14 Jan *382*	14 Mar *242*	13 Dec *250*	17 Dec *384*	26 Dec *457*	27 Sep *294*	28 Feb *536*	28 Jan *441*	20 Aug *369*	22 Apr *475*	5 Nov *505*	15 Apr *528*	18 Feb *410*	18 Mar *282*	31 Jan *286*	25 Apr *263*	22 Oct *425*	29 Aug *394*		4 Feb *468*	11 Mar *342*	1 Nov *331*
Tooting & Mitcham	18 Mar *233*	4 Mar *255*	17 Sep *229*	25 Feb *255*	12 Nov *316*	29 Aug *248*	14 Apr *448*	8 Oct *313*	26 Dec *398*	1 Apr *272*	19 Nov *319*	20 Aug *320*	11 Feb *552*	20 Sep *251*	25 Oct *185*	7 Mar *166*	29 Oct *214*	17 Dec *246*	14 Jan *372*	3 Dec *365*		22 Apr *258*	27 Sep *206*
Walton Casuals	15 Apr *56*	17 Sep *89*	6 Dec *72*	28 Mar *55*	20 Aug *117*	28 Jan *74*	14 Jan *87*	1 Apr *228*	4 Mar *109*	8 Oct *108*	29 Oct *137*	26 Nov *177*	26 Dec *241*	29 Apr *112*	25 Feb *81*	20 Dec *101*	27 Sep *167*	14 Feb *76*	4 Feb *92*	19 Nov *138*	10 Dec *143*		18 Mar *65*
Whyteleafe	14 Jan *176*	20 Sep *134*	20 Aug *146*	22 Nov *119*	3 Dec *173*	29 Oct *222*	27 Dec *236*	20 Dec *215*	17 Sep *224*	11 Feb *200*	12 Nov *231*	14 Apr *336*	29 Aug *295*	8 Apr *211*	19 Nov *151*	4 Mar *163*	25 Feb *152*	10 Sep *151*	28 Jan *195*	28 Mar *202*	25 Mar *306*	1 Oct *184*	

ISTHMIAN LEAGUE DIVISION ONE NORTH

CONSTITUTION FOR 2006-07

AFC HORNCHURCH
Colours: Red, white & black
Hornchurch Stadium, Bridge Avenue, Upminster, Essex RM14 2LX
Tel: 01708 220080

AFC SUDBURY
Colours: Yellow & blue
Kingsmarsh Stadium, Brundon Lane, Sudbury, Suffolk CO10 6XR
Tel: 01787 376213

ARLESEY TOWN
Colours: Navy & sky blue
Hitchin Road, Arlesey, Bedfordshire SG15 6RS
Tel: 01462 734504

AVELEY
Colours: Blue
Mill Field, Mill Road, Aveley, Essex RM15 4SJ
Tel: 01708 865940

BURY TOWN
Colours: Blue
Ram Meadow, Cotton Lane, Bury St Edmonds, Suffolk IP33 1XP
Tel: 01284 754721

CANVEY ISLAND
Colours: Yellow, blue & white
Park Lane, Canvey Island, Essex SS8 7PX
Tel: 01268 682991

ENFIELD
Colours: White & blue
Ware FC, Wodson Park, Wadesmill Road, Ware, Hertfordshire SG12 0HZ
Tel: 01920 463247

ENFIELD TOWN
Colours: White & blue
Brimsdown Rovers FC, Goldsdown Road, Enfield, Middlesex EN3 7RP
Tel: 020 8804 5491

FLACKWELL HEATH
Colours: Red & black
Wilks Park, Magpie Lane, Flackwell Heath, High Wycombe HP10 9E
01628 523892

GREAT WAKERING ROVERS
Colours: Green & white
Burroughs Park, Little Wakering Hall Lane, Gt Wakering, Southend-on-Sea, Essex SS3 0HH
Tel: 01702 217812

HARLOW TOWN
Colours: Red & white
Harlow Sportscentre, Hammarskjold Road, Harlow, Essex CM20 2JF
Tel: 01279 445319
will be moving to Barrows Farm, Elizabeth Way, Harlow, Essex CM19 5BE *during the season*
Tel: 01279 445319

ILFORD
Colours: Royal blue & white hoops
Cricklefield Stadium, 486 High Road, Seven Kings, Ilford, Essex IG1 1UB
Tel: 020 8514 8352

MALDON TOWN
Colours: Blue & white
Wallace Binder Ground, Park Drive, Maldon, Essex CM9 5XX
Tel: 01621 853762

POTTERS BAR TOWN
Colours: Red & royal blue
Parkfield, Watkins Rise, The Walk, Potters Bar, Hertfordshire EN6 1QN
Tel: 01707 654833

REDBRIDGE
Colours: Blue
Oakside Stadium, Station Road, Barkingside, Ilford, Essex IG6 1NA
Tel: 020 8550 3611

TILBURY
Colours: Black & white
Chadfields, St Chad's Road, Tilbury, Essex RM18 8NL
Tel: 01375 843093

WALTHAM ABBEY
Colours: White & green
Capershotts, Sewardstone Road, Waltham Abbey, Essex EN9 1LU
Tel: 01992 711287

WALTHAM FOREST
Colours: White & navy blue
Wadham Lodge Sports Ground, Kitchener Road, Walthamstow, London E17 4JP
Tel: 020 8527 2444

WARE
Colours: Blue & white
Wodson Park, Wadesmill Road, Ware SG12 0HZ
Tel: 01920 463247

WINGATE & FINCHLEY
Colours: Blue & white
The Abrahams Stadium, Summers Lane, Finchley, London N12 0PD
Tel: 020 8446 2217

WITHAM TOWN
Colours: Red, black & white
Spa Road, Witham, Essex CM8 1UN
Tel: 01376 511198

WIVENHOE TOWN
Colours: Blue & yellow
Broad Lane Sports Ground, Elmstead Road, Wivenhoe, Essex CO7 7HA
Tel: 01206 825380

NEW DIVISION FORMED BY: AFC Hornchurch (P – Essex Senior League), AFC Sudbury (P – Eastern Counties League Premier Division), Arlesey Town (S – Southern League Division One West), Aveley (S – Southern League Division One East), Bury Town (P – Eastern Counties League Premier Division One), Canvey Island (W – Football Conference), Enfield (S – Southern League Division One East), Enfield Town (S – Southern League Division One East), Flackwell Heath (P), Great Wakering Rovers (S – Southern League Division One East), Harlow Town (S – Southern League Division One East), Ilford (S – Southern League Division One East), Maldon Town (R), Potters Bar Town (S – Southern League Division One East), Redbridge (R), Tilbury (P – Essex Senior League), Waltham Abbey (P – Essex Senior League), Waltham Forest (S – Isthmian League Division One), Ware (P), Wingate & Finchley (S – Southern League Division One East), Witham Town (P), Wivenhoe Town (S – Southern League Division One East)

ISTHMIAN LEAGUE DIVISION ONE SOUTH

CONSTITUTION FOR 2006-07

ASHFORD TOWN
Colours: Green & navy blue
The Homelands, Ashford Road, Kingsnorth, Ashford, Kent TN26 1NJ
Tel: 01233 611838

BURGESS HILL TOWN
Colours: Yellow & black
Leylands Park, Maple Drive, Burgess Hill, West Sussex RH15 8DL
Tel: 01444 242429

CHATHAM TOWN
Colours: Red & black
Sports Ground, Maidstone Road, Bourneville Avenue, Chatham, Kent ME4 6EJ
Tel: 01634 812194

CORINTHIAN CASUALS
Colours: Chocolate, pink & sky blue
King Georges Field, Queen Mary Close, Tolworth, Surrey KT6 7NA
Tel: 020 8397 3368

CRAY WANDERERS
Colours: Amber & black
Bromley FC, Hayes Lane, Bromley, Kent BR2 9EF
Tel: 020 8460 5291

CROYDON ATHLETIC
Colours: Maroon & white
Mayfields, Mayfield Road, Thornton Heath, Surrey CR7 6DN
Tel: 020 8664 8343

DARTFORD
Colours: White & black
Gravesend & Northfleet FC, Stonebridge Road, Northfleet, Gravesend, Kent DA11 9BA
Tel: 01474 533796

DOVER ATHLETIC
Colours: White & Black
Crabble Athletic Ground, Lewisham Road, River, Dover, Kent CT17 0PB
Tel: 01304 822373

DULWICH HAMLET
Colours: Navy blue & pink
Champion Hill Stadium, Edgar Kail Way, Dog Kennel Hill, East Dulwich, London SE22 8BD
Tel: 020 7274 8707

FLEET TOWN
Colours: Navy & sky blue
Calthorpe Park, Crookham Road, Fleet, Hampshire GU51 5FA
Tel: 01252 623804

GODALMING TOWN
Colours: Yellow & green
Wey Court, Meadrow, Godalming, Surrey GU7 3JE
Tel: 01483 417520

HASTINGS UNITED
Colours: Claret & blue
The Pilot Field, Elphinstone Road, Hastings, East Sussex TN34 2AX
Tel: 01424 444635

HORSHAM YMCA
Colours: White & black
Gorings Mead, off Queen Street, Horsham, West Sussex RH13 5BP
Tel: 01403 252689

KINGSTONIAN
Colours: Red & white
AFC Wimbledon, Kingsmeadow, Jack Goodchild Way, 422a Kingston Road, Kingston-upon-Thames, Surrey KT1 3PB
Tel: 020 8547 3528

LEATHERHEAD
Colours: Green & white
Fetcham Grove, Guildford Road, Leatherhead, Surrey KT22 9AS
Tel: 01372 360151

MAIDSTONE UNITED
Colours: Amber & black
Sittingbourne FC, Eurolink Industrial Estate, Church Road, Sittingbourne, Kent ME10 3SB
Tel: 01795 435077

METROPOLITAN POLICE
Colours: Blue
Imber Court Sports Club, Ember Lane, East Molesey, Surrey KT8 0BT
Tel: 020 8398 7358

MOLESEY
Colours: Black & white
412 Walton Road, West Molesey, Surrey KT8 2JG
Tel: 020 8979 4823

SITTINGBOURNE
Colours: Red & black
Central Park Stadium, Church Road, Eurolink, Sittingbourne, Kent ME10 3SB
Tel: 01795 435077

TOOTING & MITCHAM UNITED
Colours: White & black
Imperial Fields, Bishopsford Road, Morden, Surrey SM4 6BF
Tel: 020 8648 3248

WALTON CASUALS
Colours: Tangerine & black
Franklyn Road Sports Ground, Waterside Drive, Walton-on-Thames, Surrey KT12 2JP
Tel: 01932 787749

WHYTELEAFE
Colours: Green & white
15 Church Road, Whyteleafe, Surrey CR3 0AR
Tel: 020 8660 5491

NEW DIVISION FORMED BY: Ashford Town (S – Isthmian League Division One), Burgess Hill Town (S – Isthmian League Division One), Chatham Town (S – Southern League Division One East), Corinthian Casuals (S – Isthmian League Division One), Cray Wanderers (S – Isthmian League Division One), Croydon Athletic (S – Isthmian League Division One), Dartford (S – Southern League Division One East), Dover Athletic (S – Isthmian League Division One), Dulwich Hamlet (S – Isthmian League Division One), Fleet Town (S – Isthmian League Division One), Godalming Town (P – Combined Counties League Premier Division), Hastings United (S – Isthmian League Division One), Horsham YMCA (P – Sussex County League Division One), Kingstonian (S – Isthmian League Division One), Leatherhead (S – Isthmian League Division One), Maidstone United (P – Kent League Premier Division), Metropolitan Police (S – Isthmian League Division One), Molesey (S – Isthmian League Division One), Sittingbourne (S – Southern League Division One East), Tooting & Mitcham United (S – Isthmian League Division One), Walton Casuals (S – Isthmian League Division One), Whyteleafe (S – Isthmian League Division One)

	Brook House	Camberley Town	Chalfont St Peter	Chertsey Town	Clapton	Croydon	Dorking	Edgware Town	Egham Town	Epsom & Ewell	Flackwell Heath	Hertford Town	Kingsbury Town	Ware	Wembley	Witham Town
Brook House		2-0	4-2	2-0	2-0	2-0	4-1	1-2	0-2	2-0	7-1	6-1	1-1	2-6	2-1	1-0
Camberley Town	0-3		1-2	1-3	2-2	1-0	0-0	2-1	3-0	0-0	1-3	2-2	1-1	2-4	1-3	0-3
Chalfont St Peter	3-2	2-0	*D*	2-0	3-1	2-3	0-2	1-1	3-0	2-3	1-2	1-0	0-3	3-1	2-1	0-2
Chertsey Town	3-1	3-1	3-2	*I*	3-0	2-1	0-2	2-1	0-1	2-2	1-3	3-0	2-2	3-1	3-0	0-0
Clapton	1-3	3-0	2-2	0-0	*V*	1-0	0-3	0-2	1-4	1-3	2-2	0-0	2-0	0-6	1-6	0-3
Croydon	1-1	1-1	0-1	3-0	8-5	*I*	2-1	0-3	0-0	3-0	1-2	2-2	1-0	1-1	1-4	1-2
Dorking	0-1	1-2	1-0	2-2	3-3	1-0	*S*	2-1	4-1	4-3	1-1	2-2	1-2	2-5	2-2	1-5
Edgware Town	1-1	1-0	6-2	1-1	0-2	1-4	3-0	*I*	0-0	1-0	4-1	2-4	0-1	0-2	3-1	2-1
Egham Town	1-2	5-1	3-2	2-1	2-1	1-1	1-0	0-1	*O*	0-2	0-1	2-1	1-1	1-0	2-0	2-1
Epsom & Ewell	2-2	0-4	0-4	4-2	2-2	0-1	2-2	0-1	0-1	*N*	2-3	0-2	1-1	1-2	1-3	1-0
Flackwell Heath	1-1	3-2	3-2	0-2	2-2	1-2	0-1	3-2	4-2	2-0		2-1	1-0	0-2	4-0	5-2
Hertford Town	0-4	0-0	3-2	0-2	0-0	0-0	1-0	3-5	2-1	2-0	1-1	*T*	0-1	1-2	2-1	0-2
Kingsbury Town	1-1	1-1	1-3	1-2	2-0	0-1	1-3	1-0	0-1	1-0	3-0	1-1	*W*	1-0	0-4	2-2
Ware	0-2	2-1	3-0	2-1	4-1	5-2	2-3	3-1	2-0	7-0	1-1	3-3	4-1	*O*	4-0	0-2
Wembley	1-1	2-0	0-1	0-1	1-0	0-2	2-0	0-0	1-2	4-2	0-0	1-0	2-2	0-2		2-2
Witham Town	1-0	4-1	2-0	0-0	3-0	3-1	3-3	3-0	1-1	3-1	3-2	6-1	1-0	1-1	0-2	

Division Two		P	W	D	L	F	A	Pts
Ware		30	19	4	7	77	36	61
Witham Town		30	17	7	6	61	30	58
Brook House		30	17	7	6	63	33	58
Flackwell Heath		30	15	7	8	54	49	52
Egham Town		30	15	5	10	39	36	50
Chertsey Town		30	14	7	9	47	37	49
Edgware Town		30	13	5	12	46	41	44
Chalfont St Peter		30	13	2	15	50	53	41
Dorking		30	11	8	11	48	51	41
Croydon		30	11	7	12	43	43	40
Wembley		30	11	6	13	44	43	39
Kingsbury Town		30	9	10	11	32	37	37
Hertford Town		30	7	10	13	35	54	31
Camberley Town		30	5	8	17	31	57	23
Epsom & Ewell		30	5	6	19	32	64	21
Clapton	*-5*	30	4	9	17	33	71	16

The Isthmian League Division One and Division Two have been disbanded and replaced by Division One North and Division One South
(see pages 86 and 87)

OUT: Brook House (P – Southern League Division One South & West), Camberley Town (S – Combined Counties League Premier Division), Chalfont St Peter (S – Spartan South Midlands League Premier Division), Chertsey Town (S – Combined Counties League Premier Division), Clapton (S – Essex Senior League), Croydon (S – Kent League Premier Division), Dorking (S – Combined Counties League Premier Division), Edgware Town (S – Spartan South Midlands League Premier Division), Egham Town (S – Combined Counties League Premier Division), Epsom & Ewell (S – Combined Counties League Premier Division), Flackwell Heath (P – Isthmian League Division One North), Hertford Town (S – Spartan South Midlands League Premier Division), Kingsbury Town (having merged with Middlesex County League Premier Division side London Tigers to form Kingsbury London Tigers) (S – Spartan South Midlands League Premier Division), Ware (P – Isthmian League Division One North), Wembley (S – Combined Counties League Premier Division), Witham Town (P – Isthmian League Division One North)

LEAGUE CUP

FIRST ROUND

Banstead Athletic 2 Corinthian Casuals 1 *aet*
Burgess Hill Town 2 **Brook House** 4
Camberley Town 0 **Edgware Town** 1
Chertsey Town 1 **Leatherhead** 2
Croydon 1 **Croydon Athletic** 3
Dover Athletic 1 Ware 0
Dulwich Hamlet 3 Bashley 1
Egham Town 2 **Fleet Town** 3 *aet*
Epsom & Ewell 0 **Hastings United** 3
Flackwell Heath 1 **Witham Town** 3
Horsham 6 Chalfont St Peter 1
Kingsbury Town 3 Molesey 1
Lymington & New Milton 2 Kingstonian 0
Metropolitan Police 4 Hertford Town 2
Ramsgate 1 **Newport IOW** 2
Tonbridge Angels 3 Clapton 1
Walton Casuals 0 **Tooting & Mitcham United** 4
Wembley 5 Ashford Town 2
Whyteleafe 1 **Dorking** 3

SECOND ROUND

Cray Wanderers 6 Kingsbury Town 0
Dorking 0 **Edgware Town** 3
Dover Athletic 5 Wembley 0
Dulwich Hamlet 3 Banstead Athletic 2 *aet*
Fleet Town 1 **Hastings United** 3
Leatherhead 4 Metropolitan Police 1
Lymington & New Milton 1 **Horsham** 4
Newport IOW 1 **Brook House** 2
Tonbridge Angels 0 **Tooting & Mitcham United** 1
Witham Town 0 **Croydon Athletic** 2

THIRD ROUND

Billericay Town 2 Maldon Town 1
Brook House 1 **Hendon** 2
Chelmsford City 3 Horsham 1
Dover Athletic 2 Leyton 0
East Thurrock United 0 **Heybridge Swifts** 3
Fisher Athletic 4 Folkestone Invicta 2
Hampton & Richmond Borough 1 Dulwich Hamlet 0 *aet*
Harrow Borough 1 Windsor & Eton 0
Hastings United 2 **Braintree Town** 3
Leatherhead 5 Cray Wanderers 3 *aet*
Margate 2 **Bromley** 3 *aet*
Slough Town 3 Redbridge 2
Staines Town 0 **AFC Wimbledon** 2
Tooting & Mitcham United 3 Edgware Town 0
Wealdstone 1 Croydon Athletic 0
Worthing 2 Walton & Hersham 2 *aet* (5-4p)

FOURTH ROUND

AFC Wimbledon 0 **Hendon** 1
Billericay Town 3 Tooting & Mitcham United 1
Braintree Town 1 **Wealdstone** 2
Dover Athletic 0 **Bromley** 2
Fisher Athletic 2 Hampton & Richmond Borough 1
Harrow Borough 1 **Worthing** 2
Heybridge Swifts 2 Chelmsford City 0
Leatherhead 0 **Slough Town** 2

QUARTER-FINALS

Bromley 3 Wealdstone 2
Hendon 0 **Fisher Athletic** 1
Slough Town 3 Heybridge Swifts 0
Worthing 1 **Billericay Town** 3

SEMI-FINALS
(played over two legs)

Fisher Athletic 5 Slough Town 2, Slough Town 3 **Fisher Athletic** 1
Bromley 2 Billericay Town 2, **Billericay Town** 2 Bromley 1

FINAL
(April 12th at Grays Athletic)

Billericay Town 0 **Fisher Athletic** 4

ASSOCIATE MEMBERS TROPHY

(Division Two clubs)

GROUP ONE

	P	W	D	L	F	A	Pts
Hertford Town	6	4	0	2	12	8	9
Clapton	6	4	0	2	9	7	12
Witham Town	6	3	0	3	16	16	9
Ware	6	1	0	5	11	17	3

Clapton 0 Hertford Town 1
Clapton 1 Ware 0
Clapton 2 Witham Town 0
Hertford Town 1 Clapton 2
Hertford Town 4 Ware 1
Hertford Town 3 Witham Tn 1
Ware 0 Clapton 1
Ware 2 Hertford Town 3
Ware 6 Witham Town 3
Witham Town 5 Clapton 3
Witham Town 2 Hertford Tn 0
Witham Town 5 Ware 2

GROUP TWO

	P	W	D	L	F	A	Pts
Croydon	6	4	1	1	11	3	13
Epsom & Ewell	6	4	1	1	10	5	13
Dorking	6	3	0	3	11	9	9
Camberley Town	6	0	0	6	1	16	0

Camberley Town 0 Croydon 1
Camberley Town 0 Dorking 3
Camberley Tn 0 Epsom & E 3
Croydon 3 Camberley Town 0
Croydon 3 Dorking 0
Croydon 1 Epsom & Ewell 1
Dorking 4 Camberley Town 0
Dorking 1 Croydon 3
Dorking 2 Epsom & Ewell 3
Epsom & E 2 Camberley Tn 1
Epsom & Ewell 1 Croydon 0
Epsom & Ewell 0 Dorking 1

GROUP THREE

	P	W	D	L	F	A	Pts
Brook House	6	4	1	1	21	11	13
Chalfont St Peter	6	4	1	1	14	11	13
Flackwell Heath	6	1	2	3	8	11	5
Chertsey Town	6	0	2	4	7	17	2

Brook House 3 Chal. St Peter 3
Brook House 5 Chertsey Tn 1
Brook House 4 Flackwell Hth 1
Chal. St Peter 3 Brook House 2
Chal. St Peter 2 Chertsey Tn 1
Chal. St Peter 2 Flackwell Hth 1
Chertsey Tn 2 Brook House 5
Chertsey Tn 1 Chal. St Peter 3
Chertsey Tn 2 Flackwell Heath 2
Flackwell Hth 1 Brook House 2
Flackwell Hth 3 Chalfont St P 1
Flackwell Hth 0 Chertsey Tn 0

GROUP FOUR

		P	W	D	L	F	A	Pts
Egham Town		6	4	1	1	10	9	13
Edgware Town		6	2	2	2	13	7	8
Kingsbury Town	*-3*	6	3	0	3	8	8	6
Wembley		6	1	1	4	4	11	4

Edgware Tn 2 Egham Town 2
Edgware Tn 4 Kingsbury Tn 1
Edgware Town 5 Wembley 0
Egham Tn 2 Edgware Town 1
Egham Tn 0 Kingsbury Tn 4
Egham Town 2 Wembley 1
Kingsbury Tn 1 Edgware Tn 0
Kingsbury Tn 1 Egham Tn 2
Kingsbury Tn 1 Wembley 0
Wembley 1 Edgware Town 1
Wembley 0 Egham Town 2
Wembley 2 Kingsbury Tn 0

QUARTER-FINALS

Brook House 3 Epsom & Ewell 2
Croydon 2 Clapton 1
Egham Town 1 **Chalfont St Peter** 2
Hertford Town 3 Edgware Town 0

SEMI-FINALS

Chalfont St Peter 1 **Brook House** 2 *aet*
Croydon 0 **Hertford Town** 1 *(at Whyteleafe)*

FINAL *(April 5th at Brook House)*

Brook House 3 Hertford Town 1

KENT COUNTY LEAGUE

	Bearsted	Bromley Green	Cray Valley Paper Mills	Crockenhill	Faversham Town	Fleet Leisure	Lewisham Borough (Community)	Lydd Town	Milton Athletic	Norton Sports	Old Roan	Rusthall	Sheerness East	Snodland	Stansfeld Oxford & Bermondsey Club
Bearsted		1-3	3-1	1-2	3-2	2-5	4-1	1-0	1-0	0-1	1-4	1-2	0-3	4-1	0-0
Bromley Green	1-1		2-3	3-3	0-1	3-0	1-4	1-1	4-3	4-1	1-6	1-1	3-2	5-2	6-0
Cray Valley Paper Mills	5-0	3-0	*P*	5-0	3-4	1-2	0-1	2-0	0-0	3-1	2-4	2-1	2-2	1-0	2-2
Crockenhill	0-0	1-7	2-1	*R*	2-1	2-2	3-4	0-1	0-4	1-0	3-3	1-1	1-4	0-1	1-0
Faversham Town	1-0	2-1	2-2	0-0	*E*	0-0	0-2	3-1	2-3	4-2	3-0	1-0	2-0	2-1	1-1
Fleet Leisure	0-2	3-4	3-3	4-0	0-2	*M*	0-3	0-1	2-4	0-2	1-1	3-4	1-2	1-1	0-1
Lewisham Borough (Community)	2-1	4-1	1-0	3-0	1-2	1-1	*I*	3-0	1-0	1-2	1-0	2-1	1-2	3-0	4-2
Lydd Town	0-1	0-1	0-3	1-1	0-1	0-3	2-0	*E*	1-2	0-0	1-0	1-3	1-2	1-2	1-3
Milton Athletic	3-1	2-1	1-4	4-2	3-2	6-3	2-2	3-0	*R*	3-0	1-1	5-2	1-0	0-1	0-2
Norton Sports	2-2	2-1	0-0	1-2	1-2	4-2	1-5	0-1	2-1		2-1	1-0	5-1	2-1	2-2
Old Roan	1-1	2-4	2-2	0-0	2-0	0-2	0-2	2-1	0-4	1-4	*D*	1-1	3-2	3-4	1-4
Rusthall	1-3	0-2	1-0	5-1	1-3	1-2	0-2	1-2	3-0	1-1	3-0	*I*	5-3	2-0	1-1
Sheerness East	2-0	1-3	2-2	4-2	1-2	3-3	2-0	3-0	3-2	1-0	1-0	4-2	*V*	3-1	1-0
Snodland	1-0	4-1	0-2	2-1	1-2	2-3	2-2	0-0	3-2	1-3	1-3	1-0	2-1		2-2
Stansfeld Oxford & Bermondsey Club	4-0	1-3	0-0	2-0	1-0	2-1	1-1	1-1	5-1	2-1	1-0	2-2	0-1	1-0	

Premier Division		P	W	D	L	F	A	Pts
Lewisham Borough (Community)		28	18	4	6	57	30	58
Faversham Town	*-1*	28	17	4	7	47	32	54
Sheerness East		28	16	3	9	56	44	51
Bromley Green		28	14	4	10	67	54	46
Stansfeld Oxford & Bermondsey Club		28	12	10	6	43	33	46
Milton Athletic		28	14	3	11	60	48	45
Cray Valley Paper Mills		28	11	9	8	54	36	42
Norton Sports		28	12	5	11	43	43	41
Snodland		28	10	4	14	37	50	34
Rusthall		28	9	6	13	45	46	33
Bearsted		28	9	5	14	34	48	32
Fleet Leisure		28	7	7	14	47	57	28
Old Roan		28	7	7	14	41	53	28
Crockenhill		28	6	8	14	31	64	26
Lydd Town		28	6	5	17	18	42	23

CHAMPIONS TROPHY

(Premier Division champions v Inter-Regional Challenge Cup holders)

(August 31st at Sevenoaks Town)

Cray Valley Paper Mills 2 **Orpington** 4

KENT COUNTY LEAGUE PREMIER DIVISION CONSTITUTION 2006-07

BEARSTED . . . . Otham Sports Ground, Honey Lane, Otham, Maidstone ME15 8RG 07831 251657
BROMLEY GREEN . . . . The Swan Centre, Cudworth Road, South Willesborough, Ashford TN24 0BB 01233 645982
CRAY VALLEY PAPER MILLS . . . . . Badgers Sports Ground, Middle Park Avenue, Eltham SE9 5HT. 020 8850 4273
CROCKENHILL . . . . Wested, Eynsford Road, Crockenhill, Swanley BR8 8EH 01322 662067
FLEET LEISURE . . . . Beauwater Leisure Sports Club, Nelson Road, Northfleet DA11 7EE 01474 359222
HOLLANDS & BLAIR . . . . . . Rochagas Sports & Social, Star Meadow, Dartford Avenue, Gillingham ME7 3AN 01634 573839
HOLMESDALE . . . . Holmesdale Sports & Social, Oakley Road, Bromley Common BR9 8HG 020 8462 4440
LEWISHAM BOROUGH . . . . Ladywell Arena, Doggett Road, Catford SE6 4QX. 020 8314 1986
MILTON ATHLETIC . . . . UK Paper Sports Ground, Gore Court Road, Sittingbourne ME10 1QN 01795 564213
NORTON SPORTS . . . . Norton Park, Provender Lane, Norton, Faversham ME9 9JU 07989 581062
OLD ROAN . . . . The Playing Fields, John Roan School, Kidbrooke Park Road SE3 9NF. 020 8856 1915
RUSTHALL . . . . Jockey Farm, Nellington Lane, Rusthall, Tunbridge Wells TN4 8SH 07940 277138
SHEERNESS EAST . . . . Sheerness East WMC, 47 Queensborough Road, Halfway, Sheerness ME12 3BZ 01795 662049
SNODLAND . . . . Potyn's Field, Paddlesworth Road, Snodland ME6 5DL. 01634 243961
STANSFELD OXFORD & BERMONDSEY CLUB . .Greenwich University Sports Ground, Kidbrooke Lane, Eltham SE9 6TA. . 020 8850 0210

IN: Hollands & Blair (P – Division One East), Holmesdale (P – Division One West)

OUT: Faversham Town (P – Kent League Premier Division), Lydd Town (R – Division One East)

	APM Mears	Betteshanger W	Borden Village	Hollands & Blair	Kennington	New Romney	Oakwood	Sheppey United	St Margarets	Tenterden Town	Tyler Hill	Uniflo	University of Kent
APM Mears	*D*	1-3	3-0	1-6	2-4	1-2	2-1	2-0	2-3	3-3	1-2	2-2	0-3
Betteshanger Welfare	3-0	*I*	1-2	0-3	0-0	1-0	0-4	1-2	0-2	4-1	0-1	2-1	2-1
Borden Village	6-1	4-4	*V*	0-4	2-3	3-1	1-3	1-3	3-3	6-4	4-6	2-1	2-0
Hollands & Blair	4-0	2-3	3-1		2-1	2-2	2-1	2-0	2-1	4-1	1-1	3-0	3-2
Kennington	3-3	2-4	2-1	1-2	*O*	2-4	2-1	1-2	1-2	1-1	5-3	2-1	2-1
New Romney	5-0	3-0	4-3	2-1	3-4	*N*	2-2	4-2	3-2	5-0	3-1	6-0	3-1
Oakwood	1-0	2-0	1-1	3-4	2-1	1-1	*E*	2-0	3-0	6-0	2-2	2-2	2-0
Sheppey United	2-0	0-0	4-1	1-1	1-2	2-2	1-1		8-4	5-5	3-3	3-2	3-3
St Margarets	7-1	4-5	3-0	1-1	5-1	4-5	2-2	2-3	*E*	W-L	0-3	2-4	1-1
Tenterden Town	1-5	0-4	2-1	0-7	2-4	1-4	0-0	2-3	2-5	*A*	0-0	2-2	0-2
Tyler Hill	0-1	5-0	7-3	0-1	4-4	1-2	2-9	6-2	4-2	6-3	*S*	3-2	3-2
Uniflo	4-0	3-3	1-6	3-3	1-2	2-1	1-2	1-3	2-1	8-0	1-5	*T*	4-2
University of Kent	4-0	0-1	3-3	0-4	1-0	5-1	2-1	4-4	1-1	5-1	1-2	2-0	

Division One East		P	W	D	L	F	A	Pts
Hollands & Blair		24	17	5	2	67	25	56
New Romney		24	15	4	5	68	41	49
Tyler Hill		24	13	5	6	70	52	44
Oakwood		24	11	8	5	54	28	41
Sheppey United		24	10	8	6	57	52	38
Betteshanger Welfare		24	11	4	9	41	43	37
Kennington	*-3*	24	11	4	9	50	50	34
University of Kent		24	8	5	11	46	43	29
St Margarets		24	8	5	11	57	57	29
Borden Village		24	7	4	13	56	67	25
Uniflo		24	6	5	13	48	59	23
APM Mears		24	5	3	16	31	69	18
Tenterden Town		24	1	6	17	31	90	9

KENT COUNTY LEAGUE DIVISION ONE EAST CONSTITUTION 2006-07

ASHFORD BOROUGH............ Sandyacres Sports & Social, Sandyhurst Lane, Ashford TN25 4NT 01233 627373

BETTESHANGER WELFARE......... Welfare Ground, Cavell Square, Mill Hill, Deal CT14 9HR 01304 372080

BORDEN VILLAGE .... Borden Playstool, Wises Lane, Borden, Sittingbourne ME9 8LP 07903 016794

KENNINGTON .... Kennington Cricket Club, Ulley Road, Kennington, Ashford TN24 9HY.................. 07887 995219

LYDD TOWN.................. The Lindsey Field, Dengemarsh Road, Lydd, Romney Marsh TN29 9JH.................. 01797 321904

NEW ROMNEY .... The Maud Pavilion, Station Road, New Romney TN28 8SR 01797 364858

OAKWOOD .... Honey Lane, Otham, Maidstone ME15 8RG.............................. 07745 383328

SHEPPEY UNITED......... Medway Ports Authority Ground, Holm Place, Halfway, Sheerness ME12 3AT............... 01795 668054

ST MARGARETS .... Alexander Field, Kingsdown Rd, St Margarets-at-Cliffe, Dover CT15 6BD................ 01304 852386

STAPLEHURST & MONARCHS UNITED ... The Old County Ground, Norman Road, West Malling ME19 6RL.................. None

TYLER HILL................ Hersden Recreation Ground, The Avenue, Hersden, Canterbury CT3 4HY................ 07930 100034

UNIFLO.......................... The County Ground, Norman Road, West Malling ME19 6RL.......................... None

UNIVERSITY OF KENT ... The Oast House, Park Wood Road, Giles Lane, University of Kent, Canterbury CT2 7SY 01227 827430

IN: Ashford Borough (P – Division Two East), Lydd Town (R), Staplehurst & Monarchs United (P – Division Two East)

OUT: APM Mears (R – Division Two East), Hollands & Blair (P), Tenterden Town (R – Division Two East)

	Belvedere	Bly Spartans	Bromleians Sports	Eynsford	Fleetdown United	Greenways	Halls	Holmesdale	Larkfield & New Hythe Wanderers	Metrogas	Orpington	Phoenix Sports	Samuel Montagu Youth Club
Belvedere	*D*	0-2	1-4	3-3	3-0	2-0	4-2	1-1	3-1	1-2	0-2	0-1	2-0
Bly Spartans	0-0	*I*	2-1	0-0	0-1	3-2	3-0	0-4	1-0	1-3	1-1	1-4	1-5
Bromleians Sports	2-0	0-6	*V*	2-0	0-2	1-4	1-0	0-9	0-2	2-1	1-5	0-1	1-2
Eynsford	2-2	4-3	1-1		0-2	2-4	4-3	0-3	2-2	0-1	1-6	0-1	3-2
Fleetdown United	1-2	0-0	2-1	1-0	*O*	1-1	1-1	1-8	2-1	1-2	2-7	0-1	1-2
Greenways	2-2	3-1	0-1	5-2	2-0	*N*	5-2	0-1	2-2	2-1	2-3	1-1	2-6
Halls	4-3	1-2	1-5	2-3	0-1	1-3	*E*	0-2	0-5	4-3	2-5	0-2	2-2
Holmesdale	4-1	5-1	0-1	6-1	2-0	6-0	3-0		3-0	1-0	5-0	2-1	2-0
Larkfield & New Hythe Wanderers	2-2	1-0	4-2	5-0	1-0	1-2	0-3	3-4	*W*	0-1	0-6	1-0	0-0
Metrogas	1-2	1-1	3-2	2-1	1-3	2-0	4-3	1-1	1-2	*E*	4-1	2-0	3-0
Orpington	1-0	6-0	1-0	5-0	3-1	1-1	4-0	0-2	2-0	1-0	*S*	4-2	3-0
Phoenix Sports	2-1	3-2	3-0	1-0	0-3	3-1	1-0	4-2	3-0	2-0	0-2	*T*	1-1
Samuel Montagu Youth Club	1-2	3-2	0-2	0-0	1-3	1-1	2-0	0-2	1-4	0-1	1-3	0-6	

Division One West		P	W	D	L	F	A	Pts
Holmesdale		24	20	2	2	78	15	62
Orpington		24	19	2	3	72	25	59
Phoenix Sports		24	16	2	6	43	23	50
Metrogas		24	13	2	9	40	31	41
Greenways		24	9	6	9	45	46	33
Fleetdown United		24	10	3	11	29	39	33
Larkfield & New Hythe Wanderers		24	9	4	11	37	40	31
Belvedere		24	8	6	10	37	40	30
Bromleians Sports		24	9	1	14	30	50	28
Bly Spartans		24	7	5	12	33	48	26
Samuel Montagu Youth Club		24	6	5	13	30	47	23
Eynsford	*-1*	24	4	6	14	29	62	17
Halls		24	3	2	19	31	68	11

KENT COUNTY LEAGUE DIVISION ONE WEST CONSTITUTION 2006-07

BELVEDERE.................... Memorial Ground, 101a Woolwich Road, Abbey Wood SE2 0DY.................... 01322 436724
BLY SPARTANS................. Bly Spartans Sports Ground, Rede Court Road, Strood ME2 3TU.................... 01634 710577
BRIDON ROPES.................. Meridian Sports Club, Charlton Park Road, Charlton SE7 8QS.................... 020 8856 1923
BROMLEIANS SPORTS .... Scrubbs Farm, Lower Gravel Road, Bromley BR2 8LL 020 8462 5068
FLEETDOWN UNITED .... Heath Lane Open Space, Heath Lane (Lower), Dartford BA1 2QD 01322 273848
GREENWAYS .... Fleet Leisure & Sports Club, Nelson Road, Northfleet DA11 7EE.................... 01474 359222
HALLS.............................. Bexley Park S & S Club, Calvert Drive, Bexley DA2 7GU .... None
LARKFIELD & NEW HYTHE WANDERERS ... Larkfield Sports Ground, New Hythe Lane, Larkfield, Aylesford ME20 6PU.. 01732 873310
METROGAS .... Marathon Playing Fields, Forty Foot Way, New Eltham SE9 2HL.................... 020 8859 1579
ORPINGTON............... Westcombe Park & Orpington SC, Goddington Lane, Orpington BR6 9SH 01689 834902
PHOENIX SPORTS .... Phoenix Sports Club, Mayplace Road East, Bexleyheath DA7 6JT 01322 526159
SAMUEL MONTAGU YOUTH CLUB ... Samuel Montagu Youth Club, Broadwalk, Kidbrooke SE3 8ND 020 8856 1126
WESTERHAM .... Westerham Sports Association, King George V PF, Costells Meadow, Westerham TN16 1BL.......... 01959 561106

IN: Bridon Ropes (P – Division Two West), Westerham (P – Division Two West)
OUT: Eynsford (W – Sevenoaks & District League), Holmesdale (P)

	Ashford Borough	Atcost	Guru Nanak	Lanes End	New Ash Green	Otford United	Pembury	Platt United	Putlands Athletic	Staplehurst & M United	Sutton Athletic	UK Paper	Woodstock Park
Ashford Borough	*D*	4-2	4-3	3-3	6-5	0-2	1-0	10-1	3-0	2-1	4-1	2-8	5-1
Atcost	1-4	*I*	5-0	1-1	n/a	1-1	2-3	6-0	0-4	0-3	1-1	0-1	3-1
Guru Nanak	2-2	1-4	*V*	2-0	1-2	2-1	2-0	4-2	1-3	2-1	0-0	1-4	2-3
Lanes End	3-4	5-2	5-2		2-3	1-0	2-2	3-0	3-0	1-1	1-0	2-0	4-2
New Ash Green	8-5	n/a	n/a	n/a	*T*	3-3	2-0	8-0	n/a	0-4	3-1	0-1	3-4
Otford United	3-1	2-2	2-0	2-3	10-0	*W*	3-0	5-0	0-0	1-1	1-1	4-0	3-0
Pembury	0-4	3-1	2-1	2-2	n/a	3-0	*O*	4-0	0-4	0-3	1-3	0-3	0-0
Platt United	0-8	1-5	2-5	1-7	n/a	0-5	0-6		0-3	0-2	1-6	0-1	2-6
Putlands Athletic	1-4	0-2	2-1	2-5	3-2	2-2	0-3	3-1	*E*	0-2	3-1	3-2	2-2
Staplehurst & Monarchs United	1-1	4-1	2-2	4-3	2-0	1-0	5-0	7-0	2-1	*A*	1-0	3-0	2-1
Sutton Athletic	4-3	1-3	2-2	2-1	3-2	1-1	2-1	12-0	4-1	2-1	*S*	4-1	1-1
UK Paper	2-3	2-1	1-1	2-1	1-2	4-1	6-1	L-W	0-3	1-2	1-2	*T*	0-2
Woodstock Park	1-2	1-0	4-2	2-3	1-1	2-1	1-0	3-3	0-3	2-0	1-2	1-1	

Note – New Ash Green withdrew during the course of the season
Their results are shown above but are expunged from the league table

Division Two East		P	W	D	L	F	A	Pts
Staplehurst & Monarchs United		22	14	4	4	49	20	46
Ashford Borough	*-3*	22	15	3	4	74	40	45
Lanes End		22	12	5	5	59	36	41
Sutton Athletic		22	11	6	5	52	30	39
Putlands Athletic		22	10	3	9	40	38	33
Otford United		22	8	7	7	40	25	31
UK Paper		22	9	2	11	40	37	29
Woodstock Park		22	8	5	9	37	41	29
Atcost		22	7	4	11	43	43	25
Pembury		22	7	3	12	31	45	24
Guru Nanak		22	6	5	11	38	51	23
Platt United		22	1	1	20	14	111	4

New Ash Green – record expunged

KENT COUNTY LEAGUE DIVISION TWO EAST CONSTITUTION 2006-07

APM MEARS .... **Cobdown Sports & Social Club, Ditton Corner, Station Road, Aylesford ME20 6AU** **01622 716824**
ATCOST .... **Pippin Road, Bramley Gardens, East Peckham, Tonbridge TN12 5BT** **07932 792188**
GURU NANAK .... **AEI Henley Sports Club, Dunkirk Close, Gravesend DA12 5NN** .... **None**
LANES END .... **Waller Park, Wood Lane, Darenth, Dartford DA2 7LR** **01322 221006**
OTFORD UNITED .... **Otford Recreation Ground, High Street, Otford, Sevenoaks TN14 5PG** **01959 524405**
PEMBURY .... **Woodside Recreation Ground, Henwoods Mount, Woodside Road, Pembury TN2 4BH** **07970 026628**
PLATT UNITED .... **Stonehouse Field, Longmill Lane (off A25), Platt TN15 8QS** **07702 634344**
PUTLANDS ATHLETIC .... **Putlands Sports Centre, Mascalls Road, Paddock Wood TN12 6NZ** **01892 838290**
SAGA SPORTS & SOCIAL .... **Canteen Meadow, The Street, Bishopsbourne, Canterbury CT4 5HX** .... **None**
SUTTON ATHLETIC .... **The Roaches, Parsonage Lane, Sutton-at-Hone, Dartford DA4 9HD** **01322 280507**
TENTERDEN TOWN .... **Recreation Ground Road, High Street, Tenterden TN30 6RA** **07786 932151**
UK PAPER .... **UK Paper Sports Ground, Gore Court Road, Sittingbourne ME10 1QN** **01795 477047**
WOODSTOCK PARK .... **Sittingbourne Research Centre, Broadoak Road, Sittingbourne ME9 8AG** **07774 654912**

IN: APM Mears (R – Division One East), Saga Sports & Social (P – Ashford & District League), Tenterden Town (R – Division One East)
OUT: Ashford Borough (P – Division One East), New Ash Green (WS), Staplehurst & Monarchs United (P – Division One East)

Reserve Division East	P	W	D	L	F	A	Pts
Bromley Green Res.	24	18	2	4	78	32	56
Bearsted Res.	24	16	4	4	54	18	52
Oakwood Res.	24	14	5	5	55	34	47
Chipstead Res.	24	13	5	6	67	44	44
Kennington Res.	24	13	2	9	51	45	41
Otford United Res.	24	11	5	8	48	33	38
Lydd Town Res.	24	10	6	8	32	33	36
Larkfield & New Hythe Wanderers Res.	24	9	3	12	46	69	30
University of Kent Res.	24	8	4	12	51	57	28
New Romney Res.	24	8	3	13	44	48	27
Putlands Athletic Res.	24	6	2	16	31	58	20
Borden Village Res.	24	5	1	18	37	82	16
APM Mears Res.	24	3	2	19	23	64	11

	Borough United	Bridon Ropes	Chipstead	Chislehurst	Eltham Palace	Farnborough Old Boys Guild	Meridian Sports	New Bromleians	Old Addeyans	Old Bexleians	Tonbridge Invicta	Westerham	Wickham Park
Borough United	*D*	1-3	1-4	8-1	5-3	4-2	5-4	5-1	2-3	2-0	2-1	2-2	3-1
Bridon Ropes	2-1	*I*	0-0	5-1	4-0	3-0	4-3	1-1	3-1	4-1	2-2	0-5	3-1
Chipstead	2-2	1-2	*V*	2-1	1-0	4-0	2-3	0-1	W-L	7-1	2-3	0-5	7-6
Chislehurst	1-3	0-5	0-2		2-2	2-3	1-3	1-4	4-2	0-1	0-3	0-4	1-5
Eltham Palace	3-4	1-4	0-5	0-2	*T*	1-3	3-1	0-0	3-0	1-8	2-3	2-2	3-3
Farnborough Old Boys Guild	6-4	1-4	2-1	1-2	3-1	*W*	1-0	1-0	3-0	4-1	1-0	0-2	4-1
Meridian Sports	2-0	0-7	1-4	0-2	6-1	2-0	*O*	1-2	2-4	1-2	0-3	0-4	0-6
New Bromleians	3-5	0-4	2-1	1-1	2-1	2-0	2-2		2-1	3-0	3-3	2-1	3-2
Old Addeyans	3-3	1-2	0-2	4-2	3-1	0-0	2-3	1-3	*W*	2-1	3-3	2-8	3-2
Old Bexleians	3-2	0-2	1-2	1-0	3-0	0-6	3-0	1-4	3-2	*E*	1-4	0-5	1-4
Tonbridge Invicta	1-1	0-5	1-0	3-1	9-1	0-0	6-2	2-3	5-1	3-1	*S*	2-1	2-2
Westerham	4-0	2-1	2-1	4-1	3-0	1-0	1-1	1-0	2-0	2-0	1-0	*T*	4-0
Wickham Park	8-6	2-5	3-0	1-1	4-1	3-1	2-1	2-2	4-2	5-1	1-3	0-3	

Division Two West		P	W	D	L	F	A	Pts
Westerham		24	19	3	2	69	14	60
Bridon Ropes		24	19	3	2	75	25	60
Tonbridge Invicta		24	13	6	5	62	36	45
New Bromleians		24	13	6	5	46	37	45
Chipstead		24	12	2	10	50	37	38
Farnborough Old Boys Guild		24	12	2	10	42	38	38
Borough United		24	11	4	9	71	63	37
Wickham Park		24	10	4	10	68	60	34
Old Bexleians		24	8	0	16	34	65	24
Meridian Sports		24	6	2	16	38	67	20
Old Addeyans	*-3*	24	6	3	15	40	63	18
Chislehurst		24	4	3	17	27	67	15
Eltham Palace		24	2	4	18	30	80	10

KENT COUNTY LEAGUE DIVISION TWO WEST CONSTITUTION 2006-07

BOROUGH UNITED............... Princes Golf & Leisure Club, Darenth Road, Dartford DA1 1LZ.......................... 01322 276565
CHIPSTEAD...................... Chipstead Rec, Chevening Road, Chipstead, Sevenoaks TN13 2RZ.......................... 07753 603944
CHISLEHURST................ Coldharbour Leisure Centre, Chaple Farm Road, New Eltham SE9 3LX.................. 020 8851 8692
CRAY W & NB .... Coney Hall Recreation Ground, Church Drive, West Wickham, Bromley BR4 9JJ....................... None
ELTHAM PALACE .... Beaverwood Lodge, Beaverwood Road, Chislehurst BR7 6HF..................... 020 8300 1385
ERITH '147.......................... STC Sports Ground, Ivor Grove, New Eltham SE9 2AJ.. None
FARNBOROUGH OLD BOYS GUILD . . . Farnborough (Kent) Sports Club, High Street, Farnborough BR6 7BA 01689 826949
MERIDIAN SPORTS............ Meridian Sports & Social, 110 Charlton Park Lane, Charlton SE7 8QS.................. 020 8856 1923
OLD ADDEYANS .... Blackheath Park, Blackheath SE3 0HB.. 07958 408850
OLD BEXLEIANS............. Seven Acre Sports Club, Church Manor Avenue, Abbey Wood SE2 0HY................................. None
TONBRIDGE INVICTA .... Swanmead Sports Ground, Swanwead Way, off Cannon Lane, Tonbridge TN9 1PP 01732 350473
TUDOR SPORTS .... 31 Eltham Road, Lee Green SE12 8ES .... None
WICKHAM PARK ...... Wickham Park Sports Club, 228-230 Pickhurst Rise, West Wickham, Bromley BR4 0AQ 020 8777 2550

IN: Erith '147 (P – Bromley & District League Premier Division), Tudor Sports (South London Alliance Premier Division)
OUT: Bridon Ropes (P – Division One West), Westerham (P – Division One West)
New Bromleians become Cray W & NB

Reserve Division West		P	W	D	L	F	A	Pts
Westerham Res.		24	16	4	4	60	29	52
Greenways Res.		24	14	5	5	56	30	47
Holmesdale Res.		24	14	4	6	58	35	46
Stansfeld Oxford & Bermondsey Club Res.		24	13	6	5	47	22	45
Orpington Res.		24	11	12	1	45	26	45
Belvedere Res.		24	12	4	8	35	30	40
Fleet Leisure Res.		24	11	6	7	42	32	39
Fleetdown United Res.		24	10	6	8	45	41	36
Bly Spartans Res.	*-2*	24	4	8	12	32	42	18
Borough United Res.		24	4	5	15	35	68	17
Bromleians Sports Res.	*-3*	24	4	6	14	35	52	15
Wickham Park Res.	*-3*	24	4	6	14	29	63	15
Halls Res.		24	2	2	20	23	72	8

BILL MANKELOW INTER-REGIONAL CHALLENGE CUP

(All clubs in league)

FIRST ROUND EAST
Hollands & Blair 1 **Bromley Green** 2
Sheerness East 3 Bearsted 1
St Margarets 2 Betteshanger Welfare 1
University of Kent 4 Kennington 3
FIRST ROUND WEST
Bromleians Sports 3 Fleetdown United 2
Eynsford 2 **Bly Spartans** 8
Halls 1 **Larkfield & New Hythe Wanderers** 4
Holmesdale 1 Snodland 0
Lewisham Borough (Community) 6 Fleet Leisure 3
SECOND ROUND EAST
APM Mears 0 **Norton Sports** 5
Borden Village 2 New Romney 1
Bromley Green 1 **Tyler Hill** 2
Faversham Town 5 Uniflo 2
Sheerness East 2 Milton Athletic 0
Sheppey United 3 Lydd Tn 3 *aet* (5-4p)
St Margarets 1 Oakwood 0
Tenterden Town (w/o) v University of Kent (scr.)
SECOND ROUND WEST
Belvedere 5 Larkfield & New Hythe Wanderers 2
Bly Spartans 1 **Phoenix Sports** 2
Cray Valley Paper Mills 1 **Orpington** 6
Greenways 1 **Stansfeld Oxford & Bermondsey Club** 3
Holmesdale 3 Crockenhill 1
Metrogas 2 Lewisham Borough (Community) 1
Old Roan 3 Bromleians Sports 1
Samuel Montagu Youth Club 2 Rusthall 0
THIRD ROUND EAST
Borden Village 0 **Norton Sports** 2
Sheerness East 10 Tenterden Town 0
St Margarets 3 Faversham Town 1
Tyler Hill 1 **Sheppey United** 2
THIRD ROUND WEST
Metrogas 1 **Holmesdale** 2
Old Roan 3 **Samuel Montagu Youth Club** 4
Phoenix Sports 1 **Belvedere** 2
Stansfeld Oxford & Bermondsey Club 1 Orpington 0
QUARTER-FINALS
Belvedere 1 **Sheerness East** 4
Sheppey United 5 **Norton Sports** 6
St Margarets 5 Samuel Montagu Youth Club 1
Stansfeld Oxford & Bermondsey Club 2 **Holmesdale** 3
SEMI-FINALS
Norton Sports 4 Sheerness East 3
St Margarets 0 **Holmesdale** 4
FINAL
(May 4th at Chatham Town)
Norton Sports 3 Holmesdale 2 *aet*

LES LECKIE CUP

(Eastern region clubs from outside the Premier Division)

FIRST ROUND
Ashford Borough 2 **Sutton Athletic** 3
Atcost 2 University of Kent 2 *aet* (4-3p)
Borden Village (w/o) v Platt United (scr.)
New Ash Green 2 Guru Nanak 1
Otford United 1 **Lanes End** 3
Putlands Athletic 2 Hollands & Blair 1
Sheppey United 3 Tyler Hill 0
Staplehurst & Monarchs United 2 Kennington 1
UK Paper 2 St Margarets 1 *aet*
Woodstock Park 1 **Pembury** 3
SECOND ROUND
APM Mears 1 UK Paper 1 *aet* (5-3p)
Atcost 3 Lanes End 2
Borden Village 0 **Sutton Athletic** 0 *aet* (2-4p)
New Romney 6 Staplehurst & Monarchs United 1
Oakwood 6 Pembury 4
Sheppey United 4 New Ash Green 1
Tenterden Town 3 Putlands Athletic 2
Uniflo 3 Betteshanger Welfare 2
QUARTER-FINALS
Atcost 6 Tenterden Town 1
Sheppey United 3 New Romney 1
Sutton Athletic 4 APM Mears 3
Uniflo 1 **Oakwood** 5
SEMI-FINALS
Sheppey United 2 Oakwood 2 *aet* (5-4p)
Sutton Athletic 4 Atcost 2
FINAL *(April 18th at Lordswood)*
Sutton Athletic 1 **Sheppey United** 1 *aet* (5-6p)

WEST KENT CHALLENGE SHIELD

(Western region clubs from outside the Premier Division)

FIRST ROUND
Belvedere 1 **Metrogas** 3
Borough United 7 Chislehurst 1
Bridon Ropes 0 **Orpington** 2
Chipstead 1 **Phoenix Sports** 4
Farnborough Old Boys Guild 3 Eltham Palace 0
Greenways 1 **Samuel Montagu Youth Club** 2
Holmesdale 2 Tonbridge Invicta 2 *aet* (4-2p)
New Bromleians 2 Old Addeyans 1
Westerham 3 Old Bexleians 0
Wickham Park 7 Meridian Sports 0
SECOND ROUND
Bromleians Sports 4 Borough United 1
Larkfield & New Hythe Wanderers 4 Holmesdale 2 *aet*
Metrogas 4 Eynsford 2
New Bromleians 1 Westerham 0
Orpington 6 Halls 2
Phoenix Sports 3 Farnborough Old Boys Guild 1
Samuel Montagu Youth Club 2 **Fleetdown United** 3
Wickham Park 4 Bly Spartans 2 *aet*
QUARTER-FINALS
Bromleians Sports 4 New Bromleians 1
Fleetdown United 1 Metrogas 0
Larkfield & New Hythe Wanderers 0 **Orpington** 2
Wickham Park 2 **Phoenix Sports** 5
SEMI-FINALS
Fleetdown United 1 Phoenix Sports 0
Orpington 1 Bromleians Sports 0
FINAL *(April 25th at Welling United)*
Orpington 2 Fleetdown United 2 *aet* (4-3p)

FLOODLIGHT CUP

(All Eastern teams from Premier Division and selected teams from Div One East – all games played at Faversham Tn)

FIRST ROUND
APM Mears 0 **Milton Athletic** 3
Bearsted 0 **Bromley Green** 5
Betteshanger Welfare 2 **New Romney** 3
Borden Village 1 **Faversham Town** 6
Kennington 2 Lydd Town 1
Norton Sports 2 **Hollands & Blair** 5 *aet*
Tyler Hill 4 Uniflo 2
QUARTER-FINALS
Faversham Tn 2 **Bromley Gn** 2 *aet* (2-3p)
Milton Athletic 2 Kennington 1
New Romney 1 **Tyler Hill** 2 *aet*
Sheerness East 2 Hollands & Blair 1
SEMI-FINALS
Milton Athletic 1 **Sheerness East** 3
Tyler Hill 0 **Bromley Green** 2
FINAL *(April 5th)*
Sheerness East 0 **Bromley Green** 1

KENT LEAGUE

	Beckenham Town	Deal Town	Erith Town	Erith & Belvedere	Greenwich Borough	Herne Bay	Hythe Town	Lordswood	Maidstone United	Sevenoaks Town	Slade Green	Sporting Bengal Utd	Thamesmead Town	Tunbridge Wells	VCD Athletic	Whitstable Town
Beckenham Town	*P*	5-1	4-0	2-1	4-1	1-3	0-0	4-0	2-3	9-0	4-0	3-1	8-0	3-0	4-0	6-2
Deal Town	0-2	*R*	5-1	2-3	7-3	1-4	2-1	1-2	1-5	0-0	4-0	3-2	1-0	1-3	1-3	2-2
Erith Town	1-2	1-2	*E*	0-4	0-3	0-1	1-2	2-4	1-1	1-0	0-1	1-3	1-2	0-1	1-1	0-0
Erith & Belvedere	1-1	2-1	2-0	*M*	3-1	1-2	3-1	2-0	0-1	2-1	2-2	3-2	1-2	0-0	0-0	1-0
Greenwich Borough	0-7	2-0	1-1	0-1	*I*	1-2	2-1	0-0	0-2	1-0	0-2	1-2	4-3	0-2	0-1	3-5
Herne Bay	0-1	0-1	3-0	1-2	0-2	*E*	3-2	3-2	0-1	3-0	4-0	8-0	1-1	1-1	0-1	1-1
Hythe Town	1-2	1-1	3-3	1-1	3-1	0-3	*R*	1-0	2-2	1-0	1-2	4-0	1-3	2-3	0-1	0-2
Lordswood	0-5	2-0	6-0	2-2	3-2	1-1	2-2		0-5	4-0	0-0	7-0	0-3	1-0	1-2	3-2
Maidstone United	1-1	3-1	5-0	2-1	4-1	1-0	5-2	0-1	*D*	5-0	2-0	9-0	5-0	2-1	3-0	1-2
Sevenoaks Town	2-6	1-1	0-1	2-1	1-3	2-2	0-1	1-1	0-4	*I*	1-3	1-0	0-3	0-1	3-3	1-5
Slade Green	0-2	1-2	1-0	1-2	1-1	1-0	2-1	0-1	1-2	2-1	*V*	2-2	0-4	2-0	1-7	2-5
Sporting Bengal United	0-3	1-2	2-3	1-1	4-1	2-2	0-6	1-1	1-5	0-1	1-1	*I*	0-7	0-0	1-5	0-7
Thamesmead Town	2-1	6-1	2-1	2-3	3-2	6-0	3-0	1-1	1-1	2-0	1-1	5-0	*S*	2-0	1-0	0-0
Tunbridge Wells	2-2	3-4	0-1	1-2	3-0	0-2	2-1	1-1	2-3	2-0	1-1	5-1	2-3	*I*	0-1	2-1
VCD Athletic	0-2	1-2	0-1	0-1	2-0	0-1	1-0	1-2	1-1	1-0	3-0	7-0	2-2	3-0	*O*	1-3
Whitstable Town	2-0	2-3	3-0	0-2	2-0	1-1	1-0	3-1	1-1	2-0	2-1	3-0	4-3	1-1	0-2	*N*

Premier Division	P	W	D	L	F	A	Pts
Maidstone United	30	22	6	2	85	23	72
Beckenham Town	30	22	4	4	96	24	70
Thamesmead Town	30	18	6	6	73	41	60
Erith & Belvedere	30	17	7	6	50	31	58
Whitstable Town	30	16	7	7	64	38	55
VCD Athletic	30	15	5	10	51	30	50
Herne Bay	30	14	7	9	52	33	49
Lordswood	30	12	9	9	49	45	45
Deal Town	30	13	4	13	53	62	43
Tunbridge Wells	30	10	7	13	39	41	37
Slade Green	30	9	7	14	31	56	34
Hythe Town	30	7	6	17	41	51	27
Greenwich Borough	30	7	3	20	36	69	24
Erith Town	30	5	5	20	21	65	20
Sporting Bengal United	30	3	6	21	27	107	15
Sevenoaks Town	30	3	5	22	18	70	14

CHALLENGE SHIELD

(Premier Division champions v League Cup holders)

Herne Bay qualify as Premier Division runners-up as Ramsgate won both in 2004-05

(August 6th at Ramsgate)

Ramsgate 3 Herne Bay 1

KENT LEAGUE PREMIER DIVISION CONSTITUTION 2006-07

BECKENHAM TOWN	Eden Park Avenue, Beckenham BR3 3JJ	020 8650 1066
CROYDON	Croydon Sports Arena, Albert Road, South Norwood SE25 4QL	020 8654 8555/3462
DEAL TOWN	Charles Sports Ground, St Leonards Road, Deal CT14 9BB	01304 375623
ERITH TOWN	Erith Sports Centre, Avenue Road, Erith DA8 3AJ	01322 350271
ERITH & BELVEDERE	Welling United FC, Park View Road, Welling DA16 1SY	020 8304 0333
FAVERSHAM TOWN	Salter Lane, Faversham ME13 8ND	None
GREENWICH BOROUGH	Harrow Meadow, Eltham Green Road, Eltham SE9 6BA	020 8859 5788
HERNE BAY	Winchs Field, Stanley Gardens, Herne Bay CT6 5SG	01227 374156
HYTHE TOWN	Reachfields Stadium, Fort Road, Hythe CT21 6JS	01303 264932
LORDSWOOD	Martyn Grove, Northdane Way, Walderslade ME5 8YE	01634 669138
SEVENOAKS TOWN	Greatness Park, Seal Road (on main A25), Sevenoaks TN14 5BL	01732 741987
SLADE GREEN	The Small Glenn, 35 Moat Lane, Slade Green, Erith BA8 2ND	01322 351077
SPORTING BENGAL UNITED	Mile End Stadium, Rhodeswell Road, Burdett Road, Poplar E14 7TW	020 8980 1885
THAMESMEAD TOWN	Bayliss Avenue, Thamesmead SE28 8NJ	020 8311 4211
TUNBRIDGE WELLS	Culverden Stadium, Culverden Down, Tunbridge Wells TN4 9SH	01892 520517
VCD ATHLETIC	Lordswood FC, Martyn Grove, Northdane Way, Walderslade ME5 8YE.	01634 669138
WHITSTABLE TOWN	Belmont Road, Whitstable CT5 1QP	01227 266012

IN: Croydon (S – Isthmian League Division Two), Faversham Town (P – Kent County League Premier Division)

OUT: Maidstone United (P – Isthmian League Division One South)

PREMIER DIVISION CUP

GROUP A

	P	W	D	L	F	A	Pts
Herne Bay	6	4	1	1	12	3	13
Hythe Town	6	3	1	2	18	8	10
Erith & Belvedere	6	3	1	2	11	9	10
Sporting Bengal United	6	0	1	5	4	25	1

Erith & Belvedere 2 Herne Bay 0
Erith & Belvedere 2 Hythe Town 4
Erith & Belvedere 5 Sporting Bengal United 0
Herne Bay 2 Hythe Town 1
Herne Bay 3 Sporting Bengal United 0
Herne Bay 4 Erith & Belvedere 0
Hythe Town 0 Erith & Belvedere 1
Hythe Town 0 Herne Bay 0
Hythe Town 7 Sporting Bengal United 1
Sporting Bengal United 0 Herne Bay 3
Sporting Bengal United 1 Erith & Belvedere 1
Sporting Bengal United 2 Hythe Town 6

GROUP B

	P	W	D	L	F	A	Pts
Lordswood	6	4	1	1	12	10	13
Whitstable Town	6	3	2	1	12	7	11
Erith Town	6	2	0	4	7	8	6
Greenwich Borough	6	1	1	4	7	13	4

Erith Town 1 Lordswood 2
Erith Town 2 Whitstable Town 0
Erith Town 3 Greenwich Borough 0
Greenwich Borough 0 Whitstable Town 2
Greenwich Borough 1 Lordswood 2
Greenwich Borough 2 Erith Town 1
Lordswood 2 Erith Town 0
Lordswood 3 Greenwich Borough 2
Lordswood 3 Whitstable Town 3
Whitstable Town 2 Erith Town 0
Whitstable Town 2 Greenwich Borough 2
Whitstable Town 3 Lordswood 0

GROUP C

	P	W	D	L	F	A	Pts
Maidstone United	6	5	0	1	16	6	15
VCD Athletic	6	3	2	1	9	7	11
Tunbridge Wells	6	2	2	2	8	8	8
Deal Town	6	0	0	6	7	19	0

Deal Town 0 Tunbridge Wells 2
Deal Town 1 Maidstone United 3
Deal Town 3 VCD Athletic 4
Maidstone United 0 VCD Athletic 2
Maidstone United 3 Tunbridge Wells 2
Maidstone United 5 Deal Town 1
Tunbridge Wells 0 Maidstone United 3
Tunbridge Wells 0 VCD Athletic 0
Tunbridge Wells 3 Deal Town 1
VCD Athletic 0 Maidstone United 2
VCD Athletic 1 Tunbridge Wells 1
VCD Athletic 2 Deal Town 1

GROUP D

	P	W	D	L	F	A	Pts
Thamesmead Town	6	3	3	0	11	5	12
Beckenham Town	6	2	4	0	11	5	10
Slade Green	6	2	2	2	8	7	8
Sevenoaks Town	6	0	1	5	2	15	1

Beckenham Town 0 Slade Green 0
Beckenham Town 2 Sevenoaks Town 0
Beckenham Town 3 Thamesmead Town 3
Sevenoaks Town 0 Beckenham Town 4
Sevenoaks Town 0 Slade Green 1
Sevenoaks Town 0 Thamesmead Town 1
Slade Green 0 Thamesmead Town 2
Slade Green 1 Beckenham Town 1
Slade Green 6 Sevenoaks Town 1
Thamesmead Town 1 Beckenham Town 1
Thamesmead Town 1 Sevenoaks Town 1
Thamesmead Town 3 Slade Green 0

Top two teams from each group qualify for knockout stage

QUARTER-FINALS

Herne Bay 2 Whitstable Town 1
Lordswood 0 **VCD Athletic** 1
Maidstone United 4 Beckenham Town 3 *aet*
Thamesmead Town 1 **Hythe Town** 2

SEMI-FINALS
(played over two legs)

Hythe Town 1 Maidstone United 2, **Maidstone United** 2 Hythe Town 1
VCD Athletic 1 Herne Bay 1, Herne Bay 0 **VCD Athletic** 1

FINAL
(April 29th at Folkestone Invicta)

Maidstone United 4 VCD Athletic 0

Division One	P	W	D	L	F	A	Pts
Thamesmead Town Res.	22	15	5	2	50	23	50
Whitstable Town Res.	22	13	3	6	46	32	42
Cray Wanderers Res.	22	11	5	6	51	34	38
Bromley Res.	22	12	2	8	42	34	38
Dartford Res.	22	10	5	7	39	27	35
Erith Town Res.	22	10	4	8	50	42	34
Ramsgate Res.	22	8	6	8	38	45	30
Ashford Town Res.	22	8	4	10	38	47	28
Erith & Belvedere Res.	22	7	6	9	43	47	27
Maidstone United Res.	22	6	4	12	31	53	22
Herne Bay Res.	22	3	5	14	25	46	14
Deal Town Res.	22	3	3	16	20	43	12

Division Two	P	W	D	L	F	A	Pts
Folkestone Invicta Res.	20	14	4	2	53	16	46
Sevenoaks Town Res.	20	11	4	5	32	22	37
Chatham Town Res.	20	11	1	8	47	42	34
Slade Green Res.	20	9	6	5	36	22	33
Tunbridge Wells Res.	20	8	7	5	42	34	31
Lordswood Res.	20	8	4	8	42	39	28
Greenwich Borough Res.	20	6	5	9	26	37	23
VCD Athletic Res.	20	6	4	10	27	46	22
Tilbury Res.	20	5	5	10	26	33	20
Sittingbourne Res.	20	4	5	11	24	42	17
Hythe Town Res.	20	3	5	12	24	46	14

DIVISION ONE/TWO CUP

FINAL
(April 26th at Folkestone Invicta)

Dartford Res. 3 Whitstable Town Res. 1

LEICESTERSHIRE SENIOR LEAGUE

	Anstey Nomads	Aylestone Park Old Boys	Barrow Town	Birstall United	Blaby & Whetstone Athletic	Downes Sports	Ellistown	Friar Lane & Epworth	Highfield Rangers	Holwell Sports	Ibstock United	Kirby Muxloe SC	Ratby Sports	Rothley Imperial	St Andrews SC	Stapenhill	Thurmaston Town	Thurnby Rangers
Anstey Nomads		1-0	1-5	0-5	0-2	2-2	0-2	1-6	0-1	0-3	0-6	1-1	3-1	0-1	0-3	0-0	3-2	2-5
Aylestone Park Old Boys	6-0	*P*	1-2	1-2	2-3	0-0	2-0	0-2	3-1	1-1	0-1	1-3	1-2	0-3	2-6	1-3	2-3	1-5
Barrow Town	2-1	1-6	*R*	1-0	3-1	2-0	5-0	2-1	4-0	2-0	3-0	2-1	4-2	3-1	2-1	4-1	5-1	0-6
Birstall United	3-1	4-2	1-3	*E*	3-3	0-1	2-1	0-1	1-1	2-1	2-3	0-0	1-0	1-0	0-3	3-2	1-1	0-2
Blaby & Whetstone Athletic	4-2	1-2	2-6	1-0	*M*	0-0	2-0	0-4	2-1	0-0	1-0	0-2	1-2	0-4	3-1	1-4	1-1	1-1
Downes Sports	4-1	2-1	2-0	1-0	2-3	*I*	5-2	0-2	0-0	4-1	5-2	0-2	1-0	1-1	1-2	0-2	0-1	1-2
Ellistown	5-1	4-0	0-6	1-3	1-1	1-6	*E*	1-2	2-3	0-7	0-3	0-0	2-3	3-1	2-3	2-3	3-4	0-1
Friar Lane & Epworth	5-1	5-1	7-0	3-0	1-0	3-0	1-1	*R*	2-1	3-2	4-1	2-6	6-3	1-0	3-1	3-3	3-2	2-0
Highfield Rangers	5-1	5-1	0-0	2-1	2-1	1-2	4-1	1-1		1-0	5-2	1-2	3-4	4-0	1-1	3-1	2-0	1-0
Holwell Sports	6-0	4-0	0-4	3-1	4-1	0-1	0-1	0-2	0-2	*D*	0-2	1-0	1-1	0-1	0-1	1-0	4-1	3-1
Ibstock United	11-1	3-4	2-1	2-0	3-2	2-1	2-1	5-2	0-2	0-0	*I*	0-1	5-0	2-2	0-1	0-4	1-0	2-1
Kirby Muxloe SC	4-1	2-1	1-2	6-2	0-0	2-1	7-0	2-2	2-4	1-1	1-2	*V*	0-1	2-1	5-2	1-1	2-3	0-1
Ratby Sports	1-2	3-2	0-5	1-2	0-1	0-2	1-3	0-2	0-2	1-1	2-4	0-2	*I*	1-5	5-3	1-1	1-1	1-1
Rothley Imperial	2-0	4-3	1-1	2-2	4-0	0-0	4-1	0-3	1-2	4-0	1-6	0-0	1-2	*S*	0-0	2-1	2-0	1-0
St Andrews SC	5-1	4-0	3-2	2-1	9-2	1-1	4-0	3-0	1-2	0-2	3-0	2-2	3-2	1-2	*I*	3-4	5-4	2-0
Stapenhill	2-0	4-0	1-0	2-0	4-0	1-1	8-0	2-0	5-0	0-1	4-0	1-4	0-1	3-0	2-1	*O*	0-3	0-0
Thurmaston Town	2-0	2-1	5-0	0-2	1-2	2-3	3-3	0-3	2-0	0-3	1-3	1-0	2-0	2-3	1-3	2-4	*N*	0-3
Thurnby Rangers	3-1	3-1	1-2	0-0	3-1	1-1	4-0	3-1	1-1	2-1	2-1	2-1	3-1	4-2	1-3	3-3	2-0	

Premier Division	P	W	D	L	F	A	Pts
Friar Lane & Epworth	34	24	4	6	88	42	76
Barrow Town	34	24	2	8	84	50	74
St Andrews SC	34	20	4	10	86	53	64
Thurnby Rangers	34	19	7	8	67	37	64
Highfield Rangers	34	19	6	9	64	44	63
Stapenhill	34	18	7	9	76	41	61
Ibstock United	34	19	2	13	76	57	59
Kirby Muxloe SC	34	15	9	10	65	39	54
Rothley Imperial	34	15	7	12	56	49	52
Downes Sports	34	14	9	11	51	40	51
Holwell Sports	34	13	6	15	51	40	45
Birstall United	34	12	6	16	45	53	42
Blaby & Whetstone Athletic	34	11	7	16	43	72	40
Thurmaston Town	34	11	4	19	53	70	37
Ratby Sports	34	9	5	20	43	76	32
Ellistown	34	6	4	24	43	101	22
Aylestone Park Old Boys	34	6	2	26	49	89	20
Anstey Nomads	34	4	3	27	28	115	15

LEICESTERSHIRE SENIOR LEAGUE PREMIER DIVISION CONSTITUTION 2006-07

ANSTEY NOMADS .... Llimah International Park, Cropston Road, Anstey LE7 7BY 0116 236 4868
AYLESTONE PARK OLD BOYS .... Dorset Avenue, Wigston, Leicester LE18 4WB 0116 277 5307
BARDON HILL SPORTS .... Bardon Close, Coalville LE67 4BS 01530 815569
BARROW TOWN............. Riverside Park, Meynell, Barrow Road, Quorn, Loughborough LE12 8PJ 01509 620650
BIRSTALL UNITED.............................. Meadow Lane, Birstall LE4 4FN 0116 267 1230
BLABY & WHETSTONE ATHLETIC ... Blaby & Whetstone Boys Club, Warwick Road, Whetstone LE8 6LW 0116 286 4852
DOWNES SPORTS................... The Sports Ground, Leicester Road, Hinckley LE10 1TP 01455 615062
ELLISTOWN .... 1 Terrace Road, Ellistown, Coalville LE67 1GD 01530 230159
HIGHFIELD RANGERS .... 443 Gleneagles Avenue, Rushey Mead, Leicester LE4 7YJ 0116 266 0009
HOLWELL SPORTS.................. Welby Road, Asfordby Hill, Melton Mowbray LE14 3RD 01664 812715
IBSTOCK UNITED...................... The Welfare, Leicester Road, Ibstock LE67 6HN...................... 01530 260656
KIRBY MUXLOE SC...................... Ratby Lane, Kirby Muxloe, Leicester LE9 9AQ...................... 0116 239 3201
RATBY SPORTS .... Desford Lane, Ratby, Leicester LE6 0LF...................... 0116 239 2474
ROTHLEY IMPERIAL .... Loughborough Road, Mountsorrell, Leicester LE12 7AU...................... 0116 237 4003
ST ANDREWS SC .... Canal Street, Aylestone, Leicester LE2 8LX 0116 283 9298
STAPENHILL .... Maple Grove, Stapenhill, Burton-on-Trent DE15 9NN 01283 562471
THURMASTON TOWN .... Elizabeth Park, Checkland Road, Thurmaston, Leicester LE4 8FN 0116 260 2519
THURNBY RANGERS .... Dakyn Road, Thurnby Lodge Estate, Leicester LE5 2ED...................... 0116 243 3698

IN: Bardon Hill Sports (P)
OUT: Friar Lane & Epworth (P – Midland Alliance)

	Anstey Town	Asfordby Amateurs	Ashby Ivanhoe	Bardon Hill Sports	Cottesmore Amateurs	Earl Shilton Albion	HM Desford Sports	Huncote Sports & Social	Leics Constabulary	Lutterworth Athletic	Lutterworth Town	Narborough & Littlethorpe	North Kilworth	Ravenstone	Saffron Dynamo	Sileby Town
Anstey Town		1-0	7-4	2-0	3-0	6-1	1-0	2-0	4-0	2-2	3-0	2-1	3-1	1-0	0-1	1-0
Asfordby Amateurs	3-1		2-0	0-1	4-2	2-1	1-1	2-3	1-1	1-1	5-1	3-1	4-0	0-0	2-1	4-3
Ashby Ivanhoe	2-0	1-1	*D*	3-3	1-1	1-1	4-2	5-0	3-1	4-2	4-4	3-1	6-2	3-2	5-2	3-2
Bardon Hill Sports	1-1	3-2	2-2	*I*	4-2	3-1	1-0	2-0	3-0	1-2	1-1	4-2	6-2	2-1	3-2	2-3
Cottesmore Amateurs	0-1	3-1	2-3	0-4	*V*	3-3	1-0	1-0	3-0	0-0	1-3	1-3	10-0	3-2	5-1	0-1
Earl Shilton Albion	4-2	2-0	1-2	3-4	2-3	*I*	4-0	0-2	4-4	0-2	1-2	1-1	4-3	2-1	1-1	0-1
HM Desford Sports	0-2	0-1	1-3	1-3	0-3	0-2	*S*	4-3	1-0	1-1	1-0	0-2	3-1	1-3	1-3	1-1
Huncote Sports & Social	0-1	0-1	0-3	1-4	0-4	2-2	2-2	*I*	4-1	2-3	1-1	0-1	2-0	4-5	1-1	1-2
Leics Constabulary	2-4	0-1	2-4	0-3	1-4	5-0	3-0	1-0	*O*	0-4	0-1	0-3	1-1	3-0	0-2	1-4
Lutterworth Athletic	1-2	0-3	1-0	4-3	6-1	5-0	2-1	0-1	1-0	*N*	3-1	0-2	2-0	1-1	4-1	1-2
Lutterworth Town	2-2	2-0	2-3	2-4	0-2	8-2	2-2	2-1	1-0	2-2		2-0	5-3	3-3	4-3	1-1
Narborough & Littlethorpe	1-4	1-3	2-2	1-3	2-1	5-2	0-0	1-0	1-0	0-5	0-5	*O*	2-1	2-1	0-2	0-0
North Kilworth	1-6	0-1	0-1	0-8	1-5	1-4	3-5	1-2	1-3	1-6	1-3	0-2	*N*	0-2	1-3	1-7
Ravenstone	1-2	0-0	0-2	2-3	3-1	2-1	3-1	2-2	2-1	1-6	0-4	2-0	8-1	*E*	3-1	0-3
Saffron Dynamo	1-3	0-2	1-1	3-2	2-0	4-1	3-0	3-1	2-0	1-1	4-1	1-1	2-0	3-1		1-2
Sileby Town	2-2	2-1	2-2	1-2	1-0	1-0	5-1	4-0	4-0	0-1	5-1	2-4	3-0	5-4	3-1	

Division One	P	W	D	L	F	A	Pts
Anstey Town	30	22	4	4	71	31	70
Bardon Hill Sports	30	21	4	5	85	44	67
Ashby Ivanhoe	30	18	9	3	80	49	63
Sileby Town	30	19	5	6	72	36	62
Lutterworth Athletic	30	17	7	6	69	34	58
Asfordby Amateurs	30	16	6	8	51	32	54
Lutterworth Town	30	13	8	9	66	58	47
Saffron Dynamo	30	14	5	11	56	49	47
Narborough & Littlethorpe	30	13	5	12	42	50	44
Cottesmore Amateurs	30	13	3	14	62	52	42
Ravenstone	30	10	5	15	55	61	35
Earl Shilton Albion	30	7	6	17	50	76	27
Huncote Sports & Social	30	6	5	19	35	61	23
HM Desford Sports	30	5	6	19	30	63	21
Leics Constabulary	30	5	3	22	30	66	18
North Kilworth	30	0	1	29	27	119	1

LEICESTERSHIRE SENIOR LEAGUE DIVISION ONE CONSTITUTION 2006-07

ANSTEY TOWN .... Leicester Road, Thurcaston, Leicester LE7 7JH 0116 236 8231
ASFORDBY AMATEURS .... Hoby Road Sports Ground, Hoby Road, Asfordby, Melton Mowbray LE14 3TL 01664 434545
ASHBY IVANHOE .... Hood Park, North Street, Ashby-de-la-Zouch LE65 1HU .... None
COTTESMORE AMATEURS .... Rogues Park, Main Street, Cottesmore, Oakham LE15 4DH 01572 813486
EARL SHILTON ALBION .... Stoneycroft Park, New Street, Earl Shilton LE9 7FR 01455 844277
FC BRAUNSTONE VICTORIA .... Braunstone Park, Hinckley Road, Leicester LE3 1HX .... None
HATHERN .... Pasture Lane, Hathern, Loughborough LE12 5LJ .... None
HUNCOTE SPORTS & SOCIAL .... Enderby Lane, Thurlaston 01455 888430
LEICS CONSTABULARY .... Police Headquarters, St Johns, Enderby .... 0116 248 2198 (matchdays only)
LUTTERWORTH ATHLETIC .... Dunley Way, Lutterworth LE17 4NA .... None
LUTTERWORTH TOWN .... Hall Lane, Bitteswell, Lutterworth LE17 4LN 01455 554046
NARBOROUGH & LITTLETHORPE .... Leicester Road, Narborough LE19 2DG 0116 275 1855
RAVENSTONE .... Ravenslea, Ravenstone, Coalville LE67 2AW .... None
SAFFRON DYNAMO .... Cambridge Road, Whetstone LE8 2LH 0116 284 9695
SILEBY TOWN .... Memorial Park, Seagrave Road, Sileby, Loughborough LE12 7TP 01509 816104
SYSTON FOSSE SPORTS .... Co-operative Sports Ground, Birstall Road, Birstall, Leicester LE4 4DE 0116 267 4059

IN: FC Braunstone Victoria (P – Leicester City League Division One), Hathern (P – North Leicestershire League Premier Division),
OUT: Bardon Hill Sports (P), North Kilworth (R – Leicester & District League Premier Division)
HM Desford Sports become Syston Fosse Sports

LEAGUE CUP

PREMIER DIVISION SECTION

PRELIMINARY ROUND

Rothley Imperial 0 **Ibstock United** 1
Thurmaston Town 1 **Blaby & Whetstone Athletic** 1 (4-5p)

FIRST ROUND

Anstey Nomads 1 Ratby Sports 0
Birstall United 1 **Holwell Sports** 4
Blaby & Whetstone Athletic 1 **Barrow Town** 4
Downes Sports 1 **Highfield Rangers** 1 (12-13p)
Ellistown 0 **Kirby Muxloe SC** 1
Ibstock United 2 Aylestone Park Old Boys 1
Stapenhill 1 **St Andrews SC** 1 (4-5p)
Thurnby Rangers 3 Friar Lane & Epworth 2

SECOND ROUND

Holwell Sports 5 Anstey Nomads 0
Ibstock United 5 St Andrews SC 2
Kirby Muxloe SC 2 Barrow Town 2 (4-2p)
Thurnby Rangers 5 Highfield Rangers 1

DIVISION ONE SECTION

FIRST ROUND

Asfordby Amateurs 5 Ravenstone 0
Bardon Hill Sports 2 Lutterworth Athletic 1
Cottesmore Amateurs 2 Sileby Town 1
Earl Shilton Albion 1 **Huncote Sports & Social** 3
Leics Constabulary 4 HM Desford Sports 0
Lutterworth Town 5 North Kilworth 2
Narborough & Littlethorpe 0 **Anstey Town** 2
Saffron Dynamo 6 Ashby Ivanhoe 0

SECOND ROUND

Anstey Town 0 **Leics Constabulary** 1
Bardon Hill Sports 1 **Saffron Dynamo** 3
Cottesmore Amateurs 3 Huncote Sports & Social 1
Lutterworth Town 2 Asfordby Amateurs 1

QUARTER-FINALS

Cottesmore Amateurs 2 **Holwell Sports** 5
Ibstock United 3 Saffron Dynamo 1
Kirby Muxloe SC 4 Leics Constabulary 1
Thurnby Rangers 2 Lutterworth Town 0

SEMI-FINALS

Holwell Sports 4 Kirby Muxloe SC 0
Ibstock United 2 Thurnby Rangers 1

FINAL

(May 8th at Barrow Town)

Holwell Sports 2 Ibstock United 0

Combination One		P	W	D	L	F	A	Pts
Barrow Town Res.		30	21	5	4	89	29	68
Highfield Rangers Res.		30	20	5	5	59	25	65
Thurmaston Town Res.		30	19	5	6	59	33	62
Ibstock United Res.		30	16	4	10	60	47	52
Anstey Town Res.		30	13	7	10	61	42	46
Friar Lane & Epworth Res.		30	13	6	11	53	38	45
Downes Sports Res.		30	12	8	10	44	45	44
Aylestone Park Old Boys Res.		30	12	4	14	44	65	40
Kirby Muxloe SC Res.		30	12	3	15	38	57	39
Birstall United Res.		30	12	2	16	45	46	38
Blaby & Whetstone Athletic Res.		30	9	8	13	55	56	35
Ratby Sports Res.		30	8	9	13	58	59	33
Rothley Imperial Res.		30	8	7	15	42	64	31
Leics Constabulary Res.		30	8	5	17	39	56	29
St Andrews SC Res.		30	6	6	18	40	68	24
Thurnby Rangers Res.		30	5	8	17	33	89	23

Combination Two		P	W	D	L	F	A	Pts
Lutterworth Athletic Res.		30	22	7	1	88	26	73
Sileby Town Res.		30	18	9	3	89	37	63
Narborough & Littlethorpe Res.		30	18	8	4	75	33	62
Ashby Ivanhoe Res.		30	16	6	8	81	49	54
Lutterworth Town Res.		30	16	4	10	76	45	52
Asfordby Amateurs Res.		30	13	10	7	67	43	49
Holwell Sports Res.	*-1*	30	14	6	10	89	45	47
Earl Shilton Albion Res.		30	13	7	10	78	49	46
Saffron Dynamo Res.		30	14	3	13	83	55	45
Bardon Hill Sports Res.		30	12	6	12	63	58	42
Anstey Nomads Res.		30	10	4	16	46	67	34
Huncote Sports & Social Res.		30	9	4	17	53	78	31
Ellistown Res.		30	7	5	18	50	79	26
Cottesmore Amateurs Res.	*-1*	30	8	2	20	26	78	25
North Kilworth Res.		30	6	1	23	39	113	19
HM Desford Sports Res.	*-1*	30	2	2	26	31	179	7

PRESIDENT'S CUP

FINAL

(May 9th at Aylestone Park Old Boys)

Downes Sports Res. 2 Thurmaston Town Res. 1

LINCOLNSHIRE LEAGUE

Note – Limestone Rangers withdrew during the course of the season. Their results are shown herein but are expunged from the league table	CGB Humbertherm	Caistor Rovers	Grimsby Borough Res.	Horncastle Town	Hykeham Town	LSS Lucarly's Res.	Limestone Rangers	Lincoln Moorlands Res.	Lincoln United Juniors	Louth United	Retford Town	Ruston Sports	Skegness Town	Wyberton
CGB Humbertherm		1-0	6-1	0-1	3-2	3-1	n/a	4-0	2-0	2-4	3-1	2-2	1-1	1-0
Caistor Rovers	0-1		2-0	1-1	1-5	3-0	4-1	2-2	5-2	1-0	2-1	2-1	1-1	0-2
Grimsby Borough Res.	1-5	0-1		0-6	1-4	0-2	n/a	0-3	2-0	1-1	1-1	1-2	1-0	1-2
Horncastle Town	1-0	3-2	5-1		0-2	2-0	n/a	2-0	5-0	2-2	6-0	0-1	2-2	0-1
Hykeham Town	1-2	4-1	7-0	4-2		7-0	8-0	2-1	2-1	4-1	7-0	5-0	4-0	5-1
LSS Lucarly's Res.	1-6	0-3	1-6	2-5	1-5		5-0	4-5	5-1	0-3	2-1	1-2	2-2	0-6
Limestone Rangers	0-2	n/a	2-2	n/a	n/a	0-1		1-5	n/a	n/a	0-0	n/a	0-3	n/a
Lincoln Moorlands Res.	0-1	4-0	5-1	1-8	0-2	2-4	n/a		2-1	1-3	0-2	2-2	1-1	1-4
Lincoln United Juniors	2-3	0-0	2-1	1-3	0-3	1-1	7-1	1-7		2-1	2-3	0-1	2-0	0-2
Louth United	0-3	3-0	1-4	1-4	0-1	2-1	11-0	3-2	4-0		5-2	2-3	4-0	3-2
Retford Town	0-1	2-1	3-2	2-4	0-3	2-2	9-0	0-0	2-1	1-3		2-3	2-2	0-2
Ruston Sports	2-2	4-0	2-1	0-2	2-1	2-0	4-2	1-0	1-2	2-5	1-0		0-8	2-4
Skegness Town	0-3	2-1	3-3	0-5	1-2	5-1	n/a	1-2	3-0	2-2	3-1	3-0		1-1
Wyberton	2-1	7-2	3-2	3-1	1-2	3-3	6-0	W-L	3-2	1-1	5-0	1-3	4-2	

		P	W	D	L	F	A	Pts
Hykeham Town		24	21	0	3	84	19	63
CGB Humbertherm		24	17	3	4	56	23	54
Horncastle Town		24	16	3	5	70	26	51
Wyberton		24	16	3	5	60	33	51
Ruston Sports		24	13	3	8	39	46	42
Louth United		24	12	4	8	54	41	40
Caistor Rovers		24	8	4	12	31	46	28
Skegness Town		24	6	9	9	43	45	27
Lincoln Moorlands Res.	*-3*	24	7	4	13	41	49	22
Retford Town		24	5	4	15	28	61	19
Grimsby Borough Res.		24	4	3	17	31	67	15
Lincoln United Juniors		24	4	2	18	23	61	14
LSS Lucarly's Res.	*-3*	24	4	4	16	34	77	13

Limestone Rangers – record expunged

LINCOLNSHIRE LEAGUE CONSTITUTION 2006-07

BOSTON TOWN COLTS .... **The Stadium, Tattershall Road, Boston PE21 9LR** **01205 365470**
CGB HUMBERTHERM .... **Chartdale Club, Love Lane Corner, Clee Road, Grimsby DN12 8QL** .... **None**
CAISTOR ROVERS .... **Brigg Road, Caistor, Market Rasen LN7 6RX** .... **None**
GRIMSBY BOROUGH RESERVES .. **King George V Ath. Stadium, Weelsby Road, Grimsby DN32 9RU** .... **01472 602192 Fax: 323228**
HORNCASTLE TOWN .... **The Wong, Boston Road, Horncastle LE9 6EY** .... **None**
HYKEHAM TOWN .... **Memorial Hall Ground, Newark Road, North Hykeham, Lincoln LN6 9RJ** **01522 880035**
KEELBY UNITED .... **Keelby Village Green, Keelby** .... **None**
LSS LUCARLY'S RESERVES .... **Wilton Road, Humberston, Grimsby DN36 4AW** **01472 812936**
LINCOLN UNITED COLTS .... **Ashby Avenue, Hartsholme, Lincoln LN6 0DY** **01522 696400**
LOUTH UNITED RESERVES .... **Park Avenue, Louth LN6 8BY** **01507 607351**
RUSTON SPORTS .... **Ruston Marconi Sports Club, Newark Road, Lincoln** **01522 882111**
SKEGNESS TOWN .... **Burgh Road, Skegness PE25 2RJ** **01754 764385**

IN: Boston Town Colts (P – Boston League Premier Division), Keelby United (N), Louth United Reserves (N)
OUT: Limestone Rangers (WS – Scunthorpe & District League Division One), Lincoln Moorlands (S – Central Midlands League Reserve Division Two), Louth United (P – Central Midlands League Premier Division), Retford United (S – Doncaster Senior League), Wyberton (W – Boston League Premier Division)
Lincoln United Juniors become Lincoln United Colts

LEAGUE CUP

FIRST ROUND
CGB Humbertherm 3 Retford Town 1
Horncastle Town 4 Caistor Rovers 0
Limestone Rgrs 2 LSS Lucarly's Res. 1 *aet*
Ruston Sports 1 Louth United 0
Skegness Town 2 **Lincoln Utd Juniors** 3
Wyberton 2 **Hykeham Town** 3 *aet*

QUARTER-FINALS
CGB Humbertherm 0 **Horncastle Town** 2
Lincoln Moorlands Res. 2 **Hykeham Tn** 4
Lincoln Utd Jun. 1 **Grimsby Boro' Res.** 2
Ruston Spts (w/o) v Limestone Rgrs (scr.)

SEMI-FINALS
Grimsby Borough Res. 1 **Hykeham Tn** 3
Horncastle Town 1 **Ruston Sports** 2

FINAL
(April 6th at Lincoln Moorlands)
Hykeham Town 0 **Ruston Sports** 2

SUPPLEMENTARY CUP

PRELIMINARY ROUND
CGB Humbertherm 0 **Louth United** 3
Hykeham Town 4 Caistor Rovers 1
Lincoln Moorlands Res. 2 **Horncastle Tn** 4
Lincoln Utd Jun. 2 Grimsby Boro' Res. 0
Ruston Sports 5 Wyberton 2
Skegness Town 2 Limestone Rangers 1

QUARTER-FINALS
Hykeham Town 5 LSS Lucarly's Res. 2
Louth United 3 Ruston Sports 1
Retford Town 2 Lincoln United Juniors 1
Skegness Town 2 **Horncastle Town** 3

SEMI-FINALS
Hykeham Town 1 Horncastle Town 0
Louth United 3 **Retford Town** 4

FINAL
(April 12th at Louth United)
Hykeham Town 5 Retford Town 3 *aet*

LIVERPOOL COUNTY COMBINATION

	Aigburth People's Hall	Birchfield	Bootle	Cheshire Lines	Ford Motors	Halewood Village	Kingsley United	Lucas Sports	Mossley Hill Athletic	Penlake	South Liverpool	South Sefton Borough	Speke	St Aloysius	St Dominics	Waterloo Dock
Aigburth People's Hall		2-1	0-1	2-3	0-2	n/a	2-2	4-2	0-0	2-2	1-3	2-2	4-4	1-2	0-5	1-2
Birchfield	4-3		1-3	2-0	0-1	n/a	5-1	2-1	3-1	3-2	0-0	1-0	0-1	2-2	1-1	1-0
Bootle	4-0	2-4		5-1	2-1	n/a	8-1	2-2	1-1	3-2	3-2	3-0	3-1	0-1	0-2	3-2
Cheshire Lines	1-1	0-2	1-2		1-3	n/a	3-0	3-3	2-2	1-4	0-2	0-3	0-1	0-0	0-2	2-3
Ford Motors	3-0	2-3	3-4	3-1		n/a	4-0	3-5	0-5	1-1	0-1	1-1	0-3	1-3	0-2	2-2
Halewood Village	0-9	n/a	n/a	n/a	1-6		n/a	n/a	n/a	n/a	n/a	0-4	0-8	2-7	n/a	n/a
Kingsley United	1-2	1-0	1-6	1-2	1-3	3-0		1-5	0-4	1-3	2-2	0-7	0-4	1-5	1-2	2-5
Lucas Sports	0-3	1-0	5-3	5-2	1-0	3-2	2-0		2-3	3-2	4-2	3-4	0-2	0-0	2-1	5-2
Mossley Hill Athletic	2-1	0-2	2-3	2-2	0-2	4-1	1-2	1-5		4-0	1-3	0-2	2-1	1-2	3-3	0-1
Penlake	6-3	3-1	2-1	4-0	1-2	3-2	6-2	1-3	5-1		2-2	1-0	1-4	5-1	2-2	3-2
South Liverpool	2-0	0-1	2-0	1-4	1-2	n/a	6-0	0-0	4-3	3-3		1-2	0-0	2-0	4-1	1-2
South Sefton Borough	2-0	1-3	2-1	5-1	1-3	n/a	2-2	3-2	2-0	1-3	2-0		1-0	3-4	2-0	1-1
Speke	3-0	1-1	1-0	3-0	3-0	n/a	6-0	0-1	1-0	2-1	2-1	3-0		2-1	2-2	2-1
St Aloysius	3-0	0-3	1-0	2-1	2-3	5-1	4-0	1-1	2-1	2-0	0-2	0-3	0-5		0-1	1-2
St Dominics	0-2	2-0	1-2	0-1	1-1	n/a	5-0	1-2	0-0	3-0	1-0	2-1	2-1	0-0		0-1
Waterloo Dock	1-0	2-1	1-0	4-0	1-1	n/a	7-1	4-1	4-1	7-1	0-0	2-2	0-1	2-4	3-1	

Note – Halewood Village withdrew during the course of the season; their results are shown above but are expunged from the league table

		P	W	D	L	F	A	Pts
Speke		28	19	4	5	59	21	61
Waterloo Dock		28	16	5	7	64	38	53
Bootle		28	16	2	10	65	43	50
Lucas Sports		28	15	5	8	66	50	50
Birchfield		28	15	4	9	47	33	49
South Sefton Borough		28	14	5	9	55	39	47
St Dominics		28	12	7	9	43	31	43
Penlake		28	12	5	11	66	60	41
Ford Motors		28	12	5	11	47	46	41
St Aloysius	*-3*	28	13	5	10	43	42	41
South Liverpool		28	11	7	10	47	36	40
Mossley Hill Athletic		28	6	6	16	41	55	24
Aigburth People's Hall		28	5	6	17	36	63	21
Cheshire Lines		28	5	5	18	32	67	20
Kingsley United		28	2	3	23	24	111	9

Halewood Village – record expunged

LORD MAYOR'S CHARITY SHIELD

(September 12th at LCFA, Walton Hall Avenue)

East Villa 0 **Waterloo Dock** 2

The LIVERPOOL COUNTY COMBINATION and the I ZINGARI LEAGUE have merged to form the LIVERPOOL COUNTY PREMIER LEAGUE

(see page 240 for the I ZINGARI tables)

LIVERPOOL COUNTY PREMIER LEAGUE PREMIER DIVISION (formerly LIVERPOOL COUNTY COMBINATION) CONSTITUTION 2006-07

BIRCHFIELD .... Edge Hill College, St Helens Road, Ormskirk L39 4QP 01695 584745
COLLEGIATE OLD BOYS .... Holly Lodge Playing Fields, Mill Lane, West Derby Road, Liverpool .... None
CROXTETH RED RUM .... Croxteth Community Comprehensive School, Parkstile Lane, Liverpool L11 0PB 0151 546 4168
EAST VILLA .... MYA Jeffreys Humble, Long Lane, Walton, Liverpool L9 9AQ .... None
FORD MOTORS .... Ford Sports & Social Club, Cronton Lane, Widnes WA8 5AJ 0151 424 7078
LUCAS SPORTS .... William Collins Memorial Ground, Commercial Road, Liverpool .... None
MACKETS .... Great Lakes, Lower Road, Halebank, Widnes WA8 8NT .... None
NELTC .... Edinburgh Park, Townsend Lane, Liverpool L13 9DY .... None
OLD XAVERIANS .... St Francis Xaviers College, Beconsfield Road, Liverpool L25 6EG 0151 288 1000
PENLAKE .... Edge Hill College, St Helens Road, Ormskirk L39 4QP 01695 584745
ROMA .... Kirkby Sports Centre, Valley Road, Kirkby L20 9PQ 0151 443 4404
SOUTH SEFTON BOROUGH .... Mill Dam Field, Bridges Lane, Sefton .... None
SPEKE .... Speke Hall Avenue, Speke, Liverpool L24 1YD 0151 486 1588
ST ALOYSIUS .... King George V Sports Complex, Long View Lane, Huyton, Liverpool L36 7UN 0151 443 5712
ST DOMINICS .... St Dominics School, Lordens Road, Huyton L14 8UD 0151 489 8279
WATERLOO DOCK .... Edinburgh Park, Townsend Lane, Liverpool L6 0BB 0151 263 5267

IN: Collegiate Old Boys (P), Croxteth Red Rum (formerly Red Rum) (P), East Villa (P), Mackets (P), NELTC (P), Old Xaverians (P), Roma (P)

OUT: Aigburth People's Hall (R), Bootle (P – North West Counties League Division One), Cheshire Lines (R), Halewood Village (WS), Kingsley United (R), Mossley Hill Athletic (R), South Liverpool (R)

PETER COYNE/GEORGE MAHON CUP

FIRST ROUND
Aigburth People's Hall 1 **South Liverpool** 2
Kingsley United 0 **St Dominics** 4
Lucas Sports (w/o) v Halewood Village (scr.)
Mossley Hill Athletic 5 St Aloysius 1
Penlake 3 Cheshire Lines 2
South Sefton Borough 4 Ford Motors 2
Speke 3 Birchfield 0
Waterloo Dock 3 Bootle 0

QUARTER-FINALS
Penlake 2 **Mossley Hill Athletic** 3
South Liverpool 1 **Lucas Sports** 6
Speke 1 **St Dominics** 4
Waterloo Dock 1 South Sefton Borough 0

SEMI-FINALS
Lucas Sports 2 **St Dominics** 5 *aet*
Mossley Hill Athletic 2 **Waterloo Dock** 3

FINAL *(May 5th at Merseyside Police)*
St Dominics 2 Waterloo Dock 2 *aet* (4-1p)

LORD WAVERTREE CUP

FIRST ROUND
Ford Motors 5 Aigburth People's Hall 2 *aet*
Kingsley United 1 **South Liverpool** 3
Mossley Hill Athletic 1 **St Aloysius** 2
Penlake 2 Lucas Sports 1
Speke 4 Bootle 3 *aet*
St Dominics 4 Cheshire Lines 1
Waterloo Dock 4 Birchfield 0
South Sefton Borough (w/o) v Halewood Village (scr.)

QUARTER-FINALS
Ford Motors 0 **South Liverpool** 3
Penlake 1 **Waterloo Dock** 2
St Aloysius 2 Speke 0
St Dominics 5 South Sefton Borough 3

SEMI-FINALS
South Liverpool 1 **St Aloysius** 2
Waterloo Dock 1 **St Dominics** 4 *aet*

FINAL *(May 3rd at Ford Motors)*
St Dominics 2 St Aloysius 2 *aet* (8-7p)

FRED MICKLESFIELD CUP

(Peter Coyne/George Mahon Cup First Round losers)

FIRST ROUND
Aigburth People's Hall (w/o) v Halewood Village (scr.)
Birchfield 8 Kingsley United 2
Bootle 3 Ford Motors 2
Cheshire Lines 4 St Aloysius 2

SEMI-FINALS
Aigburth People's Hall 2 **Birchfield** 3
Cheshire Lines 1 **Bootle** 3

FINAL *(May 1st at Bootle)*
Bootle 0 **Birchfield** 1

LIVERPOOL COUNTY PREMIER LEAGUE DIVISION ONE (formerly I ZINGARI LEAGUE PREMIER DIVISION) CONSTITUTION 2006-07

AIGBURTH PEOPLE'S HALL	Cheshire Lines FC, Southmead Road, Allerton, Liverpool L19 5NB	0151 427 7176
ALSOP OLD BOYS	MYA Jeffreys Humble, Long Lane, Walton, Liverpool L9 9AQ	None
BRNESC	Melling Road, Aintree, Liverpool	None
CHESHIRE LINES	Southmead Road, Allerton, Liverpool L19 5NB	0151 427 7176
COPPERAS HILL	Breckside Park, Liverpool	None
HILL ATHLETIC	Litherland Park Sports Centre, Liverpool L21 7LA	0151 288 6288
KINGSLEY UNITED	Edinburgh Park, Townsend Lane, Liverpool L6 0BB	0151 263 5267
LIVERPOOL NALGO	Alder Road Sports Club, Alder Road, Liverpool	None
MOSSLEY HILL ATHLETIC	Mossley Hill Athletic Club, Mossley Hill Road, Liverpool L18 8DX	0151 724 4377
PAGE CELTIC	King George V Sports Complex, Long View Lane, Huyton, Liverpool L36 7UN	0151 443 5712
QUARRY BANK OLD BOYS	Greenhill Road, Liverpool	None
SOUTH LIVERPOOL	Jericho Lane, Aigburth, Liverpool L17 5AR	None
ST AMBROSE	Little Heath Playing Fields, Little Heath Road/Central Way, Liverpool L24 2TJ	None
STOCKBRIDGE VISION	Lower Breck Road Playing Flds, Lower Breck Road, Liverpool	None
STONEYCROFT	Maiden Lane Playing Fields, Maiden Lane, Liverpool L13 9AN	None
WARBRECK	Playfootball.com, Drummond Road, Thornton L20 6DX	None

***IN:** Aigburth People's Hall (R), Cheshire Lines (R), Copperas Hill (P), Kingsley United (R), Mossley Hill Athletic (R), Page Celtic (P), South Liverpool (R), St Ambrose (P), Stoneycroft (P), Stockbridge Vision (formerly The Angus Vision) (P)*
***OUT:** Collegiate Old Boys (P), East Villa (P), Mackets (P), NELTC (P), Old Xaverians (P), Red Rum (now Croxteth Red Rum) (P), Roma (P), Turpins Devonshire (W)*
The Angus Vision become Stockbridge Vision

LIVERPOOL COUNTY PREMIER LEAGUE DIVISION TWO (formerly I ZINGARI LEAGUE DIVISION ONE) CONSTITUTION 2006-07

ALBANY ATHLETIC	Millbank College, Bankfield Road, Liverpool	None
BLUELINE	Buckley Hill Playing Fields, Buckley Hill Lane, Netherton, Bootle L29 1YB	None
EDGE HILL BCOB	Simpson Ground, Hillfoot Road, Liverpool	0151 486 3166
ELI LILLY	Thomas Lane Playing Fields, Thomas Lane, Liverpool	None
ESSEMAY OLD BOYS	Jericho Lane Playing Field, Jericho Lane, Liverpool L17 5AR	None
FINN HARPS	Thomas Lane Playing Fields, Thomas Lane, Liverpool	None
JUBILEE TRIANGLE	Buckley Hill Playing Fields, Buckley Hill Lane, Netherton, Bootle L29 1YB	None
LEISURE SPORTS ORCHARD	Clarence House School, West Lane, Formby, Liverpool	None
LEYFIELD	Thomas Lane Playing Fields, Thomas Lane, Liverpool	None
LIOBIANS	Mersey Road, Aigburth, Liverpool	None
LYDIATE WELD	Sandy Lane Playing Fields, Sandy Lane, Lydiate	None
OLD HOLTS	Simpson Ground, Hillfoot Road, Liverpool	0151 486 3166
REMYCA UNITED	Playfootball.com, Drummond Road, Thornton L20 6DX	None
REDGATE ROVERS	Clarence House, West Lane, Formby L37 7AZ	None
ROCKVILLE WALLESEY	Belvidere Recreation Ground, Belvidere Road, Liscard, Wallesey CH45 4RY	None
ROLLS ROYCE	Litherland Park Sports Centre, Liverpool L21 7LA	0151 288 6288
SACRE COUER FORMER PUPILS	Playfootball.com, Drummond Road, Thornton L20 6DX	None

***IN:** Eli Lilly (P – I Zingari League Division Two), Jubilee Triangle (P – I Zingari League Division Two), Leisure Sports Orchard (P – I Zingari League Division Two), Leyfield (P – I Zingari League Combination One), Liobians (P – I Zingari League Combination Two), Lydiate Weld (P – I Zingari League Division Two), Redgate Rovers (P – I Zingari League Division Two), REMYCA United (P – I Zingari League Division Two), Rockville Wallesey (P – I Zingari League Division Two), Sacre Couer Former Pupils (P – I Zingari League Combination Three)*
***OUT:** Copperas Hill (P), Padua (W), Page Celtic (P), St Ambrose (P), Stoneycroft (P), The Angus Vision (P)*
The Albany become Albany Athletic

MANCHESTER LEAGUE

Note – Old Altrinchamians withdrew during the course of the season. Their results are shown herein but are expunged from the league table	AFC Blackley	Atherton Town	Avro	Breightmet United	Dukinfield Town	East Manchester	Hindsford	Irlam Mitchell Shackleton	Leigh Athletic	Monton Amateurs	Old Altrinchamians	Prestwich Heys	Rochdale Sacred Heart	Royton Town	Springhead	Stockport Georgians	Wilmslow Albion	Wythenshawe Amateur
AFC Blackley		3-0	1-3	5-1	4-1	0-1	1-1	3-2	1-3	2-2	n/a	0-3	1-4	1-2	1-0	2-2	3-1	0-1
Atherton Town	1-1	*P*	1-4	7-2	1-5	1-6	0-1	0-7	2-1	0-1	n/a	0-0	1-4	2-1	4-3	2-2	2-1	3-2
Avro	1-5	3-1	*R*	3-0	1-0	1-1	2-0	1-0	2-3	3-0	n/a	0-3	2-1	3-1	3-3	2-1	2-1	3-1
Breightmet United	2-3	3-1	0-0	*E*	3-3	3-2	3-0	5-0	2-3	2-2	n/a	3-2	0-1	1-0	0-1	1-2	4-1	4-1
Dukinfield Town	3-2	0-0	0-0	2-1	*M*	5-1	3-3	2-1	0-1	3-2	n/a	1-0	3-0	2-2	2-3	2-1	7-0	2-3
East Manchester	3-2	6-1	0-0	5-2	4-1	*I*	2-0	2-1	2-1	6-3	n/a	2-2	1-2	2-3	3-3	1-1	3-2	1-0
Hindsford	4-1	2-3	2-0	1-4	2-1	2-2	*E*	3-0	1-1	1-0	n/a	0-2	2-0	1-1	2-1	2-3	2-1	1-3
Irlam Mitchell Shackleton	5-1	6-0	1-4	7-2	1-2	2-1	3-2	*R*	2-3	4-10	n/a	0-5	2-3	1-2	0-2	1-1	4-3	1-1
Leigh Athletic	1-2	3-1	1-0	5-0	2-1	3-1	1-1	0-4		2-5	n/a	2-2	1-2	1-1	1-1	1-0	2-0	1-1
Monton Amateurs	2-2	3-3	2-2	2-0	2-3	2-3	2-1	3-3	0-2	*D*	n/a	2-3	3-2	5-0	2-1	0-2	0-2	0-1
Old Altrinchamians	n/a	1-1	n/a	n/a	n/a	0-5	2-3	n/a	n/a	n/a	*I*	n/a	n/a	n/a	1-4	n/a	n/a	n/a
Prestwich Heys	3-1	2-0	2-2	3-2	3-1	3-0	3-0	2-0	1-0	4-3	n/a	*V*	2-3	3-1	2-2	2-1	5-1	1-0
Rochdale Sacred Heart	3-0	4-2	0-1	4-2	1-3	2-3	1-3	5-2	0-3	1-1	n/a	2-0	*I*	3-2	2-2	2-4	1-2	1-3
Royton Town	1-0	2-0	1-5	0-3	0-4	2-0	3-2	5-0	2-3	1-0	n/a	1-3	1-3	*S*	2-3	1-2	1-3	0-7
Springhead	4-3	2-2	1-1	3-3	4-1	1-1	5-1	1-1	1-3	4-2	n/a	0-2	2-2	1-1	*I*	3-0	3-0	0-0
Stockport Georgians	4-1	0-0	4-1	4-0	2-1	0-1	5-0	1-2	0-3	2-0	n/a	2-1	0-2	1-1	2-1	*O*	2-1	0-3
Wilmslow Albion	3-2	1-4	1-4	0-2	0-4	1-2	2-2	4-3	1-2	2-2	n/a	1-1	0-1	3-0	0-4	0-1	*N*	0-3
Wythenshawe Amateur	1-1	2-0	1-2	2-1	5-0	1-5	3-1	2-1	2-1	3-1	n/a	2-1	3-2	1-0	1-1	0-1	2-0	

Premier Division		P	W	D	L	F	A	Pts
Prestwich Heys		32	20	6	6	71	35	66
Wythenshawe Amateur		32	19	5	8	61	36	62
Avro		32	18	8	6	61	39	62
East Manchester		32	17	7	8	73	53	58
Leigh Athletic	*-3*	32	18	6	8	60	41	57
Stockport Georgians		32	16	3	13	64	57	51
Rochdale Sacred Heart	*-3*	32	16	6	10	53	40	51
Dukinfield Town		32	15	5	12	68	55	50
Springhead		32	11	14	7	66	50	47
Breightmet United		32	11	4	17	61	75	37
Hindsford		32	10	7	15	46	62	37
AFC Blackley		32	9	6	17	55	68	33
Monton Amateurs		32	8	8	16	64	70	32
Royton Town		32	9	5	18	41	69	32
Irlam Mitchell Shackleton		32	9	4	19	67	81	31
Atherton Town		32	8	7	17	45	83	31
Wilmslow Albion		32	6	3	23	38	80	21

Old Altrinchamians – record expunged

MANCHESTER LEAGUE PREMIER DIVISION CONSTITUTION 2006-07

AFC BLACKLEY	White House Social Club, Middleton Road, Crumpsall M8 4JZ	None
ATHERTON TOWN	Howe Bridge Sports Centre, Leigh Road, Atherton M46 0PJ	01942 884882
AVRO	Lancaster Club, Broadway, Failsworth, Oldham M35 0DX	0161 681 3083
BREIGHTMET UNITED	Moss Park, Bury Road, Breightmet, Bolton BL2 6QB	01204 533930
DUKINFIELD TOWN	Blocksages Playing Fields, Birch Lane, Dukinfield SK16 5AP	0161 343 4529
EAST MANCHESTER	Longsight Sports & Social, Kirkmanshulme Lane, Gorton M12 4WB	0161 224 3213
GREGORIANS	Manchester City FC Platt Lane Complex, Yew Tree Road, Fallowfield	None
HINDSFORD	Squires Lane, Tyldesley M29 8JH	None
HOLLINWOOD	Lime Lane, Hollinwood, Oldham OL8 3TB	0161 681 3385
IRLAM	Silver Street, Irlam M44 6JL	None
LEIGH ATHLETIC	Leigh Harriers AC, Madley Park, Charles Street, Leigh WN7 1BG	01942 673500
MONTON AMATEURS	Granary Lane, Worsley M28 2PH	None
PRESTWICH HEYS	Sandgate Road, Prestwich Heys M45 6WG	0161 773 8888
ROCHDALE SACRED HEART	Fox Park, Belfield Mill Lane, Rochdale OL16 2UB	None
ROYTON TOWN	Crompton Cricket Club Complex, Glebe Street, Shaw, Oldham OL2 7SF	01706 847421
SPRINGHEAD	St John Street, Lees, Oldham OL4 4DB	0161 627 0260
STOCKPORT GEORGIANS	Cromley Road, Woodsmoor, Stockport SK6 8BP	0161 483 6581
WHITWORTH VALLEY	Rawston Street Stadium, Whitworth, Rochdale OL12 8BA	None
WYTHENSHAWE AMATEUR	Longley Lane, Northendon, Wythenshawe M22 4LA	0161 998 7268

IN: Gregorians (P), Hollinwood (P), Whitworth Valley (P)
OUT: Old Altrinchamians (WS), Wilmslow Albion (R)
Irlam Mitchell Shackleton become Irlam

	Ashton Athletic	Chapel Town	Elton Vale	Fives Athletic	Gregorians	Heywood St James	Hollinwood	Manchester Juniors	Manchester Titans	Milton	Pennington	Salford AFC	Stand Athletic	Tintwistle Villa	Walshaw Sports	Whitworth Valley	Wigan Robin Park	Wythenshawe Town
Ashton Athletic		2-0	1-1	2-1	1-0	1-0	0-2	1-3	6-0	2-1	5-0	1-2	4-0	3-0	0-0	1-4	2-0	1-2
Chapel Town	2-2		1-1	3-1	1-8	5-4	5-0	1-1	7-1	5-2	3-0	6-1	3-1	0-1	1-1	3-4	3-1	2-1
Elton Vale	1-2	5-1		1-0	0-2	3-0	4-3	1-1	3-0	6-1	2-2	4-1	0-1	3-1	1-2	0-1	1-0	3-1
Fives Athletic	0-1	3-2	0-2	*D*	2-5	1-4	0-9	0-1	2-1	3-1	4-3	2-1	1-2	3-0	2-1	0-6	2-1	1-3
Gregorians	1-1	0-0	2-1	7-1	*I*	3-1	1-2	1-2	5-0	5-2	2-1	2-0	6-3	0-1	0-0	1-1	1-2	0-2
Heywood St James	1-5	5-2	7-4	2-1	1-1	*V*	3-3	1-1	1-0	8-4	3-1	3-0	4-1	3-3	4-2	0-2	1-3	1-2
Hollinwood	3-2	2-1	2-0	7-2	3-2	3-0	*I*	2-0	7-3	6-2	7-3	0-2	4-2	3-0	1-3	0-6	2-3	3-2
Manchester Juniors	1-0	0-1	2-0	0-2	1-1	2-4	0-3	*S*	3-2	4-0	3-1	3-5	3-0	3-1	0-3	2-2	1-3	4-2
Manchester Titans	0-4	4-4	2-4	2-3	2-4	2-5	2-6	1-2	*I*	6-3	3-2	5-1	3-7	0-0	1-1	0-3	1-5	1-7
Milton	1-4	0-2	0-4	2-2	0-3	2-6	0-4	2-0	2-1	*O*	1-4	0-2	1-4	0-1	2-2	0-4	1-3	0-5
Pennington	2-3	2-2	0-5	3-2	0-3	0-4	2-3	0-1	2-2	0-0	*N*	0-2	2-2	0-2	2-0	0-9	0-0	1-0
Salford AFC	0-1	1-3	1-2	3-3	1-10	2-1	2-1	2-1	1-3	2-1	5-1		1-2	4-0	2-0	2-1	2-1	4-1
Stand Athletic	1-2	0-1	2-3	1-2	2-3	1-0	1-3	3-5	1-1	5-0	0-1	0-2	*O*	1-1	1-4	0-3	0-5	4-3
Tintwistle Villa	1-2	3-2	1-3	2-4	2-3	W-L	1-4	0-2	4-1	1-2	1-1	1-0	4-1	*N*	2-1	1-6	2-3	1-1
Walshaw Sports	4-2	1-2	2-0	1-1	0-0	7-0	2-1	0-0	5-0	6-0	7-0	3-2	4-3	3-2	*E*	0-3	2-1	4-4
Whitworth Valley	0-0	2-0	5-2	2-2	0-2	4-1	4-2	5-1	3-0	4-1	2-2	4-2	4-1	0-0	0-0		2-1	1-3
Wigan Robin Park	3-0	2-2	2-1	4-1	0-2	1-1	1-3	3-1	5-0	1-0	2-0	4-1	1-2	2-0	0-2	2-2		0-4
Wythenshawe Town	1-1	0-2	3-0	6-0	1-3	W-L	1-2	3-0	3-2	3-2	1-1	3-1	0-0	6-1	4-2	1-2	1-0	

Division One		P	W	D	L	F	A	Pts
Whitworth Valley		34	23	8	3	101	33	77
Hollinwood		34	24	1	9	106	62	73
Gregorians		34	20	7	7	89	37	67
Ashton Athletic		34	19	6	9	65	38	63
Wythenshawe Town		34	18	5	11	80	50	59
Walshaw Sports		34	16	10	8	75	44	58
Elton Vale		34	17	4	13	71	52	55
Wigan Robin Park		34	17	4	13	65	46	55
Chapel Town	*-3*	34	16	8	10	78	62	53
Manchester Juniors		34	15	6	13	54	56	51
Heywood St James		34	14	5	15	79	72	47
Salford AFC	*-3*	34	16	1	17	60	73	46
Fives Athletic	*-1*	34	12	4	18	54	91	39
Tintwistle Villa	*-3*	34	10	6	18	41	70	33
Stand Athletic		34	9	4	21	55	84	31
Pennington		34	5	9	20	39	91	24
Manchester Titans		34	4	5	25	52	121	17
Milton		34	3	3	28	36	118	12

MANCHESTER LEAGUE DIVISION ONE CONSTITUTION 2006-07

CHAPEL TOWN .... **Rowton Ground, Willow Drive, Chapel-en-le-Frith, Stockport** .... **None**
ELTON VALE .... **Elton Vale Road, Bury BL8 2RZ** **0161 762 0666**
FIVES ATHLETIC .... **Harriet Street, Walkden** .... **None**
HEYWOOD ST JAMES .... **Phoenix Ground, Heywood OL10 2JG** .... **None**
MANCHESTER JUNIORS .... **Ford Lane, Northenden** .... **None**
MANCHESTER TITANS .... **Nicholls College, Hyde Road, Ardwick M12 6BA** **0161 455 2434**
MILTON .... **Milton Recreation Ground, The Sycamores, Milton, Cambridge CB4 6ZN** **01706 53339**
PENNINGTON .... **Jubilee Park, Leigh Road, Atherton M46 0RN** .... **None**
SALFORD AFC .... **Agecroft Farm, Agecroft Road, Pendlebury, Swinton** .... **None**
SALFORD VICTORIA .... **Salford Sports Village, Littleton Road, Salford** .... **None**
STAND ATHLETIC .... **The Elms, Whitefield, Manchester M45 7FD** .... **None**
TINTWISTLE VILLA .... **West Drive, Tintwistle, Glossop SK13 1LX** .... **None**
WALSHAW SPORTS .... **Walshaw Sports Club, Sycamore Road, Tottington, Bury BL8 3EG** **01204 882448**
WEST DIDSBURY & CHORLTON .... **Brookburn Road, Chorlton-cum-Hardy M21 8EH** .... **None**
WIGAN ROBIN PARK .... **Robin Park, Newton (adj Wigan Athletic FC), Wigan WN5 0UZ** .... **None**
WILMSLOW ALBION .... **Oakwood Farm, Styal Road, Wilmslow SK9 4HP** **01625 535823**
WYTHENSHAWE TOWN .... **Ericstan Park, Timpson Road, Baguley M23 9LL** **0161 998 5076**

IN: Salford Victoria (P – Lancashire & Cheshire League), West Didsbury & Chorlton (P – Lancashire & Cheshire League), Wilmslow Albion (R)
OUT: Ashton Athletic (P – North West Counties League Division Two), Gregorians (P), Hollinwood (P), Whitworth Valley (P)

GILGRYST CUP

(Premier Division teams)

PRELIMINARY ROUND

Stockport Georgians 5 Prestwich Heys 3
Wythenshawe Amateur 1 **East Manchester** 3

FIRST ROUND

AFC Blackley 4 Breightmet United 3
Atherton Town 5 Wilmslow Albion 4
Dukinfield Town 0 **Stockport Georgians** 1
East Manchester 2 Avro 2 *aet* (4-2p)
Hindsford 2 **Leigh Athletic** 3
Irlam Mitchell Shackleton 5 Monton Amateurs 1
Rochdale Sacred Heart (w/o) v Old Altrinchamians (scr.)
Springhead 5 Royton Town 2

QUARTER-FINALS

AFC Blackley 1 **East Manchester** 2
Leigh Athletic 3 Atherton Town 0
Springhead 0 **Rochdale Sacred Hearts** 2
Stockport Georgians 2 **Irlam Mitchell Shackleton** 3

SEMI-FINALS

Leigh Athletic 5 Irlam Mitchell Shackleton 1
Rochdale Sacred Heart 2 **East Manchester** 4

FINAL

(May 1st at Woodley Sports)

Leigh Athletic 2 East Manchester 1

MURRAY SHIELD

(Division One teams)

PRELIMINARY ROUND

Manchester Juniors 0 **Wigan Robin Park** 2
Walshaw Sports 7 Chapel Town 0

FIRST ROUND

Ashton Athletic 4 Tintwistle Villa 1
Fives Athletic 0 **Walshaw Sports** 1
Heywood St James 13 Pennington 0
Hollinwood 4 **Gregorians** 4 *aet* (3-4p)
Milton 1 **Wythenshawe Town** 4
Salford 2 **Manchester Titans** 3
Stand Athletic 0 **Whitworth Valley** 6
Wigan Robin Park 0 Elton Vale 0 *aet* (4-2p)

QUARTER-FINALS

Ashton Athletic 3 Heywood St James 1
Walshaw Sports 1 Gregorians 0
Whitworth Valley 1 **Wigan Robin Park** 2 *aet*
Wythenshawe Town 4 Manchester Titans 0

SEMI-FINALS

Ashton Athletic 1 **Walshaw Sports** 2
Wigan Robin Park 4 Wythenshawe Town 0

FINAL

(May 5th at Woodley Sports)

Walshaw Sports 3 Wigan Robin Park 3 *aet* (4-3p)

Division Two	P	W	D	L	F	A	Pts
East Manchester Res.	26	21	3	2	78	32	66
Leigh Athletic Res.	26	17	4	5	77	36	55
Gregorians Res.	26	15	2	9	54	37	47
Prestwich Heys Res.	26	14	2	10	57	56	44
Wythenshawe Amateur Res.	26	12	6	8	49	33	42
Springhead Res.	26	12	2	12	62	48	38
Monton Amateurs Res.	26	11	2	13	48	53	35
Stockport Georgians Res.	26	9	8	9	32	39	35
Elton Vale Res.	26	9	5	12	48	60	32
Dukinfield Town Res.	26	10	2	14	40	43	32
Hindsford Res.	26	9	4	13	49	66	31
Avro Res.	26	8	4	14	49	66	28
Breightmet United Res.	26	6	1	19	36	74	19
Atherton Town Res.	26	5	3	18	31	67	18

Division Three		P	W	D	L	F	A	Pts
Walshaw Sports Res.		22	14	3	5	50	42	45
Ashton Athletic Res.		22	12	3	7	59	36	39
Dukinfield Town 'A'		22	10	6	6	61	33	36
Leigh Athletic 'A'		22	9	6	7	52	45	33
Milton Res.	*+3*	22	9	2	11	49	45	32
Holllinwood Res.	*-1*	22	9	6	7	46	37	32
Rochdale Sacred Heart Res.		22	9	2	11	57	57	29
Stand Athletic Res.		22	8	3	11	42	58	27
Springhead 'A'		22	7	6	9	38	43	27
Gregorians 'A'		22	6	7	9	41	55	25
Wilmslow Albion Res.		22	7	3	12	24	79	24
Salford AFC Res.		22	6	5	11	45	34	23

Division Four	P	W	D	L	F	A	Pts
Wythenshawe Town Res.	18	13	3	2	63	36	42
Whitworth Valley Res.	18	12	1	5	64	34	37
AFC Blackley Res.	18	10	2	6	56	38	32
Walshaw Sports 'A'	18	10	1	7	40	39	31
Stockport Georgians 'A'	18	9	2	7	44	37	29
Heywood St James Res.	18	7	2	9	41	40	23
Royton Town Res.	18	6	3	9	43	47	21
Gregorians 'B'	18	5	3	10	26	50	18
Pennington Res.	18	5	1	12	38	67	16
Monton Amateurs 'A'	18	4	0	14	32	59	12

OPEN TROPHY

FINAL

(May 6th at Stockport Georgians)

Leigh Athletic Res. 6 Wythenshawe Amateurs Res. 1

LEAGUE CUP

FINAL

(May 10th at Irlam Mitchell Shackleton)

AFC Blackley Res. 4 Whitworth Valley Res. 3 *aet*

MID-CHESHIRE LEAGUE

	Barnton	Bollington Athletic	Crosfields	Daten	Eagle Sports	Garswood United	Greenalls Padgate St Oswalds	Knutsford	Linotype & Cheadle HN	Middlewich Town	Pilkington	Poynton	Rylands	Styal	Trafford Res.	Witton Albion Res.
Barnton		2-2	0-2	4-1	1-1	0-8	3-1	0-1	1-2	0-3	2-2	0-1	2-1	2-1	3-3	0-2
Bollington Athletic	3-1		3-0	1-2	2-2	3-2	0-2	2-1	2-2	0-7	3-1	3-2	1-1	1-1	3-4	0-1
Crosfields	5-0	2-2	*D*	1-1	2-1	2-2	1-2	2-5	3-1	0-4	2-2	3-1	1-2	2-1	4-0	4-2
Daten	0-1	8-0	0-3	*I*	2-2	0-1	2-3	2-2	1-1	0-3	4-1	6-1	1-2	0-2	1-2	0-2
Eagle Sports	2-1	1-1	1-1	1-2	*V*	2-1	0-2	1-2	3-1	0-4	0-1	0-2	1-2	3-3	3-2	3-3
Garswood United	7-0	2-3	0-0	0-0	3-0	*I*	1-1	2-1	0-2	0-3	0-2	1-3	1-1	3-3	1-1	2-0
Greenalls Padgate St Oswalds	1-1	2-5	2-2	1-1	2-0	1-2	*S*	1-3	1-1	1-1	4-1	2-0	2-1	2-1	5-3	2-3
Knutsford	1-1	4-1	1-0	0-2	6-3	4-3	1-2	*I*	2-0	1-3	7-2	0-1	3-0	2-2	3-0	2-5
Linotype & Cheadle HN	2-2	1-0	3-0	2-1	0-3	1-3	3-2	2-4	*O*	0-0	3-1	3-3	1-1	1-0	2-1	0-0
Middlewich Town	7-0	9-0	1-1	4-1	2-1	1-0	2-1	2-3	5-2	*N*	2-1	3-0	3-1	0-0	4-0	1-1
Pilkington	5-5	1-1	1-2	2-1	0-0	0-2	1-1	1-1	3-2	1-2		5-2	3-2	0-1	2-1	1-4
Poynton	1-2	5-2	1-1	2-0	3-2	0-1	3-3	1-2	2-2	0-0	0-0	*O*	0-2	0-1	0-1	4-4
Rylands	0-3	1-0	0-2	0-1	2-0	0-2	2-1	1-1	0-3	0-3	2-2	1-2	*N*	0-3	0-0	2-2
Styal	4-4	2-2	0-0	4-0	1-0	2-2	1-3	3-1	2-0	2-1	2-2	2-0	5-1	*E*	1-0	0-4
Trafford Res.	4-1	0-2	3-1	0-0	1-2	1-0	1-2	0-0	3-2	2-1	2-2	2-4	3-0	3-2		1-2
Witton Albion Res.	4-0	5-2	0-0	3-2	3-0	1-3	1-0	1-1	3-1	1-2	2-0	0-1	3-1	3-1	1-1	

Division One		P	W	D	L	F	A	Pts
Middlewich Town		30	21	6	3	83	20	69
Witton Albion Res.		30	17	8	5	66	37	59
Knutsford		30	15	7	8	65	46	52
Greenalls Padgate St Oswalds		30	13	8	9	55	47	47
Styal		30	12	10	8	53	42	46
Garswood United		30	12	8	10	55	38	44
Crosfields	*-3*	30	11	11	8	49	42	41
Linotype & Cheadle HN		30	10	9	11	46	52	39
Poynton		30	10	7	13	45	54	37
Trafford Res.		30	10	7	13	45	54	37
Bollington Athletic		30	9	9	12	50	74	36
Pilkington		30	7	11	12	46	62	32
Barnton		30	7	9	14	42	77	30
Daten		30	7	7	16	42	51	28
Rylands		30	7	7	16	29	55	28
Eagle Sports		30	6	8	16	38	58	26

J B PARKER DIVISION ONE CUP

FIRST ROUND

Barnton 0 **Styal** 6

Linotype & Cheadle HN 1 **Eagle Sports** 2

Middlewich Town 3 Greenalls Padgate St Oswalds 1

Pilkington 2 **Garswood Utd** 4

Poynton 1 **Daten** 2

Rylands 3 Crosfields 2

Trafford Res. 0 **Bollington Athletic** 2

Witton Albion Res. 1 **Knutsford** 2

QUARTER-FINALS

Bollington Ath 3 Rylands 0

Daten 0 **Middlewich Town** 4

Eagle Sports 2 **Styal** 3

Garswood United 4 Knutsford 1

SEMI-FINALS

Bollington Athletic 0 **Middlewich Town** 2

Garswood United 1 Styal 0

FINAL *(March 30th at Trafford)*

Garswood United 3 Middlewich Town 1

MID-CHESHIRE LEAGUE DIVISION ONE CONSTITUTION 2006-07

BARNTON .... Townfield, Townfield Lane, Barnton, Northwich CW8 4LH .... None
CROSFIELDS .... Crosfields Recreation Ground, Hood Lane, Great Sankey, Warrington WA5 1ES 01925 411730
DATEN .... Culcheth Sports Ground, Charnock Road, Culcheth, Warrington WA3 5SH 01925 763096
GAMESLEY .... Melandra Park, Melandra Castle Road, Gamesley, Glossop SK13 6UQ .... None
GARSWOOD UNITED ... The Wooders, Simms Lane End, Garswood Road, Garswood, Ashton-in-Makerfield WN4 0XF 01744 892258
GREENALLS PADGATE ST OSWALDS.... Walkers Club, Long Lane, Warrington WA2 8PU .... None
KNUTSFORD .... Manchester Road, Knutsford WA16 0NU .... None
LINOTYPE & CHEADLE HN ... The Heath, Norbreck Avenue, Norbreck Avenue, Cheadle, Stockport SK8 2ET 0161 282 6574
MIDDLEWICH TOWN .... Seddon Street, Middlewich CW10 9DT 01606 835842
PILKINGTON .... Ruskin Drive, Dentons Green, St Helens WA10 6RP 01744 28866
POYNTON .... London Road North, Poynton, Stockport SK12 1AG 01625 875765
RYLANDS .... Rylands Recreation Club, Gorsey Lane, Warrington WA2 7RZ 01925 625700
STYAL .... Altrincham Road, Styal, Wilmslow SK9 4JE 01625 529303
TRAFFORD RESERVES .... Shawe View, Pennybridge Lane, Flixton, Urmston M41 5DL 0161 747 1727
WITTON ALBION RESERVES ... CMB Stadium, Wincham Park, Chapel Street, Wincham, Northwich CW9 6DA 01606 43008
WOODLEY SPORTS RESERVES ... Lambeth Grove Stadium, Lambeth Grove, Woodley, Stockport SK6 1QX 0161 406 6896

IN: Gamesley (P), Woodley Sports Reserves (P)

OUT: Bollington Athletic (W – East Cheshire League), Eagle Sports (R)

	Billinge	Broadheath C.	Club AZ	Crewe	Curzon A. Res.	Fearnhead	Gamesley	Glossop N E Res.	Golborne Sports	Lostock Gralam	Maine Road Res.	Malpas	Monk Sports	Warrington Town Res.	Whitchurch Alport	Woodley Sports Res.
Billinge		1-2	0-2	1-2	1-4	1-1	2-1	0-0	1-2	2-0	1-1	4-3	3-1	0-3	3-1	1-4
Broadheath C.	4-1		3-2	1-4	2-2	5-0	4-2	2-1	0-0	2-2	1-1	1-3	5-0	1-1	2-2	5-2
Club AZ	1-3	2-4	*D*	1-1	2-1	5-1	0-4	5-1	2-1	3-3	8-1	2-0	3-1	1-0	1-2	0-2
Crewe	0-1	3-1	0-2	*I*	4-3	0-2	3-2	2-1	1-1	4-0	1-3	2-1	4-1	1-3	0-1	2-2
Curzon A. Res.	5-0	2-0	5-1	1-2	*V*	6-0	3-3	5-1	2-4	2-1	4-1	3-1	4-0	0-1	3-3	1-1
Fearnhead	2-1	1-2	1-4	0-5	0-4	*I*	0-5	3-3	0-2	2-4	0-1	0-4	0-1	1-2	3-4	1-4
Gamesley	4-1	2-3	7-0	2-1	6-1	6-0	*S*	5-0	4-2	3-0	2-0	5-1	3-1	0-1	3-1	2-3
Glossop N E Res.	2-2	3-1	1-1	1-1	1-4	2-1	1-2	*I*	4-2	4-0	0-2	2-0	0-1	1-0	0-5	2-0
Golborne Sports	2-0	2-3	0-2	1-1	0-0	3-2	2-2	2-1	*O*	4-1	5-5	2-0	4-1	1-2	4-1	3-2
Lostock Gralam	3-3	2-1	1-4	0-3	3-1	6-1	0-4	3-3	2-9	*N*	1-2	3-2	2-6	3-1	1-0	1-1
Maine Road Res.	0-3	4-3	3-2	0-4	3-1	6-0	2-5	4-0	0-2	2-0		3-3	1-3	1-3	5-1	3-6
Malpas	3-0	0-3	5-5	0-6	1-0	4-3	1-1	2-1	0-2	4-3	0-2	*T*	2-2	0-1	0-4	1-1
Monk Sports	4-3	1-2	2-1	3-1	1-4	5-1	1-6	2-2	3-3	2-3	0-3	2-2	*W*	2-3	2-1	2-2
Warrington Tn Res.	2-1	0-0	1-3	1-2	4-0	2-0	0-0	0-2	1-1	0-0	0-1	2-1	1-1	*O*	3-0	0-0
Whitchurch Alport	4-2	2-2	4-1	1-3	1-1	0-4	2-2	4-0	0-1	4-0	1-0	0-0	3-1	0-2		1-2
Woodley Sports Res.	5-0	4-2	2-2	1-2	3-2	9-0	1-3	4-2	2-2	4-0	3-1	4-0	4-1	1-0	2-2	

Reserve Division	P	W	D	L	F	A	Pts
Linotype & Cheadle HN Res.	30	22	5	3	69	35	71
Broadheath Central Res.	30	21	4	5	68	31	67
Styal Res.	30	17	7	6	86	42	58
Pilkington Res.	30	14	9	7	58	36	51
Witton Albion Youth	30	13	5	12	50	38	44
Poynton Res.	30	10	11	9	63	49	41
Garswood United Res.	30	10	11	9	52	39	41
Middlewich Town Res.	30	11	7	12	49	45	40
Daten Res.	30	11	7	12	45	52	40
Golborne Sports Res.	30	10	7	13	50	60	37
Rylands Res.	30	10	4	16	60	63	34
Greenalls Padgate St Oswalds Res.	30	9	6	15	49	66	33
Billinge Res.	30	7	9	14	39	56	30
Eagle Sports Res.	30	8	6	16	42	97	30
Crosfields Res.	30	7	4	19	36	78	25
Gamesley Res.	30	6	6	18	42	71	24

RESERVES CUP

FINAL *(March 22nd at Trafford)*
Linotype & Cheadle HN Res. 3 Poynton Res. 1

Division Two	P	W	D	L	F	A	Pts
Gamesley	30	19	5	6	96	37	62
Woodley Sports Res.	30	16	9	5	81	44	57
Crewe	30	17	5	8	65	38	56
Golborne Sports	30	15	9	6	69	45	54
Warrington Town Res.	30	15	7	8	40	25	52
Broadheath Central	30	14	8	8	67	52	50
Club AZ	30	14	5	11	68	60	47
Maine Road Res.	30	14	4	12	61	63	46
Curzon Ashton Res.	30	13	6	11	74	51	45
Whitchurch Alport	30	11	7	12	55	53	40
Monk Sports	30	9	6	15	53	76	33
Glossop North End Res.	30	8	7	15	42	65	31
Lostock Gralam	30	8	6	16	48	83	30
Billinge	30	8	5	17	42	68	29
Malpas	30	7	7	16	44	69	28
Fearnhead	30	3	2	25	30	106	11

DIVISION TWO CUP

FIRST ROUND
Broadheath Central 1 Curzon Ashton Res. 0
Crewe 1 Billinge 0
Gamesley 5 Lostock Gralam 1
Glossop North End Res. 0 **Malpas** 3
Maine Road Res. 1 **Club AZ** 2
Warrington Tn Res. 1 **Golborne Sports** 3
Whitchurch Alport 2 Fearnhead 0
Woodley Sports Res. 4 Monk Sports 1

QUARTER-FINALS
Broadh'th Central 3 **Malpas** 3 *aet* (2-3p)
Club AZ 2 Gamesley 0
Crewe 0 **Woodley Sports Res.** 1
Whitchurch Alport 1 Golborne Sports 1 *aet* (4-3p)

SEMI-FINALS
Club AZ 3 **Woodley Sports Res.** 4
Malpas 0 **Whitchurch Alport** 1

FINAL
(May 6th at Congleton Town)
Woodley Sports Res. 2 Whitchurch Alport 1

PRESIDENT'S CUP

(First Round losers from Division One, Two and Reserve Cups)

FIRST ROUND
Barnton 2 Warrington Town Res. 2 *aet* (3-1p)
Crosfields Res. 0 **Crosfields** 6
Fearnhead 0 **Billinge** 4
Gamesley Res. 1 **Glossop North End Res.** 3
Golborne Sports Res. 1 Middlewich Town Res. 0
Greenalls Padgate St Oswalds 2 Trafford Res. 1
Monk Sports 4 **Lostock Gralam** 5
Pilkington 2 Witton Youth 1

SECOND ROUND
Billinge 1 **Witton Albion Res.** 1 *aet* (2-3p)
Curzon Ashton Res. 1 **Crosfields** 3 *(at Crosfields)*
Glossop North End Res. 3 **Poynton** 4
Golborne Sports Res. 5 Eagle Sports 0
Greenalls Padgate St Oswalds 4 Maine Road Res. 3
Linotype & Cheadle HN 1 **Barnton** 2
Lostock Gralam 0 **Pilkington Res.** 3
Pilkington 2 Witton Albion Youth 1

QUARTER-FINALS
Barnton 1 **Witton Albion Res.** 2
Crosfields 3 Pilkington Res. 2
Greenalls Padgate St Oswalds 1 **Poynton** 2
Pilkington 2 **Golborne Sports Res.** 4

SEMI-FINALS
Crosfields 0 **Witton Albion Res.** 2
Golborne Sports Res. 1 **Poynton** 2

FINAL *(May 11th at Congleton Town)*
Poynton 1 Witton Albion Res. 0

MID-CHESHIRE LEAGUE DIVISION TWO CONSTITUTION 2006-07

BILLINGE .... Edleston Playing Fields, Billinge .... None
BROADHEATH CENTRAL .... Viaduct Road, Broadheath, Altrincham WA14 5DX 0161 928 5849
CLUB AZ .... Mulberries Sports Centre, Astra Zeneca (off 34), Macclesfield 01625 514040
CONGLETON TOWN RESERVES ... Booth Street Ground, off Crescent Road, Congleton CW12 4DG 01260 274460
CREWE .... Cumberland Sports Ground, Thomas Street, Crewe CW1 2BD 01270 537913
CURZON ASHTON RESERVES ... The Tameside Stadium, Richmond Street, Ashton-under-Lyne OL7 9HG 0161 330 6033
EAGLE SPORTS .... Penketh & Sankey S & S Club, Warrington Road, Penketh, Warrington WA5 2BP 01925 482448/722523
FEARNHEAD .... Tetley Walker Club, Long Lane, Warrington WA2 8PU 01925 634971
GOLBORNE SPORTS .... Simpson Playing Fields, Stone Cross Road, Lowton WA3 2FL 01942 510161
LOSTOCK GRALAM .... Rear of Slow & Easy Hotel, Manchester Road, Lostock Gralam CW9 7PJ .... None
MAINE ROAD RESERVES .. Manchester County FA Ground, Branthingham Road, Chorlton-cum-Hardy M21 0TT 0161 881 0299
MALPAS .... Malpas & District Sports Club, Oxheys, Wrexham Road, Malpas SY14 7EJ 01948 860662
MONK SPORTS .... Hillock Lane, Woolston, Warrington WA1 4QL .... None
STALYBRIDGE CELTIC RESERVES ..... Bower Fold, Mottram Road, Stalybridge SK15 2RT 0161 338 2828
TARPORLEY VICTORIA .... Tattenhall Recreation Club, Field Lane, Tattenhall, Chester CH3 9QF 01829 770710
WARRINGTON TOWN RESERVES ..... Cantilever Park, Common Lane, Warrington WA4 2RS 01925 631932
WHITCHURCH ALPORT .... Yockings Park, Blackpark Road, Whitchurch SY13 1PG 01948 667415

IN: Congleton Town Reserves (N), Eagle Sports (R), Stalybridge Celtic Reserves (N), Tarporley Victoria (P – Chester & District League)
OUT: Cheadle Town Reserves (WN), Gamesley (P), Glossop North End Reserves (S – North West Counties League Reserve Division), Woodley Sports Reserves (P)

MIDDLESEX COUNTY LEAGUE

Note – Bethnal Green United withdrew during the course of the season

Their results are shown herein but are expunged from the league table

	Battersea Ironsides	Bedfont Sports	Bethnal Green United	Brazilian Sports Club	CB Hounslow United	Crown & Manor	Ealing	FC Deportivo Galicia	London Tigers	Marsh Rangers	Mauritius Sports (CMB)	Neasden Foundations	Spelthorne Sports	Stonewall	Walthamstow Ave & P	Willesden Constantine	Wraysbury
Battersea Ironsides	*P*	1-0	n/a	0-5	1-0	1-0	3-0	4-2	2-1	5-2	W-L	3-0	2-3	7-1	W-L	3-0	1-1
Bedfont Sports	0-1	*R*	4-1	1-1	2-2	1-2	2-1	0-1	1-5	7-0	3-1	1-4	1-0	5-1	3-2	2-3	1-4
Bethnal Green United	3-3	n/a	*E*	1-2	0-2	3-0	n/a	1-1	4-1	n/a	6-3	n/a	n/a	n/a	n/a	5-5	n/a
Brazilian Sports Club	0-1	4-4	n/a	*M*	1-2	6-0	1-0	1-0	3-1	3-0	1-1	1-3	0-1	1-2	2-3	0-2	2-4
CB Hounslow United	1-1	1-1	W-L	4-0	*I*	2-0	4-3	3-2	2-2	5-0	W-L	1-3	1-0	3-0	1-1	2-1	4-3
Crown & Manor	0-2	3-2	n/a	4-1	0-3	*E*	3-0	1-2	1-2	4-0	1-1	1-0	2-2	6-0	2-0	2-2	0-3
Ealing	1-3	2-3	1-1	1-3	1-1	1-4	*R*	4-2	1-4	4-2	4-1	2-1	0-1	1-2	2-3	0-2	2-2
FC Deportivo Galicia	0-3	2-2	1-4	3-2	0-3	1-2	3-1		1-3	2-1	2-3	0-2	0-1	2-0	0-2	3-2	0-3
London Tigers	1-1	2-0	n/a	4-0	2-2	2-0	5-0	1-3		W-L	5-0	1-1	3-3	6-0	0-1	4-3	8-1
Marsh Rangers	0-0	1-2	2-5	0-3	2-6	0-2	1-1	0-1	0-5	*D*	W-L	0-2	0-1	4-0	2-3	0-4	2-1
Mauritius Sports (CMB)	L-W	4-0	n/a	3-6	0-4	2-4	0-4	1-4	2-1	1-3	*I*	1-8	0-0	0-4	1-4	0-6	2-5
Neasden Foundations	1-0	0-1	2-1	1-2	2-2	2-0	0-1	5-0	3-2	W-L	2-1	*V*	1-0	4-1	L-W	3-2	5-3
Spelthorne Sports	1-2	1-1	3-4	3-5	1-6	W-L	2-0	3-2	3-1	W-L	3-0	0-0	*I*	2-0	0-1	2-1	1-1
Stonewall	0-3	1-5	1-2	0-4	1-2	1-4	2-4	0-2	1-4	0-2	1-2	1-2	0-3	*S*	0-2	0-2	1-2
Walthamstow Avenue & Pennant	1-1	0-0	n/a	3-1	2-0	1-4	W-L	0-3	0-0	2-2	0-2	1-1	2-0	5-1	*I*	1-1	0-3
Willesden Constantine	0-3	1-0	n/a	2-2	2-3	2-6	3-4	1-1	3-2	0-3	1-4	6-4	2-1	4-1	1-1	*O*	0-0
Wraysbury	1-1	0-2	n/a	2-0	1-1	4-2	9-3	0-3	2-3	5-0	6-2	3-0	2-0	0-0	3-3	2-0	*N*

Premier Division	P	W	D	L	F	A	Pts
Battersea Ironsides	30	21	6	3	55	22	69
CB Hounslow United	30	18	9	3	71	35	63
Neasden Foundation	30	17	4	9	60	37	55
London Tigers	30	16	6	8	80	40	54
Wraysbury	30	15	8	7	76	49	53
W'stow Avenue/Pennant	30	14	9	7	44	36	51
Crown & Manor	30	15	3	12	60	46	48
Spelthorne Sports	30	14	6	10	38	36	48
FC Deportivo Galicia	30	13	2	15	47	54	41
Brazilian Sports Club	30	12	4	14	61	55	40
Bedfont Sports	30	11	7	12	53	51	40
Willesden Constantine	30	11	6	13	59	59	39
Ealing	30	8	3	19	48	72	27
Marsh Rangers	30	6	3	21	27	69	21
Mauritius Sports (CMB)	30	6	3	21	35	82	21
Stonewall	30	3	1	26	22	93	10

Bethnal Green United – record expunged

MIDDLESEX FEDERATION LEAGUE CUP

FINAL *(April 29th at Yeading)*
Walthamstow Avenue & Pennant 1 Willesden Constantine 0

ALEC SMITH PREMIER DIVISION CUP

FIRST ROUND
Bethnal Green United 2 Willesden Constantine 0

SECOND ROUND
Battersea Ironsides 0 **Walthamstow Avenue & Pennant** 1
Bedfont Sports 4 Marsh Rangers 1
Bethnal Green United 6 Stonewall 1
Brazilian Sports Club 0 **Crown & Manor** 1 *(at Crown & Manor)*
CB Hounslow United 1 **Wraysbury** 4
FC Deportivo Galicia 3 **London Tigers** 5
Mauritius Sports 2 **Ealing** 4
Neasden Foundation 2 Spelthorne Sports 1

QUARTER-FINAL
Bedfont Sports 0 **Walthamstow Avenue & Pennant** 3
Bethnal Green United 1 **Wraysbury** 3
London Tigers 3 Ealing 0
Neasden Foundation 3 **Crown & Manor** 4

SEMI-FINALS
Walthamstow Avenue & Pennant 0 **Crown & Manor** 1
London Tigers 4 Wraysbury 4 *aet* (6-5p)

FINAL
(April 15th at Yeading)
London Tigers 1 Crown & Manor 0

MIDDLESEX COUNTY LEAGUE PREMIER DIVISION CONSTITUTION 2006-07

BEDFONT SPORTS . . . . Bedfont Sports Club, Hatton Road, Feltham . . . . None
BISON . . . . Conquest Sports & Social Club, Wood Lane, Isleworth TW7 5EJ 020 8560 2892
BRAZILIAN SPORTS CLUB . . Waltham Forest FC, Wadham Lodge, Kitchener Road, Walthamstow E17 4JP 020 8527 2444
EALING . . . . Osterley Sports Club, Tentelow Lane, Osterley, Southall UB2 4LW 020 8574 3774
FC DEPORTIVO GALICIA . . . . Osterley Sports Club, Tentelow Lane, Osterley, Southall UB2 4LW 020 8574 3774
KINGS MEADOW . . . . Chertsey Town FC, Alwyns Lane, Chertsey, Surrey KT16 9DN. 01932 561774
MARSH RANGERS . . . . Stockley Park, Chestnut Avenue, West Drayton . . . . None
MAURITIUS SPORTS (CMB) . . . . Fredrick Knight Sports Ground, Willoughby Lane, Tottenham N17 0SL 020 8801 8233
NEASDEN FOUNDATION . . . . Conquest Sports & Social Club, Wood Lane, Isleworth TW7 5EJ 020 8560 2892
PARKFIELD YOUTH OLD BOYS . . . . RCT Sports Ground, Headstone Lane, Harrow . . . . None
SOUTHALL . . . . Viking Greenford FC, Avenue Park, Western Avenue, Greenford 020 8578 2706
SPELTHORNE SPORTS . . . . Spelthorne Sports Club, 296 Staines Road West, Ashford TW15 1RY 01932 783625
SPORT LONDON E BENFICA . . . Hanwell Town FC, Reynolds Field, Perivale Lane, Greenford UB6 8TL. 020 8998 1701
WALTHAMSTOW AVENUE & PENNANT . . . Town Mead Leisure Park, Brooker Road, Waltham Abbey EN9 1JH. 01992 714949
WILLESDEN CONSTANTINE . . . . Alperton Sports Ground, Alperton Lane, Wembley HA0 1JH 020 8997 9909
WRAYSBURY . . . . Memorial Ground, The Green, Wraysbury, Staines TW19 5NA 01784 482155

IN: Bison (P), Kings Meadow (N), Parkfield Youth Old Boys (P), Southall (S – Combined Counties League Premier Division), Sport London E Benfica (P)

OUT: Battersea Ironsides (W), Bethnal Green United (WS), CB Hounslow United (P – Combined Counties League Division One), Crown & Manor (W), London Tigers (S – Spartan South Midlands League Premier Division having merged with Kingsbury Town to form Kingsbury London Tigers), Stonewall (R)

Division One		P	W	D	L	F	A	Pts
Sport London E Benfica		22	15	5	2	46	19	50
Parkfield Youth Old Boys		22	14	4	4	58	25	46
Bison		22	14	4	4	60	27	46
Fenerbahce		22	11	5	6	50	34	38
The Wilberforce Wanderers		22	10	4	8	48	44	34
North Greenford Utd Social		22	8	6	8	39	40	30
St John's Athletic		22	9	2	11	32	45	29
Harefield Ex-Servicemens		22	7	6	9	31	49	27
Hounslow Wanderers	-3	22	6	5	11	34	43	20
Islington Shooting Stars		22	5	5	12	41	62	20
South Kilburn		22	5	4	13	28	39	19
FC Ealing Assyrians		22	3	0	19	24	64	9

JIM ROGERS DIVISION ONE PRESIDENT'S CUP FINAL
(April 22nd at Yeading)
Bison 4 Fenerbahce 1

Division Two		P	W	D	L	F	A	Pts
Signcraft		20	12	6	2	70	25	42
North Hayes Academicals		20	11	5	4	45	35	38
Bridge Rovers	-3	20	12	2	6	39	27	35
Puma 2000		20	9	6	5	54	39	33
LPOSSA		20	8	6	6	52	48	30
Brentham		20	8	6	6	39	40	30
Harefield Wednesday		20	8	5	7	43	37	29
Haringey Town		20	3	10	7	38	45	19
South Acton		20	5	4	11	27	47	19
Brunel University		20	3	5	12	36	65	14
Barn Elms		20	2	3	15	30	65	9

SIR JOHN SALMOND DIVISION TWO CUP FINAL
(April 8th at Yeading)
Brentham 6 Signcraft 1

Division Three		P	W	D	L	F	A	Pts
Harrow St Mary's Youth Old Boys		26	18	5	3	79	32	59
Imperial College Old Boys		26	17	5	4	93	41	56
Camden & Ampthill Football Academy		26	17	4	5	92	45	55
Amis-BK/London United		26	17	2	7	46	27	53
Blue Marlin		26	15	5	6	81	48	50
FC Tilburg Regents		26	12	3	11	55	57	39
Harlington		26	12	1	13	54	56	37
Stedfast United		26	10	5	11	66	72	35
Renegades		26	8	6	12	53	44	30
Greens United	-3	26	7	6	13	52	63	24
Samba Soccer School	-3	26	8	2	16	50	63	23
Warren		26	5	6	15	41	89	21
Hayes Town		26	5	5	16	30	62	20
ACA		26	2	3	21	22	115	9

P D MARDON DIVISION THREE CUP FINAL
(April 26th at Yeading)
Imperial College Old Boys 3 Harrow St Mary's Youth Old Boys 0

Senior Reserve Division		P	W	D	L	F	A	Pts
CB Hounslow United Res.		21	15	1	5	41	13	46
Spelthorne Sports Res.		21	13	1	7	38	29	40
Harefield Ex-Servicemens Res.		21	9	5	7	39	36	32
North Greenford United Social Res.	-3	21	10	4	7	30	26	31
Hendon 'A'		21	9	3	9	30	24	30
London Tigers Res.		21	8	6	7	37	34	30
Hanworth Villa Res.		21	4	3	14	26	57	15
Bedfont Sports Res.		21	3	3	15	34	56	12

SENIOR RESERVE DIVISION CUP FINAL
(April 5th at Yeading)
Hendon 'A' 4 Spelthorne Sports Res. 1

Junior Reserve Division	P	W	D	L	F	A	Pts
Eastcote-Richings Park	18	14	4	0	60	12	46
CB Hounslow United 'A'	18	14	3	1	65	18	45
North Hayes Academicals Res.	18	10	4	4	50	26	34
Brunel University Res.	18	10	2	6	45	34	32
Kentish Town Res.	18	9	1	8	47	31	28
Brentham Res.	18	9	0	9	61	45	27
Harefield Wednesday Res.	18	5	4	9	31	51	19
Stonewall Res.	18	3	3	12	22	60	12
Hounslow Wanderers Res.	18	1	4	13	17	63	7
FC Tilburg Regents Res.	18	1	3	14	11	69	6

JEFF NARDIN JUNIOR RESERVE DIVISION TROPHY FINAL
(April 1st at Yeading)
CB Hounslow United 'A' 4 North Hayes Academicals Res. 1

MIDLAND ALLIANCE

	Alvechurch	Barwell	Biddulph V	Boldmere	Causeway	Chasetown	Coalville Tn	Cradley Tn	Leamington	Loughboro'	Malvern Tn	Oadby Tn	Oldbury U	Quorn	Racing C W	Rocester	Romulus	Stourbridge	Stratford T	Studley	Tipton Tn	Westfields
Alvechurch		3-3	2-1	1-0	5-0	1-2	3-2	2-1	1-4	0-1	0-1	3-1	2-0	0-2	0-2	3-0	1-3	2-2	1-1	3-0	1-0	2-1
Barwell	2-1		3-1	0-4	2-1	1-1	3-0	2-1	0-4	2-0	0-2	0-3	1-1	1-2	1-2	6-0	1-2	1-0	1-2	4-1	2-4	2-0
Biddulph Victoria	2-1	1-4		1-3	5-0	0-2	1-0	1-1	1-1	2-2	3-1	2-1	2-1	0-1	1-0	2-2	1-2	0-4	0-2	0-0	3-5	1-1
Boldmere St Michaels	2-0	3-3	3-1		0-0	1-2	1-2	1-1	2-3	1-1	0-1	1-1	1-1	0-0	1-0	3-1	1-1	0-1	2-0	2-3	1-1	2-1
Causeway United	0-3	1-3	0-1	1-1		0-1	1-3	4-0	0-3	1-4	1-2	3-0	0-0	0-2	2-0	3-3	1-2	3-3	0-2	2-2	1-2	1-0
Chasetown	3-2	2-1	2-0	3-0	2-1		1-1	5-0	0-2	1-0	3-1	0-0	1-2	1-2	2-1	1-0	2-0	1-0	1-0	1-1	1-1	2-0
Coalville Town	3-1	0-4	2-1	0-0	1-2	0-1		1-0	1-0	1-1	1-0	5-1	0-2	1-0	0-2	2-1	1-2	3-4	1-1	4-2	3-2	1-0
Cradley Town	1-3	0-2	1-2	2-0	1-3	1-4	1-3		0-4	1-3	1-3	1-1	0-0	0-2	1-2	3-3	1-1	0-2	1-0	3-5	0-0	1-1
Leamington	1-1	1-1	5-0	0-0	3-1	1-3	2-0	4-1		1-3	0-2	1-0	2-0	1-1	2-1	4-0	1-1	1-2	1-0	3-0	3-0	3-0
Loughborough Dynamo	4-0	1-2	1-1	3-1	3-0	0-1	0-1	0-2	0-0		0-1	1-0	0-2	0-3	4-2	0-0	0-1	0-1	3-1	0-1	1-0	3-1
Malvern Town	5-0	5-3	5-0	3-2	1-3	3-1	2-3	6-2	4-1	2-1		2-0	1-0	2-1	2-3	2-0	2-2	6-3	1-1	2-1	0-2	3-1
Oadby Town	0-1	0-1	3-3	0-1	5-2	1-2	2-1	1-1	0-3	1-1	1-1		0-0	1-4	0-3	1-0	0-3	3-3	2-1	6-0	0-2	4-2
Oldbury United	1-0	2-1	2-3	1-2	2-0	0-3	2-4	2-1	4-1	2-3	2-1	2-3		1-2	0-2	4-1	1-0	0-3	2-1	4-0	3-1	3-3
Quorn	3-0	1-2	2-1	1-2	3-0	1-1	0-2	6-0	1-1	2-0	3-5	0-2	1-2		1-2	1-3	0-1	1-5	0-1	2-0	3-2	3-3
Racing Club Warwick	0-0	4-4	2-0	1-0	1-1	3-1	2-2	2-1	0-1	2-0	3-1	1-2	2-2	0-1		3-1	1-2	1-3	2-1	0-0	4-1	2-2
Rocester	1-1	4-5	1-3	0-2	0-1	0-2	0-2	1-0	0-0	0-2	1-2	2-2	2-1	1-3	0-2		4-2	0-5	1-4	0-1	0-0	1-3
Romulus	0-2	2-2	5-0	0-2	4-2	1-1	4-0	2-0	2-2	4-0	1-1	0-0	1-1	2-1	2-5	5-0		0-2	1-1	3-0	1-0	4-0
Stourbridge	2-0	1-0	3-1	0-2	4-1	0-2	4-2	3-2	2-1	4-1	2-1	1-1	3-0	2-4	6-1	4-1	0-4		1-2	5-1	3-2	4-1
Stratford Town	2-1	2-1	2-1	2-3	1-2	1-3	0-2	0-1	1-3	1-1	1-0	2-0	0-1	0-2	1-2	2-0	1-3	0-2		2-2	1-0	3-0
Studley	2-4	0-2	3-1	1-2	3-2	0-1	3-0	1-0	3-1	2-0	0-2	0-0	2-0	0-1	1-2	2-0	2-3	0-4	1-0		2-3	1-0
Tipton Town	2-2	1-4	2-2	2-5	3-0	2-0	0-0	6-1	2-2	0-2	1-4	1-1	2-2	2-2	2-1	3-0	4-1	2-2	2-1	4-2		2-1
Westfields	1-0	0-0	0-3	2-0	3-2	0-5	1-2	0-2	3-2	2-3	2-4	1-0	0-0	1-0	0-1	3-1	2-4	1-5	1-2	3-3	1-1	

	P	W	D	L	F	A	Pts
Chasetown	42	29	7	6	74	32	94
Stourbridge	42	29	5	8	110	55	92
Malvern Town	42	27	4	11	95	56	85
Romulus	42	23	11	8	84	49	80
Leamington	42	21	11	10	79	44	74
Racing Club Warwick	42	22	7	13	72	55	73
Quorn	42	21	6	15	71	51	69
Coalville Town	42	21	6	15	63	60	69
Barwell	42	20	8	14	83	66	68
Boldmere St Michaels	42	17	12	13	60	48	63
Tipton Town	42	15	13	14	74	69	58
Oldbury United	42	16	10	16	58	58	58
Loughborough Dynamo	42	16	8	18	53	53	56
Alvechurch	42	16	7	19	59	64	55
Stratford Town	42	15	6	21	49	55	51
Studley	42	14	7	21	54	81	49
Biddulph Victoria	42	12	9	21	55	83	45
Oadby Town	42	10	14	18	50	64	44
Causeway United	42	9	7	26	49	89	34
Westfields	42	8	9	25	48	88	33
Cradley Town	42	5	9	28	38	94	24
Rocester	42	4	8	30	36	100	20

LEAGUE CUP

FIRST ROUND

Alvechurch 1 Boldmere St Mich. 0
Barwell 2 Stratford Town 1
Cradley Town 2 **Studley** 4
Romulus 1 **Tipton Town** 2
Stourbridge 1 Loughboro' Dyn 0
Westfields 2 Oldbury United 1

SECOND ROUND

Barwell 3 Westfields 0
Chasetown 3 Oadby Town 0
Coalville Town 3 Causeway Utd 0
Leamington 4 Rocester 1
Malvern Town 2 **Alvechurch** 3
Quorn 1 **Tipton Town** 2
R C Warwick 1 Biddulph Vic 0
Stourbridge 5 Studley 0

QUARTER-FINALS

Barwell 2 Alvechurch 0
Chasetown 5 Stourbridge 2
Leamington 2 Coalville Town 2
aet (5-4p)
Tipton Town 2 Racing Club Warwick 0

SEMI-FINALS

(played over two legs)
Chasetown 1 Leamington 3,
Leamington 0 Chasetown 1
Tipton Town 0 Barwell 1,
Barwell 1 Tipton Town 0

FINAL

(May 16th at Walsall)
Barwell 3 Leamington 1

JOE McGORRIAN CUP

(League champions v League Cup holders)

(August 6th at Rushall Olympic)
Rushall Olympic 1 **Racing Club Warwick** 2

MIDLAND ALLIANCE CONSTITUTION 2006-07

ALVECHURCH. . . . . Lye Meadow, Redditch Road, Alvechurch B48 7RS 0121 445 2929
ATHERSTONE TOWN . . . . . Sheepy Road, Sheepy, Atherstone CV9 3AD. 01827 717829
BARWELL . . . . . Kirkby Road, Barwell LE9 8FQ. 01455 843067
BIDDULPH VICTORIA. . . . . Tunstall Road, Knypersley, Stoke-On-Trent ST8 7AQ 01782 522737
BOLDMERE ST MICHAELS . . . Trevor Brown Memorial Ground, Church Road, Boldmere, Sutton Coldfield B73 5RY 0121 384 7531
CAUSEWAY UNITED . . . . . Tividale FC, The Beeches, Packwood Road, Tividale, Oldbury B69 1UL. 01384 211743
COALVILLE TOWN . . . . . Owen Street Sports Ground, Owen Street, Coalville LE67 3DA. 01530 833365
CRADLEY TOWN. . . . . Beeches View Avenue, Cradley, Halesowen B63 2HB 01384 569658
FRIAR LANE & EPWORTH . . . . . Knighton Lane East, Aylestone Park, Leicester LE2 6FT. 0116 283 3629
LEAMINGTON . . . . . New Windmill Ground, Harbury Lane, Whitnash, Leamington Spa CV33 9JR 01926 334934
LOUGHBOROUGH DYNAMO . . Nanpantan Sports Ground, Nanpantan Road, Loughborough LE11 3YD 01509 237148
MARKET DRAYTON TOWN. . . . . Greenfield Sports Club, Greenfield Lane, Market Drayton TF9 3SL 01630 655088
OADBY TOWN . . . . . Topps Park, Wigston Road, Oadby LE2 5QG. 0116 271 5728
OLDBURY UNITED. . . . . The Cricketts, York Road, Oldbury, Warley B65 0RT 0121 559 5564
QUORN. . . . . Sutton Park, Farley Way, Quorn, Loughborough LE12 8RB. 01509 620232
RACING CLUB WARWICK . . . . . Townsend Meadow, Hampton Road, Warwick CV34 6JP 01926 495786
ROCESTER. . . . . Hillsfield, Mill Street, Rocester, Uttoxeter ST14 5TX 01889 590463
ROMULUS . . . . . Sutton Coldfield Town FC, Central Ground, Coles Lane, Sutton Coldfield B72 1NL 0121 354 2997
STRATFORD TOWN. . . . . Masons Road, Stratford-on-Avon CV37 9NF 01789 297479
STUDLEY . . . . . The Bee Hive, Abbeyfield Drive, off Birmingham Road, Studley B80 7BE 01527 853817
TIPTON TOWN . . . . . Tipton Sports Academy, Wednesbury Oak Road, Tipton DY4 0BS. 0121 502 5534/556 5067
WESTFIELDS . . . . . Allpay Park, Widemarsh Common, Hereford HR4 9NA. 07860 410548

IN: Atherstone Town (P – Midland Combination Premier Division), Friar Lane & Epworth (P – Leicestershire Senior League Premier Division), Market Drayton Town (P – West Midlands (Regional) League Premier Division)

OUT: Chasetown (P – Southern League Division One Midlands), Malvern Town (P – Southern League Division One Midlands), Stourbridge (P – Southern League Division One Midlands)

MIDLAND COMBINATION

	Alveston	Atherstone Town	Barnt Green Spartak	Bolehall Swifts	Bridgnorth Town	Brocton	Cadbury Athletic	Castle Vale	Coleshill Town	Continental Star	Coventry Copsewood	Coventry Sphinx	Dudley Sports	Feckenham	Highgate United	Massey-Ferguson	Meir KA	Nuneaton Griff	Pershore Town	Pilkington XXX	Shifnal Town	Southam United
Alveston		0-3	0-3	0-1	1-1	1-0	3-1	1-2	3-4	3-0	1-2	3-2	1-2	1-3	5-2	1-0	1-2	3-1	5-2	1-0	1-2	0-2
Atherstone Town	3-1		6-0	2-2	0-0	2-0	0-2	3-0	4-1	9-0	1-0	2-2	2-0	2-2	3-0	1-0	5-0	1-1	7-0	0-1	3-1	0-0
Barnt Green Spartak	0-1	1-2		1-0	4-1	1-0	1-0	3-0	3-3	2-1	2-0	0-2	3-0	1-2	2-0	3-1	4-2	4-2	3-0	3-1	1-0	2-1
Bolehall Swifts	4-3	0-6	4-1	*P*	3-1	2-0	5-1	2-1	3-1	2-0	3-0	2-4	4-1	4-1	3-0	2-0	7-0	0-3	2-1	2-2	0-4	2-1
Bridgnorth Town	1-0	0-2	1-1	3-0	*R*	0-1	2-1	6-1	4-2	3-2	2-0	0-2	3-2	1-0	1-0	0-1	3-0	1-1	2-1	4-1	0-2	5-2
Brocton	2-0	0-1	2-0	1-1	0-1	*E*	3-3	3-3	0-3	3-0	2-2	1-0	0-2	3-0	1-1	5-3	3-0	1-4	0-1	1-2	1-1	2-1
Cadbury Athletic	1-2	0-3	1-3	3-1	0-1	3-3	*M*	2-5	2-4	2-0	1-2	4-7	3-2	1-3	1-2	1-1	1-1	4-3	0-1	3-2	2-0	1-2
Castle Vale	0-3	3-3	2-3	0-0	2-0	2-1	1-1	*I*	1-1	1-0	2-1	1-2	2-1	1-3	4-2	3-2	0-1	1-4	5-0	0-2	2-1	1-1
Coleshill Town	1-0	1-4	0-5	2-2	1-2	4-3	0-1	2-3	*E*	1-1	3-0	1-3	4-2	0-4	1-2	5-2	1-3	0-1	1-1	0-0	3-1	2-1
Continental Star	1-3	0-7	0-3	1-6	1-6	1-1	1-2	2-3	2-5	*R*	1-5	0-4	1-1	3-7	0-1	1-0	1-2	2-0	2-3	1-1	0-2	1-4
Coventry Copsewood	0-3	0-1	2-1	2-1	0-3	0-1	2-2	2-1	3-1	4-1		0-1	1-4	0-4	2-1	1-1	2-2	2-2	2-1	1-3	1-2	1-1
Coventry Sphinx	5-1	2-3	6-1	3-4	1-1	3-0	6-4	1-4	4-1	7-3	4-1	*D*	5-1	2-1	5-0	11-0	5-3	6-1	4-3	6-1	1-1	2-0
Dudley Sports	0-4	0-5	1-1	0-2	0-1	2-2	1-3	0-1	0-2	2-2	1-1	1-2	*I*	0-0	3-4	5-0	1-0	2-0	1-2	1-2	0-0	2-2
Feckenham	1-1	1-3	3-2	3-1	1-2	3-0	3-1	5-2	5-5	3-2	2-0	2-5	3-0	*V*	4-1	0-1	2-0	3-0	1-1	5-1	1-0	5-1
Highgate United	1-0	1-7	1-2	2-1	2-2	1-3	0-4	0-1	0-0	2-0	4-0	1-1	0-0	2-0	*I*	0-4	1-2	2-0	2-1	3-3	2-5	1-7
Massey-Ferguson	0-0	0-4	0-1	0-1	3-1	3-2	1-1	2-1	0-5	2-2	3-2	1-3	0-1	0-4	0-3	*S*	3-1	0-4	4-0	0-2	0-4	1-2
Meir KA	1-4	0-4	1-2	0-4	2-1	1-1	0-0	3-3	1-0	0-3	0-2	1-2	1-1	7-3	1-0	1-0	*I*	4-5	0-0	2-2	0-0	3-2
Nuneaton Griff	1-2	2-1	0-1	1-0	1-3	0-1	1-0	1-0	5-2	5-3	3-1	2-5	0-3	0-4	1-1	2-0	3-0	*O*	2-1	3-1	1-1	3-1
Pershore Town	2-0	2-3	1-0	0-3	3-1	0-1	3-0	0-3	3-0	3-6	3-4	0-1	0-1	1-3	4-0	1-2	5-3	0-3	*N*	3-1	3-5	2-0
Pilkington XXX	0-1	0-8	0-5	3-3	0-3	6-2	3-2	1-3	3-3	2-3	1-3	3-4	1-2	2-6	1-0	1-4	2-3	1-0	0-4		1-6	2-1
Shifnal Town	2-1	0-2	0-1	0-1	1-1	5-0	4-1	5-2	5-1	5-0	2-0	1-3	0-1	4-1	1-1	2-1	1-0	0-0	3-1	3-1		3-2
Southam United	0-0	1-3	1-2	1-0	0-1	1-0	4-2	0-0	1-2	1-0	1-2	1-6	1-1	0-0	0-2	1-0	2-1	4-1	2-0	0-0	0-1	

Premier Division		P	W	D	L	F	A	Pts
Atherstone Town		42	32	7	3	131	27	103
Coventry Sphinx		42	33	4	5	150	61	103
Barnt Green Spartak		42	28	3	11	82	51	87
Feckenham		42	25	6	11	107	64	81
Bridgnorth Town		42	24	7	11	75	48	79
Bolehall Swifts		42	24	6	12	90	59	78
Shifnal Town		42	23	8	11	86	44	77
Nuneaton Griff		42	19	6	17	73	72	63
Castle Vale		42	18	8	16	73	76	62
Alveston		42	18	4	20	65	61	58
Coleshill Town		42	14	9	19	79	93	51
Brocton		42	13	10	19	56	70	49
Southam United		42	13	9	20	56	65	48
Highgate United		42	13	8	21	51	86	47
Coventry Copsewood	*-3*	42	14	7	21	56	79	46
Pershore Town		42	14	3	25	63	88	45
Meir KA		42	12	9	21	55	92	45
Dudley Sports		42	11	11	20	51	71	44
Pilkington XXX		42	11	8	23	62	108	41
Massey-Ferguson		42	11	5	26	46	91	38
Cadbury Athletic	*-4*	42	11	8	23	68	92	37
Continental Star		42	5	6	31	51	128	21

TONY ALLDEN MEMORIAL CUP

(Premier Division champions v Challenge Cup holders)

(October 18th at Leamington)

Leamington 5 Coventry Sphinx 1

Reserve Division		P	W	D	L	F	A	Pts
Rushall Olympic Res.		28	19	4	5	.72	25	61
Mickleover Sports Res.		28	17	4	7	56	43	55
Hinckley United Res.		28	16	5	7	71	42	53
Oadby Town Res.		28	16	3	9	61	45	51
Boldmere St Michaels Res.		28	15	4	9	54	36	49
Quorn Res.		28	15	3	10	61	52	48
Tipton Town Res.		28	12	9	7	55	39	45
Bromsgrove Rovers Res.		28	13	5	10	75	75	44
Gresley Rovers Res.		28	13	4	11	47	51	43
Shepshed Dynamo Res.		28	11	4	13	53	59	37
Barwell Res.		28	10	4	14	36	48	34
Chasetown Res.		28	8	3	17	40	58	27
Loughborough Dynamo Res.	*-3*	28	9	3	16	51	74	27
Atherstone Town Res.		28	2	1	25	30	94	7
Rugby Town Res.	*-12*	28	4	4	20	51	72	4

CHALLENGE TROPHY

FINAL

(May 9th at Chasetown)

Chasetown Res. 2 Mickleover Sports Res. 1

CHALLENGE BOWL

FINAL

(May 8th at Oadby Town)

Oadby Town Res. 1 **Hinckley United Res.** 1 *aet* (1-3p)

MIDLAND COMBINATION PREMIER DIVISION CONSTITUTION 2006-07

ALVESTON	Home Guard Club, Main Street, Tiddington, Stratford-upon-Avon CV37 7AY	01789 297718
BARNT GREEN SPARTAK	Bromsgrove Rovers FC, Victoria Park, Birmingham Road, Bromsgrove B61 0DJ	01527 876949
BOLEHALL SWIFTS	Rene Road, Bolehall, Tamworth B77 3NN	01827 62637
BRERETON SOCIAL	Red Lion Ground, Armitage Lane, Rugeley WS15 1ED	01889 585526
BROCTON	Heath Hayes FC, Coppice Coll., Newlands Lane, Heath Hayes, Cannock WS12 3HH	07791 841774
CADBURY ATHLETIC	Triplex Sports Ground, Eckersall Road, Kings Norton, Birmingham B38 8SR	0121 458 4570
CASTLE VALE	Vale Stadium, Farnborough Road, Castle Vale, Warwick, Birmingham B35 7DA	0121 747 6969
COLESHILL TOWN	Pack Meadow, Packington Lane, Coleshill B46 3JQ	01675 463259
CONTINENTAL STAR	Oldbury Leisure Centre, Newbury Road, Oldbury, Warley B69 1HE	0121 552 4497
COVENTRY COPSEWOOD	Copsewood Sports & Social Club, Allard Way, Binley, Coventry CV3 1HQ	02476 635992
COVENTRY SPHINX	Sphinx Sports & Social Club, Siddeley Avenue, Stoke Aldermoor, Coventry CV3 1WA	024 7645 1361
FECKENHAM	Redditch United FC, Valley Stadium, Bromsgrove Road, Redditch B97 4RN	01527 67450
HEATH HAYES	Coppice Colliery Ground, Newlands Lane, Heath Hayes, Cannock WS12 3HH	01543 279022
HIGHGATE UNITED	The Coppice, Tythe Barn Lane, Shirley, Solihull B90 1PH	0121 744 4194
MASSEY-FERGUSON	Banner Lane, Tile Hill, Coventry CV4 9LA	07985 000222
MEIR KA	Kings Park, Hilderstone Road, Meir Heath, Stoke-on-Trent ST3 7NT	07888 750532
NUNEATON GRIFF	The Pingles Stadium, Avenue Road, Nuneaton CV11 4LX	024 7637 0688
PERSHORE TOWN	King George V Playing Fields, King George's Way, Pershore WR10 1AA	01386 556902
PILKINGTON XXX	Triplex Sports Ground, Eckersall Road, Kings Norton, Birmingham B38 8SR	0121 458 4570
SOUTHAM UNITED	Banbury Road, Southam, Leamington Spa CV47 2BJ	01926 812091
WALSALL WOOD	Oak Park, Lichfield Road, Walsall Wood WS9 9NP	01543 361084

IN: Brereton Social (P – West Midlands (Regional) League Division One), Heath Hayes (S – West Midlands (Regional) League Premier Division), Walsall Wood (P – West Midlands (Regional) League Division One)

OUT: Atherstone Town (P – Midland Alliance), Bridgnorth Town (S – West Midlands (Regional) League Premier Division), Dudley Sports (S – West Midlands (Regional) League Premier Division), Shifnal Town (S – West Midlands (Regional) League Premier Division)

CHALLENGE CUP

(Premier and Division One teams)

FIRST ROUND

Alveston 1 **Feckenham** 2
Archdale 2 **Meir KA** 3
Atherstone Town 4 Bridgnorth Town 1
Bolehall Swifts 2 Cadbury Athletic 1
Castle Vale 1 Pilkington XXX 0
Kenilworth Town KH 0 **Massey-Ferguson** 2
Newhall United 0 **Southam United** 1
Shifnal Town 2 Stockingford AA 0
Shifnal Town 3 Stockingford AA 0 *rematch*

SECOND ROUND

Atherstone Town 5 Continental Star 1
Barnt Green Spartak 2 Leamington Hibernian 1
Brocton 1 **Feckenham** 2
Burntwood Town 3 Meir KA 1
Castle Vale 1 **Ettington** 2
Coleshill Town 1 **Nuneaton Griff** 3
Coventry Copsewood 2 Dudley Sports 1 *aet*
Fairfield Villa 6 Polesworth North Warwick 5
Handsworth United 6 Southam United 1
Heather Athletic 1 **Massey-Ferguson** 4
Highgate United 0 **Northfield Town** 1
Knowle 1 **Mile Oak Rovers** 2
Loughborough 3 Littleton 2
Pershore Town 3 Bolehall Swifts 2
Shifnal Town 4 Thimblemill REC 3
West Midlands Police 0 **Coventry Sphinx** 1

THIRD ROUND

Coventry Copsewood 1 **Barnt Green Spartak** 2
Fairfield Villa 5 Burntwood Town 1
Handsworth United 1 **Feckenham** 3
Massey-Ferguson 1 Ettington 1 *aet* (3-2p)
Northfield Town 0 **Atherstone Town** 3
Nuneaton Griff 0 **Coventry Sphinx** 4
Pershore Town 4 Mile Oak Rovers 0
Shifnal Town 10 Loughborough 0

QUARTER-FINALS

Barnt Green Spartak 1 **Atherstone Town** 5
Coventry Sphinx 3 **Feckenham** 4
Massey-Ferguson 0 **Pershore Town** 4
Shifnal Town 5 Fairfield Villa 1

SEMI-FINALS

(played over two legs)

Atherstone Town 3 Shifnal Town 0, Shifnal Town 0 **Atherstone Town** 0
Pershore Town 1 Feckenham 1, **Feckenham** 3 Pershore Town 3 *aet* (5-3p)

FINAL

(May 10th at West Bromwich Albion)

Feckenham 1 **Atherstone Town** 2

	Archdale	Burntwood Town	Ettington	Fairfield Villa	Handsworth United	Heather Athletic	Kenilworth Town KH	Knowle	Leamington Hibernian	Littleton	Loughborough	Mile Oak Rovers	Newhall United	Northfield Town	Polesworth Nth Warwick	Stockingford AA	Thimblemill REC	West Midlands Police
Archdale		4-2	3-1	1-0	2-4	0-0	2-1	1-5	1-1	3-2	1-2	0-0	1-0	0-1	1-7	2-2	4-2	3-1
Burntwood Town	2-4		1-1	0-2	3-2	3-1	1-1	0-1	3-2	1-3	3-2	1-4	3-0	1-0	1-3	3-2	0-1	2-1
Ettington	2-0	0-2		2-4	1-4	3-1	4-1	1-2	3-0	1-0	3-1	1-1	1-2	0-3	1-0	1-0	1-1	0-2
Fairfield Villa	4-0	0-0	1-2	*D*	2-1	1-2	0-2	1-2	2-4	1-0	1-2	1-2	7-0	1-1	2-1	2-1	4-2	4-0
Handsworth United	0-3	7-3	1-3	5-1	*I*	1-1	2-2	1-3	0-4	4-2	4-2	0-3	2-2	0-11	3-0	2-2	2-2	2-0
Heather Athletic	1-0	0-2	5-2	3-0	4-2	*V*	3-0	0-2	4-2	2-2	0-0	0-1	0-1	2-3	1-1	0-1	2-1	0-3
Kenilworth Town KH	2-0	1-3	0-5	0-5	1-8	0-3	*I*	1-0	0-2	4-3	4-1	0-1	4-0	2-2	2-2	0-5	0-4	4-2
Knowle	2-1	4-2	5-0	0-2	4-2	3-0	2-0	*S*	0-0	1-1	0-0	3-0	5-0	1-0	4-0	2-2	0-1	2-1
Leamington Hibernian	2-2	0-2	1-3	0-1	0-1	0-1	1-0	1-0	*I*	1-3	2-2	2-0	1-1	0-5	1-2	1-3	2-1	2-1
Littleton	1-2	0-4	2-3	6-0	0-3	1-3	5-2	0-1	1-4	*O*	4-3	2-0	1-1	3-0	1-0	4-1	1-4	0-2
Loughborough	2-0	2-1	0-2	1-2	1-3	2-1	0-0	0-2	2-0	1-3	*N*	2-1	2-3	0-2	2-1	0-5	0-2	2-0
Mile Oak Rovers	3-0	1-1	2-0	0-2	1-3	0-1	3-0	0-1	5-0	3-0	1-2		3-1	2-1	0-1	2-2	3-0	1-2
Newhall United	0-3	1-1	1-4	0-1	4-1	1-1	5-0	1-1	0-1	5-1	0-0	1-1	*O*	1-2	2-2	3-2	0-2	3-1
Northfield Town	2-1	2-0	2-2	0-0	3-0	2-0	3-0	0-0	3-2	2-0	6-0	4-0	2-2	*N*	3-3	2-1	8-0	2-2
Polesworth North Warwick	4-0	1-2	0-1	1-2	2-0	0-0	1-2	0-2	2-0	3-1	1-1	0-0	6-1	4-2	*E*	2-2	2-1	2-1
Stockingford AA	0-1	0-1	2-5	0-0	3-2	5-0	4-0	1-1	3-2	4-3	4-0	5-0	7-2	0-0	0-4		1-3	W-L
Thimblemill REC	2-2	3-3	0-1	0-0	0-9	2-1	3-0	0-0	2-0	1-4	5-1	0-4	3-0	0-4	4-2	4-2		3-2
West Midlands Police	0-0	2-0	0-2	2-3	2-0	2-2	3-2	2-1	2-1	0-1	3-4	4-1	2-2	0-1	3-4	0-3	1-0	

Division One		P	W	D	L	F	A	Pts
Knowle		34	21	8	5	62	22	71
Northfield Town		34	20	9	5	84	30	69
Ettington		34	19	4	11	62	50	61
Fairfield Villa		34	18	5	11	59	43	59
Burntwood Town		34	15	6	13	57	58	51
Thimblemill REC		34	15	6	13	59	66	51
Stockingford AA		34	14	8	12	75	54	50
Polesworth North Warwick		34	14	8	12	64	49	50
Mile Oak Rovers		34	14	6	14	49	43	48
Archdale		34	13	7	14	48	60	46
Handsworth United	*-3*	34	14	5	15	81	77	44
Heather Athletic		34	12	8	14	45	49	44
Littleton		34	12	3	19	61	70	39
Loughborough		34	11	6	17	42	70	39
West Midlands Police		34	11	4	19	49	59	37
Leamington Hibernian		34	10	5	19	42	61	35
Newhall United	*-3*	34	8	11	15	46	74	32
Kenilworth Town KH		34	8	5	21	38	88	29

PRESIDENT'S CUP

FIRST ROUND

Burntwood Town 0 **Loughborough** 2
Leamington Hibernian 2 **Ettington** 3

SECOND ROUND

Ettington 2 **Polesworth North Warwick** 5 *aet*
Fairfield Villa 3 West Midlands Police 1
Handsworth United 2 **Archdale** 4
Kenilworth Town KH 0 **Heather Athletic** 1
Littleton 2 Loughborough 1
Newhall United 3 **Knowle** 5
Stockingford AA 0 **Mile Oak Rovers** 1
Thimblemill REC 2 Northfield Town 1

QUARTER-FINALS

Archdale 2 Knowle 2 *aet* (9-8p)
Fairfield Villa 2 Littleton 1
Mile Oak Rovers 1 **Polesworth North Warwick** 2
Thimblemill REC 0 **Heather Athletic** 1

SEMI-FINALS

(played over two legs)

Archdale 2 Heather Athletic 1, **Heather Athletic** (w/o) v Archdale (scr.)
Polesworth North Warwick 1 Fairfield Villa 2, **Fairfield Villa** 2 Polesworth North Warwick 1 *aet*

FINAL

(May 3rd at Boldmere St Michaels)

Heather Athletic 0 **Fairfield Villa** 1

MIDLAND COMBINATION DIVISION ONE CONSTITUTION 2006-07

ARCHDALE .... County Sports Ground, Claines Lane, Worcester WR3 7SS 07736 309670
BARTLEY GREEN .... Illey Lane, Halesowen B62 0HF 0121 475 5443
BURNTWOOD TOWN .... Memorial Ground, Rugeley Road, Burntwood WS7 9BE 07946 269153
ETTINGTON .... Community Centre, Rogers Lane, Ettington, Stratford-upon-Avon CV37 7SX .... None
FAIRFIELD VILLA .... Recreation Ground, Stourbridge Road, Fairfield, Bromsgrove B61 9LZ 01527 877049
HEATHER ATHLETIC .... St John's Park, Ravenstone Road, Heather LE67 2QJ 01530 263986
KENILWORTH TOWN KH .... Gypsy Lane, off Rouncil Lane, Kenilworth CV8 1FQ 01926 850851
KNOWLE .... Hampton Road, Knowle, Solihull B93 0NX 01564 779807
LEAMINGTON HIBERNIAN .. Racing Club Warwick FC, Townsend Meadow, Hampton Road, Warwick CV34 6JP 01926 495786
LITTLETON .... Five Acres, Pebworth Road, North Littleton, Evesham WR11 8QL 07966 297971
MILE OAK ROVERS .... Mile Oak Community Ground, Price Avenue, Mile Oak, Tamworth B78 3NL 01827 289614
NEWHALL UNITED .... The Hadfields, St Johns Drive, Newhall, Swadlincote DE11 0SU 01283 551029
NORTHFIELD TOWN .... Shenley Lane, Northfield, Birmingham B29 4HZ 0121 478 3900/475 3870
STOCKINGFORD AA .... The Pavilion, Ansley Road, Stockingford, Nuneaton CV10 8LP 024 7638 7743
THIMBLEMILL REC .... Thimblemill Road, Smethwick, Warley B66 6NR 0121 429 2459
UNIVERSITY OF BIRMINGHAM .. Munrow Sports Centre, Univ. of Birmingham, Edgbaston, Birmingham B15 2TT 0121 414 7948
WEST MIDLANDS POLICE ... Tally Ho! Sports Ground, Pershore Road, Edgbaston, Birmingham B5 7RD 0121 626 8228

IN: Bartley Green (P), University of Birmingham (P)

OUT: Handsworth United (now Birmingham Academy) (R), Loughborough (W – North Leicestershire League Premier Division), Polesworth North Warwick (F)

	Bartley Green	Cadbury Athletic Res.	Castle Vale Res.	Chelmsley Town	Continental Star Res.	Coton Green	Droitwich Spa	Earlswood Town	Enville Athletic	Feckenham Res.	Himley Athletic	Nunnery Wood Sports	University of Birmingham	Warwick Town	West Hagley
Bartley Green		6-0	2-0	4-0	3-2	2-1	1-1	3-3	3-1	5-1	4-1	1-2	1-1	2-0	3-0
Cadbury Athletic Res.	0-4	*D*	8-2	0-1	0-3	3-1	0-2	0-1	3-2	2-0	3-0	n/a	3-1	2-1	1-0
Castle Vale Res.	0-2	2-1	*I*	4-4	2-2	0-1	2-1	0-4	4-3	2-0	n/a	4-1	1-2	0-2	1-1
Chelmsley Town	1-2	3-2	1-2	*V*	6-0	1-3	0-2	3-1	1-1	1-2	2-3	2-1	1-4	2-2	5-2
Continental Star Res.	1-3	2-0	1-2	5-5	*I*	2-2	0-0	1-1	5-2	0-4	6-0	n/a	1-1	2-1	3-1
Coton Green	1-1	1-1	2-2	1-5	1-2	*S*	1-1	0-0	0-0	3-2	4-2	n/a	2-2	2-2	4-3
Droitwich Spa	1-2	3-0	2-1	3-0	2-0	0-3	*I*	0-1	1-2	1-1	n/a	n/a	0-2	1-1	1-4
Earlswood Town	1-1	2-1	1-2	2-1	2-0	3-2	2-1	*O*	0-0	1-0	3-0	n/a	2-0	1-1	3-3
Enville Athletic	1-6	2-2	6-2	4-0	6-1	1-2	0-1	3-2	*N*	3-1	1-0	n/a	1-5	5-3	2-2
Feckenham Res.	3-2	2-1	4-1	2-0	2-1	1-2	0-2	0-5	2-1		6-0	n/a	0-4	2-1	0-1
Himley Athletic	3-1	n/a	1-1	n/a	n/a	0-2	0-2	1-4	2-3	1-2		n/a	n/a	n/a	2-3
Nunnery Wood Sports	n/a	n/a	n/a	n/a	n/a	n/a	n/a	n/a	n/a	n/a	3-4	*T*	n/a	n/a	n/a
University of Birmingham	2-2	0-0	2-0	8-0	3-1	3-1	4-1	2-0	4-1	0-2	11-0	n/a	*W*	3-1	1-0
Warwick Town	0-1	0-1	2-0	3-0	5-1	1-2	2-0	0-1	0-4	1-1	4-4	n/a	0-3	*O*	0-3
West Hagley	1-1	1-5	5-1	2-2	4-0	2-3	1-2	2-1	2-3	2-1	1-2	3-1	3-1	2-2	

Note – Nunnery Wood Sports withdrew during the course of the season
Their results are shown above but are expunged from the league table

Himley Athletic resigned but their results stand

Division Two		P	W	D	L	F	A	Pts
Bartley Green		26	17	7	2	67	26	58
University of Birmingham		25	16	5	4	69	24	53
Earlswood Town		26	14	7	5	47	27	49
Coton Green		26	11	9	6	47	42	42
Enville Athletic		26	11	5	10	58	54	38
Feckenham Res.		26	12	2	12	41	43	38
Droitwich Spa		25	10	5	10	31	30	35
Cadbury Athletic Res.		25	10	3	12	39	42	33
West Hagley	*-3*	26	9	6	11	51	50	30
Continental Star Res.		25	7	6	12	42	58	27
Castle Vale Res.		25	7	5	13	34	60	26
Chelmsley Town		25	6	5	14	45	64	23
Warwick Town		25	5	7	13	35	45	22
Himley Athletic		19	3	2	14	22	63	11

Nunnery Wood Sports – record expunged

Himley Athletic – resigned

CHALLENGE VASE

FIRST ROUND

Bartley Green 4 Feckenham Res. 2
Chelmsley Town (w/o) v Nunnery Wood Sports (scr.)
Continental Star Res. 2 Cadbury Athletic Res. 0
Coton Green (w/o) v Kenilworth Town KH Res. (scr.)
Droitwich Spa 0 **University of Birmingham** 1
Enville Athletic 4 Himley Athletic 3
Warwick Town 1 Castle Vale Res. 0
West Hagley 3 Earlswood Town 1

QUARTER-FINALS

Continental Star Res. 0 **Bartley Green** 2
Coton Green 5 West Hagley 1
Enville Athletic 2 Chelmsley Town 1
Warwick Town 0 **University of Birmingham** 8

SEMI-FINALS

(played over two legs)

Coton Green 2 Enville Athletic 1, **Enville Athletic** 3 Coton Green 1
University of Birmingham 0 Bartley Green 1, Bartley Green (scr.) v **University of Birmingham** (w/o)

FINAL

(April 29th at Pilkington XXX)

Enville Athletic 3 University of Birmingham 2

MIDLAND COMBINATION DIVISION TWO CONSTITUTION 2006-07

BIRMINGHAM ACADEMY .... Mile Flat Sports Ground, Mile Flat, Wall Heath, Kingswinford .... None
CADBURY ATHLETIC RESERVES ... Cadbury Recreation Ground, Bournville Lane, Bournville, Birmingham 0121 458 2000x3316
CHELMSLEY TOWN .... The Pavilions, Coleshill Road, Marston Green, Birmingham B37 7HW 0121 779 5400
CONTINENTAL STAR RESERVES .. Holly Lane Sports & Social Club, Holly Lane, Erdington B24 9LH 0121 373 0979
COTON GREEN .... New Mill Lane, Fazeley, Tamworth B78 3RX .... None
COVENTRY SPHINX RESERVES .. Sphinx Sports & Social Club, Siddeley Ave., Stoke Aldermoor, Coventry CV3 1WA 024 7645 1361
DROITWICH SPA .... Droitwich Spa Leisure Centre, Briar Mill, Droitwich WR9 8UE 07360 561091
EARLSWOOD TOWN .... The Pavilions, Malthouse Lane, Earlswood, Solihull B94 5DX 01564 703989
ENVILLE ATHLETIC .... Enville Athletic Club, Hall Drive, Enville, Stourbridge DY7 5HB 01384 872368
FECKENHAM RESERVES .... The Playing Fields, The Square, Mill Lane, Feckenham B96 6HY 01527 892611
PERRYWOOD .... Neel Park, Droitwich Road, Perdiswell, Worcester WR3 7SN 01905 756617
WARWICK TOWN .... Ajax Park, Hampton Road, Warwick CV34 6HX 01926 496295
WERNLEY ATHLETIC .... Oldbury Leisure Centre, Newbury Lane, Oldbury, Warley B69 1HE 0121 552 4497
WORCESTER CITY RESERVES .. Worcester City Football Development Ground, Bilford Road, Worcester WR3 8QA 07778 216579

IN: Coventry Sphinx Reserves (P), Handsworth United (now Birmingham Academy) (R), Perrywood (P), Wernley Athletic (N), Worcester City Reserves (P)

OUT: Bartley Green (P), Castle Vale Reserves (now Castle Vale JKS) (R), Himley Athletic (WS), Kenilworth Town KH Reserves (WN), Nunnery Wood Sports (WS), University of Birmingham (P), West Hagley (W)

	Barnt Green Spartak Res.	Bolehall Swifts Res.	Chelmsley Town Res.	Coleshill Town Res.	Coventry Sphinx Res.	Droitwich Spa Res.	Ettington Res.	Greenhill	Halesowen Town Res.	Heather Athletic Res.	Knowle Res.	Northfield Town Res.	Perrywood	Shipston Excelsior	Wellesbourne	Worcester City Res.
Barnt Green Spartak Res.		n/a	2-1	1-2	2-2	5-2	1-1	4-3	3-2	2-1	1-0	2-1	3-2	2-0	4-0	1-2
Bolehall Swifts Res.	0-15	*D*	n/a	n/a	n/a	n/a	n/a	n/a	n/a	n/a	n/a	n/a	n/a	n/a	n/a	n/a
Chelmsley Town Res.	2-2	n/a	*I*	0-1	0-3	1-2	0-0	1-4	2-4	0-1	2-2	0-1	3-5	2-1	1-4	0-3
Coleshill Town Res.	1-3	n/a	3-0	*V*	0-1	0-0	4-1	1-0	1-1	0-0	3-2	2-2	2-1	6-2	1-1	5-0
Coventry Sphinx Res.	0-2	n/a	4-0	0-1	*I*	4-0	8-1	0-1	0-3	3-0	6-0	4-2	2-2	2-2	5-0	0-0
Droitwich Spa Res.	3-1	7-1	4-2	3-1	0-5	*S*	4-2	2-1	0-1	1-1	1-5	3-4	1-3	7-2	6-5	1-4
Ettington Res.	1-3	3-1	0-0	0-1	1-3	1-4	*I*	1-2	2-3	2-2	1-1	3-2	1-2	0-1	8-2	1-1
Greenhill	2-3	n/a	4-3	3-2	0-4	0-1	W-L	*O*	1-0	0-2	1-0	2-1	2-3	3-1	3-1	0-1
Halesowen Town Res.	1-0	n/a	1-0	3-3	1-1	4-0	4-1	3-3	*N*	4-0	7-2	8-1	0-0	6-0	9-0	0-1
Heather Athletic Res.	2-2	3-1	1-1	0-2	0-2	1-1	4-2	1-2	0-4		1-1	3-1	0-3	0-1	1-0	0-4
Knowle Res.	2-0	n/a	1-0	1-1	0-4	2-1	3-0	1-2	1-4	2-1	*T*	3-1	1-5	3-3	4-0	3-1
Northfield Town Res.	4-0	n/a	4-0	1-2	0-3	0-2	7-1	0-3	1-0	0-0	1-2	*H*	2-4	3-3	1-1	0-6
Perrywood	0-1	n/a	5-0	1-0	1-1	1-1	5-0	4-2	2-2	1-0	3-2	1-0	*R*	3-1	2-1	2-1
Shipston Excelsior	1-4	n/a	5-2	3-2	1-4	1-1	2-2	0-2	0-3	0-1	4-2	2-1	4-1	*E*	2-0	2-0
Wellesbourne	1-3	n/a	0-4	0-3	1-5	4-0	4-4	1-2	0-3	1-2	0-2	1-2	1-3	3-1	*E*	0-2
Worcester City Res.	2-1	n/a	4-0	4-3	1-3	1-1	1-1	1-1	0-3	1-0	3-2	3-0	2-1	0-2	5-3	

Note – Bolehall Swifts Res. withdrew during the course of the season
Their results are shown above but are expunged from the league table

Division Three		P	W	D	L	F	A	Pts
Halesowen Town Res.		28	18	6	4	84	25	60
Coventry Sphinx Res.		28	18	6	4	79	22	60
Perrywood		28	18	5	5	66	36	59
Barnt Green Spartak Res.		28	17	4	7	58	41	55
Worcester City Res.		28	16	5	7	54	36	53
Greenhill		28	16	2	10	49	42	50
Coleshill Town Res.		28	14	7	7	53	34	49
Droitwich Spa Res.		28	11	6	11	52	62	39
Knowle Res.		28	11	5	12	50	57	38
Shipston Excelsior		28	10	5	13	47	65	35
Heather Athletic Res.		28	7	8	13	25	43	29
Northfield Town Res.		28	7	4	17	43	64	25
Wellesbourne		28	3	3	22	35	88	12
Chelmsley Town Res.		28	2	5	21	27	71	11
Ettington Res.	*-6*	28	2	9	17	38	74	9

Bolehall Swifts Res. – record expunged

CHALLENGE URN

FIRST ROUND

Chelmsley Town Res. 1 **Halesowen Town Res.** 2
Coleshill Town Res. 2 Perrywood 0
Droitwich Spa Res. 3 Heather Athletic Res. 2
Greenhill 0 **Worcester City Res.** 1
Knowle Res. 4 Barnt Green Spartak Res. 2
Northfield Town Res. 3 **Ettington Res.** 4
Shipston Excelsior (w/o) v Bolehall Swifts Res. (scr.)
Wellesbourne 1 **Coventry Sphinx Res.** 1 *aet* (4-5p)

QUARTER-FINALS

Coleshill Town Res. 2 **Halesowen Town Res.** 2 *aet* (3-4p)
Coventry Sphinx Res. 2 Worcester City Res. 1
Ettington Res. 3 Droitwich Spa Res. 1
Knowle Res. 1 **Shipston Excelsior** 4

SEMI-FINALS

(played over two legs)

Coventry Sphinx Res. 2 Halesowen Town Res. 2, Halesowen Town Res. (scr.) v **Coventry Sphinx Res.** (w/o)
Ettington Res. 0 Shipston Excelsior 1, Shipston Excelsior (scr.) v **Ettington Res.** (w/o)

FINAL

(May 2nd at Studley)

Coventry Sphinx Res. 0 Ettington Res. 0 *aet* (8-7p)

MIDLAND COMBINATION DIVISION THREE CONSTITUTION 2006-07

BNJS MANN & CO . . . . Coneygre Arts Centre, Sedgley Road East, Tipton DY4 8UH 0121 557 3585
BURNTWOOD TOWN RESERVES . . . . . Memorial Ground, Rugeley Road, Burntwood WS7 9BE 07946 269153
CASTLE VALE JKS . . . . Vale Stadium, Farnborough Road, Castle Vale, Warwick, Birmingham B35 7DA 0121 747 6969
CHELMSLEY TOWN RESERVES . . The Pavilions, Coleshill Road, Marston Green, Birmingham B37 7HW 0121 779 5400
DOSTHILL COLTS . . . . Bolehall Swifts FC, Rene Road, Bolehall, Tamworth B77 3NN 01827 62637
DROITWICH SPA RESERVES . . . . . . Droitwich Spa Leisure Centre, Briar Mill, Droitwich WR9 8UE 07360 561091
ETTINGTON RESERVES . . . . . Community Centre, Rogers Lane, Ettington, Stratford-upon-Avon CV37 7SX . . . . None
GREENHILL . . . . Cradley Town FC, Beeches View Avenue, Cradley, Halesowen B63 2HB 01384 569658
HEATHER ATHLETIC RESERVES . . . . . . St John's Park, Ravenstone Road, Heather LE67 2QJ 01530 263986
KENILWORTH TOWN KH RESERVES . . . Gypsy Lane, off Rouncil Lane, Kenilworth CV8 1FQ 01926 850851
KNOWLE RESERVES . . . . Hampton Road, Knowle, Solihull B93 0NX 01564 779807
NORTHFIELD TOWN RESERVES . . . . Shenley Lane, Northfield, Birmingham B29 4HZ 0121 478 3900/475 3870
SHIPSTON EXCELSIOR . . . . Shipston Sports Club, London Road, Shipston-on-Stour CV36 4EP 01608 661139
STUDLEY ATHLETIC . . . . Studley Sports & Social Club, Eldorado Close, Studley B80 7HP 01527 852671

IN: BNJS Mann & Co (N), Burntwood Town Reserves (N), Castle Vale Reserves (now Castle Vale JKS) (R), Dosthill Colts (N), Kenilworth Town KH Reserves (N), Studley Athletic (N)

OUT: Barnt Green Spartak Reserves (W), Bolehall Swifts Reserves (WS), Coleshill Town Reserves (W), Coventry Sphinx Reserves (P), Halesowen Town Reserves (W), Perrywood (P), Worcester City Reserves (P)

NORTH BERKS LEAGUE

	Ardington & Lockinge	Blewbury	Coleshill United	Drayton	East Hendred	Faringdon Town	Grove Rangers	Harwell International	Lambourn Sports	Marcham	Saxton Rovers	Steventon
Ardington & Lockinge	*D*	4-2	3-2	5-2	2-1	2-0	2-2	1-0	0-2	4-1	2-2	1-1
Blewbury	2-2	*I*	2-5	2-0	0-3	2-2	2-2	4-2	2-6	5-1	2-1	3-2
Coleshill United	2-3	7-0	*V*	3-4	2-1	5-1	0-0	4-2	6-5	4-4	2-1	2-2
Drayton	3-1	6-1	0-1	*I*	2-0	2-0	2-2	1-0	1-1	5-2	2-1	4-2
East Hendred	0-3	4-2	0-1	0-2	*S*	1-0	2-3	2-1	0-1	0-0	4-1	1-2
Faringdon Town	0-0	1-0	3-1	1-2	4-0	*I*	3-1	2-1	1-0	2-1	3-1	2-1
Grove Rangers	1-2	1-2	1-2	0-1	3-2	0-4	*O*	3-2	2-3	2-0	0-1	2-3
Harwell International	0-1	1-0	1-3	1-4	3-3	2-5	2-1	*N*	0-1	0-1	1-1	4-1
Lambourn Sports	1-0	4-0	3-0	6-3	4-1	3-2	4-0	4-1		W-L	1-3	4-2
Marcham	1-2	2-2	1-4	0-5	5-2	1-0	1-0	1-0	1-4	*O*	0-2	5-2
Saxton Rovers	0-3	3-1	0-3	1-2	2-0	0-2	1-3	2-1	1-0	1-1	*N*	2-3
Steventon	1-3	4-1	4-4	1-1	1-2	0-2	3-0	0-2	5-7	1-1	0-3	*E*

Division One	P	W	D	L	F	A	Pts
Lambourn Sports	22	17	1	4	64	31	52
Drayton	22	15	3	4	54	31	48
Ardington & Lockinge	22	14	5	3	46	26	47
Coleshill United	22	13	4	5	63	41	43
Faringdon Town	22	13	2	7	40	26	41
Saxton Rovers	22	8	3	11	30	36	27
Marcham	22	6	5	11	30	47	23
Blewbury	22	6	4	12	37	63	22
Steventon	22	5	5	12	41	56	20
East Hendred	22	6	2	14	29	44	20
Grove Rangers	22	5	4	13	29	44	19
Harwell International	22	4	2	16	27	45	14

NORTH BERKS LEAGUE DIVISION ONE CONSTITUTION 2006-07

ARDINGTON & LOCKINGE . . . . White Road, Ardington, Wantage . . . . None
BLEWBURY . . . . Bohams Road, Blewbury, Didcot OX11 9QF . . . . None
COLESHILL UNITED . . . . Bottom of the Hill, Coleshill . . . . None
DRAYTON . . . . Recreation Ground, Lockway, Drayton, Abingdon OX14 4LG . . . . None
EAST HENDRED . . . . Hendred Sports & Social Club, Mill Lane, East Hendred OX12 8JS . . . . None
FARINGDON TOWN . . . . Tucker Park, Park Road, Faringdon SN7 7BP 01235 821008
GROVE RANGERS . . . . Recreation Ground, Cane Lane, Grove, Wantage OX12 0AA 01367 241759
LAMBOURN SPORTS . . . . Bockhampton Road, Lambourn, Hungerford RG17 8PS . . . . None
MARCHAM . . . . Moreland Road, Marcham, Abingdon OX13 6PY 01488 72214
SAXTON ROVERS . . . . Recreation Ground, Caldecott Road, Abingdon OX14 5ET . . . . None
STEVENTON . . . . Steventon Green, Milton Lane, Steventon, Abingdon OX13 6SA . . . . None
WALLINGFORD ATHLETIC . . . . The Recreation Ground, Brightwell-cum-Sotwell, Wallingford . . . . None

IN: Wallingford Athletic (formerly AFC Wallingford 'A') (P)
OUT: Harwell International (R)

NORTH BERKS CUP

FIRST ROUND

Appleton Abingdon 7 Warborough & Shillingford 1
Ardington & Lockinge 1 **Faringdon Town** 3
Bampton & Buckland 0 **Blewbury** 10
Botley United 2 Didcot Casuals 1
Crowmarsh & Gifford 1 **Steventon** 2
Drayton 4 Long Wittenham Athletic 1
Grove Rangers 5 Benson Lions 1
Hagbourne United 1 **Benson** 3
Kingsclere 0 **Challow United** 6
Lambourn Sports 2 Marcham 1 *aet*
Saxton Rovers 4 Harwell Village 0
Stanford-in-the-Vale 4 Hanney United 3
Sutton Courtenay 1 **Harwell International** 4
Uffington United 1 **Northcroft** 3
Wootton & Dry Sandford 3 East Hendred 0

SECOND ROUND

Appleton Abingdon 5 Blewbury 2
Benson 1 **Harwell International** 5
Challow United 0 **Grove Rangers** 7
Drayton 4 Coleshill United 2
Lambourn Sports 4 Faringdon Town 3
Northcroft 2 **Steventon** 3
Saxton Rovers 1 Wootton & Dry Sandford 0
Stanford-in-the-Vale 2 Botley United 1

QUARTER-FINALS

Appleton Abingdon 0 **Drayton** 1
Harwell International 2 Grove Rangers 0
Lambourn Sports 5 Stanford-in-the-Vale 1
Saxton Rovers 2 Steventon 1

SEMI-FINALS

Drayton 2 Harwell International 1
(at Lambourn Sports)
Lambourn Sports 2 Saxton Rovers 0
(at Ardington & Lockinge)

FINAL

(April 29th at Abingdon United)
Lambourn Sports 2 Drayton 2 *aet* (4-3p)

CHARITY SHIELD

FIRST ROUND
Ardington & Lockinge 3 Stanford-in-the-Vale 1
Bampton & Buckland 1 **Steventon** 7
Benson Lions 1 **Marcham** 5
Botley United 5 Long Wittenham Ath 1
Challow United 1 **Sutton Courtenay** 3
Coleshill United 4 Blewbury 2
Didcot Casuals 3 **Kingsclere** 5
Drayton 2 East Hendred 0
Grove Rangers 2 Uffington United 0
Hanney United (w/o) v Appleton Abingdon (scr.)
Harwell International 1 Faringdon Tn 0
Northcroft 2 Crowmarsh Gifford 1
Saxton Rovers 2 Benson 1
Warborough & Shillingford 2 Hagbourne United 1
Wootton & Dry Sandford 0 **Lambourn Sports** 5

SECOND ROUND
Ardington & Lockinge 4 Marcham 0
Botley United 4 Hanney United 0
Coleshill United 2 **Grove Rangers** 3
Harwell International 2 **Drayton** 3
Harwell Village 2 Warborough & Shillingford 0
Kingsclere 1 **Steventon** 5
Lambourn Sports 7 Northcroft 1
Sutton Courtenay 2 Saxton Rovers 0

QUARTER-FINALS
Grove Rangers 0 **Botley United** 1
Harwell Village 1 **Drayton** 2
Lambourn Sports 2 Ardington & Lockinge 1
Sutton Courtenay 2 Steventon 4
(Steventon expelled)

SEMI-FINAL
Lambourn Sports 2 Botley United 0
(at Faringdon Town)
Sutton Courtenay 0 **Drayton** 5
(at Saxton Rovers)

FINAL
(May 13th at Wantage Town)
Lambourn Sports 1 Drayton 0

Division Two	P	W	D	L	F	A	Pts
AFC Wallingford 'A'	22	19	0	3	79	20	57
Shrivenham 'A'	22	16	1	5	70	32	49
Appleton Abingdon	22	14	2	6	58	34	44
Kintbury Rangers Res.	22	13	2	7	59	32	41
Sutton Courtenay	22	12	1	9	44	37	37
Harwell Village	22	11	2	9	55	49	35
Bampton & Buckland	22	10	1	11	47	55	31
Saxton Rovers Res.	22	7	1	14	32	64	22
Benson	22	6	3	13	43	65	21
Northcroft	22	6	2	14	42	64	20
Long Wittenham Athletic	22	6	1	15	42	87	19
Lambourn Sports Res.	22	3	2	17	25	57	11

Division Three	P	W	D	L	F	A	Pts
Wootton & Dry Sandford	24	21	2	1	82	9	65
Blewbury Res.	24	14	7	3	54	32	49
Stanford-in-the-Vale	24	13	3	8	51	34	42
Faringdon Town Res.	24	11	5	8	46	33	38
Didcot Casuals	24	11	5	8	59	47	38
Benson Lions	24	12	1	11	55	42	37
Ardington & Lockinge Res.	24	9	5	10	46	41	32
Kingsclere	24	9	4	11	39	43	31
Marcham Res.	24	8	2	14	25	46	26
Drayton Res.	24	8	1	15	32	72	25
Warborough & Shillingford	24	6	6	12	35	57	24
East Hendred Res.	24	6	5	13	34	51	23
Hagbourne United	24	4	2	18	20	71	14

Division Four	P	W	D	L	F	A	Pts
Coleshill United Res.	22	19	1	2	81	19	58
Crowmarsh Gifford	22	17	2	3	59	19	53
Challow United	22	15	2	5	76	41	47
Botley United	22	14	3	5	64	34	45
Uffington United	22	11	5	6	66	46	38
Hanney United	22	6	6	10	44	52	24
Grove Rangers Res.	22	7	3	12	40	62	24
Harwell International Res.	22	5	6	11	40	51	21
Bampton & Buckland Res.	22	6	3	13	29	59	21
Stanford-in-the-Vale Res.	22	5	4	13	40	58	19
Long Wittenham Athletic Res.	22	4	4	14	22	61	16
Sutton Courtenay Res.	22	2	3	17	34	93	9

Division Five	P	W	D	L	F	A	Pts
Wootton & Dry Sandford Res.	20	16	3	1	68	18	51
Steventon Res.	20	13	1	6	58	44	40
Uffington United Res.	20	11	4	5	53	34	37
Benson Res.	20	10	5	5	52	25	35
Coleshill United 'A'	20	9	5	6	40	40	32
Didcot Casuals Res.	20	9	4	7	53	39	31
Faringdon Town 'A'	19	7	2	10	25	27	23
Hanney United Res.	19	6	2	11	30	38	20
Harwell Village Res.	20	6	0	14	44	73	18
Challow United Res.	20	4	3	13	30	64	15
Hagbourne United Res.	20	3	1	16	23	74	10

Faringdon Town 'A' v Hanney United Res. not played

WAR MEMORIAL CUP

FINAL
(April 21st at Wantage Town)
Appleton Abingdon 2 Wootton & Dry Sandford 1

A G KINGHAM CUP

FINAL
(April 8th at Abingdon United)
Kintbury Rangers Res. 5 Shrivenham 'A' 0

LEAGUE CUP

FINAL
(April 1st at Milton United)
Bampton & Buckland Res. 3 Benson Res. 0

NAIRNE PAUL CUP

FINAL
(April 29th at AFC Wallingford)
AFC Wallingford 'A' 2 Blewbury Res. 0

NORTH WEST COUNTIES LEAGUE

	Abbey Hey	Alsager Town	Atherton C.	Atherton LR	Bacup Borough	Cammell Laird	Colne	Congleton Town	Curzon Ashton	Formby	Glossop N End	Maine Road	Nantwich Town	Newcastle Tn	Ramsbottom U	Salford City	Silsdens	Skelmersdale U	Squires Gate	St Helens Town	Stone Dominoes	Trafford
Abbey Hey		0-0	3-2	3-1	0-0	0-4	1-4	2-3	2-2	2-2	4-1	2-1	0-5	2-1	1-3	0-1	3-0	3-1	1-1	2-1	3-1	2-1
Alsager Town	3-0		3-1	4-1	1-0	0-1	0-1	4-0	2-1	2-1	4-2	3-1	2-0	0-4	2-2	5-1	3-1	1-1	1-0	0-1	4-2	1-1
Atherton Collieries	0-3	1-4		2-2	2-1	1-4	1-3	0-2	2-1	3-0	2-3	1-1	0-1	2-2	1-0	0-2	3-3	0-8	1-1	0-2	0-0	2-3
Atherton LR	0-4	1-2	1-5		0-5	0-9	0-1	1-4	2-4	3-3	0-0	0-2	0-3	0-8	1-0	0-0	0-1	1-0	1-2	0-2	3-0	0-2
Bacup Borough	2-1	0-2	2-1	0-0		1-3	1-3	0-0	2-2	3-1	2-1	0-2	1-4	0-3	2-0	0-2	2-0	0-4	0-1	0-2	3-2	0-0
Cammell Laird	4-1	1-1	1-0	3-0	1-2	*D*	4-3	3-0	3-0	7-1	2-0	3-2	2-0	2-4	4-2	4-2	1-0	1-1	5-1	3-1	10-0	3-2
Colne	4-0	1-4	3-0	2-3	2-0	2-3	*I*	2-0	1-0	4-2	6-0	2-3	2-3	1-1	2-1	1-2	2-1	4-1	3-1	3-2	0-1	0-4
Congleton Town	2-0	2-1	2-0	1-1	2-1	0-2	3-2	*V*	0-1	6-4	0-2	0-1	0-0	0-0	1-2	1-2	1-2	1-1	0-1	1-3	0-1	2-1
Curzon Ashton	2-1	3-1	4-1	4-3	3-1	1-4	5-0	0-1	*I*	1-0	2-1	2-2	1-5	1-0	2-1	2-2	0-1	1-0	1-1	2-0	4-0	1-3
Formby	0-1	1-4	2-0	1-1	1-2	0-2	1-6	0-2	4-1	*S*	2-2	2-3	0-3	1-4	0-1	0-2	0-2	0-5	0-1	0-1	3-1	1-1
Glossop North End	1-1	0-2	2-0	1-2	1-1	1-4	0-1	1-2	1-2	2-0	*I*	2-2	0-5	0-3	1-1	2-4	3-1	2-1	2-0	3-3	5-2	1-1
Maine Road	1-1	1-0	1-1	3-1	1-0	1-3	2-0	1-2	1-2	1-0	2-2	*O*	0-4	0-1	3-0	0-4	1-3	0-1	4-0	1-2	3-0	2-0
Nantwich Town	3-1	0-2	4-1	7-0	2-0	0-2	1-0	1-1	5-0	1-0	2-1	1-1	*N*	3-1	3-0	1-0	2-0	1-2	1-2	2-1	5-0	3-0
Newcastle Town	0-0	0-1	4-1	4-2	2-1	1-2	2-0	5-2	3-1	3-0	1-2	0-1	2-0		1-1	2-2	3-2	1-2	1-1	4-4	6-1	1-1
Ramsbottom United	2-2	1-1	1-1	1-0	2-2	1-0	2-3	2-1	1-1	1-2	0-3	1-1	0-3	1-3	*O*	2-2	2-0	2-0	0-0	0-0	1-1	1-0
Salford City	3-1	0-1	2-0	4-0	2-1	0-1	1-1	2-0	2-4	4-0	2-0	1-1	1-1	1-0	1-1	*N*	3-2	2-2	0-1	1-2	6-0	3-2
Silsden	2-1	2-2	4-0	3-0	1-1	1-5	1-2	1-1	2-3	6-3	1-1	2-1	2-1	1-3	0-0	0-1	*E*	1-5	5-2	4-2	3-0	2-2
Skelmersdale United	3-3	6-1	1-1	6-2	2-0	2-1	2-0	3-0	2-1	1-1	0-2	3-1	4-1	5-1	2-1	2-1	4-1		4-0	6-1	9-0	5-3
Squires Gate	2-1	0-2	5-0	1-2	3-1	0-3	0-0	0-0	0-0	1-1	1-0	0-0	2-2	2-5	1-1	1-3	1-1	0-1		1-1	3-0	2-1
St Helens Town	1-1	1-4	0-1	2-2	0-2	1-3	6-1	1-2	2-0	2-1	2-1	2-1	2-0	2-1	2-0	0-2	3-2	2-5	1-0		2-1	1-0
Stone Dominoes	0-2	0-6	0-2	4-0	0-1	0-3	1-3	2-1	0-3	3-2	3-5	2-7	1-2	0-6	3-3	0-1	1-7	2-4	1-1	3-3		0-3
Trafford	0-0	0-1	2-1	2-3	0-1	0-0	4-3	4-1	1-1	4-0	2-2	0-2	0-0	1-0	1-1	2-2	1-2	1-2	5-0	2-1	8-0	

Division One		P	W	D	L	F	A	Pts
Cammell Laird	*-6*	42	35	3	4	126	36	102
Skelmersdale United		42	28	7	7	119	48	91
Alsager Town		42	27	7	8	87	43	88
Nantwich Town		42	26	6	10	91	37	84
Salford City		42	23	10	9	79	46	79
Newcastle Town		42	21	9	12	97	52	72
Curzon Ashton		42	20	8	14	72	66	68
St Helens Town		42	20	7	15	70	68	67
Colne	*-6*	42	22	3	17	84	70	63
Maine Road		42	17	10	15	65	56	61
Abbey Hey		42	14	12	16	61	70	54
Congleton Town		42	15	8	19	50	63	53
Squires Gate		42	12	15	15	43	62	51
Silsden	*-6*	42	16	8	18	76	75	50
Trafford	*-3*	42	13	13	16	71	56	49
Glossop North End		42	12	11	19	62	78	47
Bacup Borough		42	13	8	21	44	62	47
Ramsbottom United		42	9	18	15	45	60	45
Atherton Collieries		42	7	9	26	43	93	30
Atherton LR		42	7	8	27	40	115	29
Stone Dominoes		42	5	5	32	39	146	20
Formby		42	4	7	31	43	105	19

NORTH WEST COUNTIES LEAGUE DIVISION ONE CONSTITUTION 2006-07

ABBEY HEY .... Abbey Stadium, Goredale Avenue, Gorton M18 7HD 0161 231 7147
ATHERTON COLLIERIES .... Alder House, Alder Street, Atherton M46 9EY 07729 374641
ATHERTON LR .... Crilly Park, Spa Road, Atherton M46 9XX 01942 883950
BACUP BOROUGH .... West View, Cowfoot Lane, Blackthorn, Bacup OL13 8EE 01706 878655
COLNE .... Holt House Stadium, Harrison Drive, Colne BB8 9SE 01282 862545
CONGLETON TOWN .... Booth Street Ground, off Crescent Road, Congleton CW12 4DG 01260 274460
CURZON ASHTON .... The Tameside Stadium, Richmond Street, Ashton-under-Lyne OL7 9HG 0161 330 6033
FC UNITED OF MANCHESTER .... Bury FC, Gigg Lane, Bury BL9 9HR 0161 764 4881
FLIXTON .... Valley Road, Flixton, Manchester M41 8RQ 0161 747 7757
FORMBY .... Altcar Road, Formby L37 8DL 01704 833505
GLOSSOP NORTH END .... Arthur Goldthorpe Stadium, Surrey Street, Glossop SK13 7AJ 01457 855469
MAINE ROAD .... Manchester County FA Ground, Branthingham Road, Chorlton-cum-Hardy M21 0TT 0161 881 0299
NANTWICH TOWN .... Jackson Avenue, Nantwich CW5 6LL 01270 621771
NELSON .... Victoria Park, Lomeshaye Way, Nelson BB9 7AF 01282 613820
NEWCASTLE TOWN .. Lyme Valley Parkway Stadium, Buckmaster Ave., Clayton, Newcastle-under-Lyne ST5 3BF 01782 662351
RAMSBOTTOM UNITED .... Riverside Ground, Acre Bottom, Ramsbottom BL8 3JH 01706 822799
SALFORD CITY .... Moor Lane, Kersal, Salford M7 3PZ 0161 792 6287
SILSDEN .... Keighley Cougars RFC, Cougar Park, Hard Ings, Keighley BD21 3RF 01535 213111
SQUIRES GATE .... School Road, Marton, Blackpool FY4 3DS 01253 798584
ST HELENS TOWN .... St Helens RLFC, Knowsley Road, Dunriding Lane, St Helens WA10 4AD 08707 565252
STONE DOMINOES .... Springbank Park, Yarnfield Road, Stone ST15 0NF 01782 761891
TRAFFORD .... Shawe View, Pennybridge Lane, Flixton, Urmston M41 5DL 0161 747 1727

IN: FC United of Manchester (P), Flixton (P), Nelson (P)

OUT: Alsager Town (P – Northern Premier League Division One), Cammell Laird (P – Northern Premier League Division One), Skelmersdale United (P – Northern Premier League Division One)

	Ashton Town	Blackpool Mechanics	Castleton Gabriels	Chadderton	Cheadle Town	Daisy Hill	Darwen	Eccleshall	FC United of Manchester	Flixton	Great Harwood Town	Holker Old Boys	Leek CSOB	Nelson	New Mills	Norton United	Oldham Town	Padiham	Winsford United
Ashton Town		0-4	2-0	2-1	0-1	3-2	2-2	4-3	0-4	2-1	1-2	2-1	4-2	0-2	1-0	1-1	1-0	2-4	1-0
Blackpool Mechanics	1-3		4-3	2-1	0-1	0-0	3-2	1-2	2-4	0-2	1-0	2-2	1-0	1-2	2-0	0-0	0-0	3-1	2-0
Castleton Gabriels	1-1	3-2		1-4	1-2	1-2	4-3	0-1	0-3	2-6	0-6	1-4	1-2	3-7	0-5	1-4	0-1	0-1	1-3
Chadderton	1-3	2-2	4-2	*D*	0-3	1-0	2-0	1-0	2-3	0-0	2-2	1-1	1-0	2-2	1-2	4-3	3-1	1-4	0-1
Cheadle Town	0-0	2-0	6-0	1-2	*I*	0-2	1-2	2-0	3-3	0-4	2-3	3-4	4-1	1-2	1-0	0-0	0-2	3-3	0-1
Daisy Hill	0-3	0-0	1-1	1-2	1-2	*V*	1-0	1-4	0-3	2-5	0-2	3-2	2-0	1-2	2-3	2-1	0-3	1-2	1-1
Darwen	0-2	3-1	3-1	2-1	1-2	3-2	*I*	1-2	1-2	1-2	2-1	3-1	2-1	0-1	5-0	0-1	2-1	1-4	2-3
Eccleshall	3-1	1-2	5-1	2-0	0-3	2-0	1-0	*S*	0-0	1-1	1-2	3-1	1-2	1-1	1-2	2-0	1-1	1-3	2-2
FC United of Manchester	2-1	4-2	10-2	4-0	1-1	6-0	2-0	7-1	*I*	1-2	0-1	4-1	8-1	5-0	6-1	1-2	1-0	3-2	2-1
Flixton	3-2	2-0	4-2	1-1	4-1	2-2	2-0	6-0	1-1	*O*	1-2	5-0	5-1	2-3	2-0	1-1	6-1	2-1	3-0
Great Harwood Town	1-2	0-0	1-1	3-0	2-0	2-3	3-2	2-0	1-1	1-2	*N*	1-0	0-0	3-5	0-0	1-0	0-0	1-0	0-1
Holker Old Boys	2-2	2-1	6-0	1-2	3-1	2-1	2-0	1-1	0-2	0-0	2-1		3-2	3-3	3-1	2-0	2-2	0-1	0-4
Leek CSOB	1-1	5-0	2-0	1-3	2-4	2-2	0-0	0-0	2-5	1-4	0-1	5-1		0-2	2-0	1-2	0-2	1-1	3-2
Nelson	3-2	0-3	3-0	4-1	1-0	3-1	3-2	7-2	1-3	1-2	1-2	5-0	3-1	*T*	4-0	2-2	1-3	1-0	2-1
New Mills	0-3	1-1	3-1	1-0	1-1	3-0	1-0	0-1	0-2	0-5	1-0	1-1	5-4	1-2	*W*	1-1	3-1	2-2	2-1
Norton United	0-2	0-0	1-0	1-1	4-3	1-0	0-2	4-1	1-3	0-1	0-0	2-1	2-1	1-1	1-1	*O*	2-1	2-1	2-2
Oldham Town	4-1	1-1	3-2	0-2	0-1	3-1	3-0	1-0	0-1	0-1	0-2	2-1	3-2	2-0	1-4	2-1		1-1	0-1
Padiham	4-1	1-2	3-1	4-0	1-0	3-1	1-0	2-3	1-2	5-3	2-0	4-2	6-2	0-2	1-0	1-2	2-1		1-2
Winsford United	1-1	1-2	4-1	2-2	2-0	2-0	2-0	2-1	2-2	2-0	0-2	3-1	1-1	2-0	3-1	4-0	3-0	3-3	

Division Two		P	W	D	L	F	A	Pts
FC United of Manchester		36	27	6	3	111	35	87
Flixton		36	24	7	5	93	37	79
Nelson		36	23	5	8	82	53	74
Winsford United		36	19	8	9	65	41	65
Padiham		36	19	5	12	76	52	62
Great Harwood Town		36	18	8	10	51	33	62
Ashton Town		36	17	7	12	59	57	58
Norton United		36	13	12	11	45	47	51
Blackpool Mechanics		36	13	10	13	48	51	49
Oldham Town		36	14	6	16	46	49	48
Eccleshall		36	13	7	16	50	64	46
New Mills		36	13	7	16	46	62	46
Chadderton	*-3*	36	13	8	15	51	62	44
Cheadle Town	*-6*	36	14	6	16	55	53	42
Holker Old Boys		36	11	8	17	58	74	41
Darwen		36	11	2	23	47	61	35
Leek CSOB		36	7	7	22	51	82	28
Daisy Hill		36	7	6	23	38	75	27
Castleton Gabriels	*-8*	36	2	3	31	38	122	1

Reserve Division		P	W	D	L	F	A	Pts
Formby Res.		32	25	3	4	72	21	78
Nantwich Town Res.		31	21	6	4	94	40	69
Skelmersdale United Res.		32	21	5	6	79	32	68
Padiham Res.		32	20	4	8	77	46	64
Flixton Res.		32	18	4	10	75	44	58
New Mills Res.		32	15	6	11	73	47	51
Colne Res.	*-6*	31	15	4	12	70	58	43
Nelson Res.		30	12	4	14	65	59	40
Darwen Res.	*-3*	29	12	5	12	68	72	38
Winsford United Res.		32	11	5	16	54	64	38
Squires Gate Res.	*-6*	31	12	7	12	58	72	37
Blackpool Mechanics Res.		32	10	5	17	60	81	35
Daisy Hill Res.	*-4*	32	11	5	16	75	65	34
Chadderton Res.	*-3*	31	10	5	16	57	75	32
Atherton LR Res.		32	6	3	23	34	104	21
Ashton Town Res.	*-3*	32	4	6	22	57	95	15
Bacup Borough Res.	*-4*	29	3	3	23	31	124	8

Bacup Borough Res. v Colne Res., Bacup Borough Res. v Darwen Res., Chadderton Res. v Darwen Res., Nantwich Town Res. v Darwen Res., Nelson Res. v Bacup Borough Res. and Nelson Res. v Squires Gate Res. not played

RESERVES CUP

FINAL *(May 24th at Nelson)*

Nelson Res. 1 Nantwich Town Res. 0

NORTH WEST COUNTIES LEAGUE DIVISION TWO CONSTITUTION 2006-07

ASHTON ATHLETIC .... Brocstedes Park, Farm Road, Ashton-in-Makerfield WN4 0NQ 01942 716360
ASHTON TOWN .... Edge Green Street, Ashton-in-Makerfield, Wigan WN4 8SL 01942 510677
BLACKPOOL MECHANICS .... Jepson Way, Common Edge Road, Blackpool FY4 5DY 01253 761721
BOOTLE .... New Bucks Park, Bootle, Liverpool 07866 912625
CASTLETON GABRIELS .... Butterworth Park, Heywood Road, Castleton, Rochdale OL11 3BY 01706 527103
CHADDERTON .... Andrew Street, Chadderton, Oldham OL9 0JT 0161 624 9733
CHEADLE TOWN .... Park Road Stadium, Park Road, Cheadle, Stockport SK8 2AN 0161 428 2510
DAISY HILL .... New Sirs, St James Street, Westhoughton, Bolton BL5 2EB 01942 818544
DARWEN .... Anchor Ground, Anchor Road, Darwen BB3 0BB 01254 705677
ECCLESHALL .... Pershall Park, Chester Road, Eccleshall ST21 6NE 01785 851351
HOLKER OLD BOYS .... Rakesmoor Lane, Hawcoat, Barrow-in-Furness LA14 4QB 01229 828176
LEEK CSOB .... Leek Town FC, Harrison Park, Macclesfield Road, Leek ST13 8LD 01538 399278
NEW MILLS .... Church Lane, Church Road, New Mills SK22 4NP 01663 747435
NORTON UNITED .... Norton CC & MW Institute, Community Drive, Smallthorne, Stoke-on-Trent ST6 1QF 01782 838290
OLDHAM TOWN .... Whitebank Stadium, Whitebank Road, Hollins, Oldham OL8 3JH 0161 624 2689
PADIHAM .... Arbories Memorial Sports Ground, Well Street, Padiham BB12 8LE 01282 773742
RUNCORN LINNETS .... Witton Albion FC, Wincham Park, Chapel Street, Wincham, Northwich CW9 6DA 01606 43008
WINSFORD UNITED .... Barton Stadium, Kingsway, Winsford CW7 3AE 01606 558447

IN: Ashton Athletic (P – Manchester League Division One), Bootle (P – Liverpool County Combination), Runcorn Linnets (N)
OUT: FC United of Manchester (P), Flixton (P), Great Harwood Town (F), Nelson (P)

LEAGUE CUP

FIRST ROUND

Blackpool Mechanics 3 Ashton Town 1
Cheadle Town 1 **FC United of Manchester** 5
(at Curzon Ashton)
Darwen 2 Chadderton 0
Flixton 4 Castleton Gabriels 1
Holker Old Boys 1 **Norton United** 2
Leek CSOB 2 Daisy Hill 0
Nelson 3 Eccleshall 2
New Mills 1 **Oldham Town** 7
Padiham 0 **Silsden** 1

SECOND ROUND

Abbey Hey 2 Skelmersdale United 1
Bacup Borough 1 **Salford City** 7 *(at Salford City)*
Blackpool Mechanics 0 **Ramsbottom United** 1
Cammell Laird 2 Winsford United 1
Colne 2 FC United of Manchester 1 *(at Accrington Stanley)*
Congleton Town 4 Nantwich Town 1
Curzon Ashton 4 Squires Gate 0 *(at Squires Gate)*
Darwen 0 **Alsager Town** 3
Flixton 2 Silsden 1
Glossop North End 1 Trafford 0
Great Harwood Town 2 **Atherton Collieries** 1
(Great Harwood Town expelled)
Nelson 2 Formby 0
Newcastle Town 2 **Leek CSOB** 3
Norton United 2 **Stone Dominoes** 4 *aet*
Oldham Town 3 Maine Road 1
St Helens Town 4 Atherton LR 1

THIRD ROUND

Abbey Hey 0 **Ramsbottom United** 1
Cammell Laird 14 Nelson 0
Colne 0 **Oldham Town** 1
Congleton Town 3 Leek CSOB 2
Curzon Ashton 3 Atherton Collieries 2
Glossop North End 2 Salford City 2 *aet*
Salford City 5 Glossop North End 2 *replay*
St Helens Town 1 **Alsager Town** 3
Stone Dominoes 0 **Flixton** 1

QUARTER-FINALS

Cammell Laird 4 Curzon Ashton 2 *aet*
Flixton 3 Congleton Town 1
Oldham Town 2 Alsager Town 1 *aet*
Ramsbottom United 1 **Salford City** 2

SEMI-FINALS

(played over two legs)
Cammell Laird 5 Flixton 0, Flixton 1 **Cammell Laird** 5
Oldham Town 1 Salford City 0, **Salford City** 2 Oldham Town 0

FINAL *(April 27th at Skelmersdale United)*
Salford City 3 Cammell Laird 2

DIVISION TWO TROPHY

FIRST ROUND

Nelson 0 Blackpool Mechanics 2 *(Blackpool Mechanics expelled)*
New Mills 2 Chadderton 1
Norton United 1 **Oldham Town** 2

SECOND ROUND

Ashton Town 2 Oldham Town 1
Castleton Gabriels 3 **Flixton** 4
Daisy Hill 2 Holker Old Boys 1
Darwen 2 **Cheadle Town** 0 *(Darwen expelled)*
Leek CSOB 0 **Winsford United** 5
Nelson 2 Eccleshall 1
New Mills 0 **FC United of Manchester** 5
Padiham 1 **Great Harwood Town** 3

QUARTER-FINALS

Ashton Town 3 Flixton 3 *aet*
Flixton 5 Ashton Town 0 *replay*
Cheadle Town 4 Great Harwood Town 3
FC United of Manchester 0 **Nelson** 1 *aet*
Winsford United 5 Daisy Hill 0

SEMI-FINALS

(played over two legs)
Cheadle Tn 1 Winsford Utd 3, **Winsford United** 2 Cheadle Tn 2
Flixton 2 Nelson 0, Nelson 1 **Flixton** 0

FINAL

(April 20th at Trafford)
Winsford United 1 **Flixton** 2

NORTHAMPTONSHIRE COMBINATION

	Caledonian Strip Mills	Corby Hellenic Fisher	Corby St Brendans	Crick Athletic	Harpole	Heyford Athletic	Kettering Nomads	Kislingbury	Milton	Moulton	Priors Marston	Roade	Rushden Rangers	Stanion United	Weedon
Caledonian Strip Mills		1-5	12-0	2-2	1-0	0-2	2-1	5-2	5-1	2-2	2-0	1-3	4-0	0-5	3-0
Corby Hellenic Fisher	5-1		6-2	6-0	0-3	2-1	2-2	3-4	1-2	1-2	1-1	4-1	4-1	3-0	5-0
Corby St Brendans	3-1	0-5	*P*	3-2	1-5	1-0	3-2	4-4	2-4	0-5	3-1	4-1	4-0	5-2	3-0
Crick Athletic	3-4	0-1	4-1	*R*	0-1	0-5	0-4	1-1	1-5	0-4	2-4	1-6	4-3	4-4	1-2
Harpole	1-3	1-1	3-1	1-0	*E*	0-0	4-0	3-1	3-1	2-0	4-0	2-0	1-3	2-1	5-1
Heyford Athletic	1-7	1-4	8-1	2-0	2-1	*M*	1-1	1-0	0-4	2-3	0-3	1-1	2-1	5-3	5-1
Kettering Nomads	2-1	1-1	2-1	0-0	0-3	1-0	*I*	0-1	2-4	0-1	0-0	0-2	2-5	1-2	3-1
Kislingbury	3-1	3-3	4-4	2-0	2-1	3-0	3-2	*E*	2-3	0-0	1-1	1-1	5-4	8-0	3-0
Milton	2-1	0-3	4-3	3-0	1-0	1-2	0-2	1-1	*R*	1-1	3-0	2-4	3-1	2-0	3-3
Moulton	0-1	0-3	4-3	1-0	1-0	2-0	2-0	1-1	0-1		3-0	4-0	3-3	3-2	2-1
Priors Marston	W-L	1-4	2-1	2-2	2-1	0-3	2-1	1-4	1-2	1-7	*D*	2-2	5-1	4-2	0-1
Roade	2-4	2-4	3-2	4-1	1-3	0-1	1-3	0-1	1-0	2-3	2-2	*I*	0-1	7-1	3-1
Rushden Rangers	3-1	3-3	6-2	6-0	3-2	2-2	0-0	0-1	0-2	1-1	5-1	2-2	*V*	1-4	2-2
Stanion United	1-1	0-4	0-0	2-1	0-4	1-3	1-2	0-2	5-3	3-0	1-1	4-0	4-2		3-2
Weldon United	1-4	1-6	1-1	3-3	0-5	1-2	1-0	0-4	2-4	0-1	2-3	2-3	3-3	2-1	

Premier Division	P	W	D	L	F	A	Pts
Corby Hellenic Fisher	28	18	6	4	90	34	60
Moulton	28	17	6	5	56	30	57
Kislingbury	28	15	9	4	67	40	54
Milton	28	17	3	8	62	46	54
Harpole	28	17	2	9	61	26	53
Heyford Athletic	28	14	4	10	52	44	46
Caledonian Strip Mills *-3*	28	14	3	11	70	50	42
Roade	28	10	5	13	54	57	35
Priors Marston	28	9	7	12	40	60	34
Rushden Rangers	28	8	8	12	62	67	32
Stanion United	28	9	4	15	52	72	31
Kettering Nomads	28	8	6	14	34	44	30
Corby St Brendans *-3*	28	9	4	15	58	91	28
Weldon United	28	4	5	19	34	81	17
Crick Athletic	28	2	6	20	32	82	12

NORTHANTS COMBINATION/ NORTHAMPTON TOWN LEAGUE CHAMPIONS CUP

(30th November at Raunds Town)

Caledonian Strip Mills 3 Airflow 0

PREMIER DIVISION CUP

FIRST ROUND

Corby Hellenic Fisher 6 Stanion United 4
Crick Athletic 1 **Caledonian Strip Mills** 3
Harpole 4 Weldon United 1
Heyford Athletic 2 Milton 1
Moulton 5 Rushden Rangers 1
Priors Marston 1 **Corby St Brendans** 2
Roade 3 Kettering Nomads 0

QUARTER-FINALS

Caledonian Strip Mills 2 **Corby Hellenic Fisher** 3
Harpole 1 Roade 0
Heyford Athletic 2 Corby St Brendans 0
Kislingbury 2 Moulton 1

SEMI-FINALS

Corby Hellenic Fisher 2 **Harpole** 5 *aet*
Kislingbury 1 **Heyford Athletic** 2

FINAL

(April 22nd at Northampton Town)
Harpole 3 **Heyford Athletic** 4 *aet*

NORTHAMPTONSHIRE COMBINATION PREMIER DIVISION CONSTITUTION 2006-07

BRIXWORTH ALL SAINTS .... St Davids Close, off Froxhill Crescent, Brixworth NN6 9EA 01604 880073
CALEDONIAN STRIP MILLS...... West Glebe South Pitch One, Cottingham Road, Corby NN17 1EL 01536 401659
CORBY GRAMPIAN .... West Glebe South, Cottingham Road, Corby NN17 1EL.......... 01536 401659
CORBY HELLENIC FISHER .... Burghley Drive, Corby NN18 8DY.......... 01536 402290
CORBY ST BRENDANS.......... Corby Rugby Club, Rockingham Road, Corby NN17 2AE.......... None
HARPOLE .... Playing Field, Larkhall Lane, Harpole NN7 4DP.......... None
HEYFORD ATHLETIC.......... Nether Heyford Playing Field, Nether Heyford NN7 3LL .... None
KETTERING NOMADS .... Orlingbury Road, Isham, Kettering NN14 1HY 01536 420068
KISLINGBURY .... Beech Lane, Kislingbury, Northampton NN7 4AL 01604 831225
MILTON .... Collingtree Road, Milton Mansor NN7 3AF .... None
MOULTON.......... Brunting Road, Milton, Northampton NN3 7QX.......... 01604 492675
PRIORS MARSTON .... Priors Sports Ground, Priors Marston CV47 7RR .... None
ROADE.......... Connolly Way, Hyde Road, Roade NN7 2LU 01604 862814
RUSHDEN RANGERS.......... Hayden Road, Rushden NN10 0HY 01933 410036
STANION UNITED.......... Village Hall, Brigstock Road, Stanion NN14 1BX.......... None

IN: Brixworth All Saints (P), Corby Grampian (P)
OUT: Crick Athletic (R), Weldon United (R)

Division One	P	W	D	L	F	A	Pts
Corby Grampian *+2*	28	21	6	1	113	35	71
Brixworth All Saints	28	18	2	8	80	49	56
Bective Wanderers	28	17	3	8	86	53	54
Whitefield Norpol	28	16	4	8	82	50	52
Ravensthorpe Athletic	28	16	4	8	83	59	52
Spratton	28	12	5	11	58	63	41
Corby Pegasus	28	12	4	12	65	63	40
Harborough Spencer United	28	12	4	12	53	53	40
Stanwick Rovers	28	11	6	11	71	71	39
Queen Eleanor Great Houghton	28	10	6	12	69	74	36
Earls Barton United	28	10	5	13	54	56	35
Ringstead Rangers	28	8	5	15	39	55	29
Weedon	28	6	3	19	51	92	21
Corby Locomotives	28	5	2	21	32	91	17
Gretton *-10*	28	5	3	20	38	110	8

Division Two	P	W	D	L	F	A	Pts
Welford Victoria	24	16	6	2	63	23	54
Medbourne	24	15	4	5	74	41	49
Clipston	24	14	6	4	51	33	48
AFC Corby Town *-9*	24	18	1	5	92	37	46
Wootton St George	24	13	2	9	63	47	41
Burton United	24	13	1	10	69	61	40
Islip United	24	8	7	9	46	64	31
Wellingborough R'way Staff *-3*	24	9	6	9	64	57	30
Wilbarston	24	9	2	13	56	58	29
Finedon Volta	24	5	7	12	45	61	22
Wollaston Victoria	24	5	4	15	39	75	19
Wilby	24	5	2	17	39	82	17
Ristee Towers	24	0	4	20	23	85	4

Geddington WMC – record expunged

DIVISION ONE CUP FINAL

(April 29th at Rushden & Diamonds Pitch Two)

Ravensthorpe Athletic 1 Corby Grampian 0

DIVISION TWO CUP FINAL

(April 29th at Rushden & Diamonds Pitch Two)

AFC Corby Town 2 Medbourne 2 *aet* (4-3p)

Division Three	P	W	D	L	F	A	Pts
Corby Kingfisher Athletic	22	17	4	1	83	31	55
Rushden Corner Flag *-6*	22	16	2	4	80	30	44
Kettering Orchard Park	22	14	1	7	68	31	43
Wellingborough Old Grammarians	22	12	2	8	50	38	38
Corby Flamingo	22	9	5	8	50	53	32
Great Doddington	22	9	3	10	43	51	30
Dainite Sports	22	10	0	12	46	60	30
Weavers Old Boys	22	7	5	10	36	41	26
Corby Danesholme Vikings *-3*	22	9	1	12	55	67	25
Kettering Park Rovers	22	4	4	14	46	72	16
Yardley United	22	4	2	16	38	65	14
Wellingborough Wincanton SAS *-6*	22	5	3	14	42	98	12

Division Four	P	W	D	L	F	A	Pts
Cold Ashby Rovers	20	18	2	0	72	14	56
West Haddon	20	11	1	8	49	33	34
Harlestone Park Wanderers	20	9	5	6	50	36	32
Northampton Sapphires *-3*	20	11	2	7	57	47	32
Weekley Vale United	20	9	2	9	32	39	29
Wellingborough Raffertys *-6*	20	11	1	8	73	49	28
Wellingborough Oak Rangers	20	8	1	11	51	53	25
Brafield United	20	8	1	11	48	61	25
AFC Sovereigns	20	6	3	11	35	52	21
Raunds Academy *-3*	20	7	1	12	41	55	19
Wellingborough Rising Sun	20	2	1	17	15	84	7

DIVISION THREE CUP FINAL

(April 25th at Raunds Town)

Great Doddington 6 Dainite Sports 5 *aet*

DIVISION FOUR CUP FINAL

(April 6th at Bugbrooke St Michaels)

Harlestone Park Wanderers 2 Northampton Sapphires 1

Reserve Division One	P	W	D	L	F	A	Pts
Corby Hellenic Fisher Res.	28	21	4	3	108	39	67
James King Blisworth Res.	28	20	4	4	118	37	64
Roade Res.	28	15	8	5	63	46	53
Harpole Res.	28	15	5	8	67	29	50
Kettering Nomads Res.	28	13	9	6	67	48	48
Corby St Brendans Res.	28	13	4	11	76	64	43
Caledonian Strip Mills Res.	28	11	7	10	59	60	40
Rushden Rangers Res.	28	11	6	11	77	69	39
Stanion United Res.	28	10	8	10	51	55	38
Queen Eleanor Gt Houghton Res.	28	9	7	12	54	62	34
Bugbrooke St Michaels 'A'	28	7	8	13	64	80	29
Heyford Athletic Res. *-3*	28	9	5	14	52	73	29
Moulton Res. *-9*	28	10	4	14	64	71	25
Corby Locomotives Res.	28	3	1	24	43	147	10
Crick Athletic Res.	28	2	2	24	44	127	8

Reserve Division Two	P	W	D	L	F	A	Pts
Weldon United Res.	28	23	3	2	123	23	72
Corby Pegasus Res.	28	18	5	5	98	41	59
Milton Res.	28	18	4	6	89	34	58
Gretton Res.	28	16	7	5	73	52	55
Harborough Spencer United Res.	28	15	6	7	79	47	51
Kislingbury Res.	28	13	9	6	77	45	48
Brixworth All Saints Res.	28	12	7	9	89	57	43
Northampton ON Chenecks 'A'	28	12	6	10	82	71	42
James King Blisworth 'A'	28	12	4	12	58	62	40
Bugbrooke St Michaels 'B' *-3*	28	10	4	14	59	77	31
Harpole 'A'	28	8	6	14	61	81	30
Ringstead Rangers Res.	28	6	2	20	45	110	20
Wollaston Victoria Res.	28	5	4	19	53	100	19
Earls Barton United Res.	28	4	0	24	41	126	12
Weedon Res. *-6*	28	4	1	23	42	143	7

RESERVE DIVISION ONE CUP FINAL

(April 29th at Rushden & Diamonds Pitch Two)

Corby Hellenic Fisher Res. 3 Harpole Res. 1

RESERVE DIVISION TWO CUP FINAL

(April 11th at Rushden Rangers)

Northampton ON Chenecks 'A' 3 Corby Pegasus Res. 1

Reserve Division Three	P	W	D	L	F	A	Pts
Finedon Volta Res.	24	16	2	6	69	39	50
Corby Danesholme Vikings Res. *-3*	24	17	1	6	49	33	49
Whitefield Norpol Res.	24	13	3	8	93	48	42
Spratton Res.	24	12	5	7	64	56	41
Islip United Res.	24	13	2	9	70	64	41
Queen Eleanor Gt.Houghton 'A'	24	11	4	9	58	55	37
Welford Victoria Res.	24	7	9	8	34	36	30
Wellingboro' Old Gramm. Res.	24	9	2	13	63	88	29
Stanwick Rovers Res.	24	7	4	13	34	46	25
Dainite Sports Res.	24	7	4	13	64	77	25
Rushden Corner Flag Res. *-3*	24	8	3	13	60	64	24
Weldon United 'A'	24	7	3	14	55	80	24
Kettering Orchard Park Res.	24	5	6	13	42	69	21

RESERVE DIVISION THREE CUP FINAL

(April 18th at Wellingborough Town)

Weldon United 'A' 1 **Welford Victoria Res.** 2

NORTHERN ALLIANCE

	Alnmouth	Blyth Town	Carlisle City	Easington Colliery	Harraby Catholic Club	Heaton Stannington	Heddon	Murton	Newcastle University	Northbank Carlisle	Percy Main Amateurs	Ponteland United	Seaton Delaval Amateurs	Shankhouse	Team Northumbria	Walker Central
Alnmouth	*P*	0-6	1-4	0-0	1-3	0-1	4-1	2-1	1-4	1-5	1-2	4-2	3-2	0-3	1-5	0-1
Blyth Town	1-1	*R*	1-3	2-2	3-3	3-2	1-0	3-4	2-2	1-2	7-0	1-3	4-1	1-1	0-0	2-1
Carlisle City	10-0	1-2	*E*	3-0	1-0	1-1	1-3	1-0	1-1	3-3	3-1	2-1	0-3	0-0	0-2	0-1
Easington Colliery	2-1	0-2	0-1	*M*	6-1	1-2	4-3	0-3	0-2	1-2	2-2	1-0	3-2	0-3	1-5	2-4
Harraby Catholic Club	3-4	1-3	2-2	3-2	*I*	1-2	1-3	2-1	2-2	2-1	2-0	1-1	1-1	0-3	0-2	1-1
Heaton Stannington	4-1	2-0	0-2	5-2	3-2	*E*	2-1	4-1	0-1	4-1	0-0	0-5	4-1	1-2	3-2	3-1
Heddon	5-6	1-3	1-0	0-2	1-2	1-1	*R*	1-2	2-0	2-0	1-1	2-1	1-0	2-0	2-3	1-6
Murton	1-2	0-1	1-6	4-3	1-1	2-2	3-1		1-1	1-1	0-3	2-4	0-1	0-2	3-5	1-6
Newcastle University	5-1	2-3	0-3	1-2	1-1	0-1	0-1	4-2	*D*	2-0	1-1	0-3	2-2	0-1	1-4	2-2
Northbank Carlisle	1-1	3-2	2-3	6-2	4-6	0-1	2-3	2-0	1-2	*I*	2-0	3-0	2-0	2-1	3-2	1-0
Percy Main Amateurs	1-4	2-7	0-4	2-1	1-3	0-2	1-3	5-0	0-2	0-7	*V*	2-3	2-3	0-3	0-7	1-2
Ponteland United	2-7	0-0	0-3	3-0	3-0	1-0	1-0	4-2	1-2	0-5	3-0	*I*	4-3	1-1	0-3	0-4
Seaton Delaval Amateurs	2-2	1-1	0-3	2-0	2-1	1-2	2-1	5-1	2-2	4-2	2-1	5-2	*S*	0-5	3-6	3-4
Shankhouse	1-1	1-0	1-2	4-2	1-0	1-0	4-0	3-2	1-1	1-1	6-0	3-2	0-0	*I*	0-1	3-1
Team Northumbria	4-1	2-0	2-4	4-0	2-2	0-1	4-1	7-1	2-1	3-1	7-0	4-1	3-1	1-1	*O*	5-2
Walker Central	1-1	1-3	2-1	4-0	1-0	2-0	2-1	1-2	1-1	0-2	6-1	3-1	0-2	0-1	0-2	*N*

Premier Division		P	W	D	L	F	A	Pts
Team Northumbria		30	23	3	4	99	34	72
Shankhouse		30	18	8	4	57	21	62
Carlisle City		30	18	5	7	68	31	59
Heaton Stannington	*-3*	30	18	4	8	53	36	55
Northbank Carlisle		30	15	4	11	67	48	49
Walker Central		30	15	4	11	60	43	49
Blyth Town	*-3*	30	14	8	8	65	42	47
Seaton Delaval Amateurs		30	11	6	13	56	62	39
Ponteland United		30	12	3	15	52	63	39
Heddon		30	11	2	17	45	59	35
Harraby Catholic Club		30	8	9	13	47	59	33
Alnmouth		30	9	6	15	52	83	33
Newcastle University	*-6*	30	9	11	10	45	44	32
Easington Colliery		30	7	3	20	41	76	24
Murton		30	6	4	20	42	83	22
Percy Main Amateurs		30	4	4	22	29	94	16

CHALLENGE CUP

(Premier Division teams)

FIRST ROUND

Carlisle City 5 Easington Colliery 1
Harraby Catholic Club 0 **Team Northumbria** 2
Heaton Stannington 2 Murton 1
Heddon 2 **Blyth Town** 3
Newcastle University 0 **Northbank Carlisle** 1
Ponteland United 2 Percy Main Amateurs 2 *aet* (10-9p)
Shankhouse 1 **Seaton Delaval Amateurs** 2
Walker Central 1 **Alnmouth** 1 *aet* (3-5p)

QUARTER-FINALS

Blyth Town 2 **Seaton Delaval Amateurs** 3
Carlisle City (w/o) Alnmouth (scr.)
Ponteland United 3 Northbank Carlisle 0 *aet*
Team Northumbria 2 Heaton Stannington 1

SEMI-FINALS

Carlisle City 2 Ponteland United 0
Seaton Delaval Amateurs 1 **Team Northumbria** 2 *aet*

FINAL *(May 16th at Haydon Bridge United)*
Carlisle City 2 Team Northumbria 2 *aet* (4-3p)

NORTHERN ALLIANCE PREMIER DIVISION CONSTITUTION 2006-07

ALNMOUTH .... Morpeth Town FC, Craik Park, Morpeth Common, Morpeth NE61 2YX 01670 513785
ASHINGTON COLLIERS .... Hirst Welfare, Alexandra Road, Ashington .... None
BLYTH TOWN .... South Newsham Sports Ground, Blyth .... None
CARLISLE CITY .... Sheepmount Sports Complex, Sheepmount, Carlisle CA3 8XL 01228 625599
EASINGTON COLLIERY ... Welfare Park Ground, Paradise Gardens, Easington Colliery, Peterlee NE32 4SH 0191 489 6930
HARRABY CATHOLIC CLUB .... Harraby Community Centre, Edghill Road, Carlisle CA1 3PP .... None
HEATON STANNINGTON ..... Grounsell Park, Newton Road, High Heaton, Heaton, Newcastle-upon-Tyne .... None
HEDDON .... Wheatsheaf Ground, Woolsington, Newcastle-upon-Tyne .... None
NEWCASTLE UNIVERSITY ...... Cochrane Park, Etherstone Avenue, Newcastle-upon-Tyne NE7 7JX .... None
NORTHBANK CARLISLE .... Sheepmount Sports Complex, Sheepmount, Carlisle CA3 8XL 01228 625599
PETERLEE TOWN .... Eden Lane, Peterlee SR8 2PH 0191 586 3004
PONTELAND UNITED .... The Leisure Centre Ground, Callerton Lane, Ponteland NE20 9EG 01661 825441
SEATON DELAVAL AMATEURS .... Wheatridge Park, Seaton Delaval, Whitley Bay .... None
SHANKHOUSE .... Northburn Community & Sports Complex, Crowhall Road, Cramlington NE23 7AA 01670 714154
WALKER CENTRAL .... Monkchester Road, Walker, Newcastle-upon-Tyne NE6 2LJ 0191 265 7230
WALLSEND .... Shibdon Park, Shibdon Road, Blaydon-on-Tyne .... None

IN: Ashington Colliers (P), Peterlee Town (formerly Peterlee Newtown) (R – Northern League Division Two), Wallsend (P)
OUT: Murton (R), Percy Main Amateurs (R), Team Northumbria (P – Northern League Division Two)

	Ashington Colliers	Chopwell Top Club	Cramlington Town	Gosforth Bohemians Garnett	Haydon Bridge United	Hebburn Reyrolle	Newcastle East End Railway Club	Penrith United	Rutherford Newcastle	Spittal Rovers	Walker Fosse	Wallington	Wallsend	Wark
Ashington Col.		3-0	1-1	1-2	1-0	4-0	0-2	1-3	2-1	2-0	n/a	1-4	1-2	2-1
Chopwell T C	1-3	*D*	1-0	1-4	3-2	1-2	4-2	4-1	1-1	6-1	n/a	1-1	2-1	0-0
Cramlington Tn	0-2	2-0	*I*	0-1	1-1	2-2	4-2	1-4	1-2	2-0	2-6	1-1	1-2	1-3
Gosforth Boh. G	1-5	4-3	3-2	*V*	4-2	2-0	1-1	1-0	2-0	1-0	n/a	1-1	0-2	2-3
Haydon Bridge	0-3	0-2	0-2	2-2	*I*	1-3	0-2	1-3	0-5	3-2	0-4	1-3	1-4	2-1
Hebburn Rey.	2-4	0-4	2-0	3-2	2-0	*S*	2-2	0-5	0-3	1-2	n/a	3-0	0-1	2-5
Newcastle EERC	1-4	3-4	3-1	1-1	2-2	0-1	*I*	2-2	2-5	2-0	n/a	3-1	0-2	1-1
Penrith United	1-3	4-1	0-1	1-3	4-3	8-3	1-0	*O*	1-0	2-0	n/a	2-1	0-0	5-1
Rutherford N.	0-0	1-5	2-2	2-1	6-0	2-2	2-1	3-0	*N*	1-1	n/a	6-4	1-0	5-3
Spittal Rovers	1-2	1-2	0-2	2-1	1-3	1-1	4-1	1-5	0-2		0-3	1-3	0-3	5-1
Walker Fosse	3-0	4-1	4-1	4-0	n/a	n/a	n/a	4-0	4-3	n/a	*O*	5-0	n/a	n/a
Wallington	1-0	1-2	2-2	2-2	2-1	1-1	2-1	1-1	3-0	3-1	3-3	*N*	3-3	4-2
Wallsend	1-1	4-1	4-0	5-0	4-2	3-1	6-1	2-1	2-0	3-0	4-1	5-5	*E*	2-3
Wark	1-0	2-3	1-3	3-4	4-2	4-1	8-1	4-1	1-1	3-0	1-4	3-1	2-3	

Note – Walker Fosse withdrew during the course of the season
Their results are shown above but are expunged from the league table

Division One		**P**	**W**	**D**	**L**	**F**	**A**	**Pts**
Wallsend	*-3*	**24**	**17**	**4**	**3**	**64**	**26**	**52**
Ashington Colliers		**24**	**14**	**3**	**7**	**46**	**26**	**45**
Penrith United		**24**	**13**	**3**	**8**	**55**	**37**	**42**
Rutherford Newcastle		**24**	**12**	**6**	**6**	**51**	**34**	**42**
Chopwell Top Club		**24**	**13**	**3**	**8**	**52**	**43**	**42**
Gosforth Bohemians Garnett		**24**	**12**	**5**	**7**	**45**	**42**	**41**
Wark		**24**	**11**	**3**	**10**	**60**	**51**	**36**
Wallington		**24**	**9**	**9**	**6**	**50**	**44**	**36**
Cramlington Town		**24**	**7**	**6**	**11**	**32**	**39**	**27**
Hebburn Reyrolle		**24**	**7**	**5**	**12**	**34**	**57**	**26**
Newcastle East End Railway Club		**24**	**5**	**6**	**13**	**36**	**58**	**21**
Spittal Rovers		**24**	**4**	**2**	**18**	**24**	**55**	**14**
Haydon Bridge United		**24**	**3**	**3**	**18**	**29**	**66**	**12**

Walker Fosse – record expunged

COMBINATION CUP

(Division One teams)

FIRST ROUND

Ashington Colliers 1 **Wallington** 3
Chopwell Top Club 3 **Penrith United** 4 *aet*
Cramlington Town 3 Spittal Rovers 1
Newbiggin Central Welfare (w/o) v Eppleton Colliery Welfare (scr.)
Newcastle East End Rail Club 1 Gosforth Garnett Bohemians 4
(Gosforth Garnett Bohemians expelled)
Walker Fosse 5 Hebburn Reyrolle 1 *aet*
Wallsend 6 Haydon Bridge United 2
Wark 2 Rutherford Newcastle 0

QUARTER-FINALS

Cramlington Tn 2 **Wallington** 2 *aet* (2-4p)
Penrith United 1 **Newcastle East End Rail Club** 2
Wark (w/o) v Walker Fosse (scr.)
Wallsend (w/o) v Newbiggin Central Welfare (scr.)

SEMI-FINALS

Wallington 0 **Newcastle East End Rail Club** 1
Wark 1 **Wallsend** 4

FINAL *(May 15th at Prudhoe Town)*

Newcastle East End Railway Club 4 Wallsend 2 *aet*

LEAGUE CUP

FIRST ROUND

Ashington Colliers 1 Walker Central 0
Carlisle City 6 Harraby Catholic Club 0
Cramlington Town 2 **Alnmouth** 4 *aet*
Easington Colliery 0 **Heddon** 1
Eppleton Colliery Welfare (scr.) v **Wark** (w/o)
Haydon Bridge United 3 **Wallington** 6
Heaton Stannington 2 Blyth Town 1
Newbiggin Central Welfare (scr.) v **Penrith United** (w/o)
Newcastle E E R'way Club 4 Gosforth Garnett Bohemians 3
Newcastle University 6 Murton 3
Ponteland United 1 Percy Main Amateurs 0 *aet*
Rutherford Newcastle 2 Seaton Delaval Amateurs 1 *aet*
Spittal Rovers 1 **Chopwell Top Club** 7
Team Northumbria 1 Shankhouse 0
Walker Fosse 4 Hebburn Reyrolle 1
Wallsend 1 **Northbank Carlisle** 2 *aet*

SECOND ROUND

Ashington Colliers 4 Wark 0
Carlisle City 3 Ponteland United 0
Chemfica 2 **Stocksfield** 7
Chopwell Top Club 4 Highfields United 0
Gillford Park Spartans 4 Adderstone Jesmond 0
Heaton Stannington 1 Newcastle British Telecom 0
Lowick 5 Wallsend Town 1

NORTHERN ALLIANCE DIVISION ONE CONSTITUTION 2006-07

BERWICK UNITED .... Swan Leisure Centre, Northumberland Road, Tweedmouth, Berwick-on-Tweed TD15 2AS........... 01289 330603
CHOPWELL TOP CLUB .... Welfare Park, Chopwell, Newcastle-upon-Tyne .... None
CRAMLINGTON TOWN .... Sporting Club of Cramlington, Highburn, Cramlington NE23 6BN 01670 591970
GILLFORD PARK SPARTANS .... Gillford Park Railway Club, Petteril Bank Road, Carlisle CA1 3AF................ 01228 526449
GOSFORTH BOHEMIANS GARNETT....... Benson Park, Gosforth, Newcastle-upon-Tyne .... None
HAYDON BRIDGE UNITED .... Low Hall Park, Haydon Bridge, Hexham NE47 6AF .... None
HEBBURN REYROLLE............ Hebburn Sports Ground, 16 South Drive, Hebburn NE31 1UN............................ None
MURTON......................... Recreation Park, Church Lane, Murton, Seaham SR7 9RD 07814 523289
NEWCASTLE EAST END RAILWAY CLUB ... Swan Hunter Rec Ground, Stotts Road, Walkergate, Newcastle-upon-Tyne NE6 4UD .. None
PENRITH UNITED .... Frenchfields Sports Centre, Brougham, Penrith CA11 8UA .... None
PERCY MAIN AMATEURS........... Purvis Park, St John's Green, Percy Main, North Shields........................ 0191 257 4831
RUTHERFORD NEWCASTLE .. Farnacres, Beggarswood Park, Coach Road, Lobley Hill, Gateshead NE11 8HJ.................. None
SEATON BURN...................... Seaton Burn Welfare, Seaton Burn, Newcastle-upon-Tyne............................ None
WALLINGTON.......................... Oakford Park, Scots Gap, Morpeth .... None
WARK................................ Wark Sports Club, Wark, Hexham NE48 3NP.. 01434 230259
WHITLEY BAY 'A' .... Hillheads Park, Rink Way, Whitley Bay NE25 8HR 0191 291 3636

IN: Gillford Park Spartans (P), Murton (R), Percy Main Amateurs (R), Seaton Burn (P), Whitley Bay 'A' (P)
OUT: Ashington Colliers (P), Eppleton Colliery Welfare (WN), Newbiggin Central Welfare (WN), Walker Fosse (WS), Wallsend (P)
Spittal Rovers merge with Highfields United (Division Two) to become Berwick United

	Addlestone Jesmond	Chemfica	Felling Fox	Gillford Park Spartans	Highfields United	Lowick	Newcastle British Telecom	Red Row Welfare	Seaton Burn	Sport Benfield	Stocksfield	Swarland	Wallsend Town	Westerhope	Whitley Bay 'A'
Addlestone Jesmond		3-3	2-2	0-4	4-2	0-1	3-1	1-3	0-3	2-0	0-0	2-3	4-2	0-1	0-4
Chemfica	2-2	*D*	0-1	5-1	3-1	1-4	3-1	1-2	1-4	3-6	2-2	0-1	4-2	2-2	0-2
Felling Fox	1-3	2-2	*I*	0-2	3-2	3-1	0-2	3-2	1-1	0-2	1-0	3-2	1-3	1-1	0-3
Gillford Park Spartans	3-2	4-1	8-1	*V*	6-2	3-2	2-1	2-2	6-0	3-4	4-1	4-2	7-1	5-3	3-1
Highfields United	1-2	1-1	5-1	5-5	*I*	2-4	6-1	1-3	0-1	2-1	0-7	0-2	5-4	0-3	2-3
Lowick	1-2	2-2	2-1	1-4	0-0	*S*	3-1	2-1	1-2	4-0	1-0	3-3	1-1	2-2	2-0
Newcastle British Telecom	1-4	1-4	1-0	2-2	5-0	2-3	*I*	3-2	0-3	2-2	1-3	2-1	1-1	0-2	2-1
Red Row Welfare	2-0	1-3	5-2	1-2	2-2	2-0	2-2	*O*	4-1	4-4	1-3	4-1	3-3	1-3	1-1
Seaton Burn	0-0	1-0	2-1	1-6	2-1	0-0	2-1	2-1	*N*	5-1	0-4	3-2	2-0	2-2	1-1
Sport Benfield	0-0	3-2	4-2	4-3	1-1	2-2	5-1	0-0	5-1		2-0	4-2	2-1	2-6	1-5
Stocksfield	0-3	2-0	3-1	3-2	1-1	1-1	6-0	0-0	2-2	5-4		8-0	2-1	3-0	0-1
Swarland	1-1	2-3	1-3	2-1	4-3	2-4	5-3	1-3	3-6	6-0	0-3	*T*	0-3	3-2	0-1
Wallsend Town	1-2	3-2	1-3	0-3	2-0	1-2	1-4	3-1	0-2	5-2	0-3	0-3	*W*	2-1	1-2
Westerhope	1-3	1-2	2-1	1-4	5-0	3-0	3-0	1-0	2-4	3-3	1-1	2-3	5-3	*O*	2-3
Whitley Bay 'A'	2-0	2-0	0-4	5-0	3-1	3-2	3-2	6-1	2-0	3-1	1-1	3-0	4-1	1-1	

Newcastle East End Railway Club 0 **Walker Fosse** 5
Newcastle University 2 **Team Northumbria** 3
Northbank Carlisle 4 Swarland 0
Penrith United 2 Whitley Bay 'A' 1
Red Row Welfare 0 **Alnmouth** 1 *aet*
Seaton Burn 2 Sport Benfield 0
Wallington 1 **Rutherford Newcastle** 3
Westerhope 3 Felling Fox 0
Wetheral (scr.) v **Heddon** (w/o)

THIRD ROUND

Alnmouth 0 **Heddon** 4
Ashington Colliers 4 Seaton Burn 2
Chopwell Top Club 1 **Team Northumbria** 5
Heaton Stannington 1 **Westerhope** 2
Northbank Carlisle 4 Lowick 0
Penrith United 0 **Gillford Park Spartans** 1
Rutherford Newcastle 2 **Carlisle City** 5
Walker Fosse (scr.) v **Stocksfield** (w/o)

QUARTER-FINALS

Ashington Colliers 3 Gillford Park Spartans 2
Carlisle City 3 Westerhope 0
Northbank Carlisle 3 Stocksfield 0
Team Northumbria 2 Heddon 1

SEMI-FINALS

Northbank Carlisle 1 **Carlisle City** 5
Team Northumbria 2 Ashington Colliers 0

FINAL

(May 22nd at Haydon Bridge United)
Carlisle City 2 Team Northumbria 1

Division Two		P	W	D	L	F	A	Pts
Whitley Bay 'A'		28	20	4	4	66	29	64
Gillford Park Spartans	*-3*	28	19	3	6	99	53	57
Seaton Burn		28	16	6	6	53	47	54
Stocksfield		28	14	8	6	64	30	50
Lowick	*-3*	28	12	8	8	51	44	41
Westerhope		28	11	7	10	61	51	40
Sport Benfield		28	11	7	10	65	73	40
Red Row Welfare		28	9	8	11	54	53	35
Addlestone Jesmond	*-6*	28	11	7	10	45	45	34
Swarland		28	10	2	16	55	74	32
Chemfica		28	8	7	13	52	59	31
Felling Fox		28	9	4	15	42	62	31
Newcastle British Telecom		28	7	4	17	43	72	25
Wallsend Town		28	7	3	18	46	71	24
Highfields United		28	4	6	18	46	79	18

AMATEUR CUP

(Division Two teams)

FIRST ROUND

Addlestone Jesmond 2 Lowick 0
Chemfica 2 **Felling Fox** 4
Gillford Pk Sp 1 **Seaton Burn** 2
Highfields 2 **Whitley Bay 'A'** 3
Newcastle British Telecom 1 **Westerhope** 3
Sport Benfield 4 Swarland 0
Wallsend Town 2 **Stocksfield** 3

QUARTER-FINALS

Addlestone Jesmond 2 **Red Row Welfare** 3
Seaton Burn 4 Felling Fox 1
Sport Benfield 1 **Stocksfield** 4
Westerhope 3 **Whitley Bay 'A'** 3 *aet* (3-4p)

SEMI-FINALS

Stocksfield 4 Seaton Burn 1
Whitley Bay 'A' 3 Red Row Welfare 1

FINAL

(May 12th at Prudhoe Town)
Stocksfield 4 Whitley Bay 'A' 2

NORTHERN ALLIANCE DIVISION TWO CONSTITUTION 2006-07

AMBLE .... Amble Welfare Ground, Amble-by-the-Sea .... None
BLAYDON .... Shibdon Park, Shibdon Road, Blaydon-on-Tyne .... None
CULLERCOATS .... Links Avenue, Cullercoats .... None
FELLING FOX .... Northumbria Centre, Stephenson Road, Stephenson Industrial Estate, Washington NE37 3HR .... None
HEXHAM .... Wentworth Leisure Centre, Hexham NE46 9PD 01434 607080
JESMOND .... Miller's Dene, Fossway, Walkerdene, Newcastle-upon-Tyne .... None
LOWICK .... New Barber Park, Lowick .... None
MORPETH TOWN 'A' .... Morpeth Common Ground, Morpeth .... None
NEWCASTLE BRITISH TELECOM .... Burradon Welfare Ground, Burradon .... None
NEWCASTLE CHEMFICA .. Benfield School of Sporting Excellence, Benfield Road, Newcastle-upon-Tyne NE6 4NQ .... None
NORTH SHIELDS ATHLETIC ..... Collingwood View Playing Field, West Percy Road, North Shields .... None
RED ROW WELFARE .... Red Row Welfare Ground, Red Row, Amble .... None
STOCKSFIELD .... Stocksfield Sports Field, Main Road, Stocksfield, Prudhoe NE42 5DH .... None
WALLSEND TOWN .... Langdale School Ground, Wallsend, Newcastle-upon-Tyne NE28 0HG .... None
WESTERHOPE .... Westerhope Institute, Westerhope, Newcastle-upon-Tyne .... None
WHITLEY BAY VENTURE .. Churchill Playing Fields, Hartley Avenue, Monkseaton, Whitley Bay NE26 3NS .... None

***IN:** Blaydon (N), Cullercoats (N), Hexham (N), North Shields Athletic (N), Whitley Bay Venture (P – Tyneside Amateur League Division One)*
***OUT:** Gillford Park Spartans (P), Seaton Burn (P), Sport Benfield (W), Whitley Bay 'A' (P)*
Addlestone Jesmond become Jesmond, Chemfica become Newcastle Chemfica, Swarland become Amble
Highfields United have merged with Division One side Spittal Rovers to become Berwick United

NORTHERN COUNTIES EAST LEAGUE

	Armthorpe Welfare	Arnold Town	Brodsworth Miners Welfare	Buxton	Eccleshill United	Garforth Town	Glapwell	Glasshoughton Welfare	Hallam	Harrogate Railway Athletic	Liversedge	Long Eaton United	Maltby Main	Mickleover Sports	Pickering Town	Selby Town	Sheffield	Shirebrook Town	Sutton Town	Thackley
Armthorpe Welfare		0-2	3-1	0-5	1-2	1-5	1-2	1-0	2-0	0-2	1-3	3-0	1-2	1-1	1-0	4-2	1-2	3-2	0-6	5-1
Arnold Town	1-1		2-0	0-2	7-2	3-3	0-2	4-0	2-1	1-2	3-1	2-2	0-1	2-1	0-1	2-1	1-0	3-1	1-2	3-1
Brodsworth Miners Welfare	0-2	0-1	*P*	0-3	1-5	1-2	1-3	4-2	2-3	0-6	2-3	3-0	4-3	2-3	1-2	2-2	0-4	0-5	0-1	0-1
Buxton	2-1	2-1	3-3	*R*	3-1	2-1	9-0	2-0	4-0	3-0	1-0	4-0	2-1	2-1	2-3	4-0	5-0	2-1	1-6	4-2
Eccleshill United	1-1	0-2	1-1	0-0	*E*	3-1	2-2	2-1	2-1	2-3	2-3	1-1	7-1	0-1	0-1	1-0	2-3	6-0	2-1	1-2
Garforth Town	2-2	3-1	1-2	0-1	1-0	*M*	2-2	1-0	1-2	0-0	1-4	2-3	1-1	0-0	0-2	1-2	2-0	0-0	4-1	0-3
Glapwell	1-1	0-2	2-1	0-0	0-4	1-1	*I*	0-4	1-2	1-4	2-1	0-3	2-0	0-0	1-4	0-1	0-0	3-2	2-2	2-0
Glasshoughton Welfare	3-1	1-3	5-0	1-2	1-2	6-3	3-0	*E*	0-2	2-3	1-2	2-1	1-0	2-1	1-1	1-0	0-1	0-1	2-2	1-1
Hallam	1-4	0-1	3-2	1-1	1-0	1-5	2-2	2-2	*R*	1-2	0-3	2-1	1-1	0-0	3-1	2-2	1-4	0-1	1-1	0-1
Harrogate Railway Athletic	5-3	3-2	5-0	1-4	1-1	1-2	2-0	8-1	5-1		0-1	2-2	1-2	6-1	1-1	3-1	1-0	2-5	2-2	4-1
Liversedge	2-3	1-1	4-0	1-1	6-1	5-3	7-2	2-0	3-2	1-0	*D*	7-2	2-1	2-3	2-2	5-1	1-2	8-2	2-3	5-4
Long Eaton United	2-0	1-5	2-4	0-2	4-2	2-4	1-1	2-0	1-0	0-3	1-1	*I*	0-1	0-1	0-1	2-0	2-2	1-2	1-1	3-2
Maltby Main	2-2	2-2	2-2	0-3	1-1	2-2	2-1	0-0	1-0	2-4	0-2	2-1	*V*	2-3	1-1	1-3	2-2	5-2	1-2	0-1
Mickleover Sports	2-5	2-2	4-2	0-6	2-0	0-1	0-3	3-1	4-3	4-1	1-2	3-2	0-4	*I*	0-0	0-1	1-3	3-2	0-2	1-3
Pickering Town	3-3	1-2	2-0	0-1	3-2	2-1	0-0	2-1	4-1	0-0	0-1	4-2	2-0	2-0	*S*	1-0	1-1	6-1	0-1	5-1
Selby Town	5-2	3-1	4-1	0-3	2-0	0-0	2-1	0-4	2-0	1-3	0-0	3-0	3-1	2-0	4-1	*I*	1-2	1-4	3-2	0-2
Sheffield	0-0	0-3	4-0	1-0	3-2	4-1	1-0	3-1	0-1	0-4	0-4	8-0	1-1	1-1	1-0	1-1	*O*	2-0	2-1	1-0
Shirebrook Town	3-5	1-1	2-4	0-4	0-3	2-3	1-2	4-1	1-1	1-0	0-4	2-0	2-1	3-2	1-2	0-2	0-0	*N*	1-2	1-2
Sutton Town	3-0	0-1	5-0	1-3	6-2	5-0	1-2	4-0	0-2	0-0	0-5	2-2	2-1	1-1	4-2	3-2	1-1	0-1		1-2
Thackley	1-0	1-2	1-1	0-4	2-1	1-1	2-3	0-1	4-0	0-2	1-0	2-0	4-2	2-1	1-0	0-1	1-3	1-2	5-1	

Premier Division		P	W	D	L	F	A	Pts
Buxton		38	30	5	3	102	27	95
Liversedge		38	25	5	8	106	49	80
Harrogate Railway Athletic		38	22	7	9	92	49	73
Sheffield		38	20	10	8	63	43	70
Arnold Town	*-3*	38	21	7	10	72	45	67
Pickering Town		38	19	9	10	63	42	66
Sutton Town		38	17	9	12	78	57	60
Selby Town		38	17	5	16	58	60	56
Thackley	*-3*	38	18	3	17	59	62	54
Garforth Town		38	12	11	15	61	68	47
Armthorpe Welfare		38	13	8	17	65	77	47
Glapwell		38	12	11	15	46	71	47
Mickleover Sports		38	12	8	18	51	73	44
Eccleshill United		38	12	7	19	66	70	43
Shirebrook Town		38	13	4	21	59	85	43
Glasshoughton Welfare		38	11	5	22	52	70	38
Hallam		38	10	8	20	44	73	38
Maltby Main	*-1*	38	9	11	18	52	70	37
Long Eaton United	*-3*	38	8	8	22	47	86	29
Brodsworth Miners Welfare		38	6	5	27	47	106	23

NORTHERN COUNTIES EAST LEAGUE PREMIER DIVISION CONSTITUTION 2006-07

ARMTHORPE WELFARE .... Church Street, Armthorpe, Doncaster DN3 3AG.................. 07775 915503
ARNOLD TOWN.................... King George V Playing Field, Gedling Road, Arnold NG5 6NQ 0115 926 3660
BRODSWORTH MINERS WELFARE...... Welfare Ground, Woodlands, Doncaster DN6 7PP 01302 728380
CARLTON TOWN .... Stoke Lane, Gedling, Nottingham NG4 2QS 0115 940 2531
ECCLESHILL UNITED .... Plumpton Park, Kingsway, Wrose, Bradford BD2 1PN 01274 615739
GARFORTH TOWN.............. Wheatley Park Stadium, Cedar Ridge, Garforth, Leeds LS25 2PF 0113 286 4083
GLAPWELL .... Hall Corner, Park Avenue, Glapwell, Chesterfield S44 5NJ 01623 812213
GLASSHOUGHTON WELFARE .... Leeds Road, Glasshoughton, Castleford WF10 4PF.................. 01977 518981
HALLAM .... Sandygate Road, Crosspool, Sheffield S10 5SD 0114 230 9484
LIVERSEDGE .... Clayborn Ground, Quaker Lane, Hightown Road, Cleckheaton BD19 3RJ 01274 862108
LONG EATON UNITED .... Grange Park, Station Road, Long Eaton NG10 2EF 0115 973 5700
MALTBY MAIN .... Maltby Miners Welfare, Muglet Lane, Maltby, Rotherham S66 7JQ............. 07941 057883
MICKLEOVER SPORTS.......... Mickleover Sports Club, Station Road, Mickleover, Derby DE3 5FE 01332 521167
PICKERING TOWN .... Recreation Ground, off Mill Lane, Malton Road, Pickering YO18 8DR 01751 473317
RETFORD UNITED .... Canon Park, Leverton Road, Retford DN22 6QF.................... 01777 710300
SELBY TOWN .... Flaxley Road Ground, Richard Street, Scott Road, Selby YO8 0BS 01757 210900
SHEFFIELD .... Coach & Horses Ground, Stubley Hollow, Sheffield Road, Dronfield S18 2GD 01246 413269
SHIREBROOK TOWN............. BRSA Sports Ground, Langwith Road, Shirebrook NG20 8TF................ 01623 742535
SUTTON TOWN............ The Hoisery Mills Ground, Huthwaite Road, Sutton-in-Ashfield NG17 2HB 01623 552376
THACKLEY .... Dennyfield, Ainsbury Avenue, Thackley, Bradford BD10 0LL 01274 615571

IN: Carlton Town (P), Retford United (P)

OUT: Buxton (P – Northern Premier League Division One), Harrogate Railway Athletic (P – Northern Premier League Division One)

	Borrowash Victoria	Carlton Town	Gedling Town	Hall Road Rangers	Lincoln Moorlands	Parkgate	Pontefract Collieries	Retford United	Rossington Main	South Normanton Athletic	Staveley Miners Welfare	Tadcaster Albion	Teversal	Winterton Rangers	Worsbrough Bridge MW	Yorkshire Amateur
Borrowash Victoria		1-3	1-1	0-1	3-0	0-2	3-2	2-4	0-2	3-2	0-5	3-2	2-0	1-3	0-0	4-0
Carlton Town	3-1		3-2	1-1	0-2	2-0	3-0	0-0	1-0	3-1	4-0	1-0	1-0	1-5	3-0	6-0
Gedling Town	1-0	0-3	*D*	3-1	3-1	2-0	1-0	1-3	3-1	3-0	4-1	2-1	1-1	3-2	5-1	6-0
Hall Road Rangers	1-4	0-3	0-6	*I*	1-0	2-2	0-1	0-2	2-3	1-3	1-2	2-3	5-1	0-0	0-2	3-3
Lincoln Moorlands	1-3	1-2	1-4	9-1	*V*	2-0	1-0	3-0	1-0	2-0	1-0	1-2	3-0	0-2	3-1	1-2
Parkgate	5-1	1-2	4-0	4-0	4-2	*I*	6-3	2-0	5-1	4-0	1-1	1-2	6-0	4-2	4-1	3-0
Pontefract Collieries	0-2	0-0	0-6	5-0	0-2	2-3	*S*	1-3	3-3	3-0	1-2	2-1	0-0	2-2	1-1	4-2
Retford United	0-0	2-0	1-1	2-1	2-0	2-2	5-1	*I*	4-1	1-2	2-0	1-2	7-1	1-0	6-2	3-0
Rossington Main	0-2	1-2	2-2	2-3	1-5	2-0	3-1	0-3	*O*	1-2	0-1	1-2	0-2	0-5	1-4	1-1
South Normanton Athletic	2-5	1-4	2-1	6-4	1-2	2-8	1-1	1-3	2-2	*N*	0-5	0-2	2-0	1-3	0-2	4-1
Staveley Miners Welfare	0-1	0-2	1-2	2-3	1-3	2-2	1-3	1-3	0-4	4-2		0-2	2-1	0-3	1-1	1-2
Tadcaster Albion	0-3	0-3	1-1	3-0	2-1	0-3	3-1	1-0	4-0	4-0	2-1	*O*	2-0	2-1	3-1	2-0
Teversal	0-1	3-4	0-4	3-2	1-1	0-3	2-1	0-6	4-1	4-4	3-3	0-1	*N*	0-4	0-4	1-0
Winterton Rangers	0-0	4-5	2-0	1-1	2-1	1-1	2-0	1-1	0-0	5-1	2-1	3-1	3-0	*E*	2-0	5-0
Worsbrough Bridge MW	4-2	1-1	1-4	5-0	0-3	4-3	4-3	1-4	2-4	2-2	1-3	2-3	4-0	0-4		3-1
Yorkshire Amateur	1-2	0-2	0-3	1-2	2-3	2-4	2-2	1-3	1-0	3-1	1-3	1-2	1-1	0-2	1-3	

Division One	P	W	D	L	F	A	Pts
Carlton Town	30	23	4	3	68	27	73
Retford United	30	20	5	5	74	28	65
Tadcaster Albion	30	21	1	8	55	35	64
Gedling Town	30	19	5	6	75	34	62
Winterton Rangers	30	18	7	5	71	27	61
Parkgate	30	18	5	7	87	40	59
Lincoln Moorlands	30	16	1	13	56	40	49
Borrowash Victoria	30	15	4	11	50	45	49
Worsbrough Bridge MW	30	11	5	14	57	67	38
Staveley Miners Welfare	30	9	4	17	44	57	31
Pontefract Collieries	30	6	7	17	43	64	25
South Normanton Athletic	30	7	4	19	45	86	25
Rossington Main	30	6	5	19	37	67	23
Hall Road Rangers	30	6	5	19	38	82	23
Teversal	30	5	6	19	28	78	21
Yorkshire Amateur	30	4	4	22	29	80	16

NORTHERN COUNTIES EAST LEAGUE DIVISION ONE CONSTITUTION 2006-07

AFC EMLEY .... Emley Welfare Sports Ground, Emley, Huddersfield HD8 9RE 01924 848398
BORROWASH VICTORIA .... Robinson Construction Bowl, Borrowash Road, Spondon, Derby DE21 7PH 01332 669688
DINNINGTON TOWN .... Resource Centre, 131 Laughton Road (The Stute), Dinnington S25 2HA 01909 518555
GEDLING TOWN .... Ferryboat Ground, Stoke Lane, Stoke Bardolph, Gedling NG14 5HX......................... 0115 940 2145
HALL ROAD RANGERS .... Dene Park, Dene Close, Beverley Road, Dunswell, Hull HU6 0AB 01482 850101
LINCOLN MOORLANDS .... Moorlands Sports Ground, Newark Road, Lincoln LN6 8RT 01522 520184
NOSTELL MINERS WELFARE ... Miners Welfare Ground, Middle Lane, New Crofton, Wakefield WF4 1LB 01924 862348
PARKGATE .... Roundwood Sports Complex, Green Lane, Rawmarsh, Rotherham S62 7LA 01709 826600
PONTEFRACT COLLIERIES .... Abstract Stadium, Skinner Lane, Pontefract WF8 4QE 01977 600818
ROSSINGTON MAIN .... Welfare Ground, Oxford Street, Rossington DN11 0DU 01302 865524
SOUTH NORMANTON ATHLETIC....ExChem Sports Ground, Lees Lane, South Normanton DE55 2AD 01773 581491
STAVELEY MINERS WELFARE .... Inkersall Road, Staveley, Chesterfield S43 3JL 01246 471441
TADCASTER ALBION .... The Park, Ings Lane, off Centre Lane, Tadcaster LS24 9AY 01937 834119
TEVERSAL .... Teversal Grange S & S Centre, Carnarvon Street, Teversal, Sutton-in-Ashfield NG17 3HJ 01623 555944
WINTERTON RANGERS .... 54 West Street, Winterton, Scunthorpe DN15 9QF 01724 732628
WORSBROUGH BRIDGE MW .... Park Road, Worsbrough Bridge, Barnsley S70 5LJ 01226 284452
YORKSHIRE AMATEUR .... Bracken Edge Ground, Roxholme Road, Leeds LS8 4JG 0113 262 4093

IN: AFC Emley (P – West Yorkshire League Division One), Dinnington Town (P – Central Midlands League Supreme Division), Nostell Miners Welfare (P – West Yorkshire League Premier Division)

OUT: Carlton Town (P), Retford United (P)

LEAGUE CUP

(All sides in league)

FIRST ROUND

Hall Road Rangers 5 Retford United 3
Lincoln Moorlands 2 Rossington Main 1
Parkgate 7 South Normanton Athletic 1
Staveley Miners Welfare 2 **Carlton Town** 4

SECOND ROUND

Armthorpe Welfare 3 **Carlton Town** 5
Arnold Town 0 **Gedling Town** 1
Brodsworth Miners Welfare 1 **Buxton** 7 *(at Buxton)*
Glapwell 2 Borrowash Victoria 0
Glasshoughton Welfare 0 **Long Eaton United** 2
Harrogate Railway Athletic 3 Hallam 1
Lincoln Moorlands 2 Hall Road Rangers 1
Mickleover Sports 2 Winterton Rangers 4
(Winterton Rangers expelled)
Parkgate 2 Garforth Town 0
Pontefract Collieries 1 **Thackley** 7
Selby Town 4 Sutton Town 3
Sheffield 5 Eccleshill United 1
Tadcaster Albion 1 **Maltby Main** 2
Teversal 1 **Liversedge** 3
Worsbrough Bridge MW 2 Shirebrook Town 1
Yorkshire Amateur 1 **Pickering Town** 2

THIRD ROUND

Carlton Town 4 Parkgate 4 *aet*
Parkgate 3 Carlton Town 3 *aet* (4-1p) *replay*
Gedling Town 1 Harrogate Railway Athletic 1 *aet*
Harrogate Railway Athletic 3 **Gedling Town** 3
aet (3-5p) *replay*
Lincoln Moorlands 3 **Buxton** 1
(Lincoln Moorlands expelled)
Liversedge 2 Mickleover Sports 0
Maltby Main 3 Long Eaton United 2 *aet*
Pickering Town 1 Glapwell 0
Selby Town 1 Thackley 1 *aet*
Thackley 1 **Selby Town** 4 *replay*
Sheffield 3 Worsbrough Bridge MW 1

QUARTER-FINALS

Liversedge 8 Parkgate 1
Maltby Main 0 **Buxton** 2
Selby Town 1 Pickering Town 1 *aet*
Pickering Town 2 **Selby Town** 4 *replay*
Sheffield 6 Gedling Town 1

SEMI-FINALS

Buxton 0 Liversedge 1
Sheffield 3 Selby Town 1

FINAL

(played over two legs)
(May 4th)
Sheffield 0 Liversedge 2
(May 6th)
Liversedge 3 Sheffield 1

PRESIDENT'S CUP

(Top eight finishers from Premier and Division One)

FIRST ROUND

Buxton 2 Carlton Town 1
Garforth Town 2 Tadcaster Albion 1
Gedling Town 4 Shirebrook Town 1
Pickering Town 1 **Selby Town** 3
Retford United 3 Harrogate Railway Athletic 0
Sheffield 3 Liversedge 1
Sutton Town 1 Lincoln Moorlands 0
Thackley 5 Yorkshire Amateur 0

QUARTER-FINALS

Gedling Town 1 **Garforth Town** 2
Selby Town 1 Sheffield 0
Sutton Town 1 Retford United 0
Thackley 0 **Buxton** 1

SEMI-FINALS

Garforth Town 1 **Selby Town** 2
Sutton Town 1 **Buxton** 4

FINAL

(played over two legs)
(April 13th)
Buxton 1 Selby Town 0
(April 27th)
Selby Town 0 **Buxton** 1

WILKINSON SWORD SHIELD

(Division One sides)

FIRST ROUND

Carlton Town 5 Borrowash Victoria 2
Gedling Town 1 **Rossington Main** 2
Hall Road Rangers 0 **Yorkshire Amateur** 2
Lincoln Moorlands 0 **South Normanton Athletic** 1
Retford United 3 Tadcaster Albion 1
Teversal 0 **Parkgate** 6
Winterton Rangers 3 Staveley Miners Welfare 1
Worsbrough Bridge MW 2 Pontefract Collieries 1

QUARTER-FINALS

Carlton Town 3 **Yorkshire Amateur** 1 *(Carlton Tn expelled)*
Retford United 1 South Normanton Athletic 0
Winterton Rangers 1 Rossington Main 0
Worsbrough Bridge MW 2 Parkgate 0

SEMI-FINALS

Winterton Rangers 1 **Retford United** 2
Yorkshire Amateur 3 Worsbrough Bridge MW 1

FINAL

(played over two legs)
(April 4th)
Retford United 3 Yorkshire Amateur 0
(April 18th)
Yorkshire Amateur 2 **Retford United** 3

NORTHERN LEAGUE

	Ashington	Bedlington Terriers	Billingham Synthonia	Billingham Town	Brandon United	Chester-le-Street Town	Dunston Federation Brewery	Durham City	Esh Winning	Horden Colliery Welfare	Jarrow Roofing Boldon CA	Morpeth Town	Newcastle Benfield Bay Pla.	Newcastle Blue Star	Shildon	Sunderland Nissan	Thornaby	Tow Law Town	West Allotment Celtic	West Auckland Town	Whitley Bay
Ashington		1-3	0-1	0-1	6-1	1-2	3-3	1-1	4-0	1-1	3-1	0-3	1-2	0-2	1-1	1-2	6-1	0-1	3-1	1-0	0-2
Bedlington Terriers	0-3		1-0	2-1	5-0	1-1	0-1	1-0	3-2	1-0	3-2	0-1	3-2	1-0	5-3	4-3	3-0	3-3	3-2	0-1	0-0
Billingham Synthonia	1-0	4-3		1-1	3-0	4-1	1-1	1-0	4-0	1-1	3-2	1-4	4-2	1-1	0-1	1-0	0-3	3-0	1-0	2-1	3-3
Billingham Town	0-0	4-4	3-3		5-0	2-1	1-2	2-1	3-0	4-1	2-2	1-2	1-2	1-2	3-2	0-0	4-2	2-1	4-2	4-1	3-1
Brandon United	1-3	3-2	0-3	1-0	*D*	0-3	0-6	1-5	2-2	0-5	3-4	1-1	0-3	0-4	1-6	0-2	0-5	0-8	1-1	1-2	1-5
Chester-le-Street Town	1-1	2-2	2-0	2-2	3-1	*I*	2-3	3-2	2-0	2-1	2-0	2-0	1-0	1-1	2-0	0-1	0-1	3-2	3-5	2-2	1-4
Dunston Federation Brewery	1-1	2-3	3-3	1-1	3-2	3-0	*V*	0-2	6-0	4-1	2-1	1-0	2-0	0-0	3-2	1-1	0-0	3-1	4-0	0-1	5-2
Durham City	4-0	2-1	0-1	0-2	2-1	3-1	1-1	*I*	0-0	0-0	2-2	1-0	2-4	1-0	2-2	2-1	5-0	0-0	2-1	2-1	0-0
Esh Winning	1-4	0-5	4-0	0-0	0-2	1-3	0-2	0-0	*S*	1-1	1-1	0-3	0-2	1-2	0-2	0-2	1-4	0-1	1-4	1-3	2-1
Horden Colliery Welfare	1-4	0-1	2-2	0-2	3-0	0-1	2-1	1-0	2-0	*I*	1-2	3-3	2-1	1-1	0-0	1-2	2-1	2-2	1-0	0-0	1-2
Jarrow Roofing Boldon CA	2-1	2-3	2-1	2-2	4-2	4-0	0-3	1-0	2-1	0-3	*O*	3-0	0-3	1-2	2-2	3-4	1-1	5-1	2-0	1-1	0-3
Morpeth Town	2-0	2-1	0-1	1-4	3-2	1-1	2-0	0-0	2-3	5-1	4-1	*N*	0-3	2-3	2-0	3-3	4-1	0-2	1-0	2-0	2-1
Newcastle Benfield Bay Plastics	2-1	2-2	1-1	0-3	2-1	1-1	2-0	3-3	1-1	8-2	1-0	1-1		1-2	1-2	0-3	6-3	1-1	6-2	3-0	2-2
Newcastle Blue Star	3-0	1-2	2-1	2-1	8-0	5-1	1-0	3-2	4-0	1-0	4-1	3-1	1-0		2-1	7-2	0-3	1-1	0-1	3-1	3-1
Shildon	0-0	0-2	1-0	1-1	3-2	1-3	2-0	1-4	2-1	1-4	1-2	0-0	2-1	0-0	*O*	1-1	2-4	3-1	3-3	1-1	2-2
Sunderland Nissan	1-2	0-4	3-3	4-0	3-1	0-2	2-2	2-2	6-2	0-1	3-0	0-2	1-6	0-1	0-0	*N*	0-4	2-4	0-1	2-1	1-2
Thornaby	1-3	1-5	4-2	1-1	8-1	1-1	0-2	0-1	4-2	3-1	1-0	2-3	0-2	0-2	1-3	4-3	*E*	0-4	2-1	1-6	0-1
Tow Law Town	0-3	0-0	3-0	1-2	1-2	1-2	1-7	2-1	3-2	3-0	1-0	0-2	2-1	3-2	0-0	3-1	2-2		0-3	1-2	0-0
West Allotment Celtic	5-1	3-3	1-1	1-4	4-1	4-1	1-1	1-1	5-1	1-5	2-6	1-1	4-0	1-4	3-1	1-2	2-2	3-1		1-2	1-5
West Auckland Town	2-2	5-1	1-2	2-2	7-0	3-2	3-1	3-1	3-1	3-1	4-0	2-2	3-0	0-2	1-0	1-0	1-0	1-2	2-3		1-2
Whitley Bay	3-2	2-0	1-1	3-2	4-0	0-1	0-2	0-1	3-0	1-1	0-1	1-1	2-3	0-2	4-0	0-1	2-1	1-0	1-2	1-2	

Division One	P	W	D	L	F	A	Pts
Newcastle Blue Star	40	28	6	6	87	34	90
Bedlington Terriers	40	22	8	10	86	61	74
Dunston Federation Brewery	40	20	11	9	82	45	71
Billingham Town	40	18	13	9	81	54	67
West Auckland Town	40	20	7	13	76	53	67
Morpeth Town	40	19	10	11	68	50	67
Billingham Synthonia	40	17	12	11	65	58	63
Chester-le-Street Town	40	18	9	13	64	64	63
Newcastle Benfield Bay Plastics	40	18	8	14	81	62	62
Whitley Bay	40	17	9	14	68	51	60
Durham City	40	15	13	12	58	44	58
Tow Law Town	40	15	9	16	63	65	54
West Allotment Celtic	40	14	8	18	77	83	50
Sunderland Nissan	40	14	8	18	64	73	50
Jarrow Roofing Boldon CA	40	14	7	19	65	76	49
Ashington	40	13	9	18	64	60	48
Thornaby	40	14	6	20	72	85	48
Horden Colliery Welfare	40	12	11	17	55	65	47
Shildon	40	11	14	15	55	65	47
Esh Winning	40	3	7	30	32	103	16
Brandon United	40	4	3	33	35	147	15

J R CLEATOR CUP

(League champions v League Cup holders)

Billingham Synthonia qualified this season as Division One runners-up because Dunston Federation Brewery completed the double in 2004-05

(August 15th at Dunston Federation Brewery)

Dunston Federation Brewery 2

Billingham Synthonia 1

NORTHERN LEAGUE DIVISION ONE CONSTITUTION 2006-07

ASHINGTON .... Portland Park, Lintonville Terrace, Ashington NE63 9XG........ 01670 811991
BEDLINGTON TERRIERS .... Dr Pitt Welfare Ground, Park Road, Bedlington NE22 5DP 01670 825485
BILLINGHAM SYNTHONIA .... The Stadium, Central Avenue, Billingham TS23 1LR........ 01642 532348
BILLINGHAM TOWN........ Bedford Terrace, Billingham TS23 4AF........ 01642 560043
BISHOP AUCKLAND........ Shildon FC, Dean Street, Shildon, Durham DL4 1EZ........ 01388 773877
CHESTER-LE-STREET TOWN........ Moor Park, Chester Moor, Chester-le-Street DH2 3RW........ 07729 527973
CONSETT .... Belle Vue Park, Ashdale Road, Consett DH8 5SR 01207 503788
DARLINGTON RAILWAY ATHLETIC ... Darlington Rail Athletic Club, Brinkburn Road, Darlington DL3 9LF........ 01325 468125
DUNSTON FEDERATION BREWERY ... Federation Park, Wellington Road, Dunston, Gateshead NE11 9EE 0191 493 2935
DURHAM CITY........ Archibald Stadium, Belmont Industrial Estate, Durham DH1 1GG 0191 386 9616
HORDEN COLLIERY WELFARE.... Welfare Park Ground, Park Road, Horden, Peterlee SR8 4LW 0191 587 3549
JARROW ROOFING BOLDON CA .. Boldon CA Sports Club, New Road, Boldon Colliery NE35 9DS........ 0191 489 9825
MORPETH TOWN .... Craik Park, Morpeth Common, Morpeth NE61 2YX........ 01670 513785
NEWCASTLE BENFIELD BP Benfield School Sports Ground, Benfield Road, Newcastle-upon-Tyne NE6 4NU 0191 265 9357
NEWCASTLE BLUE STAR....... Wheatsheaf Sports Ground, Woolsington, Main, Callerton NE13 8DF 0191 286 0425
NORTHALLERTON TOWN...... Calvert Stadium, Ainderby Road, Romanby, Northallerton DL7 8HA........ 01609 772418
SHILDON........ Dean Street, Shildon DL4 1EZ 01388 773877
SUNDERLAND NISSAN .... Nissan Sports Complex, Washington Road, Sunderland SR5 3NS 0191 415 2354
TOW LAW TOWN........ Ironworks Road, Tow Law, Bishop Auckland DL13 4DH 01388 731443
WEST ALLOTMENT CELTIC ... Whitley Park, Whitley Road, Benton, Newcastle-upon-Tyne NE12 9SF........ 0191 270 0885
WEST AUCKLAND TOWN ...... Darlington Road Ground, Darlington Road, West Auckland DL14 9JT 07800 796630
WHITLEY BAY .... Hillheads Park, Rink Way, Whitley Bay NE25 8HR........ 0191 291 3636

IN: Bishop Auckland (R – Northern Premier League Division One), Consett (P), Darlington Railway Athletic (P), Northallerton Town (P)
OUT: Brandon United (R), Esh Winning (R), Thornaby (R)

	Alnwick Town	Consett	Crook Town	Darlington Railway Athletic	Guisborough Town	Hebburn Town	Kennek Ryhope CA	Marske United	North Shields	Northallerton Town	Norton & Stockton Ancients	Penrith	Peterlee Newtown	Prudhoe Town	Ryton	Seaham Red Star	South Shields	Spennymoor Town	Washington	Whickham
Alnwick Town		1-3	0-2	1-4	3-2	2-1	4-0	1-0	1-2	1-2	1-3	2-1	10-0	1-3	1-3	2-1	2-2	2-3	1-2	1-2
Consett	5-0		2-1	1-1	12-1	6-0	2-0	4-1	5-0	2-0	4-1	3-1	6-2	1-0	1-0	2-1	3-0	5-1	2-2	5-0
Crook Town	4-1	1-3		3-0	3-1	0-1	1-1	5-0	3-1	0-0	3-3	3-0	6-1	2-1	6-0	3-3	2-1	6-1	3-0	4-1
Darlington Railway Athletic	2-1	1-2	1-1		1-0	2-0	2-0	1-2	3-1	0-0	4-3	1-4	5-2	2-1	0-1	3-0	1-2	0-0	2-0	3-0
Guisborough Town	0-2	1-0	1-2	0-5	*D*	0-1	0-0	1-1	1-2	0-2	1-1	2-3	0-3	1-0	2-1	3-2	0-2	1-1	1-2	0-2
Hebburn Town	4-1	0-7	1-1	0-2	1-0	*I*	0-0	0-1	2-2	0-3	2-1	1-0	4-5	1-0	0-2	1-3	2-0	2-2	1-2	1-1
Kennek Ryhope CA	2-0	2-5	2-3	0-3	2-2	0-2	*V*	2-2	0-2	1-3	1-2	0-2	1-0	0-0	1-2	1-1	1-2	5-2	0-0	1-1
Marske United	1-2	2-2	0-5	2-3	2-0	1-1	1-1	*I*	2-3	2-2	3-2	1-1	8-2	0-1	0-3	1-1	1-0	0-0	2-3	1-1
North Shields	3-1	1-3	2-1	0-3	4-0	0-0	1-1	0-2	*S*	0-3	0-2	1-1	4-0	1-1	5-0	1-3	2-1	3-1	1-6	1-1
Northallerton Town	6-0	3-0	3-1	2-0	2-1	2-0	1-1	1-2	4-0	*I*	0-0	2-3	3-0	1-4	2-1	1-1	8-0	1-1	4-1	4-1
Norton & Stockton Ancients	3-1	1-2	3-2	1-8	2-2	2-3	2-1	2-1	4-1	1-3	*O*	3-4	5-1	3-1	1-1	1-1	3-0	1-4	4-4	3-3
Penrith	4-1	1-3	1-0	4-1	1-0	0-0	1-0	2-2	2-1	0-1	1-2	*N*	4-0	2-2	0-0	2-2	1-0	5-1	2-1	1-1
Peterlee Newtown	1-4	0-5	0-7	1-3	0-2	1-2	0-5	2-4	0-4	3-4	2-6	2-3		0-0	3-5	1-3	3-1	0-5	0-3	2-5
Prudhoe Town	3-0	0-5	1-1	1-3	5-1	4-2	1-1	1-1	2-1	0-1	0-1	0-0	0-2	*T*	2-1	1-0	1-2	0-0	1-0	2-3
Ryton	1-4	0-6	2-1	0-4	5-1	0-0	2-1	1-2	2-1	1-1	1-2	0-2	4-1	0-0	*W*	3-3	2-2	2-0	1-2	1-4
Seaham Red Star	0-3	1-2	0-0	1-3	0-3	4-1	3-0	2-3	1-1	2-1	1-4	1-1	4-0	1-2	1-1	*O*	3-1	1-3	1-1	1-0
South Shields	4-1	1-8	0-4	1-2	7-1	1-6	3-4	1-3	1-3	0-3	1-1	2-1	2-4	3-1	2-1	0-3		2-2	1-0	2-3
Spennymoor Town	5-0	1-2	1-1	3-2	3-1	2-1	4-2	4-1	2-2	0-2	2-1	2-6	4-2	2-1	0-1	2-1	2-0		1-1	1-0
Washington	3-2	1-3	0-0	1-1	0-0	5-2	7-1	1-1	1-0	0-3	1-2	0-2	6-2	2-0	1-0	1-0	4-1	1-0		3-3
Whickham	6-1	1-2	4-4	4-1	1-2	2-0	7-0	5-3	1-0	0-2	2-1	2-4	8-0	1-2	0-0	0-3	3-0	2-2	3-0	

Division Two		P	W	D	L	F	A	Pts
Consett		38	33	3	2	134	31	102
Northallerton Town		38	25	8	5	86	30	83
Darlington Railway Athletic		38	23	5	10	83	46	74
Penrith		38	20	10	8	73	46	70
Crook Town		38	19	11	8	95	43	68
Washington		38	17	10	11	68	54	61
Norton & Stockton Ancients		38	17	9	12	83	73	60
Spennymoor Town		38	16	11	11	70	66	59
Whickham		38	16	10	12	84	64	58
Marske United		38	12	13	13	62	69	49
Ryton		38	13	9	16	51	65	48
North Shields		38	13	8	17	57	67	47
Prudhoe Town		38	12	10	16	45	49	46
Seaham Red Star		38	11	12	15	60	59	45
Hebburn Town		38	12	9	17	46	67	45
Alnwick Town	*-3*	38	12	1	25	62	93	34
Kennek Ryhope CA		38	5	13	20	41	76	28
South Shields	*-6*	38	10	4	24	51	95	28
Guisborough Town		38	7	7	24	35	86	28
Peterlee Newtown		38	5	1	32	48	155	16

NORTHERN LEAGUE DIVISION TWO CONSTITUTION 2006-07

ALNWICK TOWN .... St James Park, Weavers Way, Alnwick NE66 1BG 01665 603162
BRANDON UNITED .... Welfare Ground, Commercial Street, Brandon DH7 8PL 0191 378 1730
CROOK TOWN .... Millfield Ground, West Road, Crook DL15 9PW 01388 762959
ESH WINNING .... West Terrace, Waterhouses, Esh Winning DH7 9BQ 0191 373 3872
GUISBOROUGH TOWN .... King George V Playing Fields, Howlbeck Road, Guisborough TS14 6LE 01287 636925
HEBBURN TOWN .... Hebburn Sports & Social Club, Victoria Road West, Hebburn NE31 1UN 0191 483 5101
MARSKE UNITED .... Mount Pleasant, Mount Pleasant Avenue, Marske-by-Sea TS11 7BW 01642 471091
NORTH SHIELDS .... Ralph Gardner Park, West Percy Road, Chirton, North Shields NE29 7RG .... None
NORTON & STOCKTON ANCIENTS ... Norton Sports Complex, Station Road, Norton, Stockton-on-Tees TS20 1PE 01642 530203
PENRITH .... Southend Road Ground, Penrith CA11 8JH 01768 859990
PRUDHOE TOWN .... Kimberley Park, Broomhouse Road, Prudhoe NE42 5EH 01661 835900
RYTON .... Kingsley Park, Stannerford Road, Crawcock, Ryton NE40 3SN 0191 413 4448
SEAHAM RED STAR .... Seaham Town Park, Stockton Road, Seaham SR7 0JT 0191 581 1347
SOUTH SHIELDS .... Filtrona Park, Shaftsbury Avenue, Simonside Industrial Estate NE32 3UP 0191 427 9839
SPENNYMOOR TOWN .... Brewery Field, Durham Road, Spennymoor DL16 6UU 01388 811934
STOKESLEY SPORTS CLUB .. Stokesley Sports Club, Broughton Road, Stokesley, Middlesbrough TS9 5AQ 01642 710051
SUNDERLAND RYHOPE CA ... Meadow Park, Beechbrook, off Waterworks Road, Ryhope, Sunderland SR2 0NZ 0191 523 6555
TEAM NORTHUMBRIA ... Bullock Steads Sports Ground, Ponteland Rd, Kenton Bank Foot, Newcastle-upon-Tyne NE13 8AH ...... None
THORNABY .... Teesdale Park, Acklam Road, Thornaby, Stockton-on-Tees TS17 7JU 01642 606803
WASHINGTON .... Albany Park, Spout Lane, Concord, Washington N37 2AB 0191 417 7779
WHICKHAM .... Glebe Ground Sports, Rectory Lane, Whickham, Newcastle-upon-Tyne NE16 4NA 0191 420 0186

IN: Brandon United (R), Esh Winning (R), Stokesley Sports Club (P – Wearside League), Team Northumbria (P – Northern Alliance Premier Division), Thornaby (R)

OUT: Consett (P), Darlington Railway Athletic (P), Northallerton Town (P), Peterlee Newtown (now Peterlee Town) (R – Northern Alliance Premier Division)

Kennek Ryhope CA become Sunderland Ryhope CA

LEAGUE CUP

(All clubs in League)

FIRST ROUND

Alnwick Town 1 **Billingham Town** 4
Brandon United 1 **Morpeth Town** 3
Peterlee Newtown 2 **Sunderland Nissan** 4
Ryton 1 **Crook Town** 3
South Shields 2 North Shields 0
West Allotment Celtic 4 Hebburn Town 0
West Auckland Town 3 Durham City 1
Whickham 2 Chester-le-Street Town 0
Whitley Bay 2 **Northallerton Town** 4

SECOND ROUND

Ashington 2 Shildon 1
Bedlington Terriers 3 Horden Colliery Welfare 2
Consett 2 Billingham Town 1
Crook Town 2 **Jarrow Roofing Boldon CA** 4
Darlington Railway Athletic 3 South Shields 2
Dunston Federation Brewery 5 Washington 4 *aet*
Esh Winning 4 **Newcastle Blue Star** 4 *aet* (1-3p)
Kennek Ryhope CA 2 **Norton & Stockton Ancients** 2 *aet* (1-3p)
Morpeth Town 1 Billingham Synthonia 0
Penrith 3 Sunderland Nissan 2
Prudhoe Town 0 **Tow Law Town** 3
Seaham Red Star 5 Marske United 2
Thornaby 4 Northallerton Town 1
West Allotment Celtic 0 **Newcastle BBP** 1
West Auckland Town 3 Spennymoor Town 1
Whickham 5 Guisborough Town 0

THIRD ROUND

Ashington 0 **Dunston Federation Brewery** 1
Bedlington Terriers 0 **Darlington Railway Athletic** 2
Jarrow Roofing Boldon CA 4 Seaham Red Star 1
Morpeth Town 4 Tow Law Town 1 *aet*
Norton & Stockton Ancients 1 **Newcastle Blue Star** 2
Penrith 2 Newcastle BBP 1
Thornaby 1 **Consett** 5
Whickham 0 **West Auckland Town** 1

QUARTER-FINALS

Darlington Railway Athletic 2 **Consett** 2 *aet* (3-4p)
Jarrow Roofing Boldon CA 1 **Dunston Federation Brewery** 2
Morpeth Town 1 **West Auckland Town** 2 *aet*
Newcastle Blue Star 2 Penrith 1

SEMI-FINALS

Consett 0 **Newcastle Blue Star** 1
Dunston Federation Brewery 4 West Auckland Town 0

FINAL

(May 5th at Durham City)

Newcastle Blue Star 1 Dunston Federation Brewery 0

CRAVEN CUP

(Division Two clubs)

FIRST ROUND

Guisborough Town 1 **Spennymoor Town** 2
North Shields 1 **Crook Town** 2
Penrith 3 Alnwick Town 0
Prudhoe Town 2 **Consett** 5

SECOND ROUND

Consett 4 Ryton 3
Crook Town 1 **Whickham** 2
Darlington Railway Athletic 6 Kennek Ryhope CA 3
Hebburn Town 0 **Northallerton Town** 1
Norton & Stockton Ancients 2 Marske United 0
Peterlee Newtown 4 South Shields 3 *aet*
Seaham Red Star 0 **Spennymoor Town** 3
Washington 1 **Penrith** 0 *(Washington expelled)*

QUARTER-FINALS

Darlington Railway Athletic 3 Whickham 1
Penrith 4 Consett 1
Peterlee Newtown 1 **Northallerton Town** 11
Spennymoor Town 2 **Norton & Stockton Ancients** 4

SEMI-FINALS

Northallerton Town 0 **Penrith** 2 *aet*
Norton & Stockton Ancients 2 **Darlington Railway Athletic** 3 *aet*

FINAL

(May 6th at Crook Town)

Penrith 5 Darlington Railway Athletic 1

NORTHERN PREMIER LEAGUE

	AFC Telford United	Ashton United	Blyth Spartans	Bradford Park Avenue	Burscough	Farsley Celtic	Frickley Athletic	Gateshead	Guiseley	Ilkeston Town	Leek Town	Lincoln United	Marine	Matlock Town	North Ferriby United	Ossett Town	Prescot Cables	Radcliffe Borough	Runcorn FC Halton	Wakefield-Emley	Whitby Town	Witton Albion
AFC Telford United		2-1	1-1	3-6	0-1	1-0	1-3	1-1	0-0	0-0	1-0	2-0	1-1	2-1	2-1	1-1	3-2	2-1	3-1	2-3	3-1	2-2
Ashton United	0-0		2-3	3-0	1-3	1-1	0-1	3-1	2-2	2-2	3-1	3-0	1-2	1-1	2-4	0-3	1-3	3-0	6-0	4-0	4-2	0-2
Blyth Spartans	1-1	2-0		2-0	1-0	0-1	1-0	1-1	3-1	1-1	2-1	0-1	1-0	2-2	4-2	4-4	2-0	1-0	0-0	3-0	1-0	5-1
Bradford Park Avenue	0-1	1-1	2-1	*P*	3-4	4-3	1-4	0-1	1-3	2-2	0-0	1-1	1-3	1-2	0-4	2-0	1-0	1-2	8-0	2-1	0-0	2-3
Burscough	0-1	3-0	0-0	0-1	*R*	0-3	0-1	2-3	3-2	2-1	1-2	1-1	0-3	1-1	3-2	4-1	2-3	3-0	2-2	3-2	2-1	1-1
Farsley Celtic	2-0	3-0	1-1	3-0	2-4	*E*	0-1	4-2	1-1	1-1	3-2	3-0	0-1	3-1	1-1	3-0	2-0	3-0	5-0	6-1	1-3	0-3
Frickley Athletic	1-0	2-2	3-2	6-2	4-1	1-0	*M*	1-2	2-1	2-0	2-1	2-2	0-0	1-0	1-1	1-0	0-1	0-2	1-0	0-0	3-0	2-0
Gateshead	1-1	3-2	1-2	2-1	2-0	0-5	2-2	*I*	0-2	1-2	2-0	1-1	0-1	1-5	2-3	2-1	0-3	0-0	2-4	3-2	3-2	3-2
Guiseley	1-0	1-3	0-2	0-3	3-1	0-3	2-0	1-0	*E*	2-2	1-1	1-2	1-0	1-0	0-2	0-2	2-5	3-2	1-1	0-1	0-2	3-1
Ilkeston Town	2-0	2-0	0-0	2-0	2-1	1-1	0-2	3-1	0-1	*R*	2-2	1-2	1-0	0-1	1-1	0-1	0-2	3-1	2-0	2-0	0-0	2-0
Leek Town	1-1	1-0	0-3	3-0	3-0	1-1	0-2	0-0	0-2	0-3		1-0	1-1	1-1	0-0	1-1	1-1	0-3	2-3	0-0	3-0	2-2
Lincoln United	1-2	0-0	0-1	3-2	0-1	0-1	3-7	2-2	1-0	2-2	3-3	*D*	1-1	0-1	0-1	0-0	0-2	1-1	0-0	1-2	2-0	1-2
Marine	1-1	2-2	0-1	3-1	2-1	1-0	1-0	0-0	2-0	4-2	1-2	5-1	*I*	0-0	1-0	4-0	1-0	3-0	2-0	0-0	0-0	0-1
Matlock Town	1-1	0-0	0-1	1-0	3-0	0-0	1-2	1-2	1-0	2-0	0-2	0-3	2-5	*V*	1-1	1-0	3-1	1-1	2-1	0-1	4-1	0-4
North Ferriby United	1-0	1-0	1-4	5-2	0-1	0-1	1-2	1-0	2-2	2-1	4-0	0-0	0-2	3-2	*I*	2-1	3-0	2-1	3-1	3-3	0-0	5-1
Ossett Town	1-1	3-2	3-1	3-2	0-0	0-1	2-4	3-1	1-0	1-0	0-1	1-3	0-2	4-4	2-3	*S*	3-1	2-0	2-1	2-0	2-3	1-0
Prescot Cables	0-0	2-1	1-3	2-2	1-2	1-1	0-2	2-1	0-2	0-0	0-2	1-3	0-1	2-1	0-2	2-1	*I*	1-0	0-0	2-0	5-1	1-1
Radcliffe Borough	2-2	1-2	0-3	1-0	0-2	0-5	0-3	4-0	0-0	3-1	2-3	4-0	2-0	0-1	1-2	0-1	4-0	*O*	8-1	3-0	0-1	1-3
Runcorn FC Halton	0-7	1-2	0-5	2-2	1-3	0-7	1-1	2-1	0-0	2-1	0-2	0-1	0-0	0-4	2-4	0-2	5-1	2-2	*N*	2-1	1-1	0-4
Wakefield-Emley	1-1	0-1	0-3	1-1	2-1	0-1	0-0	1-0	1-3	1-0	1-3	1-1	0-2	2-3	1-0	0-1	1-0	0-0	2-0		2-3	0-2
Whitby Town	4-1	2-0	0-4	3-3	1-2	1-1	2-0	2-0	1-0	2-0	1-0	2-1	1-1	2-1	4-2	2-1	0-1	1-1	4-0	4-2		0-2
Witton Albion	4-0	0-1	1-1	2-3	2-3	0-1	1-0	2-2	4-0	3-1	0-1	3-0	0-2	2-4	2-2	2-0	0-0	0-1	2-0	1-2	0-0	

Premier Division		HOME					AWAY					TOTAL					
	P	**W**	**D**	**L**	**F**	**A**	**W**	**D**	**L**	**F**	**A**	**W**	**D**	**L**	**F**	**A**	**Pts**
Blyth Spartans	42	13	6	2	37	16	13	5	3	42	16	26	11	5	79	32	89
Frickley Athletic	42	13	5	3	35	17	13	3	5	37	19	26	8	8	72	36	86
Marine	42	12	6	3	33	12	11	6	4	28	13	23	12	7	61	25	81
Farsley Celtic	42	12	4	5	47	22	11	6	4	37	12	23	10	9	84	34	79
North Ferriby United	42	12	4	5	39	24	9	6	6	38	30	21	10	11	77	54	73
Whitby Town	42	13	4	4	39	23	5	6	10	21	36	18	10	14	60	59	64
Burscough	42	8	5	8	33	31	11	1	9	31	33	19	6	17	64	64	63
Witton Albion	42	7	5	9	31	24	10	4	7	37	31	17	9	16	68	55	60
Matlock Town	42	8	5	8	24	26	8	6	7	36	29	16	11	15	60	55	59
AFC Telford United	42	10	7	4	33	27	4	10	7	21	25	14	17	11	54	52	59
Ossett Town	42	11	3	7	36	30	6	4	11	21	31	17	7	18	57	61	58
Leek Town	42	5	10	6	21	24	9	4	8	29	29	14	14	14	50	53	56
Prescot Cables	42	7	6	8	23	26	8	2	11	26	34	15	8	19	49	60	53
Guiseley	42	8	3	10	23	33	6	6	9	22	25	14	9	19	45	58	51
Ashton United	42	8	5	8	42	31	5	5	11	20	32	13	10	19	62	63	49
Ilkeston Town	42	10	5	6	26	16	2	8	11	22	35	12	13	17	48	51	49
Gateshead	42	8	4	9	31	41	4	6	11	21	36	12	10	20	52	77	46
Radcliffe Borough	42	8	2	11	36	30	4	6	11	18	32	12	8	22	54	62	44
Lincoln United	42	3	8	10	21	31	7	6	8	23	33	10	14	18	44	64	44
Wakefield-Emley	42	6	5	10	17	26	5	4	12	21	43	11	9	22	38	69	42
Bradford Park Avenue	42	6	5	10	33	36	4	4	13	31	50	10	9	23	64	86	39
Runcorn FC Halton	42	4	6	11	21	51	2	5	14	15	57	6	11	25	36	108	29

PLAY-OFFS

SEMI-FINALS

(May 1st)

Frickley Athletic 0 **North Ferriby United** 0 *aet* (2-4p) ***Att*** 593

Marine 0 **Farsley Celtic** 1 ***Att*** 477

FINAL

(May 6th at Farsley Celtic)

Farsley Celtic 2 North Ferriby United 1 *aet* ***Att*** 933

DATES & GATES

	AFC Telford United	Ashton United	Blyth Spartans	Bradford Park Avenue	Burscough	Farsley Celtic	Frickley Athletic	Gateshead	Guiseley	Ilkeston Town	Leek Town	Lincoln United	Marine	Matlock Town	North Ferriby United	Ossett Town	Prescot Cables	Radcliffe Borough	Runcorn FC Halton	Wakefield-Emley	Whitby Town	Witton Albion
AFC Telford United		14 Apr *1,720*	10 Dec *1,388*	3 Sep *1,385*	23 Aug *1,686*	25 Feb *1,572*	1 Oct *1,627*	28 Jan *1,601*	8 Apr *1,556*	25 Oct *1,629*	11 Oct *1,250*	4 Mar *1,556*	20 Sep *1,424*	3 Dec *1,192*	29 Apr *2,323*	4 Feb *1,451*	22 Oct *1,564*	27 Aug *1,471*	1 Nov *1,342*	8 Oct *1,402*	25 Mar *1,835*	2 Jan *1,782*
Ashton United	1 Apr *442*		4 Feb *180*	20 Mar *151*	12 Sep *250*	21 Jan *178*	2 Sep *230*	10 Oct *214*	5 Nov *227*	1 Oct *210*	19 Sep *233*	24 Sep *172*	2 Jan *223*	29 Aug *202*	20 Aug *120*	13 Mar *128*	10 Dec *172*	17 Apr *207*	29 Apr *202*	25 Mar *151*	25 Feb *178*	8 Apr *164*
Blyth Spartans	18 Feb *561*	27 Aug *313*		17 Apr *658*	25 Feb *418*	23 Aug *322*	13 Sep *361*	26 Dec *767*	27 Apr *1,024*	8 Apr *592*	1 Oct *486*	3 Dec *314*	3 Sep *295*	29 Oct *430*	4 Apr *659*	7 Jan *359*	25 Mar *537*	15 Apr *525*	11 Oct *352*	29 Apr *1,250*	20 Sep *460*	28 Jan *402*
Bradford Park Avenue	22 Apr *423*	17 Sep *191*	28 Sep *144*		4 Feb *216*	5 Oct *287*	26 Oct *320*	29 Mar *177*	2 Jan *370*	12 Nov *235*	10 Dec *278*	29 Aug *213*	15 Mar *169*	21 Jan *246*	19 Apr *215*	14 Apr *244*	20 Aug *244*	5 Nov *287*	12 Apr *173*	22 Oct *250*	5 Sep *236*	25 Feb *261*
Burscough	27 Sep *305*	1 Nov *236*	20 Aug *264*	29 Oct *355*		10 Dec *526*	4 Apr *193*	21 Jan *252*	18 Mar *240*	26 Nov *231*	7 Mar *187*	18 Feb *256*	17 Apr *387*	8 Apr *218*	17 Sep *702*	28 Mar *172*	2 Jan *443*	6 Sep *215*	8 Nov *350*	28 Jan *224*	22 Apr *195*	29 Aug *349*
Farsley Celtic	29 Oct *279*	18 Mar *202*	20 Dec *201*	20 Sep *365*	1 Oct *200*		2 Jan *335*	13 Sep *178*	29 Aug *576*	18 Feb *221*	3 Sep *205*	1 Apr *295*	22 Apr *245*	21 Feb *172*	5 Nov *235*	14 Jan *151*	19 Nov *295*	28 Jan *225*	25 Apr *202*	28 Mar *176*	11 Oct *211*	20 Aug *191*
Frickley Athletic	14 Jan *460*	28 Feb *334*	4 Oct *392*	27 Jan *454*	29 Apr *407*	6 Sep *287*		18 Mar *251*	21 Mar *230*	29 Oct *310*	27 Aug *197*	7 Oct *357*	22 Oct *299*	1 Apr *324*	14 Apr *908*	17 Dec *244*	17 Sep *212*	26 Nov *246*	18 Feb *319*	26 Dec *348*	23 Aug *220*	19 Nov *263*
Gateshead	17 Sep *289*	22 Oct *144*	14 Apr *715*	14 Jan *200*	1 Apr *120*	15 Mar *87*	29 Aug *201*		5 Oct *137*	29 Apr *194*	29 Oct *153*	20 Aug *136*	26 Apr *102*	4 Feb *184*	11 Mar *126*	28 Sep *118*	8 Oct *126*	17 Dec *130*	3 Dec *113*	7 Sep *121*	2 Jan *194*	24 Apr *103*
Guiseley	21 Jan *363*	7 Feb *151*	6 Sep *282*	11 Oct *473*	27 Aug *198*	26 Dec *517*	10 Dec *274*	23 Aug *231*		28 Jan *238*	26 Nov *215*	29 Apr *145*	15 Apr *225*	25 Mar *200*	27 Sep *223*	28 Feb *113*	17 Apr *205*	17 Sep *252*	29 Oct *295*	11 Feb *212*	19 Apr *93*	18 Feb *213*
Ilkeston Town	6 Sep *513*	4 Mar *352*	17 Sep *378*	17 Dec *332*	25 Mar *412*	27 Aug *331*	22 Apr *393*	5 Nov *368*	22 Oct *323*		23 Aug *397*	2 Jan *442*	21 Mar *293*	17 Apr *470*	19 Nov *373*	25 Feb *313*	4 Oct *348*	8 Oct *258*	21 Jan *378*	27 Sep *265*	4 Feb *395*	20 Apr *279*
Leek Town	29 Aug *615*	22 Apr *297*	15 Feb *235*	18 Mar *293*	21 Feb *173*	8 Apr *246*	25 Mar *323*	18 Feb *253*	20 Aug *248*	14 Jan *317*		17 Apr *306*	28 Jan *231*	2 Jan *394*	26 Apr *232*	17 Sep *269*	5 Nov *256*	27 Sep *200*	12 Nov *247*	4 Oct *243*	24 Apr *209*	6 Sep *286*
Lincoln United	11 Mar *266*	17 Dec *138*	21 Jan *135*	8 Nov *115*	3 Sep *128*	18 Oct *85*	7 Apr *167*	22 Apr *115*	13 Sep *117*	14 Apr *193*	27 Dec *134*		4 Feb *83*	20 Sep *140*	4 Oct *175*	23 Aug *135*	25 Feb *101*	18 Mar *102*	1 Oct *135*	26 Nov *92*	27 Aug *142*	29 Oct *135*
Marine	4 Oct *364*	8 Oct *218*	18 Mar *403*	8 Apr *303*	26 Dec *452*	14 Feb *216*	5 Nov *354*	27 Aug *267*	14 Jan *353*	3 Dec *490*	4 Mar *387*	17 Sep *440*		17 Dec *246*	25 Mar *337*	29 Apr *642*	6 Sep *270*	23 Aug *261*	18 Oct *273*	18 Feb *285*	21 Jan *355*	14 Apr *394*
Matlock Town	18 Mar *559*	18 Feb *273*	25 Apr *259*	27 Aug *280*	14 Jan *221*	17 Sep *228*	24 Apr *265*	10 Dec *215*	22 Apr *204*	26 Dec *541*	15 Apr *404*	6 Sep *265*	4 Apr *231*		28 Jan *402*	26 Nov *186*	27 Apr *185*	4 Oct *294*	27 Sep *234*	23 Aug *295*	22 Oct *276*	5 Nov *315*
North Ferriby United	17 Dec *333*	12 Nov *226*	2 Jan *386*	23 Aug *212*	11 Apr *201*	4 Feb *252*	20 Sep *251*	1 Oct *262*	25 Feb *194*	14 Sep *188*	21 Jan *286*	21 Mar *230*	29 Oct *279*	11 Oct *248*		6 Sep *231*	25 Oct *216*	14 Jan *169*	27 Aug *118*	3 Dec *153*	17 Apr *211*	22 Apr *171*
Ossett Town	20 Aug *440*	28 Jan *164*	11 Apr *200*	26 Dec *256*	25 Apr *54*	25 Mar *175*	11 Oct *280*	17 Apr *114*	20 Sep *191*	29 Aug *97*	19 Apr *82*	25 Oct *43*	1 Oct *112*	13 Sep *103*	10 Dec *81*		4 Mar *151*	18 Feb *122*	3 Sep *78*	22 Apr *135*	4 Apr *82*	21 Jan *178*
Prescot Cables	14 Mar *335*	23 Aug *138*	22 Feb *132*	6 Mar *167*	14 Apr *304*	29 Apr *182*	21 Jan *190*	11 Feb *132*	2 Sep *210*	18 Mar *150*	13 Sep *132*	28 Jan *133*	11 Oct *320*	1 Oct *187*	18 Feb *145*	27 Aug *156*		28 Feb *152*	26 Dec *227*	29 Oct *165*	26 Nov *165*	27 Sep *186*
Radcliffe Borough	19 Apr *303*	26 Dec *213*	21 Mar *188*	29 Apr *366*	20 Sep *188*	3 Dec *166*	25 Feb *239*	4 Apr *123*	24 Sep *228*	1 Apr *217*	4 Feb *230*	10 Dec *153*	13 Sep *145*	20 Aug *230*	3 Sep *160*	29 Oct *160*	29 Aug *189*		14 Apr *253*	21 Jan *167*	1 Oct *209*	11 Oct *220*
Runcorn FC Halton	17 Apr *349*	6 Sep *181*	22 Apr *154*	8 Oct *108*	4 Oct *173*	27 Apr *101*	20 Aug *147*	19 Nov *73*	4 Feb *154*	10 Dec *104*	4 Apr *135*	10 Apr *77*	29 Aug *203*	25 Feb *142*	22 Oct *116*	8 Apr *79*	20 Sep *244*	2 Jan *166*		17 Sep *101*	1 Apr *115*	22 Mar *145*
Wakefield-Emley	24 Apr *159*	14 Jan *99*	5 Nov *131*	15 Nov *153*	17 Dec *106*	21 Mar *79*	18 Apr *289*	20 Sep *115*	1 Oct *216*	2 Sep *159*	25 Feb *84*	11 Oct *147*	20 Aug *107*	25 Oct *138*	29 Aug *144*	2 Jan *212*	4 Feb *98*	19 Nov *104*	24 Sep *104*		18 Mar *91*	10 Dec *127*
Whitby Town	5 Nov *386*	29 Oct *296*	29 Aug *306*	18 Feb *337*	19 Nov *265*	16 Nov *206*	26 Apr *272*	22 Mar *262*	14 Apr *355*	20 Aug *318*	29 Apr *315*	14 Jan *291*	10 Dec *232*	3 Sep *264*	26 Dec *386*	5 Oct *246*	29 Mar *271*	8 Apr *264*	28 Jan *286*	19 Oct *256*		17 Sep *271*
Witton Albion	26 Dec *617*	4 Oct *240*	19 Apr *214*	1 Oct *303*	11 Mar *237*	17 Apr *255*	12 Nov *301*	3 Sep *214*	17 Dec *245*	20 Sep *225*	31 Jan *282*	22 Oct *206*	21 Feb *196*	29 Apr *260*	26 Nov *259*	18 Mar *193*	14 Jan *298*	26 Apr *184*	23 Aug *309*	27 Aug *258*	3 Dec *243*	

NORTHERN PREMIER LEAGUE PREMIER DIVISION

CONSTITUTION FOR 2006-07

AFC TELFORD UNITED

New Bucks Head Stadium, Watling Street, Wellington, Telford, Shropshire TF1 2TU
Tel: 01952 640064 Fax: 01952 640021
Manager: Rob Smith www.telfordunited.com Colours: White & black

ASHTON UNITED

Hurst Cross, Surrey Street, Ashton-under-Lyne, Lancashire OL6 8DY
Tel: 0161 339 4158 Club: 0161 330 1511 Fax: 0161 339 4158
Manager: Scott Green www.ashtonunited.com Colours: Red, white & black

BURSCOUGH

Victoria Park, Mart Lane, Burscough, Ormskirk, Lancashire L40 0SD
Tel: 01704 893237 Fax: 01704 893237
Manager: Liam Watson www.burscoughfc.co.uk Colours: Green & white

FLEETWOOD TOWN

Highbury Stadium, Park Avenue, Fleetwood, Lancashire FY7 6TX
Tel: 01253 770702
Manager: Tony Greenwood www.fleetwoodtownfc.co.uk Colours: Red & black

FRICKLEY ATHLETIC

Westfield Lane, South Elmsall, Pontefract, West Yorkshire WF9 2EQ
Tel: 01977 642460 Fax: 01977 642460
Manager: Gary Morrow www.frickleyafc.co.uk Colours: Blue

GATESHEAD

The International Stadium, Neilson Road, Gateshead, Tyne & Wear NE10 0EF
Tel: 0191 478 3883 Fax: 0191 477 1315
Manager: Tony Lee www.gateshead-fc.com Colours: Black & white

GRANTHAM TOWN

South Kesteven Sports Stadium, Trent Road, Grantham, Lincolnshire NG31 7XQ
Tel: 01476 402224 Club: 01476 402225
Manager: Lee Glover www.granthamtownfc.co.uk Colours: Black & white

GUISELEY

Nethermoor Park, Otley Road, Guiseley, Leeds, West Yorkshire LS20 8BT
Tel: 01943 873223 Club: 01943 872872
Manager: Neil Parsley www.guiseleyafc.co.uk Colours: White & navy blue

HEDNESFORD TOWN

Keys Park, Keys Park Road, Hednesford, Staffs WS12 2DZ
Tel: 01543 422870 Fax: 01543 428180
Manager: Phil Starbuck www.hednesfordtown.com Colours: White & black

ILKESTON TOWN

The New Manor Ground, Awsworth Road, Ilkeston, Derbyshire DE7 8JF
Tel: 0115 932 4094 Club: 0115 930 5622
Manager: Nigel Jemson www.whiteballproject.co.uk Colours: Red & black

KENDAL TOWN

Parkside, Parkside Road, Kendal, Cumbria LA9 7BL
Tel: 01539 727472 Club: 01539 722469 Fax: 01539 727472
Manager: Tony Hesketh www.kendaltownfc.co.uk Colours: Black & white

LEEK TOWN

Harrison Park, Macclesfield Road, Leek, Staffordshire ST13 8LD
Tel: 01538 399278 Club: 01538 383734 Fax: 01538 399826
Manager: Mark Cartwright www.leektown.co.uk Colours: Blue & white

LINCOLN UNITED

Ashby Avenue, Hartsholme, Lincoln, Lincolnshire LN6 0DY
Tel: 01522 696400 Club: 01522 690674 Fax: 01522 696400
Manager: John Wilkinson www.comeonyouwhites.com Colours: White

MARINE

Rossett Park, College Road, Crosby, Liverpool, Merseyside L23 3AS
Tel: 0151 924 1743 Club: 0151 924 4046 Fax: 0151 924 1743
Manager: Alvin McDonald www.marinefc.com Colours: White & black

MATLOCK TOWN

Causeway Lane, Matlock, Derbyshire DE4 3AR
Tel: 01629 583866 Club: 01629 553362 Fax: 01629 583866
Manager: Gareth Williams/Phil Brown www.matlocktownfc.co.uk Colours: Royal blue

MOSSLEY

Seel Park, Market Street, Mossley, Ashton-under-Lyne, Lancashire OL5 0ES
Tel: 01457 835989 Club: 01457 836104
Manager: Jason Beckford None Colours: White & black

NORTH FERRIBY UNITED

Grange Lane, Church Road, North Ferriby, East Yorkshire HU14 3AA
Tel: 01482 634601 Fax: 01482 634601
Manager: Brian France www.northferribyunited.co.uk Colours: White & green

OSSETT TOWN

Ingfield, Prospect Road, Ossett, Wakefield, West Yorkshire WF5 9HA
Tel: 01924 272960
Manager: Steve Kittrick www.ossett-town.com Colours: Red & white

PRESCOT CABLES

Valerie Park, Hope Street, Prescot, Merseyside L34 6HD
Tel: 0151 430 0507
Manager: Andy Gray www.prescotcablesfc.co.uk Colours: Gold & black

RADCLIFFE BOROUGH

Stainton Park, Pilkington Road, Radcliffe, Manchester M26 3PE
Tel: 0161 724 8346 Club: 0161 724 5937 Fax: 0161 723 3178
Manager: Kevin Glendon www.radcliffeborough.com Colours: Blue & white

WHITBY TOWN

Turnbull Ground, Upgang Lane, Whitby, North Yorkshire YO21 3HZ
Tel: 01947 604847 Club: 01947 603193 Fax: 01947 603779
Manager: Lee Nogan www.whitby-town.com Colours: Royal blue

WITTON ALBION

CMB Stadium, Wincham Park, Chapel Street, Wincham, Northwich, Cheshire CW9 6DA
Tel: 01606 43008 Club: 01606 47117 Fax: 01606 43008
Manager: Jim Vince www.wittonalbion.co.uk Colours: Red & white

IN: Fleetwood Town (P), Grantham Town (S – Southern League Premier Division), Hednesford Town (R – Football Conference North), Kendal Town (P), Mossley (P)
OUT: Blyth Spartans (P – Football Conference North), Bradford Park Avenue (R), Farsley Celtic (P – Football Conference North), Runcorn Halton (F), Wakefield (formerly Wakefield-Emley) (R)

	Bamber Bridge	Belper Town	Bishop Auckland	Bridlington Town	Brigg Town	Chorley	Clitheroe	Colwyn Bay	Eastwood Town	Fleetwood Town	Goole	Gresley Rovers	Kendal Town	Kidsgrove Athletic	Mossley	Ossett Albion	Rossendale United	Shepshed Dynamo	Spalding United	Stocksbridge Park Steels	Warrington Town	Woodley Sports
Bamber Bridge		0-1	7-2	1-1	3-4	3-1	2-2	2-1	3-1	2-1	1-0	1-1	0-5	2-4	1-2	0-0	0-1	2-1	4-0	1-1	2-1	1-1
Belper Town	1-0		2-1	2-3	1-1	3-1	2-0	2-1	2-1	1-4	2-0	2-1	3-4	0-0	4-0	1-4	0-1	0-1	2-2	0-1	1-1	1-0
Bishop Auckland	1-1	1-3		2-1	0-3	1-4	1-2	0-1	0-1	1-3	0-2	1-2	2-2	2-1	1-2	1-2	1-1	0-4	0-2	1-4	2-3	0-3
Bridlington Town	2-0	2-1	1-0		3-1	4-1	1-0	0-0	2-3	1-1	3-1	2-2	1-2	1-1	2-1	2-1	1-2	1-0	1-0	1-1	1-1	0-2
Brigg Town	3-2	1-2	2-0	3-2		1-0	2-2	1-1	2-2	3-1	1-0	2-1	2-1	2-3	0-1	2-3	2-2	0-1	3-1	0-0	3-2	1-2
Chorley	0-1	1-0	2-1	2-2	1-2	*D*	1-2	1-1	0-1	1-1	0-1	2-2	1-1	1-2	1-2	3-0	2-3	1-2	1-1	1-1	3-0	1-4
Clitheroe	1-0	0-2	4-1	2-0	2-2	0-1	*I*	1-0	0-3	1-0	1-0	3-3	0-3	2-2	3-2	4-2	2-0	1-1	2-1	0-1	2-3	3-2
Colwyn Bay	1-1	0-1	2-0	1-3	0-0	1-2	0-0	*V*	0-0	2-0	4-1	6-0	0-1	4-3	3-0	2-0	0-4	2-0	3-0	1-1	3-0	2-1
Eastwood Town	1-1	2-0	2-0	0-3	2-0	0-4	3-1	4-1	*I*	0-1	3-3	2-3	3-3	2-1	2-2	3-2	4-0	1-1	0-0	1-1	3-3	4-0
Fleetwood Town	0-0	2-0	3-2	2-3	5-1	2-1	4-0	2-1	3-2	*S*	0-1	1-1	1-2	0-2	1-1	2-2	2-2	1-0	2-1	1-1	1-0	2-0
Goole	3-3	1-0	1-0	2-2	2-2	2-2	1-0	3-0	0-3	3-3	*I*	2-3	2-4	1-1	0-0	1-4	1-1	0-5	1-6	0-4	2-3	1-4
Gresley Rovers	3-1	3-1	3-1	2-1	3-2	2-1	3-1	3-2	2-0	0-2	4-0	*O*	0-1	0-0	3-1	3-1	1-1	0-0	3-0	1-1	2-3	2-5
Kendal Town	2-0	2-2	3-3	2-1	1-4	1-2	1-4	0-0	1-1	2-1	3-1	0-3	*N*	4-0	1-1	0-1	4-0	1-2	3-0	1-1	3-1	2-1
Kidsgrove Athletic	0-2	1-0	3-0	3-2	1-4	1-0	5-0	6-0	0-0	0-3	3-3	0-1	0-2		2-3	1-3	2-1	2-3	3-0	0-3	3-3	2-1
Mossley	1-1	4-2	2-1	6-1	1-0	2-1	1-0	1-2	4-0	0-1	3-0	3-1	5-2	2-1	*O*	7-0	2-1	2-3	3-1	2-0	1-1	2-2
Ossett Albion	3-2	0-2	2-2	5-2	1-2	1-2	2-1	1-0	0-0	1-2	0-1	2-1	1-2	0-1	0-2	*N*	1-0	1-1	1-2	1-0	1-1	2-1
Rossendale United	1-1	2-2	3-0	5-0	1-1	0-1	2-1	2-1	1-0	0-1	2-2	1-4	3-2	1-1	0-0	0-1	*E*	2-4	3-3	0-0	2-2	2-3
Shepshed Dynamo	0-5	0-1	0-0	0-0	1-1	1-0	5-0	0-0	0-2	4-0	0-4	1-2	0-3	2-1	2-1	1-1	2-2		0-0	0-1	2-1	1-2
Spalding United	1-1	0-0	2-1	2-0	1-1	1-2	1-2	2-3	0-0	0-4	0-2	4-3	3-0	2-1	0-4	1-1	0-0	2-2		2-2	2-2	1-0
Stocksbridge Park Steels	1-1	4-1	4-2	1-0	3-0	1-3	4-0	1-1	3-1	1-2	1-2	2-1	0-1	2-0	2-3	1-0	2-3	3-1	0-0		2-1	0-0
Warrington Town	0-3	0-0	4-2	3-0	1-1	2-1	1-0	1-2	1-2	2-4	2-1	0-0	0-1	3-2	1-1	2-0	0-0	2-2	1-2	2-2		1-3
Woodley Sports	3-1	3-0	0-2	1-2	2-2	0-2	2-2	2-1	4-1	0-0	2-1	2-1	2-2	2-1	5-0	0-0	2-0	5-1	3-0	4-2	4-1	

Division One			HOME					AWAY					TOTAL					
		P	W	D	L	F	A	W	D	L	F	A	W	D	L	F	A	Pts
Mossley		42	15	3	3	54	21	8	6	7	29	34	23	9	10	83	55	78
Fleetwood Town		42	11	6	4	37	23	11	4	6	35	25	22	10	10	72	48	76
Kendal Town		42	9	6	6	37	29	13	4	4	44	29	22	10	10	81	58	76
Woodley Sports		42	13	5	3	48	22	9	3	9	37	31	22	8	12	85	53	74
Gresley Rovers		42	13	4	4	43	25	7	6	8	36	39	20	10	12	79	64	70
Stocksbridge Park Steels		42	11	4	6	38	23	6	12	3	28	20	17	16	9	66	43	67
Eastwood Town		42	9	8	4	42	30	7	6	8	24	28	16	14	12	66	58	62
Brigg Town		42	10	5	6	36	29	6	9	6	34	35	16	14	12	70	64	62
Belper Town		42	10	4	7	32	27	7	4	10	21	29	17	8	17	53	56	59
Shepshed Dynamo		42	6	7	8	22	27	9	6	6	35	29	15	13	14	57	56	58
Bridlington Town		42	11	6	4	32	21	5	4	12	29	47	16	10	16	61	68	58
Colwyn Bay		42	11	5	5	37	18	4	6	11	19	35	15	11	16	56	53	56
Bamber Bridge		42	9	6	6	38	31	4	9	8	27	28	13	15	14	65	59	54
Ossett Albion		42	8	4	9	26	27	7	5	9	28	37	15	9	18	54	64	54
Rossendale United		42	6	9	6	33	30	6	8	7	25	31	12	17	13	58	61	53
Clitheroe		42	11	4	6	34	29	4	4	13	20	44	15	8	19	54	73	53
Kidsgrove Athletic		42	9	3	9	38	34	5	6	10	28	35	14	9	19	66	69	51
Chorley		42	4	7	10	26	30	10	1	10	32	29	14	8	20	58	59	50
Warrington Town		42	7	7	7	29	29	4	8	9	33	45	11	15	16	62	74	48
Spalding United		42	6	9	6	27	31	4	6	11	22	39	10	15	17	49	70	45
Goole	*-1*	42	4	8	9	29	50	7	3	11	26	35	11	11	20	55	85	43
Bishop Auckland		42	2	3	16	18	47	1	3	17	21	52	3	6	33	39	99	15

PLAY-OFFS

SEMI-FINALS

(May 2nd)

Kendal Town 1 Stocksbridge Park Steels 1 *aet* (4-2p) ***Att*** 415

Woodley Sports 0 **Gresley Rovers** 4 ***Att*** 214

FINAL

(May 6th at Kendal Town)

Kendal Town 2 Gresley Rovers 1 ***Att*** 852

DATES & GATES

	Bamber Bridge	Belper Town	Bishop Auckland	Bridlington Town	Brigg Town	Chorley	Clitheroe	Colwyn Bay	Eastwood Town	Fleetwood Town	Goole	Gresley Rovers	Kendal Town	Kidsgrove Athletic	Mossley	Ossett Albion	Rossendale United	Shepshed Dynamo	Spalding United	Stocksbridge Park Steels	Warrington Town	Woodley Sports
Bamber Bridge		20 Aug *126*	21 Jan *147*	17 Dec *148*	8 Apr *138*	17 Apr *255*	11 Oct *237*	29 Aug *141*	22 Oct *152*	2 Jan *392*	22 Apr *135*	20 Sep *121*	13 Sep *165*	3 Sep *136*	31 Jan *211*	5 Nov *187*	4 Apr *138*	18 Mar *163*	3 Dec *136*	1 Oct *154*	25 Feb *175*	27 Apr *159*
Belper Town	4 Feb *158*		8 Apr *112*	8 Oct *112*	20 Sep *121*	22 Apr *142*	29 Oct *174*	10 Dec *166*	17 Apr *207*	17 Sep *154*	2 Jan *255*	11 Feb *225*	1 Apr *178*	11 Oct *133*	17 Dec *205*	25 Mar *144*	22 Oct *128*	23 Aug *151*	6 Sep *129*	16 Mar *136*	1 Oct *143*	14 Jan *148*
Bishop Auckland	18 Feb *103*	5 Apr *72*		8 Feb *103*	7 Sep *101*	11 Oct *122*	26 Dec *138*	20 Aug *144*	23 Apr *111*	11 Mar *136*	29 Mar *101*	25 Apr *84*	24 Aug *141*	17 Sep *128*	29 Oct *159*	22 Mar *65*	14 Apr *132*	14 Jan *133*	27 Apr *77*	28 Jan *109*	20 Apr *79*	29 Apr *91*
Bridlington Town	29 Oct *169*	3 Sep *112*	17 Apr *207*		2 Jan *190*	22 Oct *158*	1 Oct *145*	19 Mar *121*	28 Jan *164*	4 Feb *166*	15 Oct *311*	10 Sep *128*	14 Jan *152*	25 Mar *111*	19 Nov *209*	11 Oct *127*	26 Dec *205*	3 Dec *136*	20 Sep *117*	22 Apr *137*	20 Aug *157*	10 Dec *142*
Brigg Town	14 Jan *176*	11 Apr *135*	5 Nov *173*	28 Sep *113*		18 Mar *184*	3 Dec *186*	24 Sep *169*	15 Mar *114*	25 Feb *164*	17 Apr *245*	26 Oct *116*	25 Mar *191*	1 Oct *202*	28 Jan *201*	24 Aug *191*	1 Apr *171*	10 Dec *165*	11 Oct *154*	14 Sep *117*	22 Apr *175*	3 Sep *122*
Chorley	26 Dec *460*	12 Nov *172*	7 Jan *164*	29 Apr *129*	26 Nov *161*		18 Oct *205*	4 Oct *180*	25 Feb *171*	14 Apr *397*	1 Oct *174*	11 Mar *165*	27 Sep *168*	28 Jan *182*	20 Sep *221*	3 Dec *141*	23 Aug *211*	29 Oct *192*	5 Nov *169*	18 Feb *182*	4 Apr *99*	25 Mar *148*
Clitheroe	29 Apr *228*	14 Apr *173*	3 Sep *173*	11 Mar *303*	20 Aug *238*	2 Jan *334*		4 Apr *153*	8 Apr *199*	27 Sep *311*	25 Feb *258*	4 Feb *224*	21 Jan *303*	22 Oct *262*	8 Oct *323*	13 Sep *160*	22 Apr *214*	18 Feb *324*	29 Aug *211*	5 Nov *261*	14 Mar *236*	4 Oct *282*
Colwyn Bay	25 Mar *287*	18 Feb *343*	18 Mar *259*	8 Apr *232*	29 Oct *407*	21 Jan *839*	14 Jan *426*		1 Oct *335*	8 Oct *415*	1 Apr *249*	17 Dec *275*	17 Apr *321*	27 Sep *274*	3 Sep *304*	10 Sep *256*	25 Feb *288*	26 Nov *202*	2 Jan *401*	12 Nov *359*	3 Dec *251*	23 Aug *265*
Eastwood Town	17 Sep *140*	26 Dec *249*	8 Oct *116*	18 Oct *118*	17 Dec *127*	20 Aug *169*	7 Mar *119*	4 Feb *145*		21 Jan *166*	13 Sep *164*	15 Nov *242*	11 Mar *171*	14 Jan *140*	14 Apr *245*	18 Feb *174*	29 Oct *141*	12 Nov *157*	29 Apr *150*	26 Nov *126*	25 Mar *161*	22 Apr *120*
Fleetwood Town	19 Nov *602*	28 Jan *523*	25 Mar *507*	11 Feb *583*	29 Apr *523*	14 Jan *573*	23 Aug *321*	20 Sep *412*	4 Mar *521*		17 Dec *414*	20 Aug *408*	26 Dec *584*	21 Mar *317*	11 Oct *511*	1 Oct *483*	21 Feb *371*	3 Sep *318*	10 Sep *306*	23 Apr *486*	17 Apr *516*	29 Oct *508*
Goole	26 Nov *208*	11 Mar *167*	20 Sep *179*	23 Aug *272*	26 Dec *251*	8 Apr *166*	10 Dec *213*	14 Apr *189*	18 Mar *219*	5 Nov *191*		6 Sep *258*	4 Feb *254*	19 Nov *198*	4 Mar *254*	25 Apr *171*	20 Aug *229*	21 Jan *252*	18 Oct *153*	8 Oct *166*	17 Sep *194*	18 Feb *214*
Gresley Rovers	10 Dec *228*	21 Mar *183*	25 Feb *220*	21 Jan *225*	4 Oct *289*	1 Apr *243*	17 Sep *260*	19 Nov *328*	2 Sep *440*	18 Feb *249*	25 Mar *259*		5 Nov *287*	23 Aug *260*	29 Apr *359*	22 Oct *274*	14 Jan *281*	26 Dec *349*	13 Sep *216*	17 Apr *259*	8 Apr *213*	14 Mar *199*
Kendal Town	21 Mar *308*	3 Dec *198*	18 Oct *219*	14 Apr *298*	17 Sep *250*	8 Oct *209*	20 Sep *199*	22 Oct *192*	2 Jan *414*	4 Oct *301*	29 Oct *248*	11 Apr *262*		17 Dec *307*	21 Feb *302*	28 Jan *363*	3 Sep *274*	29 Apr *527*	20 Aug *274*	18 Mar *224*	30 Mar *188*	19 Nov *219*
Kidsgrove Athletic	8 Oct *127*	25 Oct *142*	10 Dec *102*	1 Apr *151*	4 Feb *166*	25 Apr *101*	24 Sep *151*	6 Sep *161*	4 Oct *169*	27 Apr *137*	29 Apr *141*	18 Mar *130*	8 Apr *139*		2 Jan *260*	21 Jan *117*	20 Sep *110*	24 Jan *125*	18 Feb *100*	20 Aug *144*	5 Nov *155*	17 Apr *127*
Mossley	4 Oct *207*	13 Sep *184*	22 Apr *231*	17 Sep *231*	18 Feb *242*	21 Mar *173*	17 Apr *268*	11 Mar *203*	5 Nov *232*	24 Sep *325*	22 Oct *225*	3 Dec *217*	6 Sep *225*	4 Apr *177*		20 Aug *224*	4 Feb *232*	24 Apr *313*	1 Oct *202*	25 Mar *218*	14 Jan *214*	26 Dec *271*
Ossett Albion	11 Mar *104*	26 Nov *82*	5 Oct *82*	7 Sep *84*	5 Apr *83*	4 Feb *121*	18 Mar *102*	22 Apr *74*	21 Sep *110*	8 Apr *186*	14 Jan *169*	29 Aug *122*	10 Dec *83*	29 Oct *115*	25 Feb *158*		29 Mar *79*	8 Oct *105*	17 Apr *82*	2 Jan *139*	27 Apr *75*	17 Sep *107*
Rossendale United	27 Sep *86*	5 Nov *90*	2 Jan *207*	18 Feb *172*	29 Aug *101*	25 Oct *135*	25 Mar *257*	28 Jan *199*	10 Dec *124*	6 Sep *159*	3 Dec *148*	1 Oct *110*	11 Oct *138*	11 Mar *165*	18 Mar *245*	29 Apr *151*		17 Apr *170*	12 Nov *193*	17 Sep *143*	21 Jan *106*	20 Apr *115*
Shepshed Dynamo	28 Jan *144*	29 Mar *122*	4 Feb *103*	24 Sep *112*	26 Apr *155*	17 Sep *130*	11 Feb *139*	5 Nov *112*	7 Sep *88*	22 Apr *145*	12 Oct *60*	2 Jan *353*	1 Oct *108*	14 Sep *85*	8 Apr *173*	14 Apr *142*	4 Mar *145*		25 Mar *105*	17 Dec *121*	22 Oct *133*	22 Mar *95*
Spalding United	15 Apr *85*	25 Feb *81*	22 Oct *133*	25 Oct *116*	21 Jan *147*	24 Sep *107*	1 Apr *92*	17 Sep *112*	23 Aug *103*	18 Mar *98*	11 Feb *135*	8 Oct *126*	22 Apr *95*	26 Dec *89*	10 Dec *117*	19 Nov *109*	26 Nov *88*	4 Oct *91*		14 Jan *112*	3 Sep *82*	8 Apr *70*
Stocksbridge Park Steels	24 Sep *165*	21 Jan *175*	3 Dec *172*	4 Oct *178*	14 Apr *190*	10 Dec *168*	27 Apr *189*	29 Apr *179*	6 Apr *123*	22 Oct *191*	3 Sep *175*	29 Oct *198*	25 Apr *198*	20 Apr *193*	23 Aug *204*	26 Dec *203*	8 Apr *142*	20 Sep *162*	10 Apr *148*		4 Feb *190*	11 Oct *157*
Warrington Town	23 Aug *101*	29 Apr *115*	13 Apr *88*	18 Mar *113*	8 Oct *106*	6 Sep *123*	25 Apr *102*	26 Dec *129*	18 Apr *85*	10 Dec *122*	28 Jan *132*	14 Apr *128*	18 Feb *116*	28 Mar *96*	27 Sep *125*	24 Sep *114*	4 Oct *93*	11 Mar *103*	29 Oct *112*	21 Mar *108*		20 Sep *85*
Woodley Sports	6 Sep *101*	18 Mar *86*	1 Oct *97*	5 Nov *105*	22 Oct *98*	21 Feb *88*	4 Mar *168*	28 Mar *159*	3 Dec *97*	4 Apr *181*	25 Oct *127*	28 Jan *133*	24 Sep *110*	14 Apr *117*	21 Jan *276*	27 Sep *75*	25 Apr *112*	20 Aug *134*	4 Feb *127*	28 Feb *98*	2 Jan *110*	

NORTHERN PREMIER LEAGUE DIVISION ONE

CONSTITUTION FOR 2006-07

ALSAGER TOWN
Colours: Black & white
The Town Ground, Woodland Court, Alsager,
Staffordshire ST7 2DP
Tel: 01270 882336

BAMBER BRIDGE
Colours: White & black
Irongate, Brownedge Road, Bamber Bridge, Preston,
Lancashire PR5 6UX
Tel: 01772 909690

BELPER TOWN
Colours: Yellow & black
Christchurch Meadow, Bridge Street, Belper,
Derbyshire DE56 1BA
Tel: 01773 825549

BRADFORD PARK AVENUE
Colours: White
Horsfall Stadium, Cemetary Road, Low Moor,
Bradford, West Yorkshire BD6 2NG
Tel: 01274 604578

BRIDLINGTON TOWN
Colours: Red
Queensgate Stadium, Queensgate, Bridlington,
East Yorkshire YO16 5LN
Tel: 01262 606879

BRIGG TOWN
Colours: White & black
The Hawthorns, Hawthorn Avenue, Brigg,
North Lincs DN20 8PG
Tel: 01652 651605

BUXTON
Colours: Blue & white
The Silverlands, Buxton, Derbyshire SK17 6QH
Tel: 01298 23197

CAMMELL LAIRD
Colours: Royal blue
Kirklands, St Peters Road, Rock Ferry, Birkenhead,
Merseyside CH42 1PY
Tel: 0151 645 3121

CHORLEY
Colours: Black & white
Victory Park, Duke Street, Chorley, Lancs PR7 3DU
Tel: 01257 263406

CLITHEROE
Colours: Blue
Shawbridge, off Pendle Road, Clitheroe,
Lancashire BB7 1DP
Tel: 01200 423344

COLWYN BAY
Colours: Sky blue
Llanelian Road, Old Colwyn, Colwyn,
Clwyd LL29 8UN
Tel: 01492 514581

EASTWOOD TOWN
Colours: Black & white
Coronation Park, Chewton Street, Eastwood,
Nottinghamshire NG16 3GL
Tel: 01773 712301

GOOLE TOWN
Colours: Red & white
Victoria Pleasure Grounds, Marcus Street, Goole,
East Yorkshire DN14 6TW
Tel: 01405 762794

GRESLEY ROVERS
Colours: Red & white
Moat Ground, Moat Street, Church Gresley,
Swadlincote, Derbyshire DE11 9RE
Tel: 01283 216315

HARROGATE RAILWAY ATHLETIC
Colours: Red & green
Station View, Station View Road, Starbeck, Harrogate,
North Yorkshire HG2 7JA
Tel: 01423 883104

KIDSGROVE ATHLETIC
Colours: Blue & white
Hollinwood Stadium, Hollinwood Road, Kidsgrove,
Stoke-on-Trent, Staffordshire ST7 1BQ
Tel: 01782 782412

OSSETT ALBION
Colours: Gold & black
Queens Terrace, Dimple Wells, Ossett, Wakefield,
West Yorkshire WF5 8JU
Tel: 01924 280450

ROSSENDALE UNITED
Colours: Blue & white
Dark Lane, Staghills Road, Newchurch, Rossendale,
Lancashire BB4 7UA
Tel: 01706 215119

SHEPSHED DYNAMO
Colours: Black & white
The Dovecote, Butt Hole Lane, Shepshed,
Loughborough, Leicestershire LE12 9BN
Tel: 01509 650992

SKELMERSDALE UNITED
Colours: Blue
Westgate Interactive Stadium, Selby Place,
Stanley Ind. Est., Skelmersdale, Lancashire WN8 8EF
Tel: 01695 722123

STOCKSBRIDGE PARK STEELS
Colours: Yellow & royal blue
Bracken Moor Lane, Stocksbridge, Sheffield,
South Yorkshire S36 5AN
Tel: 0114 288 8305

WAKEFIELD
Colours: Claret & blue
College Grove, Eastmore Road, Wakefield,
West Yorkshire WF1 3RR
Tel: 01924 365007

WARRINGTON TOWN
Colours: Yellow & blue
Cantilever Park, Common Lane, Warrington,
Cheshire WA4 2RS
Tel: 01925 631932

WOODLEY SPORTS
Colours: Blue, red & white
Lambeth Grove Stadium, Lambeth Grove, Woodley,
Stockport, Cheshire SK6 1QX
Tel: 0161 494 6429

IN: Alsager Town (P – North West Counties League Division One), Bradford Park Avenue (R), Buxton (P – Northern Counties East League Division One), Cammell Laird (P – North West Counties League Division One), Harrogate Railway Athletic (P – North West Counties League Division One), Skelmersdale United (P – North West Counties League Division One), Wakefield (formerly Wakefield-Emley) (R)
OUT: Bishop Auckland (R – Northern League Division One), Fleetwood Town (P), Kendal Town (P), Mossley (P), Spalding United (S – Southern League Division One Midlands)
Goole become Goole Town

LEAGUE CUP

FIRST ROUND
Blyth Spartans 1 **Goole** 2
Bridlington Town 2 Ossett Albion 1
Clitheroe 4 Woodley Sports 2
Colwyn Bay 2 Warrington Town 0
Kidsgrove Athletic 4 Chorley 2
Lincoln United 1 Frickley Athletic 1 *aet* (2-0p)
Marine 3 Bamber Bridge 1
Ossett Town 0 **Gateshead** 1
Rossendale United 2 **Fleetwood Town** 4
Shepshed Dynamo 0 **Stocksbridge Park Steels** 3
Spalding United 1 Belper Town 0
Wakefield-Emley 4 Bishop Auckland 2

SECOND ROUND
AFC Telford United 3 Gresley Rovers 2
Bridlington Town 1 Lincoln United 0
Brigg Tn 0 **Stocksbridge Park Steels** 0 *aet* (7-8p)
Clitheroe 3 **Kendal Town** 4
Farsley Celtic 2 Bradford Park Avenue 2 *aet* (4-1p)
Fleetwood Town 2 Burscough 1
Gateshead 2 **Guiseley** 4 *aet*
Kidsgrove Athletic 1 **Eastwood Town** 1 *aet* (4-5p)
Leek Town 3 Ilkeston Town 1
Marine 3 Prescot Cables 2
Mossley 0 **Witton Albion** 2
North Ferriby United 3 Matlock Town 2
Radcliffe Borough 3 Colwyn Bay 1
Runcorn Halton 1 Ashton United 0
Wakefield-Emley 3 Spalding United 0
Whitby Town 4 Goole 3 *aet*

THIRD ROUND
AFC Telford United 0 **Witton Albion** 1
Farsley Celtic 4 North Ferriby United 0
Fleetwood Town 0 **Radcliffe Borough** 1
Guiseley 1 **Whitby Town** 3
Kendal Town 0 **Runcorn Halton** 1
Marine 3 Leek Town 0
Stocksbridge Park Steels 3 Bridlington Town 1
Wakefield-Emley 0 **Eastwood Town** 1

QUARTER-FINALS
Farsley Celtic 2 Whitby Town 1
Marine 3 Eastwood Town 0
Radcliffe Borough 3 **Stocksbridge Park Steels** 4
Witton Albion 1 **Runcorn Halton** 3

SEMI-FINALS
Farsley Celtic 5 Runcorn Halton 2
Stocksbridge Park Steels 2 Marine 1

FINAL
(April 3rd at Farsley Celtic)
Farsley Celtic 1 Stocksbridge Park Steels 0

PETER SWALES CHALLENGE CUP
(League champions v League Cup holders)

2004-05 *(July 29th at Matlock Town)*
Hyde United 2 Matlock Town 0

2005-06 *(May 9th at Blyth Spartans)*
Blyth Spartans 1 Farsley Celtic 0

PRESIDENT'S CUP
(League Cup Second Round losers)

FIRST ROUND
Ashton United 0 **Bradford Park Avenue** 1
Brigg Town 2 Gateshead 0
Colwyn Bay 4 Clitheroe 2
Goole 2 **Ilkeston Town** 4
Kidsgrove Athletic 0 **Mossley** 1
Lincoln United 2 Spalding United 1
Matlock Town 4 Gresley Rovers 0
Prescot Cables 0 **Burscough** 1

QUARTER-FINALS
Burscough 1 **Bradford Park Avenue** 2
Ilkeston Town 1 Mossley 0
Lincoln United 1 **Brigg Town** 1 *aet* (4-5p)
Matlock Town 2 Colwyn Bay 0

SEMI-FINALS
Brigg Town 1 **Bradford Park Avenue** 1 *aet* (3-5p)
Matlock Town 3 **Ilkeston Town** 4 *aet*

FINAL
(April 25th at Ilkeston Town)
Ilkeston Town 0 **Bradford Park Avenue** 1

CHAIRMAN'S CUP
(League Cup First Round losers)

FIRST ROUND
Bamber Bridge 2 Belper Town 1 *aet*
Ossett Albion 4 Shepshed Dynamo 1
Rossendale United 1 **Frickley Athletic** 3
Warrington Town 0 **Woodley Sports** 1

QUARTER-FINALS
Bamber Bridge 0 **Ossett Town** 2 *aet*
Blyth Spartans 1 Ossett Albion 0
Frickley Athletic 4 Chorley 2
Woodley Sports 2 Bishop Auckland 0

SEMI-FINALS
Frickley Athletic 2 **Blyth Spartans** 2 *aet* (3-5p)
Woodley Sports 2 **Ossett Town** 4

FINAL
(May 1st at Blyth Spartans)
Blyth Spartans 2 Ossett Town 0

NOTTS SENIOR LEAGUE

	Arnold Southb.	Attenborough	Awsworth Villa	Bestwood M W	Boots Athletic	Calverton M W	Caribbean Cav.	Clifton	Cotgrave C W	Keyworth Utd	Kimberley M W	Linby C W	Magdala Am.	Notts Police	Ruddington Utd	Sandhurst	Siemens EWS	Wollaton
Arnold Southbank		0-1	4-0	2-1	0-1	2-2	1-4	0-1	5-1	2-2	1-2	2-1	4-1	3-2	0-0	3-0	1-0	1-1
Attenborough	0-2	*S*	4-2	4-2	0-2	0-1	3-2	2-1	3-2	1-1	2-3	3-1	2-1	3-0	3-0	0-0	3-2	0-0
Awsworth Villa	1-1	3-2	*E*	1-6	2-7	2-3	1-4	1-3	2-6	0-3	0-4	1-0	3-4	0-5	4-3	8-2	4-4	0-5
Bestwood Miners Welfare	1-4	1-2	2-3	*N*	3-3	1-0	1-1	1-1	2-1	0-1	1-2	3-1	0-1	2-0	0-0	1-0	3-1	0-2
Boots Athletic	2-1	1-0	2-2	1-3	*I*	1-3	3-2	2-3	1-2	5-1	2-4	5-0	2-2	4-7	4-0	5-1	5-1	1-2
Calverton Miners Welfare	0-4	1-1	0-1	0-1	1-1	*O*	2-1	1-3	7-0	1-3	1-4	3-0	4-3	3-1	0-1	6-0	5-5	1-2
Caribbean Cavaliers	1-2	1-3	5-1	2-0	2-1	1-3	*R*	2-5	0-1	3-0	2-0	0-2	1-1	1-1	1-1	5-0	0-2	1-1
Clifton	3-2	1-2	5-1	4-1	1-1	4-0	2-2		0-0	2-1	3-1	1-2	2-1	2-2	8-0	7-1	2-0	2-3
Cotgrave Colliery Welfare United	2-3	2-2	2-0	5-1	7-1	3-0	1-0	2-3		2-1	2-0	2-1	3-2	2-1	3-0	5-1	4-2	2-1
Keyworth United	3-1	3-3	0-1	1-1	4-0	2-0	1-1	1-1	3-1	*D*	1-2	0-4	2-1	7-1	1-1	3-3	1-0	2-4
Kimberley Miners Welfare	1-1	0-3	1-2	2-0	2-0	1-2	2-2	0-2	0-0	1-1	*I*	2-2	4-4	0-0	5-1	1-0	1-4	0-0
Linby Colliery Welfare	0-1	0-1	3-1	0-1	4-0	2-3	3-2	0-3	2-1	3-0	2-1	*V*	5-0	4-3	4-0	3-0	1-2	2-1
Magdala Amateurs	4-3	1-2	2-5	0-2	0-1	0-2	0-0	3-1	1-1	1-2	2-1	4-3	*I*	3-0	5-0	5-3	3-1	0-3
Notts Police	2-6	3-1	4-1	1-5	3-1	0-2	1-1	1-4	1-2	0-2	2-0	0-2	2-1	*S*	5-1	3-1	1-3	0-1
Ruddington United	1-10	2-3	1-6	4-2	2-0	0-7	0-3	2-5	0-7	1-2	4-1	1-3	2-0	1-2	*I*	0-4	0-5	0-0
Sandhurst	0-3	1-4	1-0	1-0	0-7	1-6	3-4	2-2	0-2	0-3	1-7	3-4	3-3	1-6	2-4	*O*	0-3	0-1
Siemens EWS	1-1	1-1	4-2	1-2	3-1	1-0	0-2	2-3	1-2	2-3	1-6	0-0	5-1	1-2	4-2	3-0	*N*	1-1
Wollaton	1-1	4-0	3-1	4-1	1-2	1-0	1-0	0-1	2-1	2-0	0-0	1-0	7-1	6-0	4-1	8-0	3-1	

Senior Division		P	W	D	L	F	A	Pts
Wollaton		34	22	8	4	76	23	74
Clifton		34	22	7	5	91	42	73
Cotgrave Colliery Welf. Utd	*-2*	34	21	4	9	79	49	65
Attenborough		34	19	7	8	64	47	64
Arnold Southbank		34	17	8	9	77	43	59
Keyworth United		34	15	9	10	61	51	54
Linby Colliery Welfare		34	17	2	15	64	51	53
Calverton Miners Welfare		34	16	4	14	70	53	52
Kimberley Miners Welfare		34	13	9	12	61	51	48
Boots Athletic		34	14	5	15	75	69	47
Bestwood Miners Welfare		34	13	5	16	51	56	44
Caribbean Cavaliers		34	11	10	13	59	49	43
Siemens EWS		34	12	6	16	67	66	42
Notts Police	*-3*	34	12	4	18	62	77	37
Magdala Amateurs	*-2*	34	10	6	18	61	81	34
Awsworth Villa		34	10	3	21	62	105	33
Ruddington United		34	6	5	23	36	113	23
Sandhurst		34	3	4	27	35	125	13

Division One	P	W	D	L	F	A	Pts
Wollaton Res.	32	24	4	4	97	28	76
Arnold Southbank Res.	32	22	5	5	105	36	71
Kimberley Miners Welfare Res.	32	19	5	8	80	56	62
Keyworth United Res.	32	18	6	8	77	40	60
Bestwood Miners Welfare Res.	32	18	4	10	77	44	58
Boots Athletic Res.	32	17	6	9	71	37	57
Notts Police Res.	32	16	8	8	78	55	56
Cotgrave Colliery Welfare Utd Res.	32	13	5	14	57	54	44
Calverton Miners Welfare Res.	32	14	1	17	69	66	43
Attenborough Res.	32	14	1	17	63	72	43
Linby Colliery Welfare Res.	32	10	12	10	59	53	42
Clifton Res.	32	13	2	17	62	78	41
Awsworth Villa Res.	32	11	6	15	56	75	39
Caribbean Cavaliers Res.	32	10	8	14	54	51	38
Magdala Amateurs Res.	32	6	4	22	37	97	22
Siemens EWS Res.	32	7	1	24	43	106	22
Sandhurst Res.	32	0	2	30	17	154	2

SENIOR CUP

PRELIMINARY ROUND

Cotgrave Colliery Welfare United 0 **Keyworth United** 2
Kimberley Miners Welfare 3 Arnold Southbank 0

FIRST ROUND

Awsworth Villa 2 **Keyworth United** 3
Bestwood Miners Welfare 1 Calverton Miners Welfare 1 *aet* (4-2p)
Boots Athletic 5 Magdala Amateurs 2
Caribbean Cavaliers 3 Siemens EWS 2
Clifton 4 Ruddington United 1 *aet*
Linby Colliery Welfare 2 Kimberley Miners Welfare 0
Sandhurst 0 **Attenborough** 2
Wollaton 1 Notts Police 1 *aet* (3-1p)

QUARTER-FINALS

Boots Athletic 2 Wollaton 1
Caribbean Cavaliers 0 **Attenborough** 2
Clifton 4 Bestwood Miners Welfare 1
Keyworth United 1 **Linby Colliery Welfare** 4

SEMI-FINALS *(both at Cotgrave Colliery Welfare United)*

Attenborough 2 Boots Athletic 0
Clifton 2 Linby Colliery Welfare 1

FINAL *(May 18th at Calverton Miners Welfare)*

Clifton 2 Attenborough 1

JUNIOR CUP

FINAL

(May 10th at Calverton Miners Welfare)

Boots Athletic Res. 2 Attenborough Res. 0

NOTTS SENIOR LEAGUE SENIOR DIVISION CONSTITUTION 2006-07

ATTENBOROUGH .... Village Green, The Strand, Attenborough NG9 6AU 0115 925 7439
AWSWORTH VILLA .... Shilo Park, Attewell Road, Awsworth NG16 2SY 0115 849 8741
BASFORD UNITED .... Greenwich Avenue, Bagnall Road, Basford, Nottingham NG6 0LE 0115 942 3918
BESTWOOD MINERS WELFARE ... Bestwood Workshops, Park Road, Bestwood Village, Nottingham NG6 8TQ .... None
BOOTS ATHLETIC .... Trent Vale Road, Beeston, Nottingham NG9 1ND 0115 981 9201
CARIBBEAN CAVALIERS .... Carrington Sports Ground, Mansfield Road, Nottingham NG5 2EJ .... None
CLIFTON .... Green Lane, Clifton Estate, Nottingham NG12 3PJ 0115 984 4903
COTGRAVE COLLIERY WELFARE UTD ..... The Woodview, Cotgrave, Nottingham 0115 989 2414
GEDLING SOUTHBANK .... Carlton Recreation Ground, Carlton Hill, Nottingham .... None
KEYWORTH UNITED .... Platt Lane Sports Complex, Keyworth, Nottingham NG12 5GE 0115 937 5998
KIMBERLEY MINERS WELFARE .... Digby Street, Kimberley, Nottingham NG16 2HP 07966 964458
LINBY COLLIERY WELFARE .... Church Lane, Linby Village, Linby NG15 8AB .... None
MAGDALA AMATEURS .... ROKO Health Club, Nottingham 0115 982 7799
NOTTS POLICE .... Rolls Royce Leisure, Nottingham 0115 982 7799
RUDDINGTON UNITED .... The Elms Park, Loughborough Road, Ruddington NG11 6NX 0115 984 4976
SANDHURST .... Walesby Sports & Social Club, Retford Road, Walesby NG22 9PE 01623 860456
SIEMENS EWS .... Sports Ground, Trent Vale Road, Beeston Rylands NG9 1ND 0115 943 3700
WOLLATON .... Wollaton Sports Association, Wollaton Road, Wollaton, Nottingham NG8 2AA 0115 928 3875

IN: Basford United (P – Nottinghamshire Amateur League)
OUT: Calverton Miners Welfare (P – Central Midlands League Premier Division)
Arnold Southbank become Gedling Southbank

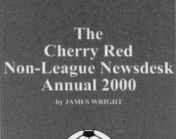

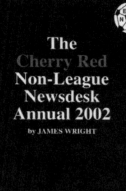

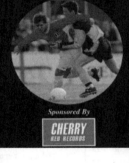

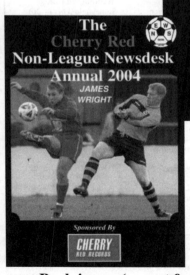

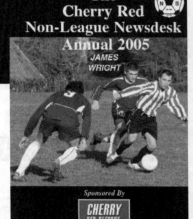

OXFORDSHIRE SENIOR LEAGUE

	Adderbury Park	BCS Bardwell	Berinsfield	Chadlington	Charlton United	Eynsham Association	Garsington	Haddenham	Kidlington Old Boys	Launton Sports	Long Crendon	Oxford University Press	Rover Cowley	Watlington Town
Adderbury Park		0-2	0-2	3-4	0-5	1-4	1-1	2-2	2-1	0-3	1-0	0-7	0-5	4-1
BCS Bardwell	5-1	*P*	1-2	4-1	4-2	3-4	2-1	4-5	3-0	5-2	6-0	2-0	3-0	1-0
Berinsfield CA	2-2	0-0	*R*	3-1	0-0	3-4	1-3	4-1	3-2	1-3	3-0	0-2	5-1	2-1
Chadlington	1-1	0-0	0-1	*E*	0-2	0-2	5-1	1-2	1-1	2-3	4-0	1-1	4-3	1-0
Charlton United	1-3	3-0	1-5	1-0	*M*	2-3	2-4	0-3	0-1	2-4	3-2	0-3	3-4	2-1
Eynsham Association	1-1	5-0	0-1	2-0	1-1	*I*	1-1	1-2	1-0	1-1	3-0	2-1	3-2	2-3
Garsington	2-1	2-2	3-1	5-1	4-0	1-1	*E*	0-0	1-1	1-0	2-1	1-1	0-1	5-2
Haddenham	1-2	1-1	0-1	1-1	1-3	0-0	3-2	*R*	5-2	3-3	1-0	1-3	2-1	4-3
Kidlington Old Boys	5-2	1-2	1-5	2-2	2-2	0-2	3-1	1-2		0-3	2-1	0-5	0-2	1-1
Launton Sports	2-2	1-3	W-L	2-5	1-2	2-2	4-2	3-2	9-0		5-1	1-2	3-2	0-1
Long Crendon	3-2	1-2	3-4	2-2	3-0	0-0	0-2	0-3	1-2	0-1	*D*	1-2	4-1	5-2
Oxford University Press	5-1	2-1	3-4	5-1	1-2	1-1	5-3	2-4	1-0	2-2	3-1	*I*	5-2	1-0
Rover Cowley	5-1	5-0	3-2	1-3	1-0	1-3	2-2	2-2	6-1	1-1	2-3	4-1	*V*	4-1
Watlington Town	3-3	5-3	2-1	W-L	3-0	2-1	5-2	1-5	2-1	4-0	0-0	0-6	2-1	

Premier Division	P	W	D	L	F	A	Pts
Oxford Univ. Press	26	16	4	6	70	35	52
Eynsham Association	26	13	9	4	50	29	48
Berinsfield CA	26	15	3	8	56	37	48
BCS Bardwell	26	14	4	8	59	44	46
Haddenham	26	13	7	6	56	43	46
Launton Sports	26	12	6	8	59	46	42
Garsington	26	10	8	8	52	46	38
Rover Cowley	26	11	3	12	62	54	36
Watlington Town	26	11	3	12	45	55	36
Charlton United	26	9	3	14	39	54	30
Chadlington	26	7	7	12	41	48	28
Adderbury Park	26	5	7	14	36	73	22
Kidlington Old Boys	26	5	5	16	30	65	20
Long Crendon	26	5	3	18	32	58	18

BEN TURNER CUP

FINAL

(May 1st at Enstone Sports)

Fritwell 3 Middleton Cheney 1

PRESIDENT'S CUP

FIRST ROUND

BCS Bardwell (w/o) v Rover Cowley (scr,)

Enstone Sports 1 Middleton Cheney 0

Eynsham Association 0 **Charlton United** 0 *aet* (3-4p)

Horspath 2 **Adderbury Park** 3

Kings Sutton 4 Garden City 0

Launton Sports 1 Watlington Tn 0

Long Crendon 0 **Garsington** 2

Marston Saints 1 Fritwell 1 *aet* (3-2p)

Oakley 4 **Yarnton** 1 *(Oakley expelled)*

Old Salesians 1 **Kennington United** 8

Oxford University Press 3 Chadlington 0

SECOND ROUND

BCS Bardwell 3 Adderbury Park 2

Enstone Sports 3 Garsington 0

Kidlington Old Boys 0 **Oxford University Press** 5

Kennington United 3 Stonesfield 3 *aet* (4-3p)

Kings Sutton 2 **Yarnton** 3 *aet*

Launton Sports 3 Charlton United 0

Marston Saints 3 Haddenham 0

Worcester College Old Boys & Bletchington 2 **Berinsfield CA** 4

QUARTER-FINALS

Berinsfield CA 2 Kennington United 1

Enstone Sports 2 Marston Saints 1

Launton Sports 2 BCS Bardwell 1

Yarnton 0 **Oxford University Press** 6

SEMI-FINALS

Berinsfield CA 1 Oxford University Press 0

Launton Sports 1 **Enstone Sports** 2

FINAL

(April 17th at Oxford University Press)

Berinsfield CA 1 Enstone Sports 0

OXFORDSHIRE SENIOR LEAGUE PREMIER DIVISION CONSTITUTION 2006-07

ADDERBURY PARK .... Adderbury Park Playing Fields, Round Close Road, Adderbury, Banbury OX17 .... None
BCS BARDWELL .... Rodney House Sports & Social, London Road, Bicester OX26 6HD 01869 243280
BERINSFIELD CA .... Green Furlong, Berinsfield, Wallingford OX8 1SX 01865 340201
CHADLINGTON .... Chapel Row, Chadlington OX7 3NA .... None
CHARLTON UNITED .... Charlton PF, Oddington Road, Charlton-on-Otmoor, Kidlington OX5 2TJ .... None
EYNSHAM ASSOCIATION .... Oxford Road, Eynsham, Witney OX29 4DA .... None
GARSINGTON .... Garsington Sports Club, Denton Lane, Garsington, Oxford OX44 9EL 01865 361720
HADDENHAM .... Woodways, Haddenham, Aylesbury HP17 8DS .... None
HORSPATH .... Brookes University Campus, Wheatley, Oxford OX4 6LB .... None
KENNINGTON UNITED .... Playfield Road, Kennington, Oxford OX1 5RS .... None
LAUNTON SPORTS .... Launton Sports & Social Club, Bicester Road, Bicester OX26 5DP 01869 242007
OXFORD UNIVERSITY PRESS .... Jordan Hill, Banbury Road, Oxford OX2 8EF .... None
ROVER COWLEY .... Pressed Steel Sports Ground, Roman Way, Beckley, Oxford OX3 9UA .... None
WATLINGTON TOWN .... Shirburn Road, Watlington OX49 5BZ .... None

IN: Horspath (P), Kennington United (P)

OUT: Kidlington Old Boys (R), Long Crendon (R)

	Enstone Sports	Fritwell	Garden City	Horspath	Kennington United	Kings Sutton	Marston Saints	Middleton Cheney	Oakley United	Old Salesians	Stonesfield	Worcester COB & Bletchington	Yarnton
Enstone Sports	*D*	1-2	5-1	0-2	1-2	3-1	1-3	3-3	1-0	8-0	1-1	4-3	1-1
Fritwell	1-1	*I*	5-0	1-3	4-2	6-1	2-2	2-2	6-2	9-0	2-4	3-3	1-0
Garden City	0-2	L-W	*V*	2-3	1-4	2-0	2-7	W-L	0-0	1-5	0-4	2-1	3-1
Horspath	2-0	3-2	6-0	*I*	1-2	4-1	3-0	1-1	4-0	8-0	4-2	3-3	4-1
Kennington United	3-3	3-3	1-0	2-0	*S*	4-0	0-0	6-2	3-0	7-1	2-2	5-2	2-1
Kings Sutton	1-2	3-2	2-1	1-3	1-2	*I*	1-1	0-2	5-2	6-0	0-2	2-2	6-2
Marston Saints	W-L	0-3	4-1	2-1	0-4	1-0	*O*	1-1	4-1	4-0	1-3	1-1	1-0
Middleton Cheney	1-0	2-1	4-0	1-3	1-3	1-2	3-1	*N*	5-1	6-0	3-2	2-1	1-0
Oakley United	L-W	1-5	6-1	2-9	1-5	2-2	1-0	3-5		1-2	0-2	3-1	3-2
Old Salesians	1-0	1-8	0-2	0-4	0-10	5-2	1-5	1-7	2-5		1-7	2-3	L-W
Stonesfield	2-1	3-4	10-0	1-2	2-3	6-1	3-2	3-1	2-0	7-0	*O*	1-3	7-0
Worcester College Old Boys & Bletchington	1-1	3-2	9-1	2-1	1-6	3-4	1-2	3-1	2-2	2-2	2-4	*N*	4-3
Yarnton	1-1	0-5	2-1	0-3	4-4	0-5	0-4	4-1	3-2	3-1	2-2	2-2	*E*

Division One	P	W	D	L	F	A	Pts
Kennington United	24	18	5	1	85	31	59
Horspath	24	18	2	4	77	26	56
Stonesfield	24	15	3	6	82	35	48
Fritwell	24	13	5	6	79	40	44
Marston Saints	24	12	5	7	46	33	41
Middleton Cheney	24	12	4	8	56	41	40
Enstone Sports	24	8	7	9	40	32	31
Worcester College Old Boys & Bletchington	24	7	8	9	58	59	29
Kings Sutton	24	8	3	13	47	58	27
Yarnton	24	5	5	14	32	64	20
Oakley United	24	5	3	16	38	71	18
Garden City	24	5	1	18	21	81	16
Old Salesians	24	4	1	19	25	115	13

Division Two A	P	W	D	L	F	A	Pts
Marston Saints Res.	20	15	1	4	51	20	46
Kidlington Old Boys Res.	20	11	4	5	69	29	37
Oxford University Press Res. *-3*	20	13	1	6	51	38	37
BCS Bardwell Res.	20	10	2	8	50	61	32
Horspath Res.	20	10	1	9	64	43	31
Launton Sports Res. *-2*	20	10	3	7	46	36	31
Eynsham Association Res.	20	9	3	8	48	45	30
Berinsfield CA Res.	20	8	4	8	47	42	28
Chadlington Res.	19	5	4	10	37	45	19
Watlington Town Res.	20	2	3	15	21	76	9
Oakley United Res.	19	2	2	15	25	74	8

Chadlington Res. v Oakley United Reserves – not played

Division Two B	P	W	D	L	F	A	Pts
Garsington Res.	22	18	3	1	83	18	57
Fritwell Res.	22	15	3	4	73	46	48
Haddenham Res.	22	15	2	5	64	37	47
Worc. Coll. OB & B Res.	22	13	1	8	60	42	40
Yarnton Res.	22	10	6	6	39	44	36
Stonesfield Res.	22	11	2	9	45	27	35
Middleton Cheney Res.	22	9	2	11	59	59	29
King Sutton Res.	22	7	3	12	28	63	24
Charlton United Res.	22	6	3	13	41	47	21
Enstone Sports Res.	22	5	2	15	27	49	17
Long Crendon Res.	22	5	1	16	36	76	16
Kennington United Res.	22	2	4	16	35	82	10

CLARENDON CUP

FINAL

(April 17th at Oxford University Press)

Kidlington Old Boys Res. 3 Garsington Res. 0

IVOR GUBBINS CUP

FINAL

((May 6th at Garsington)

Haddenham Res. 2 Marston Saints Res. 0

OXFORDSHIRE SENIOR LEAGUE DIVISION ONE CONSTITUTION 2006-07

ENSTONE SPORTS . . . . Charlbury Road, Enstone, Oxford OX2 6UT 01608 677823
FRITWELL . . . . Playing Field, Fewcott Road, Fritwell OX27 7QA. . . . . None
KIDLINGTON OLD BOYS . . . . Exeter Close, Crown Road, Kidlington OX5 1AP. . . . . None
KINGS SUTTON . . . . Longburrow Park, The Lane, Kings Sutton, Banbury. . . . . None
LONG CRENDON . . . . Rec Ground, Chearsley Road, Long Crendon, Aylesbury HP18 9AP. . . . . None
MARSTON SAINTS. . . . . Boults Lane, Old Marston, Oxford OX3 0PW 01865 203970
MIDDLETON CHENEY . . . . Astrop Road, Middleton Cheney, Banbury OX17 2PG . . . . None
MIDDLE BARTON. . . . . Worton Road, Middle Barton, Chipping Norton OX7 7EF. 01869 347597
OAKLEY UNITED . . . . Playfield Fields, Oxford Road, Oakley, Aylesbury HP18 9RE. . . . . None
OLD SALESIANS. . . . . . . John Radcliffe Sports Ground, Osler Road, Headington *(possible new ground for 2006-07)* . . . . None
STONESFIELD. . . . . Stonesfield Playing Field, off Longmore, Stonesfield . . . . None
WHEATLEY '84. . . . . Holton Playing Fields, Wheatley, Oxford OX33 1QL . . . . None
WORCESTER COLLEGE OLD BOYS & BLETCHINGTON . . . Rover Cowley Sports Ground, Oxford 01865 775463
YARNTON. . . . . Green Lane, Yarnton 01865 842037

IN: Kidlington Old Boys (R), Long Crendon (R), Middle Barton (W – Hellenic League Division One West), Wheatley '84 (P – Oxford City League Premier Division)

OUT: Garden City (W), Horspath (P), Kennington United (P)

PETERBOROUGH & DISTRICT LEAGUE

	Alconbury	Crowland Town	Hotpoint	Leverington Sports	Long Sutton Athletic	Moulton Harrox	Ortonians	Oundle Town	Parson Drove	Perkins Sports	Peterborough Sports	Pinchbeck United	Stamford Belvedere	Uppingham Town	Whittlesey United	Wimblington Old Boys
Alconbury	*P*	0-4	0-3	3-0	7-0	4-3	1-2	1-1	1-0	6-0	3-1	1-2	3-3	2-2	1-0	5-2
Crowland Town	1-3	*R*	2-2	4-0	7-1	0-1	2-3	1-0	2-1	2-3	4-3	5-1	1-1	2-3	2-1	3-2
Hotpoint	2-2	1-1	*E*	7-0	11-1	1-0	3-3	4-2	3-2	2-1	2-3	2-1	3-0	10-3	3-0	7-3
Leverington Sports	2-1	2-2	3-1	*M*	1-0	0-1	0-1	3-1	1-3	0-2	4-1	1-0	1-4	2-0	1-2	3-0
Long Sutton Athletic	0-1	0-4	0-6	1-2	*I*	1-4	1-5	2-5	0-1	1-3	1-3	2-1	0-0	3-6	0-1	5-0
Moulton Harrox	1-1	1-1	0-2	3-1	4-0	*E*	1-2	2-2	0-1	0-0	2-1	1-0	3-2	3-3	1-1	3-4
Ortonians	1-0	1-1	3-1	4-0	3-2	0-1	*R*	3-0	0-1	4-1	1-0	2-1	2-1	7-0	1-2	5-1
Oundle Town	3-0	2-0	0-3	0-2	4-0	2-3	2-5		2-0	2-1	2-2	2-1	4-2	4-2	1-5	5-2
Parson Drove	1-0	0-1	0-2	1-0	4-0	1-2	3-5	3-0	*D*	1-0	6-0	3-1	1-0	2-1	1-1	6-1
Perkins Sports	3-1	3-3	2-3	0-1	1-1	0-1	0-5	2-3	0-3	*I*	2-1	5-0	0-2	2-2	1-2	1-0
Peterborough Sports	1-2	2-3	0-6	3-1	5-1	3-7	2-5	1-2	2-3	4-3	*V*	0-2	0-1	3-1	2-0	4-1
Pinchbeck United	1-2	1-4	1-4	1-1	0-2	1-2	0-2	1-3	3-2	1-0	2-1	*I*	1-2	3-2	3-2	1-3
Stamford Belvedere	0-6	4-1	1-5	0-4	3-0	0-2	1-2	1-0	0-4	1-3	1-3	1-1	*S*	3-1	1-0	2-2
Uppingham Town	1-4	1-2	0-6	3-2	6-0	0-0	3-3	2-1	2-7	2-2	1-7	0-4	0-0	*I*	2-3	1-1
Whittlesey United	2-2	1-2	0-3	2-2	3-1	4-1	0-4	4-1	0-3	2-0	3-2	1-1	0-2	2-1	*O*	0-0
Wimblington Old Boys	0-4	0-2	0-5	1-2	1-1	2-4	0-5	0-4	2-1	1-3	0-5	2-5	0-1	2-2	2-4	*N*

Premier Division	P	W	D	L	F	A	Pts
Ortonians	30	24	3	3	89	31	75
Hotpoint	30	23	4	3	113	34	73
Parson Drove	30	19	1	10	65	32	58
Moulton Harrox	30	16	7	7	57	40	55
Crowland Town *-3*	30	16	7	7	69	44	52
Alconbury	30	15	6	9	67	42	51
Oundle Town	30	14	3	13	60	58	45
Whittlesey United	30	13	6	11	48	47	45
Leverington Sports	30	13	3	14	42	52	42
Stamford Belvedere	30	11	6	13	40	53	39
Peterborough Sports	30	11	1	18	65	72	34
Perkins Sports	30	9	5	16	44	57	32
Pinchbeck United	30	9	3	18	41	60	30
Uppingham Town	30	5	9	16	53	92	24
Wimblington Old Boys	30	3	5	22	35	99	14
Long Sutton Athletic	30	3	3	24	27	102	12

JACK HOGG CHARITY SHIELD

(League champions v Peterborough Senior Cup holders)

(August 20th at Chestnut Avenue)

Whittlesey United 0 **Ortonians** 7

PETERBOROUGH SENIOR CUP

(Premier Division teams and top eight Division One first teams)

FIRST ROUND

Chatteris Town 5 Ryhall United 0
Deeping Sports 2 Oundle Town 1
Hotpoint 6 Pinchbeck United 2
Kings Cliffe United 2 **Parson Drove** 3
Perkins Sports 4 Alconbury 2
Wimblington Old Boys 3 Ketton 0

SECOND ROUND

Chatteris Town 5 Ryhall United 0
Deeping Sports 2 Oundle Town 1
Moulton Harrox 2 Hotpoint 1
Perkins Sports 4 Alconbury 2
Peterborough Sports 0 Leverington Sports 0 *aet* (4-3p) *(at Perkins Sports)*
Stamford Belvedere 1 **Parson Drove** 3
Uppingham Town 2 **Crowland Town** 3 *aet*
Woodlands 8 **Wimblington Old Boys** 0 *(Woodlands expelled)*

QUARTER-FINALS

Crowland Town 3 Parson Drove 2
Deeping Sports 9 Wimblington Old Boys 0
Perkins Sports 0 **Moulton Harrox** 1
Peterborough Sports 5 Chatteris Town 1

SEMI-FINALS

Crowland Town 2 Moulton Harrox 0
Peterborough Sports 1 **Deeping Sports** 3

FINAL

(May 1st at Peterborough United)

Deeping Sports 3 Crowland Town 0

PETERBOROUGH & DISTRICT LEAGUE PREMIER DIVISION CONSTITUTION 2006-07

ALCONBURY .... Great North Road, Alconbury, Huntingdon PE28 4EX 01480 891313
CROWLAND TOWN .... Snowden Field, Thorney Road, Crowland PE6 0AL 01733 211548
DEEPING SPORTS .... Outgang Road, Towngate East, Market Deeping PE6 8LQ 01778 344701
HOTPOINT .... Celta Road, Peterborough PE2 9JD 01733 556104
LEVERINGTON SPORTS .... Church Road, Leverington, Wisbech PE13 5DE 01945 465082
MOULTON HARROX .... Broad Lane, Moulton Harrox 01406 371991
ORTONIANS .... Thomas Cook Leisure Centre, Thorpe Wood, Peterborough 01733 503008
OUNDLE TOWN .... Station Road, Oundle, Peterborough PE8 4DE 01832 274188
PARSON DROVE .... Main Road, Parson Drove, Wisbech PE13 4LF .... None
PERKINS SPORTS .... Perkins Sports Pavilion, Oxney Road, Peterborough PE1 5NA 01733 310578
PETERBOROUGH SPORTS ..... Peterborough Sports & Leisure, Lincoln Road, Peterborough PE1 3HA 01733 567835
PINCHBECK UNITED .... Glebe Playing Fields, Knight Street, Pinchbeck, Spalding PE11 3RB 01775 762057
STAMFORD BELVEDERE .... Queen Eleanor School, Green Lane, Stamford PE9 1HE 01780 751011
UPPINGHAM TOWN .... North Street East, Uppingham LE15 9QJ 01572 821446
WHITTLESEY UNITED .... Manor Leisure Centre, Station Road, Whittlesey, Peterborough PE7 1UE 01733 202298
WOODLANDS .... Woodlands Sports Centre, Splash Lane, Peterborough CB7 5AA 01733 475000

IN: Deeping Sports (P), Woodlands (P)

OUT: Long Sutton Athletic (R), Wimblington Old Boys (R)

Division One		P	W	D	L	F	A	Pts
Woodlands		30	25	4	1	147	35	79
Deeping Sports		30	23	3	4	104	26	72
Chatteris Town		30	21	3	6	73	26	66
Netherton United		30	19	5	6	66	33	62
Rutland Rangers		30	18	5	7	82	39	59
Wimblington Harriers		29	18	3	8	79	47	57
Werrington Town		30	11	7	12	56	59	40
Kings Cliffe United		30	12	3	15	42	59	39
Gedney Hill		30	9	6	15	53	60	33
Ramsey Town		30	8	9	13	49	56	33
Langtoft United		30	10	2	18	39	82	32
Sutton Bridge United	*-3*	30	7	7	16	49	83	25
Ketton		30	5	7	18	43	89	22
Silver Jubilee	*-6*	30	8	2	20	32	95	20
Castor & Ailsworth		30	4	6	20	45	99	18
Ryhall United	*-3*	29	2	6	21	19	90	9

Wimblington Harriers v Ryhall United – not played

Division Two		P	W	D	L	F	A	Pts
Thorney		26	21	2	3	98	29	65
Griffin Park		26	19	4	3	106	46	61
Coates Athletic		26	17	5	4	113	34	56
Stilton United		26	17	2	7	107	31	53
Manea United		26	15	4	7	54	38	49
Farcet United		26	15	3	8	74	58	48
Doddington United		26	12	2	12	55	43	38
Guyhirn		26	11	1	14	73	62	34
Chatteris Fen Tigers		26	11	1	14	67	85	34
Warboys	*-3*	26	9	4	13	53	72	28
Peterborough Rovers		26	7	1	18	43	106	22
March St Marys	*-3*	26	7	0	19	32	103	18
Emneth Seniors	*-1*	26	3	1	22	39	113	9
Eye Sports & Social		26	3	0	23	30	124	9

Combination One		P	W	D	L	F	A	Pts
Perkins Sports Res.		26	18	5	3	78	31	59
Hotpoint Res.		26	17	1	8	85	53	52
Deeping Sports Res.	*-6*	26	18	3	5	88	32	51
Oundle Town Res.		26	14	3	9	65	47	45
Leverington Sports Res.		25	11	8	6	50	37	41
Stamford Belvedere Res.		26	13	2	11	53	53	41
Moulton Harrox Res.		26	12	3	11	54	48	39
Ortonians Res.	*-3*	26	10	7	9	69	47	34
Parson Drove Res.		26	9	6	11	39	43	33
Whittlesey United Res.		25	9	3	13	56	62	30
Peterborough Northern Star Res.		26	8	6	12	51	61	30
Ramsey Town Res.		26	5	4	17	31	87	19
Werrington Town Res.		26	5	3	18	29	82	18
Long Sutton Athletic Res.		26	4	2	20	34	99	14

Whittlesey United Res. v Leverington Sports Res. – not played

Combination Two		P	W	D	L	F	A	Pts
Chatteris Town Res.		24	20	3	1	99	22	63
Woodlands Res.		24	17	4	3	75	35	55
Peterborough Sports Res.		24	16	4	4	83	40	52
Netherton United Res.		24	13	5	6	74	35	44
Gedney Hill Res.		24	12	6	6	74	45	42
Crowland Town Res.	*-3*	23	11	3	9	58	43	33
Alconbury Res.	*-3*	24	10	4	10	47	42	31
Uppingham Town Res.	*-3*	24	7	4	13	36	74	22
Langtoft United Res.		23	6	3	14	33	60	21
Wimblington Harriers Res.	*-3*	24	7	1	16	42	76	19
Leverington Sports 'A'		24	5	2	17	34	80	17
Kings Cliffe United Res.	*-3*	24	6	1	17	39	81	16
Ketton Res.		24	4	2	18	46	107	14

Crowland Town Res. v Langtoft United Res. – not played

Combination Three		P	W	D	L	F	A	Pts
Pinchbeck United Res.		22	17	2	3	93	35	53
Doddington United Res		22	14	3	5	61	29	45
Eye Sports & Social Res.		22	11	4	7	55	49	37
Sutton Bridge United Res.		22	9	6	7	48	49	33
Stamford Belvedere 'A'		22	8	7	7	44	48	31
Coates Athletic Res.		22	8	4	10	44	48	28
Silver Jubilee Res.	*-3*	22	8	5	9	59	58	26
Rutland Rangers Res.		22	8	2	12	47	60	26
Ramsey Town 'A'		22	7	4	11	45	52	25
Netherton United 'A'		22	7	4	11	35	54	25
Chatteris Town 'A'		22	6	5	11	45	67	23
Manea United Res.		22	4	4	14	33	60	16

PETERBOROUGH CHALLENGE CUP

FINAL

(May 5th at Chestnut Avenue)

Castor & Ailsworth 3 Werrington Town 2 *aet*

PETERBOROUGH JUNIOR CUP

FINAL

(April 28th at Chestnut Avenue)

Leverington Sports Res. 1 Perkins Sports Res. 1 *aet*

FINAL REPLAY

(May 6th at Chestnut Avenue)

Perkins Sports Res. 3 Leverington Sports Res. 0

PETERBOROUGH MINOR CUP

FINAL

(April 22nd at Chestnut Avenue)

Woodlands Res. 4 Crowland Town Res. 0

READING LEAGUE

	Ascot United	Berks County Sports	Cookham Dean	Forest Old Boys	Highmoor/IBIS	Hurst	Marlow United	Mortimer	Reading Old Blues	Reading YMCA	Royal Mail	West Reading	Westwood United	Woodley Town
Ascot United		1-0	0-1	6-0	1-0	1-2	1-3	5-0	7-1	7-2	1-2	9-0	3-1	1-1
Berks County Sports	1-3		0-1	7-0	0-2	2-0	1-2	4-1	5-0	0-2	1-1	5-1	4-0	2-1
Cookham Dean	2-1	4-0	*S*	1-0	1-0	4-0	2-0	0-0	10-0	4-0	2-0	7-0	2-0	0-1
Forest Old Boys	0-2	1-5	1-8	*E*	0-5	2-0	0-4	1-4	2-0	2-2	0-2	5-4	L-W	2-3
Highmoor/IBIS	3-2	4-0	1-1	3-1	*N*	5-1	1-0	2-1	3-0	1-0	0-1	1-0	4-1	7-1
Hurst	0-5	0-1	1-3	2-2	0-2	*I*	0-3	2-4	1-1	3-1	0-2	3-1	0-2	0-0
Marlow United	4-1	2-1	2-3	7-2	1-0	2-1	*O*	2-1	W-L	5-2	4-0	4-1	1-0	3-2
Mortimer	1-3	1-1	0-2	3-1	0-4	0-3	0-5	*R*	2-0	0-5	4-2	4-2	1-0	1-3
Reading Old Blues	1-7	0-2	1-5	4-1	1-7	3-2	0-2	0-3		1-0	1-6	3-4	2-3	0-1
Reading YMCA	1-3	1-1	0-1	0-1	0-1	2-2	0-3	3-1	4-3	*D*	0-3	5-0	3-1	2-3
Royal Mail	2-3	3-0	4-4	0-2	1-1	2-0	0-2	1-0	3-2	4-1	*I*	6-0	2-2	1-2
West Reading	1-3	0-5	0-6	1-5	L-W	1-2	1-2	1-2	7-2	3-2	2-3	*V*	1-6	0-5
Westwood United	1-2	2-1	0-3	4-2	3-4	1-5	2-4	1-1	1-5	1-3	0-0	2-1		2-1
Woodley Town	3-2	1-1	0-3	1-1	1-3	1-1	1-2	0-0	3-3	3-2	1-2	1-5	0-0	

SENIOR CUP

(Senior and Premier Division teams)

FIRST ROUND

Finchampstead 'A' 0 **Marlow Utd** 4
Hurst 2 **Spencers Wood** 2 *aet* (4-5p)
Mortimer 0 **Ascot United** 3
Reading YMCA 7 The Old Bell 1
Rides Dynamoes 3 Forest Old Boys 1
Royal Mail 3 Westwood United 2
Shinfield 2 Goring United 1
Sonning Common 0 **Berks County Sports** 5
Woodcote & Stoke Row 1 **Cookham Dean** 6

SECOND ROUND

Cookham Dean 0 Berks County Sports 0 *aet* (4-3p)
Newtown Henley 1 **Ascot United** 4
Rabson Rovers 3 West Reading 0
Reading Old Blues 0 **Woodley Tn** 4
Rides Dynamoes 0 **Highmoor/IBIS** 3
Royal Mail 3 **Reading YMCA** 4
Shinfield 1 **Marlow United** 4
Spencers Wood 0 **Reading Town Res.** 2

QUARTER-FINALS

Cookham Dean 2 Reading YMCA 0 *aet*
Highmoor/IBIS 2 Ascot United 1
Marlow United 3 **Rabson Rovers** 6
Reading Town Res. 2 Woodley Town 1 *aet*

SEMI-FINALS

Cookham Dean 0 **Woodley Town** 1
Highmoor/IBIS 2 Rabson Rovers 1

FINAL

(May 4th at Reading)

Highmoor/IBIS 5 Woodley Town 2

Senior Division	P	W	D	L	F	A	Pts
Cookham Dean	26	22	3	1	80	12	69
Marlow United	26	23	0	3	69	23	69
Highmoor/IBIS	26	20	2	4	64	18	62
Ascot United	26	17	1	8	80	33	52
Royal Mail	26	14	5	7	53	35	47
Berks County Sports	26	11	4	11	50	34	37
Woodley Town	26	9	8	9	40	46	35
Mortimer	26	9	4	13	35	53	31
Westwood United	26	8	4	14	36	55	28
Reading YMCA	26	7	3	16	43	57	24
Hurst	26	6	5	15	31	53	23
Forest Old Boys	26	6	3	17	34	78	21
Reading Old Blues	26	4	2	20	34	91	14
West Reading	26	4	0	22	37	98	12

INTERMEDIATE CUP

FINAL

(May 20th at Reading Town)

Taplow United 3 **AFC Corinthians** 3 *aet* (3-4p)

JUNIOR CUP

FINAL

(May 20th at Reading Town)

Taplow United Res. 2 **Berks County Sports Res.** 3

READING LEAGUE SENIOR DIVISION CONSTITUTION 2006-07

ASCOT UNITED .... **Ascot Race Course Car Park 10, Winkfield Road, Ascot SL5 7LJ** .... **None**
BERKS COUNTY SPORTS .... **Berks Co. Sports & Social Club, Sonning Lane, Sonning, Reading RG4 6ST** .... **None**
COOKHAM DEAN .... **Alfred Major Rec Ground, Hillcrest Avenue, Cookham Rise, Maidenhead SL6 9NB** **01628 819423**
FOREST OLD BOYS .... **Holme Park (Adwest), Sonning Lane, Sonning, Reading RG4 6ST** **01734 690356**
HIGHMOOR/IBIS .... **Prudential IBIS Sports Club, Scours Lane, Reading RG3 6AY** .... **None**
HURST .... **Cantley Park, Twyford Road, Wokingham RG40 5QT** .... **None**
MORTIMER .... **Alfred Palmer Memorial PF, West End Road, Mortimer, Reading RG7 3TJ** .... **None**
RABSON ROVERS .... **Lower Whitley Rec, Basingstoke Road, Reading RG2 0JA** .... **None**
READING YMCA .... **Reading Town FC, Scours Lane, Tilehurst, Reading RG30 6AY** **0118 945 3555**
ROYAL MAIL .... **Prospect Park, Leibenwood Road, Reading RG30 2ND** .... **None**
WESTWOOD UNITED .... **Cotswold Sports Centre, Downs Way, Tilehurst, Reading RG31 6LX** .... **None**
WOODLEY TOWN .... **East Park Farm, Park Lane, Charvil, Reading** .... **None**

IN: Rabson Rovers (P)

OUT: Marlow United (P – Hellenic League Division One East), Reading Old Blues (W), West Reading (R)

Note – The Old Bell withdrew during the course of the season. Their results are shown herein but are expunged from the league table	Finchampstead 'A'	Goring United	Hurst Res.	Newtown Henley	Rabson Rovers	Reading Town Res.	Rides Dynamos	Shinfield	Sonning Common	Spencers Wood	The Old Bell	Woodcote & Stoke Row
Finchampstead 'A'	*P*	3-0	2-2	2-2	1-12	1-4	0-4	0-1	1-2	2-5	2-1	0-2
Goring United	0-5	*R*	0-2	3-4	5-5	1-7	0-7	0-4	1-0	0-5	2-2	3-2
Hurst Res.	1-1	1-1	*E*	0-3	1-9	0-7	1-2	1-4	2-1	0-2	7-1	0-1
Newtown Henley	2-2	2-2	3-2	*M*	0-5	1-2	2-3	3-1	0-2	5-3	n/a	1-1
Rabson Rovers	5-0	10-2	7-0	9-0	*I*	1-1	2-0	2-3	5-3	4-2	n/a	0-2
Reading Town Res.	W-L	W-L	3-2	2-1	4-0	*E*	4-1	1-0	3-0	4-1	4-0	5-3
Rides Dynamos	L-W	2-0	4-0	3-1	1-2	1-2	*R*	6-1	0-1	2-3	n/a	4-1
Shinfield	2-0	2-1	3-2	4-3	3-3	3-2	1-1		4-1	5-4	2-0	2-2
Sonning Common	4-0	1-0	3-2	2-3	0-4	0-0	0-4	0-2		0-3	5-0	1-1
Spencers Wood	2-2	L-W	2-0	4-2	0-6	1-3	3-1	0-2	2-1	*D*	1-0	0-3
The Old Bell	1-1	1-3	n/a	n/a	2-5	n/a	n/a	n/a	0-2	n/a	*I*	0-1
Woodcote & Stoke Row	2-1	3-0	2-1	2-0	1-4	0-0	6-2	5-1	4-0	1-3	n/a	*V*

Premier Division	P	W	D	L	F	A	Pts
Reading Town Res.	20	16	3	1	54	17	51
Rabson Rovers	20	14	3	3	95	29	45
Shinfield	20	13	3	4	48	37	42
Woodcote & Stoke Row	20	11	4	5	44	28	37
Rides Dynamos	20	10	1	9	48	30	31
Spencers Wood	20	10	1	9	45	43	31
Newtown Henley	20	6	4	10	38	54	22
Sonning Common	20	6	2	12	22	41	20
Finchampstead 'A'	20	3	5	12	23	52	14
Goring United	20	3	3	14	19	65	12
Hurst Res.	20	2	3	15	20	60	9

The Old Bell – record expunged

READING LEAGUE PREMIER DIVISION CONSTITUTION 2006-07

AFC CORINTHIANS .... Civil Service Club, James Lane, Burghill, Reading RG30 3RS.............. 0118 983 3423
COOKHAM DEAN RESERVES . . Alfred Major Rec Ground, Hillcrest Avenue, Cookham Rise, Maidenhead SL6 9NB 01628 819423
MARLOW UNITED RESERVES .... Gossmore Park, Gossmore Lane, Marlow SL7 1QF.............. None
NEWTOWN HENLEY .... Harpsden Hall, Harpsden Village, Henley-on-Thames RG9 4HH .... None
RIDES DYNAMOS .... Rides Community Centre, Gorse Ride South, Finchampstead RG40 4EH .... None
SHINFIELD .... Millworth Lane, Shinfield, Reading RG2 9EN .... None
SONNING COMMON .... Bishopswood, Horsepond Road, Peppard, Reading RG4 9BT.............. None
SPENCERS WOOD .... Coley Recreation Ground, Saviours Road, Coley, Reading RG1 6EJ.............. None
TADLEY CALLEVA RESERVES .... The Green, Tadley RG26 3PD.............. None
TAPLOW UNITED .... Berry Hill, Taplow SL6 0DA .... None
WEST READING .... Victoria Recreation Ground, Kentwood Hill, Tilehurst, Reading RG31 6DE 01628 621745
WOODCOTE & STOKE ROW .... Woodcote Recreation Ground, Woodcote, Reading .... None

IN: AFC Corinthians (P), Cookham Dean Reserves (P), Marlow United Reserves (P), Tadley Calleva Reserves (P), Taplow United (P), West Reading (R)
OUT: Finchampstead 'A' (R), Goring United (R), Hurst Reserves (R), Rabson Rovers (P), Reading Town Reserves (W), The Old Bell (WS)

Division One	P	W	D	L	F	A	Pts
Cookham Dean Res.	22	15	4	3	53	21	49
Marlow United Res.	22	14	2	6	50	40	44
AFC Corinthians	22	12	5	5	45	24	41
OLA Newbury	22	10	4	8	60	51	34
Radstock	22	10	4	8	41	42	34
Tadley Calleva Res.	22	9	3	10	40	38	30
Taplow United	22	9	3	10	45	44	30
Wokingham & Emmbrook 'A'	22	8	4	10	32	40	28
Frilsham & Yattendon	22	8	2	12	38	45	26
Highmoor/IBIS Res.	22	7	1	14	42	59	22
Unity	22	5	4	13	35	46	19
REME Arborfield	22	5	4	13	31	62	19

Division Two	P	W	D	L	F	A	Pts
Whitley Wood	20	15	3	2	68	29	48
Ascot United Res.	20	13	3	4	42	20	42
Prospect United	20	12	2	6	58	32	38
Twyford & Ruscombe	20	10	5	5	39	21	35
SRCC	20	10	0	10	60	40	30
Whitley Rovers	20	8	3	9	34	44	27
Westwood United Res.	20	7	2	11	39	49	23
Newtown Henley Res.	20	5	5	10	26	42	20
Crowthorne Sports	20	5	3	12	27	61	18
Woodcote & Stoke Row Res.	20	4	5	11	22	51	17
Woodley Town Res.	20	2	7	11	19	45	13

Division Three	P	W	D	L	F	A	Pts
Marlow United 'A'	22	18	2	2	80	29	56
Ashridge Park	22	18	1	3	107	25	55
Park United	22	17	3	2	72	16	54
Theale	22	13	3	6	63	36	42
Taplow United Res.	22	11	1	10	48	42	34
Mortimer Res.	22	10	3	9	47	46	33
Wokingham Wanderers	22	10	1	11	51	55	31
Englefield	22	7	2	13	48	91	23
Sonning	22	6	4	12	37	50	22
Highmoor/IBIS 'A'	22	6	2	14	56	86	20
Goring United Res.	22	1	4	17	28	93	7
Sonning Sports	22	1	2	19	31	99	5

Division Four	P	W	D	L	F	A	Pts
South Reading	26	24	0	2	144	18	72
Royal Mail Res.	26	20	3	3	114	40	63
Berks County Sports Res.	26	17	2	7	82	24	53
Wokingham & Emmbrook 'B'	26	16	3	7	81	55	51
Theale Res.	26	14	3	9	60	58	45
Wargrave	26	12	7	7	70	52	43
Compton	26	12	1	13	78	69	37
Rides Dynamos Res.	26	10	4	12	82	58	34
Woodley Town 'A'	26	10	4	12	33	59	34
Taplow United 'A'	26	8	4	14	36	66	28
The Hop Leaf	26	7	1	18	45	109	22
Hurst 'A'	26	6	3	17	38	78	21
Sonning Res.	26	3	3	20	17	128	12
Linear United	26	3	2	21	30	96	11

SHROPSHIRE COUNTY LEAGUE

	Broseley Juniors	Church Stretton Town	Clee Hill United	Hanwood United	Haughmond	Highley Welfare	Hopesgate United	Meole Brace	Morda United	Shawbury United Colts	Shifnal United	Tibberton United	Wellington Amateurs	Wem Town
Broseley Juniors		2-3	3-1	0-0	2-1	3-1	2-0	2-1	10-0	1-2	4-4	1-3	1-1	2-1
Church Stretton Town	2-3	*P*	1-1	2-4	1-2	0-0	2-2	4-0	5-0	3-0	0-0	2-5	3-2	2-3
Clee Hill United	1-6	1-5	*R*	1-4	1-2	1-2	2-5	1-2	5-1	3-1	3-8	2-2	1-2	1-4
Hanwood United	1-1	3-1	6-2	*E*	4-2	3-1	1-0	2-1	7-0	6-0	4-0	5-4	1-0	6-1
Haughmond	3-3	2-1	5-1	0-6	*M*	2-0	1-1	3-2	0-1	2-1	6-1	0-0	0-0	0-2
Highley Welfare	1-2	2-2	3-3	1-2	5-1	*I*	3-0	6-3	5-4	2-0	0-2	0-1	1-3	1-0
Hopesgate United	2-2	3-1	9-2	0-1	1-3	0-2	*E*	3-0	6-1	3-0	0-0	3-0	0-0	3-4
Meole Brace	0-2	0-1	2-1	0-4	3-9	1-4	1-4	*R*	1-2	1-5	0-3	5-3	2-2	0-3
Morda United	1-3	2-2	3-0	0-7	1-4	1-4	1-5	4-2		0-4	0-3	2-0	0-3	1-2
Shawbury United Colts	0-1	1-2	2-2	0-3	2-1	0-6	1-4	0-2	1-4		1-4	2-4	0-0	3-0
Shifnal United	1-1	0-1	3-1	1-2	2-1	1-0	1-0	5-0	4-0	2-2	*D*	2-0	2-2	3-1
Tibberton United	0-4	2-0	1-0	2-3	5-1	3-3	3-3	4-1	4-3	4-0	2-1	*I*	0-2	3-0
Wellington Amateurs	0-1	3-1	8-1	4-6	4-3	1-0	1-1	4-1	4-0	4-0	2-1	0-2	*V*	1-0
Wem Town	5-0	1-3	2-2	1-1	2-2	2-2	0-1	5-1	4-0	2-0	1-0	3-1	1-2	

Premier Division	P	W	D	L	F	A	Pts
Hanwood United	26	23	3	0	92	25	72
Broseley Juniors	26	15	7	4	62	35	52
Wellington Amateurs	26	14	7	5	55	29	49
Shifnal United	26	13	6	7	54	34	45
Tibberton United	26	13	4	9	58	48	43
Hopesgate United	26	11	7	8	59	35	40
Wem Town	26	12	4	10	50	41	40
Highley Welfare	26	11	5	10	55	41	38
Haughmond	26	11	5	10	56	52	38
Church Stretton Town	26	10	6	10	50	44	36
Morda United	26	6	1	19	32	95	19
Shawbury United Colts	26	5	3	18	28	66	18
Meole Brace	26	4	1	21	32	86	13
Clee Hill United	26	2	5	19	40	92	11

PREMIER DIVISION CUP

FIRST ROUND

Church Stretton Town 0 **Hanwood United** 1
Clee Hill United 4 Tibberton United 2
Haughmond 3 Hopesgate United 2
Shawbury United Colts 2 Highley Welfare 0
Shifnal United 0 **Broseley Juniors** 3
Wellington Amateurs 2 Wem Town 0

QUARTER-FINALS

Broseley Juniors 1 Haughmond 0
Clee Hill United 3 **Morda United** 4 *aet*
Hanwood United 4 Wellington Amateurs 0
Meole Brace 3 Shawbury United Colts 2 *aet*

SEMI-FINALS

Hanwood United 1 Broseley Juniors 0
Morda United 3 Meole Brace 2

FINAL

(May 6th at Bridgnorth Town)
Hanwood United 4 Morda United 0

SHROPSHIRE COUNTY LEAGUE PREMIER DIVISION CONSTITUTION 2006-07

BROSELEY JUNIORS .... Birchmeadow, Broseley TF12 5LP .... None
CHURCH STRETTON TOWN .... Russell Meadow, Church Stretton .... None
CLEE HILL UNITED .... Knowle Sports Ground, Tenbury Road, Clee Hill, Ludlow SY8 3NE .... None
HANWOOD UNITED .... Hanwood Recreation Ground, Hanwood .... None
HAUGHMOND .... Mereside, Springfield, Shrewsbury .... None
HIGHLEY WELFARE .... Welfare Ground, Main Road, Highley WV16 6NQ .... None
HOPESGATE UNITED .... The Cotes, Snailbeach .... None
JFF TELFORD .... Grainger Road, Leegomery, Telford TF1 6UJ .... None
MEOLE BRACE .... Church Road, Meole Brace, Shrewsbury SY3 9HF .... None
MORDA UNITED .... Weston Road, Morda, Oswestry SY10 9NS 01691 659621
SHIFNAL UNITED .... Idsall Sports Centre, Shifnal .... None
TELFORD JUNIORS .... Ironbridge Power Station, Buildwas Road, Ironbridge TF8 7BL .... None
TIBBERTON UNITED .... Doseley Road, Dawley, Telford TF4 .... None
WELLINGTON AMATEURS .... Grainger Road, Leegomery, Telford TF1 6UJ .... None
WEM TOWN .... Butler Sports Centre, Bowens Field, Wem SY4 5AW 01939 233287

IN: JFF Telford (P), Telford Juniors (P)

OUT: Shawbury United Colts (R)

	Brown Clee	Craven Arms Town	Dawley Wanderers	Ellesmere Rangers Res.	JFF Telford	Market Drayton Town Res.	Morda United Res.	Oakengates Athletic	Springvale Rovers	St Martins	Telford Juniors	Wrockwardine Wood	Wroxeter Rovers
Brown Clee	*D*	2-1	1-3	3-2	1-0	0-1	6-1	0-2	1-1	4-3	1-3	2-0	2-3
Craven Arms Town	0-0	*I*	1-2	1-5	0-1	2-2	2-2	1-5	0-0	2-5	2-6	4-3	1-1
Dawley Wanderers	0-2	1-1	*V*	2-2	2-0	3-2	1-0	0-4	0-2	1-4	1-3	2-3	1-2
Ellesmere Rangers Res.	3-2	6-2	3-2	*I*	0-0	6-0	6-0	1-4	5-0	1-1	2-6	6-3	1-1
JFF Telford	2-1	1-1	3-1	3-1	*S*	2-2	12-0	5-1	2-1	6-0	5-1	6-2	3-0
Market Drayton Town Res.	0-0	5-1	1-3	1-2	4-2	*I*	7-1	4-0	0-0	5-1	0-4	0-0	2-0
Morda United Res.	4-3	4-3	1-5	0-2	0-8	0-7	*O*	1-4	0-3	2-3	2-7	1-3	1-4
Oakengates Athletic	1-1	5-2	2-2	4-4	1-6	1-0	1-1	*N*	2-2	4-1	1-3	0-1	2-2
Springvale Rovers	2-1	3-0	2-1	3-3	1-0	7-1	4-2	1-2		1-0	1-1	4-2	1-0
St Martins	1-1	3-5	3-1	5-2	0-4	3-1	4-3	1-4	5-0		3-1	4-1	1-3
Telford Juniors	0-1	3-1	3-0	5-2	1-2	2-2	4-0	5-3	4-2	3-0	*O*	2-0	5-0
Wrockwardine Wood	0-1	1-2	3-1	0-0	0-2	2-1	10-0	1-2	2-3	2-3	1-5	*N*	2-2
Wroxeter Rovers	4-1	2-2	2-2	1-1	4-2	1-2	9-1	4-1	3-1	1-0	2-4	4-3	*E*

DIVISION ONE CUP

FIRST ROUND
Craven Arms Town 1 **Brown Clee** 4
Dawley Wanderers 2 **Market Drayton Town Res.** 3
JFF Telford 2 St Martins 0
Springvale Rovers 1 Ellesmere Rangers Res. 0
Wrockwardine Wood 1 **Telford Juniors** 3

QUARTER-FINALS
Brown Clee 4 Oakengates Athletic 2
Morda United Res. 1 **Springvale Rovers** 5
Telford Juniors 0 **JFF Telford** 5
Wroxeter Rovers 3 Market Drayton Town Res. 0

SEMI-FINALS
Brown Clee 3 Springvale Rovers 2
JFF Telford 0 **Wroxeter Rovers** 1

FINAL
(May 18th at Bridgnorth Town)
Brown Clee 3 Wroxeter Rovers 1

Division One	P	W	D	L	F	A	Pts
Telford Juniors	24	18	2	4	81	34	56
JFF Telford	24	16	3	5	77	25	51
Springvale Rovers	24	12	6	6	45	37	42
Wroxeter Rovers	24	11	7	6	55	42	40
Oakengates Athletic	24	11	6	7	56	49	39
Ellesmere Rangers Res.	24	10	8	6	66	49	38
St Martins	24	11	2	11	54	58	35
Market Drayton Tn Res.	24	9	6	9	50	43	33
Brown Clee	24	9	5	10	37	37	32
Dawley Wanderers	24	7	4	13	37	50	25
Wrockwardine Wood	24	6	3	15	45	57	21
Craven Arms Town	24	3	8	13	37	68	17
Morda United Res.	24	2	2	20	27	118	8

RON JONES MEMORIAL CUP

FIRST ROUND
Broseley Juniors 0 **Highley Welfare** 2
Brown Clee 2 **Wroxeter Rovers** 2 *aet* (3-4p)
Clee Hill United 4 Craven Arms Town 3
Dawley Wanderers 2 Market Drayton Town 1
Ellesmere Rangers Res. 2 Church Stretton Town 0
Hopesgate United 0 **Shifnal United** 4
JFF Telford 0 **St Martins** 2
Meole Brace 5 Morda United Res. 1
Morda United 1 **Oakengates Athletic** 3
Shawbury United Colts 3 Hanwood United 2
Wem Town 1 Tibberton United 0

SECOND ROUND
Clee Hill United 2 **Springvale Rovers** 3
Dawley Wanderers 0 **Highley Welfare** 1
Meole Brace 0 **Haughmond** 2
Oakengates Athletic 2 **Shifnal United** 2 *aet* (4-5p)
Shawbury United Colts 0 **Wellington Amateurs** 4
St Martins 7 Wrockwardine Wood 2
Telford Juniors 1 **Ellesmere Rangers Res.** 3 *aet*
Wroxeter Rovers 1 **Wem Town** 2

QUARTER-FINALS
Ellesmere Rangers Res. 0 **Shifnal United** 1
Springvale Rovers 1 **Haughmond** 3
St Martins 2 **Highley Welfare** 4
Wem Town 1 Wellington Amateurs 0

SEMI-FINALS
Haughmond 3 **Shifnal United** 6
Wem Town 4 Highley Welfare 3 *aet*

FINAL
(May 20th at Bridgnorth Town)
Shifnal United 4 Wem Town 1

SHROPSHIRE COUNTY LEAGUE DIVISION ONE CONSTITUTION 2006-07

BOBBINGTON .... **Recreation Ground, Bobbington** .... **None**
BROWN CLEE .... **Hall Meadow, Cleobury North, Bridgnorth WV16 6RP** .... **None**
CRAVEN ARMS TOWN .... **Craven Arms Playing Fields, Shrewsbury, Craven Arms** .... **None**
DAWLEY WANDERERS .... **Doseley Road, Dawley, Telford TF5** .... **None**
ELLESMERE RANGERS RESERVES .... **Beech Grove Playing Fields, Ellesmere SY12 0BT** .... **None**
MARKET DRAYTON TOWN RESERVES .... **Greenfield Sports Club, Greenfield Lane, Market Drayton TF9 3SL** **01630 655088**
MORDA UNITED RESERVES .... **Weston Road, Morda, Oswestry SY10 9NS** **01691 659621**
OAKENGATES ATHLETIC .... **School Road, Oakengates** .... **None**
SHAWBURY UNITED COLTS .... **Butlers Sports Centre, Bowens Field, Wem SY4 5AW** **01939 233287**
SHIFNAL TOWN RESERVES .... **Phoenix Park, Coppice Green Lane, Shifal TF11 8PB** **01952 463667**
SPRINGVALE ROVERS .... **Cleobury Mortimer PF, Love Lane, Cleobury Mortimer DY14 8PE** .... **None**
ST MARTINS .... **St Martins Playing Fields, Overton Road, St Martins, Oswestry SY11 3DG** .... **None**
WROCKWARDINE WOOD .... **New Road, Wrockwardine Wood TF2 7AB** **01952 613086**
WROXETER ROVERS .... **Springfield, Wroxeter** .... **None**

IN: Bobbington (formerly Royal Oak) (P – Telford Combination (subject to ground grading)), Shawbury United Colts (R)

OUT: JFF Telford (P), Meole Brace Reserves (WN), Oswestry Boys Club (WN), Telford Juniors (P)

SOMERSET COUNTY LEAGUE

	Backwell United Res.	Bridgwater Town Res.	Burnham United	Castle Cary	Cheddar	Cleeve West Town	Fry Club	Hengrove Athletic	Ilminster Town	Mangotsfield United Res.	Nailsea United	Oldland Abbotonians	Paulton Rovers Res.	Stockwood Green	Timsbury Athletic	Wells City	Welton Rovers Res.	Winscombe
Backwell United Res.		0-3	1-5	1-3	3-3	0-5	3-4	0-3	0-1	1-3	0-5	0-3	0-5	0-0	4-0	1-6	1-1	2-1
Bridgwater Town Res.	9-0	*P*	1-1	4-1	1-0	4-0	1-1	2-2	2-0	3-1	0-1	1-1	0-2	2-2	1-0	3-0	1-1	1-1
Burnham United	2-1	2-0	*R*	1-2	3-2	2-1	2-0	1-1	1-1	0-0	1-1	0-0	1-1	5-2	2-1	3-2	1-0	1-1
Castle Cary	2-0	0-2	2-3	*E*	1-1	2-1	2-3	0-5	0-1	1-2	1-3	0-3	0-4	3-1	2-1	2-2	1-1	1-1
Cheddar	7-0	0-2	0-2	1-3	*M*	5-1	1-2	0-1	4-1	1-1	1-3	2-1	1-1	1-2	2-2	0-5	2-3	1-1
Cleeve West Town	5-1	1-2	1-1	1-1	3-2	*I*	2-1	0-2	3-0	0-4	0-2	0-1	0-3	3-1	1-0	2-0	2-3	2-3
Fry Club	2-0	1-2	2-2	2-1	3-1	1-3	*E*	0-2	0-1	0-3	0-5	1-4	0-1	0-2	2-2	2-1	2-3	1-2
Hengrove Athletic	3-2	2-2	5-0	6-0	4-0	4-1	3-2	*R*	4-0	3-1	2-1	3-0	1-0	2-2	2-1	2-1	2-0	4-0
Ilminster Town	4-2	1-5	0-2	0-5	1-3	1-0	2-4	0-4		1-1	1-1	0-3	0-2	3-3	0-0	2-2	1-4	0-2
Mangotsfield United Res.	11-0	1-0	3-1	0-0	8-1	0-0	6-2	0-1	1-2	*D*	2-2	0-2	1-0	5-0	2-0	3-0	1-0	3-2
Nailsea United	4-0	3-0	0-3	1-2	1-1	3-0	3-1	0-1	5-0	1-1	*I*	0-1	2-1	3-0	0-1	2-3	2-2	2-2
Oldland Abbotonians	2-0	1-1	1-0	0-1	6-0	2-1	2-0	1-1	0-1	1-1	1-5	*V*	1-0	1-0	3-0	0-2	2-1	2-1
Paulton Rovers Res.	5-0	1-4	0-3	2-3	1-0	1-0	2-1	0-1	0-1	2-1	1-2	3-0	*I*	1-1	3-1	1-1	2-3	1-1
Stockwood Green	3-0	0-5	0-0	0-0	3-2	0-0	0-1	1-4	0-1	0-2	0-1	2-1	0-2	*S*	1-2	3-3	1-4	3-1
Timsbury Athletic	2-0	1-1	0-1	3-2	2-3	0-3	3-2	1-2	4-0	4-2	2-3	0-2	1-1	2-0	*I*	2-2	1-1	2-1
Wells City	2-1	5-2	2-8	3-2	3-2	2-1	3-2	0-0	2-1	W-L	2-1	0-0	0-0	2-1	1-3	*O*	5-2	2-0
Welton Rovers Res.	2-0	1-1	1-0	1-1	3-0	3-1	1-0	1-2	1-1	1-3	2-1	0-1	1-2	1-1	2-3	2-1	*N*	0-2
Winscombe	1-3	1-2	2-3	3-1	1-3	4-1	3-0	0-4	4-2	0-3	4-3	0-2	2-0	3-0	0-1	2-3	3-2	

Premier Division		P	W	D	L	F	A	Pts
Hengrove Athletic		34	28	6	0	88	20	90
Oldland Abbotonians		34	20	6	8	51	27	66
Burnham United		34	18	11	5	63	37	65
Mangotsfield Utd Res.	*-1*	34	18	8	8	76	32	61
Wells City		34	17	8	9	68	58	59
Bridgwater Town Res.	*-4*	34	17	11	6	70	35	58
Nailsea United		34	17	7	10	72	39	58
Paulton Rovers Res.		34	15	7	12	51	34	52
Welton Rovers Res.		34	13	9	12	54	50	48
Timsbury Athletic		34	12	7	15	48	54	43
Winscombe		34	12	6	16	55	61	42
Castle Cary		34	11	8	15	48	63	41
Cleeve West Town		34	10	4	20	45	61	34
Ilminster Town		34	9	7	18	31	74	34
Fry Club	*-1*	34	9	3	22	45	74	29
Cheddar		34	7	7	20	53	78	28
Stockwood Green		34	6	10	18	35	66	28
Backwell United Res.	*-3*	34	3	3	28	27	117	9

PREMIER/DIVISION ONE CUP

FIRST ROUND

Backwell United Res. 0 **Castle Cary** 3
Brislington Res. 1 **Winscombe** 2
Hengrove Athletic 2 Glastonbury 1
Tunley Athletic 2 **Westland United** 4

SECOND ROUND

Bridgwater Town Res. 4 Bishop Sutton Res. 0
Castle Cary 1 Stockwood Green 0
Churchill Club 3 Frome Town Res. 2
Cleeve West Town 2 **Taunton Blackbrook** 4
Crewkerne 0 **Hengrove Athletic** 4
Ilminster Town 3 **Keynsham Town Res.** 4
Nailsea Town 1 **Odd Down Res.** 3
Nailsea United 1 **Westland United** 5
Oldland Abbotonians 3 Cheddar 0
Paulton Rovers Res. 1 Shirehampton 0
Shepton Mallet Res. 1 **Burnham United** 4 *aet*
St George Easton-in-Gordano 0 **Welton Rovers Res.** 3
Timsbury Athletic 8 Robinsons 0
Watchet Town 0 **Mangotsfield United Res.** 2

SOMERSET COUNTY LEAGUE PREMIER DIVISION CONSTITUTION 2006-07

BRIDGWATER TOWN RESERVES . . . Fairfax Park, College Way, Bath Road, Bridgwater TA6 4TZ . . . 01278 446899
BURNHAM UNITED . . . Burnham Road Playing Fields, Cassis Close, Burnham-on-Sea TA8 1NN . . . 01278 794615
CASTLE CARY . . . Donald Pither Memorial PF, Castle Cary . . . 01963 351538
CHEDDAR . . . Bowdens Park, Draycott Road, Cheddar BS27 3RL . . . 01934 743736
CLEEVE WEST TOWN . . . King George V Playing Fields, Meeting House Lane, Cleeve . . . 01934 832173
FROME TOWN RESERVES . . . Badgers Hill, Berkley Road, Frome BA11 2EH . . . 01373 464087
FRY CLUB . . . Fry Club, Somerdale, Keynsham, Bristol . . . 0117 937 6500/6501
GLASTONBURY TOWN . . . Abbey Moor Stadium, Godney Road, Glastonbury BA6 9AF . . . 01458 831460
ILMINSTER TOWN . . . Recreation Ground, Ilminster . . . 01460 54756
MANGOTSFIELD UNITED RESERVES . . . Cossham Street, Mangotsfield, Bristol BS17 3EN . . . 0117 956 0119
NAILSEA UNITED . . . Grove Sports Ground, Old Church, Nailsea BS48 4ND . . . 01275 856892
OLDLAND ABBOTONIANS . . . Aitchinson Playing Field, Castle Road, Oldland Common BS30 9SZ . . . 0117 932 8263
PAULTON ROVERS RESERVES . . . Athletic Ground, Winterfield Road, Paulton BS39 7RF . . . 01761 412907
SHIREHAMPTON . . . Recreation Ground, Penpole Lane, Shirehampton, Bristol BS11 0EA . . . 0117 923 5461
TIMSBURY ATHLETIC . . . Recreation Ground, North Road, Timsbury, Bath BA2 0JH . . . 01761 472523
WELLS CITY . . . The Athletic Ground, Rowdens Road, Wells BA5 1TU . . . 01749 679971
WELTON ROVERS RESERVES . . . West Clewes, North Road, Midsomer Norton BA3 2QD . . . 01761 412097
WINSCOMBE . . . Recreation Ground, The Lynch, Winscombe BS25 1AP . . . 01934 842720 (cricket club)

IN: Frome Town Reserves (P), Glastonbury Town (P), Shirehampton (P)

OUT: Backwell United Reserves (R), Hengrove Athletic (P – Western League Division One), Stockwood Green (having merged with Division One side Robinsons to form Stockwood Green Robinsons) (R)

	Bishop Sutton Res.	Brislington Res.	Churchill Club	Crewkerne	Frome Town Res.	Glastonbury Town	Keynsham Town Res.	Nailsea Town	Odd Down Res.	Robinsons	Shepton Mallet Res.	Shirehampton	St George Easton-in-Gordano	Taunton Blackbrook	Tunley Athletic	Watchet Town	Westland United	Worle
Bishop Sutton Res.		0-1	2-2	1-3	1-2	0-3	0-2	1-0	1-4	2-3	1-1	0-5	2-2	1-2	1-0	0-1	2-3	2-2
Brislington Res.	3-1		7-1	2-0	1-1	0-1	4-2	0-1	0-0	2-0	3-1	1-6	1-0	1-1	2-1	2-1	0-0	3-2
Churchill Club	4-2	1-3		3-0	2-1	0-0	2-1	1-0	1-0	2-1	1-2	1-1	3-2	0-0	5-1	4-1	1-4	1-1
Crewkerne	0-2	0-2	2-0	*D*	0-2	2-5	4-5	2-1	1-2	2-1	2-2	2-4	2-1	0-3	1-3	1-1	0-0	3-2
Frome Town Res.	1-0	0-0	0-1	3-0	*I*	0-0	4-2	1-0	3-0	2-0	5-0	0-2	0-1	1-0	3-2	2-0	1-0	4-1
Glastonbury Town	1-1	1-0	5-1	2-1	0-0	*V*	6-3	2-1	1-2	6-0	2-1	3-6	2-2	2-2	1-0	3-3	1-1	3-0
Keynsham Town Res.	0-0	2-1	2-1	3-2	1-3	1-1	*I*	3-2	1-1	1-1	2-2	5-2	1-3	0-1	2-1	3-0	3-1	2-1
Nailsea Town	1-3	2-4	1-1	1-1	0-3	0-4	1-1	*S*	1-2	2-0	2-2	1-0	0-1	0-1	2-3	1-0	1-3	8-0
Odd Down Res.	0-1	0-3	3-1	2-0	2-4	0-1	0-2	0-3	*I*	3-0	2-0	1-2	1-0	4-2	2-0	2-2	1-1	2-1
Robinsons	0-4	0-3	0-4	2-2	0-2	1-3	0-1	0-1	0-3	*O*	1-1	0-3	0-2	1-5	5-0	0-4	3-2	0-4
Shepton Mallet Res.	3-2	4-1	1-1	2-0	2-3	0-0	2-0	0-0	2-2	2-0	*N*	0-6	0-2	1-2	2-1	1-1	2-3	1-3
Shirehampton	6-0	1-0	2-0	2-0	3-0	3-1	2-2	6-0	7-4	1-1	5-0		2-1	2-1	2-1	4-1	4-2	1-0
St George Easton-in-Gordano	2-2	1-1	3-3	2-0	1-2	1-2	1-0	3-0	4-1	2-1	4-1	3-1	*O*	2-0	1-1	3-0	0-0	2-4
Taunton Blackbrook	1-2	5-2	4-1	3-1	3-4	3-2	2-1	1-1	5-1	1-2	2-1	0-0	2-2	*N*	1-3	3-0	0-4	0-1
Tunley Athletic	1-1	1-3	2-0	2-2	0-3	1-3	1-1	1-4	1-4	1-0	0-0	2-0	2-2	4-2	*E*	3-0	1-4	3-1
Watchet Town	3-1	3-0	7-2	1-1	0-3	0-4	4-2	1-1	2-0	4-0	1-0	2-0	0-0	2-1	5-0		1-0	1-1
Westland United	2-1	2-6	2-1	2-2	1-1	1-3	0-1	3-0	2-1	1-3	4-0	3-3	1-0	4-1	1-1	4-2		1-2
Worle	2-1	0-7	1-1	1-1	1-2	3-2	4-4	1-4	5-2	0-0	3-2	0-8	2-5	4-0	0-0	1-3	1-1	

Wells City 3 **Winscombe** 4
Worle 3 **Fry Club** 4

THIRD ROUND

Churchill Club 6 Taunton Blackbrook 0
Fry Club 0 **Odd Down Res.** 1
Keynsham Town Res. 1 **Timsbury Athletic** 3
Oldland Abbotonians 0 **Bridgwater Town Res.** 2
Paulton Rovers Res. 0 **Hengrove Athletic** 2
Welton Rovers Res. 0 **Mangotsfield United Res.** 2
Westland United 5 Castle Cary 1
Winscombe 0 **Burnham United** 4

QUARTER-FINALS

Churchill Club 3 Westland United 2 *aet*
Hengrove Athletic 2 **Bridgwater Town Res.** 2 *aet* (1-4p)
Mangotsfield United Res. 1 **Timsbury Athletic** 2
Odd Down Res. 1 **Burnham United** 3

SEMI-FINALS

Burnham United 0 **Bridgwater Town Res.** 4
Churchill Club 0 **Timsbury Athletic** 2

FINAL

(May 11th at Shepton Mallet)
Bridgwater Town Res. 1 Timsbury Athletic 0

Division One		P	W	D	L	F	A	Pts
Shirehampton		34	24	5	5	102	38	77
Frome Town Res.		34	24	5	5	66	27	77
Glastonbury Town		34	19	10	5	76	40	67
Brislington Res.		34	19	6	9	69	42	63
St George Easton-in-Gordano		34	15	10	9	61	40	55
Westland United		34	14	10	10	63	50	52
Watchet Town		34	14	8	12	57	53	50
Keynsham Res.	*-2*	34	14	9	11	62	60	49
Taunton Blackbrook		34	14	6	14	60	57	48
Odd Down Res.		34	14	5	15	54	60	47
Churchill Club		34	12	9	13	53	64	45
Worle		34	10	9	15	55	80	39
Nailsea Town		34	9	7	18	43	55	34
Tunley Athletic	*-2*	34	9	8	17	44	66	33
Shepton Mallet Res.	*-2*	34	7	11	16	41	67	30
Bishop Sutton Res.		34	7	8	19	41	66	29
Crewkerne		34	6	9	19	40	70	27
Robinsons		34	5	5	24	26	78	20

SOMERSET COUNTY LEAGUE DIVISION ONE CONSTITUTION 2006-07

BACKWELL UNITED RESERVES . . . The Playing Fields, West Town Road, Backwell, Bristol BS48 3HG 01275 462612
BISHOP SUTTON RESERVES . . . . Lake View, Wick Road, Bishop Sutton, Bristol BS39 5XP 01275 333097
BISHOPS LYDEARD . . . . Darby Way, Bishops Lydeard TA4 3BE . . . . None
BRISLINGTON RESERVES . . . . Ironmould Lane, Brislington, Bristol BS4 5SA 0117 977 4030
CHURCHILL CLUB . . . . Ladymead Lane, Churchill, Winscombe BS25 5NH 01934 852739
CUTTERS FRIDAY . . . . The Cutters Club, Stockwood Lane, Stockwood, Bristol BS41 8LN 01275 839830
DUNDRY ATHLETIC . . . . Dundry Playing Field, Crabtree Lane, Dundry, Bristol 0117 964 5536
KEYNSHAM TOWN RESERVES . . . . Crown Field, Bristol Road, Keynsham, Bristol BS31 2BE 0117 986 5876
NAILSEA TOWN . . . . Fryth Way, Pound Lane, Nailsea BS48 2AS . . . . None
ODD DOWN RESERVES . . . . . . Lew Hill Memorial Ground, Combe Hay Lane, Odd Down, Bath BA2 8PH 01225 832491
SHEPTON MALLET RESERVES . . . West Shepton Playing Fields, Old Wells Road, Shepton Mallet BA4 5XN 01749 344609
ST GEORGE EASTON-IN-GORDANO . . . . . Court Hay, Easton-in-Gordano, Bristol BS20 0PY 01275 374235
STOCKWOOD GREEN ROBINSONS . . . Hursley Lane, Woolard Lane, Whitchurch, Bristol BS14 0QY 01275 891300
TAUNTON BLACKBROOK . . . . Taunton Town FC, Wordsworth Drive, Taunton TA1 2HG 01823 278191
TUNLEY ATHLETIC . . . . The Recreation Centre, Bath Road, Tunley . . . . None
WATCHET TOWN . . . . Memorial Ground, Doniford Road, Watchet TA23 0TG 01984 631041
WESTLAND UNITED . . . . Westland Sports Club, Winterstoke Road, Weston-super-Mare BS24 9AA 01934 632037
WORLE . . . . Worle Recreation Ground, Station Road, Worle, Weston-super-Mare BS22 6AU . . . . None

IN: Backwell United Reserves (R), Bishops Lydeard (P), Cutters Friday (P), Dundry Athletic (P), Stockwood Green (having merged with Robinsons to form Stockwood Green Robinsons) (R)
OUT: Crewkerne (R – Division Two West), Frome Town Reserves (P), Glastonbury Town (P), Shirehampton (P)

	Bishops Lydeard	Burnham United Res.	Clevedon United Res.	Combe St Nicholas	Congresbury	Cutters Friday	Dundry Athletic	Frome Collegians	Larkhall Athletic Res.	Nailsea United Res.	Peasedown Athletic	Portishead Res.	Saltford	Street Res.	Wells City Res.	Weston St Johns Res.	Wincanton Town
Bishops Lydeard		5-0	1-1	2-0	1-1	1-1	0-1	6-0	4-0	1-0	11-0	2-3	2-1	1-1	2-0	7-0	3-0
Burnham United Res.	0-5		2-0	2-1	0-5	2-0	1-1	1-2	0-2	1-2	4-0	2-2	3-2	2-2	1-2	4-0	2-2
Clevedon United Res.	2-1	0-0	*D*	2-0	2-2	0-5	1-0	1-1	2-2	3-0	5-2	0-1	0-5	1-3	2-1	2-0	3-0
Combe St Nicholas	2-0	5-4	0-1	*I*	4-1	1-4	4-0	0-0	3-2	0-0	3-4	2-0	2-0	1-3	1-0	3-0	4-1
Congresbury	0-0	5-2	3-2	1-0	*V*	0-2	1-2	0-0	1-3	2-1	6-1	2-2	5-1	1-1	0-1	3-0	1-2
Cutters Friday	2-1	3-1	3-0	0-1	8-0	*I*	3-0	5-0	1-1	4-2	13-0	2-1	1-0	1-0	2-0	2-1	4-1
Dundry Athletic	0-2	6-1	1-0	1-1	3-1	2-2	*S*	1-0	1-0	1-2	2-0	1-1	2-1	2-1	0-0	10-0	2-2
Frome Collegians	2-1	1-2	0-3	1-0	0-2	0-1	1-2	*I*	1-2	0-5	4-1	0-2	0-2	2-0	2-3	2-0	0-0
Larkhall Athletic Res.	1-2	4-1	3-0	3-2	2-0	4-1	1-2	0-3	*O*	4-2	5-2	2-1	5-1	2-2	1-4	2-0	7-2
Nailsea United Res.	1-1	4-0	3-2	0-0	0-3	0-0	0-0	0-1	1-1	*N*	6-1	2-1	1-0	1-3	0-0	0-2	1-3
Peasedown Athletic	0-3	4-4	4-0	0-0	2-5	1-5	0-7	2-2	1-1	1-4		0-0	1-4	1-1	0-5	2-3	0-1
Portishead Res.	1-3	2-1	2-0	0-0	1-0	0-4	2-2	5-0	2-1	1-2	7-0		4-3	2-1	4-1	2-0	3-2
Saltford	0-2	1-2	2-4	1-2	0-1	2-3	0-0	1-0	2-2	1-2	1-1	0-3	*T*	3-1	0-4	3-2	1-0
Street Res.	2-3	0-2	0-1	0-3	3-1	1-4	0-2	0-0	0-1	4-1	5-1	4-2	2-3	*W*	0-0	4-1	3-1
Wells City Res.	0-3	4-1	2-0	2-0	2-2	5-0	1-1	0-0	0-1	1-4	5-4	1-0	1-1	2-1	*O*	2-1	3-4
Weston St Johns Res.	1-4	4-0	4-1	1-5	2-1	3-3	5-2	4-4	1-1	3-3	4-2	0-4	1-1	2-14	2-0		1-1
Wincanton Town	2-1	1-1	3-0	2-1	2-4	1-3	1-5	5-2	0-4	0-1	6-1	1-3	2-3	4-1	2-5	3-0	

Division Two		P	W	D	L	F	A	Pts
Cutters Friday		32	23	5	4	92	32	74
Bishops Lydeard		32	19	6	7	81	25	63
Dundry Athletic		32	16	10	6	62	35	58
Larkhall Athletic Res.		32	17	7	8	70	45	58
Portishead Res.		32	17	6	9	64	41	57
Wells City Res.		32	15	7	10	57	42	52
Nailsea United Res.		32	13	8	11	51	45	47
Combe St Nicholas	*-2*	32	14	6	12	51	38	46
Congresbury		32	13	7	12	60	52	46
Clevedon United Res.	*-1*	32	12	5	15	41	56	40
Wincanton Town		32	11	5	16	57	73	38
Street Res.	*-3*	32	10	7	15	63	54	34
Burnham United Res.		32	9	7	16	49	77	34
Saltford		32	9	5	18	46	61	32
Frome Collegians		32	8	8	16	31	57	32
Weston St Johns Res.	*-3*	32	8	6	18	48	97	27
Peasedown Athletic	*-8*	32	2	7	23	39	132	5

Divisions Two and Three have been regionalised into Division Two East and Division Two West

DIVISION TWO/THREE CUP

FIRST ROUND

Banwell 1 **Weston St Johns Res.** 3
Burnham United Res. 0 **Nailsea United Res.** 1
Cheddar Res. 0 **Hengrove Athletic Res.** 4
Clutton 0 **Imperial** 1
Dundry Athletic 1 Timsbury Athletic Res. 1 *aet* (5-3p)
Fry Club Res. 6 Yatton Athletic 2
Langford Rovers 1 **Cutters Friday** 3
Peasedown Athletic 0 **Larkhall Athletic Res.** 2
Portishead Res. 2 Berrow 1
Robinsons Res. 1 **Frome Collegians** 5
Saltford 2 **Clevedon United Res.** 3
Street Res. 1 **Congresbury** 4
Taunton Blackbrook Res. 1 **Bishops Lydeard** 2 *aet*
Wincanton Town 3 Long Ashton 0
Wrington-Redhill 1 **Combe St Nicholas** 2 *aet*

SECOND ROUND

Bishops Lydeard 6 Weston St Johns Res. 0
Clevedon United Res. 5 Fry Club Res. 2
Combe St Nicholas 2 Nailsea United Res. 0
Congresbury 0 **Dundry Athletic** 1
Cutters Friday 3 **Larkhall Athletic Res.** 4
Frome Collegians 0 **Portishead Res.** 7
Hengrove Athletic Res. 0 **Wincanton Town** 3
Wells City Res. 1 **Imperial** 2

QUARTER-FINALS

Clevedon United Res. 0 **Bishops Lydeard** 2
Combe St Naicholas 0 **Dundry Athletic** 1
Imperial 3 Wincanton Town 0
Portishead Res. 0 **Larkhall Athletic Res.** 1

SEMI-FINALS

Dundry Athletic 2 Larkhall Athletic Res. 0
Imperial 2 **Bishops Lydeard** 3

FINAL *(May 9th at Cheddar)*

Bishops Lydeard 2 Dundry Athletic 0

SOMERSET COUNTY LEAGUE DIVISION TWO EAST CONSTITUTION 2006-07

CHEDDAR RESERVES .... Bowdens Park, Draycott Road, Cheddar BS27 3RL 01934 743736
CLUTTON .... Warwick Fields, Upper Bristol Road (A37), Clutton, Bristol BS39 5TA .... None
FROME COLLEGIANS .... Selwood School, Berkley Road, Frome BA11 2EF .... None
FRY CLUB RESERVES .... Fry Club, Somerdale, Keynsham, Bristol 0117 937 6500/6501
HENGROVE ATHLETIC RESERVES .... Norton Lane, Whitchurch, Bristol BS14 0BT 01275 832894
IMPERIAL .... Bristol Imperial Sports Club, West Town Lane, Whitchurch, Brislington BS4 5DT 01275 546000
LARKHALL ATHLETIC RESERVES .... Plain Ham, Charlcombe Lane, Larkhall, Bath BA1 8DJ 01225 334952
LONG ASHTON .... Long Ashton Rec., Keedwell Hill, Long Ashton BS41 9DP .... None
PEASEDOWN ATHLETIC .... Miners Welfare Park, Peasedown St John, Bath 01761 437319
SALTFORD .... Playing Fields, Norman Road, Saltford BS31 0BQ 01225 873725
STOCKWOOD GREEN ROBINSONS RESERVES .. Hursley Lane, Woolard Lane, Whitchurch, Bristol BS14 0QY 01275 891300
STREET RESERVES .... The Tannery Ground, Middlebrooks, Street BA16 0TA 01458 444987
TIMSBURY ATHLETIC RESERVES .... Recreation Ground, North Road, Timsbury, Bath BA2 0JH 01761 472523
WELLS CITY RESERVES .... The Athletic Ground, Rowdens Road, Wells BA5 1TU 01749 679971

IN: Cheddar Reserves (Division Three), Clutton (Division Three), Frome Collegians (Division Two), Fry Club Reserves (Division Three), Hengrove Athletic Reserves (Division Three), Imperial (Division Three), Larkhall Athletic Reserves (Division Two), Long Ashton (Division Three), Peasedown Athletic (Division Two), Saltford (Division Two), Stockwood Green Robinsons Reserves (formerly Robinsons Reserves) (Division Three), Street Reserves (Division Two), Timsbury Athletic Reserves (Division Three), Wells City Reserves (Division Two)

OUT FROM DIVISION TWO: Bishops Lydeard (P), Cutters Friday (P), Dundry Athletic (P)

	Banwell	Berrow	Cheddar Res.	Clutton	Fry Club Res.	Hengrove Athletic Res.	Imperial	Langford Rovers	Long Ashton	Robinsons Res.	Taunton Blackbrook Res.	Timsbury Ath. Res.	Wrington-Redhill	Yatton Athletic
Banwell	*D*	0-0	2-2	1-0	5-4	2-4	1-0	1-4	0-2	0-5	0-2	1-7	0-3	1-5
Berrow	2-1	*I*	5-0	3-2	3-1	1-1	2-3	2-0	3-1	11-0	2-5	2-0	5-0	3-1
Cheddar Res.	1-4	0-3	*V*	0-1	4-3	2-2	3-1	5-3	0-2	2-3	2-3	1-3	0-1	3-1
Clutton	2-0	0-5	2-0	*I*	5-0	1-2	1-0	4-1	2-2	3-0	2-3	1-2	2-1	0-4
Fry Club Res.	3-1	3-2	0-1	5-2	*S*	0-0	1-1	4-1	1-2	4-0	1-5	0-4	2-6	2-1
Hengrove Athletic Res.	6-0	0-4	5-3	0-2	3-2	*I*	3-1	0-1	4-4	0-0	0-5	1-2	1-2	3-1
Imperial	4-1	2-1	2-1	3-2	3-2	2-0	*O*	1-4	0-1	6-1	0-3	2-1	2-1	6-1
Langford Rovers	1-2	6-1	2-2	4-2	3-0	2-0	1-2	*N*	3-2	7-0	0-5	5-0	1-0	2-1
Long Ashton	6-0	1-1	2-2	3-1	5-3	1-1	5-1	1-2		4-2	3-2	4-1	0-1	2-3
Robinsons Res.	7-5	0-2	0-1	0-2	0-3	0-4	0-2	0-0	0-4	*T*	0-5	1-2	1-4	3-2
Taunton Blackbrook Res.	5-0	1-1	3-0	3-1	2-2	1-1	3-0	3-1	1-2	6-0	*H*	3-1	3-1	3-1
Timsbury Athletic Res.	3-2	3-0	3-1	0-2	4-1	3-2	3-4	4-1	3-2	2-1	0-3	*R*	3-2	2-2
Wrington-Redhill	2-2	2-1	4-1	2-3	2-1	1-0	2-2	2-1	2-0	4-1	1-1	2-1	*E*	3-1
Yatton Athletic	6-2	2-2	1-0	0-5	4-1	0-4	3-2	1-3	0-3	2-0	1-6	2-2	1-1	*E*

Division Three		P	W	D	L	F	A	Pts
Taunton Blackbrook Res.		26	20	4	2	85	23	64
Wrington-Redhill		26	15	4	7	52	36	49
Berrow		26	14	5	7	67	35	47
Long Ashton		26	14	5	7	64	39	47
Timsbury Athletic Res.		26	15	2	9	59	48	47
Langford Rovers		26	14	2	10	59	45	44
Imperial	-1	26	14	2	10	52	47	43
Clutton		26	13	1	12	50	44	40
Hengrove Athletic Res.		26	9	7	10	47	43	34
Yatton Athletic		26	8	4	14	47	64	28
Fry Club Res.		26	7	3	16	49	69	24
Cheddar Res.		26	6	4	16	37	61	22
Banwell		26	5	3	18	34	86	18
Robinsons Res.	-3	26	4	2	20	25	87	11

DIVISION THREE SUBSIDIARY CUP

GROUP A

		P	W	D	L	F	A	Pts
Yatton Athletic		6	5	0	1	14	9	15
Hengrove Athletic Res.		6	4	1	1	16	9	13
Taunton Blackbrook Res.		6	3	1	2	14	7	10
Fry Club Res.		6	3	1	2	19	13	10
Long Ashton		6	2	1	3	8	13	7
Timsbury Athletic Res.		6	1	0	5	7	18	3
Imperial	*-3*	6	1	0	5	3	12	0

Fry Club Res. 2 Taunton Blackbrook Res. 4
Fry Club Res. 5 Hengrove Athletic Res. 2
Fry Club Res. 6 Timsbury Athletic Res. 2
Hengrove Athletic Res. 3 Imperial 0
Hengrove Athletic Res. 3 Long Ashton 2
Hengrove Athletic Res. 4 Timsbury Athletic Res. 0
Imperial 0 Fry Club Res. 2
Imperial 1 Taunton Blackbrook Res. 0
Imperial 1 Yatton Athletic 3
Long Ashton 0 Yatton Athletic 2
Long Ashton 2 Fry Club Res. 2
Long Ashton 2 Imperial 1
Taunton Blackbrook Res. 1 Hengrove Athletic Res. 1
Taunton Blackbrook Res. 3 Timsbury Athletic Res. 1
Taunton Blackbrook Res. 5 Long Ashton 0
Timsbury Athletic Res. 0 Long Ashton 2
Timsbury Athletic Res. 2 Imperial 0
Timsbury Athletic Res. 2 Yatton Athletic 3
Yatton Athletic 1 Hengrove Athletic Res. 3
Yatton Athletic 2 Taunton Blackbrook Res. 1
Yatton Athletic 3 Fry Club Res. 2

GROUP B

		P	W	D	L	F	A	Pts
Clutton		6	5	1	0	27	7	16
Cheddar Res.		6	4	0	2	11	14	12
Langford Rovers		6	3	0	3	20	11	9
Wrington-Redhill		6	2	2	2	7	8	8
Robinsons Res.		6	1	2	3	7	14	5
Berrow	*-2*	6	1	3	2	8	14	4
Banwell		6	0	2	4	8	20	2

Banwell 1 Clutton 4
Banwell 2 Cheddar Res. 3
Banwell 3 Wrington-Redhill 4
Berrow 0 Clutton 6
Berrow 1 Banwell 1
Berrow 1 Wrington-Redhill 1
Cheddar Res. 3 Berrow 1
Cheddar Res. 1 Robinsons Res. 0
Cheddar Res. 2 Langford Rovers 1
Clutton 4 Robinsons Res. 2
Clutton 5 Langford Rovers 2
Clutton 8 Cheddar Res. 2
Langford Rovers 1 Berrow 3
Langford Rovers 3 Wrington-Redhill 0
Langford Rovers 7 Banwell 0
Robinsons Res. 1 Banwell 1
Robinsons Res. 1 Langford Rovers 6
Robinsons Res. 2 Berrow 2
Wrington-Redhill 0 Clutton 0
Wrington-Redhill 0 Robinsons Res. 1
Wrington-Redhill 2 Cheddar Res. 0

FINAL *(May 10th at Radstock Town)*
Clutton 2 Yatton Athletic 2 *aet* (3-1p)

SOMERSET COUNTY LEAGUE DIVISION TWO WEST CONSTITUTION 2006-07

BANWELL .... Riverside Ground, Riverside, Banwell BS29 6EE 01934 820773
BERROW .... Red Road Playing Fields, Berrow, Burnham-on-Sea TA8 2LY .... None
BURNHAM UNITED RESERVES ... Burnham Road Playing Fields, Cassis Close, Burnham-on-Sea TA8 1NN 01278 794615
CLEVEDON UNITED RESERVES .... Coleridge Vale, Clevedon 01275 871878
COMBE ST NICHOLAS .... Slades Cross, Combe St Nicholas TA20 3HQ 01460 234743
CONGRESBURY .... Broadstones Playing Fields, Stonewell Lane, Congresbury BS49 5DL 01934 832150
CREECH ST MICHAEL .... Creech St Michael Rec, Hyde Lane, Creech St Michael, Taunton TA3 5QJ .... None
CREWKERNE .... Henhayes, South Street, Crewkerne TA18 7JJ 01460 76422
LANGFORD ROVERS .... Westland United FC, Winterstoke Road, Weston-super-Mare BS24 9AA 01934 632037
NAILSEA UNITED RESERVES .... Grove Sports Ground, Old Church, Nailsea BS48 4ND 01275 856892
PORTISHEAD RESERVES .... Bristol Road Playing Fields, Portishead, Bristol BS20 6QB 01275 847136
WESTON ST JOHNS RESERVES ... Coleridge Road, Bournville Estate, Weston-super-Mare BS23 3UP 01934 612862
WRINGTON-REDHILL .... Recreation Ground, Silver Street, Wrington BS40 5QE .... None
YATTON ATHLETIC .... Hangstones Playing Fields, Stowey Road, Yatton BS49 4QT .... None

IN: Banwell (Division Three), Berrow (Division Three), Burnham United Reserves (Division Two), Clevedon United Reserves (Division Two), Combe St Nicholas (Division Two), Congresbury (Division Two), Creech St Michael (formerly Taunton Blackbrook Reserves) (Division Three), Crewkerne (R – Division One), Langford Rovers (Division Three), Nailsea United Reserves (Division Two), Portishead Reserves (Division Two), Weston St Johns Reserves (Division Two), Wrington-Redhill (Division Three), Yatton Athletic (Division Three)

SOUTH WALES AMATEUR LEAGUE

	AFC Bargoed	Aber Valley YMCA	Baglan Red Dragons	Caerau United	Cardiff Cosmos Portos	Cardiff Draconians	Corus Steel	Cwmaman Institute	Kenfig Hill	Llangeinor	Llangynwyd Rangers	Llantwit Major	Pantyscallog Village Juniors	Taffs Well Res.	Ton & Gelli Boys Club	Ynysddu Welfare Crusaders
AFC Bargoed		0-2	1-4	3-0	4-1	2-2	1-4	4-1	0-2	1-7	0-1	2-1	1-2	2-1	3-1	2-1
Aber Valley YMCA	3-1		2-0	2-5	1-1	9-1	0-5	0-2	8-1	1-1	5-2	4-3	1-1	2-1	1-3	1-1
Baglan Red Dragons	1-1	1-5	*D*	0-4	5-3	1-0	0-2	3-2	1-2	2-2	9-3	1-3	2-3	1-1	9-0	2-1
Caerau United	3-0	4-1	1-0	*I*	3-2	1-0	0-2	1-3	5-1	2-2	1-0	2-2	2-1	3-1	9-0	3-2
Cardiff Cosmos Portos	0-1	1-2	5-1	1-1	*V*	0-1	0-2	1-2	3-1	3-4	2-3	1-5	0-1	1-0	7-1	5-3
Cardiff Draconians	1-1	1-1	2-4	2-2	3-0	*I*	2-0	0-7	4-0	2-3	1-1	0-3	2-2	2-4	8-1	6-6
Corus Steel	4-2	1-1	0-1	6-2	3-0	4-1	*S*	1-1	2-2	1-2	7-0	5-2	2-1	3-1	6-0	7-0
Cwmaman Institute	2-0	1-1	5-0	3-0	15-0	4-5	2-1	*I*	10-0	0-1	3-2	0-1	3-4	1-1	4-1	2-1
Kenfig Hill	0-2	2-2	1-1	0-5	0-1	3-4	1-4	0-1	*O*	0-1	0-2	1-2	3-4	1-2	5-1	0-2
Llangeinor	2-2	3-1	0-2	2-0	3-1	4-3	1-1	1-3	4-0	*N*	3-2	1-2	1-0	5-2	2-1	2-0
Llangynwyd Rangers	1-3	1-0	1-2	2-3	3-1	1-3	1-2	0-2	0-1	0-4		0-3	3-1	3-2	4-0	2-3
Llantwit Major	1-0	1-1	3-1	4-0	6-0	2-2	2-4	4-1	5-1	4-1	7-1	*O*	0-2	4-2	5-0	4-2
Pantyscallog Village Juniors	2-3	4-0	3-0	2-4	7-4	3-0	0-4	4-5	4-1	2-3	5-1	3-3	*N*	1-2	3-0	3-4
Taffs Well Res.	2-1	2-1	4-1	2-4	4-4	3-2	2-1	1-2	3-2	0-2	3-5	1-5	0-1	*E*	1-0	4-4
Ton & Gelli Boys Club	1-1	1-1	0-1	0-4	3-4	2-3	0-4	1-4	2-1	0-5	0-0	0-4	0-6	4-0		3-4
Ynysddu Welfare Crusaders	3-0	0-3	5-0	1-1	5-1	6-2	1-5	1-3	2-3	1-2	1-1	3-3	2-2	4-1	3-1	

Division One		P	W	D	L	F	A	Pts
Llangeinor		30	21	5	4	74	39	68
Corus Steel		30	21	4	5	93	29	67
Llantwit Major		30	20	5	5	94	42	65
Cwmaman Institute		30	20	3	7	94	40	63
Caerau United	*-3*	30	18	5	7	75	47	56
Pantyscallog Village Juniors		30	15	4	11	77	56	49
Aber Valley YMCA		30	11	10	9	62	51	43
Baglan Red Dragons		30	12	4	14	56	65	40
AFC Bargoed		30	11	5	14	44	56	38
Cardiff Draconians		30	9	8	13	65	80	35
Ynysddu Welfare Crusaders	*-3*	30	10	7	13	72	74	34
Taffs Well Res.		30	10	4	16	53	72	34
Llangynwyd Rangers		30	9	3	18	46	77	30
Cardiff Cosmos Portos		30	7	3	20	53	93	24
Kenfig Hill	*-3*	30	5	3	22	35	87	15
Ton & Gelli Boys Club		30	3	3	24	27	112	12

CORINTHIAN CUP

FIRST ROUND

Aber Valley YMCA 2 Taffs Well Res. 1
AFC Bargoed 3 Pencoed Athletic 0
Cardiff Draconians 1 **Llangynwyd Rangers** 4
Caerau United (scr.) v **Cardiff Cosmos Portos** (w/o)
Carnetown 4 Llanharry 1
Corus Steel 2 Turberville Arms 0
Cwmaman Institute 4 Ton & Gelli Boys Club 0
FC Abercwmboi 7 Graig Castle Ivor 2
Ferndale Boys Club 3 Llangeinor 2 *aet*
Hirwaun Welfare 4 **Kenfig Hill** 5 *aet*
Llantwit Major 7 Tonyrefail Welfare 1
Osborne Athletic 3 Abercynon Athletic 0
Pantyscallog Village Juniors 4 Splott Albion 2
Rhydyfelin 1 **Trelewis Welfare** 2
Treforest 1 **Trefelin BGC** 3
Ynysddu Welfare Crusaders 2 Baglan Red Dragons 1

SOUTH WALES AMATEUR LEAGUE DIVISION ONE CONSTITUTION 2006-07

AFC BARGOED .... Bargoed Park, Bargoed .... None
ABER VALLEY YMCA .... Abertridwr Park, Tridwr Road, Abertridwr, Caerphilly CF83 4DN.......... None
ABERCYNON ATHLETIC.................. Cae Carnetown, Grovers Lane, Carnetown .... None
BAGLAN RED DRAGONS .... Evans Bevans, Baglan, Port Talbot.................. None
BLAENRHONDDA.................. Blaenrhondda Park, Blaenrhondda 01443 774772
CAERAU UNITED .... Athletic Ground, Humphries Terrace, Caerau, Bridgend CF34 0SG.......... 01656 732471
CARDIFF DRACONIANS.................. Llanidloes Road, Gabalfa, Cardiff CF14 2ST .... None
CARNETOWN .... Cae Carnetown, Grovers Lane, Carnetown .... None
CORUS STEEL .... Corus Playing Fields, Margam, Port Talbot.................. 01639 882066
CWMAMAN INSTITUTE .... Canolfan, Cwmaman, Rhondda.................. 01685 887100
LLANGYNWYD RANGERS .... Llangynwyd Playing Fields, Llangynwyd, Maesteg .... None
LLANTWIT MAJOR.................. Windmill Lane, Llantwit Major CF61 2SU .... None
PANTYSCALLOG VILLAGE JUNIORS.......... ICI Riflefields, Pant, Merthyr Tydfil.................. None
RHYDYFELIN .... Upper Boat Playing Field, Hawthorn, Rhondda .... None
TAFFS WELL RESERVES .... Rhiw Dda'r, Parish Road, Taffs Well CF15 7QB.................. 02920 811080
YNYSDDU WELFARE CRUSADERS.................. Ynysddu Welfare Park, Ynysddu .... None

IN: Abercynon Athletic (P), Blaenrhondda (R – Welsh League Division Three), Carnetown (P), Rhydyfelin (P)

OUT: Cardiff Cosmos Portos (E), Kenfig Hill (R), Llangeinor (P – Welsh League Division Three), Ton & Gelli Boys Club (R)

	Abercynon Athletic	Carnetown	FC Abercwmboi	Ferndale Boys Club	Graig Castle Ivor	Hirwaun Welfare	Llanharry	Osborne Athletic	Pencoed Athletic	Rhydyfelin	Splott Albion	Tonyrefail Welfare	Trefelin BGC	Treforest	Trelewis Welfare	Turberville Arms
Abercynon Athletic		1-0	1-0	4-1	3-2	1-0	2-1	4-1	5-0	2-3	3-4	4-1	2-1	0-0	1-0	3-3
Carnetown	2-2		3-0	5-0	8-1	1-0	2-2	5-0	1-1	0-1	5-4	6-1	0-2	8-1	6-1	5-2
FC Abercwmboi	1-5	1-1	*D*	3-0	2-1	4-4	5-1	1-2	3-1	1-3	4-1	2-4	3-2	5-3	1-0	3-0
Ferndale Boys Club	4-0	0-2	7-3	*I*	1-2	1-2	0-2	2-2	5-1	3-3	8-3	1-4	3-2	0-3	5-3	0-2
Graig Castle Ivor	2-1	0-2	4-3	0-2	*V*	2-4	1-3	1-4	2-1	0-3	1-5	0-1	5-2	1-1	0-2	3-0
Hirwaun Welfare	1-4	1-2	0-1	3-3	3-3	*I*	2-0	6-1	3-1	3-3	3-3	4-7	1-2	1-2	0-1	0-1
Llanharry	5-1	1-5	1-0	9-1	2-3	2-1	*S*	5-1	3-0	1-1	4-2	2-1	1-2	3-3	2-1	3-1
Osborne Athletic	0-1	0-4	1-1	1-5	2-3	2-3	2-3	*I*	5-0	1-1	1-3	1-0	0-1	0-9	0-1	1-1
Pencoed Athletic	1-5	2-2	1-4	1-1	2-3	1-2	2-6	0-4	*O*	0-6	1-5	1-0	0-4	1-3	1-4	0-3
Rhydyfelin	1-1	3-0	4-0	2-2	5-2	6-1	1-1	2-1	7-1	*N*	3-0	3-0	1-1	2-0	3-0	1-0
Splott Albion	1-3	2-4	3-6	6-0	3-4	6-1	1-2	3-1	1-2	0-3		7-4	3-3	1-6	1-1	3-5
Tonyrefail Welfare	6-5	1-4	0-1	5-1	3-2	1-0	2-3	3-0	2-3	3-5	3-4	*T*	1-4	4-0	3-2	2-2
Trefelin BGC	2-1	2-1	6-0	3-3	7-1	7-3	0-1	3-1	4-2	1-3	8-2	5-0	*W*	2-2	4-2	1-2
Treforest	1-3	0-4	1-5	5-2	3-4	2-1	2-2	2-1	3-1	1-2	2-0	3-0	1-3	*O*	2-0	2-2
Trelewis Welfare	0-1	3-6	4-1	1-1	3-1	1-2	0-6	3-1	3-1	0-1	3-2	1-1	2-2	1-4		1-3
Turberville Arms	1-2	2-2	4-2	4-2	4-1	7-2	3-3	2-2	5-3	1-0	7-0	5-3	1-5	3-3	3-2	

SECOND ROUND

Cardiff Cosmos Portos 2 Carnetown 1
Cwmaman Institute 2 Corus Steel 1
Llangynwyd Rangers 2 AFC Bargoed 0
Llantwit Major 3 Ferndale Boys Club 2
Osborne Athletic 2 FC Abercwmboi 1
Pantyscallog Village Juniors 2 **Aber Valley YMCA** 3 *aet*
Trelewis Welfare 1 **Trefelin BGC** 4
Ynysddu Welfare Crusaders 1 **Kenfig Hill** 3

QUARTER-FINALS

Cwmaman Institute 7 Llantwit Major 1
Kenfig Hill 1 **Aber Valley YMCA** 3
Llangynwyd Rangers 3 **Cardiff Cosmos Portos** 6
Osborne Athletic 0 **Trefelin BGC** 2

SEMI-FINALS

Aber Valley YMCA 2 Trefelin BGC 0
Cwmaman Institute 5 Cardiff Cosmos Portos 0

FINAL

(May 12th at Pontypridd Town)
Cwmaman Institute 3 Aber Valley YMCA 1

Division Two		P	W	D	L	F	A	Pts
Rhydyfelin	*-3*	30	21	8	1	82	27	68
Carnetown		30	19	6	5	96	37	63
Abercynon Athletic		30	19	4	7	71	45	61
Trefelin BGC		30	18	5	7	91	48	59
Llanharry	*-3*	30	18	6	6	80	48	57
Turberville Arms	*-3*	30	15	8	7	79	60	50
Treforest		30	13	7	10	70	62	46
FC Abercwmboi		30	14	3	13	66	68	45
Tonyrefail Welfare		30	11	2	17	66	81	35
Graig Castle Ivor		30	11	2	17	55	85	35
Trelewis Welfare		30	9	4	17	46	65	31
Hirwaun Welfare		30	8	5	17	57	78	29
Splott Albion	*-3*	30	9	3	18	79	101	27
Ferndale Boys Club	*-9*	30	8	7	15	64	86	22
Osborne Athletic		30	5	5	20	39	78	20
Pencoed Athletic		30	3	3	24	32	104	12

SOUTH WALES AMATEUR LEAGUE DIVISION TWO CONSTITUTION 2006-07

BRYNNA .... Brynna Welfare Ground, Heol Dewi, Brynna, Pontyclun CF72 9SP 01443 226646
FC ABERCWMBOI .... Recreation Ground, Abercwmboi, Rhondda .... None
FERNDALE BOYS CLUB .... Recreation Ground, Ferndale, Rhondda .... None
GRAIG .... Pontypridd Town FC, Ynysangharad Park, Pontypridd 01443 486571
HIRWAUN WELFARE .... Manchester Place, Hirwaun, Aberdare CF44 9RB 01685 811900
KENFIG HILL .... Central Athletic Ground, Croft Goch, Kenfig Hill, Bridgend CF33 .... None
LLANHARRY .... Recreation Ground, Llanharry .... None
OSBORNE ATHLETIC .... Pentwyn Fields, Penrhiwceiber, Mountain Ash CF45 4RJ 01443 473737
PENCOED ATHLETIC .... Recreation Ground, Felindre Road, Pencoed, Bridgend CF35 5PB .... None
SPLOTT ALBION .... University Playing Field, Llanrumney, Cardiff .... None
TON & GELLI BOYS CLUB .... Ton Pentre FC, Ynys Park, Sawmill Villas, Ton Pentre CF41 7AF 01443 432813
TONYREFAIL WELFARE .... The Welfare Park, Tonyrefail .... None
TREFELIN BGC .... Ynys Park, Cwmavon Road, Port Talbot SA12 8RD 01639 882609
TREFOREST .... White Tips Stadium, Treforest 01443 485532
TRELEWIS WELFARE .... Welfare Ground, Brondeg, Trelewis .... None
TURBERVILLE ARMS .... Ely Playing Fields, Penygraig, Rhondda .... None

IN: Brynna (P – Bridgend & District League Premier Division), Kenfig Hill (R), Ton & Gelli Boys Club (R)
OUT: Abercynon Athletic (P), Carnetown (P), Rhydyfelin (P)
Graig Castle Ivor become Graig

SOUTH WALES SENIOR LEAGUE

	Bridgend Street	Cascade	Cogan Coronation	Cwm Welfare	Fairwater	Fochriw Rising Sun	Grange Albion	Lisvane/Llanishen	Nelson Cavaliers	Pant Yr Awel	Penydarren Boys Club	Stanleytown	Sully Sports	Tonyrefail BGC	Ynyshir Albion
Bridgend Street		3-0	5-1	4-2	0-5	3-2	2-0	4-4	3-1	5-1	3-2	2-0	0-2	4-3	2-1
Cascade	1-2	*D*	1-0	1-2	1-4	1-4	0-3	2-1	2-2	0-0	6-3	3-1	2-5	0-2	1-3
Cogan Coronation	1-4	5-1	*I*	1-1	1-1	3-2	1-3	5-2	1-1	0-1	2-0	3-1	0-2	3-3	5-1
Cwm Welfare	1-2	0-2	1-3	*V*	2-3	1-1	0-0	2-0	2-2	0-4	0-1	4-1	2-2	4-2	4-1
Fairwater	2-1	8-1	0-5	5-0	*I*	2-1	2-3	4-2	2-5	3-4	2-0	3-2	1-2	6-3	6-1
Fochriw Rising Sun	1-2	4-1	5-5	3-4	3-0	*S*	5-1	0-3	1-1	2-0	4-0	5-0	0-0	1-1	3-1
Grange Albion	4-3	1-1	2-0	2-1	1-2	3-1	*I*	0-0	3-2	0-2	1-1	2-0	0-4	0-1	0-0
Lisvane/Llanishen	2-3	2-2	1-4	1-4	4-1	2-1	2-1	*O*	0-2	4-5	4-1	3-2	1-1	1-1	6-3
Nelson Cavaliers	3-1	3-1	1-0	2-2	6-3	2-3	2-0	1-3	*N*	6-2	0-1	3-1	2-4	2-2	4-1
Pant Yr Awel	2-3	2-0	2-2	1-1	4-7	5-1	4-3	5-1	6-2		3-1	2-1	1-5	2-3	2-1
Penydarren Boys Club	3-4	3-2	1-1	2-1	4-2	2-1	1-1	1-3	1-5	2-0		1-2	0-4	2-2	2-1
Stanleytown	0-2	1-3	4-3	1-4	1-7	0-5	1-2	0-2	2-2	0-2	2-0	*O*	1-3	0-0	1-2
Sully Sports	0-2	4-1	2-0	0-1	1-4	4-0	1-0	5-0	4-2	3-1	5-0	2-0	*N*	2-0	9-1
Tonyrefail BGC	0-1	3-2	1-2	3-2	0-1	1-1	0-2	2-0	3-4	1-4	3-2	1-4	0-5	*E*	4-2
Ynyshir Albion	2-3	2-1	2-5	1-3	5-3	2-7	0-0	5-0	4-4	1-2	2-1	2-2	1-3	1-2	

Division One	P	W	D	L	F	A	Pts
Sully Sports	28	22	3	3	84	23	69
Bridgend Street	28	22	1	5	73	46	67
Fairwater	28	17	1	10	89	63	52
Pant Yr Awel	28	16	3	9	69	58	51
Nelson Cavaliers	28	12	8	8	72	58	44
Cogan Coronation	28	11	7	10	62	51	40
Grange Albion	28	11	7	10	38	39	40
Fochriw Rising Sun	28	11	6	11	67	50	39
Cwm Welfare	28	10	7	11	51	51	37
Lisvane/Llanishen	28	10	5	13	54	67	35
Tonyrefail BGC	28	9	7	12	47	60	34
Penydarren Boys Club	28	8	4	16	38	66	28
Cascade	28	6	4	18	39	73	22
Ynyshir Albion	28	6	4	18	49	85	22
Stanleytown	28	4	3	21	31	73	15

SOUTH WALES SENIOR LEAGUE DIVISION ONE CONSTITUTION 2006-07

BRIDGEND STREET . . . Willows High School, Willows Avenue, Splott, Cardiff CF24 2YE *(May move to new ground)* . . . . None
CAERPHILLY TOWN . . . . Llanbradach Park, Llanbradach, Caerphilly CF83 1AB . . . . None
COGAN CORONATION . . . . Cogan Recreation Field, Leisure Centre, Hewell Street, Penarth CF64 2JZ 029 2033 7588
CWM WELFARE . . . . Mount Pleasant Park, Beddau, Pontypridd . . . . None
CWMBACH ROYAL STARS . . . . Blaennant-Y-Groes Rec Ground, Cwmbach, Aberdare CF44 0EA . . . . None
FAIRWATER . . . . Poplar Park, Poplar Road, Fairwater, Cardiff CF5 3PU . . . . None
FOCHRIW RISING SUN . . . . Fochriw Recreation Ground, Fochriw, Bargoed . . . . None
GRANGE ALBION . . . . Coronation Park, Sloper Road, Cardiff CF11 . . . . None
LISVANE/LLANISHEN . . . . The Village Field, Heol Y Delyn, Lisvane, Cardiff CF14 0SQ . . . . None
LLANRUMNEY UNITED . . . . Riverside Park, Llanrumney, Cardiff . . . . None
NELSON CAVALIERS . . . . Wern Field, Nelson, Treharris . . . . None
PANT YR AWEL . . . . Lewistown, Ogmore Vale, Bridgend . . . . None
PENRHIWFER . . . . Penrhiwfer Park, Ashdale Road, Tonypandy CF40 1RT 01443 433736
PENYDARREN BOYS CLUB . . . . The Bont, Rockery Road, Penydarren, Merthyr Tydfil 01685 375241
SULLY SPORTS . . . . Sully Sports & Leisure Club, South Road, Sully, Penarth CF64 5SP 02920 530629
TONYREFAIL BGC . . . . Tynybryn Park, Tonyrefail, Porth, Rhondda CF39 8DA . . . . None

IN: Caerphilly Town (P), Cwmbach Royal Stars (P), Llanrumney United (P), Penrhiwfer (R – Welsh League Division Three)

OUT: Cascade (R), Stanleytown (R), Ynyshir Albion (R)

	AFC Butetown	AFC Llwynypia	AFC Whitchurch	Brecon Corinthians	Butetown	Cadoxton Cons	Caerphilly Town	Cwmbach Royal Stars	Hopkinstown	Llanrumney United	Margam Youth Centre	Mountain Ash Town	St Josephs	Tongwynlais	Trebanog Rangers
AFC Butetown		2-1	3-0	3-0	2-1	3-1	1-2	0-2	2-0	2-0	4-0	6-0	4-0	3-1	3-0
AFC Llwynypia	3-5	*D*	2-1	6-1	4-7	1-2	2-1	1-3	5-1	2-1	0-0	3-1	3-0	1-2	2-4
AFC Whitchurch	2-2	3-1	*I*	2-1	1-3	2-1	2-1	1-2	1-6	1-3	5-2	7-3	4-2	2-2	4-2
Brecon Corinthians	0-0	2-1	3-3	*V*	0-5	2-3	2-3	0-2	3-0	1-2	2-1	3-2	1-2	1-1	1-2
Butetown	2-3	2-0	2-0	3-2	*I*	3-2	0-1	2-0	4-2	1-3	4-2	3-1	4-3	2-2	2-3
Cadoxton Cons	2-4	4-1	2-5	0-2	6-3	*S*	3-3	4-3	8-3	6-1	6-0	2-1	4-2	3-4	5-4
Caerphilly Town	2-6	4-1	5-2	2-0	3-1	2-2	*I*	3-1	1-3	0-1	6-1	4-0	5-1	4-5	9-1
Cwmbach Royal Stars	2-0	4-0	3-2	7-4	2-2	3-2	3-1	*O*	8-4	3-3	10-1	4-2	3-3	3-0	3-1
Hopkinstown	1-1	1-0	1-0	1-4	0-1	5-1	1-3	2-5	*N*	0-2	4-1	5-5	3-0	2-3	4-2
Llanrumney United	1-1	2-0	3-2	7-0	3-2	4-0	2-4	0-1	4-1		4-0	16-1	3-2	2-0	4-1
Margam Youth Centre	3-0	3-1	2-6	2-2	1-2	1-4	2-6	1-3	1-2	1-5		0-4	1-5	2-3	3-1
Mountain Ash Town	2-0	2-9	1-2	1-3	2-5	0-5	2-4	4-4	4-1	2-4	2-1	*T*	3-1	0-5	0-3
St Josephs	2-2	2-2	1-4	0-0	3-2	2-4	3-4	0-5	3-2	4-3	4-1	4-2	*W*	2-2	1-4
Tongwynlais	1-4	2-0	2-4	0-2	3-4	3-2	1-5	0-3	3-1	0-1	2-2	7-2	5-3	*O*	1-1
Trebanog Rangers	1-3	2-4	1-1	3-2	3-5	3-3	1-8	2-6	3-4	1-3	4-4	1-2	6-3	5-11	

Division Two		P	W	D	L	F	A	Pts
Cwmbach Royal Stars		28	21	4	3	98	45	67
Llanrumney United		28	20	2	6	87	39	62
Caerphilly Town		28	19	2	7	96	50	59
AFC Butetown		28	18	5	5	69	32	59
Butetown		28	17	2	9	77	57	53
Cadoxton Cons		28	14	3	11	87	70	45
AFC Whitchurch		28	13	4	11	69	62	43
Tongwynlais		28	12	6	10	71	66	42
Hopkinstown		28	10	2	16	60	78	32
AFC Llwynypia		28	9	2	17	56	64	29
Brecon Corinthians		28	8	5	15	44	64	29
St Josephs		28	7	5	16	58	86	26
Trebanog Rangers	*-3*	28	7	4	17	65	101	22
Mountain Ash Town		28	6	2	20	51	112	20
Margam Youth Centre		28	3	4	21	39	101	13

SOUTH WALES SENIOR LEAGUE DIVISION TWO CONSTITUTION 2006-07

AFC BUTETOWN .... **Bute Park, Loudoun Square, Butetown, Cardiff** .... **None**
AFC CAERPHILLY .... **Owain Glyndwr Fields, Crescent Road, Caerphilly** .... **None**
AFC LLWYNYPIA .... **Ynyscynon Park, Llwynypia, Rhondda** .... **None**
AFC WHITCHURCH .... **Whitchurch Hospital, Park Road, Whirchurch, Cardiff CF14 7XB** .... **None**
BRECON CORINTHIANS .... **The Rich Field, The Watton, Brecon LD3 7PF** **01874 624033**
BUTETOWN .... **The Marl, Grangetown, Cardiff** .... **None**
CADOXTON CONS .... **Parc Bryn-Y-Don, Dinas Powys *(May move to new ground)*** .... **None**
CASCADE .... **Trosnant Crescent, Penybryn, Hengoed CF82 7FU** .... **None**
HOPKINSTOWN .... **Western Field, Hopkinstown, Pontypridd** .... **None**
MOUNTAIN ASH TOWN .... **Deep Duffryn, Mountain Ash** .... **None**
ST ATHAN .... **St Athan Community Centre, Glyndwr Avenue, St Athan CF64 4PP** .... **None**
ST JOSEPHS .... **Maes-Y-Coed Road, Heath, Cardiff CF14 4HH** .... **None**
STANLEYTOWN .... **Tylorstown Rec, Tylorstown, Rhondda** .... **None**
TONGWYNLAIS .... **Ironbridge Road, Tongwynlais, Cardiff CF15 7NH** .... **None**
TREBANOG RANGERS .... **Trebanog Fields, Trebanog, Rhondda *(May move to new ground)*** .... **None**
YNYSHIR ALBION .... **Ynyshir Oval, Ynyshir, Rhondda** .... **None**

IN: AFC Caerphilly (P – Taff Ely Rhymney Alliance), Cascade (R), St Athan (P – Vale of Glamorgan League), Stanleytown (R), Ynyshir Albion (R)
OUT: Caerphilly Town (P), Cwmafan Phoenix (WN), Cwmbach Royal Stars (P), Llanrumney United (P), Margam Youth Centre (R – Port Talbot League)

C W BRUTY CUP

(All South Wales Senior League teams)

FIRST ROUND

AFC Butetown 4 Caerphilly Town 1
AFC Llwynypia 3 Llanrumney United 3 *aet* (4-2p)
AFC Whitchurch 0 **Nelson Cavaliers** 2
Brecon Corinthians 1 **Butetown** 2
Cadoxton Cons (w/o) v Cwmafan Phoenix (scr.)
Cogan Coronation 4 Margam Youth Centre 0
Cwmbach Royal Stars 3 St Josephs 1
Fochriw Rising Sun 3 Tongwynlais 1
Hopkinstown 2 **Stanleytown** 3
Lisvane/Llanishen 2 **Fairwater** 5 *aet*
Mountain Ash Town 4 **Pant Yr Awel** 10 aet
Penydarren Boys Club 3 Cascade 0 *aet*
Sully Sports 4 Trebanog Rangers 0
Tonyrefail BGC 3 Grange Albion 1
Ynyshir Albion 2 Bridgend Street 1

SECOND ROUND

AFC Butetown 1 Fairwater 0
AFC Llwynypia (scr.) v **Ynyshir Albion** (w/o)
Cadoxton Cons 2 **Cwmbach Royal Stars** 3
Nelson Cavaliers 3 Cwm Welfare 1
Pant Yr Awel 4 Cogan Coronation 0
Penydarren Boys Club 0 **Butetown** 2
Stanleytown 1 **Tonyrefail BGC** 4
Sully Sports 1 **Fochriw Rising Sun** 3

QUARTER-FINALS

Fochriw Rising Sun 5 Cwmbach Royal Stars 3 *aet*
Pant Yr Awel 0 AFC Butetown 0 *aet* (4-1p)
Tonyrefail BGC 2 Butetown 1
Ynyshir Albion 1 **Nelson Cavaliers** 3

SEMI-FINALS

Fochriw Rising Sun 3 Pant Yr Awel 1
Nelson Cavaliers 4 Tonyrefail BGC 1

FINAL

(May 6th at Penydarren Boys Club)
Nelson Cavaliers 2 Fochriw Rising Sun 1

SOUTH WALES SENIOR CUP

(All South Wales Amateur and Senior League teams)

FIRST ROUND

Aber Valley YMCA 1 **Penydarren Boys Club** 3
AFC Bargoed 3 Mountain Ash Town 0 *aet*
AFC Llwynypia 1 **Fairwater** 5
AFC Whitchurch 3 **Abercynon Athletic** 5
FC Abercwmboi 4 Hirwaun Welfare 3
Llanrumney United 3 Cwmbach Royal Stars 2
Pantyscallog Village Juniors 0 **Turberville Arms** 2
Splott Albion 1 **Baglan Red Dragons** 6
St Josephs 3 **Butetown** 3 *aet* (2-4p)
Sully Sports 2 Llangynwyd Rangers 1

SECOND ROUND

Abercynon Athletic 2 Rhydyfelin 1
Brecon Corinthians 1 **AFC Bargoed** 3
Butetown 4 Cascade 2
Caerau United 1 **Bridgend Street** 2
Caerphilly Town 1 **Turberville Arms** 2 *aet*
Carnetown 3 **Grange Albion** 3 *aet* (2-4p)
Fairwater 6 Llanrumney United 1
Graig Castle Ivor 1 **Ferndale Boys Club** 3
Margam Youth Centre 1 **Llanishen/Lisvane** 2
Osborne Athletic 0 **FC Abercwmboi** 4
Stanleytown 2 **Nelson Cavaliers** 3
Sully Sports 2 Llantwit Major 1
Tonyrefail Welfare 1 **Baglan Red Dragon** 6
Trebanog Rangers 3 Penydarren Boys Club 2
Treforest 1 **Cwm Welfare** 3
Ynyshir Albion 0 **Trelewis Welfare** 2

THIRD ROUND

Baglan Red Dragons 2 **AFC Bargoed** 2 *aet* (2-4p)
Bridgend Street 5 FC Abercwmboi 3
Cwm Welfare 6 Ferndale Boys Club 0
Nelson Cavaliers 0 **Fairwater** 2
Sully Sports 3 Lisvane/Llanishen 0
Trebanog Rangers 3 Abercynon Athletic 1
Trelewis Welfare 1 **Grange Albion** 2
Turberville Arms 4 Butetown 1

QUARTER-FINALS

AFC Bargoed 4 **Bridgend Street** 5 *aet*
Cwm Welfare 5 Fairwater 2
Sully Sports 0 **Turberville Arms** 2
Trebanog Rangers 2 **Grange Albion** 3

SEMI-FINALS

Cwm Welfare 1 Bridgend Street 0
Turberville Arms 2 **Grange Albion** 2 *aet* (4-5p)

FINAL

(May 4th at Caerau Ely)
Grange Albion 2 Cwm Welfare 1

SOUTH WESTERN LEAGUE

	Bodmin Town	Callington Town	Falmouth Town	Goonhavern	Launceston	Liskeard Athletic	Millbrook	Newquay	Penryn Athletic	Penzance	Plymouth Parkway	Porthleven	St Austell	St Blazey	Tavistock	Torpoint Athletic	Truro City	Wadebridge Town
Bodmin Town		7-3	2-2	3-1	4-0	4-3	2-0	5-0	0-1	4-2	5-1	1-0	5-1	1-1	4-1	5-1	0-0	2-0
Callington Town	2-5		0-1	0-1	0-2	0-7	1-1	1-2	1-3	4-1	1-2	0-1	2-1	1-4	1-1	2-0	0-0	0-2
Falmouth Town	1-0	5-0		0-0	3-4	1-1	2-2	5-2	0-3	2-1	5-2	3-2	5-1	2-1	6-1	1-0	2-3	7-0
Goonhavern	0-2	0-1	2-1		2-0	0-4	0-2	1-1	1-5	1-3	2-2	1-2	0-2	1-1	0-5	1-2	1-3	2-1
Launceston	0-1	1-0	1-3	2-1		1-2	1-1	2-2	3-1	3-0	0-2	0-0	1-1	0-1	1-3	1-1	1-1	2-4
Liskeard Athletic	2-2	3-1	2-1	3-1	3-2		4-0	2-2	1-0	2-0	0-2	6-0	8-1	2-3	2-2	1-1	1-2	0-0
Millbrook	0-1	2-1	0-3	2-1	6-2	1-1		2-0	1-4	0-2	2-2	0-2	2-0	2-2	0-0	1-0	0-4	1-2
Newquay	1-2	1-2	1-4	1-0	0-1	0-2	0-0		1-2	2-2	1-1	0-2	3-1	2-2	2-3	1-1	1-2	2-4
Penryn Athletic	0-2	2-0	0-1	6-0	4-2	2-4	2-2	8-1		3-4	2-2	3-1	4-0	2-3	3-1	5-0	0-4	6-0
Penzance	0-1	6-1	0-2	0-0	1-2	0-3	3-0	1-4	1-1		2-4	2-0	5-0	1-6	1-3	2-0	0-3	0-1
Plymouth Parkway	1-2	3-0	3-2	6-1	4-1	2-1	0-2	7-0	2-3	3-1		1-0	4-3	3-3	2-1	2-1	3-2	1-1
Porthleven	2-4	4-0	2-2	3-1	4-2	0-0	2-0	1-0	1-7	2-2	1-2		8-1	1-3	0-1	4-1	1-4	0-1
St Austell	1-3	4-2	3-4	1-3	0-4	0-10	3-1	2-3	1-7	0-2	0-2	4-0		0-3	0-6	2-1	1-3	1-2
St Blazey	0-0	6-1	1-4	7-0	5-1	2-2	3-1	1-0	0-2	4-1	3-3	4-1	3-1		4-2	4-1	1-1	1-1
Tavistock	1-4	2-1	1-3	1-1	1-2	0-2	0-2	2-4	3-1	5-3	3-1	0-2	2-1	1-1		4-2	1-2	2-0
Torpoint Athletic	1-5	2-1	0-4	1-4	1-3	0-6	0-1	1-1	0-3	0-2	0-1	0-0	2-2	0-5	1-5		0-3	1-0
Truro City	1-0	4-0	1-0	5-0	3-2	0-1	3-0	4-2	2-3	3-0	2-2	4-0	6-0	1-1	0-0	0-1		1-0
Wadebridge Town	1-1	2-1	0-1	2-1	1-1	1-2	1-0	0-1	2-0	5-1	1-0	2-1	1-0	2-3	0-3	3-0	4-1	

		P	W	D	L	F	A	Pts
Bodmin Town		34	25	6	3	89	31	81
Truro City	*-3*	34	22	7	5	78	29	70
Falmouth Town	*-1*	34	22	5	7	88	42	70
Liskeard Athletic		34	20	9	5	93	34	69
St Blazey		34	19	12	3	92	44	69
Penryn Athletic		34	21	3	10	98	47	66
Plymouth Parkway		34	19	8	7	78	54	65
Wadebridge Town		34	17	5	12	47	46	56
Tavistock		34	15	6	13	67	59	51
Porthleven		34	12	5	17	50	62	41
Launceston		34	11	7	16	51	66	40
Millbrook		34	10	9	15	37	54	39
Penzance		34	10	4	20	52	74	34
Newquay		34	7	9	18	44	76	30
Goonhavern		34	6	6	22	31	80	24
Callington Town		34	5	3	26	31	88	18
St Austell		34	5	2	27	39	117	17
Torpoint Athletic	*-6*	34	4	6	24	23	85	12

LEAGUE CUP

PRELIMINARY ROUND

St Blazey 4 Penzance 2
Torpoint Athletic 0 **Porthleven** 2

FIRST ROUND

Launceston 3 St Blazey 1 *aet*
Liskeard Athletic 5 Newquay 3
Millbrook 0 **Falmouth Town** 2
Penryn Athletic 5 Callington Town 1
Plymouth Parkway 2 Tavistock 1
Porthleven 0 **Goonhavern** 1
St Austell 1 **Wadebridge Town** 6
Truro City 1 **Bodmin Town** 2

QUARTER-FINALS

Falmouth Town 1 **Plymouth Parkway** 2
Launceston 3 Wadebridge Town 1
Liskeard Athletic 0 **Bodmin Town** 1
Penryn Athletic 5 Goonhavern 3

SEMI-FINALS

Bodmin Town 1 Launceston 0 *(at Tavistock)*
Penryn Athletic 2 Plymouth Parkway 0 *(at St Blazey)*

FINAL *(May 1st at Truro City)*

Penryn Athletic 1 Bodmin Town 1 *aet*

FINAL REPLAY *(May 4th at Truro City)*

Bodmin Town 1 Penryn Athletic 0

SOUTH WESTERN LEAGUE DIVISION CONSTITUTION 2006-07

BODMIN TOWN .... Priory Park, Bodmin PL31 2PP 01208 78165
CALLINGTON TOWN .... The Marsh, Callington Community College, Launceston Road, Callington PL17 7DR 01579 382647
FALMOUTH TOWN .... Bickland Park, Bickland Water Road, Falmouth TR11 4PB 01326 377736
GOONHAVERN .... Reen Manor Parc, Reen, Perranporth TR6 0AN 01872 572493
LAUNCESTON .... Pennygillam, Pennygillam Industrial Estate, Launceston PL15 7ED 01566 773279
LISKEARD ATHLETIC .... Lux Park, Coldstyle Lane, Liskeard PL14 3HZ 01579 342665
MILLBROOK .... Mill Park, off Southdown Road, Millbrook, Torpoint PL11 1EN 01752 822113
NEWQUAY .... Mount Wise, Clevedon Road, Newquay TR7 2BU 01637 872935
PENRYN ATHLETIC .... Kernick, Kernick Road, Penryn TR10 8NT 01326 375182
PENZANCE .... Penlee Park, Alexandra Place, Penzance TR18 4NE 01736 361964
PLYMOUTH ARGYLE 'A' . . Plymouth Parkway FC, Bolitho Park, St Peters Road, Manadon, Plymouth PL5 3DL .... None
PLYMOUTH PARKWAY .... Bolitho Park, St Peters Road, Manadon, Plymouth PL5 3DL .... None
PORTHLEVEN .... Gala Parc, Mill Lane, Porthleven TR13 9LQ 01326 574754
SALTASH UNITED .... Kimberley Stadium, Callington Road, Saltash PL12 6DX 01752 845746
ST AUSTELL .... Poltair Park, Poltair Road, St Austell PL25 4LR 01726 66099
ST BLAZEY .... Blaise Park, Station Road, St Blazey PL24 2ND 01726 814110
TAVISTOCK .... Langsford Park, Crowndale Road, Tavistock PL19 8DD 01822 614447
TORPOINT ATHLETIC .... The Mill, Mill Lane, Torpoint PL11 2RE 01752 812889
WADEBRIDGE TOWN .... Bodieve Park, Bodieve Road, Wadebridge PL27 6EA 01208 812537

IN: Saltash United (S – Western League Division One), Plymouth Argyle 'A' (N)
OUT: Truro City (P – Western League Division One)

SOUTHAMPTON LEAGUE

	AFC Arrow	AFC Target	Botley Village	Brendon & Northend United	Classic Comrades	Forest Town NFC	Hamble Harriers	Hythe Aztecs	Nursling	Otterbourne Res.	Wellow
AFC Arrow	*P*	0-1	0-3	1-5	1-1	2-1	4-1	8-1	L-W	1-1	1-5
AFC Target	0-2	*R*	2-4	2-2	3-5	3-1	5-1	5-3	2-6	1-8	4-2
Botley Village	2-4	0-5	*E*	2-1	2-2	0-2	2-0	9-0	1-2	5-0	1-1
Brendon & Northend United	0-1	4-1	1-2	*M*	3-3	2-3	3-2	4-4	0-5	2-0	1-1
Classic Comrades	1-3	2-1	2-0	2-0	*I*	4-3	1-1	5-0	0-2	0-1	0-2
Forest Town NFC	4-0	3-2	0-2	3-2	2-4	*E*	2-1	3-3	1-1	1-0	6-0
Hamble Harriers	3-4	0-2	0-1	2-2	3-0	1-4	*R*	2-0	0-1	2-0	0-5
Hythe Aztecs	1-1	1-7	1-2	0-8	2-4	0-3	0-7		0-7	1-4	2-7
Nursling	6-2	W-L	3-2	8-2	2-2	3-1	2-0	6-1	*D*	2-0	4-0
Otterbourne Res.	1-1	3-1	2-6	5-2	2-0	0-3	3-3	3-1	1-2	*I*	3-5
Wellow	1-0	4-3	2-2	3-1	1-2	3-0	6-1	1-2	1-3	3-0	*V*

Premier Division		P	W	D	L	F	A	Pts
Nursling	*-3*	20	18	2	0	65	16	53
Botley Village		20	11	3	6	48	30	36
Wellow		20	11	3	6	53	36	36
Forest Town NFC		20	11	2	7	46	33	35
Classic Comrades		20	9	5	6	40	34	32
AFC Arrow		20	8	4	8	36	38	28
AFC Target		20	8	1	11	50	51	25
Otterbourne Res.		20	7	3	10	37	42	24
Brendon Northend		20	5	5	10	45	50	20
Hamble Harriers		20	4	3	13	30	47	15
Hythe Aztecs		20	1	3	16	23	96	6

SENIOR CUP

FINAL

(April 20th at AFC Totton)

Bush Hill 2 Botley Village 1

SOUTHAMPTON LEAGUE PREMIER DIVISION CONSTITUTION 2006-07

AFC TARGET .... Cutbush Lane, West End, Southampton SO18 2GF 023 8046 2371
ACADEMICALS .... Wide Lane, Eastleigh SO50 5PE .... None
BOTLEY VILLAGE .... Botley Recreation Ground, High Street, Botley, Southampton SO30 2EA 01489 780440
BURRIDGE SPORTS .... Allotment Road, Sarisbury SO31 7AP .... None
BUSH HILL .... Millbrook Rec (Vida), Millbrook Road, Southampton .... None
COMRADES .... BTC Sports Ground, Stoneham Lane, Eastleigh SO16 2PA .... None
FOREST TOWN NFC .... Gang Warily, Newlands Road, Blackfield, Southampton SO45 1GA 02380 893603
HAMBLE HARRIERS .... Mount Pleasant Rec, Hamble-le-Rice, Southampton .... None
MALVERN .... Cutbush Lane, West End, Southampton SO18 5RY .... None
NORTHEND UNITED .... Test Park, Porlock Road, Millbrook, Southampton .... None
NURSLING .... Nursling Recreation Ground, Nursling Street (off Romsey Road), Nursling .... None
OTTERBOURNE RESERVES .... Oakwood Park, Oakwood Avenue, Otterbourne SO21 2ED 01962 714681
SOLENT WTL .... Itchen College, Middle Road, Sholing .... None

IN: Academicals (P), Burridge Sports (P), Bush Hill (P), Malvern (P), Solent WTL (P)

OUT: AFC Arrow (W), Hythe Aztecs (R), Wellow (P – Wessex League Division Three)

Classic Comrades become Comrades

Senior Division One	P	W	D	L	F	A	Pts
Solent WTL	20	15	3	2	63	18	48
Malvern	20	12	4	4	49	25	40
Academicals	20	12	3	5	48	23	39
Burridge Sports	20	13	0	7	47	39	39
Spartans	20	11	4	5	41	25	37
Capital	20	8	2	10	35	46	26
Ordnance Survey Res.	20	6	4	10	26	43	22
Burridge AFC	20	5	4	11	31	45	19
Classic Comrades Res.	20	4	5	11	23	49	17
Priory Rovers	20	4	2	14	25	41	14
Cadnam United	20	4	1	15	31	65	13

Senior Division Two		P	W	D	L	F	A	Pts
Bush Hill		20	16	3	1	77	20	51
BTC Southampton		20	14	4	2	58	27	46
AFC Solent		20	13	2	5	52	27	41
Bishopstoke WMC	*-1*	20	9	4	7	40	28	30
M & T Awbridge Res..		20	9	3	8	31	45	30
Compton		20	7	7	6	44	39	28
Capital Res.		20	8	4	8	44	46	28
AFC Hop		20	7	3	10	35	37	24
Brendon/N'end Utd Res.	*-1*	20	4	2	14	33	74	13
Braishfield		20	3	1	16	21	59	10
Mottisfont Res.		20	2	3	15	22	55	9

Junior Division One		P	W	D	L	F	A	Pts
Team Solent		16	15	1	0	78	8	46
Hedge End Rangers		16	11	3	2	46	15	36
Otterbourne 'A'		16	10	3	3	41	22	33
AP Sports		16	10	1	5	45	32	31
Langley Manor		16	6	1	9	26	35	19
Hythe & Dibden Res		16	4	2	10	27	45	14
Durley Res.		16	4	2	10	24	43	14
Phoenix Mortgages		16	1	4	11	16	64	7
Bacardi	*-1*	16	0	5	11	21	60	4

Junior Division Two		P	W	D	L	F	A	Pts
WEB		18	11	3	4	40	21	36
Hythe Aztecs Res.		18	10	5	3	42	27	35
Redbridge FC	*-6*	18	11	4	3	52	26	31
Keywords Direct		18	9	2	7	62	37	29
Ordnance Survey 'A'		18	9	2	7	40	45	29
Spar Tec Wessex		18	8	4	6	51	40	28
Lowford		18	6	4	8	29	38	22
Wellow Res.	*-1*	18	5	5	8	39	46	19
London Airways		18	2	7	9	32	57	13
Inter		18	1	0	17	14	64	3

Junior Division Three		P	W	D	L	F	A	Pts
Inmar		18	13	1	4	59	23	40
Freemantle AFC		18	12	1	5	41	23	37
BTC Southampton Res.		18	11	3	4	45	21	36
Inter Northam		18	11	3	4	53	30	36
Sholing Sports		18	11	2	5	45	27	35
Cadnam United Res.		18	8	4	6	30	29	28
Dibden Minster Harriers	*-3*	18	6	2	10	20	32	17
Monks Brook		18	4	4	10	36	37	16
Priory Rovers Res.		18	2	4	12	19	63	10
Keywords Direct Res.		18	0	0	18	14	77	0

Junior Division Four		P	W	D	L	F	A	Pts
Saint Denys		20	13	3	4	45	31	42
Beaney Park	*-3*	20	13	3	4	53	30	39
Rownhams	*-6*	20	13	3	4	68	35	36
Norleywood		20	9	3	8	53	36	30
Oakley		20	9	3	8	45	31	30
Hedge End Town		20	9	3	8	41	37	30
Hamble Harriers Res.		20	8	3	9	44	39	27
AFC Energy	*-3*	20	9	0	11	51	56	24
Burridge Sport Res.		20	5	5	10	37	53	20
Alma	*-1*	20	3	4	13	29	64	12
M & T Awbridge 'A'		20	2	4	14	24	78	10

Junior Division Five		P	W	D	L	F	A	Pts
East Boldre		20	16	3	1	78	19	51
AFC Redbridge		20	15	2	3	95	29	47
FC Flames		20	9	7	4	40	24	34
AC Sholing		20	9	5	6	46	43	32
Compton Res.		20	8	6	6	54	36	30
Bronco & Snax	*-3*	20	8	4	8	36	43	25
TBCC		20	7	4	9	35	46	25
Botley Village Res.		20	7	4	9	38	63	25
Bishops Waltham		20	5	2	13	36	70	17
Ordnance Survey 'B'		20	3	3	14	26	67	12
Braishfield Res.		20	2	2	16	21	65	8

Junior Division Six		P	W	D	L	F	A	Pts
Gardeners AFC		18	18	0	0	111	15	54
S & B Sports		18	13	0	5	69	30	39
Academicals Res.		18	12	2	4	76	31	38
Forest Town NFC Res.		18	11	0	7	82	40	33
Keywords Direct 'A'	*-3*	18	10	3	5	53	39	30
AFC Aldermoor		18	7	1	10	41	59	22
Sparky Albion		18	6	3	9	40	38	21
AFC Brookwood		18	4	0	14	26	87	12
AFC Terminal		18	3	1	14	23	80	10
Southampton KC		18	1	0	17	13	115	3

ROY WIGHTMAN JUNIOR CUP

FINAL

(May 1st at Clayfields, Dibden)

Otterbourne 'A' 1 Hythe Aztecs Res. 0

ROY VALLANCE JUNIOR PLATE

FINAL

(May 1st at Clayfields, Dibden)

Freemantle 3 S & B Sports 2

SOUTHERN LEAGUE

	Aylesbury United	Banbury United	Bath City	Bedford Town	Chesham United	Cheshunt	Chippenham Town	Cirencester Town	Evesham United	Gloucester City	Grantham Town	Halesowen Town	Hitchin Town	King's Lynn	Mangotsfield United	Merthyr Tydfil	Northwood	Rugby Town	Salisbury City	Team Bath	Tiverton Town	Yate Town
Aylesbury United		2-0	1-5	1-2	0-1	1-0	1-1	1-0	2-2	0-1	0-2	2-1	1-3	1-0	1-1	0-2	3-0	1-1	1-3	1-2	0-5	3-0
Banbury United	2-1		2-3	3-2	0-1	1-1	4-2	2-1	3-2	1-0	1-1	1-0	2-2	4-2	2-4	4-2	0-1	2-1	1-2	1-1	3-1	1-1
Bath City	3-2	0-3		1-1	1-0	2-0	0-2	3-0	2-0	0-0	2-0	0-0	2-1	1-1	1-2	2-0	3-0	1-0	0-2	3-1	1-0	1-2
Bedford Town	2-1	3-2	1-0	*P*	2-3	1-1	2-1	2-1	1-1	5-3	1-1	0-0	0-2	3-2	1-0	0-1	4-0	1-1	1-0	1-1	3-0	2-0
Chesham United	1-1	1-1	0-1	0-3	*R*	4-2	0-1	0-2	0-2	0-2	2-2	0-2	0-0	1-0	2-0	2-2	3-1	1-2	1-4	0-2	3-3	2-5
Cheshunt	0-1	2-0	1-0	0-3	4-1	*E*	1-1	1-2	1-0	1-1	3-2	2-3	1-2	0-1	2-2	3-3	5-2	2-3	0-1	2-1	1-0	2-3
Chippenham Town	1-1	1-0	2-0	1-2	3-0	1-1	*M*	2-0	2-0	3-0	1-0	0-0	2-2	1-1	3-1	2-1	3-1	4-0	2-1	4-2	0-1	4-2
Cirencester Town	2-1	1-3	1-2	5-1	0-1	0-2	1-1	*I*	0-1	0-1	0-1	2-1	2-1	0-2	0-3	1-1	0-0	1-2	2-5	1-0	2-1	1-3
Evesham United	2-0	0-0	1-2	1-1	3-1	0-1	0-2	0-4	*E*	0-0	0-2	1-1	2-0	1-1	2-3	1-2	4-0	3-0	2-2	0-1	1-1	0-1
Gloucester City	1-1	1-1	0-2	0-0	3-1	3-2	0-1	0-1	1-1	*R*	4-1	1-0	1-0	1-2	1-3	1-1	4-1	5-2	1-2	3-0	4-5	2-0
Grantham Town	2-0	2-3	0-3	3-0	0-0	0-1	1-1	0-1	1-1	2-1		1-1	1-1	0-1	1-2	0-0	2-0	2-2	1-0	0-1	1-1	2-0
Halesowen Town	1-1	2-2	2-1	1-1	1-0	1-1	1-2	1-1	2-0	1-0	0-2	*D*	1-1	0-0	2-0	1-3	4-1	3-2	0-1	1-3	4-2	7-2
Hitchin Town	3-2	3-0	2-2	1-4	1-1	4-1	3-3	1-3	2-2	2-2	0-2	1-0	*I*	0-5	0-0	1-2	4-2	1-0	0-3	2-1	3-2	4-3
King's Lynn	1-1	2-0	0-2	1-0	2-0	2-0	3-1	2-1	2-1	4-0	3-1	0-1	3-0	*V*	1-1	0-3	3-2	1-1	1-3	4-2	4-1	1-0
Mangotsfield United	0-0	1-2	0-2	0-2	4-3	2-1	1-2	3-0	2-2	5-4	0-1	1-1	1-0	1-3	*I*	3-0	1-3	1-3	0-0	3-3	1-1	0-3
Merthyr Tydfil	2-4	1-0	0-0	1-3	1-4	2-0	4-0	3-1	3-0	2-2	2-1	2-3	1-2	0-1	1-0	*S*	0-1	1-1	0-1	1-0	1-1	3-0
Northwood	2-1	2-1	0-3	2-3	1-1	3-1	2-1	3-0	1-2	0-1	0-2	3-0	0-0	0-1	3-5	2-3	*I*	0-0	2-2	1-1	2-4	3-2
Rugby Town	4-0	3-0	1-2	5-2	3-0	1-5	0-0	1-2	1-3	0-1	0-2	0-0	4-1	0-3	2-2	1-0	1-2	*O*	1-3	1-0	3-1	0-0
Salisbury City	3-0	1-3	0-0	1-0	6-0	5-0	2-1	3-0	1-0	2-0	3-0	0-1	3-0	1-0	2-2	2-0	3-0	3-0	*N*	0-1	1-0	3-1
Team Bath	1-1	2-2	0-4	1-2	2-0	0-1	2-0	4-2	2-1	1-0	1-2	0-2	1-0	1-3	0-1	2-3	2-3	1-3	1-2		0-2	5-3
Tiverton Town	1-1	0-0	1-2	0-1	4-0	1-1	0-2	0-4	3-0	1-0	3-1	0-0	6-2	1-2	2-3	2-0	4-1	2-2	0-1	2-0		3-2
Yate Town	3-0	0-3	1-1	4-0	5-2	4-1	1-2	3-1	1-1	3-1	3-1	2-1	2-1	3-2	2-2	3-2	1-0	1-0	1-0	0-3	2-1	

Premier Division		HOME					AWAY					TOTAL					
	P	**W**	**D**	**L**	**F**	**A**	**W**	**D**	**L**	**F**	**A**	**W**	**D**	**L**	**F**	**A**	**Pts**
Salisbury City	42	16	2	3	45	9	14	3	4	38	18	30	5	7	83	27	95
Bath City	42	12	4	5	29	17	13	4	4	37	16	25	8	9	66	33	83
King's Lynn	42	14	3	4	40	21	11	4	6	33	20	25	7	10	73	41	82
Chippenham Town	42	14	5	2	42	16	8	6	7	27	29	22	11	9	69	45	77
Bedford Town	42	12	6	3	36	21	10	4	7	33	32	22	10	10	69	53	76
Yate Town	42	15	3	3	45	25	6	2	13	33	49	21	5	16	78	74	68
Banbury United	42	11	5	5	40	31	6	6	9	26	30	17	11	14	66	61	62
Halesowen Town	42	9	7	5	36	26	6	8	7	18	19	15	15	12	54	45	60
Merthyr Tydfil	42	9	4	8	31	25	8	5	8	31	33	17	9	16	62	58	60
Mangotsfield United	42	6	6	9	30	36	9	7	5	37	31	15	13	14	67	67	58
Grantham Town	42	6	8	7	22	20	9	3	9	27	29	15	11	16	49	49	56
Tiverton Town	42	9	5	7	36	25	5	5	11	33	40	14	10	18	69	65	52
Gloucester City	42	9	5	7	37	27	5	5	11	20	33	14	10	18	57	60	52
Hitchin Town	42	9	6	6	38	40	4	6	11	21	36	13	12	17	59	76	51
Rugby Town	42	8	4	9	32	29	5	7	9	26	37	13	11	18	58	66	50
Cheshunt	42	8	4	9	34	32	5	5	11	23	38	13	9	20	57	70	48
Team Bath	42	7	2	12	29	37	7	4	10	26	31	14	6	22	55	68	48
Cirencester Town	42	6	3	12	22	33	8	1	12	27	35	14	4	24	49	68	46
Northwood	42	7	5	9	32	34	5	1	15	21	54	12	6	24	53	88	42
Evesham United	42	5	7	9	24	25	4	7	10	22	33	9	14	19	46	58	41
Aylesbury United	42	7	4	10	23	32	2	8	11	20	37	9	12	21	43	69	39
Chesham United	42	4	6	11	23	38	5	3	13	20	46	9	9	24	43	84	36

PLAY-OFFS

SEMI-FINALS

(May 1st)

Bath City 0 **Bedford Town** 1 ***Att*** 1,691

King's Lynn 1 **Chippenham Town** 3 ***Att*** 1,065

FINAL

(May 6th at Chippenham Town)

Chippenham Town 2 **Bedford Town** 3 ***Att*** 2,029

DATES & GATES	Aylesbury United	Banbury United	Bath City	Bedford Town	Chesham United	Cheshunt	Chippenham Town	Cirencester Town	Evesham United	Gloucester City	Grantham Town	Halesowen Town	Hitchin Town	King's Lynn	Mangotsfield United	Merthyr Tydfil	Northwood	Rugby Town	Salisbury City	Team Bath	Tiverton Town	Yate Town
Aylesbury United		4 Mar *432*	22 Apr *301*	2 Jan *493*	11 Mar *827*	15 Nov *187*	13 Aug *333*	22 Nov *168*	14 Jan *271*	25 Mar *267*	17 Sep *349*	1 Apr *287*	28 Jan *313*	23 Aug *307*	26 Nov *281*	20 Dec *241*	17 Apr *268*	18 Feb *272*	21 Mar *214*	10 Dec *254*	17 Dec *270*	27 Aug *294*
Banbury United	25 Oct *418*		11 Mar *508*	25 Feb *454*	17 Sep *444*	29 Aug *425*	1 Nov *411*	3 Dec *341*	8 Nov *378*	29 Apr *426*	16 Aug *352*	4 Feb *418*	14 Jan *333*	2 Jan *543*	18 Feb *372*	28 Jan *371*	29 Oct *389*	17 Apr *356*	1 Apr *588*	17 Dec *419*	20 Aug *380*	19 Nov *379*
Bath City	14 Feb *405*	2 Sep *718*		7 Jan *661*	20 Aug *610*	17 Dec *561*	17 Apr *2,268*	11 Oct *417*	2 Jan *585*	29 Oct *583*	10 Dec *490*	22 Oct *580*	11 Feb *588*	28 Jan *631*	27 Sep *618*	25 Feb *643*	18 Mar *718*	1 Apr *773*	27 Aug *787*	7 Mar *579*	16 Aug *800*	25 Mar *960*
Bedford Town	15 Apr *556*	27 Aug *474*	17 Sep *399*		16 Aug *407*	10 Dec *453*	4 Mar *550*	8 Apr *452*	18 Feb *489*	1 Oct *472*	31 Dec *517*	19 Nov *505*	31 Jan *480*	24 Sep *439*	8 Nov *372*	14 Jan *501*	11 Feb *463*	29 Apr *482*	18 Mar *479*	29 Oct *439*	28 Jan *387*	20 Aug *357*
Chesham United	27 Dec *458*	31 Dec *320*	4 Feb *304*	13 Dec *241*		23 Aug *209*	2 Sep *333*	13 Aug *249*	5 Nov *277*	17 Dec *223*	8 Oct *283*	21 Jan *308*	15 Apr *367*	27 Aug *258*	22 Apr *269*	18 Mar *333*	25 Oct *243*	11 Feb *223*	27 Sep *252*	7 Jan *195*	3 Dec *253*	25 Feb *295*
Cheshunt	16 Aug *138*	21 Jan *149*	8 Apr *220*	4 Oct *167*	17 Apr *227*		18 Mar *128*	31 Dec *110*	27 Aug *107*	20 Aug *110*	4 Feb *117*	29 Oct *149*	25 Oct *100*	3 Sep *115*	7 Jan *114*	1 Oct *115*	21 Feb *114*	3 Dec *114*	10 Jan *136*	25 Feb *135*	18 Feb *145*	29 Apr *155*
Chippenham Town	21 Jan *652*	25 Mar *601*	27 Dec *1,612*	3 Dec *632*	18 Feb *543*	1 Apr *578*		29 Aug *651*	17 Sep *522*	16 Aug *605*	7 Jan *626*	29 Apr *610*	11 Mar *548*	4 Feb *568*	31 Dec *663*	25 Oct *743*	20 Aug *550*	29 Oct *734*	11 Oct *851*	14 Mar *384*	15 Apr *662*	1 Oct *633*
Cirencester Town	4 Feb *140*	21 Mar *148*	18 Feb *325*	11 Mar *166*	29 Oct *196*	28 Jan *127*	17 Dec *394*		17 Apr *239*	19 Nov *230*	20 Aug *208*	16 Aug *253*	1 Oct *186*	20 Dec *171*	17 Sep *239*	10 Dec *202*	29 Apr *158*	25 Oct *168*	7 Mar *188*	27 Aug *174*	1 Apr *201*	2 Jan *276*
Evesham United	3 Sep *193*	10 Dec *303*	15 Apr *396*	22 Oct *235*	29 Apr *289*	11 Feb *184*	25 Feb *304*	27 Dec *270*		11 Oct *219*	29 Aug *245*	27 Sep *200*	18 Mar *201*	26 Nov *180*	8 Apr *195*	31 Dec *226*	19 Nov *196*	7 Jan *179*	20 Aug *238*	16 Aug *223*	11 Mar *269*	29 Oct *199*
Gloucester City	3 Dec *299*	5 Nov *341*	21 Jan *521*	1 Apr *384*	8 Apr *338*	26 Nov *234*	6 Dec *261*	27 Sep *329*	4 Feb *340*		18 Feb *339*	17 Apr *471*	22 Apr *391*	13 Aug *372*	29 Aug *425*	23 Aug *355*	8 Oct *264*	3 Sep *223*	2 Jan *551*	11 Mar *347*	7 Jan *392*	21 Mar *366*
Grantham Town	11 Feb *248*	11 Oct *298*	13 Aug *472*	27 Sep *263*	28 Jan *271*	22 Oct *272*	22 Apr *232*	18 Mar *212*	17 Jan *236*	14 Jan *366*		3 Sep *270*	23 Aug *264*	17 Apr *523*	5 Nov *319*	11 Mar *241*	27 Aug *266*	2 Jan *398*	3 Dec *282*	1 Apr *266*	25 Feb *234*	17 Dec *277*
Halesowen Town	25 Feb *309*	23 Aug *416*	31 Dec *403*	22 Apr *355*	1 Oct *386*	11 Mar *347*	14 Jan *463*	5 Nov *367*	28 Jan *402*	27 Dec *468*	25 Oct *291*		13 Aug *371*	3 Dec *360*	18 Mar *216*	15 Apr *349*	8 Apr *301*	29 Aug *375*	17 Sep *401*	11 Feb *343*	28 Mar *288*	11 Oct *243*
Hitchin Town	29 Oct *349*	22 Oct *367*	3 Dec *282*	17 Apr *508*	29 Aug *336*	2 Jan *278*	22 Nov *146*	4 Mar *270*	17 Dec *222*	25 Feb *338*	25 Mar *268*	7 Jan *293*		27 Sep *223*	4 Feb *249*	17 Sep *333*	16 Aug *257*	19 Nov *249*	21 Jan *388*	20 Aug *231*	29 Apr *307*	1 Apr *237*
King's Lynn	5 Nov *759*	15 Apr *841*	29 Apr *1,079*	29 Aug *835*	4 Mar *871*	14 Jan *820*	21 Feb *810*	22 Apr *787*	1 Oct *771*	12 Nov *690*	27 Dec *1,118*	20 Aug *801*	31 Dec *928*		10 Dec *832*	8 Apr *843*	25 Mar *1,026*	16 Aug *889*	4 Apr *1,821*	22 Oct *734*	17 Sep *710*	11 Feb *868*
Mangotsfield United	20 Aug *315*	1 Oct *413*	14 Jan *661*	25 Mar *209*	19 Nov *242*	4 Mar *196*	28 Jan *569*	11 Feb *243*	21 Jan *269*	25 Oct *332*	29 Apr *190*	27 Aug *309*	3 Sep *251*	1 Apr *303*		11 Apr *199*	25 Feb *225*	17 Dec *300*	16 Aug *395*	2 Jan *324*	29 Oct *434*	17 Apr *421*
Merthyr Tydfil	29 Apr *402*	7 Jan *420*	17 Jan *467*	17 Dec *395*	1 Apr *387*	27 Apr *302*	27 Aug *466*	2 Sep *432*	4 Apr *310*	11 Feb *411*	29 Oct *541*	2 Jan *512*	18 Feb *408*	21 Jan *442*	21 Feb *251*		3 Dec *405*	20 Aug *412*	13 Dec *394*	17 Apr *336*	7 Feb *343*	16 Aug *321*
Northwood	30 Aug *243*	22 Apr *171*	5 Nov *222*	23 Aug *159*	2 Jan *253*	15 Apr *132*	17 Jan *215*	7 Jan *151*	1 Apr *178*	4 Mar *182*	21 Jan *201*	10 Dec *182*	11 Oct *209*	17 Dec *202*	22 Oct *183*	13 Aug *227*		12 Nov *162*	18 Feb *234*	3 Sep *127*	4 Feb *193*	11 Mar *138*
Rugby Town	31 Dec *354*	27 Dec *505*	1 Oct *246*	5 Nov *304*	11 Oct *247*	17 Sep *225*	8 Apr *256*	25 Feb *212*	23 Aug *259*	10 Dec *214*	15 Apr *265*	21 Mar *207*	27 Aug *302*	11 Mar *293*	13 Aug *327*	26 Nov *295*	28 Jan *208*		11 Apr *262*	22 Apr *204*	17 Jan *202*	14 Jan *233*
Salisbury City	7 Jan *763*	21 Feb *494*	28 Mar *1,478*	13 Aug *571*	10 Dec *557*	22 Apr *1,327*	11 Feb *1,907*	23 Aug *506*	25 Mar *774*	15 Apr *1,609*	1 Oct *875*	4 Mar *787*	8 Apr *978*	29 Oct *922*	11 Mar *826*	29 Aug *761*	31 Dec *759*	22 Oct *587*		28 Jan *690*	27 Dec *980*	2 Sep *800*
Team Bath	1 Oct *102*	8 Apr *117*	29 Aug *632*	4 Feb *98*	26 Mar *141*	13 Aug *85*	22 Aug *417*	27 Nov *83*	24 Oct *84*	17 Sep *114*	4 Mar *101*	30 Jan *82*	5 Nov *108*	18 Feb *287*	15 Apr *154*	27 Dec *196*	14 Jan *83*	21 Jan *102*	29 Apr *337*		31 Dec *161*	20 Feb *145*
Tiverton Town	8 Apr *387*	11 Feb *549*	4 Mar *649*	3 Sep *416*	14 Jan *536*	5 Nov *521*	2 Jan *796*	21 Jan *731*	13 Aug *584*	27 Aug *471*	19 Nov *408*	15 Feb *359*	10 Dec *442*	18 Mar *351*	24 Aug *546*	22 Apr *422*	1 Oct *475*	25 Mar *372*	17 Apr *629*	11 Oct *334*		16 Nov *380*
Yate Town	18 Mar *220*	13 Aug *210*	23 Aug *575*	21 Jan *215*	22 Oct *262*	8 Oct *167*	10 Dec *380*	15 Apr *270*	22 Apr *222*	31 Dec *340*	8 Apr *154*	18 Feb *270*	26 Nov *175*	7 Jan *210*	27 Dec *710*	4 Feb *220*	17 Sep *220*	4 Mar *207*	5 Nov *320*	27 Sep *165*	29 Aug *295*	

SOUTHERN LEAGUE PREMIER DIVISIO

CONSTITUTION FOR 2006-07

BANBURY UNITED

Spencer Stadium, Station Approach, Banbury, Oxfordshire OX16 5TA

Tel: 01295 263354 Club: 01295 261899

Manager: Kevin Brock www.banburyunited.co.uk Colours: Red & gold

BATH CITY

Twerton Park, Twerton, Bath, North Somerset BA2 1DB

Tel: 01225 423087 Club: 01225 313247 Fax: 01225 481391

Manager: John Relish www.bathcityfc.com Colours: Black & white

CHESHUNT

The Stadium, Theobalds Lane, Cheshunt, Hertfordshire EN8 8RU

Tel: 01992 633500 Fax: 01992 626752

Manager: Tom Loizou www.cheshuntfc.com Colours: Amber & black

CHIPPENHAM TOWN

Hardenhuish Park, Bristol Road, Chippenham, Wiltshire SN14 6LR

Tel: 01249 650400 Fax: 01249 650400

Manager: Darren Perrin www.chippenhamtownfc.co.uk Colours: Royal blue

CIRENCESTER TOWN

Corinium Stadium, Kingshill Lane, Cirencester, Gloucestershire GL7 1HS

Tel: 01285 654543 Fax: 01285 654474

Manager: Neil Hards www.cirentownfc.com Colours: Red & black

CLEVEDON TOWN

The Hand Stadium, Davis Lane, Clevedon, North Somerset BS21 6TG

Tel: 01275 341913 Club: 01275 871600

Manager: Phil Bater www.clevedontownafc.co.uk Colours: Blue & white

CORBY TOWN

Rockingham Triangle Stadium, Rockingham Road, Corby, Northants NN17 2AE

Tel: 01536 401007 Club: 01536 406640 Fax: 01536 406640

Manager: Rob Dunion www.corbytownfc.com Colours: White & black

GLOUCESTER CITY

Meadow Park, Sudmeadow Road, Hempsted, Gloucester, Gloucestershire GL2 5HS

Tel: 01452 421400 Club: 01452 311060 Fax: 01452 301330

Manager: Tim Harris www.t-ender.co.uk Colours: Yellow & black

HALESOWEN TOWN

The Grove, Old Hawne Lane, Halesowen, West Midlands B63 3TB

Tel: 0121 550 2179 Club: 0121 602 2210

Manager: Paul Holleran www.halesowentownfc.co.uk Colours: Blue

HEMEL HEMPSTEAD TOWN

Vauxhall Road, Adeyfield, Hemel Hempstead, Hertfordshire HP2 4HW

Tel: 01442 259777

Manager: Steve Bateman www.hemelhempsteadtownfc.com Colours: Red & white

HITCHIN TOWN

Top Field, Fishponds Road, Hitchin, Hertfordshire SG5 1NU

Tel: 01462 434483 Fax: 01462 482463

Manager: Darren Salton www.hitchintownfc.co.uk Colours: Yellow & green

KING'S LYNN

The Walks Stadium, Tennyson Road, King's Lynn, Norfolk PE30 5PB

Tel: 01553 760060

Manager: Tommy Taylor www.thelinnets.co.uk Colours: Blue & gold

MAIDENHEAD UNITED

York Road, Maidenhead, Berkshire SL6 1SQ

Tel: 01628 636314 Club: 01628 624739

Manager: Carl Taylor www.maidenheadunitedfc.co.uk Colours: Black & white

MANGOTSFIELD UNITED

Cossham Street, Mangotsfield, Bristol, Gloucestershire BS17 3EN

Tel: 0117 956 0119

Manager: Lee Howells mangos.freehosting.net Colours: Sky blue & maroon

MERTHYR TYDFIL

Pennydarren Park, Merthyr Tydfil, Mid-Glamorgan CF47 9YE

Tel: 01685 384102 Fax: 01685 382882

Manager: Paul Sugrue/John Lewis www.themartyrs.com Colours: White & black

NORTHWOOD

Northwood Park, Chestnut Avenue, Northwood, Middlesex HA6 1HR

Tel: 01923 827148 Fax: 020 8428 1533

Manager: Colin Payne www.northwoodfc.com Colours: Red

RUGBY TOWN

Butlin Road, Rugby, Warwickshire CV21 3ST

Tel: 01788 844806 Club: 01788 844806 Fax: 01788 540202

Manager: Billy Jeffrey www.rugbytownfc.co.uk Colours: Sky blue & white

STAMFORD

Vic Couzens Stadium, Kettering Road, Stamford, Lincolnshire PE9 2JR

Tel: 01780 763079

Manager: Graham Drury www.stamfordafc.moonfruit.com Colours: Red & white

TEAM BATH

Bath City FC, Twerton Park, Twerton, Bath, North Somerset BA2 1DB

Tel: 01225 423087 Club: 01225 313247 Fax: 01225 481391

Manager: Ged Roddy www.teambath.com Colours: Yellow & blue

TIVERTON TOWN

Ladysmead, Bolham Road, Tiverton, Devon EX16 6SG

Tel: 01884 252397 Fax: 01884 258840

Manager: Martyn Rogers www.tiverton-town-fc.com Colours: Yellow & black

WEALDSTONE

Northwood FC, Northwood Park, Chestnut Avenue, Northwood, Middlesex HA6 1HR

Tel: 01923 827148

Manager: Gordon Bartlett www.come-to-wealdstonefc.co.uk Colours: Blue & white

YATE TOWN

Lodge Road, Yate, Bristol, South Glos BS17 5LE

Club: 01454 228103

Manager: Richard Thompson www.yatetownfc.com Colours: White & navy blue

IN: Clevedon Town (P – Division One West), Corby Town (P – Division One East), Hemel Hempstead Town (P – Division One West), Maidenhead United (R – Football Conference South), Stamford (P – Division One East), Wealdstone (S – Isthmian League Premier Division)

OUT: Aylesbury United (R – Division One Midlands), Bedford Town (P – Football Conference South), Chesham United (R – Division One South & West), Evesham United (R – Division One Midlands), Grantham Town (S – Northern Premier League Premier Division), Salisbury City (P – Football Conference South)

	Arlesey Town	Aveley	Barking & East Ham United	Barton Rovers	Berkhamsted Town	Boreham Wood	Chatham Town	Corby Town	Dartford	Enfield	Enfield Town	Great Wakering Rovers	Harlow Town	Ilford	Potters Bar Town	Rothwell Town	Sittingbourne	Stamford	Uxbridge	Waltham Forest	Wingate & Finchley	Wivenhoe Town
Arlesey Town		1-0	1-3	2-2	2-0	0-2	0-1	0-1	0-1	1-0	2-4	2-5	0-2	3-3	4-0	1-0	1-3	2-2	2-1	1-0	1-1	2-0
Aveley	1-2		0-1	1-0	1-0	0-2	2-2	3-0	1-3	1-1	0-0	1-1	2-0	1-0	0-2	1-0	2-2	0-3	2-0	1-4	2-1	1-1
Barking & East Ham United	4-2	2-1	*D*	2-0	1-0	0-0	1-1	0-1	2-2	2-1	1-2	2-0	2-0	2-1	3-1	1-0	1-2	0-1	2-3	1-1	2-1	2-1
Barton Rovers	3-0	2-1	0-0	*I*	3-2	0-1	1-0	0-3	0-2	0-1	1-2	1-2	2-2	2-3	1-2	4-1	0-2	2-1	1-1	1-0	3-1	0-0
Berkhamsted Town	2-2	2-1	0-7	1-6	*V*	1-2	1-0	2-2	3-1	0-1	1-2	2-2	1-1	1-1	2-3	2-2	1-3	3-1	2-0	0-2	0-2	1-1
Boreham Wood	1-3	7-3	3-0	2-2	2-0	*I*	3-0	2-1	3-1	1-1	1-0	0-0	1-1	4-2	3-1	1-1	2-0	5-0	1-1	6-1	1-2	4-0
Chatham Town	0-1	3-2	1-1	3-2	3-0	2-0	*S*	0-0	1-0	3-0	0-2	3-2	1-1	1-2	3-2	3-1	2-3	0-1	1-2	0-1	3-1	2-2
Corby Town	1-2	1-0	3-1	5-0	2-1	2-0	2-0	*I*	4-1	3-0	1-0	1-1	2-1	1-1	1-3	1-0	2-1	1-0	0-0	1-0	1-0	3-0
Dartford	0-0	5-1	2-2	2-1	1-1	2-2	3-1	1-1	*O*	4-2	0-1	3-2	1-1	3-1	1-2	0-1	0-0	2-1	1-2	1-1	2-1	3-0
Enfield	1-0	1-2	1-0	3-0	1-2	1-2	0-2	2-1	2-2	*N*	1-2	0-0	2-3	1-1	3-2	1-3	4-3	0-1	2-2	2-1	0-0	0-0
Enfield Town	4-1	0-0	3-0	3-2	0-2	0-2	2-1	0-1	0-1	2-2		1-0	1-2	1-0	2-0	1-2	1-1	4-2	2-2	2-0	1-1	2-1
Great Wakering Rovers	2-1	2-2	3-1	5-1	2-1	0-1	2-0	1-3	0-1	6-1	0-5	*O*	2-3	1-0	3-2	1-0	2-0	2-1	1-2	2-3	2-2	2-2
Harlow Town	1-1	2-2	0-2	3-0	3-2	2-1	1-1	0-0	1-1	0-1	1-5	1-1	*N*	3-2	2-0	2-1	1-0	4-1	2-2	2-0	1-2	2-2
Ilford	1-1	0-0	0-1	0-2	0-0	1-4	0-0	1-0	0-2	0-1	0-0	1-0	2-0	*E*	1-1	2-2	1-0	1-0	0-0	1-3	0-0	1-0
Potters Bar Town	1-1	4-1	0-1	3-1	4-2	1-1	1-1	0-1	1-4	0-0	4-2	2-1	0-0	2-2		0-0	4-4	1-0	2-3	1-2	2-0	1-2
Rothwell Town	2-2	0-0	1-5	0-0	2-2	1-1	1-2	0-0	3-0	2-0	2-2	3-3	3-2	2-1	1-0	*E*	1-0	1-0	1-4	1-1	0-2	1-0
Sittingbourne	0-1	0-4	1-1	2-4	3-1	1-1	2-1	0-0	1-0	1-0	2-4	2-1	1-1	0-0	1-1	1-0	*A*	4-2	1-3	1-1	0-0	0-2
Stamford	3-1	2-2	1-1	3-0	2-2	2-2	1-1	2-0	2-0	2-1	0-0	2-0	1-0	5-0	1-0	1-0	6-2	*S*	3-1	4-0	2-2	4-2
Uxbridge	1-3	1-1	4-1	1-2	0-0	2-3	2-1	0-1	3-1	2-5	1-2	4-0	1-1	3-0	0-2	0-3	3-0	1-1	*T*	0-1	0-1	1-2
Waltham Forest	2-2	6-2	1-0	0-4	1-0	0-1	3-1	4-5	2-2	3-1	0-1	1-1	1-2	4-0	1-1	3-1	4-2	0-1	1-0		3-2	0-3
Wingate & Finchley	3-1	1-3	1-1	3-3	1-4	0-2	2-0	0-3	3-2	0-3	1-4	1-1	2-0	2-2	2-0	0-0	2-1	2-2	4-2	4-2		1-2
Wivenhoe Town	1-3	3-0	0-1	2-0	5-1	3-1	1-0	3-1	1-1	2-2	1-3	2-1	1-0	0-0	2-1	0-2	1-0	1-3	2-1	2-0	0-0	

Division One East		HOME					AWAY					TOTAL					
	P	**W**	**D**	**L**	**F**	**A**	**W**	**D**	**L**	**F**	**A**	**W**	**D**	**L**	**F**	**A**	**Pts**
Boreham Wood	42	13	6	2	53	20	11	6	4	31	21	24	12	6	84	41	84
Corby Town	42	16	3	2	38	12	9	6	6	25	21	25	9	8	63	33	84
Enfield Town	42	10	5	6	32	23	14	4	3	43	20	24	9	9	75	43	81
Stamford	42	14	7	0	49	17	6	3	12	24	36	20	10	12	73	53	70
Barking & East Ham United	42	12	4	5	33	21	8	6	7	30	26	20	10	12	63	47	70
Wivenhoe Town	42	12	4	5	33	21	5	7	9	23	33	17	11	14	56	54	62
Dartford	42	9	8	4	37	24	7	5	9	28	33	16	13	13	65	57	61
Waltham Forest	42	10	4	7	40	32	7	4	10	24	34	17	8	17	64	66	59
Harlow Town	42	9	8	4	34	27	5	8	8	23	29	14	16	12	57	56	58
Arlesey Town	42	8	4	9	28	31	7	7	7	30	34	15	11	16	58	65	56
Rothwell Town	42	8	9	4	28	27	5	5	11	20	26	13	14	15	48	53	53
Wingate & Finchley	42	8	6	7	35	38	5	8	8	22	26	13	14	15	57	64	53
Great Wakering Rovers	42	11	3	7	41	32	2	9	10	24	35	13	12	17	65	67	51
Uxbridge	42	6	4	11	30	31	7	7	7	32	33	13	11	18	62	64	50
Potters Bar Town	42	7	8	6	34	29	6	3	12	26	37	13	11	18	60	66	50
Enfield	42	7	6	8	28	29	6	5	10	24	35	13	11	18	52	64	50
Chatham Town	42	10	4	7	35	26	3	6	12	16	31	13	10	19	51	57	49
Sittingbourne	42	7	8	6	24	28	5	4	12	29	41	12	12	18	53	69	48
Barton Rovers	42	8	4	9	27	27	5	4	12	32	46	13	8	21	59	73	47
Aveley	42	8	6	7	23	25	3	7	11	28	45	11	13	18	51	70	46
Ilford	42	6	9	6	13	17	2	8	11	22	42	8	17	17	35	59	41
Berkhamsted Town	42	5	7	9	28	42	3	5	13	23	39	8	12	22	51	81	36

PLAY-OFFS

SEMI-FINALS

(May 1st)

Enfield Town 1 **Wivenhoe Town** 3 *aet* ***Att*** 326

Stamford 3 Barking & East Ham United 2 ***Att*** 375

FINAL

(May 6th at Stamford)

Stamford 2 Wivenhoe 1 ***Att*** 561

DATES & GATES

DATES & GATES	Arlesey Town	Aveley	Barking & East Ham United	Barton Rovers	Berkhamsted Town	Boreham Wood	Chatham Town	Corby Town	Dartford	Enfield	Enfield Town	Gt Wakering Rovers	Harlow Town	Ilford	Potters Bar Town	Rothwell Town	Sittingbourne	Stamford	Uxbridge	Waltham Forest	Wingate & Finchley	Wivenhoe Town
Arlesey Town		26 Nov *116*	24 Sep *171*	27 Sep *122*	27 Dec *132*	14 Mar *120*	25 Mar *97*	14 Jan *151*	13 Aug *153*	22 Apr *161*	31 Dec *298*	11 Mar *132*	5 Nov *135*	15 Apr *120*	10 Dec *138*	23 Aug *134*	28 Jan *102*	25 Oct *161*	8 Oct *93*	8 Apr *77*	18 Feb *131*	3 Sep *122*
Aveley	20 Aug *129*		21 Jan *149*	10 Dec *56*	8 Apr *115*	18 Feb *119*	29 Aug *116*	4 Mar *102*	27 Dec *310*	17 Sep *166*	17 Apr *275*	31 Dec *174*	26 Oct *84*	7 Jan *103*	1 Oct *66*	29 Oct *78*	19 Nov *117*	4 Feb *70*	29 Apr *115*	17 Aug *110*	25 Mar *74*	10 Oct *139*
Barking & East Ham Utd	29 Apr *86*	22 Oct *123*		11 Feb *85*	5 Nov *89*	24 Jan *103*	16 Aug *105*	8 Apr *110*	25 Feb *132*	11 Oct *78*	20 Aug *184*	14 Apr *80*	11 Mar *84*	27 Dec *142*	21 Feb *71*	18 Mar *76*	17 Sep *107*	1 Oct *75*	28 Jan *86*	3 Dec *91*	10 Sep *82*	7 Jan *87*
Barton Rovers	2 Jan *180*	11 Mar *84*	21 Mar *83*		21 Jan *74*	14 Feb *136*	17 Sep *63*	17 Apr *125*	29 Apr *160*	14 Jan *106*	25 Oct *140*	25 Mar *92*	4 Feb *98*	16 Aug *78*	8 Apr *87*	3 Dec *59*	3 Sep *90*	11 Oct *86*	25 Feb *71*	20 Aug *72*	1 Oct *73*	29 Oct *75*
Berkhamsted Town	11 Feb *94*	27 Sep *63*	1 Apr *131*	22 Oct *101*		29 Aug *126*	14 Jan *98*	10 Dec *128*	18 Feb *147*	28 Mar *74*	29 Apr *236*	8 Oct *137*	17 Sep *119*	20 Aug *102*	25 Mar *100*	17 Apr *102*	21 Feb *64*	2 Jan *134*	16 Aug *106*	29 Oct *122*	19 Nov *103*	4 Mar *101*
Boreham Wood	17 Sep *202*	23 Aug *125*	27 Sep *94*	8 Oct *101*	3 Dec *146*		22 Oct *131*	21 Feb *107*	3 Sep *162*	5 Nov *202*	11 Feb *369*	22 Apr *179*	2 Jan *180*	20 Mar *104*	7 Mar *117*	1 Apr *180*	7 Feb *114*	20 Dec *127*	17 Apr *176*	28 Jan *134*	11 Mar *181*	13 Aug *107*
Chatham Town	3 Dec *158*	2 Jan *175*	18 Feb *199*	26 Nov *144*	3 Sep *119*	4 Mar *210*		13 Aug *140*	27 Sep *200*	23 Aug *121*	18 Mar *284*	5 Nov *214*	31 Jan *113*	22 Apr *189*	24 Sep *233*	8 Oct *159*	17 Apr *338*	21 Jan *182*	1 Apr *186*	7 Jan *139*	4 Feb *205*	12 Nov *141*
Corby Town	17 Aug *103*	1 Apr *185*	4 Feb *171*	27 Dec *147*	12 Oct *105*	5 Apr *203*	11 Mar *151*		17 Sep *144*	29 Aug *104*	21 Jan *335*	18 Feb *185*	19 Nov *145*	31 Dec *141*	7 Jan *145*	26 Oct *405*	20 Aug *84*	15 Apr *407*	3 Dec *145*	29 Apr *1,340*	29 Oct *196*	1 Oct *94*
Dartford	7 Jan *280*	5 Nov *263*	25 Oct *259*	28 Jan *267*	1 Oct *261*	8 Apr *315*	15 Apr *369*	25 Mar *266*		10 Dec *263*	4 Mar *434*	16 Aug *285*	22 Apr *327*	11 Oct *235*	11 Mar *268*	11 Feb *310*	2 Jan *407*	20 Aug *272*	7 Feb *254*	30 Aug *233*	17 Dec *250*	14 Jan *283*
Enfield	29 Oct *123*	3 Dec *83*	3 Sep *107*	4 Mar *101*	31 Dec *85*	21 Aug *166*	19 Nov *111*	8 Oct *92*	17 Apr *159*		27 Dec *522*	25 Feb *112*	8 Apr *122*	4 Feb *116*	21 Jan *136*	24 Sep *129*	16 Aug *109*	10 Sep *93*	27 Sep *87*	25 Mar *103*	25 Oct *108*	29 Apr *111*
Enfield Town	25 Feb *253*	28 Jan *278*	10 Dec *281*	17 Dec *251*	26 Nov *250*	11 Oct *355*	1 Oct *279*	22 Oct *295*	23 Aug *315*	15 Apr *802*		29 Aug *343*	13 Aug *355*	18 Feb *317*	5 Nov *294*	14 Jan *252*	25 Mar *311*	1 Apr *403*	14 Feb *192*	16 Sep *387*	2 Jan *326*	11 Mar *258*
Great Wakering Rovers	1 Oct *120*	18 Mar *118*	2 Jan *151*	1 Apr *106*	13 Aug *122*	7 Jan *131*	11 Feb *120*	3 Sep *110*	19 Nov *146*	17 Dec *102*	29 Oct *245*		23 Aug *132*	21 Jan *129*	4 Feb *106*	29 Apr *95*	25 Oct *111*	24 Sep *83*	28 Mar *95*	11 Oct *113*	3 Dec *85*	17 Apr *131*
Harlow Town	4 Mar *85*	25 Feb *106*	29 Oct *127*	24 Sep *82*	18 Mar *81*	15 Apr *150*	12 Oct *68*	11 Feb *107*	3 Dec *139*	1 Oct *77*	7 Jan *237*	22 Oct *87*		18 Jan *77*	20 Aug *101*	31 Dec *86*	29 Apr *165*	17 Aug *124*	29 Aug *87*	15 Feb *106*	28 Jan *79*	1 Apr *68*
Ilford	19 Nov *82*	13 Aug *92*	17 Apr *131*	18 Mar *57*	25 Feb *52*	26 Oct *115*	10 Dec *62*	23 Nov *74*	1 Apr *163*	2 Jan *105*	8 Oct *173*	28 Sep *82*	3 Sep *61*		29 Apr *64*	28 Jan *56*	29 Oct *72*	17 Dec *52*	11 Feb *46*	11 Mar *63*	14 Jan *62*	24 Aug *104*
Potters Bar Town	29 Aug *115*	22 Apr *112*	13 Aug *144*	18 Feb *108*	25 Oct *105*	29 Oct *152*	28 Jan *101*	23 Aug *90*	8 Oct *143*	1 Apr *151*	10 Jan *254*	17 Sep *84*	14 Jan *114*	3 Dec *85*		4 Mar *113*	11 Feb *101*	18 Mar *118*	2 Jan *116*	19 Nov *85*	17 Apr *128*	17 Dec *93*
Rothwell Town	11 Oct *130*	17 Dec *81*	19 Nov *102*	15 Apr *121*	7 Jan *87*	21 Jan *142*	20 Aug *106*	2 Jan *247*	22 Oct *165*	11 Mar *119*	8 Apr *252*	10 Dec *91*	25 Mar *119*	17 Sep *95*	16 Aug *140*		25 Feb *114*	13 Sep *135*	5 Nov *103*	1 Oct *135*	22 Apr *104*	4 Feb *95*
Sittingbourne	1 Apr *164*	15 Apr *176*	4 Mar *211*	7 Jan *166*	6 Dec *69*	1 Oct *231*	27 Dec *280*	5 Nov *271*	24 Sep *299*	18 Mar *152*	3 Dec *332*	10 Jan *139*	21 Jan *190*	29 Aug *146*	11 Oct *200*	13 Aug *194*		22 Apr *203*	22 Oct *195*	31 Jan *131*	23 Aug *179*	18 Feb *212*
Stamford	17 Apr *242*	3 Sep *182*	14 Jan *213*	23 Aug *186*	11 Mar *233*	29 Apr *316*	8 Apr *208*	27 Sep *210*	29 Oct *235*	22 Oct *213*	19 Nov *302*	28 Jan *221*	18 Feb *234*	4 Mar *252*	31 Dec *218*	27 Dec *268*	8 Oct *201*		17 Sep *199*	11 Feb *207*	13 Aug *168*	3 Dec *200*
Uxbridge	21 Jan *69*	14 Jan *99*	23 Aug *122*	13 Aug *132*	4 Feb *79*	27 Dec *110*	29 Oct *101*	22 Apr *120*	31 Dec *127*	18 Feb *105*	4 Oct *156*	8 Apr *101*	10 Dec *105*	1 Oct *91*	15 Apr *115*	3 Sep *83*	11 Mar *124*	25 Mar *88*		25 Oct *66*	11 Oct *80*	19 Nov *107*
Waltham Forest	17 Dec *74*	8 Oct *70*	22 Apr *108*	5 Nov *64*	23 Aug *70*	4 Oct *94*	25 Feb *60*	26 Nov *75*	21 Jan *153*	13 Aug *75*	4 Feb *165*	14 Jan *72*	17 Apr *74*	22 Oct *77*	2 Sep *110*	18 Feb *63*	27 Sep *60*	10 Dec *64*	18 Mar *56*		1 Apr *68*	2 Jan *73*
Wingate & Finchley	22 Oct *76*	24 Sep *62*	8 Oct *66*	31 Dec *54*	15 Apr *51*	16 Aug *73*	29 Apr *54*	25 Feb *53*	18 Mar *83*	11 Feb *93*	3 Sep *154*	20 Aug *86*	27 Sep *63*	8 Apr *46*	20 Dec *67*	26 Nov *45*	10 Dec *63*	5 Nov *57*	7 Jan *54*	4 Mar *50*		21 Jan *51*
Wivenhoe Town	18 Mar *97*	11 Feb *113*	25 Mar *136*	18 Oct *75*	22 Apr *150*	10 Dec *121*	28 Feb *104*	28 Jan *114*	22 Nov *105*	26 Nov *102*	16 Aug *210*	7 Feb *101*	8 Oct *103*	5 Nov *104*	22 Oct *155*	27 Sep *82*	8 Apr *121*	25 Feb *139*	20 Aug *87*	14 Apr *189*	17 Sep *107*	

	Ashford Town (Middx)	Beaconsfield SYCOB	Bedworth United	Brackley Town	Bracknell Town	Bromsgrove Rovers	Burnham	Cinderford Town	Clevedon Town	Dunstable Town	Hemel Hempstead Town	Leighton Town	Marlow	Paulton Rovers	Rushall Olympic	Solihull Borough	Stourport Swifts	Sutton Coldfield Town	Swindon Supermarine	Taunton Town	Thame United	Willenhall
Ashford Town (Middx)		3-1	2-0	1-0	0-2	1-1	2-0	0-1	3-0	1-1	1-1	1-0	1-0	4-2	2-1	1-2	4-0	1-2	1-0	5-1	5-0	2-2
Beaconsfield SYCOB	0-2		1-1	0-2	2-1	1-2	3-0	2-0	2-4	3-0	0-5	1-1	2-2	2-2	1-1	0-0	1-1	2-1	1-3	3-2	1-0	2-1
Bedworth United	1-2	1-2	*D*	2-1	1-0	1-1	1-3	0-3	0-2	1-2	0-1	1-1	1-2	1-1	2-1	1-1	0-1	1-0	1-0	0-4	4-0	2-0
Brackley Town	0-1	5-0	0-0	*I*	2-0	1-0	5-2	2-2	2-0	0-0	1-0	3-0	2-1	1-0	0-2	0-1	5-0	0-1	1-2	1-0	5-0	1-1
Bracknell Town	2-1	0-0	0-4	1-3	*V*	1-2	2-1	3-1	0-2	4-4	0-3	1-3	1-2	3-1	0-1	0-2	1-5	2-0	1-5	1-1	6-0	3-0
Bromsgrove Rovers	1-3	2-0	1-2	1-1	0-0	*I*	2-0	6-2	3-0	4-0	0-4	0-2	0-2	2-0	4-1	0-0	2-1	3-6	0-2	1-2	4-0	1-4
Burnham	0-4	1-1	2-0	2-4	0-2	1-2	*S*	1-1	1-3	1-1	0-3	2-0	3-1	1-0	0-2	0-1	0-1	0-1	3-2	4-2	1-0	2-1
Cinderford Town	3-1	3-4	1-2	1-1	2-0	1-3	2-4	*I*	0-2	3-1	1-2	0-1	0-1	4-2	3-2	1-3	0-1	2-0	4-0	1-1	2-1	1-4
Clevedon Town	3-1	1-0	3-0	0-1	2-1	2-0	3-2	5-1	*O*	2-1	2-3	1-0	0-1	3-0	3-3	4-0	3-1	0-0	3-2	3-1	4-1	2-5
Dunstable Town	2-5	0-3	1-1	3-2	2-4	0-4	0-3	0-0	0-1	*N*	1-0	1-1	0-0	2-0	1-1	1-0	0-1	0-1	1-1	5-4	4-2	1-1
Hemel Hempstead Town	1-3	1-1	1-1	1-3	2-3	1-0	5-1	2-1	0-0	5-0		6-2	1-1	0-1	1-3	1-1	2-0	0-1	2-1	4-2	3-0	3-2
Leighton Town	1-4	3-0	2-0	0-2	2-1	1-1	0-1	0-1	1-2	2-1	2-1	*O*	1-2	0-1	3-1	1-0	1-1	1-0	0-1	3-0	1-2	1-0
Marlow	2-0	4-3	1-3	1-2	2-1	0-0	1-3	3-3	1-0	4-0	0-4	0-2	*N*	0-2	0-4	1-0	2-1	3-2	0-2	2-1	2-0	1-2
Paulton Rovers	1-2	4-0	2-1	0-0	0-0	0-2	2-2	1-4	2-2	2-0	2-1	1-1	1-3	*E*	2-0	0-1	3-1	1-3	1-3	2-2	3-0	2-3
Rushall Olympic	1-2	2-1	2-0	0-0	3-0	1-1	3-1	1-1	1-3	4-0	0-2	2-1	3-3	1-1		3-1	2-0	0-3	0-1	3-0	5-0	2-2
Solihull Borough	2-1	0-0	0-1	1-1	6-1	1-1	2-0	2-0	2-2	4-0	1-3	1-2	1-2	2-0	0-4	*W*	0-0	0-3	2-1	0-0	2-0	2-2
Stourport Swifts	4-0	1-5	1-0	0-2	2-2	1-1	0-0	3-3	0-3	5-1	1-3	1-1	1-2	2-3	1-3	1-1	*E*	3-3	0-0	3-3	1-2	2-2
Sutton Coldfield Town	2-2	1-4	3-1	4-0	2-1	1-1	3-2	1-1	1-4	2-4	1-1	1-3	2-3	7-1	4-1	2-0	4-0	*S*	2-3	2-0	8-0	3-1
Swindon Supermarine	1-3	1-0	2-2	1-2	3-0	1-0	1-0	1-2	2-2	3-1	0-0	2-2	0-2	3-0	2-0	2-2	1-0	4-2	*T*	1-1	2-1	0-0
Taunton Town	1-1	0-0	1-2	0-2	2-0	0-1	1-3	6-4	0-2	3-2	3-0	0-3	1-0	1-3	2-2	2-0	4-0	1-5	2-3		4-0	1-2
Thame United	2-2	1-4	0-2	0-5	0-2	0-4	1-3	1-4	0-1	0-0	4-4	1-2	0-1	2-2	3-1	1-3	1-3	2-1	0-3	1-3		1-1
Willenhall	3-3	1-1	3-1	2-0	1-0	2-1	0-2	3-1	0-2	3-1	0-3	0-1	3-1	4-1	0-0	5-0	4-4	3-0	0-2	1-2	4-0	

Division One West		HOME					AWAY					TOTAL					
	P	W	D	L	F	A	W	D	L	F	A	W	D	L	F	A	Pts
Clevedon Town	42	15	2	4	49	24	13	4	4	37	21	28	6	8	86	45	90
Ashford Town (Middx)	42	13	4	4	41	17	11	4	6	43	33	24	8	10	84	50	80
Brackley Town	42	12	4	5	37	13	11	5	5	34	21	23	9	10	71	34	78
Hemel Hempstead Town	42	10	5	6	42	27	12	4	5	44	20	22	9	11	86	47	75
Swindon Supermarine	42	10	7	4	33	22	12	2	7	37	25	22	9	11	70	47	75
Marlow	42	10	2	9	30	35	12	4	5	32	24	22	6	14	62	59	72
Sutton Coldfield Town	42	11	4	6	56	33	10	2	9	35	29	21	6	15	91	62	69
Leighton Town	42	10	2	9	26	22	9	6	6	29	26	19	8	15	55	48	65
Willenhall Town	42	11	4	6	42	26	6	8	7	36	35	17	12	13	78	61	63
Rushall Olympic	42	10	6	5	39	23	7	5	9	34	34	17	11	14	73	57	62
Bromsgrove Rovers	42	9	3	9	37	32	8	8	5	28	18	17	11	14	65	50	62
Solihull Borough	42	8	7	6	31	24	7	6	8	19	27	15	13	14	50	51	58
Beaconsfield SYCOB	42	8	7	6	30	31	6	6	9	30	35	14	13	15	60	66	55
Burnham	42	8	3	10	25	32	8	2	11	33	39	16	5	21	58	71	53
Cinderford Town	42	8	2	11	35	36	6	7	8	36	43	14	9	19	71	79	51
Bedworth United	42	7	4	10	22	28	7	5	9	24	29	14	9	19	46	57	51
Paulton Rovers	42	7	6	8	32	31	5	4	12	23	45	12	10	20	55	76	46
Taunton Town	42	8	3	10	35	35	4	6	11	32	46	12	9	21	67	81	45
Bracknell Town	42	7	3	11	32	41	5	3	13	21	36	12	6	24	53	77	42
Stourport Swifts	42	3	10	8	33	40	6	4	11	22	40	9	14	19	55	80	41
Dunstable Town	42	6	7	8	25	35	2	5	14	20	56	8	12	22	45	91	36
Thame United	42	2	5	14	21	51	2	0	19	9	71	4	5	33	30	122	17

PLAY-OFFS

SEMI-FINALS

(May 1st)

Brackley Town 2 Marlow 1 ***Att*** 317

Hemel Hempstead Town 3 Swindon Supermarine 0 ***Att*** 371

FINAL

(May 6th at Brackley Town)

Brackley Town 2 **Hemel Hempstead Town** 3 ***Att*** 655

DATES & GATES

	Ashford Town (Middx)	Beaconsfield SYCOB	Bedworth United	Brackley Town	Bracknell Town	Bromsgrove Rovers	Burnham	Cinderford Town	Clevedon Town	Dunstable Town	Hemel Hempstead Tn	Leighton Town	Marlow	Paulton Rovers	Rushall Olympic	Solihull Borough	Stourport Swifts	Sutton Coldfield Tn	Swindon Supermarine	Taunton Town	Thame United	Willenhall
Ashford Town (Middx)	*112*	23 Aug *97*	1 Apr *102*	5 Nov *103*	17 Apr *151*	7 Feb *112*	2 Jan *101*	21 Jan *132*	22 Apr *78*	22 Oct *151*	11 Feb *63*	3 Sep *131*	11 Oct *111*	11 Mar *110*	3 Dec *97*	18 Mar *95*	7 Jan *95*	28 Jan *101*	13 Aug *135*	17 Dec *123*	25 Feb *163*	1 Oct
Beaconsfield SYCOB	4 Mar *80*		20 Aug *56*	17 Sep *75*	2 Jan *85*	3 Dec *92*	17 Apr *112*	22 Apr *48*	4 Feb *51*	10 Oct *78*	15 Aug *142*	5 Nov *56*	29 Aug *120*	1 Oct *59*	14 Jan *62*	6 Feb *62*	19 Nov *54*	8 Apr *72*	22 Oct *70*	21 Jan *64*	18 Feb *65*	25 Mar *70*
Bedworth United	10 Jan *91*	25 Feb *84*		23 Aug *161*	17 Sep *137*	25 Oct *226*	14 Jan *142*	11 Mar *100*	8 Apr *123*	11 Feb *130*	28 Jan *112*	22 Apr *107*	1 Oct *133*	29 Oct *135*	11 Oct *101*	10 Dec *118*	25 Mar *133*	27 Dec *225*	7 Feb *98*	13 Aug *125*	3 Sep *81*	15 Apr *138*
Brackley Town	29 Apr *572*	25 Oct *90*	18 Feb *204*		25 Feb *112*	20 Aug *183*	21 Jan *117*	10 Dec *112*	7 Jan *135*	12 Nov *79*	29 Aug *175*	27 Dec *215*	29 Oct *120*	8 Apr *166*	4 Feb *108*	16 Aug *166*	8 Oct *74*	31 Dec *112*	22 Nov *99*	26 Nov *106*	15 Apr *148*	18 Mar *144*
Bracknell Town	17 Jan *101*	15 Apr *102*	5 Nov *121*	13 Aug *155*		7 Jan *129*	18 Feb *133*	26 Nov *78*	22 Oct *142*	23 Aug *85*	31 Dec *115*	27 Sep *87*	11 Mar *123*	12 Nov *85*	8 Apr *109*	4 Feb *110*	10 Dec *98*	3 Sep *82*	21 Jan *125*	8 Oct *126*	18 Mar *86*	22 Apr *121*
Bromsgrove Rovers	10 Dec *353*	13 Aug *260*	27 Sep *231*	28 Jan *327*	4 Mar *306*		17 Sep *317*	27 Dec *350*	31 Dec *343*	22 Apr *266*	8 Apr *323*	28 Feb *201*	10 Jan *232*	14 Jan *354*	23 Aug *232*	22 Nov *168*	15 Apr *314*	11 Feb *312*	3 Sep *212*	18 Mar *319*	11 Mar *267*	5 Nov *385*
Burnham	15 Apr *93*	27 Dec *227*	6 Dec *116*	11 Feb *121*	11 Oct *123*	19 Nov *135*		25 Mar *84*	10 Dec *121*	7 Jan *100*	10 Jan *138*	31 Dec *113*	4 Mar *179*	28 Jan *101*	1 Oct *104*	25 Feb *108*	1 Apr *87*	13 Aug *168*	31 Jan *121*	22 Apr *132*	23 Aug *110*	3 Sep *117*
Cinderford Town	17 Sep *98*	29 Oct *94*	29 Apr *118*	3 Sep *76*	1 Apr *85*	18 Feb *146*	17 Dec *90*		11 Oct *118*	28 Jan *98*	1 Oct *117*	11 Apr *117*	19 Nov *83*	3 Dec *101*	25 Oct *111*	2 Jan *135*	4 Feb *88*	15 Apr *117*	18 Mar *106*	23 Aug *140*	13 Aug *94*	4 Apr *126*
Clevedon Town	18 Feb *257*	1 Apr *163*	17 Jan *156*	19 Nov *157*	28 Jan *162*	25 Feb *221*	20 Aug *128*	16 Aug *151*		3 Sep *118*	14 Jan *163*	25 Mar *188*	17 Dec *154*	2 Jan *251*	11 Mar *214*	25 Oct *153*	29 Oct *181*	8 Oct *144*	27 Sep *105*	17 Apr *303*	29 Apr *198*	17 Sep *138*
Dunstable Town	29 Aug *115*	31 Dec *53*	8 Oct *99*	14 Jan *98*	19 Nov *119*	1 Oct *156*	16 Aug *71*	8 Apr *87*	18 Mar *68*		27 Dec *208*	15 Apr *147*	3 Dec *91*	20 Aug *81*	17 Sep *81*	29 Oct *100*	29 Apr *190*	18 Feb *103*	10 Dec *91*	4 Feb *85*	25 Oct *69*	4 Mar *110*
Hemel Hempstead Town	27 Sep *96*	8 Oct *137*	17 Dec *132*	11 Mar *162*	3 Dec *115*	21 Jan *197*	4 Feb *129*	7 Jan *104*	13 Aug *136*	17 Apr *165*		23 Aug *127*	2 Jan *167*	18 Mar *132*	18 Feb *202*	1 Apr *188*	3 Sep *95*	13 Dec *67*	22 Apr *178*	5 Nov *164*	4 Oct *114*	22 Oct *160*
Leighton Town	25 Oct *124*	28 Jan *114*	18 Mar *106*	17 Apr *145*	14 Jan *110*	29 Apr *120*	4 Oct *98*	20 Aug *100*	1 Oct *143*	2 Jan *191*	22 Nov *116*		16 Aug *117*	21 Feb *72*	19 Nov *97*	3 Dec *98*	11 Mar *95*	17 Sep *89*	8 Apr *120*	25 Feb *110*	29 Oct *112*	11 Feb *122*
Marlow	31 Dec *146*	10 Dec *107*	7 Jan *141*	25 Mar *165*	25 Oct *104*	4 Feb *158*	15 Nov *143*	24 Sep *98*	5 Nov *105*	25 Feb *122*	15 Apr *189*	8 Oct *105*		3 Sep *70*	21 Jan *112*	22 Apr *135*	13 Aug *98*	18 Mar *114*	23 Aug *114*	8 Apr *154*	27 Dec *159*	26 Nov *166*
Paulton Rovers	8 Oct *100*	26 Nov *100*	4 Feb *121*	4 Mar *122*	25 Apr *115*	6 Apr *122*	12 Dec *107*	29 Aug *98*	15 Apr *231*	5 Nov *133*	17 Sep *126*	21 Jan *135*	22 Oct *129*		13 Aug *150*	7 Jan *115*	22 Aug *128*	22 Apr *129*	27 Dec *150*	31 Oct *286*	13 Mar *78*	10 Dec *139*
Rushall Olympic	20 Aug *110*	3 Sep *114*	16 Aug *141*	22 Oct *84*	11 Feb *61*	25 Mar *188*	18 Mar *97*	27 Sep *114*	24 Sep *111*	26 Nov *94*	29 Oct *112*	1 Apr *118*	29 Apr *186*	25 Feb *90*		15 Apr *118*	31 Dec *103*	10 Dec *92*	8 Oct *82*	7 Jan *109*	28 Jan *88*	27 Dec *230*
Solihull Borough	19 Nov *124*	19 Oct *87*	22 Oct *188*	12 Oct *95*	1 Oct *171*	17 Apr *207*	8 Apr *112*	5 Nov *137*	24 Aug *127*	21 Jan *127*	25 Mar *133*	13 Aug *128*	11 Feb *154*	29 Apr *109*	4 Mar *268*		22 Mar *100*	11 Mar *137*	15 Feb *113*	3 Sep *110*	22 Feb *73*	31 Dec *163*
Stourport Swifts	8 Apr *74*	18 Mar *74*	30 Aug *100*	22 Apr *123*	20 Aug *95*	2 Jan *301*	26 Nov *72*	17 Apr *90*	11 Feb *87*	17 Dec *75*	4 Mar *78*	22 Oct *95*	14 Jan *78*	11 Oct *84*	5 Nov *93*	28 Jan *107*		27 Sep *84*	25 Feb *88*	12 Nov *89*	17 Sep *80*	16 Aug *123*
Sutton Coldfield Town	29 Oct *125*	7 Jan *61*	17 Apr *157*	1 Oct *100*	17 Dec *91*	15 Aug *194*	6 Feb *101*	25 Feb *137*	4 Mar *157*	24 Sep *112*	29 Apr *118*	4 Feb *127*	20 Aug *90*	19 Nov *115*	2 Jan *255*	29 Aug *165*	21 Jan *190*		25 Mar *107*	22 Oct *79*	1 Apr *108*	10 Oct *180*
Swindon Supermarine	14 Jan *254*	11 Mar *89*	4 Mar *149*	24 Jan *124*	16 Aug *127*	29 Oct *173*	29 Apr *136*	11 Feb *116*	29 Aug *191*	1 Apr *138*	19 Nov *175*	18 Feb *91*	28 Jan *146*	17 Apr *169*	17 Dec *85*	17 Sep *159*	1 Oct *126*	25 Oct *100*		2 Jan *197*	11 Oct *94*	20 Aug *129*
Taunton Town	25 Mar *198*	11 Feb *196*	19 Nov *221*	1 Apr *254*	29 Apr *234*	12 Oct *138*	29 Oct *266*	31 Dec *138*	27 Dec *405*	11 Mar *208*	20 Aug *236*	10 Dec *212*	17 Sep *262*	17 Aug *277*	29 Aug *223*	18 Feb *208*	26 Oct *204*	14 Jan *217*	15 Apr *280*		1 Oct *244*	28 Jan *211*
Thame United	16 Aug *112*	24 Sep *82*	21 Jan *89*	3 Jan *85*	10 Sep *104*	4 Apr *92*	29 Nov *64*	12 Nov *86*	27 Nov *110*	12 Apr *91*	11 Dec *123*	7 Jan *105*	18 Apr *116*	11 Feb *69*	25 Apr *42*	20 Aug *116*	3 Dec *86*	5 Nov *75*	4 Feb *73*	5 Mar *75*		8 Apr *85*
Willenhall	4 Feb *163*	29 Apr *104*	2 Jan *195*	17 Dec *127*	29 Oct *129*	29 Aug *246*	11 Mar *110*	8 Oct *81*	21 Jan *159*	13 Aug *103*	14 Mar *100*	24 Sep *113*	1 Apr *149*	25 Oct *94*	17 Apr *210*	27 Sep *91*	18 Feb *132*	23 Aug *135*	7 Jan *135*	14 Feb *118*	19 Nov *123*	

SOUTHERN LEAGUE DIVISION ONE MIDLANDS

CONSTITUTION FOR 2006-07

AYLESBURY UNITED
Colours: Green & white
Aylesbury Vale FC, Haywood Way, Aylesbury, Buckinghamshire HP19 9WZ
Tel: 01296 423324

BARTON ROVERS
Colours: Royal blue
Sharpenhoe Road, Barton-le-Clay, Beds MK45 4SD
Tel: 01582 707772

BEDWORTH UNITED
Colours: Green & white
The Oval, Welfare Park, Coventry Road, Bedworth, Warwickshire CV12 8NN
Tel: 024 7631 4302

BERKHAMSTED TOWN
Colours: White & black
Broadwater, Lower Kings Road, Berkhamsted, Hertfordshire HP4 2AA
Tel: 01442 862815

BISHOPS CLEEVE
Colours: Green & black
Kayte Lane, Bishops Cleeve, Cheltenham, Gloucestershire GL52 3PD
Tel: 07866 077291

BRACKLEY TOWN
Colours: Red & white
St James's Park, Churchill Way, Brackley, Northants NN13 7EJ
Tel: 01280 704077

BROMSGROVE ROVERS
Colours: Green & white
Victoria Ground, Birmingham Road, Bromsgrove, Worcestershire B61 8DR
Tel: 01527 876949

CHASETOWN
Colours: Royal blue
The Scholars Ground, Church Street, Chasetown, Walsall, Staffs WS7 8QL
Tel: 01543 682222

CINDERFORD TOWN
Colours: White & black
Causeway Ground, Edge Hills Road, Hilldene, Cinderford, Gloucestershire GL14 2QH
Tel: 01594 822039 Club: 01594 827147

DUNSTABLE TOWN
Colours: Blue & white
Creasey Park Stadium, Brewers Hill Road, Dunstable, Bedfordshire LU6 1BB
Tel: 01582 667555

EVESHAM UNITED
Colours: Red, white & black
Worcester City FC, St George's Lane, Barbourne, Worcester, Worcestershire WR1 1QT
Tel: 01905 23003

LEIGHTON TOWN
Colours: Red & white
Bell Close, Lake Street, Leighton Buzzard, Bedfordshire LU7 1RX
Tel: 01525 373311

MALVERN TOWN
Colours: Sky blue & claret
Langland Stadium, Langland Avenue, Malvern, Worcestershire WR14 2EQ
Tel: 01684 574068

ROTHWELL TOWN
Colours: Blue
Home Close, Cecil St, Rothwell, Northants NN14 2EZ
Tel: 01536 710694

RUSHALL OLYMPIC
Colours: Amber & black
Dales Lane, off Daw End Lane, Rushall, Walsall, West Midlands WS4 1LJ
Tel: 01922 641021

SOLIHULL BOROUGH
Colours: Red & white
Damson Park, Damson Parkway, Solihull, West Midlands B91 2PP
Tel: 0121 705 6770

SPALDING UNITED
Colours: Tangerine & black
Sir Halley Stewart Field, Winfrey Avenue, Spalding, Lincolnshire PE11 1DA
Tel: 01775 713328

STOURBRIDGE
Colours: Red & white
War Memorial Athletic Ground, High Street, Amblecote, Stourbridge, West Midlands DY8 4HN
Tel: 01384 394040

STOURPORT SWIFTS
Colours: Yellow
Walshes Meadow, Harold Davies Drive, Stourport-on-Severn, Worcestershire DY13 0AA
Tel: 01299 825188

SUTTON COLDFIELD TOWN
Colours: Blue
Central Ground, Coles Lane, Sutton Coldfield, West Midlands B72 1NL
Tel: 0121 354 2997

WILLENHALL TOWN
Colours: Red
Noose Lane, Willenhall, West Midlands WV13 3BB
Tel: 01902 636586

WOODFORD UNITED
Colours: Red
Byfield Road, Woodford Halse, Daventry, Northants NN11 3PZ
Tel: 01327 263734

DIVISION ONE MIDLANDS (formerly DIVISION ONE WEST)

IN: Aylesbury United (R), Barton Rovers (S – Southern League Division One East), Berkhamsted Town (S – Southern League Division One East), Bishops Cleeve (P – Hellenic League Premier Division), Chasetown (P – Midland Alliance), Evesham United (R), Malvern Town (P – Midland Alliance), Rothwell Town (S – Southern League Division One East), Spalding United (S – Northern Premier League Division One), Stourbridge (P – Midland Alliance), Woodford United (P – United Counties League Premier Division)

OUT: Ashford Town (Middx) (P – Isthmian League Premier Division), Beaconsfield SYCOB (S – Southern League Division One South & West), Bracknell Town (S – Southern League Division One South & West), Burnham (S – Southern League Division One South & West), Clevedon Town (P), Hemel Hempstead Town (P), Marlow (S – Southern League Division One South & West), Paulton Rovers (S – Southern League Division One South & West), Swindon Supermarine (S – Southern League Division One South & West), Taunton Town (S – Southern League Division One South & West), Thame United (R – Hellenic League Premier Division)

SOUTHERN LEAGUE DIVISION ONE SOUTH & WEST

CONSTITUTION FOR 2006-07

ABINGDON UNITED
Colours: Yellow & blue
Northcourt Road, Abingdon, Oxfordshire OX14 1PL
Tel: 01235 203203

ANDOVER
Colours: Red & black
The Portway Stadium, West Portway Ind. Estate, Andover, Hampshire SP10 3LF
Tel: 01264 351302

BASHLEY
Colours: Gold & black
Bashley Recreation Ground, Bashley Road, New Milton, Hampshire BH25 5RY
Tel: 01425 620280

BEACONSFIELD SYCOB
Colours: Red, white & black
Holloway Park, Slough Road, Beaconsfield, Buckinghamshire HP9 2SG
Tel: 01494 676868

BRACKNELL TOWN
Colours: Red & white
Larges Lane, Bracknell, Berkshire RG12 9AN
Tel/Fax: 01344 300933

BROOK HOUSE
Colours: Blue & white
Farm Park, Kingshill Avenue, Hayes, Middx UB4 8DD
Tel: 020 8845 0110

BURNHAM
Colours: Blue & white
The Gore, Wymers Wood Road, Burnham SL1 8JG
Tel: 01628 602697

CHESHAM UNITED
Colours: Claret & sky blue
Meadow Park, Amy Lane, Amersham Road, Chesham, Buckinghamshire HP5 1NE
Tel: 01494 783964

DIDCOT TOWN
Colours: Red & white
Loop Meadow Stadium, Bowmont Water, off Avon Way, Didcot, Oxfordshire OX11 7GA
Tel: 01235 813138

HANWELL TOWN
Colours: Black & white
Reynolds Field, Perivale Lane, Perivale, Greenford, Middlesex UB6 8TL
Tel: 020 8998 1701

HILLINGDON BOROUGH
Colours: White & royal blue
Middlesex Stadium, Breakspear Road, Ruislip, Middlesex HA4 7SB
Tel: 01895 639544

LYMINGTON & NEW MILTON
Colours: Maroon & blue
Fawcetts Field, Christchurch Road, New Milton, Hampshire BH25 6QB
Tel: 01425 628191

MARLOW
Colours: Royal blue & white
Alfred Davis Ground, Oak Tree Road, Marlow, Buckinghamshire SL7 3ED
Tel: 01628 483970

NEWPORT IOW
Colours: Yellow & blue
St George's Park, St George's Way, Newport, Isle of Wight PO30 2QH
Tel: 01983 525027

OXFORD CITY
Colours: Blue & white
Court Place Farm, Marsh Lane, Marston, Oxford, Oxfordshire OX3 0NQ
Tel: 01865 744493

PAULTON ROVERS
Colours: Maroon & white
Athletic Ground, Winterfield Road, Paulton, North Somerset BS39 7RF
Tel: 01761 412907

SWINDON SUPERMARINE
Colours: Blue & white
Hunts Copse, Highworth Road, South Marston, Swindon, Wiltshire SN3 4SY
Tel: 01793 828778

TAUNTON TOWN
Colours: Burgundy & sky blue
Wordsworth Drive, Taunton, Somerset TA1 2HG
Tel: 01823 278191

THATCHAM TOWN
Colours: Blue & white
Waterside Park, Crookham Road, Thatcham, Berkshire RG19 4PA
Tel: 01635 862016

UXBRIDGE
Colours: Red & white
Honeycroft, Horton Road, West Drayton, Middlesex UB7 8HX
Tel: 01895 443557

WINCHESTER CITY
Colours: Red & black
The City Ground, Hillier Way, Abbotts Barton, Winchester, Hampshire SO23 7EF
Tel: 01962 810200

WINDSOR & ETON
Colours: Red & green
Stag Meadow, St Leonards Road, Windsor, Berkshire SL4 3DR
Tel: 01753 860656

For movements please see overleaf

DIVISION ONE SOUTH & WEST (formerly DIVISION ONE EAST)

IN: Abingdon United (P – Hellenic League Premier Division), Andover (P – Wessex League Division One), Bashley (S – Isthmian League Division One), Beaconsfield SYCOB (S – Southern League Division One West), Bracknell Town (S – Southern League Division One West), Brook House (P – Isthmian League Division Two), Burnham (S – Southern League Division One West), Chesham United (R), Didcot Town (P – Hellenic League Premier Division), Hanwell Town (P – Spartan South Midlands League Premier Division), Hillingdon Borough (P – Spartan South Midlands League Premier Division), Lymington & New Milton (S – Isthmian League Division One), Marlow (S – Southern League Division One West), Newport IOW (S – Isthmian League Division One North), Oxford City (P – Spartan South Midlands League Premier Division), Paulton Rovers (S – Southern League Division One West), Swindon Supermarine (S – Southern League Division One West), Taunton Town (S – Southern League Division One West), Thatcham Town (P – Wessex League Division One), Winchester City (P – Wessex League Division One), Windsor & Eton (R – Isthmian League Premier Division)

OUT: Arlesey Town (S – Isthmian League Division One North), Aveley (S – Isthmian League Division One North), Barking & East Ham United (F), Barton Rovers (S – Southern League Division One Midlands), Berkhamsted Town (Southern League Division One Midlands), Boreham Wood (P – Isthmian League Premier Division), Chatham Town (S – Isthmian League Division One South), Corby Town (P), Dartford (S – Isthmian League Division One South), Enfield (S – Isthmian League Division One North), Enfield Town (S – Isthmian League Division One North), Great Wakering Rovers (S – Isthmian League Division One North), Harlow Town (S – Isthmian League Division One North), Ilford (S – Isthmian League Division One North), Potters Bar Town (S – Isthmian League Division One North), Rothwell Town (S – Southern League Division One Midlands), Sittingbourne (S – Isthmian League Division One South), Stamford (P), Waltham Forest (S – Isthmian League Division One North), Wingate & Finchley (S – Isthmian League Division One North), Wivenhoe Town (S – Isthmian League Division One North),

LEAGUE CUP

FIRST ROUND

Aveley 0 **Potters Bar Town** 0 *aet* (3-5p)
Barking & East Ham United 2 Sittingbourne 1
Boreham Wood 1 **Ashford Town (Middx)** 4
Bracknell Town 1 **Marlow** 2
Bromsgrove Rovers 2 Stourport Swifts 1
Burnham 2 Beaconsfield SYCOB 0
Corby Town 4 Brackley Town 1 *aet*
Dartford 0 **Chatham Town** 1
Dunstable Town 6 Stamford 5 *aet*
Enfield Town 0 **Wivenhoe Town** 0 *aet* (4-5p)
Great Wakering Rovers 3 **Enfield** 4 *aet*
Harlow Town 2 Ilford 1
Leighton Town 1 Barton Rovers 0
Rothwell Town 4 Arlesey Town 0
Solihull Borough 4 Bedworth United 0
Sutton Coldfield Town 2 Cinderford Town 1
Swindon Supermarine 2 Paulton Rovers 0
Taunton Town 0 **Clevedon Town** 2
Thame United 0 **Berkhamsted Town** 4
Uxbridge 0 **Hemel Hempstead Town** 5
Willenhall Town 0 **Rushall Olympic** 1
Wingate & Finchley 2 **Waltham Forest** 3

SECOND ROUND

Ashford Town (Middx) 5 Burnham 0
Barking & East Ham United 2 **Chatham Town** 3
Berkhamsted Town 1 **Marlow** 2 *aet*
Dunstable Town 0 **Hitchin Town** 1
Enfield 0 **Potters Bar Town** 3
Hemel Hempstead Town 6 Leighton Town 0
Rothwell Town 1 **Corby Town** 2
Rushall Olympic 1 Sutton Coldfield Town 0
Solihull Borough 0 **Bromsgrove Rovers** 2
Swindon Supermarine 1 Clevedon Town 0
Waltham Forest 1 **Cheshunt** 5
Wivenhoe Town 1 Harlow Town 2
(Harlow Town expelled)

THIRD ROUND

Banbury United 2 Halesowen Town 1
Bedford Town 1 Grantham Town 0
Chesham United 0 **Cheshunt** 1
Chippenham Town 1 Swindon Supermarine 0 *aet*
Evesham United 0 **Bromsgrove Rovers** 5
Gloucester City 2 **Cirencester Town** 4
Hemel Hempstead Town 1 **Potters Bar Town** 4
Hitchin Town 2 Marlow 1 *aet*
King's Lynn 5 Corby Town 0
Mangotsfield United 4 Merthyr Tydfil 1
Northwood 1 **Ashford Town (Middx)** 2
Rushall Olympic 2 Rugby Town 0
Salisbury City 3 Aylesbury United 0
Team Bath 4 Yate Town 1
Tiverton Town 1 **Bath City** 2
Wivenhoe Town 1 **Chatham Town** 4

FOURTH ROUND

Ashford Town (Middx) 1 **Hitchin Town** 4
Banbury United 1 Rushall Olympic 0
Bedford Town 1 Cheshunt 0
Bromsgrove Rovers 1 King's Lynn 0
Chatham Town 2 Potters Bar Town 0
Chippenham Town 2 Team Bath 0
Mangotsfield United 2 Bath City 1 *aet*
Salisbury City 3 **Cirencester Town** 4

QUARTER-FINALS

Banbury United 0 **Bromsgrove Rovers** 4
Chatham Town 0 **Bedford Town** 2
Chippenham Town 2 Mangotsfield United 0
Cirencester Town 0 **Hitchin Town** 7

SEMI-FINALS

Chippenham Town 1 **Bromsgrove Rovers** 2
Hitchin Town 2 Bedford Town 0

FINAL

(played over two legs)
(1st leg Apr 11th)
Hitchin Town 1 Bromsgrove Rovers 0
(2nd leg Apr 25th)
Bromsgrove Rovers 1 **Hitchin Town** 2

SPARTAN SOUTH MIDLANDS LEAGUE

	Atlesbury Vale	Biggleswade Tn	Biggleswade Utd	Broxbourne Boro'	Hanwell Town	Harefield United	Haringey Boro'	Harpenden Tn	Hillingdon Boro'	Holmer Green	Langford	Leverstock Gn	London Colney	Oxford City	Oxhey Jets	Royston Town	Ruislip Manor	St Margaretsb'y	Tring Athletic	Welwyn G'den Cy
Aylesbury Vale		2-1	1-0	1-4	2-0	3-1	3-2	1-0	0-1	2-0	6-0	1-5	3-2	1-0	2-1	8-0	1-1	2-0	4-2	3-2
Biggleswade Town	0-0		2-1	0-3	1-2	0-7	2-2	2-1	1-3	2-1	1-2	3-3	2-1	1-3	2-1	2-1	2-1	0-4	0-1	1-0
Biggleswade United	1-2	3-1	*P*	2-0	1-6	1-1	3-2	2-2	0-0	1-2	0-1	0-3	3-0	1-2	1-3	2-0	1-0	3-1	0-0	1-1
Broxbourne Borough V & E	2-3	3-3	1-3	*R*	1-3	1-2	2-0	2-0	2-3	3-1	2-3	3-4	1-3	1-1	3-0	4-0	2-1	0-0	2-1	1-0
Hanwell Town	2-1	3-1	1-2	1-0	*E*	0-2	3-1	4-1	3-1	4-2	8-1	4-0	6-1	1-2	3-1	8-1	3-2	3-2	2-0	1-2
Harefield United	1-0	2-1	2-0	4-1	0-1	*M*	3-0	0-0	2-1	2-3	3-1	0-0	4-0	2-3	1-0	6-0	0-0	3-0	2-3	3-1
Haringey Borough	0-1	1-1	2-1	1-3	2-1	1-2	*I*	0-1	1-3	1-2	0-3	0-0	1-0	0-3	2-1	3-1	1-3	2-1	1-0	0-3
Harpenden Town	1-4	1-0	1-3	4-2	1-3	0-0	1-2	*E*	0-1	2-3	2-4	0-0	2-1	0-6	1-3	1-2	1-0	1-1	2-1	1-2
Hillingdon Borough	3-1	1-0	2-2	3-2	2-1	1-2	4-0	3-1	*R*	2-1	5-2	3-0	2-3	2-2	2-1	2-0	2-1	1-2	3-1	1-1
Holmer Green	0-0	3-5	1-4	1-1	1-1	1-1	7-1	4-0	1-2		2-0	1-4	3-1	0-1	2-1	1-1	3-1	0-3	2-1	1-2
Langford	3-4	0-4	0-3	1-6	0-3	0-3	1-0	3-0	0-2	1-4	*D*	1-2	0-2	1-3	3-4	3-1	1-2	1-1	0-1	2-0
Leverstock Green	1-4	1-4	1-2	3-0	0-3	2-2	5-0	2-0	2-1	1-1	3-1	*I*	4-1	0-3	3-2	1-0	2-2	1-0	2-2	1-1
London Colney	1-1	4-2	0-3	2-1	1-1	1-1	3-0	3-1	0-3	1-2	2-2	1-0	*V*	0-0	2-0	3-4	0-2	1-2	0-1	0-1
Oxford City	3-2	5-1	3-1	1-0	1-1	6-3	4-0	2-0	2-3	1-1	6-3	1-0	3-1	*I*	1-4	1-0	6-3	1-3	2-1	2-0
Oxhey Jets	2-2	1-0	1-1	3-1	3-0	3-4	2-1	0-0	0-3	1-2	1-2	2-1	1-1	0-2	*S*	5-2	0-0	2-1	0-0	0-3
Royston Town	1-0	3-2	2-1	1-1	0-2	1-2	3-0	3-1	0-1	1-4	3-0	0-1	1-1	2-2	2-1	*I*	1-2	0-1	0-4	0-0
Ruislip Manor	0-3	1-1	1-3	2-1	0-1	1-2	2-1	3-1	2-3	0-3	1-1	0-1	5-0	0-1	2-0	0-2	*O*	2-1	1-1	0-1
St Margaretsbury	2-4	2-0	1-3	1-2	2-2	0-1	4-1	7-1	1-2	1-2	9-0	0-3	0-4	0-3	2-2	1-0	0-0	*N*	0-1	1-1
Tring Athletic	2-0	0-0	3-0	0-2	1-1	1-1	2-2	2-1	0-1	0-1	0-2	1-0	0-0	0-1	0-0	2-0	2-0	1-2		1-1
Welwyn Garden City	5-1	1-1	2-1	1-0	3-3	0-4	2-0	3-0	1-2	3-0	3-2	1-2	0-2	2-2	0-2	7-0	1-0	1-2	1-1	

Premier Division	P	W	D	L	F	A	Pts
Oxford City	38	27	7	4	91	41	88
Hillingdon Borough	38	28	4	6	80	41	88
Hanwell Town	38	24	6	8	95	45	78
Harefield United	38	23	9	6	81	38	78
Aylesbury Vale	38	23	5	10	79	52	74
Leverstock Green	38	18	9	11	64	51	63
Holmer Green	38	18	7	13	69	59	61
Welwyn Garden City	38	16	10	12	59	45	58
Biggleswade United	38	16	7	15	60	54	55
Tring Athletic	38	12	12	14	40	39	48
Broxbourne Borough V & E	38	14	5	19	66	63	47
St Margaretsbury	38	13	7	18	61	57	46
Oxhey Jets	38	12	8	18	54	60	44
London Colney	38	11	8	19	49	68	41
Biggleswade Town	38	11	8	19	52	74	41
Ruislip Manor	38	10	8	20	44	56	38
Langford	38	11	3	24	51	102	36
Royston Town	38	10	5	23	39	86	35
Haringey Borough	38	8	4	26	34	86	28
Harpenden Town	38	6	6	26	33	84	24

PREMIER DIVISION CUP

FIRST ROUND

Harefield United 2 Haringey Borough 1

Langford 0 **Tring Athletic** 1

Royston Town 0 **Hillingdon Borough** 4

St Margaretsbury 3 Welwyn Garden City 0

SECOND ROUND

Aylesbury Vale 2 Harpenden Town 1

Biggleswade United 1 **Leverstock Green** 2

Broxbourne Borough V & E 3 Tring Athletic 1

Harefield United 3 Oxhey Jets 0

Hillingdon Borough 4 Hanwell Town 1

Holmer Gn 2 London Colney 1

Oxford City 3 Biggleswade Tn 2

Ruislip Manor 1 St Margaretsbury 0

QUARTER-FINALS

Aylesbury V 0 **Ruislip Manor** 1

Broxbourne Borough V & E 1 **Harefield United** 4 *aet*

Holmer Green 1 **Oxford City** 2

Leverstock Green 2 Hillingdon Borough 1

SEMI-FINALS

Leverstock Green 3 Harefield United 1

Ruislip Manor 0 **Oxford City** 1

FINAL

(April 18th at Hillingdon Borough)

Oxford City 1 Leverstock Green 0

SPARTAN SOUTH MIDLANDS LEAGUE PREMIER DIVISION CONSTITUTION 2006-07

AYLESBURY VALE .... Haywood Way, Aylesbury HP19 9WZ 01296 423324
BIGGLESWADE TOWN .. Beford United & Valerio FC, McMullen Park, Meadow Lane, Cardington, Bedford MK44 3LW..... 01234 831024
BIGGLESWADE UNITED .... Second Meadow, Fairfield Road, Biggleswade SG18 0AA 01767 600408
BROXBOURNE BOROUGH V & E .... The V & E Club, Goffs Lane, Cheshunt EN7 5QN 01992 624281
CHALFONT ST PETER......... Mill Meadow, Gravel Hill, Amersham Road, Chalfont St Peter SL9 9QX.............. 01753 885797
COLNEY HEATH.............. The Recreation Ground, High Street, Colney Heath, St Albans AL4 0NN 01727 826188
EDGWARE TOWN.................. White Lion Ground, High Street, Edgware HA8 5AQ 020 8952 6799
HARFFIELD UNITED.................. Preston Park, Breakspeare Road, Harefield UB9 6BH.................. 01895 823474/822275
HARINGEY BOROUGH .... Coles Park, White Hart Lane, Wood Green, Tottenham N17 7JP 020 8889 1415
HERTFORD TOWN.................. Hertingfordbury Park, West Street, Hertford SG13 8EZ 01992 583716
HOLMER GREEN.................. Watchet Lane, Holmer Green, High Wycombe HP15 6UF 01494 711485
KINGSBURY LONDON TIGERS ...... Silver Jubilee Park, Townsend Lane, Kingsbury NW9 7NE 020 8205 1645/5204
LANGFORD .... Forde Park, Langford Road, Henlow SG16 6AF 01462 816106
LEVERSTOCK GREEN............ Pancake Lane, Leverstock Green, Hemel Hempstead HP2 4BN.................. 01442 246280
LONDON COLNEY.................. Cotlandswick Playing Fields, London Colney AL2 1EH.................. 01727 822132
OXHEY JETS .... The Boundary Stadium, Altham Way, South Oxhey WD19 6FW.................. 020 8421 6277
ROYSTON TOWN .... Garden Walk, Royston SG8 7HP 01763 241204
RUISLIP MANOR .... Grosvenor Vale, off West End Road, Ruislip HA4 6JQ.................. 01895 676168/637487
ST MARGARETSBURY .... Station Road, Stanstead St Margarets, near Ware SG12 8EH 01920 870473
TRING ATHLETIC.................. Pendley Sports Centre, Cow Lane, Tring HP23 3NR 01442 828331
WELWYN GARDEN CITY .... Herns Way, Welwyn Garden City AL7 1TA.................. 01707 329358

IN: Chalfont St Peter (S – Isthmian League Division Two), Colney Heath (P), Edgware Town (S – Isthmian League Division Two), Hertford Town (S – Isthmian League Division Two), Kingsbury Town (having merged with Middlesex County League Premier Division side London Tigers to form Kingsbury London Tigers) (S – Isthmian League Division Two)

OUT: Hanwell Town (P – Southern League Division One South & West), Harpenden Town (R), Hillingdon Borough (P – Southern League Division One South & West), Oxford City (P – Southern League Division One South & West)

	Amersham Town	Ampthill Town	Arlesey Athletic	Bedford United & Valerio	Brache Sparta	Brimsdown Rovers	Buckingham Athletic	Cockfosters	Colney Heath	Cranfield United	Dunstable Town '98	Hoddesdon Town	Kentish Town	New Bradwell St Peter	Stony Stratford Town	Sun Postal Sports	Winslow United
Amersham Town		3-2	1-5	1-1	0-1	0-0	0-2	0-2	1-3	1-3	3-1	3-0	1-2	0-4	1-5	2-3	1-2
Ampthill Town	0-0		2-2	0-3	1-4	2-1	2-3	0-1	1-5	4-0	0-1	1-0	0-2	1-3	3-6	2-3	0-5
Arlesey Athletic	1-0	4-3	*D*	14-0	0-4	4-0	3-1	3-6	1-1	4-1	2-1	1-7	1-3	2-0	3-0	0-0	2-3
Bedford United & Valerio	4-1	1-4	1-0	*I*	1-0	4-1	1-3	1-2	0-6	1-0	4-2	2-1	4-1	1-0	0-2	1-0	2-5
Brache Sparta	1-0	6-1	2-1	2-1	*V*	5-3	3-0	1-1	1-0	2-3	4-2	2-1	4-1	5-2	1-3	2-0	2-0
Brimsdown Rovers	5-3	1-1	1-0	3-1	3-1	*I*	0-2	0-4	1-4	2-0	3-0	1-2	1-1	1-2	3-2	2-1	2-0
Buckingham Athletic	2-0	2-1	2-4	0-2	2-0	2-1	*S*	4-5	0-3	0-1	1-3	2-0	0-3	3-4	1-2	1-0	3-0
Cockfosters	4-1	5-2	0-2	2-3	1-3	2-3	2-1	*I*	1-3	1-1	0-3	0-0	3-2	0-2	1-1	2-2	3-1
Colney Heath	1-0	4-1	4-2	4-1	1-0	1-1	0-2	3-0	*O*	3-1	4-1	4-0	6-0	3-0	3-4	6-2	4-1
Cranfield United	2-0	2-3	0-2	0-3	0-2	1-2	1-1	2-4	0-2	*N*	2-1	0-1	2-4	0-1	0-3	3-0	3-3
Dunstable Town '98	4-1	4-0	0-2	2-1	2-2	1-3	3-3	2-2	2-4	2-0		1-2	1-1	2-3	3-2	3-2	3-2
Hoddesdon Town	2-1	6-1	2-0	8-1	1-1	0-1	2-1	3-1	0-3	1-1	3-1		3-3	3-2	1-1	6-1	2-1
Kentish Town	1-2	3-0	5-1	1-1	2-3	1-3	3-0	1-2	0-4	3-4	1-1	2-1	*O*	6-0	3-3	1-1	1-2
New Bradwell St Peter	7-2	3-2	1-1	2-1	1-2	0-0	2-1	4-2	2-5	3-0	0-2	3-0	1-2	*N*	3-1	0-1	1-1
Stony Stratford Town	4-0	4-0	4-0	9-2	3-5	2-2	2-0	3-0	0-0	2-0	2-0	3-2	4-0	2-2	*E*	3-1	4-1
Sun Postal Sports	1-1	2-1	0-2	9-0	0-3	0-2	1-1	2-3	1-4	4-1	2-1	3-2	6-3	2-1	1-0		3-2
Winslow United	2-0	1-2	2-2	1-3	1-2	1-0	0-0	2-1	0-8	3-2	1-3	2-2	3-3	0-1	0-4	0-4	

Division One	P	W	D	L	F	A	Pts
Colney Heath	32	26	3	3	106	27	81
Brache Sparta	32	23	3	6	76	38	72
Stony Stratford Town	32	20	6	6	90	42	66
New Bradwell St Peter	32	16	4	12	60	54	52
Brimsdown Rovers	32	15	6	11	52	50	51
Arlesey Athletic	32	15	5	12	71	57	50
Hoddesdon Town	32	14	6	12	64	50	48
Cockfosters	32	14	6	12	63	61	48
Sun Postal Sports	32	13	5	14	58	61	44
Bedford United & Valerio *-3*	32	15	2	15	52	86	44
Kentish Town	32	11	8	13	65	68	41
Dunstable Town '98	32	12	5	15	58	62	41
Buckingham Athletic	32	12	4	16	46	54	40
Winslow United	32	9	6	17	48	73	33
Cranfield United	32	7	4	21	36	68	25
Ampthill Town	32	6	3	23	43	90	21
Amersham Town	32	4	4	24	30	77	16

DIVISION ONE CUP

FIRST ROUND

Bedford United & Valerio 0 **Colney Heath** 5
Brache Sparta 4 Amersham Town 1

SECOND ROUND

Brache Sparta 1 Cockfosters 0
Brimsdown Rovers 1 Sun Postal Sports 0
Buckingham Athletic 2 Colney Heath 0
Cranfield United 4 Dunstable Town '98 2
Hoddesdon Town 1 **Winslow United** 2
Kentish Town 1 **Arlesey Athletic** 3
Shillington (scr.) v **New Bradwell St Peter** (w/o)
Stony Stratford Town 1 Ampthill Town 0

QUARTER-FINALS

Brimsdown Rovers 4 Arlesey Athletic 2 *aet*
Buckingham Athletic 2 Winslow United 1
Cranfield United 0 **New Bradwell St Peter** 1
Stony Stratford Town 3 Brache Sparta 2

SEMI-FINALS

Brimsdown Rovers 4 Stony Stratford Town 3
Buckingham Athletic 1 New Bradwell St Peter 0

FINAL

(April 25th at Tring Athletic)
Buckingham Athletic 0 **Brimsdown Rovers** 1

SPARTAN SOUTH MIDLANDS LEAGUE DIVISION ONE CONSTITUTION 2006-07

AMERSHAM TOWN .... Spratleys Meadow, School Lane, Amersham HP7 0EJ 01494 727428
AMPTHILL TOWN .... Ampthill Park, Woburn Road, Ampthill MK45 2HX 01525 404440
ARLESEY ATHLETIC .... Arlesey Town FC, Hitchin Road, Arlesey SG15 6RS 01462 734504
BEDFORD UNITED & VALERIO... McMullen Park, Meadow Lane, Cardington, Bedford MK44 3LW 01234 831024
BRACHE SPARTA .... Foxdell Recreation Ground, Dallow Road, Luton LU1 1TG 01582 720751
BRIMSDOWN ROVERS .... Brimsdown Sports & Social, Goldsdown Road, Enfield EN3 7RP 020 8804 5491
BUCKINGHAM ATHLETIC .... Stratfields Fields, Stratford Road, Buckingham KM18 1NY 01280 816945
COCKFOSTERS .... Chalk Lane, Cockfosters, Barnet EN4 9JG 0208 449 5833
CRANFIELD UNITED .... Crawley Road, Cranfield, Bedford MK43 0AA 01234 751444
HARPENDEN TOWN .... Rothamsted Park, Amenbury Lane, Harpenden AL5 2EF 01582 715724
HODDESDON TOWN .... Lowfield, Park View, Hoddesdon EN11 8PX 01707 870816
KENTISH TOWN .... Potters Bar Town FC, Parkfield, Watkins Rise, The Walk, Potters Bar EN6 1QN 01707 654833
NEW BRADWELL ST PETER .... Bradwell Road Rec Ground, New Bradwell, Milton Keynes 01908 313835
STONY STRATFORD TOWN .... Ostlers Lane, Stony Stratford, Milton Keynes MK11 1AR 01908 562267
SUN POSTAL SPORTS .... Bellmount Wood Avenue, Watford WD17 3BN 01923 227453
WINSLOW UNITED .... Rec. Ground, Elmfields Gate, Winslow, Buckingham MK18 3JQ 01296 713057

IN: Harpenden Town (R)
OUT: Colney Heath (P), Dunstable Town '98 (W), Shillington (WS)

	AFC Dunstable	Aston Clinton	Caddington	Crawley Green	Flamstead	Kent Athletic	Kings Langley	Loughton Orient	MK Scot	Markyate	Mursley United	Old Bradwell Utd	Padbury United	Pitstone & Ivinghoe	Risborough Rangers	The 61 FC (Luton)	Totternhoe	Tring Corinthians
AFC Dunstable		0-3	3-0	3-1	1-0	3-1	0-1	8-0	2-0	4-1	2-0	3-1	6-0	5-0	5-1	3-1	2-2	0-2
Aston Clinton	1-2		4-2	3-0	7-0	4-0	2-4	7-0	4-0	6-2	3-1	8-1	10-1	8-0	2-2	1-0	5-0	5-2
Caddington	2-3	1-7		1-4	1-2	2-3	1-1	5-1	4-0	3-0	1-0	0-1	2-0	4-2	1-1	1-4	4-1	0-2
Crawley Green	1-2	3-3	2-0	*D*	4-0	0-0	1-1	7-0	4-1	3-0	2-0	1-2	6-3	3-1	2-1	1-0	2-0	2-5
Flamstead	2-4	2-3	1-2	1-0	*I*	1-3	4-0	6-2	0-3	3-1	1-0	3-0	1-0	0-0	2-2	0-1	2-4	0-3
Kent Athletic	3-0	0-2	0-0	1-1	4-0	*V*	2-1	5-1	3-0	1-0	1-0	2-0	3-0	2-0	2-1	2-1	0-0	3-1
Kings Langley	1-2	1-3	1-0	3-1	2-3	3-1	*I*	8-0	0-0	2-1	3-2	1-2	3-1	0-2	3-4	1-0	5-1	3-1
Loughton Orient	L-W	0-6	2-5	1-2	0-5	0-6	1-3	*S*	2-3	0-2	2-3	1-2	4-2	2-7	0-1	1-2	2-3	2-8
MK Scot	2-2	0-3	2-2	3-1	4-1	0-1	3-5	3-0	*I*	8-2	1-1	4-2	5-0	3-0	1-1	2-3	1-2	2-6
Markyate	0-5	1-4	1-6	1-5	2-2	0-7	1-2	0-1	0-5	*O*	1-3	0-2	4-2	0-2	0-2	0-3	0-4	0-4
Mursley United	1-2	1-7	1-2	3-1	3-3	0-1	1-3	4-0	1-1	0-0	*N*	0-4	2-3	1-1	3-2	1-6	1-4	1-3
Old Bradwell United	1-2	1-3	2-1	2-3	2-2	3-1	2-1	0-1	2-2	1-0	2-1		6-0	4-0	6-1	1-2	3-7	2-0
Padbury United	3-8	1-4	1-5	1-1	0-5	2-7	0-3	2-4	0-3	4-4	1-0	2-4	*T*	3-0	0-0	0-5	4-5	1-3
Pitstone & Ivinghoe	0-4	0-5	3-2	1-3	1-1	3-4	2-4	2-0	1-4	1-1	0-1	3-2	1-1	*W*	1-3	3-1	0-4	0-4
Risborough Rangers	0-7	0-4	2-0	0-1	1-4	0-2	0-1	7-0	2-2	6-0	3-4	3-2	9-2	4-1	*O*	4-2	1-2	2-2
The 61 FC (Luton)	0-5	1-2	2-2	1-2	3-5	0-3	0-0	3-0	3-1	0-2	2-0	1-3	2-1	0-0	3-3		3-0	1-1
Totternhoe	1-4	1-3	2-0	1-4	1-1	1-2	0-0	2-2	0-4	4-1	3-0	1-2	9-1	1-1	1-0	1-0		1-1
Tring Corinthians	3-2	0-0	3-0	2-3	5-2	1-3	1-0	16-1	0-3	12-1	1-1	3-1	3-1	0-0	4-1	2-2	2-1	

Division Two	P	W	D	L	F	A	Pts
Aston Clinton	34	29	3	2	142	30	90
AFC Dunstable	34	27	2	5	159	35	83
Kent Athletic	34	25	4	5	79	31	79
Tring Corinthians	34	20	7	7	106	47	67
Crawley Green	34	20	5	9	77	47	65
Kings Langley	34	19	5	10	70	45	62
Old Bradwell United	34	18	2	14	71	63	56
Totternhoe	34	15	7	12	70	63	52
MK Scot	34	14	8	12	76	60	50
Flamstead	34	13	7	14	65	69	46
The 61 FC (Luton)	34	13	6	15	58	54	45
Risborough Rangers	34	11	8	15	70	72	41
Caddington	34	12	5	17	62	64	41
Pitstone & Ivinghoe	34	7	8	19	39	84	29
Mursley United	34	7	6	21	41	72	27
Markyate	34	3	4	27	29	117	13
Padbury United	34	3	4	27	43	137	13
Loughton Orient	34	4	1	29	33	200	13

DIVISION TWO CUP

FIRST ROUND

Mursley United 1 **Loughton Orient** 2
Pitstone & Ivinghoe 1 Tring Corinthians 0

SECOND ROUND

AFC Dunstable 4 MK Scot 2
Aston Clinton 10 Markyate 2
Crawley Green 1 **Risborough Rangers** 2
Loughton Orient 1 **Kings Langley** 7
Padbury United 1 **Kent Athletic** 5
Pitstone & Ivinghoe 0 **Old Bradwell United** 4
The 61FC (Luton) 1 **Caddington** 2
Totternhoe 3 Flamstead 3 *aet* (4-3p)

QUARTER-FINALS

AFC Dunstable 4 Kings Langley 1
Caddington 1 **Aston Clinton** 5
Old Bradwell United 3 Risborough Rangers 2
Totternhoe 2 Kent Athletic 2 *aet* (4-1p)

SEMI-FINALS

Old Bradwell United 0 **AFC Dunstable** 3
Totternhoe 3 Aston Clinton 2

FINAL

(April 19th at Ampthill Town)
AFC Dunstable 2 Totternhoe 0

SPARTAN SOUTH MIDLANDS LEAGUE DIVISION TWO CONSTITUTION 2006-07

AFC DUNSTABLE .... Lancot Park, Dunstable Road, Totternhoe, Dunstable LU6 1QP 01582 663735
ASTON CLINTON .... London Road, Aston Clinton HP22 5HL 01296 631818
CADDINGTON .... Caddington Recreation Club, Manor Road, Caddington, Luton LU1 4HH 01582 450151
CRAWLEY GREEN .... Crawley Green Rec Ground, Crawley Green Road, Luton LU2 9HA 01582 700883
FLAMSTEAD .... Flamstead Sports Association, Friendless Lane, Flamstead, St Albans AL3 8DE 01582 841307
KENT ATHLETIC .... Kent Social Club, Tenby Drive, Leagrave, Luton LU4 9BN 01582 582723
KINGS LANGLEY .... Hempstead Road, Kings Langley WD4 8BS .... None
LOUGHTON ORIENT .... Loughton Sports & Social Club, Linceslade Grove, Milton Keynes MK5 8DL 01908 690668
MK SCOT .... Scot Sports & Social Club, Selbourne Avenue, Bletchley, Milton Keynes MK3 5BX 01908 368881
MARKYATE .... The Playing Fields, Cavendish, Markyate 01582 841731
MURSLEY UNITED .... Station Road, Mursley, Milton Keynes MK17 0SA .... None
OLD BRADWELL UNITED .... Abbey Road, Bradwell Village, Milton Keynes MK13 9AR 01908 312355
PADBURY UNITED .... Playing Fields, Springfields, Padbury MK18 2AS .... None
PITSTONE & IVINGHOE .... Recreation Ground, Pitstone, Leighton Buzzard 01296 661271
RISBOROUGH RANGERS .... Windsor, Horsenden Lane, Princes Risborough HP27 9NE 01844 274176
THE 61 FC (LUTON) .... Kingsway Ground, Beverley Road, Luton LU4 8EU 01582 495417
TOTTERNHOE .... Totternhoe Recreation Ground, Castle Hill Road, Totternhoe, Dunstable LU6 1RG 01582 606738
TRING CORINTHIANS .... Icknield Way, Tring HP23 5HJ 07985 726431

No change

CHALLENGE TROPHY

FIRST ROUND

Arlesey Athletic 0 **Winslow United** 3
Aston Clinton 1 **AFC Dunstable** 2
Aylesbury Vale 6 Amersham Town 0
Bedford United & Valerio 1 **Ampthill Town** 4
Biggleswade Town 3 Welwyn Garden City 1
Biggleswade United 2 MK Scot 1
Brache Sparta 3 Kentish Town 0
Broxbourne Borough V & E 1 **Ruislip Manor** 3
Dunstable Town '98 6 Loughton Orient 0
Flamstead 0 **Brimsdown Rovers** 2
Harefield United 3 Colney Heath 1
Haringey Borough 0 **Crawley Green** 1
Harpenden Town 0 **Hillingdon Borough** 4
Holmer Green 3 Caddington 1
Kent Athletic 3 The 61FC (Luton) 0
Leverstock Green 3 **St Margaretsbury** 4
New Bradwell St Peter 6 Markyate 1
Oxhey Jets (w/o) v Hanwell Town (scr.)
Padbury United 0 **Oxford City** 9
Royston Town 1 **Buckingham Athletic** 2 *aet*
Stony Stratford Town 0 **Langford** 2
Sun Postal Sports 1 **Cockfosters** 5
Totternhoe 1 **Mursley United** 2
Tring Corinthians 0 **Kings Langley** 1

SECOND ROUND

Ampthill Town 1 **Buckingham Athletic** 6
Biggleswade United 3 **AFC Dunstable** 4 *aet*
Cockfosters 5 Brimsdown Rovers 4
Crawley Green 2 Pitstone & Ivinghoe 1
Hoddesdon Town 4 Cranfield United 0
Holmer Green 1 Biggleswade Town 0
Langford 2 Dunstable Town '98 1
London Colney 4 Risborough Rangers 0
New Bradwell St Peter 3 Kings Langley 1
Old Bradwell United 1 **Brache Sparta** 3
Oxford City 3 Harefield United 2
Ruislip Manor 5 Kent Athletic 1
Shillington (scr.) v **Oxhey Jets** (w/o)
St Margaretsbury 0 **Hillingdon Borough** 1
Tring Athletic 2 Mursley United 1
Winslow United 0 **Aylesbury Vale** 1

THIRD ROUND

AFC Dunstable 3 Cockfosters 1
Aylesbury Vale 2 Brache Sparta 0
Buckingham Athletic 1 **Ruislip Manor** 4
Crawley Green 1 Hoddesdon Town 0
Holmer Green 5 New Bradwell St Peter 2
Langford 0 **London Colney** 4
Oxford City 1 **Hillingdon Borough** 3
Oxhey Jets 1 **Tring Athletic** 2

QUARTER-FINALS

AFC Dunstable 2 **London Colney** 5
Aylesbury Vale 1 **Ruislip Manor** 2 *aet*
Crawley Green 1 **Tring Athletic** 2
Holmer Green 1 **Hillingdon Borough** 4

SEMI-FINALS

Hillingdon Borough 2 London Colney 2 *aet* (2-1p)
Ruislip Manor 1 Tring Athletic 0

FINAL

(May 1st at Hanwell Town)
Ruislip Manor 2 Hillingdon Borough 1

Reserve Division One	P	W	D	L	F	A	Pts
Sawbridgeworth Town Res.	30	22	3	5	71	28	69
Welwyn Garden City Res.	30	20	5	5	72	25	65
New Bradwell St Peter Res.	30	16	4	10	46	47	52
St Margaretsbury Res.	30	15	6	9	77	52	51
Tring Athletic Res.	30	14	8	8	58	45	50
Oxhey Jets Res.	30	14	7	9	82	52	49
Leverstock Green Res.	30	14	6	10	51	49	48
Hertford Town Res.	30	12	9	9	51	35	45
Holmer Green Res.	30	13	6	11	43	48	45
Aylesbury Vale Res.	30	10	4	16	57	65	34
Buckingham Athletic Res.	30	8	8	14	34	54	32
Harpenden Town Res.	30	10	2	18	51	75	32
Mursley United Res.	30	10	2	18	45	81	32
Colney Heath Res.	30	8	7	15	32	49	31
Hoddesdon Town Res.	30	6	4	20	46	74	22
Haringey Borough Res.	30	5	5	20	34	71	20

Reserve Division Two	P	W	D	L	F	A	Pts
Sun Postal Sports Res.	26	20	3	3	68	17	63
Stony Stratford Town Res.	26	19	3	4	96	32	60
London Colney Res.	26	16	4	6	86	30	52
Cockfosters Res.	26	13	8	5	76	33	47
Risborough Rangers Res.	26	11	5	10	43	38	38
Royston Town Res.	26	10	7	9	48	41	37
Amersham Town Res.	26	11	4	11	49	53	37
Caddington Res.	26	10	6	10	56	52	36
Tring Corinthians Res.	26	10	5	11	53	55	35
Kings Langley Res.	26	8	5	13	36	56	29
MK Scot Res.	26	5	10	11	42	64	25
Winslow United Res.	26	4	7	15	32	60	19
Old Bradwell United Res.	26	5	4	17	31	89	19
Loughton Orient Res.	26	2	5	19	23	119	11

RESERVES TROPHY

FINAL

(May 3rd at Royston Town)
Welwyn Garden City Res. 1 Sawbridgeworth Town Res. 1
aet (4-3p)

STAFFORDSHIRE COUNTY SENIOR LEAGUE

Note – Audley & District withdrew during the course of the season Their results are shown herein but are expunged from the league table	Abbey Hulton U	Alsager Tn Res.	Audley & District	Ball Haye Green	Eccleshall AFC	Fegg Hayes	Florence Colliery	Foley	Goldenhill Wdrs	Hanford	Hanley Town	Newcastle Tn Rs.	Norton	Redgate Clayton	Rocester Res.	Stallington	Stone Dom. Res.	Wolstanton Utd
Abbey Hulton United		1-1	2-1	0-2	0-0	2-1	1-2	0-0	0-7	1-3	1-2	0-1	2-0	0-2	0-2	2-1	4-1	6-0
Alsager Town Res.	0-1	*P*	2-1	1-0	3-0	1-2	1-0	0-2	3-2	2-1	1-0	1-1	1-1	0-0	2-1	3-2	5-0	5-0
Audley & District	n/a	n/a	*R*	n/a	3-1	n/a	0-0	n/a	n/a	1-0	2-1	n/a	n/a	n/a	1-3	1-1	5-0	n/a
Ball Haye Green	1-0	4-1	n/a	*E*	1-1	2-1	1-0	0-0	2-0	2-0	0-4	3-4	3-0	0-1	3-0	4-2	2-0	2-2
Eccleshall AFC	2-0	1-1	0-1	1-4	*M*	3-1	2-1	0-5	3-0	5-3	0-4	2-0	1-0	1-1	2-1	3-0	2-1	5-2
Fegg Hayes	0-6	1-3		4-1	5-3	*I*	0-4	2-1	3-1	1-1	0-3	2-2	0-0	0-3	2-1	4-3	0-1	5-2
Florence Colliery	0-3	1-3	1-3	1-1	0-1	3-1	*E*	0-0	1-3	2-1	0-2	1-4	1-0	0-5	2-1	2-1	0-4	0-0
Foley	3-2	1-3	0-1	1-2	2-2	4-0	4-0	*R*	5-1	3-0	1-1	0-1	2-0	3-2	3-2	1-0	1-5	2-2
Goldenhill Wanderers	2-0	0-3	n/a	3-2	3-1	5-2	1-0	1-0		1-2	2-2	0-1	4-1	3-0	1-0	4-2	9-2	1-1
Hanford	2-1	0-3	1-3	0-3	5-2	2-1	1-0	2-4	4-2	*D*	3-4	1-2	0-2	0-2	1-0	5-2	9-0	2-1
Hanley Town	3-1	4-0	n/a	2-0	4-1	9-2	5-2	1-0	6-0	3-1	*I*	5-1	3-2	1-0	3-1	8-0	7-0	4-1
Newcastle Town Res.	3-2	4-0	3-1	1-1	1-2	1-0	6-1	2-0	2-1	0-1	1-2	*V*	2-0	0-0	4-0	4-0	8-0	0-1
Norton	2-2	1-0	0-0	1-5	4-1	0-0	0-3	0-4	0-0	0-2	1-1	1-1	*I*	1-3	3-0	0-0	0-1	0-0
Redgate Clayton	1-4	1-1	n/a	0-1	0-0	3-0	1-2	0-4	1-1	1-3	2-3	2-1	0-1	*S*	3-0	0-2	0-2	3-0
Rocester Res.	1-0	0-3	2-1	0-2	0-0	0-0	1-1	0-1	1-2	1-3	1-3	0-1	2-0	1-2	*I*	3-2	2-0	3-1
Stallington	2-3	0-1	2-0	1-1	0-4	3-1	0-0	0-2	1-2	1-0	0-3	2-1	0-2	0-4	3-0	*O*	1-0	2-0
Stone Dominoes Res.	1-2	1-5	n/a	0-2	1-1	1-2	1-2	2-5	0-1	1-3	0-2	0-0	1-1	1-8	3-3	3-2	*N*	5-0
Wolstanton United	1-3	1-1	n/a	0-0	1-3	3-2	0-2	2-0	2-2	3-2	0-4	1-4	3-2	1-1	2-0	1-1	2-0	

Premier Division	P	W	D	L	F	A	Pts
Hanley Town	32	28	3	1	108	25	87
Ball Haye Green	32	18	7	7	57	32	61
Alsager Town Res.	32	18	7	7	58	34	61
Newcastle Town Res.	32	18	6	8	64	32	60
Foley	32	17	6	9	64	35	57
Goldenhill Wanderers	32	16	5	11	65	53	53
Eccleshall AFC	32	15	8	9	55	54	53
Hanford	32	16	1	15	63	56	49
Redgate Clayton	32	13	7	12	52	37	46
Abbey Hulton United	32	12	4	16	50	49	40
Florence Colliery	32	11	5	16	34	55	38
Fegg Hayes	32	9	5	18	45	77	32
Wolstanton United	32	7	10	15	36	72	31
Norton	32	6	10	16	26	48	28
Stallington	32	7	4	21	36	71	25
Stone Dominoes Res.	32	7	4	21	38	91	25
Rocester Res.	32	6	4	22	28	58	22

Audley & District – record expunged

LEAGUE CUP

FIRST ROUND

Congleton Vale 0 Holditch Grandy's 1
(Holditch Grandy's expelled)

SECOND ROUND

Abbey Hulton United 3 Holt JCB 0
Alsager Town Res. 2 Manor Inne 0
Audley & District 5 Newcastle Town Youth 0
Brocton Res. 1 **Stone Dominoes Res.** 2
Congleton Vale 1 Rocester Res. 0
Foley 0 **Hanley Town** 2
Foley Res. 7 Abbey Hulton U Res. 0
Hanford 4 Ball Haye Gn Res. 2 *aet*
Hanley Tn Res. 4 Eccleshall AFC 0
Newcastle Town Res. 1 Florence 0
Redgate Clayton 1 Wedgwood Sports & Social 0
Redgate Clayton Res. (w/o) v Alsagers Bank (scr.)
Stafford Rangers Stripes 1 Fegg Hayes 0
Stallington 0 **Norton** 2
Stone Old Alleynians 2 Goldenhill Wanderers 1
Wolstanton Utd 1 **Ball Haye Gn** 4

THIRD ROUND

Abbey Hulton United 1 **Redgate Clayton** 2
Alsager Town Res. 4 Stone Old Alleynians 0
Audley & District 2 Stone Dominoes Res. 1
Ball Haye Green 5 Norton 0
Congleton Vale 3 Hanford 1
Foley Res. 1 Hanley Town Res. 1 *aet* (3-2p)
Newcastle Town Res. 1 Hanley Town 1 *aet* (5-4p)
Stafford Rangers Stripes 3 **Redgate Clayton Res.** 5 *aet*

QUARTER-FINALS

Alsager Tn Res. 3 Congleton Vale 2
Audley & District 1 **Newcastle Town Res.** 2
Foley Res. 0 **Redgate Clayton** 3
Redgate Clayton Res. 0 **Ball Haye Green** 1

SEMI-FINALS

Ball Haye Gn 4 Newcastle Tn Res. 1
Redgate Clayton 0 **Alsager Tn Res.** 2

FINAL *(March 13th at Norton Utd)*
Alsager Tn Res. 2 **Ball Haye Gn** 4 *aet*

STAFFORDSHIRE COUNTY LEAGUE PREMIER DIVISION CONSTITUTION 2006-07

ABBEY HULTON UNITED........... Birches Head Road, Abbey Hulton, Stoke-on-Trent ST2 8DD 01782 544232
ALSAGER TOWN RESERVES.......... The Town Ground, Woodland Court, Alsager ST7 2DP........................ 01270 882336
ASHBOURNE UNITED........... Rocester FC, Riversfield, Mill Street, Rocester, Uttoxeter ST14 5TX 01889 590463
BALL HAYE GREEN........... Ball Haye Green WMC, Ball Haye Green, Leek ST13 6BH........................ 01538 371926
ECCLESHALL AFC........... Pershall Park, Chester Road, Eccleshall ST21 6NE........................ 01785 851351
FLORENCE COLLIERY........ Florence Miners Welfare, Lightwood Road, Stoke-on-Trent ST3 4JS 01782 312887
FOLEY........... Whitcombe Road, Meir, Stoke-on-Trent ST3 6NU 01782 595274
GOLDENHILL WANDERERS.. Sandyford Cricket Club, Shelford Road, Sandyford, Stoke-on-Trent ST6 5LA 01782 811977
HANFORD........... Northwood Stadium, Keelings Road, Hanley, Stoke-on-Trent ST1 6PA 01782 234400
HANLEY TOWN........... Abbey Lane, Abbey Hulton, Bucknall, Stoke-on-Trent ST8 8AJ 01782 267234
NEWCASTLE TOWN RESERVES Lyme Valley Parkway Stadium, Buckmaster Ave., Clayton, Newcastle-under-Lyne ST5 3BF. 01782 662351
NORTON........... Norton CC & MW Institute, Community Drive, Smallthorne, Stoke-on-Trent 01782 838290
REDGATE CLAYTON........... Northwood Lane, Clayton, Newcastle-under-Lyme 01782 717409
ROCESTER RESERVES........... Hillsfield, Mill Street, Rocester, Uttoxeter ST14 5TX 01889 590463
STAFFORD RANGERS STRIPES.. Monkton Playing Field, Pinfold Lane, Penkridge, Stafford ST16 3BX 01785 602430
STALLINGTON........... Stallington Hospital, Fulford Lane, Stallington Road, Blythe Bridge ST11 9PD 07785 338804
STONE DOMINOES RESERVES........... Springbank Park, Yarnfield Road, Stone ST15 0NF 01782 761891
WOLSTANTON UNITED.. Bradwell Community Centre, Riceyman Road, Bradwell, Newcastle-under-Lyne ST5 8LF 01782 660818

IN: Ashbourne United (S – West Midlands (Regional) League Premier Division), Stafford Rangers Stripes (P)
OUT: Audley & District (WS), Fegg Hayes (F)

	Abbey Hulton United Res.	Alsagers Bank	Ball Haye Green Res.	Brocton Res.	Congleton Vale	Featherstone	Foley Res.	Hanley Town Res.	Holditch Grandy's	Holt JCB	Manor Inne	Newcastle Town Youth	Redgate Clayton Res.	Stafford Rangers Stripes	Stone Old Alleynians	Wedgwood Sports & Social
Abbey Hulton United Res.		1-5	1-2	0-1	0-1	0-9	1-2	1-3	n/a	2-3	0-1	3-0	1-2	1-3	2-2	2-0
Alsager Bank	2-0		3-1	6-0	1-1	4-2	3-1	2-3	n/a	6-0	1-3	2-2	1-3	0-0	3-3	2-8
Ball Haye Green Res.	8-1	2-1	*D*	1-0	0-1	3-3	2-5	0-0	3-0	4-2	0-2	1-1	0-1	0-4	4-0	0-3
Brocton Res.	4-1	0-2	4-1	*I*	1-5	1-6	3-2	2-1	n/a	5-1	1-0	0-2	2-3	0-7	1-1	1-3
Congleton Vale	1-1	2-1	5-1	3-0	*V*	5-0	2-0	2-1	n/a	2-1	4-1	4-0	4-0	0-1	4-1	0-0
Featherstone	6-1	1-3	1-3	4-0	0-5	*I*	2-5	5-3	n/a	3-1	1-0	6-3	0-7	0-3	2-1	2-0
Foley Res.	1-2	3-2	3-3	1-1	0-1	8-1	*S*	3-2	n/a	0-1	0-3	2-0	3-2	0-3	6-1	2-2
Hanley Town Res.	4-0	4-1	2-2	1-1	1-1	3-3	3-4	*I*	n/a	1-2	4-0	1-1	1-4	3-1	1-1	2-4
Holditch Grandy's	n/a	0-4	n/a	n/a	n/a	1-5	0-3	n/a	*O*	n/a	1-3	n/a	n/a	n/a	n/a	3-3
Holt JCB	0-1	0-3	3-1	4-0	1-1	0-2	0-4	1-4	n/a	*N*	0-1	2-1	0-2	0-4	0-5	2-2
Manor Inne	0-2	1-0	1-5	3-2	0-1	4-7	1-1	1-3	n/a	2-1		2-1	5-1	1-5	2-2	1-7
Newcastle Town Youth	3-2	2-3	0-5	1-1	2-4	2-6	4-4	0-9	n/a	3-3	0-3	*O*	1-0	1-10	0-1	3-0
Redgate Clayton Res.	6-0	1-1	4-1	1-1	3-1	3-0	1-2	1-3	2-0	1-1	2-1	4-1	*N*	2-3	2-2	1-1
Stafford Rangers Stripes	4-1	2-0	5-2	3-1	0-1	5-1	2-1	4-2	3-0	2-0	1-0	7-0	2-0	*E*	2-0	3-2
Stone Old Alleynians	0-2	1-3	3-0	2-2	0-1	1-2	1-1	1-4	n/a	2-2	0-0	3-1	0-1	0-2		1-3
Wedgwood Sports & Social	4-1	1-0	5-2	4-3	1-1	4-1	2-3	4-1	n/a	6-0	5-0	1-5	1-1	1-3	1-0	

Note – Holditch Grandy's withdrew during the course of the season
Their results are shown above but are expunged from the league table

Division One		P	W	D	L	F	A	Pts
Stafford Rangers Stripes		28	25	1	2	91	20	76
Congleton Vale		28	20	6	2	63	18	66
Wedgwood Sports & Social		28	15	6	7	75	43	51
Redgate Clayton Res.		28	14	6	8	59	39	48
Foley Res.		28	13	6	9	67	51	45
Featherstone		28	14	2	12	76	78	44
Alsagers Bank		28	12	5	11	61	48	41
Hanley Town Res.		28	11	7	10	70	52	40
Manor Inne	*-3*	28	11	3	14	39	57	33
Ball Haye Green Res.		28	9	5	14	54	64	32
Brocton Res.		28	7	6	15	38	69	27
Holt JCB		28	6	5	17	31	70	23
Stone Old Alleynians		28	4	10	14	35	54	22
Newcastle Town Youth		28	5	6	17	40	89	21
Abbey Hulton United Res.		28	6	2	20	30	77	20

Holditch Grandy's – record expunged

STAFFORDSHIRE COUNTY LEAGUE DIVISION ONE CONSTITUTION 2006-07

ABBEY HULTON UNITED RESERVES .... Birches Head Road, Abbey Hulton, Stoke-on-Trent ST2 8DD 01782 544232
ALSAGERS BANK .... The Drive, Alsagers Bank, Stoke-on-Trent ST7 8BB .... None
AUDLEY & DISTRICT .... Town Fields, Old Road, Bignall, Stoke-on-Trent ST7 8QH 01782 723482
BARLASTON .... Wedgwood Sports & Social, Barlaston Park, Barlaston, Stoke-on-Trent ST12 9ES 01782 373442
BIDDULPH TOWN .... Tunstall Road, Knypersley, Stoke-On-Trent ST8 7AQ 01782 522737
BROCTON RESERVES ... Heath Hayes FC, Coppice Colliery Ground, Newlands Lane, Heath Hayes, Cannock WS12 3HH .... None
CHESTERTON .... Red Street Community Centre, Talke Road, Newcastle-under-Lyme .... None
CONGLETON VALE .... Back Lane Playing Fields, Congleton CW12 .... 01260 276975
FEATHERSTONE .... HMP Featherstone, New Road, Featherstone, Wolverhampton WV10 7PU 01902 703132
FOLEY RESERVES .... Whitcombe Road, Meir, Stoke-on-Trent ST3 6NU 01782 595274
HANLEY TOWN RESERVES .... Abbey Lane, Abbey Hulton, Bucknall, Stoke-on-Trent ST8 8AJ 01782 267234
HOLT JCB .... JCB Lakeside Club, Station Road, Rocester, Uttoxeter ST14 5LS 01889 591057
MANOR INNE .... Sandyford Cricket Club, Shelford Road, Sandyford, Stoke-on-Trent ST6 5LA .... None
NEW PENNY .... Northwood Stadium, Keelings Road, Hanley, Stoke-on-Trent ST1 6PA 01782 234400
REDGATE CLAYTON RESERVES .... Northwood Lane, Clayton, Newcastle-under-Lyme 01782 717409
STONE OLD ALLEYNIANS .... Springbank Park, Yarnfield Road, Yarnfield, Stone ST15 0NF 01785 761891

IN: Audley & District (N), Biddulph Town (P), Chesterton (P), New Penny (P)
OUT: Ball Haye Green Reserves (W), Holditch Grandy's (WS), Stafford Rangers Stripes (P)
Wedgwood Sports & Social become Barlaston

	Ball Green Y & A	Biddulph Town	Cheadle Town Old Boys	Chesterton	Chesterton Youth & Adult	Fegg Hayes Res.	Hawkins Sport Youth	Holt JCB Res.	Milton United	New Penny	Screwfix Direct	Stone Old Alleynians Res.	Tunstall Town
Ball Green Y & A	*D*	2-3	0-2	0-3	3-1	0-0	1-2	6-1	1-4	1-1	5-2	6-2	8-2
Biddulph Town	4-1	*I*	4-2	1-2	1-1	5-0	2-0	5-1	3-0	1-1	2-1	3-2	15-2
Cheadle Town Old Boys	2-3	1-1	*V*	2-4	2-2	4-0	2-0	2-1	2-1	1-1	7-0	3-0	6-1
Chesterton	3-2	1-1	2-0	*I*	5-3	3-0	3-1	6-0	3-0	1-3	5-1	2-1	9-0
Chesterton Youth & Adult	0-4	1-5	1-2	0-3	*S*	3-1	1-1	1-1	4-4	2-3	1-3	3-3	6-1
Fegg Hayes Res.	1-2	0-3	2-3	0-6	5-0	*I*	2-5	2-0	3-3	3-4	4-1	3-5	6-0
Hawkins Sport Youth	1-1	1-1	2-1	1-2	1-1	2-2	*O*	0-1	1-2	3-3	4-0	5-0	6-0
Holt JCB Res.	0-2	1-2	0-2	1-6	0-2	2-2	1-3	*N*	2-2	1-6	1-0	0-2	3-1
Milton United	0-2	1-3	1-1	0-2	2-2	3-3	1-3	4-1		1-1	3-0	1-2	7-1
New Penny	4-0	0-0	2-1	2-2	1-0	7-5	2-1	4-0	0-0		10-0	4-1	8-2
Screwfix Direct	0-4	1-2	0-6	0-6	0-7	1-8	0-8	0-5	1-6	1-2	*T*	1-3	2-2
Stone Old Alleynians Res.	2-1	1-3	1-3	3-0	1-2	3-3	2-1	4-0	0-2	1-1	4-0	*W*	14-0
Tunstall Town	1-10	0-7	1-9	0-9	0-5	2-8	0-6	0-5	0-4	0-11	2-4	1-5	*O*

Division Two	P	W	D	L	F	A	Pts
Chesterton	24	20	2	2	88	22	62
Biddulph Town	24	17	6	1	77	23	57
New Penny	24	15	9	0	81	28	54
Cheadle Town Old Boys	24	14	4	6	66	30	46
Ball Green Y & A	24	12	3	9	65	41	39
Hawkins Sport Youth	24	10	6	8	58	31	36
Stone Old Alleynians Res.	24	11	3	10	62	48	36
Milton United	24	8	8	8	52	41	32
Chesterton Youth & Adult	24	6	8	10	49	52	26
Fegg Hayes Res.	24	6	6	12	63	67	24
Holt JCB Res.	24	5	3	16	28	64	18
Screwfix Direct	24	2	1	21	19	107	7
Tunstall Town	24	0	1	23	19	173	1

DIVISION TWO CUP

FIRST ROUND

Ball Green Y & A 3 Stone Old Alleynians 1

Cheadle Town Old Boys 0 **Biddulph Town** 0 *aet* (1-4p)

Chesterton Youth & Adult 3 Screwfix 1

Hawkins Spts Yth 1 **Chesterton** 2

Tunstall Town 0 **Milton United** 5

QUARTER-FINALS

Ball Green Y & A 7 Fegg Hayes Res. 0

Biddulph Town 4 Milton United 1

Chesterton 4 Chesterton Youth & Adult 0

Holt JCB Res. 0 **New Penny** 1

SEMI-FINALS

Biddulph Town 2 **New Penny** 3

Chesterton 1 **Ball Green Y & A** 2

FINAL

(March 20th at Newcastle Town)

New Penny 2 Ball Green Y & A 0

STAFFORDSHIRE COUNTY LEAGUE DIVISION TWO CONSTITUTION 2006-07

BALL GREEN Y & A. .... **Wilding Road, Ball Green, Stoke-on-Trent ST6 8BA** .... **None**
CHEADLE TOWN OLD BOYS .... **Cheadle Leisure Centre, Allen Street, Cheadle ST10 1HJ** **01538 753331**
CHESTERTON YOUTH & ADULT .... **Loomer Road, Chesterton, Newcastle-under-Lyme ST5 7LB** .... **None**
HAWKINS SPORT YOUTH ...... **Hawkins Sports Club, Coppice Lane, Cheslyn Hay, Walsall WS6 7EY** .... **None**
LEEK CSOB RESERVES .... **Birchall Playing Field, Cheddleton Road, Leek.** .... **None**
LICHFIELD ENOTS .... **Brownsfield Road, off Eastern Avenue, Lichfield WS13 6SB** **01543 254361**
MILTON UNITED .... **Leek Road, Milton, Stoke-on-Trent ST9 9NJ** .... **None**
REAL MACOT .... **Watery Lane, Longton, Stoke-on-Trent.** .... **None**
SCREWFIX DIRECT .... **Blurton High School, Beaconsfield Drive, Trentham, Stoke-on-Trent ST3 3HU** .... **None**
STAFFORD RANGERS STRIPES RESERVES .. **Monkton Playing Field, Pinfold Lane, Penkridge, Stafford ST16 3BX.** **01785 602430**
STALLINGTON RESERVES .. **Stallington Hospital, Fulford Lane, Stallington Road, Blythe Bridge ST11 9PD** **07785 338804**
STONE OLD ALLEYNIANS RESERVES ... **Springbank Park, Yarnfield Road, Yarnfield, Stone ST15 0NF** **01785 761891**
STRETTON EAGLES 2004 .... **Pirelli Sports Ground, Burton-on-Trent** .... **None**
TUNSTALL TOWN .... **Kidsgrove Athletic FC, Hollinwood Road, Kidsgrove, Stoke-on-Trent ST7 1BQ** **01782 782412**
WOLSTANTON UNITED RESERVES ... **Bradwell Community Centre, Riceyman Road, Bradwell, Stoke-on-Trent** **01782 660818**

IN: Leek CSOB Reserves (P – Youth football), Lichfield Enots (P – Burton & District FA Division One), Real Macot (Sunday football), Stafford Rangers Stripes Reserves (N), Stallington Reserves (N), Stretton Eagles 2004 (P – Burton & District FA Division One), Wolstanton United Reserves (N)
OUT: Biddulph Town (P), Chesterton (P), Holt JCB Reserves (W), New Penny (P)

TROPHY *(Division One and Two teams)*

FIRST ROUND

Chesterton 0 **Stone Old Alleynians Res.** 1

Hanley Town Res. 6 Chesterton Youth & Adult 2

Hawkins Sports Youth 1 **Cheadle Town Old Boys** 2

Holt JCB 0 **Brocton Res.** 1 *aet*

Holt JCB Res. 4 Biddulph Town 1

New Penny 5 Holditch Grandy's 1

Newcastle Town Youth 5 Ball Green Y & A 1

Redgate Clayton Res. 2 Foley Res. 1

Stafford Rangers Stripes 4 Ball Haye Green Res. 0

Stone Old Alleynians 4 Milton United 0

Tunstall Town 0 **Manor Inne** 4

Wedgwood Sports & Social 4 Alsagers Bank 0

SECOND ROUND

Abbey Hulton Unted Res. 4 Screwfix 0

Cheadle Town Old Boys 5 Newcastle Town Youth 0

Congleton Vale 4 Manor Inne 2

Fegg Hayes Res. 1 **Wedgwood Sports & Social** 3 *aet*

New Penny 3 Hanley Town Res. 2

Redgate Clayton Res. 3 Stone Old Alleynians Res. 2

Stafford Rangers Stripes 4 Brocton Res. 1

Stone Old Alleynians 0 **Holt JCB Res.** 3

QUARTER-FINALS

Cheadle Town Old Boys 2 Holt JCB Res. 2 *aet* (4-3p)

Congleton Vale 3 **Wedgwood Sports & Social** 6

Redgate Clayton Res. 0 **New Penny** 1

Stafford Rangers Stripes 10 Abbey Hulton United Res. 1

SEMI-FINALS

Cheadle Town Old Boys 1 **New Penny** 2

Stafford Rangers Stripes 3 Wedgwood Sports & Social 0

FINAL *(April 5th at Newcastle Town)*

Stafford Rangers Stripes 3 New Penny 2 *aet*

SUFFOLK & IPSWICH LEAGUE

	Achilles	Brantham Athletic	Capel Plough	Cockfield United	Crane Sports	East Bergholt United	Felixstowe United	Framlingham Town	Grundisburgh	Haughley United	Ipswich Athletic	Leiston St Margarets	Melton St Audrys	Ransomes Sports	Stonham Aspal	Westerfield United
Achilles	*S*	2-1	1-1	1-1	2-2	0-1	3-3	2-2	2-2	4-2	2-0	5-0	7-0	2-0	4-2	2-3
Brantham Athletic	2-3	*E*	0-0	1-4	1-5	2-6	0-2	1-1	0-6	0-0	2-1	1-3	1-1	1-1	1-0	1-5
Capel Plough	3-5	1-0	*N*	1-1	0-1	0-2	5-2	3-1	1-0	1-1	3-1	2-0	1-3	1-2	2-2	2-1
Cockfield United	0-0	1-3	1-1	*I*	1-1	0-3	2-0	1-1	4-1	1-1	3-2	2-2	5-1	0-0	0-0	1-3
Crane Sports	2-3	2-1	4-1	1-1	*O*	1-2	3-1	3-1	2-0	1-3	2-1	0-0	1-0	0-0	1-0	2-2
East Bergholt United	1-3	3-3	0-0	2-0	0-1	*R*	2-0	2-2	0-1	0-3	1-0	1-0	3-0	3-0	4-1	1-0
Felixstowe United	1-0	1-3	3-2	3-1	1-1	0-3		1-3	0-2	1-3	0-2	1-0	2-2	1-4	3-2	0-0
Framlingham Town	2-2	2-2	1-1	1-3	1-1	2-0	1-4		2-3	1-2	1-1	2-3	1-0	2-4	1-2	2-3
Grundisburgh	3-3	3-0	3-3	2-0	1-0	2-0	0-1	0-0	*D*	0-1	1-0	2-3	1-0	2-3	2-0	1-1
Haughley United	2-2	2-4	2-0	2-2	0-0	0-1	4-2	1-0	3-5	*I*	0-0	2-1	2-0	5-1	2-2	4-1
Ipswich Athletic	3-3	5-4	0-3	3-0	2-3	0-0	3-1	2-2	1-0	2-0	*V*	3-0	4-1	1-1	3-3	3-5
Leiston St Margarets	1-5	2-1	3-2	3-0	2-1	0-4	2-3	3-2	1-4	2-2	2-1	*I*	1-0	1-2	5-2	2-4
Melton St Audrys	1-0	0-2	3-1	1-1	3-1	3-2	3-0	1-0	3-2	2-0	1-1	2-1	*S*	3-1	2-2	2-3
Ransomes Sports	0-1	2-2	1-1	3-0	1-2	2-2	1-3	1-1	1-0	2-0	2-1	3-1	6-0	*I*	1-0	1-2
Stonham Aspal	3-2	2-4	3-1	4-7	1-5	0-1	4-1	0-3	1-1	1-4	1-4	2-2	2-5	1-3	*O*	0-2
Westerfield United	1-2	0-3	0-5	1-5	2-1	7-1	2-2	2-1	0-2	3-4	1-1	1-1	3-2	1-2	5-1	*N*

Senior Division		P	W	D	L	F	A	Pts
East Bergholt United		30	17	5	8	51	33	56
Achilles		30	14	11	5	73	45	53
Crane Sports		30	14	9	7	50	34	51
Ransomes Sports		30	14	8	8	51	40	50
Grundisburgh		30	14	6	10	52	36	48
Westerfield United		30	14	6	10	64	57	48
Haughley United	*-4*	30	14	9	7	57	42	47
Leiston St Margarets		30	11	5	14	47	62	38
Capel Plough		30	9	10	11	48	47	37
Cockfield United		30	8	13	9	48	48	37
Ipswich Athletic		30	9	9	12	51	48	36
Melton St Audrys	*-6*	30	12	5	13	45	57	35
Felixstowe United		30	10	5	15	43	63	35
Brantham Athletic		30	8	8	14	47	66	32
Framlingham Town		30	4	12	14	42	54	24
Stonham Aspal		30	4	7	19	44	81	19

Division One		P	W	D	L	F	A	Pts
Coplestonians		26	17	5	4	71	30	56
Stowupland		26	15	8	3	60	35	53
BT Trimley		26	16	3	7	54	27	51
Old Newton United		26	13	8	5	58	35	47
Thurston		26	14	2	10	84	48	44
Stanton		26	11	7	8	48	44	40
St Edmunds '65		26	11	6	9	56	54	39
Needham Market 'A'	*-6*	26	13	6	7	38	38	39
Woodbridge Athletic		26	8	7	11	34	47	31
Willis		26	6	7	13	36	64	25
Wickham Market		26	7	3	16	35	54	24
Bramford United		26	6	6	14	31	51	24
Ipswich Exiles		26	4	5	17	36	72	17
Wenhaston United	*-3*	26	3	3	20	24	66	9

SUFFOLK & IPSWICH LEAGUE SENIOR DIVISION CONSTITUTION 2006-07

ACHILLES .... **Pauls Social Club, Selmet Close, Ipswich IP2 9BA** **01473 604874**
BRANTHAM ATHLETIC..... **Athletic & Social Club, New Village, Brantham, near Manningtree CO11 1RZ** **01206 392506**
CAPEL PLOUGH.......................... **Friars, Capel St Mary, Ipswich IP9 2XS** .... **None**
COCKFIELD UNITED.......................... **Green Green, Cockfield, Bury St Edmunds IP30 0HJ**.......................... **None**
COPLESTONIANS.......................... **Copleston High School, Copleston Road, Ipswich IP4 5HD**.......................... **01473 244178**
CRANE SPORTS.......................... **King George V Playing Field, Old Norwich Road, Ipswich IP1 6LE**.......................... **01473 464030**
EAST BERGHOLT UNITED.......................... **Gandish Road, East Bergholt, Colchester CO7 6TP**.......................... **07775 691526**
FELIXSTOWE UNITED.......................... **Kirton Recreation Ground, Back Road, Kirton, Ipswich IP10 0PW**.......................... **None**
GRUNDISBURGH.......................... **The Playing Field, Ipswich Road, Grundisburgh, Woodbridge IP13 6TJ**.......................... **01473 738234**
HAUGHLEY UNITED.......................... **King George V Playing Field, Green Road, Haughley IP14 3RA**.......................... **01449 673460**
IPSWICH ATHLETIC .... **Bourne Vale Social Ground, Halifax Road, Ipswich IP2 8RE**.......................... **None**
LEISTON ST MARGARETS .... **Junction Meadow, Abbey Road, Leiston IP16 4RD**.......................... **01728 831239**
MELTON ST AUDRYS..... **St Audrys Sports & Social Club, Lodge Farm Lane, Melton, Woodbridge IP12 1LX**.......................... **None**
RANSOMES SPORTS.......................... **Ransomes Sports & Social Club, Sidegate Avenue, Ipswich IP4 4JJ**.......................... **01473 726134**
STOWUPLAND FALCONS .... **The Village Hall, Church Road, Stowupland IP14 4BQ**.......................... **01449 771010**
WESTERFIELD UNITED...... **Rushmere Sports Club, The Street, Rushmere St Andrew, Ipswich IP5 1DE**.......................... **01473 272525**

IN: Coplestonians (P), Stowupland Falcons (formerly Stowupland) (P)

OUT: Framlingham Town (R), Stonham Aspal (R)

LEAGUE CUP

THIRD ROUND
Albion Mills 3 Trimley Red Devils 0
Bildeston Rangers 1 **Framlingham Town** 2
Bramford Road Old Boys 1 **Ransomes Sports** 4
Bramford United 0 **Stonham Aspal** 2
Capel Plough 1 **Achilles** 3 *(at Achilles)*
Cockfield United 11 Stowmarket Stag 0
Coplestonians 4 Claydon 0
East Bergholt United 1 Leiston St Margarets 0
Felixstowe United 2 **Crane Sports** 3
Grundisburgh 3 Stradbroke United 0
Haughley United 2 **St Johns** 5
Ipswich Athletic 2 Ipswich Exiles 1
Ipswich Postals 1 **Willis** 3
Old Newton United 4 Brantham Athletic 0
Saxmundham Sports 3 **St Edmunds '65** 5
Westerfield United 3 Melton St Audrys 0
FOURTH ROUND
Achilles 4 Grundisburgh 0
Cockfield United 0 **Old Newton United** 2
Crane Sports 4 Stonham Aspal 0
East Bergholt United 0 Willis 0 *aet* (4-3p)
Ipswich Athletic 4 Framlingham Town 2
Ransomes Sports 10 Albion Mills 0
St Edmonds '65 2 **Coplestonians** 3
St Johns 1 Westerfield United 1 *aet* (8-7p)
QUARTER-FINALS
Achilles 3 East Bergholt United 2
Coplestonians 5 St Johns 1
Crane Sports 2 **Old Newton United** 4
Ransomes Sports 2 Ipswich Athletic 0
SEMI-FINALS
Coplestonians 2 **Achilles** 4 *(at Westerfield United)*
Old Newton United 0 **Ransomes Sports** 3 *(at Grundisburgh)*
FINAL
(May 9th at Woodbridge Town)
Ransomes Sports 2 Achilles 1 *aet*

Division Two		P	W	D	L	F	A	Pts
St Johns		26	22	0	4	92	21	66
Mendlesham Kings Head		26	18	2	6	79	47	56
Halesworth Town		26	13	1	12	52	65	40
AFC Hoxne	-3	26	11	9	6	56	53	39
Bacton United		26	10	7	9	74	72	37
Dennington United		26	10	7	9	53	55	37
Bramford Road Old Boys		26	10	6	10	52	45	36
Claydon		26	10	6	10	51	46	36
Stradbroke United		26	10	3	13	64	62	33
John Bull United		26	10	3	13	58	69	33
Coddenham		26	8	7	11	44	48	31
Salvation Army		26	9	4	13	47	58	31
Somersham		26	9	2	15	41	50	29
Murray Rangers	-3	26	3	1	22	33	105	7

Division Three		P	W	D	L	F	A	Pts
Bildeston Rangers		26	21	0	5	101	46	63
Peasenhall United		26	19	3	4	90	38	60
Sporting '87		26	15	4	7	63	35	49
Parkside United		26	15	2	9	82	57	47
Albion Mills		26	11	4	11	56	56	37
Elmswell		26	12	1	13	46	57	37
Sproughton Sports		26	9	4	13	53	64	31
Martlesham Athletic		26	9	4	13	49	78	31
Coplestonians 'A'	-6	26	11	3	12	57	56	30
Ipswich United	-3	26	10	3	13	71	75	30
Ufford Sports		26	9	3	14	35	70	30
St Clements Hospital	-6	26	10	4	12	31	44	28
Walsham-le-Willows 'A'		26	6	2	18	26	65	20
Henley Athletic		26	3	7	16	32	51	16

Division Four		P	W	D	L	F	A	Pts
Saxmundham Sports		26	22	3	1	113	27	69
Alstons		26	20	0	6	99	51	60
Tacket Street BBOB		26	13	6	7	70	40	45
Sizewell & Aldeburgh		26	13	5	8	80	66	44
Great Blakenham		26	14	1	11	55	48	43
Benhall St Mary		26	12	5	9	53	56	41
Ipswich Postals		26	11	3	12	73	68	36
Henley Athletic Res.		26	10	6	10	45	50	36
Tattingstone United		26	9	5	12	60	67	32
Waterside		26	8	6	12	52	65	30
East Bergholt United 'A'	-3	26	9	2	15	67	91	26
Claydon Res.	-3	26	8	4	14	51	63	25
Bramford Road Old Boys Res.		26	5	3	18	39	80	18
Haughley United 'A'		26	2	3	21	23	108	9

Division Five		P	W	D	L	F	A	Pts
Meadlands		26	21	3	2	118	29	66
Stowmarket Stag		26	20	4	2	82	31	64
Somersham Res.		26	17	6	3	77	34	57
Trimley Red Devils	-6	26	19	3	4	109	24	54
St Clements Hospital Res.		26	11	7	8	67	50	40
Stonham Aspal 'A'		26	12	4	10	54	46	40
Bacton United Res.		26	11	2	13	62	87	35
Stowupland 'A'		26	9	3	14	61	86	30
Needham Market Youth		26	7	4	15	40	62	25
Stradbroke United Res.		26	6	4	16	40	76	22
Salvation Army Res.		26	5	4	17	43	86	19
Mendlesham Kings Head Res.		26	4	7	15	43	87	19
Old Newton United 'A'		26	6	1	19	36	91	19
AFC Hoxne Res.	-6	26	7	2	17	42	85	17

Division Six		P	W	D	L	F	A	Pts
Woolverstone United		24	19	0	5	74	31	57
Claydon 'A'		24	16	2	6	81	35	50
Coddenham Res.		24	14	6	4	68	32	48
Sproughton Sports Res.		24	14	1	9	50	38	43
Elmswell Res.		24	11	5	8	50	54	38
Needham Market Vets		24	11	2	11	61	55	35
Peasenhall United Res.		24	9	4	11	41	58	31
St Johns Res.		24	9	2	13	64	80	29
Albion Mills Res.		24	8	4	12	50	62	28
Tacket Street BBOB Res.		24	7	5	12	40	54	26
BT Trimley 'A'	-4	24	9	2	13	48	67	25
Halesworth Town Res.		24	6	6	12	42	57	24
Dennington United Res.		24	3	1	20	33	79	10

Intermediate Division A		P	W	D	L	F	A	Pts
Haughley United Res.		26	20	2	4	83	25	62
Felixstowe United Res.		26	12	5	9	46	56	41
Capel Plough Res.		26	11	5	10	46	46	38
East Bergholt United Res.	-3	25	13	1	11	59	50	37
Crane Sports Res.		25	11	4	10	49	55	37
Westerfield United Res.		26	10	6	10	67	67	36
Grundisburgh Res.		26	11	3	12	73	88	36
Leiston St Margarets Res.		26	10	5	11	48	48	35
Coplestonians Res.	-6	26	12	4	10	57	43	34
Old Newton United Res.		26	10	4	12	50	61	34
Ipswich Athletic Res.		26	9	6	11	58	44	33
Achilles Res.		26	9	6	11	55	49	33
Stanton Res.		26	8	3	15	39	69	27
Stowupland Res.		26	6	4	16	39	68	22

Crane Sports Res. v East Bergholt Res. not played

RESERVES CUP

FINAL
(May 5th at Needham Market)
Melton St Audrys Res. 1 Debenham Leisure Centre Res. 0

JUNIOR CUP

FINAL
(April 28th at Framlingham Town)
Coplestonians 'A' 1 Somersham Res. 0

Intermediate Division B		P	W	D	L	F	A	Pts
Cockfield United Res.		28	18	7	3	77	36	61
Brantham Athletic Res.		28	17	5	6	79	33	56
Framlingham Town Res.		28	17	5	6	77	38	56
Debenham Leisure Centre Res.		28	15	7	6	61	28	52
Melton St Audrys Res.		27	14	6	7	68	46	48
BT Trimley Res.		28	14	2	12	58	68	44
Woodbridge Athletic Res.	-3	28	14	3	11	56	45	42
Ransomes Sports Res.		28	11	8	9	73	49	41
Stonham Aspal Res.		28	12	4	12	47	66	40
Willis Res.		28	10	2	16	66	77	32
Thurston Res.		28	10	1	17	60	95	31
Bramford United Res.	-3	28	10	3	15	41	51	30
Wenhaston United Res.		27	8	4	15	39	56	28
Wickham Market Res.		28	5	0	23	35	90	15
Ipswich Exiles Res.	-3	28	4	3	21	34	93	12

Melton St Audrys Res. v Wenhaston Utd Res. not played

SUSSEX COUNTY LEAGUE

	Arundel	Chichester City U	Crowborough Ath	East Preston	Eastbourne Town	Eastbourne U Ass	Hailsham Town	Hassocks	Horsham YMCA	Littlehampton Tn	Redhill	Ringmer	Rye & Iden Utd	Shoreham	Sidley United	Southwick	Three Bridges	Whitehawk	Wick	Worthing United
Arundel		2-0	2-0	2-2	3-2	1-1	0-0	2-0	1-0	1-1	4-0	0-1	1-3	4-1	2-1	6-1	2-2	3-1	4-2	1-1
Chichester City United	1-1		2-1	1-0	0-4	1-2	2-2	2-3	0-1	2-1	3-1	2-1	2-1	3-2	4-0	2-2	1-4	1-2	1-0	2-2
Crowborough Athletic	1-1	2-3		1-2	0-0	5-2	2-0	2-1	0-2	0-1	4-0	2-3	3-0	1-0	7-0	4-1	3-0	1-0	2-1	1-0
East Preston	2-0	1-0	2-2		0-0	1-1	2-2	1-0	2-6	1-1	1-2	1-1	2-2	1-1	2-1	1-2	2-2	0-0	2-4	0-0
Eastbourne Town	0-1	0-1	1-1	3-3	*D*	1-1	3-2	0-1	0-1	0-0	3-1	1-0	2-1	3-2	5-2	6-0	1-0	1-3	3-1	2-1
Eastbourne United Association	0-1	1-2	1-2	1-0	2-1	*I*	1-1	1-1	1-4	0-4	2-1	0-1	2-1	2-3	0-1	2-2	1-2	2-1	0-1	1-2
Hailsham Town	0-3	1-1	2-0	0-0	1-1	1-2	*V*	0-0	0-1	2-0	2-0	0-0	3-2	1-3	2-1	1-0	0-0	0-2	1-3	0-2
Hassocks	1-1	0-1	3-2	2-1	5-2	2-2	2-2	*I*	1-2	2-4	2-0	0-0	6-1	0-1	6-2	2-0	3-0	2-1	2-0	0-1
Horsham YMCA	4-2	1-1	5-1	0-0	2-1	3-1	0-0	2-0	*S*	2-0	2-0	1-2	2-2	1-2	5-2	5-0	0-1	1-1	3-0	2-0
Littlehampton Town	1-1	2-0	3-1	2-0	2-1	0-3	2-1	2-2	1-2	*I*	2-1	1-2	2-1	3-1	4-0	2-0	2-2	2-1	0-0	1-0
Redhill	2-1	1-3	0-0	1-2	0-3	0-2	1-3	0-5	1-2	2-1	*O*	1-3	3-0	1-4	4-1	2-0	2-1	0-4	0-0	1-2
Ringmer	1-1	2-0	3-4	3-0	0-2	3-1	0-1	4-0	1-1	2-1	4-1	*N*	2-1	2-1	3-0	3-0	1-0	0-0	1-1	2-0
Rye & Iden United	1-1	0-5	0-3	2-0	0-2	1-2	2-2	1-1	1-3	0-6	1-2	0-2		0-1	L-W	2-2	0-1	0-1	1-1	2-0
Shoreham	0-0	1-1	0-0	3-0	1-1	3-1	2-4	3-3	0-1	2-1	2-1	0-1	4-2	*O*	2-3	1-0	0-3	0-2	0-2	2-3
Sidley United	2-0	2-0	2-2	3-1	1-4	4-0	0-1	4-2	1-1	0-1	1-0	4-0	5-3	2-1	*N*	6-1	2-0	0-2	0-3	3-2
Southwick	0-1	2-2	0-2	2-0	0-4	0-5	1-2	1-1	0-4	2-3	2-2	1-3	1-1	0-1	1-3	*E*	0-0	0-2	0-1	2-2
Three Bridges	1-2	2-2	0-1	3-1	4-1	0-1	0-1	0-1	0-2	1-2	1-1	1-2	2-0	1-3	3-1	3-1		1-1	2-4	0-0
Whitehawk	5-1	3-2	1-2	1-0	0-1	2-0	1-2	0-1	2-3	3-0	4-1	3-1	2-0	2-1	1-1	2-0	1-1		2-0	5-0
Wick	1-1	0-2	1-1	1-2	1-3	2-0	3-0	0-0	2-3	1-2	0-1	1-2	3-0	3-1	3-2	4-1	1-1	4-1		1-2
Worthing United	1-1	2-3	0-2	2-3	0-1	1-1	1-0	0-0	1-3	2-0	1-2	0-6	1-3	0-3	2-2	5-0	1-1	1-1	0-0	

Division One	P	W	D	L	F	A	Pts
Horsham YMCA	38	27	7	4	83	31	88
Ringmer	38	24	7	7	68	34	79
Whitehawk	38	20	7	11	66	36	67
Littlehampton Town	38	20	7	11	63	44	67
Eastbourne Town	38	19	8	11	69	44	65
Crowborough Athletic	38	19	8	11	68	45	65
Arundel	38	16	15	7	61	43	63
Chichester City United	38	17	9	12	61	55	60
Hassocks	38	15	12	11	63	48	57
Hailsham Town	38	13	13	12	43	46	52
Sidley United	38	16	4	18	65	80	52
Wick	38	14	9	15	56	49	51
Shoreham	38	15	6	17	58	59	51
Eastbourne Utd Assoc.	38	12	8	18	48	62	44
Three Bridges	38	10	12	16	46	50	42
East Preston	38	8	15	15	41	60	39
Worthing United	38	9	12	17	41	60	39
Redhill	38	10	4	24	39	78	34
Rye & Iden United	38	4	8	26	38	83	20
Southwick	38	2	9	27	28	98	15

JOHN O'HARA LEAGUE CUP

(Division One and Two teams)

FIRST ROUND

Eastbourne United Association 2 Storrington 0

Hailsham Town 1 Lancing 0

Littlehampton Town 2 **Oakwood** 3

Midhurst & Easebourne Utd 3 **Chichester City United** 4

Saltdean Utd 3 **Crowborough Athletic** 4

Three Bridges 2 Bexhill United 0

SECOND ROUND

Arundel 1 **Selsey** 2

East Grinstead Town 2 Ringmer 1

East Preston 3 Sidlesham 2

Eastbourne Utd Association 1 **Whitehawk** 4

Hailsham Town 2 Seaford Town 0

Hassocks 6 Crawley Down 0

Mile Oak 0 **Worthing United** 3

Oakwood 1 **Sidley United** 2

Pagham 0 **Chichester City United** 3

Redhill 0 **Three Bridges** 1

Shoreham 5 Broadbridge Heath 0

Southwick 3 **Crowborough Athletic** 4

St Francis Rangers 0 **Rye & Iden Utd** 1

Steyning Town 0 **Eastbourne Town** 3

Wealden 3 Wick 0

Westfield 1 **Horsham YMCA** 5

THIRD ROUND

East Grinstead Tn 1 **Worthing United** 3

Hailsham Town 1 **East Preston** 2

Hassocks 1 Eastbourne Town 1 *aet*

Eastbourne Town 1 **Hassocks** 3 *replay*

Rye & Iden United 0 **Shoreham** 3

Selsey 3 Chichester City United 1

Three Bridges 3 **Crowborough Athletic** 4

Wealden 2 Horsham YMCA 1

Whitehawk 1 Sidley United 0

QUARTER-FINALS

Hassocks 1 **Crowborough Athletic** 2

Selsey 0 **Whitehawk** 2

Shoreham 6 East Preston 2

Worthing United 1 **Wealden** 6

SEMI-FINALS

Shoreham 2 Crowborough Athletic 1

(at Three Bridges)

Wealden 0 **Whitehawk** 1 *aet*

(at Ringmer)

FINAL

(April 14th at Three Bridges)

Whitehawk 1 **Shoreham** 2

SUSSEX COUNTY LEAGUE DIVISION ONE CONSTITUTION 2006-07

ARUNDEL .... Mill Road, Arundel BN18 9PA 01903 882548
CHICHESTER CITY UNITED .... Portfield, Church Road, Chichester PO19 4HN 01243 779875
CROWBOROUGH ATHLETIC .. Alderbrook Recreation Ground, Fermor Road, Crowborough TN6 3BT 01892 661893
EAST PRESTON .... Roundstone Recreation Ground, Lashmar Road, East Preston BN16 1ES 01903 776026
EASTBOURNE TOWN .... The Saffrons Sports Club, Compton Place Road, Eastbourne BN21 1EA 01323 723734
EASTBOURNE UNITED ASSOCIATION .. The Oval, Channel View Road, Eastbourne BN22 7LN 01323 726989
HAILSHAM TOWN .... The Beaconsfield, Western Road, Hailsham BN27 3DN 01323 840446
HASSOCKS .... The Beacon, Brighton Road, Hassocks BN6 9LY 01273 846040
LITTLEHAMPTON TOWN .... The Sportsfield, St Flora's Road, Littlehampton BN17 6BB 01903 732030
OAKWOOD .... Oakwood Sports & Social Club, Tinsley Lane, Three Bridges RH10 8AW 01293 515742
REDHILL .... Kiln Brow, Three Arch Road, Redhill RH1 1HL 01737 762129
RINGMER .... Caburn Ground, Anchor Field, Ringmer BN8 5QN 01273 812738
RYE UNITED .... Rye Cricket & Football Salts, Fishmarket Road, Rye TN31 7LP 01797 223855
SELSEY .... High Street Ground, Selsey, Chichester PO20 0QG 01243 603420
SHOREHAM .... Middle Road, Shoreham BN43 6LT 01273 454261
SIDLEY UNITED .... Gullivers, North Road, Bexhill TN39 5BL 01424 217078
THREE BRIDGES .... Jubilee Field, Jubilee Way, Three Bridges, Crawley RH10 1LQ 01293 442000
WHITEHAWK .... Enclosed Ground, East Brighton Park, Brighton BN2 5TS 01273 609736
WICK .... Crabtree Park, Coomes Way, Wick, Littlehampton BN17 7LS 01903 713535
WORTHING UNITED .... Robert Albon Memorial Ground, Lyons Way, Worthing BN14 9JF 01903 234466

IN: Oakwood (P), Selsey (P)

OUT: Horsham YMCA (P – Isthmian League Division One South), Southwick (R)

Rye & Iden United become Rye United

	Bexhill United	Broadbridge Heath	Crawley Down	East Grinstead Town	Lancing	Midhurst & Easebourne Utd	Mile Oak	Oakwood	Pagham	Saltdean United	Seaford Town	Selsey	Sidlesham	St Francis Rangers	Steyning Town	Storrington	Wealden	Westfield
Bexhill United		2-3	1-3	0-2	1-3	2-2	1-1	0-5	1-1	1-2	0-4	0-4	2-1	1-5	0-2	2-1	1-3	1-3
Broadbridge Heath	3-0		1-2	0-0	0-2	3-0	2-1	0-5	2-2	3-2	2-4	1-2	2-1	0-3	0-1	3-0	1-2	1-0
Crawley Down	4-1	4-0		3-0	2-1	2-0	1-2	0-1	0-0	4-1	3-1	2-0	1-1	1-2	5-1	3-2	2-0	2-3
East Grinstead Town	5-1	2-1	0-0	*D*	2-1	4-2	1-1	0-3	1-4	1-3	4-1	0-3	1-2	0-4	4-1	4-1	1-4	4-2
Lancing	2-0	3-1	0-1	1-3	*I*	2-2	1-0	1-2	2-1	2-0	1-2	1-0	2-2	0-0	0-1	4-0	1-3	0-5
Midhurst & Easebourne United	5-0	0-1	1-1	0-5	2-0	*V*	2-0	0-0	0-1	2-1	3-2	3-3	1-1	1-5	2-1	3-2	1-2	0-3
Mile Oak	3-3	8-2	3-0	2-5	5-1	2-0	*I*	0-2	4-1	2-2	1-0	2-1	5-2	2-0	3-1	0-1	2-1	2-3
Oakwood	0-1	3-0	1-1	3-1	3-1	3-2	4-0	*S*	4-2	4-0	4-0	1-4	3-1	3-1	7-2	1-0	0-1	2-1
Pagham	9-0	1-1	3-2	0-5	1-1	1-1	1-1	1-1	*I*	0-1	2-0	1-1	1-1	1-4	6-1	2-2	1-3	1-2
Saltdean United	1-0	2-3	2-2	0-1	0-1	2-1	1-2	1-4	3-1	*O*	2-2	0-2	3-0	3-2	2-1	0-2	0-3	0-2
Seaford Town	3-0	1-1	1-1	5-0	2-1	1-0	0-1	0-4	4-1	1-6	*N*	2-3	3-1	1-3	2-2	0-1	4-0	1-3
Selsey	9-0	1-2	2-0	2-0	3-0	2-0	2-0	0-0	3-0	8-1	3-2		1-1	1-2	2-0	1-0	2-0	2-1
Sidlesham	4-2	4-3	5-0	1-0	2-0	3-0	1-1	0-1	1-2	0-2	0-0	1-5	*T*	2-4	2-1	3-2	1-1	0-1
St Francis Rangers	3-0	3-3	1-0	3-1	1-1	3-1	6-1	1-5	2-1	6-0	5-0	1-2	1-1	*W*	3-2	0-0	4-0	3-1
Steyning Town	1-1	2-1	1-4	2-4	1-1	1-2	2-3	1-0	1-4	1-0	3-1	1-1	1-1	3-3	*O*	3-0	0-1	3-1
Storrington	4-1	1-0	2-2	1-5	0-2	3-1	1-0	0-4	1-1	5-0	2-2	2-3	3-1	0-0	0-3		0-2	4-1
Wealden	3-1	2-6	2-2	1-2	2-2	3-2	1-1	1-1	3-9	4-1	1-2	1-1	0-5	3-0	3-3	4-0		4-2
Westfield	5-1	3-1	1-1	3-2	3-1	5-0	1-0	1-3	4-2	2-1	0-3	0-1	1-1	1-1	0-0	2-4	1-0	

Division Two		P	W	D	L	F	A	Pts
Oakwood		34	25	5	4	87	25	80
Selsey		34	23	6	5	80	28	75
St Francis Rangers	*+3*	34	20	8	6	85	42	71
Westfield		34	18	4	12	67	52	58
Crawley Down		34	15	10	9	61	43	55
Wealden		34	16	7	11	64	62	55
East Grinstead Town		34	17	3	14	70	61	54
Mile Oak	*-3*	34	15	7	12	61	53	49
Seaford Town		34	12	6	16	57	64	42
Sidlesham		34	10	11	13	53	56	41
Broadbridge Heath		34	12	5	17	53	69	41
Lancing		34	11	7	16	42	53	40
Pagham		34	9	12	13	65	63	39
Storrington		34	11	6	17	47	63	39
Steyning Town		34	10	8	16	50	69	38
Saltdean United		34	11	3	20	45	75	36
Midhurst & Easebourne United		34	8	7	19	42	70	31
Bexhill United		34	3	5	26	28	109	14

DIVISION TWO CUP

FIRST ROUND

Saltdean United 2 **Wealden** 3
St Francis Rangers 8 Steyning Town 1

SECOND ROUND

Broadbridge Hth 0 **Mile Oak** 3
Lancing 0 **Midhurst & Easebourne United** 2
Oakwood 0 **St Francis Rangers** 1
Pagham 0 **Sidlesham** 1
Seaford Town 4 Bexhill United 1
Selsey 2 **Crawley Down** 3
Storrington 0 **Wealden** 2
Westfield 2 **East Grinstead Town** 3 *aet*

QUARTER-FINALS

Mile Oak 4 East Grinstead Town 0
Seaford Town 1 **Wealden** 2
Sidlesham 2 Midhurst & Easebourne United 1
St Francis Rangers 0 **Crawley Down** 3

SEMI-FINALS

Mile Oak 2 Wealden 2 *aet* (5-4p) *(at Ringmer)*
Sidlesham 3 Crawley Down 1 *(at Wick)*

FINAL

(April 14th at Wick)
Sidlesham 0 **Mile Oak** 1

SUSSEX COUNTY LEAGUE DIVISION TWO CONSTITUTION 2006-07

BROADBRIDGE HEATH . . . . The Leisure Centre, Broadbridge Heath, Horsham RH12 3YS 01403 211311
CRAWLEY DOWN . . . . Haven Sportsfield, Hophurst Lane, Crawley Down RH10 4JL 01342 717140
EAST GRINSTEAD TOWN . . . . East Court, Hollye Road, East Grinstead RH19 3XB 01342 325885
LANCING . . . . Culver Road, Lancing BN15 9AX 01903 764398
LINGFIELD . . . . Godstone Road, Lingfield RH7 6SA 01342 834269
MIDHURST & EASEBOURNE UTD . . . . . . Rotherfield, Dodsley Lane, Easebourne GU29 9AS 01730 816557
MILE OAK . . . . Mile Oak Recreation Ground, Chalky Road, Mile Oak BN41 2WT 01273 423854
PAGHAM . . . . Nyetimber Lane, Pagham, Bognor Regis PO21 3JY 01243 266112
PEACEHAVEN & TELSCOMBE . . . . Piddinghoe Avenue, Peacehaven BN10 8RH 01273 582471
SALTDEAN UNITED . . . . Hill Park, Coombe Vale, Saltdean, Brighton BN2 8HJ 01273 309898
SEAFORD . . . . The Crouch, Bramber Road, Seaford BN25 1AG 01323 892221
SIDLESHAM . . . . Recreation Ground, Selsey Road, Sidlesham, Chichester PO20 7RD 01243 641538
SOUTHWICK . . . . Old Barn Way, Manor Hall Road, Southwick, Brighton BN43 4NT 01273 701010
ST FRANCIS RANGERS . . . . Lewes Road, Haywards Heath RH16 4EX 01444 457726
STEYNING TOWN . . . . The Shooting Field, Shooting Field Estate, Steyning BN44 3RP 01903 812228
STORRINGTON . . . . Recreation Ground, Pulborough Road, Storrington RH20 4HJ 01903 745860
WEALDEN . . . . Wealden Sports Club, Old Eastbourne Road, Uckfield TN22 5QL 01825 890905
WESTFIELD . . . . Main Road, Westfield, Hastings TN35 4SB 01424 751011

IN: Lingfield (P), Peacehaven & Telscombe (P), Southwick (R)
OUT: Bexhill United (R), Oakwood (P), Selsey (P)

ROY HAYDEN TROPHY

(Sussex Senior Cup holders v Div One champions)

(August 6th at Horsham YMCA)

Crawley Town 2 Horsham YMCA 1

NORMAN WINGATE TROPHY

(Division One champions v John O'Hara Cup holders)

(August 13th at Horsham YMCA)

Horsham YMCA 5 Rye & Iden United 2

	Bosham	Forest	Haywards Heath Tn	Hurstpierpoint	Ifield Edwards	Lingfield	Little Common	Newhaven	Peacehaven & Telsco.	Pease Pottage Village	Rustington	Uckfield Town	Upper Beeding	Wadhurst United
Bosham		1-0	3-2	2-2	3-2	1-2	1-2	1-3	0-4	2-2	0-4	0-0	6-0	4-1
Forest	4-0		3-1	2-1	2-0	2-1	1-1	3-1	0-5	4-1	0-2	1-1	4-0	1-1
Haywards Heath Town	4-2	3-4	*D*	2-0	0-1	0-2	3-0	1-1	1-2	2-2	1-1	3-0	3-0	8-2
Hurstpierpoint	4-3	0-3	1-1	*I*	2-5	2-2	0-1	2-1	0-7	3-4	3-2	2-0	5-0	5-1
Ifield Edwards	7-0	2-2	5-2	1-2	*V*	1-3	6-3	4-3	3-5	5-1	1-2	0-2	3-1	2-1
Lingfield	0-0	3-1	3-3	1-2	2-0		3-1	3-1	1-0	2-1	4-1	5-0	2-0	7-1
Little Common	0-1	1-1	2-5	2-1	3-1	0-1		2-3	1-5	3-1	0-4	2-3	6-1	4-1
Newhaven	4-1	1-1	1-1	3-2	2-1	4-0	2-0	*T*	2-1	5-1	1-1	2-0	5-0	2-1
Peacehaven & Telscombe	1-0	3-3	4-2	1-0	3-1	4-2	3-0	2-2	*H*	2-0	4-2	3-2	5-1	3-2
Pease Pottage Village	3-2	4-1	1-1	0-1	2-3	0-1	1-2	1-0	2-1	*R*	1-2	1-2	3-1	1-1
Rustington	1-1	2-1	1-0	1-1	5-0	2-6	0-2	1-0	2-0	2-0	*E*	3-2	6-1	5-1
Uckfield Town	3-4	1-3	0-2	1-2	0-2	1-2	1-0	1-3	1-2	0-0	0-2	*E*	2-0	1-0
Upper Beeding	2-3	0-2	0-2	2-2	0-9	0-11	0-4	0-7	0-6	1-5	1-7	2-3		1-2
Wadhurst United	1-3	1-2	0-4	1-2	1-3	1-4	1-1	0-2	1-5	2-1	0-4	0-3	9-0	

Division Three		P	W	D	L	F	A	Pts
Peacehaven & Telscombe		26	20	2	4	81	31	62
Lingfield		26	19	3	4	73	29	60
Rustington		26	17	4	5	65	31	55
Newhaven		26	15	5	6	61	31	50
Forest		26	13	7	6	51	37	46
Ifield Edwards		26	13	1	12	68	52	40
Hurstpierpoint		26	11	5	10	47	49	38
Haywards Heath Town		26	10	7	9	57	41	37
Little Common		26	10	3	13	43	50	33
Bosham	*-3*	26	9	5	12	44	58	29
Uckfield Town		26	8	3	15	30	46	27
Pease Pottage Village		26	7	5	14	39	51	26
Wadhurst United		26	3	3	20	33	78	12
Upper Beeding	*+3*	26	0	1	25	14	122	4

DIVISION THREE CUP

FIRST ROUND

Bosham 1 Little Common 0
Ifield Edwards 2 Uckfield Town 1
Lingfield 3 Pease Pottage Village 0
Peacehaven & Telscombe 4 Haywards Heath Town 0
Rustington 3 Forest 0
Wadhurst United 0 **Newhaven** 3
Upper Beeding 0 **Hurstpierpoint** 7

QUARTER-FINALS

Lingfield 2 Ifield Edwards 0
Newhaven 3 Bosham 1
Rustington 3 Peacehaven & Telscombe 0

SEMI-FINALS

Hurstpierpoint 0 **Lingfield** 2
(at Haywards Heath Town)
Rustington 4 Newhaven 0
(at Shoreham)

FINAL

(April 14th at Horsham YMCA)
Lingfield 1 **Rustington** 1
aet (11-12)

SUSSEX COUNTY LEAGUE DIVISION THREE CONSTITUTION 2006-07

BEXHILL UNITED .... Brockley Road, Bexhill-on-Sea TN39 3EX 01424 220732
BOSHAM .... Recreation Ground, Walton Lane, Bosham PO18 8QF 01243 574011
FOREST .... Roffey Sports & Social Club, Spooners Road, Roffey RH12 4EB 01403 210221
HAYWARDS HEATH TOWN .... Hanbury Park Stadium, Allen Road, Haywards Heath RH16 3PT 01444 412837
HURSTPIERPOINT .... Fairfield Recreation Ground, Cuckfield Road, Hurstpierpoint BN6 9SD 01273 834783
IFIELD EDWARDS .... Edwards Sports & Social Club, Ifield Green, Rusper Road, Crawley 01293 420598
LITTLE COMMON .... Peartree Lane, Little Common, Bexhill TN39 4PH 01424 845861
LOXWOOD .... Loxwood Sports Association, Sports Pavilion, Billingshurst RH14 0SX 01403 753185
NEWHAVEN .... Recreation Ground, Fort Road, Newhaven BN9 9EE 01273 513940
PEASE POTTAGE VILLAGE .... Finches Field, Pease Pottage RH11 9AH 01293 538651
ROTTINGDEAN VILLAGE .... Rotttingdean Field, Wilkinson Close, Rottingdean, Brighton BN2 7EG .... None
RUSTINGTON .... Recreation Ground, Jubilee Avenue, Rustington BN16 3NB 01903 770495
UCKFIELD TOWN .... Victoria Pleasure Grounds, New Town, Uckfield TN22 5DJ 01825 769400
WADHURST UNITED .... Sparrow Green Rec., South View Road, Wadhurst TN5 6TP 01892 783527

***IN:** Bexhill United (R), Loxwood (P – West Sussex League Premier Division), Rottingdean Village (P – Brighton, Hove & District League Premier Division)*
***OUT:** Lingfield (P), Peacehaven & Telscombe (P), Upper Beeding (R – West Sussex League Premier Division)*

Reserve Premier Division		P	W	D	L	F	A	Pts
Eastbourne Town Res.		26	16	6	4	74	33	54
Crowborough Res.		26	16	5	5	72	24	53
Hailsham Town Res.		26	14	5	7	52	38	47
Horsham YMCA Res.		26	14	4	8	44	34	46
Chichester City Utd Res.		26	12	3	11	32	41	39
Hassocks Res.		26	9	8	9	46	36	35
Arundel Res.		26	10	4	12	53	48	34
East Grinstead Tn Res.		26	9	7	10	41	39	34
Sidley United Res.		26	9	7	10	46	45	34
Worthing United Res.		26	9	6	11	47	56	33
Oakwood Res.		26	8	6	12	44	55	30
Whitehawk Res.		26	9	3	14	41	59	30
East Preston Res.		26	6	4	16	29	68	22
Lancing Res.		26	5	4	17	34	79	19

Reserve Section East		P	W	D	L	F	A	Pts
Ringmer Res.		24	13	7	4	59	32	46
Westfield Res.		24	13	7	4	60	36	46
Crawley Down Res.	*-3*	24	13	7	4	72	31	43
Redhill Res.		24	11	7	6	41	39	40
Eastbourne Utd Ass. Res.		24	11	5	8	49	43	38
Seaford Town Res.		24	10	7	7	36	29	37
Saltdean United Res.	*+3*	24	9	4	11	41	41	34
Peacehaven/Tels. Res.		24	9	5	10	47	53	32
Wealden Res.		24	7	6	11	50	49	27
Bexhill United Res.		24	7	5	12	37	55	26
Haywards Heath Tn Res.		24	6	5	13	40	55	23
Newhaven Res.		24	6	5	13	34	65	23
Lingfield Res.		24	3	6	15	31	69	15

Reserve Section West		P	W	D	L	F	A	Pts
Shoreham Res.		22	16	3	3	59	18	51
Storrington Res.		22	13	2	7	56	38	41
St Francis Rangers Res.		22	11	5	6	51	33	38
Sidlesham Res.	*-3*	22	12	5	5	59	42	38
Pagham Res.	*+3*	22	10	4	8	46	43	37
Wick Res.		22	11	3	8	60	39	36
Broadbridge Heath Res.		22	11	1	10	42	40	34
Midhurst/Ease. Utd Res.		22	7	6	9	44	64	27
Selsey Res.		22	6	4	12	24	42	22
Mile Oak Res.		22	5	6	11	23	41	21
Forest Res.		22	5	3	14	31	63	18
Steyning Town Res.		22	3	2	17	18	50	11

RESERVE SECTION CUP

FINAL *(April 12th at East Preston)*
Storrington Res. 1 Shoreham Res. 0

TEESSIDE LEAGUE

	BEADS	Billingham Wanderers	Carlin How WMC	Dormans Athletic	Fishburn Park	Grangetown Boys Club	Hartlepool	Hartlepool Chester Hotel	Nunthorpe Athletic	Richmond Mavericks	Richmond Town	Thornaby Athletic	Thornaby Res.	Thornaby Youth Club	Whinney Banks
BEADS		6-0	1-2	1-4	2-1	2-5	3-0	2-2	1-1	3-1	4-0	3-1	8-0	0-2	7-0
Billingham Wanderers	1-7	*D*	2-11	7-4	2-2	2-3	0-4	0-3	1-1	2-9	2-3	2-3	3-5	1-3	2-4
Carlin How WMC	8-1	6-3	*I*	3-0	1-2	2-1	2-1	2-2	4-0	4-0	4-0	2-0	5-0	1-1	2-1
Dormans Athletic	0-1	6-2	0-4	*V*	1-4	2-1	3-3	0-1	0-3	2-5	3-2	2-3	2-4	1-1	0-0
Fishburn Park	3-2	7-1	0-2	2-0	*I*	2-2	1-0	6-0	0-1	3-4	5-0	2-1	2-2	2-0	1-1
Grangetown Boys Club	4-2	7-1	1-4	4-2	3-0	*S*	2-1	2-3	4-1	2-2	4-1	1-2	4-4	2-1	8-3
Hartlepool	2-1	6-2	0-4	2-5	0-1	3-2	*I*	0-3	0-2	3-4	3-0	1-3	0-1	5-0	3-3
Hartlepool Chester Hotel	0-2	1-4	3-4	8-1	0-2	3-0	1-2	*O*	1-1	0-2	7-0	1-1	1-1	2-1	3-2
Nunthorpe Athletic	2-2	3-0	1-6	3-0	2-1	2-1	1-2	1-1	*N*	4-1	5-0	0-4	2-0	0-3	4-3
Richmond Mavericks	4-6	7-3	0-1	2-5	2-1	0-1	5-0	3-2	1-2		4-0	2-1	1-0	1-1	5-0
Richmond Town	0-4	3-1	0-4	3-4	0-1	1-0	1-3	2-4	4-2	1-1		0-3	2-0	1-3	3-3
Thornaby Athletic	2-3	3-0	1-0	4-2	0-0	3-2	1-1	1-2	0-2	3-0	6-0	*O*	3-1	0-1	3-1
Thornaby Res.	1-2	2-1	0-3	5-4	1-1	1-3	3-3	2-1	0-1	3-0	2-0	0-4	*N*	1-0	1-1
Thornaby Youth Club	4-3	5-1	5-2	10-0	2-1	2-0	2-2	2-3	4-1	3-1	0-0	3-1	4-0	*E*	8-0
Whinney Banks	3-4	1-1	0-2	3-2	1-1	3-9	2-3	1-1	6-2	0-4	0-0	2-2	0-1	2-4	

Division One		P	W	D	L	F	A	Pts
Carlin How WMC		28	23	2	3	95	26	71
Thornaby Youth Club		28	17	5	6	75	34	56
BEADS		28	16	3	9	83	53	51
Thornaby Athletic		28	15	4	9	59	36	49
Fishburn Park		28	13	7	8	54	33	46
Grangetown Boys Club		28	14	3	11	78	55	45
Richmond Mavericks		28	14	3	11	71	56	45
Nunthorpe Athletic	*-3*	28	14	5	9	50	50	44
Hartlepool Chester Hotel	*-3*	28	12	7	9	59	47	40
Thornaby Res.		28	10	6	12	41	61	36
Hartlepool		28	10	5	13	53	58	35
Whinney Banks		28	3	10	15	46	86	19
Richmond Town		28	5	4	19	27	82	19
Dormans Athletic	*-9*	28	7	3	18	55	91	15
Billingham Wanderers		28	2	3	23	47	125	9

LOU MOORE MEMORIAL SHIELD

(Division One sides)

FIRST ROUND

Billingham Wanderers 0 **Thornaby Youth Club** 5

Carlin How WMC 3 Thornaby Athletic 1

Dormans Athletic 2 **Hartlepool** 3

Grangetown Boys Club 5 Richmond Mavericks 2

Hartlepool Chester Hotel 3 Richmond Town 2

Thornaby Res. 1 **Nunthorpe Ath** 3

Whinney Banks 4 **BEADS** 5

QUARTER-FINALS

BEADS 1 **Hartlepool Chester Hotel** 2

Carlin How WMC 4 Fishburn Park 0

Grangetown Boys Club 0 **Thornaby Youth Club** 2

Hartlepool 2 Nunthorpe Athletic 1

SEMI-FINALS

Carlin How WMC 4 Hartlepool 4 *aet (3-4p) (Hartlepool expelled)*

Thornaby Youth Club 2 Hartlepool Chester Hotel 1

FINAL

(May 3rd at Stokesley Sports Club)

Carlin How WMC 5 Thornaby Youth Club 2

TEESSIDE LEAGUE DIVISION ONE CONSTITUTION 2006-07

BEADS .... Beechwood/Easterside SC, Marton Road, Middlesbrough 01642 311304
CARLIN HOW WMC .... Kilton Lane, Carlin How, Saltburn TS13 4DG .... None
DARLINGTON RUGBY CLUB .... Darlington Rugby Club, Grange Road, Darlington DL1 5NR .... None
FISHBURN PARK .... Eskdale School, Broomfield Park, Whitby YO22 4HS .... None
GRANGETOWN BOYS CLUB ... Grangetown YCC, Trunk Road, Grangetown, Middlesbrough TS6 7HP 01642 455435
HARTLEPOOL CHESTER HOTEL .... Grayfield Enclosure, Jesmond Road, Hartlepool TS25 3PB .... None
HARTLEPOOL RESERVES .... NTL College, Owton Manor Lane, Hartlepool TS25 3PS .... None
NUNTHORPE ATHLETIC .... Recreation Club, Guisborough Lane, Nunthorpe TS7 0LD 01642 313251
REDCAR RUGBY CLUB .... Redcar Rugby Club, Green Lane, Redcar TS10 3RW ....
RICHMOND MAVERICKS .... Catterick Garrison, Wavell Road, Catterick DL9 3BJ .... None
RICHMOND TOWN .... Earls Orchard Playing Fields, Sleegill, Richmond DL10 4RH .... None
THORNABY RESERVES .... Teesdale Park, Acklam Road, Thornaby, Stockton-on-Tees TS17 7JU 01642 606803
THORNABY ATHLETIC .... Harold Wilson Rec Ground, Thornaby Road, Thornaby TS17 8PH .... None
THORNABY DUBLINERS .... Grangefield Community Centre, Oxbridge Lane, Stockton-on-Tees TS18 4DA .... None
WHINNEY BANKS .... Hall Garth School, Hall Drive, Middlesbrough TS5 7JX .... None

IN: Darlington Rugby Club (P), Hartlepool Reserves (P), Mackinlay Park (now Redcar Rugby Club) (P)
OUT: Billingham Wanderers (R), Dormans Athletic (W), Hartlepool (P – Wearside League)

J V MADDEN TROPHY

(League champions v McMillan Bowl holders)

Hartlepool qualified this season as Division One runners-up as Carlin How WMC completed the double in 2004-05

(August 6th at Carlin How WMC)

Carlin How WMC 2 Hartlepool 1

	Bedale Athletic	Darlington RA Res.	Darlington Rugby Club	Darlington Simpson	Guisborough B Swan	Hartlepool Res.	Mackinlay Park	New Marske SC Res.	Nth Ormesby Sports	Pickering Town CFC	Spraire Lads	Stokesley SC Res.	Teesside Athletic Res.	Yorkshire Cobbles
Bedale Athletic		5-1	5-5	5-1	1-3	2-2	4-3	3-3	4-5	2-2	7-3	0-2	6-1	4-3
Darlington RA Res.	0-1	*D*	0-2	1-0	1-3	5-1	2-0	7-3	6-0	3-0	6-1	0-1	2-0	5-8
Darlington Rugby Club	3-3	7-1	*I*	1-0	2-1	4-0	1-3	2-1	3-0	5-1	3-0	0-0	2-1	9-0
Darlington Simpson RM	1-2	2-3	0-2	*V*	1-4	4-0	0-5	1-0	3-5	7-1	3-1	3-4	4-1	0-2
Guisborough Black Swan	7-2	2-1	2-2	4-1	*I*	2-1	3-5	3-4	5-1	4-1	2-0	1-1	4-1	5-1
Hartlepool Res.	2-4	4-0	2-1	2-3	1-3	*S*	1-3	3-1	2-2	2-0	1-2	1-2	12-2	2-1
Mackinlay Park	4-0	4-1	2-0	5-0	4-3	2-3	*I*	9-0	4-6	3-1	8-1	2-0	3-0	2-0
New Marske Spts Club Res.	0-5	0-10	1-8	0-3	2-11	2-5	0-2	*O*	1-6	6-3	1-0	2-4	0-2	0-5
North Ormesby Sports	1-3	1-4	2-2	1-4	4-3	1-4	4-4	5-1	*N*	4-3	11-3	6-3	8-1	5-5
Pickering Town CFC	3-3	1-0	1-2	2-0	1-1	2-1	1-4	4-1	6-6		2-1	1-3	11-0	2-2
Spraire Lads	1-5	3-5	3-2	2-0	6-2	0-7	1-5	4-3	1-6	0-2	*T*	0-5	4-4	3-2
Stokesley Sports Club Res.	0-2	2-1	0-3	0-1	0-4	2-2	0-1	6-0	2-2	2-1	1-1	*W*	2-2	0-2
Teesside Athletic Res.	0-7	5-4	0-6	4-1	0-4	2-2	0-6	0-2	7-4	3-2	1-1	2-3	*O*	1-5
Yorkshire Cobble	4-5	4-2	0-3	2-5	0-3	3-2	4-3	1-0	1-1	5-3	3-1	3-0	2-0	

Division Two		P	W	D	L	F	A	Pts
Mackinlay Park		26	20	1	5	96	36	61
Darlington Rugby Club		26	17	5	4	80	29	56
Guisborough Black Swan		26	17	3	6	89	44	54
Bedale Athletic		26	15	6	5	90	60	51
North Ormesby Sports		26	11	7	8	97	85	40
Stokesley Sports Club Res.		26	11	6	9	45	43	39
Darlington Railway Athletic Res.		26	12	0	14	71	60	36
Yorkshire Coble	*-6*	26	13	3	10	68	66	36
Hartlepool Res.		26	10	4	12	65	55	34
Darlington Simpson RM		26	10	0	16	48	59	30
Pickering Town CFC		26	7	5	14	57	70	26
Spraire Lads	-3	26	6	3	17	43	97	18
Teesside Athletic Res.	-3	26	5	4	17	40	107	16
New Marske Sports Club Res.	-3	26	4	1	21	34	112	10

TEESSIDE LEAGUE DIVISION TWO CONSTITUTION 2006-07

BEDALE ATHLETIC............ Leyburn Road, Bedale DL8 1HA .... None
BILLINGHAM WANDERERS ...... Billingham Rugby Club, Greenwood Road, Billingham TS23 4AZ .... None
DARLINGTON RAILWAY ATHLETIC RESERVES ... Darlington RA Club, Brinkburn Road, Darlington DL3 9LF.......... 01325 468125
DARLINGTON SIMPSON RM.......... Longfield School, Longfield Road, Darlington DL3 0HT............ None
GUISBOROUGH BLACK SWAN RESERVES .. King George V Playing Fields, Howlbeck Road, Guisborough TS14 6LE 01287 636925
GUISBOROUGH QUOIT........ King George V Playing Fields, Howlbeck Road, Guisborough TS14 6LE.......... 01287 636925
KIRKBYMOORSIDE .... Kirby Mills, Kirkbymoorside, York .... None
NORTH ORMESBY SPORTS........... Pallister Park, Ormesby Road, Middlesbrough TS3 7AP .... None
SPRAIRE LADS .... Queen Elizabeth College, Abbey Road, Darlington DL3 8ND............ None
STOKESLEY SPORTS CLUB RESERVES ... Stokesley SC, Broughton Road, Stokesley, Middlesbrough TS9 5AQ............ 01642 710051
TEESSIDE ATHLETIC RESERVES .... Green Lane, Redcar TS10 3RW............ None
YORKSHIRE COBLE.................... Ayton Road, Roseberry Square, Redcar TS10 4EL .... None

IN: Billingham Wanderers (R), Guisborough Black Swan Reserves (N), Guisborough Quoit (P – Eskvale & Cleveland League), Kirkbymoorside (P – Scarborough & District League)

OUT: Darlington Rugby Club (P), Guisborough Black Swan (P – Wearside League), Hartlepool Reserves (W), Mackinlay Park (now Redcar Rugby Club) (P), New Marske Sports Club Reserves (W), Pickering Town CFC (W)

McMILLAN BOWL *(All teams)*

FIRST ROUND

Bedale Athletic 4 Whinney Banks 3
Darlington Rugby Club 3 Darlington Simpson RM 1
Dormans Athletic 4 Teesside Athletic Res. 3
Grangetown Boys Club 1 **Hartlepool Chester Hotel** 2
Pickering Town CFC (w/o) v Billingham Wanderers (scr.)
Richmond Mavericks 3 BEADS 0
Richmond Town 2 Hartlepool 1
Spraire Lads 0 **Darlington RA Res.** 1
Stokesley Sports Club Res. 2 **Fishburn Park** 3
Thornaby Athletic Res. 0 **Yorkshire Coble** 2
Thornaby Res. 3 North Ormesby Sports 1
Thornaby Youth Club 3 Guisborough Black Swan 0

SECOND ROUND

Bedale Athletic 4 Darlington RA Res. 3
Darlington Rugby Club 4 Pickering Town CFC 3
Dormans Athletic 3 **Mackinlay Park** 5
Fishburn Park 0 **Thornaby Youth Club** 2
New Marske Sports Club Res. 1 **Thornaby Res.** 2
Nunthorpe Athletic 0 **Carlin How WMC** 2
Richmond Town 0 **Hartlepool Chester Hotel** 2
Yorkshire Coble 2 **Richmond Mavericks** 3

QUARTER-FINALS

Carlin How WMC 4 Mackinlay Park 0
Darlington Rugby Club 3 Bedale Athletic 0
Thornaby Res. 3 Richmond Mavericks 1
Thornaby Youth Club 5 Hartlepool Chester Hotel 3

SEMI-FINALS

Carlin How WMC 2 **Thornaby Youth Club** 3
Darlington Rugby Club 0 **Thornaby Res.** 1

FINAL

(May 15th at Thornaby)

Thornaby Res. 0 **Thornaby Youth Club** 1

R T RAINE TROPHY

(Teams knocked out in 1st Round of the McMillan Bowl)

FIRST ROUND

Guisborough Black Swan 6 North Ormesby Sports 4
Hartlepool 2 BEADS 1
Spraire Lads 4 Billingham Wanderers 0
Thornaby Athletic 2 Stokesley Sports Club Res. 0
Whinney Banks 2 **Darlington Simpson RM** 3

QUARTER-FINALS

Darlington Simpson RM 3 Spraire Lads 0
Hartlepool 1 **Guisborough Black Swan** 2
Hartlepool Res. 2 **Grangetown Boys Club** 7
Teesside Athletic Res. 1 **Thornaby Athletic** 2

SEMI-FINALS

Grangetown Boys Club 1 **Thornaby Athletic** 2 *aet* (1-3p)
Guisborough Black Swan 1 **Darlington Simpson RM** 1 *aet* (3-4p)

FINAL

(April 17th at Stokesley Sports Club)

Thornaby Athletic 2 Darlington Simpson RM 1

ALEX BURNESS PLATE

(Division Two teams)

FIRST ROUND

Bedale Ath 1 **Yorkshire Coble** 3
Darlington RA Res. 1 **Spraire Lads** 3
Guisborough Black Swan 4 Teesside Athletic Res. 2
Hartlepool Res. 3 **North Ormesby Sports** 4
New Marske Sports Club Res. 4 Darlington Simpson RM 0
Stokesley Sports Club Res. 1 Mackinlay Park 0

QUARTER-FINALS

North Ormesby Sports 5 Spraire Lads 0
Pickering Town CFC 0 **Guisborough Black Swan** 2
Stokesley Sports Club Res. 3 New Marske Sports Club Res. 1
Yorkshire Coble 3 Darlington RC 2

SEMI-FINALS

North Ormesby Sports 1 **Guisborough Black Swan** 3
Yorkshire Coble 2 Stokesley Sports Club Res. 1

FINAL

(May 1st at Darlington Railway Ath)

Stokesley Sports Club Res. 1 Guisborough Black Swan 0

UNITED COUNTIES LEAGUE

	Blackstones	Boston Town	Bourne Town	Buckingham	Cogenhoe United	Deeping Rangers	Desborough	Ford Sports Daventry	Harrowby United	Holbeach United	Long Buckby	Newport Pagnell Town	Northampton Spencer	Potton United	Raunds Town	St Ives Town	St Neots Town	Stewart/Lloyds Corby	Stotfold	Woodford United	Wootton Blue Cross	Yaxley
Blackstones		2-3	1-3	1-2	4-1	3-0	1-1	5-2	7-0	2-0	3-3	2-1	0-5	1-1	5-1	3-4	3-2	2-2	3-2	0-0	3-0	2-2
Boston Town	1-0		1-0	1-0	2-2	1-0	5-5	1-0	4-0	2-0	2-1	4-1	5-1	1-3	1-1	4-0	4-1	1-2	2-1	1-1	3-0	1-0
Bourne Town	0-1	1-4		0-0	1-4	0-3	3-2	3-2	6-0	2-1	1-1	3-1	1-3	1-2	1-2	1-2	2-0	3-1	2-4	1-1	1-1	2-4
Buckingham Town	1-1	3-2	2-2	*P*	1-3	1-0	0-3	3-2	8-1	0-2	2-0	3-4	1-4	1-1	0-0	1-4	0-1	2-3	3-2	0-5	0-2	1-3
Cogenhoe United	2-3	4-4	3-2	4-1	*R*	3-2	2-1	2-0	3-0	2-2	2-0	1-1	3-0	2-3	4-1	2-1	1-0	2-1	1-1	1-4	1-1	0-2
Deeping Rangers	3-2	4-3	1-4	0-2	2-6	*E*	4-1	3-3	2-3	3-1	3-0	1-0	0-5	1-2	2-2	0-1	0-3	1-1	1-1	0-2	3-1	0-0
Desborough Town	1-1	4-2	1-2	3-5	1-3	2-1	*M*	1-4	4-0	1-0	2-1	4-0	1-3	3-3	1-0	1-2	0-1	2-0	2-0	1-6	2-0	1-3
Ford Sports Daventry	1-1	0-1	0-1	5-2	0-1	1-0	3-0	*I*	2-3	1-2	4-1	3-1	0-4	2-1	1-3	2-0	2-2	0-1	1-1	0-4	2-1	0-1
Harrowby United	2-3	0-7	2-2	0-8	0-3	1-4	1-1	0-4	*E*	2-2	0-6	3-3	0-2	1-2	1-9	0-4	1-7	2-2	1-5	3-5	1-3	2-6
Holbeach United	2-2	6-0	0-0	1-3	3-3	2-4	0-0	5-1	5-0	*R*	0-1	1-0	1-1	3-1	1-2	0-2	0-3	5-0	2-3	0-1	0-4	1-3
Long Buckby	1-1	4-3	1-3	1-5	0-3	1-2	2-0	1-2	6-1	2-3		4-1	0-6	1-3	4-2	0-1	1-2	1-1	1-2	2-3	2-4	3-1
Newport Pagnell Town	1-0	0-3	0-0	0-0	0-1	1-0	2-1	2-2	3-0	2-1	1-1	*D*	0-3	2-5	1-0	1-2	0-2	1-0	1-1	0-1	2-0	3-0
Northampton Spencer	1-0	1-0	0-1	0-2	3-2	0-0	4-2	2-0	7-1	1-0	3-1	1-0	*I*	1-1	1-2	2-1	1-2	2-1	5-0	1-0	1-1	1-1
Potton United	2-1	1-1	5-2	4-2	2-1	2-1	3-0	4-1	4-1	2-1	2-1	1-0	2-1	*V*	0-0	1-2	3-1	4-2	1-0	4-0	2-2	4-1
Raunds Town	1-1	1-1	3-0	3-1	0-1	2-0	3-1	2-3	2-1	0-1	1-0	1-1	1-3	0-2	*I*	3-1	1-0	4-1	1-1	0-2	1-0	1-1
St Ives Town	2-1	1-3	0-5	2-4	2-2	1-1	1-1	3-0	2-0	1-3	0-2	4-0	0-2	3-1	0-0	*S*	1-2	1-4	1-2	1-0	4-1	1-3
St Neots Town	2-1	4-1	2-0	2-1	0-1	1-1	3-1	4-1	3-0	1-1	2-2	2-1	1-0	4-1	0-2	2-1	*I*	3-1	2-5	2-1	3-1	1-2
Stewarts & Lloyds Corby	0-2	0-1	2-0	2-2	2-0	2-1	1-1	3-0	3-1	1-2	1-3	0-4	0-5	1-4	0-2	2-1	3-2	*O*	2-0	2-0	1-0	1-3
Stotfold	3-1	1-1	2-3	1-2	4-2	1-1	1-3	5-0	9-0	2-2	5-0	2-3	0-3	0-1	3-1	3-1	2-4	3-2	*N*	0-4	2-2	0-2
Woodford United	3-2	1-1	3-0	5-2	3-0	2-0	3-0	0-0	10-0	4-0	4-1	3-1	2-0	1-0	2-2	6-0	1-2	0-0	0-0		1-0	2-0
Wootton Blue Cross	1-2	1-0	1-1	3-0	4-1	2-1	4-1	3-0	5-1	0-0	0-0	0-1	0-2	1-2	4-2	4-1	0-0	3-0	1-2	2-4		1-3
Yaxley	3-0	2-0	4-2	1-0	0-1	1-0	0-1	1-2	7-1	5-1	0-2	0-1	0-1	0-0	0-1	1-2	1-0	1-1	3-2	0-2	0-1	

Premier Division		P	W	D	L	F	A	Pts
Woodford United		42	28	8	6	102	32	92
Potton United		42	28	8	6	92	51	92
Northampton Spencer		42	28	5	9	92	36	89
St Neots Town		42	25	5	12	81	52	80
Cogenhoe United		42	23	8	11	86	64	77
Boston Town		42	22	9	11	88	60	75
Yaxley	-3	42	21	6	15	71	49	66
Raunds Town		42	18	11	13	66	54	65
St Ives Town		42	18	4	20	64	76	58
Blackstones		42	15	12	15	79	68	57
Stotfold		42	15	10	17	84	74	55
Wootton Blue Cross		42	15	9	18	65	59	54
Bourne Town		42	15	9	18	68	73	54
Buckingham Town	-1	42	15	7	20	77	84	51
Newport Pagnell Town		42	14	8	20	48	66	50
Stewarts & Lloyds Corby		42	14	8	20	55	77	50
Holbeach United		42	12	10	20	63	70	46
Desborough Town	-1	42	13	8	21	64	83	46
Ford Sports Daventry		42	13	6	23	59	84	45
Deeping Rangers		42	11	9	22	56	73	42
Long Buckby		42	11	7	24	65	87	40
Harrowby United		42	2	5	35	37	190	11

UNITED COUNTIES LEAGUE PREMIER DIVISION CONSTITUTION 2006-07

BLACKSTONES .... Blackstones Sports & Social, Lincoln Road, Stamford PE9 1SH 01780 757835
BOSTON TOWN .... The Stadium, Tattershall Road, Boston PE21 9LR 01205 365470
BOURNE TOWN .... Abbey Lawn, Abbey Road, Bourne PE10 9EN 01778 422292
BUCKINGHAM TOWN .... Ford Meadow, Ford Street, Buckingham MK18 1AG 01280 816257
COGENHOE UNITED .... Compton Park, Brafield Road, Cogenhoe NN7 1ND 01604 890521
DEEPING RANGERS .... Outgang Road, Towngate East, Market Deeping PE6 8LQ 01778 344701
DESBOROUGH TOWN .... Waterworks Field, Braybrooke Road, Desborough NN14 2PT 01536 761350
FORD SPORTS DAVENTRY .... Royal Oak Way, Daventry NN11 5NT 01327 704914
HOLBEACH UNITED .... Carters Park, Park Road, Holbeach PE12 7EE 01406 424761
LONG BUCKBY .... Station Road, Long Buckby NN6 7PQ 01327 842682
NEWPORT PAGNELL TOWN .... Willen Road Sports Ground, Newport Pagnell MK16 0DF 01908 611993
NORTHAMPTON SPENCER .... Kingsthorpe Mill, Studland Road, Kingsthorpe, Northampton NN2 6NE 01604 718898
POTTON UNITED .... The Hollow, Biggleswade Road, Potton SG19 2LU 01767 261100
RAUNDS TOWN .... Kiln Park, London Road, Raunds, Wellingborough NN9 6EQ 01933 623351
ST IVES TOWN .... Westwood Road, St Ives PE27 6WU 01480 463207
ST NEOTS TOWN .... Rowley Park, Cambridge Road, St Neots PE19 6SN 01480 470012
STEWARTS & LLOYDS CORBY .... Recreation Ground, Occupation Road, Corby NN17 1EH 01536 401497
STOTFOLD .... Roker Park, The Green, Stotfold, Hitchin SG5 4BX 01462 730765
WELLINGBOROUGH TOWN .... Dog & Duck, London Road, Wellingborough NN8 2DP 01933 441388
WOOTTON BLUE CROSS .... Weston Park, Bedford Road, Wootton MK43 9JT 01234 767662
YAXLEY .... Leading Drove, Holme Road, Yaxley, Peterborough PE7 3NA 01733 244928

IN: Wellingborough Town (P)

OUT: Harrowby United (W – Grantham League), Woodford United (P – Southern League Division One Midlands)

	AFC Kempston Rovers	Blisworth	Bugbrooke St Michaels	Burton Park Wanderers	Daventry Town	Eynesbury Rovers	Higham Town	Huntingdon Town	Irchester United	Northampton ON Chenecks	Olney Town	Peterborough Northern Star	Rothwell Corinthians	Sileby Rangers	Sleaford Town	Thrapston Town	Wellingborough Town	Wellingborough Whitworths
AFC Kempston Rovers		4-1	4-1	1-1	3-1	2-3	4-0	0-0	1-1	1-2	2-0	2-2	1-1	5-1	1-0	2-1	0-0	0-5
Blisworth	2-0		5-0	3-1	2-2	2-3	1-2	5-3	1-2	3-3	3-4	1-4	2-0	0-3	1-2	0-3	0-3	1-1
Bugbrooke St Michaels	0-1	0-1		3-2	3-1	1-2	1-0	1-1	2-1	1-1	1-1	1-0	4-3	0-3	1-4	2-1	1-1	1-2
Burton Park Wanderers	0-2	0-4	1-1	*D*	1-1	2-1	0-2	2-3	0-4	0-1	1-1	0-8	0-5	0-5	1-2	0-1	1-2	1-3
Daventry Town	1-0	3-3	3-0	0-1	*I*	4-1	1-0	1-1	1-0	1-1	4-3	3-1	2-2	3-2	2-0	2-1	1-1	1-4
Eynesbury Rovers	1-3	3-1	0-3	2-0	1-1	*V*	2-3	3-0	2-0	1-0	1-5	3-3	3-1	1-1	2-4	3-1	0-3	4-2
Higham Town	1-5	1-1	1-1	3-2	1-6	2-7	*I*	3-1	1-4	0-4	0-4	3-0	0-2	1-1	1-6	3-5	1-2	1-2
Huntingdon Town	0-1	3-2	1-3	2-0	0-0	3-1	0-0	*S*	1-0	0-1	2-3	0-1	3-1	0-1	1-2	3-0	1-3	1-0
Irchester United	2-4	0-0	2-3	1-0	2-1	1-1	3-1	3-1	*I*	0-2	0-3	1-2	2-3	3-0	3-1	2-5	0-5	0-3
Northampton ON Chenecks	1-0	2-3	4-1	4-0	1-3	3-4	3-1	0-2	2-1	*O*	4-0	3-1	5-2	3-1	0-1	4-4	1-2	2-0
Olney Town	0-1	1-1	5-1	1-0	4-1	2-1	4-0	1-2	4-1	1-2	*N*	4-2	1-2	7-1	1-3	2-0	1-3	0-2
Peterborough Northern Star	2-0	2-5	3-2	2-2	2-1	1-0	7-1	2-1	2-2	2-3	1-1		1-2	4-0	1-2	2-1	0-0	2-2
Rothwell Corinthians	0-3	3-3	1-2	4-1	4-1	0-1	4-1	1-0	2-0	2-2	1-1	2-2	*O*	1-0	0-1	3-0	0-3	0-3
Sileby Rangers	2-5	1-1	1-2	1-2	1-7	1-2	3-1	2-3	5-3	2-0	4-0	3-1	2-1	*N*	1-4	3-1	0-2	1-4
Sleaford Town	0-1	4-2	4-1	8-0	2-1	3-0	8-0	2-0	3-1	2-0	6-2	7-1	2-2	8-2	*E*	6-2	1-2	3-2
Thrapston Town	1-1	1-2	2-0	1-1	1-5	3-3	2-0	1-2	1-2	0-1	2-1	2-5	0-4	3-4	0-4		1-1	2-3
Wellingborough Town	5-0	0-0	1-1	3-1	5-1	3-1	7-0	4-2	2-0	0-1	1-1	1-0	4-0	0-0	0-0	1-1		2-0
Wellingborough Whitworths	0-1	7-1	2-0	3-2	4-1	4-0	2-0	3-2	0-1	1-0	3-0	2-2	1-0	3-1	1-1	2-2	1-2	

Division One		P	W	D	L	F	A	Pts
Sleaford Town		34	26	3	5	106	36	81
Wellingborough Town		34	22	11	1	74	19	77
Wellingborough Whitworths		34	21	5	8	77	38	68
AFC Kempston Rovers		34	19	7	8	61	38	64
Northampton ON Chenecks		34	19	5	10	66	43	62
Daventry Town		34	14	9	11	67	58	51
Eynesbury Rovers		34	15	5	14	63	68	50
Olney Town		34	14	6	14	69	59	48
Peterborough Northern Star		34	13	9	12	71	63	48
Rothwell Corinthians		34	13	7	14	59	57	46
Bugbrooke St Michaels		34	12	7	15	45	65	43
Huntingdon Town		34	12	5	17	45	53	41
Sileby Rangers		34	12	4	18	59	81	40
Blisworth	*-1*	34	10	10	14	63	71	39
Irchester United		34	11	4	19	48	65	37
Thrapston Town		34	7	7	20	52	79	28
Higham Town		34	6	4	24	35	105	22
Burton Park Wanderers		34	3	6	25	26	88	15

UNITED COUNTIES LEAGUE DIVISION ONE CONSTITUTION 2006-07

AFC KEMPSTON ROVERS .... Hillgrounds Road, Kempston, Bedford MK42 8QU.......................... 01234 852346
BUGBROOKE ST MICHAELS ...... Birds Close, Gayton Road, Bugbrooke, Northampton NN7 3PH 01604 830707
BURTON PARK WANDERERS......... Latimer Park, Polwell Lane, Burton Latimer NN15 5PS............................ 01536 725841
DAVENTRY TOWN .... Elderstubbs, Browns Road, Daventry NN11 4NS.............................. 01327 706286
EYNESBURY ROVERS .... Alfred Hall Memorial Ground, Hall Road, Eynesbury, St Neots PE19 2SF 01480 477449
HIGHAM TOWN .... Vine Hall Drive, Higham Ferrers, Rushden NN10 8EF 01933 353751
HUNTINGDON TOWN................ Jubilee Park, Kings Ripton Road, Huntingdon PE28 2NU.............................. 07929 651226
IRCHESTER UNITED .... Alfred Street, Irchester NN29 7DR.. 01933 312877
NORTHAMPTON ON CHENECKS ... Old Northamptonians, Billing Road, Northampton NN1 5RX 01604 634045
OLNEY TOWN .... Recreation Ground, East Street, Olney MK46 4DW 01234 712227
PETERBOROUGH NORTHERN STAR... Chestnut Avenue, Dogsthorpe, Peterborough PE7 4NB 01733 564894
ROTHWELL CORINTHIANS .... Seargents Lawn, Desborough Road, Rothwell NN14 6JG 01536 418688
SILEBY RANGERS .... Fernie Fields Sports Ground, Woodford Chase, Moulton, Northampton NN3 7BD.............. 01604 670366
SLEAFORD TOWN.. RAF Cranwell, Sleaford NG34 8HB 07748 434445
THRAPSTON TOWN.......................... Chancery Lane, Thrapston, Kettering NN14 4JL...................................... 01832 732470
WHITWORTHS.. London Road, Wellingborough NN8 2DT.. 01933 227324

OUT: Blisworth (W – Northamptonshire Combination Division Two) are now James King Blisworth, Wellingborough Town (P)

Wellingborough Whitworths become Whitworths

LEAGUE CUP

PRELIMINARY ROUND

Blackstones 5 Rothwell Corinthians 2
Blackstones 5 Rothwell Corinthians 3 *rematch*
Blisworth 0 **Stotfold** 3
Deeping Rangers 1 **Yaxley** 3
Irchester United 0 **Peterborough Northern Star** 2
Long Buckby 1 **Ford Sports Daventry** 5
Potton United 2 Huntingdon Town 1
Raunds Town 2 Eynesbury Rovers 1
St Ives Town 0 **Wellingborough Town** 1

FIRST ROUND

Boston Town 2 Holbeach United 2 *aet* (5-4p)
Bourne Town 1 **Stotfold** 1 *aet* (2-4p)
Buckingham Town 1 **Ford Sports Daventry** 0 *(Buckingham Town expelled)*
Cogenhoe United 3 Blackstones 2
Daventry Town 1 AFC Kempston Rovers 0
Harrowby United 2 **Sileby Rangers** 2 *aet* (2-4p)
Higham Town 0 **St Neots Town** 4
Newport Pagnell Town 1 Bugbrooke St Michaels 0
Northampton Spencer 3 Wellingborough Whitworths 0
Peterborough Northern Star 2 Northampton ON Chenecks 0
Potton United 5 Burton Park Wanderers 0
Raunds Town 0 **Stewarts & Lloyds Corby** 2
Thrapston Town 1 **Desborough Town** 2
Woodford United 4 Olney Town 0
Wootton Blue Cross 1 **Sleaford Town** 2
Yaxley 4 Wellingborough Town 0

SECOND ROUND

Boston Town 2 **St Neots Town** 3
Cogenhoe United 10 Daventry Town 0
Desborough Town 3 Stewarts & Lloyds Corby 1 *aet*
Peterborough Northern Star 2 Newport Pagnell Town 1
Sileby Rangers 1 **Northampton Spencer** 5
Sleaford Town 2 **Ford Sports Daventry** 2 *aet* (4-5p)
Stotfold 2 **Yaxley** 4
Woodford United 1 Potton United 0

QUARTER-FINALS

Cogenhoe United 5 Desborough Town 2
Peterborough Northern Star 1 **Northampton Spencer** 2
St Neots Town 2 Woodford United 2 *aet* (3-2p)
Yaxley 5 Ford Sports Daventry 3

SEMI-FINALS

Northampton Spencer 1 **Yaxley** 3
St Neots Town 4 Cogenhoe United 1

FINAL

(April 28th at Raunds Town)
Yaxley 2 St Neots Town 1

Reserve Division One		P	W	D	L	F	A	Pts
Bourne Town Res.		30	20	5	5	69	26	65
Blackstones Res.		30	18	7	5	69	35	61
Northampton Spencer Res.	*-1*	30	15	6	9	58	46	50
Raunds Town Res.		30	13	8	9	52	37	47
Stotfold Res.		30	14	5	11	62	49	47
Desborough Town Res.		30	13	8	9	61	53	47
Stewarts & Lloyds Corby Res.		30	14	4	12	46	42	46
Deeping Rangers Res.		30	12	7	11	45	46	43
Ford Sports Daventry Res.		30	10	12	8	50	47	42
Wellingborough Whitworths Res.		30	11	8	11	57	48	41
Sileby Rangers Res.		30	11	6	13	33	49	39
Newport Pagnell Town Res.		30	10	5	15	39	49	35
Cogenhoe United Res.		30	9	5	16	40	55	32
Yaxley Res.		30	9	5	16	45	62	32
Rothwell Town Res.	*-3*	30	7	9	14	50	60	27
Eynesbury Rovers Res.		30	4	0	26	26	98	12

Reserve Division Two	P	W	D	L	F	A	Pts
Woodford United Res.	26	16	6	4	70	36	54
Rothwell Corinthians Res.	26	15	6	5	70	33	51
Bugbrooke St Michaels Res.	26	16	2	8	75	43	50
Thrapston Town Res.	26	15	2	9	63	38	47
Wellingborough Town Res.	26	14	5	7	57	40	47
Olney Town Res.	26	14	2	10	42	33	44
Northampton ON Chenecks Res.	26	12	5	9	60	52	41
Huntingdon Town Res.	26	10	5	11	33	47	35
Long Buckby Res.	26	9	6	11	53	63	33
Irchester United Res.	26	8	5	13	45	55	29
Spalding United Res.	26	7	4	15	41	81	25
Holbeach United Res.	26	4	10	12	37	67	22
Higham Town Res.	26	4	6	16	25	48	18
Burton Park Wanderers Res.	26	4	4	18	31	66	16

RESERVES CUP

FINAL

(April 20th at Wellingborough Town)
Sileby Rangers Res. 2 Raunds Town Res. 1

WEARSIDE LEAGUE

	Annfield Plain	Birtley Town	Boldon Comm. Assoc.	Cleator Moor Celtic	Coxhoe Athletic	Ferryhill Athletic	Gateshead Low Fell	Jarrow	New Marske Spts Club	Nissan SSC Sunderland	Ryhope Colliery Welfare	Shotton Comrades	Sth Shields Cleadon SC	Sth Shields Harton & W	Stokesley Sports Club	Teesside Athletic	Whitehaven Amateurs	Willington	Windscale	Wolviston
Annfield Plain		1-2	2-1	2-0	5-0	6-0	2-3	3-2	4-1	3-1	2-5	n/a	2-4	2-2	0-1	3-1	1-5	0-1	1-3	2-1
Birtley Town	3-0		2-0	1-0	1-1	4-1	1-0	3-2	3-2	4-1	6-1	n/a	1-0	1-1	1-1	1-4	0-0	4-3	0-2	2-2
Boldon Community Association	0-2	1-0		1-5	2-1	6-0	3-0	2-0	1-1	2-0	3-0	n/a	0-3	1-1	0-2	3-1	2-1	2-1	0-1	3-0
Cleator Moor Celtic	8-0	1-1	0-1		2-0	1-0	3-0	4-1	1-0	2-0	1-1	n/a	3-0	6-0	1-3	2-1	1-3	8-0	1-0	1-1
Coxhoe Athletic	0-1	0-4	2-3	0-3		1-1	0-2	2-5	2-4	4-0	3-1	n/a	2-1	0-2	0-0	0-2	0-4	1-2	1-2	4-0
Ferryhill Athletic	1-1	0-9	2-4	0-4	3-1		1-10	0-3	2-6	4-5	2-2	n/a	n/a	0-5	n/a	0-3	n/a	0-3	0-1	n/a
Gateshead Low Fell	1-1	1-3	0-1	1-3	1-1	3-2		3-1	6-2	1-2	0-1	n/a	3-3	1-3	2-2	1-4	1-2	2-0	1-0	2-2
Jarrow	1-3	1-0	0-0	0-1	6-0	3-2	1-1		5-2	2-1	6-0	n/a	1-2	2-0	0-1	1-0	1-0	3-4	0-3	1-0
New Marske Sports Club	1-4	0-1	2-3	0-1	2-1	n/a	2-0	0-1		6-0	1-1	n/a	2-3	2-1	1-5	0-2	0-2	1-4	1-1	2-0
Nissan SSC Sunderland	1-4	0-2	0-5	0-3	0-3	1-2	0-0	2-2	0-6		1-3	n/a	2-2	0-1	0-4	1-5	1-3	4-0	0-4	1-3
Ryhope Colliery Welfare	0-1	1-3	2-0	0-1	5-1	5-3	2-3	3-0	2-2	2-1		2-1	0-3	0-0	2-3	1-2	2-5	0-5	0-2	2-1
Shotton Comrades	n/a	n/a	n/a	n/a	n/a	n/a	n/a	n/a	n/a	n/a	n/a		n/a	n/a	1-1	0-2	n/a	n/a	n/a	n/a
South Shields Cleadon SC	0-3	1-1	1-2	2-2	4-1	7-2	1-0	1-0	2-1	3-2	2-0	n/a		4-0	0-2	0-4	1-4	1-0	2-0	3-0
South Shields Harton & Westoe	2-1	0-5	0-3	1-1	0-1	4-5	2-2	1-1	3-2	2-2	4-2	n/a	2-3		2-4	0-5	0-10	2-2	2-1	1-4
Stokesley Sports Club	0-1	1-0	2-1	1-0	3-1	6-0	3-0	2-1	2-2	6-1	2-1	n/a	1-2	1-1		3-2	0-1	1-0	4-2	1-0
Teesside Athletic	3-0	1-1	1-2	1-0	3-1	n/a	2-1	3-1	0-2	2-1	1-2	n/a	0-1	3-0	0-0		2-2	1-0	2-1	1-2
Whitehaven Amateurs	7-1	2-2	6-1	0-2	4-1	n/a	6-0	8-0	7-0	3-1	2-1	n/a	3-1	5-0	3-1	0-1		6-0	2-2	6-0
Willington	2-4	0-3	2-0	1-0	4-0	1-0	1-0	2-3	0-1	3-2	2-3	n/a	1-3	2-2	0-4	0-1	0-1		0-1	3-1
Windscale	2-1	0-1	3-1	2-1	2-0	2-0	4-1	0-0	5-1	4-0	4-1	4-1	1-2	5-0	2-2	1-2	0-1	3-1		2-3
Wolviston	3-1	1-4	3-0	0-3	1-2	4-0	5-1	1-1	1-1	2-0	0-1	n/a	2-3	6-2	0-2	0-1	1-4	0-2	1-4	

Note – Ferryhill Athletic and Shotton Comrades withdrew during the course of the season
Their results are shown above but are expunged from the league table

		P	W	D	L	F	A	Pts
Whitehaven Amateurs		34	26	4	4	118	27	82
Stokesley Sports Club		34	23	7	4	70	30	76
Birtley Town		34	20	9	5	67	32	69
South Shields Cleadon SC		34	21	4	9	64	48	67
Teesside Athletic		34	21	3	10	64	34	66
Cleator Moor Celtic		34	20	5	9	71	25	65
Windscale		34	19	4	11	69	36	61
Boldon Community Association	*-3*	34	18	3	13	50	47	54
Annfield Plain		34	17	2	15	63	67	53
Jarrow		34	12	6	16	52	58	42
Willington		34	12	2	20	48	68	38
Ryhope Colliery Welfare		34	11	4	19	48	73	37
Wolviston		34	9	5	20	47	69	32
South Shields Harton & Westoe		34	7	11	16	40	90	32
New Marske Sports Club	*-3*	34	9	6	19	53	74	30
Gateshead Low Fell		34	7	8	19	41	69	29
Coxhoe Athletic		34	7	3	24	36	81	24
Nissan SSC Sunderland		34	2	4	28	28	101	10

Ferryhill Athletic and Shotton Comrades – records expunged

WEARSIDE LEAGUE CONSTITUTION 2006-07

ANNFIELD PLAIN.......................... Derwent Park, West Road, Annfield Plain.......................... None
BIRTLEY TOWN............ Birtley Sports Complex, Durham Road, Birtley, Chester-le-Street DH3 2TB .... None
BOLDON COMMUNITY ASSOCIATION ... Boldon Welfare, New Road, Boldon Colliery NE35 9DS.......... 0191 536 4180 (Cricket Club)
CLEATOR MOOR CELTIC .... Celtic Club, Birks Road, Cleator Moor CA25 5HR.................. 01946 812476
COXHOE ATHLETIC .... Beechfield Park, Coxhoe DH6 4SD.......................... None
GUISBOROUGH BLACK SWAN... King George V Playing Fields, Howlbeck Road, Guisborough TS14 6LE.............. 01287 636925
HARTLEPOOL .... Grayfields Enclosure, Jesmond Gardens, Hartlepool .... None
JARROW.................... Perth Green Community Association, Inverness Road, Jarrow NE32 4AQ 0191 489 3743
NEW MARSKE SPORTS CLUB .... Gurney Street, New Marske, Redcar TS11 8EG 01642 479808
NISSAN SSC SUNDERLAND .... Nissan Sports Complex, Washington Road, Sunderland SR5 3NS 0191 415 2354
RYHOPE COLLIERY WELFARE ... Ryhope Recreation Park, Ryhope Street, Ryhope, Sunderland SR2 0AG 0191 521 2843
SOUTH SHIELDS CLEADON SC..... Jack Clark Park, Horsley Hill Road, South Shields NE33 3HE 0191 454 2023
SOUTH SHIELDS HARTON & WESTOE ... Harton Colliery Welfare, Boldon Lane, South Shields NE34 0NA.............. 0191 456 6166
TEESSIDE ATHLETIC .... Green Lane, Redcar TS10 3RW ....
WHITEHAVEN AMATEURS......... County Sports Field, Coach Road, Whitehaven CA22 2DD.......................... None
WILLINGTON.......................... Hall Lane Ground, Hall Lane Estate, Willington DL15 0QF 01388 746221
WINDSCALE.......................... Falcon Field, Smithfield, Egremont CA22 2QN 01946 820421
WOLVISTON.................. Metcalfe Park, Wynyard Road, Wolviston, Billingham TS22 5NE.................. 07768 321651

IN: Guisborough Black Swan (P – Teesside League Division Two), Hartlepool (P – Teesside League Division One)
OUT: Ferryhill Athletic (WS – Durham Alliance), Gateshead Low Fell (W), Shotton Comrades (WS), Stokesley Sports Club (P – Northern League Division Two)

LEAGUE CUP

FIRST ROUND

Gateshead Low Fell 2 Ryhope Colliery Welfare 1
Jarrow 3 South Shields Harton & Westoe 2
New Marske Sports Club 4 **Wolviston** 4 *aet* (4-5p)
Shotton Comrades 2 **Boldon Community Association** 6

SECOND ROUND

Annfield Plain 6 Nissan SSC Sunderland 0
Birtley Town 3 Gateshead Low Fell 2
Jarrow (w/o) v Ferryhill Athletic (scr.)
South Shields Cleadon SC 4 Coxhoe Athletic 1
Stokesley Sports Club 5 Cleator Moor Celtic 1
Whitehaven Amateurs 1 **Boldon Community Association** 3
Willington 3 Teesside Athletic 2
Wolviston 0 **Windscale** 1

QUARTER-FINALS

Annfield Plain 1 **Jarrow** 2
Birtley Town 1 Boldon Community Association 0
South Shields Cleadon SC 2 Stokesley Sports Club 0
Willington 0 **Windscale** 4

SEMI-FINALS

South Shields Cleadon SC 2 Jarrow 1
Windscale 2 **Birtley Town** 2 *aet* (3-4p)

FINAL

(May 19th at Boldon Community Association)
Birtley Town 1 South Shields Cleadon SC 0

MONKWEARMOUTH CHARITY CUP

FIRST ROUND

Annfield Plain 3 Willington 0
Boldon Community Association 1 **Gateshead Low Fell** 2
Nissan SSC Sunderland 2 Ferryhill Athletic 0
Whitehaven Amateurs (w/o) v Shotton Comrades (scr.)

SECOND ROUND

Coxhoe Athletic 2 **Cleator Moor Celtic** 4
Gateshead Low Fell 0 **Annfield Plain** 6
Jarrow 1 Birtley Town 0
Nissan SSC Sunderland 0 **Ryhope Colliery Welfare** 8
South Shields Harton & Westoe 3 Windscale 2 *aet*
Stokesley Sports Club 4 New Marske Sports Club 2
Teesside Athletic 2 Wolviston 1
Whitehaven Amateurs 4 South Shields Cleadon SC 3 *aet*

QUARTER-FINALS

Cleator Moor Celtic 4 South Shields Harton & Westoe 1
Ryhope Colliery Welfare 2 Annfield Plain 1
Stokesley Sports Club 0 **Teesside Athletic** 0 *aet* (3-4p)
Whitehaven Amateurs 0 **Jarrow** 3

SEMI-FINALS

Jarrow 2 Ryhope Colliery Welfare 1
Teesside Athletic 2 Cleator Moor Celtic 1

FINAL

(May 26th at Jarrow)
Jarrow 0 **Teesside Athletic** 2

SUNDERLAND SHIPOWNERS CUP

FIRST ROUND

Boldon Community Association 5 Gateshead Low Fell 0
Jarrow 0 **Cleator Moor Celtic** 1
Nissan SSC Sunderland (w/o) v Shotton Comrades (scr.)
South Shields Cleadon SC 3 Windscale 2

SECOND ROUND

Annfield Plain 2 **Cleator Moor Celtic** 5 *aet*
Birtley Town 4 Willington 1
Boldon Community Association 2 South Shields Cleadon SC 1
New Marske Sports Club 0 **Stokesley Sports Club** 6
Nissan SSC Sunderland 1 **Coxhoe Athletic** 3
Teesside Athletic 2 South Shields Harton & Westoe 1
Whitehaven Amateurs 2 Ryhope Colliery Welfare 0
Wolviston 5 Ferryhill Athletic 3

QUARTER-FINALS

Cleator Moor Celtic 4 Birtley Town 2
Coxhoe Athletic 0 **Stokesley Sports Club** 3
Whitehaven Amateurs 5 Boldon Community Association 0
Wolviston 0 **Teesside Athletic** 2 *(at Teesside Athletic)*

SEMI-FINALS

Cleator Moor Celtic 1 Whitehaven Amateurs 1 *aet* (4-3p)
Stokesley Sports Club 1 Teesside Athletic 0

FINAL

(May 1st at Stokesley Sports Club)
Stokesley Sports Club 2 Cleator Moor Celtic 1

WELSH ALLIANCE

	Bethesda Athletic	Caerwys	Cemaes Bay	Conwy United	Denbigh Town	Glan Conwy	Llanberis	Llandudno Junction	Llanrug United	Llanrwst United	Nefyn United	Penmaenmawr Phoenix	Prestatyn Town	Rhydymwyn	Rhyl Res.	Sealand Rovers
Bethesda Athletic		5-0	5-1	4-1	3-2	1-1	3-0	3-2	3-1	2-0	2-1	3-2	1-3	6-2	2-3	3-1
Caerwys	1-6		5-4	0-1	1-5	3-1	1-3	0-2	4-0	1-3	2-1	7-3	0-6	5-3	1-2	3-1
Cemaes Bay	2-10	2-7		0-3	3-6	0-0	0-7	1-2	3-1	1-0	1-4	4-3	2-4	6-2	0-3	1-1
Conwy United	2-3	2-1	4-0		0-1	1-2	1-0	0-0	0-1	0-3	1-1	1-3	2-4	0-3	1-1	1-2
Denbigh Town	2-4	3-0	7-0	3-0		1-0	3-0	2-0	3-2	4-1	2-0	7-0	1-1	6-1	4-2	4-0
Glan Conwy	0-2	2-3	4-1	1-2	0-5		2-3	2-3	3-3	1-2	0-2	2-1	2-5	0-0	0-4	5-0
Llanberis	2-1	6-2	1-2	4-3	1-2	3-1		3-3	1-3	0-1	2-3	2-2	0-2	3-1	1-1	3-2
Llandudno Junction	0-0	3-0	5-1	1-1	2-5	1-1	1-3		3-1	1-1	4-3	5-2	1-4	3-0	2-3	3-2
Llanrug United	1-1	2-1	3-0	2-0	2-1	4-2	1-0	0-0		1-4	1-3	4-1	1-1	3-1	2-3	3-3
Llanrwst United	1-0	5-2	7-0	0-1	0-2	5-0	0-0	3-2	3-0		2-1	6-0	2-3	4-0	2-2	2-0
Nefyn United	0-8	1-0	4-1	3-2	1-2	2-0	3-2	2-0	0-0	0-3		5-3	0-4	6-2	3-2	5-2
Penmaenmawr Phoenix	3-8	2-3	2-2	0-5	1-2	0-1	0-1	0-2	1-2	0-5	1-4		1-4	1-1	0-2	1-3
Prestatyn Town	3-0	4-1	14-0	1-1	1-1	4-1	5-2	3-0	3-0	4-0	6-1	2-0		2-0	2-2	9-1
Rhydymwyn	0-2	3-1	1-0	1-2	1-3	2-1	1-0	4-0	4-0	1-4	1-0	2-0	2-3		1-1	3-2
Rhyl Res.	2-4	2-1	8-0	3-2	2-0	7-0	4-0	2-0	5-1	6-1	1-0	4-2	2-4	5-0		6-0
Sealand Rovers	4-6	0-4	4-0	2-1	2-1	2-3	1-2	1-2	0-2	0-4	0-1	3-2	1-3	0-5	0-4	

		P	W	D	L	F	A	Pts
Prestatyn Town		30	25	5	0	114	28	80
Denbigh Town		30	23	2	5	90	31	71
Bethesda Athletic		30	22	3	5	101	43	69
Rhyl Res.		30	21	5	4	94	36	68
Llanrwst United		30	19	3	8	74	35	60
Nefyn United		30	16	2	12	60	57	50
Llandudno Junction		30	12	7	11	53	53	43
Llanrug United		30	12	6	12	47	57	42
Llanberis		30	12	4	14	55	55	40
Rhydymwyn		30	11	3	16	48	69	36
Caerwys		30	11	0	19	60	83	33
Conwy United		30	9	5	16	41	50	32
Glan Conwy		30	6	5	19	38	72	23
Sealand Rovers		30	6	2	22	40	92	20
Cemaes Bay		30	5	3	22	38	127	18
Penmaenmawr Phoenix	*-3*	30	1	3	26	37	102	3

COOKSON CUP

FIRST ROUND

Bethesda Athletic 3 Nefyn United 0
Caerwys 1 **Denbigh Town** 1 *aet* (2-4p)
Conwy United 3 **Llandudno Junction** 1
(Conwy United expelled)
Glan Conwy 1 **Sealand Rovers** 2
Llanrug United 0 **Rhyl Res.** 2
Llanrwst United 3 Locomotive Llanberis 0
Penmaenmawr Phoenix 4 **Cemaes Bay** 7
Prestatyn Town 3 Rhydymwyn 0

QUARTER-FINALS

Cemaes Bay 0 **Sealand Rovers** 2
Llandudno Junction 0 **Denbigh Town** 4
Llanrwst United 2 Bethesda Athletic 0
Prestatyn Town 1 **Rhyl Res.** 5

SEMI-FINALS

Denbigh Town 8 Sealand Rovers 0
Llanrwst United 0 **Rhyl Res.** 2

FINAL

(April 24th at Prestatyn Town)
Denbigh Town 2 Rhyl Res. 1

WELSH ALLIANCE CONSTITUTION 2006-07

BETHESDA ATHLETIC .... Parc Meurig Park, Bethesda, Bangor LL57 3NT .... None
CAERWYS.................. Lon Yr Ysgol, Caerwys, Mold CH7 5PZ .... None
CONWY UNITED.................. The Morfa, Penmaen Road, Conwy LL32 8HA 01492 573080
DENBIGH TOWN.................. Central Park, Park Street, Denbigh LL16 3DD 01745 812505
GLAN CONWY .... Cae Ffwt, Llanrwst Road, Glan Conwy, Colwyn Bay LL28 5SP.................. None
HALKYN UNITED .... Pant Newydd, Halkyn.................. 01352 780576
HOLYWELL TOWN .... Halkyn Road, Holywell CH8 7SJ .... None
LLANDUDNO JUNCTION .... The Flyover, Victoria Drive, Llandudno Junction LL31 9PG.................. None
LLANRUG UNITED .... Eithin Duon, Llanrug, Caernarfon LL55 4DA 01286 677543
LLANRWST UNITED .... Gwydyr Park, Llanrwst LL26 0PN.................. None
LLANBERIS .... Ffordd Padarn, Llanberis, Caernarfon LL55 4SU .... None
NEFYN UNITED .... Caer Delyn, Nefyn, Pwllheli .... None
PWLLHELI .... Dwyfor Leisure Centre, Recreation Road, Pwllheli LL53 5PF 01758 613437
RHYDYMWYN .... Vicarage Road, Rhydymwyn, Mold CH7 5HL .... None
RHYL.................. Belle Vue, Grange Road, Rhyl LL18 4BT 01745 338327
SEALAND ROVERS .... Welsh Road Playing Fields, Garden City, Deeside CH5 2HX .... None

IN: Halkyn United (R – Cymru Alliance), Holywell Town (R – Cymru Alliance), Pwllheli (Gwynedd League Premier Division)
OUT: Cemaes Bay (R – Gwynedd League Premier Division), Penmaenmawr Phoenix (R – Clwyd League Premier Division), Prestatyn Town (P – Cymru Alliance)

WELSH LEAGUE

	AFC Llwydcoed	Afan Lido	Barry Town	Bettws	Bridgend Town	Briton Ferry Athletic	Bryntirion Athletic	Caerleon	Dinas Powys	Ely Rangers	Goytre United	Maesteg Park Athletic	Neath Athletic	Newport YMCA	Pontardawe Town	Taffs Well	Ton Pentre	UWIC Inter Cardiff
AFC Llwydcoed		2-1	0-0	0-0	0-2	3-0	2-1	1-5	1-0	0-2	0-4	1-3	2-3	5-4	1-2	1-2	2-0	1-2
Afan Lido	2-0		3-0	2-0	2-2	2-1	3-1	1-0	3-1	1-0	2-2	2-2	1-1	0-2	0-1	0-1	1-2	0-1
Barry Town	5-0	1-0		2-1	3-1	1-1	1-1	1-0	0-0	3-3	0-0	3-5	1-2	2-2	2-1	2-2	1-1	2-1
Bettws	5-1	1-2	1-0	*D*	2-0	3-2	1-2	2-0	3-1	4-0	2-4	0-2	2-4	0-3	2-0	1-1	4-1	2-3
Bridgend Town	3-1	1-0	0-1	4-1	*I*	4-2	2-0	3-0	0-3	1-2	2-1	0-2	1-0	2-2	3-3	3-2	1-0	3-2
Briton Ferry Athletic	1-0	0-2	1-2	2-1	1-2	*V*	0-3	1-2	2-0	2-1	1-1	1-2	1-3	0-0	1-2	1-2	2-1	1-3
Bryntirion Athletic	2-1	3-3	5-2	6-0	3-1	5-0	*I*	2-0	2-2	2-1	1-4	2-2	1-2	1-1	2-4	0-2	1-2	3-1
Caerleon	2-0	1-0	1-0	1-0	1-2	0-0	1-4	*S*	0-0	2-1	0-2	1-0	0-2	3-0	0-1	3-2	0-0	2-1
Dinas Powys	1-0	2-2	1-0	2-2	1-0	3-2	1-2	2-0	*I*	4-2	1-2	2-1	0-2	4-0	3-1	1-2	1-0	2-2
Ely Rangers	3-2	1-0	0-1	3-0	1-1	2-4	4-0	3-0	0-2	*O*	1-3	2-0	2-2	1-0	3-1	3-2	0-1	1-0
Goytre United	0-2	2-1	2-2	2-0	1-1	5-3	2-0	7-3	2-0	2-1	*N*	2-2	1-4	4-2	1-1	7-3	4-0	2-1
Maesteg Park Athletic	2-1	1-0	4-0	2-0	1-0	2-2	2-2	1-1	2-0	2-2	1-2		3-3	4-2	2-0	2-0	1-2	0-2
Neath Athletic	3-1	1-2	3-0	1-0	2-0	1-2	3-2	6-1	4-0	2-0	0-0	1-2	*O*	0-1	1-1	4-0	4-0	3-1
Newport YMCA	1-1	0-1	0-1	3-0	2-0	0-3	2-0	2-0	0-0	2-0	0-3	0-0	1-1	*N*	3-3	2-1	1-6	3-1
Pontardawe Town	3-0	1-1	3-0	1-1	1-0	1-0	2-0	1-0	2-0	1-0	1-2	1-2	1-1	1-1	*E*	5-0	4-1	2-0
Taffs Well	2-0	2-2	2-0	1-1	2-4	0-1	1-0	4-1	0-1	1-1	1-1	0-1	0-2	2-2	0-2		1-2	2-2
Ton Pentre	1-2	2-3	1-0	5-1	0-4	1-1	2-3	4-1	2-0	6-1	1-2	1-2	1-3	1-2	0-1	2-2		1-1
UWIC Inter Cardiff	2-1	3-1	2-0	0-3	2-2	4-1	1-0	2-1	1-1	5-0	2-3	2-1	1-2	3-2	2-2	2-1	3-1	

Division One	P	W	D	L	F	A	Pts
Goytre United	**34**	**22**	**9**	**3**	**82**	**42**	**75**
Neath Athletic	**34**	**22**	**7**	**5**	**76**	**32**	**73**
Pontardawe Town	**34**	**18**	**9**	**7**	**57**	**35**	**63**
Maesteg Park Athletic	**34**	**18**	**9**	**7**	**61**	**40**	**63**
UWIC Inter Cardiff	**34**	**16**	**6**	**12**	**61**	**52**	**54**
Bridgend Town	**34**	**16**	**6**	**12**	**55**	**47**	**54**
Afan Lido	**34**	**13**	**8**	**13**	**46**	**41**	**47**
Dinas Powys	**34**	**13**	**8**	**13**	**42**	**44**	**47**
Bryntirion Athletic	**34**	**13**	**6**	**15**	**62**	**58**	**45**
Newport YMCA	**34**	**11**	**11**	**12**	**48**	**54**	**44**
Barry Town	**34**	**11**	**10**	**13**	**39**	**50**	**43**
Ely Rangers	**34**	**12**	**5**	**17**	**47**	**59**	**41**
Ton Pentre	**34**	**11**	**5**	**18**	**51**	**60**	**38**
Caerleon	**34**	**11**	**4**	**19**	**33**	**58**	**37**
Taffs Well	**34**	**9**	**9**	**16**	**46**	**62**	**36**
Bettws	**34**	**10**	**5**	**19**	**46**	**63**	**35**
Briton Ferry Athletic	**34**	**9**	**6**	**19**	**43**	**64**	**33**
AFC Llwydcoed	**34**	**8**	**3**	**23**	**35**	**69**	**27**

Reserve Division East		P	W	D	L	F	A	Pts
UWIC Inter Cardiff Res.	*-3*	30	26	1	3	108	25	76
Caerleon Res.		30	18	6	6	65	43	60
Newport YMCA Res.		30	17	5	8	66	46	56
Ely Rangers Res.		30	17	5	8	62	42	56
Grange Harlequins Res.	*-3*	30	16	6	8	84	52	51
Treowen Stars Res.		30	15	5	10	66	50	50
Croesyceiliog Res.		30	14	4	12	62	67	46
Caldicot Town Res.	*-3*	30	14	4	12	72	51	43
Bryntirion Athletic Res.		30	12	3	15	71	88	39
Dinas Powys Res.		30	11	3	16	50	73	36
Cardiff Corinthians Res.		30	8	5	17	52	77	29
Caerau Ely Res.		30	8	4	18	51	77	28
Chepstow Town Res.		30	7	7	16	41	71	28
Pontyclun Res.		30	7	6	17	52	77	27
Risca & Gelli United Res.		30	6	8	16	37	57	26
Llantwit Fardre Res.		30	6	4	20	55	98	22

Reserve Division West	P	W	D	L	F	A	Pts
Neath Athletic Res.	28	25	2	1	111	20	77
Garden Village Res.	28	22	1	5	107	35	67
Goytre United Res.	28	19	3	6	109	52	60
Afan Lido Res.	28	16	4	8	77	46	52
Pontardawe Town Res.	28	15	0	13	76	59	45
AFC Llwydcoed Res.	28	13	4	11	72	66	43
Briton Ferry Athletic Res.	28	11	7	10	60	67	40
Porthcawl Town Res.	28	12	4	12	50	69	40
Maesteg Park Athletic Res.	28	10	4	14	31	59	34
Ammanford Res.	28	9	6	13	55	61	33
Morriston Town Res.	28	6	9	13	43	76	27
Cwmamman United Res.	28	7	4	17	44	87	25
Newcastle Emlyn Res.	28	7	4	17	44	87	25
Ystradgynlais Res.	28	7	3	18	49	83	24
Seven Sisters Res.	28	2	3	23	28	89	9

WELSH LEAGUE DIVISION ONE CONSTITUTION 2006-07

AFAN LIDO .... **Runtech Stadium, Princess Margaret Way, Aberavon Beach, Port Talbot SA12 6QW** **01639 892960**
BARRY TOWN .... **Jenner Park Athletic Stadium, Barry Road, Barry CF62 9BG** **01446 746870**
BRIDGEND TOWN .... **Coychurch Road, Bridgend CF31 3AP** **01656 655097**
BRYNTIRION ATHLETIC .... **Bryntirion Park, Bryntirion, Bridgend** **01656 652702**
CAERLEON .... **Cold Bath Road, Caerleon, Newport NP18 1NF** **01633 420074**
CROESYCEILIOG .... **Woodland Road, Croesyceiliog, Cwmbran NP11 2DZ** **01633 485157**
DINAS POWYS .... **Murchfield, Sunnycroft Lane, Dinas Powys CF64 4QP** **07745 457848**
ENTO ABERAMAN ATHLETIC .... **Aberaman Park, Cardiff Road, Aberaman CF44 6AA** **07966 597567**
ELY RANGERS .... **Station Road, Wenvoe CF5 6AG** **02920 598725**
GOYTRE UNITED .... **Glen Hafod Park, Goytre, Port Talbot SA13 2YP** **01639 898983**
GRANGE HARLEQUINS .... **Leckwith Stadium, Leckwith, Cardiff CF11 8AZ** **02920 225345**
MAESTEG PARK ATHLETIC .... **Tudor Park, Maesteg CF34 0SW** **01656 730005**
NEATH ATHLETIC .... **Llandarcy Park, Llandarcy, Neath** **01792 812036**
NEWPORT YMCA .... **Mendalgief Road, Newport NP20 2HF** **01633 266872**
PONTARDAWE TOWN .... **Recreation Ground, Alloy Industrial Estate, Pontardawe SA8 4EN** **01792 862228**
PONTYPRIDD TOWN .... **Ynysangharad Park, Pontypridd** **01443 486571**
TAFFS WELL .... **Rhiw Dda'r, Parish Road, Taffs Well CF15 7QB** **02920 811080**
TON PENTRE .... **Ynys Park, Sawmill Villas, Ton Pentre CF41 7AF** **01443 442625**
UWIC INTER CARDIFF .... **Cyncoed Road, Cardiff CF23 6XD** **02920 416155**

IN: Grange Harlequins (R – Welsh Premier League), Croesyceiliog (P), ENTO Aberaman Athletic (P), Pontypridd Town (P)
OUT: AFC Llwydcoed (R), Bettws (R), Briton Ferry Athletic (R)

	Abertillery Exscelsior	Ammanford	Caerau Ely	Caldicot Town	Cardiff Corinthians	Croesyceiliog	ENTO Aberaman Athletic	Garden Village	Garw Athletic	Gwynfi United	Merthyr Saints	Morriston Town	Penrhiwceiber Rangers	Pontyclun	Pontypridd Town	Porthcawl Town	Tredegar Town	Troedyrhiw
Abertillery Excelsior		0-0	2-3	2-2	0-2	2-3	0-2	1-3	0-1	3-3	2-2	1-2	0-3	3-0	2-1	2-2	1-2	1-2
Ammanford	3-1		1-0	4-4	4-3	1-3	2-0	2-3	1-3	3-0	3-2	0-2	1-1	0-1	1-3	1-0	3-0	2-2
Caerau Ely	1-1	3-1		6-2	4-1	2-4	0-2	2-0	0-2	4-0	2-5	5-5	2-4	2-1	1-1	5-2	3-3	4-0
Caldicot Town	2-0	3-1	1-0	*D*	4-1	4-0	1-1	1-0	2-1	8-3	3-2	1-0	1-4	1-3	0-0	2-1	2-1	0-1
Cardiff Corinthians	1-3	0-0	4-2	1-1	*I*	1-2	1-3	1-0	0-1	0-1	4-1	1-3	4-0	2-0	0-6	7-2	0-2	1-3
Croesyceiliog	3-1	3-2	5-3	4-3	4-0	*V*	1-2	3-3	1-6	7-1	3-2	3-2	5-3	2-0	0-2	3-2	4-1	2-1
ENTO Aberaman Athletic	3-0	1-0	0-0	1-1	3-1	4-1	*I*	1-1	0-1	4-0	2-1	2-2	1-1	0-1	0-1	2-0	5-0	1-1
Garden Village	2-1	2-0	3-0	0-0	1-0	3-2	1-2	*S*	2-3	3-1	6-0	1-2	0-2	1-0	1-2	3-2	2-2	1-0
Garw Athletic	6-1	2-0	3-0	0-4	1-1	2-1	0-2	2-2	*I*	1-2	4-0	3-1	3-1	5-2	0-2	2-0	3-1	1-0
Gwynfi United	1-5	0-2	2-2	1-5	2-2	2-5	0-2	1-1	0-2	*O*	0-2	1-6	1-1	3-2	0-7	0-1	0-6	0-2
Merthyr Saints	5-1	2-0	2-1	1-0	0-1	2-3	1-1	0-2	0-2	3-0	*N*	1-0	0-1	1-1	1-3	4-0	3-2	0-4
Morriston Town	2-3	1-2	3-0	3-2	1-0	1-2	1-2	0-1	1-2	2-0	1-2		4-1	3-1	0-3	0-0	2-0	5-2
Penrhiwceiber Rangers	5-1	3-2	9-1	1-1	3-1	2-4	1-2	1-2	8-0	7-0	0-0	2-2	*T*	5-4	1-1	0-3	4-2	2-0
Pontyclun	1-1	3-0	1-3	1-1	0-3	2-4	0-0	1-2	0-2	3-0	6-0	1-2	0-1	*W*	2-0	0-3	1-2	0-5
Pontypridd Town	5-1	7-1	5-0	4-2	4-1	0-0	1-1	3-0	1-0	4-0	4-0	3-3	3-1	1-0	*O*	7-0	1-0	3-1
Porthcawl Town	0-0	0-0	1-4	1-3	2-0	1-2	1-2	0-3	1-2	3-1	2-2	1-2	1-3	0-2	0-1		0-1	1-0
Tredegar Town	2-2	0-0	0-0	3-2	3-2	2-2	0-3	0-3	1-3	4-3	2-1	1-2	1-0	3-1	0-1	3-0		0-5
Troedyrhiw	2-1	3-1	4-0	2-2	4-0	0-1	2-0	2-0	1-0	11-1	3-1	1-2	4-3	4-2	0-1	3-1	2-0	

Division Two		P	W	D	L	F	A	Pts
Pontypridd Town		34	26	6	2	91	20	84
Croesyceiliog		34	24	3	7	92	65	75
ENTO Aberaman Athletic		34	19	10	5	57	25	67
Troedyrhiw		34	20	3	11	77	40	63
Garden Village		34	18	6	10	58	40	60
Morriston Town		34	17	5	12	68	51	56
Penrhiwceiber Rangers		34	16	7	11	84	57	55
Caldicot Town		34	15	10	9	71	54	55
Tredegar Town		34	12	6	16	50	66	42
Garw Athletic	*-33*	34	24	2	8	69	39	41
Merthyr Saints		34	11	5	18	49	69	38
Ammanford		34	10	7	17	44	61	37
Cardiff Corinthians		34	9	4	21	47	70	31
Caerau Ely	*-10*	34	11	7	16	65	80	30
Pontyclun		34	8	4	22	43	65	28
Abertillery Excelsior		34	5	9	20	45	77	24
Porthcawl Town		34	6	5	23	34	72	23
Gwynfi United	*-6*	34	3	5	26	30	123	8

RESERVES CUP

FINAL

(May 10th at Taffs Well)

Neath Athletic Res. 3 Chepstow Town Res. 1

LEAGUE CUP

FIRST ROUND

Abertillery Excelsior 2 Newport YMCA 1

Barry Town 0 **Garden Village** 3

Briton Ferry Athletic 0 **Merthyr Saints** 1

Caerau Ely 4 Bridgend Town 3

Cambrian & Clydach Vale BC 2 Cwmbran Celtic 1

Cardiff Corinthians 3 **Penrhiwceiber Rangers** 4

Croesyceiliog 1 Caerleon 0

Cwmamman United 2 Gwynfi United 1

ENTO Aberaman Athletic 1 **Pontypridd Town** 3

Goytre 0 **Pontardawe Town** 3

Llantwit Fardre 2 Treharris Athletic 1 *aet*

Maesteg Park Athletic 5 Ely Rangers 2

Morriston Town 2 Afan Lido 0

Newcastle Emlyn 3 **Neath Athletic** 5 *aet*

Penrhiwfer 2 **AFC Porth** 5

Porthcawl Tn 1 **Pontyclun** 2 *aet*

Risca & Gelli United 0 **AFC Llwydcoed** 0 *aet* (1-3p)

Seven Sisters 1 **Ystradgynlais** 2

Ton Pentre 4 Dinas Powys 1

Tredegar Town 1 **Caldicot Town** 5

Troedyrhiw 2 Bryntirion Athletic 0

UWIC Inter Cardiff (w/o) v Garw Athletic (scr.)

SECOND ROUND

AFC Porth 1 **Taffs Well** 2

Blaenrhondda 0 **Maesteg Park Athletic** 3

Caerau Ely 2 Abertillery Excelsior 1

Cambrian & Clydach Vale BC 1 **Neath Athletic** 3

WELSH LEAGUE DIVISION TWO CONSTITUTION 2006-07

AFC LLWYDCOED . . . . . Welfare Ground, Llwydcoed, Aberdare 01685 873924
AMMANFORD . . . . . Rice Road, Colonel Road, Betws, Ammanford SA18 2HP 01269 592407
BETTWS . . . . . North Site, Bettws Road, Bettws, Bridgend CF32 8YD 07887 530804
BRITON FERRY ATHLETIC . . . . . Old Road, Briton Ferry, Neath SA11 2HA 07817 048195
CAERAU ELY . . . . . Cwrt-y-Ala, Caerau, Cardiff CF64 4HE 07790 084636
CALDICOT TOWN . . . . . Jubilee Way, Caldicot NP9 1XX 01291 423519
CAMBRIAN & CLYDACH VALE BC . . . . . King George V New Field, Clydach Vale 01443 442649
CARDIFF CORINTHIANS . . . . . Riverside Ground, Through Station Road, Radyr, Cardiff CF15 8AA 02920 843407
GARDEN VILLAGE . . . . . Stafford Common, Victoria Road, Gowerton, Swansea SA4 3AB 01792 894933
GARW ATHLETIC . . . . . Blandy Park, Pontycymmer, Bridgend CF32 8LD 07779 956926
MERTHYR SAINTS . . . . . ICI Pavilion, Pant, Merthyr Tydfil 01685 386140
MORRISTON TOWN . . . . . The Dingle, Clydach Road, Morriston, Swansea SA6 6QH 01792 702033
PENRHIWCEIBER RANGERS . . Glasbrook, Glasbrook Terrace, Penrhiwceiber, Mountain Ash CF45 3SY 01443 473368
PONTYCLUN . . . . . Ivor Park, Cowbridge Road, Pontyclun CF72 9EE 01443 222182
TREDEGAR TOWN . . . . . Tredegar Leisure Complex, Stable Lane, Tredegar NP22 3BH 01495 723554
TREHARRIS ATHLETIC . . . . . Athletic Ground, Commercial Terrace, Treharris CF46 5PY 07790 511985
TROEDYRHIW . . . . . The Willows, Bridge Street, Troedyrhiw, Merthyr Tydfil CF48 4DX 01443 692198
WEST END . . . . . Pryderri Park, Townhill, Swansea SA1 6LD . . . . . None

IN: AFC Llwydcoed (R), Bettws (R), Briton Ferry Athletic (R), Cambrian & Clydach Vale BC (P), Treharris Athletic (P), West End (P)

OUT: Abertillery Excelsior (R), Croesyceiliog (P), ENTO Aberaman Athletic (P), Gwynfi United (R), Pontypridd Town (P), Porthcawl Town (R)

	AFC Porth	Blaenrhondda	Cambrian/Clydach Vale BC	Chepstow Town	Cwmamman United	Cwmbran Celtic	Goytre	Llantwit Fardre	Llanwern	Newcastle Emlyn	Penrhiwfer	Pentwyn Dynamo	Risca & Gelli United	Seven Sisters	Treharris Athletic	Treowen Stars	West End	Ystradgynlais
AFC Porth		2-0	1-2	3-2	1-1	2-2	1-1	2-0	2-4	3-2	2-1	3-2	2-4	1-0	1-1	1-1	1-1	0-3
Blaenrhondda	2-1		1-1	1-2	1-0	0-2	0-0	1-1	2-0	2-3	1-0	3-1	3-2	1-0	3-4	2-0	1-0	4-0
Cambrian & Clydach Vale BC	1-0	0-0	*D*	3-0	1-2	1-0	1-2	1-1	6-3	4-2	4-1	0-0	2-1	4-0	5-0	2-0	5-2	3-1
Chepstow Town	1-2	1-0	2-2	*I*	3-2	1-2	2-4	4-2	1-3	0-1	3-0	0-3	5-1	2-2	1-1	2-3	0-3	3-1
Cwmamman United	2-1	8-2	1-2	2-5	*V*	4-1	2-1	2-3	2-0	4-0	0-0	1-1	1-0	0-1	2-1	3-3	2-6	0-1
Cwmbran Celtic	1-2	3-0	0-2	0-2	2-4	*I*	1-3	1-0	0-2	1-2	3-0	2-2	3-0	3-1	2-1	4-1	1-3	0-3
Goytre	1-2	3-0	2-2	0-1	2-3	4-0	*S*	2-1	1-1	2-3	2-2	1-2	5-0	0-2	3-3	3-0	2-4	2-1
Llantwit Fardre	1-0	2-2	0-3	0-0	2-2	2-0	0-0	*I*	2-0	1-5	2-2	0-1	2-3	2-0	1-2	1-0	0-4	2-3
Llanwern	2-1	4-1	1-3	3-0	2-1	1-0	4-1	1-2	*O*	3-0	4-0	4-2	4-3	2-0	0-3	6-3	2-1	4-4
Newcastle Emlyn	2-1	4-1	1-0	5-2	5-2	1-0	1-0	2-1	0-0	*N*	3-1	1-2	0-1	5-3	0-1	4-2	4-2	5-2
Penrhiwfer	2-4	3-0	2-6	3-5	1-1	1-1	1-0	0-0	3-2	2-4		4-1	2-3	4-9	2-5	0-1	1-2	3-4
Pentwyn Dynamo	4-2	4-2	4-2	4-2	1-1	3-0	1-1	3-0	4-1	3-3	2-2	*T*	5-2	2-0	2-0	0-0	3-1	3-2
Risca & Gelli United	1-1	1-0	0-1	1-1	1-1	3-1	4-0	2-1	2-0	3-2	1-3	1-1	*H*	1-1	2-5	2-1	3-1	1-0
Seven Sisters	3-2	3-2	0-3	2-1	3-3	1-4	3-1	0-2	0-1	4-3	2-1	1-0	1-0	*R*	0-1	0-1	0-2	1-1
Treharris Athletic	3-0	4-1	4-3	3-0	4-3	3-0	1-0	2-2	2-0	1-3	6-1	4-0	5-1	6-1	*E*	1-1	2-3	3-1
Treowen Stars	0-1	1-0	0-1	3-2	2-0	0-1	0-1	0-1	0-1	1-2	1-0	2-1	3-2	2-1	0-2	*E*	0-1	1-1
West End	4-1	1-1	1-5	5-2	5-2	4-2	4-1	2-1	5-0	6-0	8-1	2-1	3-1	3-2	2-1	2-0		3-2
Ystradgynlais	2-1	3-2	1-2	2-1	2-3	1-0	3-1	1-0	3-2	1-1	4-3	2-2	2-1	1-0	1-2	3-1	0-2	

Chepstow Town 0 **Troedyrhiw** 4
Croesyceiliog 2 **Llanwern** 3
Cwmamman Utd 0 **Ton Pentre** 5
Garden Village 1 Pontyclun 0
Goytre United 3 Pontypridd Town 0
Llantwit Fardre 4 Caldicot Town 1
Penrhiwceiber Rangers 3 AFC Llwydcoed 1
Pontardawe Town 4 Ammanford 1
Treowen Stars 2 **Bettws** 4
UWIC Inter Cardiff 2 Pentwyn Dynamo 1 *aet*
West End 0 **Morriston Town** 4
Ystradgynlais 2 **Merthyr Saints** 5

THIRD ROUND

Bettws 2 **Pontardawe Tn** 3 *aet*
Garden Village 6 Caerau Ely 1
Goytre United 1 **UWIC Inter Cardiff** 1 *aet* (0-3p)
Maesteg Park Athletic 2 Taffs Well 0
Merthyr Saints 0 **Llanwern** 1
Morriston Town 0 Troedyrhiw 0 *aet* (4-2p)
Neath Athletic 3 Ton Pentre 1
Penrhiwceiber Rangers 3 Llantwit Fardre 1

QUARTER-FINALS

Llanwern 2 **Garden Village** 3
Maesteg Park Athletic 1 **Morriston Town** 3
Pontardawe Town 2 Neath Athletic 0
UWIC Inter Cardiff 2 **Penrhiwceiber Rangers** 3

SEMI-FINALS

(both at Afan Lido)

Morriston Town 1 **Pontardawe Town** 2
Penrhiwceiber Rangers 2 Garden Village 1

FINAL

(May 30th at Afan Lido)

Pontardawe Town 1 **Penrhiwceiber Rangers** 2 *aet*

Division Three	P	W	D	L	F	A	Pts
West End	34	25	2	7	98	50	77
Cambrian & Clydach Vale BC	34	23	6	5	83	36	75
Treharris Athletic	34	22	5	7	87	47	71
Newcastle Emlyn	34	21	3	10	79	62	66
Pentwyn Dynamo	34	16	10	8	70	52	58
Llanwern	34	18	3	13	67	60	57
Ystradgynlais	34	16	5	13	62	62	53
Cwmamman United	34	12	9	13	67	66	45
Risca & Gelli United	34	13	5	16	54	68	44
AFC Porth	34	12	7	15	50	59	43
Goytre	34	10	8	16	52	56	38
Chepstow Town	34	11	5	18	59	72	38
Seven Sisters	34	11	4	19	47	67	37
Llantwit Fardre	34	9	9	16	38	53	36
Cwmbran Celtic	34	11	3	20	43	60	36
Blaenrhondda	34	10	6	18	42	64	36
Treowen Stars	34	10	5	19	34	54	35
Penrhiwfer	34	5	7	22	52	96	22

WELSH LEAGUE DIVISION THREE CONSTITUTION 2006-07

AFC PORTH . . . . **Dinas Park, Dinas, Rhondda** **07840 294842**
ABERBARGOED BUDS . . . . **Recreation Ground, Aberbargoed** . . . . **None**
ABERTILLERY EXCELSIOR . . . . **Woodland Field, Cwmtillery, Abertillery NP13 1LA** **01495 217839**
CHEPSTOW TOWN . . . . **Larkfield Ground, Newport Road, Chepstow NP16 5PR** **01291 629220**
CWMAMMAN UNITED . . . . **Grenig Park, Glanamman, Ammanford SA18 1YU** . . . . **None**
CWMBRAN CELTIC . . . . **Cwmbran Stadium, Henllys Way, Cwmbran NP44 3XL** . . . . **Celtic Club: 01633 774019**
GOYTRE . . . . **Plough Road, Penperlleni, Pontypool NP4 0AL** . . . . **None**
GWYNFI UNITED . . . . **Gwynfi Welfare, Margaret Terrace, Blaengwynfi, Port Talbot SA13 3UY** **01639 852089**
LLANGEINOR . . . . **Llangeinor Park, Llangeinor, Bridgend** **01656 871676**
LLANSAWEL . . . . **Neath Abbey Road, Neath SA10 7BR** **01639 635013**
LLANTWIT FARDRE . . . . **Tonteg Park, Church Village, Pontypridd CF31 1ND** **01443 207393**
LLANWERN . . . . **Newport Stadium, Spytty Park, Newport NP19 4PT** **07762 013310**
NEWCASTLE EMLYN . . . . **Parc Emlyn, New Road, Newcastle Emlyn SA38 9BA** **01239 710007**
PENTWYN DYNAMO . . . . **Parc Coed-y-Nant, Pentwyn, Cardiff** **02920 549211**
PORTHCAWL TOWN . . . . **Locks Lane, Porthcawl CF36 3HY** **07866 545830**
RISCA UNITED . . . . **Ty Isaf Park, Pontymister Road, Risca NP11 6ND** **01633 615081 Club:01633 615689**
SEVEN SISTERS . . . . **Welfare Ground, Seven Sisters, Neath** **01639 700354**
YSTRADGYNLAIS . . . . **Recreation Ground, Ynyscedwyn Road, Ystradgynlais, Swansea SA9 1BH** . . . . **None**

IN: Aberbargoed Buds (P – Gwent County League Division One), Abertillery Excelsior (R), Gwynfi United (R), Llangeinor (P – South Wales Amateur League Division One), Llansawel (P – Neath Senior League Premier Division), Porthcawl Town (R)

OUT: Blaenrhondda (R – South Wales Senior League Division One), Cambrian & Clydach Vale BC (P), Penrhiwfer (R – South Wales Senior League Division One), Treharris Athletic (P), Treowen Stars (R – Gwent County League Division One), West End (P)

WELSH NATIONAL LEAGUE (WREXHAM AREA)

	Acrefair Youth	Borras Park Albion	Brickfield Rangers	Brynteg Village	Cefn United	Chirk AAA	Coedpoeth United	Corwen Amateurs	Hawarden Rangers	Llangollen Town	Llay Welfare	Mold Alexandra	Mynydd Isa	Penycae	Rhos Aelwyd	Ruthin Town Res.	Summerhill Brymbo
Acrefair Youth	*P*	1-0	0-5	2-2	2-2	1-1	3-1	5-2	2-0	3-2	3-0	5-3	0-1	1-1	1-1	3-0	1-2
Borras Park Albion	1-2	*R*	0-1	2-4	0-2	0-3	3-4	0-4	2-1	1-3	2-4	0-2	1-4	0-1	3-1	1-1	1-4
Brickfield Rangers	0-2	3-1	*E*	3-1	3-0	1-6	1-1	6-2	6-2	0-0	4-1	1-1	1-0	1-2	2-2	2-1	2-0
Brynteg Village	2-2	3-1	1-2	*M*	2-2	4-2	0-0	4-0	1-2	3-3	3-7	2-2	3-4	2-1	5-4	4-1	3-2
Cefn United	0-1	5-0	1-1	1-1	*I*	0-1	4-2	1-0	2-3	1-0	3-0	5-1	1-2	3-1	1-2	2-0	0-0
Chirk AAA	1-3	3-0	2-1	1-1	2-1	*E*	1-1	3-0	5-0	7-2	3-1	3-2	0-2	3-0	3-0	1-0	1-3
Coedpoeth United	1-2	2-2	1-2	1-1	1-5	2-1	*R*	1-0	0-2	3-3	5-2	3-4	0-2	4-0	1-5	2-0	3-1
Corwen Amateurs	1-4	1-0	0-1	2-0	1-0	3-6	2-3		3-2	0-1	4-4	3-1	0-1	1-1	1-6	0-0	2-4
Hawarden Rangers	3-1	7-2	2-3	2-1	2-1	1-4	2-2	2-2		1-2	4-0	4-2	0-4	5-1	2-4	4-2	1-0
Llangollen Town	2-2	1-3	1-3	7-3	0-1	6-3	0-4	4-1	2-4	*D*	4-2	4-2	2-3	3-1	2-5	2-3	1-2
Llay Welfare	2-0	2-4	4-1	3-3	2-2	0-4	5-3	4-4	4-5	3-7	*I*	2-1	2-4	0-2	1-2	6-2	1-1
Mold Alexandra	3-0	1-3	1-3	4-3	4-0	1-1	2-2	10-0	3-0	1-1	5-1	*V*	2-1	2-1	1-4	3-4	4-4
Mynydd Isa	2-0	3-1	2-2	3-0	5-0	4-1	3-1	6-0	2-0	3-2	8-4	1-1	*I*	3-0	2-2	5-1	3-0
Penycae	7-0	2-2	0-4	6-4	2-2	1-7	0-1	1-1	2-1	0-1	4-3	1-3	2-0	*S*	0-2	4-2	3-1
Rhos Aelwyd	4-0	2-1	2-1	6-3	4-1	5-0	5-3	1-1	4-2	2-0	2-3	4-2	2-0	3-3	*I*	5-0	2-2
Ruthin Town Res.	3-0	0-2	1-3	1-3	0-2	1-5	0-2	2-1	0-3	0-2	2-1	2-4	1-6	1-6	0-1	*O*	1-5
Summerhill Brymbo	3-1	4-2	2-0	1-2	1-0	1-2	2-3	3-1	3-2	4-1	3-1	4-3	1-4	5-0	4-4	5-0	*N*

Premier Division		P	W	D	L	F	A	Pts
Rhos Aelwyd		32	21	7	4	98	51	70
Mynydd Isa	*-9*	32	25	3	4	93	33	69
Chirk AAA		32	20	4	8	86	48	64
Brickfield Rangers		32	19	6	7	69	42	63
Summerhill Brymbo		32	17	5	10	77	55	56
Acrefair Youth		32	14	7	11	53	58	49
Hawarden Rangers		32	15	2	15	71	72	47
Coedpoeth United		32	12	8	12	63	65	44
Mold Alexandra		32	12	7	13	81	72	43
Cefn United		32	12	7	13	51	46	43
Llangollen Town		32	12	5	15	71	74	41
Brynteg Village		32	10	10	12	74	80	40
Penycae		32	11	6	15	56	71	39
Llay Welfare		32	8	5	19	75	104	29
Corwen Amateurs		32	6	7	19	43	87	25
Borras Park Albion		32	6	3	23	41	81	21
Ruthin Town Res.		32	5	2	25	32	95	17

PREMIER DIVISION CUP

PRELIMINARY ROUND

Coedpoeth United 1 **Acrefair Youth** 2

FIRST ROUND

Brickfield Rangers 2 Corwen Amateurs 1
Cefn United 8 Penycae 2
Chirk AAA 3 Summerhill Brymbo 2
Hawarden Rangers 1 Acrefair Youth 0
Llangollen Town 3 **Mynydd Isa** 4
Llay Welfare 1 **Ruthin Town Res.** 2
Mold Alexandra 3 Brynteg Village 1
Rhos Aelwyd 4 Borras Pk Albion 0

QUARTER-FINALS

Cefn United 1 Hawarden Rangers 0
Chirk AAA 3 Mold Alexandra 1
Rhos Aelwyd 1 Brickfield Rangers 0
Ruthin Town Res. 0 **Mynydd Isa** 5

SEMI-FINALS

(played over two legs)

Chirk AAA 1 Rhos Aelwyd 4, **Rhos Aelwyd** 2 Chirk AAA 0
Mynydd Isa 0 Cefn United 0, Cefn United 0 **Mynydd Isa** 2

FINAL

(May 2nd at Newi Cefn Druids)

Mynydd Isa 4 Rhos Aelwyd 3

WELSH NATIONAL LEAGUE (WREXHAM AREA) PREMIER DIVISION CONSTITUTION 2006-07

ACREFAIR YOUTH .... The Bont Playing Field, Froncysyllte, Wrexham .... None
BORRAS PARK ALBION .... Dean Road, Wrexham LL13 9EF .... None
BRICKFIELD RANGERS .... Court Road, Wrexham LL13 7SN .... None
BRYNTEG VILLAGE .... Solway Banks, Southsea, Wrexham .... None
CASTELL ALUN COLTS .... Castell Alun Sports Centre, Fagl Lane, Hope, Wrexham LL12 9PY .... None
CEFN UNITED .... Church Field, Rhosymedre, Wrexham .... None
CHIRK AAA .... Holyhead Road, Chirk, Wrexham LL14 5NA 01691 773676
COEDPOETH UNITED .... Pengelli Playing Fields, Coedpoeth, Wrexham .... None
CORWEN AMATEURS .... War Memorial Park, Corwen .... None
HAWARDEN RANGERS .... Gladstone Playing Fields, Hawarden .... None
LLANGOLLEN TOWN .... Tower Field, Dinbren Road, Llangollen LL20 8TF .... None
LLAY WELFARE .... The Ring, Llay, Wrexham .... None
MOLD ALEXANDRA .... Alyn Park, Denbigh Road, Mold CH7 .... None
PENYCAE .... Afoneitha Road, Penycae, Wrexham LL14 2PF .... None
RHOS AELWYD .... Ponciau Park, Clarke Street, Ponciau, Wrexham LL14 1RT .... None
SUMMERHILL BRYMBO .... Brymbo Sports Complex, College Hill, Tanyfron, Wrexham LL11 5TF 01978 752577

IN: Castell Alun Colts (P)

OUT: Borras Park Albion (R), Mynydd Isa (P – Cymru Alliance), Ruthin Town Reserves (R)

Division One		P	W	D	L	F	A	Pts
Castell Alun Colts		24	18	4	2	82	29	58
Airbus UK Res.		24	17	1	6	67	38	52
Gresford Athletic Res.		24	16	3	5	65	30	51
Overton Recreation		24	15	2	7	77	42	47
Llanuwchllyn		24	13	1	10	70	62	40
New Brighton Villa		24	11	2	11	80	50	35
Glyn Ceiriog		24	10	4	10	55	67	34
Cefn United Res.		24	9	3	12	48	59	30
Ruabon Villa		24	7	4	13	60	75	25
Ruthin Town Colts		24	6	5	13	34	83	23
Rhos Aelwyd Res.		24	6	4	14	35	55	22
Penycae Res.		24	4	7	13	40	73	19
Bradley Villa		24	2	4	18	28	78	10

DIVISION ONE CUP

FINAL

(May 11th at Llay Welfare)

Gresford Athletic Res. 1 Castell Alun Colts 0

Division Two		P	W	D	L	F	A	Pts
Bala Town Res.		22	16	4	2	59	21	52
Penyffordd		22	14	3	5	53	34	45
Penley		22	13	3	6	58	35	42
Buckley Town Res.	*-6*	22	15	1	6	66	38	40
Mold Juniors		22	13	1	8	53	31	40
Llangollen Town Res.		22	13	1	8	42	33	40
Johnstown Youth		22	9	3	10	43	36	30
Llay Welfare Res.		22	8	2	12	44	56	26
Mold Alexandra Res.		22	7	1	14	33	49	22
Corwen Amateurs Res.		22	5	1	16	29	60	16
Acrefair Youth Res.		22	4	1	17	29	71	13
Borras Park Albion Res.		22	4	1	17	29	74	13

DIVISION TWO CUP

FINAL

(May 15th at Llangollen Town)

Bala Town Res. 1 Mold Juniors 0

Division Three		P	W	D	L	F	A	Pts
Venture		22	16	2	4	113	34	50
Holt Nomads		22	15	4	3	59	30	49
Brickfield Rangers Res.		22	14	4	4	66	33	46
Garden Village	*-3*	22	13	6	3	46	28	42
Chirk AAA Res.		22	11	4	7	70	39	37
Hawarden Rangers Res.		22	9	4	9	58	69	31
Coedpoeth United Res.		22	8	6	8	48	52	30
Overton Recreation Res.		22	7	5	10	54	64	26
New Brighton Villa Res.		22	6	4	12	51	72	22
Brynteg Village Res.		22	4	3	15	55	66	15
Borras Park Albion Colts		22	3	2	17	24	99	11
Hightown Rangers		22	2	4	16	28	86	10

DIVISION THREE CUP

FINAL

(May 8th at Llay Welfare)

Venture 3 Garden Village 1

HORACE WYNNE CUP

FINAL

(May 12th at Brymbo Broughton)

Venture 3 New Brighton Villa 1

WELSH PREMIER LEAGUE

	Aberystwyth Town	Airbus	Bangor City	Caernarfon Town	Caersws	Carmarthen Town	Connah's Quay Nomads	Cwmbran Town	Grange Harlequins	Haverfordwest County	Llanelli	NEWI Cefn Druids	Newtown	Port Talbot Town	Porthmadog	Rhyl	Total Network Solutions	Welshpool Town
Aberystwyth Town		2-2	1-0	1-1	0-0	1-1	1-2	3-1	0-0	1-1	4-1	2-1	3-1	0-3	4-1	1-2	2-0	6-2
Airbus UK	0-1		2-1	1-2	1-1	1-3	2-2	1-3	3-0	1-2	1-0	3-2	0-2	0-1	0-1	1-2	0-5	0-2
Bangor City	3-1	1-2		1-0	1-2	1-2	0-2	3-0	5-1	0-1	1-3	2-1	0-1	3-2	1-2	0-3	2-3	2-4
Caernarfon Town	4-2	0-1	1-1		6-0	0-2	4-2	2-2	2-1	0-2	0-3	1-1	0-0	0-1	1-2	0-2	1-3	1-1
Caersws	1-1	3-1	0-6	3-4		1-2	1-0	1-2	2-2	1-0	1-4	1-0	2-1	1-1	2-1	1-1	0-2	0-2
Carmarthen Town	1-0	2-1	0-2	1-1	1-3		1-1	1-1	8-0	2-3	0-1	3-0	6-0	1-1	3-1	1-1	2-1	2-0
Connah's Quay Nomads	1-0	3-0	0-1	2-1	1-3	0-1		2-2	1-0	1-1	1-0	1-0	0-2	0-1	0-2	0-1	0-2	2-0
Cwmbran Town	1-3	1-1	1-2	0-1	2-2	3-2	2-1		1-1	3-2	0-1	1-2	0-1	2-5	3-1	1-7	1-4	1-2
Grange Harlequins	2-5	0-1	2-3	4-1	0-5	0-6	1-4	1-1		1-0	0-5	3-1	0-1	0-5	0-2	0-2	0-3	0-5
Haverfordwest County	1-1	1-1	1-1	2-2	0-0	1-2	2-0	3-0	7-0		0-2	0-0	1-1	1-3	1-1	2-2	0-1	2-1
Llanelli	2-1	3-0	5-0	3-1	5-0	0-2	2-0	0-1	1-0	0-1		1-0	2-2	3-1	2-2	1-1	0-2	0-0
NEWI Cefn Druids	2-2	0-0	2-2	3-2	2-0	1-2	2-2	0-0	7-0	0-1	2-5		3-0	0-0	1-1	1-1	0-6	1-0
Newtown	1-3	0-3	0-1	1-2	0-2	2-1	1-1	4-1	5-0	2-3	0-3	2-3		0-1	3-1	1-4	0-3	1-1
Port Talbot Town	0-0	4-0	0-2	1-1	0-0	3-0	0-0	2-1	0-1	1-1	0-1	1-0	3-2		2-1	1-0	1-1	1-1
Porthmadog	0-2	3-1	1-2	2-3	3-3	3-0	2-2	5-1	4-0	1-4	1-2	5-0	1-1	1-1		2-1	2-2	2-0
Rhyl	4-1	1-1	4-1	2-1	0-0	1-0	2-1	1-2	5-2	1-1	0-1	1-1	3-1	3-0	3-0		0-0	3-0
Total Network Solutions	5-0	3-0	2-0	2-1	2-0	4-1	2-0	1-0	7-0	2-0	0-0	4-1	3-1	3-0	7-0	1-0		1-1
Welshpool Town	1-4	3-3	2-0	0-0	2-2	3-0	4-1	5-1	2-1	1-1	3-2	3-2	1-2	2-1	1-0	3-1	1-2	

		P	W	D	L	F	A	W	D	L	F	A	W	D	L	F	A	Pts
Total Network Solutions		34	15	2	0	47	5	12	3	2	40	12	27	5	2	87	17	86
Llanelli		34	9	4	4	30	14	12	1	4	34	14	21	5	8	64	28	68
Rhyl		34	10	5	2	34	13	8	5	4	31	17	18	10	6	65	30	64
Carmarthen Town		34	8	5	4	35	17	9	1	7	27	25	17	6	11	62	42	57
Port Talbot Town		34	7	7	3	20	12	8	4	5	27	18	15	11	8	47	30	56
Welshpool Town		34	10	4	3	37	23	5	5	7	22	25	15	9	10	59	48	54
Aberystwyth Town		34	8	6	3	32	19	6	4	7	27	29	14	10	10	59	48	52
Haverfordwest County		34	4	9	4	25	18	8	5	4	24	18	12	14	8	49	36	50
Bangor City		34	6	0	11	26	30	8	3	6	25	24	14	3	17	51	54	45
Caersws		34	6	4	7	21	30	5	8	4	23	26	11	12	11	44	56	45
Porthmadog		34	7	5	5	38	25	5	3	9	19	34	12	8	14	57	59	44
Connah's Quay Nomads		34	7	2	8	15	17	3	6	8	21	29	10	8	16	36	46	38
Caernarfon Town		34	4	5	8	23	26	5	5	7	24	29	9	10	15	47	55	37
Newtown		34	4	2	11	23	33	6	4	7	19	28	10	6	18	42	61	36
NEWI Cefn Druids		34	5	8	4	27	24	2	3	12	15	34	7	11	16	42	58	32
Airbus UK		34	4	2	11	17	30	4	6	7	18	30	8	8	18	35	60	32
Cwmbran Town	*-13*	34	4	3	10	23	38	4	5	8	19	35	8	8	18	42	73	19
Grange Harlequins	*-1*	34	3	1	13	14	50	1	3	13	9	60	4	4	26	23	110	15

DATES & GATES	Aberystwyth Town	Airbus UK	Bangor City	Caernarfon Town	Caersws	Carmarthen Town	Connah's Quay Nomads	Cwmbran Town	Grange Harlequins	Haverfordwest County	Llanelli	NEWI Cefn Druids	Newtown	Port Talbot Town	Porthmadog	Rhyl	Total Network Solutions	Welshpool Town
Aberystwyth Town		17 Dec *292*	18 Mar *315*	24 Sep *470*	18 Nov *450*	31 Mar *448*	3 Dec *320*	14 Apr *379*	30 Aug *320*	9 Sep *412*	18 Feb *365*	7 Jan *344*	14 Mar *301*	29 Oct *331*	26 Dec *520*	22 Jan *623*	25 Apr *402*	14 Oct *408*
Airbus UK	22 Apr *118*		28 Oct *240*	7 Feb *159*	17 Mar *135*	19 Nov *92*	31 Mar *172*	29 Apr *104*	27 Aug *143*	21 Jan *121*	24 Sep *106*	26 Dec *137*	20 Sep *167*	17 Apr *107*	11 Apr *137*	30 Aug *346*	14 Oct *240*	17 Feb *140*
Bangor City	12 Nov *353*	14 Mar *195*		26 Dec *701*	11 Feb *291*	8 Oct *327*	24 Feb *301*	22 Oct *320*	26 Nov *298*	10 Dec *342*	7 Jan *346*	21 Mar *201*	22 Apr *251*	25 Mar *226*	4 Apr *350*	11 Apr *451*	22 Jan *427*	30 Aug *353*
Caernarfon Town	11 Feb *247*	17 Sep *219*	2 Jan *822*		27 Aug *220*	14 Jan *269*	7 Sep *187*	28 Jan *180*	25 Feb *130*	11 Mar *152*	5 Apr *172*	7 Oct *266*	12 Nov *253*	17 Dec *197*	18 Nov *372*	21 Oct *487*	14 Apr *497*	29 Apr *212*
Caersws	24 Mar *305*	12 Nov *201*	24 Sep *305*	7 Jan *225*		25 Feb *215*	22 Oct *190*	4 Apr *140*	8 Apr *210*	22 Apr *202*	30 Aug *252*	25 Apr *186*	26 Dec *713*	7 Feb *145*	18 Feb *255*	10 Dec *355*	10 Sep *365*	21 Jan *335*
Carmarthen Town	28 Feb *232*	25 Mar *210*	19 Feb *304*	4 Sep *301*	15 Oct *364*		29 Apr *242*	12 Nov *313*	10 Dec *311*	26 Dec *578*	20 Jan *741*	8 Apr *296*	7 Jan *316*	24 Sep *360*	15 Apr *273*	22 Apr *376*	4 Apr *341*	10 Sep *313*
Connah's Quay Nomads	8 Apr *117*	25 Nov *184*	14 Oct *202*	20 Jan *174*	28 Mar *105*	29 Oct *122*		25 Mar *111*	22 Apr *108*	7 Jan *110*	25 Apr *104*	9 Dec *175*	30 Aug *142*	4 Apr *101*	17 Mar *104*	26 Dec *342*	23 Sep *223*	3 Feb *165*
Cwmbran Town	9 Dec *210*	8 Apr *102*	17 Apr *117*	19 Mar *121*	29 Oct *156*	17 Mar *247*	19 Nov *165*		4 Jan *192*	31 Aug *175*	8 Feb *181*	22 Apr *177*	21 Jan *145*	15 Oct *135*	19 Apr *132*	7 Jan *174*	17 Feb *199*	24 Sep *135*
Grange Harlequins	14 Jan *143*	7 Jan *142*	30 Apr *122*	15 Oct *175*	3 Dec *175*	11 Apr *186*	17 Dec *154*	28 Feb *110*		24 Sep *153*	21 Mar *129*	4 Sep *147*	18 Feb *144*	28 Mar *88*	4 Feb *107*	17 Apr *62*	19 Mar *221*	29 Oct *162*
Haverfordwest County	27 Jan *320*	4 Sep *193*	15 Apr *312*	29 Oct *225*	17 Dec *202*	2 Jan *582*	27 Aug *201*	21 Feb *225*	10 Feb *210*		17 Mar *347*	17 Sep *189*	4 Mar *211*	2 Dec *243*	15 Oct *291*	8 Oct *182*	31 Mar *301*	19 Nov *284*
Llanelli	7 Oct *431*	11 Feb *309*	27 Aug *523*	17 Apr *259*	14 Jan *418*	7 Sep *744*	28 Jan *302*	16 Sep *407*	21 Dec *148*	12 Nov *361*		25 Feb *336*	19 Apr *224*	2 Jan *447*	8 Apr *294*	29 Apr *304*	17 Dec *375*	15 Apr *392*
NEWI Cefn Druids	27 Aug *135*	2 Jan *235*	18 Nov *154*	17 Feb *233*	1 Apr *182*	17 Apr *80*	14 Apr *238*	17 Dec *85*	22 Jan *115*	29 Apr *93*	16 Oct *301*		23 Sep *253*	18 Mar *91*	30 Aug *115*	20 Sep *301*	28 Oct *439*	28 Mar *113*
Newtown	17 Sep *395*	28 Jan *182*	17 Dec *210*	17 Mar *155*	2 Jan *820*	27 Aug *210*	11 Apr *150*	4 Sep *250*	8 Oct *315*	22 Oct *325*	19 Nov *305*	11 Feb *195*		15 Apr *225*	29 Oct *310*	4 Apr *195*	3 Dec *350*	25 Apr *295*
Port Talbot Town	10 Mar *263*	22 Oct *164*	28 Jan *152*	22 Apr *170*	17 Sep *108*	11 Feb *230*	8 Oct *60*	24 Feb *136*	18 Nov *127*	20 Apr *270*	26 Dec *502*	12 Nov *144*	10 Dec *220*		21 Jan *125*	26 Nov *305*	30 Aug *171*	27 Aug *101*
Porthmadog	2 Jan *312*	10 Dec *167*	17 Sep *376*	25 Mar *287*	8 Oct *167*	14 Mar *139*	12 Nov *174*	26 Nov *137*	28 Jan *159*	25 Feb *178*	28 Mar *136*	14 Jan *144*	11 Mar *166*	4 Sep *237*		25 Sep *403*	27 Aug *435*	22 Apr *233*
Rhyl	4 Sep *464*	13 Jan *536*	4 Dec *694*	29 Mar *382*	15 Apr *472*	17 Dec *353*	2 Jan *585*	10 Sep *380*	17 Sep *384*	18 Feb *449*	29 Oct *471*	27 Jan *517*	15 Oct *487*	25 Apr *361*	11 Feb *491*		18 Nov *620*	17 Mar *447*
Total Network Solutions	22 Oct *317*	26 Feb *353*	4 Sep *382*	10 Dec *221*	27 Jan *823*	17 Sep *237*	10 Feb *362*	9 Oct *260*	12 Nov *288*	11 Apr *287*	22 Apr *383*	19 Apr *234*	7 Apr *382*	14 Jan *343*	7 Jan *233*	26 Mar *434*		2 Jan *534*
Welshpool Town	18 Apr *311*	7 Oct *156*	14 Jan *140*	8 Apr *272*	4 Sep *220*	28 Jan *380*	16 Sep *130*	11 Feb *390*	11 Mar *306*	25 Mar *307*	10 Dec *85*	21 Oct *110*	26 Nov *170*	7 Jan *111*	17 Dec *105*	12 Nov *155*	26 Dec *290*	

WELSH PREMIER LEAGUE CONSTITUTION 2006-07

ABERYSTWYTH TOWN
Park Avenue, Maesgogerddan, Aberystwyth, Ceredigion SY23 2EY
Tel: 01970 617939 Fax: 01970 617939
Manager: Brian Coyne www.atfc.org.uk Colours: Green, black & white

AIRBUS UK
The Airfield, Broughton, Chester, Cheshire CH4 0BA
Tel: 01244 522356
Manager: Gareth Owen www.sportnetwork.net/main/s356.htm Colours: White & navy blue

BANGOR CITY
The Stadium, Farrar Road, Bangor, Gwynedd LL57 3HU
Tel: 01248 355852 Fax: 01248 716873
Manager: Clayton Blackmore www.bangorcityfc.com Colours: Blue

CAERNARFON TOWN
The Oval, Marcus Street, Caernarfon, Gwynedd LL55 2RT
Tel: 01286 676885 Club: 01286 674620 Fax: 01286 675002
Manager: Waynne Phillips www.caernarfontown.net Colours: Yellow & green

CAERSWS
Recreation Ground, Bridge Street, Caersws, Powys SY17 5DT
Tel: 01686 688753
Manager: Mickey Evans www.caersws-fc.com Colours: Blue & white

CARMARTHEN TOWN
Richmond Park, Priory Street, Carmarthen, Carmarthenshire SA31 1LR
Tel: 01267 232101 Fax: 01267 222851
Manager: Mark Jones www.carmarthentownafc.net Colours: Old gold & black

CONNAH'S QUAY NOMADS
Flint Town United FC, Cae-y-Castell, Marsh Lane, Flint, Flintshire CH6 5PJ
Tel: 01352 730982 Club: 01352 762804
Manager: Neville Powell www.sportnetwork.net/main/s493.htm Colours: White & black

CWMBRAN TOWN
Cwmbran Stadium, Henllys Way, Cwmbran, Gwent NP44 3XL
Tel: 01633 627100 Fax: 01633 863324
Manager: Sean Wharton www.cwmbrantownafc.org.uk Colours: Blue & white

HAVERFORDWEST COUNTY
New Bridge Meadow, Bridge Meadow Lane, Haverfordwest, Pembrokeshire SA61 2EX
Tel: 01437 769048 Fax: 01437 769048
Manager: Deryn Brace www.haverfordwestcounty.com Colours: Royal blue

LLANELLI
Stebonheath Park, Penallt Road, Stebonheath, Llanelli, Carmarthenshire SA15 1EY
Tel: 01554 772973 Club: 01554 773847 Fax: 01554 772973
Manager: Peter Nicholas www.llanelliafc.com Colours: Red

NEWI CEFN DRUIDS
Plas Kynaston Lane, Plas Kynaston, Cefn Mawr, Wrexham, Denbighshire LL14 3PY
Tel: 01978 824332 Club: 01978 824279 Fax: 01978 824332
Manager: Dixie McNeil/Graham Jones www.cefndruidsafc.co.uk Colours: Black & white

NEWTOWN
Latham Park, Park Lane, Newtown, Powys SY1 6XX
Tel: 01686 623120/622666 Club: 01686 626159 Fax: 01686 623813
Manager: Roger Preece www.newtownafc.co.uk Colours: Red

PORT TALBOT TOWN
The Remax Stadium, Victoria Road, Aberavon, Port Talbot, West Glamorgan SA12 6AD
Tel: 01639 882465 Fax: 01639 886991
Manager: Wayne Davies www.porttalbottown.com Colours: Blue

PORTHMADOG
Y Traeth, Porthmadog, Gwynedd LL49 9PP
Tel: 01766 514687
Manager: Viv Williams/Osian Roberts www.porthmadogfc.com Colours: Red & black

RHYL
Belle Vue, Grange Road, Rhyl, Clwyd LL18 4BT
Tel: 01745 338327 Fax: 01745 338327
Manager: John Hulse www.rhylfc.com Colours: White & black

THE NEW SAINTS
Recreation Park, Treflan, Llansantffraid, Powys SY22 6AE
Tel: 01691 828112 Fax: 01691 828862
Manager: Ken McKenna www.saints-alive.co.uk Colours: Green & white

WELSHPOOL TOWN
Maesydre Recreation Grounds, Howells Drive, Welshpool, Powys SY21 7SU
Tel: 01938 553027
Manager: Tomi Morgan www.welshpooltownfc.co.uk Colours: White & black

OUT: Grange Harlequins (R – Welsh League Division One)
Total Network Solutions become The New Saints

CHALLENGE CUP

PRELIMINARY ROUND
Grange Harlequins 1 Caernarfon Town 0
NEWI Cefn Druids 2 **Airbus UK** 5 *aet*

FIRST ROUND
Bangor City 2 **Rhyl** 4 *(aet)*
Connah's Quay Nomads 0 **Newtown** 3
Cwmbran Town 1 Haverfordwest County 0
Grange Harlequins 3 Caersws 1 *(at Caersws)*
Llanelli 3 Aberystwyth Town 0
Port Talbot Town 1 Carmarthen Town 0
Porthmadog 2 **Airbus UK** 3
Welshpool Town 0 **Total Network Solutions** 2

QUARTER-FINALS
Airbus UK 3 Rhyl 2 *(aet)*
Llanelli 5 Grange Harlequins 2 *(aet)*
Port Talbot Town 2 Cwmbran Town 1 *(aet)*
Total Network Solutions 6 Newtown 1

SEMI-FINALS
Airbus UK 1 Total Network Solutions 2, **Total Network Solutions** 2 Airbus UK 0
Port Talbot Town 0 Llanelli 1, Llanelli 0 **Port Talbot Town** 1 *aet* (6-7p)

FINAL *(30th April at Aberystwyth Town)*
Port Talbot Town 0 **Total Network Solutions** 4

WELSH PREMIER TEAMS IN EUROPE

CHAMPIONS LEAGUE
FIRST QUALIFYING ROUND
Liverpool 3 TOTAL NETWORK SOLUTIONS 0,
TOTAL NETWORK SOLUTIONS 0 Liverpool 3
(at Wrexham)

INTERTOTO CUP
FIRST ROUND
BANGOR CITY 1 FC Dinaburg 2 *(at Rhyl)*
FC Dinaburg 2 BANGOR CITY 0

U E F A CUP
FIRST QUALIFYING ROUND
Longford Town 2 CARMARTHEN TOWN 0,
CARMARTHEN TOWN 5 Longford Tn 1 *(at Newtown)*
RHYL 2 FK Atlantis 1, FK Atlantis 3 **RHYL** 2
(Rhyl win on away goals)

SECOND QUALIFYING ROUND
FC Copenhagen 2 CARMARTHEN TOWN 0,
CARMARTHEN TOWN 0 FC Copenhagen 2
RHYL 0 Viking 1, Viking 2 RHYL 1

WESSEX LEAGUE

	AFC Newbury	AFC Totton	Alton Town	Andover	BAT Sports	Bemerton Heath H.	Bournemouth	Brockenhurst	Christchurch	Cowes Sports	Fareham Town	Gosport Borough	Hamble ASSC	Hamworthy United	Lymington Town	Moneyfields	Poole Town	Portland United	Thatcham Town	VTFC	Wimborne Town	Winchester City
AFC Newbury		0-5	2-1	2-1	0-4	0-1	2-1	1-0	0-5	3-0	0-4	0-7	1-1	0-1	4-1	2-4	0-1	2-0	1-2	1-4	1-3	1-2
AFC Totton	1-1		4-1	5-1	3-0	4-1	2-0	1-0	3-0	5-0	1-1	2-2	2-1	2-1	0-0	1-1	1-1	8-1	1-2	1-2	0-1	0-4
Alton Town	1-1	0-4		1-3	1-2	2-0	1-4	4-0	1-4	5-0	1-3	0-4	1-1	2-0	2-2	2-1	1-3	2-2	1-2	1-4	3-1	1-5
Andover	6-0	4-2	2-0		4-1	3-1	1-0	4-1	1-3	2-1	3-1	6-3	1-0	3-1	4-1	4-1	3-3	8-0	1-2	4-0	2-1	0-2
BAT Sports	1-3	1-8	2-2	1-4		3-3	3-6	3-2	2-3	1-0	1-3	0-3	0-2	1-2	2-1	0-2	2-4	0-2	0-3	0-1	5-4	0-4
Bemerton Heath Harlequins	5-0	3-3	1-1	2-2	3-1	*D*	3-1	3-2	1-2	1-0	0-3	1-2	2-1	1-6	1-3	1-1	1-2	7-0	3-3	2-1	1-3	1-6
Bournemouth	3-0	1-2	4-0	1-3	2-2	3-2	*I*	1-0	3-1	4-0	3-1	1-2	0-1	1-0	1-1	0-2	3-1	4-0	0-2	1-1	1-1	0-1
Brockenhurst	1-1	0-3	3-1	0-4	2-3	0-2	2-3	*V*	2-3	1-1	0-1	0-0	1-1	1-1	0-1	0-1	1-3	3-0	0-3	1-4	1-2	0-3
Christchurch	3-0	2-2	2-2	4-0	2-0	2-2	0-3	3-1	*I*	1-0	3-1	1-1	2-0	0-2	1-2	0-0	0-1	6-0	1-4	2-2	1-1	0-1
Cowes Sports	2-0	1-3	1-1	3-0	2-3	2-1	2-2	1-0	3-1	*S*	1-2	1-2	3-2	2-2	0-0	0-2	2-1	2-0	1-2	2-2	0-1	0-1
Fareham Town	2-0	1-2	1-1	2-1	1-3	1-0	2-3	3-2	4-2	0-3	*I*	0-0	1-0	0-1	2-2	1-1	0-1	1-1	1-3	3-3	3-1	3-3
Gosport Borough	5-0	0-1	4-1	1-3	4-1	1-0	0-0	3-1	1-0	2-0	2-0	*O*	3-1	4-1	1-1	0-1	2-2	6-0	0-1	1-0	1-1	1-2
Hamble ASSC	4-0	0-3	2-1	2-2	2-0	2-0	0-2	3-0	2-0	0-1	1-5	4-1	*N*	1-0	1-0	1-1	2-1	3-1	0-1	0-1	1-0	0-3
Hamworthy United	1-0	1-0	2-0	2-2	2-1	4-0	0-0	2-1	5-2	4-1	1-2	0-0	1-1		0-0	1-0	2-1	4-0	0-0	0-2	2-0	0-1
Lymington Town	0-0	0-2	1-2	0-6	1-1	2-1	1-2	1-3	1-4	1-1	0-3	0-1	2-1	0-2	*O*	1-1	4-2	1-0	0-4	0-0	3-1	2-3
Moneyfields	1-1	0-3	3-0	4-4	2-2	1-3	0-1	1-0	1-0	1-1	0-2	0-1	1-0	1-1	0-0	*N*	0-4	3-2	0-1	3-2	1-1	2-1
Poole Town	3-1	1-1	3-0	2-3	4-1	3-0	0-1	3-3	1-1	0-3	3-5	3-1	2-1	0-1	1-2	0-0	*E*	2-1	1-0	3-1	1-0	1-1
Portland United	1-1	1-3	0-2	1-4	3-3	3-4	0-1	1-5	0-1	1-1	0-2	1-5	2-1	0-1	0-1	1-3	1-5		0-4	1-1	3-4	0-8
Thatcham Town	1-1	1-0	4-0	3-1	2-0	2-3	0-2	3-2	2-1	1-1	0-0	2-4	1-1	1-2	4-1	2-0	4-1	6-1		2-0	5-0	0-1
VTFC	6-1	0-3	3-1	1-7	1-3	1-1	1-1	1-0	0-0	0-1	2-2	1-3	2-1	2-2	5-1	0-0	0-4	3-0	2-2		1-1	0-1
Wimborne Town	1-0	0-3	5-0	1-2	4-1	1-2	0-0	5-0	1-2	4-1	2-0	0-0	2-1	2-2	0-0	1-1	0-1	2-1	0-2	2-1		0-1
Winchester City	0-1	2-1	4-1	2-1	2-1	3-0	2-2	5-0	3-1	2-1	4-1	4-1	3-1	2-2	2-1	1-0	4-0	6-0	2-3	1-1	4-0	

Division One	P	W	D	L	F	A	Pts
Winchester City	42	34	5	3	112	31	107
Thatcham Town	42	29	7	6	92	37	94
Andover	42	27	5	10	120	64	86
AFC Totton	42	25	9	8	101	40	84
Gosport Borough	42	23	10	9	85	44	79
Hamworthy United	42	21	12	9	65	40	75
Bournemouth	42	21	10	11	72	45	73
Poole Town	42	21	8	13	79	60	71
Fareham Town	42	19	10	13	74	61	67
Christchurch	42	17	9	16	72	62	60
Moneyfields	42	14	16	12	48	49	58
Wimborne Town	42	15	10	17	60	61	55
VTFC	42	13	15	14	65	66	54
Bemerton Heath Harlequins	42	14	8	20	70	86	50
Hamble ASSC	42	14	7	21	50	56	49
Cowes Sports	42	12	10	20	48	67	46
Lymington Town	42	10	14	18	42	71	44
BAT Sports	42	10	6	26	61	109	36
AFC Newbury	42	9	8	25	35	96	35
Alton Town	42	8	9	25	51	99	33
Brockenhurst	42	4	6	32	42	93	18
Portland United	42	2	6	34	32	139	12

WESSEX LEAGUE PREMIER DIVISION (formerly DIVISION ONE) CONSTITUTION 2006-07

AFC TOTTON .... Testwood Park, Testwood Place, Totton, Southampton SO40 3BE 023 8086 8981
ALTON TOWN .... Bass Sports Ground, Anstey Road, Alton GU34 2LS 01420 82465
BEMERTON HEATH HARLEQUINS ... Westwood Recreation Ground, Western Way, Bemerton Heath, Salisbury SP2 9DR ... 01722 331925
BOURNEMOUTH .... Victoria Park, Namu Road, Winton, Bournemouth BH9 2RA 01202 515123
BRADING TOWN .... Vicarage Lane, Brading PO36 0AR 01983 405217
BROCKENHURST .... Grigg Lane, Brockenhurst SO42 7RE 01590 623544
CHRISTCHURCH .... Hurn Bridge Sports Club, Avon Causeway, Christchurch BH23 6DY 01202 473792
COWES SPORTS .... Westwood Park, Reynolds Close, off Park Road, Cowes PO31 7NT 01983 293793
DOWNTON .... Brian Whitehead Sports Centre, Wick Lane, Downton, Salisbury SP5 3NF 01725 512162
FAREHAM TOWN .... Cams Alders Sports Stadium, Highfield Avenue, Fareham PO15 5NL 01329 231151
GOSPORT BOROUGH .... Privett Park, Privett Road, Gosport PO12 3SX 023 9250 1042
HAMBLE ASSC .... Folland Park, Kings Avenue, Hamble-le-Rice, Southampton SO31 4NF 023 8045 2173
HAMWORTHY UNITED .... The County Ground, Blandford Close, Hamworthy, Poole BH15 4BF 01202 674974
HORNDEAN .... Five Heads Park, Five Heads Road, Horndean PO8 9NZ 023 9259 1363
LYMINGTON TOWN .... Sports Ground, Southampton Road, Lymington SO41 0UU 01590 671305
MONEYFIELDS .... Moneyfields Sports & Social Club, Moneyfields Avenue, Copnor, Portsmouth PO3 6LA 023 9266 5260
POOLE TOWN .... Tatnam Farm, School Road, off Stanley Green/Palmer Road, Poole BH15 3AT 07771 604289
RINGWOOD TOWN .... The Clubhouse, Long Lane, Ringwood BH24 3BX 01425 473448
VTFC .... VT Sports Ground, Portsmouth Road, Sholing SO19 9PW 023 8040 3829
WIMBORNE TOWN .... The Cuthbury, Cowgrove Road, Wimborne BH21 2EL 01202 884821

IN: Brading Town (P), Downton (P), Horndean (P), Ringwood Town (P)

OUT: AFC Newbury (R – Division Two), Andover (P – Southern League Division One South & West), BAT Sports (R – Division Two), Portland United (R – Dorset Premier League), Thatcham Town (P – Southern League Division One South & West), Winchester City (P – Southern League Division One South & West)

	Alresford Town	Amesbury Town	Andover New Street	Bishops Waltham Town	Blackfield & Langley	Brading Town	Downton	East Cowes Victoria Ath	Farnborough North End	Fawley	Hayling United	Horndean	Hythe & Dibden	Liss Athletic	Locks Heath	Petersfield Town	Ringwood Town	Romsey Town	Shaftesbury	Stockbridge	Utd Services Portsmouth	Whitchurch United
Alresford Town		1-2	2-1	3-0	0-5	0-1	1-2	3-0	0-1	2-2	1-1	0-0	1-4	0-3	1-2	2-5	0-2	0-1	1-1	4-0	1-1	0-6
Amesbury Town	3-0		2-4	1-1	0-3	1-2	1-2	2-3	2-1	1-4	0-2	1-6	2-1	1-4	0-3	2-1	1-5	0-2	1-1	2-1	2-2	3-2
Andover New Street	0-2	1-0		3-2	1-1	1-2	2-3	2-2	2-1	2-5	0-2	2-2	7-1	3-1	0-7	4-5	0-1	0-1	1-2	0-2	1-1	4-0
Bishops Waltham Town	0-0	3-1	0-2		3-0	0-3	2-8	2-4	1-6	3-1	0-5	1-4	1-4	0-1	0-1	0-3	0-1	1-0	5-2	0-3	2-2	1-1
Blackfield & Langley	1-1	5-1	4-0	4-2		2-3	4-4	1-2	3-3	0-1	0-3	1-1	1-1	0-1	0-0	3-2	0-2	2-3	5-3	2-1	3-1	6-1
Brading Town	1-0	3-2	3-0	6-1	3-0	*D*	2-3	5-1	1-0	0-1	3-3	2-3	2-1	2-1	1-2	3-1	2-4	2-1	3-1	1-1	2-2	4-3
Downton	2-1	0-1	1-1	2-0	2-1	0-1	*I*	1-0	2-1	2-0	2-4	2-1	8-1	2-1	2-0	1-3	0-0	3-2	3-2	1-1	2-0	2-0
East Cowes Victoria Athletic	1-2	3-1	5-0	1-1	4-1	1-1	1-3	*V*	4-3	2-2	1-0	3-3	1-2	4-0	1-3	5-3	0-2	4-3	3-0	0-2	1-1	4-0
Farnborough North End	4-1	2-1	3-3	6-2	2-1	2-4	4-3	2-2	*I*	1-2	0-2	2-1	1-2	0-3	0-2	5-0	5-0	3-2	4-1	2-2	1-3	2-0
Fawley	1-0	2-0	5-0	3-2	1-1	0-1	1-1	0-1	1-0	*S*	1-3	1-2	3-0	3-2	0-1	0-0	2-1	2-2	6-0	2-4	3-1	4-1
Hayling United	6-0	3-0	2-1	4-1	0-0	1-2	2-1	0-0	4-1	3-0	*I*	3-2	3-0	2-2	0-3	2-3	3-0	0-0	3-0	1-0	2-1	5-2
Horndean	4-2	4-1	3-0	3-2	3-3	0-1	5-9	4-0	3-2	0-1	1-0	*O*	6-0	0-1	0-4	4-2	3-0	1-2	4-1	1-2	1-0	5-3
Hythe & Dibden	1-1	1-3	0-0	0-5	0-2	1-3	1-4	4-2	0-4	1-1	3-1	0-3	*N*	0-0	1-3	2-2	1-2	1-2	0-2	2-1	0-4	2-0
Liss Athletic	3-1	5-1	4-1	3-0	0-2	3-2	5-1	3-1	6-2	4-3	1-3	0-1	3-1		4-1	1-0	2-4	3-2	2-1	3-2	2-2	1-1
Locks Heath	3-0	3-0	2-1	3-1	5-1	1-0	0-1	3-1	0-1	2-1	1-1	4-2	3-0	2-0	*T*	0-1	2-2	2-0	0-0	0-1	4-1	3-0
Petersfield Town	2-1	5-4	1-2	3-2	3-3	0-3	0-4	0-4	1-4	0-0	1-1	2-0	0-2	1-1	0-2	*W*	0-3	1-0	0-2	2-5	1-4	1-1
Ringwood Town	5-3	0-4	4-0	2-1	1-3	1-1	3-1	2-1	0-1	2-2	1-2	3-1	1-2	4-2	0-3	0-1	*O*	3-2	3-5	0-0	2-4	3-4
Romsey Town	2-3	6-1	3-2	1-1	2-0	0-0	2-2	1-1	1-1	1-2	2-1	1-2	0-3	0-4	0-3	2-0	1-0		1-0	1-1	1-2	1-0
Shaftesbury	4-3	2-1	3-3	1-2	0-0	0-4	1-5	1-0	1-1	2-1	2-3	2-1	1-0	0-2	0-4	0-0	1-3	1-1		0-3	3-3	0-1
Stockbridge	1-1	2-0	1-1	4-1	1-1	2-2	0-4	0-0	4-1	2-1	0-2	1-1	1-1	1-2	2-2	2-0	2-0	1-2	5-2		4-1	10-0
United Services Portsmouth	2-1	5-0	5-1	3-1	2-1	3-2	5-1	1-0	2-3	0-2	0-5	0-1	5-3	0-3	1-2	2-1	2-2	2-2	4-1	3-1		2-0
Whitchurch United	0-3	3-3	0-2	4-4	0-5	0-7	1-6	0-2	1-5	0-3	0-6	0-3	3-0	0-7	0-5	3-1	1-7	0-0	1-1	0-3	1-1	

Division Two	P	W	D	L	F	A	Pts
Locks Heath	42	31	5	6	96	28	98
Hayling United	42	27	8	7	99	39	89
Brading Town	42	27	7	8	96	50	88
Downton	42	27	6	9	108	64	87
Liss Athletic	42	26	5	11	99	57	83
Horndean	42	22	6	14	95	67	72
Fawley	42	20	9	13	76	53	69
Stockbridge	42	18	13	11	82	52	67
Ringwood Town	42	20	6	16	81	71	66
United Services Portsmouth	42	18	11	13	86	72	65
Farnborough North End	42	19	6	17	93	76	63
East Cowes Victoria Athletic	42	16	10	16	76	70	58
Romsey Town	42	15	11	16	59	61	56
Blackfield & Langley	42	14	13	15	81	69	55
Petersfield Town	42	12	8	22	58	91	44
Shaftesbury	42	10	10	22	53	96	40
Hythe & Dibden	42	11	7	24	50	98	40
Andover New Street	42	10	9	23	61	96	39
Amesbury Town	42	10	4	28	55	109	34
Alresford Town	42	8	9	25	49	86	33
Bishops Waltham Town	42	7	7	28	57	112	28
Whitchurch United	42	5	8	29	44	137	23

WESSEX LEAGUE DIVISION ONE (formerly DIVISION TWO) CONSTITUTION 2006-07

ALRESFORD TOWN........................ Alrebury Park, The Avenue, Alresford SO24 9EP 01962 735100
AMESBURY TOWN.............. Amesbury Recreation Ground, Recreation Road, Amesbury SP4 7BB.............. 01980 623489
ANDOVER NEW STREET........... Foxcotte Park, Hatherton Road, Charlton, Andover SP11 0HS.............. 01264 358358
BLACKFIELD & LANGLEY .... Gang Warily Community Centre, Newlands Road, Blackfield SO45 1GA.......... 023 8089 3603
EAST COWES VICTORIA ATHLETIC .. Beatrice Avenue, Whippingham, East Cowes PO32 6PA.................. 01983 297165
FARNBOROUGH NORTH END .. Cody Sports & Social Club, Old Iveley Road, Pyestock, Farnborough GU14 0LS .... None
FAWLEY.................... Waterside Sports & Social, Long Lane, Holbury, Southampton SO45 2PA 023 8089 3750
HAYLING UNITED............. Hayling Sports Centre, Mengham Park, Hayling Island PO11 9BG 023 9263 7758
HYTHE & DIBDEN .... Ewart Recreation Ground, Jones Lane, Hythe, Southampton SO45 6DG 023 8084 5264
LAVERSTOCK & FORD ... The Dell, Laverstock & Ford SC, 23 Church Road, Laverstock, Salisbury SP1 1QX............ 01722 327401
LISS ATHLETIC .... Newman Collard Ground, Hill Brow Road, Liss GU33 7NS 01730 894022
LOCKS HEATH.............. Locksheath Rec, Warsash Road, Titchfield Common, Fareham PO14 4JX.............. 01489 600932
PETERSFIELD TOWN .... Love Lane, Petersfield GU31 4BW............................ 01730 233416
ROMSEY TOWN .... The By-Pass Ground, South Front, Romsey SO51 4GJ 01794 512003
SHAFTESBURY .... Cockrams, Coppice Street, Shaftesbury SP7 8PD.......................... 01747 853990
STOCKBRIDGE..................... Recreation Ground, High Street, Stockbridge SO20 6HG .... None
UNITED SERVICES PORTSMOUTH .... Victory Stadium, Burnaby Road, Portsmouth PO1 2EJ 023 9272 5315
VERWOOD TOWN...................... Potterne Park, Potterne Way, Verwood BH21 6RS.................................. None
WARMINSTER TOWN .... Weymouth Street, Warminster BA12 9NS.......................... 01985 217828

IN: Laverstock & Ford (P), Verwood Town (P), Warminster Town (P – Wiltshire League Premier Division)

OUT: Bishops Waltham Town (R), Brading Town (P), Downton (P), Horndean (P), Ringwood Town (P), Whitchurch United (R)

	AFC Aldermaston	AFC Portchester	Clanfield	Colden Common	Fleet Spurs	Fleetlands	Hamble Club	Laverstock & Ford	Micheldever	Netley Central Sports	Ordnance Survey	Otterbourne	Overton United	Paulsgrove	QK Southampton	Tadley Calleva	Verwood Town
AFC Aldermaston		4-2	5-2	3-2	3-3	2-0	5-3	2-3	2-1	0-1	1-1	0-5	2-2	3-1	4-1	0-2	0-3
AFC Portchester	4-1	*D*	6-1	3-1	1-3	1-4	2-1	1-2	n/a	0-0	1-4	2-2	0-2	0-2	7-1	2-1	3-2
Clanfield	1-2	4-1	*I*	1-5	2-1	1-2	4-0	2-0	3-1	0-1	2-0	0-3	2-0	2-5	7-1	4-2	2-3
Colden Common	2-2	5-0	2-1	*V*	6-0	3-1	2-0	1-2	n/a	2-0	4-2	3-0	1-1	3-1	2-2	0-2	1-4
Fleet Spurs	5-2	1-3	2-0	3-2	*I*	0-1	8-0	0-2	5-0	1-3	3-5	2-3	2-3	2-2	3-0	1-2	0-2
Fleetlands	4-3	3-3	0-2	1-3	2-1	*S*	7-0	2-3	5-2	2-2	2-1	2-0	3-0	1-1	2-0	3-0	1-0
Hamble Club	0-5	0-3	0-1	1-8	1-4	0-4	*I*	2-5	4-0	2-1	0-2	1-3	1-1	0-7	1-3	1-1	1-5
Laverstock & Ford	1-4	0-0	0-0	1-3	2-1	2-0	2-1	*O*	n/a	2-2	5-4	1-1	2-1	1-0	5-0	4-0	3-1
Micheldever	n/a	1-6	0-3	0-9	4-8	0-5	1-1	2-4	*N*	0-7	2-1	1-5	0-6	n/a	6-3	0-2	0-3
Netley Central Sports	3-1	3-2	4-1	1-1	3-0	0-2	4-0	2-1	10-0		4-2	1-0	2-1	0-1	9-0	1-2	1-3
Ordnance Survey	5-1	2-3	1-1	3-3	5-4	1-1	3-0	1-4	4-0	2-4		2-5	1-1	4-0	5-0	0-1	2-2
Otterbourne	1-3	3-1	1-1	1-4	3-2	0-0	3-0	0-0	n/a	2-3	6-2	*T*	4-1	1-1	3-1	0-2	1-2
Overton United	2-1	2-1	4-2	2-4	2-2	3-1	4-0	0-2	5-1	4-0	1-4	0-1	*H*	0-2	2-2	3-1	6-1
Paulsgrove	4-0	1-0	3-2	3-1	5-0	3-3	10-1	2-2	n/a	3-0	2-0	4-0	7-0	*R*	7-2	1-0	2-1
QK Southampton	3-1	0-4	1-6	0-7	0-2	0-5	0-0	1-2	1-2	0-7	1-3	2-3	0-5	1-5	*E*	1-5	1-5
Tadley Calleva	1-3	3-0	2-1	3-2	4-2	1-0	3-0	1-3	n/a	0-0	4-1	2-0	0-0	2-2	2-0	*E*	1-2
Verwood Town	1-1	3-1	5-1	1-3	6-2	0-0	2-0	2-0	n/a	4-0	2-1	0-1	2-1	2-4	4-0	3-2	

Note – Micheldever withdrew during the course of the season
Their results are shown above but are expunged from the league table

Division Three	P	W	D	L	F	A	Pts
Paulsgrove	30	20	6	4	91	34	66
Laverstock & Ford	30	19	6	5	62	37	63
Verwood Town	30	19	3	8	73	42	60
Colden Common	30	17	5	8	86	45	56
Netley Central Sports	30	16	5	9	62	41	53
Fleetlands	30	15	7	8	59	36	52
Tadley Calleva	30	16	4	10	52	40	52
Otterbourne	30	14	6	10	56	45	48
AFC Aldermaston	30	12	5	13	64	68	41
Overton United	30	11	7	12	54	53	40
AFC Portchester	30	11	4	15	57	61	37
Ordnance Survey	30	10	6	14	69	68	36
Clanfield	30	11	3	16	56	62	36
Fleet Spurs	30	8	3	19	60	75	27
QK Southampton	30	2	3	25	24	123	9
Hamble Club	30	1	3	26	17	112	6

Micheldever – record expunged

WESSEX LEAGUE DIVISION TWO (formerly DIVISION THREE) CONSTITUTION 2006-07

AFC ALDERMASTON. . Aldermaston Rec Society, Atomic Weapons Establishment, Aldermaston, Reading RG7 4PR 0118 982 4544
AFC NEWBURY . . . . St Bartholomew's School, Andover Road, Newbury RG14 6JP 01635 521255
AFC PORTCHESTER . . . . Portchester Community School, White Hart Lane, Fareham PO16 9BD. 023 9236 4399
BAT SPORTS. . . . . BAT Sports Ground, Southern Gardens, Ringwood Road, Totton SO40 8RW 023 8086 2143
BISHOPS WALTHAM TOWN . . . Priory Park, Elizabeth Way, Bishops Waltham, Southampton SO32 1SQ 01489 894269
CLANFIELD . . . . Peel Park, Charlton Lane, Clanfield, Waterlooville PO8 0RJ. . . . . None
COLDEN COMMON. . . . . Colden Common Rec., Main Road, Colden Common, Winchester SO21 1RP 01962 712365
FLEET SPURS . . . . Kennels Lane, Southwood, Farnborough GU14 0LT . . . . None
FLEETLANDS . . . . DARA Fleetlands, Fareham Road, Gosport PO13 0AA 01329 239723
HAMBLE CLUB. . . . . Shell Mex Ground, Hamble Lane, Hamble-le-Rice, Southampton SO31 4QJ 07881 766085
OTTERBOURNE . . . . Oakwood Park, Oakwood Avenue, Otterbourne SO21 2ED 01962 714681
OVERTON UNITED. . . . . Lordsfield Gardens, Bridge Street, Overton RG25 3EW. 01256 770561
PAULSGROVE . . . . The Grove Club, Marsden Road, off Allaway Avenue, Paulsgrove, Portsmouth PO6 4JB 023 9232 4102
QK SOUTHAMPTON . . . . Lordshill Recreation Centre, Redbridge Lane, Southampton SO16 9BP. 023 8073 2531
STONEHAM . . . . Stoneham Lane, Eastleigh, Southampton SO16 2PA . . . . None
TADLEY CALLEVA . . . . The Green, Tadley RG26 3PD. . . . . None
WELLOW . . . . Hatches Farm, Romsey Road, West Wellow, Romsey SO51 6EA . . . . None
WHITCHURCH UNITED. . . . . Longmeadow, Winchester Road, Whitchurch RG28 7RB 01256 892493

IN: AFC Newbury (R – Premier Division), BAT Sports (R – Premier Division), Bishops Waltham Town (R), Wellow (P – Southampton League Premier Division), Whitchurch United (R)

OUT: Laverstock & Ford (P), Micheldever (WS), Netley Central Sports (R – Hampshire League), Verwood Town (P)

Ordnance Survey become Stoneham

LEAGUE CUP

FIRST ROUND

AFC Newbury 2 AFC Aldermaston 1
AFC Totton 1 East Cowes Victoria Athletic 0
Alresford Town 3 **Colden Common** 6
Alton Town 2 Paulsgrove 1
Andover 3 Fleet Spurs 0
Andover New Street 4 Amesbury Town 2
Bemerton Heath Harlequins 3 Shaftesbury 2
Bishops Waltham Town 0 **Fleetlands** 2
Brockenhurst 6 BAT Sports 0
Cowes Sports 3 Brading Town 1
Downton 3 Hythe & Dibden 1
Fawley 4 Verwood Town 3
Gosport Borough 6 Hayling United 1
Hamble ASSC 1 Ordnance Survey 0
Hamworthy United 2 Bournemouth 1
Laverstock & Ford 0 **Christchurch** 1
Liss Athletic 1 Otterbourne 0
Locks Heath 2 AFC Portchester 0
Moneyfields 6 Clanfield 1
Netley Central Sports 2 Horndean 1
Petersfield Town 6 Overton United 4
Portland United 5 Ringwood Town 2
Romsey Town 7 QK Southampton 1
Stockbridge 2 Farnborough North End 1
Thatcham Town 2 **Tadley Calleva** 3
United Services Portsmouth 3 Hamble Club 1
VTFC 3 Fareham Town 1
Whitchurch United 1 **Winchester City** 3
Wimborne Town 1 Lymington Town 0

SECOND ROUND

AFC Totton 4 Fleetlands 1
Alton Town 1 **AFC Newbury** 2
Andover 7 Colden Common 3
Andover New Street 1 United Services Portsmouth 0
Blackfield & Langley 0 **Christchurch** 5
Brockenhurst 4 **Portland United** 4 *aet* (9-10p)
Downton (w/o) v Micheldever (scr.)
Gosport Borough 8 Liss Athletic 0
Hamble ASSC 0 **Moneyfields** 1
Hamworthy United 3 Bemerton Heath Harlequins 1
Netley Central Sports 0 **VTFC** 3
Petersfield Town 3 Tadley Calleva 3 *aet* (7-6p)
Poole Town 5 Fawley 0
Romsey Town 2 Cowes Sports 1
Wimborne Town 7 Stockbridge 0
Winchester City 2 Locks Heath 0

THIRD ROUND

AFC Newbury 0 **Poole Town** 1
AFC Totton 5 Portland United 0
Andover 1 Moneyfields 0
Andover New Street 1 **VTFC** 3
Hamworthy United 1 Christchurch 0
Petersfield Town 3 Romsey Town 2
Wimborne Town 2 Gosport Borough 0
Winchester City 3 Downton 0

QUARTER-FINALS

AFC Totton 6 Petersfield Town 0
Andover 3 Hamworthy United 3 *aet* (4-1p)
Poole Town 2 VTFC 0
Winchester City 4 Wimborne Town 2

SEMI-FINALS
(played over two legs)

Andover 2 Poole Town 1, Poole Town 2 **Andover** 3
Winchester City 0 AFC Totton 0, **AFC Totton** 3 Winchester City 2

FINAL
(May 1st at Thatcham Town)

AFC Totton 1 Andover 0 *aet*

Combination One	P	W	D	L	F	A	Pts
Gosport Borough Res.	40	35	2	3	140	27	107
Winchester City Res.	40	29	3	8	129	37	90
Moneyfields Res.	40	29	2	9	128	55	89
VTFC Res.	40	27	6	7	102	39	87
BAT Sports Res.	40	24	8	8	113	64	80
AFC Totton Res.	40	23	5	12	96	58	74
Christchurch Res.	40	23	5	12	92	62	74
Bemerton Heath Harlequins Res.	40	22	6	12	100	68	72
Andover Res.	40	19	10	11	109	79	67
Cowes Sports Res.	40	18	5	17	83	70	59
Hamble ASSC Res.	40	18	5	17	81	71	59
Bashley Res.	40	17	7	16	83	60	58
Horndean Res.	40	17	5	18	91	90	56
Lymington Town Res.	40	13	8	19	51	61	47
Locks Heath Res.	40	11	8	21	74	98	41
Brockenhurst Res.	40	12	4	24	68	110	40
Alton Town Res.	40	9	3	28	53	121	30
Lymington & New Milton Res.	40	8	4	28	58	132	28
Alresford Town Res.	40	6	3	31	39	135	21
Downton Res.	40	4	3	33	35	133	15
Blackfield & Langley Res.	40	5	0	35	45	200	15

Combination Two	P	W	D	L	F	A	Pts
Fleetlands Res.	30	20	2	8	81	43	62
Paulsgrove Res.	30	18	3	9	94	55	57
Hayling United Res.	30	17	6	7	71	44	57
Laverstock & Ford Res.	30	17	6	7	65	48	57
United Services Portsmouth Res.	30	16	6	8	90	60	54
Ringwood Town Res.	30	16	5	9	60	53	53
AFC Portchester Res.	30	13	6	11	75	63	45
Romsey Town Res.	30	12	7	11	52	51	43
Clanfield Res.	30	10	7	13	66	55	37
Fawley Res.	30	12	1	17	64	66	37
Overton United Res.	30	10	7	13	39	71	37
Liss Athletic Res.	30	10	5	15	68	81	35
Colden Common Res.	30	8	5	17	56	79	29
Petersfield Town Res.	30	7	6	17	41	69	27
Fleet Spurs Res.	30	8	3	19	35	77	27
Andover New Street Res.	30	7	3	20	41	83	24

Whitchurch United Res. – record expunged

COMBINATION CUP

FINAL
(April 28th at Bemerton Heath Harlequins)

Gosport Borough Res. 1 BAT Sports Res. 1 *aet* (5-3p)

WEST CHESHIRE LEAGUE

	Aintree Villa	Ashville	Cammell Laird Res.	Castrol Social	Christleton	Ellesmere Port	Heswall	Maghull	Mallaby	Merseyside Police	New Brighton	Newton	Poulton Victoria	Runcorn Town	Vauxhall Motors Res.	West Kirby
Aintree Villa		2-0	3-2	5-0	3-1	1-1	0-0	1-0	7-0	4-2	4-0	2-0	3-1	0-4	4-1	0-1
Ashville	2-3		3-1	1-3	1-4	0-2	0-2	1-1	1-3	2-3	4-3	2-1	1-2	2-1	2-0	1-2
Cammell Laird Res.	2-3	0-1	*D*	0-1	3-3	7-0	0-1	1-0	1-2	1-0	1-3	0-2	1-1	2-0	3-2	0-0
Castrol Social	0-3	1-1	2-0	*I*	0-0	1-2	0-1	2-5	0-4	0-0	0-2	1-1	1-2	2-0	1-4	0-0
Christleton	0-1	1-3	2-1	0-1	*V*	1-2	0-1	3-3	5-1	1-0	1-1	3-3	1-2	5-1	1-2	1-1
Ellesmere Port	3-1	1-1	1-1	1-1	0-1	*I*	1-1	1-3	2-1	0-1	1-2	0-0	0-6	2-1	0-2	1-1
Heswall	0-5	0-1	4-1	3-2	1-0	1-0	*S*	1-0	1-1	3-3	3-1	2-0	0-3	1-2	2-2	1-2
Maghull	2-2	4-0	2-0	4-0	2-2	0-0	0-3	*I*	4-0	0-1	0-0	2-2	0-1	2-1	1-3	2-2
Mallaby	0-2	0-3	0-3	1-4	3-4	1-2	0-0	1-5	*O*	0-4	1-1	1-0	2-4	3-4	1-1	0-3
Merseyside Police	1-1	0-0	0-0	4-2	1-4	0-1	0-3	4-1	3-2	*N*	1-3	0-2	4-1	2-2	2-0	1-4
New Brighton	1-2	1-0	2-3	2-1	1-1	2-0	1-0	0-1	0-0	0-1		1-2	3-2	4-0	4-5	1-2
Newton	1-2	1-0	1-3	1-2	3-5	0-0	2-0	1-4	4-0	0-4	1-1	*O*	0-0	0-1	3-3	4-2
Poulton Victoria	2-2	1-0	1-0	6-0	2-1	0-0	3-3	0-0	3-0	4-1	5-1	2-0	*N*	1-0	4-2	2-1
Runcorn Town	2-1	0-2	2-1	1-2	1-3	3-3	2-5	1-1	3-0	2-3	3-3	4-5	2-4	*E*	1-2	0-1
Vauxhall Motors Res.	0-1	2-1	2-3	6-1	1-1	4-1	2-0	4-0	1-0	1-1	4-1	2-0	2-0	1-2		5-2
West Kirby	1-1	2-2	3-1	5-0	2-2	3-0	1-2	1-0	0-0	0-0	4-3	2-1	0-1	3-3	3-0	

Division One		P	W	D	L	F	A	Pts
Poulton Victoria		30	20	6	4	66	31	66
Aintree Villa	*-3*	30	20	6	4	69	30	63
Vauxhall Motors Res.		30	16	5	9	66	46	53
West Kirby		30	14	11	5	54	35	53
Heswall		30	15	7	8	45	35	52
Merseyside Police		30	12	8	10	47	44	44
Christleton		30	10	10	10	57	47	40
Maghull		30	10	10	10	49	39	40
New Brighton		30	10	7	13	48	53	37
Ashville		30	10	5	15	38	47	35
Ellesmere Port		30	8	11	11	28	47	35
Cammell Laird Res.		30	9	5	16	42	47	32
Newton		30	8	8	14	41	51	32
Castrol Social		30	8	6	16	31	65	30
Runcorn Town		30	8	5	17	49	66	29
Mallaby		30	4	6	20	28	75	18

BILL WEIGHT MEMORIAL CUP

(Divisional champions and Pyke Cup holders)

SEMI-FINALS

New Brighton 0 **Runcorn Town** 4

Vauxhall Motors Res. 4 Heswall 0

FINAL

(September 6th at Cammell Laird)

Vauxhall Motors Res. 1 **Runcorn Town** 1 *(Trophy shared)*

PYKE CUP

(Division One clubs)

FIRST ROUND

Ashville 1 **West Kirby** 3

Ellesmere Port 0 Castrol Social 0 *aet*

Castrol Social 2 Ellesmere Port 2 *aet* (4-3p) *replay*

Heswall 3 **Poulton Victoria** 4

Maghull 5 New Brighton 2

Mallaby 1 **Cammell Laird Res.** 4

Merseyside Police 1 **Vauxhall Motors Res.** 2

Newton 4 Christleton 2

Runcorn Town 0 Aintree Villa 0 *aet*

Aintree Villa 4 Runcorn Town 3 *replay*

QUARTER-FINALS

Aintree Villa 0 **Vauxhall Motors Res.** 5

Cammell Laird Res. 1 **Maghull** 2

Newton 0 **Poulton Victoria** 5 *(at Poulton Victoria)*

West Kirby 6 Castrol Social 1

SEMI-FINALS

Maghull 0 **Poulton Victoria** 1 *(at Ashville)*

Vauxhall Motors Res. 2 **West Kirby** 3 *(at Ashville)*

FINAL

(April 14th at Vauxhall Motors)

Poulton Victoria 2 **West Kirby** 3

WEST CHESHIRE LEAGUE DIVISION ONE CONSTITUTION 2006-07

AINTREE VILLA .... **Aintree Racecourse, Melling Road, Aintree L9 5AB** .... **None**
ASHVILLE .... **Villa Park, Cross Lane, Wallasey Village, Wallasey CH45 8RH** **0151 638 2127**
BLACON YOUTH CLUB .... **Cairns Crescent Playing Fields, Blacon, Chester CH1 5JF** .... **None**
CAMMELL LAIRD RESERVES ..... **Kirklands, St Peters Road, Rock Ferry, Birkenhead CH42 1PY** **0151 645 3121**
CASTROL SOCIAL .... **Castrol Sports & Social Club, Chester Road, Whitby, Ellesmere Port CH66 2NZ** **0151 357 3712**
CHRISTLETON .... **Little Heath Road, Christleton, Chester CH3 7AH** **01244 332153**
ELLESMERE PORT .... **Chester Road, Whitby, Ellesmere Port** **0151 200 7080/7050**
HESWALL .... **Gayton Park, Brimstage Road, Heswall CH60 1XG** **0151 342 8172**
MAGHULL .... **Old Hall Field, Hall Lane, Maghull LE31 7BB** **0151 526 7320**
MARINE RESERVES .... **Rossett Park, College Road, Crosby, Liverpool L23 3AS** **0151 924 1743/4046**
MERSEYSIDE POLICE .... **Police Club, Fairfield, Prescot Road, Liverpool L7 0JD** **0151 228 2352**
NEW BRIGHTON .... **Harrison Drive, Wallasey Village, Wallasey CH45 3PH** .... **None**
NEWTON .... **Millcroft, Frankby Road, Greasby CH47 0NB** **0151 677 8282**
POULTON VICTORIA .... **Victoria Park, Rankin Street, Wallasey CH44 5SR** **0151 638 3559**
UPTON ATHLETIC ASSOCIATION .. **Cheshire County S & S Club, Plas Newton Lane, Chester CH2 1PR** **01244 318167**
VAUXHALL MOTORS RESERVES .. **Vauxhall Sports Ground, Rivacre Road, Hooton, Ellesmere Port CH66 1NJ** **0151 328 1114**
WEST KIRBY .... **Marine Park, Greenbank Road, West Kirby CH48 5HL** .... **None**

IN: Blacon Youth Club (P), Marine Reserves (S – Lancashire League), Upton Athletic Association (P)

OUT: Mallaby (R), Runcorn Town (R)

	Ashville Res.	Blacon Youth Club	Capenhurst Villa	Chester Nomads	Christleton Res.	FC Pensby	Halton	Helsby	Heswall Res.	MANWEB	Maghull Res.	Poulton Victoria Res.	Runcorn Town Res.	Upton Athletic Assoc.	Willaston
Ashville Res.		4-6	2-2	3-4	2-3	1-1	4-0	1-1	4-1	1-2	0-1	1-1	3-3	2-3	2-1
Blacon Youth Club	2-1	*D*	1-0	5-2	6-0	4-2	5-0	3-2	5-1	4-1	2-1	2-0	9-2	2-3	2-2
Capenhurst Villa	1-0	0-0	*I*	3-0	5-0	2-0	3-1	2-4	4-0	5-0	4-1	1-0	1-2	2-0	2-3
Chester Nomads	2-1	2-4	2-0	*V*	6-2	2-2	3-2	1-1	8-4	1-3	3-3	0-1	0-1	1-2	2-3
Christleton Res.	2-1	0-7	1-1	2-10	*I*	1-2	1-0	0-5	0-2	0-4	1-4	3-0	1-4	2-3	1-2
FC Pensby	2-7	1-2	1-2	1-2	3-1	*S*	2-0	5-5	3-3	1-4	1-2	0-1	2-4	0-3	2-1
Halton	2-0	2-2	0-4	1-1	3-2	1-0	*I*	3-4	1-2	3-3	0-1	0-3	1-1	3-1	1-1
Helsby	1-3	0-3	2-2	3-5	3-2	0-1	4-1	*O*	4-1	5-0	0-2	2-3	3-3	2-3	1-5
Heswall Res.	2-1	0-2	1-3	0-0	3-3	1-1	2-2	4-1	*N*	4-0	0-3	5-5	1-1	1-1	1-1
MANWEB	5-1	1-4	0-1	5-2	1-0	1-2	1-2	1-1	4-0		1-2	3-1	1-3	0-5	1-1
Maghull Res.	3-1	3-1	0-1	4-2	2-0	3-1	1-1	3-1	3-0	3-1		2-1	7-2	2-1	4-2
Poulton Victoria Res.	1-1	3-2	3-0	3-3	6-0	3-2	2-1	7-1	4-1	1-1	1-0	*T*	2-3	1-2	2-0
Runcorn Town Res.	3-0	1-5	3-3	5-3	2-0	3-2	1-1	6-2	3-3	2-1	0-3	0-3	*W*	0-2	1-1
Upton Athletic Association	5-0	2-3	4-0	4-3	2-1	3-0	3-0	2-0	4-2	4-0	2-2	2-1	4-2	*O*	3-1
Willaston	1-1	2-0	0-1	1-1	5-0	1-3	3-0	4-3	3-0	4-0	2-2	1-2	1-0	1-2	

Division Two		P	W	D	L	F	A	Pts
Upton Athletic Association		28	22	2	4	75	34	68
Blacon Youth Club		28	21	3	4	93	38	66
Maghull Res.		28	20	4	4	67	32	64
Capenhurst Villa		28	16	5	7	55	31	53
Poulton Victoria Res.		28	15	5	8	61	39	50
Runcorn Town Res.		28	12	8	8	61	65	44
Willaston	*-3*	28	11	8	9	53	40	38
Chester Nomads		28	9	7	12	71	69	34
MANWEB		28	9	4	15	45	63	31
Helsby		28	7	6	15	61	76	27
FC Pensby		28	7	5	16	43	63	26
Heswall Res.		28	5	10	13	45	74	25
Halton		28	5	8	15	32	60	23
Ashville Res.		28	5	7	16	48	61	22
Christleton Res.		28	4	2	22	29	94	14

WEST CHESHIRE BOWL

(Division Two clubs)

FIRST ROUND

Capenhurst Villa 3 Ashville Res. 1
Christleton Res. 1 Chester Nomads 0
FC Pensby 2 Poulton Victoria Res. 2 *aet*
MANWEB (w/o) v FC Building Boards (scr.)
Poulton Victoria Res. 4 FC Pensby 1 *replay*
Helsby 4 Halton 1
Heswell Res. 1 **Upton Athletic Association** 3
Runcorn Town Res. 2 Blacon Youth Club 1
Willaston 0 **Maghull Res.** 2

QUARTER-FINALS

Capenhurst Villa 0 **Helsby** 2 *(at Helsby)*
Christleton Res. 1 **Maghull Res.** 4
MANWEB 3 Runcorn Town Res. 1
Poulton Victoria Res. 8 Upton Athletic Association 2

SEMI-FINALS

Helsby 1 **Poulton Victoria Res.** 2 *(at Vauxhall Motors)*
Maghull Res. 1 **MANWEB** 0 *(at Poulton Victoria)*

FINAL

(May 5th at Ashville)
Maghull Res. 1 **Poulton Victoria Res.** 2

WEST CHESHIRE LEAGUE DIVISION TWO CONSTITUTION 2006-07

ASHVILLE RESERVES .... Villa Park, Cross Lane, Wallasey Village, Wallasey CH45 8RH 0151 638 2127
CAPENHURST VILLA .... Capenhurst Sports Ground, Capenhurst Lane, Capenhurst CH1 6HE .... None
CHESTER NOMADS .... Boughton Hall Cricket Club, Boughton, Chester CH3 5EL 01244 326072
CHRISTLETON RESERVES .... Little Heath Road, Christleton, Chester CH3 7AH 01244 332153
FC PENSBY .... Ridgewood Park, Fishers Lane, Pensby .... None
HALTON .... Picow Farm Road, Runcorn .... None
HELSBY .... Helsby Sports & Social Club, Chester Road, Helsby WA6 0DL 01928 722267
HESWALL RESERVES .... Gayton Park, Brimstage Road, Heswall CH60 1XG 0151 342 8172
MANWEB .... MANWEB Sports & Social Club, Thingwall Lane, Liverpool L15 7LB 0151 281 5364
MAGHULL RESERVES .... Old Hall Field, Hall Lane, Maghull LE31 7BB 0151 526 7320
MALLABY .... Unilever Sports Ground, Bromborough .... None
NEW BRIGHTON RESERVES .... Harrison Drive, Wallasey Village, Wallasey CH45 3PH .... None
POULTON VICTORIA RESERVES .... Victoria Park, Rankin Street, Wallasey CH44 5SR 0151 638 3559
RUNCORN TOWN .... Pavilions Club, Sandy Lane, Weston Point, Runcorn WA7 4EX 01928 590508/07734 558 8795
WEST KIRBY RESERVES .... Marine Park, Greenbank Road, West Kirby CH48 5HL .... None
WILLASTON .... Johnston Recreation Ground, Neston Road, Willaston CH64 2TL .... None

IN: Mallaby (R), New Brighton Reserves (P), Runcorn Town (R), West Kirby Reserves (P)

OUT: Blacon Youth Club (P), FC Building Boards (WN), Runcorn Town Reserves (R), Upton Athletic Association (P)

	AFC Bebington Athletic	Bronze Social	Capenhurst Villa Res.	Ellesmere Port Res.	FOCUS	Grange Athletic	MANWEB Res.	MBNA	Manor Athletic	Mersey Royal	Merseyside Police Res.	New Brighton Res.	Shaftesbury	St Werburghs	Upton Athletic Ass. Res.	West Kirby Res.
AFC Bebington Athletic		4-2	3-0	2-1	5-1	7-2	1-2	1-1	1-1	3-2	1-1	0-7	6-4	4-0	2-3	1-4
Bronze Social	0-4	*D*	4-3	3-2	2-4	2-2	6-5	3-2	1-1	0-3	1-2	1-3	3-0	0-0	0-3	2-2
Capenhurst Villa Res.	0-2	1-1	*I*	3-4	0-2	3-3	0-2	0-1	0-0	2-0	1-2	0-7	4-3	0-0	0-2	0-2
Ellesmere Port Res.	0-4	3-3	4-0	*V*	1-0	3-3	3-2	0-1	1-1	1-0	1-2	0-3	4-3	2-3	3-0	0-1
FOCUS	1-0	0-3	4-2	1-0	*I*	5-2	2-2	1-1	1-1	1-3	3-1	0-0	1-0	0-0	6-1	1-1
Grange Athletic	1-2	2-1	2-0	0-4	1-2	*S*	4-1	2-1	4-1	4-3	2-1	3-4	2-1	1-4	1-0	1-9
MANWEB Res.	0-5	2-3	1-2	3-4	2-1	1-1	*I*	2-0	5-1	2-1	1-3	1-6	9-1	2-3	4-3	0-3
MBNA	1-6	6-3	0-2	5-1	1-3	3-1	3-4	*O*	5-0	3-3	1-1	0-4	1-0	4-6	0-6	2-4
Manor Athletic	2-3	0-7	2-3	0-3	1-3	1-1	2-5	0-4	*N*	1-2	2-1	3-5	2-1	2-3	0-4	1-5
Mersey Royal	5-0	0-3	1-2	0-3	1-3	0-2	3-3	2-0	3-0		0-4	1-2	2-2	1-5	3-1	0-5
Merseyside Police Res.	0-0	1-1	2-1	1-3	4-1	12-0	1-0	3-3	4-1	3-3	*T*	1-2	2-0	3-4	6-2	0-3
New Brighton Res.	3-0	3-1	3-0	2-2	1-4	1-2	3-2	2-2	4-0	1-0	2-2	*H*	7-0	3-1	4-1	2-0
Shaftesbury	1-1	2-2	1-2	2-2	2-3	2-4	0-0	4-1	4-2	3-4	2-3	1-2	*R*	1-4	4-5	0-3
St Werburghs	0-6	7-1	0-2	7-1	3-0	4-1	7-3	2-2	1-2	1-1	0-5	1-4	5-1	*E*	0-0	1-3
Upton Athletic Association Res.	1-3	2-2	0-0	4-1	2-1	3-3	4-3	3-0	1-1	6-0	2-5	2-2	1-3	2-1	*E*	1-3
West Kirby Res.	2-1	6-5	1-1	2-0	3-0	2-3	9-1	2-0	1-0	2-0	4-1	1-0	4-0	2-2	3-1	

Division Three		P	W	D	L	F	A	Pts
West Kirby Res.		30	24	4	2	92	27	76
New Brighton Res.		30	22	5	3	92	32	71
AFC Bebington Athletic		30	17	5	8	78	48	56
Merseyside Police Res.		30	15	7	8	77	47	52
FOCUS		30	15	6	9	55	46	51
St Werburghs		30	14	7	9	75	59	49
Grange Athletic		30	13	6	11	60	83	45
Upton Ath. Assoc. Res.		30	12	6	12	66	64	42
Ellesmere Port Res.		30	12	5	13	57	61	41
Bronze Social		30	9	9	12	66	75	36
MANWEB Res.		30	10	4	16	70	85	34
Capenhurst Villa Res.		30	8	6	16	34	59	30
Mersey Royal		30	8	5	17	47	68	29
MBNA	*-3*	30	8	7	15	54	71	28
Manor Athletic		30	3	7	20	31	86	16
Shaftesbury		30	3	5	22	48	91	14

WEST CHESHIRE SHIELD

(Division Three clubs)

FIRST ROUND

AFC Bebington Athletic 3 St Werburghs 3 *aet*
St Werburghs 0 **AFC Bebington Athletic** 6
Bronze Social 2 **West Kirby Res.** 4
Ellesmere Port Res. 2 MBNA 1
Grange Athletic 4 Capenhurst Villa Res. 1
Mersey Royal 4 FOCUS 3 *aet*
Merseyside Police Res. 0 **MANWEB Res.** 3
New Brighton Res. 3 Shaftesbury 3 *aet*
Shaftesbury 2 **New Brighton Res.** 4
Upton Athletic Association Res. 2 Manor Athletic 0

QUARTER-FINALS

AFC Bebington Athletic 1 **New Brighton Res.** 2
MANWEB Res. 1 Ellesmere Port Res. 0
Upton Athletic Association Res. 3 Mersey Royal 1
West Kirby Res. 3 Grange Athletic 1

SEMI-FINALS

MANWEB Res. 1 **New Brighton Res.** 2 *(at Poulton Victoria)*
Upton Athletic Association Res. 2 **West Kirby Res.** 5 *(at Ashville)*

FINAL

(May 2nd at Poulton Victoria)
West Kirby Res. 2 New Brighton Res. 1

WEST CHESHIRE LEAGUE DIVISION THREE CONSTITUTION 2006-07

AFC BEBINGTON ATHLETIC .... Unilever Sports Ground, Bromborough. .... None
BLACON YOUTH CLUB RESERVES .... Cairns Crescent Playing Fields, Blacon, Chester .... None
BRONZE SOCIAL .... Unilever Sports Ground, Bromborough. .... None
CAPENHURST VILLA RESERVES .. Capenhurst Sports Ground, Capenhurst Lane, Capenhurst CH1 6HE .... None
ELLESMERE PORT RESERVES .... Chester Road, Whitby, Ellesmere Port 0151 200 7080/7050
FOCUS .... Riversdale Police Ground, Liverpool L19 3QN 0151 724 5214
GRANGE ATHLETIC ...... Greyhound Stadium, Thornton Road, Stanney Grange, Ellesmere Port CH65 5DE 0151 355 1717
MANWEB RESERVES .... MANWEB Sports & Social Club, Thingwall Lane, Liverpool L15 7LB 0151 281 5364
MANOR ATHLETIC .... Octel Sports & Social Club, 28 Bridle Road, Bromborough CH62 6AR 0151 3566159
MERSEY ROYAL .... Unilever Sports Ground, Bromborough. .... None
MERSEYSIDE POLICE RESERVES ..... Police Club, Fairfield, Prescot Road, Liverpool L7 0JD. 0151 228 2352
RUNCORN TOWN RESERVES ...... Pavilions Club, Sandy Lane, Weston Point, Runcorn WA7 4EX 01928 590508/07734 558 8795
SHAFTESBURY .... Memorial Ground, Borough Road, Birkenhead CH42 9PY 0151 608 7165
ST WERBURGHS .... West Cheshire College, Old Wrexham Road, Handbridge, Chester CH4 7HS .... None
UPTON ATHLETIC ASSOCIATION RESERVES .. Cheshire County S & S Club, Plas Newton Lane, Chester CH2 1PR 01244 318167
WILLASTON RESERVES .... Johnston Recreation Ground, Neston Road, Willaston CH64 2TL .... None

IN: Blacon Youth Club Reserves (P – Chester & District League), Runcorn Town Reserves (R), Willaston Reserves (P – Wirral & Birkenhead League)

OUT: MBNA (F), New Brighton Reserves (P), West Kirby Reserves (P)

WEST LANCS LEAGUE

	Barnoldswick Town	Blackpool Wren Rovers	Blackrod Town	Burnley United	Charnock Richard	Coppull United	Dalton United	Eagley	Euxton Villa	Fleetwood Hesketh	Freckleton	Fulwood Amateurs	Hesketh Bank	Kirkham & Wesham	Turton	Wyre Villa
Barnoldswick Town	*P*	2-2	1-4	2-1	1-1	2-2	1-0	1-1	2-1	0-0	0-0	1-4	5-0	2-6	1-1	1-3
Blackpool Wren Rovers	3-0	*R*	3-0	2-4	0-5	0-1	0-3	3-4	0-1	2-0	3-1	2-2	1-0	0-1	1-0	0-2
Blackrod Town	5-1	3-3	*E*	3-0	0-2	1-1	0-0	1-4	3-0	0-0	1-0	0-0	1-2	0-1	1-2	1-1
Burnley United	4-0	0-1	2-2	*M*	1-1	4-2	1-1	5-1	2-2	0-0	2-1	1-3	5-2	0-6	2-1	0-3
Charnock Richard	6-1	4-1	6-0	4-1	*I*	3-1	0-0	0-3	6-2	4-1	3-1	2-2	8-1	0-0	5-2	4-1
Coppull United	1-1	2-0	1-2	2-1	1-4	*E*	0-4	1-2	2-0	0-1	0-0	0-2	1-0	0-2	3-0	2-0
Dalton United	2-2	7-0	3-2	3-1	2-0	1-1	*R*	2-1	1-1	0-6	1-0	2-2	3-0	2-3	7-1	0-0
Eagley	1-4	1-0	0-4	1-2	1-2	0-1	3-2		3-0	1-2	1-4	5-3	1-0	2-4	1-1	5-2
Euxton Villa	3-0	0-0	3-0	3-2	1-1	0-0	4-2	0-2	*D*	3-3	1-1	2-1	3-0	1-1	0-0	3-1
Fleetwood Hesketh	1-2	1-2	1-1	1-0	2-1	1-1	0-0	0-1	2-4	*I*	0-1	0-0	3-1	1-2	0-1	3-1
Freckleton	2-1	1-1	2-0	1-4	1-2	0-1	1-2	1-7	3-2	0-0	*V*	1-2	2-1	0-2	1-0	4-1
Fulwood Amateurs	4-1	2-0	2-2	0-2	3-1	1-2	2-3	1-1	0-2	1-0	2-1	*I*	0-6	2-5	1-1	0-4
Hesketh Bank	0-0	1-2	3-0	0-0	0-0	1-1	1-4	0-2	2-2	3-3	0-1	0-3	*S*	1-5	1-2	4-0
Kirkham & Wesham	4-0	6-0	4-0	5-0	3-3	6-1	2-0	2-0	1-1	2-0	2-0	3-1	2-0	*I*	5-0	8-1
Turton	2-1	1-4	1-1	2-3	1-4	1-1	4-2	4-3	1-1	2-2	1-4	1-2	3-2	0-2	*O*	3-4
Wyre Villa	3-1	0-0	3-0	1-3	0-4	0-3	1-2	1-1	3-1	0-1	4-2	1-2	3-0	1-1	0-3	*N*

Premier Division		P	W	D	L	F	A	Pts
Kirkham & Wesham		30	25	5	0	96	19	80
Charnock Richard		30	18	8	4	86	34	62
Dalton United		30	14	9	7	61	40	51
Eagley		30	14	4	12	59	53	46
Fulwood Amateurs		30	12	8	10	50	52	44
Euxton Villa		30	10	12	8	47	45	42
Burnley United		30	12	6	12	53	56	42
Coppull United		30	11	9	10	35	40	42
Blackpool Wren Rovers		30	10	6	14	36	55	36
Fleetwood Hesketh		30	8	11	11	35	36	35
Freckleton		30	10	5	15	37	47	35
Wyre Villa	*-3*	30	10	5	15	45	62	32
Turton		30	8	8	14	42	65	32
Blackrod Town		30	7	10	13	38	52	31
Barnoldswick Town		30	6	10	14	37	67	28
Hesketh Bank		30	4	6	20	32	66	18

WEST LANCASHIRE LEAGUE PREMIER DIVISION CONSTITUTION 2006-07

BARNOLDSWICK TOWN	Victory Park, West Close, Barnoldswick, Colne BB18 5EN	01282 815817
BLACKPOOL WREN ROVERS	Bruce Park, School Road, Marton, Blackpool FY4 5EL	01253 760570
BLACKROD TOWN	Blackrod Community Centre, Vicarage Road, Blackrod, Bolton BL6 5DD	01204 692614
BURNLEY UNITED	Barden Sports Ground, Barden Lane, Burnley BB10 1JQ	None
CHARNOCK RICHARD	Charter Lane, Charnock Richard, Chorley PR7 5LY	01257 794288
COPPULL UNITED	Springfield Road, Coppull PR7 5EJ	01257 795190
DALTON UNITED	Railway Meadow, Beckside Road, Dalton-in-Furness LA15 8DP	01229 462799
EAGLEY	Eagley Sports Complex, Dunscar Bridge, Bolton BL7 9PF	01204 306830
EUXTON VILLA	Runshaw Hall Lane, Euxton, Chorley PR7 6HQ	None
FLEETWOOD HESKETH	Fylde Road, Southport PR9 9XH	01704 227968
FRECKLETON	Hodgson Memorial Ground, Bush Lane, Freckleton, Preston PR1 1SB	01772 679139
FULWOOD AMATEURS	Lightfoot Lane, Fulwood, Preston PR2 3LP	01772 861827
HASLINGDEN ST MARY'S	Townsend Street, Haslingden, Rossendale BB4 5DF	01706 221814
KIRKHAM & WESHAM	Birley Arms, Church Road, Warton, Kirkham	None
TURTON	Thomasson Fold, Turton, Edgworth, Bolton BL7 0PD	07929 965160
WYRE VILLA	Hallgate Park, Stalmine Village, near Knott End	01253 701468

IN: Haslingden St Mary's (P)

OUT: Hesketh Bank (R)

	BAE Barrow Sports Club	Bootle	Crooklands Casuals	Crosshills	Furness Rovers	Garstang	Haslingden St Mary's	Millom	Milnthorpe Corinthians	Norcross & Warbreck	Poulton Town	Springfields	Stoneclough	Tempest United	Whinney Hill
BAE Barrow Sports Club		1-1	2-2	3-1	1-0	2-1	1-3	3-0	4-1	4-3	3-1	0-4	6-1	3-3	2-1
Bootle	0-1	*D*	2-0	6-3	3-2	2-3	0-1	1-0	1-5	2-1	4-7	2-2	2-1	2-2	4-3
Crooklands Casuals	4-1	2-1	*I*	0-1	2-2	1-2	1-2	3-1	2-0	3-4	0-1	1-3	0-3	0-2	0-1
Crosshills	1-5	5-5	3-3	*V*	2-5	3-3	1-4	4-2	4-1	3-0	2-3	0-2	0-2	1-3	0-0
Furness Rovers	1-2	1-2	2-2	2-1	*I*	1-3	3-4	1-4	0-0	0-0	2-1	1-2	1-3	0-1	1-2
Garstang	3-0	0-0	2-1	2-2	1-3	*S*	2-0	2-2	1-1	1-2	1-4	2-2	3-2	3-3	1-2
Haslingden St Mary's	2-1	5-0	2-1	4-1	6-3	5-1	*I*	6-1	5-1	1-1	3-0	1-3	4-5	3-0	2-2
Millom	0-2	1-3	1-2	2-1	2-4	5-1	6-4	*O*	9-1	1-2	6-5	1-4	1-1	2-3	3-2
Milnthorpe Corinthians	2-3	3-0	0-2	1-2	0-0	1-1	0-3	2-4	*N*	0-1	1-4	1-4	1-2	1-0	1-0
Norcross & Warbreck	1-3	0-1	3-0	4-1	2-3	2-4	1-2	3-1	6-1		3-4	1-4	2-2	4-1	5-2
Poulton Town	3-6	2-1	1-0	0-2	2-0	5-0	2-3	7-2	3-0	2-1		3-2	1-1	1-2	3-1
Springfields	2-2	n/a	1-2	4-2	0-0	2-2	1-4	5-0	7-1	2-0	1-1	*O*	0-1	3-2	4-0
Stoneclough	6-1	5-0	3-0	2-2	4-2	2-1	1-3	3-0	9-2	2-1	5-0	0-5	*N*	3-3	3-4
Tempest United	3-2	4-1	3-1	2-3	4-2	2-0	1-3	4-1	3-0	2-3	0-4	0-0	3-3	*E*	3-2
Whinney Hill	0-3	4-2	3-0	4-1	3-2	2-1	0-3	6-0	0-3	0-5	2-1	0-2	1-3	1-1	

Note – Bootle withdrew during the course of the season
Their results are shown above but are expunged from the league table

Division One	P	W	D	L	F	A	Pts
Haslingden St Mary's	26	20	2	4	82	40	62
Springfields	26	16	6	4	69	28	54
Stoneclough	26	15	6	5	72	47	51
BAE Barrow Sports Club	26	16	3	7	65	49	51
Poulton Town	26	14	2	10	62	49	44
Tempest United	26	12	6	8	54	49	42
Norcross & Warbreck	26	12	3	11	60	49	39
Whinney Hill	26	10	3	13	41	53	33
Garstang	26	7	8	11	44	57	29
Crosshills	26	7	5	14	44	63	26
Millom	26	8	2	16	57	81	26
Furness Rovers	26	6	6	14	41	54	24
Crooklands Casuals	26	6	4	16	33	49	22
Milnthorpe Corinthians	26	3	4	19	23	79	13

Bootle – record expunged

WEST LANCASHIRE LEAGUE DIVISION ONE CONSTITUTION 2006-07

BAE BARROW SPORTS CLUB .... Vickers Sports Club, Hawcoat Lane, Barrow-in-Furness LA14 4HF 01229 825296
CROOKLANDS CASUALS .... Longlands Park, Greystone Lane, Dalton-in-Furness 01229 465010
CROSSHILLS .... Holme Lane, Crosshills, Keighley BD20 7RL .... None
CROSTON SPORTS .... Old Emmanuel School, Westhead Road, Croston, Leyland PR26 9RR 01772 600261
FURNESS ROVERS .... Wilkie Road, Barrow-in-Furness LA14 5UQ .... None
GARSTANG .... Riverside Community Centre, off High Street, Garstang PR3 1FA 01995 601586
HESKETH BANK .... Hesketh Sports Field, Station Road, Hesketh Bank PR4 6SR .... None
MILLOM .... Millom RL Club, Devonshire Road, Millom LA18 4PG 01229 772030
NORCROSS & WARBRECK .... Anchorsholme Lane, Thornton Cleveleys, near Blackpool FY5 .... 01253 859836
POULTON TOWN .... Cottam Hall Playing Fields, Blackpool Old Road, Poulton-le-Fylde FY6 7RS 01253 896150
STONECLOUGH .... Brook Street, opposite Europa Business Park, Stoneclough, Kearsley, Bolton .... None
TEMPEST UNITED .... Tempest Road, Chew Moor Village, Lostock, near Bolton BL6 4EL 01942 811938
TRIMPELL .... Trimpell Sports & Social Club, Out Moss Lane, Morecambe LA4 4UP 01524 412984
WHINNEY HILL .... Clayton-le-Moors, Accrington .... None

IN: Croston Sports (P), Hesketh Bank (R), Trimpell (P)

OUT: Bootle (WS), Haslingden St Mary's (P), Milnthorpe Corinthians (R), Springfields (R – having merged with BAC/EE Preston to form Springfields BAC Preston)

	Askam United	BAC/EE Preston	BAE Canberra	Bolton County	Burnley Belvedere	Croston Sports	Furness Cavaliers	Glaxo Ulverston Rangers	Lancashire Constabulary	Lostock St Gerards	Mill Hill St Peters	Thornton Cleveleys	Todmorden Borough	Trimpell
Askam United		2-1	0-1	1-2	0-1	1-2	2-0	1-1	0-0	2-0	2-0	0-3	2-2	0-3
BAC/EE Preston	0-4	*D*	2-2	0-3	2-3	1-5	0-4	1-4	0-4	0-4	5-3	0-3	0-1	1-5
BAE Canberra	1-2	7-1	*I*	2-1	2-0	2-2	1-2	0-0	2-3	3-4	0-1	5-2	3-1	2-1
Bolton County	3-1	5-0	0-2	*V*	5-5	2-1	3-1	0-2	3-1	1-1	1-0	1-2	3-2	1-5
Burnley Belvedere	0-3	4-1	2-3	3-1	*I*	2-2	4-5	1-1	2-3	2-1	2-2	5-2	1-1	2-0
Croston Sports	3-1	5-0	1-1	4-2	5-0	*S*	1-0	2-4	0-0	1-1	1-0	4-0	1-0	3-3
Furness Cavaliers	3-3	5-0	1-1	0-0	2-1	0-3	*I*	0-2	1-0	4-2	2-2	1-2	1-1	0-2
Glaxo Ulverston Rangers	0-3	4-1	1-1	0-3	1-2	2-5	1-1	*O*	2-2	2-1	3-1	2-3	0-0	1-3
Lancashire Constabulary	3-3	1-1	2-2	1-2	2-4	0-2	1-0	0-1	*N*	3-1	4-2	5-2	1-3	1-5
Lostock St Gerards	6-2	3-1	2-2	0-5	1-1	2-0	0-2	2-1	1-3		0-2	1-5	0-2	1-1
Mill Hill St Peters	2-1	3-0	3-0	1-0	2-1	1-1	3-3	2-2	1-1	2-4	*T*	3-1	1-1	2-2
Thornton Cleveleys	2-0	6-1	1-1	1-1	6-1	2-2	3-1	4-1	4-1	2-1	2-2	*W*	2-0	4-1
Todmorden Borough	3-0	7-0	1-1	3-1	1-0	0-2	2-0	1-0	1-0	0-0	0-0	2-2	*O*	0-5
Trimpell	3-2	4-1	4-2	5-2	3-1	3-2	5-1	2-2	1-0	6-1	3-1	4-1	4-1	

Division Two	P	W	D	L	F	A	Pts
Trimpell	26	19	4	3	83	35	61
Croston Sports	26	14	8	4	60	30	50
Thornton Cleveleys	26	15	5	6	67	46	50
Bolton County	26	12	4	10	51	44	40
Todmorden Borough	26	10	9	7	36	30	39
BAE Canberra	26	9	10	7	49	40	37
Mill Hill St Peters	26	8	10	8	42	42	34
Glaxo Ulverston Rangers	26	8	9	9	40	42	33
Burnley Belvedere	26	9	6	11	50	57	33
Lancs Constabulary	26	8	7	11	42	46	31
Furness Cavaliers	26	8	7	11	40	45	31
Askam United	26	8	5	13	38	45	29
Lostock St Gerards	26	7	6	13	40	55	27
BAC/EE Preston	26	1	2	23	20	101	5

WEST LANCASHIRE LEAGUE DIVISION TWO CONSTITUTION 2006-07

ASKAM UNITED .... **Duddon Road, James Street, Askam-in-Furness LA16 7AH** **01229 464576**
BAE CANBERRA .... **Samlesbury Works, Whalley Road, Samlesbury PR5 0UN** **01254 768888**
BOLTON COUNTY .... **Radcliffe Road, Darcy Lever, Bolton BL3 1RU** .... **None**
BURNLEY BELVEDERE .... **Belvedere & Caldervale SC, Holden Road, Burnley BL10 2LE** **01282 433171**
FURNESS CAVALIERS .... **Rampside Road, Barrow-in-Furness LA13 0HN** .... **None**
GLAXO ULVERSTON RANGERS .... **off North Lonsdale Road, Ulverston LA12 9DZ** **01229 582261**
LANCASHIRE CONSTABULARY .... **Police HQ, Saunders Lane, Hutton, Preston PR4 5SG** **01772 410591**
LOSTOCK ST GERARDS .... **Wateringpool Lane, Lostock Hall PR5 5UA** .... **None**
MILL HILL ST PETERS ..... **Opposite Mill Hill Hotel, Bridge Street, off Buncer Lane, Blackburn BB2 2QY** **01254 675557**
MILNTHORPE CORINTHIANS .... **Strands Lane, Milnthorpe** **01539 562135**
SPRINGFIELDS BAC PRESTON ...... **BAC Sports Ground, South Meadow Lane, Preston PR1 8JP** **01772 464351**
THORNTON CLEVELEYS .... **Bourne Road, Cleveleys, Thornton Cleveleys FY5 4AB** **01253 869666**
TODMORDEN BOROUGH .... **Bellholme, Walsden Road (off A6033), Todmorden** .... **None**
VICKERS TOWN .... **Park Vale, Mill Lane, Walney, Barrow-in-Furness LA14 3ND** .... **None**

IN: Milnthorpe Corinthians (R), Springfields (R – having merged with BAC/EE Preston to form Springfields BAC Preston), Vickers Town (N)
OUT: Croston Sports (P), Rivington (WS), Trimpell (P)

RICHARDSON CUP

(Premier Division teams)

FIRST ROUND

Blackpool Wren Rovers 4 Blackrod Town 1
Eagley 1 **Freckleton** 5
Euxton Villa 1 **Burnley United** 3
Fleetwood Hesketh 1 Barnoldswick Town 0
Fulwood Amateurs 2 **Wyre Villa** 5
Hesketh Bank 0 **Dalton United** 3
Kirkham & Wesham 2 Coppull United 1
Turton 1 **Charnock Richard** 3

QUARTER-FINALS

Charnock Richard 4 Blackpool Wren Rovers 2
Dalton United 0 **Kirkham & Wesham** 4
Freckleton 2 **Fleetwood Hesketh** 3
Wyre Villa 3 **Burnley United** 5

SEMI-FINALS

Burnley United 1 **Kirkham & Wesham** 4
(at Eagley)
Charnock Richard 1 **Fleetwood Hesketh** 1 *aet* (6-7p)
(at Croston Sports)

FINAL

(April 26th at LCFA, Leyland)
Kirkham & Wesham 3 Fleetwood Hesketh 1

PRESIDENT'S CUP

(First Division teams)

FIRST ROUND

Bootle 4 Crosshills 0
Crooklands Casuals 3 **BAE Barrow Sports Club** 4
Furness Rovers (w/o) v Rivington (scr.)
Garstang 5 Millom 1
Norcross & Warbreck 5 Milnethorpe Corinthians 3
Springfields 4 Tempest United 0
Stoneclough 3 Poulton Town 2
Whinney Hill 0 **Haslingden St Mary's** 5

QUARTER-FINALS

Garstang 4 Stoneclough 2
Haslingden St Mary's 0 **Bootle** 0 *aet* (5-6p)
Norcross & Warbreck 0 **Furness Rovers** 1
Springfields 2 BAE Barrow Sports Club 2 *aet* (6-5p)

SEMI-FINALS

Furness Rovers 1 **Garstang** 3
(at Trimpell)
Springfields 3 Bootle 1
(at Crooklands Casuals)

FINAL

(April 19th at Lancaster City)
Garstang 0 **Springfields** 0 *aet* (4-5p)

CHALLENGE CUP

(Second Division teams)

FIRST ROUND

Askam United 1 BAE Canberra 0
BAC/EE Preston 2 Mill Hill St Peters 1
Bolton County 5 Furness Cavaliers 1
Glaxo Ulverston Rangers 4 Lancashire Constabulary 3 *aet*
Lostock Gralam 2 **Croston Sports** 3 *aet*
Todmorden Borough 1 Burnley Belvedere 0

QUARTER-FINALS

Croston Sports 1 **Bolton County** 3
Glaxo Ulverston Rangers 2 Todmorden Borough 0
Thornton Cleveleys 3 Askam United 0
Trimpell 3 **BAC/EE Preston** 3 *aet* (4-5p)

SEMI-FINALS

BAC/EE Preston 0 **Glaxo Ulverston Rangers** 4
(at Fulwood Amateurs)
Thornton Cleverleys 0 **Bolton County** 2
(at Freckleton)

FINAL

(April 20th at Blackpool Mechanics)
Bolton County 2 Glaxo Ulverston Rangers 0

Reserve Division One		P	W	D	L	F	A	Pts
Blackrod Town Res.		28	19	6	3	69	33	63
Euxton Villa Res.		28	18	3	7	70	28	57
Kirkham & Wesham Res.		28	15	8	5	66	39	53
Norcross & Warbreck Res.		28	14	6	8	53	50	48
Eagley Res.		28	11	10	7	48	38	43
Poulton Town Res.		28	11	10	7	65	61	43
Charnock Richard Res.		28	12	6	10	52	38	42
Burnley United Res.		28	12	4	12	52	43	40
Fulwood Amateurs Res.		28	11	5	12	58	41	38
Freckleton Res.		28	10	4	14	40	67	34
Tempest United Res.	*-3*	28	9	8	11	61	66	32
Thornton Cleveleys Res.		28	9	5	14	48	64	32
Turton Res.	*-3*	28	7	3	18	54	77	21
Coppull United Res.		28	5	5	18	39	78	20
Hesketh Bank Res.		28	4	3	21	35	87	15

Reserve Division Two		P	W	D	L	F	A	Pts
Blackpool Wren Rovers Res.		28	20	5	3	99	37	65
Fleetwood Hesketh Res.		28	18	5	5	65	41	59
Springfields Res.		28	16	5	7	79	45	53
Barnoldswick Town Res.		28	16	3	9	65	44	51
Garstang Res.		28	14	7	7	62	30	49
Whinney Hill Res.		28	14	4	10	63	46	46
Wyre Villa Res.		28	14	4	10	58	49	46
Stoneclough Res.		28	12	7	9	59	55	43
Haslingden St Mary's Res.		28	10	7	11	63	46	37
Burnley Belvedere Res.		28	10	7	11	61	68	37
Bolton County Res.		28	9	5	14	62	70	32
Mill Hill St Peters Res.		28	6	4	18	36	84	22
Crosshills Res.	*-3*	28	6	4	18	53	82	19
Todmorden Borough Res.		28	4	7	17	30	61	19
Milnthorpe Corinthians Res.		28	3	2	23	26	123	11

HOUSTON CUP

FINAL

(May 3rd at Croston Sports)
Kirkham & Wesham Res. 3 Eagley Res. 1

WEST MIDLANDS (REGIONAL) LEAGUE

	Bewdley Town	Brierley & Hagley	Bromyard Town	Bustleholme	Dudley Town	Goodrich	Gornal Athletic	Great Wyrley	Heath Hayes	Kington Town	Ledbury Town	Ludlow Town	Lye Town	Market Drayton Tn	Pelsall Villa	Shawbury United	Smethwick Rangers	Tividale	Wednesfield	Wellington	Wolverhampton Cas	Wyrley Rangers
Bewdley Town		2-2	1-1	5-0	4-0	3-1	3-0	2-1	2-1	3-1	3-1	2-2	2-2	1-0	4-1	5-1	1-1	1-0	4-1	2-3	1-0	0-2
Brierley & Hagley	2-0		1-4	1-0	1-2	1-1	0-1	0-5	0-0	1-0	6-0	3-7	0-1	1-5	0-2	4-0	1-0	0-1	2-0	1-2	1-2	2-2
Bromyard Town	1-1	2-1		0-1	1-3	2-6	0-2	1-3	1-2	3-0	1-3	0-0	2-3	1-1	2-0	1-2	2-0	1-2	0-3	1-0	1-4	0-5
Bustleholme	1-4	2-0	1-0	*P*	1-1	2-2	1-1	1-5	3-1	7-1	3-2	2-2	3-0	0-1	0-1	3-1	1-3	2-3	1-2	0-0	2-1	0-2
Dudley Town	4-3	1-2	2-1	4-0	*R*	2-2	0-0	3-5	1-0	1-3	4-0	5-1	0-6	1-4	2-0	3-1	2-1	3-1	1-1	3-0	3-1	0-2
Goodrich	0-0	2-0	0-3	3-2	3-2	*E*	1-0	0-3	1-1	2-1	6-0	1-1	0-0	2-6	2-1	5-2	4-1	3-1	0-4	2-2	4-1	2-2
Gornal Athletic	2-0	3-0	2-0	1-0	2-0	1-3	*M*	1-1	2-1	1-1	1-1	4-0	1-0	2-2	0-0	1-0	5-2	2-1	0-1	4-0	4-0	2-0
Great Wyrley	1-1	3-1	2-0	0-0	4-1	3-3	0-0	*I*	4-1	5-0	4-0	4-1	1-0	1-1	2-1	2-0	4-0	4-1	0-1	1-2	1-1	1-1
Heath Hayes	2-1	0-1	3-2	0-3	1-3	1-1	2-1	0-0	*E*	3-2	3-0	3-1	2-1	0-3	0-1	2-0	1-0	1-1	1-0	2-1	0-0	2-2
Kington Town	0-7	0-0	0-0	2-2	2-1	0-1	2-1	0-2	3-2	*R*	2-2	1-2	0-2	0-1	1-4	0-4	0-2	0-4	1-0	0-3	4-2	3-5
Ledbury Town	2-4	1-0	3-3	0-2	0-1	1-1	0-2	1-1	5-0	1-3		0-0	1-2	1-2	4-2	1-2	5-1	1-2	0-1	0-1	3-0	1-0
Ludlow Town	1-2	2-1	1-2	1-4	1-1	2-2	1-4	0-3	0-1	3-1	3-3	*D*	2-0	0-2	2-0	0-0	4-2	0-3	5-0	2-4	3-2	0-1
Lye Town	2-1	4-1	1-1	4-2	3-2	2-1	2-2	2-1	0-0	0-0	2-0	3-0	*I*	0-1	1-0	0-0	1-0	1-1	0-1	1-1	4-1	0-2
Market Drayton Town	3-2	1-1	2-1	6-1	1-0	2-1	0-1	2-2	4-2	1-1	4-2	3-0	2-1	*V*	1-0	3-1	2-1	0-0	3-0	3-0	4-0	0-0
Pelsall Villa	1-3	1-0	3-2	2-3	1-1	0-3	1-2	2-2	1-1	4-2	6-0	4-2	1-1	1-2	*I*	2-1	4-1	1-0	0-3	2-0	0-1	0-1
Shawbury United	1-2	5-1	0-1	0-0	1-1	2-5	2-4	0-3	2-4	6-1	8-1	1-2	1-1	0-5	4-1	*S*	2-1	1-2	2-1	3-2	7-0	0-4
Smethwick Rangers	0-7	0-3	5-2	3-1	3-2	2-2	1-2	1-1	3-1	1-2	2-1	5-0	1-3	1-4	1-2	1-2	*I*	0-2	0-1	0-1	2-1	2-1
Tividale	2-1	5-2	3-0	2-1	0-2	2-2	1-2	1-2	1-1	2-1	4-1	1-2	1-2	1-3	1-2	1-1	4-0	*O*	4-0	3-0	5-0	1-1
Wednesfield	0-4	1-4	1-1	2-2	2-1	2-1	0-3	0-2	1-1	4-0	3-1	6-0	0-2	0-4	1-3	1-2	0-4	3-0	*N*	2-2	2-0	2-0
Wellington	2-1	3-1	4-3	0-2	2-2	1-1	1-1	0-1	2-1	1-0	1-0	1-3	3-1	1-4	4-1	2-3	4-1	0-1	2-0		3-1	0-0
Wolverhampton Casuals	1-3	3-1	1-3	3-2	3-1	2-3	0-3	2-2	2-2	2-0	3-2	1-1	1-2	1-2	5-2	1-2	8-2	0-2	2-1	0-2		1-2
Wyrley Rangers	3-2	7-0	1-0	1-2	1-2	0-1	1-1	1-2	2-1	4-0	2-1	2-2	2-1	1-2	1-0	7-1	2-0	0-0	1-2	2-1	5-0	

Premier Division		P	W	D	L	F	A	Pts
Market Drayton Town		42	32	8	2	102	33	104
Gornal Athletic		42	25	11	6	74	32	86
Great Wyrley	*-1*	42	24	14	4	94	36	85
Bewdley Town		42	23	8	11	100	52	77
Wyrley Rangers		42	22	10	10	81	40	76
Lye Town		42	20	11	11	64	44	71
Goodrich		42	18	16	8	86	66	70
Tividale		42	20	8	14	73	50	68
Wellington		42	19	8	15	64	62	65
Dudley Town		42	18	8	16	74	71	62
Wednesfield		42	18	5	19	56	66	59
Bustleholme		42	15	9	18	66	73	54
Heath Hayes		42	14	12	16	53	64	54
Pelsall Villa		42	16	5	21	61	69	53
Shawbury United		42	15	6	21	74	87	51
Ludlow Town	*-2*	42	12	11	19	62	90	45
Brierley & Hagley		42	11	6	25	50	83	39
Bromyard Town		42	10	8	24	53	79	38
Wolverhampton Casuals		42	11	5	26	60	99	38
Smethwick Rangers	*-1*	42	11	3	28	57	98	35
Kington Town		42	8	7	27	41	102	31
Ledbury Town		42	7	7	28	52	101	28

PREMIER DIVISION CUP

FIRST ROUND

Bromyard Tn 4 Wednesfield 2
Brierley & Hagley 1 **Pelsall Villa** 2
Heath Hayes 3 Tividale 1
Kington Town 2 Gornal Athletic 0
Market Drayton Town 3 Ledbury Town 1
Wyrley Rangers 1 Ludlow Town 0

SECOND ROUND

Bromyard Town 3 Smethwick Rangers 2
Bustleholme 1 **Pelsall Villa** 2
Dudley Town 3 Bewdley Town 2
Great Wyrley 3 Wolverhampton Casuals 0
Kington Town 0 **Goodrich** 8
Market Drayton Town 2 Wellington 0
Shawbury United 2 Lye Tn 0
Wyrley Rangers 3 Heath Hayes 0

QUARTER-FINALS

Dudley Town 1 **Wyrley Rangers** 1 *aet* (2-3p)
Goodrich 1 **Market Drayton Tn** 5
Pelsall Villa 0 **Great Wyrley** 3
Shawbury Utd 0 **Bromyard Tn** 1

SEMI-FINALS

(played over two legs)

Market Drayton Town 0 Great Wyrley 2, **Great Wyrley** 1 Market Drayton Town 1
Wyrley Rangers 3 Bromyard Town 1, Bromyard Town 0 **Wyrley Rangers** 3

FINAL

(May 15th at Goodrich)

Wyrley Rangers 2 Great Wyrley 0

WEST MIDLANDS (REGIONAL) LEAGUE PREMIER DIVISION CONSTITUTION 2006-07

BEWDLEY TOWN .... Ribbesford Meadows, Ribbesford, Bewdley 01299 405837
BRIDGNORTH TOWN .... Crown Meadow, Innage Lane, Bridgnorth WV16 4HS 01746 762747
BRIERLEY & HAGLEY ...... Lye Town FC, Sports Ground, Stourbridge Road, Lye, Stourbridge DY9 7DH 01384 422672
BROMYARD TOWN .... Delahay Meadow, Stourport Road, Bromyard H47 4NT 01885 483974
BUSTLEHOLME .... Bilston Town FC, Queen Street, Bilston WV14 7EX 01902 491498
DUDLEY SPORTS .... Dudley Employees S&S, Hillcrest Avenue, Brierley Hill DY5 3QH 01384 826420
DUDLEY TOWN ..... Stourbridge FC, War Memorial Athletic Ground, High Str, Amblecote, Stourbridge DY8 4HN 01384 394040
ELLESMERE RANGERS .... Beech Grove Playing Fields, Ellesmere, Shropshire SY12 0BT .... None
GOODRICH .... Goodrich Sports Ground, Stafford Road, Fordhouses, Wolverhampton WV10 7EH .... None
GORNAL ATHLETIC .... Garden Walk Stadium, Garden Walk, Lower Gornal, Dudley DY3 2NH 01384 358398
GREAT WYRLEY .... Hazelbrook, Hazel Lane, Great Wyrley, Walsall WS6 6AA 01922 410366
LEDBURY TOWN .... New Street Ground, New Street, Ledbury HR8 2EL 07879 268205
LUDLOW TOWN .... Coors Stadium, Bromfield Road, Ludlow SY8 2BY 01584 876000
LYE TOWN .... Sports Ground, Stourbridge Road, Lye, Stourbridge DY9 7DH. 01384 422672
PELSALL VILLA .... The Bush Ground, Walsall Road, Heath End, Pelsall WS3 4ET 01922 692748/682018
SHAWBURY UNITED .... Butlers Sports Centre, Bowens Field, Wem SY4 5AW. 01939 233287
SHIFNAL TOWN .... Phoenix Park, Coppice Green Lane, Shifnal TF11 8PB 01952 463667
TIVIDALE .... The Beeches, Packwood Road, Tividale, Oldbury B69 1UL 01384 211743
WEDNESFIELD .... Cottage Ground, Amos Lane, Wednesfield WV11 1ND 01902 735506
WELLINGTON .... Wellington Playing Fields, Wellington, Hereford HR4 8AZ .... None
WOLVERHAMPTON CASUALS .... Brinsford Lane, Coven Heath, WV10 7PR 01902 783214
WYRLEY RANGERS .... Long Lane Park, Long Lane, Essington, Wolverhampton WV11 2AA 01922 406604

IN: Bridgnorth Town (S – Midland Combination Premier Division), Dudley Sports (S – Midland Combination Premier Division), Ellesmere Rangers (P), Shifnal Town (S – Midland Combination Premier Division)

OUT: Heath Hayes (S – Midland Combination Premier Division), Kington Town (R – Herefordshire League Premier Division), Market Drayton Town (P – Midland Alliance), Smethwick Rangers (W)

	Ashbourne United	Bilston Town	Blackheath Town	Brereton Social	Bridgnorth Town Res.	Cresswell Wanderers	Darlaston Town	Ellesmere Rangers	Hinton	Ludlow Town Res.	Malvern Rangers	Malvern Town Res.	Parkfield Leisure	Riverway	Sporting Khalsa	Stafford Town	Tenbury United	Walsall Wood	Wolverhampton United
Ashbourne United		1-3	0-0	2-1	1-1	1-0	4-1	1-2	1-2	2-0	3-4	1-0	0-9	1-1	1-0	1-3	2-4	1-2	2-2
Bilston Town	2-1		4-0	3-0	3-4	3-0	3-2	0-3	3-2	3-0	5-1	6-2	1-5	2-2	2-1	3-0	5-0	4-3	1-3
Blackheath Town	2-0	1-2		2-0	2-1	5-2	2-0	2-4	4-1	1-2	4-2	2-0	0-3	4-1	4-1	3-1	1-0	1-2	2-0
Brereton Social	3-0	3-1	1-1	*D*	3-0	1-0	6-1	3-1	3-0	6-1	7-0	3-0	3-1	7-1	5-1	9-0	3-1	0-4	2-0
Bridgnorth Town Res.	3-1	1-4	1-0	1-3	*I*	4-2	3-0	0-2	1-1	1-2	5-2	2-0	5-2	1-3	4-1	1-2	3-0	1-3	2-0
Cresswell Wanderers	2-1	0-5	3-2	0-6	2-4	*V*	4-0	0-0	2-3	1-1	4-1	1-1	0-4	3-1	3-3	4-2	1-3	3-4	3-1
Darlaston Town	1-3	2-3	2-10	1-6	0-3	0-4	*I*	0-4	1-3	4-2	4-0	0-10	1-5	0-2	1-2	1-3	3-1	0-5	3-1
Ellesmere Rangers	1-2	2-1	1-1	1-4	2-0	4-0	4-1	*S*	1-0	4-0	2-1	0-0	3-0	1-0	4-0	4-1	4-0	0-0	2-0
Hinton	1-2	3-1	4-1	1-2	6-3	0-2	4-1	1-4	*I*	6-0	3-0	3-2	0-3	3-3	4-3	1-1	1-1	0-5	1-4
Ludlow Town Res.	1-1	0-2	3-5	2-2	1-1	2-3	8-1	0-2	3-5	*O*	2-1	3-2	2-4	3-3	1-1	4-2	1-0	0-2	1-2
Malvern Rangers	1-0	0-2	0-2	3-2	4-2	3-1	1-3	2-0	0-1	0-0	*N*	1-3	1-3	0-4	3-2	2-4	6-1	0-4	2-2
Malvern Town Res.	4-2	0-4	0-1	1-2	2-0	3-1	3-1	1-4	6-2	2-1	3-1		2-3	2-0	2-4	3-2	5-4	3-2	1-2
Parkfield Leisure	1-0	5-2	3-3	1-3	1-0	1-0	3-2	2-2	4-0	5-1	4-1	4-2		1-0	2-1	2-0	3-1	0-2	3-0
Riverway	4-0	3-2	0-1	2-3	2-2	2-4	3-1	0-2	3-2	5-1	3-0	2-4	1-0	*O*	0-3	2-2	4-1	0-3	3-0
Sporting Khalsa	1-0	1-4	0-1	0-5	2-4	2-2	3-0	0-1	6-2	2-3	4-3	2-1	0-5	0-6	*N*	2-5	5-1	1-5	5-1
Stafford Town	1-1	5-4	0-1	4-1	3-2	1-3	4-2	0-2	3-3	3-4	3-1	5-0	4-4	0-1	5-0	*E*	2-1	1-2	4-2
Tenbury United	1-3	4-3	0-1	0-2	1-2	2-1	0M0	1-3	4-5	2-2	2-1	1-1	0-3	2-1	4-1	1-0		2-1	2-3
Walsall Wood	3-0	0-5	0-1	3-1	2-3	5-1	4-0	1-1	4-1	2-2	2-1	4-0	2-0	3-1	1-2	2-1	3-1		2-2
Wolverhampton United	3-1	3-2	0-2	0-1	4-0	0-2	1-1	0-1	1-1	1-1	3-2	1-0	0-3	4-2	3-2	1-1	2-2	0-0	

Division One		P	W	D	L	F	A	Pts
Ellesmere Rangers		36	26	6	4	78	25	84
Brereton Social		36	27	2	7	112	40	83
Parkfield Leisure		36	26	3	7	102	45	81
Walsall Wood		36	24	5	7	92	40	77
Blackheath Town		36	23	4	9	75	44	73
Bilston Town		36	23	1	12	103	63	70
Bridgnorth Town Res.		36	16	4	16	71	69	52
Riverway		36	14	6	16	71	68	48
Stafford Town		36	14	6	16	78	80	48
Hinton		36	14	6	16	76	88	48
Malvern Town Res.		36	14	3	19	71	77	45
Wolverhampton United		36	12	9	15	52	65	45
Cresswell Wanderers		36	13	5	18	64	81	44
Ludlow Town Res.		36	9	10	17	60	89	37
Ashbourne United		36	10	6	20	43	70	36
Sporting Khalsa	*-3*	36	11	3	22	64	98	33
Tenbury United		36	9	5	22	51	87	32
Malvern Rangers		36	8	2	26	51	99	26
Darlaston Town		36	5	2	29	41	127	17

DIVISION ONE CUP

FIRST ROUND

Ashbourne United 0 **Ellesmere Rangers** 1
Blackheath Town 3 Wolverhampton United 1
Walsall Wood 3 Cresswell Wanderers 0

SECOND ROUND

Bilston Town 1 **Stafford Town** 2
Brereton Social 1 Walsall Wood 0
Bridgnorth Town Res. 2 **Malvern Rangers** 3
Ellesmere Rangers 2 Sporting Khalsa 1
Hinton 4 Blackheath Town 2 *aet*
Ludlow Town Res. 2 **Darlaston Town** 3 *aet*
Malvern Town Res. 1 **Tenbury United** 2
Riverway 1 **Parkfield Leisure** 3

QUARTER-FINALS

Darlaston Town 0 **Brereton Social** 3
Hinton 2 **Tenbury United** 3
Malvern Rangers 0 **Stafford Town** 5
Parkfield Leisure 2 Ellesmere Rangers 1

SEMI-FINALS

(played over two legs)
Brereton Soc. 0 Parkfield Leis. 3, **Parkfield Leisure** 5 Brereton Social 1
Stafford Tn 2 Tenbury Utd 1, **Stafford Tn** 1 Tenbury Utd 0 *aet* (3-4p)

FINAL

(May 12th at Wolverhampton Casuals)
Stafford Town 1 Parkfield Leisure 0

WEST MIDLANDS (REGIONAL) LEAGUE DIVISION ONE CONSTITUTION 2006-07

AFC WULFRUNIANS . . . Wolverhampton Casuals FC, Brinsford Lane, Coven Heath, Wolverhampton WV10 7PR. 01902 783214
BILBROOK. . . . . Pendeford Lane, Wolverhampton WV9 5HQ . . . . None
BILSTON TOWN . . . . Queen Street, Bilston WV14 7EX 01902 491498
BLACKHEATH TOWN. . . . . Oldbury United FC, Cricketts, York Road, Oldbury, Warley B65 0RT 0121 559 5564
BRIDGNORTH TOWN RESERVES . . . . . . Crown Meadow, Innage Lane, Bridgnorth WV16 4HS 01746 762747
CRESSWELL WANDERERS . . . Abbey Park, Glastonbury Crescent, Mossley, Bloxwich, Walsall WS3 2RQ. 01922 477640
DARLASTON TOWN . . . . City Ground, Waverley Road, Darlaston WS10 8ED. 0121 526 4423
HINTON . . . . Broomy Hill, Hereford. . . . . None
LUDLOW TOWN RESERVES . . . . Coors Stadium, Bromfield Road, Ludlow SY8 2BY. 01584 876000
MALVERN TOWN RESERVES . . . . Langland Stadium, Langland Avenue, Malvern WR14 2EQ 01684 574068
PARKFIELD LEISURE. . . . . Rooker Avenue, Parkfield, Wolverhampton WV2 2DT . . . . None
RIVERWAY. . . . . Wyrley Rangers FC, Long Lane Park, Long Lane, Essington WV11 2AA 01922 406604
SPORTING KHALSA. . . . . Abbey Park, Glastonbury Crescent, Mossley, Bloxwich, Walsall WS3 2RQ. 01922 477640
STAFFORD TOWN . . . . Rowley Park Stadium, Averill Road, West Road, Stafford ST17 9XX 01785 251060
TENBURY UNITED. . . . . Palmers Meadow, Burford, Tenbury Wells . . . . None
WOLVERHAMPTON UNITED . . . . . Prestwood Road West, Wednesfield, Wolverhampton WV11 1HL. 01902 730881

IN: AFC Wulfrunians (P), Bilbrook (P)

OUT: Ashbourne United (S – Staffordshire County Senior League Premier Division), Brereton Social (P – Midland Combination Premier Division), Ellesmere Rangers (P), Malvern Rangers (W), Walsall Wood (P – Midland Combination Premier Division)

	AFC Wulfrunians	Bewdley Town Res.	Bilbrook	Brereton Town	Bromyard Town Res.	Bustleholme Res.	Chaddesley Corbett	Darlaston Town Res.	Dudley United	Mahal	Penkridge Town	Sedgley Town	Shenstone Pathfinder	Wednesbury Town	Wolverhampton Development	Wyrley
AFC Wulfrunians	*P*	2-0	1-1	3-1	12-0	4-0	4-0	n/a	5-1	6-0	5-1	n/a	1-1	2-0	3-1	3-0
Bewdley Town Res.	0-3	*R*	1-8	2-1	4-0	0-0	2-1	n/a	2-1	3-1	2-3	1-0	3-1	1-3	3-2	2-1
Bilbrook	0-3	1-2	*E*	8-0	7-3	2-1	0-7	n/a	5-2	1-1	2-3	n/a	3-2	5-1	2-4	4-0
Brereton Town	0-3	5-1	0-3	*M*	3-2	2-3	4-3	n/a	3-4	3-3	0-1	5-1	0-1	2-3	3-0	5-0
Bromyard Town Res.	0-6	3-2	0-3	1-2	*I*	1-7	0-5	n/a	0-1	1-1	0-2	2-3	3-7	2-0	1-0	2-4
Bustleholme Res.	0-7	4-1	0-3	3-0	3-0	*E*	2-0	n/a	2-1	5-0	2-2	n/a	3-1	2-2	0-0	3-1
Chaddesley Corbett	0-1	2-2	4-1	1-0	4-1	1-1	*R*	n/a	1-0	3-2	3-2	4-0	0-2	2-2	5-2	0-2
Darlaston Town Res.	n/a	n/a	n/a	n/a	1-0	n/a	1-8		n/a	n/a	n/a	n/a	n/a	n/a	n/a	1-7
Dudley United	0-1	2-0	0-3	5-1	7-0	1-1	1-2	n/a	*D*	3-0	0-1	n/a	0-1	2-1	1-2	6-1
Mahal	0-3	2-3	1-4	2-3	3-3	2-5	2-2	n/a	3-0	*I*	4-0	7-2	1-2	1-1	1-1	0-3
Penkridge Town	0-1	0-0	1-3	0-0	5-0	3-2	3-0	n/a	1-0	1-2	*V*	3-2	1-2	5-3	1-0	3-1
Sedgley Town	n/a	n/a	0-6	0-2	8-2	n/a	0-3	n/a	n/a	1-2	1-2	*I*	1-3	1-5	1-1	n/a
Shenstone Pathfinder	0-1	3-2	0-1	2-2	6-0	3-0	3-2	n/a	7-0	4-4	2-1	n/a	*S*	3-1	3-1	2-1
Wednesbury Town	1-1	4-4	5-0	2-2	11-0	3-1	3-3	n/a	2-1	5-0	4-0	n/a	5-1	*I*	4-1	2-2
Wolverhampton Development	0-0	1-2	2-1	2-2	5-0	1-1	1-0	n/a	4-2	0-0	1-2	n/a	0-0	2-2	*O*	0-1
Wyrley	0-2	0-0	0-4	2-2	7-0	3-2	0-1	n/a	4-2	3-0	0-1	3-0	1-1	1-5	3-1	*N*

Note – Darlaston Town Res. and Sedgley Town withdrew during the course of the season
Their results are shown above but are expunged from the league table

Division Two	P	W	D	L	F	A	Pts
AFC Wulfrunians	26	22	4	0	83	7	70
Bilbrook	26	16	2	8	75	44	50
Shenstone Pathfinder	26	15	5	6	60	37	50
Penkridge Town	26	14	3	9	43	39	45
Wednesbury Town	26	11	9	6	75	46	42
Bustleholme Res.	26	11	7	8	53	44	40
Chaddesley Corbett	26	11	5	10	52	43	38
Bewdley Town Res.	26	11	5	10	44	54	38
Wyrley	26	9	4	13	41	53	31
Brereton Town	26	7	6	13	46	60	27
Wolverhampton Development	26	6	8	12	34	43	26
Dudley United	26	8	1	17	43	53	25
Mahal	26	3	9	14	36	68	18
Bromyard Town Res.	26	3	2	21	23	117	11

Darlaston Town Res. and Sedgley Town – records expunged

DIVISION TWO CUP

FIRST ROUND

AFC Wulfrunians 3 Bilbrook 1
Bewdley Town Res. 2 Wednesbury Town 0
Brereton Town 2 Bromyard Town Res. 0
Darlaston Town Res. (scr.) v **Bustleholme Res.** (w/o)
Penkridge Town 2 **Mahal** 3
Sedgley Town 1 **Shenstone Pathfinder** 4
Wolverhampton Development 3 Dudley United 1
Wyrley 2 Chaddesley Corbett 1

QUARTER-FINALS

Bewdley Town Res. 2 **Shenstone Pathfinder** 3
Brereton Town 2 Wyrley 1
Bustleholme Res. 0 **AFC Wulfrunians** 1
Wolverhampton Development 5 Mahal 0

SEMI-FINALS

(played over two legs)
Brereton Town 0 AFC Wulfrunians 2,
AFC Wulfrunians (w/o) v Brereton Town (scr.)
Wolverhampton Development 1 Shenstone Pathfinder 0,
Shenstone Pathfinder 1 **Wolverhampton Development** 1

FINAL

(May 9th at Gornal Athletic)
AFC Wulfrunians 2 Wolverhampton Development 0

WEST MIDLANDS (REGIONAL) LEAGUE DIVISION TWO CONSTITUTION 2006-07

BEWDLEY TOWN RESERVES .... Ribbesford Meadows, Ribbesford, Bewdley 01299 405837
BRERETON TOWN .... Ravenhill Park, Brereton, Rugeley WS15 1DF 01889 578255
BUSTLEHOLME RESERVES .... Ray Hall Lane, Great Barr, Birmingham B43 6JF 01902 491498
CHADDESLEY CORBETT .. Chaddesley Sports Club, Longmore, Chaddesley Corbett, Kidderminster DY10 4RE 01562 777691
DUDLEY UNITED .... Mile Flat Sports Ground, Mile Flat, Wall Heath, Kingswinford .... None
GORNAL ATHLETIC RESERVES .. Garden Walk Stadium, Garden Walk, Lower Gornal, Dudley DY3 2NH 01384 358398
HEATH TOWN RANGERS ...... Wednesfield FC, Cottage Ground, Amos Lane, Wednesfield WV11 1ND 01902 735506
MAHAL .... Hadley Stadium, Wilson Road, Smethwick, Warley B68 9JW 0121 434 4848
PENKRIDGE TOWN .... Monkton Recreation Centre, Pinfold Lane, Penkridge, Stafford ST19 5QP .... None
PENN COLTS .... Fordhouses Cricket Club, Wobaston Road, Pendeford, Wolverhampton WV9 5HH 01902 397038
SHENSTONE PATHFINDER .. Shenstone PF (Pavilion Club), Birmingham Road, Shenstone, Lichfield WS14 0LR 01543 481658
WARSTONE WANDERERS ... Parkfield Leisure FC, Rooker Avenue, Parkfield, Wolverhampton WV2 2DT .... None
WEDNESBURY TOWN .... Darlaston Town FC, City Ground, Waverley Road, Darlaston WS10 8ED 0121 526 4423
WOLVERHAMPTON DEVELOPMENT ...... Four Ashes, Stafford Road, Wolverhampton .... None
WYRLEY .... Yates Sports & Social Club, Lime Lane, Pelsall, Walsall WS3 5AS 01543 373458

IN: Gornal Athletic Reserves (N), Heath Town Rangers (N), Penn Colts (N), Warstone Wanderers (N)
OUT: AFC Wulfrunians (P), Bilbrook (P), Bromyard Town Reserves (W), Darlaston Town Reserves (WS), Sedgley Town (WS)

WEST RIDING COUNTY AMATEUR LEAGUE

	Ardsley Celtic	Bay Athletic	Brighouse Town	Campion	Eastmoor	Golcar United	Halifax Irish Club	Heckmondwike Town	Hemsworth Miners Welfare	Otley Town	Ovenden West Riding	Storthes Hall	Tyersal	Wibsey
Ardsley Celtic		0-3	3-2	1-4	3-2	0-2	1-3	2-1	1-2	1-0	2-1	1-1	2-0	1-1
Bay Athletic	4-0	*P*	0-1	3-0	1-0	1-3	7-1	6-1	2-1	3-0	3-1	0-0	3-1	1-1
Brighouse Town	4-2	1-1	*R*	2-2	5-1	2-0	2-1	4-0	3-2	3-0	4-2	3-1	1-1	1-2
Campion	4-0	2-0	5-2	*E*	2-0	4-1	6-2	5-1	5-0	3-3	3-2	2-3	4-0	2-3
Eastmoor	1-3	1-3	0-2	0-1	*M*	2-1	1-0	4-1	1-0	2-1	2-4	0-1	0-0	1-2
Golcar United	1-0	1-3	1-2	2-4	2-1	*I*	2-2	3-2	2-0	3-2	1-2	1-0	2-4	4-1
Halifax Irish Club	2-1	0-1	1-3	0-7	3-0	4-6	*E*	2-0	1-2	1-4	1-2	3-2	3-1	2-3
Heckmondwike Town	1-5	0-1	0-7	1-6	1-1	1-2	1-0	*R*	4-3	3-2	0-4	0-0	1-4	0-3
Hemsworth Miners Welfare	2-1	1-5	1-3	1-6	2-2	2-2	0-1	5-2		2-2	1-2	2-0	2-1	3-2
Otley Town	1-1	1-2	4-3	0-2	1-1	2-3	0-3	3-0	1-1		1-3	1-1	1-1	1-1
Ovenden West Riding	2-0	1-3	0-1	0-5	0-0	3-0	3-2	3-2	3-0	3-1	*D*	1-0	1-1	3-2
Storthes Hall	4-0	0-5	3-2	1-9	3-1	1-1	4-3	2-4	3-1	2-1	2-0	*I*	1-2	1-5
Tyersal	3-1	1-3	1-0	1-5	1-4	0-1	2-1	5-2	4-1	2-1	3-2	0-3	*V*	1-3
Wibsey	1-2	0-2	3-3	5-2	3-0	2-4	2-2	5-0	3-1	2-1	3-1	1-2	1-1	

Premier Division	P	W	D	L	F	A	Pts
Bay Athletic	26	20	3	3	66	19	63
Campion	26	20	2	4	100	34	62
Brighouse Town	26	16	4	6	66	37	52
Wibsey	26	13	6	7	60	42	45
Golcar United	26	14	3	9	51	47	45
Ovenden West Riding	26	14	2	10	49	43	44
Storthes Hall	26	11	5	10	41	49	38
Tyersal	26	10	5	11	41	49	35
Ardsley Celtic	26	9	3	14	34	52	30
Halifax Irish Club	26	8	2	16	44	63	26
Hemsworth Miners Welfare	26	7	4	15	38	62	25
Eastmoor	26	6	5	15	28	46	23
Otley Town	26	3	8	15	35	52	17
Heckmondwike Town	26	4	2	20	29	87	14

PREMIER DIVISION CUP

FIRST ROUND

Bay Athletic 2 Ardsley Celtic 0
Brighouse Town 2 Wibsey 1
Campion 2 Ovenden West Riding 1 *aet*
Golcar United 3 Eastmoor 0
Hemsworth Miners Welfare 0 Heckmondwike Town 0 *aet* (3-1p)
Otley Town 1 Tyersal 1 *aet* (3-2p)

QUARTER-FINALS

Bay Athletic 2 Storthes Hall 0
Golcar United 0 **Brighouse Town** 1
Hemsworth Miners Welfare 0 **Halifax Irish Club** 1
Otley Town 0 **Campion** 3

SEMI-FINALS

Bay Athletic 1 **Brighouse Town** 3
(at Dudley Hill Athletic)
Campion 2 Halifax Irish Club 1
(at Brighouse Town)

FINAL

(May 1st at Littletown)
Brighouse Town 1 **Campion** 2

WEST RIDING COUNTY AMATEUR LEAGUE PREMIER DIVISION CONSTITUTION 2006-07

ARDSLEY CELTIC	Cave Lane, Main Street, East Ardsley, Wakefield WF3 2BB	07950 131889
BAY ATHLETIC	University of Huddersfield, Salendine Nook, Huddersfield	07796 511243
BRIGHOUSE TOWN	St Giles Road, Hove Edge, Brighouse HD6 2RX	None
CAMPION	Manningham Mills Sports Ground, Scotchman Road, Manningham, Bradford BD9 4SH	01274 546726
EASTMOOR	King George V Playing Fields, Woodhouse Road, Eastmoor, Wakefield WF1 4RD	01924 375367
GOLCAR UNITED	Longfield Recreation Ground, Golcar, Huddersfield HD7 4AZ	07779 700098
HALIFAX IRISH CLUB	Natty Lane, Illingworth, Halifax HX2 9DS	01422 360134
HALL GREEN UNITED	Crigglestone Sports Club, Painthorpe Lane, Crigglestone, Wakefield WF4 3JU	01924 254544
HEMSWORTH MINERS WELFARE	Fitzwilliam Sports Complex, Wakefield Road, Fitzwilliam, Pontefract	01977 610444
LOWER HOPTON	Woodend Road, Lower Hopton, Mirfield WF14 8PP	01924 492048
OVENDEN WEST RIDING	Natty Lane, Illingworth, Halifax HX2 9DS	01422 244350
STORTHES HALL	Woodfield Park, Police Sports Ground, Lockwood, Huddersfield	07957 691189
TYERSAL	Arkwright Street, off Dick Lane, Tyersal, Bradford BD4 8JL	07710 006241
WIBSEY	Westwood Park, Cooper Lane, Bradford BD6 3NN	None

IN: Hall Green United (P), Lower Hopton (P)

OUT: Heckmondwike Town (R), Otley Town (S – West Yorkshire League Division One)

	Altofts	Dudley Hill Rangers	Farnley	Hall Green United	Keighley Shamrocks	Kirkburton	Littletown	Lower Hopton	Marsden	Salts	South Bradford	Steeton	Wakefield City	Westwood
Altofts		4-0	0-3	2-2	6-1	2-2	0-2	3-3	4-0	5-1	4-2	2-1	1-1	1-1
Dudley Hill Rangers	2-2	*D*	0-3	2-1	2-3	3-0	0-3	3-2	3-1	2-0	1-0	0-1	1-2	1-3
Farnley	2-2	4-0	*I*	1-2	4-1	2-3	2-1	1-8	2-3	1-1	2-4	2-0	3-1	1-3
Hall Green United	7-0	4-2	1-0	*V*	5-1	1-3	1-0	0-0	7-1	2-1	2-1	4-3	1-0	2-2
Keighley Shamrocks	1-2	3-1	1-2	1-4	*I*	2-8	2-2	2-4	14-1	4-0	1-3	1-3	1-3	0-2
Kirkburton	7-3	3-0	2-2	1-2	0-2	*S*	1-3	1-0	4-1	4-1	2-1	1-0	0-1	5-0
Littletown	0-0	2-2	1-1	1-3	2-0	4-1	*I*	1-1	0-1	4-0	2-0	0-1	0-5	0-0
Lower Hopton	5-1	5-0	2-2	4-1	5-0	3-3	2-2	*O*	4-0	5-2	2-0	1-4	0-0	2-0
Marsden	4-4	3-3	1-3	0-1	2-1	0-4	1-1	1-5	*N*	1-0	3-1	3-4	2-1	0-3
Salts	0-1	0-1	1-1	1-3	1-1	0-2	1-3	0-5	0-0		0-3	4-2	3-7	1-0
South Bradford	4-0	2-0	1-3	1-3	2-1	4-2	1-5	0-4	5-3	1-1	*O*	2-4	2-2	5-2
Steeton	8-2	6-4	0-3	3-2	3-4	2-3	1-2	1-2	3-0	4-3	3-1	*N*	3-1	1-6
Wakefield City	0-1	0-3	4-0	1-2	1-0	2-0	3-1	0-1	4-2	3-1	2-1	1-1	*E*	3-2
Westwood	3-1	1-1	1-2	2-3	2-1	2-2	4-0	0-2	3-0	2-0	1-4	1-4	0-2	

Division One	P	W	D	L	F	A	Pts
Hall Green United	26	19	3	4	66	34	60
Lower Hopton	26	16	7	3	77	28	55
Kirkburton	26	14	4	8	64	43	46
Wakefield City	26	14	4	8	50	32	46
Steeton	26	14	1	11	66	55	43
Farnley	26	12	6	8	52	44	42
Littletown	26	10	8	8	42	34	38
Altofts	26	9	9	8	53	62	36
Westwood	26	10	5	11	46	44	35
South Bradford	26	10	2	14	51	55	32
Dudley Hill Rangers	26	8	4	14	37	58	28
Marsden	26	6	4	16	34	84	22
Keighley Shamrocks	26	6	2	18	49	70	20
Salts	26	2	5	19	23	67	11

DIVISION ONE CUP

FIRST ROUND

Dudley Hill Rangers 3 Altofts 1 *aet*
Farnley 3 **Westwood** 3 *aet* (1-3p)
Hall Green United 1 **South Bradford** 2 *aet*
Kirkburton 6 Keighley Shamrocks 2
Marsden 1 **Lower Hopton** 2
Salts 0 **Wakefield City** 1

QUARTER-FINALS

Dudley Hill Rangers 2 **Steeton** 5
Kirkburton 0 **Westwood** 1
Lower Hopton 6 Littletown 0
Wakefield City 6 South Bradford 0

SEMI-FINALS

Lower Hopton 1 **Steeton** 2
(at Campion)
Wakefield City 2 Westwood 0
(at Heckmondwike Town)

FINAL

(May 12th at Littletown)
Wakefield City 1 **Steeton** 4

WEST RIDING COUNTY AMATEUR LEAGUE DIVISION ONE CONSTITUTION 2006-07

DUDLEY HILL RANGERS .... Newhall Park School, Newhall Road, Bierley, Bradford BD4 6AF 07967 359883
FARNLEY .... Farnley Cricket Club, Church Lane, Farnley 0113 253 5950
HECKMONDWIKE TOWN .... Cemetary Road, Heckmondwike WF16 9ED 01924 442907
KEIGHLEY SHAMROCKS .... Marley Stadium, Aireworth Road, Keighley BD21 4DB 01535 609910
KIRKBURTON .... Gregory Playing Fields, Kirkburton, Huddersfield HD8 0XH .... None
LITTLETOWN .... Beck Lane, Heckmondwike WF16 0JZ 07930 852796
MARSDEN .... Fell Lane, Marsden, Huddersfield 01484 844191
MELTHAM ATHLETIC .... Broadlands Recreation Ground, Meltham, Huddersfield .... None
SALTS .... Salts Playing Fields, Hirst Lane, Saltaire, Shipley BD18 4DD 01274 583427
SOUTH BRADFORD .... Broadstone Way, Holmewood, Bradford BD4 9BU 01274 751160
STEETON .... Summer Hill Lane, Steeton BD20 6RX 01585 683387
VENTUS & YEADON CELTIC .... Dam Lane, Yeadon, Leeds 07721 468967
WAKEFIELD CITY .... West Yorks Sports & Social, Walton Lane, Sandal, Wakefield WF2 6NG 01924 258760
WESTBROOK YMCA .... Lawnswood YMCA, Westbrook, Leeds 0113 267 8158

IN: Heckmondwike Town (R), Meltham Athletic (P), Ventus & Yeadon Celtic (P), Westbrook YMCA (P)
OUT: Altofts (S – West Yorkshire League Division One), Hall Green United (P), Lower Hopton (P), Westwood (S – Sunday football)

	Barclays	Crag Road United	Dudley Hill Athletic	Dynamoes	Hunsworth	Keighley Lifts	Meltham Athletic	Morley Town	Overthorpe Sports	Roberttown	Ventus /Yeadon Celtic	Westbrook YMCA
Barclays	*D*	2-2	3-0	0-3	6-2	2-1	2-7	0-4	0-1	n/a	4-4	1-3
Crag Road United	1-1	*I*	5-3	1-1	3-0	3-3	4-4	2-7	3-0	n/a	1-2	2-2
Dudley Hill Athletic	0-1	1-3	*V*	2-1	2-6	4-1	1-9	1-5	0-11	n/a	2-5	1-2
Dynamoes	2-2	0-5	0-3	*I*	4-3	2-0	0-5	2-3	1-0	3-1	0-5	0-4
Hunsworth	2-3	1-1	2-4	6-2	*S*	2-0	2-4	3-1	2-1	n/a	2-6	3-0
Keighley Lifts	2-1	1-5	2-2	4-3	2-3	*I*	0-15	1-5	1-5	n/a	3-3	0-5
Meltham Athletic	6-0	1-1	8-0	6-1	8-0	3-1	*O*	5-0	1-1	n/a	8-1	5-2
Morley Town	2-4	2-4	4-2	3-2	0-2	3-0	2-7	*N*	1-5	n/a	3-1	0-2
Overthorpe Sports	2-2	6-5	3-1	3-1	1-0	3-1	3-5	2-4		5-0	3-2	1-2
Roberttown	n/a	n/a	3-0	n/a	2-4	2-6	n/a	n/a	2-3	*T*	n/a	1-2
Ventus & Yeadon Celtic	6-1	7-0	1-3	0-2	5-4	8-0	1-3	6-4	6-3	n/a	*W*	4-1
Westbrook YMCA	4-1	5-3	3-2	5-2	3-0	6-0	2-3	4-3	0-0	n/a	1-2	*O*

Note – Roberttown withdrew during the course of the season
Their results are shown above but are expunged from the league table

Division Two	P	W	D	L	F	A	Pts
Meltham Athletic	20	17	3	0	113	24	54
Westbrook YMCA	20	13	2	5	56	33	41
Ventus & Yeadon Celtic	20	12	2	6	75	48	38
Overthorpe Sports	20	10	3	7	54	38	33
Morley Town	20	10	0	10	56	55	30
Crag Road United	20	7	8	5	54	49	29
Hunsworth	20	8	1	11	45	56	25
Barclays	20	6	5	9	36	54	23
Dynamoes	20	5	2	13	29	60	17
Dudley Hill Athletic	20	5	1	14	34	75	16
Keighley Lifts	20	2	3	15	23	83	9

Roberttown – record expunged

DIVISION TWO CUP

FIRST ROUND

Barclays 4 **Westbrook YMCA** 4 *aet* (2-4p)
Dudley Hill Athletic 2 Roberttown 1
Morley Town 1 **Overthorpe Sports** 3 *aet*
Ventus & Yeadon Celtic 0 **Crag Road United** 4

QUARTER-FINALS

Crag Road United 3 Keighley Lifts 2
Dynamoes 1 **Hunsworth** 4
Overthorpe Sports 1 **Meltham Athletic** 4
Westbrook YMCA 7 Dudley Hill Athletic 0

SEMI-FINALS

Crag Road United 2 Hunsworth 2 *aet* (4-3p)
(at Crag Road United)
Meltham Athletic 3 Westbrook YMCA 1 *(at Ardsley Celtic)*

FINAL

(May 10th at Lower Hopton)
Meltham Athletic 7 Crag Road United 1

Reserve Division One	P	W	D	L	F	A	Pts
Lower Hopton Res.	26	18	2	6	78	41	56
Storthes Hall Res.	26	17	3	6	62	36	54
Tyersal Res.	26	17	3	6	62	39	54
Brighouse Town Res.	25	15	3	7	58	42	48
Campion Res.	26	13	6	7	68	60	45
Wibsey Res.	26	12	7	7	59	50	43
Hall Green United Res.	26	8	7	11	48	56	31
Hemsworth Miners Welfare Res.	26	8	6	12	39	45	30
Ovenden West Riding Res.	26	8	5	13	48	61	29
Bay Athletic Res.	26	8	3	15	52	54	27
Ardsley Celtic Res.	25	7	5	13	55	60	26
Steeton Res.	26	7	5	14	52	61	26
Keighley Shamrocks Res.	26	8	1	17	56	86	25
Dudley Hill Rangers Res.	26	6	2	18	40	86	20

Brighouse Town Res. v Ardsley Celtic Res. – not played

Reserve Division Two	P	W	D	L	F	A	Pts
Golcar United Res.	18	14	1	3	59	23	43
Otley Town Res.	18	13	2	3	61	23	41
Westbrook YMCA Res.	18	13	2	3	46	25	41
Farnley Res.	18	10	4	4	55	25	34
Littletown Res.	18	8	4	6	45	37	28
Wakefield City Res.	18	9	0	9	36	42	27
Salts Res.	18	6	3	9	35	47	21
Kirkburton Res.	18	3	4	11	35	44	13
Hunsworth Res.	18	3	2	13	30	67	11
Barclays Res.	18	0	0	18	18	87	0

Heckmondwike Town Res. – record expunged

RESERVES CUP

FINAL

(May 3rd at Campion)
Brighouse Town Res. 1 Otley Town Res. 0 *aet*

WEST RIDING COUNTY AMATEUR LEAGUE DIVISION TWO CONSTITUTION 2006-07

BARCLAYS .... Crawshaw Street, Ravensthorpe, Dewsbury WF13 3ER 01924 497020
BRIGHOUSE TOWN RESERVES .... St Giles Road, Hove Edge, Brighouse HD6 2RX .... None
BRONTE WANDERERS .... Marley Stadium, Aireworth Road, Keighley BD21 4DB 01535 609910
CAMPION RESERVES ... Manningham Mills Sports Ground, Scothman Road, Manningham, Bradford BD9 4SH 01274 546726
CRAG ROAD UNITED .... Apperley Road, Greengates, Bradford BD10 0PX 07781 808212
DUDLEY HILL ATHLETIC .... Hunsworth Lane, East Bierley BD4 6RN .... None
DYNAMOES .... Dudley Hill Athletic FC, Hunsworth Lane, East Bierley BD4 6RN 01274 823576
HALL GREEN UNITED RESERVES .. Crigglestone Sports Club, Painthorpe Lane, Crigglestone, Wakefield 01924 254544
HUNSWORTH .... Birkenshaw Middle School, Bradford Road, Gomersal, Cleckheaton BD19 4BE 07711 197741
LOWER HOPTON RESERVES .... Woodend Road, Lower Hopton, Mirfield WF14 8PP 01924 492048
MORLEY TOWN .... Glen Road, Morley, Leeds 07709 727085
OVERTHORPE SPORTS .... Overthorpe Park, Edge Top Road, Dewsbury WF12 0BG 01924 464164
RAWDON OLD BOYS .... Hanson Field, Rawdon, Leeds .... None
STORTHES HALL RESERVES ..... Woodfield Park, Police Sports Ground, Lockwood, Huddersfield 07957 691189
TYERSAL RESERVES .... Arkwright Street, off Dick Lane, Tyersal, Bradford BD4 8JL 07710 006241
WIBSEY RESERVES .... Westwood Park, Cooper Lane, Bradford BD6 3NN .... None

IN: Brighouse Town Reserves (P – Reserve Division One), Bronte Wanderers (P – Craven & District League Premier Division (having merged with Keighley Lifts)), Campion Reserves (P – Reserve Division One), Hall Green United Reserves (P – Reserve Division One), Lower Hopton Reserves (P – Reserve Division One), Rawdon Old Boys (Leeds Red Triangle League Premier Division), Storthes Hall Reserves (P – Reserve Division One), Tyersal Reserves (P – Reserve Division One), Wibsey Reserves (P – Reserve Division One)
OUT: Meltham Athletic (P), Roberttown (WS), Ventus & Yeadon Celtic (P), Westbrook YMCA (P)

WEST YORKSHIRE LEAGUE

	Aberford Albion	Bardsey	Beeston St Anthony's	Boroughbridge	Carlton Athletic	Horsforth St Margaret's	Howden Clough	Knaresborough Town	Leeds Metropolitan Carnegie	Nostell Miners Welfare	Ossett Common Rovers	Pontefract Sports & Social Club	Rothwell Athletic	Tadcaster Magnet Sports	Wetherby Athletic	Whitkirk Wanderers
Aberford Albion	*P*	0-2	1-6	2-1	0-1	1-3	0-3	3-0	1-1	2-3	0-1	0-0	1-2	3-3	3-0	3-1
Bardsey	2-0	*R*	0-3	5-2	1-0	1-3	3-1	4-0	2-5	0-1	2-0	3-1	2-1	3-3	2-3	4-4
Beeston St Anthony's	2-0	4-1	*E*	1-0	3-3	0-2	1-2	1-0	2-3	0-1	3-0	1-0	6-0	3-0	2-3	5-2
Boroughbridge	4-0	1-1	0-1	*M*	1-3	3-3	3-0	2-2	1-0	0-1	1-1	1-3	4-0	0-0	1-2	2-0
Carlton Athletic	1-2	1-2	1-4	1-1	*I*	3-2	1-2	1-2	1-3	1-2	1-0	5-0	2-0	2-0	3-1	2-2
Horsforth St Margaret's	0-0	0-2	1-3	0-1	1-0	*E*	1-2	0-1	2-2	1-4	1-4	1-7	0-3	1-2	0-1	2-4
Howden Clough	1-1	2-2	1-2	2-1	1-2	4-2	*R*	1-1	2-2	5-3	1-0	1-3	4-1	2-2	0-0	2-0
Knaresborough Town	0-1	0-0	0-3	0-1	0-1	3-2	1-0		1-3	0-2	2-1	1-0	3-1	0-1	1-2	1-2
Leeds Metropolitan Carnegie	3-3	5-0	0-0	2-1	6-1	7-2	3-0	4-1	*D*	1-2	6-0	7-0	4-2	2-0	4-0	0-1
Nostell Miners Welfare	2-1	2-1	0-1	4-2	0-1	8-0	1-2	1-1	1-1	*I*	4-0	1-4	0-2	3-0	1-0	3-2
Ossett Common Rovers	1-1	2-1	1-1	0-4	0-1	0-0	3-2	3-0	0-6	0-4	*V*	3-2	2-3	1-1	1-1	2-0
Pontefract Sports & Social Club	1-0	2-2	0-4	4-1	2-2	3-2	1-0	2-0	0-6	0-1	3-0	*I*	2-3	3-3	4-3	2-1
Rothwell Athletic	1-2	1-0	0-1	1-5	1-2	0-2	2-6	0-0	2-2	0-4	4-4	0-1	*S*	2-0	2-1	0-1
Tadcaster Magnet Sports	1-3	0-0	2-1	2-0	1-4	1-2	2-5	0-2	0-2	1-5	0-1	0-1	2-0	*I*	3-0	2-6
Wetherby Athletic	1-2	2-2	1-5	0-2	1-3	4-5	3-3	3-2	0-4	1-7	1-1	1-1	3-1	1-0	*O*	2-3
Whitkirk Wanderers	3-2	0-5	0-3	2-1	2-1	0-2	2-3	3-2	0-2	1-1	2-2	3-0	3-1	4-1	0-1	*N*

Premier Division	P	W	D	L	F	A	Pts
Leeds Metropol. Carnegie	30	20	7	3	96	28	67
Beeston St Anthony's	30	21	3	6	72	25	66
Nostell Miners Welfare	30	21	3	6	72	31	66
Howden Clough	30	14	7	9	60	49	49
Carlton Athletic	30	15	4	11	51	43	49
Pontefract Sports & Social	30	14	5	11	52	56	47
Bardsey	30	12	8	10	55	49	44
Whitkirk Wanderers	30	13	4	13	54	59	43
Boroughbridge	30	10	6	14	47	43	36
Aberford Albion	30	9	7	14	38	50	34
Ossett Common Rovers	30	8	9	13	34	58	33
Wetherby Athletic	30	9	6	15	42	68	33
Knaresborough Town	30	8	5	17	27	48	29
Horsforth St Margaret's	30	8	4	18	43	74	28
Rothwell Athletic	30	8	3	19	36	69	27
Tadcaster Magnet Sports	30	6	7	17	33	62	25

Premier Alliance Division	P	W	D	L	F	A	Pts
Rothwell Athletic Res.	22	17	2	3	77	28	53
Whitkirk Wanderers Res.	22	16	4	2	77	23	52
Boroughbridge Res.	22	15	4	3	57	34	49
Nostell Miners Welfare Res.	22	13	5	4	57	34	44
Beeston St Anthony's Res.	22	13	3	6	52	37	42
Bardsey Res.	22	9	6	7	47	34	33
Ossett Common Rovers Res.	22	6	4	12	32	44	22
Knaresborough Town Res.	22	6	1	15	32	49	19
Tadcaster Magnet Sports Res.	22	5	3	14	20	47	18
Wetherby Athletic Res.	22	4	4	14	28	57	16
Pontefract Sports & Social Club Res.	22	4	3	15	34	92	15
Aberford Albion Res.	22	3	3	16	36	70	12

Reserve Division	P	W	D	L	F	A	Pts
Churwell Lions Res.	26	20	4	2	95	31	64
Ripon City Magnets Res.	26	16	4	6	79	33	52
Rothwell Town Res.	26	13	9	4	56	34	48
Sherburn White Rose Res.	26	14	4	8	63	38	46
Ilkley Res.	26	14	2	10	58	47	44
Woodhouse Hill WMC Res.	26	11	4	11	53	62	37
Old Headingley Res.	26	11	3	12	54	63	36
Sandy Lane Res.	26	10	5	11	55	63	35
Robin Hood Athletic Res.	26	9	7	10	58	64	34
Hartshead Res.	26	9	5	12	48	62	32
Horbury Town Res.	26	7	5	14	62	66	26
Kippax Welfare Res.	26	8	0	18	40	68	24
Baildon Trinity Athletic Res.	26	7	2	17	41	75	23
Barwick Res.	26	5	2	19	39	95	17

WEST YORKSHIRE LEAGUE PREMIER DIVISION CONSTITUTION 2006-07

ABERFORD ALBION .... Bunkers Hill, Main Street (South), Aberford LS25 3DE .... None
BARDSEY .... The Sportsfield, Keswick Lane, Bardsey LS17 9AQ 01937 574286
BEESTON ST ANTHONY'S .... Beggars Hill, Sunnyview Gdns, Beeston Road, Beeston, Leeds 0113 270 7223
BOROUGHBRIDGE .... Aldborough Road, Boroughbridge, York YO51 9EA 01423 324206
CARLTON ATHLETIC .... Carlton Cricket Club, Town Street, Carlton, Wakefield WF3 3QU 0113 282 1114
HORSFORTH ST MARGARET'S .... Cragg Hill Recreation Ground, off Ring Road, Horsforth, Leeds .... None
HOWDEN CLOUGH .... Batley Sports Centre, Windmill Lane, Batley WF17 0QD 01924 326181
KNARESBOROUGH TOWN .... Manse Lane, Knaresborough HG5 8LF 0777 367 9971
LEEDS METROPOLITAN CARNEGIE .. LMU Headingley Campus, Headlingley, Leeds LS6 3QS. 0113 2833160
OSSETT COMMON ROVERS .... Illingworth Park, Monor Road, Ossett .... None
PONTEFRACT SPORTS & SOCIAL CLUB .. Willow Park School, Harewood Avenue, Pontefract WF8 2ER .... None
ROTHWELL ATHLETIC .... Royds Lane, Rothwell, Leeds LS26 0BE .... Club HQ: 0113 282 0723
SHERBURN WHITE ROSE .... Recreation Ground, Finkle Hill, Sherburn-in-Elmet, Leeds LS25 6EB .... None
STREET WORK SOCCER .... Buslingthorpe Rec Ground, Chapeltown, Leeds .... None
WETHERBY ATHLETIC ..... Wetherby Sports Association, The Ings, Boston Road, Wetherby LS22 5HA 01937 585699
WHITKIRK WANDERERS ...... Whitkirk Sports & Social Club, Selby Road, Whitkirk, Leeds LS15 0AA 0113 264 6623

IN: Sherburn White Rose (P), Street Work Soccer (P)
OUT: Nostell Miners Welfare (P – Northern Counties East League Division One), Tadcaster Magnet Sports (R)

	AFC Emley	Baildon Trinity Athletic	Barwick	Churwell Lions	Hartshead	Ilkley	Kellingley Welfare	Mount St Mary's	Pool	Ripon City Magnets	Robin Hood Athletic	Sandy Lane	Sherburn White Rose	Street Work Soccer	Woodhouse Hill WMC
AFC Emley		3-1	2-2	2-3	7-1	0-2	1-0	4-1	3-2	1-0	1-3	8-3	0-3	0-0	4-1
Baildon Trinity Athletic	1-2	*D*	1-1	1-2	2-2	2-3	1-5	2-3	2-1	1-0	1-2	0-1	0-3	0-0	1-2
Barwick	1-5	1-1	*I*	0-1	L-W	0-3	3-0	0-3	5-1	1-1	4-2	4-0	1-3	1-4	2-3
Churwell Lions	4-1	1-2	0-3	*V*	2-1	4-0	2-0	3-1	6-4	2-2	3-1	2-2	1-1	3-4	2-2
Hartshead	3-2	4-6	1-2	3-1	*I*	2-2	4-0	W-L	0-3	2-1	2-4	3-2	2-3	0-2	1-3
Ilkley	1-2	0-5	3-0	1-1	1-1	*S*	1-0	7-0	2-3	4-2	2-5	2-3	0-3	0-2	4-2
Kellingley Welfare	3-7	4-0	1-3	0-3	1-0	1-4	*I*	5-2	2-2	0-1	0-1	2-0	0-4	1-2	1-2
Mount St Mary's	0-1	2-5	3-1	0-3	0-5	0-3	0-1	*O*	0-0	1-3	0-5	2-1	0-3	0-7	2-4
Pool	2-2	7-2	2-2	2-3	1-4	1-1	6-1	6-0	*N*	3-3	4-3	2-0	0-4	0-1	2-2
Ripon City Magnets	0-2	1-1	1-1	4-3	2-3	4-2	1-1	10-0	1-3		1-1	3-0	1-6	1-2	7-1
Robin Hood Athletic	0-4	4-3	3-3	1-4	1-5	3-1	2-1	5-1	2-1	1-2		3-1	1-1	0-0	4-3
Sandy Lane	0-6	2-1	1-0	3-1	2-1	0-4	1-2	5-3	3-5	0-5	2-3	*O*	0-4	1-2	4-3
Sherburn White Rose	6-0	1-0	6-0	6-1	1-0	1-1	1-0	8-0	2-0	1-0	1-1	3-1	*N*	1-0	0-2
Street Work Soccer	0-9	2-1	8-3	1-1	2-1	1-1	4-3	1-1	5-1	3-2	3-1	5-0	1-0	*E*	3-1
Woodhouse Hill WMC	1-7	2-2	2-4	2-2	2-2	0-2	1-4	6-1	3-1	3-2	2-2	0-2	2-4	1-2	

Division One	P	W	D	L	F	A	Pts
Sherburn White Rose	28	22	4	2	80	15	70
Street Work Soccer	28	20	6	2	67	34	66
AFC Emley	28	18	3	7	86	44	57
Churwell Lions	28	14	7	7	64	50	49
Robin Hood Athletic	28	14	6	8	64	56	48
Ilkley	28	12	6	10	57	48	42
Hartshead	28	11	4	13	53	55	37
Ripon City Magnets	28	9	7	12	61	49	34
Pool	28	9	7	12	65	64	34
Woodhouse Hill WMC	28	9	6	13	58	74	33
Barwick	28	8	7	13	48	61	31
Sandy Lane	28	9	1	18	40	79	28
Kellingley Welfare	28	8	2	18	39	59	26
Baildon Trinity Athletic	28	6	6	16	45	61	24
Mount St Mary's	28	4	2	22	26	104	14

LEAGUE CUP

FIRST ROUND

AFC Emley 2 Wetherby Athletic 0
Bardsey 6 Barwick 0
Beeston St Anthony's 0 Boroughbridge 2
(Boroughbridge expelled)
Field Sports & Social 0 **Howden Clough** 5
Knaresborough Town 6 Kippax Athletic 2
Leeds Metropolitan Carnegie 3 Rothwell Athletic 1
Mount St Mary's 5 Featherstone Colliery 4
Ossett Common Rovers 3 Ilkley 1
Pontefract Sports & Social Club 3 Boston Spartans 1
Pool 0 **Sherburn White Rose** 6
Sandy Lane 8 Hunslet 4
Swillington Saints 1 **Stanley United** 2
Upper Armley Old Boys 0 **Kippax Welfare** 5
Victoria BC Rothwell 1 **Nostell Miners Welfare** 10
Whitkirk Wanderers 0 **Churwell Lions** 1

SECOND ROUND

Aberford Albion 0 **Knaresborough Town** 2
Baildon Trinity Athletic 3 **Nostell Miners Welfare** 4
Beeston St Anthony's 10 Pontefract Sports & Social Club 1
Churwell Lions 2 **Hartshead** 3
Dewsbury Moor Athletic 0 **AFC Emley** 10
East End Park WMC 2 **Bardsey** 4
Horsforth St Margaret's 4 Ripon City Magnets 2
Kellingley Welfare 3 **Howden Clough** 4
Kippax Welfare 0 **Tadcaster Magnet Sports** 3

WEST YORKSHIRE LEAGUE DIVISION ONE CONSTITUTION 2006-07

ALTOFTS .... Altofts Sports Club, Lock Lane, Altofts, Normanton WF6 2QJ 01924 892708
BARWICK .... Back of Village Hall, Chapel Lane, Barwick-in-Elmet, Leeds LS15 4HL .... Club HQ: 0113 281 3065
CHURWELL LIONS .... Bruntcliffe High School, Bruntcliffe Lane, Morley, Leeds LS27 0LZ .... None
FIELD SPORTS & SOCIAL .... Field Sports Ground, Hollingwood Lane, Bradford 01274 546726
HARTSHEAD .... Littletown Recreation Ground, Hartshead 01274 873365
ILKLEY .... Benton Road, Ilkley .... None
KELLINGLEY WELFARE .. Kellingley (Knottingley) SC, Marine Villa Road, Knottingley, Wakefield WF11 8ER 01977 673113
KIPPAX ATHLETIC .... Kippax Common, Valley Road, Kippax, Leeds LS25 7DA .... None
OLD HEADINGLEY .. Collingham & Linton Sports Association, Harewood Avenue, Collingham, Wetherby LS22 5BL .... None
OTLEY TOWN .... Old Show Ground, Pool Road, Otley LS20 1DY 01943 451025
POOL .... Arthington Lane, Pool-in-Wharfedale, Otley LS21 .... 0113 284 3932
RIPON CITY MAGNETS .... Mallorie Park Drive, Ripon HG4 2QD 01765 600542
ROBIN HOOD ATHLETIC .... Behind Coach & Horses, Rothwell Haigh, Leeds LS26 0SF 0113 282 1021
SANDY LANE .... Haworth Road Rec. Ground, Bradford .... None
TADCASTER MAGNET SPORTS .... Queens Gardens, Tadcaster LS24 9HD 01937 833435
WOODHOUSE HILL WMC .... Woodlands School Playing Field, Woodhouse Hill, Leeds LS10 2DN .... None

IN: Altofts (S – West Riding County Amateur League Division One), Field Sports & Social (P), Kippax Athletic (P), Old Headlingley (P), Otley Town (S – West Riding County Amateur League Premier Division), Tadcaster Magnet Sports (R)

OUT: AFC Emley (Northern Counties East League Division One), Baildon Trinity Athletic (R), Mount St Mary's (R), Ryhill & Havercroft Sports (WN), Sherburn White Rose (P), Street Work Soccer (P)

Note – Victoria BC Rothwell withdrew during the course of the season. Their results are shown herein but are expunged from the league table	Acle United	Dewsbury Moor Athletic	East End Park WMC	Featherstone Colliery	Field Sports & Social	Great Preston	Horbury Town	Hunslet	Kippax Athletic	Kippax Welfare	Old Headingley	Rothwell Town	Stanley United	Swillington Saints	Upper Armley Old Boys	Victoria BC Rothwell
Boston Spartans		2-0	0-1	4-1	0-4	4-0	1-2	0-11	2-4	0-2	2-4	1-2	2-2	4-2	1-1	n/a
Dewsbury Moor Athletic	1-5		4-7	0-2	0-8	3-3	0-4	3-6	2-3	2-5	0-1	2-6	5-1	1-4	1-2	2-4
East End Park WMC	3-2	3-0	*D*	4-2	1-2	3-1	1-3	1-1	1-5	2-5	2-2	5-1	3-3	4-0	5-0	n/a
Featherstone Colliery	4-0	2-0	1-2	*I*	0-6	1-1	1-1	2-8	2-4	5-0	0-6	1-2	2-1	3-2	8-5	n/a
Field Sports & Social	11-1	5-1	6-4	4-0	*V*	2-1	3-0	5-1	4-1	3-1	1-0	0-0	0-1	5-0	5-1	n/a
Great Preston	2-2	1-0	1-1	0-4	1-6	*I*	2-5	0-11	1-4	1-1	2-4	W-L	2-1	1-0	1-1	n/a
Horbury Town	2-2	4-2	1-1	2-0	1-3	3-0	*S*	5-2	3-2	0-0	2-4	4-1	2-3	6-2	2-1	5-0
Hunslet	5-0	2-0	2-4	3-3	6-0	8-4	3-3	*I*	2-3	3-1	0-3	0-1	3-1	6-3	1-1	n/a
Kippax Athletic	7-1	7-0	4-1	6-5	0-2	4-0	1-1	4-5	*O*	2-4	3-2	4-1	2-1	2-1	4-5	n/a
Kippax Welfare	3-1	4-1	1-2	1-0	0-0	0-2	2-2	7-2	2-1	*N*	1-2	6-1	0-4	2-0	1-0	n/a
Old Headingley	4-3	2-1	1-0	4-0	3-2	2-1	3-0	1-3	2-3	5-0		2-2	5-1	2-0	3-1	8-0
Rothwell Town	4-1	L-W	1-3	1-5	0-4	6-1	3-3	1-2	2-4	2-3	1-1	*T*	3-1	2-1	2-0	1-1
Stanley United	0-1	5-2	1-0	4-0	0-2	4-3	0-1	2-0	4-3	2-0	0-3	1-1	*W*	3-0	6-0	0-2
Swillington Saints	2-5	2-1	1-5	2-4	1-4	1-1	1-3	2-2	1-5	1-6	1-3	4-2	3-3	*O*	2-5	1-4
Upper Armley Old Boys	2-2	5-3	0-3	3-2	1-4	3-3	0-2	L-W	2-6	1-4	0-1	2-5	1-2	2-5		1-0
Victoria BC Rothwell	n/a	n/a	n/a	1-4	n/a	n/a	n/a	n/a	n/a	n/a	1-7	1-4	n/a	7-0	n/a	

Leeds Metropolitan Carnegie 5 Stanley United 1
Mount St Mary's 1 **Woodhouse Hill WMC** 3
Ossett Common Rovers 1 Old Headingley 0
Robin Hood Athletic 3 Street Works Soccer 2
Rothwell Town 1 **Horbury Town** 2
Sandy Lane 3 Great Preston 0
Sherburn White Rose 0 **Carlton Athletic** 1

THIRD ROUND

AFC Emley 2 Carlton Athletic 1
Hartshead 2 Horbury Town 1
Horsforth St Margaret's 0 **Howden Clough** 1
Knaresborough Town 0 **Robin Hood Athletic** 2
Leeds Metropolitan Carnegie 2 **Beeston St Anthony's** 3
Ossett Common Rovers 1 **Tadcaster Magnet Sports** 2
Sandy Lane 0 **Nostell Miners Welfare** 3
Woodhouse Hill WMC 0 **Bardsey** 5

QUARTER-FINALS

Hartshead 2 **AFC Emley** 2 *aet* (2-3p)
Howden Clough 0 **Beeston St Anthony's** 3
Robin Hood Athletic 2 **Nostell Miners Welfare** 6
Tadcaster Magnet Sports 0 **Bardsey** 0 *aet* (2-3p)

SEMI-FINALS

Beeston St Anthony's 3 AFC Emley 2
(at Nostell Miners Welfare)
Nostell Miners Welfare 2 **Bardsey** 3
(at AFC Emley)

FINAL *(May 10th at Nostell Miners Welfare)*
Beeston St Anthony's 2 Bardsey 1

Division Two	P	W	D	L	F	A	Pts
Field Sports & Social	28	23	2	3	101	26	71
Old Headingley	28	21	3	4	75	32	66
Kippax Athletic	28	19	1	8	98	59	58
Horbury Town	28	15	8	5	67	44	53
Hunslet	28	15	5	8	98	60	50
East End Park WMC	28	15	5	8	72	51	50
Kippax Welfare	28	15	4	9	62	47	49
Stanley United	28	13	4	11	57	49	43
Rothwell Town	28	10	5	13	53	61	35
Featherstone Colliery	28	10	3	15	60	76	33
Boston Spartans	28	7	5	16	49	86	26
Great Preston	28	5	8	15	36	84	23
Upper Armley Old Boys	28	5	5	18	45	84	20
Swillington Saints	28	4	3	21	44	92	15
Dewsbury Moor Athletic	28	2	1	25	35	101	7

Victoria BC Rothwell – record expunged

LEAGUE TROPHY

FINAL
(May 3rd at AFC Emley)
Whitkirk Wanderers Res. 2 Beeston St Anthony's 0

WEST YORKSHIRE LEAGUE DIVISION TWO CONSTITUTION 2006-07

BAILDON TRINITY ATHLETIC .... The Dell, Cliffe Lane, West Baildon, Shipley BD17 5LB .... None
BOSTON SPARTANS .... Stables Lane, Boston Spa, Wetherby LS23 6BX .... None
EAST END PARK WMC .... Skelton Road, Leeds LS9 9EP .... None
FEATHERSTONE COLLIERY .. Featherstones Miners Welfare, Cresseys Corner, Green Lane, Featherstone WF7 6EH .... None
GREAT PRESTON .... Berry Lane, Great Preston LS26 8AU .... None
HORBURY TOWN .... Slazengers Sports Complex, Engine Lane, Horbury, Wakefield WF4 5NH 01924 274228
HUNSLET .... Community Sports Club, Hunslet Green, Leeds .... None
KIPPAX WELFARE .... Long Dyke Lane, Kippax, Leeds LS25 7BP 0113 286 4908
LEEDS CITY .... Adel WMA, Church Lane, Adel, Leeds LS16 .... None
MOUNT ST MARY'S .... Welfare Sports Ground, Wakefield Road, Swillington, Leeds LS26 8DT .... None
NOSTELL MINERS WELFARERESERVES .. Miners Welfare Ground, Middle Lane, New Crofton, Wakefield WF4 1LB 01924 862348
ROTHWELL TOWN .... off Fifth Avenue, Leeds Road, Rothwell, Leeds LS26 0HG .... None
STANLEY UNITED .... John O'Gaunts, Sixth Avenue, Leeds Road, Rothwell, Leeds LS26 0JF .... None
SWILLINGTON SAINTS .... Welfare Sports Ground, Wakefield Road, Swillington, Leeds LS26 8DT .... None
UPPER ARMLEY OLD BOYS .... Churwell Hill, Morley, Leeds .... None
WYKE WANDERERS .... The Albert Morton Memorial Playing Field, White Chapel Road, Cleckheaton .... None

IN: Baildon Trinity Athletic (R), Leeds City (P – Yorkshire Old Boys League (merger of Abbey Grange Old Boys (Senior Division A) and Adel (Senior Division B))), Mount St Mary's (R), Nostell Miners Welfare Reserves (P – Premier Alliance Division), Wyke Wanderers (P – Spen Valley League Division One)

OUT: Dewsbury Moor Athletic (W), Field Sports & Social (P), Kippax Athletic (P), Old Headlingley (P), Victoria BC Rothwell (WS)

WESTERN LEAGUE

Note – Exmouth Town withdrew during the course of the season Their results are shown herein but are expunged from the league table	Backwell United	Barnstaple Town	Bideford	Bishop Sutton	Bitton	Bridgwater Town	Brislington	Bristol Manor Farm	Calne Town	Corsham Town	Devizes Town	Exmouth Town	Frome Town	Hallen	Keynsham Town	Melksham Town	Odd Down	Radstock Town	Torrington	Welton Rovers	Willand Rovers
Backwell United		2-2	1-1	1-3	1-3	0-9	0-5	0-0	1-4	1-4	0-2	n/a	0-0	0-2	1-0	3-1	0-4	3-6	0-4	1-1	2-4
Barnstaple Town	1-1		1-3	0-0	3-1	0-2	3-1	1-2	0-2	0-2	1-1	3-1	1-2	2-4	3-0	4-1	1-0	5-2	5-1	0-1	2-2
Bideford	2-0	7-0	*P*	2-0	2-0	5-1	0-0	3-0	2-1	1-0	8-1	4-0	4-2	0-0	5-2	5-0	5-1	3-1	3-0	1-1	0-0
Bishop Sutton	1-1	2-0	0-1	*R*	1-1	2-2	3-1	1-3	0-3	1-4	5-1	n/a	0-0	0-0	2-2	1-0	0-0	0-1	1-1	0-2	2-2
Bitton	1-0	1-1	0-1	2-0	*E*	2-1	3-1	0-1	0-1	0-0	7-1	n/a	1-1	3-1	1-1	2-0	0-1	1-1	3-1	4-1	0-1
Bridgwater Town	0-1	0-3	1-2	4-0	1-1	*M*	2-1	0-2	2-2	0-1	2-1	5-0	1-2	4-2	2-1	1-3	1-1	2-2	5-0	0-2	0-0
Brislington	4-1	2-1	0-0	2-1	2-1	0-1	*I*	0-2	1-3	1-1	2-1	0-0	1-3	1-2	1-2	1-1	1-0	3-1	1-3	1-3	1-0
Bristol Manor Farm	1-1	1-1	2-3	2-1	6-0	2-1	1-2	*E*	1-1	2-4	4-0	n/a	0-2	1-2	6-1	0-1	5-0	3-0	5-1	4-2	2-1
Calne Town	2-1	6-0	1-1	1-0	0-1	1-1	0-5	1-2	*R*	1-1	4-0	n/a	2-0	3-2	1-0	4-3	0-1	5-2	4-0	0-0	2-0
Corsham Town	2-1	3-0	4-0	2-1	2-0	1-0	4-1	3-0	1-1		5-3	n/a	1-1	5-0	4-1	2-0	2-0	2-1	3-0	0-1	1-1
Devizes Town	1-0	1-0	0-3	1-0	0-2	0-2	0-2	1-5	0-3	0-0		n/a	2-0	0-2	0-1	1-0	1-0	0-1	0-0	1-1	1-4
Exmouth Town	1-0	2-3	1-2	2-3	0-3	4-3	n/a	n/a	1-5	n/a	n/a	*D*	n/a	n/a	n/a	n/a	n/a	0-1	n/a	0-3	n/a
Frome Town	1-0	3-2	2-3	2-0	1-2	1-0	1-2	2-5	2-1	2-1	2-1	1-0	*I*	3-4	0-0	0-0	0-1	1-1	0-0	2-2	4-1
Hallen	2-1	1-1	0-2	0-0	1-1	3-1	1-1	2-1	2-2	2-2	8-1	n/a	1-3	*V*	2-0	1-2	0-0	3-2	6-0	0-1	0-2
Keynsham Town	1-1	0-2	0-5	1-3	0-4	1-2	0-1	1-2	0-0	2-2	4-1	n/a	0-4	1-1	*I*	1-1	1-4	0-1	1-1	0-2	1-2
Melksham Town	4-1	1-0	0-3	1-0	1-3	2-6	1-1	1-0	1-1	1-2	0-0	2-2	0-1	0-6	1-1	*S*	2-0	0-5	2-3	0-2	3-1
Odd Down	3-0	1-2	0-1	1-2	0-2	0-2	0-0	0-2	3-2	1-1	2-0	n/a	0-3	1-1	1-1	0-1	*I*	1-0	2-0	0-1	0-1
Radstock Town	4-1	1-3	1-3	1-0	0-4	1-2	3-2	1-3	2-1	0-2	3-2	1-4	1-1	2-1	1-2	4-2	0-2	*O*	0-1	3-1	2-2
Torrington	1-1	2-0	0-1	1-1	2-4	0-2	2-3	0-3	0-2	0-1	4-0	n/a	0-3	1-4	1-3	0-3	1-1	1-4	*N*	0-1	0-1
Welton Rovers	5-1	0-3	0-1	2-1	1-1	2-0	1-1	2-4	3-0	3-1	4-0	3-1	1-2	1-1	2-1	1-1	1-1	2-1	4-1		1-1
Willand Rovers	2-0	0-0	2-1	1-1	2-1	4-3	1-0	0-1	0-2	0-2	3-1	n/a	3-2	3-1	5-0	1-2	1-1	3-0	6-0	0-0	

Premier Division	P	W	D	L	F	A	Pts
Bideford	38	29	7	2	93	25	94
Corsham Town	38	24	10	4	78	30	82
Bristol Manor Farm	38	24	4	10	86	43	76
Welton Rovers	38	19	12	7	61	39	69
Calne Town	38	19	10	9	70	41	67
Willand Rovers	38	18	11	9	63	42	65
Frome Town	38	18	10	10	61	45	64
Bitton	38	18	9	11	63	41	63
Hallen	38	15	12	11	71	54	57
Brislington	38	15	8	15	55	53	53
Bridgwater Town	38	15	7	16	66	54	52
Radstock Town	38	14	5	19	62	73	47
Barnstaple Town	38	12	9	17	54	62	45
Melksham Town	38	12	8	18	43	68	44
Odd Down	38	11	10	17	34	44	43
Bishop Sutton	38	7	13	18	36	52	34
Keynsham Town	38	5	11	22	34	78	26
Devizes Town	38	7	5	26	27	94	26
Torrington	38	6	7	25	33	89	25
Backwell United	38	3	10	25	30	93	19

Exmouth Town – record expunged

LES PHILLIPS CUP

PRELIMINARY ROUND

Bideford 1 **Willand Rovers** 2

Bishop Sutton 1 Dawlish Town 0

Bridport 1 **Westbury United** 4

Brislington 1 **Barnstaple Town** 2

Chard Town 4 Bradford Town 1

Clevedon United 2 Calne Town 1 *aet*

Elmore 3 **Bridgwater Town** 4

Ilfracombe Town 1 **Bitton** 2

Shrewton United 1 Shepton Mallet 0

Wellington 1 **Weston St Johns** 3

Welton Rovers 4 Saltash United 0

FIRST ROUND

Almondsbury 2 Street 0

Barnstaple Town 1 **Bridgwater Town** 2

Bishop Sutton 3 Weston St Johns 1

Bitton 1 **Bristol Manor Farm** 2

Chard Town 0 Odd Down 0 *aet* (7-6p)

Corsham Town 4 Cadbury Heath 0

Frome Town 3 Clyst Rovers 0

Keynsham Tn 1 **Devizes Town** 5

Longwell Green Sports 0 **Hallen** 1 *(at Hallen)*

Melksham Town 2 Backwell United 1

Minehead Town 0 **Biddestone** 3

Radstock Town 1 **Larkhall Athletic** 2

WESTERN LEAGUE PREMIER DIVISION CONSTITUTION 2006-07

BARNSTAPLE TOWN	Mill Road, Barnstaple EX31 1JQ	01271 343469
BIDEFORD	The Sports Ground, Kingsley Road, Bideford EX39 2LH	01237 474974
BISHOP SUTTON	Lake View, Wick Road, Bishop Sutton, Bristol BS39 5XP	01275 333097
BITTON	Recreation Ground, Bath Road, Bitton, Bristol BS30 6HX	0117 932 3222
BRIDGWATER TOWN	Fairfax Park, College Way, Bath Road, Bridgwater TA6 4TZ	01278 446899
BRISLINGTON	Ironmould Lane, Brislington, Bristol BS4 5SA	0117 977 4030
BRISTOL MANOR FARM	The Creek, Portway, Sea Mills, Bristol BS9 2HS	0117 968 4916
CALNE TOWN	Lickhill Road, Bremhill View, Calne SN11 8AE	01249 819186
CHARD TOWN	Denning Sports Field, Zembard Lane, Chard TA20 1JL	01460 61402
CORSHAM TOWN	Southbank Ground, Lacock Road, Corsham SN13 9HS	01249 715609
DAWLISH TOWN	Playing Fields, Sandy Lane, Exeter Road, Dawlish EX7 0AF	01626 863110
DEVIZES TOWN	Nursteed Road, Devizes SN10 3EJ	01380 722817
FROME TOWN	Badgers Hill, Berkley Road, Frome BA11 2EH	01373 464087
HALLEN	Hallen Centre, Moorhouse Lane, Hallen, Bristol BS10 7RU	0117 950 5559
KEYNSHAM TOWN	Crown Field, Bristol Road, Keynsham, Bristol BS31 2BE	0117 986 5876
MELKSHAM TOWN	The Conigre, Market Place, Melksham SN12 6ES	01225 702843
ODD DOWN	Lew Hill Memorial Ground, Combe Hay Lane, Odd Down, Bath BA2 8PH	01225 832491
RADSTOCK TOWN	Southfield Recreation Ground, Frome Hill, Radstock BA3 3NZ	01761 435004
STREET	The Tannery Ground, Middlebrooks, Street BA16 0TA	01458 444987
TORRINGTON	Vicarage Field, School Lane, Great Torrington EX38 7AJ	01805 622853
WELTON ROVERS	West Clewes, North Road, Midsomer Norton BA3 2QD	01761 412097
WILLAND ROVERS	Silver Street, Willand, Cullompton EX15 2SL	01884 33885

IN: Chard Town (P), Dawlish Town (P), Street (P)
OUT: Backwell United (R), Exmouth Town (WS)

	Almondsbury	Biddestone	Bradford Town	Bridport	Cadbury Heath	Chard Town	Clevedon United	Clyst Rovers	Dawlish Town	Elmore	Ilfracombe Town	Larkhall Athletic	Longwell Green Sports	Minehead Town	Portishead	Saltash United	Shepton Mallet	Shrewton United	Street	Wellington Town	Westbury United	Weston St Johns
Almondsbury		3-0	2-2	1-2	2-2	1-2	1-2	0-0	0-7	3-2	1-4	1-2	0-2	1-1	0-1	3-0	0-2	0-0	1-1	1-2	1-0	0-2
Biddestone	0-0		1-1	1-0	1-0	1-1	1-2	6-0	2-4	2-0	1-2	0-0	2-1	1-2	1-3	1-2	3-1	0-2	1-2	3-0	0-0	4-2
Bradford Town	1-3	1-1		2-6	1-0	1-1	1-1	3-1	2-4	3-3	2-2	2-2	1-1	2-2	0-0	1-0	2-0	2-8	3-1	6-1	1-2	1-0
Bridport	2-1	2-0	0-1		0-2	1-3	2-2	4-1	0-2	0-0	2-1	2-1	1-0	3-1	4-3	5-2	2-1	1-0	1-2	4-2	3-2	8-0
Cadbury Heath	2-1	1-2	4-0	4-1		0-1	3-1	2-1	1-4	5-0	0-2	1-1	4-0	3-0	0-1	2-2	2-0	4-4	2-2	1-2	1-1	0-0
Chard Town	3-0	1-0	3-0	1-0	3-0	*D*	5-0	3-0	4-1	5-2	2-1	1-3	0-0	6-0	0-0	2-0	5-0	1-0	0-0	3-2	2-1	1-0
Clevedon United	2-2	4-1	1-2	0-2	1-0	0-2	*I*	1-4	1-0	4-0	0-0	2-2	1-1	3-0	1-0	2-0	2-0	2-2	2-3	4-1	4-2	3-0
Clyst Rovers	2-3	3-1	2-3	1-2	2-0	0-2	0-2	*V*	0-4	3-0	3-3	1-1	0-1	4-0	2-2	4-0	0-1	0-2	0-5	1-4	1-2	0-1
Dawlish Town	4-0	0-0	4-0	2-2	3-2	2-1	2-1	0-0	*I*	6-1	3-1	2-0	2-0	3-0	1-1	4-1	5-0	5-1	2-1	1-0	0-0	7-0
Elmore	0-2	2-1	1-1	0-2	0-4	2-4	1-1	0-1	1-4	*S*	1-5	1-4	1-2	1-3	1-2	1-6	3-2	0-3	2-5	4-2	0-3	1-3
Ilfracombe Town	0-1	2-1	0-4	2-2	2-1	1-2	3-1	3-2	0-1	3-2	*I*	1-0	2-1	2-0	1-0	3-0	1-0	2-0	1-0	3-3	1-1	3-1
Larkhall Athletic	0-0	1-1	2-1	1-0	1-0	1-3	1-1	5-0	1-1	11-0	0-2	*O*	0-0	9-1	3-1	8-0	3-1	1-2	4-2	1-0	1-3	1-1
Longwell Green Sports	2-1	2-2	0-4	2-1	3-0	1-2	0-0	1-1	0-1	3-1	0-0	1-2	*N*	5-0	0-3	1-2	1-0	2-0	1-0	1-2	3-2	1-2
Minehead Town	1-0	0-1	6-1	1-1	0-5	1-1	1-1	3-1	0-2	4-0	1-1	2-3	3-1		0-4	1-2	3-1	1-3	0-2	1-1	1-2	3-1
Portishead	2-1	0-0	2-0	4-2	2-1	1-3	1-1	2-2	0-1	3-2	1-1	1-3	0-1	1-0	*O*	1-1	1-0	1-0	1-1	1-2	2-0	1-1
Saltash United	4-2	2-2	1-2	0-1	1-2	2-1	3-1	3-0	1-2	1-2	1-2	4-3	3-1	0-0	2-3	*N*	3-2	2-1	1-1	4-2	1-2	3-4
Shepton Mallet	0-0	0-2	3-1	1-1	1-3	0-3	1-0	2-1	0-3	2-1	0-6	1-4	1-4	3-2	1-0	0-5	*E*	1-0	0-1	0-0	0-0	2-1
Shrewton United	2-4	2-3	3-1	1-5	1-0	1-1	5-0	3-2	3-7	7-1	4-5	4-1	1-0	3-1	2-3	2-2	3-1		2-2	3-1	2-0	4-2
Street	1-0	1-0	4-2	1-0	1-1	0-0	2-1	3-0	1-3	4-0	1-0	2-0	1-0	8-1	1-0	1-1	2-0	1-1		4-1	2-0	1-2
Wellington Town	1-2	3-2	2-3	1-2	1-3	1-1	0-1	6-0	1-0	6-1	0-6	0-3	0-1	0-0	1-1	2-0	2-1	4-0	1-1		1-2	4-2
Westbury United	0-0	4-0	1-1	4-2	6-0	0-0	7-3	1-0	3-4	6-0	3-2	3-1	1-1	5-0	5-0	3-1	3-2	5-0	1-3	3-3		2-0
Weston St Johns	5-1	0-2	0-3	3-0	4-2	0-2	3-0	2-1	0-2	7-1	1-0	4-2	2-1	3-0	0-3	1-2	1-0	2-1	0-3	0-1	0-4	

Shrewton United 2 **Westbury United** 2 *aet* (3-4p)
Torrington 5 Exmouth Town 2
Welton Rovers 2 Portishead 2 *aet* (3-2p)
Willand Rovers 6 Clevedon United 0

SECOND ROUND

Biddestone (w/o) v Torrington (scr.)
Bishop Sutton 2 Larkhall Athletic 0
Bridgwater Town 0 **Hallen** 1
Chard Town 0 **Bristol Manor Farm** 1
Corsham Town 2 Frome Town 0
Devizes Town 1 **Westbury United** 6
Melksham Town 1 **Welton Rovers** 3
Willand Rovers 1 Almondsbury 0

QUARTER-FINALS

Biddestone 0 **Welton Rovers** 1 *aet (at Corsham Town)*
Hallen 3 Bishop Sutton 0
Westbury United 2 **Corsham Town** 3 *aet*
Willand Rovers 3 Bristol Manor Farm 2 *aet*

SEMI-FINALS

Hallen 0 **Corsham Town** 2
Willand Rovers 2 Welton Rovers 1

FINAL

(May 6th at Frome Town)

Willand Rovers 0 **Corsham Town** 1

Division One	P	W	D	L	F	A	Pts
Dawlish Town	42	33	6	3	115	33	105
Chard Town	42	29	10	3	87	27	97
Street	42	24	11	7	80	39	83
Ilfracombe Town	42	23	9	10	82	50	78
Westbury United	42	22	10	10	95	50	76
Bridport	42	22	6	14	81	60	72
Larkhall Athletic	42	19	11	12	93	56	68
Portishead	42	18	12	12	59	49	66
Shrewton United	42	18	7	17	88	79	61
Bradford Town	42	15	13	14	71	81	58
Clevedon United	42	15	12	15	62	67	57
Longwell Green Sports	42	15	9	18	49	52	54
Weston St Johns *-3*	42	18	3	21	63	81	54
Cadbury Heath	42	15	8	19	70	62	53
Saltash United	42	15	7	20	71	84	52
Biddestone	42	13	11	18	54	59	50
Wellington Town	42	14	8	20	69	81	50
Almondsbury	42	10	11	21	46	70	41
Minehead Town	42	9	9	24	47	100	36
Shepton Mallet	42	10	4	28	34	85	34
Clyst Rovers	42	7	7	28	47	92	28
Elmore	42	4	4	34	42	148	16

WESTERN LEAGUE DIVISION ONE CONSTITUTION 2006-07

ALMONDSBURY .... **Almondsbury Sports & Social Centre, Gloucester Road, Almondsbury BS34 4AA** **01454 612240**
BACKWELL UNITED .... **The Playing Fields, West Town Road, Backwell, Bristol BS48 3HG** **01275 462612**
BIDDESTONE .... **The Sports Ground, Yatton Road, Biddestone, Chippenham SN14 7BZ** **01249 716622**
BRADFORD TOWN .... **Avon Sports Ground, Trowbridge Road, Bradford-on-Avon BA15 1EE** **01225 866649**
BRIDPORT .... **St Marys Field, Skilling Hill Road, Bridport DT6 5LN** **01308 423834**
CADBURY HEATH .... **Springfield, Cadbury Heath Road, Warmley, Bristol BS30 8BX** **0117 967 5731**
CLEVEDON UNITED .... **Clevedon Town FC, The Hand Stadium, Davis Way, Clevedon BS21 6TG** **01275 341913**
CLYST ROVERS .... **Waterslade Park, Clyst Honiton EX5 2BA** **01392 366424**
ELMORE .... **Horsdon Park, Heathcoat Way, Tiverton EX16 4DB** **01884 252341**
HENGROVE ATHLETIC .... **Norton Lane, Whitchurch, Bristol BS14 0BT** **01275 832894**
ILFRACOMBE TOWN .... **Marlborough Park, Marlborough Road, Ilfracombe EX34 8JB** **01271 865939**
LARKHALL ATHLETIC .... **Plain Ham, Charlcombe Lane, Larkhall, Bath BA1 8DJ** **01225 334952**
LONGWELL GREEN SPORTS ... **Longwell Green Comm. Centre, Shellards Road, Longwell Green BS30 9DU** **0117 932 5111**
MINEHEAD TOWN .... **Recreation Ground, Irnham Road, Minehead TA24 5DP** **01643 704989**
PORTISHEAD .... **Bristol Road Playing Fields, Portishead, Bristol BS20 6QB** **01275 847136**
SHEPTON MALLET **West Shepton Playing Fields, Old Wells Road, Shepton Mallet BA4 5XN** **01749 344609**
SHERBORNE TOWN .... **Raleigh Grove, The Terrace Playing Fields, Sherborne DT9 5NS** **01935 816110**
SHREWTON UNITED .... **Recreation Ground, Mill Lane, Shrewton, Salisbury SP3 4JU** **07796 098122**
TRURO CITY .... **Treyew Road, Truro TR1 2TH** **01872 278853**
WELLINGTON TOWN .... **Wellington Playing Field, North Street, Wellington TA1 8NA** **01823 664810**
WESTBURY UNITED .... **Meadow Lane, Westbury BA13 3AF** **01373 823409**
WESTON ST JOHNS .... **Coleridge Road, Bournville Estate, Weston-super-Mare BS23 3UP** **01934 612862**

IN: Backwell United (R), Hengrove Athletic (P – Somerset County League Premier Divisiom), Sherborne Town (P – Dorset Premier League), Truro City (P – South Western League)

OUT: Chard Town (P), Dawlish Town (P), Saltash United (S – South Western League), Street (P)

WESTMORLAND LEAGUE

	Ambleside United	Appleby	Carleton Rovers	Coniston	Greystoke	Ibis	Kendal County	Kendal Town Res.	Keswick	Lunesdale United	Sedbergh Wanderers	Staveley United	Wetheriggs United	Windermere SC
Ambleside United		0-4	0-2	4-4	3-5	1-1	2-9	2-2	2-4	6-1	3-0	4-2	1-3	1-3
Appleby	5-0	*D*	3-1	1-0	2-0	4-1	0-0	1-2	1-0	4-1	1-0	4-1	1-1	3-4
Carleton Rovers	6-3	4-5	*I*	4-2	1-1	2-1	1-5	3-1	0-2	1-4	3-0	4-0	1-2	5-1
Coniston	2-3	5-3	2-0	*V*	4-0	4-1	2-3	2-2	3-0	2-1	1-0	2-1	0-2	1-0
Greystoke	1-0	3-4	1-1	0-9	*I*	2-3	2-3	0-2	2-2	0-4	2-2	3-1	1-3	1-1
Ibis	5-4	2-1	5-0	1-7	1-2	*S*	1-8	0-4	2-5	4-2	3-3	5-1	2-6	3-4
Kendal County	5-3	5-1	5-0	0-0	2-0	1-3	*I*	0-0	1-0	3-0	4-2	7-1	3-0	2-0
Kendal Town Res.	1-0	2-0	7-1	0-3	3-0	2-3	0-1	*O*	2-1	1-2	3-0	4-0	1-1	0-3
Keswick	5-1	1-3	2-1	1-2	0-3	3-2	1-1	1-1	*N*	3-5	0-4	2-0	1-1	1-2
Lunesdale United	1-1	3-4	1-2	0-4	1-2	3-1	2-2	1-2	2-2		5-0	5-0	0-5	1-7
Sedbergh Wanderers	1-2	3-0	6-2	1-3	3-1	1-4	1-1	4-1	3-1	4-6	*O*	9-1	2-3	2-2
Staveley United	2-2	0-4	0-6	0-6	2-2	4-5	0-7	2-5	1-3	2-4	1-5	*N*	0-5	3-4
Wetheriggs United	6-1	4-0	3-1	4-1	3-1	3-1	1-0	2-0	3-0	8-1	6-0	9-1	*E*	2-2
Windermere SC	6-1	3-1	5-2	3-3	1-2	2-3	2-4	4-1	2-1	4-0	4-1	3-1	1-2	

Division One		P	W	D	L	F	A	Pts
Wetheriggs United		26	21	4	1	88	23	67
Kendal County		26	18	6	2	82	25	60
Coniston		26	16	4	6	74	35	52
Windermere SC		26	15	4	7	73	47	49
Appleby		26	15	2	9	60	46	47
Kendal Town Res.	*-3*	26	12	5	9	49	37	38
Ibis		26	11	2	13	63	79	35
Carleton Rovers		26	10	2	14	54	67	32
Lunesdale United		26	9	3	14	56	74	30
Keswick		26	8	5	13	42	50	29
Sedbergh Wanderers		26	8	4	14	57	63	28
Greystoke		26	7	6	13	37	61	27
Ambleside United		26	5	5	16	50	86	20
Staveley United		26	0	2	24	27	119	2

WESTMORLAND LEAGUE DIVISION ONE CONSTITUTION 2006-07

APPLEBY .... The Board Close, Chapel Street, Bolton, Appleby-in-Westmorland CA16 6QR .... None
BURNESIDE.................. Cricket Pavilion, Hollins Lane, Burneside, Kendal LA9 6QL.................. None
CARLETON ROVERS .... Frenchfield, Penrith CA11 8TW.................. None
CONISTON .... Shepherds Bridge, Coniston LA21 8AL.................. None
GREYSTOKE .... Greystoke Playing Field, Greystoke .... None
IBIS .... Millennium Field, Kendal .... None
KENDAL COUNTY .... Netherfield Cricket Club, Parkside Road, Kendal LA9 7BL 01539 724051
KENDAL TOWN RESERVES .... Parkside, Parkside Road, Kendal LA9 7BL 01539 727472/722469
KESWICK .... Walker Park, Keswick.................. None
LUNESDALE UNITED.................. Recreation Ground, Orton Road, Tebay, Penrith CA10 3TL.................. None
NORTHBANK CARLISLE RESERVES .. Sheepmount Sports Complex, Sheepmount, Carlisle CA3 8XL 01228 625599
SEDBERGH WANDERERS.................. Havera Playing Field, Sedbergh LA10 5HD.................. None
WETHERIGGS UNITED.................. Gilwilly Recreation Ground, Castletown, Penrith.................. None
WINDERMERE SC.................. Queen's Park, Windermere.................. None

IN: Burneside (P), Northbank Carlisle Reserves (P)
OUT: Ambleside United (R), Staveley United (R)

HIGH SHERIFF'S CUP

FIRST ROUND
Ambleside United 4 Sedbergh Wanderers 3
Ibis 0 **Coniston** 4
Kendal County 2 Appleby 1
Keswick 2 **Wetheriggs United** 5
Lunesdale United 1 **Greystoke** 3
Windermere SC 4 Staveley United 0

QUARTER-FINALS
Greystoke 4 Carleton Rovers 1
Kendal Town Res. 2 Coniston 1 *aet*
Wetheriggs United (w/o) v Ambleside United (scr.)
Windermere SC 0 **Kendal County** 4

SEMI-FINALS
Kendal County 4 Kendal Town Res. 0
Wetheriggs United 2 Greystoke 0

FINAL
(May 11th at Penrith)
Wetheriggs United 3 Kendal County 0

Division Two	P	W	D	L	F	A	Pts
Northbank Carlisle Res.	24	18	2	4	75	29	56
Burneside	24	16	5	3	68	26	53
Kendal County Res.	24	14	5	5	53	33	47
Penrith Rangers	24	14	1	9	72	49	43
Kirkoswald	24	13	1	10	58	43	40
Carvetii United	24	12	4	8	65	57	40
Wetheriggs United Res.	24	10	4	10	61	56	34
Kendal Celtic	24	9	4	11	51	51	31
Keswick Res.	24	7	4	13	46	80	25
Ullswater United	24	6	4	14	32	54	22
Windermere SC Res.	24	4	8	12	35	72	20
Dent	24	5	3	16	36	71	18
Shap	24	4	3	17	39	70	15

MASON & FREEMAN CUP

FINAL

(May 8th at Penrith)

Carvetii United 1 Wetheriggs United Res. 1 *aet* (5-4p)

Division Three	P	W	D	L	F	A	Pts
Sedbergh Wanderers Res.	22	16	3	3	70	30	51
Ibis Res.	22	16	3	3	61	26	51
Carleton Rovers Res.	22	15	2	5	75	40	47
Burneside Res.	22	10	5	7	57	37	35
Carvetii United Res.	22	9	8	5	40	30	35
Endmoor KGR	22	9	3	10	52	43	30
Ambleside United Res. *-3*	22	10	2	10	43	61	29
Appleby Res.	22	6	7	9	38	43	25
Braithwaite	22	7	2	13	33	51	23
Penrith Rangers Res.	22	7	1	14	46	64	22
Wetheriggs United 'A'	22	6	3	13	53	65	21
Staveley United Res.	22	1	1	20	16	94	4

Grasmere – record expunged

PETER DAWS MEMORIAL SHIELD

FINAL

(May 12th at Carvetii United)

Sedbergh Wanderers Res. 3 Wetheriggs United 'A' 2

Division Four		P	W	D	L	F	A	Pts
Lunesdale United Res.		20	15	1	4	58	29	46
Penrith United Res.		20	14	0	6	72	37	42
Coniston Res.	*-3*	20	13	2	5	67	29	38
Kendal Celtic Res.	*-3*	20	13	1	6	61	32	37
Burneside Academy		20	9	3	8	59	46	30
Kendal United		20	9	3	8	52	51	30
Greystoke Res.		20	9	2	9	43	49	29
Shap Res.		20	9	0	11	43	50	27
Windermere SC 'A'		20	5	2	13	27	55	17
Dent Res.		20	3	3	14	24	77	12
Endmoor KGR Res.		20	2	1	17	32	83	7

AUSTIN WREN CUP

FINAL

(May 5th at Penrith)

Penrith United Res. 3 Kendal Celtic Res. 1

WILTSHIRE LEAGUE

	AFC Trowbridge Town Youth	Aldbourne	Bromham	Calne Town Res.	Corsham Town Res.	Devizes Town Res.	Down Ampney	Malmesbury Victoria Res.	Marlborough Town	Melksham Town Res.	New College	Pewsey Vale Res.	Purton Res.	Shrewton United Res.	Warminster Town	Westbury United Res.	Westside
AFC Trowbridge Town Youth	*P*	0-2	3-2	6-0	0-1	0-1	4-1	7-1	5-4	3-3	3-0	1-0	7-1	5-0	1-1	0-1	2-3
Aldbourne	1-2	*R*	5-2	1-2	1-0	1-1	2-0	2-0	0-1	1-5	4-2	4-3	3-0	7-0	0-1	0-1	7-0
Bromham	0-4	0-2	*E*	1-0	2-3	0-4	0-1	1-1	2-1	1-6	2-5	4-3	2-4	4-0	0-3	1-1	4-1
Calne Town Res.	0-2	5-1	1-1	*M*	2-2	4-0	0-3	3-1	1-2	1-1	2-2	4-2	5-0	0-0	2-1	2-2	1-3
Corsham Town Res.	6-0	2-1	3-0	3-1	*I*	5-2	2-2	4-0	2-0	3-0	1-0	3-0	3-1	6-0	1-1	2-1	1-2
Devizes Town Res.	2-4	1-3	2-3	2-0	1-4	*E*	0-7	2-0	1-0	0-1	1-2	1-0	9-1	1-1	1-3	0-3	3-3
Down Ampney	6-0	2-0	5-1	3-2	1-4	4-1	*R*	1-0	0-2	2-0	3-0	4-0	7-0	4-1	2-5	5-0	0-8
Malmesbury Victoria Res.	0-1	1-0	4-2	2-2	0-3	1-6	1-2		0-2	0-1	3-2	0-4	3-5	0-4	1-3	1-3	1-3
Marlborough Town	1-2	0-0	1-0	3-2	0-4	2-3	1-3	0-0		1-1	0-0	1-1	9-0	7-0	2-1	1-1	0-4
Melksham Town Res.	0-3	0-1	2-1	3-0	1-1	1-3	2-5	4-1	1-1	*D*	2-1	2-1	1-0	1-2	1-2	5-1	2-3
New College	1-1	0-0	2-2	2-1	1-1	0-3	0-1	2-1	1-1	3-4	*I*	0-0	4-2	4-0	0-2	2-0	2-2
Pewsey Vale Res.	1-1	0-1	2-3	1-8	0-0	4-3	3-2	1-1	1-0	1-2	0-5	*V*	2-0	1-4	0-5	0-1	0-2
Purton Res.	1-0	2-3	5-3	0-4	1-5	1-5	2-1	1-1	0-4	1-3	1-4	1-2	*I*	0-5	1-2	1-5	2-3
Shrewton United Res.	2-3	1-3	3-1	2-3	0-1	5-0	11-1	1-3	0-3	4-3	3-4	2-0	6-1	*S*	2-3	1-1	2-4
Warminster Town	0-0	1-0	2-0	1-1	0-0	1-2	3-1	7-0	2-0	4-0	5-0	1-2	2-0	1-1	*I*	1-1	6-1
Westbury United Res.	1-1	3-0	2-1	4-1	2-0	0-2	2-0	9-0	2-0	1-3	1-1	0-0	6-3	2-0	2-1	*O*	1-0
Westside	1-4	1-1	7-2	4-0	0-4	6-1	4-2	3-0	2-2	0-2	5-3	5-1	2-0	3-1	2-1	3-0	*N*

Premier Division		P	W	D	L	F	A	Pts
Corsham Town Res.		32	22	7	3	80	23	73
Westside		32	21	4	7	90	58	67
Warminster Town		32	19	7	6	72	27	64
AFC Trowbridge Town Youth		32	18	6	8	75	44	60
Westbury United Res.		32	17	8	7	60	38	59
Down Ampney	*-2*	32	19	1	12	81	61	56
Melksham Town Res.		32	16	5	11	63	52	53
Aldbourne		32	16	4	12	57	39	52
Devizes Town Res.	*-1*	32	14	3	15	64	70	44
Marlborough Town		32	11	9	12	52	42	42
New College		32	10	10	12	55	57	40
Calne Town Res.	*-1*	32	10	8	14	60	61	37
Shrewton United Res.		32	10	4	18	64	80	34
Pewsey Vale Res.	*-2*	32	7	6	19	36	71	25
Bromham		32	7	4	21	48	88	25
Malmesbury Victoria Res.		32	4	5	23	28	91	17
Purton Res.	*-1*	32	5	1	26	38	121	15

WILTSHIRE LEAGUE PREMIER DIVISION CONSTITUTION 2006-07

AFC TROWBRIDGE TOWN YOUTH	Woodmarsh, North Bradley, Trowbridge BA14 0SA	None
ALDBOURNE	Farm Lane, Aldbourne, Marlborough SN8 2DS	None
BLUEPRINT CHISELDON	Chiseldon Sports & Social Club, 6 Draycott Road, Chiseldon, Swindon SN4 0LS	01793 740274
BRADFORD TOWN RESERVES	Avon Sports Ground, Trowbridge Road, Bradford-on-Avon BA15 1EE	01225 866649
BROMHAM	Jubilee Field, Bromham, Chippenham	01380 850671
CALNE TOWN RESERVES	Lickhill Road, Bremhill View, Calne SN11 8AE	01249 819186
CORSHAM TOWN RESERVES	Southbank Ground, Lacock Road, Corsham SN13 9HS	01249 715609
DEVIZES TOWN RESERVES	Nursteed Road, Devizes SN10 3EJ	01380 722817
MALMESBURY VICTORIA RESERVES	Flying Monk Ground, Gloucester Road, Malmesbury SN16 0AJ	01666 822141
MARLBOROUGH TOWN	Elcot Lane, Marlborough SN8 2BG	01672 513340
MELKSHAM TOWN RESERVES	The Conigre, Market Place, Melksham SN12 6ES	01225 702843
NEW COLLEGE	Swindon Supermarine FC, Highworth Road, South Marston, Swindon SN3 4SF	01793 828778
PEWSEY VALE RESERVES	Recreation Ground, Kings Corner, Ball Road, Pewsey SN9 5GF	01672 562990
PURTON RESERVES	The Red House, Church Street, Purton SN5 4DT	01793 770262
SHREWTON UNITED RESERVES	Recreation Ground, Mill Lane, Shrewton, Salisbury SP3 4JU	07796 098122
WESTBURY UNITED RESERVES	Meadow Lane, Westbury BA13 3AF	01373 823409
WESTSIDE	Southbrook Recreation Ground, Pinehurst Road, Swindon	None
WROUGHTON	The Weir Field, Wroughton WMC, Devizes Road, Wroughton SN4 0SA	01793 812319

IN: Blueprint Chiseldon (P – Division Two following merger of Division Two sides Blueprint and Chiseldon Castrol), Bradford Town Reserves (P – Trowbridge & District League Division Three), Wroughton (P)

OUT: Warminster Town (P – Wessex League Division One)

SENIOR CUP

(Premier Division teams)

FIRST ROUND

Cricklade Town Res. (scr.) v **Westside** (w/o)

Melksham Town Res. 4 Devizes Town Res. 3

SECOND ROUND

AFC Trowbridge Town Youth 0 New College 4 *(New College expelled)*

Aldbourne 6 Pewsey Vale Res. 1

Bromham 0 **Warminster Town** 3

Calne Town Res. 0 **Marlborough Town** 0 *aet* (4-3p) *(Calne Town Res. expelled)*

Purton Res. 1 **Corsham Town Res.** 4

Shrewton United Res. 2 **Melksham Town Res.** 3 *aet*

Westbury United Res. 1 **Down Ampney** 1 *aet* (1-3p)

Westside 1 Malmesbury Victoria Res. 0

QUARTER-FINALS

Aldbourne 0 **Melksham Town Res.** 1

Corsham Town Res. 2 Marlborough Town 0

Down Ampney 0 **Warminster Town** 0 *aet* (4-5p)

Westside 1 **AFC Trowbridge Town Youth** 2

SEMI-FINALS

AFC Trowbridge Town Youth 0 **Melksham Town Res.** 2

Warminster Town 1 **Corsham Town Res.** 2

FINAL

(April 29th at Corsham Town)

Corsham Town Res. 2 Melksham Town 0

Division One		P	W	D	L	F	A	Pts
Wroughton		28	27	0	1	132	20	81
Pinehurst Old Boys		28	19	3	6	87	52	60
Stratton Rovers		28	17	3	8	81	48	54
Barron Heating		28	17	3	8	79	57	54
AFC Abbey Rodbourne	*-3*	28	17	0	11	76	70	48
AFC Stratton		28	14	5	9	57	55	47
Westlecot United		28	13	3	12	65	66	42
Swindon Asians	*-3*	28	14	1	13	77	65	40
Castle Combe		28	11	5	12	51	67	38
Blunsdon United	*-1*	28	10	5	13	59	55	34
SKS Blyskawica	*-2*	28	10	2	16	62	85	30
Biddestone Res.	*-2*	28	7	4	17	57	80	23
Minety	*-3*	28	6	6	16	68	96	21
Marlborough Town Res.	*-1*	28	5	3	20	34	94	17
Lower Stratton		28	1	1	26	43	118	4

Division Two		P	W	D	L	F	A	Pts
Chiseldon Castrol		24	21	3	0	77	12	66
AFC Rodbourne		24	16	3	5	71	41	51
Aldbourne Res.	*-1*	24	14	4	6	71	32	45
CHQ United		24	13	2	9	53	39	41
Blunsdon United Res		24	10	6	8	58	48	36
Stratton Rovers Res.		24	10	3	11	40	52	33
Westlecot United Res.	*-1*	24	9	5	10	45	54	31
QT Swindon	*-1*	24	9	4	11	44	65	30
Bromham Res.	*-1*	24	7	6	11	42	57	26
Wroughton Res.		24	6	7	11	49	70	25
Blueprint	*-4*	24	6	7	11	44	54	21
Purton 'A'	*-3*	24	6	5	13	41	60	20
Westside Res.		24	0	3	21	23	74	3

JUNIOR CUP

(Division One and Two teams)

FINAL

(April 29th at Corsham Town)

Wroughton 3 Stratton Rovers 1

OTHER LEAGUES

All league tables in this section are final.
It is the policy of some competitions to leave some oft postponed matches as unplayed if they do not affect end of season issues.

ABERYSTWYTH & DISTRICT LEAGUE

Division One	P	W	D	L	F	A	Pts
Penrhyncoch Res.	24	20	1	3	64	37	61
Tywyn & Bryncrug	24	19	2	3	93	25	59
Bow Street	24	19	2	3	84	31	59
Penparcau	24	15	2	7	75	39	47
Bont	24	10	2	12	57	43	32
Llanrhystud	24	9	5	10	53	58	32
Dolgellau	24	9	4	11	56	58	31
Llannon	24	9	3	12	45	57	30
Llanilar	24	7	4	13	38	54	25
Padarn United	24	6	2	16	36	77	20
Aberdyfi	24	5	4	15	43	80	19
UW Aberystwyth Res.	24	4	6	14	38	66	18
Machynlleth *-3*	24	5	1	18	30	87	13

Division Two	P	W	D	L	F	A	Pts
Tregaron Turfs	20	16	1	3	101	20	49
Talybont	20	14	4	2	70	31	46
Bow Street Res.	20	13	1	6	44	34	40
Tywyn/Bryncrug Res.	20	12	3	5	61	28	39
Dolgellau Res.	20	9	4	7	44	40	31
Penparcau Res.	20	8	3	9	51	67	27
UW Aberystwyth 'A'	20	7	2	11	26	44	23
Penrhyncoch 'A'	20	7	2	11	36	62	23
Llanilar Res.	20	4	4	12	34	74	16
Corris United	20	3	4	13	42	70	13
Trawsgoed	20	2	2	16	24	63	8

ACCRINGTON & DISTRICT LEAGUE

Division One	P	W	D	L	F	A	Pts
Bridge Inn	18	17	1	0	89	29	52
Rhoden Inn	18	10	4	4	54	32	34
Baileys	18	9	3	6	46	39	30
Crown Rovers *-15*	18	12	2	4	64	27	23
Wellington	18	7	2	9	49	50	23
Brittania Padiham	18	5	6	7	49	48	21
Whinney Hill 'A'	18	5	2	11	36	53	17
Railway *-3*	18	6	2	10	42	61	17
Foxhill Falcons *-3*	18	5	2	11	40	76	14
Oswaldtwistle S M Res.	18	1	2	15	20	74	5

King Street – record expunged

Division Two	P	W	D	L	F	A	Pts
Bold Street	18	16	2	0	72	15	50
Church Town	18	12	3	3	49	20	39
Clarence Hotel	18	12	0	6	79	43	36
Baxenden	18	10	2	6	49	49	32
Crown Rovers Res.	18	8	4	6	44	45	28
Sydney Street WMC	18	5	3	10	30	46	18
Black Horse *-6*	18	6	4	8	41	44	16
Red Star *-3*	18	4	5	9	40	48	14
Railway Res.	18	2	0	16	29	83	6
Accr. Loy. Am. 'C' *-7*	18	2	3	13	19	59	2

ALTRINCHAM & DISTRICT LEAGUE

Division One	P	W	D	L	F	A	Pts
Broadh'th Central 'A'	16	11	2	3	63	32	35
King George	16	10	3	3	52	29	33
Old York Victoria	16	9	5	2	58	30	32
Quarry Bank	16	6	2	8	38	38	20
Trafford 'A'	16	5	3	8	28	55	18
Knutsford Res.	16	5	2	9	31	36	17
Wythenshawe Am 'A'	16	5	2	9	22	40	17
Stretford Victoria	16	4	4	8	38	52	16
Atlantic	16	4	3	9	30	48	15

Division Two	P	W	D	L	F	A	Pts
AFC Sale	22	17	2	3	104	30	53
Kartel Sports	22	15	2	5	78	32	47
Brooklands	22	13	5	4	56	44	44
Sale Amateurs	22	14	1	7	80	43	43
Styal 'A'	22	12	3	7	58	42	39
Timperley Wanderers	22	11	3	8	53	34	36
Northenden Victoria	22	11	3	8	67	50	36
O Altrinchamians Res.	22	8	1	13	45	55	25
Sale Rovers	22	6	1	15	40	66	19
NCC Group	22	4	3	15	35	70	15
Trafford United	22	5	0	17	34	111	15
Northern Moor	22	4	0	18	45	118	12

AMATEUR COMBINATION

(Higher divisions on page 8)

Int Division North	P	W	D	L	F	A	Pts
Mill Hill Village	20	17	2	1	77	25	53
Southgate County Res.	20	13	3	4	52	39	42
Enfield O Gram Res.	20	12	2	6	57	37	38
Bealonians Res.	20	8	5	7	33	28	29
Old Woodhouseians	20	7	4	9	43	43	25
Egbertian	20	6	6	8	39	44	24
UCL Academicals 'A'	20	7	3	10	42	50	24
Old Camdenians	20	7	2	11	33	48	23
Old Edmontonians	20	6	4	10	39	48	22
Old Buckwellians Res.	20	4	4	12	34	59	16
Old Parmiterians Res.	20	2	7	11	36	64	13

Int Division South	P	W	D	L	F	A	Pts
Hon Artillery Co Res.	20	13	6	1	65	23	45
Old Belgravians	20	12	2	6	78	44	38
Centymca	20	9	5	6	43	44	32
Witan	20	8	6	6	52	50	30
Kings Old Boys Res.	20	8	5	7	50	41	29
Old Thorntonians	20	7	6	7	37	39	27
Old Suttonians Res.	20	7	5	8	35	39	26
Old Josephians	20	7	3	10	60	63	24
Mickleham O Box.	20	6	6	8	46	53	24
Old Tenisonians Res.	20	5	5	10	41	73	20
Old St Marys	20	1	5	14	31	69	8

Int Division West	P	W	D	L	F	A	Pts
Old Meadonians 'A'	20	14	1	5	64	37	43
Old Manorians Res.	20	13	3	4	63	36	42
Brent	20	13	2	5	66	33	41
London Welsh	20	10	6	4	52	40	36
Cardinal Manning OB	20	11	1	8	48	39	34
Old Challoners Res.	20	10	2	8	40	32	32
Old Vaughanians Res.	20	6	3	11	47	51	21
Parkfield 'A'	20	5	4	11	29	46	19
Old Danes Res. *-3*	20	5	5	10	42	86	17
Old Salvatorians 'A'	20	3	4	13	34	58	13
Phoenix Old Boys	20	3	3	14	25	52	12

Division One North	P	W	D	L	F	A	Pts
Old Parmiterians 'A'	20	13	5	2	58	38	44
William Fitt	20	13	2	5	54	25	41
O Edmontonians Res.	20	12	3	5	60	37	39
Old Aloysians 'A'	20	10	4	6	57	43	34
Egbertian Res.	20	9	3	8	45	44	30
UCL Academicals 'B'	20	9	2	9	44	42	29
Old Tollingtonians	20	8	4	8	51	37	28
Old Ignatian Res.	20	6	3	11	26	52	21
University of Hertford	20	6	1	13	32	47	19
QM College OB Res.	20	6	1	13	38	60	19
Latymer OB Res.	20	4	0	16	27	67	12

Division One South	P	W	D	L	F	A	Pts
Economicals Res.	18	14	3	1	101	29	45
Fulham Compton OB	18	12	4	2	51	19	40
Old Wokingians Res.	18	9	3	6	57	37	30
Sinjuns Gramms Res.	18	9	3	6	36	30	30
Clapham O Xavs Res.	18	9	2	7	47	31	29
Reigatians Res.	18	6	3	9	28	46	21
Old Bromleians	18	6	2	10	37	55	20
Valley Park Rangers	18	5	3	10	38	41	18
Pegasus Res.	18	5	3	10	29	39	18
Inland Revenue	18	2	0	16	11	108	6

Division One West	P	W	D	L	F	A	Pts
Old Vaughanians 'A'	17	12	3	2	57	37	39
Old Hamptonians 'A'	18	12	1	5	56	34	37
Old Magdalenians	18	11	3	4	59	34	36
Parkfield 'B'	18	9	3	6	59	37	30
Old Uxonians *-3*	17	9	2	6	43	42	26
Old Uffingtonians	18	7	2	9	41	40	23
Old Manorians 'A'	18	7	1	10	31	51	22
Old Kingsburians	18	6	3	9	37	50	21
Old Salvatorians 'B'	18	2	4	12	33	63	10
O Isleworthians Res.	18	3	0	15	30	58	9

Division Two North	P	W	D	L	F	A	Pts
Old Aloysians 'B'	18	13	3	2	78	23	42
Leyton County OB	18	12	3	3	52	19	39
Wood Green OB Res.	18	11	3	4	59	27	36
Albanian 'A'	18	8	4	6	35	39	28
Bealonians 'A'	18	7	4	7	38	34	25
O Woodhouseians Res.	18	7	3	8	25	33	24
London Hospital OB	18	6	3	9	36	44	21
Egbertian 'A'	18	5	3	10	35	58	18
O Edmontonians 'A'	18	4	3	11	27	52	15
Old Parmiterians 'B'	18	2	1	15	22	78	7

Division Two South	P	W	D	L	F	A	Pts
Chertsey O Salesians	20	18	0	2	86	23	54
Old Suttonians 'A'	20	13	2	5	60	36	41
Old Whitgiftians	20	11	5	4	54	31	38
City of London	20	11	2	7	46	45	35
Glyn Old Boys Res.	20	10	3	7	48	37	33
The Comets	20	7	3	10	41	61	24
Clapham O Xavs 'A'	20	7	1	12	48	52	22
Old Tiffinians Res.	20	6	3	11	47	60	21
Sinjuns Gramms 'A'	20	5	4	11	36	51	19
Old Dorkinians Res.	20	4	7	9	44	75	19
O Bromleians Res. *-3*	20	2	2	16	30	69	5

Division Two West	P	W	D	L	F	A	Pts
O Uffingtonians Res.	18	14	4	0	58	23	46
Old Kolsassians	18	13	1	4	65	27	40
Parkfield 'C'	18	11	3	4	55	38	36
Old Meadonians 'B'	18	8	2	8	41	38	26
Brent Res.	18	7	4	7	48	49	25
Old Uxonians Res.	18	6	6	6	40	48	24
H'stead Heathens Res.	18	6	1	11	31	42	19
Old Manorians 'B'	18	4	4	10	36	48	16
Old Salvatorians 'C'	18	4	1	13	33	67	13
London Airways	18	3	2	13	30	57	11

Division Three North	P	W	D	L	F	A	Pts
Ravenscroft O Boys	18	14	1	3	62	33	43
Enfield O Gramms 'A'	18	13	1	4	42	21	40
Davenant Wdrs OB	18	9	5	4	46	31	32
O Woodhouseians 'A'	18	8	5	5	47	41	29
Albanian 'B'	18	8	2	8	46	41	26
Southgate County 'A'	18	7	4	7	39	34	25
Hale End Athletic 'A'	18	6	4	8	44	46	22
Old Ignatian 'A'	18	5	2	11	45	60	17
Old Camdenians Res.	18	3	3	12	30	55	12
Latymer OB 'A'	18	2	3	13	25	64	9

Division Three South	P	W	D	L	F	A	Pts
Old Tenisonians 'A'	18	13	4	1	56	19	43
Old Meadonians 'C'	18	13	3	2	50	31	42
Old Paulines Res.	18	9	6	3	51	34	33
John Fisher OB Res.	18	7	6	5	47	29	27
Sinjuns Gramms 'B'	18	7	4	7	38	44	25
Old Wokingians 'A'	18	6	5	7	32	40	23
Old Suttonians 'B'	18	3	5	10	18	31	14
BBC	18	3	5	10	28	48	14
O Tiffinians 'A' *-3*	18	3	7	8	38	45	13
Old Sedcopians Res.	18	3	1	14	28	65	10

Division Three West	P	W	D	L	F	A	Pts
Old Challoners 'A'	20	11	6	3	68	37	39
Old Vaughanians 'B'	20	11	6	3	61	41	39
O Kingsburians Res. *-3*	20	10	8	2	64	38	35
Old Danes 'A' *-3*	20	11	4	5	62	37	34
Phoenix OB Res.	20	10	2	8	56	49	32
Old Meadonians 'D'	20	9	3	8	63	56	30
Parkfield 'D'	20	8	3	9	45	55	27
O Isleworthians 'A'	20	6	1	13	35	54	19
Old Manorians 'C'	20	6	0	14	37	55	18
Old Salvatorians 'D'	20	3	6	11	34	63	15
Holland Park OB	20	3	5	12	39	79	14

Division Four North	P	W	D	L	F	A	Pts
Mill Hill County OB	18	15	0	3	59	23	45
Leyton C'nty OB Res.	18	9	5	4	52	37	32
O Minchendenians Res	18	9	4	5	56	34	31
Old Aloysians 'C'	18	8	3	7	50	50	27
Old Buckwellians 'A'	18	7	5	6	42	45	26
Mayfield Athletic	18	8	1	9	43	37	25
Mill Hill Village Res.	18	6	4	8	42	40	22
Wood Green OB 'A'	18	5	4	9	35	44	19
Bealonians 'B'	18	5	2	11	40	63	17
Old Ignatian 'B'	18	3	2	13	28	74	11

Division Four South	P	W	D	L	F	A	Pts
Witan Res.	18	13	1	4	60	33	40
Old Strandians	18	11	1	6	56	40	34
Centymca Res.	18	10	4	4	36	24	34
Wandsworth Boro' Res.	18	10	3	5	67	38	33
Economicals 'A'	18	8	3	7	46	37	27
Old Josephians Res.	18	8	3	7	42	47	27
Old St Marys Res.	18	6	3	9	36	50	21
Old Wokingians 'B'	18	5	3	10	42	49	18
Old Suttonians 'C'	18	4	1	13	29	62	13
Sinjuns Gramms 'C'	18	3	2	13	34	68	11

Division Four West	P	W	D	L	F	A	Pts
Phoenix OB 'A'	16	13	3	0	83	20	42
Birkbeck College	16	12	0	4	70	34	36
C'l Manning OB Res.	16	10	1	5	60	40	31
Old Kingsburians 'A'	16	8	2	6	58	48	26
Ealing Association	16	7	2	7	35	35	23
O Magdalenians Res.	16	7	2	7	33	45	23
Old Challoners 'B'	16	5	1	10	25	53	16
Old Vaughanians 'C'	16	2	1	13	25	67	7
London Welsh Res.	16	1	2	13	18	65	5

Old Salvatorians 'E' – record expunged

Division Five North	P	W	D	L	F	A	Pts
Old Parmiterians 'C'	18	14	1	3	74	29	43
Mill Hill C'nty OB Res.	18	13	0	5	69	30	39
Old Aloysians 'D'	18	11	1	6	52	32	34
Bealonians 'C'	18	9	4	5	39	29	31
Enfield O Gramms 'B'	18	9	3	6	44	42	30
UCL Academicals 'C'	18	8	1	9	48	40	25
Wood Green OB 'B'	17	7	2	8	45	35	23
Old Hendonians	18	6	1	11	37	72	19
O W'dh'seians 'B' -3	17	4	1	12	25	52	10
Mayfield Ath Res.	18	1	0	17	17	89	3

Division Five South	P	W	D	L	F	A	Pts
Old Josephians 'A'	18	14	0	4	67	37	42
O Guildfordians Res.	18	11	1	6	46	33	34
Reigatians 'A'	18	10	2	6	46	38	32
F'ham C'mpt'n OB Res	18	8	4	6	36	41	28
Sinjuns Gramms 'D'	18	9	0	9	48	54	27
Clapham O Xavs 'B'	18	7	3	8	40	44	24
Old Wokingians 'C'	18	6	4	8	32	35	22
Glyn Old Boys 'A'	18	7	0	11	39	48	21
Old Dorkinians 'A'	18	5	3	10	51	60	18
John Fisher OB 'A'	18	3	3	12	42	57	12

Division Five West	P	W	D	L	F	A	Pts
Ealing Assoc. Res.	18	14	2	2	78	35	44
Old Kolsassians Res.	18	14	1	3	80	31	43
Brent 'A'	18	12	3	3	57	31	39
Phoenix OB 'B'	18	11	1	6	69	37	34
Old Vaughanians 'D'	18	8	2	8	50	50	26
Old Manorians 'D'	18	7	2	9	39	43	23
Cardinal Man. OB 'A'	18	6	4	8	53	75	22
Old Isleworthians 'B'	18	5	2	11	36	60	17
Old Kingsburians 'B'	18	2	2	14	35	89	8
Old Uffingtonians 'A'	18	1	1	16	35	81	4

Division Six North	P	W	D	L	F	A	Pts
Old Buckwellians 'B'	18	13	3	2	60	31	42
Southgate County 'B'	18	13	0	5	66	25	39
Old Camdenians 'A'	18	11	5	2	55	30	38
O Minchendenians 'A'	18	9	3	6	67	52	30
Albanian 'C'	18	7	6	5	50	45	27
Egbertian 'B'	18	6	3	9	48	48	21
Mill Hill C'y OB 'A'	18	6	3	9	47	49	21
Old Edmontonians 'B'	18	6	0	12	50	73	18
QM College OB 'A'	18	4	5	9	46	68	17
Ravenscroft OB Res.	18	0	2	16	31	99	2

Division Six South	P	W	D	L	F	A	Pts
Shene O Grams Res.	18	15	3	0	72	18	48
Old Thorntonians Res.	18	10	3	5	59	32	33
Glyn Old Boys 'B'	18	10	3	5	38	37	33
Old Tiffinians 'B'	18	9	3	6	43	34	30
Chertsey O Sales. Res.	18	7	5	6	49	44	26
John Fisher OB 'B'	18	7	1	10	51	65	22
Old Suttonians VI	18	5	5	8	54	53	20
Sinjuns Gramms 'E'	18	6	2	10	38	55	20
Old Josephians 'B'	18	3	3	12	31	56	12
BBC Res. -3	18	4	0	14	29	70	9

Division Seven North	P	W	D	L	F	A	Pts
O Tollingtonians Res.	18	13	4	1	68	22	43
Mill Hill C'ty OB 'B'	18	10	5	3	63	47	35
Old Gladstonians	18	9	5	4	65	40	32
Leyton County OB 'A'	18	9	5	4	49	30	32
Mill Hill Village 'A'	18	10	1	7	59	45	31
Old Pamiterians 'D'	18	9	2	7	53	41	29
UCL Academicals 'D'	18	6	0	12	45	66	18
L'dn Hosp OB Res. -3	18	5	3	10	37	54	15
Bealonians 'D'	18	4	1	13	22	68	13
Southgate County 'C'	18	1	2	15	28	76	5

Division Seven South	P	W	D	L	F	A	Pts
Old Paulines 'A'	18	10	4	4	45	33	34
Old Suttonians 'E'	18	11	0	7	59	38	33
Old Meadonians 'E'	18	9	3	6	38	34	30
Clapham O Xavs 'C'	18	8	4	6	46	42	28
City of London Res.	18	8	3	7	28	25	27
O Guildfordians 'A'	18	7	3	8	34	43	24
Centymca 'A'	18	7	2	9	34	36	23
Old Bromleians 'A'	18	6	4	8	42	44	22
Old Wokingians 'D'	18	5	7	6	35	49	22
Reigatians 'B'	18	3	2	13	26	43	11

Division Eight North	P	W	D	L	F	A	Pts
Wood Green OB 'C'	16	11	3	2	52	25	36
Leyton C'nty OB 'B'	16	10	2	4	39	31	32
O Minchendenians 'B'	16	9	2	5	69	35	29
O Woodhouseians 'C'	16	7	5	4	32	23	26
Davenant W Res. -1	16	8	2	6	56	41	25
Latymer OB 'B' -6	16	7	3	6	32	38	18
Albanian 'D'	16	4	3	9	40	63	15
UCL Academicals 'E'	16	3	1	12	27	50	10
Old Camdenians 'B'	16	2	1	13	25	66	7

Division Eight South	P	W	D	L	F	A	Pts
Old Guildfordians 'B'	18	11	3	4	40	23	36
Old Sedcopians 'A'	18	11	2	5	54	31	35
Old Meadonians 'F'	18	9	6	3	52	22	33
Old Thorntonians 'A'	18	9	4	5	46	34	31
Glyn Old Boys 'C'	18	8	5	5	47	36	29
W'dsworth Boro 'A'	18	5	5	8	34	37	20
Old Dorkinians 'B'	18	5	4	9	26	45	19
F'ham C'mpt'n OB 'A'	18	5	3	10	24	40	18
Old Wokingians 'E'	18	5	2	11	30	56	17
Old Suttonians 'F'	18	4	2	12	31	60	14

Division Nine North	P	W	D	L	F	A	Pts
Old Parmiterians 'D'	14	10	0	4	34	18	30
O Minchendenians 'C'	14	8	0	6	61	49	24
Ravenscroft OB 'A'	14	7	1	6	40	42	22
Enfield O Gramms 'C'	14	6	2	6	37	34	20
Bealonians 'E'	14	6	0	8	38	46	18
Old Ignatian 'C'	14	5	1	8	31	37	16
O Edmontonians 'C' -3	14	6	1	7	39	46	16
Mill Hill C'ty OB 'C'	14	4	3	7	37	45	15

Division Nine South	P	W	D	L	F	A	Pts
Economicals 'B'	18	11	3	4	67	36	36
M'ham O Box Res.	18	10	3	5	62	46	33
Old Whitgiftians Res.	18	9	2	7	50	37	29
Old Bromleians 'B'	18	9	1	8	37	38	28
Old St Marys 'A'	18	8	2	8	35	33	26
BBC 'A'	18	7	5	6	38	42	26
Shene Old Grams 'A'	18	7	4	7	31	30	25
Reigatians 'C'	18	6	2	10	26	40	20
Old Dorkinians 'C'	18	6	2	10	40	68	20
Old Tiffinians 'C'	18	4	2	12	41	57	14

Division Ten South	P	W	D	L	F	A	Pts
John Fisher OB 'C'	18	12	3	3	70	27	39
Old Tenisonians 'B'	18	11	2	5	57	38	35
Old Sedcopians 'B'	18	10	4	4	53	32	34
Old St Marys 'B'	18	9	2	7	55	45	29
Old Meadonians 'G'	18	8	2	8	34	54	26
Old Guildfordians 'C'	18	7	2	9	41	35	23
Sinjuns Gramms 'F'	18	7	2	9	36	46	23
Old Paulines 'B'	18	6	1	11	46	54	19
Old Wokingians 'F'	18	4	4	10	29	61	16
Reigatians 'D'	18	4	2	12	36	65	14

Division Eleven South	P	W	D	L	F	A	Pts
Kings Old Boys 'A'	21	18	0	3	86	24	54
F'm Compton OB 'B'	21	16	1	4	78	33	49
Old Strandians Res.	21	16	0	5	75	31	48
Old Meadonians 'H'	21	11	2	8	51	47	35
Old Guildfordians 'D'	21	6	1	14	39	76	19
Sinjuns Gramms 'G'	21	5	2	14	34	48	17
Reigatians 'E'	21	4	4	13	40	75	16
Old Suttonians 'G'	21	3	0	18	33	102	9

ANDOVER & DISTRICT LEAGUE

	P	W	D	L	F	A	Pts
Borough Arms	24	21	1	2	89	36	64
Wherwell	24	18	2	4	108	46	56
Ludgershall Res.	24	17	2	5	83	28	53
Chestnut Tree +1	24	15	2	7	94	40	48
ABC United	24	13	5	6	82	42	44
Burghclere	24	11	6	7	83	62	39
Picket Piece Spts/Soc	24	9	6	9	48	58	33
Parkes Brown -3	24	8	4	12	57	84	25
Vitacress	24	6	4	14	37	65	22
King's Somborne	24	5	6	13	37	83	21
Stannah -1	24	5	4	15	35	58	18
Whitchurch Utd 'A'	24	5	1	18	31	98	16
Over Wallop	24	1	1	22	26	110	4

ANGLESEY LEAGUE

	P	W	D	L	F	A	Pts
Amlwch Town	20	14	5	1	78	31	47
Pentraeth	20	13	5	2	72	33	44
Gwalchmai	20	11	4	5	63	42	37
Holyhead Gwelfor Ath.	20	10	6	4	65	39	36
Llanerchymedd	20	9	6	5	57	30	33
Bodedern Res.	20	10	3	7	40	39	33
Conwy United Res.	20	7	2	11	47	80	23
Llandudno Junc. Res.	20	5	4	11	37	53	19
Llangoed & District	20	4	2	14	29	66	14
Llandegfan	20	3	3	14	37	67	12
Llanfairpwll Res.	20	2	4	14	38	83	10

AYLESBURY & DISTRICT LEAGUE

Premier Division	P	W	D	L	F	A	Pts
Bedgrove United	20	15	2	3	45	16	47
Aston Park	20	13	3	4	65	29	42
Long Marston	20	13	3	4	66	34	42
Aston Clinton Res.	20	12	3	5	54	32	39
Rockwood	20	11	2	7	70	51	35
Wingrave	20	8	1	11	37	47	25
Elmhurst	20	7	3	10	49	54	24
Bierton	20	6	4	10	44	62	22
Northchurch	20	4	5	11	37	64	17
Halifax	20	3	4	13	29	60	13
Jakeman Sports	20	1	4	15	22	69	7

Division One	P	W	D	L	F	A	Pts
Wendover	22	16	2	4	78	33	50
Bedgrove Dynamos	22	16	2	4	70	33	50
St Johns	22	13	6	3	69	35	45
Bedgrove Utd Res.	22	14	2	6	52	42	44
Mandeville Old Boys	22	13	2	7	66	56	41
Bierton Res.	22	9	1	12	53	78	28
Oving	22	8	2	12	49	57	26
Cheddington	22	7	5	10	37	53	26
Waddesdon	22	7	2	13	53	51	23
Brittania	22	7	1	14	37	46	22
Long Marston Res.	22	4	5	13	43	65	17
Cross Keys	22	3	0	19	22	80	9

Division Two	P	W	D	L	F	A	Pts
Dairy Maid	24	17	3	4	94	31	54
Black Horse	24	14	4	6	75	43	46
Fairford Leys	24	14	4	6	71	39	46
Bedgrove Dyn. Res.	24	14	3	7	81	47	45
Aston Clinton 'A'	24	13	6	5	76	45	45
Quainton	24	13	5	6	70	51	44
New Zealand	24	14	1	9	77	42	43
Wingrave Res.	24	12	2	10	52	56	38
Kimble Cricketers	24	9	2	13	50	43	29
Ludgershall	24	7	2	15	34	90	23
AC Meadowcroft	24	5	1	18	21	70	16
St Johns Res.	24	3	3	18	38	90	12
Waddesdon Res.	24	2	2	20	23	115	8

BANBURY & LORD JERSEY FA

Premier Division	P	W	D	L	F	A	Pts
Chasewell Park	22	17	5	0	67	22	56
Steeple Aston	22	16	5	1	58	27	53
Bishops Itchington	22	14	4	4	83	39	46
Bodicote Sports	22	14	4	4	55	25	46
Hethe	22	11	2	9	70	56	35
Cropredy	22	8	6	8	44	44	30
Hanwell Atletico	22	8	0	14	43	47	24
Deddington	22	7	3	12	39	54	24
Arncott	22	6	3	13	34	55	21
Kineton SC	22	5	3	14	30	70	18
Wroxton Sports	22	4	2	16	34	72	14
Broughton/N New'ton	22	2	3	17	27	73	9

Division One	P	W	D	L	F	A	Pts
Finmere	22	18	4	0	83	15	58
Hornton	22	16	2	4	65	37	50
St Johns	22	11	3	8	47	58	36
Barford United	22	10	5	7	64	56	35
Heyford Athletic 'A'	22	11	1	10	73	49	34
Merton Mustangs	22	9	3	10	51	47	30
Fenny Compton	22	9	3	10	45	57	30
Cropredy Res.	22	8	3	11	30	60	27
Drayton Village	22	7	4	11	53	53	25
Bishops Itchington Res.	22	7	1	14	45	67	22
Decoma Sybex	22	4	7	11	55	69	19
Abba Athletic	22	3	2	17	40	83	11

Division Two	P	W	D	L	F	A	Pts
Heyford United	26	21	1	4	112	47	64
Souldern	26	21	0	5	80	30	63
Ruscote	26	20	1	5	87	39	61
KEA	26	16	2	8	79	58	50
Wroxton Res.	26	13	2	11	62	61	41
Bloxham	26	12	4	10	60	55	40
Banbury Irish	26	8	9	9	56	56	33
Steeple Aston Res.	26	9	5	12	40	53	32
Deddington Res.	26	9	4	13	56	63	31
Bodicote Res.	26	9	3	14	45	65	30
Heyford Athletic 'B'	26	6	7	13	56	86	25
Cropredy 'A'	26	6	4	16	40	88	22
Adderbury Park Res.	26	6	3	17	46	63	21
Finmere Res.	26	3	1	22	49	104	10

BASINGSTOKE & DISTRICT LEAGUE

Premier Division	P	W	D	L	F	A	Pts
New Inn	16	13	3	0	66	15	42
R & B Sports	16	13	1	2	47	14	40
Oakley Athletic	16	8	2	6	30	34	26
Bramley United	16	7	2	7	41	35	23
B'stoke Labour Club	16	6	3	7	30	43	21
Hook	16	6	2	8	27	36	20
AFC Aldermaston Res.	16	5	2	9	28	42	17
Oakridge West	16	3	3	10	18	32	12
Preston Candover	16	1	2	13	14	50	5

Division One	P	W	D	L	F	A	Pts
Sainsbury Staff Ass.	16	12	2	2	71	29	38
Rangers	16	12	1	3	47	15	37
Bramley United Res.	16	9	4	3	39	27	31
AFC Aldermaston 'A'	16	7	5	4	32	22	26
AFC Popley	16	5	3	8	33	50	18
Laarsens	16	5	2	9	34	37	17
Tadley Calleva 'A'	16	5	2	9	20	28	17
Silchester United *-1*	16	3	5	8	20	37	13
Headley Athletic	16	1	2	13	22	73	5

Division Two	P	W	D	L	F	A	Pts
Oakley Athletic Res.	22	17	5	0	70	16	56
Hook Res.	22	17	3	2	97	30	54
AFC Berg	22	16	0	6	94	49	48
R & B Sports Res. *-1*	22	13	2	7	74	34	40
Herriard Sports	22	10	4	8	45	59	34
Rangers Res.	22	9	4	9	57	58	31
Chineham	22	9	3	10	45	59	30
AFC Aldermaston 'B'	22	8	5	9	45	40	29
Overton United 'A'	22	6	3	13	38	60	21
Sherborne St John Ath	22	4	3	15	36	76	15
Sherfield	22	3	3	16	31	75	12
Heathpark	22	2	1	19	19	95	7

BATH & DISTRICT LEAGUE

Division One	P	W	D	L	F	A	Pts
Crown Sports	16	14	2	0	62	8	44
University of Bath	16	12	1	3	49	19	37
Cutters Friday Res.	16	9	2	5	41	32	29
WESA	16	7	4	5	39	29	25
Bath Spa University	16	6	2	8	29	41	20
Oval Sports	16	6	1	9	32	50	19
Aces SSJ	16	5	3	8	28	36	18
Sportzcoach United	16	2	3	11	34	63	9
Keynsham Town 'A'	16	1	2	13	9	45	5

Odd Down 'A' – record expunged

Division Two	P	W	D	L	F	A	Pts
University of Bath Res.	22	17	2	3	75	22	53
CCB United	22	17	1	4	105	44	52
Saltford Res.	22	17	1	4	55	21	52
Odd Down 'B'	22	13	3	6	86	49	42
Fry Club Old Boys	22	10	0	12	42	46	30
Oldfield Sports	22	9	3	10	31	44	30
C S Filos	22	7	3	12	32	46	24
Stothert & Pitt	22	8	0	14	32	59	24
Chew Valley	22	7	1	14	30	56	22
Freshford Sports	22	7	1	14	44	73	22
Timsbury Ath 'A'	22	7	0	15	32	63	21
Oval Sports Res.	22	5	1	16	29	70	16

Newton & Corston – record expunged

Division Three	P	W	D	L	F	A	Pts
Bath Arsenal	24	20	1	3	95	36	61
Fairfield Pk Rangers	24	15	5	4	93	45	50
Claverton Academical	24	14	4	6	76	42	46
AFC Bath Rangers	24	13	5	6	67	47	44
Westwood United	24	14	1	9	101	60	43
FILOS	24	12	3	9	79	70	39
Cutters Friday 'A'	24	9	7	8	43	54	34
Wesco United	24	10	3	11	55	62	33
Aces SSJ Res.	24	9	3	12	63	65	30
Westfield 'A'	24	7	4	13	30	69	25
Bath Post Office	24	6	1	17	50	77	19
Staplemead Sports	24	5	1	18	38	87	16
Crown/Anch W'on Res.	24	2	2	20	39	115	8

BIRMINGHAM AMATEUR FOOTBALL ALLIANCE

Premier Division	P	W	D	L	F	A	Pts
BBGR	26	18	5	3	64	33	59
Sutton United	26	15	7	4	48	25	52
Handsworth GSOB	26	15	6	5	62	26	51
Wake Green Amateurs	26	15	3	8	43	32	48
Village	26	13	5	8	49	46	44
Penncroft	26	9	7	10	39	41	34
Ajax United	26	8	6	12	42	45	30
CPA Erdington Star	26	8	6	12	36	41	30
Shirley Athletic	26	6	9	11	34	55	27
Silhill	26	6	8	12	44	47	26
Cresconians	26	7	5	14	34	58	26
Colinthians	26	6	5	15	36	47	23
Old Wulfrunians *-8*	26	6	11	9	37	46	21
Kynoch IMI	26	4	9	13	28	54	21

Division One	P	W	D	L	F	A	Pts
Boldmere Steelers	26	18	6	2	80	18	60
Woodbourne Sports	26	18	4	4	94	28	58
Smiths Wood	25	13	4	8	80	51	43
Sutton United Res.	26	12	6	8	57	40	42
Kings Norton Celtic	26	11	8	7	57	44	41
Village Res.	26	11	8	7	45	42	41
AFC Somers	26	10	6	10	47	56	36
West Midlands Travel	26	9	8	9	52	44	35
Solihull Gas	26	10	4	12	49	59	34
Parkfield Amateurs	26	8	6	12	56	62	30
Britannic Assurance	26	7	9	10	47	55	30
Aston Rangers	25	6	6	13	49	79	24
West Hagley Res.	26	4	3	19	30	124	15
Old Nortonians	26	3	4	19	46	87	13

Division Two	P	W	D	L	F	A	Pts
Billesley United	22	17	0	5	67	31	51
Walsall Phoenix	22	13	7	2	68	31	46
Acocks Green	22	14	2	6	45	31	44
University Barbarians	22	13	4	5	48	20	43
Wake Green Am Res.	22	12	2	8	41	39	38
Handsw'th GSOB Res.	22	11	2	9	42	38	35
Old Wulfrunians Res.	22	9	3	10	38	52	30
Eccleston & Hart	22	5	6	11	43	53	21
Village 'A'	22	6	3	13	31	45	21
Britannia Old Boys	22	4	5	13	48	70	17
Airmark	22	5	1	16	25	51	16
Silhill Res.	22	4	3	15	33	68	15

Moxley Old Boys, Welwyn – records expunged

Division Three	P	W	D	L	F	A	Pts
Erin Go Bragh	26	20	2	4	95	33	62
Flamengo	25	18	4	3	87	26	58
Malremo Rangers	26	18	1	7	63	36	55
Wondervaults	23	14	4	5	55	35	46
FCS Lasermail	26	12	1	13	69	72	37
Wake Green Ams 'A'	25	9	6	10	58	57	33
Ilsley Old Boys	26	9	4	13	49	56	31
Sutton United 'A'	26	8	7	11	44	56	31
Shirley Athletic Res.	25	8	4	13	53	73	28
Silhill 'A'	26	7	4	15	54	77	25
Colinthians Res.	24	7	2	15	33	57	23
Dosthill Boys Club	26	6	5	15	48	76	23
GNG Smethwick *-6*	22	8	4	10	38	59	22
Walsall Phoenix Res.	26	6	4	16	49	82	22

Division Four	P	W	D	L	F	A	Pts
Cresconians Res.	24	17	4	3	88	29	55
Aston Detached	24	17	3	4	99	44	54
Aston Youth F & N	24	16	3	5	72	37	51
Inter Vaughans	24	12	4	8	66	47	40
Castle Bromwich Alb	24	11	6	7	45	48	39
MG Star	24	12	2	10	52	41	38
Willclare Sports	24	11	4	9	55	64	37
Welwyn Res.	24	11	2	11	50	63	35
Village 'B'	24	8	3	13	39	58	27
CPA Erd'ton Star Res.	24	8	2	14	37	61	26
Parkfield Am Res.	24	4	4	16	36	61	16
Old Wulfrunians 'A'	24	3	4	17	33	82	13
Glades Athletic *-3*	24	4	3	17	43	80	12

Division Five	P	W	D	L	F	A	Pts
St Francis FC	26	19	7	0	79	15	64
Britannic Res.	26	17	5	4	59	29	56
Sikh Hunter NBoys *-3*	26	17	6	3	71	36	54
Crusaders	26	16	5	5	74	39	53
Desi 2	26	10	8	8	60	49	38
Shere Punjab	26	12	2	12	58	47	38
Shirley Athletic 'A'	26	10	8	8	54	47	38
Manchester Wdrs	26	11	2	13	47	74	35
Pathfinder	26	10	3	13	40	48	33
Sutton United 'B'	26	7	5	14	41	60	26
Wood Wanderers	26	6	6	14	32	57	24
Old Nortonians Res.	26	5	5	16	49	71	20
Birmingham Citadel	26	4	5	17	42	92	17
Wylde Gn Wdrs *-3*	26	2	5	19	33	75	8

Division Six	P	W	D	L	F	A	Pts
Great Barr	24	18	5	1	61	27	59
IDQ	24	18	3	3	70	29	57
Inter Quinton	24	17	0	7	87	45	51
Bearwood Athletic	24	14	1	9	66	44	43
Bustleholme Athletic	24	12	6	6	75	40	42
Willclare Fujitsu Res.	24	12	2	10	67	57	38
Handsw'th GSOB 'A'	24	10	2	12	66	57	32
Acocks Green Ath.	24	9	5	10	65	58	32
Cresconians 'A'	24	10	1	13	54	69	31
Silhill 'B'	24	8	2	14	43	69	26
Colinthians 'A'	24	5	2	17	40	79	17
The Clock	24	4	4	16	32	80	16
Kingshurst Phoenix	24	2	1	21	32	104	7

Division Seven	P	W	D	L	F	A	Pts
Athletic Sparkhill	24	21	2	1	75	23	65
Coleshill Celtic	24	16	2	6	93	44	50
Cable & Wireless	24	15	3	6	77	40	48
Rubery	24	14	3	7	89	41	45
Asgard Rovers	24	13	6	5	69	32	45
Coton Green Res.	24	12	3	9	44	41	39
Alcoa Europe	24	12	2	10	85	47	38
Walsall Phoenix 'A'	24	10	4	10	73	55	34
Wythall Athletic	24	9	1	14	61	78	28
Handsw'th GSOB 'B'	24	7	3	14	48	76	24
Tamworth QEOB	24	3	3	18	30	108	12
Birmingham Stars	24	3	3	18	36	128	12
Aston '76	24	3	1	20	26	93	10

BOSTON LEAGUE

Premier Division	P	W	D	L	F	A	Pts
Billinghay Athletic	20	17	2	1	53	15	53
Croft United	20	13	2	5	55	35	41
Spilsby Town	20	12	1	7	54	45	37
Coningsby	20	8	7	5	44	40	31
Swineshead Institute	20	9	2	9	44	42	29
Skegness Town Res.	20	7	4	9	47	42	25
Boston Town Colts	20	7	3	10	30	29	24
Wyberton Res.	20	8	0	12	43	53	24
Kirton Town	20	5	4	11	34	58	19
Wrangle United	20	4	4	12	34	57	16
North Sea United	20	3	5	12	37	59	14

Division One	P	W	D	L	F	A	Pts
Sleaford Town Res.	22	20	1	1	100	17	61
Gedney Drove End	22	18	0	4	81	22	54
Old Doningtonians	22	13	1	8	62	54	40
Swineshead Inst. Res.	22	11	3	8	47	41	36
Spalding Town	22	12	0	10	44	54	36
Fishtoft *+1*	22	9	4	9	38	40	32
Old Leake	22	9	3	10	45	50	30
Spilsby Town Res.	22	8	2	12	51	57	26
Tydd St Mary	22	8	1	13	47	52	25
Holbeach Bank	22	6	2	14	44	87	20
Fosdyke	22	5	2	15	38	88	17
Sutterton	22	3	1	18	28	63	10

Division Two	P	W	D	L	F	A	Pts
West End Tigers	20	16	2	2	56	26	50
Westside Rangers	20	11	7	2	74	32	40
Spalding Harriers	20	10	7	3	39	25	37
Mareham United	20	11	3	6	59	41	36
Park Road Old Boys	20	10	5	5	56	42	35
Wainfleet United	20	8	1	11	45	48	25
Freiston	20	6	5	9	40	59	23
Park United	20	7	0	13	42	54	21
Coningsby Res.	20	5	3	12	33	52	18
Black Bull United	20	4	2	14	28	59	14
Holbeach St Marks	20	2	5	13	31	65	11

Croft United Res. – record expunged

Division Three	P	W	D	L	F	A	Pts
Woodhall Spa Utd	22	18	3	1	92	22	57
Shodfriars	22	18	2	2	117	31	56
Kirton Town Res.	22	16	2	4	77	29	50
Old Doningtonians Res.	22	12	4	6	58	45	40
Holbeach United SC	22	8	4	10	46	49	28
East Region	22	8	3	11	62	59	27
Wrangle United Res.	22	8	2	12	57	77	26
Billinghay Ath Res.	22	7	4	11	54	62	25
West Pinchbeck	22	6	1	15	39	92	19
Park United Res.	22	4	6	12	32	88	18
Friskney	22	4	5	13	33	66	17
Mareham Utd Res.	22	2	6	14	32	79	12

Sibsey – record expunged

BOURNEMOUTH LEAGUE

Division One	P	W	D	L	F	A	Pts
Southbourne	20	15	2	3	47	18	47
Suttoners Civil	20	15	1	4	47	20	46
West Moors	20	13	2	5	54	29	41
Sway	20	11	5	4	43	24	38
Westover B'mouth	20	10	6	4	44	24	36
B'mouth Electric	20	8	7	5	32	25	31
Hamworthy Rec Res.	20	6	4	10	28	43	22
Redlynch/Woodfalls U	20	4	4	12	27	41	16
Redhill Rangers	20	2	7	11	27	49	13
Trinidad Dorset Knob	20	3	3	14	23	50	12
Fordingbridge Turks	20	1	3	16	16	65	6

Division Two	P	W	D	L	F	A	Pts
Lymington/Pennington	22	15	2	5	69	29	47
Bournemouth Res. -2	22	12	7	3	55	27	41
Old Oakmeadians	22	11	7	4	62	32	40
Magpies/Woolsbridge	22	10	5	7	49	41	35
B'mouth Electric Res.	22	9	7	6	48	40	34
AFC Burton	22	8	5	9	45	40	29
Verwood Town Res.	22	8	3	11	47	47	27
Westover B'mouth Res.	22	7	4	11	52	70	25
AFC Highcliffe	22	7	2	13	42	58	23
Mploy	22	7	2	13	45	84	23
Urban B'mouth *-3*	22	6	5	11	36	59	20
Parley Sports	22	5	5	12	36	59	20

Division Three	P	W	D	L	F	A	Pts
Ferndown Town	22	16	4	2	70	27	52
Suttoners Civil Res. -3	22	16	4	2	58	23	49
Harrington United	22	13	2	7	50	32	41
Bisterne United	22	11	4	7	51	35	37
Sway Res.	22	9	6	7	43	42	33
St Mary's FC	22	9	4	9	42	43	31
JP Morgan	22	9	3	10	46	51	30
Holt United Res.	22	8	5	9	44	36	29
Lym/New Milton 'A'	22	7	4	11	36	42	25
Redlynch/W'df's Res.	22	5	4	13	29	57	19
Queens Park Athletic	22	2	7	13	29	60	13
B'mouth Sports Res.	22	2	3	17	34	84	9

Division Four	P	W	D	L	F	A	Pts
Slades Farm	20	16	2	2	87	28	50
Mudeford Mens Club	20	14	4	2	62	20	46
AFC Branksome *-3*	20	12	5	3	73	36	38
Moordown United	20	11	2	7	69	47	35
Westover B'm'th 'A'	20	9	4	7	48	36	31
AFC Bluebird	20	8	3	9	47	54	27
Talbot Rise	20	8	2	10	45	46	26
Queens Park Ath Res.	20	7	1	12	36	68	22
Old Oakmeadians Res.	20	5	3	12	40	60	18
Magpies/W'dge U Res.	20	4	2	14	45	68	14
Duke Of Wellington	20	2	0	18	35	124	6

Division Five	P	W	D	L	F	A	Pts
Twynham Rangers	24	18	2	4	133	49	56
Portcastrian *+3*	24	16	2	6	76	35	53
Walkford Stores	24	16	2	6	91	68	50
Stourvale	24	15	4	5	74	36	49
Alderholt	24	12	5	7	57	43	41
Burley	24	11	5	8	58	54	38
Winton CC	24	10	5	9	54	55	35
Phoenix	24	9	7	8	65	54	34
Griffin	24	7	6	11	55	79	27
Boscombe Celtic	24	5	4	15	52	85	19
Winton United	24	3	8	13	40	104	17
AFC Highcl. Res. *-3*	24	4	5	15	40	78	14
Parley Sports Res.	24	2	1	21	22	77	7

Division Six	P	W	D	L	F	A	Pts
St Andrews FC	24	20	2	2	109	40	62
Parkside Wanderers	24	18	4	2	77	33	58
Wessex Lions	24	15	3	6	78	32	48
Bisterne United Res.	24	15	1	8	76	41	46
N Milton Eag Res. *-1*	24	13	4	7	80	57	42
ELE	24	13	3	8	57	45	42
Pilot Sports Flyers	24	10	3	11	43	70	33
Southbourne Res.	24	9	2	13	63	70	29
Fifa Standards *-1*	24	9	2	13	63	68	28
Redlynch/W'df's 'A'	24	7	2	15	33	52	23
F'dingbridge T'ks Res.	24	5	3	16	36	73	18
Magpies/W'dge U 'A'	24	3	2	19	31	79	11
Phoenix Res.	24	3	1	20	30	116	10

BRIGHTON, HOVE & DISTRICT LEAGUE

Premier Division	P	W	D	L	F	A	Pts
Rottingdean Village	20	17	3	0	65	17	54
Montpelier Villa	20	16	1	3	75	24	49
Hanover	20	12	5	3	37	24	41
Master Tiles	20	10	5	5	39	31	35
Alpha Sports	20	10	3	7	49	44	33
American Express	20	6	8	6	31	31	26
O & G United	20	4	8	8	27	45	20
AFC St Georges	20	6	1	13	34	56	19
Rottingdean United	20	3	7	10	30	36	16
Brighton Electricity	20	2	4	14	33	66	10
Portslade Athletic	20	1	1	18	20	66	4

Division One	P	W	D	L	F	A	Pts
Blue House	18	14	2	2	68	28	44
Montpelier Villa Res.	18	11	3	4	50	24	36
Brighton Rangers	18	10	3	5	53	42	33
Legal & General	18	9	3	6	49	38	30
Southern Rangers OB	18	7	4	7	47	46	25
Coversure Athletic	18	6	5	7	31	43	23
FC Midlothians	18	6	1	11	38	70	19
Rottingdean Vill Res.	18	4	6	8	32	29	18
Midway	18	4	3	11	29	53	15
Harbour View	18	3	2	13	30	54	11

Division Two	P	W	D	L	F	A	Pts
Ovingdean	20	15	0	5	73	41	45
Real Conqueror	20	13	2	5	76	53	41
AFC Stadium	20	13	1	6	69	52	40
Brighton BBOB	20	10	4	6	68	57	34
Portslade Rangers	20	10	2	8	58	53	32
Four Corners	20	9	3	8	56	49	30
Whitehawk 'A'	20	7	6	7	43	56	27
Midway Res.	20	7	0	13	41	71	21
Lectern Sports	20	6	1	13	51	62	19
Portslade Ath Res.	20	4	3	13	37	57	15
AFC Cosmos	20	4	2	14	39	60	14

Division Three	P	W	D	L	F	A	Pts
Brighton Rangers Res.	18	12	3	3	56	23	39
CCK	18	11	2	5	47	27	35
PJ Panthers	18	8	5	5	60	45	29
Autopaints	18	9	2	7	48	43	29
AFC Stanley	18	8	4	6	39	45	28
Grand Parade	18	6	5	7	44	42	23
Portslade Sports	18	7	2	9	36	48	23
Ricardo	18	6	4	8	35	45	22
Rottingdean Dynamos	18	6	2	10	29	33	20
Montpelier Villa 'A'	18	2	1	15	25	68	7

BRISTOL & AVON LEAGUE

	P	W	D	L	F	A	Pts
Backwell Utd Colts	26	22	3	1	104	27	69
Dundry Athletic Res.	26	21	2	3	106	20	65
Long Ashton Res.	26	14	6	6	63	39	48
Broadwalk	26	13	5	8	73	46	44
Mendip United Res.	26	13	3	10	76	64	42
Lawrence Rovers	26	12	6	8	54	52	42
Hartwood Fathers	26	12	1	13	68	67	37
Crown Parkway *-3*	26	11	6	9	50	51	36
Bideford Old Boys	26	7	8	11	42	44	29
Henleaze Rovers	26	8	5	13	48	79	29
Severn Beach Fusion	26	6	5	15	33	67	23
Queens Sq. Wed *-3*	26	7	2	17	61	79	20
Wessex Wdrs Res.	26	6	2	18	39	80	20
AFC Apex	26	1	4	21	37	139	7

BRISTOL & DISTRICT LEAGUE

Senior Division	P	W	D	L	F	A	Pts
Talbot Knowle *+3*	24	18	2	4	90	27	59
Frampton Ath Rgrs	24	16	4	4	78	23	52
Nicholas Wdrs Res.	24	12	3	9	43	26	39
Shirehampton Res.	24	12	3	9	43	36	39
Crosscourt United	24	11	6	7	45	54	39
Pucklechurch Spts Res.	24	11	4	9	39	29	37
Westerleigh Sports	24	10	5	9	50	42	35
Knowle United	24	8	8	8	38	38	32
Mendip United	24	7	8	9	44	38	29
Sea Mills Park Res.	24	9	2	13	41	48	29
AXA Res.	24	7	3	14	47	59	24
Oldland Abb. Res. *-3*	24	7	5	12	45	60	23
DRG Stapleton Res.	24	1	1	22	23	146	4

Division One	P	W	D	L	F	A	Pts
Avonmouth Village	26	23	1	2	63	21	70
Longwell Gn Spts Res.	26	21	4	1	72	17	67
Hanham Athletic Res.	26	16	3	7	75	41	51
Bitton 'A'	26	15	2	9	58	45	47
Hallen 'A'	26	13	5	8	48	39	44
Made for Ever	26	11	5	10	46	48	38
Hartcliffe Res.	26	10	4	12	45	44	34
Hartcliffe C'nity Centre	26	9	4	13	48	66	31
FM Sports	26	9	1	16	49	61	28
Iron Acton Res.	26	8	2	16	36	49	26
Bendix	26	8	1	17	45	69	25
Highridge United 'A'	26	7	3	16	46	78	24
Stockw'd Breakaways	26	5	6	15	40	66	21
Hillfields OB Res.	26	4	5	17	42	69	17

Division Two	P	W	D	L	F	A	Pts
Lawrence Rovers Res.	26	22	2	2	76	24	68
Coalpit Heath	26	20	2	4	100	37	62
Soundwell Victoria	26	19	4	3	74	30	61
Cemex Wick Res.	26	18	3	5	58	31	57
Hambrook	26	14	5	7	68	49	47
Chipping Sodbury Res.	26	12	2	12	67	51	38
Shaftesbury Crus. Res.	26	10	3	13	45	58	33
St Pancras	26	8	3	15	60	66	27
Henbury OB 'A'	26	8	3	15	47	68	27
Seymour United Res.	26	7	3	16	47	68	24
Nicholas Wdrs 'A'	26	6	5	15	36	58	23
Sth Bristol C'ral Res.	26	7	2	17	34	80	23
AEK Boco Res.	26	5	5	16	36	73	20
Tilly Rangers	26	4	2	20	36	91	14

Division Three	P	W	D	L	F	A	Pts
Greyfriars Ath Res.	22	17	0	5	69	30	51
Roman Glass St G 'A'	22	16	3	3	63	27	51
Patchway Town 'A'	22	12	4	6	49	43	40
Longwell Gn Spts 'A'	22	12	2	8	52	41	38
Fry Club 'A'	22	11	4	7	57	48	37
Rangeworthy Res.	22	10	3	9	62	43	33
Miners Rangers	22	7	3	12	33	57	24
Winterbourne Utd 'A'	22	6	5	11	38	49	23
Totterdown Utd Res.	22	6	4	12	34	46	22
Frampton Ath Rgrs Res.	22	5	6	11	35	55	21
Brimsham Green Res.	22	4	8	10	34	46	20
Brislington Cricketers	22	3	4	15	27	68	13

Division Four	P	W	D	L	F	A	Pts
Hallen 'B'	26	20	1	5	74	26	61
Shirehampton 'A'	26	19	2	5	82	34	59
Old Sodbury	26	15	7	4	66	35	52
Olveston United Res.	26	14	5	7	49	29	47
Fishponds Ath Res.	26	14	3	9	66	57	45
Oakland	26	12	5	9	66	50	41
Hanham Athletic 'A'	26	10	7	9	55	57	37
AXA 'A'	26	9	7	10	52	52	34
Pucklechurch Spts 'A'	26	10	3	13	56	52	33
Westerleigh Spts Res.	26	8	7	11	46	50	31
Warmley Saints Res.	26	9	2	15	55	74	29
Hartcliffe 'A'	26	7	2	17	37	70	23
Fry Club 'B'	26	4	5	17	40	74	17
Henbury Old Boys 'B'	26	2	2	22	30	114	8

Division Five	P	W	D	L	F	A	Pts
Eden Grove	24	19	4	1	93	15	61
Stockwood Wanderers	24	17	1	6	87	46	52
Chipping Sodbury 'A'	24	16	2	6	65	25	50
Frampton Ath Rgrs 'A'	24	15	4	5	76	42	49
Made for Ever Res.	24	13	4	7	73	53	43
Oldland Abbot's 'A'	24	13	2	9	71	51	41
Bendix Res.	24	8	5	11	54	46	29
AEK Boco 'A'	24	8	3	13	36	57	27
Soundwell Vic. Res.	24	7	4	13	57	75	25
Cemex Wick 'A'	24	7	4	13	39	65	25
St Nicholas	24	6	3	15	55	74	21
St Pancras Res.	24	5	3	16	36	88	18
Sth Bristol Central 'A'	24	1	3	20	20	125	6

Division Six	P	W	D	L	F	A	Pts
Longwell Gn Spts 'B'	26	20	3	3	102	43	63
BAWA Aces	26	19	3	4	96	42	60
Air	26	18	4	4	89	48	58
Talbot Knowle Res.	26	14	5	7	67	51	47
Shaftesbury Crus. 'A'	26	12	6	8	71	48	42
AXA 'B'	26	11	5	10	60	61	38
Greyfriars Ath 'A'	26	11	4	11	71	60	37
Bradley Stoke Town	26	11	4	11	69	66	37
Coalpit Heath Res.	26	10	1	15	52	80	31
Impact Squad	26	8	2	16	55	70	26
Seymour United 'A'	26	8	2	16	39	78	26
Crosscourt Utd Res.	26	6	6	14	53	64	24
Little Thatch	26	7	0	19	50	87	21
Fishponds Ath 'A'	26	4	1	21	36	112	13

BRISTOL & SUBURBAN LEAGUE

Premier Division One	P	W	D	L	F	A	Pts
St Aldhelms	26	21	4	1	91	19	67
Broad Plain House OB	26	19	3	4	84	36	60
Glenside Five	26	17	7	2	67	16	58
Almondsbury Res.	26	16	2	8	65	34	50
Teyfant Athletic	26	13	6	7	56	33	45
B & W Avonside	26	12	5	9	67	50	41
De Veys	26	12	2	12	67	55	38
Fishponds Old Boys	26	10	5	11	47	39	35
Ashton United	26	9	2	15	54	62	29
Ridings High	26	8	4	14	44	52	28
Avonmouth	26	6	8	12	46	60	26
Bristol Telephones	26	7	3	16	47	80	24
Old Cothamians	26	4	4	18	47	77	16
Lawrence Weston	26	0	1	25	15	184	1

Premier Division Two	P	W	D	L	F	A	Pts
Stoke Gifford	28	20	5	3	83	24	65
Potterswood	28	19	2	7	78	36	59
Almondsbury Tn Res.	28	17	6	5	67	31	57
Golden Hill	28	17	4	7	67	40	55
Bristol Manor Fm Res.	28	14	4	10	69	45	46
Ashton Rangers	28	14	4	10	62	66	46
Cadbury Heath Res.	28	13	3	12	64	50	42
B'l Builders Supplies	28	12	4	12	54	52	40
Brislington 'A'	28	12	2	14	59	65	38
Whitchurch	28	11	2	15	51	73	35
Longwell Green OB	28	9	3	16	53	87	30
Totterdown P of B Res.	28	7	7	14	49	63	28
Hartcliffe Old Boys	28	7	6	15	49	77	27
Little Stoke	28	5	5	18	37	72	20
Corinthian Sports	28	3	3	22	24	85	12

Division One	P	W	D	L	F	A	Pts
Old Georgians	30	23	3	4	116	27	72
St Aldhelms Res.	30	22	6	2	101	35	72
Filton Athletic	30	18	4	8	86	52	58
Glenside Five Res.	30	17	5	8	65	49	56
T C Sports	30	16	5	9	68	47	53
Tyndalls Pk Rangers	30	14	2	14	67	51	44
Broad Plain H OB Res.	30	13	3	14	51	57	42
B & W Avonside Res.	30	12	5	13	53	59	41
Hengrove BC	30	10	10	10	49	50	40
Bristol Telephones Res.	30	10	8	12	54	64	38
Lockleaze	30	9	9	12	48	55	36
Ashton United Res.	30	9	7	14	59	68	34
Ridings High Res.	30	8	4	18	44	73	28
Bristol North West	30	9	0	21	59	73	27
Imperial Saints	30	6	7	17	52	94	25
Sefton Park	30	4	2	24	32	150	14

Division Two	P	W	D	L	F	A	Pts
CTK Southside	30	25	2	3	128	38	77
South Glos Old Boys	30	23	3	4	91	39	72
Astra Zeneca	30	19	4	7	101	43	61
Stoke Gifford Res.	30	18	7	5	73	43	61
Almondsbury 'A'	30	18	4	8	92	52	58
St Aldhelms 'A'	30	13	5	12	59	59	44
Fishponds OB Res.	30	12	5	13	65	74	41
Oldbury Crusaders	30	12	4	14	59	56	40
Tyth' Rocks Res. -6	30	13	4	13	66	61	37
Hengrove Old Boys	30	11	4	15	75	81	37
Avonmouth Res.	30	10	4	16	59	77	34
Cadbury Heath 'A'	30	9	4	17	52	78	31
Old Cothamians Res.	30	8	3	19	43	88	27
Rolls Royce	30	7	4	19	45	76	25
Thrissells Nomads	30	7	4	19	45	97	25
Parson Street OB	30	3	3	24	44	135	12

Division Three	P	W	D	L	F	A	Pts
Southmead Athletic	22	19	3	0	118	14	60
Totterdown P of B 'A'	22	15	4	3	70	40	49
Hartcliffe OB Res.	22	14	3	5	72	30	45
Ingleside	22	14	3	5	77	45	45
Wessex Wanderers	22	12	5	5	52	29	41
Little Stoke Res.	22	10	6	6	54	45	36
Unathletico	22	11	2	9	78	56	35
Teyfant Athletic Res.	22	5	4	13	36	63	19
Ashton United 'A'	22	6	1	15	30	79	19
Ridings High 'A'	22	4	0	18	34	84	12
Broad Plain H OB 'A'	22	2	4	16	34	87	10
St Annes Town	22	1	3	18	30	113	6

Division Four	P	W	D	L	F	A	Pts
Potterswood Res.	20	18	1	1	92	31	55
Brandon TT Sports	20	18	1	1	80	34	55
Old Georgians Res.	20	13	1	6	65	37	40
Fishponds OB 'A'	20	11	1	8	48	40	34
Astra Zeneca Res.	20	8	2	10	48	47	26
Bristol Telephones 'A'	20	8	2	10	64	68	26
Wanderers	20	7	3	10	47	58	24
Glenside Five 'A'	20	6	4	10	52	49	22
Lockleaze Res.	20	6	1	13	48	65	19
Oldbury Crusaders Res	20	6	0	14	35	73	18
Longwell Gn OB Res.	20	1	0	19	18	95	3

Division Five	P	W	D	L	F	A	Pts
Avonmouth Rangers	20	18	0	2	83	29	54
Fishponds OB 'B'	20	15	0	5	67	32	45
Southmead Ath Res.	20	13	3	4	72	35	42
T C Sports Res.	20	11	2	7	58	40	35
Whitchurch Res.	20	8	2	10	62	64	26
Stoke Gifford 'A'	20	5	8	7	38	44	23
Thrissells Nom. Res.	20	7	2	11	45	57	23
Filton Athletic Res.	20	6	4	10	39	48	22
Stoke Rangers	20	6	3	11	54	56	21
Imperial Saints Res.	20	6	3	11	33	82	21
Parson Street OB Res.	20	1	1	18	26	90	4

BRISTOL DOWNS LEAGUE

Division One	P	W	D	L	F	A	Pts
Retainers	26	19	3	4	64	22	60
Sneyd Park	26	17	4	5	64	23	55
Lawes Juniors	26	14	7	5	54	34	49
Portland Old Boys	26	13	5	8	55	51	44
Easton Cowboys	26	11	4	11	49	46	37
Durdham Down	26	10	6	10	52	54	36
Sporting Greyhound	26	9	7	10	44	44	34
Clifton St Vincents -3	26	10	7	9	39	39	34
Ashley	26	9	5	12	58	57	32
Bristol Juve	26	9	5	12	40	42	32
Clifton Rockets	26	8	7	11	27	48	31
Cotswool	26	7	4	15	35	52	25
Torpedo	26	6	6	14	38	47	24
Bristol Dynamos	26	4	2	20	28	88	14

Division Two	P	W	D	L	F	A	Pts
Hare-on-the-Hill	26	19	2	5	80	31	59
Bristol Barcelona	26	18	1	7	57	25	55
Sneyd Park Res.	26	15	3	8	51	39	48
Bohemia	26	14	4	8	69	49	46
Red Lion	26	15	1	10	63	60	46
Saints Old Boys	26	14	3	9	59	53	45
St Andrews	26	10	9	7	42	40	39
Torpedo Res.	26	8	7	11	35	50	31
Tebby	26	9	3	14	49	56	30
Luccombe Garage	26	8	5	13	48	50	29
Clifton St Vins Res.	26	8	4	14	45	56	28
Jamaica Bell	26	8	3	15	52	64	27
Portland OB Res.	26	7	5	14	45	64	26
Cotham Old Boys	26	2	4	20	21	79	10

Division Three	P	W	D	L	F	A	Pts
Hydez	26	20	2	4	54	24	62
Cabot Asset Finance	26	19	1	6	92	35	58
Bohemia Res.	26	16	3	7	84	53	51
Torpedo 'A'	26	14	3	9	64	40	45
Sneyd Park 'A'	26	14	0	12	74	58	42
LA Cricket	26	10	9	7	52	46	39
Retaines Res.	26	10	5	11	60	54	35
Cotswool Res.	26	11	2	13	40	55	35
Sporting Gr'yh'nd Res.	26	10	3	13	61	63	33
Easton Cowboys Res.	26	10	2	14	51	56	32
Clifton St Vincents 'A'	26	8	6	12	47	56	30
Ashley Res.	26	8	4	14	54	69	28
Bengal Tigers	26	7	1	18	46	84	22
Penpole Inn	26	3	3	20	34	120	12

Division Four	P	W	D	L	F	A	Pts
Jersey Rangers	30	22	4	4	102	41	70
Evergreen	30	18	3	9	97	64	57
Clifton Rockets Res.	30	17	5	8	86	53	56
Red Lion Res.	30	16	7	7	76	54	55
Saville Freights	30	17	4	9	75	57	55
Durdham Down Res.	30	13	6	11	71	62	45
Retainers 'A'	30	12	5	13	63	62	41
Hare-on-the-Hill Res.	30	11	5	14	58	72	38
Tebby Res.	30	11	4	15	65	74	37
Sneyd Park 'B'	30	10	7	13	58	67	37
West Town United	30	9	8	13	58	79	35
Beachcroft	30	11	1	18	52	76	34
Clifton St Vincents 'B'	30	8	8	14	61	80	32
Hydez Res.	30	8	6	16	75	87	30
Luccombe Garage Res.	30	8	5	17	51	81	29
Conham Rangers	30	7	6	17	47	86	27

BRISTOL PREMIER COMBINATION

Premier Division	P	W	D	L	F	A	Pts
Hanham Athletic	24	22	1	1	61	21	67
Hallen Res.	24	17	3	4	64	29	54
Bitton Res.	24	12	9	3	54	23	45
Shaftesbury Crusade	24	9	7	8	41	37	34
AEK Boco	24	10	4	10	36	40	34
Longshore	24	10	4	10	39	48	34
Cemex Wick	24	8	8	8	33	30	32
Totterdown United	24	9	3	12	39	39	30
Brimsham Green	24	8	4	12	30	37	28
Nicholas Wanderers	24	6	8	10	31	38	26
Highridge Utd Res.	24	6	3	15	23	49	21
Rangeworthy	24	5	2	17	44	73	17
Hartcliffe	24	4	4	16	32	63	16

Division One	P	W	D	L	F	A	Pts
Chipping Sodbury	26	19	3	4	61	29	60
Roman Glass St G Res.	26	14	3	9	46	37	45
Winterbourne Utd Res.	26	14	2	10	57	35	44
St Philips Marsh A S	26	13	1	12	54	50	40
Hillfields Old Boys	26	12	4	10	43	52	40
Patchway Town Res.	26	11	5	10	41	38	38
Olveston United	26	10	8	8	40	37	38
South Bristol Central	26	10	5	11	45	48	35
Greyfriars Athletic	26	10	4	12	61	54	34
Henbury OB Res.	26	9	7	10	46	45	34
Fishponds Athletic	26	9	7	10	47	48	34
Seymour United	26	8	4	14	43	47	28
Iron Acton	26	7	6	13	39	59	27
Warmley Saints	26	4	5	17	28	72	17

BROMLEY & DISTRICT LEAGUE

Premier Division	P	W	D	L	F	A	Pts
Erith '147	16	14	1	1	37	14	43
Hollington YPC	16	10	1	5	31	22	31
Unity FC	16	10	0	6	45	25	30
Anerley Athletic	16	6	3	7	34	38	21
Phoenix Sports Res. -1	16	7	1	8	32	38	21
Univ of Greenwich	16	6	1	9	28	34	19
Elite Res.	16	5	3	8	14	20	18
Stansfeld O/B 'A' -1	16	3	4	9	14	24	12
Old Addeyans Res.	16	3	2	11	18	38	11

Division One	P	W	D	L	F	A	Pts
Old Addeyans 'A'	18	13	2	3	52	18	41
Old Colfeians Res.	18	10	5	3	44	26	35
Seven Acre Spts Res.	18	10	5	3	38	30	35
South East Athletic	18	11	1	6	52	22	34
Rotherhithe	18	8	5	5	58	37	29
Erith '147 Res.	18	6	3	9	37	46	21
AFC Bromley	18	6	3	9	30	42	21
Hayeswood	18	5	2	11	35	51	17
Ex-Blues	18	5	0	13	25	59	15
Farnboro' OB G'ld 'B'	18	2	2	14	23	63	8

Division Two	P	W	D	L	F	A	Pts
AFC Mottingham Res.	22	17	1	4	96	29	52
Latter Day Saints	22	16	2	4	98	49	50
Barnet Wood	22	15	3	4	76	41	48
Chislehurst Dynamoes	22	11	6	5	62	42	39
New Bromleians Res.	22	12	3	7	65	46	39
South East 4	22	11	4	7	61	50	37
Highfield Rovers	22	8	1	13	42	56	25
Ex-Blues Res.	22	8	1	13	44	70	25
Heathfield	22	7	2	13	51	55	23
South Star	22	6	4	12	43	58	22
Old Colfeians 'B'	22	4	6	12	38	64	18
Penhill Standard Res.	22	0	1	21	24	140	1

BURTON & DISTRICT FA

Division One	P	W	D	L	F	A	Pts
Barton United	14	11	1	2	36	11	34
Stretton Eagles 2004	14	10	3	1	37	14	33
Lichfield Enots	14	10	1	3	31	15	31
Castle Hotel	14	5	2	7	32	31	17
Rolleston Cricket Club	14	5	2	7	31	33	17
Ashbourne Utd Res	14	4	3	7	24	30	15
Stretton Eagles	14	1	4	9	21	35	7
Lichfield Brenstar	14	1	2	11	11	54	5

Division Two	P	W	D	L	F	A	Pts
The Dart	16	14	2	0	82	20	44
Red Lion Horninglow	16	12	1	3	63	31	37
Barton United Res.	16	11	1	4	57	27	34
Jubilee Winshill	16	10	0	6	60	45	30
Newhall United Res.	16	5	2	9	37	55	17
Overseal St Matthews	16	4	4	8	36	50	16
The Sump	16	4	2	10	27	46	14
Branston Arms	16	2	3	11	28	68	9
The Wyggeston Hotel	16	2	1	13	28	76	7

Division Three	P	W	D	L	F	A	Pts
Netherseal St Peters	16	14	1	1	50	17	43
Beacon Park	16	11	2	3	40	14	35
Gresley Rovers Yth	16	10	1	5	54	33	31
Hammerwich	16	7	1	8	42	37	22
Red Lion H'glow Res.	16	7	1	8	43	50	22
The Seal Inn	16	6	2	8	34	40	20
Shobnall Sports	16	5	3	8	34	47	18
Madina	16	3	3	10	19	37	12
Ridware Swifts	16	2	0	14	26	67	6

BURY & DISTRICT LEAGUE

Division One	P	W	D	L	F	A	Pts
Black Eagles	18	15	1	2	91	19	46
The Rising Sun	18	11	1	6	43	32	34
Lawshall Sun	18	10	2	6	55	44	32
Karooze	18	9	3	6	43	33	30
Barons	18	9	2	7	54	42	29
The Bushell	18	8	3	7	42	40	27
Silver Spoon	18	6	3	9	34	46	21
The Fox	18	6	2	10	40	48	20
Brandon Town 'A'	18	4	1	13	30	82	13
Ixworth Pykkerell	18	2	2	14	26	72	8

Division Two	P	W	D	L	F	A	Pts
Westbury United	20	17	0	3	77	20	51
Jubilee '96	20	14	4	2	75	30	46
Priors Inn	20	13	3	4	67	21	42
Bartons	20	13	3	4	58	47	42
Elveden Phoenix	20	9	4	7	55	46	31
Sporting '87 Res.	20	8	4	8	33	33	28
The Rising Sun Res.	20	7	3	10	41	61	24
Ipswich Arms	20	6	3	11	39	61	21
Elephant & Castle	20	6	2	12	33	55	20
Black Boy	20	4	0	16	33	63	12
Beck Row	20	0	0	20	15	89	0

CAERNARFON & DISTRICT LEAGUE

Division One	P	W	D	L	F	A	Pts
Llanllyfni *-3*	28	20	6	2	85	43	63
Llanystumdwy	28	19	5	4	81	43	62
Trefor	28	17	7	4	84	43	58
Caernarfon Borough	28	16	3	9	78	39	51
Machno United	28	16	2	10	87	50	50
Rhiwlas	28	14	5	9	58	51	47
Llanrug Utd Res. *-3*	28	14	4	10	67	47	43
Pwllheli Res.	28	11	5	12	76	63	38
Llanberis Res.	28	10	4	14	61	64	34
Talysarn Celts	28	9	4	15	79	83	31
Mynydd Llandegai *-3*	28	9	6	13	51	56	30
Blaenau Amateurs Res.	28	8	5	15	52	86	29
Nefyn United Res.	28	7	6	15	44	56	27
Deiniolen *-3*	28	4	3	21	37	135	12
Penrhyndeudraeth	28	2	3	23	33	114	9

CENTRAL & SOUTH NORFOLK LEAGUE

Division One	P	W	D	L	F	A	Pts
Great Ryburgh	20	17	2	1	91	28	53
Yaxham	20	13	2	5	60	41	41
Toftwood United	20	12	3	5	75	37	39
Redgrave Rangers	20	10	4	6	51	32	34
Dereham Town 'A'	20	8	5	7	38	33	29
Hingham Athletic	20	8	2	10	49	44	26
Longham	20	6	5	9	45	52	23
Stoke Ferry	20	7	1	12	42	79	22
Swaffham Town 'A'	20	6	2	12	40	63	20
Tacolneston	20	5	4	11	37	57	19
Dickleburgh	20	2	2	16	37	99	8

Division Two	P	W	D	L	F	A	Pts
North Elmham	22	15	4	3	85	26	49
Feltwell United	22	14	5	3	59	20	47
Saham Toney	22	13	7	2	59	17	46
Mulbarton Wanderers	22	12	5	5	51	25	41
Rockland United	22	12	5	5	33	23	41
Bridgham United	22	10	5	7	71	49	35
Shropham United	22	11	2	9	67	66	35
East Harling Res.	22	5	6	11	49	66	21
Wendling	22	6	2	14	46	58	20
Necton Res.	22	6	2	14	32	59	20
Attleborough Tn 'A'	22	3	2	17	24	107	11
Morley Village Res.	22	2	1	19	26	86	7

Division Three	P	W	D	L	F	A	Pts
Shipdham	22	17	2	3	100	27	53
Dereham Posties	22	17	2	3	80	17	53
Yaxham Res.	24	17	1	6	90	48	52
Saham Toney Res.	24	15	3	6	57	39	48
Wymondham Tn 'A'	24	12	5	7	59	22	41
Palgrave United	24	12	2	10	93	68	38
Watton United 'A'	20	12	2	6	48	28	38
Hingham Ath Res.	24	9	3	12	77	80	30
Mattishall 'A'	24	9	2	13	48	65	29
West End	24	6	4	14	58	82	22
North Elmham Res.	24	6	2	16	49	74	20
Bawdeswell	24	3	6	15	43	70	15
Beetley	24	0	0	24	15	197	0

Shipdham and Dereham Posties declared joint champions, their results against Watton United 'A' being declared void

Division Four	P	W	D	L	F	A	Pts
Thetford Athletic	24	19	4	1	90	19	61
Foulsham Res.	24	16	6	2	79	34	54
Cherry Tree	24	16	2	6	66	45	50
Bunwell	24	13	5	6	86	50	44
Toftwood Utd Res.	24	12	4	8	62	46	40
Shipdham Res.	24	11	2	11	48	58	35
Rockland United Res.	24	10	4	10	35	50	34
Shropham United Res.	24	7	3	14	53	63	24
Longham Res.	24	7	3	14	38	74	24
Bintree	24	7	2	15	63	74	23
Cockers	24	6	3	15	44	82	21
Great Cressingham	24	4	6	14	39	71	18
Scarning	24	5	2	17	48	85	17

CHELTENHAM ASSOCIATION LEAGUE

Division One	P	W	D	L	F	A	Pts
Star	24	16	6	2	72	30	54
Winchcombe Town	24	12	7	5	59	31	43
Endsleigh	24	14	1	9	56	36	43
Hatherley Rangers *-1*	24	11	7	6	61	39	39
Bishops Cleeve 'A'	24	12	3	9	52	45	39
Newton *-3*	24	12	4	8	46	40	37
Kings	24	11	3	10	53	44	36
Belmore Jags	24	10	5	9	48	53	35
Northway	24	9	7	8	56	47	34
Shipton Oliffe	24	6	4	14	34	57	22
Dynamos	24	5	3	16	37	66	18
Prestbury Rovers	24	3	7	14	19	50	16
Tewkesb'y YMCA *-6*	24	5	3	16	47	102	12

Division Two	P	W	D	L	F	A	Pts
Cheltenham C S Res.	24	17	4	3	69	36	55
Andoversford Nomads	24	17	3	4	76	36	54
Naunton Park	24	16	2	6	88	36	50
Smiths Ath Res. *-3*	24	14	4	6	61	47	43
Moreton Rangers	24	13	2	9	65	49	41
Bredon Res. *-4*	24	10	4	10	56	55	30
Star Res.	24	8	5	11	48	60	29
Chelt. Saracens 'A'	24	7	7	10	46	59	28
Northleach Town	24	7	2	15	49	80	23
Finlay Rovers *-7*	24	8	3	13	63	81	20
Gala Wilton Res.	24	4	5	15	27	61	17
Bourton Rovers Res.	24	4	1	19	26	75	13
St Marks CA *-33*	24	8	4	12	49	48	-5

Division Three	P	W	D	L	F	A	Pts
Hi Tech Rangers	24	19	2	3	88	37	59
Woodmancote	24	16	4	4	69	34	52
FC Electrics	24	14	5	5	67	45	47
St Marks CA Res. *-3*	24	15	2	7	77	40	44
Belmore Jags Res.	24	10	7	7	59	51	37
Smiths Athletic 'A'	24	7	8	9	53	54	29
Charlton Rovers *-3*	24	7	8	9	48	54	26
Northway Res.	24	6	7	11	40	73	25
Gas Green	24	7	3	14	47	73	24
Andoversford N Res.	24	5	8	11	60	79	23
Prestbury Rvrs Res. *-6*	24	6	5	13	44	61	17
Falcons *-3*	24	4	8	12	33	54	17
Brockworth Albion 'A'	24	4	5	15	31	61	17

Division Four	P	W	D	L	F	A	Pts
AC Olympia	22	16	3	3	85	33	51
Winchcombe Tn Res.	22	15	3	4	66	41	48
Tewkesbury Dynamos	22	13	5	4	64	26	44
Bishops Cleeve 'B'	22	12	3	7	62	42	39
Phoenix United	22	11	4	7	51	49	37
Cheltenham C S 'A'	22	10	4	8	48	35	34
Kings Res.	22	9	4	9	46	42	31
Gaffers	22	9	3	10	48	57	30
Elmbridge Old Boys	22	6	4	12	46	70	22
Gas Green Res.	22	6	1	15	35	63	19
Charlton Kings *-3*	22	4	2	16	42	77	11
Smiths Athletic 'B'	22	2	2	18	23	81	8

Division Five	P	W	D	L	F	A	Pts
Tewkesbury Town	26	26	0	0	109	14	78
Naunton Park Res.	26	20	1	5	86	33	61
Belmore Jags 'A'	26	16	1	9	62	56	49
Chelt. Saracens 'B'	26	14	4	8	85	53	46
Charlton Rovers Res.	26	12	5	9	81	62	41
Bredon 'A'	26	12	5	9	58	60	41
Star 'A'	26	12	2	12	59	43	38
Northleach Tn Res.	26	10	2	14	47	59	32
Churchdown Panthers	26	8	5	13	64	72	29
Cleevonians	26	8	5	13	35	55	29
Sherborne Harriers	26	7	7	12	52	73	28
Cheltenham C S 'B'	26	5	7	14	33	58	22
Finlay Rovers Res. *-3*	26	5	5	16	41	104	17
Southside	26	2	1	23	34	104	7

CLWYD LEAGUE

Premier Division	P	W	D	L	F	A	Pts
Castle Rhuddlan	20	13	4	3	71	30	43
Holywell Town Res.	20	13	4	3	54	40	43
Prestatyn Town Res.	20	11	5	4	57	24	38
Rhuddlan Town	20	12	1	7	47	30	37
Mochdre Sports	20	7	5	8	31	30	26
Aston Park Rgrs *-1*	20	7	4	9	41	49	24
Bro Cernyw	20	6	5	9	32	32	23
Rhyl Youth	20	7	2	11	31	48	23
Halkyn United Res.	20	5	5	10	30	52	20
Llansannan	20	5	4	11	27	48	19
Denbigh Tn Res. *-3*	20	3	3	14	24	62	9

Division One	P	W	D	L	F	A	Pts
Flint Town Utd Res.	18	11	7	0	55	22	40
Rhydymwyn Res.	18	12	4	2	47	20	40
Llandyrnog Utd Res.	18	9	5	4	47	31	32
Brynford United	18	10	2	6	54	44	32
Trefnant Village	18	8	1	9	31	33	25
Mochdre Sports Res.	18	7	3	8	30	25	24
Point of Ayr	18	6	1	11	37	39	19
Cerrigydrudion	18	4	3	11	29	49	15
Caerwys Res.	18	4	3	11	26	50	15
Mostyn	18	4	1	13	22	65	13

Division Two	P	W	D	L	F	A	Pts
Abergele Rovers	18	15	1	2	64	12	46
Castle Rhuddlan Res.	18	12	2	4	57	27	38
Greenfield	18	11	2	5	54	26	35
Aztec Sports	18	9	3	6	37	49	30
Northop Hall	18	7	2	9	37	37	23
Aston Park Rgrs Res.	18	6	3	9	44	56	21
Y Glannau	18	5	3	10	30	52	18
Sychdyn	18	4	5	9	34	45	17
The George	18	5	2	11	33	62	17
Rhuddlan Town Res.	18	4	1	13	32	56	13

COLCHESTER & EAST ESSEX LEAGUE

Premier Division	P	W	D	L	F	A	Pts
Posties	20	16	3	1	54	13	51
Kirby Athletic	20	14	1	5	57	28	43
Univ of Essex Res.	20	12	3	5	66	26	39
Clacton United	20	10	3	7	66	26	33
Harwich & Park. 'A'	20	9	3	8	63	41	30
Tollesbury	20	8	5	7	41	44	29
Harwich Rangers	20	7	4	9	45	51	25
Forty Fives	20	7	3	10	36	44	24
Cinque Port	20	5	5	10	48	64	20
Fox Ash Res.	20	5	4	11	32	43	19
Clacton Town 'A'	20	0	0	20	15	143	0

Division One	P	W	D	L	F	A	Pts
Colchester Hotspurs	20	15	3	2	62	20	48
Monkwick Wanderers	20	14	4	2	68	24	46
Worming'd Wdrs *-1*	20	12	5	3	57	25	40
AXA FC	20	10	3	7	48	31	33
St Ives	20	9	3	8	32	37	30
Univ of Essex 'A' *-1*	20	7	8	5	47	25	28
Castle	20	7	3	10	47	61	24
Lawford Lads 'A'	20	5	4	11	32	59	19
Ardleigh United	20	5	2	13	29	63	17
Stoke-by-Nayland	20	1	8	11	32	60	11
Feering United	20	2	3	15	12	61	9

Division Two	P	W	D	L	F	A	Pts
Univ of Essex 'B'	14	9	3	2	42	18	30
Wimpole	14	8	4	2	42	23	28
Colchester Athletic	14	8	3	3	37	21	27
Devon FC	14	7	3	4	41	29	24
Tollesbury Res.	14	5	4	5	39	30	19
Oyster Rangers	14	4	3	7	30	50	15
Royal London	14	1	4	9	24	40	7
Nayland Rangers	14	1	2	11	14	58	5

Division Three	P	W	D	L	F	A	Pts
Whitehall	20	15	1	4	63	18	46
Tiptree Heath Res.	20	14	0	6	57	37	42
Colne Engaine	20	13	2	5	73	38	41
Monkwick Wdrs Res.	20	10	3	7	36	43	33
Weeley Athletic 'A'	20	9	5	6	43	30	32
New Field	20	8	4	8	35	35	28
Mistley United 'A'	20	6	5	9	46	43	23
Informa Athletic	20	7	2	11	35	47	23
Univ of Essex 'C'	20	6	3	11	31	49	21
Bradfield Rovers Res.	20	5	2	13	30	47	17
Wormingford W Res.	20	3	1	16	20	82	10

COVENTRY ALLIANCE

Premier Division	P	W	D	L	F	A	Pts
Mount Nod Highway	28	21	2	5	77	37	65
Witherley United	28	19	3	6	60	30	60
Bedworth Ex-Serv *-7*	28	19	6	3	59	26	56
Christ The King	28	14	6	8	52	29	48
Brooklands-Jaguar	28	13	5	10	53	41	44
Woodlands WMC	28	13	4	11	40	29	43
Coundon Court OB	28	10	11	7	46	40	41
Folly Lane BCOB	28	11	7	10	42	45	40
Whitnash Town	28	10	6	12	54	56	36
Bulkington Spts/Soc	28	8	8	12	29	47	32
Stockton	28	6	10	12	46	54	28
Cov. Copsewood Res.	28	8	3	17	36	75	27
Peugeot	28	6	8	14	41	62	26
Dunlop	28	5	6	17	42	60	21
Triumph Athletic	28	2	5	21	39	85	11

Division One	P	W	D	L	F	A	Pts
Stockingford AA Pav.	22	16	3	3	44	19	51
Alvis	22	15	3	4	53	28	48
AEI Rugby	22	11	4	7	37	34	37
Nuneaton Griff /Coton	22	10	5	7	43	30	35
Folly Lane BCOB Res.	22	9	3	10	48	58	30
Coventry University	22	8	4	10	43	34	28
Collycroft Sports	22	7	6	9	44	47	27
Hawkes Mill Sports	22	6	7	9	42	46	25
Ambleside Sports	22	6	5	11	32	46	23
Coventry Colliery	22	5	7	10	28	37	22
Kenilworth Wardens	22	5	6	11	28	48	21
Bourton & Frankton	22	5	5	12	35	50	20

Division Two	P	W	D	L	F	A	Pts
Brooklands-Jaguar Res.	22	15	6	1	61	27	51
Potters Green	22	12	8	2	55	20	44
Triumph Athletic Res.	22	12	4	6	54	42	40
Christ The King Res.	22	10	5	7	58	42	35
Fillongley	22	10	3	9	50	56	33
Newdigate *-1*	22	10	2	10	49	75	31
Dunlop Res.	22	8	5	9	47	39	29
Mount Nod H'way Res	22	8	4	10	51	54	28
Coundon C'rt OB Res.	22	7	6	9	48	36	27
Shilton	22	6	4	12	45	50	22
AEI Rugby Res.	22	5	1	16	34	64	16
Bulkington Spts/S Res.	22	4	2	16	30	77	14

Division Three	P	W	D	L	F	A	Pts
Peugeot Res.	22	13	4	5	58	35	43
Alvis Res.	22	12	3	7	58	49	39
F'y Lane BCOB 'A' *-7*	22	14	3	5	57	32	38
Cov. Copsewood 'A'	22	12	2	8	71	56	38
Balsall & Berkswell	22	11	4	7	55	43	37
Stockton Res.	22	9	6	7	62	47	33
PR Sporting GNP	22	10	3	9	51	51	33
Hillmorton	22	7	5	10	43	53	26
Christ The King 'A'	22	7	4	11	46	63	25
Bedw'th Ex-Serv Res.	22	6	4	12	33	54	22
Coventry Univ Res.	22	5	6	11	42	60	21
W'dlands WMC Res.	22	3	2	17	24	57	11

Division Four	P	W	D	L	F	A	Pts
Brinklow	22	18	3	1	109	24	57
Potters Green Res.	22	13	6	3	61	31	45
Witherley Utd Res.	22	13	5	4	69	27	44
Kenilw'th W'dens Res.	22	10	4	8	46	46	34
Hawkes Mill Spts Res.	22	8	7	7	55	38	31
Ambleside Spts Res.	22	9	4	9	32	42	31
Heart Athletic	22	8	6	8	48	59	30
Collycroft Sports Res.	22	8	3	11	50	57	27
Bilton Social	22	7	2	13	36	74	23
AEI Rugby 'A'	22	5	4	13	35	57	19
Fillongley Res.	22	5	3	14	38	73	18
Shilton Res.	22	2	5	15	21	72	11

Division Five	P	W	D	L	F	A	Pts
The Hub	16	14	2	0	66	19	44
Cov. Colliery Res.	16	12	1	3	44	16	37
Peugeot 'A'	16	9	0	7	44	35	27
Balsall/Berkswell Res.	16	8	2	6	44	36	26
Coventry Univ 'A'	16	6	3	7	42	39	21
Bourton/Frankton Res.	16	6	3	7	37	43	21
Bermuda WMC	16	5	1	10	30	41	16
Parkgate	16	3	2	11	20	59	11
Hillmorton Res.	16	1	2	13	15	54	5

CRAVEN & DISTRICT LEAGUE

Premier Division	P	W	D	L	F	A	Pts
Oxenhope Recreation	22	18	3	1	91	33	57
Bronte Wanderers	22	16	4	2	84	35	52
Skipton LMS	22	16	2	4	86	44	50
Embsay	22	11	2	9	53	45	35
Gargrave	22	10	3	9	42	38	33
Waddington *-3*	22	9	7	6	60	48	31
WFC Clitheroe	22	9	3	10	64	73	30
Cononley Sports	22	7	4	11	54	55	25
Grassington United	22	5	6	11	36	52	21
Carleton	22	5	1	16	47	80	16
Grindleton	22	3	6	13	38	72	15
Crosshills 'A'	22	1	3	18	32	112	6

Skipton Bulldogs – record expunged

Division One	P	W	D	L	F	A	Pts
Bradley	22	14	6	2	52	23	48
Hellifield Sports	22	13	5	4	61	39	44
Clitheroe Lions *-2*	22	12	7	3	55	27	41
Skipton Town	22	11	3	8	56	49	36
Ox'hope Rec Res. *-3*	22	10	5	7	41	42	32
Craven College OB *-3*	22	9	4	9	45	56	28
Embsay Res.	22	7	5	10	42	44	26
Intake	22	6	7	9	38	41	25
Rolls Royce FC	22	6	6	10	36	42	24
Silsden 2004 Res. *-4*	22	7	6	9	39	38	23
Skipton LMS Res.	22	6	2	14	37	57	20
Barrowford United	22	2	2	18	29	73	8

Division Two	P	W	D	L	F	A	Pts
Pendle Athletic	22	18	0	4	92	36	54
Long Lee Juniors	22	13	4	5	68	31	43
Cowling	22	11	5	6	52	42	38
Keighley	22	10	7	5	65	54	37
Intake Res.	22	10	2	10	62	74	32
Gargrave Res.	22	8	6	8	63	58	30
Rolls Royce FC Res.	22	8	3	11	47	62	27
Horton	22	8	2	12	47	57	26
Waddington Res.	22	8	2	12	42	71	26
Cononley Sports Res.	22	7	3	12	44	59	24
Grindleton Res.	22	7	3	12	51	71	24
Earby Town	22	4	3	15	63	81	15

McBrides – record expunged

Division Three	P	W	D	L	F	A	Pts
Grassington Utd Res.	22	16	4	2	68	24	52
Oakworth	22	16	2	4	93	27	50
Earby	22	15	2	5	72	44	47
Silsden White Star *-3*	22	13	4	5	61	40	40
Pendle Renegades *-1*	22	9	5	8	52	59	31
Barnoldswick Barons	22	8	5	9	59	47	29
Long Lee Juniors Res.	22	8	4	10	45	54	28
Carleton Res.	22	8	4	10	45	73	28
Bradley Res.	22	8	2	12	38	62	26
Ingleton 'A'	22	5	4	13	48	64	19
Hellifield Sports Res.	22	5	3	14	40	68	18
Cowling Res.	22	0	3	19	32	91	3

Skipton Bulldogs Res. – record expunged

CRAWLEY & DISTRICT LEAGUE

Premier Division	P	W	D	L	F	A	Pts
Merstham Newton	24	18	2	4	87	32	56
Boca Elite	24	16	1	7	55	35	49
South Park *-1*	24	14	6	4	66	32	47
Ifield Edwards Res.	24	14	4	6	58	46	46
Phoenix	24	11	9	4	48	31	42
Three Bridges 'A'	24	11	3	10	55	56	36
Horley Albion	24	9	5	10	44	64	32
Oakwood 'A'	24	9	4	11	54	57	31
Trumpton Town	24	9	2	13	53	56	29
Holland Sports	24	6	6	12	42	60	24
Cent. Sussex College	24	7	2	15	51	71	23
St Francis Flyers	24	4	3	17	32	53	15
Trident FC	24	4	1	19	21	73	13

Division One	P	W	D	L	F	A	Pts
Windmill	16	13	1	2	81	17	40
FC Spartak	16	12	1	3	64	31	37
Sporting Crawley	16	12	0	4	53	24	36
St Francis Flyers Res.	16	10	1	5	61	33	31
South Park Res.	16	7	1	8	36	43	22
Real Hydraquip	16	6	1	9	37	39	19
Worth Park Rangers	16	4	2	10	34	66	14
Horley Albion Res.	16	2	2	12	25	62	8
Virgin Holidays	16	1	1	14	24	100	4

Division Two	P	W	D	L	F	A	Pts
County Oak	18	15	0	3	90	21	45
Broadfield	18	13	3	2	74	26	42
Greets Inn	18	11	3	4	80	28	36
Maidenbower Village	18	11	3	4	65	25	36
Black Dog	18	11	1	6	68	51	34
Ifield Edwards 'A'	18	8	3	7	65	50	27
Phoenix Res.	18	6	1	11	44	53	19
Wingspan	18	4	0	14	25	99	12
Seebrook Rovers	18	1	3	14	19	106	6
Stones	18	1	1	16	21	92	4

Division Three	P	W	D	L	F	A	Pts
Sussex Elite *+2*	20	17	2	1	69	14	55
GSK Sports & Social	20	14	2	4	70	35	44
Ifield Edwards 'B'	20	9	4	7	43	36	31
Southside Rovers *-1*	20	9	4	7	47	30	30
Boca Elite Res.	20	9	1	10	32	39	28
Virgin Holidays Res.	20	8	2	10	46	58	26
Rowfant Village	20	7	4	9	43	40	25
Pelham Wanderers	20	7	4	9	36	39	25
Real Hydraquip Res.	20	6	4	10	48	50	22
Sporting Crawley Res.	20	4	3	13	32	58	15
Border Wanderers	20	4	2	14	20	87	14

DONCASTER & DISTRICT SENIOR LEAGUE

Premier Division	P	W	D	L	F	A	Pts
Hemsworth St Patrick	26	22	3	1	107	27	69
Kinsley Boys	26	20	2	4	101	28	62
Moorland	26	18	2	6	107	69	56
Pontefract Coll's Res.	26	16	3	7	68	48	51
Swinton Station	26	14	7	5	69	35	49
Thorne Town	26	12	4	10	72	63	40
Mexborough Athletic	26	12	2	12	60	57	38
Rossington Main Res.	26	9	6	11	56	82	33
South Kirkby Colliery	26	9	4	13	43	57	31
Askern Welfare Res.	26	7	6	13	41	70	27
Upton/Harew'd Social	26	7	4	15	58	72	25
Ackworth United	26	7	3	16	49	82	24
Eden Grove	26	2	3	21	29	84	9
Bawtry Town	26	2	1	23	31	117	7

Division One	P	W	D	L	F	A	Pts
Tickhill Athletic	18	15	1	2	75	27	46
Maltby Sheppey	18	10	3	5	43	23	33
AFC Beeches	18	10	1	7	44	38	31
Edlington Rangers	18	9	2	7	44	31	29
Sutton Rovers	18	9	2	7	47	48	29
The Star	18	8	4	6	36	35	28
Donc. College Deaf	18	7	4	7	33	28	25
Hemsworth St Pat Res.	18	4	6	8	30	42	18
Wickersley OB Res.	18	5	1	12	27	48	16
Cooplands United	18	0	2	16	23	82	2

DRIFFIELD & DISTRICT LEAGUE

Premier Division	P	W	D	L	F	A	Pts
Yorkies	16	12	4	0	50	18	40
Brid .Sports Club Res.	16	10	5	1	54	18	35
Driffield Rangers	16	10	2	4	40	26	32
Driffield EI	16	10	1	5	41	36	31
Nafferton	16	5	3	8	34	37	18
Bridlington Excelsior	16	4	3	9	35	52	15
Hutton Cranswick SRA	16	4	1	11	22	32	13
Burton Agnes	16	3	2	11	25	48	11
Bridlington Rovers	16	2	3	11	21	55	9

DUCHY LEAGUE

Premier Division	P	W	D	L	F	A	Pts
St Columb Major	26	20	1	5	96	40	61
Bere Alston United	26	17	6	3	95	43	57
Lanreath	26	17	4	5	75	40	55
Polperro	26	15	4	7	64	38	49
St Newlyn East	26	13	3	10	68	53	42
Boscastle	26	13	3	10	63	59	42
Gunnislake	26	11	6	9	50	44	39
Bude Town *-3*	26	12	3	11	53	50	36
St Dominick	26	9	8	9	51	45	35
St Mawgan *+3*	26	7	4	15	43	70	28
Sticker Res. *-3*	26	9	3	14	47	69	27
St Minver	26	7	2	17	51	74	23
St Blazey Res.	26	7	2	17	49	87	23
St Stephen Res.	26	0	1	25	18	111	1

Division One	P	W	D	L	F	A	Pts
Lamerton	26	19	2	5	97	31	59
St Dennis Res.	25	16	4	5	87	43	52
St Merryn	26	15	6	5	66	32	51
Pensilva	26	15	5	6	71	34	50
Dobwalls Res.	26	16	2	8	77	47	50
Mevagissey	26	12	7	7	64	51	43
Launceston United	26	13	3	10	66	64	42
Maker-with-Rame	26	13	2	11	73	56	41
Altarnun	26	13	2	11	79	63	41
Mary Tavy	26	12	4	10	62	49	40
St Teath	26	7	4	15	37	73	25
St Columb Minor	25	4	4	17	40	89	16
Gerrans	26	2	0	24	29	104	6
St Cleer Res.	26	1	1	24	19	131	4

Division Two	P	W	D	L	F	A	Pts
Edgcumbe *-1*	28	20	4	4	120	24	63
Torpoint Athletic 'A'	28	19	4	5	97	40	61
St Stephens Borough	28	17	8	3	64	20	59
Roseland	28	17	7	4	58	27	58
Tywardreath RBL	28	15	6	7	79	50	51
St Anns Chapel *+3*	28	14	4	10	73	60	49
Callington Tn 'A' *-3*	28	13	7	8	57	44	43
Delabole United	28	10	7	11	67	72	37
Polperro Res.	28	9	7	12	37	63	34
Foxhole Stars Res.	28	10	3	15	58	63	33
Newmoor Rovers *+2*	28	8	7	13	41	49	33
Menheniot	28	8	5	15	47	72	29
Pelynt	28	6	3	19	38	82	21
Queens Rangers *-3*	28	4	2	22	35	115	11
Fowey United *-3*	28	3	0	25	44	134	6

Division Three	P	W	D	L	F	A	Pts
Lanivet	26	23	1	2	123	27	70
Godolphin Atlantic Res	26	20	2	4	83	37	62
Looe	26	15	4	7	80	51	49
St Dominick Res.	26	12	5	9	69	55	41
Camelford Res.	26	11	5	10	41	40	38
Roche Res.	26	11	5	10	32	42	38
Biscovey Res.	26	9	6	11	49	60	33
Probus Res. *-3*	26	10	4	12	71	80	31
St Breward	26	8	7	11	46	60	31
Grampound	26	7	8	11	33	42	29
Calstock	26	7	7	12	54	75	28
North Hill	26	6	4	16	53	71	22
St Mawgan Res. *+3*	26	5	3	18	36	95	21
South Petherwin *-6*	26	6	3	17	41	76	15

Division Four	P	W	D	L	F	A	Pts
Holywell Bay/Cubert	26	25	1	0	111	24	76
Saltash United 'A'	26	23	0	3	117	16	69
Garrison Club *-3*	26	14	5	7	59	40	44
Wadebridge Tn 'A'	26	13	3	10	78	44	42
Lewdown Rovers *-3*	26	13	4	9	66	58	40
Padstow United Res.	26	12	3	11	58	45	39
Gorran	26	10	5	11	66	66	35
Bere Alston U Res. *-3*	26	12	1	13	58	69	34
St Newlyn East Res.	26	7	6	13	52	55	27
Pensilva Res.	26	7	6	13	48	66	27
Lifton Res.	26	6	4	16	40	96	22
Boscastle Res.	26	4	7	15	31	77	19
Altarnun Res.	26	4	7	15	25	96	19
Tintagel	26	5	2	19	28	85	17

Division Five	P	W	D	L	F	A	Pts
Week St Mary *-3*	28	23	2	3	121	29	68
Lanreath Res.	28	21	3	4	111	40	66
Nanpean Rovers Res.	28	21	2	5	126	34	65
Lostwithiel *+2*	28	17	5	6	90	59	58
Newmoor Rovers Res.	28	17	6	5	85	50	57
Porthia *-2*	28	13	8	7	79	63	45
St Merryn Res.	28	13	4	11	71	63	43
St Col. Maj Res. *+5*	28	9	4	15	43	67	36
Grampound Res.	28	9	7	12	70	72	34
Biscovey 'A' *-1*	28	10	4	14	65	68	33
Pelynt Res.	28	8	7	13	57	83	31
St Teath Res. *+2*	28	8	1	19	57	109	27
Mount Charles SC	28	4	2	22	50	95	14
St Minver Res.	28	3	5	20	28	114	14
Delabole Utd Res.	28	3	2	23	27	134	11

EAST BERKSHIRE LEAGUE

Premier Division	P	W	D	L	F	A	Pts
Red Lion	22	17	3	2	84	21	54
Spital Old Boys	22	15	2	5	73	27	47
Chalvey (WMC) Spts	22	14	5	3	51	35	47
Orchard Park Rgrs	22	12	2	8	46	40	38
Old Windsor	22	11	2	9	40	37	35
Running Horse	22	11	2	9	58	58	35
New Windsor OB	22	10	2	10	56	55	32
FC Wraysbury	22	10	2	10	46	49	32
Waltham	22	7	3	12	45	60	24
Holland Park	22	5	3	14	30	51	18
Bagshot	22	3	3	16	37	72	12
Slough Heating	22	1	3	18	22	83	6

Division One	P	W	D	L	F	A	Pts
Slough Heating Res.	20	17	2	1	65	33	53
Datchet	20	13	2	5	67	43	41
Slough Laurencians	20	12	4	4	69	35	40
Orchard Pk Rgrs Res.	20	13	1	6	71	39	40
Cippenham Sports	20	10	5	5	78	46	35
ICI (Slough)	20	9	3	8	61	53	30
Frontline	20	6	5	9	45	50	23
Burnham Athletic	20	6	2	12	35	62	20
Windsor Cricket Club	20	5	3	12	31	44	18
Holland Park Res.	20	3	3	14	23	75	12
Alpha Arms Acad'als	20	0	2	18	25	90	2

Division Two	P	W	D	L	F	A	Pts
Iver Heath Rovers	22	18	3	1	79	28	57
Maidenhead Town	22	17	2	3	81	34	53
Stoke Green	22	11	7	4	53	37	40
Foxes	22	12	4	6	55	41	40
Burnham United	22	10	2	10	57	46	32
Windsor Gt Park *+3*	22	8	5	9	50	57	32
Britwell	22	9	4	9	60	60	31
Englefield Gn Rov 'A'	22	9	2	11	36	44	29
Braybrooke	22	7	4	11	41	48	25
Chalvey (WMC) Res.	22	5	2	15	41	74	17
Slough Heating 'A' *-3*	22	4	5	13	37	53	14
Red Lion Res.	22	2	0	20	27	95	6

New Windsor Old Boys Res. – record expunged

Division Three	P	W	D	L	F	A	Pts
Stoke Poges	24	15	5	4	71	39	50
Boyne Hill	24	15	3	6	73	39	48
Falcons	24	13	5	6	57	39	44
Sl'gh Laurencians Res.	24	12	6	6	63	63	42
Hayes Villa Old Boys	24	12	3	9	55	44	39
Crowthorne Royals	24	11	5	8	64	46	38
Bagshot Res.	24	12	1	11	54	31	37
Windsor G P Res. *+3*	24	10	4	10	37	41	37
Running Horse Res.	24	11	2	11	61	58	35
Mercian United	24	7	4	13	53	77	25
Reading Athletic *-3*	24	8	3	13	47	34	24
Willow Wanderers	24	3	4	17	41	80	13
KS Gryf	24	4	1	19	36	121	13

EAST GWENT LEAGUE

Division One	P	W	D	L	F	A	Pts
Tintern Abbey	21	18	1	2	91	24	55
Underwood Spts/Soc	21	17	1	3	88	24	52
Monmouth Tn Res.	21	17	0	4	70	37	51
Caldicot Town 'A'	21	11	0	10	60	51	33
Rockfield Rovers	21	8	2	11	51	57	26
Chepstow Town 'A'	21	5	1	15	29	85	16
Portskewett/Sudbrook	21	4	0	17	34	72	12
Undy Athletic Res.	21	1	1	19	22	95	4

Division Two	P	W	D	L	F	A	Pts
Caldicot Castle Res.	21	16	3	2	91	26	51
Chepstow Athletic	21	16	2	3	61	28	50
Thornwell Red/W Res.	21	12	4	5	49	38	40
Sudbrook Crckt C Res.	21	7	6	8	51	51	27
Rogiet & Tippling	21	7	4	10	38	49	25
Underwood S/S Res.	21	7	4	10	52	65	25
Portskewett/Sud Res.	21	2	4	15	36	67	10
Bulwark	21	2	3	16	29	83	9

Division Three	P	W	D	L	F	A	Pts
Monmouth Tn 'A'	20	16	2	2	79	24	50
Devauden Green	20	11	4	5	59	35	37
Mathern Wanderers	20	10	5	5	62	42	35
Rockfield Rvrs Res.	20	7	3	10	52	58	24
Sudbrook Crckt C 'A'	20	5	3	12	33	69	18
Caldicot Castle 'A'	20	2	1	17	25	82	7

EAST LANCASHIRE LEAGUE

Division One	P	W	D	L	F	A	Pts
Rimington	26	19	1	6	70	30	58
Hurst Green	26	14	8	4	67	35	50
Stacksteads St Josephs	26	14	8	4	61	34	50
Colne United	26	13	6	7	73	50	45
Goodshaw United	26	11	7	8	65	53	40
Settle United	26	11	5	10	61	53	38
Rock Rovers	26	10	7	9	49	44	37
Worsthorne	26	10	6	10	62	57	36
Silsden 2004	26	8	8	10	45	47	32
Langho	26	8	8	10	49	56	32
Kelbrook	26	7	5	14	38	59	26
Enfield	26	7	4	15	35	59	25
Padiham 'A'	26	7	2	17	38	79	23
Oswaldtwistle SM	26	2	7	17	34	91	13

EAST RIDING COUNTY AMATEUR LEAGUE

Premier Division	P	W	D	L	F	A	Pts
North Cave	18	10	4	4	45	33	34
Sculcoates Ams Res.	18	9	4	5	40	39	31
Rawcliffe Bridge Utd	18	9	3	6	49	32	30
Northfield Athletic	18	9	1	8	41	33	28
Long Riston	18	8	2	8	31	33	26
Howden Amateurs	18	7	4	7	34	45	25
Old George	18	6	5	7	31	25	23
Reckitts Res.	18	5	6	7	27	31	21
Poachers	18	6	3	9	25	33	21
FC Ridings	18	3	4	11	24	43	13

Division One	P	W	D	L	F	A	Pts
Boothferry Rgrs *+3*	20	12	4	4	60	35	43
Holme Rovers	20	10	7	3	47	25	37
Skidby Millers	20	11	3	6	52	42	36
Easington Utd Res.	20	8	7	5	46	40	31
Warter	20	9	3	8	44	50	30
Westella/Willerby Res.	20	8	5	7	43	42	29
North Ferriby Ath *-3*	20	9	4	7	61	51	28
Beverley Town Res.	20	6	6	8	35	35	24
Hornsea Town Res.	20	6	5	9	45	53	23
Hutton Cranswick Res.	20	3	5	12	27	52	14
Hall Road Rgrs Res.	20	2	3	15	26	61	9

Division Two	P	W	D	L	F	A	Pts
Dales Tigers YC	22	16	4	2	71	24	52
Anlaby United Res.	22	15	1	6	47	33	46
Alborough United	21	13	4	4	55	36	43
Lord Nelson Beverley	22	12	4	6	66	41	40
FC Swallow	22	11	4	7	63	44	37
South Cave United	22	10	3	9	67	54	33
Patrington United *-3*	22	8	8	6	40	40	29
Gilberdyke	22	9	2	11	38	44	29
Hedon Utd Res. *+3*	22	6	2	14	32	65	23
Leven Members Club	22	6	3	13	40	58	21
North Frodingham	21	3	2	16	36	68	11
North Newbald	22	2	3	17	19	67	9

Division Three	P	W	D	L	F	A	Pts
Brandesburton Res.	18	13	2	3	53	31	41
Beaver	18	12	4	2	49	25	40
Hodgsons	18	13	1	4	51	40	40
Howden Ams Res.	18	8	4	6	44	34	28
Boothferry Rgrs Res.	18	7	3	8	38	35	24
Market Weighton Utd	18	7	1	10	42	48	22
Haltemprice OB	18	6	1	11	30	45	19
Withernsea Res.	18	5	3	10	43	60	18
Plexus Networking	18	4	2	12	34	48	14
Molescroft Rangers	18	3	3	12	33	51	12

Division Four	P	W	D	L	F	A	Pts
FC Peacock	22	19	1	2	87	29	58
West Hull Amateurs	22	18	3	1	77	25	57
North Cave Res.	22	15	3	4	72	39	48
Keysign Solutions	22	14	0	8	54	49	42
Roos	22	12	3	7	46	40	39
Long Riston Res.	22	12	1	9	45	64	37
Skidby Millers Res.	22	9	2	11	45	56	29
Cross Keys Howden	22	7	2	13	40	73	23
Holme Rovers Res.	22	4	5	13	23	39	17
Leven MC Res.	22	4	4	14	39	66	16
Westella/Willerby Jun	22	4	0	18	21	33	12
Shiptonthorpe Utd *-2*	22	2	0	20	12	48	4

Division Five	P	W	D	L	F	A	Pts
Dads FC	26	17	6	3	86	38	57
Withernsea 'A'	26	15	7	4	58	33	52
Easington Utd Casuals	26	12	6	8	50	44	42
Molescroft Rgrs Res.	26	13	3	10	62	65	42
FC Peacock Res.	26	12	5	9	78	68	41
Howden Town	26	12	4	10	75	61	40
Patrington Stanley	26	11	7	8	54	43	40
Market Weighton Res.	26	10	7	9	52	49	37
Hornsea Town 'A'	26	10	5	11	53	68	35
Skirlaugh	26	10	2	14	61	64	32
Brandesburton 'A'	26	9	3	14	69	78	30
Easington Village	26	7	4	15	50	66	25
Shiptonthorpe Utd Res.	26	7	4	15	51	79	25
Haltemprice Rangers	26	4	3	19	32	75	15

EAST SUSSEX LEAGUE

Premier Division	P	W	D	L	F	A	Pts
Hawkhurst United	22	18	2	2	84	24	56
Hollington United *-3*	22	15	3	4	80	29	45
St Leonards Social	22	13	2	7	70	39	41
Bodiam	22	12	3	7	49	50	39
AFC Peasmarsh	22	11	3	8	45	43	36
Eastbourne WMC	22	8	5	9	53	55	29
Peche Hill Select	22	9	1	12	44	48	28
Mountfield United	22	8	2	12	52	59	26
Rock-a-Nore	22	7	3	12	59	60	24
Ticehurst	22	5	8	9	35	51	23
Punnetts Town	22	6	4	12	43	77	22
Rye & Iden Utd 'A'	22	1	2	19	19	98	5

Division One	P	W	D	L	F	A	Pts
Hollington Utd Res.	20	16	3	1	60	26	51
Heathfield Hotspurs	20	15	2	3	76	18	47
Ridge West Garage	20	14	4	2	69	20	46
Sedlescombe	20	13	4	3	49	24	43
Jun. Club Tackleway	20	11	0	9	40	33	33
Sandhurst	20	10	2	8	43	44	32
Hooe Sports	20	8	2	10	36	44	26
Ninfield United	20	6	3	11	36	45	21
Firehills Seniors	20	3	1	16	36	69	10
Wadhurst Utd Res.	20	2	1	17	26	86	7
Rye & Iden Utd 'B'	20	1	0	19	13	75	3

Division Two	P	W	D	L	F	A	Pts
Icklesham Casuals	20	15	2	3	67	17	47
Bexhill AAC	20	14	2	4	60	20	44
Northiam	20	13	2	5	41	34	41
Crowhurst	20	13	1	6	56	27	40
White Knight *-3*	20	12	1	7	59	42	34
Little Common Res.	20	9	3	8	49	36	30
Old Hastonians	20	8	1	11	41	40	25
Hastings Rangers	20	8	0	12	46	49	24
Burfield Tyres	20	7	1	12	38	39	22
Mayfield	20	2	1	17	21	122	7
Cranbrook Town	20	2	0	18	25	77	6

Hillcrest – record expunged

Division Three	P	W	D	L	F	A	Pts
Athletico	20	14	2	4	62	28	44
Jun. Club T'way Res.	20	11	6	3	62	36	39
Herstmonceux *-5*	20	11	5	4	51	34	33
Little Common 'A'	20	9	4	7	58	48	31
Burwash	20	9	4	7	41	35	31
Magham Down	20	8	4	8	54	42	28
Catsfield	20	8	3	9	38	41	27
Beulah Baptists	20	5	8	7	37	39	23
Wittersham	20	6	4	10	42	51	22
Pebsham Sibex	20	6	2	12	27	45	20
Westfield 'A'	20	2	0	18	23	96	6

Division Four	P	W	D	L	F	A	Pts
Hastings Rgrs Res. *-3*	22	18	1	3	108	49	52
Battle Baptists	22	12	7	3	64	32	43
Red Lion	22	11	5	6	71	54	38
Hawkhurst Utd Res.	22	9	8	5	46	40	35
Victoria Baptists	22	9	5	8	48	57	32
Battle Rangers *-3*	22	8	6	8	56	63	27
St Helens	22	6	7	9	55	48	25
Bodiam Res.	22	7	3	12	36	58	24
Punnetts Town Res.	22	5	6	11	49	64	21
Northiam Res.	22	6	3	13	35	65	21
Old Centmodians *-6*	22	7	3	12	41	53	18
Travaux *-3*	22	5	4	13	46	72	16

Division Five	P	W	D	L	F	A	Pts
Eastbourne Fishermen	20	18	1	1	64	18	55
Robertsbridge Utd	20	15	1	4	72	22	46
Benbow *-3*	20	16	1	3	69	19	46
Bexhill AAC Res.	20	10	2	8	50	44	32
Hthfield Hotspurs Res.	20	9	1	10	42	44	28
Icklesham Cas. Res.	20	7	5	8	42	57	26
Mountfield Utd Res.	20	6	5	9	39	57	23
Sedlescombe Res.	20	5	3	12	27	51	18
Jun.Club T'way 'A'	20	4	3	13	30	53	15
Sandhurst Res. *-3*	20	4	4	12	16	54	13
Wadhurst United 'A'	20	2	2	16	23	55	8

Oceans – record expunged

Division Six	P	W	D	L	F	A	Pts
Panako	20	13	6	1	69	37	45
Cinque Ports	20	12	5	3	64	42	41
Beulah Baptists Res.	20	12	2	6	50	33	38
Orington	20	10	2	8	72	58	32
Herstmonceux Res. *-3*	20	10	4	6	46	47	31
White Knight Res.	20	8	2	10	53	57	26
Peche Hill Select Res.	20	6	6	8	38	40	24
Hastings Rangers 'A'	20	6	4	10	48	54	22
Pelham *-9*	20	8	4	8	58	52	19
Hastings APF *-1*	20	3	3	14	36	69	11
Magham Down Res.	20	3	0	17	24	69	9

ESSEX & HERTS BORDER COMBINATION

	P	W	D	L	F	A	Pts
Canvey Island Res.	36	30	5	1	144	22	95
Leyton Res.	36	27	4	5	134	36	85
Heybridge Swifts Res.	36	26	6	4	107	40	84
Romford Res.	36	22	5	9	72	37	71
Thurrock Res.	36	22	2	12	89	56	68
Harlow Town Res.	36	18	7	11	71	49	61
Brentwood Tn Res.	36	18	5	13	64	62	59
Ilford Res.	36	16	8	12	64	48	56
Barking/E H U Res.	36	14	7	15	57	64	49
Basildon United Res.	36	12	11	13	49	61	47
Burnham Ramb. Res.	36	13	5	18	49	64	44
Waltham Abbey Res.	36	12	5	19	55	83	41
Bowers & P Res. *-6*	36	14	4	18	59	86	40
E Thurrock Utd Res.	36	11	3	22	58	92	36
Chelmsford Cy Res. *-1*	36	9	9	18	53	85	35
Maldon Town Res.	36	9	6	21	39	76	33
Concord Rangers Res.	36	6	9	21	46	76	27
Gt Wakering Rvrs Res.	36	8	3	25	54	95	27
Stansted Res.	36	2	2	32	26	158	8

ESSEX BUSINESS HOUSES LEAGUE

Premier Division	P	W	D	L	F	A	Pts
Sungate	22	16	2	4	69	30	50
M & B Club	22	15	5	2	61	26	50
Toby	22	11	6	5	58	47	39
Bancroft	22	11	5	6	56	49	38
Brampton Park	22	11	2	9	60	35	35
East Ham Baptist	22	10	4	8	50	35	34
West Essex	22	10	3	9	47	42	33
Newham United	22	8	3	11	45	55	27
Old Barkabbeyans	22	7	5	10	42	44	26
Globe Rangers	22	7	5	10	53	66	26
Melbourne Sports	22	4	2	16	35	65	14
Glory House	22	1	0	21	23	105	3

Millwall Albion, Sembhy – records expunged

Division One	P	W	D	L	F	A	Pts
Rainham Athletic	22	16	4	2	50	24	52
Euro Dagenham	22	13	4	5	52	38	43
Heath Park	22	11	7	4	51	32	40
Rainham WMC	22	9	6	7	58	37	33
M & B Club Res.	22	10	3	9	52	39	33
P L A Vets	22	8	6	8	38	38	30
Beaumont Athletic	22	8	5	9	39	34	29
Platinium	22	8	3	11	35	47	27
Barking Borough	22	6	8	8	43	49	26
Fairbairn House	22	6	6	10	41	51	24
O Barkabbeyans Res.	22	5	4	13	36	59	19
Harold Park	22	2	4	16	28	75	10

Division Two	P	W	D	L	F	A	Pts
Old Barkabbeyans 'A'	24	18	2	4	83	29	56
West Green	24	16	2	6	67	33	50
P L A Res.	24	15	4	5	54	42	49
Sungate Res.	24	14	5	5	69	49	47
Snaresbrook	24	13	5	6	67	41	44
Romford Town Res.	24	12	4	8	72	66	40
Frenford Vets	24	11	2	11	41	45	35
Barking Borough Res.	24	8	4	12	55	58	28
West Essex Res.	24	8	3	13	49	54	27
Newham United Res.	24	6	5	13	48	64	23
Ford Athletic	24	4	4	16	40	63	16
Newark Youth	24	4	3	17	30	73	15
Glory House Res.	24	4	3	17	41	99	15

Division Three	P	W	D	L	F	A	Pts
Forest Glade	22	17	3	2	71	26	54
Doddinghurst Olympics	22	14	5	3	43	14	47
Stags Head	22	15	0	7	59	27	45
Westhamians Vets	22	14	1	7	65	40	43
Sungate 'A'	22	12	1	9	55	41	37
S S Barking	22	9	5	8	43	33	32
Globe Rangers Vets	22	9	4	9	44	57	31
Clarendon	22	8	3	11	46	52	27
Frenford Senior 'C'	22	7	4	11	40	44	25
Barking Borough 'A'	22	4	4	14	25	63	16
Old Barkabbeyans 'B'	22	3	2	17	25	55	11
Newham United 'A'	22	2	4	16	20	84	10

FALMOUTH-HELSTON LEAGUE

Division One	P	W	D	L	F	A	Pts
St Day	28	21	4	3	89	32	67
Porthleven Res.	28	19	4	5	113	43	61
St Agnes Res.	28	17	5	6	62	42	56
Falmouth Athletic *-3*	28	16	2	10	79	55	47
Penryn Athletic 'A'	28	14	5	9	65	49	47
Mousehole Res.	28	13	5	10	62	62	44
Mawnan	28	13	4	11	70	60	43
Chacewater	28	12	5	11	65	71	41
Wendron CC Utd Res.	28	12	3	13	51	53	39
Helston Athletic Res.	28	10	4	14	50	62	34
Falmouth Albion	28	8	7	13	44	58	31
Holmans S C Res. *+3*	28	4	9	15	33	70	24
Hayle Res.	28	5	8	15	31	70	23
Stithians	28	4	8	16	35	85	20
Constantine	28	4	3	21	49	86	15

Division Two	P	W	D	L	F	A	Pts
Mawnan Res.	30	26	2	2	105	21	80
Lizard *-3*	30	23	2	5	91	28	68
Trispen	30	20	4	6	69	37	64
Truro City 'A' *-3*	30	18	9	3	74	30	60
Pendeen Rovers	30	18	4	8	59	35	58
Perranwell Res.	30	16	5	9	62	40	53
Marazion Blues	30	15	3	12	55	61	48
St Keverne	30	14	3	13	48	57	45
Mawgan 'A'	30	11	6	13	69	70	39
Penryn Athletic 'B'	30	10	6	14	39	52	36
Wendron CC Utd 'A'	30	10	6	14	61	66	36
Perranporth Res.	30	9	4	17	42	71	31
Hayle 'A' *+2*	30	5	4	21	37	89	21
Helston Athletic 'A'	30	5	2	23	34	77	17
Rosudgeon-Ken. *-3*	30	4	5	21	39	88	14
Ruan Minor	30	2	3	25	38	100	9

Division Three	P	W	D	L	F	A	Pts
St Day Res. *+3*	30	25	3	2	118	31	81
Carharrack *+3*	30	24	2	4	83	40	77
Hayle 'B' *-3*	30	20	4	6	109	29	61
Falmouth Tn 'A' *+3*	30	18	2	10	97	57	59
RNAS Culdrose Res.	30	17	1	12	89	50	52
Mullion Res. *-6*	30	17	3	10	63	35	48
Falmouth Ath Res. *+2*	30	12	4	14	56	89	42
Frogpool-Cusgarne	30	11	6	13	68	56	39
Camborne Park *+6*	30	9	6	15	53	57	39
Constantine Res. *-6*	30	12	4	14	63	67	34
Lanner	30	10	2	18	56	78	32
Lizard Res.	30	8	8	14	47	74	32
Praze-an-Beeble *-6*	30	11	3	16	68	90	30
Porthleven R Res. *+2*	30	6	4	20	50	97	24
Cury *+5*	30	5	2	23	50	161	22
Stithians Res. *-3*	30	6	4	20	40	99	19

GRAVESEND LEAGUE

Premier Division	P	W	D	L	F	A	Pts
Craggs Farm TT	16	11	4	1	43	17	37
Viewpoint	16	11	2	3	48	31	35
Lullingstone Castle	16	7	5	4	37	26	26
The O Prince of Or'ge	16	8	2	6	31	35	26
Canal Tavern	16	7	4	5	33	35	25
South Darenth	16	4	4	8	24	28	16
Istead Rise	16	4	2	10	29	38	14
Woodlands Athletic	16	3	4	9	19	39	13
A & Z Sports	16	3	1	12	25	40	10

GREAT YARMOUTH & DISTRICT LEAGUE

Division One	P	W	D	L	F	A	Pts
Catfield	22	20	2	0	117	13	62
Freethorpe	22	16	0	6	75	32	48
Gapton Car Hire	22	13	4	5	83	43	43
White Horse	22	11	6	5	69	46	39
Town Hall	22	11	4	7	60	44	37
MK United	22	9	7	6	70	54	34
Arches *-3*	22	7	6	9	34	41	24
Prince FC	22	7	1	14	73	75	22
Feathers	22	6	3	13	72	112	21
Gorleston Rangers	22	5	5	12	38	73	20
Bohemians	22	4	0	18	32	116	12
SWS Roofing	22	3	2	17	42	116	11

Division Two	P	W	D	L	F	A	Pts
MK United Res. *-3*	22	17	1	4	70	34	49
Yarmouth Peelers	22	16	1	5	68	36	49
Freethorpe Res.	22	14	4	4	87	46	46
Martham Res.	22	10	5	7	65	39	35
Salisbury Arms	22	10	5	7	66	57	35
Feathers Res.	22	10	4	8	55	59	34
Caister United 'A'	22	8	3	11	51	63	27
Prince Consort	22	7	3	12	60	66	24
Reedham	22	6	6	10	44	50	24
Peggottys (Yarmouth)	22	6	2	14	34	87	20
Hemsby	22	3	8	11	32	50	17
Peggottys (Gorleston)	22	3	2	17	30	75	11

GUILDFORD & WOKING ALLIANCE

Premier Division	P	W	D	L	F	A	Pts
Woking Phoenix	22	16	3	3	52	23	51
University of Surrey	22	14	5	3	49	16	47
Lightwater United	22	13	3	6	57	41	42
Burpham	22	12	5	5	65	29	41
Hambledon	22	11	5	6	71	36	38
Bedfont Green 'A'	22	10	7	5	37	29	37
Milford & Witley 'A'	22	10	4	8	64	42	34
Shalford 'A'	22	9	2	11	41	55	29
Weybrook Wanderers	22	6	2	14	24	65	20
Elstead	22	5	2	15	35	45	17
Bisley Sports 'A'	22	5	2	15	33	54	17
Merrow 'A'	22	1	0	21	12	105	3

Division One	P	W	D	L	F	A	Pts
Hersham	22	17	2	3	72	22	53
Addlestone Town	22	15	4	3	68	32	49
Holmbury St Mary	22	14	3	5	86	44	45
AFC Chilworth	22	13	2	7	56	37	41
Emmanuel	22	11	4	7	39	28	37
Univ of Surrey Res.	22	10	2	10	35	46	32
G'ford R'y OB 'A' *-3*	22	9	1	12	40	48	25
Guildford City Shere	22	7	3	12	42	68	24
Surrey Athletic	22	7	1	14	41	55	22
G'ford City Weys. 'A'	22	5	3	14	38	63	18
Oatlands	22	6	0	16	35	63	18
Lightwater Utd Res.	22	4	3	15	32	78	15

Division Two	P	W	D	L	F	A	Pts
West Byfleet Albion	20	18	1	1	62	12	55
Millmead	20	14	2	4	75	34	44
Pirbright Sports	20	11	3	6	59	34	36
New Haw Wanderers	20	11	2	7	62	32	35
Staines Lammas 'A'	20	10	4	6	58	32	34
Milford & Witley 'B'	20	8	4	8	54	47	28
Shottermill/Hasl. 'A'	20	7	5	8	42	40	26
Border/Hth End Spts	20	7	1	12	42	57	22
Dynamo Hindhead	20	5	5	10	44	59	20
Horsley 'A'	20	2	3	15	22	77	9
Elstead Res.	20	1	2	17	24	120	5

Division Three	P	W	D	L	F	A	Pts
AFC Bourne	18	16	2	0	106	13	50
Shepperton FB	18	14	0	4	66	21	42
Staines Lammas 'B'	18	11	1	6	29	24	34
Badshot Lea 'A'	18	10	2	6	63	46	32
Univ of Surrey 'A'	18	9	4	5	45	45	31
G'ford Ciyy Weys. 'B'	18	6	3	9	35	53	21
Christchurch Woking	18	4	4	10	45	61	16
Shottermill/Hasl. 'B'	18	4	4	10	24	46	16
Queen Street Rangers	18	3	1	14	36	81	10
Byfleet	18	2	1	15	20	79	7

Division Four	P	W	D	L	F	A	Pts
Burpham Res.	26	21	2	3	83	35	65
Emmanuel Res.	26	18	7	1	79	31	61
Abbey Rangers	26	18	4	4	72	34	58
Hersham Res.	26	18	1	7	98	38	55
Guildford Park	26	11	7	8	58	47	40
Knaphill 'A'	26	11	5	10	56	47	38
Bedfont Green 'B'	26	12	2	12	59	54	38
Holmbury St M'y Res.	26	9	4	13	44	64	31
Woking Pk/Horsell 'A'	26	7	7	12	48	57	28
Weybrook Wdrs Res.	26	8	1	17	38	65	25
Milford & Witley 'C'	26	6	3	17	38	81	21
Hambledon Res.	26	6	2	18	39	81	20
Shalford 'B'	26	4	7	15	41	78	19
Woking Phoenix Res.	26	5	4	17	35	76	19

GWENT CENTRAL LEAGUE

Division One	P	W	D	L	F	A	Pts
Tranch Res.	26	19	4	3	86	37	61
Clydach Wasps Res.	26	17	3	6	80	40	54
Goytre Res.	26	14	6	6	52	29	48
Govilon Res.	26	14	3	9	90	54	45
Cwmffrwdoer Sp. Res.	26	14	2	10	61	41	44
Llanarth	26	13	4	9	70	59	43
Usk Town *-3*	26	14	3	9	73	59	42
Blaenavon Blues Res.	26	12	6	8	63	58	42
Pontypool Town	26	7	7	12	54	67	28
Gilwern & District	26	7	2	17	47	80	23
Panteg Res.	26	6	5	15	39	78	23
Lower New Inn	26	6	3	17	56	88	21
Race Res.	26	6	2	18	48	83	20
Mardy Res. *-3*	26	6	4	16	52	98	19

Division Two	P	W	D	L	F	A	Pts
Prescoed	28	23	2	3	156	48	71
Pandy	28	21	4	3	143	50	67
Crickhowell Res.	28	18	2	8	105	68	56
PILCS Res.	28	17	3	8	108	50	54
New Inn Res. *-6*	28	18	5	5	95	46	53
Fairfield United Res.	28	14	6	8	96	61	48
Pontypool Town Res.	28	12	7	9	83	67	43
Sebastopol Res.	28	12	5	11	81	79	41
Llanfoist	28	8	3	17	66	107	27
Llanarth Res.	28	9	0	19	53	122	27
Clydach Wasps 'A' *-3*	28	8	5	15	57	85	26
Gilwern/Dist. Res. *-4*	28	9	2	17	50	80	25
Abergavenny Th. Res.	28	5	5	18	48	121	20
Usk Town Res. *-3*	28	5	4	19	38	107	16
Mardy 'A' *-3*	28	3	3	22	35	123	9

GWYNEDD LEAGUE

	P	W	D	L	F	A	Pts
Pwllheli	30	24	2	4	107	39	74
Llangefni Town Res.	30	17	6	7	73	53	57
Barmouth/Dyffryn U	30	18	2	10	85	51	56
Univ. of Wales Bangor	30	17	1	12	60	37	52
Bontnewydd	30	16	4	10	71	55	52
Nantlle Vale	30	15	5	10	84	61	50
Gaerwen	30	14	5	11	63	56	47
Beaumaris Town	30	13	4	13	60	51	43
Bethel	30	13	4	13	55	62	43
Holyhead Hotspur Res.	30	12	4	14	84	85	40
Blaenau Amateurs	30	10	6	14	53	63	36
Porthmadog Res.	30	10	6	14	55	67	36
Llanfairfechan	30	10	5	15	62	76	35
West Shore	30	7	4	19	37	96	25
Llanrwst United Res.	30	6	5	19	29	84	23
Y Felinheli	30	5	3	22	42	84	18

HALIFAX & DISTRICT FA

Premier Division	P	W	D	L	F	A	Pts
Hebden Royd Red Star	22	17	5	0	81	17	56
Stainland United	22	15	3	4	69	40	48
Wheatsheaf	22	13	5	4	54	31	44
Elland United	22	11	5	6	71	42	38
Brighouse Old Boys	22	10	3	9	44	40	33
Halifax Irish Centre	22	9	6	7	45	47	33
Shelf United	22	7	7	8	55	47	28
Ryburn United	22	8	4	10	41	54	28
Midgley United	22	7	5	10	48	47	26
Denholme United	22	6	1	15	49	65	19
St Andrews	22	4	4	14	43	83	16
Greetland CC	22	0	2	20	20	107	2

Wadsworth United – record expunged

Division One	P	W	D	L	F	A	Pts
Holmfield	20	17	2	1	92	32	53
Sowerby United	20	12	2	6	52	34	38
Warley Rangers	20	11	4	5	63	36	37
Brigh'se OB Res. *+2*	20	11	2	7	58	49	37
Mixenden United	20	9	9	2	46	26	36
Salem	20	8	2	10	55	44	26
Calder '76	20	7	4	9	44	31	25
Northowram *-2*	20	6	8	6	64	46	24
Sowerby Bridge *+2*	20	5	2	13	38	65	19
Friendly	20	4	2	14	27	69	14
Stump Cross	20	1	1	18	21	128	4

AFC Lords, Boothtown – records expunged

Division Two	P	W	D	L	F	A	Pts
Martins Nest	24	20	2	2	97	28	62
Sowerby Br. Res. *+3*	24	16	3	5	77	44	54
FC Fold	24	16	4	4	96	53	52
Volunteer Arms	24	14	2	8	107	67	44
Junction	24	11	6	7	68	59	39
Shelf United Res.	24	12	2	10	68	61	38
Ryburn Utd Res. *-3*	24	11	4	9	71	63	34
Hal. Irish Centre Res.	24	11	1	12	56	62	34
Warley Rangers Res.	24	7	4	13	53	60	25
Copley United *-1*	24	7	3	14	55	103	23
Denholme Utd Res.	24	5	3	16	60	99	18
Stainland Utd Res. *+2*	24	2	6	16	55	108	14
Midgley United Res.	24	3	2	19	41	97	11

Division Three	P	W	D	L	F	A	Pts
Golden Lion	20	17	0	3	107	26	51
Pellon United	20	12	4	4	57	36	40
Hebden Royd R S Res.	20	11	4	5	53	28	37
Hipperholme Athetic	20	11	4	5	56	42	37
Bowling Green *+3*	20	10	2	8	66	52	35
Wheatsheaf Res.	20	7	7	6	41	39	28
Stafford	20	8	4	8	46	46	28
Calder '76 Res. *-3*	20	4	8	8	32	51	17
Wadsworth Utd Res.	20	4	4	12	28	57	16
Salem Res.	20	3	2	15	19	73	11
Sowerby United Res.	20	3	1	16	26	81	10

Friendly Res., Ovenden Friendly Athletic – records expunged

HEREFORDSHIRE LEAGUE

Premier Division	P	W	D	L	F	A	Pts
Ewyas Harold	24	19	0	5	92	33	57
Sutton United	24	17	6	1	76	26	57
Wellington Rangers	24	15	6	3	68	29	51
Woofferton	24	13	3	8	51	39	42
Westfields Res.	24	11	6	7	54	42	39
Ledbury Town Res.	24	9	3	12	45	51	30
Pegasus Juniors Res.	24	8	3	13	40	47	27
Leominster Town	24	7	5	12	46	48	26
Hereford Lads Club	24	7	5	12	46	79	26
Fownhope	24	7	4	13	55	84	25
Hinton Res.	24	5	9	10	34	44	24
Weston	24	6	4	14	36	69	22
Kington Town Res.	24	4	2	18	31	83	14

Division One	P	W	D	L	F	A	Pts
Colwall Rangers	18	13	4	1	65	15	43
Bartestree	18	12	3	3	42	22	39
Ewyas Harold Res.	18	11	1	6	53	34	34
Bringsty Sports	18	10	2	6	47	47	32
Widemarsh Rangers	18	10	0	8	41	37	30
Orcop Juniors	18	6	3	9	43	44	21
Shobdon	18	5	2	11	37	46	17
Wellington Rgrs Colts	18	4	3	11	28	53	15
Skenfrith United	18	4	2	12	33	58	14
Woofferton Res.	18	3	4	11	23	56	13

Allpay – record expunged

Division Two	P	W	D	L	F	A	Pts
Ross Town Res.	20	16	0	4	57	27	48
Holme Lacy	20	12	2	6	60	36	38
Orleton	20	9	5	6	50	46	32
Burghill	20	9	3	8	38	36	30
Leintwardine Colts	20	9	3	8	49	51	30
Stoke Prior	20	8	4	8	48	43	28
Hereford Civil Service	20	8	4	8	38	41	28
Bartestree Res.	20	7	3	10	46	45	24
Weobley	20	6	5	9	32	37	23
Weston Res.	20	5	7	8	37	43	22
Pencombe	20	2	2	16	26	76	8

Division Three	P	W	D	L	F	A	Pts
Fownhope Res. -3	18	16	0	2	76	13	45
H'f'd Lads Club Colts	18	13	0	5	59	34	39
Hinton Colts -3	18	13	2	3	77	22	38
H'f'd Civil Serv. Res.	18	10	1	7	46	39	31
Pegasus Juniors Colts	18	8	3	7	37	36	27
Holme Lacy Res.	18	6	4	8	37	47	22
Bartestree Colts	18	4	5	9	40	61	17
Presteigne St And. Res.	18	5	0	13	26	63	15
Dore Valley	18	3	2	13	37	63	11
Kingstone Rovers	18	2	3	13	35	92	9

HERTFORD & DISTRICT LEAGUE

Premier Division	P	W	D	L	F	A	Pts
Bengeo Trinity	22	14	5	3	67	24	33
Royals	22	16	1	5	66	33	33
Westmill	22	12	5	5	49	30	29
Hertford Heath	22	12	5	5	52	35	29
County Hall Rangers	22	12	4	6	55	47	28
Wodson Park	22	12	3	7	55	45	27
John Warner	22	9	3	10	43	44	21
Inter	22	9	3	10	37	42	21
Little Munden Sports	22	6	2	14	36	52	14
Greenbury United	22	4	3	15	28	55	11
Watton-at-Stone	22	5	0	17	35	68	10
Elizabeth Allen OB	22	3	2	17	41	89	8

Division One	P	W	D	L	F	A	Pts
Waltham Abbey 'A'	18	13	3	2	50	28	29
Much Hadham	18	11	5	2	47	22	27
Westmill Res.	18	9	5	4	40	24	23
Thundridge United	18	8	4	6	61	46	20
Wodson Park Res.	18	7	6	5	47	42	20
Bengeo Trinity Res.	18	5	5	8	34	48	15
Buntingford Tn 'A'	18	7	1	10	31	47	15
Kings Sports Res.	18	5	4	9	36	40	14
Mangrove	18	4	1	13	21	56	9
Eliz. Allen OB Res.	18	3	2	13	28	42	8

Division Two	P	W	D	L	F	A	Pts
Ware Lions	22	20	2	0	102	26	42
Broxbourne Badgers	22	14	3	5	79	49	31
Cottered	22	13	4	5	66	41	30
Parklands	22	12	3	7	63	42	27
John Warner Res.	22	10	4	8	53	47	24
Standon & Puck. 'A'	22	8	7	7	66	46	23
Inter Res.	22	10	3	9	56	45	23
Much Hadham Res.	22	7	5	10	53	56	19
Watton-at-Stone Res.	22	6	4	12	49	63	16
Wodson Park 'A'	22	5	1	16	35	75	11
Eliz. Allen OB 'A'	22	4	1	17	32	93	9
Mangrove Res.	22	3	3	16	29	100	9

Division Three	P	W	D	L	F	A	Pts
Baldock Cannon	22	21	0	1	85	24	42
County Hall Rgrs Res.	22	16	2	4	86	41	34
Saracens	22	16	1	5	53	22	33
Bengeo Tigers	22	13	5	4	57	34	31
Mangrove 'A'	22	9	3	10	40	46	21
Deaconsfield	22	9	2	11	42	53	20
Eliz. Allen OB 'B'	22	8	4	10	45	60	20
Buntingford Tn 'B'	22	8	3	11	36	49	19
Cottered Res.	22	6	4	12	26	37	16
Kings Sports 'B'	22	4	2	16	27	53	10
Braughing Rovers	22	4	2	16	46	75	10
Hoddesdon United	22	2	4	16	34	83	8

HOUNSLOW & DISTRICT LEAGUE

Premier Division	P	W	D	L	F	A	Pts
Northfield Shamrocks	21	16	4	1	71	21	52
Sligo Rovers	21	15	3	3	62	30	48
Bedham	21	15	1	5	57	22	46
Eutectic	21	9	2	10	46	52	29
Hanworth	21	7	2	12	43	48	23
CB Hounslow Utd 'B'	21	7	2	12	36	50	23
AFC Explorers	21	5	4	12	46	59	19
Bedfont Town	21	0	2	19	34	113	2

Division One	P	W	D	L	F	A	Pts
Northfield Sham. Res.	20	17	2	1	94	25	53
Spelthorne Sports 'A'	20	17	1	2	95	29	52
West London Wdrs	20	13	0	7	57	47	39
AFC Hampton	20	12	2	6	101	36	38
AFC Ashford	20	12	2	6	74	34	38
CB Hounslow Utd 'C'	20	9	1	10	74	50	28
Surrey Fire	20	8	3	9	60	53	27
Heathrow Seniors	20	7	4	9	44	51	25
Locomotive	20	5	0	15	43	79	15
Bedham Res.	20	1	1	18	24	157	4
Whitton Tn Seniors	20	1	0	19	14	119	3

I ZINGARI LEAGUE

Premier Division	P	W	D	L	F	A	Pts
Old Xaverians	26	23	2	1	75	25	71
East Villa	26	23	1	2	72	18	70
Red Rum	26	15	3	8	74	49	48
Roma	26	13	2	11	40	37	41
NELTC	26	10	7	9	36	41	37
Collegiate Old Boys	26	10	4	12	50	44	34
Mackets	26	11	1	14	41	59	34
Warbreck	26	10	3	13	47	44	33
Hill Athletic	26	9	6	11	41	39	33
Turpins Devonshire	26	9	3	14	40	57	30
Quarry Bank OB	26	8	3	15	30	66	27
Alsop Old Boys	26	6	6	14	31	49	24
Liverpool NALGO	26	7	2	17	45	65	23
BRNESC	26	3	7	16	31	60	16

Division One	P	W	D	L	F	A	Pts
St Ambrose	24	22	0	2	94	15	66
Page Celtic	24	18	2	4	77	44	56
Stoneycroft	24	17	1	6	88	39	52
The Angus Vision	24	15	2	7	87	40	47
Copperas Hill	24	14	3	7	82	57	45
Rolls Royce	24	11	4	9	58	43	37
The Albany	24	11	3	10	54	48	36
Essemmay Old Boys	24	10	2	12	48	50	32
Old Holts	24	9	2	13	40	65	29
Finn Harps	24	7	3	14	48	74	24
Blueline	24	4	4	16	29	62	16
Padua	24	2	1	21	29	121	7
Edge Hill BCOB	24	1	3	20	21	97	6

Division Two	P	W	D	L	F	A	Pts
REMYCA United	24	19	4	1	83	25	61
Eli Lilly	24	17	3	4	81	39	54
Leisure Spts Orchard	24	12	3	9	53	40	39
Lydiate Weld	24	12	2	10	70	58	38
Jubilee Triangle	24	11	3	10	53	60	36
Rockville Wallasey	24	10	4	10	65	47	34
Downholland	24	8	3	13	62	67	27
Redgate Rovers	24	5	2	17	43	81	17
Rhein	24	1	2	21	21	114	5

Combination Div One	P	W	D	L	F	A	Pts
Old Xaverians Res.	16	12	2	2	49	17	38
Speke Res.	16	11	4	1	68	24	37
Collegiate OB Res.	16	7	4	5	37	40	25
Leyfield	16	7	2	7	26	38	23
Birchfield Res.	16	6	4	6	35	30	22
NELTC Res.	16	5	5	6	28	29	20
Aintree Villa Res.	16	4	4	8	36	44	16
Alsop Old Boys Res.	16	5	1	10	26	49	16
Warbreck Res. -1	16	0	4	12	26	60	3

Combination Div Two	P	W	D	L	F	A	Pts
South Liverpool Res.	15	12	1	2	50	10	37
Liobians	15	9	2	4	39	30	29
Old Xaverians 'A'	15	8	4	3	34	20	28
L'pool NALGO Res.	15	6	0	9	29	44	18
Rockville Wall. Res.	15	3	1	11	22	44	10
Stoneycroft Res.	15	2	2	11	21	47	8

Combination Div Three	P	W	D	L	F	A	Pts
Sacre Coeur Former P	21	13	5	3	62	33	44
Birchfield 'A'	21	12	5	4	60	35	41
Edge Hill BCOB Res.	21	10	2	9	70	46	32
Quarry Bank OB Res.	21	8	3	10	41	64	27
Jubilee Tri. Res. -3	21	8	4	9	53	51	25
Mexoc -3	21	7	6	8	44	49	24
Essemmay OB Res.	21	6	4	11	42	62	22
Rockville Wall. 'A'	21	4	3	14	31	63	15

ILFORD & DISTRICT LEAGUE

Premier Division	P	W	D	L	F	A	Pts
St Francis	16	13	1	2	52	19	40
Clapton Res.	16	12	2	2	46	15	38
Broadwater United	16	10	2	4	46	20	32
Woodberry Downs PF	16	8	3	5	45	25	27
Border Rangers	16	7	4	5	35	30	25
London APSA Res.	16	4	3	9	28	60	15
Westill	16	4	0	12	24	53	12
Ryan 'A'	16	1	5	10	23	53	8
Melbourne Sports Res.	16	1	4	11	20	44	7

Division One	P	W	D	L	F	A	Pts
AC Leyton PF	16	13	2	1	70	25	41
St Vincents	16	11	1	4	64	32	34
Titans United	16	11	1	4	62	47	34
Forest United	16	7	1	8	61	41	22
East London Celtic	16	7	0	9	55	57	21
St Francis Res.	16	7	0	9	34	62	21
Ryan 'B'	16	5	1	10	34	52	16
Warriors	16	4	2	10	28	50	14
HB Wanderers	16	2	2	12	26	68	8

Division Two	P	W	D	L	F	A	Pts
London & Essex	16	11	4	1	45	21	37
Baronsmere	16	11	3	2	54	25	36
Trelawny	16	10	2	4	47	28	32
Avondale Rangers	16	6	5	5	44	38	23
Debden Colts	16	7	1	8	40	40	22
Denmark	16	4	3	9	30	41	15
Cowley Leyton	16	4	3	9	28	42	15
Old Ludlows	16	3	4	9	35	64	13
Newham Royals	16	2	3	11	37	61	9

Division Three	P	W	D	L	F	A	Pts
Castle United	18	13	2	3	74	35	41
Alliance United	18	11	3	4	68	39	36
Mile End East -3	18	13	0	5	58	32	36
Ascot United	18	9	4	5	53	27	31
Glendale	18	9	3	6	51	34	30
Durning	18	8	3	7	50	43	27
Midland	18	7	2	9	49	46	23
Renegades	18	4	3	11	43	57	15
East Ham Inter	18	4	2	12	42	67	14
Forest United Res.	18	0	2	16	13	121	2

ISLE OF WIGHT LEAGUE

Division One	P	W	D	L	F	A	Pts
Shanklin	22	17	2	3	55	27	53
West Wight	22	16	4	2	67	21	52
Red Star Spartans	22	11	4	7	48	26	37
Ventnor	22	11	4	7	45	32	37
Oakfield	22	11	2	9	38	38	35
Whitecroft/Barton Spts	22	9	2	11	42	51	29
Binstead & COB	22	8	5	9	40	55	29
Cowes Sports 'A' -2	22	8	2	12	52	45	24
Yarmouth/Calb. -2	22	6	4	12	48	62	20
Sandown	22	6	2	14	22	46	20
E Cowes Vic Ath Res.	22	5	4	13	27	53	19
Niton -2	22	5	3	14	31	59	16

Division Two	P	W	D	L	F	A	Pts
Newport IOW Res.	22	17	0	5	69	25	51
Brading Town Res.	22	15	5	2	70	21	50
Ryde Saints	22	16	1	5	62	24	49
Northwood St John	22	11	3	8	50	47	36
St Helens Blue Star	22	10	5	7	65	36	35
GKN Westlands	22	11	2	9	52	40	35
Plessey Sports	22	7	6	9	52	60	27
Vics Veterans	22	7	4	11	47	62	25
Shanklin VYCC	22	5	6	11	17	34	21
Seaview	22	6	1	15	43	74	19
Carisbrooke United	22	5	3	14	30	71	18
Medina	22	2	4	16	27	90	10

Division Three	P	W	D	L	F	A	Pts
Newchurch	24	23	1	0	93	19	70
Brighstone	24	14	3	7	63	39	45
Wroxall	24	13	3	8	85	54	42
Kyngs Towne	24	13	3	8	64	46	42
Wakes	24	12	2	10	66	43	38
Osborne Coburg	24	9	1	14	48	47	28
Cowes Old Boys	24	8	1	15	44	80	25
Arreton Athletic -4	24	4	4	16	33	57	12
Rookley	24	3	0	21	14	125	9

KIDDERMINSTER & DISTRICT LEAGUE

Premier Division	P	W	D	L	F	A	Pts
Wyre Forest	26	20	6	0	91	29	66
Two Gates	26	16	5	5	61	29	53
Gemini	26	16	2	8	78	50	50
Cradley Heath	26	14	6	6	55	27	48
Blackheath Tn Res.	26	15	2	9	60	40	47
Brintons	26	13	7	6	60	50	46
Areley Kings	26	13	3	10	51	39	42
KS Athletic	26	11	3	12	60	52	36
Kinver	26	9	4	13	48	50	31
Cookley Social	26	9	4	13	57	66	31
Quarry Bank	26	8	4	14	35	62	28
Oldswinford Harriers	26	5	6	15	48	74	21
Parkdale Rovers	26	3	3	20	31	84	12
George/Dragon Colts	26	1	3	22	23	106	6

Division One	P	W	D	L	F	A	Pts
Gigmill	30	24	4	2	144	31	76
Albron	30	24	3	3	124	32	75
Burlish Olympic	30	20	5	5	101	46	65
Millstar Sports	30	20	3	7	117	43	63
Quarry Bank Rangers	30	19	3	8	124	53	60
Birch Coppice	30	19	3	8	95	48	60
Furnace Sports	30	18	3	9	125	55	57
Duke of York -3	30	16	1	13	112	89	46
Dudley Wood Ath	30	14	3	13	127	81	45
Wilden	30	11	4	15	79	94	37
GDIS	30	10	2	18	55	88	32
Rising Sun	30	7	4	19	58	110	25
Dudley Hearts	30	7	1	22	47	84	22
Kings Heath OB	30	3	5	22	49	154	14
Tenbury United Res.	30	3	3	24	40	165	12
Libertys Sports	30	1	1	28	30	254	4

KINGSLEY LEAGUE

	P	W	D	L	F	A	Pts
North Petherwin	20	19	0	1	95	20	57
Holsworthty 'A'	20	17	0	3	68	21	51
Morwenstow Res.	20	15	1	4	71	26	46
Bridgerule	20	13	2	5	71	21	41
Woolsery Res.	20	11	2	7	56	37	35
Merton	20	6	2	12	49	62	20
Kilkhampton Res. -2	20	7	0	13	42	46	19
Week St Mary Res.	20	6	1	13	39	65	19
Stratton United Res.	20	5	1	14	61	86	16
Black Torrington	20	5	1	14	36	70	16
Hartland 'A'	20	1	0	19	21	155	3

KINGSTON & DISTRICT LEAGUE

Premier Division	P	W	D	L	F	A	Pts
Westminster Casuals	18	14	1	3	62	23	43
Maori Park	18	12	3	3	74	25	39
Chessington KC	18	12	1	5	50	38	37
Molesey Villa	18	10	2	6	48	38	32
Kingston Albion	18	8	3	7	39	29	27
Robin Hood	18	7	4	7	49	39	25
Dynamo Pimlico	18	7	1	10	22	32	22
Albert Royals	18	6	3	9	35	41	21
Stoneleigh Park	18	4	1	13	21	52	13
Walton Athletic Res.	18	0	1	17	13	96	1

Division One	P	W	D	L	F	A	Pts
Kingston Academicals	18	13	2	3	60	26	41
Hook Venturers	18	12	1	5	70	31	37
Summerstown	18	11	3	4	43	28	36
Westside Res.	18	9	3	6	43	38	30
Repton	18	7	5	6	36	39	26
Refectory Sports Res.	18	8	1	9	50	49	25
Merton Social	18	6	3	9	28	50	21
Heathfield	18	5	3	10	26	40	18
Fulham Deaf	18	3	3	12	28	61	12
Esher United	18	2	4	12	23	45	10

Division Two	P	W	D	L	F	A	Pts
Wandsworth Corinth.	18	12	2	4	44	40	38
Thornton Heath	18	11	3	4	50	26	36
Spartak Molesey	18	10	1	7	44	39	31
International FC	18	8	5	5	43	31	29
Maori Park Res.	18	8	3	7	42	33	27
Old Rutlishians 'A'	18	7	3	8	27	31	24
AC Malden	18	6	5	7	35	42	23
Teddington BC	18	6	2	10	31	39	20
Barnslake	18	3	4	11	39	58	13
Chessington KC Res.	18	2	6	10	29	45	12

Division Three	P	W	D	L	F	A	Pts
Wandsworth Town	14	9	3	2	36	11	30
MMB	14	8	6	0	27	5	30
Kingston Albion Res.	14	7	4	3	28	19	25
Wandle	14	7	4	3	24	17	25
NPL 'A'	14	5	3	6	23	23	18
Red Star	14	3	4	7	14	20	13
Oxshott Royals	14	2	4	8	15	26	10
Egham Saints	14	0	2	12	9	55	2

Division Four	P	W	D	L	F	A	Pts
Riverdale	16	14	0	2	69	19	42
Surrey Fire Res.	16	13	2	1	55	11	41
NPL 'B'	16	10	2	4	55	32	32
Claygate Swans	16	10	1	5	57	34	31
Hook Vent. Res. -1	16	5	6	5	31	33	20
Surbiton Eagles	16	4	2	10	25	42	14
Merton Social Res.	16	4	2	10	24	58	14
Westside 'A'	16	2	2	12	30	70	8
Heathfield Res. -1	16	1	1	14	16	63	3

Division Five	P	W	D	L	F	A	Pts
Claygate Royals	18	14	1	3	68	27	43
Hersham Royal BL 'A'	18	12	3	3	35	25	39
Darkside	18	12	0	6	62	26	36
Victoire	18	11	3	4	42	23	36
AFC Kingston	18	10	2	6	39	34	32
Outcasts	18	8	2	8	32	35	26
MMB Res.	18	6	4	8	25	30	22
Dynamo Kingston	18	2	5	11	27	50	11
New Malden All Stars	18	2	1	15	21	52	7
Westside 'B'	18	1	3	14	13	62	6

LANCASHIRE AMATEUR LEAGUE

Premier Division	P	W	D	L	F	A	Pts
Little Lever SC	26	18	2	6	72	49	56
Old Mancunians	26	15	5	6	78	39	50
Old Boltonians	26	15	4	7	56	41	49
Rochdale St Clements	26	14	5	7	68	42	47
Mostonians	26	14	4	8	52	38	46
Prairie United	26	12	4	10	67	61	40
Bury GSOB	26	11	6	9	63	64	39
Radcliffe Town	26	11	3	12	58	60	36
Rossendale Amateurs	26	9	5	12	43	52	32
Bolton Lads Club	26	10	1	15	45	42	31
Lymm	26	7	9	10	45	50	30
Chaddertonians	26	7	7	12	48	50	28
Broughton Amateurs	26	6	5	15	39	61	23
Oldham Hulmeians	26	2	2	22	29	114	8

Division One	P	W	D	L	F	A	Pts
Hindley Juniors	26	20	2	4	93	37	62
Bury Amateurs	26	18	4	4	75	27	58
Chaddertonians Res.	26	16	3	7	75	44	51
Old Blackburnians	26	15	5	6	66	40	50
Little Lever	26	14	3	9	77	62	45
Bolton Ambassadors	26	12	4	10	72	64	40
Bolton Wyresdale	26	11	5	10	57	54	38
Tonge United	26	10	3	13	58	63	33
Thornleigh	26	9	4	13	48	54	31
Hesketh Casuals	26	9	4	13	47	55	31
Horwich RMI	26	8	6	12	58	56	30
Tyldesley United	26	9	1	16	50	66	28
Accrington Loyal Am.	26	7	2	17	60	92	23
Fairfield	26	1	0	25	29	151	3

Division Two	P	W	D	L	F	A	Pts
Spotland Methodists	26	18	3	5	119	55	57
Little Lever SC Res.	26	15	3	8	77	49	48
Tottington United	26	14	6	6	72	48	48
Rossendale Am. Res.	26	13	6	7	61	50	45
Bromley Cross	26	11	9	6	60	51	42
Radcliffe Boys	26	12	3	11	77	77	39
Ashtonians	26	10	8	8	63	56	38
Acc. Loyal Am. Res.	26	10	6	10	38	49	36
Lymm Res.	26	10	6	10	44	57	36
Old Boltonians Res.	26	8	7	11	45	62	31
Newman College	26	7	7	12	50	66	28
Bacup United	26	7	2	17	47	65	23
Mostonians Res.	26	5	7	14	50	77	22
Ainsworth	26	5	1	20	45	86	16

Division Three	P	W	D	L	F	A	Pts
O Blackburnians Res.	20	15	2	3	75	29	47
Rochdale St Clem Res.	20	14	2	4	73	31	44
Broughton Amat Res.	20	13	3	4	69	55	42
Hesketh Casuals Res.	20	10	2	8	55	40	32
Bury GSOB Res.	20	8	4	8	44	37	28
Old Mancunians Res.	20	7	6	7	51	39	27
Prairie United Res.	20	8	3	9	41	45	27
Bolton Wyresdale Res.	20	8	2	10	44	45	26
Radcliffe Town Res.	20	5	4	11	31	59	19
Thornleigh Res.	20	4	2	14	31	68	14
Oldham Hulm. Res.	20	2	2	16	23	89	8

Division Four	P	W	D	L	F	A	Pts
Hesketh Casuals 'A'	20	16	2	2	63	32	50
Old Blackburnians 'A'	20	15	1	4	62	30	46
Rochdale St Clem. 'A'	20	12	3	5	44	26	39
Little Lever SC 'A'	20	9	5	6	53	43	32
Spotland Meth. Res.	20	8	5	7	40	47	29
Tottington Utd Res.	20	7	6	7	53	45	27
Tonge United Res.	20	7	4	9	45	54	25
Bury Amateurs Res.	20	7	3	10	36	42	24
Newman College Res.	20	3	5	12	30	51	14
Horwich RMI Res.	20	4	1	15	22	51	13
Bolton Lads Club Res.	20	2	5	13	23	50	11

Division Five	P	W	D	L	F	A	Pts
Radcliffe Boys Res.	20	12	5	3	66	32	41
Old Boltonians 'A'	20	13	2	5	48	30	41
Chaddertonians 'A'	20	11	3	6	59	41	36
Old Blackburnians 'B'	20	9	3	8	44	41	30
Rossendale Am. 'A'	20	8	5	7	44	36	29
Thornleigh 'A'	20	9	2	9	52	50	29
Ashtonians Res.	20	9	2	9	41	41	29
Little Lever SC 'B'	20	9	2	9	42	51	29
Ainsworth Res.	20	7	5	8	33	38	26
Acc'n Loyal Am. 'A'	20	6	2	12	44	60	20
Bolton Ambass. Res.	20	0	3	17	32	85	3

Division Six	P	W	D	L	F	A	Pts
Rochdale St Clem 'B'	22	17	2	3	92	41	53
Acc'n Loyal Am. 'B'	22	15	2	5	80	51	47
Old Boltonians 'B'	22	10	6	6	59	45	36
Mostonians 'A'	22	10	5	7	46	27	35
Old Mancunians 'A'	22	10	5	7	55	44	35
Bolton Wyresdale 'A'	22	11	2	9	59	52	35
Broughton Amat 'A'	22	11	2	9	53	47	35
Horwich RMI 'A'	22	10	2	10	39	51	32
Oldham Hulmeians 'A'	22	6	3	13	47	78	21
Radcliffe Town 'A'	22	5	3	14	39	63	18
Lymm 'A'	22	4	5	13	48	64	17
Thornleigh 'B'	22	3	3	16	34	88	12

Division Seven	P	W	D	L	F	A	Pts
Rossendale Amat 'B'	24	20	2	2	91	30	62
Bury GSOB 'A'	24	19	3	2	79	30	60
Hesketh Casuals 'B'	24	14	2	8	63	41	44
Bury Amateurs 'A'	24	13	1	10	89	61	40
Old Mancunians 'B'	24	12	4	8	61	41	40
Chaddertonians 'B'	24	9	4	11	46	60	31
Lymm 'B'	24	9	3	12	69	61	30
Mostonians 'B' -4	24	8	7	9	50	44	27
Broughton Amat 'B'	24	8	3	13	72	91	27
Spotland Method. 'A'	24	8	0	16	71	66	24
Bury GSOB 'B'	24	7	3	14	52	88	24
Bolton Wyresdale 'B'	24	6	5	13	34	68	23
Oldham Hulmeians 'B'	24	4	1	19	44	140	13

LANCASHIRE LEAGUE

	P	W	D	L	F	A	Pts
Morecambe Res. -3	30	21	4	5	91	31	64
Marine Res.	30	21	1	8	80	30	64
Fleetwood Town Res.	30	19	5	6	82	43	62
Altrincham Res.	30	18	5	7	101	48	59
Southport Res.	30	17	3	10	84	49	54
Leigh RMI Res.	30	14	6	10	47	44	48
Bradford Pk Ave Res.	30	14	5	11	56	68	47
Bamber Bridge Res.	30	14	3	13	66	67	45
Guiseley Res.	30	12	4	14	51	77	40
Burscough Res. -1	30	13	0	17	68	71	38
Lancaster City Res. -7	30	13	3	14	67	58	35
Barrow Res.	30	8	8	14	54	68	32
Workington Res.	30	8	3	19	52	82	27
Ossett Albion Res.	30	6	7	17	38	62	25
Chorley Res.	30	6	6	18	47	88	24
Clitheroe Res.	30	3	3	24	34	132	12

LEEDS RED TRIANGLE LEAGUE

Premier Division	P	W	D	L	F	A	Pts
Rawdon Old Boys	22	17	1	4	81	27	52
Wykebeck Arms Utd	22	14	5	3	58	30	47
Swinnow Athletic	22	14	3	5	69	40	45
Churwell New Inn	22	12	3	7	64	46	39
Arla Foods	22	12	2	8	52	45	38
Yew Tree	22	9	6	7	75	61	33
Farnley Nags Head	22	8	6	8	73	66	30
East Leeds	22	8	2	12	60	65	26
Garforth	22	6	3	13	56	80	21
Amaranth	22	5	2	15	39	65	17
Middleton Park	22	4	3	15	37	110	15
Elhaya African S&CC	22	4	2	16	44	73	14

Park – record expunged

Division One	P	W	D	L	F	A	Pts
Queen	26	19	3	4	91	46	60
Halton Moor	26	17	3	6	96	70	54
Seacroft WMC	26	15	5	6	76	48	50
Skinners Arms	26	15	5	6	85	60	50
Drighlington Adwalton	26	12	6	8	54	51	42
New Farnley CC	26	12	5	9	57	51	41
Farsley Bay Horse	26	11	7	8	61	54	40
Bainbridge United	26	11	2	13	51	59	35
Farnley Sports	26	9	5	12	54	58	32
Leodis	26	8	6	12	49	66	30
Red Lion	26	8	4	14	73	82	28
Dynamo Turbot	26	8	2	16	47	60	26
Golden Fleece	26	3	5	18	26	63	14
Leeds Deaf	26	4	2	20	28	80	14

South Leeds – record expunged

LEICESTER & DISTRICT LEAGUE

Premier Division	P	W	D	L	F	A	Pts
Cosby United	24	17	4	3	73	29	55
Desford	24	16	5	3	67	34	53
Barlestone St Giles	24	15	5	4	58	27	50
Belgrave Blackbird	24	14	2	8	60	37	44
Dunton & Broughton	24	11	4	9	55	43	37
Thringstone M W	24	12	1	11	72	67	37
Birstall RBL	24	10	5	9	56	46	35
Welby Lane United	24	9	5	10	49	40	32
Glenfield Town	24	10	0	14	53	54	30
Magna '73	24	7	8	9	52	42	29
Guru Nanak Gurdwar	24	7	3	14	47	72	24
Glen Villa	24	5	2	17	37	94	17
Syston Fosse	24	1	0	23	24	118	3

Division One	P	W	D	L	F	A	Pts
FC Kirkland	22	19	1	2	79	33	58
Blaby United	22	12	7	3	60	33	43
Queniborough	22	10	7	5	60	49	37
St Patricks	22	11	1	10	60	53	34
Ashby Athletic	22	8	7	7	49	47	31
Oadby Boys Club	22	9	3	10	56	57	30
Earl Shilton Town	22	8	4	10	49	51	28
Barwell Ath. Sporting	22	8	4	10	36	43	28
Burbage Old Boys	22	7	6	9	43	40	27
Broughton Astley	22	6	4	12	37	64	22
Braunstone Tn OB	22	4	5	13	45	64	17
Oakham Imperial *-3*	22	4	3	15	30	70	12

Division Two	P	W	D	L	F	A	Pts
Mountsorrel Amateurs	24	21	0	3	117	35	63
South Leicester	24	15	1	8	62	46	46
W'dgate/N WMC *-3*	24	15	2	7	63	52	44
County Hall	24	13	4	7	50	37	43
Northbridge *-6*	24	15	2	7	76	50	41
Melton Mowbray	24	12	1	11	75	50	37
Houghton Rangers	24	9	7	8	49	43	34
Sapcote United	24	9	3	12	52	58	30
Thurlaston Magpies	24	9	2	13	42	53	29
Kingsway Motel	24	9	1	14	45	75	28
Fleckney Athletic	24	5	3	16	37	63	18
Huncote	24	4	3	17	39	93	15
Midland Syston SP *-3*	24	5	1	18	35	87	13

Reserve Premier Div.	P	W	D	L	F	A	Pts
FC Kirkland Res.	20	13	4	3	46	25	43
Belgrave B'bird Res.	20	13	3	4	57	35	42
Barlestone St G Res.	20	12	3	5	48	33	39
Glenfield Town Res.	20	11	4	5	56	42	37
Cosby United Res.	20	10	2	8	52	40	32
Magna '73 Res.	20	9	3	8	50	40	30
Mountsorrel Am Res.	20	7	3	10	48	47	24
Glen Villa Res.	20	6	2	12	56	56	20
Earl Sh'n Tn Res. *-3*	20	6	3	11	45	71	18
Dunton/B'ton Rg Res.	20	2	7	11	29	39	13
Syston Fosse Res.	20	3	2	15	26	85	11

Reserve Division One	P	W	D	L	F	A	Pts
Oakham Imperial Res.	20	15	2	3	57	33	47
Guru Nanak G. Res.	20	12	3	5	49	27	39
Birstall RBL Res.	20	10	5	5	47	32	35
Burbage OB Res.	20	9	6	5	56	41	33
Thringstone MW Res.	20	9	5	6	38	27	32
Queniborough Res.	20	9	2	9	51	50	29
Broughton Astley Res.	20	7	4	9	32	39	25
Welby Lane Utd Res.	20	6	2	12	29	54	20
St Patricks Res.	20	5	4	11	38	49	19
Oadby Boys Club Res.	20	5	3	12	38	62	18
County Hall Res.	20	4	2	14	36	57	14

LEICESTER CITY LEAGUE

Premier Division	P	W	D	L	F	A	Pts
FC Braunstone Victoria	18	14	2	2	85	29	44
FC Khalsa	18	9	6	3	49	28	33
FC Knighton	18	8	2	8	54	50	26
Sporting United	18	7	4	7	35	45	25
FC Belgrave	18	7	2	9	46	54	23
L'r Sikh Centre YMCA	18	4	4	10	27	55	16
Parva Wayfarers	18	3	2	13	36	71	11

Division One	P	W	D	L	F	A	Pts
Park End '74	16	13	2	1	68	23	41
Ponte	16	13	1	2	53	32	40
South Wigston Wdrs	16	11	1	4	66	29	34
Bharat	16	7	2	7	48	48	23
Brock Design	16	6	3	7	55	44	21
Aylestone/Dist. WMC	16	4	5	7	39	41	17
FC Khalsa Res.	16	4	2	10	26	63	14
Kibworth Town	16	4	0	12	26	60	12
Castle SA	16	1	2	13	24	65	5

Division Two	P	W	D	L	F	A	Pts
FC Rowlatts	22	21	1	0	180	27	64
Mayflower	22	16	2	4	93	61	50
S Wigston W Res. *-3*	22	16	1	5	91	56	46
Generous Briton	22	11	5	6	75	53	38
Glen Villa 'A'	22	10	5	7	68	49	35
Park End '74 Res.	22	10	2	10	61	72	32
Kirkland	22	8	3	11	56	68	27
Cosby Victory	22	7	2	13	49	66	23
Brocks Design Res.	22	5	2	15	51	102	17
FC Knighton Res.	22	5	2	15	48	116	17
FC GNG	22	5	1	16	49	94	16
The Charlotte	22	3	4	15	38	95	13

LINCOLN LEAGUE

	P	W	D	L	F	A	Pts
Heckington United	22	18	1	3	69	14	55
Ivy Tavern	22	17	3	2	82	25	54
Lincoln Railway	22	15	3	4	62	28	48
FC Rustons United	22	13	3	6	49	26	42
Fulbeck United	22	11	3	8	50	33	36
Plough Skellingthorpe	22	11	2	9	55	26	35
Metheringham	22	9	4	9	50	58	31
Horncastle Tn Res.	22	9	2	11	51	51	29
RMSC Athletic	22	6	3	13	37	69	21
FC Maze	22	5	2	15	42	72	17
Metheringham Wed.	22	3	2	17	24	65	11
Harby	22	1	0	21	11	115	3

LIVERPOOL OLD BOYS LEAGUE

Division One	P	W	D	L	F	A	Pts
Bankfield Old Boys	18	15	2	1	56	21	47
Collegiate OB 'A'	18	10	5	3	40	27	35
Old Bootleians	18	10	2	6	49	36	32
FC Salle *-6*	18	9	4	5	41	31	25
Old Xaverians 'B' *-3*	18	8	4	6	38	38	25
NALGO Students *-3*	18	8	1	9	35	53	22
Croxteth Comp OB	18	5	3	10	36	40	18
Hope Park	18	4	5	9	39	47	17
Wavertree WD OB *-3*	18	4	2	12	23	42	11
Business School	18	2	2	14	31	53	8

Division Two	P	W	D	L	F	A	Pts
Naylorsfield *-1*	20	17	2	1	66	28	52
Old Instonians *-5*	20	13	3	4	54	28	37
De La Salle Old Boys	20	11	1	8	37	41	34
Old Bootleians Res.	20	10	2	8	52	40	32
Waterloo GSOB	20	8	4	8	56	46	28
Cardinal Newman *-3*	20	10	0	10	52	45	27
Old Xaverians 'C'	20	7	5	8	39	44	26
Quarry Bank OB 'A'	20	7	3	10	45	49	24
Corinthian	20	8	0	12	42	52	24
Alsop Old Boys 'A'	20	7	1	12	35	46	22
Convocation	20	1	1	18	19	78	4

Division Three	P	W	D	L	F	A	Pts
Sacre Coeur F P Res.	22	17	3	2	59	20	54
Old Xaverians 'D'	22	15	4	3	64	33	49
Alsop Old Boys 'B'	22	15	1	6	67	44	46
Bootech Old Boys	22	11	6	5	62	37	39
Collegiate OB 'B'	22	13	0	9	61	49	39
Waterloo GSOB Res.	22	8	7	7	76	58	31
Gateacre	22	8	6	8	63	58	30
Old Bootleians 'A'	22	7	2	13	50	73	23
Oaks Institute OB	22	5	4	13	51	72	19
Essemmay OB 'A'	22	5	4	13	48	81	19
Quarry Bank OB 'B'	22	4	3	15	42	64	15
Old Cathinians	22	3	2	17	47	101	11

LONDON COMMERCIAL LEAGUE

Division One	P	W	D	L	F	A	Pts
British Airways	18	13	3	2	67	25	42
Kodak Harrow	18	11	4	3	47	20	37
New Hanford	18	12	1	5	51	25	37
Indian Gymkhana	18	11	4	3	35	18	37
Hillingdon Irish	18	9	2	7	44	43	29
Northolt Villa	18	6	3	9	31	40	21
Travaux	18	5	4	9	29	57	19
Chiswick Homefields	18	4	2	12	22	45	14
Sporting Hackney	18	3	3	12	38	60	12
Roxeth	18	1	4	13	28	59	7

Division Two	P	W	D	L	F	A	Pts
Old Alpertonians	20	15	1	4	60	30	46
British Airways Res.	20	15	1	4	55	32	46
East Fulham	20	14	2	4	64	25	44
AC New Team	20	13	2	5	59	30	41
Wadadiya	20	11	4	5	52	38	37
Acton Spts Club Mens	20	10	3	7	42	38	33
Somerville Old Boys	20	4	5	11	29	48	17
Sandgate Old Boys	20	5	2	13	26	47	17
Camden Sports Club	20	3	6	11	35	62	15
Sudbury Court	20	2	3	15	23	57	9
Kodak Harrow Res.	20	2	3	15	15	53	9

LONDON FINANCIAL FA

Division One	P	W	D	L	F	A	Pts
Marsh	16	11	4	1	41	15	37
Nat West Bank Res.	16	8	5	3	38	31	29
Dresdner Kleinwort W	16	5	4	7	29	33	19
Chislehurst Sports	16	4	5	7	26	36	17
National West. Bank	16	0	6	10	16	35	6

Division Two	P	W	D	L	F	A	Pts
Credit Suisse	14	11	2	1	54	17	35
Royal Bank of Scot.	14	10	3	1	44	25	33
Chislehurst S Res. *-1*	14	6	5	3	39	25	22
Coutts & Co	14	5	2	7	39	41	17
Zurich Eagle Star	14	5	2	7	39	41	17
Marsh Res.	14	4	3	7	31	39	15
Nat West Bank 'A'	14	4	2	8	43	61	14
JP Morgan Chase	14	1	1	12	24	64	4

Division Three	P	W	D	L	F	A	Pts
Nat West Bank 'B'	16	13	3	0	47	12	42
Royal Bk of Scot Res.	16	10	3	3	36	16	33
Chislehurst Sp 'A' *-1*	16	7	6	3	31	25	26
British Council	16	7	2	7	25	30	23
Citigroup CIB	16	6	2	8	29	30	20
Royal Sun Alliance	16	6	2	8	24	32	20
Temple Bar	16	5	3	8	34	38	18
Foreign/Com. Office	16	4	1	11	26	53	13
Royal Sun All. Res.	16	2	2	12	25	41	8

LUTON & SOUTH BEDS LEAGUE

Premier Division	P	W	D	L	F	A	Pts
Christians in Sport	18	15	2	1	83	20	47
Luton Irish	18	12	4	2	64	20	40
St Josephs	18	12	2	4	54	27	38
Dunstable United	18	11	4	3	55	29	37
Eaton Bray	18	8	3	7	24	43	27
Ewe & Lamb	18	7	3	8	43	42	24
Yeoman Luton	18	5	3	10	27	49	18
Lewsey Park	18	3	4	11	31	48	13
Hansom Cab	18	3	1	14	28	51	10
The 61 FC (L'n) Res.	18	0	2	16	15	95	2

Division One	P	W	D	L	F	A	Pts
Club Lewsey	14	13	1	0	79	12	40
AC Bellini	14	9	1	4	48	28	28
Luton Eagles	14	8	0	6	49	39	24
St Josephs Res.	14	7	3	4	33	42	24
Christians in Spt Res.	14	7	2	5	32	28	23
Crown Sundon	14	4	0	10	30	41	12
Vauxhall Aftersales	14	2	2	10	18	58	8
Luton Leagrave	14	1	1	12	16	57	4

Sportsman – record expunged

MATLOCK & DISTRICT LEAGUE

Division One	P	W	D	L	F	A	Pts
Cotes Park	22	18	3	1	102	18	57
Shirland MW	22	15	3	4	68	36	48
Kings Arms	22	13	3	6	64	39	42
Cromford Res.	22	13	2	7	69	41	41
Somerlea	22	11	4	7	56	33	37
Pinxton North End	22	10	5	7	60	46	35
Laburnum Saints	22	11	2	9	50	56	35
Peak United	22	9	3	10	44	47	30
Darley Dale Lions	22	6	2	14	47	72	20
J B United	22	3	2	17	26	71	11
AFC Lea Holloway *-3*	22	3	4	15	31	80	10
Bell Inn	22	2	3	17	20	98	9

MIDLAND AMATEUR ALLIANCE

Premier Division	P	W	D	L	F	A	Pts
Underwood Villa	24	21	0	3	119	47	63
Racing Athletic	24	15	4	5	58	30	49
Ashland Rovers	24	15	4	5	58	40	49
Woodborough Utd	24	14	2	8	87	48	44
Beaufort United	24	13	5	6	68	39	44
Steelers	24	13	3	8	61	39	42
Old Elizabethans	24	11	6	7	49	46	39
Wollaton 'A'	24	10	4	10	66	59	34
Beeston OB Assoc.	24	9	4	11	48	53	31
Lady Bay	24	6	2	16	47	80	20
Bassingfield	24	5	2	17	29	99	17
Derbyshire Am Res.	24	2	4	18	32	78	10
Sherwood Forest	24	1	2	21	25	89	5

Division One	P	W	D	L	F	A	Pts
Monty Hind OB	26	19	7	0	73	27	64
County NALGO	26	17	5	4	64	34	56
Brunts Old Boys	26	14	3	9	66	64	45
Clinphone	26	11	7	8	61	50	40
Radcliffe Olympic 'A'	26	11	4	11	47	45	37
PASE	26	10	7	9	59	63	37
Old Bemrosians	26	11	3	12	46	40	36
Nottinghamshire	26	11	3	12	50	53	36
Old Elizabethans Res.	26	11	1	14	57	62	34
Keyworth United 'A'	26	8	7	11	56	58	31
Southwell Amateurs	26	7	6	13	47	58	27
Wollaton 'B'	26	7	6	13	44	59	27
Broadmeadows	26	6	5	15	57	60	23
West Bridgford Utd	26	5	4	17	40	94	19

Division Two	P	W	D	L	F	A	Pts
FC '05	26	26	0	0	178	20	78
Acorn Athletic	26	20	2	4	128	62	62
Top Club	26	19	3	4	105	54	60
Calverton MW 'A'	26	15	1	10	80	62	46
Ashland Rovers Res.	26	14	3	9	75	80	45
Hickling	26	14	1	11	88	69	43
EMTEC	26	12	3	11	86	67	39
Nottinghamshire Res.	26	10	4	12	60	70	34
Cambridge Knights	26	9	1	16	93	80	28
Derbyshire Am 'A'	26	8	3	15	50	98	27
Ashfield Athletic	26	5	6	15	68	105	21
Old Bemrosians Res.	26	6	2	18	34	92	20
Tibshelf Old Boys	26	5	3	18	47	110	18
Hare & Hounds	26	2	2	22	41	164	8

MIDLAND REGIONAL ALLIANCE

Premier Division	P	W	D	L	F	A	Pts
Ashover	32	20	8	4	97	56	68
Derby Rolls R Leisure	32	19	6	7	82	34	63
Carlton Town Res.	32	19	6	7	77	44	63
Wirksworth Town	32	16	5	11	74	46	53
Holbrook St Michaels	32	15	7	10	61	41	52
Ilkeston Town Res.	32	15	7	10	49	42	52
Rowsley	32	15	4	13	74	61	49
Cromford	32	14	7	11	62	61	49
Allestree	32	12	8	12	45	59	44
Belper United	32	12	7	13	49	55	43
Melbourne Dynamo	32	13	3	16	58	65	42
Borrowash Vic Res.	32	13	3	16	65	76	42
Shirebrook Tn Res.	32	12	4	16	59	69	40
Belper Town Res.	32	9	7	16	60	69	34
Eastwood Town Res.	32	10	4	18	55	85	34
Chesterfield Athletic	32	5	9	18	45	90	24
Long Eaton Utd Res.	32	4	3	25	39	98	15

Division One	P	W	D	L	F	A	Pts
Dronfield Town	32	28	1	3	130	21	85
Newmount	32	20	8	4	96	33	68
Castle Donington Tn	32	20	2	10	98	47	62
Ripley *-1*	32	18	7	7	79	47	60
Pastures	32	16	7	9	74	46	55
Swanwick Pentrich Rd	32	16	7	9	62	46	55
Dovedale Long Eaton	32	14	9	9	56	58	51
Derbyshire Amateurs	32	13	9	10	58	63	48
Sutton Town Res.	32	12	6	14	50	65	42
Shirebrook Town 'A'	32	11	8	13	58	62	41
Holbrook St M Res.	32	11	5	16	50	70	38
Little Eaton *-1*	32	10	5	17	52	72	34
Derby RR Leis Res.	32	7	8	17	49	76	29
Bargate Rovers	32	8	5	19	53	85	29
Woolley Moor Utd	32	7	7	18	45	77	28
Beeston AFC	32	7	5	20	48	106	26
Rowsley Res.	32	2	5	25	33	117	11

MID-SOMERSET LEAGUE

Premier Division	P	W	D	L	F	A	Pts
Meadow Rangers	20	14	3	3	46	23	45
Radstock Town Res.	20	11	4	5	43	27	37
Coleford Athletic	20	9	2	9	50	34	29
Westfield	20	8	4	8	42	36	28
Wookey	20	8	4	8	37	33	28
Chew Magna	20	7	7	6	29	38	28
Mells & Vobster Utd	20	7	5	8	30	27	26
Chilcompton	20	6	5	9	27	34	23
Littleton Sports	20	6	5	9	35	45	23
Farrington Gurney	20	6	3	11	27	42	21
Stoke Rovers	20	5	4	11	29	56	19

Division One	P	W	D	L	F	A	Pts
Purnells Sports	20	16	3	1	105	13	51
Belrose	20	15	1	4	72	32	46
Glastonbury Tn Res.	20	13	2	5	60	29	41
Frome Collegians Res.	20	12	2	6	52	22	38
Norton Hill Rangers	20	10	3	7	60	37	33
Welton Arsenal	20	8	4	8	28	41	28
Littleton Sports Res.	20	7	3	10	30	52	24
Evercreech Rovers	20	7	3	10	45	69	24
Welton Rovers 'A'	20	6	2	12	42	46	20
Oakhill	20	3	2	15	31	103	11
Pilton United	20	0	1	19	21	102	1

Division Two	P	W	D	L	F	A	Pts
Pensford	20	20	0	0	104	12	60
Temple Cloud	20	14	0	6	51	34	42
Purnells Sports Res.	20	11	4	5	52	23	37
Wells City 'A'	20	8	8	4	51	45	32
Clutton Res. *-1*	20	9	6	5	36	40	32
Frome Tn Sports Res.	20	6	5	9	36	45	23
Farmborough	20	6	2	12	50	55	20
Tunley Athletic Res.	20	5	4	11	34	60	19
Chilcompton Res.	20	5	3	12	32	62	18
Frome Collegians 'A'	20	5	2	13	37	53	17
Radstock Town 'A'	20	0	8	12	25	79	8

Division Three	P	W	D	L	F	A	Pts
Mells/Vobster U Res.	24	19	3	2	87	25	60
Westfield Res.	24	17	3	4	90	40	54
Interhound	24	16	4	4	59	35	52
Farrington Gurn. Res.	24	12	4	8	59	53	40
Chew Magna Res.	24	10	5	9	51	39	35
Meadow Rangers Res.	24	8	7	9	60	63	31
Belrose Res.	24	8	6	10	45	46	30
Coleford Ath Res.	24	8	6	10	50	65	30
Chilcompton United	24	7	5	12	51	56	26
Wookey Res.	24	7	4	13	42	62	25
Stoke Rovers Res.	24	5	7	12	46	67	22
Pensford Res.	24	4	8	12	44	66	20
Evercreech Rvrs Res.	24	3	2	19	25	92	11

MID-SUSSEX LEAGUE

Premier Division	P	W	D	L	F	A	Pts
East Grinstead Utd	26	20	2	4	76	23	62
Maresfield Village	26	18	5	3	72	27	59
Old Varndeanians	26	19	1	6	83	28	58
Willingdon Athletic	26	14	7	5	48	31	49
Wisdom Sports	26	13	5	8	57	40	44
Jarvis Brook	26	13	2	11	45	39	41
Balcombe	26	12	3	11	44	34	39
Hassocks 'A'	26	9	7	10	56	52	34
Lewes Bridgeview	26	9	3	14	42	41	30
Lindfield	26	8	2	16	34	67	26
Cuckfield Town	26	7	2	17	24	66	23
Newick	26	6	4	16	37	72	22
Nutley	26	5	4	17	36	96	19
Buxted	26	3	5	18	31	69	14

Division One	P	W	D	L	F	A	Pts
Felbridge *-1*	24	16	3	5	76	39	50
Plumpton Ath *+2*	24	13	7	4	56	42	48
Forest Row	24	14	5	5	58	36	47
Barcombe *+2*	24	10	7	7	68	55	39
Heath Pilgrims	24	9	5	10	42	46	32
O Varndeanians Res.	24	8	7	9	56	48	31
Sporting Lindfield	24	8	6	10	56	64	30
Wisdom Sports Res.	24	7	7	10	48	55	28
Wivelsfield Green	24	6	9	9	50	57	27
Turners Hill	24	7	6	11	52	72	27
Village of Ditchling	24	7	5	12	47	69	26
Ardingly	24	6	5	13	42	59	23
Uckfield Tn Res. *-1*	24	5	8	11	50	59	22

Division Two	P	W	D	L	F	A	Pts
Horsted Keynes	24	19	3	2	113	31	60
Hartfield	24	15	6	3	55	27	51
Rotherfield	24	12	4	8	50	37	40
Hurstpierpoint Res.	24	12	4	8	57	44	40
Franklands Village	24	11	3	10	64	52	36
Burgess Hill Albion	24	11	2	11	56	44	35
Crawley Dn 'A' *+2*	24	9	6	9	44	45	35
Peacehaven Utd *+3*	24	10	2	12	40	62	35
Handcross Village	24	10	4	10	67	52	34
Pease P Vill Res. *-3*	24	11	4	9	58	61	34
E Grinstead Utd Res.	24	6	7	11	46	70	25
E G'stead Tn 'A' *-1*	24	5	2	17	42	114	16
Maresfield Vill Res.	24	0	3	21	20	73	3

Division Three	P	W	D	L	F	A	Pts
Willingdon Ath Res.	22	21	0	1	103	10	63
Ashurst Wood	22	14	2	6	74	35	44
Cuckfield Wheatsheaf	22	13	4	5	65	42	43
Horley Athletico	22	12	5	5	51	35	41
Roffey	22	11	3	8	59	35	36
Scaynes Hill	22	11	2	9	68	43	35
E Grinstead Mariners	22	9	3	10	44	54	30
Cuckfield Town Res.	22	8	2	12	44	64	26
Lindfield Res. *+2*	22	5	4	13	33	52	21
West Hoathly *-1*	22	6	4	12	31	65	21
Burgess Hill Athletic	22	4	1	17	32	109	13
Plumpton Ath Res.	22	2	2	18	26	86	8

Division Four	P	W	D	L	F	A	Pts
AFC Ringmer	20	17	2	1	81	21	53
East Court	20	14	2	4	93	35	44
Fletching	20	14	1	5	49	29	43
Dormansland Rockets	20	10	3	7	45	33	33
Lewes Bridgeview Res.	20	10	1	9	37	48	31
Wealden 'A'	20	8	1	11	36	58	25
O V'deanians 'A' *+3*	20	5	4	11	35	54	22
Crowborough Ath 'A'	20	6	3	11	47	58	21
Uckfield Town 'A'	20	6	2	12	42	64	20
Ardingly Res.	20	5	0	15	44	68	15
Nutley Res. *-3*	20	4	3	13	24	65	12

Division Five	P	W	D	L	F	A	Pts
Keymer & Hassocks	22	17	0	5	70	29	51
Roffey Res.	22	14	3	5	50	24	45
Danehill	22	11	4	7	68	52	37
Lingfield 'A'	22	11	4	7	54	43	37
Scaynes Hill Res.	22	12	1	9	55	47	37
Turners Hill Res.	22	11	3	8	61	38	36
Fairwarp	22	10	2	10	54	54	32
Newick Res.	22	9	1	12	42	43	28
Fairfield	22	6	6	10	38	45	24
Handcross Vill Res.	22	7	3	12	30	68	24
Buxted Res.	22	4	5	13	29	57	17
Vill of Ditchling Res.	22	3	2	17	25	76	11

Division Six	P	W	D	L	F	A	Pts
Wisdom Sports 'A'	22	14	3	5	74	43	45
Burgess Hill Alb Res.	22	14	2	6	51	34	44
Barcombe Res.	22	11	6	5	51	24	39
Willingdon Ath 'A'	22	11	5	6	53	43	38
Jarvis Brook Res.	22	11	3	8	50	39	36
Rotherfield Res.	22	10	4	8	52	47	34
E Grinstead Utd 'A'	22	10	3	9	53	67	33
E G'stead Mar. Res.	22	8	3	11	46	57	27
Wivelsfield Gn Res.	22	7	3	12	47	57	24
Ansty Spts & Social	22	6	3	13	37	51	21
Heath Pilgrims Res.	22	6	1	15	40	71	19
Cuckfield Town 'A'	22	3	6	13	32	53	15

Division Seven	P	W	D	L	F	A	Pts
St Francis Rgrs 'A'	22	20	1	1	82	13	61
Copthorne Rovers	22	17	2	3	99	25	53
Horsted Keynes Res.	22	15	3	4	72	33	48
Ashurst Wood Res.	22	10	8	4	45	29	38
Bolney Rovers	22	9	4	9	43	44	31
Burgess Hill Res. *-1*	22	9	4	9	55	50	30
Maresfield Village 'A'	22	8	4	10	35	59	28
Hartfield Res.	22	8	3	11	58	65	27
Dormansland Rkts Res.	22	6	2	14	34	49	20
Lindfield 'A' *+2*	22	5	2	15	32	83	19
Cuckfield Wh'f Res.	22	4	6	12	37	63	18
Danehill Res.	22	1	1	20	16	95	4

Division Eight	P	W	D	L	F	A	Pts
Copthorne Rvrs Res.	22	19	0	3	104	23	57
Felbridge Res.	22	14	2	6	62	34	44
Uckfield Tn 'B' *+3*	22	13	2	7	60	42	44
Balcombe Res.	22	12	5	5	77	41	41
Fletching Res.	22	12	3	7	45	34	39
Scaynes Hill 'A'	22	11	6	5	43	34	39
Forest Row Res.	22	11	3	8	42	34	36
Chailey Res.	22	9	1	12	44	36	28
Vill of Ditchling 'A'	22	5	2	15	28	85	17
Handcross Vill 'A'	22	4	4	14	33	87	16
Wealden 'B'	22	4	0	18	35	73	12
Lindfield 'B' *-3*	22	3	2	17	25	75	8

Division Nine	P	W	D	L	F	A	Pts
Wivelsfield Gn 'A'	22	20	0	2	90	30	60
Crowborough Ath 'B'	22	17	2	3	82	31	53
Fairwarp Res.	22	12	1	9	57	47	37
Maresfield Village 'B'	22	11	3	8	47	34	36
Burgess Hill Alb 'A'	22	11	2	9	56	61	35
Lindfield 'C'	22	10	2	10	54	61	32
Ardingly 'A' *+3*	22	8	2	12	53	49	29
Plumpton Ath 'A' *+3*	22	8	2	12	50	47	29
W Hoathly Res. *-3*	22	9	3	10	52	55	27
Cuckfield Tn 'B' *-6*	22	8	4	10	65	53	22
Scaynes Hill 'B' *+3*	22	4	1	17	22	91	16
Buxted 'A'	22	3	0	19	31	100	9

MID-WALES LEAGUE

	P	W	D	L	F	A	Pts
Llanrhaeadr	30	21	4	5	83	44	67
Presteigne St Andrews	30	21	2	7	67	42	65
Aberystwyth Tn Res.	30	20	4	6	71	38	64
Kerry	30	17	2	11	57	36	53
Llanfyllin Town	30	16	5	9	65	48	53
Caersws Res.	30	14	8	8	46	33	50
UW Aberystwyth	30	12	10	8	66	46	46
Berriew	30	13	6	11	47	39	45
Rhayader Town	30	12	8	10	68	54	44
Welshpool Tn Res.	30	10	7	13	39	49	37
Llanidloes Town	30	9	7	14	51	53	34
Four Crosses	30	9	4	17	41	61	31
Newtown Res.	30	8	4	18	43	74	28
Knighton Town	30	5	8	17	42	67	23
Waterloo Rovers	30	6	1	23	33	74	19
Carno	30	5	4	21	31	92	19

MONTGOMERYSHIRE & DISTRICT LEAGUE

Division One	P	W	D	L	F	A	Pts
Total Network S. Res.	22	17	3	2	68	18	54
Dyffryn Banw	22	14	5	3	65	29	47
Llanfair United	22	13	1	8	54	37	40
Llanfyllin Town Res.	22	12	3	7	47	32	39
Guilsfield Res.	22	12	2	8	46	34	38
Llangedwyn	22	9	2	11	42	49	29
Abermule	22	8	4	10	35	40	28
Montgomery Town	22	7	5	10	33	54	26
Bishops Castle	22	6	7	9	36	39	25
Bettws	22	6	5	11	31	48	23
Meifod	22	6	1	15	41	61	19
Llanwddyn	22	2	2	18	26	83	8

Division Two	P	W	D	L	F	A	Pts
Waterloo Rvrs Res.	22	17	3	2	55	18	54
Severn Valley	22	14	5	3	76	31	47
Newtown Rangers	22	14	5	3	69	27	47
Churchstoke	22	14	4	4	75	37	46
Llanidloes Tn Res.	22	10	2	10	37	35	32
Llanfair United Res.	22	10	1	11	49	49	31
Bishops Castle Res.	22	8	6	8	37	38	30
Llanfechain	22	8	4	10	51	58	28
Dyffryn Banw Res.	22	8	4	10	34	58	28
Defaid Du	22	4	5	13	24	58	17
Abermule Res.	22	2	3	17	43	83	9
Kerry Res.	22	0	4	18	14	72	4

NEWPORT & DISTRICT LEAGUE

Premier Division X	P	W	D	L	F	A	Pts
Pioneer	26	22	3	1	146	42	69
Malpas Gladiator	26	22	2	2	137	29	68
Pill	26	18	6	2	84	33	60
Villa Dino	26	18	3	5	97	28	57
Ship & Pilot	26	15	4	7	97	54	49
New Lysaghts Club	26	12	2	12	63	68	38
Pill Hibernians	26	10	2	14	59	75	32
Contour	26	10	1	15	56	98	31
Merry Miller	26	9	1	16	66	108	28
Pontnewydd United	26	8	2	16	50	94	26
Duffryn	26	6	2	18	42	78	20
Caerleon Town	26	5	5	16	36	84	20
Malpas	26	4	3	19	40	97	15
Henllys Rangers	26	4	2	20	29	114	14

Premier Division Y	P	W	D	L	F	A	Pts
Coed Eva Ath Res.	24	19	2	3	84	36	59
Cwmbran Celtic Res.	24	15	5	4	63	31	50
Lliswerry Res.	24	13	4	7	78	41	43
Trethomas B'birds Res.	24	11	6	7	66	43	39
AC Pontymister Res.	24	11	5	8	58	42	38
Albion Rovers Res.	24	11	4	9	52	51	37
Spencer Yth/Boys Res.	24	10	4	10	57	54	34
Cromwell Youth Res.	24	10	4	10	59	54	34
W Pontnewydd Res.	24	9	3	12	47	60	30
Rogerstone Welf Res.	24	9	3	12	53	70	30
Newport C Serv Res.	24	7	4	13	44	78	25
Lucas Cwmbran Res.	24	4	5	15	40	70	17
Croesyceiliog 'A'	24	0	5	19	29	100	5

Division One	P	W	D	L	F	A	Pts
Malpas Gladiator Res.	22	17	4	1	74	29	55
Llanwern Sports	22	16	4	2	87	26	52
Marshfield	22	13	5	4	72	34	44
Spencer Old Boys	22	12	4	6	59	49	40
Shaftesbury Youth	22	9	7	6	60	42	34
Six in Hand	22	8	7	7	53	55	31
Newport Cor. Res.	22	8	3	11	51	70	27
Gaer Inn	22	5	4	13	45	49	19
Lliswerry 'A'	22	5	4	13	44	66	19
Villa Dino Res.	22	6	1	15	37	75	19
Albion Rovers 'A'	22	4	4	14	29	70	16
Pill Res.	22	3	5	14	34	80	14

NORTH DEVON LEAGUE

Premier Division	P	W	D	L	F	A	Pts
Boca Seniors	30	27	0	3	124	28	81
Morwenstow	30	23	3	4	96	33	72
Georgeham/Croyde	30	19	3	8	80	45	60
Dolton Rangers	30	18	6	6	85	53	60
Braunton	30	18	4	8	94	46	58
Shamwickshire Rvrs	30	16	6	8	73	39	54
Appledore Res.	30	10	7	13	46	48	37
Barnstaple AAC	30	10	7	13	51	60	37
Bradworthy United	30	10	5	15	62	79	35
Northam Lions	30	10	5	15	51	81	35
Holsworthy Res.	30	8	8	14	37	53	32
Hartland	30	9	5	16	43	79	32
Putford	30	8	6	16	53	59	30
Kilkhampton	30	8	3	19	47	84	27
Clovelly	30	7	4	19	36	78	25
Ilfracombe Tn Res.	30	2	2	26	25	138	8

Senior Division	P	W	D	L	F	A	Pts
Woolacombe	26	21	1	4	100	30	64
Lovacott/J&A Cameras	26	16	3	7	95	49	51
Combe Martin	26	14	7	5	88	50	49
North Molton	26	14	7	5	91	57	49
Braunton Res.	26	14	5	7	83	55	47
Pilton Academicals	26	13	2	11	94	71	41
Chittlehampton	26	12	5	9	83	68	41
South Molton	26	12	5	9	61	70	41
Woolsery -3	26	10	6	10	47	56	33
Shamwickshire R Res.	26	8	6	12	57	64	30
High Bickington	26	8	3	15	54	86	27
Appledore 'A' -3	26	5	4	17	37	77	16
Wrey Arms -6	26	4	5	17	44	72	11
Bradworthy Res. -3	26	1	1	24	14	143	1

Intermediate Div One	P	W	D	L	F	A	Pts
Northam Lions Res.	30	23	2	5	125	41	71
Torrington Res.	30	22	4	4	104	42	70
Torridgeside	30	19	6	5	103	56	63
Bratton Fleming	30	18	4	8	77	50	58
Braunton 'A'	30	15	4	11	79	57	49
Bude Town Res.	30	15	1	14	62	78	46
Lynton & Lynmouth	30	14	3	13	77	76	45
Barnstaple AAC Res.	30	13	5	12	58	57	44
Stratton United -3	30	13	2	15	86	77	38
Georgeham/Cr'de Res	30	11	5	14	56	75	38
Torrington Admirals	30	10	4	16	67	95	34
Hartland Res.	30	9	3	18	56	96	30
Nth Molton Res. -3	30	10	1	19	70	90	28
Combe Martin Res.	30	8	3	19	53	107	27
Equalizers	30	7	5	18	48	74	26
Landkey	30	6	2	22	56	106	20

Intermediate Div Two	P	W	D	L	F	A	Pts
Dolton Rangers Res.	30	27	3	0	156	38	84
Sporting Barum	30	18	7	5	116	56	61
Shebbear United	30	16	6	8	100	55	54
Chittlehampton Res.	30	16	5	9	88	73	53
Pilton Acad'cals Res.	30	14	8	8	86	65	50
Lovacott/J&A C Res.	30	14	7	9	93	91	49
Clovelly Res.	30	14	6	10	70	61	48
Anchor	30	12	4	14	72	83	40
Buckland Brewer	30	9	10	11	61	61	37
South Molton Res.	30	11	3	16	72	99	36
Putford Res.	30	9	7	14	47	75	34
High Bickington Res.	30	10	3	17	76	95	33
Grosvenor	30	7	6	17	51	99	27
Lynton/Lynm'th Res.	30	7	2	21	65	102	23
Torrington 'A'	30	5	8	17	56	101	23
Landkey Res. -6	30	7	3	20	56	111	18

NORTH GWENT LEAGUE

Premier Division	P	W	D	L	F	A	Pts
Castle United	22	18	3	1	97	28	57
Abertillery Blue. Res.	22	13	4	5	78	48	43
The Woodlands	22	12	6	4	92	43	42
Southend Athletic	22	12	4	6	59	38	40
Rhymney	22	10	4	8	55	51	34
Aberbargoed Town	22	11	1	10	63	70	34
KT's Wine Bar	22	9	5	8	69	58	32
Pantside	22	7	5	10	49	49	26
Abertillery Res.	22	5	8	9	45	64	23
Abercarn Utd Res.	22	5	1	16	33	81	16
Trinant Res.	22	4	3	15	28	84	15
Pentwynmawr Res.	22	2	4	16	37	91	10

Division One	P	W	D	L	F	A	Pts
Brynmawr Town	28	23	0	5	128	48	69
Tafarn y Werin	28	19	2	7	100	53	59
Drysiog Inn	28	17	4	7	104	67	55
Cefn Forest United	28	17	3	8	92	59	54
Tredegar Athletic	28	15	4	9	64	51	49
Rhymney Res.	28	14	6	8	72	57	48
Cwm Sports	28	15	1	12	86	75	46
Nantyglo	28	13	3	12	89	75	42
Crusaders Res.	28	12	2	14	65	89	38
RTB Ebbw Vale Res.	28	10	2	16	45	79	32
Abertillery Bl'b'ds 'A'	28	9	4	15	68	75	31
Abertillery Youth	28	9	1	18	67	120	28
Llanhilleth Ath Res.	28	5	8	15	55	108	23
FC Dugout Res.	28	4	5	19	44	81	17
Cefn Forest Utd Res.	28	3	5	20	59	101	14

NORTH LANCASHIRE & DISTRICT LEAGUE

Premier Division	P	W	D	L	F	A	Pts
Storeys	24	20	2	2	60	15	62
Marsh United	24	20	1	3	68	16	61
Slyne-with-Hest	24	14	3	7	57	37	45
CCM Dynamos	24	14	1	9	57	36	43
Kirkby Lonsdale	24	11	7	6	56	32	40
Cartmel & District	24	12	4	8	42	32	40
Ingleton	24	12	2	10	53	52	38
Highgrove	24	9	2	13	46	58	29
Morecambe Royals	24	8	1	15	36	47	25
Boys Club	24	5	6	13	25	53	21
Torrisholme	24	6	3	15	35	66	21
Westgate Wanderers	24	5	3	16	29	73	18
City Contract Services	24	1	3	20	18	65	6

Division One	P	W	D	L	F	A	Pts
Galgate	28	22	2	4	78	27	68
Caton United	28	19	5	4	86	32	62
Swarthmoor Soc Club	28	18	6	4	84	40	60
Cartmel & Dist Res.	28	16	7	5	73	42	55
Bentham	28	16	5	7	82	54	53
Storeys Res.	28	15	4	9	67	51	49
Ingleton Res.	28	10	5	13	71	80	35
Grange	28	10	3	15	60	60	33
Community Spts -3	28	8	9	11	58	74	30
Burton Thistle	28	8	4	16	69	92	28
Vine	28	7	6	15	45	74	27
Slyne-with-Hest Res.	28	7	5	16	41	75	26
M'cambe Royals Res.	28	7	4	17	41	80	25
Millhead -3	28	6	6	16	62	81	21
Arnside	28	3	5	20	27	82	14

Division Two	P	W	D	L	F	A	Pts
Carnforth Rangers	28	23	2	3	104	28	71
Marsh United Res.	28	20	4	4	110	37	64
Halton Rangers	28	17	7	4	88	39	58
Morecambe Hoops	28	16	7	5	102	51	55
Bolton-le-Sands	28	16	7	5	68	37	55
Trimpell Res.	28	16	5	7	62	42	53
Freehold	28	10	6	12	48	59	36
Caton United Res.	28	10	4	14	51	79	34
Swarthmoor SC Res.	28	8	9	11	57	69	33
Torrisholme Res.	28	10	3	15	51	65	33
Holme Athletic -3	28	9	3	16	46	75	27
Westgate Rangers	28	6	4	18	31	70	22
Kirkby Lonsdale Rgrs	28	6	3	19	47	84	21
Allithwaite Rangers	28	4	4	20	46	90	16
Arnside Res.	28	2	6	20	26	112	12

Division Three	P	W	D	L	F	A	Pts
Millhead Res.	20	15	2	3	63	31	47
Highgrove Res.	20	13	3	4	63	28	42
Poulton United	20	13	2	5	56	32	41
Central Pier	20	12	3	5	65	30	39
Boys Club Res.	20	12	3	5	52	26	39
Gregson	20	7	9	4	33	32	30
AFC Moorlands	20	6	7	7	37	35	25
Galgate Res.	20	3	5	12	26	45	14
Burton Thistle Res.	20	3	4	13	28	62	13
Grange Res.	20	1	6	13	20	72	9
Allithwaite Rgrs Res.	20	1	4	15	19	69	7

Division Four	P	W	D	L	F	A	Pts
Bowerham	14	13	1	0	69	6	40
Furness Rovers Res.	14	10	2	2	59	18	32
Bolton-le-Sands Res.	14	7	2	5	37	29	23
Heysham	14	6	2	6	49	44	20
Villa Royals	14	5	3	6	28	43	18
Bentham Res.	14	4	1	9	40	58	13
Carnforth Rgrs Res.	14	1	3	10	15	31	6
Poulton Utd Res. -3	14	2	2	10	21	89	5

NORTH LEICESTERSHIRE LEAGUE

Premier Division	P	W	D	L	F	A	Pts
Hathern	20	17	2	1	71	14	53
Sileby Saints	20	15	2	3	57	19	47
Ingles	20	11	4	5	46	30	37
Gresley Miners Arms	20	10	4	6	49	35	34
Loughborough Town	20	9	7	4	48	38	34
Whitwick White Horse	20	9	4	7	39	27	31
Shepshed Amateurs	20	7	3	10	27	38	24
Woodhouse Imperial	20	5	4	11	31	61	19
Bagworth Colliery	20	4	5	11	41	55	17
Club AZ	20	2	3	15	16	53	9
Belton Villa *-6*	20	1	2	17	20	75	*-1*

Division One	P	W	D	L	F	A	Pts
Genesis	20	15	2	3	63	27	47
The Railway	20	11	4	5	58	33	37
East Leake Athletic	20	11	2	7	54	36	35
Loughboro' Dyn. 'A'	20	10	2	8	64	53	32
Melton Mowbray BS	20	10	2	8	43	36	32
Sutton Bonington	20	9	3	8	40	38	30
Caterpillar	20	8	4	8	45	48	28
Quorn United	20	6	4	10	35	50	22
Markfield	20	6	4	10	45	61	22
Hathern Res.	20	5	2	13	28	53	17
Loughborough Res.	20	3	3	14	29	69	12

Division Two	P	W	D	L	F	A	Pts
Radmoor *-3*	20	15	3	2	81	29	45
Asfordby Village	20	12	2	6	57	41	38
Birstall Old Boys	20	11	3	6	65	53	36
East Leake United	20	9	7	4	52	30	34
Whitwick Wanderers	20	10	4	6	49	37	34
Anstey Town 'A'	20	8	6	6	64	45	30
Jubilee	20	7	5	8	51	38	26
ATI Garryson	20	8	1	11	42	65	25
Shepshed Am Res.	20	6	2	12	26	55	20
Thurmaston Rangers	20	6	1	13	34	54	19
Shepshed Town *-1*	20	0	2	18	27	101	1

Division Three	P	W	D	L	F	A	Pts
Lithuanian-Scandin.	18	13	3	2	66	27	42
Charnwood Rangers	18	12	0	6	65	38	36
Sileby Saints Res.	18	10	1	7	41	28	31
Thringstone Rangers	18	9	4	5	51	43	31
Woodhouse Imp Res.	18	9	3	6	54	38	30
Bagworth Coll Res.	18	8	3	7	50	44	27
Loughborough Utd	18	6	3	9	45	51	21
Belgrave Blackbird 'A'	18	4	5	9	31	45	17
Long Clawson	18	4	2	12	36	74	14
Measham Welfare	18	3	0	15	26	77	9

Division Four	P	W	D	L	F	A	Pts
3M Loughborough	20	16	4	0	72	20	52
Ashby Ivanhoe 'A'	20	15	1	4	81	28	46
The Railway Res.	20	12	2	6	66	41	38
East Leake Ath Res.	20	11	2	7	52	32	35
Thurmaston Rgrs Res.	20	9	2	9	54	51	29
Genesis Res.	20	8	3	9	54	52	27
Caterpillar Res.	20	8	2	10	38	52	26
Birstall Old Boys Res.	20	6	4	10	56	68	22
Markfield Res.	20	7	1	12	43	68	22
ATI Garryson Res.	20	4	2	14	33	71	14
Loughboro' Utd Res.	20	1	3	16	31	97	6

NORTH NORTHUMBERLAND LEAGUE

Division One	P	W	D	L	F	A	Pts
Amble	16	12	2	2	58	19	38
North Sunderland	16	12	1	3	45	17	37
Harrow	16	9	0	7	48	31	27
Rothbury	16	9	0	7	50	53	27
Stobswood Welfare	16	8	2	6	35	20	26
Shilbottle	16	8	1	7	44	28	25
Belford	16	5	3	8	27	41	18
Craster	16	3	1	12	25	48	10
Wooler	16	1	0	15	15	90	3

Division Two	P	W	D	L	F	A	Pts
Alnmouth Res.	14	13	1	0	58	15	40
Acklington *-3*	14	9	2	3	53	23	26
Lynemouth	14	8	1	5	39	26	25
Bedlington Terr. Res.	14	8	0	6	46	39	24
Swarland Res.	14	5	1	8	24	42	16
Springhill	14	5	0	9	17	27	15
Embleton *+3*	14	4	0	10	23	42	15
Hedgeley	14	1	1	12	12	58	4

NORTH WEST NORFOLK LEAGUE

Division One	P	W	D	L	F	A	Pts
Ingoldisthorpe	24	18	3	3	117	36	57
Terrington	24	15	6	3	68	27	51
King's Lynn Royals	24	16	3	5	69	35	51
Gaywood	24	14	4	6	87	59	46
West Winch	24	13	4	7	65	40	43
King's Lynn 'A'	24	13	3	8	65	36	42
Woottons	24	12	4	8	71	63	40
Great Massingham	24	9	4	11	56	55	31
Narborough *-3*	24	6	5	13	36	55	20
Snettisham	24	6	2	16	72	113	20
Watlington	24	5	3	16	41	96	18
Heacham	24	4	1	19	41	83	13
Flitcham	24	2	4	18	26	116	10

Division Two	P	W	D	L	F	A	Pts
Wiggenhall	26	23	1	2	150	42	70
Millfleet	26	21	2	3	153	43	65
Ingoldisthorpe Res.	26	14	5	7	77	50	47
Sandringham	26	14	5	7	59	41	47
Bircham Newton	26	14	3	9	86	44	45
West Winch Res.	26	12	3	11	51	61	39
Marham Wanderers	26	11	3	12	63	66	36
Terrington Res.	26	8	9	9	64	66	33
Stanhoe	26	8	8	10	87	75	32
Lynn Docklands	26	7	3	16	62	87	24
Lynn Napier *-3*	26	8	3	15	66	102	24
South Wootton	26	6	4	16	50	122	22
Snettisham Res.	26	6	3	17	42	103	21
Castle Rising	26	3	2	21	36	144	11

Division Three	P	W	D	L	F	A	Pts
Wiggenhall Res.	24	17	4	3	108	26	55
Hunstanton	24	17	4	3	82	32	55
Gt Massingham Res.	24	17	2	5	70	54	53
Ashill	24	11	8	5	58	48	41
William Burt	24	10	5	9	54	49	35
Docking	24	11	2	11	62	65	35
Dersingham Rvrs 'A'	24	10	4	10	67	65	34
Castle Acre	24	8	6	10	54	66	30
Heacham Res.	24	8	2	14	43	92	26
Burnham Market	24	6	5	13	47	58	23
Walsingham	24	6	5	13	32	58	23
Sporle	24	5	4	15	55	77	19
Smithdon	24	2	5	17	33	75	11

Division Four	P	W	D	L	F	A	Pts
Gaywood Res.	20	15	3	2	83	33	48
Old Hunstanton	20	15	1	4	63	38	46
Narborough Ship	20	13	2	5	62	37	41
FC Walpole	20	11	2	7	44	36	35
Watlington Res.	20	9	3	8	59	49	30
Greyfriars	20	8	5	7	36	29	29
Lynn Fern	20	8	2	10	45	61	26
Fakenham Town 'A'	20	5	7	8	31	38	22
Narborough Res.	20	5	5	10	38	49	20
Dersingham Rvrs 'B'	20	2	2	16	23	56	8
Queensway Royals	20	2	2	16	33	91	8

NORTHAMPTON TOWN LEAGUE

Premier Division	P	W	D	L	F	A	Pts
Univ Coll N'hampton	18	14	2	2	102	19	44
Broadmead Saints	18	12	3	3	82	32	39
Duston United	18	12	3	3	67	33	39
Thorpland United *+1*	18	10	2	6	61	51	33
Airflow *-1*	18	10	2	6	49	40	31
Parklands	18	8	2	8	54	49	26
TWS	18	6	1	11	30	48	19
N'hampton Harlequins	18	4	3	11	26	64	15
Ashley Rovers	18	2	2	14	19	64	8
Delapre Old Boys	18	2	0	16	18	108	6

Barratts – record expunged

Division One	P	W	D	L	F	A	Pts
Airflow Res.	24	20	2	2	106	36	62
Birchfield Rovers	24	19	2	3	108	27	59
U C N'hampton Res.	24	18	2	4	81	27	56
Double Four	24	18	2	4	86	33	56
Asda George	24	10	4	10	85	59	34
FC Crispin	24	9	4	11	63	75	31
Prince of Wales	24	8	2	14	46	74	26
Ashley Rovers Res.	24	8	2	14	50	87	26
Denton	24	6	6	12	49	76	24
Hartwell	24	7	2	15	36	87	23
Kingsthorpe Wdrs	24	6	2	16	41	79	20
N'hampton Diamonds	24	4	6	14	44	86	18
Northants Police	24	3	4	17	30	79	13

OXFORD CITY FA

Premier Division	P	W	D	L	F	A	Pts
Wheatley '84	16	13	1	2	73	22	40
Crown & Thistle	16	10	3	3	45	31	33
Donnington Old Boys	16	5	1	10	36	24	16
AFC Bullnose	16	4	2	10	30	66	14
North Oxford	16	4	1	11	29	70	13

Division One	P	W	D	L	F	A	Pts
Fairview	20	17	2	1	76	21	53
Tetsworth	20	15	2	3	77	21	47
Union Street	20	7	3	10	36	39	24
Golden Ball	20	7	2	11	58	63	23
North Oxford Res.	20	5	3	12	28	92	18
Great Milton	20	2	2	16	22	61	8

PERRY STREET & DISTRICT LEAGUE

Premier Division	P	W	D	L	F	A	Pts
South Petherton	22	16	4	2	83	21	52
Lyme Regis	22	14	3	5	72	39	45
Barrington	22	13	4	5	54	40	43
Merriott Rovers	22	12	3	7	58	36	39
Farway United	22	13	0	9	53	46	39
Perry Street	22	11	2	9	45	37	35
Chard Town Res.	22	8	5	9	44	46	29
Forton Rangers	22	8	3	11	44	58	27
Ilminster Tn Res. *-1*	22	8	2	12	37	51	25
Beaminster	22	7	3	12	27	40	24
Netherbury	22	5	2	15	38	79	17
Charmouth	22	1	1	20	18	80	4

Division One	P	W	D	L	F	A	Pts
Combe St Nich. Res.	22	18	3	1	78	25	57
White Horse Sym'y	22	18	2	2	101	25	56
Lyme Regis Res.	22	14	2	6	67	32	44
Pymore	22	12	3	7	66	60	39
Chard Rangers	22	11	3	8	56	49	36
Crewkerne Res.	22	9	3	10	29	48	30
Merriott Rvrs Res. *-1*	22	9	3	10	44	56	29
Hinton St George	22	8	4	10	45	59	28
Uplyme *-1*	22	6	4	12	61	78	21
Chard United	22	4	8	10	46	54	20
Drimpton *-1*	22	4	1	17	29	81	12
Shepton Beauchamp	22	1	0	21	21	76	3

Division Two	P	W	D	L	F	A	Pts
Thorncombe	20	17	0	3	63	19	51
Winsham	20	14	1	5	52	20	43
Misterton	20	13	3	4	65	37	42
Millwey Rise	20	11	3	6	44	29	36
Haselbury	20	9	3	8	64	53	30
Combe St Nich. 'A'	20	8	2	10	44	67	26
South Petherton Res.	20	6	4	10	38	44	22
Forton Rangers Res.	20	7	1	12	38	53	22
Norton Athletic	20	5	3	12	35	49	18
Ilminster Tn Colts *-3*	20	4	5	11	33	69	14
Lyme Regis Bantams	20	2	3	15	32	68	9

Division Three	P	W	D	L	F	A	Pts
Dowlish & Donyatt	18	13	2	3	70	40	41
Hawkchurch	18	11	5	2	58	33	38
Perry Street Res.	18	11	3	4	59	32	36
Chard Rangers Res.	18	8	4	6	45	36	28
White Horse S'y Res.	18	7	1	10	33	46	22
Hinton St George Res.	18	6	3	9	51	53	21
Barrington Res.	18	5	6	7	45	48	21
Chard Town Colts	18	6	3	9	41	51	21
Shepton B'p Res. *-1*	18	5	3	10	37	42	17
Farway United Res.	18	2	2	14	27	85	8

Division Four	P	W	D	L	F	A	Pts
Combe St N 'B' *-1*	16	14	2	0	75	22	43
Fivehead United *-1*	16	11	4	1	72	24	36
Hawkchurch Res.	16	8	2	6	49	39	26
Chard United Res.	16	7	0	9	40	52	21
Charmouth Res. *-1*	16	6	3	7	38	38	20
Misterton Res.	16	5	4	7	38	52	19
Thorncombe Res.	16	3	5	8	26	45	14
Winsham Res.	16	4	2	10	28	60	14
Millwey Rise Res.	16	2	2	12	20	54	8

PLYMOUTH & WEST DEVON COMBINATION

Premier Division	P	W	D	L	F	A	Pts
Wessex Lopes Arms	24	17	5	2	61	33	56
Univ of Plymouth	24	17	4	3	70	21	55
Friary Vaults Mt G'ld	24	16	6	2	68	21	54
Tamarside	24	14	2	8	55	32	44
Plymstock Utd Res.	24	12	3	9	52	40	39
Horrabridge Rgrs SA	24	10	3	11	47	54	33
Elburton Villa Res.	24	9	3	12	45	50	30
Lee Moor	24	8	3	13	38	69	27
The Falcon	24	7	4	13	28	42	25
Plym'th P'kway Res.	24	6	6	12	43	50	24
Oddfellows Arms	24	7	3	14	44	71	24
Vospers Oak V. Res.	24	3	8	13	29	54	17
Breakwater Breakers	24	4	2	18	35	78	14

Senior Division	P	W	D	L	F	A	Pts
Tamarside Res.	24	19	3	2	85	21	60
Plymouth Rangers	24	16	3	5	96	47	51
Old Suttonians	24	16	3	5	66	45	51
Plymouth City	24	12	4	8	74	68	40
Rok	24	12	2	10	50	53	38
Yealm Green	24	11	3	10	47	55	36
Q Arms Tamerton	24	10	3	11	61	74	33
Tavistock Res. *-3*	24	11	0	13	58	79	30
CSSA Spts/Leis. *-3*	24	10	2	12	81	69	29
SWEB	24	8	5	11	59	55	29
Friendship Inn	24	5	2	17	46	99	17
Buckland Milton & C	24	4	4	16	46	64	16
Mainstone Sports	24	3	4	17	38	78	13

Intermediate Division	P	W	D	L	F	A	Pts
The Falcon Res.	28	23	3	2	115	31	72
U of Plymouth Res.	28	21	3	4	102	40	66
Old Suttonians Res.	28	19	3	6	92	46	60
Clipper Rangers	28	17	3	8	86	57	54
Bull & Bush	28	16	1	11	77	60	49
Roborough SC	28	15	2	11	84	76	47
Walton Developments	28	15	1	12	95	72	46
Royal Mail	28	13	1	14	89	79	40
Horrabridge Rgrs Res.	28	10	7	11	56	60	37
St Judes United *-3*	28	11	4	13	64	67	34
Yelverton	28	6	7	15	81	103	25
Breakwater Res. *-3*	28	6	6	16	56	83	21
Air South West.com	28	5	5	18	50	101	20
P'mouth Civil Service	28	4	3	21	47	120	15
Modbury Rovers	28	4	1	23	41	140	13

PORTSMOUTH & DISTRICT LEAGUE

Premier Division	P	W	D	L	F	A	Pts
Wymering	16	9	4	3	57	44	31
Envy	16	8	5	3	45	34	29
Old Portmuthians	16	8	4	4	36	26	28
St Helena Bobs	16	7	5	4	53	45	26
Co-op	16	6	6	4	55	40	24
Waterlooville Soc Cl	16	6	3	7	36	46	21
Casey's United	16	5	2	9	37	44	17
Royal TML	16	4	4	8	31	31	16
Southside	16	1	3	12	14	54	6

Division One	P	W	D	L	F	A	Pts
Kingston Arrows	18	15	0	3	99	37	45
Golden Hind	18	12	3	3	43	26	39
Hayling Billy	18	11	3	4	59	42	36
Segensworth	18	9	3	6	58	43	30
AFC Ventora	18	8	4	6	37	35	28
Fleur de Lys	18	7	2	9	50	57	23
Horndean United	18	6	3	9	37	39	21
Portchester	18	4	5	9	31	51	17
Purbrook Sports	18	4	0	14	37	77	12
Carberry	18	1	3	14	24	68	6

Division Two	P	W	D	L	F	A	Pts
Purbrook Spts Res. *-3*	18	14	3	1	86	34	42
Cosham Blues	18	13	1	4	67	34	40
SL Southsea	18	11	1	6	49	40	34
Fleet Support Ltd	18	8	2	8	41	43	26
Farefield Sports	18	7	3	8	39	39	24
Tardis Music	18	7	3	8	46	48	24
Harchester United	18	7	0	11	49	56	21
Westover Rangers	18	4	4	10	32	62	16
Hayling Billy Res.	18	3	6	9	35	55	15
Castle United	18	2	5	11	32	65	11

PRESTON & DISTRICT LEAGUE

Premier Division	P	W	D	L	F	A	Pts
Southport Trinity	24	21	2	1	89	26	65
Burscough Richmond	24	18	5	1	74	21	59
Leyland Town	24	14	6	4	69	32	48
CCA	24	13	6	5	61	36	45
Appley Bridge	24	11	4	9	69	43	37
Eccleston/Heskin Utd	24	11	2	11	50	42	35
Preston Wanderers	24	11	1	12	61	53	34
Hoghton West End	24	10	3	11	49	58	33
Longridge Town	24	8	4	12	43	39	28
Southport Amateurs	24	7	3	14	40	56	24
Lancaster Univ. *-6*	24	6	4	14	32	80	16
Town Green	24	4	2	18	34	82	14
Burscough Barons	24	0	2	22	17	120	2

Division One	P	W	D	L	F	A	Pts
Croston Sports Res.	22	14	6	2	66	30	48
Leyland Red Rose	22	13	2	7	73	37	41
Tarleton Corinthians	22	11	8	3	53	30	41
Baxter's	22	12	2	8	68	54	38
Burscough Bridge	22	9	7	6	56	51	34
Southport Trinity Res.	22	10	3	9	43	32	33
Appley Bridge Res.	22	10	3	9	61	52	33
Walmer Bridge	22	9	5	8	60	48	32
Burscough Rich. Res.	22	8	3	11	43	36	27
Preston GSA	22	6	4	12	50	70	22
Lostock St Ger. Res.	22	5	5	12	38	55	20
Hesketh Bank 'A' *-3*	22	1	0	21	17	133	0

Division Two East	P	W	D	L	F	A	Pts
Blessed Sacrement	22	20	1	1	109	29	61
Royal Garrison	22	17	3	2	101	31	54
New Longton Rovers	22	16	0	6	60	26	48
Chipping	22	10	5	7	66	52	35
Mawdesley	22	10	3	9	43	43	33
Walmer Bridge Res.	22	9	3	10	50	59	30
Hoole United	22	8	3	11	37	70	27
Halsall	22	7	5	10	53	53	26
Tarleton Corinth. Res.	22	7	3	12	45	65	24
Hoghton Olympic	22	4	5	13	40	63	17
Leyland Red R Res.	22	5	1	16	39	77	16
Longridge Tn Res. *-3*	22	0	6	16	24	99	3

Division Two West	P	W	D	L	F	A	Pts
Leyland St Marys	20	14	3	3	67	26	45
Top Spinners	20	14	3	3	45	24	45
CCA Res.	20	11	5	4	55	38	38
Walton-le-dale	20	9	4	7	65	61	31
New Longton Rv Res.	20	8	3	9	38	44	27
Heath Charnock	20	8	2	10	38	45	26
Muldoons	20	8	1	11	60	54	25
Highcross	20	7	3	10	49	39	24
Charnock Richard 'A'	20	7	3	10	45	59	24
Farington Villa	20	4	4	12	40	56	16
Preston GSA Res.	20	4	1	15	33	89	13

Division Three	P	W	D	L	F	A	Pts
Southport Trinity 'A'	20	18	2	0	80	23	56
Southport Ams Res.	20	14	3	3	84	38	45
Tarleton Corinth. 'A'	20	11	4	5	65	42	37
Preston United	20	9	6	5	62	45	33
Catforth	20	7	5	8	49	45	26
Gamull	20	7	4	9	61	70	25
Leyland Red Rose 'A'	20	7	3	10	43	56	24
Preston GSA 'A'	20	5	7	8	44	49	22
Leyland St Marys Res.	20	5	1	14	36	74	16
Hoole Utd Res. *-3*	20	3	4	13	37	74	10
Eccleston/H Res. *-3*	20	3	3	14	37	82	9

REDHILL & DISTRICT LEAGUE

Premier Division	P	W	D	L	F	A	Pts
Clarkson Hyde	20	16	2	2	62	23	50
Limpsfield Blues	20	11	3	6	53	31	36
Reigate Priory	20	10	4	6	40	30	34
Smallfield	20	10	2	8	47	35	32
Horley Town 'A'	20	9	4	7	36	38	31
Marlpit United	20	8	3	9	56	44	27
Kenley	20	6	8	6	39	40	26
Charlwood	20	6	6	8	34	56	24
Reigate Sala	20	4	5	11	21	41	17
Bookham 'A'	20	4	4	12	31	59	16
Brockham	20	4	3	13	27	49	15

Division One	P	W	D	L	F	A	Pts
South Godstone	20	16	2	2	88	28	50
Woodland Albion	20	13	2	5	51	36	41
Frenches Athletic	20	11	5	4	48	34	38
Reigate Priory Res.	20	9	3	8	41	40	30
Reed	20	7	8	5	46	47	29
Westcott '35	20	7	6	7	36	36	27
Caterham Old Boys	20	4	8	8	29	37	20
Smallfield Res.	20	6	2	12	31	55	20
Walton Heath	20	5	4	11	28	53	19
Reigate Hill	20	4	5	11	36	48	17
Warlingham 'A'	20	2	7	11	36	56	13

Division Two	P	W	D	L	F	A	Pts
Caterham OB Res.	20	17	1	2	64	19	52
Nutfield Res.	20	12	3	5	62	30	39
Duke of York	20	12	1	7	56	47	37
Cheam Vill War Res.	20	10	2	8	62	33	32
Merstham Newt. Res.	20	10	2	8	34	34	32
Paynes Sports	20	9	3	8	49	51	30
Oxted & District 'A'	20	9	0	11	32	46	27
Charlwood Res.	20	7	5	8	41	54	26
Godstone	20	5	5	10	36	42	20
South Park 'A'	20	4	1	15	32	77	13
Warlingham 'B'	20	3	1	16	16	51	10

Division Three	P	W	D	L	F	A	Pts
Westcott '35 Res.	18	14	3	1	65	22	45
RH123 Athletic	18	14	0	4	71	34	42
Reigate Priory 'A'	18	12	0	6	57	43	36
Limpsfield Blues Res.	18	10	2	6	47	40	32
South Godstone Res.	18	9	3	6	35	31	30
Merstham Newton 'A'	18	6	3	9	34	45	21
Park Lane	18	5	1	12	31	50	16
Cheam Village W 'A'	18	5	1	12	29	49	16
Nutfield 'A'	18	4	2	12	34	52	14
Walton Heath Res.	18	3	1	14	20	57	10

Division Four	P	W	D	L	F	A	Pts
RH123 Athletic Res.	22	16	2	4	91	41	50
Alma Tavern	22	15	2	5	88	48	47
Real Holmesdale Res.	22	14	3	5	73	38	45
Frenches Athletic Res.	22	13	4	5	50	30	43
Reigate Priory 'B'	22	11	4	7	58	48	37
Abgene Eagles	22	10	4	8	68	57	34
Westcott '35 'A'	22	8	4	10	48	59	28
Brockham Res.	22	8	3	11	48	55	27
Reigate Hill Res.	22	7	5	10	51	54	26
Caterham OB 'A'	22	6	2	14	41	66	20
Court Lodge	22	5	4	13	48	67	19
Park Lane Res.	22	0	1	21	12	113	1

ROCHESTER & DISTRICT LEAGUE

Premier Division	P	W	D	L	F	A	Pts
Gillingham Green	20	17	0	3	71	25	51
White Horse Borstal	20	17	0	3	61	26	51
Wayfield Athletic	20	12	2	6	50	24	38
Medway Queen	20	10	3	7	37	36	33
Lordswood Athletic	20	10	2	8	37	34	32
Cliffe Woods	20	9	1	10	50	43	28
Plough/Chequers Sp.	20	7	4	9	41	57	25
Hollands & Blair Res.	20	7	2	11	37	43	23
Sheerness East Res.	20	6	2	12	36	45	20
Newington	20	2	4	14	21	58	10
Emerald Star	20	1	4	15	24	74	7

Division One	P	W	D	L	F	A	Pts
Medway City	22	16	4	2	76	19	52
Roch' Prince of Wales	22	15	4	3	84	38	49
Horsted	22	12	5	5	65	32	41
Greenwich Thistle	22	11	6	5	50	31	39
FC Quayside	22	9	9	4	59	33	36
Evolution	22	10	5	7	71	61	35
Milton Athletic Res.	22	11	2	9	38	50	35
Pegasus '81	22	8	2	12	61	67	26
Veena Leisure	22	8	2	12	61	70	26
Bosun	22	3	8	11	44	71	17
Bredhurst	22	4	2	16	45	81	14
Cliffe Woods Res.	22	0	1	21	29	130	1

Division Two	P	W	D	L	F	A	Pts
Cliffe Woods 'A'	24	18	4	2	91	37	58
O'Connell's	24	14	5	5	57	40	47
Medway Knights	24	13	5	6	84	52	44
Three Sisters	24	13	3	8	66	45	42
Poachers	24	13	2	9	59	49	41
Featherby	24	12	4	8	58	50	40
Upchurch	24	11	6	7	55	38	39
Ship Frindsbury	24	9	4	11	52	54	31
Pegasus '81 Res.	24	9	3	12	57	74	30
Emerald Star Res.	24	8	4	12	45	67	28
Medway Ports	24	5	5	14	24	44	20
UK Paper Res.	24	4	2	18	33	63	14
Bosun Res.	24	3	1	20	27	95	10

Division Three	P	W	D	L	F	A	Pts
Grain Athletic	24	18	2	4	71	29	56
General at Sea	24	17	1	6	59	30	52
Frog & Toad	24	15	4	5	73	39	49
Stockbury Athletic	24	15	2	7	60	33	47
Anchorians	24	14	3	7	52	41	45
Isle of Grain	24	12	4	8	59	46	40
Plough/Chq Spts Res.	24	11	4	9	61	44	37
Athletico	24	11	4	9	39	30	37
Beechwood '76	24	6	4	14	38	61	22
Horsted Res.	24	7	1	16	40	73	22
Collyers	24	6	1	17	47	64	19
Sans Pareil	24	5	1	18	42	61	16
Valley Colts	24	3	1	20	16	106	10

Division Four	P	W	D	L	F	A	Pts
Cannon '24	24	19	1	4	144	51	58
Medway Galvanising	24	18	2	4	121	48	56
BAE Systems	24	17	2	5	111	46	53
Park Regis	24	15	2	7	97	73	47
Burnhill	24	15	0	9	80	59	45
G & M Roofing	24	12	4	8	71	53	40
Lycos	24	12	4	8	53	56	40
Roseneath Athletic	24	9	3	12	77	83	30
Insanity	24	8	2	14	48	65	26
AFC Medway	24	7	4	13	53	90	25
Rising Sun	24	6	3	15	49	84	21
Bleakwood Rangers	24	2	1	21	30	147	7
AFC Phoenix	24	1	2	21	25	104	5

Division Five	P	W	D	L	F	A	Pts
FC Cobras	26	23	2	1	123	32	71
Strood	26	23	1	2	107	36	70
Star Sports	26	15	3	8	74	48	48
Outer Fenn	26	14	4	8	69	61	46
Sturdee	26	12	9	5	58	48	45
Medway Saints	26	12	3	11	62	68	39
Emerald Star Classics	26	10	6	10	55	56	36
Lloyds	26	11	2	13	55	66	35
Rainham '84	26	7	5	14	56	88	26
Cliffe Woods 'B'	26	5	10	11	68	76	25
Riverside	26	8	1	17	57	101	25
Bowaters	26	6	4	16	53	73	22
Slade '05	26	5	2	19	42	94	17
FC Monarchs	26	2	6	18	43	75	12

SALISBURY & DISTRICT LEAGUE

Premier Division	P	W	D	L	F	A	Pts
Alderbury	20	15	1	4	68	34	46
Tisbury	20	14	1	5	49	27	43
RGV Netheravon	20	13	1	6	60	28	40
Plough FC	20	12	3	5	57	33	39
West Harnham	20	11	2	7	34	34	35
Stockton & Codford	20	10	4	6	36	36	34
Enford	20	10	1	9	60	52	31
Whiteparish	20	7	3	10	41	34	24
Damerham	20	3	3	14	24	74	12
Meadow Park	20	2	2	16	28	67	8
Porton Sports	20	1	3	16	24	62	6

Division One	P	W	D	L	F	A	Pts
Castle Street Club	22	18	2	2	77	23	56
Friends Provident	22	15	1	6	78	44	46
Chalke Valley	22	14	4	4	64	33	46
Bemerton H H 'A'	22	13	3	6	82	33	42
Nomansland	22	12	4	6	79	31	40
Beacon Sports	22	10	6	6	58	37	36
James Hay	22	9	4	9	64	57	31
Rouge Raiders	22	9	3	10	61	55	30
Boscombe Down	22	5	5	12	34	62	20
Winterslow Lions	22	5	4	13	37	56	19
Instinct	22	3	1	18	40	140	10
Phil Small Sports	22	0	1	21	25	128	1

Division Two	P	W	D	L	F	A	Pts
St Pauls Club	20	16	2	2	55	18	50
RGV Netheravon Res.	20	10	4	6	60	40	34
Porton Sports Res.	20	9	2	9	55	44	29
South Newton & W	20	8	5	7	60	58	29
West Harnham Res.	20	9	1	10	57	66	28
Tisbury Res.	20	7	6	7	38	39	27
Victoria Hotel	20	7	5	8	49	48	26
Stockton/Codford Res.	20	8	2	10	38	43	26
Devizes Inn	20	8	1	11	35	53	25
Boscombe D Rec Club	20	6	2	12	42	63	20
Langford	20	5	4	11	30	47	19

Division Three	P	W	D	L	F	A	Pts
Sth Newton/ W Res.	20	17	3	0	78	15	54
Hi-flex Sports	20	14	4	2	68	35	46
Duck Inn	20	11	5	4	57	34	38
Alderbury Res.	20	12	2	6	56	34	38
Woodisbury	20	9	1	10	35	43	28
Chalke Valley Res.	20	7	4	9	57	47	25
Enford Res.	20	8	0	12	38	66	24
Winterslow Lions Res.	20	6	4	10	52	57	22
Alderholt Res.	20	7	1	12	47	54	22
Damerham Res.	20	3	1	16	34	60	10
Hogshead	20	2	3	15	35	112	9

SCUNTHORPE & DISTRICT LEAGUE

Division One	P	W	D	L	F	A	Pts
The Mallard *-3*	20	17	1	2	73	27	49
AFC Brumby *+2*	20	13	4	3	49	25	45
Scunthonians	20	14	2	4	69	30	44
BBM	20	13	4	3	56	17	43
Epworth Town	20	10	1	9	42	47	31
Lebus Rovers *-4*	20	10	1	9	43	51	27
Scawby *+6*	20	6	1	13	36	44	25
Sherpa *-3*	20	7	1	12	37	59	19
Barnetby United *+3*	20	4	3	13	30	62	18
Crosby Colts	20	3	2	15	37	84	11
Haven	20	3	0	17	16	42	9

Bottesford Town 'A' – record expunged

Division Two	P	W	D	L	F	A	Pts
BBM Res.	22	17	2	3	94	35	53
Crowle Colts Seniors	22	16	4	2	77	22	52
AFC Brumby Res.	22	15	3	4	63	33	48
Crosby Colts Res.	22	13	3	6	99	46	42
Appleby Frod. Colts	22	13	3	6	60	40	42
New Holland Villa	22	10	4	8	62	50	34
Scawby Res.	22	10	2	10	50	73	32
Messingham T. J. *-3*	22	9	1	12	34	62	25
Scotter United *+3*	22	4	4	14	33	50	19
Deltron	22	5	3	14	43	82	18
Luddington	22	1	4	17	35	81	7
Limestone Rgrs Res.	22	2	1	19	23	99	7

Division Three	P	W	D	L	F	A	Pts
Swinefleet Juniors	26	22	2	2	90	21	68
Scunthonians Res. *+3*	26	15	4	7	77	40	52
Haxey Town	26	17	1	8	85	53	52
Barton Utd Colts *+3*	26	14	4	8	74	41	49
AC Warren *-10*	26	17	6	3	109	49	47
Scotter Utd Res. *-3*	26	14	4	8	86	65	43
College Wdrs *+2*	26	11	4	11	54	64	39
Briggensians *+3*	26	9	4	13	60	66	34
Kirton *-3*	26	11	2	13	89	72	32
Winterton Town *+2*	26	8	3	15	47	78	29
Barrow Wanderers	26	8	4	14	65	69	28
Crosby Colts Jns *+3*	26	7	2	17	47	78	26
Epworth Town Res.	26	7	3	16	59	73	24
Santon *+2*	26	0	1	25	23	196	3

SHEFFIELD & HALLAMSHIRE COUNTY SENIOR LEAGUE

Premier Division	P	W	D	L	F	A	Pts
Mexborough Main St	26	19	4	3	76	28	61
Athersley Recreation	26	16	7	3	53	16	55
Stocksbridge PS Res.	26	12	10	4	58	34	46
Roy Hancock Old Cr	26	11	8	7	54	42	41
HSBC	26	11	6	9	47	38	39
Hollinsend Amateurs	26	10	8	8	36	30	38
Houghton Main	26	10	7	9	33	36	37
Wombwell Main	26	9	8	9	42	35	35
Penistone Church	26	8	7	11	37	55	31
Edlington WMC	26	7	9	10	34	52	30
Thorpe Hesley	26	7	8	11	38	45	29
Oughtibridge WM SC	26	9	2	15	35	52	29
Sth Kirkby Colliery	26	5	5	16	24	54	20
Silkstone United	26	1	5	20	28	78	8

Division One	P	W	D	L	F	A	Pts
Sheffield Lane Top	24	15	4	5	78	36	49
Outo Kumpu S & S	24	14	4	6	71	45	46
Dinnington Tn Res.	24	12	6	6	41	30	42
Handsworth	24	10	8	6	61	50	38
Wickersley Old Boys	24	9	7	8	33	27	34
Parramore Sports	24	9	7	8	44	46	34
Georgia Pacific	24	9	6	9	42	48	33
Dearne & Swinton	24	8	7	9	66	52	31
Elm Tree	24	9	4	11	46	57	31
Ecclesfield Red Rose	24	9	4	11	45	62	31
Frecheville C. Assoc.	24	7	5	12	40	49	26
Dodworth Miners W	24	7	4	13	45	59	25
High Green Villa	24	1	8	15	21	72	11

Division Two	P	W	D	L	F	A	Pts
Parkgate Res.	26	22	2	2	110	26	68
Half Moon *-4*	26	18	6	2	62	18	56
Worsbrough Common	26	14	7	5	58	24	49
Sheffield Bankers	26	14	5	7	56	31	47
Caribbean Sports	26	13	7	6	64	42	46
AFC Cutlers	26	12	6	8	62	53	42
Worsbrough Res. *-3*	26	11	7	8	52	42	37
Phoenix	26	9	4	13	47	63	31
Sheffield Centralians	26	9	4	13	45	63	31
Everest	26	7	5	14	51	71	26
De La Salle Old Boys	26	6	7	13	44	66	25
Armthorpe Welf. Res.	26	5	5	16	41	64	20
Penistone Church Res.	26	4	7	15	45	87	19
Harworth CI Res.	26	1	2	23	13	100	5

SOUTH LONDON ALLIANCE

Premier Division	P	W	D	L	F	A	Pts
Tudor Sports	22	20	2	0	87	23	62
Kingfisher	22	14	5	3	77	26	47
Melbourne	22	12	5	5	63	33	41
Cray Valley PM Res.	22	10	5	7	46	38	35
Johnson & Phillips	22	10	5	7	38	33	35
Long Lane	22	10	4	8	43	35	34
Drummond Athletic	22	8	5	9	35	40	29
Metrogas Res.	22	8	4	10	49	45	28
Old Roan Res.	22	7	3	12	42	41	24
Middle Park	22	6	2	14	34	68	20
Eltham Town	22	3	2	17	26	77	11
Seven Acre Sports	22	3	0	19	17	98	9

Division One	P	W	D	L	F	A	Pts
Forest Hill Park	20	14	1	5	64	37	43
Peckham Town	20	14	0	6	66	35	42
Beaverwood	20	11	2	7	48	40	35
Seven Acre Spts Res.	20	11	1	8	47	38	34
Farnboro' OBG Res.	20	10	3	7	42	34	33
Crofton Albion	20	9	2	9	42	47	29
Wilmington *-3*	20	8	2	10	38	52	23
Eltham Royals	20	7	2	11	31	49	23
Blackheath Wdrs	20	7	0	13	38	50	21
Penhill Standard	20	5	3	12	43	67	18
Lewisham Seniors	20	5	2	13	35	45	17

Well Hall – record expunged

Division Two	P	W	D	L	F	A	Pts
Cray Valley P M 'A'	22	13	7	2	39	19	46
Bridon Sports Res.	22	12	2	8	49	32	38
Beckenham Royals	22	11	5	6	36	29	38
Johnson/Phillips Res	22	10	6	6	40	37	36
Parkhurst Rangers	22	10	5	7	37	34	35
Oakdale Athletic *-1*	22	8	6	8	28	29	29
Avery Hill College	22	7	6	9	40	40	27
Old Roan 'A'	22	7	4	11	44	44	25
Wickham Wdrs *-1*	22	7	4	11	40	48	24
Bexley Res.	22	6	6	10	25	39	24
Old Town New Boys	22	6	5	11	39	52	23
Old Colfeians	22	5	4	13	36	50	19

Division Three	P	W	D	L	F	A	Pts
AFC Sydenham	20	16	0	4	45	21	48
Bexlians	20	14	3	3	38	26	45
Longlands Athletic	20	13	2	5	58	31	41
New Park	20	11	0	9	61	39	33
North Kent	20	10	1	9	54	44	31
Old Roan 'B'	20	10	1	9	44	41	31
Metrogas 'A'	20	10	0	10	53	57	30
Ravens	20	9	0	11	35	45	27
Bexley 'A'	20	5	4	11	34	50	19
Desportiva Portuguese	20	3	4	13	31	48	13
Blackheath Wdrs Res.	20	0	3	17	28	79	3

Division Four	P	W	D	L	F	A	Pts
Elite	24	19	4	1	104	35	61
Long Lane Res.	24	17	4	3	91	34	55
Old Colfeians 'A'	24	16	3	5	81	54	51
Zampa Valley	24	14	4	6	68	29	46
Tudor Sports Res.	24	13	6	5	84	46	45
Farnborough OB G 'A'	24	12	3	9	64	43	39
Salmon	24	10	3	11	58	66	33
Eltham Palace Res.	24	8	2	14	51	74	26
Heath	24	6	1	17	36	78	19
Beaverwood Res.	24	5	4	15	47	90	19
Bexley Park	24	5	3	16	33	69	18
Wickham Park 'A'	24	5	3	16	40	104	18
Crofton Albion Res.	24	5	2	17	40	75	17

Forest Hill Park Res. – record expunged

SOUTH YORKSHIRE AMATEUR LEAGUE

Premier Division	P	W	D	L	F	A	Pts
Jubilee Sports *-3*	20	19	1	0	95	18	55
Thorncliffe	20	17	0	3	83	27	51
G & Ts	20	16	0	4	85	38	48
Yew Tree	20	10	4	6	48	28	34
Cross Scythes *-3*	20	10	2	8	72	34	29
Phoenix Res.	20	8	5	7	35	42	29
Bradway	20	8	2	10	50	64	26
Oxspring United *-3*	20	4	1	15	51	91	10
Civil Service	20	3	1	16	30	84	10
Norwich Union	20	2	3	15	20	72	9
De La Salle OB Res.	20	2	3	15	16	87	9

Division One	P	W	D	L	F	A	Pts
Grimethorpe Athletic	20	16	3	1	85	15	51
Grove Central	20	14	4	2	78	32	46
Athersley Rec Res.	20	14	1	5	65	19	43
Dodworth MW Res.	20	13	1	6	71	44	40
Dale Tavern	20	10	4	6	72	35	34
Bagshawe Arms	20	10	4	6	64	37	34
Kiveton Park Res.	20	7	1	12	60	51	22
Jeld-Wen	20	7	0	13	56	69	21
Sheffield Bankers Res.	20	4	4	12	30	62	16
Thurgoland Welfare	20	4	0	16	40	85	12
Bolsterstone Pagans	20	0	0	20	17	189	0

SOUTHEND BOROUGH COMBINATION

Premier Division	P	W	D	L	F	A	Pts
Ekco & Thames Park	22	17	3	2	76	20	37
Shoebury Town	22	17	3	2	74	22	37
Exhibition United	22	13	5	4	58	33	31
Old Southendian	22	10	6	6	53	33	26
Catholic United	22	10	5	7	49	41	25
Ensign	22	9	4	9	45	55	22
Leigh Town	22	9	3	10	49	43	21
Essendon	22	10	0	12	65	65	20
Borough Rovers	22	8	3	11	53	56	19
Brit Academicals	22	5	2	15	38	86	12
Battlesbridge	22	3	1	18	25	74	7
Southend Collegians	22	3	1	18	26	83	7

Division One	P	W	D	L	F	A	Pts
Shoebury Old Boys	22	15	2	5	80	43	32
Zebra Sports	22	13	4	5	46	32	30
Ekco/Thames Pk Res.	22	10	6	6	63	64	26
International PMS	22	11	3	8	75	53	25
Airborne United	22	10	4	8	55	65	24
S'end Collegians Res.	22	9	5	8	45	42	23
Thorpe Athletic	22	10	2	10	56	51	22
Bourne Athletic	22	10	1	11	60	49	21
Westcliff Amateur	22	10	1	11	40	57	21
Nubarn Athletic	22	9	2	11	47	50	20
Customs/Excise (S'd)	22	6	3	13	57	71	15
Battlesbridge Res.	22	1	3	18	25	72	5

Division Two	P	W	D	L	F	A	Pts
Weir Sports	22	16	3	3	66	21	35
Blackgate Gunners	22	17	1	4	65	24	35
Catholic United Res.	22	16	0	6	57	23	32
Southchurch Hall OS	22	13	4	5	69	33	30
Old Southendian Res.	22	13	1	8	61	34	27
Southbury	22	13	1	8	54	36	27
White Ensign 'A'	22	9	5	8	45	54	23
Little Theatre Club	22	6	4	12	49	69	16
Cupids Country Club	22	5	6	11	41	61	16
BKS Sports	22	3	3	16	30	70	9
Earls Hall United	22	3	2	17	25	66	8
Leigh Ramblers 'A'	22	3	0	19	18	89	6

Division Three	P	W	D	L	F	A	Pts
Middleway	22	17	1	4	71	32	35
Borough Rovers Res.	22	16	3	3	58	27	35
Corinthians	22	16	2	4	77	33	34
Battlesbridge 'A'	22	15	2	5	55	25	32
Ekco/Thames Pk 'A'	22	12	3	7	63	46	27
Hullbridge Sports 'A'	22	7	4	11	40	44	18
Southend Wanderers	22	5	6	11	45	45	16
Catholic United 'A'	22	6	4	12	30	55	16
Brit Academicals Res.	22	6	3	13	41	55	15
Trackback	22	7	1	14	29	44	15
Highbank	22	4	4	14	40	74	12
Southend Rangers	22	4	1	17	24	93	9

Division Four	P	W	D	L	F	A	Pts
Ashingdon Boys	22	18	1	3	64	25	37
International PMS Res.	22	15	3	4	64	37	33
Emstar United	22	15	1	6	78	34	31
Leigh Town Res.	22	13	4	5	58	27	30
Parkway Sports	22	14	1	7	79	46	29
Cupids C'try Club Res.	22	11	1	10	63	38	23
S'thchurch H O S Res.	22	10	3	9	59	57	23
S'end Collegians 'A'	22	8	3	11	46	73	19
Earls Hall Utd Res.	22	7	2	13	41	61	16
Elmwood Old Boys	22	6	2	14	45	81	14
Old Southendian 'A'	22	3	2	17	27	80	8
Battlesbridge 'B'	22	0	1	21	28	93	1

Division Five	P	W	D	L	F	A	Pts
Ekco/Thames Pk 'B'	22	20	1	1	96	32	41
Parkway Sports Res.	22	16	2	4	82	33	34
Smith's Sports	22	14	3	5	85	50	31
White Horse Rangers	22	13	1	8	73	44	27
Landwick	22	10	6	6	59	47	26
Trinity (S)	22	11	3	8	80	59	25
Heathfield	22	11	0	11	70	61	22
Little Th'tre Club Res.	22	8	2	12	64	63	18
Old Southendian 'B'	22	6	2	14	39	79	14
S'thch'ch Hall OS 'A'	22	6	1	15	42	92	13
Leigh Ramblers 'B'	22	2	3	17	28	102	7
Catholic United 'B'	22	2	2	18	29	85	6

Division Six	P	W	D	L	F	A	Pts
Southend Rangers Res.	16	13	0	3	92	21	26
Thundersley United	16	12	1	3	74	30	25
Hullbridge Athletic	16	9	1	6	55	42	19
Barnsford Hurricanes	16	9	0	7	57	46	18
Ashingdon Boys Res.	16	8	2	6	55	48	18
Trinity (S) Res.	16	7	2	7	58	43	16
Parkway Sports 'A'	16	5	1	10	46	48	11
Leigh Town 'A'	16	3	0	13	20	99	6
S'end Collegians 'B'	16	2	1	13	33	113	5

SOUTHERN AMATEUR LEAGUE

(Higher divisions on page 10)

Junior Division One	P	W	D	L	F	A	Pts
Winchmore Hill 'A'	20	14	2	4	64	34	44
Civil Service 'A'	20	13	1	6	55	33	40
Old Actonians Ass 'A'	20	12	2	6	51	40	38
Norsemen 'A'	20	12	1	7	56	40	37
Old Finchleians 'A'	20	11	1	8	48	48	34
Old Owens 'A'	20	10	2	8	42	39	32
Nottsborough 'A'	20	9	2	9	45	37	29
Weirside Rangers 'A'	20	6	4	10	31	42	22
Polytechnic 'A'	20	6	3	11	35	50	21
HSBC 'A'	20	5	3	12	42	42	18
Ibis 'A'	20	1	1	18	26	90	4

Junior Division Two	P	W	D	L	F	A	Pts
Old Stationers 'A'	20	13	3	4	84	50	42
Old Esthameians 'A'	20	14	0	6	52	34	42
West Wickham 'A'	20	10	3	7	42	45	33
Crouch End Vamp 'A'	20	10	2	8	50	35	32
E Barnet O Gram 'A'	20	10	2	8	66	56	32
Carshalton 'A' -2	20	10	2	8	48	38	30
Alleyn Old Boys 'A'	20	9	2	9	43	38	29
Bank of England 'A'	20	8	2	10	40	41	26
O W'minster Ctzn 'A'	20	6	5	9	53	54	23
Alexandra Park 'A'	20	6	3	11	43	60	21
Old Latymerians 'A'	20	1	2	17	26	96	5

Junior Division Three	P	W	D	L	F	A	Pts
S'thgate Olympic 'A'	20	16	1	3	100	24	49
Old Salesians 'A'	20	13	3	4	54	27	42
Sth Bank Cuaco 'A'	20	9	8	3	46	41	35
BB Eagles 'A'	20	10	4	6	41	33	34
Merton 'A'	20	10	4	6	41	41	34
Broomfield 'A'	20	8	1	11	34	51	25
Old Lyonians 'A'	20	7	3	10	40	57	24
Old Wilsonians 'A'	20	6	4	10	32	39	22
Old Parkonians 'A'	20	6	2	12	35	56	20
Kew Association 'A'	20	4	4	12	39	65	16
Lloyds TSB Bank 'A'	20	1	6	13	20	48	9

Minor Division One	P	W	D	L	F	A	Pts
Old Actonians Ass 'B'	20	16	1	3	61	25	49
Old Owens 'B'	20	12	3	5	45	36	39
Nottsborough 'B'	20	11	3	6	57	33	36
West Wickham 'B'	20	11	3	6	53	31	36
Old Finchleians 'B'	20	11	2	7	50	29	35
Winchmore Hill 'B'	20	10	3	7	51	28	33
Alexandra Park 'B'	20	7	2	11	41	58	23
Old Stationers 'B'	20	7	2	11	36	59	23
Civil Service 'B'	20	6	2	12	39	43	20
Old Wilsonians 'B'	20	4	2	14	27	70	14
HSBC 'B'	20	2	3	15	24	72	9

Minor Div Two North	P	W	D	L	F	A	Pts
Winchmore Hill 'C'	18	15	1	2	68	23	46
Crouch End Vamp 'B'	18	11	2	5	78	43	35
Norsemen 'B'	18	10	3	5	66	32	33
E Barnet O Gram 'B'	18	8	3	7	47	36	27
E Barnet O Gram 'C'	18	8	2	8	41	50	26
Old Finchleians 'C'	18	7	4	7	42	43	25
Old Owens 'C'	18	7	3	8	47	48	24
Old Finchleians 'D'	18	6	2	10	39	67	20
Crouch End Vamp 'C'	18	5	2	11	34	54	17
S'thgate Olympic 'B'	18	2	0	16	31	97	6

Minor Div Two South	P	W	D	L	F	A	Pts
Civil Service 'D'	20	13	3	4	59	33	42
Kew Association 'B'	20	13	2	5	58	31	41
O W'minster Ctzn 'B'	20	12	4	4	59	30	40
O Actonians Ass 'C'	20	9	4	7	47	47	31
Civil Service 'C'	20	9	3	8	48	36	30
Carshalton 'B'	20	9	3	8	38	41	30
Polytechnic 'B'	20	8	4	8	46	48	28
Polytechnic 'C'	20	6	3	11	36	52	21
Ibis 'B'	20	6	3	11	36	56	21
South Bank Cuaco 'C'	20	5	3	12	40	61	18
South Bank Cuaco 'B'	20	2	4	14	22	54	10

Minor Div Three Nth	P	W	D	L	F	A	Pts
Old Owens 'D'	20	12	5	3	55	26	41
Winchmore Hill 'D'	20	11	4	5	46	33	37
Norsemen 'D'	20	10	4	6	57	44	34
Norsemen 'C'	20	10	4	6	44	37	34
Broomfield 'B'	20	8	6	6	56	46	30
Crouch End Vamp 'D'	20	6	8	6	44	47	26
Old Esthameians 'B'	20	7	5	8	33	43	26
Old Finchleians 'E'	20	8	2	10	41	54	26
Alexandra Park 'C'	20	6	4	10	32	44	22
Old Stationers 'C'	20	5	4	11	41	45	19
Alexandra Park 'D'	20	4	0	16	37	67	12

Minor Div Three Sth	P	W	D	L	F	A	Pts
BB Eagles 'B'	18	15	0	3	66	27	45
West Wickham 'C'	18	14	0	4	56	31	42
Merton 'B'	18	11	1	6	42	23	34
Old Actonians Ass 'D'	18	11	1	6	38	30	34
HSBC 'C'	18	8	2	8	46	30	26
Kew Association 'C'	18	6	3	9	26	42	21
Polytechnic 'D'	18	6	2	10	28	41	20
Old Wilsonians 'C'	18	5	2	11	29	47	17
Weirside Rangers 'B'	18	5	2	11	32	53	17
Alleyn OB 'B' -2	18	2	1	15	17	56	5

Minor Div Four North	P	W	D	L	F	A	Pts
Winchmore Hill 'E'	20	15	2	3	73	31	47
Norsemen 'F'	20	12	2	6	61	43	38
Norsemen 'E'	20	10	7	3	61	43	37
Old Parkonians 'B'	20	11	1	8	66	43	34
Old Finchleians 'F'	20	9	3	8	54	51	30
Broomfield 'C'	20	8	3	9	48	62	27
E Barnet O Gram 'D'	20	8	2	10	49	47	26
Old Parkonians 'C'	20	8	1	11	47	52	25
S'thgate Olympic 'C'	20	6	4	10	56	67	22
Crouch End Vamp 'E'	20	4	4	12	32	61	16
Broomfield 'D'	20	4	1	15	36	83	13

Minor Div Four South	P	W	D	L	F	A	Pts
Old Actonians Ass 'E'	18	16	0	2	61	14	48
Carshalton 'C'	18	11	4	3	53	35	37
Alleyn Old Boys 'C'	18	10	2	6	57	38	32
Old Salesians 'B'	18	10	0	8	53	35	30
Carshalton 'D'	18	9	3	6	49	48	30
BB Eagles 'C'	18	7	5	6	43	39	26
Lloyds TSB Bank 'B'	18	7	1	10	37	47	22
HSBC 'D'	18	5	3	10	36	65	18
Polytechnic 'E'	18	3	2	13	33	55	11
O W'minster Ctzn 'C'	18	1	2	15	31	77	5

Minor Div Five North	P	W	D	L	F	A	Pts
Winchmore Hill 'G'	18	18	0	0	84	15	54
Winchmore Hill 'F'	18	14	0	4	100	23	42
Old Stationers 'D'	18	9	3	6	51	48	30
Old Parkonians 'D'	18	9	2	7	54	34	29
Norsemen 'G'	18	8	3	7	67	48	27
Alexandra Park 'E'	18	6	5	7	61	57	23
E Barnet O Gram 'E'	18	6	3	9	40	54	21
Alexandra Park 'F'	18	5	2	11	43	54	17
E Barnet O Gram 'F'	18	3	1	14	28	120	10
S'thgate Olympic 'D'	18	1	3	14	21	96	6

Minor Div Five South	P	W	D	L	F	A	Pts
Weirside Rangers 'C'	20	12	5	3	58	25	41
Old Wilsonians 'E'	20	13	0	7	56	30	39
Bank of England 'B'	20	12	3	5	56	36	39
Old Actonians Ass 'F'	20	12	3	5	60	45	39
Old Lyonians 'B'	20	9	5	6	53	45	32
HSBC 'E'	20	9	2	9	47	37	29
Old Wilsonians 'D'	20	8	5	7	48	48	29
Polytechnic 'F'	20	6	7	7	46	47	25
Lloyds TSB Bank 'C'	20	5	4	11	40	62	19
Old Latymerians 'B'	20	4	1	15	30	71	13
Sth Bank Cuaco 'D'	20	2	1	17	26	74	7

Minor Div Six South	P	W	D	L	F	A	Pts
Merton 'C'	20	17	2	1	85	21	53
Kew Association 'D'	20	13	3	4	72	33	42
Carshalton 'E'	20	12	3	5	54	48	39
West Wickham 'D'	20	12	1	7	71	57	37
BB Eagles 'D'	20	11	1	8	64	48	34
Civil Service 'E'	20	11	1	8	62	48	34
Lloyds TSB Bank 'D'	20	8	4	8	57	35	28
O W'minster Ctzn 'D'	20	6	2	12	40	79	20
HSBC 'F'	20	4	1	15	39	77	13
Old Wilsonians 'F'	20	2	3	15	33	78	9
Lloyds TSB Bank 'E'	20	2	3	15	30	83	9

Minor Div Seven South	P	W	D	L	F	A	Pts
Lloyds TSB Bank 'F'	20	12	5	3	61	39	41
Merton 'D'	20	11	5	4	62	36	38
Old Actonians Ass 'H'	20	11	3	6	56	53	36
Carshalton 'F'	20	10	3	7	60	48	33
Kew Association 'E'	20	7	8	5	67	57	29
Old Actonians Ass 'G'	20	8	5	7	50	42	29
Merton 'E'	20	8	4	8	57	57	28
Sth Bank Cuaco 'E'	20	6	5	9	52	72	23
Bank of England 'C'	20	6	3	11	40	48	21
Kew Association 'F'	20	5	4	11	40	45	19
Polytechnic 'G'	20	1	5	14	27	75	8

SPEN VALLEY LEAGUE

Premier Division	P	W	D	L	F	A	Pts
Salfa Rangers -3	17	16	1	0	63	15	46
Wellington Wdrs	18	10	5	3	46	32	35
Kalon	17	10	3	4	68	34	33
Hare & Hounds	18	8	4	6	64	38	28
Soothill	18	6	7	5	37	37	25
Windmill (Wibsey) -3	18	6	7	5	37	38	22
Dewsbury WS -3	18	6	4	8	43	45	19
Howden Clough Res.	18	4	6	8	24	45	18
Commonside	18	1	3	14	31	82	6
Bosnia	18	1	2	15	34	81	5

Division One	P	W	D	L	F	A	Pts
Wyke Wanderers	20	17	0	3	77	20	51
Old Bank WMC	20	15	2	3	98	35	47
Old Magnet	20	14	4	2	67	27	46
Barfield	20	10	4	6	73	49	34
Youth 2000	20	9	3	8	52	49	30
Norfolk	20	5	5	10	44	65	20
Inter Batley	20	6	2	12	30	69	20
Marsh	20	6	1	13	39	57	19
Windmill (Wibsey) Res.	20	5	2	13	50	92	17
Wellington Wdrs Res.	20	5	0	15	34	78	15
Shooters -6	20	6	1	13	56	79	13

ST HELENS COMBINATION

Premier Division	P	W	D	L	F	A	Pts
Knowsley South	24	19	3	2	94	33	60
Denton Green	24	15	4	5	63	35	49
Rainford North End	24	14	4	6	55	33	46
Clock Face Miners	24	13	7	4	41	28	46
Shoe	24	11	4	9	57	41	37
Old Congs	24	10	3	11	57	49	33
Prescot Leisure	24	9	3	12	56	70	30
British Lion -2	24	9	4	11	34	38	29
York	24	7	6	11	31	51	27
Windle Hotel	24	7	5	12	39	49	26
Stars	24	6	4	14	36	63	22
Eccleston United	24	5	3	16	39	68	18
Sidac Social	24	5	2	17	35	79	17

Division One	P	W	D	L	F	A	Pts
East Villa Res.	20	16	2	2	66	15	50
Top Nogs	20	13	4	3	60	28	43
Knowsley South Res.	20	11	3	6	44	28	36
Junction	20	11	3	6	45	38	36
Gerard Arms	20	9	3	8	44	51	30
Rainford N End Res.	20	8	5	7	44	47	29
Sidac Social 'A'	20	9	1	10	41	44	28
Sony	20	7	0	13	44	72	21
Oddfellows	20	5	2	13	34	52	17
Carr Mill -2	20	5	2	13	49	70	15
The Glassblower	20	2	3	15	37	63	9

Division Two	P	W	D	L	F	A	Pts
Wastlebridge Park	26	22	2	2	96	33	68
Greenfields	26	17	5	4	90	41	56
Boilermakers	26	16	6	4	73	38	54
Vegas	26	16	4	6	73	36	52
New Street	26	13	8	5	75	55	47
Care Trust	26	12	3	11	75	67	39
Clock Face Mnrs Res.	26	11	5	10	68	50	38
Carborundum Eagles	26	9	4	13	49	67	31
OCS	26	8	5	13	45	62	29
Orange House	26	8	5	13	38	61	29
Cricketers Arms	26	8	2	16	45	81	26
Engine	26	6	3	17	45	58	21
Prescot Leisure Res.	26	5	4	17	37	85	19
Beagle & Child	26	2	2	22	18	93	8

STOKESLEY & DISTRICT LEAGUE

	P	W	D	L	F	A	Pts
Rudds Arms	24	22	2	0	143	19	68
Sth Bank St Peters -3	24	17	2	5	115	32	50
Corus Sports Club	24	14	4	6	82	59	46
Grangetown YCC	24	12	8	4	81	45	44
Ennis Square SC -3	24	14	3	7	106	63	42
Thornaby Village	24	13	2	9	74	74	41
Coulby Newham -3	24	12	2	10	55	59	35
Acklam Steel Works	24	9	6	9	50	75	33
St Marys College OB	24	7	3	14	48	50	24
Stokesley Sp Club 'A'	24	6	3	15	66	81	21
South Park Rangers	24	5	0	19	33	130	15
The Smithy -6	24	6	1	17	41	69	13
NS Bulls Head -3	24	1	0	23	24	162	0

STROUD & DISTRICT LEAGUE

Division One	P	W	D	L	F	A	Pts
Slimbridge Res.	26	21	3	2	76	18	66
Minchinhampton RDS	26	20	5	1	73	26	65
Barnwood United -1	26	19	1	6	83	30	57
Ramblers	26	16	7	3	57	25	55
Athletico Severn	26	13	7	6	81	42	46
Leonard Stanley	26	12	3	11	61	59	39
Kings Stanley Res.	26	9	7	10	41	47	34
Shurdington Rovers	26	10	2	14	44	62	32
Longlevens Res.	26	8	5	13	41	50	29
Whitminster	26	7	7	12	44	58	28
Frampton United	26	6	4	16	31	68	22
Upton St Leonards	26	5	3	18	39	78	18
Thornbury Tn Res.	26	4	2	20	28	79	14
Brockworth Res. -3	26	3	2	21	27	84	8

Division Two	P	W	D	L	F	A	Pts
Gloucester Civ Serv	24	17	4	3	60	26	55
Coaley Rovers	24	16	2	6	61	27	50
Cashes Green	24	10	8	6	59	38	38
Longford Res.	24	12	2	10	53	51	38
Randwick	24	11	4	9	46	35	37
Whiteshill United	24	11	4	9	54	51	37
Abbeymead Rovers	24	8	8	8	55	48	32
Hardwicke Res.	24	8	6	10	50	50	30
Brimscombe/Thr Res.	24	8	5	11	40	44	29
Stratford Rangers -3	24	7	7	10	38	58	25
Stoneh'se F'way Res.	24	7	4	13	47	77	25
Wotton Rovers Res.	24	5	4	15	41	65	19
Minchinhampton Res.	24	4	6	14	30	55	18

Division Three	P	W	D	L	F	A	Pts
Marshall Langston	26	22	4	0	102	20	70
Matson	26	18	4	4	88	37	58
Shipton Moyne	26	16	4	6	91	43	52
Trident	26	13	7	6	71	62	46
Tetbury Town Res.	26	12	5	9	69	54	41
Quedgeley Rangers	26	11	7	8	56	52	40
Ebley	26	12	2	12	69	51	38
Sharpness Res.	26	10	6	10	66	61	36
Uley	26	9	5	12	57	60	32
Horsley Utd Res. +1	26	7	8	11	45	68	30
Cam Bulldogs Res.	26	9	0	17	40	62	27
Chalford Res.	26	7	0	19	31	95	21
Glevum United	26	5	0	21	23	84	15
Alkerton Rangers	26	4	2	20	36	95	14

Division Four	P	W	D	L	F	A	Pts
Tibberton United	22	15	3	4	66	23	48
Dursley Town Res.	22	12	4	6	35	27	40
Hawkesbury Upton	22	10	6	6	53	33	36
Wickwar Wanderers	22	11	3	8	44	26	36
Stonehouse F'way 'A'	22	10	5	7	43	42	35
Berkeley Town Res.	22	11	1	10	35	32	34
Frampton U Res. -1	22	9	3	10	32	48	29
North Nibley	22	7	6	9	39	34	27
Nympsfield	22	7	4	11	32	47	25
Charfield Res.	22	6	6	10	37	48	24
Uley Res.	22	7	1	14	29	70	22
Upton St Leonards Res.	22	4	4	14	35	50	16

Division Five	P	W	D	L	F	A	Pts
Kingswood Res.	24	20	0	4	78	24	60
Longlevens 'A'	24	15	4	5	88	44	49
Athletico Severn Res.	24	14	0	10	70	56	42
Thornbury Town 'A'	24	13	2	9	61	39	41
Minchinhampton 'A'	24	12	4	8	72	53	40
Shipton Moyne Res.	24	12	3	9	72	51	39
Randwick Res.	24	11	3	10	52	47	36
Glos Civil Serv Res.	24	10	2	12	53	55	32
Arlingham	24	9	4	11	48	56	31
Quedgeley Wdrs Res.	24	9	2	13	41	60	29
Dursley Town 'A'	24	6	4	14	51	86	22
Wotton Rvrs 'A' +1	24	7	0	17	36	86	22
Matchplay Reeves	24	3	2	19	33	98	11

Division Six	P	W	D	L	F	A	Pts
Ramblers Res.	24	20	1	3	90	22	61
Suttons	24	16	2	6	70	36	50
Leonard Stanley Res.	24	15	5	4	67	33	50
Barnwood Utd Res.	24	14	2	8	67	39	44
Longlevens 'B'	24	11	4	9	52	42	37
Cainscross DBs	24	11	2	11	65	62	35
Ebley Res. -1	24	9	4	11	48	63	30
Coaley Rovers Res.	24	8	4	12	53	53	28
Eastcombe Res.	24	7	6	11	44	53	27
Brockworth Alb 'B'	24	7	2	15	35	58	23
Stroud Harriers	24	7	2	15	41	86	23
Shurdington Rvrs Res.	24	7	2	15	39	86	23
NSSC	24	4	4	16	55	93	16

Division Seven	P	W	D	L	F	A	Pts
AC Royals	24	22	2	0	95	22	68
AFC Phoenix	24	19	1	4	97	44	58
BA Rangers	24	16	4	4	89	34	52
Victoria Celtic	24	14	3	7	92	40	45
Charfield 'A'	24	12	3	9	74	56	39
Glos Civil Service 'A'	24	10	3	11	47	51	33
Uley 'A'	24	9	3	12	45	89	30
Cashes Green Res.	24	9	2	13	58	65	29
Trident Res.	24	7	6	11	42	62	27
Cam Bulldogs 'A'	24	6	3	15	36	84	21
Stonehouse F'way 'B'	24	5	2	17	43	86	17
Upton St Leon. 'A'	24	4	4	16	23	62	16
North Nibley Res.	24	4	2	18	38	84	14

Division Eight	P	W	D	L	F	A	Pts
Whitminster Res.	26	22	0	4	103	31	66
Abbeymead Res. -3	26	21	2	3	138	33	62
BA Rangers Res.	26	19	0	7	87	39	57
Wickwar Wdrs Res.	26	16	3	7	98	53	51
Whiteshill Utd Res.	26	14	5	7	87	36	47
Didmarton	26	13	4	9	92	64	43
Quedgeley Wdrs 'A'	26	13	1	12	59	41	40
Ramblers 'A'	26	11	5	10	72	45	38
Essilor	26	10	6	10	54	52	36
Alkerton Rgrs Res.	26	7	3	16	45	105	24
Matchplay R'ves Res.	26	7	1	18	53	135	22
Randwick 'A'	26	6	3	17	61	79	21
Crown & Sceptre -3	26	3	2	21	35	137	8
Woodchester	26	2	1	23	23	157	7

SUBURBAN LEAGUE

Premier Division	P	W	D	L	F	A	Pts
Hemel H'pstead Res.	26	20	4	2	76	24	64
Sutton United Res.	26	18	1	7	48	27	55
Dover Athletic Res.	26	12	6	8	39	24	42
Walton & Hersh Res.	26	13	3	10	37	33	42
Basingstoke Tn Res.	26	11	8	7	37	34	41
Ashford Tn (Midx) Res.	26	11	5	10	45	46	38
Wealdstone Res.	26	11	4	11	45	49	37
Whyteleafe Res.	26	10	4	12	39	42	34
Metrop. Police Res.	26	9	6	11	43	52	33
Uxbridge Res.	26	10	2	14	42	45	32
Carshalton Ath Res.	26	10	2	14	36	52	32
B'sfield SYCOB Res.	26	7	7	12	32	44	28
Hayes Res.	26	6	7	13	35	42	25
Brook House Res.	26	3	3	20	19	59	12

Northern Division	P	W	D	L	F	A	Pts
Waltham Forest Res.	24	14	7	3	69	30	49
Harefield Utd Res.	24	15	3	6	52	34	48
Burnham Res.	24	15	2	7	53	34	47
Fleet Town Res.	24	11	6	7	48	38	39
Hillingdon Boro' Res.	24	11	8	5	48	34	41
Leighton Town Res.	24	11	5	8	65	43	38
N Greenford Utd Res.	24	8	6	10	47	50	30
Northwood Res.	24	7	6	11	45	51	27
Ruislip Manor Res.	24	7	6	11	40	49	27
Bedfont Res.	24	7	3	14	35	57	24
Broxbourne Boro Res.	24	6	5	13	32	59	23
Chalfont St Peter Res.	24	5	5	14	32	60	20
Wembley Res.	24	3	10	11	29	56	19

Southern Division	P	W	D	L	F	A	Pts
Corinthian Cas. Res.	26	16	5	5	62	25	53
Eastleigh Res.	26	16	4	6	47	24	52
Three Bridges Res.	26	15	5	6	49	32	50
Tooting/Mitcham Res.	26	15	2	9	51	31	47
Tonbridge Angels Res.	26	14	4	8	66	34	46
Merstham Res.	26	13	3	10	49	51	42
AFC Wimbledon Res.	26	11	8	7	45	25	41
Horley Town Res.	26	11	4	11	36	37	37
Chipstead Res.	26	11	3	12	38	52	36
Walton Casuals Res.	26	8	5	13	32	46	29
Molesey Res.	26	6	8	12	38	48	26
Epsom & Ewell Res.	26	7	4	15	28	51	25
Godalming Tn Res.	26	4	3	19	26	68	15
Camberley Tn Res.	26	2	8	16	18	61	14

SURREY INTERMEDIATE LEAGUE (WEST)

Premier Division	P	W	D	L	F	A	Pts
Old Rutlishians	26	18	1	7	74	30	55
Yateley -3	26	17	5	4	76	33	53
Woking Pk /Horsell	26	13	7	6	77	43	46
Hersham Royal Brit L	26	13	6	7	62	36	45
Ripley Village	26	13	5	8	48	35	44
Horsley	26	12	7	7	64	48	43
Milford & Witley	26	13	4	9	45	38	43
Pyrford	26	13	3	10	49	42	42
Chiddingfold	26	11	4	11	49	42	37
Shalford	26	10	6	10	52	48	36
Eversley Social	26	9	5	12	45	50	32
Ockham -3	26	6	3	17	33	52	18
Worplesdon	26	3	3	20	33	128	12
Unis Old Boys	26	1	1	24	23	105	4

Division One	P	W	D	L	F	A	Pts
Knaphill	26	21	2	3	101	29	65
Virginia Water	26	19	2	5	102	36	59
Elm Grove	26	17	1	8	87	33	52
Liphook	26	15	5	6	75	45	50
Royal Holloway OB	26	14	4	8	65	50	46
Ewhurst	26	12	6	8	77	48	42
Windlesham United	26	12	4	10	57	56	40
Old Salesians	26	10	4	12	47	58	34
Fairlands Wdrs -9	26	13	3	10	59	55	33
Guildford City Weys.	26	9	3	14	57	72	30
Hammer United	26	8	2	16	49	74	26
Godalming/Farncombe	26	7	4	15	49	63	25
Burymead	26	3	2	21	23	109	11
Dunsfold	26	1	0	25	20	140	3

Reserve Premier Div	P	W	D	L	F	A	Pts
Old Rutlishians Res.	26	22	1	3	87	34	67
Woking Pk & H Res.	26	19	2	5	82	36	59
Hersham R'l B L Res.	26	17	4	5	87	41	55
Eversley Social Res.	26	16	1	9	66	51	49
Shalford Res.	26	13	4	9	54	43	43
Ripley Village Res.	26	11	8	7	48	48	41
Yateley Res. -6	26	13	4	9	57	35	37
Horsley Res.	26	11	4	11	62	67	37
Milford/Witley Res.	26	10	4	12	47	52	34
Pyrford Res.	26	7	6	13	56	65	27
Chiddingfold Res.	26	7	3	16	38	69	24
Worplesdon Res.	26	6	4	16	31	62	22
Unis Old Boys Res.	26	2	3	21	32	85	9
Ockham Res. -1	26	2	4	20	24	83	9

Reserve Division One	P	W	D	L	F	A	Pts
Virginia Water Res.	26	22	2	2	92	24	68
Godalming/F Res. -3	26	21	2	3	92	33	62
Fairlands Wdrs Res.	26	19	4	3	96	35	61
Royal Holl' OB Res.	26	14	6	6	75	47	48
Knaphill Res.	26	14	5	7	56	38	47
Liphook Res.	26	12	8	6	70	58	44
Elm Grove Res.	26	13	4	9	82	53	43
Windlesham Utd Res.	26	10	3	13	51	62	33
Hammer Utd Res. -3	26	11	2	13	69	75	32
Ewhurst Res.	26	7	4	15	56	72	25
Old Salesians Res.	26	5	3	18	38	75	18
Guildford City W Res.	26	4	5	17	35	73	17
Burymead Res.	26	1	5	20	32	100	8
Dunsfold Res.	26	1	3	22	28	127	6

SURREY SOUTH EASTERN COMBINATION

Intermediate Div One	P	W	D	L	F	A	Pts
Battersea Iron. Res. -2	24	15	7	2	68	41	50
Tadworth	24	15	5	4	55	33	50
Greenside +2	24	13	6	5	70	33	47
Epsom Athletic	24	14	3	7	74	41	45
St Andrews -1	23	11	5	7	47	30	37
Sporting Kitz	23	10	5	8	50	44	35
O Plymouthians +2	24	9	5	10	48	59	34
Battersea -1	24	9	6	9	43	48	32
Continental Stars	24	8	7	9	45	43	31
NPL	24	8	6	10	58	59	30
Ashtead	24	5	6	13	36	71	21
Woodmansterne Spts	24	4	3	17	39	68	15
Cranleigh	24	1	2	21	32	95	5

Intermediate Div Two	P	W	D	L	F	A	Pts
Walton Athletic	22	15	4	3	57	26	49
Nutfield +3	22	13	1	8	56	41	43
Old Bristolians	22	12	4	6	73	39	40
SCR Kingfisher	22	12	4	6	50	38	40
Wandgas Sports	22	11	3	8	60	46	36
Merton Abbey +2	22	10	4	8	56	44	36
Oxted & District	22	9	7	6	50	36	34
Bletchingley	22	9	3	10	41	46	30
Westside	22	5	5	12	36	46	20
Croydon Postal -4	22	6	4	12	47	67	18
Thornton Hth Rvrs	22	5	2	15	41	74	17
AFC Ewell	22	3	3	16	22	86	12

Junior Division One	P	W	D	L	F	A	Pts
Refectory Sports	20	18	2	0	69	15	56
Tooting Bec	20	13	4	3	45	18	43
Clapham Town	20	11	1	8	44	48	34
Warbank Phoenix	20	9	3	8	50	43	30
New Life	20	10	0	10	44	49	30
FC Triangle	20	8	4	8	45	36	28
Yourstory +3	20	7	1	12	49	56	25
Battersea Iron. 'A' -6	20	8	2	10	37	58	20
Epsom Eagles Sn -14	20	8	4	8	65	61	14
Wilf Kroucher +3	20	3	2	15	31	78	14
Clapham Pk Utd -7	20	2	3	15	28	45	2

Junior Division Two	P	W	D	L	F	A	Pts
Trinity	22	14	5	3	54	22	47
Cheam Vill Warriors	22	14	3	5	39	25	45
Sutton High	22	12	7	3	45	28	43
Sporting Kitz Res.	22	10	6	6	60	44	36
O Plymouthians Res.	22	10	4	8	47	34	34
Continental Stars Res.	22	10	3	9	42	40	33
Worcester Park 'A'	22	9	5	8	49	40	32
NPL Res.	22	8	6	8	44	40	30
Crescent Rovers 'A'	22	8	4	10	43	60	28
St Andrews Res.	22	5	5	12	38	46	20
W'mansterne Spts Res.	22	3	3	16	31	75	12
Greenside Res.	22	2	3	17	29	67	9

Junior Division Three	P	W	D	L	F	A	Pts
Weston Green Sp Club	22	18	2	2	104	27	56
Tadworth Res.	22	16	4	2	70	28	52
Supercala	22	14	3	5	72	46	45
Fetcham	22	13	1	8	82	67	40
Norton	22	10	5	7	62	51	35
Alexander Forbes	22	9	3	10	57	66	30
Epsom Athletic Res.	22	8	4	10	44	53	28
Bletchingley Res.	22	7	4	11	39	51	25
Ashtead Res.	22	8	1	13	34	61	25
Oxted & District Res.	22	6	2	14	37	61	20
FC Maurice	22	3	3	16	33	76	12
Chessington/Hk U 'A'	22	3	2	17	29	76	11

Junior Division Four	P	W	D	L	F	A	Pts
Inter Class -3	22	16	2	4	90	31	47
Oakhill United	22	14	4	4	69	47	46
SCR Kingf'r Res. -1	22	13	5	4	55	30	43
Battersea Ir. 'B' +2	22	10	6	6	55	36	38
Old Bristolians Res.	22	11	2	9	64	48	35
Old Plymouthians 'A'	22	9	4	9	50	41	31
Croydon Athletic 'A'	22	7	7	8	42	43	28
Trinity Res.	22	8	4	10	54	60	28
Crescent Rvrs 'B' -3	22	9	2	11	55	64	26
Tooting Bec Res. +3	22	5	5	12	25	50	23
Norton Res.	22	6	4	12	29	48	22
Fetcham Res. +3	22	1	1	20	21	111	7

SUTTON & DISTRICT LEAGUE

Premier Division	P	W	D	L	F	A	Pts
Sporting Bahia	14	10	2	2	36	26	32
Alma Tavern Res.	14	10	1	3	52	21	31
AFC Inter	14	10	1	3	45	19	31
Sutton Churches	13	5	1	7	18	37	16
Wallington New For.	13	4	1	8	17	33	13
Heath Old Boys	14	3	3	8	18	29	12
Super FC	13	2	5	6	16	24	11
Real Holmesdale	13	2	2	9	25	38	8

SWINDON & DISTRICT LEAGUE

Premier Division	P	W	D	L	F	A	Pts
Shield & Dagger	16	11	1	4	40	30	34
Zurich	16	10	3	3	41	27	33
Southbrook	16	9	4	3	36	17	31
Regent	16	9	2	5	43	27	29
Queensfield	16	7	4	5	41	29	25
Green Baize	16	5	2	9	27	49	17
Ridgeway	16	4	3	9	28	38	15
Liden	16	4	1	11	28	47	13
Running Horse	16	2	2	12	25	45	8

South Marston – record expunged

Division One	P	W	D	L	F	A	Pts
Merlin	24	19	1	4	95	43	58
Down Ampney Res.	24	18	3	3	117	48	57
Eastville	24	16	5	3	91	34	53
Lower Stratton Res.	24	12	5	7	56	40	41
Spectrum	24	12	3	9	71	51	39
AFC Abbey	24	12	2	10	59	61	38
Wason & Webb	24	10	5	9	67	65	35
Walcot	24	11	2	11	54	72	35
Ramsbury	24	9	5	10	66	62	32
Trailers	24	6	3	15	50	103	21
Green Baize Res.	24	5	2	17	67	87	17
Milton Club	24	4	1	19	55	99	13
Rodbourne	24	3	1	20	44	127	10

TAUNTON & DISTRICT LEAGUE

Division One	P	W	D	L	F	A	Pts
Staplegrove	24	20	3	1	76	30	63
Bridgwater Sports	24	20	1	3	81	29	61
Porlock	24	13	3	8	47	28	42
Wyvern	24	11	6	7	58	41	39
Alcombe	24	11	5	8	59	45	38
Highbridge Town	24	10	4	10	53	41	34
Taverners	24	8	6	10	49	51	30
Bishops Lyd Res. -3	24	9	4	11	37	52	28
Norton Fitzwarren	24	8	4	12	40	64	28
Cossington	24	7	6	11	49	60	27
Sampford Blues	24	5	6	13	50	69	21
Marketeers -3	24	4	2	18	37	73	11
Wellworthy Saints -3	24	4	2	18	50	103	11

Division Two	P	W	D	L	F	A	Pts
Locomotives	24	18	5	1	81	32	59
Middlezoy Rovers	24	16	5	3	79	27	53
Dulverton Town	24	14	6	4	53	35	48
Hulan	24	13	7	4	63	37	46
Staplegrove Res.	24	13	5	6	66	36	44
Spaxton -9	24	12	4	8	62	55	31
Sydenham Rangers	24	8	3	13	41	49	27
Civil Service	24	6	7	11	37	59	25
Norton Fitzwarren Res.	24	7	3	14	58	68	24
Wellington Tn 'A' -3	24	7	3	14	45	67	21
Minehead Tn Res. -3	24	5	5	14	36	69	17
Redgate	24	4	5	15	28	67	17
Nether Stowey	24	2	4	18	23	71	10

Division Three	P	W	D	L	F	A	Pts
Westonzoyland	22	16	2	4	80	30	50
Hamilton Hawks -3	22	17	2	3	70	31	50
Staplegrove Colts	22	15	4	3	83	42	49
Predators	22	15	3	4	76	34	48
Bridgwater Spts Res.	22	12	3	7	57	41	39
Watchet Town Res.	22	10	3	9	67	42	33
Wyvern Res. -3	22	10	1	11	57	65	28
Highbridge Tn Res.	22	7	5	10	36	55	26
Victoria Rangers	22	6	2	14	57	51	20
Alcombe Rovers Res.	22	6	2	14	47	63	20
Swallowfields	22	1	1	20	16	126	4
Norton Fitz Dragon -6	22	2	2	18	39	105	2

Division Four	P	W	D	L	F	A	Pts
Milverton Rangers	24	21	1	2	105	22	64
North Petherton	24	18	3	3	94	39	57
Hemyock	24	14	4	6	76	40	46
Exmoor Rangers	24	14	4	6	71	46	46
Stogursey Greyhounds	24	12	5	7	87	55	41
Old Inn All Stars	24	12	2	10	62	51	38
Dulverton Tn Res.	24	9	4	11	53	88	31
Wembdon	24	8	4	12	47	57	28
Westonzoyland Res.	24	6	4	14	53	65	22
Hamilton Hawks Res.	24	6	2	16	51	87	20
Porlock Res. -3	24	5	4	15	43	74	16
Williton	24	4	4	16	43	99	16
Wyvern Foxes -9	24	6	1	17	49	111	10

TROWBRIDGE & DISTRICT LEAGUE

Division One	P	W	D	L	F	A	Pts
Freshford United	18	11	4	3	34	19	26
Bradford United	18	11	3	4	47	24	25
Seend United	18	7	7	4	38	29	21
Blue Circle	18	7	7	4	33	34	21
North Bradley Saints	18	6	5	7	50	46	17
Frome Town Sports	18	6	4	8	34	38	16
Rudloe -1	18	6	4	8	39	36	15
Broughton Gifford -4	18	7	4	7	40	37	14
Warminster Res. -1	18	5	4	9	25	30	13
Heytesbury	18	3	0	15	22	69	6

TYNESIDE AMATEUR LEAGUE

Division One	P	W	D	L	F	A	Pts
Winlaton Vulcan Inn	22	17	3	2	68	28	54
Whitley Bay Venture	22	15	5	2	80	36	50
Cramlington Tn Res.	22	13	5	4	59	27	44
Bellingham	22	11	4	7	62	50	37
Wallsend J'y Bowman	22	11	2	9	53	44	35
Gosforth Boh.G. Res.	22	9	4	9	44	39	31
Killingworth	22	7	4	11	34	51	25
Newcastle Medicals	22	5	4	13	43	68	19
Killingworth Soc YPC	22	5	3	14	44	77	18
Lindisfarne Athletic	22	4	4	14	37	61	16
Newcastle U Res. -12	22	7	6	9	39	43	15
Willington Q Sts -3	22	6	0	16	42	81	15

Division Two	P	W	D	L	F	A	Pts
Blyth Town Res.	22	19	2	1	82	18	59
West Jesmond	22	14	3	5	49	29	45
Wardley Durham Rgrs	22	14	2	6	74	44	44
Forest Hall	22	12	2	8	60	37	38
New York	22	12	2	8	59	50	38
Blyth Waterloo *-3*	22	12	2	8	57	53	35
Gateshead Three Tuns	22	10	1	11	58	57	31
Wallsend Tn Res. *-3*	22	10	1	11	59	56	28
N'castle Inter Dent *-3*	22	9	1	12	40	54	25
N'castle IJLW Brazil	22	5	2	15	32	63	17
Red Star Benwell	22	3	1	18	27	83	10
Proctor/Gamble Cobalt	22	2	1	19	29	82	7

WAKEFIELD & DISTRICT LEAGUE

Premier Division	P	W	D	L	F	A	Pts
Airedale Celtic	22	17	2	3	90	25	53
Sandal Athletic	22	17	2	3	74	34	53
Snydale Athletic	22	13	3	6	73	53	42
Mitres Well	22	9	3	10	69	76	30
Walton	22	7	6	9	65	65	27
Slipper	22	7	4	11	53	59	25
Altofts Res. *-3*	22	8	4	10	45	61	25
Eastmoor Res.	22	7	4	11	51	68	25
Silcoates	22	7	3	12	66	87	24
St Michaels *-6*	22	9	0	13	57	59	21
Fieldhead Hospital *-6*	22	8	3	11	47	66	21
Snydale Sports	22	4	4	14	53	90	16

Division One	P	W	D	L	F	A	Pts
White Bear Kexboro'	26	21	2	3	101	32	65
Fleece Horbury	26	19	4	3	99	41	61
AFC Thornhill	26	15	5	6	88	63	50
Wrenthorpe FC	26	14	6	6	80	47	48
Kingstone Utd WMC	26	14	1	11	73	59	43
AFC Shepherds Ar *-3*	26	12	7	7	79	50	40
Knottingley Wat. *-6*	26	15	1	10	53	39	40
Thornhill *-9*	26	11	5	10	70	65	29
Nostell M W 'A'	26	8	5	13	47	63	29
Wakefield City 'A'	26	8	3	15	42	66	27
AFC Foresters	26	8	1	17	63	107	25
Pinderfields Unison	26	6	3	17	66	92	21
Waterloo	26	5	1	20	31	97	16
Morley C & SC *-6*	26	3	2	21	45	116	5

Division Two	P	W	D	L	F	A	Pts
Ryecroft Sports	22	18	1	3	69	29	55
Ferrybridge Amateurs	22	17	2	3	79	41	53
Crofton	22	11	2	9	55	57	35
Stanley Arms *-3*	22	12	1	9	54	42	34
Gawthorpe Shoulder	22	8	5	9	66	63	29
Jolly Miller	22	9	1	12	58	59	28
AFC Cross Keys *-3*	22	9	3	10	57	54	27
Snydale Athletic Res.	22	6	7	9	47	56	25
Fleece Horb'y Res. *-6*	22	8	6	8	54	54	24
Sandal Athletic Res	22	6	3	13	49	63	21
Westgate Common	22	4	5	13	39	74	17
Ossett Panthers *-6*	22	5	2	15	51	86	11

Division Three	P	W	D	L	F	A	Pts
Stanley Utd Res. *-6*	26	21	4	1	101	28	61
White Rose	26	18	3	5	101	29	57
Wakefield United	26	16	2	8	56	40	50
Smawthorne Hotel *-12*	26	19	3	4	92	36	48
Slipper Res.	26	12	7	7	62	46	43
Park Tavern Rovers	26	13	3	10	63	50	42
Exel Knights	26	11	6	9	74	66	39
St Michaels Res.	26	12	2	12	60	52	38
Little Bull	26	11	3	12	45	53	36
Cliffe Tree *-4*	26	6	6	14	66	84	20
Altofts 'A' *-7*	26	6	5	15	37	75	16
Mitres Well Vets *-6*	26	6	3	17	40	88	15
East Ardsley General	26	3	4	19	46	115	13
Snydale Spts Res. *-3*	26	1	3	22	36	117	3

WARRINGTON & DISTRICT LEAGUE

Premier Division	P	W	D	L	F	A	Pts
Rainhill Town	22	13	7	2	68	19	46
Penlake Res.	22	11	6	5	42	27	39
Moore United	22	11	6	5	40	39	39
Halebank	22	9	6	7	46	30	33
Vulcan	22	9	6	7	36	28	33
Beeches	22	8	9	5	44	42	33
Haydock	22	8	7	7	36	32	31
Whiston Cross	22	7	7	8	46	54	28
Blackbrook	22	7	5	10	40	47	26
St Michaels DH	22	8	2	12	38	45	26
Downall Green Utd	22	5	2	15	29	64	17
Moorfield	22	3	3	16	25	63	12

Division One	P	W	D	L	F	A	Pts
Cronton Villa	20	20	0	0	86	16	60
Stockton Lane	20	13	2	5	64	34	41
Sidac Social Res.	20	13	2	5	50	38	41
Beechwood	20	9	5	6	39	42	32
Halton Borough	20	9	4	7	43	46	31
Matthiola	20	8	4	8	47	40	28
Ford Motors Res.	20	7	6	7	46	46	27
Vicars	20	6	2	12	47	60	20
Runcorn Albion	20	4	4	12	26	46	16
Avon Athletic	20	4	1	15	35	76	13
Culcheth SC	20	1	2	17	24	63	5

Division Two	P	W	D	L	F	A	Pts
Act R Sports	20	15	4	1	59	17	49
Whiston Cross Res.	20	12	6	2	52	32	42
Greenalls P St Os 'A'	20	13	3	4	42	30	42
Croft	20	11	3	6	58	47	36
Rainhill Town Res.	20	10	3	7	43	38	33
Orford Blackbourne	20	7	4	9	31	43	25
Windle Labour Club	20	7	3	10	45	51	24
Halebank Res.	20	7	3	10	32	42	24
Winwick United	20	6	3	11	38	41	21
Mill Brow	20	3	2	15	25	43	11
Runcorn Athletic	20	1	2	17	30	71	5

Division Three	P	W	D	L	F	A	Pts
Grange Safeway	20	15	2	3	62	27	47
Vulcan Res.	20	13	2	5	60	41	41
Cronton Villa Res.	20	11	4	5	56	40	37
Eagle Sports 'A'	20	9	4	7	45	50	31
Rainhill Town 'A'	20	9	2	9	57	48	29
Fife Rangers	20	8	4	8	65	53	28
Monk Sports Res.	20	7	4	9	32	39	25
Newton-le-Willows	20	6	4	10	47	45	22
Culcheth SC Res.	20	5	5	10	28	53	20
Moorfield Res.	20	5	3	12	47	66	18
Halton Borough Res.	20	2	6	12	30	67	12

Division Four	P	W	D	L	F	A	Pts
Burtonwood Albion	22	20	1	1	89	20	61
Vicars Res.	22	16	2	4	73	27	50
Lomax CC	22	12	5	5	67	37	41
Widnes Bayer	22	12	3	7	46	35	39
Village Social	22	12	0	10	68	48	36
St Michaels DH Res.	22	10	3	9	59	43	33
Whiston Cross 'A'	22	9	4	9	53	45	31
Moorfield 'A'	22	7	3	12	30	67	24
Penketh United	22	6	5	11	36	60	23
Spartak	22	6	3	13	41	72	21
Avon Athletic Res.	22	2	6	14	29	84	12
Haydock Res.	22	2	1	19	27	80	7

Division Five	P	W	D	L	F	A	Pts
Fearnhead Res.	22	14	4	4	59	40	46
Fife Rangers Res.	22	13	6	3	77	42	45
Orford BA Res.	22	10	5	7	68	51	35
Runcorn Albion Res.	22	10	5	7	54	37	35
Widnes Bayer Res.	22	11	1	10	54	46	34
Moore United Res.	22	8	7	7	52	46	31
Grange Safeway Res.	22	9	3	10	54	55	30
St Michaels DH 'A'	22	9	3	10	47	49	30
Blackbrook Res.	22	7	4	11	38	56	25
Stockton Lane Res.	22	7	3	12	32	55	24
Newton-le-Will. Res.	22	6	2	14	37	67	20
Burtonwood Alb Res.	22	6	1	15	44	72	19

WEST HERTS LEAGUE

Premier Division	P	W	D	L	F	A	Pts
Berkhamsted Sports	18	13	2	3	48	11	41
Kings Sports	18	12	4	2	56	25	40
Hemel H'stead Rvrs	18	11	2	5	45	24	35
Mill End Sports	18	9	6	3	52	25	33
Jomarth Construction	18	8	3	7	49	48	27
Wellington Arms	18	7	5	6	39	38	26
Harpenden Rovers	18	7	3	8	43	33	24
Badger Athletic	18	5	0	13	25	36	15
The Olde Bellgate	18	4	1	13	24	49	13
L'Artista	18	1	0	17	19	111	3

Division One	P	W	D	L	F	A	Pts
Oxhey Jets 'A'	22	17	3	2	83	19	54
Harpenden Rvrs Res.	22	16	0	6	94	35	48
Inter Hemel	22	13	6	3	69	34	45
Tring Athletic 'A'	22	12	3	7	53	25	39
Kings Sports 'A'	22	11	5	6	61	39	38
Hemel H'stead R Res.	22	9	7	6	57	33	34
Oxhey Wanderers	22	10	4	8	53	34	34
Rifle Volunteer	22	8	4	10	54	54	28
Oxhey	22	6	4	12	42	58	22
Glenn Sports	22	6	0	16	26	67	18
Met Pol Bushey 'A'	22	4	4	14	33	52	16
Wigginton Greyhound	22	0	0	22	11	186	0

Division Two	P	W	D	L	F	A	Pts
Red Lion Rovers	24	18	5	1	87	26	59
Hadley 'A'	24	19	1	4	71	31	58
Greenacres	24	14	5	5	78	43	47
SWR Garage Doors	24	14	5	5	60	30	47
Sun Postal Rovers	24	13	4	7	52	42	43
Oxhey Jets 'B'	24	10	3	11	39	55	33
Bovingdon 'A'	24	9	4	11	49	51	31
Potten End	24	8	3	13	40	61	27
Met Pol Bushey 'B'	24	8	1	15	44	69	25
Hunton Bridge	24	7	2	15	39	67	23
Croxley Guild 'A'	24	4	9	11	29	47	21
Langleybury CC	24	6	1	17	38	59	19
Aldenham	24	3	3	18	36	81	12

Division Three	P	W	D	L	F	A	Pts
Mill End Sports Res.	16	11	4	1	41	12	37
Tring Athletic 'B'	16	10	3	3	62	20	33
Hemel H'stead R 'A'	16	9	3	4	31	34	30
Bovingdon 'B'	16	8	4	4	39	33	28
Old Parmiterians 'A'	16	6	5	5	36	25	23
AFC Levy	16	6	4	6	41	35	22
Rickmansworth St G	16	2	4	10	22	49	10
Oxhey Res.	16	2	3	11	20	49	9
Croxley Guild 'B'	16	1	4	11	24	59	7

WEST SUSSEX LEAGUE

Premier Division	P	W	D	L	F	A	Pts
South Bersted	20	15	3	2	42	16	48
Loxwood	20	14	4	2	54	13	46
TD Shipley	20	12	3	5	50	27	39
Rogate	20	10	2	8	51	29	32
Dorking Wanderers	20	9	4	7	42	43	31
East Dean	20	7	3	10	32	37	24
Univ Coll Chichester	20	5	6	9	23	33	21
Clymping	20	5	5	10	23	50	20
Eastergate United	20	5	4	11	38	51	19
Henfield	20	5	3	12	36	48	18
Yapton	20	4	1	15	25	69	13

Division One	P	W	D	L	F	A	Pts
Predators	20	16	4	0	58	14	52
Barnham	20	14	3	3	76	22	45
West Chiltington	20	14	2	4	48	22	44
Partridge Green	20	8	3	9	39	56	27
Angmering *-3*	20	9	2	9	48	49	26
Wittering United	20	6	6	8	29	30	24
Holbrook	20	6	2	12	27	48	20
Lower Beeding	20	6	2	12	28	57	20
Southwater	20	6	1	13	24	49	19
Cowfold	20	4	5	11	20	40	17
Faygate	20	4	4	12	28	38	16

Division Two North	P	W	D	L	F	A	Pts
TD Shipley Res.	20	14	6	0	52	21	48
Fittleworth	20	11	8	1	45	21	41
Dorking Wdrs Res.	20	12	2	6	58	26	38
Billingshurst	20	8	6	6	48	37	30
Ockley	20	8	6	6	50	53	30
Ashington Rovers	20	7	4	9	44	47	25
Pulborough	20	3	11	6	27	27	20
Alfold	20	4	8	8	32	37	20
Slinfold *-1*	20	5	2	13	32	74	16
Horsham Olympic	20	3	6	11	27	54	15
Watersfield *-3*	20	4	3	13	30	48	12

Division Two South	P	W	D	L	F	A	Pts
Newtown Villa	22	16	4	2	65	23	52
Lancing United	22	15	1	6	53	33	46
Petworth	22	13	4	5	50	30	43
Rustington Res.	22	12	4	6	46	28	40
Lavant	22	9	4	9	42	40	31
Chichester Hosp Res.	22	9	4	9	33	38	31
Stedham United	22	8	6	8	37	31	30
Clymping Res.	22	7	6	9	39	36	27
Worthing BCOB	22	7	6	9	37	41	27
Lodsworth	22	7	2	13	35	46	23
Hunston CC	22	6	2	14	34	46	20
Yapton Res.	22	1	1	20	14	93	4

Division Three North	P	W	D	L	F	A	Pts
Rudgwick	22	17	2	3	77	31	53
Wisborough Green	22	16	2	4	64	27	50
Friends Provident	22	13	1	8	68	58	40
Holbrook Res.	22	12	2	8	57	48	38
Capel *-15*	22	16	2	4	73	37	35
Horsham Baptists	22	10	2	10	59	63	32
Barns Green *-2*	22	8	6	8	50	41	28
Newdigate	22	8	0	14	45	59	24
Faygate United Res.	22	6	3	13	40	65	21
Southwater Res. *-3*	22	5	3	14	47	74	15
Loxwood Res.	22	3	4	15	36	64	13
Henfield Res.	22	4	1	17	43	92	13

Division Three South	P	W	D	L	F	A	Pts
Predators Res.	16	11	2	3	70	24	35
Eastergate Utd Res.	16	10	4	2	39	21	34
Wittering Utd Res.	16	9	4	3	39	18	31
Lancing United Res.	16	9	4	3	44	27	31
Angmering Res.	16	9	3	4	44	31	30
Rogate Res.	16	5	2	9	31	37	17
Ambassadors	16	5	1	10	20	43	16
Graffham	16	3	2	11	33	57	11
Fernhurst	16	0	0	16	16	78	0

Division Four North	P	W	D	L	F	A	Pts
Billingshurst Res.	22	15	4	3	65	31	49
Horsham Trinity	22	14	2	6	73	45	44
Ockley Res.	22	10	6	6	54	38	36
Cowfold Res.	22	10	5	7	55	52	35
Storrington 'A'	22	10	3	9	79	58	33
Alfold Res.	22	10	3	9	44	51	33
TD Shipley 'A'	22	8	6	8	49	39	30
Wisborough Gn Res.	22	6	7	9	37	51	25
Fittleworth Res.	22	8	1	13	54	75	25
Horsham Olymp Res.	22	7	3	12	45	63	24
Henfield 'A'	22	5	4	13	60	88	19
Rudgwick Res.	22	4	6	12	43	67	18

Division Four South	P	W	D	L	F	A	Pts
Square Deal	20	15	4	1	86	20	49
Middleton-on-Sea	20	15	3	2	89	29	48
Newtown Villa Res.	20	13	2	5	61	30	41
Boxgrove	20	12	2	6	82	41	38
West Chiltington Res.	20	10	2	8	58	42	32
Milland	20	8	1	11	67	53	25
Coal Exchange	20	7	3	10	55	30	24
Petworth Res.	20	7	1	12	37	49	22
Pulborough Res.	20	7	0	13	50	46	21
Amberley	20	5	2	13	29	68	17
Graffham Res.	20	1	0	19	11	217	3

Division Five Central	P	W	D	L	F	A	Pts
Littleh'ton Rail Res.	16	15	0	1	58	19	45
Barnham 'A'	16	12	2	2	70	22	38
Plaistow	16	9	2	5	42	30	29
Chapel	16	9	2	5	40	44	29
Watersfield Res.	16	7	1	8	40	29	22
Lodsworth Res.	16	5	1	10	23	44	16
Fernhurst Res.	16	4	2	10	21	28	14
Holbrook 'B'	16	3	1	12	23	67	10
Harting	16	2	1	13	22	56	7

Division Five North	P	W	D	L	F	A	Pts
Warnham	22	20	0	2	97	23	60
Holbrook 'A'	22	17	1	4	79	31	52
Horsham Trinity Res.	22	16	2	4	65	34	50
Ashington Rvrs Res.	22	14	3	5	50	32	45
Partridge Green Res.	22	11	4	7	48	30	37
Norfolk Arms	22	9	2	11	39	49	29
Billingshurst 'A'	22	7	3	12	35	46	24
Horsham Baptists Res.	22	7	3	12	44	69	24
Newdigate Res.	22	7	2	13	44	62	23
Barns Green Res.	22	4	1	17	39	65	13
Slinfold Res.	22	3	4	15	27	79	13
Southwater 'A'	22	3	3	16	40	87	12

Division Five South	P	W	D	L	F	A	Pts
Barnham Res.	20	15	3	2	92	22	48
Selsey Town	20	14	4	2	87	19	46
The Wheatsheaf	20	15	1	4	81	29	46
Predators 'A'	20	13	2	5	58	32	41
General Henry	20	9	3	8	50	60	30
Bosham Res.	20	6	3	11	41	53	21
Angmering 'A'	20	6	3	11	41	67	21
Regis Veterans	20	6	3	11	41	69	21
AFC Westmead	20	5	2	13	32	67	17
Tangmere	20	4	3	13	36	74	15
Rose Green United	20	3	1	16	41	108	10

WESTON & DISTRICT LEAGUE

Division One	P	W	D	L	F	A	Pts
Blagdon	22	17	5	0	61	20	56
East Worle	22	13	5	4	46	22	44
Winscombe Res.	22	9	6	7	42	33	33
Hutton	22	8	8	6	42	36	32
Portishead 'A'	22	9	4	9	40	43	31
Clevedon United 'A'	22	8	6	8	38	44	30
Cleeve West Tn Res.	22	8	5	9	42	41	29
Bourneville Rovers	22	8	5	9	36	40	29
Kewstoke Lions	22	7	7	8	44	35	28
Portishead WMC	22	7	4	11	40	57	25
Westland Utd Res.	22	5	3	14	33	61	18
KVFC	22	2	4	16	38	70	10

Division Two	P	W	D	L	F	A	Pts
Worlebury Spartans	22	17	1	4	82	34	52
Nailsea United 'A'	22	15	4	3	57	22	49
Portishead 'B'	22	12	5	5	55	29	41
Draycott	22	11	5	6	46	32	38
Congresbury Res.	22	11	4	7	42	41	37
Selkirk United	22	5	11	6	22	35	26
Burnham United 'A'	22	8	2	12	36	59	26
Churchill Club Res.	22	7	4	11	36	46	25
Worle Res.	22	5	6	11	27	43	21
Clarence Park Rgrs	22	5	5	12	32	59	20
Locking Park	22	5	3	14	39	53	18
Wrington-Redhill Res.	22	4	4	14	33	54	16

Division Three	P	W	D	L	F	A	Pts
St George E-in-G Res.	22	16	3	3	80	25	51
Milton Crusaders	22	15	4	3	63	29	49
Hutton Res.	22	15	2	5	76	34	47
Swiss Valley	22	15	1	6	81	40	46
Clevedon United 'B'	22	12	4	6	57	47	40
Cheddar 'A'	22	12	1	9	58	63	37
Nailsea Town Res.	22	9	8	5	44	33	35
Yatton Athletic Res.	22	6	4	12	52	59	22
Banwell Res.	22	4	3	15	33	88	15
Wedmore	22	3	3	16	38	72	12
Westside	22	3	3	16	44	87	12
Winscombe 'A'	22	2	4	16	36	85	10

Division Four	P	W	D	L	F	A	Pts
South Park	22	17	4	1	60	19	55
Nailsea United 'B'	22	14	2	6	66	32	44
Kewstoke Lions Res.	22	13	2	7	53	35	41
Cleeve West Tn 'A'	22	12	4	6	55	40	40
KVFC Res.	22	13	0	9	48	47	39
Blagdon Res.	22	11	4	7	45	28	37
Berrow Res.	22	11	3	8	58	31	36
King Alfred	22	7	5	10	49	58	26
Congresbury 'A'	22	5	4	13	27	44	19
Yatton Athletic 'A'	22	5	4	13	37	62	19
Portishead 'C'	22	4	1	17	32	80	13
Cheddar 'B'	22	2	3	17	24	78	9

Division Five	P	W	D	L	F	A	Pts
Weston St Johns 'A'	22	17	3	2	92	28	54
Draycott Res.	22	14	5	3	67	26	47
Westend	22	13	2	7	83	50	41
Worlebury Spart. Res.	22	11	6	5	83	49	39
St George E-in-G 'A'	22	11	5	6	49	31	38
Nailsea United 'C'	22	9	5	8	52	52	32
Bourneville Rvrs Res.	22	9	4	9	55	58	31
BWOC	22	10	1	11	50	53	31
Athletico Wrington	22	8	1	13	43	75	25
Selkirk United Res.	22	4	6	12	40	52	18
Ellenborough Pk *-2*	22	4	1	17	47	104	11
Wedmore Res.	22	2	1	19	28	111	7

WITNEY & DISTRICT FA

Premier Division	P	W	D	L	F	A	Pts
Freeland	24	21	2	1	110	17	65
Ducklington	24	18	1	5	69	28	55
Brize Norton	24	14	6	4	52	17	48
Hanborough	24	15	2	7	54	36	47
Charlbury Town *+2*	24	13	4	7	55	34	45
Carterton FC *-10*	24	16	2	6	66	29	40
Hailey	24	10	4	10	43	44	34
Aston	24	6	4	14	41	70	22
North Leigh 'A'	24	6	4	14	51	87	22
FC Nomads	24	5	3	16	31	81	18
West Witney	24	4	5	15	28	60	17
Milton *+3*	24	4	1	19	42	106	16
Minster Lovell	24	3	4	17	37	70	13

Division One	P	W	D	L	F	A	Pts
Spartan Rangers	24	20	2	2	85	19	62
Millpark	24	14	4	6	80	46	46
Eynsham Ass 'A'	24	12	3	9	55	48	39
Ducklington Res. *+3*	24	9	8	7	49	45	38
Carterton FC Res. *-6*	24	13	4	7	63	29	37
North Leigh 'B'	24	10	4	10	43	54	34
Witney Royals	24	10	3	11	45	46	33
Witney Wanderers	24	10	0	14	53	62	30
West Witney Res.	24	8	4	12	31	48	28
FC Mills	24	7	6	11	40	53	27
Hanborough Res.	24	6	5	13	38	61	23
Brize Norton Res.	24	6	5	13	40	67	23
Kingham All Blacks	24	6	2	16	36	80	20

Division Two	P	W	D	L	F	A	Pts
Bampton	26	23	1	2	87	16	70
Real Islip	26	21	3	2	96	40	66
Cassington	26	14	7	5	50	31	49
Wootton Sports *+2*	26	14	4	8	70	47	48
Tackley	26	14	5	7	75	46	47
FC Nomads Res.	26	12	3	11	56	58	39
Spartan Rangers Res.	26	11	5	10	54	40	38
Carterton FC 'A' *-3*	26	11	6	9	56	44	36
Minster Lovell Res.	26	10	4	12	33	35	34
Burford United	26	8	4	14	55	69	28
AC Finstock	26	6	2	18	43	85	20
Chippy Swifts *-4*	26	6	4	16	37	57	18
Milton Res.	26	4	1	21	20	88	13
Hailey Res.	26	3	1	22	18	94	10

Division Three	P	W	D	L	F	A	Pts
Combe	24	20	3	1	108	20	63
Kingham All Bl Res.	24	15	3	6	50	30	48
Fieldtown Res.	24	13	3	8	77	44	42
Freeland Res.	24	11	9	4	66	39	42
Ducklington 'A'	24	12	5	7	58	43	41
Charlbury Tn Res.	24	12	5	7	65	50	41
FC Mills Res. *-3*	24	13	3	8	52	38	39
Witney Royals Res.	24	9	3	12	47	69	30
Aston Res. *+3*	24	6	4	14	38	46	25
Two Rivers	24	7	4	13	32	60	25
Southrop *+3*	24	6	2	16	52	84	23
AC Finstock Res.	24	6	2	16	34	87	20
Burford Utd Res. *-6*	24	3	0	21	26	95	3

WORTHING & DISTRICT LEAGUE

Premier Division	P	W	D	L	F	A	Pts
Worthing Wanderers	20	17	2	1	81	27	53
L & S Athletic	20	15	2	3	57	21	47
Revenue	20	13	3	4	66	26	42
Warren Sports	20	11	2	7	46	42	35
Tabernacle	20	10	4	6	48	31	34
GSK Sports	20	8	3	9	39	58	27
Adur Athletic	20	8	1	11	38	48	25
Sompting	20	7	1	12	53	75	22
Worthing Athletic	20	6	2	12	52	59	20
East Worthing	20	2	1	17	18	59	7
Ye Old Manor House	20	1	3	16	21	73	6

Division One	P	W	D	L	F	A	Pts
Northbrook	20	14	2	4	62	32	44
AFC Broadwater	20	12	6	2	45	22	42
Durrington RAFA	20	11	5	4	62	28	38
Worthing Mitsubishi	20	9	7	4	34	22	34
Goring St Theresa's	20	9	4	7	41	29	31
Worthing Albion	20	9	2	9	37	37	29
St Mary's	20	8	5	7	38	45	29
Revenue Res.	20	8	1	11	33	38	25
Sompting Res.	20	5	2	13	33	67	17
GSK Sports Res.	20	4	2	14	35	61	14
West Worthing WMC	20	2	2	16	22	61	8

Division Two	P	W	D	L	F	A	Pts
L & S Athletic Res.	16	13	3	0	63	16	42
Adur Athletic Res.	16	11	1	4	48	13	34
Montague United	16	10	2	4	47	28	32
TMG	16	9	3	4	53	27	30
Woodside	16	6	2	8	31	40	20
Athletico Wenban Sm	16	5	4	7	31	33	19
Lancing United 'A'	16	5	3	8	22	44	18
The Globe	16	2	3	11	19	44	9
Worthing BCOB Res.	16	0	1	15	6	75	1

Division Three	P	W	D	L	F	A	Pts
Shoreham RBL	22	21	0	1	110	14	63
Edge	22	16	1	5	64	33	49
Highdown Rovers	22	15	3	4	71	27	48
Worthing Wdrs Res.	22	15	0	7	73	26	45
L & L	22	13	2	7	74	31	41
West Tarring WMC	22	10	4	8	44	51	34
Upper Beeding Res.	22	7	6	9	30	50	27
AFC Phoenix	22	6	3	13	38	70	21
GSK Sports 'B'	22	5	3	14	30	85	18
Lancing United 'B'	22	4	4	14	19	73	16
RJ Cleaning	22	3	2	17	28	61	11
Northbrook Res.	22	1	4	17	23	83	7

WYCOMBE & DISTRICT LEAGUE

Senior Division	P	W	D	L	F	A	Pts
FC Beaconsfield	21	17	3	1	74	28	54
Downley Albion	21	17	1	3	68	23	52
Bucks CC	21	11	3	7	61	29	36
Winchmore Hill	21	9	4	8	49	45	31
Hambleden	21	7	0	14	46	78	21
Lane End	21	5	5	11	35	47	20
Loudwater	21	5	1	15	23	69	16
Stokenchurch	21	4	1	16	30	67	13

Premier Division	P	W	D	L	F	A	Pts
AFC Spartans	18	14	2	2	83	21	44
AC Marlow	18	13	1	4	52	25	40
FC Beaconsfield Res.	18	11	3	4	47	26	36
Holmer Gn Old Boys	18	10	3	5	55	43	33
Great Missenden	18	8	2	8	43	33	26
Lane End Res.	18	6	5	7	31	42	23
Penn & Tylers Gn 'A'	18	7	1	10	40	50	22
Wooburn Athletic	18	3	5	10	22	49	14
Loudwater Res.	18	3	3	12	27	63	12
Chinnor 'A'	18	1	3	14	21	69	6

Division One	P	W	D	L	F	A	Pts
Wycombe Judo	18	14	4	0	41	12	46
Red Lion (Wooburn)	18	11	3	4	57	29	36
Downley Albion Res.	18	8	1	9	36	34	25
AC Marlow Res.	18	5	7	6	45	51	22
Bucks CC Res.	18	5	6	7	39	36	21
Winchmore Hill Res.	18	3	4	11	32	57	13
Boca Seniors	18	2	5	11	23	54	11

Division Two	P	W	D	L	F	A	Pts
AFC Amersham	21	17	2	2	88	17	53
Walters Grp (HGSA)	21	15	2	4	82	25	47
Chinnor 'B'	21	11	5	5	39	30	38
Totteridge Wanderers	21	10	3	8	62	46	33
Coach/Horses (Marl)	21	11	0	10	52	56	33
Nash Sports	21	4	3	14	31	69	15
Prince of Wales Rgrs	21	3	5	13	34	81	14
Oxford United Deaf	21	2	2	17	22	86	8

YEOVIL & DISTRICT LEAGUE

Premier Division	P	W	D	L	F	A	Pts
Westland Sports Res.	20	17	2	1	69	15	53
Ilchester -1	20	16	3	1	101	27	50
Milborne Port	20	14	2	4	43	27	44
Normalair RSL -1	20	9	5	6	48	33	31
Stoke-sub-Hamdon	20	9	2	9	40	38	29
Henstridge United	20	7	3	10	50	69	24
Martock United	20	7	2	11	42	54	23
Keinton Mandeville	20	6	3	11	38	59	21
Yetminster Sharks	20	4	3	13	33	65	15
Victoria Sports -1	20	4	1	15	33	70	12
Pen Mill	20	2	4	14	30	70	10

Division One	P	W	D	L	F	A	Pts
Wincanton Tn Res.	20	13	4	3	58	25	43
Ilchester Tn Res. +3	20	11	2	7	43	30	38
Normalair RSL Res.	20	10	6	4	28	23	36
Milborne Port Res.	20	9	7	4	30	29	34
Ansford Rovers	20	7	11	2	38	23	32
Odcombe	20	8	7	5	48	33	31
Royal Oak Rangers	20	8	3	9	31	36	27
Castle Cary Res. -3	20	6	4	10	33	34	19
Stoke-sub-Ham. Res.	20	5	2	13	25	44	17
The Alex	20	4	2	14	24	57	14
Blue Heron	20	3	4	13	23	47	13

Division Two	P	W	D	L	F	A	Pts
Baltonsborough	20	18	2	0	78	19	56
Tor Leisure	20	12	5	3	63	31	41
Lyde United	20	8	6	6	51	36	30
Wincanton Tn Colts	20	8	5	7	40	47	29
Milborne Port 'A'	20	7	7	6	51	33	28
Pen Mill Res	20	8	4	8	47	50	28
Martock United Res.	20	7	7	6	45	48	28
Pitney	20	7	4	9	34	41	25
Montacute	20	6	4	10	35	53	22
Charlton United	20	2	4	14	33	64	10
Ansford Rovers Res.	20	1	4	15	20	75	7

Division Three	P	W	D	L	F	A	Pts
Somerton Sports	20	13	6	1	70	20	45
Templecombe Rvrs	20	14	2	4	81	38	44
Mermaid United	20	12	5	3	56	45	41
Henstridge U Res. +2	20	12	2	6	88	32	40
Yeovil Galacticos -3	20	12	4	4	68	31	37
Langport Town	20	9	4	7	46	40	31
Ilchester Colts	20	7	2	11	37	41	23
Kingsbury Episcopi	20	5	4	11	47	70	19
Bruton United	20	4	3	13	35	78	15
Baltonsborough Res.	20	3	1	16	30	103	10
Odcombe Res. -2	20	2	1	17	30	90	5

YORK LEAGUE

Premier Division	P	W	D	L	F	A	Pts
Dringhouses	28	22	1	5	86	37	67
Huntington Rovers	28	17	5	6	93	44	56
Thorpe United	28	17	5	6	72	50	56
York St Johns College	28	14	6	8	69	57	48
Kartiers (Selby)	28	14	5	9	53	40	47
Old Malton St Marys	28	15	2	11	52	49	47
Tate & Lyle Selby	28	12	3	13	54	49	39
Wigginton G'hoppers	28	12	3	13	56	61	39
Nestle Rowntree	28	11	5	12	57	50	38
Copmanthorpe	28	10	4	14	55	60	34
Dunnington	28	9	5	14	45	67	32
Pocklington Tn Res.	28	9	4	15	31	62	31
Malton Bacon Factory	28	7	7	14	33	45	28
Bishopthorpe United	28	7	6	15	44	61	27
Haxby United	28	3	1	24	20	88	10

Division One	P	W	D	L	F	A	Pts
Heslington	24	17	4	3	64	25	55
Tockwith	24	18	1	5	56	28	55
Norwich Union	24	13	6	5	64	44	45
Ouseburn United	24	12	6	6	66	52	42
Rufforth United	24	10	5	9	45	38	35
Hamilton Panthers	24	10	2	12	53	64	32
Stamford Bridge	24	10	1	13	46	57	31
Easingwold Town	24	8	5	11	46	56	29
Amotherby/Swinton	24	8	3	13	43	47	27
Wilberfoss	24	8	3	13	39	45	27
Elvington Harriers	24	7	5	12	51	53	26
New Earswick	24	6	8	10	39	45	26
Post Office	24	2	5	17	23	81	11

Division Two	P	W	D	L	F	A	Pts
Poppleton United	22	15	5	2	53	21	50
Riccall United	22	14	6	2	69	17	48
Tadcaster Albion Res.	22	14	4	4	63	30	46
Sheriff Hutton	22	12	3	7	81	57	39
York Railway Inst.	22	11	5	6	55	42	38
Wh. Horse Ch'ch Fent.	22	9	5	8	37	41	32
Fulford United	22	7	4	11	36	50	25
Selby RSSC	22	7	3	12	42	46	24
Civil Service	22	7	3	12	44	73	24
Moor Lane	22	6	4	12	41	60	22
Hemingbrough Utd	22	6	3	13	39	41	21
Barmby Moor	22	1	1	20	17	99	4

Division Three	P	W	D	L	F	A	Pts
Huby United	24	20	3	1	93	19	63
Osbaldwick	24	18	3	3	84	35	57
Cawood	24	16	3	5	70	40	51
Norton United	24	13	2	9	51	51	41
St Clements	24	11	5	8	55	52	38
LNER Builders	24	10	5	9	51	42	35
Rawcliffe Rangers	24	9	3	12	81	72	30
Stillington -3	24	10	3	11	44	37	30
Heworth	24	8	3	13	49	54	27
Strensall	24	8	2	14	61	58	26
Melbourne	24	8	1	15	37	70	25
Bishop Wilton	24	4	4	16	37	85	16
Wheldrake	24	2	1	21	32	130	7

Reserve Division A	P	W	D	L	F	A	Pts
Dringhouses Res.	22	18	2	2	85	23	56
Nestle Rowntree Res.	22	14	1	7	62	36	43
Huntington Rvrs Res.	22	13	3	6	46	40	42
York St J. College Res.	22	13	2	7	74	44	41
O Malton St M Res.	22	13	2	7	47	36	41
Dunnington Res.	22	11	1	10	42	37	34
Copmanthorpe Res.	22	9	7	6	40	41	34
Pocklington Tn 'A'	22	6	4	12	35	55	22
New Earswick Res.	22	5	4	13	28	53	19
Kartiers (Selby) Res.	22	4	6	12	32	50	18
Malton Bacon Fac Res.	22	4	2	16	31	70	14
Haxby Utd Res. -3	22	3	4	15	35	72	10

Reserve Division B	P	W	D	L	F	A	Pts
Rufforth United Res.	22	16	3	3	65	33	51
Thorpe United Res.	22	15	4	3	71	32	49
Bishopthorpe Utd Res.	22	14	4	4	68	26	46
Easingwold Tn Res.	22	13	1	8	51	32	40
Hamilton P. Res. -3	22	10	6	6	55	47	33
Poppleton Utd Res.	22	8	2	12	58	50	26
Tockwith Res.	22	8	2	12	39	54	26
Stamford Bridge Res.	22	7	3	12	29	49	24
Wigginton G Res. -3	22	7	5	10	53	67	23
Wilberfoss Res.	22	7	1	14	33	60	22
Heslington Res.	22	5	3	14	30	64	18
Wh. Horse Ch F Res.	22	3	4	15	24	62	13

Reserve Division C	P	W	D	L	F	A	Pts
Heworth Res.	22	13	1	8	53	51	40
Amotherby/Swint Res.	22	12	2	8	61	40	38
York R'way Inst Res.	22	11	5	6	60	45	38
Ouseburn Utd Res.	22	12	1	9	68	37	37
Norwich Union Res.	22	10	6	6	60	36	36
Riccall United Res.	22	9	5	8	40	37	32
Hemingbro' Utd Res.	22	9	4	9	46	50	31
Huby United Res.	22	8	6	8	46	46	30
Stillington Res.	22	8	5	9	35	60	29
Fulford United Res.	22	6	6	10	37	57	24
Civil Service Res.	22	5	5	12	31	48	20
LNER Builders Res.	22	3	6	13	28	58	15

YORKSHIRE OLD BOYS LEAGUE

Senior Division A	P	W	D	L	F	A	Pts
Yorkshire Bank	22	14	5	3	52	28	47
Old Rovers	22	11	6	5	66	52	39
Western Juniors	22	12	3	7	43	35	39
Leeds University	22	9	9	4	48	32	36
Trinity & All Saints	22	10	5	7	67	43	35
Leeds Medics	22	9	6	7	47	33	33
Stanningley	22	10	3	9	49	47	33
St Nicholas	22	8	5	9	54	45	29
Roundhegians	22	7	4	11	44	70	25
Collegians	22	5	3	14	41	69	18
Abbey Grange OB	22	5	2	15	37	71	17
Modernians	22	2	9	11	29	52	15

Senior Division B	P	W	D	L	F	A	Pts
Huddersfield Ams	22	17	2	3	71	28	53
Heckmondwike GSOB	22	17	1	4	77	25	52
Leeds Medics Res.	22	14	2	6	60	43	44
Centralians	22	10	6	6	37	26	36
FC Headingley	22	10	4	8	45	38	34
Ealandians	22	9	6	7	55	47	33
Yorkshire Am Res.	22	10	1	11	43	42	31
Griffordians	22	9	2	11	52	59	29
Calverley	22	6	6	10	46	62	24
East Ardsley Wdrs	22	4	4	14	33	80	16
Batelians	22	3	4	15	46	70	13
Adel	22	3	2	17	27	72	11

Division One	P	W	D	L	F	A	Pts
Wortley Old Boys	22	18	3	1	66	24	57
Bramley Juniors	22	17	1	4	88	31	52
Sandal Wanderers	22	14	3	5	61	45	45
Colton Academicals	22	11	2	9	59	51	35
St Bedes	22	10	5	7	44	42	35
Woodhouse Moor	22	9	5	8	52	59	32
Roundhegians Res.	22	9	1	12	52	56	28
Thornesians	22	8	2	12	40	56	26
Leeds Medics 'A'	22	6	4	12	45	49	22
Agnes Stewart	22	5	4	13	60	65	19
Modernians Res.	22	4	4	14	36	59	16
Modernians 'A'	22	2	4	16	22	88	10

Division Two	P	W	D	L	F	A	Pts
Alwoodley	22	17	3	2	79	36	54
Adel Res.	22	14	5	3	60	28	47
Wheelright	22	12	6	4	65	37	42
Almondburians	21	11	3	7	56	41	36
Leeds Independent	22	9	2	11	44	44	29
Griffordians Res.	22	9	2	11	47	52	29
Centralians Res.	22	9	2	11	46	58	29
Commonside Res.	22	7	4	11	55	58	25
Huddersf'd Am Res. -1	22	7	4	11	49	59	24
Grangefield Old Boys	21	7	2	12	40	56	23
Abbey Gr. OB Res.	22	4	4	14	33	79	16
St Bedes OB Res. -3	22	4	5	13	36	62	14

Division Three	P	W	D	L	F	A	Pts
Wortley OB Res.	22	19	1	2	88	26	58
Trinity Old Boys Res.	22	17	3	2	64	19	54
Batelians Res.	22	11	2	9	54	47	35
Heck'wike GSOB Res.	22	11	2	9	63	61	35
Horbury Tn Old Boys	22	10	3	9	47	50	33
Colton Academ. Res.	22	8	5	9	55	52	29
Thornesians Res.	22	8	3	11	36	58	27
Moortown Old Boys	22	6	7	9	51	59	25
Modernians 'B'	22	6	5	11	46	60	23
Roundhegians 'A'	22	7	2	13	36	61	23
Leeds Medics 'B'	22	6	2	14	41	68	20
Centralians 'A'	22	2	7	13	20	40	13

Division Four	P	W	D	L	F	A	Pts
Shire Academics	22	20	0	2	108	30	60
Griffordians 'A'	22	15	3	4	73	44	48
Woodhouse Moor Res.	22	13	6	3	57	33	45
Wheelright Res.	22	13	2	7	62	44	41
Batelians 'A'	22	9	4	9	62	58	31
Ealandians Res.	22	8	5	9	51	54	29
Sandal Wdrs Res.	22	8	4	10	44	52	28
Huddersfield Am 'A'	22	8	1	13	47	79	25
E Ardsley Wdrs Res.	22	6	4	12	42	57	22
Collegians Res.	22	5	5	12	32	54	20
Abbey Grange OB 'A'	22	5	2	15	32	58	17
Modernians 'C'	22	3	2	17	30	77	11

F A CHALLENGE CUP

EXTRA PRELIMINARY ROUND

(£500 to each winning club)

Newcastle Benfield Bay Plastics 2 **Bedlington Terriers** 4	153
Bacup Borough 0 **Pickering Town** 5	40
Jarrow Roofing Boldon CA 0 **Sheffield** 4	56
Blackpool Mechanics 1 **Newcastle Blue Star** 2	80
Nelson 2 **Retford United** 4	106
Esh Winning 4 Ashington 4	59
Prudhoe Town 1 **Horden Colliery Welfare** 3	32
Skelmersdale United 1 Liversedge 0	132
Curzon Ashton 1 Darwen 0	145
Oldham Town 1 Morpeth Town 0	40
Guisborough Town 1 Great Harwood Town 1	77
Cheadle Town 3 Abbey Hey 2	61
Brandon United 0 **Billingham Synthonia** 5	71
Tow Law Town 2 Squires Gate 0	108
Formby 1 Consett 1	57
Winsford United 1 Alsager Town 1	99
Flixton 1 **Hebburn Town** 2	64
Rossington Main 1 Garforth Town 1	79
Garforth Town 3 Rossington Main 0	88
Cammell Laird 4 West Allotment Celtic 1	130
West Auckland Town 2 Shildon 1	125
Winterton Rangers 1 North Shields 0	56
Studley 1 **Oadby Town** 3	67
Sutton Town 5 Loughborough Dynamo 1	108
Stourbridge 3 Glossop North End 0 *(at Halesowen Town)*	211
Borrowash Victoria 1 Ford Sports Daventry 1	79
Long Eaton United 2 Quorn 1	93
Congleton Town 2 Romulus 0	148
Norton United 1 Alvechurch 0	40
Shirebrook Town 2 **Teversal** 3	183
Oldbury United 2 Racing Club Warwick 1	72
Witham Town 1 Hadleigh United 0	51
Hullbridge Sports 2 **Wisbech Town** 5	70
Chalfont St Peter 1 Buckingham Town 0	67
Brook House 1 Leiston 1	77
Wembley 0 **St Neots Town** 2	87
Aylesbury Vale 2 Kirkley 2	105
Ware 2 Sporting Bengal United 0	207
Concord Rangers 0 **Kingsbury Town** 1	53
Harpenden Town 2 Sawbridgeworth Town 1	61
Soham Town Rangers 2 Yaxley 1	151
Stanway Rovers 4 Norwich United 1	80
Fakenham Town 2 Long Buckby 0	52
Gorleston 2 **North Greenford United** 4	84
Haringey Borough 0 **Felixstowe & Walton United** 3	73
Bowers & Pitsea 2 Stotfold 2	68
London APSA 0 **Halstead Town** 2	94
Broxbourne Borough V&E 1 **Holmer Green** 4	28
Eton Manor 0 **Leverstock Green** 1	35
St Margaretsbury 2 St Ives Town 1	60
Wootton Blue Cross 2 Desborough Town 0	67
Romford 1 **Waltham Abbey** 3	107
Biggleswade United 6 Haverhill Rovers 0	86
Harefield United 2 **Langford** 3	33
Southend Manor 0 **Woodford United** 1	34
Woodbridge Town 3 Lowestoft Town 3	121
Saffron Walden Town 1 Flackwell Heath 1	102
Erith Town 0 **Hassocks** 3	46
Thamesmead Town 2 **Abingdon United** 4	38
Saltdean United 0 Wantage Town 0	47
AFC Totton 5 Milton United 0	80
Eastbourne United Association 1 **Ash United** 2	68
Hythe Town 4 Raynes Park Vale 1	116
Moneyfields 6 Abingdon Town 1	70
Fareham Town 0 Selsey 0	90
Gosport Borough 6 Sandhurst Town 1	138
East Grinstead Town 0 **VCD Athletic** 7	73
AFC Newbury 2 Farnham Town 2	95
Farnham Town 2 **AFC Newbury** 3	90
Erith & Belvedere 4 Hamble ASSC 2	99
Lancing 1 **Whitehawk** 2	95
Westfield 1 **Godalming Town** 2	61
Chichester City United 1 **East Preston** 2	48
Sidley United 3 Pagham 1	205
Sevenoaks Town 4 Chertsey Town 2	133
Andover 4 Didcot Town 4	190
Hungerford Town 0 **North Leigh** 4	71
Horsham YMCA 1 Hailsham Town 0	80
Three Bridges 2 Shoreham 0	55
Westbury United 2 Newquay 1	78
Willand Rovers 0 **Hamworthy United** 1	167
Tuffley Rovers 0 Elmore 0	45
Bishops Cleeve 1 Corsham Town 0	94
Hallen 3 Porthleven 0	78
Calne Town 0 **Shortwood United** 2	56
Minehead 1 **Almondsbury Town** 2	49
Slimbridge 0 **Wimborne Town** 1	131
Odd Down 2 Portland United 0	50

EXTRA PRELIMINARY ROUND REPLAYS

Ashington 1 Esh Winning 0	165
Great Harwood Town 3 Guisborough Town 3 *aet* (4-2p)	95
Consett 5 Formby 1	97
Alsager Town 0 **Winsford United** 1	120
Ford Sports Daventry 1 **Borrowash Victoria** 2	50
Leiston 1 **Brook House** 3	122
Kirkley 0 **Aylesbury Vale** 3	191
Stotfold 3 Bowers & Pitsea 3 *aet* (4-2p)	65
Lowestoft Town 5 Woodbridge Town 0	238
Flackwell Heath 3 Saffron Walden Town 1	82
Wantage Town 0 **Saltdean United** 2	76
Selsey 3 Fareham Town 2	250
Didcot Town 2 Andover 0	292
Elmore 1 Tuffley Rovers 0	85

PRELIMINARY ROUND

(£1,000 to each winning club)

Bridlington Town 2 Whitley Bay 2	180
Tow Law Town 1 **Padiham** 3	112
Colne 1 **Chadderton** 2	111
Warrington Town 2 Penrith 2	84
Ramsbottom United 3 Marske United 1	169
Thornaby 3 Peterlee Newtown 0	49
Hebburn Town 1 Winterton Rangers 1	143
Cheadle Town 2 Bamber Bridge 1	71
Pontefract Collieries 2 **Bishop Auckland** 3	62
Eccleshill United 1 **Chester-le-Street Town** 2	52
Selby Town 1 **Billingham Town** 3	150
Skelmersdale United 2 Colwyn Bay 0	219
Crook Town 0 **St Helens Town** 3	103
Curzon Ashton 1 Garforth Town 0	141
Rossendale United 1 Sunderland Nissan 1	76
Norton & Stockton Ancients 0 **Great Harwood Town** 4	67
Spennymoor Town 0 **Consett** 2	284
Durham City 5 Brodsworth Miners Welfare 0	127
Seaham Red Star 2 Atherton Collieries 0	62
Cammell Laird 6 Alnwick Town 0	115
Brigg Town 4 Holker Old Boys 0	123
Retford United 4 Parkgate 3	197
Horden Colliery Welfare 1 **Kendal Town** 2	79
Tadcaster Albion 2 Chorley 2	110
Oldham Town 2 Hall Road Rangers 0	55
Pickering Town 2 Ashington 2	228
Washington 0 Stocksbridge Park Steels 0	94
Thackley 2 South Shields 0	57
Newcastle Blue Star 2 Hallam 0 *(at Alnwick Town)*	62
Sheffield 2 Mossley 2	229
Yorkshire Amateur 2 Bedlington Terriers 1	45
Glasshoughton Welfare 0 **Woodley Sports** 2	35
Maine Road 0 **Armthorpe Welfare** 2	40
Billingham Synthonia 2 Fleetwood Town 0	128
Ossett Albion 0 **Dunston Federation Brewery** 3	103
Atherton LR 1 Goole 1	70

Whickham 1 **West Auckland Town** 5	90
Harrogate Railway 1 **Clitheroe** 2	138
New Mills 0 **Salford City** 2	206
Trafford 3 Silsden 1	159
Northallerton Town 4 Winsford United 0	100
(Abandoned in 80th minute after Winsford United reduced to six players – score stands)	
Willenhall Town 1 Blackstones 0	104
Shepshed Dynamo 4 Carlton Town 1	96
Buxton 1 **Newcastle Town** 2	376
Chasetown 2 Causeway United 0	111
Congleton Town 1 **Corby Town** 2	164
Solihull Borough 2 Eccleshall 0	115
Westfields 3 Sutton Coldfield Town 0	56
Rushall Olympic 0 **Gedling Town** 2	78
Bromsgrove Rovers 4 Bourne Town 1	274
Glapwell 3 Barwell 1	46
Spalding United 0 **Staveley Miners Welfare** 1	121
Nantwich Town 3 Gresley Rovers 1	131
Long Eaton United 4 Boston Town 2	63
Coalville Town 3 Borrowash Victoria 0	117
Deeping Rangers 0 Norton United 0	77
Stourport Swifts 1 Stratford Town 2	71
Bedworth United 3 Rocester 1	107
Oadby Town 3 Stamford 3	175
Malvern Town 4 Mickleover Sports 3	136
Cradley Town 2 Biddulph Victoria 1	41
Holbeach United 0 **Boldmere St Michaels** 2	56
Teversal 1 Pegasus Juniors 1	78
Leamington 0 Sutton Town 0	538
Lincoln Moorlands 0 Eastwood Town 0	74
Belper Town 1 Leek CSOB 0	148
South Normanton Athletic 1 Arnold Town 0	84
Stourbridge 2 Kidsgrove Athletic 2	218
Ilford 0 **Brackley Town** 2	68
Long Melford 0 **AFC Sudbury** 1	448
Wootton Blue Cross 1 Barton Rovers 1	79
Barton Rovers 4 Wootton Blue Cross 1 *aet*	144
Ware 2 **Northampton Spencer** 4	103
AFC Hornchurch 0 Chalfont St Peter 0	320
Barkingside 2 Leverstock Green 2 *aet*	111
Harlow Town 4 Newport Pagnell Town 2	119
Uxbridge 2 **Great Wakering Rovers** 3	93
Tiptree United 2 **Potton United** 3	91
Bury Town 1 Ely City 1	155
Needham Market 2 **Diss Town** 5	191
Marlow 2 **Arlesey Town** 3	88
Welwyn Garden City 2 Aylesbury Vale 0	76
St Neots Town 1 **Hemel Hempstead Town** 4	145
Harwich & Parkeston 2 Holmer Green 2	110
Aveley 5 Kingsbury Town 1	53
Thame United 0 **Brentwood Town** 1	49
(at Brentwood Town)	
Fakenham Town 1 **Waltham Forest** 4	65
Berkhamsted Town 2 Newmarket Town 0	131
Mildenhall Town 3 Potters Bar Town 1	140
Stotfold 1 **Clapton** 2	70
Barking & East Ham United 1 St Margaretsbury 1	91
Leighton Town 1 Wroxham 1	113
Soham Town Rangers 1 **Enfield Town** 2	254
Cogenhoe United 4 Hanwell Town 1	78
March Town United 4 Harpenden Town 1	108
Stowmarket Town 2 Ipswich Wanderers 2	119
Oxhey Jets 1 **Lowestoft Town** 2	139
Royston Town 1 **Clacton Town** 2	83
Burnham Ramblers 4 Flackwell Heath 3	56
Southall 5 Enfield 0	48
Felixstowe & Walton United 1 **Dunstable Town** 2	123
Tilbury 0 **Wivenhoe Town** 3	38
London Colney 2 **Rothwell Town** 3	50
Raunds Town 0 **Beaconsfield SYCOB** 2	65
Woodford United 1 Wisbech Town 0	92
Boreham Wood 3 Dereham Town 0	115
Great Yarmouth Town 2 **Stanway Rovers** 3	80
Henley Town 2 **Witham Town** 4	78
Tring Athletic 1 **Biggleswade United** 2	140
North Greenford United 1 **Brook House** 6	65
Waltham Abbey 6 Wingate & Finchley 2	58
Stansted 2 Langford 1	70
(at Langford)	
Hertford Town 1 **Ruislip Manor** 2	85
Halstead Town 7 Cornard United 0	114
Lymington & New Milton 0 **Dover Athletic** 2	172
Mile Oak 1 **Camberley Town** 1	61
(Mile Oak expelled)	
Horsham YMCA 2 Corinthian Casuals 0	99
Moneyfields 4 Rye & Iden United 0	109
Lordswood 3 Saltdean United 2	60
Carterton 0 **Didcot Town** 3	109
Kingstonian 2 Ringmer 1	324
Tonbridge Angels 3 Horsham 1	457
Ashford Town 3 Slade Green 1	169
Cobham 0 **Egham Town** 2	45
Reading Town 1 **Eastbourne Town** 3	44
Molesey 2 **Burgess Hill Town** 4	121
Bashley 4 Hythe Town 0	76
Ash United 1 Leatherhead 1	111
Herne Bay 3 Sevenoaks Town 2	117
Burnham 2 Selsey 0	49
Sittingbourne 2 **Chessington & Hook United** 4	138
Erith & Belvedere 1 **Tooting & Mitcham United** 2	215
Croydon Athletic 4 Redhill 2	76
Oxford City 3 Newport IOW 2	139
East Preston 0 **Cowes Sports** 1	51
Chatham Town 2 North Leigh 0	154
Metropolitan Police 0 Bracknell Town 0	81
VCD Athletic 0 **Hastings United** 2	187
Croydon 1 Frimley Green 1	56
Mole Valley Predators 0 **Gosport Borough** 8	58
Winchester City 0 **Maidstone United** 3	452
Sidlesham 1 **Bedfont** 2	53
Thatcham Town 3 Cove 0	80
Chipstead 4 Brockenhurst 2	72
Whitstable Town 3 Fleet Town 3	162
Godalming Town 1 **Dulwich Hamlet** 2	121
Ashford Town (Middx) 3 Whyteleafe 1	102
Merstham 1 **Ramsgate** 4	85
Steyning Town 0 **Cray Wanderers** 6	80
BAT Sports 0 **Abingdon United** 3	54
Dartford 1 **Dorking** 2	281
Epsom & Ewell 6 AFC Newbury 1	81
Hillingdon Borough 0 Hassocks 0	64
Banstead Athletic 1 Alton Town 0	37
Whitehawk 0 **AFC Totton** 2	80
Three Bridges 1 Walton Casuals 0	84
Wick 1 Arundel 1	155
Littlehampton Town 1 Tunbridge Wells 1	131
(at Worthing)	
Sidley United 1 Deal Town 1	104
(at Hailsham Town)	
Elmore 2 Torrington 0	43
Shortwood United 2 **Bodmin Town** 3	93
Liskeard Athletic 2 Brislington 0	73
Melksham Town 2 Westbury United 2	112
Hamworthy United 4 Backwell United 0	122
Frome Town 0 **St Blazey** 0	211
Hallen 1 **Swindon Supermarine** 3	83
Almondsbury Town 3 **Cinderford Town** 5	81
Penzance 2 Street 2	158
Bemerton Heath Harlequins 1 Ilfracombe Town 0	64
Chard Town 0 Wimborne Town 0	93
Shepton Mallet 0 **Bournemouth** 2	69
Taunton Town 1 Bristol Manor Farm 0	268
Highworth Town 1 Welton Rovers 0	122
Bridgwater Town 0 **Paulton Rovers** 1	168
Barnstaple Town 4 Clevedon United 1	130
Odd Down 3 Exmouth Town 2	25
Bitton 2 Dawlish Town 1	127
Witney United 0 Clevedon Town 0	155
Fairford Town 0 Devizes Town 0	55

Christchurch 5 Bishop Sutton 0	55
Bishops Cleeve 3 Bideford 1	107
Bridport 0 **Falmouth Town** 3	139

PRELIMINARY ROUND REPLAYS

Whitley Bay 4 Bridlington Town 0	189
Penrith 1 **Warrington Town** 2 *aet*	118
Winterton Rangers 0 **Hebburn Town** 2	102
Sunderland Nissan 1 **Rossendale United** 4	58
Chorley 2 Tadcaster Albion 0	176
Ashington 1 **Pickering Town** 2	282
Stocksbridge Park Steels 1 Washington 1 *aet* (4-2p)	126
Mossley 1 Sheffield 0	268
Goole 2 Atherton LR 0	193
Newcastle Town 1 Buxton 1	211
Norton United 1 Deeping Rovers 0	42
Oldbury United 4 Stone Dominoes 0	62
Pegasus Juniors 3 Teversal 2	178
Sutton Town 2 **Leamington** 2 *aet* (8-9p)	205
Eastwood Town 3 Lincoln Moorlands 2 *aet*	116
Kidsgrove Athletic 5 Stourbridge 2	110
Chalfont St Peter 1 **AFC Hornchurch** 2	104
Leverstock Green 3 **Barkingside** 4	64
Ely City 0 **Bury Town** 8	218
Holmer Green 2 **Harwich & Parkeston** 5	104
St Margaretsbury 2 Barking & East Ham United 0	94
Wroxham 4 Leighton Town 1	132
Ipswich Wanderers 3 Stowmarket Town 1 *aet*	169
Leatherhead 3 Ash United 2	235
Bracknell Town 0 **Metropolitan Police** 2	131
Frimley Green 0 **Croydon** 2	68
Fleet Town 2 Whitstable Town 1	104
Hassocks 2 Hillington Borough 1 *aet*	164
Arundel 1 **Wick** 2	204
Tunbridge Wells 2 Littlehampton Town 2 *aet* (16-15p)	122
Deal Town 2 Sidley United 1	143
Westbury United 2 **Melksham Town** 3	190
St Blazey (w/o) v Frome Town (scr.)	
Street 0 **Penzance** 0 *aet* (2-4p)	135
Wimborne Town 2 Chard Town 0	200
Clevedon Town 3 Witney United 2	162
Devizes Town 0 **Fairford Town** 3	85

FIRST QUALIFYING ROUND

(£2,250 to each winning club)

Oldham Town 1 **Great Harwood Town** 2	65
Wakefield-Emley 1 **Blyth Spartans** 2	162
Armthorpe Welfare 3 Mossley 1	92
Goole 5 Clitheroe 3	207
Billingham Synthonia 4 Retford United 2	106
Trafford 4 Yorkshire Amateur 1	117
Kendal Town 2 **Witton Albion** 3	160
Durham City 0 **Hebburn Town** 2	151
Runcorn Halton 2 **Skelmersdale United** 3	129
Curzon Ashton 0 **Chester-le-Street Town** 2	110
Burscough 3 Ashton United 2	187
Pickering Town 1 **Farsley Celtic** 2	146
Cammell Laird 2 Radcliffe Borough 1	175
Stocksbridge Park Steels 1 **Ossett Town** 3	104
Chorley 0 Bishop Auckland 0	237
Dunston Federation Brewery 4 Thackley 1	140
Woodley Sports 2 **Prescot Cables** 4 *(at Hyde United)*	71
Seaham Red Star 0 **Consett** 4	87
Bradford Park Avenue 1 Padiham 1	198
Marine 4 Cheadle Town 0	191
St Helens Town 3 Northallerton Town 3	81
Frickley Athletic 2 Chadderton 0	214
Gateshead 4 Warrington Town 0	235
Guiseley 0 **Salford City** 1	192
Rossendale United 2 Billingham Town 2	107
Thornaby 4 West Auckland Town 3	62
Newcastle Blue Star 1 **Whitby Town** 2 *(at Whitby Town)*	208
North Ferriby United 3 Brigg Town 1	213
Whitley Bay 1 **Ramsbottom United** 2	162
Willenhall Town 1 Malvern Town 1	131
Bedworth United 1 Solihull Borough 1	141
Stratford Town 1 **Glapwell** 3	112
Bromsgrove Rovers 2 Newcastle Town 0	242
Ilkeston Town 1 Coalville Town 0	336
Kidsgrove Athletic 0 **Leamington** 1	429
Staveley Miners Welfare 2 Norton United 1	67
Halesowen Town 5 South Normanton Athletic 3	279
Leek Town 7 Long Eaton United 0	193
Westfields 1 **Belper Town** 2	122
Oadby Town 3 Oldbury United 3	142
Boldmere St Michaels 0 **Nantwich Town** 3	94
Matlock Town 4 Pegasus Juniors 0	160
Cradley Town 0 **Eastwood Town** 6	55
Grantham Town 4 Lincoln United 0	413
Chasetown 2 Gedling Town 1	76
AFC Telford United 1 Rugby Town 1	1,065
Corby Town 2 Shepshed Dynamo 0 *(at Kettering Town)*	184
Chesham United 0 **Brackley Town** 1	224
St Margaretsbury 0 Billericay Town 0	228
Northwood 3 March Town United 0	141
Rothwell Town 1 **Wivenhoe Town** 3	93
Welwyn Garden City 3 Beaconsfield SYCOB 2	71
Ruislip Manor 1 Redbridge 1	97
Wroxham 2 Diss Town 0	228
Woodford United 5 Harwich & Parkeston 0	76
East Thurrock United 1 **Harrow Borough** 2	96
Hampton & Richmond Borough 3 Witham Town 0	226
Halstead Town 1 **Lowestoft Town** 3	142
Aveley 1 **Burnham Ramblers** 2	76
Brentwood Town 3 Great Wakering Rovers 1	131
Barkingside 1 **Maldon Town** 6	61
Brook House 9 Clacton Town 1	91
Bedford Town 2 AFC Sudbury 2	460
AFC Hornchurch 2 Stansted 0	415
Cogenhoe United 4 Clapton 2	68
Heybridge Swifts 1 Arlesey Town 0	169
Stanway Rovers 0 Wealdstone 0	170
Chelmsford City 1 Harlow Town 1	301
Ipswich Wanderers 1 Hemel Hempstead Town 1	126
Potton United 0 **Leyton** 1	84
Hitchin Town 4 Waltham Forest 1	168
Enfield Town 3 Waltham Abbey 0	314
Bury Town 2 Boreham Wood 2	166
Northampton Spencer 1 **Aylesbury United** 2	201
Staines Town 1 Dunstable Town 1	174
Hendon 6 Biggleswade United 0	116
Southall 6 Mildenhall Town 3	75
Banbury United 2 King's Lynn 1	549
Berkhamsted Town 3 Barton Rovers 0	144
Cheshunt 1 **Braintree Town** 2	132
Slough Town 4 Oxford City 1	312
Camberley Town 1 Epsom & Ewell 0	73
Cray Wanderers 4 Kingstonian 1	225
Fleet Town 3 Thatcham Town 2	138
Lordswood 1 **AFC Totton** 2	71
Didcot Town 0 Herne Bay 0	239
Bashley 0 **Dover Athletic** 1	141
Burgess Hill Town 0 **Walton & Hersham** 4	169
Abingdon United 1 Dulwich Hamlet 1	102
Banstead Athletic 3 Moneyfields 0	72
Three Bridges 1 **Chipstead** 3	59
Croydon Athletic 1 **Ramsgate** 3	101
Bedfont 1 **Bromley** 4	128
Horsham YMCA 1 **Croydon** 2	72
AFC Wimbledon 2 Ashford Town (Middx) 2	1,619
Ashford Town 0 **Windsor & Eton** 3	163
Maidstone United 1 **Burnham** 2	347
Folkestone Invicta 3 Egham Town 1	212
Chessington & Hook United 0 **Hassocks** 3	129
Wick 0 **Worthing** 4	283
Eastbourne Town 1 **Gosport Borough** 2	160
Margate 4 Cowes Sports 0	672
Dorking 1 **Deal Town** 3	91

Fisher Athletic 6 Tooting & Mitcham United 2	159
Chatham Town 3 **Leatherhead** 4	251
Metropolitan Police 2 Tunbridge Wells 0	83
Hastings United 3 Tonbridge Angels 3	555
Swindon Supermarine 1 Melksham Town 0	101
Fairford Town 0 **Bishop's Cleeve** 1	75
Liskeard Athletic 1 Bitton 1	102
Cirencester Town 5 Wimborne Town 3	147
Bath City 1 Cinderford Town 0	404
Clevedon Town 1 Salisbury City 1	264
Taunton Town 3 Odd Down 0	283
Paulton Rovers 3 Barnstaple Town 2	102
Chippenham Town 4 Falmouth Town 0	443
Penzance 0 **Bemerton Heath Harlequins** 1	171
Gloucester City 0 Christchurch 0	280
Tiverton Town 1 Evesham United 1	392
Yate Town 2 Bodmin Town 0	170
Merthyr Tydfil 3 St Blazey 2	407
Bournemouth 1 Mangotsfield United 1	130
Hamworthy United 0 **Team Bath** 2	132
Highworth Town 2 Elmore 1	135

FIRST QUALIFYING ROUND REPLAYS

Bishop Auckland 2 Chorley 1	140
Padiham 1 **Bradford Park Avenue** 4	305
Northallerton Town 2 **St Helens Town** 3	134
Billingham Town 2 **Rossendale United** 3	166
Malvern Town 1 Willenhall Town 0	139
Solihull Borough 3 Bedworth United 2	173
Oldbury United 0 **Oadby Town** 3	62
Rugby Town 2 **AFC Telford United** 3 *aet*	265
Billericay Town 2 **St Margaretsbury** 3 *aet*	302
Redbridge 2 Ruislip Manor 1	88
AFC Sudbury 2 Bedford Town 1 *aet*	441
Wealdstone 3 Stanway Rovers 0	179
Harlow Town 0 **Chelmsford City** 1	206
Hemel Hempstead Town 4 Ipswich Wanderers 1	155
Boreham Wood 4 Bury Town 2	128
Dunstable Town 0 **Staines Town** 1 *aet*	118
Herne Bay 2 **Didcot Town** 6	211
Dulwich Hamlet 3 Abingdon United 2	115
Ashford Town (Middx) 0 **AFC Wimbledon** 2	720
Tonbridge Angels 2 Hastings United 1	454
Bitton 1 Liskeard Athletic 0	140
Salisbury City 4 Clevedon Town 2	506
Christchurch 3 Gloucester City 0	103
Evesham United 0 **Tiverton Town** 1	130
Mangotsfield United 7 Bournemouth 0	197

SECOND QUALIFYING ROUND

(£3,750 to each winning club)

Consett 1 **Ossett Town** 5	166
Billingham Synthonia 0 **North Ferriby United** 3	183
Blyth Spartans 1 Prescot Cables 0	484
Armthorpe Welfare 0 **Rossendale United** 2	110
Dunston Federation Brewery 1 Thornaby 1	124
Trafford 1 Whitby Town 1	164
Harrogate Town 3 Great Harwood Town 0	346
Chester-le-Street Town 1 **Leigh RMI** 3	193
Marine 1 Cammell Laird 1	358
Worksop Town 0 **Witton Albion** 1	348
Skelmersdale United 0 Bishop Auckland 0	509
Hyde United 2 Lancaster City 1	333
St Helens Town 0 **Alfreton Town** 2	142
Vauxhall Motors 2 Ramsbottom United 0	109
Barrow 5 Hebburn Town 1	911
Farsley Celtic 2 Bradford Park Avenue 0	403
Gainsborough Trinity 2 Goole 2	423
Frickley Athletic 1 **Northwich Victoria** 4	392
Droylsden 1 **Burscough** 2	316
Salford City 1 Gateshead 0	213
Stalybridge Celtic 0 Workington 0	448
Bromsgrove Rovers 3 Hinckley United 1	425
Leamington 2 Oadby Town 2	861
Chasetown 3 Belper Town 3	167
Brackley Town 1 Banbury United 1	680
Eastwood Town 1 Cambridge City 1	225
Nuneaton Borough 3 AFC Telford United 1	1,174
Matlock Town 2 Corby Town 0	333
Glapwell 0 **Halesowen Town** 1	171
Redditch United 1 Woodford United 1	316
Malvern Town 1 **Histon** 4	196
Hednesford Town 2 Moor Green 0	491
Leek Town 1 Grantham Town 0	371
Kettering Town 1 Stafford Rangers 0	971
Cogenhoe United 3 Staveley Miners Welfare 2	91
Solihull Borough 3 Ilkeston Town 0	237
Nantwich Town 0 **Hucknall Town** 1	190
Thurrock 3 Hemel Hempstead Town 2	93
Boreham Wood 0 **Welling United** 2	267
Wivenhoe Town 1 **Heybridge Swifts** 4	241
Bognor Regis Town 1 Basingstoke Town 1	552
Yeading 3 Maidenhead United 0	185
Hendon 0 Metropolitan Police 0	155
AFC Hornchurch 1 **Worthing** 4	544
Burnham 1 Lowestoft Town 1	110
Bromley 2 Chipstead 1	407
Staines Town 1 Croydon 1	251
Redbridge 2 Eastbourne Borough 2	113
Deal Town 1 **Hitchin Town** 3	211
Chelmsford City 1 Dover Athletic 0	404
AFC Wimbledon 0 **Walton & Hersham** 3	1,930
Cray Wanderers 4 Camberley Town 1	139
Leyton 0 **Lewes** 1	162
St Margaretsbury 0 **Folkestone Invicta** 1	212
Braintree Town 2 Didcot Town 0	306
Brentwood Town 1 **Windsor & Eton** 2	144
Wroxham 2 Slough Town 0	267
Fisher Athletic 2 **Tonbridge Angels** 3	257
Northwood 0 Aylesbury United 0	249
Margate 1 Carshalton Athletic 0	773
Hayes 1 Brook House 1	406
Welwyn Garden City 4 AFC Sudbury 2	304
Hassocks 0 **Dulwich Hamlet** 1	320
Ramsgate 1 Southall 0	251
Farnborough Town 3 Berkhamsted Town 0	456
Enfield Town 1 St Albans City 1	525
Sutton United 2 Maldon Town 0	402
Banstead Athletic 1 **Wealdstone** 4	164
Harrow Borough 2 Burnham Ramblers 1	140
Hampton & Richmond Borough 1 Leatherhead 1	357
Fleet Town 0 **Bishop's Stortford** 2	201
Highworth Town 1 **Tiverton Town** 7	284
Yate Town 0 **Salisbury City** 2	371
Christchurch 0 **Cirencester Town** 2	165
Worcester City 7 Bemerton Heath Harlequins 0	579
Taunton Town 1 Merthyr Tydfil 1	414
Gosport Borough 3 **Bath City** 4	440
Mangotsfield United 4 Swindon Supermarine 2	278
Bishops Cleeve 3 Bitton 0	211
Dorchester Town 4 Team Bath 2	317
Weston-super-Mare 2 Weymouth 2	744
Chippenham Town 4 Newport County 0	949
AFC Totton 2 Paulton Rovers 1	150
Eastleigh 0 Havant & Waterlooville 0	470

SECOND QUALIFYING ROUND REPLAYS

Thornaby 2 Dunston Federation Brewery 1	126
Whitby Town 6 Trafford 0	196
Cammell Laird 3 Marine 1	205
Bishop Auckland 1 **Skelmersdale United** 2	125
Goole 1 Gainsborough Trinity 2	298
Workington 2 Stalybridge Celtic 1 *aet*	315
Oadby 1 **Leamington** 1 *aet* (2-4p)	356
Belper Town 1 **Chasetown** 4	154
Banbury United 5 Brackley Town 2	960
Cambridge City 3 Eastwood Town 1	263
Woodford United 2 Redditch United 2 *aet* (10-9p)	207
Basingstoke Town 2 Bognor Regis Town 1	315
Metropolitan Police 1 Hendon 0	104
Lowestoft Town 1 **Burnham** 1 *aet* (2-4p)	249
Croydon 1 **Staines Town** 2	82

Eastbourne Borough 5 Redbridge 1	359
Aylesbury United 2 Northwood 0	262
Brook House 0 **Hayes** 4	342
St Albans City 3 Enfield Town 0	346
Leatherhead 2 Hampton & Richmond Borough 1	273
Merthyr Tydfil 2 Taunton Town 1	370
Weymouth 1 Weston-super-Mare 0	1,003
Havant & Waterlooville 4 Eastleigh 1	329

THIRD QUALIFYING ROUND
(£5,000 to each winning club)

Northwich Victoria 1 North Ferriby United 0	684
Vauxhall Motors 4 Skelmersdale United 3	243
Leigh RMI 1 Gainsborough Trinity 1	165
Rossendale United 0 **Blyth Spartans** 1	209
Leek Town 2 Thornaby 1	211
Matlock Town 3 **Ossett Town** 6	322
Harrogate Town 2 Witton Albion 0	402
Hucknall Town 2 Cammell Laird 2	292
Alfreton Town 2 Whitby Town 1	231
Burscough 2 Workington 0	303
Salford City 0 **Farsley Celtic** 1	195
Hyde United 2 **Barrow** 3	469
Thurrock 1 Solihull Borough 0	126
Banbury United 3 **Hednesford Town** 4	1,005
Leamington 2 Woodford United 0	1,027
Cogenhoe United 1 Chasetown 1	184
Hayes 2 Bishop's Stortford 0	231
Wroxham 1 Aylesbury United 1	220
Cambridge City 4 Hitchin Town 1	461
Heybridge Swifts 1 Braintree Town 1	360
Harrow Borough 0 **Welling United** 1	258
Wealdstone 2 **Burnham** 4	241
Halesowen Town 0 **Bromsgrove Rovers** 2	757
Histon 2 Welwyn Garden City 1	373
St Albans City 0 Kettering Town 0	882
Nuneaton Borough 1 Chelmsford City 1	915
Bishops Cleeve 1 AFC Totton 1	175
Metropolitan Police 3 Eastbourne Borough 3	201
Bromley 0 Mangotsfield United 0	488
Worcester City 3 Tonbridge Angels 0	684
Cirencester Town 2 Havant & Waterlooville 1	278
Worthing 2 **Basingstoke Town** 4	571
Yeading 1 Dorchester Town 1	151
Merthyr Tydfil 2 Salisbury City 1	615
Folkestone Invicta 2 Staines Town 0	220
Tiverton Town 2 Windsor & Eton 1	531
Leatherhead 0 **Farnborough Town** 2	609
Chippenham Town 1 Sutton United 0	727
Ramsgate 1 Walton & Hersham 0	301
Margate 0 **Cray Wanderers** 3	807
Lewes 1 Dulwich Hamlet 0	539
Weymouth 1 Bath City 0	1,232

THIRD QUALIFYING ROUND REPLAYS

Gainsborough Trinity 2 Leigh RMI 1	385
Cammell Laird 0 **Hucknall Town** 1	395
Chasetown 4 Cogenhoe United 3 *aet*	382
Aylesbury United 4 Wroxham 2	384
Braintree Town 3 Heybridge Swifts 1	479
Kettering Town 4 St Albans City 0	1,220
Chelmsford City 1 **Nuneaton Borough** 2 *aet*	379
AFC Totton 0 **Bishops Cleeve** 4	322
Eastbourne Borough 3 Metropolitan Police 2	601
Mangotsfield United 0 **Bromley** 1	403
Dorchester Town 3 Yeading 2	394

FOURTH QUALIFYING ROUND
(£10,000 to each winning club)

Harrogate Town 1 Scarborough 0	1,591
Tamworth 3 Altrincham 1	801
Southport 1 Kidderminster Harriers 0	1,108
Hucknall Town 0 Burscough 0	690
Blyth Spartans 2 Chasetown 2	926
Northwich Victoria 4 Barrow 1	1,116
Gainsborough Trinity 0 **York City** 4	1,680
Ossett Town 2 **Leamington** 3	900
Accrington Stanley 1 Worcester City 1	940
Hednesford Town 3 Vauxhall Motors 0	628
Halifax Town 2 Farsley Celtic 0	1,469
Burton Albion 2 Leek Town 0	1,467
Hereford United 0 Alfreton Town 0	1,768
Bromsgrove Rovers 0 **Morecambe** 2	919
Crawley Town 0 **Braintree Town** 1	970
Canvey Island 1 Burnham 1	363
Kettering Town 3 Gravesend & Northfleet 0	1,647
Dorchester Town 1 **Welling United** 2	533
Bromley 0 **Aldershot Town** 1	1,454
Histon 3 Hayes 1	588
Grays Athletic 2 Cray Wanderers 0	1,316
Nuneaton Borough 0 Tiverton Town 0	1,237
Exeter City 0 **Stevenage Borough** 1	3,421
Woking 3 Thurrock 0	1,486
Basingstoke Town 0 **Chippenham Town** 1	1,072
Cambridge City 2 Lewes 1	588
Merthyr Tydfil 2 Farnborough Town 0	1,019
Aylesbury United 0 **Folkestone Invicta** 2	646
Forest Green Rovers 2 **Dagenham & Redbridge** 3	751
Ramsgate 3 Cirencester Town 0	697
Weymouth 2 Cambridge United 1	1,652
Bishops Cleeve 0 **Eastbourne Borough** 1	625

FOURTH QUALIFYING ROUND REPLAYS

Burscough 6 Hucknall Town 2	415
Chasetown 1 Blyth Spartans 0	2,134
Worcester City 3 Accrington Stanley 2	1,331
Alfreton Town 1 **Hereford United** 1aet (3-4p)	740
Burnham 2 Canvey Island 1	607
Tiverton Town 0 **Nuneaton Borough** 1	885

FIRST ROUND
(£16,000 to each winning club)

Nottingham Forest 1 Weymouth 1	10,305
Southport 1 Woking 1	1,417
Bristol City 0 **Notts County** 2	4,221
Burnham 1 **Aldershot Town** 3	1,623
Rochdale 0 **Brentford** 1	2,928
Eastbourne Borough 1 Oxford United 1	3,770
Merthyr Tydfil 1 **Walsall** 2	3,046
Hartlepool United 2 Dagenham & Redbridge 1	3,655
Bradford City 2 Tranmere Rovers 1	6,116
Barnet 0 **Southend United** 1	3,545
Peterborough United 0 Burton Albion 0	3,857
Cheltenham Town 1 Carlisle United 0	2,405
Histon 4 Hednesford Town 0	1,080
York City 0 **Grays Athletic** 3	3,586
Swindon Town 2 Boston United 2	3,814
Chasetown 1 Oldham Athletic 1	1,997
AFC Bournemouth 1 **Tamworth** 2	4,559
Chester City 2 Folkestone Invicta 1	2,503
Kettering Town 1 **Stevenage Borough** 3	4,548
Nuneaton Borough 2 Ramsgate 0	2,153
Huddersfield Town 4 Welling United 1	5,578
Cambridge City 0 **Hereford United** 1	1,116
Port Vale 2 Wrexham 1	5,046
Halifax Town 1 Rushden&Diamonds 1	2,303
Barnsley 1 Darlington 0	6,059
Torquay United 1 Harrogate Town 1	2,079
Doncaster Rovers 4 Blackpool 1	4,332
Shrewsbury Town 4 Braintree Town 1	2,969
Bury 2 Scunthorpe United 2	2,940
Morecambe 1 **Northwich Victoria** 3	2,166
Burscough 3 Gillingham 2	1,927
Stockport County 2 Swansea City 0	2,978
Macclesfield Town 1 Yeovil Town 1	1,943
Chippenham Town 1 Worcester City 1	2,815
Wycombe Wanderers 1 **Northampton Town** 3	3,974
Grimsby Town 1 **Bristol Rovers** 2	2,680
Rotherham United 3 **Mansfield Town** 4	4,089
Colchester United 9 Leamington 1	3,513
Lincoln City 1 Milton Keynes Dons 1	3,508
Leyton Orient 0 Chesterfield 0	3,554

FIRST ROUND REPLAYS

Weymouth 0 **Nottingham Forest** 2	6,500
Woking 1 Southport 0 *aet*	2,298
Oxford United 3 Eastbourne Borough 0	4,396
Burton Albion 1 Peterborough United 0	2,511
Boston United 4 Swindon Town 1	2,467
Oldham Athletic 4 Chasetown 0	7,235
Rushden & Diamonds 0 Halifax Town 0 *aet* (5-4p)	2,133
Harrogate Town 0 **Torquay United** 0 *aet* (5-6p)	3,317
Scunthorpe United 1 Bury 0 *aet*	4,006
Yeovil Town 4 Macclesfield Town 0	4,456
Worcester City 1 Chippenham Town 0	4,006
Milton Keynes Dons 2 Lincoln City 1	4,029
Chesterfield 1 **Leyton Orient** 2	4,895

SECOND ROUND
(£24,000 to each winning club)

Walsall 2 Yeovil Town 0	4,580
Woking 0 Northwich Victoria 0	2,462
Burton Albion 4 Burscough 1	4,499
Aldershot Town 0 **Scunthorpe United** 1	3,584
Shrewsbury Town 1 **Colchester United** 2	3,695
Hartlepool United 1 **Tamworth** 2	3,786
Cheltenham Town 1 Oxford United 1	4,592
Mansfield Town 3 Grays Athletic 0	2,992
Hereford United 0 **Stockport County** 2	3,620
Stevenage Borough 2 Northampton Town 2	3,937
Port Vale 1 Bristol Rovers 1	4,483
Boston United 1 **Doncaster Rovers** 2	3,995
Rushden & Diamonds 0 **Leyton Orient** 1	3,245
Nuneaton Borough 2 Histon 2	3,366
Oldham Athletic 1 Brentford 1	4,365
Southend United 1 **Milton Keynes Dons** 2	5,267
Worcester City 0 **Huddersfield Town** 1	4,163
Torquay United 2 Notts County 1	2,407
Barnsley 1 Bradford City 1	7,051
Chester City 3 Nottingham Forest 0	4,732

SECOND ROUND REPLAYS

Northwich Victoria 2 Woking 1	2,302
Oxford United 1 **Cheltenham Town** 2	3,455
Northampton Town 2 Stevenage Borough 0	4,407
Bristol Rovers 0 **Port Vale** 1	5,623
Histon 1 **Nuneaton Borough** 2	3,077
Brentford 1 Oldham Athletic 0	3,146
Bradford City 3 **Barnsley** 5 *aet*	4,738

THIRD ROUND
(£40,000 to each winning club)

West Bromwich Albion 1 Reading 1	19,197
Fulham 1 **Leyton Orient** 2	13,394
Brighton & Hove Albion 0 **Coventry City** 1	6,734
Wolverhampton Wanderers 1 Plymouth Argyle 0	11,041
Port Vale 2 Doncaster Rovers 1	4,923
Sheffield Wednesday 2 **Charlton Athletic** 4	14,851
Torquay United 0 Birmingham City 0	5,974
Manchester City 3 Scunthorpe United 1	27,779
Newcastle United 1 Mansfield Town 0	41,459
Luton Town 3 **Liverpool** 5	10,170
Preston North End 2 Crewe Alexandra 1	8,386
Stoke City 0 Tamworth 0	9,366
Derby County 2 Burnley 1	12,713
Southampton 4 Milton Keynes Dons 3	15,908
Blackburn Rovers 3 Queens Park Rangers 0	12,705
Arsenal 2 Cardiff City 1	36,552
Stockport County 2 **Brentford** 3	4,078
Norwich City 1 **West Ham United** 2	23,968
Ipswich Town 0 **Portsmouth** 1	15,593
Wigan Athletic 1 Leeds United 1	10,980
Sunderland 3 Northwich Victoria 0	19,323
Chelsea 2 Huddersfield Town 1	41,650
Cheltenham Town 2 Chester City 2	4,741
Leicester City 3 Tottenham Hotpur 2	19,844
Watford 0 **Bolton Wanderers** 3	13,239
Sheffield United 1 **Colchester United** 2	11,820
Nuneaton Borough 1 Middlesbrough 1	6,000
Hull City 0 **Aston Villa** 1	17,051
Barnsley 1 Walsall 1	6,884
Burton Albion 0 Manchester United 0	6,191
Crystal Palace 4 Northampton Town 1	10,391
Millwall 1 Everton 1	16,440

THIRD ROUND REPLAYS

Reading 3 West Bromwich Albion 2 *aet*	16,723
Birmingham City 2 Torquay United 0	24,650
Tamworth 1 **Stoke City** 1 *aet* (4-5p)	3,812
Leeds United 3 **Wigan Athletic** 3 *aet* (2-4p)	15,243
Chester City 0 **Cheltenham Town** 1	5,096
Middlesbrough 5 Nuneaton Borough 2	26,255
Walsall 2 Barnsley 0	4,047
Manchester United 5 Burton Albion 0	53,564
Everton 1 Millwall 0	25,800

FOURTH ROUND
(£60,000 to each winning club)

Stoke City 2 Walsall 1	8,834
Cheltenham Town 0 **Newcastle United** 2	7,022
Coventry City 1 Middlesbrough 1	28,120
Reading 1 Birmingham City 1	23,762
Portsmouth 1 **Liverpool** 2	17,247
Leicester City 0 **Southampton** 1	20,427
Bolton Wanderers 1 Arsenal 0	13,326
Aston Villa 3 Port Vale 1	30,434
Brentford 2 Sunderland 1	11,698
Manchester City 1 Wigan Athletic 0	30,811
Everton 1 Chelsea 1	29,742
Preston North End 1 Crystal Palace 1	9,489
West Ham United 4 Blackburn Rovers 2	23,700
Colchester United 3 Derby County 1	5,933
Charlton Athletic 2 Leyton Orient 1	22,029
Wolverhampton Wanderers 0 **Manchester United** 3	28,333

FOURTH ROUND REPLAYS

Middlesbrough 1 Coventry City 0	14,131
Birmingham City 2 Reading 1	16,664
Chelsea 4 Everton 1	39,301
Crystal Palace 1 **Preston North End** 2	7,356

FIFTH ROUND
(£120,000 to each winning club)

Preston North End 0 **Middlesbrough** 2	19,877
Newcastle United 1 Southampton 0	40,975
Aston Villa 1 Manchester City 1	23,847
Chelsea 3 Colchester United 1	41,810
Charlton Athletic 3 Brentford 1	22,098
Liverpool 1 Manchester United 0	44,039
Bolton Wanderers 0 West Ham United 0	17,120
Stoke City 0 **Birmingham City** 1	18,768

FIFTH ROUND REPLAYS

Manchester City 2 Aston Villa 1	33,006
West Ham United 2 Bolton Wanderers 1	24,685

QUARTER-FINALS
(£300,000 to each winning club)

Charlton Athletic 0 Middlesbrough 0	24,187
Manchester City 1 **West Ham United** 2	39,357
Chelsea 1 Newcastle United 0	42,279
Birmingham City 0 **Liverpool** 7	27,378

QUARTER-FINAL REPLAY

Middlesbrough 4 Charlton Athletic 2	30,248

SEMI-FINALS
(£900,000 to each winning club)

Chelsea 1 **Liverpool** 2	64,575
(at Manchester United)	
Middlesbrough 0 **West Ham United** 1	39,148
(at Aston Villa)	

FINAL
(£1,000,000 to winning club)
(May 13th at Millennium Stadium, Cardiff)

Liverpool 3 West Ham United 3 *aet* (3-1p)	71,140

F A TROPHY

FIRST QUALIFYING ROUND
(£1,300 to each winning club)

Warrington Town 1 Frickley Athletic 1	132
North Ferriby United 1 Prescot Cables 1	188
Rossendale United 0 **Woodley Sports** 1	112
Guiseley 3 Chorley 1	182
Farsley Celtic 2 Runcorn Halton 0	223
Wakefield-Emley 0 **Fleetwood Town** 5	128
Mossley 3 Shepshed Dynamo 2	239
Witton Albion 1 AFC Telford United 1	404
Bradford Park Avenue 1 Gateshead 1	191
Blyth Spartans 2 Belper Town 0	372
Bamber Bridge 2 Grantham Town 2	162
Burscough 3 Leek Town 3	212
Kidsgrove Athletic 3 Ashton United 1	178
Brigg Town 0 **Matlock Town** 1	214
Radcliffe Borough 1 **Marine** 2	173
Clitheroe 3 Spalding United 1	253
Ossett Albion 0 **Kendal Town** 4	87
Ossett Town 1 Stocksbridge Park Steels 1	109
Lincoln United 2 Colwyn Bay 1	113
Whitby Town 4 Eastwood Town 2	228
Gresley Rovers 2 Ilkeston Town 2	320
Bashley 0 **Margate** 3	95
Enfield Town 3 Berkhamsted Town 0	212
Metropolitan Police 4 Maldon Town 1	105
Dover Athletic 1 Dartford 1	615
Barton Rovers 3 Potters Bar Town 2	110
AFC Wimbledon 1 King's Lynn 0	1,720
Leyton 1 Arlesey Town 0	73
Enfield 1 **Fleet Town** 2	83
Folkestone Invicta 1 Whyteleafe 1	265
Walton Casuals 0 **Harlow Town** 1	92
Slough Town 1 **Croydon Athletic** 3	286
Chelmsford City 6 Horsham 0	358
Waltham Forest 0 **Burgess Hill Town** 1	130
Kingstonian 2 Aveley 2	402
Northwood 2 **Ramsgate** 4	152
Sittingbourne 3 Chatham Town 0	284
Staines Town 2 Wivenhoe Town 0	201
Tonbridge Angels 1 Cheshunt 0	430
Leatherhead 0 **East Thurrock United** 1	141
Braintree Town 4 Great Wakering Rovers 2	210
Rothwell Town 3 Molesey 1	80
Heybridge Swifts 3 Walton & Hersham 0	202
Billericay Town 1 Wingate & Finchley 0	317
Corinthian Casuals 1 **Stamford** 4	85
Lymington & New Milton 0 **Worthing** 4	179
Hastings United 0 Corby Town 0	376
Hampton & Richmond Borough 0 **Newport IOW** 2	293
Banstead Athletic 1 **Redbridge** 2	64
Boreham Wood 1 Ilford 0	98
Dulwich Hamlet 1 Barking & East Ham United 1	228
Windsor & Eton 1 **Uxbridge** 2	172
Tooting & Mitcham United 1 **Wealdstone** 2	312
Fisher Athletic 4 Hendon 2	189
Ashford Town 0 **Bromley** 2	251
Team Bath 0 **Hitchin Town** 1	86
Thame United 0 **Aylesbury United** 5	294
Halesowen Town 0 Willenhall Town 0	326
Tiverton Town 0 Mangotsfield United 0	564
Cinderford Town 1 Chippenham Town 1	197
Dunstable Town 2 Bath City 2	122
Cirencester Town 2 Gloucester City 0	322
Evesham United 0 **Solihull Borough** 2	157
Brackley Town 1 Banbury United 1	494
Stourport Swifts 0 **Bedworth United** 1	113
Paulton Rovers 1 Salisbury City 1	285
Clevedon Town 2 Taunton Town 1	216
Hemel Hempstead Town 1 Swindon Supermarine 1	130
Merthyr Tydfil 0 **Rushall Olympic** 3	403
Leighton Town 2 Rugby Town 1	134
Bromsgrove Rovers 3 Beaconsfield SYCOB 2	347
Sutton Coldfield Town 2 Chesham United 1	107
Marlow 1 **Ashford Town (Middx)** 2	105
Burnham 2 Yate Town 0	75
Bedford Town 3 Bracknell Town 0	420

FIRST QUALIFYING ROUND REPLAYS

Frickley Athletic 1 **Warrington Town** 1 *aet* (4-5p)	265
Prescot Cables 2 North Ferriby United 2 *aet* (4-3p)	192
AFC Telford United 2 Witton Albion 1	843
Gateshead 4 Bradford Park Avenue 3 *aet*	130
Grantham Town 3 Bamber Bridge 0	230
Leek Town 1 **Burscough** 3	175
Stocksbridge Park Steels 2 **Ossett Town** 2 *aet* (1-4p)	103
Ilkeston Town 2 **Gresley Rovers** 3	349
Dartford 3 Dover Athletic 2	323
Whyteleafe 1 **Folkestone Invicta** 2	103
Aveley 0 **Kingstonian** 1	122
Corby Town 2 Hastings United 0 *(at Rothwell Town)*	100
Barking & East Ham United 2 Dulwich Hamlet 0	98
Willenhall Town 2 **Halesowen Town** 3 *aet*	210
Mangotsfield United 1 **Tiverton Town** 2	294
Chippenham Town 3 Cinderford Town 1	309
Bath City 5 Dunstable Town 0	241
Banbury United 3 Brackley Town 0	479
Salisbury City 3 Paulton Rovers 1 *aet*	336
Swindon Supermarine 0 **Hemel Hempstead Town** 1	86

SECOND QUALIFYING ROUND
(£2,000 to each winning club)

Blyth Spartans 2 Whitby Town 0	501
Gresley Rovers 1 **Mossley** 4	275
Bishop Auckland 1 **Woodley Sports** 3	85
Ossett Town 2 Clitheroe 2	108
Burscough 1 **Fleetwood Town** 2	438
Grantham Town 2 Lincoln United 1	308
Guiseley 2 Kendal Town 2	228
Gateshead 1 **Kidsgrove Athletic** 0 *(Gateshead expelled)*	127
Marine 2 Matlock Town 1	239
AFC Telford United 1 Goole 1	990
Prescot Cables 1 **Farsley Celtic** 2	214
Bridlington Town 2 Warrington Town 2	192
Harlow Town 2 Barton Rovers 1	81
Boreham Wood 4 Bromley 1	195
Fleet Town 0 **Kingstonian** 1	257
Barking & East Ham United 4 Burgess Hill Town 1	105
Cray Wanderers 4 Staines Town 3	131
Folkestone Invicta 5 Wealdstone 3	316
Enfield Town 1 Redbridge 1	268
Sittingbourne 1 Corby Town 0	178
Harrow Borough 4 Metropolitan Police 2	126
Margate 0 **Dartford** 1	549
Tonbridge Angels 2 Newport IOW 1	358
East Thurrock United 2 Leyton 1	109
Croydon Athletic 2 Rothwell Town 2	88
Heybridge Swifts 2 Billericay Town 1	326
Chelmsford City 0 **Braintree Town** 2	436
Fisher Athletic 1 **Uxbridge** 2	103
Worthing 1 Stamford 1	427
Ramsgate 1 AFC Wimbledon 1	1,047
Salisbury City 2 Clevedon Town 1	552
Hemel Hempstead Town 2 **Chippenham Town** 3	226
Burnham 3 **Leighton Town** 5	103
Rushall Olympic 3 **Ashford Town (Middx)** 4	88
Hitchin Town 1 **Bedford Town** 2	603
Solihull Borough 3 Tiverton Town 1	204
Halesowen Town 2 Aylesbury United 0	374
Banbury United 2 Cirencester Town 2	404
Bedworth United 2 **Sutton Coldfield Town** 5	146
Bath City 2 Bromsgrove Rovers 0	423

SECOND QUALIFYING ROUND REPLAYS

Clitheroe 1 Ossett Town 1 *aet* (4-2p)	188
Kendal Town 4 Guiseley 0	183
Goole 0 **AFC Telford United** 1	330
Warrington Town 1 Bridlington Town 0	135
Redbridge 2 Enfield Town 1	172
Rothwell Town 0 **Croydon Athletic** 1	98
Stamford 2 Worthing 0	203
AFC Wimbledon 2 Ramsgate 1	1,140
Cirencester Town 3 **Banbury United** 4 *aet*	186

THIRD QUALIFYING ROUND
(£3,000 to each winning club)

Leigh RMI 1 **Stafford Rangers** 4	165
Vauxhall Motors 2 Mossley 1	161
Droylsden 4 Grantham Town 0	251
Worksop Town 1 AFC Telford United 1	416
Fleetwood Town 1 **Alfreton Town** 3	552
Hucknall Town 0 Northwich Victoria 0	437
Redditch United 1 Barrow 1	289
Lancaster City 0 Workington 0	206
Kettering Town 1 Gainsborough Trinity 0	1,132
Hinckley United 2 Histon 2	446
Farsley Celtic 3 Nuneaton Borough 1	271
Marine 0 **Blyth Spartans** 1	268
Solihull Borough 1 Harrogate Town 0	199
Warrington Town 4 Kidsgrove Athletic 0	121
Clitheroe 2 Woodley Sports 1	205
Worcester City 1 Kendal Town 0	973
Sutton Coldfield Town 1 Halesowen Town 1	278
Hednesford Town 1 Moor Green 1	254
Hyde United 1 **Stalybridge Celtic** 5	906
Weston-super-Mare 4 Bedford Town 0	221
Dartford 0 AFC Wimbledon 0	1,082
Lewes 2 Dorchester Town 2	364
Dorchester Town 3 Lewes 1	235
Basingstoke Town 0 **Welling United** 2	313
Eastbourne Borough 0 **Thurrock** 3	368
Harlow Town 2 Folkestone Invicta 1	184
Ashford Town (Middx) 2 **Bognor Regis Town** 3	140
Maidenhead United 2 Bishop's Stortford 2	165
Braintree Town 0 **Hayes** 1	228
Tonbridge Angels 0 East Thurrock United 0	288
Farnborough Town 2 Banbury United 0	466
Barking & East Ham United 2 Croydon Athletic 1	101
Sittingbourne 1 **Cambridge City** 3	265
Weymouth 2 Havant & Waterlooville 1	1,018
Uxbridge 2 Sutton United 2	204
Bath City 1 **Yeading** 2	393
Leighton Town 1 Eastleigh 1	145
Boreham Wood 3 Stamford 1	146
Salisbury City 3 Newport County 0	806
Redbridge 1 Harrow Borough 1	94
Chippenham Town 0 **Carshalton Athletic** 2	510
Cray Wanderers 1 Kingstonian 1	239
Heybridge Swifts 0 **St Albans City** 1	253

THIRD QUALIFYING ROUND REPLAYS

AFC Telford United 1 **Worksop Town** 2	952
Northwich Victoria 2 Hucknall Town 1	500
Barrow 2 Redditch United 0	756
Workington 1 **Lancaster City** 2	326
Histon 2 Hinckley United 1	218
Halesowen Town 3 Sutton Coldfield Town 0	245
Moor Green 2 **Hednesford Town** 4	192
AFC Wimbledon 2 Dartford 0	1,086
Bishop's Stortford 2 Maidenhead Untied 1 *aet*	171
East Thurrock United 3 Tonbridge Angels 0	130
Sutton United 0 **Uxbridge** 1	252
Eastleigh 1 **Leighton Town** 2 *aet*	186
Harrow Borough 2 **Redbridge** 3 *aet*	101
Kingstonian 3 Cray Wanderers 1	264

FIRST ROUND
(£4,000 to each winning club)

Halesowen Town 1 **Tamworth** 2	668
York City 1 **Northwich Victoria** 2	1,372
Solihull Borough 2 Hednesford Town 1	306
Vauxhall Motors 0 **Morecambe** 4	322
Halifax Town 0 Southport 0	1,101
Warrington Town 1 Blyth Spartans 2	251
Burton Albion 0 **Worksop Town** 1	1,359
Alfreton Town 1 Histon 1	238
Barrow 2 Clitheroe 1	897
Accrington Stanley 2 Altrincham 0	810
Kidderminster Harriers 4 Scarborough 0	957
Stafford Rangers 4 Lancaster City 2	646
Stalybridge Celtic 1 Droylsden 0	598
Kettering Town 2 Farsley Celtic 1	960
Yeading 1 **Carshalton Athletic** 2	107
Salisbury City 1 Harlow Town 0	731
Aldershot Town 1 Grays Athletic 1	1,771
Weston-super-Mare 3 Barking & East Ham United 2	243
AFC Wimbledon 2 **St Albans City** 3	1,953
Stevenage Borough 0 **Crawley Town** 2	951
Exeter City 2 Bishop's Stortford 1	1,807
Bognor Regis Town 1 **Hereford United** 7	624
Dagenham & Redbridge 2 Thurrock 0	737
Uxbridge 1 **Woking** 2	471
Canvey Island 4 Kingstonian 1	413
Boreham Wood 1 Leighton Town 0	165
Worcester City 1 Hayes 0	677
Dorchester Town 3 Cambridge United 2	426
Weymouth 0 **Forest Green Rovers** 1	1,120
Farnborough Town 0 Cambridge City 2	377
East Thurrock United 0 **Gravesend & Northfleet** 2	381
Welling United 4 Redbridge 1	415

FIRST ROUND REPLAYS

Southport 0 **Halifax Town** 1	589
Histon 2 Alfreton Town 1	288
Grays Athletic 1 Aldershot Town 0 *aet*	852

SECOND ROUND
(£5,000 to each winning club)

Canvey Island 0 **Salisbury City** 1	534
Stalybridge Celtic 1 Solihull Borough 0	612
Halifax Town 0 **Hereford United** 1	1,220
Carshalton Athletic 2 Accrington Stanley 2	618
Boreham Wood 3 Gravesend & Northfleet 1	462
Tamworth 1 St Albans City 0	702
Forest Green Rovers 3 Dorchester Town 1	862
Weston-super-Mare 1 Worksop Town 1	366
Woking 1 Northwich Victoria 1	1,071
Barrow 1 **Cambridge City** 2	996
Exeter City 3 Histon 2	2,103
Dagenham & Redbridge 2 Kettering Town 1	931
Blyth Spartans 1 **Welling United** 3	784
Stafford Rangers 1 Morecambe 0	1,121
Crawley Town 3 Worcester City 1	878
Kidderminster Harriers 0 **Grays Athletic** 1	1,456

SECOND ROUND REPLAYS

Accrington Stanley 2 Carshalton Athletic 0	556
Worksop Town 2 Weston-super Mare 1	369
Northwich Victoria 1 **Woking** 2 *aet*	888

THIRD ROUND
(£6,000 to each winning club)

Hereford United 0 **Grays Athletic** 1	1,609
Stafford Rangers 2 Forest Green Rovers 1	1,178
Crawley Town 0 **Boreham Wood** 2	929
Woking 3 Welling United 2	1,244
Tamworth 0 Dagenham & Redbridge 0	920
Exeter City 1 Cambridge City 0	2,166
Accrington Stanley 1 Worksop Town 1	961
Salisbury City 0 Stalybridge Celtic 0	1,533

THIRD ROUND REPLAYS

Dagenham & Redbridge 3 Tamworth 0	922
Worksop Town 1 Accrington Stanley 1 *aet* (4-2p)	733
Stalybridge Celtic 0 **Salisbury City** 1	774

QUARTER-FINALS
(£7,000 to each winning club)

Exeter City 3 Salisbury City 1	3,653
Worksop Town 0 **Boreham Wood** 1	1,006
Woking 1 Stafford Rangers 1	2,020
Grays 1 Dagenham & Redbridge 1	2,321

QUARTER-FINAL REPLAYS

Stafford Rangers 2 **Woking** 4	1,781
Dagenham & Redbridge 2 **Grays Athletic** 4	1,526

SEMI-FINALS
(£16,000 to each winning club)
(1st leg)

Boreham Wood 0 Woking 1	1,511
Exeter City 2 Grays Athletic 1	3,051

(2nd leg)

Woking 2 Boreham Wood 0	2,080
Grays Athletic 2 Exeter City 0	2,693

FINAL
(£50,000 to winning club)
(May 14th at West Ham United)

Grays Athletic 2 Woking 0	13,800

F A VASE

FIRST QUALIFYING ROUND

(£500 to each winning club)

Horden Colliery Welfare 2 **Bacup Borough** 3	48
Hall Road Rangers 3 **Morpeth Town** 5	55
Brandon United 4 Bottesford Town 3	54
Penrith 3 Clipstone Welfare 0	73
Tow Law Town 1 Trafford 2	144
Hallam 1 **Padiham** 2	40
North Shields 1 **Cammell Laird** 4	121
Ryton 1 **Crook Town** 2	61
Esh Winning 0 **Flixton** 1 *aet*	53
Pontefract Collieries 3 Garforth Town 2	82
Winterton Rangers 3 Guisborough Town 1	70
Seaham Red Star (w/o) Shotton Comrades (scr.)	
Peterlee Newtown 2 **Retford United** 6	66
Easington Colliery 0 **Armthorpe Welfare** 6	39
Durham City 1 Eccleshill United 0	135
Ramsbottom United 1 **Squires Gate** 3	151
Yorkshire Amateur 0 **Newcastle Blue Star** 3	48
Glasshoughton Welfare 2 Chester-le-Street Town 0	60
Curzon Ashton 0 **Newcastle BBP** 1	87
Parkgate 2 Tadcaster Albion 0	26
Northallerton Town 0 **Sunderland Nissan** 1	64
Boston Town 0 **Nuneaton Griff** 2	70
Teversal 1 Norton United 1 *aet*	69
Malvern Town 4 Long Eaton United 2	99
Pilkington XXX 3 **Pegasus Juniors** 6	66
Causeway United 2 Graham Street Prims 0	75
Gedling Miners Welfare 1 **Alvechurch** 2 *aet*	56
Deeping Rangers 2 Stapenhill 1	63
Tividale 4 Highgate United 1	50
Racing Club Warwick 1 Eccleshall 0	45
Leek CSOB 2 Gornal Athletic 0	87
Studley 0 **Leamington** 1	230
Shifnal Town 4 Coventry Copsewood 0	73
Westfields 2 Stratford Town 1 *aet*	76
Bourne Town 1 **Shirebrook Town** 2	68
Blackstones 1 Dunkirk 0	41
Blaby & Whetstone Athletic 3 Loughborough Dynamo 1	88
St Andrews SC 3 Rolls Royce Leisure 1	23
Mickleover Sports 1 **Pershore Town** 2	84
Ellistown 1 **Castle Vale** 4	30
Kirby Muxloe SC 2 Sandiacre Town 2 *aet*	48
Atherstone Town 4 Ludlow Town 2	184
Friar Lane & Epworth 5 Holwell Sports 1	91
Bolehall Swifts 1 **Buxton** 5	91
Lincoln Moorlands 4 Nettleham 1	90
Biddulph Victoria 3 Brierley & Hagley 0	60
Stowmarket Town 0 **Needham Market** 5	188
Royston Town 0 Whitton United 0 *aet*	79
Southall 2 **Wroxham** 3	50
Ipswich Wanderers 2 Bowers & Pitsea 0	67
Tring Athletic 1 Stotfold 1 *aet*	83
Leiston 3 Ruislip Manor 1	122
Haverhill Rovers 2 **Welwyn Garden City** 4	139
Sawbridgeworth Town 2 Long Buckby 0	39
Tiptree United 2 London APSA 1	68
Buckingham Town 3 Barkingside 1	92
Woodbridge Town 4 Harwich & Parkeston 2	84
Harpenden Town 1 **AFC Wallingford** 2 *aet*	46
Northampton Spencer 3 Cranfield United 0	68
Huntingdon Town 1 **St Margaretsbury** 3 *aet*	53
Brimsdown Rovers 1 **Biggleswade Town** 2	60
London Colney 4 Eynesbury Rovers 1	40
Bedford United & Valerio 0 **Basildon United** 4	15
Hullbridge Sports 3 Cornard United 1	25
Hoddesdon Town 0 **Yaxley** 1	68
Flackwell Heath 1 **Gorleston** 2	65
Ware 1 **Newport Pagnell Town** 3	89
Biggleswade United 1 **Walsham-le-Willows** 2	48
Godmanchester Rovers 1 **St Neots Town** 2	85
Harefield United 2 **Witham Town** 3	71
Wootton Blue Cross 2 Stansted 0	41
Kingsbury Town 3 Saffron Walden Town 1	38
Hertford Town 1 **Dereham Town** 2	99
Camberley Town 2 **Godalming Town** 4	51
Tunbridge Wells 0 Moneyfields 0 *aet*	110
Lymington Town 3 Sidlesham 0	102
Pagham 2 **Hythe Town** 6	55
Oakwood 1 **VCD Athletic** 4	32
Epsom & Ewell 3 Petersfield Town 1	57
Hartley Wintney 1 Alton Town 0	55
Bedfont 1 **Littlehampton Town** 2	47
Greenwich Borough 2 Chertsey Town 0	56
Farnham Town 1 **Wantage Town** 2	36
VTFC 4 Wick 3	56
Bedfont Green 1 Ash United 1 *aet*	37
Cobham 0 **Sevenoaks Town** 2	23
Fareham Town 0 **Ringmer** 1	101
AFC Totton 3 Mole Valley Predators 1	87
Westfield 0 **Hungerford Town** 2	45
Maidstone United 4 Cowes Sports 2	290
East Preston 4 Redhill 1	41
Chichester City United 2 Colliers Wood United 2 *aet*	70
Eastbourne United Assoc 1 **Mile Oak** 3	65
Slimbridge 3 Chipping Norton Town 0	60
Hamworthy United (w/o) v Tuffley Rovers (scr.)	
Amesbury Town 0 **Bishop Sutton** 1	48
Harrow Hill 2 **Penryn Athletic** 5	35
Radstock Town 3 Barnstaple Town 1	79
Odd Down 2 Wadebridge Town 1	37
Westbury United 4 Shaftesbury 0	86
Fairford Town 5 Portland United 0	48
Wellington Town 3 Calne Town 1	68
Budleigh Salterton 1 Falmouth Town 1	91
Downton 1 **Street** 2	77
Truro City 3 Launceston 1	109
Exmouth Town 1 **St Blazey** 4 *aet*	125

FIRST QUALIFYING ROUND REPLAYS

Norton United 1 Teversal 0	58
Sandiacre Town 1 **Kirby Muxloe SC** 2	78
Whitton United 0 **Royston Town** 2	73
Stotford 2 Tring Athletic 0	60
Moneyfields 5 Tunbridge Wells 0	86
Ash United 4 Bedfont Green 0	106
Colliers Wood United 2 Chichester City United 1	30
Falmouth Town 0 **Budleigh Salterton** 1 *aet*	169

SECOND QUALIFYING ROUND

(£600 to each winning club)

Liversedge 1 Bacup Borough 0	102
Glasshoughton Welfare 7 Rossington Main 1	38
Abbey Hey 6 Formby 1	35
Newcastle Blue Star 1 **Seaham Red Star** 2 *(at Seaham Red Star)*	88
Cammell Laird 4 Atherton Collieries 0	74
Winsford United 2 Padiham 1 *aet*	97
Silsden 1 **Ashville** 3	108
Hebburn Town 0 **Prudhoe Town** 2	90
Whickham 5 Chadderton 1	68
Atherton LR 1 Marske United 1 *aet*	71
Sunderland Nissan 4 Whitley Bay 2	43
Washington 1 **West Auckland Town** 2 *aet*	65
Alsager Town 1 **Newcastle BBP** 4 *aet*	81
Nelson 3 Flixton 2	117
Spennymoor Town 1 **Crook Town** 4	255
Oldham Town 3 Winterton Rangers 1	45
Willington 2 **Darwen** 4	56
Norton & Stockton Ancients 2 Sheffield 0	85
Maine Road 2 **Daisy Hill** 3	57

New Mills 1 **Penrith** 2	140
Morpeth Town 1 Salford City 1 *aet*	45
Great Harwood Town 0 **Thornaby** 3	86
Poulton Victoria 1 **Parkgate** 3	49
Durham City 2 **Trafford** 4	148
Shildon 1 Alnwick Town 1 *aet*	139
South Shields 1 **Ashington** 3	105
Pontefract Collieries 2 **Darlington Railway Athletic** 3	100
Consett 5 Worsborough Bridge MW 0	87
Brodsworth Miners Welfare 2 Blackpool Mechanics 0	35
Retford United 4 Holker Old Boys 2	155
Cheadle Town 2 **Armthorpe Welfare** 4	41
Squires Gate 2 Brandon United 1	62
Buxton 2 Lincoln Moorlands 1	208
Sutton Town 0 Nuneaton Griff 0 *aet*	111
Ibstock United 0 **Arnold Town** 1	140
Shawbury United 0 **Glapwell** 4	47
Blackstones 1 **Racing Club Warwick** 2	100
Cradley Town 2 Lye Town 1	89
Highfield Rangers 2 Downes Sports 1 *aet*	31
Causeway United 2 **Kirby Muxloe SC** 3 *aet*	93
Romulus 5 Birstall United 0	65
Pershore Town 0 **Bridgnorth Town** 2	66
Barrow Town 3 Congleton Town 2 *aet*	130
Leamington (w/o) v Radcliffe Olympic (scr.)	
Glossop North End 3 Staveley Miners Welfare 2 *aet*	118
Stone Dominoes (scr.) v **Biddulph Victoria** (w/o)	
Carlton Town 2 Holbrook Miners Welfare 1	63
South Normanton Athletic 2 Wolverhampton Casuals 1	39
Barwell 3 Leek CSOB 2	66
Radford 1 **Pelsall Villa** 2	52
St Andrews SC 5 Blidworth Welfare 1	22
Oadby Town 1 **Friar Lane & Epworth** 3 *aet*	291
Ford Sports Daventry 1 Atherstone Town 0	110
Rainworth Miners Welfare 0 **Deeping Rangers** 1	51
Tividale 1 Borrowash Victoria 1 *aet*	65
Kimberley Town 1 **Alvechurch** 4	42
Blackwell Miners Welfare 0 **Shirebrook Town** 3	155
Norton United 1 Oldbury United 1 *aet*	40
Boldmere St Michaels 4 Meir KA 2	63
Malvern Town 1 **Castle Vale** 3	84
Bromyard Town 2 Heath Hayes 1	35
Barnt Green Spartak 2 **Coleshill Town** 4	26
Dudley Town 1 Anstey Nomads 0	70
Westfields 3 Pegasus Juniors 0	202
Daventry Town 0 **Wellington** 0 *aet* (2-4p)	30
Blaby & Whetstone Athletic 2 **Heanor Town** 5	85
Shifnal Town 0 **Nantwich Town** 1	99
Newark Town 4 Coventry Sphinx 2 *aet*	61
St Neots Town 0 Witham Town 0 *aet*	124
Wembley 0 **Needham Market** 4	56
Kirkley 0 **Dereham Town** 2	232
Sporting Bengal United 1 **Felixstowe & Walton United** 4	85
Biggleswade Town 1 **Tiptree United** 3	41
Downham Town 1 Leverstock Green 1 *aet*	55
Henley Town 3 Ely City 2	52
Stotfold 1 **Gorleston** 4	67
Southend Manor 3 Brentwood Town 0	21
Hullbridge Sports 4 Clacton Town 0	36
Arlesey Athletic 3 **Concord Rangers** 5 *aet*	67
Woodbridge Town 1 **Raunds Town** 4	71
Great Yarmouth Town 0 **Stanway Rovers** 1	99
Thetford Town 1 **Wootton Blue Cross** 4	42
Cockfosters 4 Holmer Green 1	67
St Ives Town 0 **Woodford United** 2	43
Bicester Town 2 Buckingham Town 0	74
Romford 2 Oxhey Jets 0	108
Basildon United 2 Buckingham Athletic 1	31
Newmarket Town 2 Walsham-le-Willows 1	91
Fakenham Town 0 **Newport Pagnell Town** 4	80
Rothwell Corinthians 1 **Welwyn Garden City** 3	49
Sawbridgeworth Town 1 **Chalfont St Peter** 3	34
Langford 0 **Leiston** 3	70
Broxbourne Borough V & E 2 St Margaretsbury 1	43
Royston Town 1 Norwich United 0	70
Bugbrooke St Michaels 0 **Long Melford** 4	45
Wroxham 0 **Yaxley** 2	126
Clapton 1 **Haringey Borough** 2	25
AFC Kempston Rovers 0 **Colney Heath** 3	40
Eton Manor 1 **Kingsbury Town** 4	20
Northampton Spencer 1 **Ipswich Wanderers** 3	66
Dunstable Town '98 1 **Wisbech Town** 7	101
London Colney 2 Hadleigh United 1	56
AFC Wallingford 1 March Town United 0	63
Mildenhall Town 4 Diss Town 0	190
Sevenoaks Town 2 **VTFC** 3 *aet*	65
Selsey 2 Lordswood 2 *aet*	220
Blackfield & Langley 4 **Abingdon Town** 5	55
Hailsham Town 2 **Cove** 5	107
Slade Green 2 East Preston 1	74
United Services Portsmouth 0 **Sidley United** 2	52
Worthing United 0 **Three Bridges** 5	58
Epsom & Ewell 3 Milton United 0	58
Lymington Town 2 **Thamesmead Town** 4	115
Colliers Wood United 3 Raynes Park Vale 0	65
Hamble ASSC 4 Steyning Town 0	68
Eastbourne Town 0 **Maidstone United** 3	324
Merstham 4 Reading Town 0	57
Peacehaven & Telscombe 1 **Godalming Town** 4 *aet*	65
North Leigh 2 Horley Town 0	74
Littlehampton Town 1 Hillingdon Borough 1 *aet*	68
Ardley United 1 **Carterton** 3	58
Mile Oak 2 BAT Sports 0	52
Shoreham 6 AFC Totton 2	72
Hassocks 3 Ash United 1	126
Guildford United 1 **Andover** 5	73
Wantage Town 3 Ringmer 2	81
Abingdon United 4 Sandhurst Town 1	69
Gosport Borough 0 **Greenwich Borough** 1 *aet*	138
Arundel 5 Frimley Green 1	96
Chipstead 1 **Brockenhurst** 2	53
Hartley Wintney 1 Hungerford Town 1 *aet*	65
Hythe Town 2 Moneyfields 1	101
East Grinstead Town 3 Lancing 1	52
Saltdean United 0 **VCD Athletic** 3	43
Erith Town 3 Andover New Street 2	86
Ilfracombe Town 2 **Bournemouth** 4	79
Pewsey Vale 1 Westbury United 0	63
Welton Rovers 5 Sherborne Town 0	72
Porthleven 0 **St Blazey** 3	197
Chard Town 4 Melksham Town 1	78
Saltash United 1 **Clevedon United** 2 *aet*	51
Devizes Town 1 Penzance 0	43
Budleigh Salterton 0 **Witney United** 6	86
Willand Rovers 4 Elmore 1	112
Wimborne Town 3 Shepton Mallet 0	213
Shortwood United 5 Cullompton Rangers 0	64
Odd Down 3 Bridport 0	29
Torrington 0 **Truro City** 4	101
Larkhall Athletic 1 **Poole Town** 4	115
Liskeard Athletic 1 **Bemerton Heath Harlequins** 4	83
Bristol Manor Farm 2 Minehead Town 1	37
Fairford Town 1 **Radstock Town** 2 *aet*	45
Wootton Bassett Town 1 Christchurch 1 *aet*	65
Millbrook 2 **Newton Abbot** 3	45
Ottery St Mary 2 **Tavistock** 5	61
Wellington Town 1 Ringwood Town 0	35
Penryn Athletic 2 Hamworthy United 1 *aet*	121
Newquay 1 **Street** 2	120
Malmesbury Victoria 0 **Slimbridge** 2	40
Almondsbury Town 0 **Dawlish Town** 1	56
Bishop Sutton 0 **Hallen** 2	43

SECOND QUALIFYING ROUND REPLAYS

Marske United 4 Atherton LR 2	168
Salford City 5 Morpeth Town 0	116
Alnwick Town 5 Shildon 2	89

Nuneaton Griff 0 **Sutton Town** 0 *aet* (4-1p)	160
Borrowash Victoria 4 Tividale 0	71
Oldbury United 2 Norton United 0	48
Witham Town 4 St Neots Town 2	96
Leverstock Green 5 Downham Town 1	56
Lordswood 0 **Selsey** 2	106
Hillingdon Borough 3 Littlehampton Town 1	73
Hungerford Town 2 Hartley Wintney 1	65
Christchurch 1 Wootton Bassett Town 0	81

FIRST ROUND

(£700 to each winning club)

Trafford 1 Prudhoe Town 0	138
Darlington Railway Ath 2 Dunston Fed'tion Brewery 2 *aet*	290
Armthorpe Welfare 0 **Norton & Stockton Ancients** 1	52
Sunderland Nissan 1 Abbey Hey 0	42
Daisy Hill 0 **Nelson** 1	46
Newcastle BBP 3 Whickham 1	97
Ashington 3 Thornaby 3 *aet*	151
Consett 0 **Cammell Laird** 1	176
Alnwick Town 1 **Glasshoughton Welfare** 3	66
Ashville 3 Penrith 1 *aet*	130
Crook Town 2 Winsford United 0	106
Squires Gate 3 Salford City 0	66
Marske United 2 **St Helens Town** 3	138
Retford United 4 Brodsworth Miners Welfare 0	180
Darwen 2 **Harrogate Railway Athletic** 4	102
Oldham Town 3 Seaham Red Star 1	40
West Auckland Town 0 **Billingham Synthonia** 2	88
Parkgate 3 Liversedge 3 *aet*	72
Wellington 0 **Alvechurch** 1	122
Holbeach United 0 **Leamington** 2	269
Biddulph Victoria 2 Castle Vale 1	76
Oldbury United 0 **Coleshill Town** 4	56
Barrow Town 4 Borrowash Victoria 3 *aet*	130
Ford Sports Daventry 2 Sutton Town 1	45
Selby Town 3 South Normanton Athletic 1	85
Deeping Rangers 0 **Buxton** 4	165
Coalville Town 7 Dudley Town 0	160
Westfields 1 Bridgnorth Town 0	64
Nantwich Town 1 Boldmere St Michaels 0	123
Heanor Town 0 **Arnold Town** 2	190
Cradley Town 4 Newark Town 2	53
Rocester 0 **Carlton Town** 2	66
Racing Club Warwick 1 Barwell 0	131
Glossop North End 6 Romulus 4	118
Friar Lane & Epworth 5 Shirebrook Town 1	229
Newcastle Town 3 Glapwell 2	101
Highfield Rangers 2 St Andrews SC 0	48
Bromyard Town 0 **Chasetown** 1	72
Kirby Muxloe 0 **Pelsall Villa** 2	72
Cockfosters 0 **Ipswich Wanderers** 3	91
Tilbury 2 Burnham Ramblers 1	71
Felixstowe & Walton United 3 Chalfont St Peter 3 *aet*	134
Wootton Blue Cross 2 Royston Town 1	64
Leiston 3 Henley Town 2	133
Long Melford 1 **Newmarket Town** 2	97
Stanway Rovers 4 Basildon United 3	75
Newport Pagnell Town 0 **Romford** 1	235
London Colney 5 Tiptree United 3 *aet*	60
Hullbridge Sports 0 **Mildenhall Town** 8	74
Yaxley 8 Southend Manor 1	93
AFC Wallingford 1 **Wisbech Town** 4	99
Hanwell Town 4 Colney Heath 1	53
Kingsbury Town 2 Haringey Borough 0	28
Woodford United 3 **Broxbourne Borough V & E** 4	48
Oxford City 1 **Welwyn Garden City** 3	162
Witham Town 5 Waltham Abbey 3	131
Aylesbury Vale 1 **Bicester Town** 2	89
Cogenhoe United 0 **AFC Hornchurch** 1	180
Gorleston 1 Raunds Town 0	106
Concord Rangers 2 Halstead Town 0 *aet*	51
Leverstock Green 3 North Greenford United 1	56
Needham Market 1 Dereham Town 0	122
VTFC 1 **Hythe Town** 2	95
Thatcham Town 4 Selsey 2 *aet*	108
Mile Oak 0 Slade Green 0 *aet*	72
Greenwich Borough 1 **Colliers Wood United** 3	21
Sidley United 3 Shoreham 0	97
Arundel 4 Croydon 2	103
Abingdon Town 0 **Egham Town** 2	84
Carterton 1 Hungerford Town 0	42
Merstham 1 **Three Bridges** 2	106
Erith Town 2 Whitehawk 0	30
Godalming Town 1 **Hassocks** 4	102
Brockenhurst 2 Abingdon United 1	51
Chessington & Hook United 1 Horsham YMCA 0	101
Herne Bay 4 Epsom & Ewell 2 *aet*	145
East Grinstead Town 3 **Rye & Iden United** 5	95
Erith & Belvedere 1 **Hillingdon Borough** 5	82
Wantage Town 1 **Thamesmead Town** 3	52
Dorking 4 Hamble ASSC 1	131
North Leigh 0 **Maidstone United** 4	276
Cove 0 **VCD Athletic** 2	72
Whitstable Town 1 **Andover** 3	180
Chard Town 1 Dawlish Town 1 *aet*	89
Poole Town 1 **Bideford** 2	226
Devizes Town 0 Pewsey Vale 0 *aet*	164
Shortwood United 0 **Bishops Cleeve** 3	70
Bristol Manor Farm 2 **Highworth Town** 3	43
Newton Abbot 1 Corsham Town 0	106
Street 0 **Christchurch** 2	78
Truro City 3 Witney United 1	235
Tavistock 3 Penryn Athletic 0	90
Bournemouth 4 Odd Down 1	69
Clevedon United 2 **St Blazey** 4 *aet*	194
Wimborne Town 3 Radstock Town 1	244
Hallen 0 **Slimbridge** 1	49
Wellington Town 1 **Bemerton Heath Harlequins** 2	45
Welton Rovers 2 **Willand Rovers** 3 *aet*	88

FIRST ROUND REPLAYS

Dunston Federation Brewery 3 Darlington Railway Ath 0	167
Thornaby 4 Ashington 3	105
Liversedge 3 Parkgate 0	117
Chalfont St Peter 2 Felixstowe & Walton United 1	84
Slade Green 1 **Mile Oak** 4	67
Dawlish Town 3 Chard Town 2 *aet*	77
Pewsey Vale 1 **Devizes Town** 1 *aet* (0-3p)	142

SECOND ROUND

(£1,000 to each winning club)

Glasshoughton Welfare 1 **Squires Gate** 2	75
Pickering Town 1 Oldham Town 0 *aet*	115
Nelson 0 **Ashville** 1	110
Sunderland Nissan 3 Bedlington Terriers 3 *aet*	94
Thackley 3 Jarrow Roofing Boldon CA 0	67
Liversedge 5 Billingham Synthonia 4 *aet*	144
Colne 4 Norton & Stockton Ancients 0	127
Crook Town 4 Billingham Town 0	161
Harrogate Railway Athletic 0 **Cammell Laird** 1	124
Newcastle BBP 5 Thornaby 1	65
St Helens Town 1 **Dunston Federation Brewery** 3	84
Skelmersdale United 4 West Allotment Celtic 3	141
Retford United 2 Trafford 1	249
Selby Town 3 Westfields 3 *aet*	65
Barrow Town 1 **Quorn** 3	420
Arnold Town 2 Pelsall Villa 0	108
Newcastle Town 1 Cradley Town 0	96
Tipton Town 0 **Racing Club Warwick** 2	80
Biddulph Victoria 1 **Leamington** 2	86
Highfield Rangers 2 **Gedling Town** 3	37
Ford Sports Daventry 4 Coleshill Town 2	40
Friar Lane & Epworth 1 **Stourbridge** 5	208
Glossop North End 3 **Carlton Town** 4	106
Desborough Town 0 **Coalville Town** 1	108

Buxton 4 Alvechurch 0	246
Chasetown 0 **Nantwich Town** 1	284
Stanway Rovers 5 Broxbourne Borough V & E 5 *aet*	65
London Colney 6 Ipswich Wanderers 3	55
AFC Hornchurch 1 **Soham Town Rangers** 3	469
Lowestoft Town 2 Wootton Blue Cross 0	240
Gorleston 0 Mildenhall Town 0 *aet*	112
Leverstock Green 0 **Chalfont St Peter** 2	74
Needham Market 3 Potton United 1	122
Newmarket Town 2 Tilbury 1 *aet*	93
Concord Rangers 1 **Welwyn Garden City** 2 *aet*	61
Wisbech Town 8 Leiston 1	330
Yaxley 3 Witham Town 0	126
AFC Sudbury 4 Romford 0	331
Bury Town 3 Hanwell Town 0	148
Colliers Wood United 2 **VCD Athletic** 3	63
Sidley United 4 Erith Town 2	92
Chessington & Hook United 2 Carterton 0	81
Mile Oak 1 **Deal Town** 3 *aet*	107
Bicester Town 0 **Dorking** 1	52
Maidstone United 4 Andover 0	423
Thamesmead Town 0 **Brook House** 4	63
Rye & Iden United 2 Hillingdon Borough 2 *aet*	86
Three Bridges 0 **Arundel** 1	92
Winchester City 5 AFC Newbury 0	184
Hythe Town 3 Thatcham Town 2	130
Didcot Town 7 Herne Bay 0	340
Brockenhurst 2 Egham Town 2 *aet*	70
Kingsbury Town 1 Hassocks 0	37
Bishops Cleeve 3 Newton Abbot 0	65
Highworth Town 0 **Wimborne Town** 1	138
Bournemouth 1 Frome Town 0 *aet*	101
Bridgwater Town 0 **Slimbridge** 1	189
Devizes Town 2 Brislington 1	54
Bodmin Town 3 Bitton 0	190
Christchurch 3 Truro City 2	142
Dawlish Town 1 Bideford 2 *aet*	162
Ledbury Town 0 **Willand Rovers** 4	72
Bemerton Heath Harlequins 2 **St Blazey** 3	134
Tavistock 4 Backwell United 2 *aet*	60

SECOND ROUND REPLAYS

Bedlington Terriers 2 Sunderland Nissan 1	121
Westfields 2 **Selby Town** 3 *aet*	28
Broxbourne Borough V & E 3 Stanway Rovers 0	41
Mildenhall Town 2 Gorleston 0	123
Hillingdon Borough 1 Rye & Iden United 0	62
Egham Town 0 **Brockenhurst** 1	45

THIRD ROUND

(£1,200 to each winning club)

Ashville 3 Racing Club Warwick 3 *aet*	160
Squires Gate 2 Skelmersdale United 1	102
Coalville Town 3 Arnold Town 3 *aet*	102
Thackley 2 Colne 1	200
Gedling Town 4 Carlton Town 3	50
Pickering Town 1 Dunston Federation Brewery 0	131
Crook Town 8 Ford Sports Daventry 2	179
Quorn 0 **Nantwich Town** 1	182
Cammell Laird 3 Retford United 0	122
Newcastle BBP 2 Stourbridge 1	82
Newcastle Town 1 **Bedlington Terriers** 3	151
Leamington 2 Liversedge 1	518
Selby Town 0 **Buxton** 1	144
Hythe Town 2 Chalfont St Peter 1	202
Needham Market 3 Devizes Town 0	120
Maidstone United 2 Broxbourne Borough V & E 2 *aet*	411
Hillingdon Borough 2 Bideford 1	91
Yaxley 2 **Winchester City** 4	212
Arundel 1 **VCD Athletic** 2	188
Soham Town Rangers 1 **Bury Town** 2	202
AFC Sudbury 3 Bodmin Town 1	331
Lowestoft Town 2 Kingsbury Town 0	265
Sidley United 1 **St Blazey** 2	146
Wisbech Town 4 Brook House 4 *aet*	371
London Colney 1 **Chessington & Hook United** 2	85
Deal Town 2 **Tavistock** 4	148
Wimborne Town 4 Bishops Cleeve 1	287
Dorking 5 Christchurch 2	164
Welwyn Garden City 3 Slimbridge 1	93
Bournemouth 1 **Brockenhurst** 2	83
Newmarket Town 1 Willand Rovers 0	105
Didcot Town 4 Mildenhall Town 4 *aet*	352

THIRD ROUND REPLAYS

Racing Club Warwick 2 **Ashville** 2 *aet* (2-4p)	125
Arnold Town 3 Coalville Town 0	124
Broxbourne Borough V&E 3 Maidstone U 3 *aet* (5-4p)	153
Brook House 2 Wisbech Town 0	155
Mildenhall Town 2 Didcot Town 1	320

FOURTH ROUND

(£1,500 to each winning club)

Crook Town 3 St Blazey 0	494
Pickering Town 3 Tavistock 0	290
Leamington 2 **Wimborne Town** 3	746
Needham Market 3 **Nantwich Town** 6 *aet*	223
Thackley 0 **Arnold Town** 2	216
Dorking 1 **Mildenhall Town** 3	449
Newcastle BBP 3 Lowestoft Town 1	239
VCD Athletic 1 Broxbourne Borough V & E 0	257
Chessington & Hook United 1 **Cammell Laird** 2	393
Buxton 1 Ashville 0	572
Brockenhurst 0 **Bury Town** 2	195
Newmarket Town 2 Welwyn Garden City 2 *aet*	284
Hillingdon Borough 2 Brook House 0	259
Squires Gate 2 Gedling Town 1 *aet*	75
Hythe Town 1 **Winchester City** 3	441
AFC Sudbury 1 Bedlington Terriers 1 *aet*	611

FOURTH ROUND REPLAYS

Welwyn Garden City 2 **Newmarket Town** 1 *aet*	353
(Welwyn Garden City expelled)	
Bedlington Terriers 1 **AFC Sudbury** 3	434

FIFTH ROUND

(£2,000 to each winning club)

AFC Sudbury 0 **Bury Town** 2	1,016
Wimborne Town 1 **Pickering Town** 2	983
Nantwich Town 1 Buxton 0	987
Cammell Laird 1 VCD Athletic 0	283
Hillingdon Borough 4 Mildenhall Town 0	233
Arnold Town 0 **Crook Town** 1	560
Winchester City 3 **Newmarket Town** 4 *aet*	533
Squires Gate 2 Newcastle BBP 1	146

QUARTER-FINALS

(£4,000 to each winning club)

Hillingdon Borough 2 Squires Gate 0	428
Crook Town 0 **Bury Town** 1	1,946
Nantwich Town 2 Pickering Town 0	700
Newmarket Town 0 **Cammell Laird** 1	750

SEMI-FINALS

(£6,000 to each winning club)

(1st leg)

Bury Town 1 Hillingdon Borough 1	1,773
Cammell Laird 0 Nantwich Town 1	525

(2nd leg)

Hillingdon Borough 2 Bury Town 1 *aet*	723
Nantwich Town 4 Cammell Laird 0	1,320

FINAL

(£15,000 to winning club)

(May 6th at Birmingham City)

Nantwich Town 3 Hillingdon Borough 1	3,286

WELSH CUP

FIRST ROUND

Afan Lido 0 **West End** 3
AFC Llwydcoed 5 Blaenrhondda 0
AFC Porth 0 **Pontyclun** 1
Bethesda Athletic 1 **Mynydd Isa** 5
Bridgend Town 1 **UWIC** 4
Briton Ferry Athletic 5 Llantwit Fadre 2
Buckley Town 4 Flint Town United 2
Caerleon 5 **Bettws** 6 *aet*
Caerwys 0 **Llanrwst United** 2
Caldicot Town 4 Porthcawl Town 0
Cefn United 0 **Connah's Quay Nomads** 2
Chirk AAA 3 Brynteg Village 2
Coedpoeth United 0 **Caernarfon Town** 3
Conwy United (w/o) v Y Felinheli (scr.)
Corwen 0 **Glantraeth** 6
Croesyceiliog 2 Garden Village 1
Cwmbran Celtic 2 **Ystradgynlais** 4
Denbigh Town 1 **Prestatyn Town** 4
Dinas Powys 0 **Port Talbot Town** 2
Ely Rangers 4 Cambrian & Clydach Boys & Girls Club 2 *aet*
Ento Aberaman 2 Barry Town 0
Garw Athletic 0 **Taffs Well** 3
Glan Conwy 0 **Bala Town** 3
Goytre United 7 Llanwern 1
Grange Harlequins 2 Penrhiwceiber Rangers 0 *aet*
Gresford Athletic 2 Bodedern 1
Hawarden Rangers 2 **Mold Alexandra** 3
Holywell Town 0 **NEWI Cefn Druids** 1
Knighton Town 0 **Penrhyncoch** 4
Llandudno Junction 0 **Airbus UK** 3
Llandyrnog United 3 Llanrhaeadr YM Mochnant 2
Llanfairpwll 1 **Llangefni Town** 3
Llanfyllin Town 2 Carno 1
Llangollen Town 0 **Llanberis** 2
Llanidloes Town 0 **Guilsfield** 7
Llanrug United 2 **Llandudno** 6
Maesteg Park Athletic 7 Ammanford 0
Morriston Town 0 **Bryntirion Athletic** 1
Neath Athletic 0 **Llanelli** 1
Nefyn United 1 Halkyn United 0
Newcastle Emlyn 1 **Cardiff Corinthians** 6
Newport YMCA 2 Caerau Ely 1
Penmaenmawr Phoenix 1 **Summerhill Brymbo** 1 *aet* (4-5p)
Penrhiwfer 2 **Risca United** 4
Pontypridd Town 3 Pontardawe Town 2
Presteigne St Andrews (w/o) v Meifod (disqualified)
Rhayader Town 5 Four Crosses 1
Rhydymwyn 0 **Holyhead Hotspur** 6
Ruthin Town 3 **Lex XI** 4
Sealand Rovers 3 Rhos Aelwyd 2
Tredegar Town 0 **Ton Pentre** 4
Treharris Athletic 4 Goytre 2
Troedyrhiw 3 Treowen Stars 0 *aet*

SECOND ROUND

Aberystwyth Town 2 Bettws 0
Airbus UK 4 Conwy United 1
Bala Town 3 Penrhyncoch 2 *aet*
Bangor City 4 Llanberis 0
Caersws 5 Grange Harlequins 3
Caldicot Town 1 **Cwmbran Town** 3
Cardiff Corinthians 0 **Carmarthen Town** 11
Chirk AAA 1 **Nefyn United** 2
Croesyceiliog 3 West End 2
Ento Aberaman 0 **Briton Ferry Athletic** 1
Glantraeth 6 Guilsfield 1
Gresford Athletic 1 **Porthmadog** 2
Haverfordwest County 1 **Goytre United** 2
Holyhead Hotspur 1 **Caernarfon Town** 3
Lex XI 4 Connah's Quay Nomads 2 *aet*
Llanelli 8 Risca United 2
Llanfyllin Town 1 **Buckley Town** 3
Llanrwst United 3 Llandudno 2
Mold Alexandra 4 Mynydd Isa 3
Newtown 5 Llandyrnog United 1
Pontyclun 2 Maesteg Park Athletic 1 *aet*
Pontypridd Town 2 Ton Pentre 2 *aet* (7-6p)
Port Talbot Town 3 Newport YMCA 2
Presteigne St Andrews 2 **Prestatyn Town** 4 *aet*
Rhayader Town 2 **Llangefni Town** 4
Rhyl 4 Sealand Rovers 0
Summerhill Brymbo 2 **NEWI Cefn Druids** 3 *aet*
Total Network Solutions 4 Welshpool Town 1
Treharris Athletic 1 **Ely Rangers** 3
Troedyrhiw 3 Taffs Well 2 *aet*
UWIC 2 AFC Llwydcoed 1
Ystradgynlais 2 **Bryntirion Athletic** 3

THIRD ROUND

Bala Town 4 Buckley Town 3 *aet*
Bangor City 4 Airbus UK 2
Caersws 3 Croesyceiliog 1
Carmarthen Town 4 Briton Ferry Athletic 0
Ely Rangers 1 **Cwmbran Town** 4
Glantraeth 2 **Rhyl** 5
Goytre United 6 Troedyrhiw 3
Llangefni Town 3 Llanrwst United 0
Mold Alexandra 0 **Prestatyn Town** 5
NEWI Cefn Druids 3 Nefyn United 1
Newtown 6 Pontyclun 0
Pontypridd Town 1 Aberystwyth Town 0 *aet*
Port Talbot Town 3 Bryntirion Athletic 0
Porthmadog 0 **Caernarfon Town** 3
Total Network Solutions 4 Lex XI 0
UWIC 1 **Llanelli** 3

FOURTH ROUND

Bangor City 2 Newtown 1
Caernarfon Town 4 Bala Town 0
Caersws 1 **Llangefni Town** 3
Cwmbran Town 1 **Port Talbot Town** 3
Llanelli 1 Total Network Solutions 0
NEWI Cefn Druids 3 **Rhyl** 5
Pontypridd Town 0 **Goytre United** 5
Prestatyn Town 1 **Carmarthen Town** 2

QUARTER-FINALS

Bangor City 1 Carmarthen Town 0
Llanelli 3 Caernarfon Town 0
Port Talbot Town 3 Llangefni Town 0
Rhyl 5 Goytre United 2

SEMI-FINALS

(both at Aberystwyth Town)
Llanelli 0 **Bangor City** 1
Rhyl 2 Port Talbot Town 2 *aet* (5-4p)

FINAL *(at Wrexham)*

Bangor City 0 **Rhyl** 2

F A W PREMIER CUP

(Top ten placed clubs from the Welsh Premier League along with the two best placed 'exiled' clubs (*Merthyr Tydfil* and *Newport County*), the Welsh Cup winners plus the three English League clubs (*Cardiff City*, *Swansea City* and *Wrexham*); *Porthmadog* qualified despite finishing 11th in the Welsh Premier as *Total Network Solutions* finished in the top ten (indeed were champions) and won the Welsh Cup)

FIRST ROUND

(£3,500 to each losing club)

Caersws 5 Aberystwyth Town 1 ***Att*** 182

Cwmbran Town 1 Merthyr Tydfil 0 ***Att*** 450

Porthmadog 1 **Carmarthen Town** 2 *aet* ***Att*** 225

Welshpool Town 0 **Newtown** 2 ***Att*** 135

SECOND ROUND

(£6,000 to each losing club)

Bangor City 1 **Carmarthen Town** 2 ***Att*** 250

Newport County 1 Caersws 0 ***Att*** 258

Newtown 2 Haverfordwest County 1 ***Att*** n/k

Rhyl 1 Cwmbran Town 0 ***Att*** 267

QUARTER-FINALS

(£15,000 to each losing club)

Carmarthen Town 2 Cardiff City 1 ***Att*** 952

Newport County 0 **Wrexham** 2 ***Att*** 442

Newtown 2 **Total Network Solutions** 5 ***Att*** 180

Rhyl 0 **Swansea City** 1 ***Att*** 860

SEMI-FINALS

(£25,000 to each losing club)

Carmarthen Town 2 **Swansea City** 3 *aet* ***Att*** 1900

Wrexham 3 Total Network Solutions 3 *aet* (5-4p) ***Att*** 1161

FINAL

(£100,000 to winning club, £50,000 to runners-up)

(29th March at Wrexham)

Wrexham 1 **Swansea City** 2 ***Att*** 3032

WELSH TROPHY

FIRST ROUND

Abercwmboi 4 Ynysddu Welfare Crusaders 3
Baglan Red Dragons (w/o) Cardiff Cosmos Portos (scr.)
Barry 1 **Ragged School** 6
Blaengwawr Inn 1 **West End** 9
Brickfield Rangers 3 Corwen 2
Brynteg Village 5 **Llangollen Town** 6
Cefn United 4 Glyn Ceiriog 1
Clydach Wasps 0 **Cwmbach Royal Stars** 2
Coedpoeth United 1 Glan Conwy 0
Cogan Coronation 6 Trelewis Welfare 1
Conwy United 4 Nefyn United 3
Cwmaman Institute 4 Llangeinor 2
Denbigh Town 3 Prestatyn Town 1
Four Crosses 2 Llanfyllin Town 1
Kenfig Hill 2 **Abertillery Excelsior** 3
Knighton Town 1 **Berriew** 4
Lisvane/Llanishen 3 Llanharry 2
Llandrindod Wells 5 Carno 0
Llandudno Junction 2 Mold Alexandra 1
Llanrhaeadr YM Mochnant 4 Llanidloes Town 0
Llanrug United 3 Mynydd Isa 2
Llanrumney United 20 ***(twenty)*** Bluestars 0
Maltsters Sports 6 Tongwynlais 4
Osborne Athletic 2 Bonymaen Colts 1
Rhayader Town 3 **Kerry** 3 *aet* (4-5p)
Rhos Aelwyd 0 **Rhydymwyn** 1 *aet*
Sealand Rovers 1 Hawarden Rangers 1 *aet* (4-3p)
South Gower 3 AFC Llwynypia 1
Summerhill Broughton 2 **Caerwys** 6 *aet*
Ton and Gelli Boys Club 1 **Corus Steel** 5
Waterloo Rovers 3 Chirk AAA 2
Y Felinheli 1 **Penycae** 3

SECOND ROUND

Abercwmboi 0 **Cwmbach Royal Stars** 3
Baglan Red Dragons 1 **Cogan Coronation** 2
Berriew 0 **Llanrhaeadr YM Mochnant** 2
Caerwys 5 Llangollen Town 2
Coedpoeth United 1 Llanrug United 0
Conwy United 1 Brickfield Rangers 0
Corus Steel 4 Llanrumney United 2
Cwmaman Institute 2 **Osborne Athletic** 4 *aet*
Kerry 3 Waterloo Rovers 2
Llandrindod Wells 7 Four Crosses 3 *aet*
Maltsters Sports 3 Abertillery Excelsior 2
Penycae 1 **Cefn United** 3
Rhydymwyn 2 Denbigh Town 1
Sealand Rovers 2 **Llandudno Junction** 3
South Gower 1 Lisvane/Llanishen 1 *aet* (5-4p)
West End 2 Ragged School 1

THIRD ROUND

Caerwys 3 **Rhydymwyn** 7 *aet*
Cefn United 3 Conwy United 2 *aet*
Corus Steel 0 **Cwmbach Royal Stars** 2
Kerry 3 Llanrhaeadr YM Mochnant 1
Llandudno Junction 6 Coedpoeth United 3 *aet*
Maltsters Sports 2 Osborne Athletic 1
South Gower 0 **Cogan Coronation** 1
West End 3 Llandrindod Wells 0

QUARTER-FINALS

Cefn United 1 Kerry 1 *aet* (5-4p)
Llandudno Junction 2 Rhydymwyn 0
Maltsters Sports 2 Cwmbach Royal Stars 1
West End 2 Cogan Coronation 2 *aet* (5-4p)

SEMI-FINALS

Cefn United 4 Maltsters Sports 1
(at Rhayader Town)
West End 3 Llandudno Junction 0
(at Newtown)

FINAL

(18th March at Caersws)
Cefn United 2 **West End** 4

MAJOR COUNTY CUP FINALS

BEDFORDSHIRE PREMIER CUP
(May 11th at Arlesey Town)
Biggleswade United 1 Leighton Town 0

BERKS & BUCKS SENIOR CUP
(May 1st at Wycombe Wanderers)
Wycombe Wanderers 2 Milton Keynes Dons 1

BIRMINGHAM SENIOR CUP
(April 25th at Willenhall Town)
Willenhall Town 1 Stourbridge 0

CAMBRIDGESHIRE INVITATION CUP
(April 11th at Cambridge United)
Great Shelford 0 **Soham Town Rangers** 1

CHESHIRE SENIOR CUP
(March 14th at Altrincham)
Stalybridge Celtic 0 **Witton Albion** 2

CORNWALL SENIOR CUP
(April 17th at St Blazey)
Bodmin Town 1 **Truro City** 4

CUMBERLAND SENIOR CUP
(May 9th at Workington)
Penrith 1 Carlisle City 0

DERBYSHIRE SENIOR CUP
1st leg *(April 4th):*
Mickleover Sports 1 Ilkeston Town 1
2nd leg *(May 2nd):*
Ilkeston Town 1 Mickleover Sports 0

DEVON St LUKES COLLEGE BOWL
(May 1st at Barnstaple Town)
Barnstaple Town 1 **Tiverton Town** 2 *aet*

DORSET SENIOR CUP
(April 19th at Wimborne Town)
Poole Town 1 **Hamworthy United** 2

DURHAM CHALLENGE CUP
(April 14th at Durham City)
Whickham 2 Billingham Synthonia 1

EAST RIDING SENIOR CUP
(April 24th at Hull City)
Hull City 2 **Sculcoates Amateurs** 2 *aet* (2-3p)

ESSEX SENIOR CUP
(March 28th at Southend United)
Waltham Forest (w/o) v Chelmsford City/Braintree Tn (scr.)

GLOUCESTERSHIRE SENIOR CUP
(April 26th at Yate Town)
Yate Town 2 Cheltenham Town 0

HAMPSHIRE SENIOR CUP
(April 24th at AFC Bournemouth)
Farnborough Town 1 Basingstoke Town 0

HEREFORDSHIRE CHALLENGE CUP
(May 3rd at Pegasus Juniors)
Hinton 0 **Westfields** 1 *aet*

HERTFORDSHIRE SENIOR CUP
(April 4th at HCFA, Letchworth)
Stevenage Borough 0 **Bishop's Stortford** 1

HUNTINGDONSHIRE SENIOR CUP
(May 1st at Somersham Town)
Ortonians 1 St Neots Town 0

KENT SENIOR CUP
(April 27th at Bromley)
Bromley 3 Gravesend & Northfleet 2 *aet*

LANCASHIRE TROPHY
(April 4th at LCFA, Leyland)
Southport 1 Lancaster City 0

LEICESTERSHIRE CHALLENGE CUP
(May 9th at Leicester City)
Leicester City 3 Coalville Town 2 *aet*

LINCOLNSHIRE SHIELD
(May 2nd at Brigg Town)
Brigg Town 0 **Lincoln United** 1

LIVERPOOL SENIOR CUP
(July 22nd at Marine)
Marine v Tranmere Rovers

LONDON SENIOR CUP
(April 25th at Tooting & Mitcham United)
Hendon 2 **Fisher Athletic** 3

MANCHESTER PREMIER CUP
(March 29th at Sportcity Athletics Arena)
Hyde United 2 Droylsden 1

MIDDLESEX SENIOR CUP
(April 17th at Harrow Borough)
Hayes 0 **Hampton & Richmond Borough** 0 *aet* (3-4p)

NORFOLK SENIOR CUP
(May 19th at Norwich City)
Dereham Town 1 Norwich United 0

NORTH RIDING SENIOR CUP 2004-05
(August 3rd at Whitby Town)
Whitby Town 3 Middlesbrough 0

NORTH RIDING SENIOR CUP
(May 2nd at York City)
York City 3 Northallerton Town 1

NORTHAMPTONSHIRE SENIOR CUP
(April 11th at Northampton Spencer)
Northampton Spencer 1 Corby Town 0

NORTHUMBERLAND SENIOR CUP
(May 3rd at Newcastle Blue Star)
Blyth Spartans 1 **Newcastle United Res.** 2

NOTTINGHAMSHIRE SENIOR CUP
(April 26th at Notts County)
Eastwood Town 3 Sutton Town 1

OXFORDSHIRE SENIOR CUP
(April 25th at Oxford United)
Carterton 0 **Banbury United** 3

SHEFFIELD & HALLAMSHIRE SENIOR CUP
(May 2nd at Sheffield Wednesday)
Sheffield 2 Parkgate 1

SHROPSHIRE SENIOR CUP
(July 29th at Shrewsbury Town)
Shrewsbury Town 4 AFC Telford United 1

SOMERSET PREMIER CUP
(April 25th at Weston-super-Mare)
Taunton Town 3 Mangotsfield United 2

STAFFORDSHIRE SENIOR CUP
(April 26th at Stoke City)
Stoke City 0 **Rushall Olympic** 1

SUFFOLK PREMIER CUP
(May 5th at Ipswich Town)
Lowestoft Town 3 Leiston 2 *aet*

SURREY SENIOR CUP
(May 12th at Woking)
AFC Wimbledon 0 **Kingstonian** 1

SUSSEX SENIOR CUP
(May 1st at Eastbourne Borough)
Horsham 1 **Lewes** 3 *aet*

WEST RIDING COUNTY CUP
(April 12th at WRCFA, Woodlesford)
Harrogate Town 1 **Farsley Celtic** 2

WESTMORLAND SENIOR CUP
(April 22nd at Kendal Town)
Kendal County 2 Windermere SC 1

WILTSHIRE PREMIER SHIELD
(April 9th at Salisbury City)
Salisbury City 0 **Chippenham Town** 1

WORCESTERSHIRE SENIOR CUP
1st leg *(April 11th)*
Moor Green 4 Halesowen Town 1
2nd leg *(April 25th)*
Halesowen Town 1 **Moor Green** 1

OTHER COUNTY & DISTRICT CUP FINALS

A F A GREENLAND CUP
(September 17th at Polytechnic)
Winchmore Hill 2 Old Meadonians 0

A F A INTERMEDIATE CUP
(March 25th at Old Actonians Association)
Civil Service Res. 0 **Mill Hill Village** 4

A F A JUNIOR CUP
(March 18th at Weirside Rangers)
Winchmore Hill 'A' 3 **Civil Service 'A'** 3 *aet* (3-4p)

A F A MINOR CUP
(March 25th at Winchmore Hill)
Old Haileyburians 2 **Old Actonians Association 'B'** 2 *aet* (4-5p)

A F A MIDDLESEX/ESSEX SENIOR CUP
(March 25th at Old Parkonians)
Broomfield 0 **Old Meadonians** 5

A F A MIDDLESEX/ESSEX INTERMEDIATE CUP
(April 1st at Polytechnic)
Old Meadonians Res. 3 Old Actonians Association Res. 1

A F A SURREY/KENT SENIOR CUP
(March 25th at Carshalton)
Clapham Old Xaverians 2 Old Salesians 0 *aet*

A F A SURREY/KENT INTERMEDIATE CUP
(April 1st at Bank of England)
Dresdner Kleinwort Wasserstein 3 Marsh 1

A F A SENIOR NOVETS CUP
(March 18th at Phoenix Old Boys)
Civil Service 'C' 1 **National Westminster Bank 'A'** 2

A F A INTERMEDIATE NOVETS CUP
(April 22nd at Polytechnic)
Old Meadonians 'D' 1 **Old Actonians Association 'D'** 3

A F A JUNIOR NOVETS CUP
(March 18th at Alleyn Old Boys)
Old Actonians Association 'E' 3 Old Meadonians 'F' 0

ALDERSHOT SENIOR CUP
(April 22nd at Aldershot Town)
Badshot Lea 0 **Sandhurst Town** 0 *aet* (5-6p)

ANCASTER CUP
(May 12th at Bourne Town)
Bourne Town Res. 3 Stamford Belvedere 0

ARTHUR DUNN CUP
(April 1st at Imperial College)
Old Carthusians 2 Old Westminsters 0

AXMINSTER HOSPITAL CUP
(April 23rd at Axminster Town)
Budleigh Salterton 1 Chard Town 0 *aet*

BARRITT CUP
(May 6th at Bangor City)
Rhyl Res. 0 **Denbigh Town** 1

BASINGSTOKE SENIOR CUP
(May 10th at Thatcham Town)
Fleet Town 2 Andover 0

BASS VASE
(August 4th at Burton Albion)
Burton Albion 1 **Notts County** 2

BEDFORDSHIRE SENIOR TROPHY
(April 25th at Stotfold)
Brache Sparta 1 Kent Athletic 0

BEDFORDSHIRE INTERMEDIATE CUP
(March 29th at Langford)
AFC Kempston Town 2 **Biggleswade United Res.** 3

BEDFORDSHIRE JUNIOR CUP
(April 21st at Cranfield United)
Henlow Italians 1 Club Lewsey 0

BEDFORDSHIRE JUNIOR TROPHY
(April 7th at Cranfield United)
Ickwell & Old Warden Res. 1 Sandy Res. 1 *aet* (5-4p)

BEDWORTH NURSING CUP
(April 14th at Bedworth United)
Bulkington Sports & Social 3 Atherstone Town Res. 1

BERKS & BUCKS TROPHY
(April 26th at Thatcham Town)
Didcot Town 4 Sandhurst Town 2

BERKS & BUCKS INTERMEDIATE CUP
(April 8th at Thatcham Town)
Chalfont Wasps 3 Eton Wick 1

BERKS & BUCKS JUNIOR CUP
(April 22nd at Aylesbury Vale)
Old Challoners 2 PB (Milton Keynes) 0

BILL SPURGEON CUP
(April 19th at Witham Town)
Witham Town Res. 3 Broomfield 1

BIRMINGHAM FLOODLIGHT CUP
(April 19th at Tamworth)
Atherstone Town 4 Pilkington XXX 1

BIRMINGHAM VASE
(April 22nd at BCFA, Great Barr)
Parkfield Leisure 2 Christ The King 0

BIRMINGHAM JUNIOR CUP
(March 3rd at BCFA, Great Barr)
Village 2 Shirley Athletic 1

BOLTON HOSPITAL CUP
(May 8th at Bolton Wanderers)
Ramsbottom United 2 Eagley 1

BRAUNTON CUP
(May 7th at Barnstaple Town)
Torridgeside 2 North Molton 2 *aet* (18-17p)

BRIGHTON CHARITY CUP
(May 3rd at Horsham)
Chichester City United 2 Ringmer 1

BUCKINGHAM CHARITY CUP
(May 1st at Buckingham Town)
Woodford United 2 **Aylesbury Vale** 4

C P O NATIONAL CHRISTIANS CUP
(May 11th at Rushden & Diamonds)
Kings Sports (Herts) 3 Leeds University CU 0

CAMBRIDGESHIRE CHALLENGE CUP
(April 17th at Histon)
Great Shelford 1 Cottenham United 0

CAMBRIDGESHIRE JUNIOR INVITATION CUP
(May 3rd at Cambridge City)
Wimblington Harriers 3 Littleport Town Res. 0

CAMBRIDGESHIRE LOWER JUNIOR CUP
(May 4th at Cambridge City)
Griffin Park 6 Witchford 1

CENTRAL WALES FLOODLIGHT CUP
(April 26th at Caersws)
Tywyn & Bryncrug 1 Four Crosses 0

CEREDIGION CUP
(May 19th at Penrhyncoch)
Bow Street 3 Tywyn & Bryncrug 0

CHESTER SENIOR CUP
(April 27th at Christleton)
Upton Athletic Association 2 Blacon Youth Club 2 *aet* (4-2p)

CHURCHMAN CUP
(May 10th at Woodbridge Town)
Leiston 3 Whitton United 0

CORNWALL CHARITY CUP
(May 18th at Launceston)
St Blazey 2 Bodmin Town 1

CORNWALL JUNIOR CUP
(April 17th at St Blazey)
St Columb 0 **St Day** 2

COVENTRY CHARITY CUP
(April 19th at Coventry City)
Coundon Court Old Boys 3 Southam United 2

COVENTRY EVENING TELEGRAPH CUP
(April 24th at Coventry City)
Coventry Sphinx 4 Coventry Copswood 1

CRAVEN & DISTRICT CUP
(May 5th at Barnoldswick Town)
Rimington 3 Barnoldswick Town 1

CRAVEN & DISTRICT MORRISON CUP
(April 28th at Settle United)
Ingleton 4 Rimington Res. 0

CRAVEN & DISTRICT NORMAN PRATT TROPHY
(April 21st at Settle United)
Gargrave Res. 4 Rimington Res. 1

CREWE & DISTRICT CUP
(May 20th at Middlewich Town)
Crewe 0 **Nantwich Town Res.** 1

DERBYSHIRE DIVISIONAL CUP NORTH
(April 25th at South Normanton Athletic)
Parkhouse 6 Wirksworth Town 2

DERBYSHIRE DIVISIONAL CUP SOUTH
(April 11th at Belper Town)
Holbrook Miners Welfare Res. 0 **Holbrook St Michaels** 2 *aet*

DERBYSHIRE JUNIOR CUP NORTH
(April 18th at Buxton)
Hayfield 2 **Whaley Thorns** 5

DERBYSHIRE JUNIOR CUP SOUTH
(March 22nd at Long Eaton United)
Heanor Jolly Colliers 2 Netherseale St Peters 0

DEVON PREMIER CUP
(May 11th at Plymouth Argyle)
Ivybridge Town 1 Plymouth Parkway 0

DEVON SENIOR CUP
(April 19th at Plymouth Parkway)
Upton Athletic Res. 2 Bere Alston 0

DEVON INTERMEDIATE CUP
(April 27th at Newton Abbot)
Plymouth University 3 Colaton Raleigh 2 *aet*

DONCASTER CHALLENGE CUP
(April 27th at Brodsworth Miners Welfare)
Askern Welfare 4 Yorkshire Main 1

DORSET INTERMEDIATE CUP
(April 27th at Bridport)
Dorchester YMCA 2 **Stalbridge** 3 *aet*

DORSET JUNIOR CUP
(April 11th at Dorchester Town)
Piddletrenthide United 1 **White Horse Symondsbury** 2

DORSET MINOR CUP
(April 6th at Hamworthy United)
Alderholt 3 Chickerell United 'A' 1

DURHAM TROPHY
(April 3rd at Durham City)
Brandon Prince Bishop 5 Whitehill 0

EAST ANGLIAN CUP
(May 6th at Harlow Town)
Harlow Town 1 Spalding United 0

EAST DEVON SENIOR CUP
(May 14th at Budleigh Salterton)
Axminster Town 3 Sidmouth Town 2

EAST DEVON FOOTBALL EXPRESS CUP
(May 9th at Crediton United)
Newtown 'A' 1 Thorverton Res. 0

EAST HAM MEMORIAL CUP
(April 15th at South Woodford CC)
Canning Town 2 Frenford Senior Res. 2 *aet* (5-4p)

EAST RIDING COUNTRY CUP
(May 6th at Bridlington Town)
Northfield Athletic 4 Malton Bacon Factory 2

EAST RIDING INTERMEDIATE COUNTRY CUP
(April 25th at Pocklington Town)
Elvington Harriers 1 Gilberdyke 0

EAST RIDING JUNIOR COUNTRY CUP
(May 1st at Pocklington Town)
Riccall Colliery 1 **Elvington Harriers Res.** 1 *aet* (3-4p)

EAST SURREY HOSPITAL CUP 2004-05
(December 20th at Redhill)
Redhill 2 **Merstham** 3

EAST SURREY HOSPITAL CUP
(May 9th at Redhill)
Chipstead 2 Merstham 0

EMRYS MORGAN CUP
(April 14th at Aberystwyth Town)
Bow Street 2 Crannog 0

ERNEST ARMSTRONG MEMORIAL TROPHY
(August 10th at Crook Town)
Crook Town 3 Consett 0

ESSEX PREMIER CUP
(April 12th at Thurrock)
Witham Town Res. 0 Harold Wood Athletic 0 *aet* (4-2p)

ESSEX THAMESSIDE TROPHY
(May 1st at Canvey Island)
Canvey Island 3 Maldon Town 0

ESSEX JUNIOR CUP
(April 5th at Billericay Town)
Potter Street 2 Brightlingsea Regent 1

ESSEX JUNIOR TROPHY
(March 29th at Great Wakering Rovers)
Southchurch Hall Old Scholars 2 Hullbridge Sports 'A' 1

FARINGDON THURSDAY MEMORIAL CUP
(May 4th at Faringdon Town)
Letcombe 5 Steventon 2

GLOUCESTERSHIRE TROPHY
(May 2nd at GCFA, Oaklands Park)
Slimbridge 1 Bitton 1 *aet* (4-3p)

GLOUCESTERSHIRE SENIOR AMATEUR CUP (NORTH)
(April 20th at Tuffley Rovers)
Dursley Town 3 Longlevens 2

GLOUCESTERSHIRE SENIOR AMATEUR CUP (SOUTH)
(April 18th at GCFA, Oaklands Park)
Glenside Five Old Boys 1 Hanham Athletic 0

GOLDLINE TROPHY
(March 20th at Bolton Wanderers)
Prestwich Heys 1 **Charnock Richard** 2 *aet*

GOLESWORTHY CUP
(May 18th at Ottery St Mary)
Farway United 3 Sidbury United Res. 2

GWENT SENIOR CUP
(May 14th at Abergavenny Thursdays)
Cwmbran Town 4 Croesceiliog 3

GWENT AMATEUR CUP
(May 6th at Abergavenny Thursdays)
Abertillery Bluebirds 4 Mardy 3

HAMPSHIRE RUSSELL COTES CUP
(April 20th at Eastleigh)
Eastleigh 0 **Gosport Borough** 1

HAMPSHIRE INTERMEDIATE CUP
(May 11th at Christchurch)
Colden Common 2 West Wight 1

HAMPSHIRE JUNIOR A CUP
(April 15th at Fareham Town)
Team Solent 4 New Inn (Basingstoke) 1

HAMPSHIRE JUNIOR B CUP
(April 15th at Fareham Town)
Twyford 3 Kyngs Towyne 1

HANSEN CUP
(May 1st at Torrington)
Torridgeside 1 Dolton Rangers Res. 0

HASTINGS SENIOR CUP
(April 11th at Hastings United)
Westfield 2 **Rye & Iden United** 3 *aet*

HASTINGS INTERMEDIATE CUP
(April 4th at Rye & Iden United)
Hollington United 2 Sidley United Res. 1

HERALD CUP
(April 14th at Buckland Athletic)
Brixham Villa 2 Upton Athletic 0

HERTFORDSHIRE CHARITY CUP
(April 25th at HCFA, Letchworth)
Boreham Wood 0 **Cheshunt** 1

HERTFORDSHIRE CENTENARY TROPHY
(March 28th at HCFA, Letchworth)
Codicote 2 Hoddesdon Town 0

HERTFORDSHIRE CHARITY SHIELD
(April 19th at HCFA, Letchworth)
Sawbridgeworth Town 2 London Colney 1

HERTFORDSHIRE INTERMEDIATE CUP
(March 22nd at HCFA, Letchworth)
Bishop's Stortford Swifts 0 Hemel Hempstead Town Res. 0 *aet* (4-2p)

HERTFORDSHIRE JUNIOR CUP
(April 14th at HCFA, Letchworth)
Bengeo Trinity 2 Park Street Village 1

HINCHINGBROOKE CUP
(May 10th at Eynesbury Rovers)
St Ives Town 2 **Barton Rovers** 3

HOLMAN CUP
(April 17th at Lynton & Lynmouth)
South Molton 2 Braunton Res. 1

HUNTINGDONSHIRE PREMIER CUP
(May 16th at Eynesbury Rovers)
Yaxley 2 St Neots Town 0 *aet*

HUNTINGDONSHIRE SCOTT GATTY CUP
(April 26th at Needingworth United)
Yaxley Res. 2 St Ives Town Res. 0

HUNTINGDONSHIRE BENEVOLENT CUP
(April 19th at Somersham Town)
St Neots Town Res. 0 Yaxley Res. 0 *aet* (5-4p)

KENT SENIOR TROPHY
(April 9th at Welling United)
VCD Athletic 1 Tunbridge Wells 1 *aet* (3-1p)

LANCASHIRE AMATEUR CUP
(April 6th at LCFA, Leyland)
Speke 3 Aintree Villa 3 *aet* (5-4p)

LAUNCESTON CUP
(May 14th at Launceston)
Bude Town 1 **Pensilva** 3

LEAGUE SYSTEMS CUP
(May 7th at Cambridge United)
Cambridgeshire County League 0 **Isle of Man League** 4

LEICESTERSHIRE SENIOR CUP
(April 25th at LCFA, Holmes Park)
Thurnby Rangers 1 Friar Lane & Epworth 0

LEICESTERSHIRE JUNIOR SHIELD
(April 11th at LCFA, Holmes Park)
Sileby Town Res. 2 Ashby Athletic 0

LINCOLNSHIRE SENIOR A CUP
(April 25th at Deeping Rangers)
Deeping Rangers 0 **Bourne Town** 1

LINCOLNSHIRE SENIOR B CUP
(April 4th at Boston Town)
Sleaford Town 2 LSS Lucarly's 1

LIVERPOOL CHALLENGE CUP
(April 9th at LCFA, Walton Hall Avenue)
Aintree Villa 0 **Waterloo Dock** 4

LIVERPOOL JUNIOR CUP
(May 2nd at LCFA, Walton Hall Avenue)
St Ambrose 0 South Liverpool Res. 0 *aet* (3-0p)

LONDON INTERMEDIATE CUP
(April 22nd at Croydon Athletic)
Metrogas 2 Corinthian Casuals Res. 1

LONDON JUNIOR CUP
(April 8th at Brimsdown Rovers)
Fenerbahce Res. 1 Bancroft 0

LONDON OLD BOYS SENIOR CUP
(April 18th at Wingate & Finchley)
Old Meadonians 3 Southgate County 2

LOUGHBOROUGH CHARITY CUP
(May 6th at Loughborough Dynamo)
Loughborough Dynamo 4 Shepshed Dynamo 3

MACCLESFIELD CUP
(May 6th at Macclesfield Town)
Astra Zeneca 1 Congleton Vale 0 *aet*

MANCHESTER CHALLENGE TROPHY
(February 9th at MCFA, Branthingham Road)
Irlam Mitchell Shackleton 2 Avro 1

MANCHESTER AMATEUR CUP
(April 13th at MCFA, Branthingham Road)
East Manchester Res. 3 Old Stretfordians 1

MARK FROWDE CUP
(May 13th Hamworthy United)
Poole Town 2 Poole Borough 1
MIDDLESEX CHARITY CUP
(April 25th at Yeading)
Enfield Town 0 **Harrow Borough** 2
MIDDLESEX PREMIER CUP
(March 15th at Staines Town)
Staines Town Res. 1 Ruislip Manor Res. 0
MIDDLESEX INTERMEDIATE CUP
(March 29th at Hillingdon Borough)
Kodak Harrow 2 Indian Gymkhana 1
MIDDLESEX JUNIOR CUP
(April 12th at Hanwell Town)
Ashton Athletic 0 **Northolt** 1
MID-CHESHIRE SENIOR CUP 2004-05
(August 2nd at Witton Albion)
Witton Albion 2 Northwich Victoria 2 *aet* (4-2p)
MID-SOMERSET CHARITY CUP
(April 28th at Shepton Mallet)
Coleford Athletic 2 Chilcompton 0 *aet*
MID-SUSSEX SENIOR CHARITY CUP
(April 26th at Burgess Hill Town)
Ifield Edwards 3 Wisdom Sports 1
MORRISON BELL CUP
(April 19th at Ottery St Mary)
Feniton 3 Sidmouth Town 2
NORFOLK JUNIOR CUP
(March 22nd at Norwich City)
Caister United 1 Mattishall Res. 0
NORTH BEDFORDSHIRE CHARITY CUP
(May 1st at Langford)
Potton United 3 Wootton Blue Cross 1
NORTH CAMBRIDGESHIRE JUNIOR CUP
(April 19th at Wisbech Town)
Chatteris Town 2 Griffin Park 2 *aet* (4-3p)
NORTH RIDING CHALLENGE CUP
(March 8th at Stokesley Sports Club)
Stokesley Sports Club 4 Thornaby Youth Club 2
NORTH WALES COAST CUP
(May 10th at Colwyn Bay)
Rhyl 2 Denbigh Town 1
NORTHAMPTON FA AREA CUP
(March 22nd at Raunds Town)
Perkins Sports Res. 3 **Rushden Corner Flag** 3 *aet* (6-7p)
NORTHAMPTON FA GORELL BARNES CUP
(May 6th at Northampton Town)
Duston United 3 **University College** 4
NORTHAMPTON FA NBC CUP
(May 6th at Northampton Town)
Birchfield Rovers 4 Double Four 1
NORTHAMPTONSHIRE JUNIOR CUP
(May 3rd at Northampton Town)
Wellingborough Town 2 Peterborough Northern Star 0 *aet*
NORTHAMPTONSHIRE LOWER JUNIOR CUP
(April 4th at Wellingborough Town)
Bugbrooke St Michaels Res. 1 Corby Grampian 0
NORTHERN CUP
(May 20th at Hanley Town)
Hanley Town 4 Top Nogs 1
NORTHUMBERLAND BENEVOLENT BOWL
(May 10th at West Allotment Celtic)
Ponteland United 3 Seaton Delaval Amateurs 2

NORTHUMBERLAND MINOR CUP
(May 19th at NFA, West Allotment Celtic)
Ashington Colliers 2 Blyth Town Res. 1 *aet*
NOTTS INTERMEDIATE CUP
(April 10th at Hucknall Town)
Basford United 2 Forest Town 1
OKEHAMPTON CUP
(May 14th at Okehampton Argyle)
Chagford 2 Heavitree Social United 1
OLD BOYS SENIOR INVITATION CUP
(April 22nd at Old Parkonians)
Old Owens 2 Old Salesians 1
ONGAR CHARITY CUP
(August 27th at Ongar Town)
Ongar Town 0 **Potter Street** 1
OXFORDSHIRE CHARITY CUP
(April 29th at Ardley United)
Rover Cowley 4 Garsington 3
OXFORDSHIRE INTERMEDIATE CUP
(April 19th at Ardley United)
Henley Town Res. 2 Enstone Sports 0
PORTSMOUTH SENIOR CUP
(April 3rd at Havant & Waterlooville)
Gosport Borough Res. 3 Moneyfields Res. 2
POTTERS BAR CHARITY CUP
(May 8th at Potters Bar Town)
Old Owens 0 **East Barnet Old Grammarians** 1
POWELL CHARITY CUP
(May 7th at Wem Town)
Shawbury United 1 Malpas 0
ROMFORD CHARITY CUP
(May 11th at Aveley)
Metropolitan Police Chigwell 1 **Harold Wood Athletic** 5
ROWE CHARITY CUP
(May 7th at Ilfracombe Town)
Barnstaple AAC 3 Barnstaple Town Res. 2
ROY BAILEY MEMORIAL TROPHY
(May 11th at Brimsdown Rovers)
Ware 1 Waltham Abbey 0
RUNCORN CHALLENGE CUP
(April 21st at Runcorn Town)
Runcorn Town 1 Helsby 0 *aet*
SEATON CUP
(May 5th at Seaton Town)
Axminster Town 3 Honiton Town 0
SHEFFIELD & HALLAMSHIRE ASSOCIATION CUP
(May 10th at Doncaster Rovers)
Kiveton Park 5 Sheffield Lane Top 0
SHROPSHIRE CHALLENGE CUP
(April 11th at Shrewsbury Town)
Market Drayton Town 1 Broseley Juniors 0
SMEDLEY CROOKE MEMORIAL CHARITY CUP
(April 20th at Bromsgrove Rovers)
Barnt Green Spartak 0 **Bartley Green** 1
SOMERSET SENIOR CUP
(May 1st at Paulton Rovers)
Broad Plain House Old Boys 2 Westland Sports 0
SOMERSET JUNIOR CUP
(April 18th at Shepton Mallet)
Mells & Vobster United 3 Meadow Rangers 2
SOMERSET INTERMEDIATE CUP
(April 27th at Clevedon Town)
Taunton Civil Service 0 **Purnells Sports** 2

SOUTHAMPTON SENIOR CUP
(April 19th at Southampton)
Mottisfont 0 **VTFC Res.** 5

SOUTHAMPTON A CUP
(April 17th at Blackfield & Langley)
Redbridge 3 **Team Solent** 5 *aet*

SOUTHAMPTON B CUP
(April 17th at Blackfield & Langley)
AFC Redbridge 4 Gardeners 3 *aet*

SOUTH MIDLANDS FLOODLIGHT CUP
(May 9th at Hillingdon Borough)
Hillingdon Borough 2 **Potters Bar Town** 4

SOUTH MIDLANDS RESERVES FLOODLIGHT CUP
(May 16th at Cockfosters)
Cockfosters Res. 3 Oxhey Jets Res. 1 *aet*

SOUTHERN COMBINATION CUP
(May 11th at Molesey)
Molesey 2 **Staines Town** 3

STAFFORDSHIRE VASE
(April 25th at Newcastle Town)
Eccleshall 0 **Redgate Clayton** 1

STAFFORDSHIRE CHALLENGE CUP
(April 10th at Eccleshall)
Great Wyrley 2 Walsall Wood 0

STAFFORDSHIRE PRESIDENT'S CUP
(March 20th at Eccleshall)
Shenstone Pathfinder 2 Biddulph Town 0

SUFFOLK SENIOR CUP
(May 3rd at Ipswich Town)
Walsham-le-Willows 4 Capel Plough 3 *aet*

SUFFOLK JUNIOR CUP
(April 25th at Ipswich Town)
AFC Sudbury Res. 1 Stowupland 0

SUPPORTERS DIRECT CUP
(July 23rd at AFC Wimbledon)
AFC Wimbledon 1 FC United of Manchester 0

SURREY PREMIER CUP
(April 12th at Leatherhead)
Sutton United Res. 3 Whyteleafe Res. 1

SURREY INTERMEDIATE CUP
(May 9th at Tooting & Mitcham United)
Holmesdale 5 Epsom Athletic 3

SURREY JUNIOR CUP
(May 4th at Molesey)
Battersea Ironsides 1 Westminster Casuals 0

SURREY LOWER JUNIOR CUP
(May 8th at Molesey)
Inter Class 6 Maori Park 2

SUSSEX R U R CHARITY CUP
(May 2nd at Lancing)
Hailsham Town 2 Whitehawk 0

SUSSEX INTERMEDIATE CUP
(April 25th at Hailsham Town)
Peacehaven & Telscombe 2 Eastbourne Town Res. 1

SUSSEX JUNIOR CUP
(March 31st at Shoreham)
Rustington Res. 2 **Legal & General (Hove)** 4

TIPTREE CHARITY CUP
(May 16th at Tiptree United)
Coggeshall Town 7 White Notley Res. 2

TORRIDGE CUP
(May 4th at Torrington)
Morwenstow 1 Shamwickshire Rovers 1 *aet* (5-4p)

U K ASIAN CHAMPIONSHIP
(May 8th at Chelsea)
London Tigers 1 London APSA 1 *aet* (3-2p)

UTTLESFORD CHARITY CUP
(May 16th at Halstead Town)
Stansted 2 Braintree Town 1

VERNON WENTWORTH CUP
(May 12th at Shoreham)
Rustington 1 Peacehaven & Telscombe 0

WALSALL SENIOR CUP
(May 15th at Walsall)
Tipton Town 0 **Boldmere St Michaels** 1

WALTHO CUP
(April 29th at Combe Martin)
Northam Lions 4 Braunton 2

WASHINGTON AGED PEOPLE'S CUP
(April 12th at Chester-le-Street Town)
Ashbrooke Belford 1 Seaham Town Community 0

WEST HERTS ST MARYS CUP
(May 1st at Leverstock Green)
Berkhamsted Town 1 Leverstock Green 1 *aet* (4-1p)

WEST RIDING CHALLENGE CUP
(May 5th at WRCFA, Woodlesford)
Bay Athletic 2 **Sherburn White Rose** 1
(Cup awarded to Sherburn White Rose)

WEST RIDING CHALLENGE TROPHY
(April 28th at WRCFA, Woodlesford)
Brighouse Town Res. 2 Golden Lion 0

WESTMORLAND BENEVOLENT TROPHY
(April 22nd at Kendal Town)
Wetheriggs United 1 Kendal County 0

WESTMORLAND JUNIOR CUP
(April 19th at Kendal Town)
Cartmel & District Res. 3 Keswick Res. 0

WILTSHIRE SENIOR CUP
(April 25th at Chippenham Town)
Corsham Town 2 Melksham Town 2 *aet* (5-3p)

WILTSHIRE JUNIOR CUP
(April 22nd at Swindon Supermarine)
Wroughton 2 Chiseldon Castrol 1

WIRRAL SENIOR CUP
(May 15th at Tranmere Rovers)
Poulton Victoria 5 Ellesmere Port 2 *aet*

WIRRAL AMATEUR CUP
(April 17th at Ashville)
Ashville Res. 1 **West Kirby Res.** 2

WORCESTER ROYAL INFIRMARY CUP
(May 9th at Bromyard Town)
Pershore Town 1 **Malvern Town** 3

WORCESTERSHIRE JUNIOR CUP
(March 29th at Worcester City)
Archdale 2 Fairfield Villa 1

WYCOMBE SENIOR CUP
(May 18th at Wycombe Wanderers)
Eton Wick 2 Holmer Green 0

WYCOMBE JUNIOR CUP
(May 4th at Holmer Green)
AFC Spartans 4 Chinnor Res. 1

Y M C A CUP
(May 13th at South Molton)
Chittlehampton 3 High Bickington 0

LEAGUE SPONSORS

	2005-06	2006-07
Anglian Combination	Lovewell Blake	Dolphin Autos
Cambridgeshire County League	Kershaw/BIS Steels	
Central Midlands League	Abacus Lighting	Abacus Lighting
Combined Counties League	Cherry Red Records	Cherry Red Records
Cornwall Combination	Jolly's	Jolly's
Cymru Alliance	Huws Gray	Huws Gray
Devon County League	Axworthys' Office Supplies	Axworthys' Office Supplies
East Cornwall League	Cornish Guardian	Cornish Guardian
Eastern Counties League	Ridgeons	Ridgeons
Essex Olympian League	Baliston	
Essex Senior League	Westview	Westview
Essex & Suffolk Border League	Kent Blaxill	Kent Blaxill
Football Conference	Nationwide	Nationwide
Gwent County League	Welsh Autoparts	Welsh Autoparts
Hellenic League	GLS Football	Sport Italia
Herts Senior County League	World Class Homes	World Class Homes
Humber Premier League	Carling	Carling
Isthmian League	Ryman	Ryman
Kent County League	British Energy	British Energy
Kent League	Kentish Times	
Mid-Cheshire League	Coors	Cheshire Building Society
Leicestershire Senior League	Everards Brewery	Everards Brewery
Lincolnshire League	Lincolnshire Echo	Lincolnshire Echo
Liverpool County Combination	Frank Armitt	Frank Armitt
Manchester League	Air Miles	
Middlesex County League	Cherry Red Records	Cherry Red Records
Midland Alliance	Harvey World Travel	Polymac Services
North West Counties League	Moore & Co. Construction Solicitors	Moore & Co. Construction Solicitors
Northamtonshire Combination	Travis Perkins	Travis Perkins
Northern Alliance	Wade Associates	Wade Associates
Northern League	Arngrove	Arngrove
Northern Premier League	Unibond	Unibond
Peterborough & District League	Marshall	Marshall
Shropshire County League	Sportsjamkits.com	Sportsjamkits.com
South Wales Amateur League	Thunder Road Motorcycles	Thunder Road Motorcycles
South Wales Senior League	Regal Travel	Regal Travel
South Western League	Carlsberg	Carlsberg
Southampton League	Drew Smith Homes	Drew Smith Homes
Southern League		British Gas Business
Suffolk & Ipswich League	Metaltec	Metaltec
Sussex County League	Badger Bitter	Badger Bitter
Teesside League	Jack Hatfield Sports	Jack Hatfield Sports
United Counties League	Eagle Bitter	Eagle Bitter
Welsh Alliance	Pentraeth Honda	Pentraeth Honda
Welsh League	Macron	None
Welsh National League (Wrexham Area)	Nizam-Druid	Nizam-Druid
Wessex League	Sydenhams	Sydenhams
West Cheshire League	Carlsberg	Carlsberg
West Lancs League	Aegon UK	Aegon UK
West Riding County Amateur League	Mumtaz	Mumtaz
Western League	Toolstation	Toolstation
Westmorland League	Talbot Insurance	Talbot Insurance
Wiltshire League	Plaister Autos	Plaister Autos

See page 276 for Division Sponsors

OTHER LEAGUE SPONSORS

Aberystwyth & District League	Cambrian Tyres
Aylesbury & District League	Perrys Peugeot
Bath & District League	Roper Rhodes Bathrooms
Bournemouth League	Hayward
Boston League	Cropley's Suzuki
Bromley & District League	Roper Rhodes Bathrooms
Burton & District FA	Marstons
Burton & District FA Division One	Pedigree
Burton & District FA Division Two	TAG Promotional Clothing
Burton & District FA Division Three	Burton Old Cottage Tavern
Central & South Norfolk League	Crown Fire
Clwyd League	McKenzie Jones
Coventry Alliance - Premier Division	Aw Engraving
Coventry Alliance - Divisions One to Five	Continental Products
East Sussex League	K & P Motoring World
Falmouth-Heston League	Whirlwind Sports
Gwent Central	Knauf Insulation
Herefordshire League	Herefordshire Times
I Zingari League	Alex Stewart Assayers
Lancashire Amateur League	Redrow
Lancashire League	Lancit Haulage
Leicester City League Premier Division	Creation
Leicester City League Division Two	Coalville Trophies
Matlock & District League Division One	Hellison
Mid-Sussex League	Robert Gray
Mid-Wales League	Spar
Montgomery & District League Division One	J T Hughes Honda
Montgomery & District League Division Two	J T Hughes Mitsubishi
North Devon League	Bideford Tool
North Gwent League	Abacus Recruitment
North Leicestershire League Premier Division	B-L Pegson
North Leicestershire League Division One	Midshires Group
North Leicestershire League Division Two	Hex Holdings Ltd
North Leicestershire League Division Three	Windmill Trophies
North Leicestershire League Division Four	RBF Fibreglass Ltd
North West Norfolk League	Thurlow-Nunn
Northampton Town League	Peter Smith Recruitment
Oxford City F.A.	R T Harris
Rochester & District League Premier Division	SKS Consultancy
Rochester & District League Divisions One & Two	HandF Finance
Rochester & District League Division Three	Asteck Ltd
Rochester & District League Division Four	Jus Cos Sports
Rochester & District League Division Five	Rainham Sports
Scunthorpe & District League	Fallen Hero
Sheffield & Hallamshire County Senior League	Windsor Food Services
St Helens Combination Premier Division	St Helens Star
St Helens Combination Division One	Bolton Mechanical Services
St Helens Combination Division Two	AVS Group
Surrey South Eastern Combination	Crown Fire
Taunton & District League	Silver Street Volkswagon
Warrington & District League Premier Division	Frontrunner
West Herts League	Arlon Printers
Weston & District League	Nightingale Removals
Worthing & District	Taulke Finance

DIVISION SPONSORS

Bedford & District League Premier Division	McGirls Money Management
Cambridgeshire County League Premier and Senior Divisions	Kershaw
Cambridgeshire County League Divisions 1-5	BIS Group
Central Midlands League Supreme Division	Stadium Services
Central Midlands League Premier Division	Vipond Fire Protection
Central Midlands League Reserve Divisions	Lee's
Leics Senior League Combination One and Two	City Goldsmiths
Northamptonshire Combination Premier Division	Dulux
Northamptonshire Combination Division One	Cuprinol
Northamptonshire Combination Division Two	Stanley Tools
Northamptonshire Combination Division Three	Makita
Northamptonshire Combination Division Four	ITW Paslode
Northamptonshire Combination Reserve Division One	Sadolin
Northamptonshire Combination Reserve Division Two	Unibond
Northamptonshire Combination Reserve Division Three	Yale, Chubb, Union
Peterborough & District League Premier Division	Peugeot
Peterborough & District League Division One	Toyota
Peterborough & District League Division Two	Honda
Peterborough & District League Division Three	Vauxhall
Peterborough & District League Division Four	Land Rover
Peterborough & District League Division Five	Jaguar

CUP SPONSORS

AFA Senior Cup	Alan Day Volkswagen
Central Midlands League Cup	Quartet Catering
Central Midlands League Floodlight Cup	Phoenix Trophies
Central Midlands League Reserve Cup	Phoenix Trophies
Cheshire Senior Cup	Unibond
Combined Counties League Cup	Captain Oi! Records
Combined Counties League Division One Cup	Lemon Recordings
Combined Counties League Reserves Premier Cup	Captain Oi! Records
Combined Counties League Reserve Division One Cup	RPM Records
Combined Counties League Reserves Shield	Shout! Records
Cymru Alliance Cup	Roger Jones Builders
Devon County League Cup	Throgmorton
Gwent County League Cup	County Motors
Hampshire Senior Cup	Computerquoteinsurance.com
Humber Premier League Cup	Grays
Football League Trophy	LDV Vans
Isthmian League Cup	Westview
Kent County League Champions Trophy	G R Roofing
Lancashire Trophy	Marsden Building Society
Leicestershire Challenge Trophy	Westerby Homes
Leicestershire Senior League Cup	Beacon Bitter
Leicestershire Combination President's Cup	Leicester Fencing
Liverpool County Combination Lord Wavertree Cup	R A Brickwork
Midland Alliance Cup	Polymac Services
Midland Combination Challenge Cup	Endsleigh Insurance
Midland Combination President's Cup	Unique Catering Services
Northamptonshire Senior Cup	Hillier
Northants Combination Premier Division Cup	John Henry Sports
Northern Alliance Premier Division Challenge Cup	Bosch Power Tools
Northern Alliance Combination Cup	Pin Point Personnel
Northern Alliance Amateur Cup	Pin Point Personnel
Northern Alliance League Cup	Longhorn Hardware
Northumberland Senior Cup	Swan Office Systems
Reading League Senior Cup	Berks Trophy Centre
Southern League Cup	Errea
Staffs County League Trophy	Bourne Sports
Suffolk Premier Cup	Club Colours
Suffolk & Ipswich League Cup	Omnico
Suffolk & Ipswich League Reserves Cup	J R Travel
Suffolk & Ipswich League Junior Cup	Harpers Intersport
Welsh League Cup	Shamrock Travel
Welsh League Reserve Shield	Harris Printers
Wiltshire League Senior Cup	Corsham Print
Wiltshire League Junior Cup	Fountain Trophies

INDEX

Page numbers point to league table
If a team's 2006-07 directory entry is on a different page, this precedes in round brackets
Teams that withdrew at the start of 2005-06 are denoted by their page number being enclosed in square brackets
Clubs subject to name changes and mergers are asterisked
Both new and old names are included in the index, and a full listing follows the index

*NAME CHANGES & MERGERS

Addlestone Jesmond become **Jesmond**
AFC Wallingford 'A' become **Wallingford Athletic**
Arnold Southbank become **Gedling Southbank**
Barwick & Stoford become **Tintinhull**
Bedford Corinthians become **Meltis Corinthians**
Berwick United are an amalgamation of **Spittal Rovers** and **Highfields United**
Blisworth become **James King Blisworth**
Blueprint Chiseldon are an amalgamation of **Blueprint** and **Chiseldon**
Bournemouth Sports CM are an amalgamation of **Bournemouth Sports** and **Corfe Mullen United**
Brendon Northend United become **Northend United**
Bronte Wanderers are an amalgamation of **Keighley Lifts** and **Bronte Wanderers**
Castle Vale Reserves become **Castle Vale JKS**
Chemfica become **Newcastle Chemfica**
Classic Comrades become **Comrades**
Exmouth Town Reserves become **Exmouth Town**
Foster Athletic become **West Lynn SSC**
Goole become **Goole Town**
Graig Castle Ivor become **Graig**
Guildford United become **Guildford City**
Handsworth United become **Birmingham Academy**
HM Desford Sports become **Syston Fosse Sports**
Irlam Mitchell Shackleton become **Irlam**
Kennek Ryhope CA become **Sunderland Ryhope CA**
Kingsbury London Tigers are an amalgamation of **Kingsbury Town** and **London Tigers**
Leeds City are an amalgamation of **Adel** and **Abbey Grange Old Boys**
M & T Awbridge become **Michelmersh & Timsbury**
Mackinlay Park become **Redcar Rugby Club**
Monotye become **Salfords**
Netherne Village become **Coulsdon Town**
New Bromleians become **Cray W & NB**
Ordnance Survey become **Stoneham**
Over Wallop are an amalgamation of **Over Wallop** and **Stockbridge Reserves**
Red Rum become **Croxteth Red Rum**
Royal Oak become **Bobbington**
Rye & Iden United become **Rye United**
Springfields BAC/EE are an amalgamation of **Springfields** and **BAC/EE Preston**
Stockwood Green Robinsons are an amalgamation of **Stockwood Green** and **Robinsons**
Stowupland become **Stowupland Falcons**
Swarland become **Amble**
Taunton Blackbrook Reserves become **Creech St Michael**
The Albany become **Albany Athletic**
Thornaby Youth Club become **Thornaby Dubliners**
Total Network Solutions become **The New Saints**
Tuffley Rovers Reserves become **Tuffley Rovers**
Wakefield & Emley become **Wakefield**
Wedgwood Sports & Social become **Barlaston**
Wellingborough Whitworths become **Whitworths**
Wincanton Sports become **Wincanton Town**
Winchester City 'A' become **Winchester Castle**

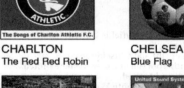